CONTENTS

VICE-COUNTIES OF BRITAIN AND IRELAND

England and Wales
1. West Cornwall
2. East Cornwall
3. South Devon
4. North Devon
5. South Somerset
6. North Somerset
7. North Wiltshire
8. South Wiltshire
9. Dorset
10. Isle of Wight
11. South Hampshire
12. North Hampshire
13. West Sussex
14. East Sussex
15. East Kent
16. West Kent
17. Surrey
18. South Essex
19. North Essex
20. Hertfordshire
21. Middlesex
22. Berkshire
23. Oxfordshire (Oxon)
24. Buckinghamshire
25. East Suffolk
26. West Suffolk
27. East Norfolk
28. West Norfolk
29. Cambridgeshire
30. Bedfordshire
31. Huntingdonshire
32. Northamptonshire
33. East Gloucestershire
34. West Gloucestershire
35. Monmouthshire
36. Herefordshire
37. Worcestershire
38. Warwickshire
39. Staffordshire
40. Shropshire (Salop)
41. Glamorganshire
42. Breconshire
43. Radnorshire
44. Carmarthenshire
45. Pembrokeshire
46. Cardiganshire
47. Montgomeryshire
48. Merionethshire
49. Caernarvonshire
50. Denbighshire
51. Flintshire
52. Anglesey
53. South Lincolnshire
54. North Lincolnshire
55. Leicestershire
56. Nottinghamshire
57. Derbyshire
58. Cheshire
59. South Lancashire
60. West Lancashire
61. South-east Yorkshire
62. North-east Yorkshire
63. South-west Yorkshire
64. Mid-west Yorkshire
65. North-west Yorkshire
66. County Durham
67. South Northumberland
68. Cheviot
69. Westmorland
70. Cumberland
71. Isle of Man
S. Channel Islands

Scotland
72. Dumfriesshire
73. Kirkcudbrightshire
74. Wigtownshire
75. Ayrshire
76. Renfrewshire
77. Lanarkshire
78. Peebleshire
79. Selkirkshire
80. Roxburghshire
81. Berwickshire
82. East Lothian
83. Midlothian
84. West Lothian
85. Fifeshire
86. Stirlingshire
87. West Perthshire
88. Mid Perthshire
89. East Perthshire
90. Angus
91. Kincardineshire
92. South Aberdeenshire
93. North Aberdeenshire
94. Banffshire
95. Moray
96. Easterness
97. Westerness
98. Main Argyll
99. Dunbarton
100. Clyde Isles
101. Kintyre
102. South Ebudes
103. Mid Ebudes
104. North Ebudes
105. West Ross
106. East Ross
107. East Sutherland
108. West Sutherland
109. Caithness
110. Outer Hebrides
111. Orkney
112. Shetland

Ireland
H1. South Kerry
H2. North Kerry
H3. West Cork
H4. Mid-Cork
H5. East Cork
H6. Co. Waterford
H7. South Tipperary
H8. Co. Limerick
H9. Co. Clare
H10. North Tipperary
H11. Co. Kilkenny
H12. Co. Wexford
H13. Co. Carlow
H14. Laois
H15. South-east Galway
H16. West Galway
H17. North-east Galway
H18. Offaly
H19. Co. Kildare
H20. Co. Wicklow
H21. Co. Dublin
H22. Meath
H23. Westmeath
H24. Co. Longford
H25. Co. Roscommon
H26. East Mayo
H27. West Mayo
H28. Co. Sligo
H29. Co. Leitrim
H30. Co. Cavan
H31. Co. Louth
H32. Co. Monaghan
H33. Fermanagh
H34. East Donegal
H35. West Donegal
H36. Tyrone
H37. Co. Armagh
H38. Co. Down
H39. Co. Antrim
H40. Co. Londonderry

0 50 100 150 km
0 50 100 miles

The *Flower Guide* is designed as a field guide to the identification of those plants found growing wild in the British Isles and neighbouring parts of northwest Europe. It covers all flowering plants, including trees, shrubs, grasses and sedges, as well as the conifers and the ferns and their allies. That is, all plants botanists classify as 'vascular plants' – those with an internal conducting system that transports water, nutrients and the products of photosynthesis around the plant.

The flora of the British Isles comprises around 3500 species, of which about 960 are apomictic 'microspecies' of brambles, hawkweeds and dandelions (*see* 'Choice of Species' below). Of the remaining 2500, about 1500 are native and 1000 are introductions (Kent, 1992). The number of species endemic to the British Isles – that is, those confined to the region and found nowhere else – is relatively small. Rich (1999) lists 470 such species, but most of these are apomicts, leaving only about 10 non-critical species. However, all these figures are only approximate as views on the status of species are constantly changing, as are views on the number of introductions.

There are three parts to the *Guide*: the species accounts, the plates and the keys. These are intended to be used together to enable the user to name with confidence plants that are met in the field. Wherever possible, characters are used that are visible to the naked eye or can be seen with a ×10 lens. However, for some critical groups certain identification depends on microscopic characters such as the structure of pollen grains or spores; in such cases this is made clear and the identification should be checked by an expert.

Choice of Species

In addition to native plants, the floras of areas such as northwest Europe include many hundreds of species growing wild that originate in other parts of the world that have a temperate climate similar to ours. The choice of which of these increasing numbers of introductions to include in a guide is necessarily somewhat arbitrary. As a rule of thumb, all those that have become well established and are able to reproduce and maintain themselves in the wild are included, whilst most of those that are simply short-term casuals have had to be omitted.

The distinction between what is a 'native' species as opposed to an 'introduction' is sometimes almost impossible to determine. For instance, many introductions arrived as weeds of agriculture in antiquity and to all intents and purposes have become established members of the native flora, so for these the distinction is merely academic. On the other hand, a large and increasing number of species are known to be more recent arrivals. These two groups are now usually distinguished by the terms *archaeophyte* and *neophyte*, which are separated by the wholly arbitrary date of about 1500. In the *Flower Guide*, the status of British plants is designated as either *native, archaeophyte* or *introduced*, the last being equivalent to those otherwise referred to as neophytes. Introduced plants that don't persist for more than a year or two are termed *casuals*. The status accorded to the individual species follows that in *New Atlas of the British and Irish Flora* by Preston, Pearman and Dines (2002).

Some groups of plants regularly produce seeds without fertilisation, these germinating into seedlings that are identical to the parent – in effect, cloning by seed. This can produce large numbers of so-called 'micro-species'. For instance, at the last count there were 412 species of hawkweeds, *Hieracium*; 232 species of dandelions, *Taraxacum*; and 320 species of brambles, *Rubus*. Such plants are termed *apomicts* and no attempt has been made here to distinguish between the micro-species.

Geographical Coverage

The *Flower Guide* covers the British Isles (the United Kingdom, the Isle of Man, the Channel Isles and Republic of Ireland), along with the neighbouring parts of northwest Europe, including Denmark, Holland, Belgium, Luxembourg, northern France south to the Loire, and northwest Germany. Altitudinal ranges are taken from Pearman and Corner (2003).

Plant Names

Many familiar wild flowers are known by different **English names** in different parts of the country. Some, such as Lords-and-ladies, have accumulated almost a hundred local and vernacular names. The English names in the *Flower Guide* follow a recommended list, *English Names of Wild Flowers* (1974) by Dony, Perring and Rob, produced by the Botanical Society of the British Isles. However, in some cases where an alternative name is equally familiar or in widespread use, this has been added. English names of non-British species, where they don't already exist, are translations of the vernacular.

Latin names have a depressing habit of changing with irritating frequency. The reasons for these changes, although often obscure, are usually perfectly good and governed by international rules that, theoretically at least, should ensure that the frequency of such changes decreases with time. Latin names in the *Flower Guide* follow those of the standard British flora, the 2nd edition of *New Flora of the British Isles* (1997) by C.A. Stace. There are two exceptions to this. First, recent research using new techniques in molecular genetics has resulted in several changes to orchid names that have been adopted, together with their more familiar synonyms. Second, a new monograph on the British sedges by Jermy *et al.* (2007) has also resulted in some revisions that have been included. Latin names of non-British species follow those in the five-volume *Flora Europaea* (Tutin *et al.*, 1964–1980).

Technical Terms

A real attempt has been made to keep unnecessary technical terms to a minimum. However, the use of a basic botanical vocabulary is unavoidable in the description of a plant. All terms are described in the Glossary (p.684) and most are illustrated. Those relating to specific groups, such as the grasses, are also illustrated and explained in the text in the introduction to the family. Readers will find that they will soon become familiar with the more common terms.

Species Accounts

The species accounts all follow a standard pattern and appear in the text opposite the relevant plate:

- English name(s) and Latin name (*see* above).
- Conservation status and legal protection (*see* 'Symbols and Abbreviations' below).
- Species description.
- Habitat.
- British distribution and status, e.g. native, archaeophyte, introduced, casual (*see* above), endemic.
- Summary of European distribution.
- Flowering time.

Using the Keys

Keys to help with identification are provided for most families and genera that contain more than four or five species. For those unfamiliar with the use of keys, they are a means of identifying species using a series of alternative descriptions (couplets) that progressively whittle down the possible options until the identity of the plant is arrived at. It's a kind of detection in which a number of clues are sorted until the identity of the individual logically emerges, and there is always a great sense of achievement when an unfamiliar plant is finally nailed down in this way!

For example, there are four species of red poppies and the key would separate them as follows:

1   Capsule glabrous (without hairs)   [go to] 2
    Capsule with long, stiff hairs   [go to] 3

2   Capsule a little longer than wide   *Papaver rhoeas*
    Capsule >2× as long as wide   *P. dubium*

3   Capsule almost spherical   *P. hybridum*
    Capsule >2× as long as wide   *P. argemone*

Be sure always to read both (or all) alternatives at each point in the key, even if the first description seems to fit your specimen perfectly. It might be that the alternative description fits it even more perfectly! If you come to a dead end, the trick is to backtrack to the last point at which you feel quite confident and to start again following an alternative route.

Identifications made through the use of a key should always be checked with the more detailed descriptions in the species accounts and by comparing the plant with the illustration on the plate. If you don't feel very confident in using keys it's a good idea to practise with a few specimens whose identity you already know.

Using a Lens

A lens is an indispensable piece of equipment for any naturalist, and the botanist is no exception. A magnification of ×10 is ideal for most purposes, and there are a number of lenses on the market offered by dealers in natural history equipment.

When using a lens for the first time, I suggest that you hold it between thumb and forefinger and bring it up to your eye such that you just touch the tip of your nose with your forefinger. You can then bring the specimen up to the lens until it comes into focus.

Conservation

Northwest Europe is one of the most densely populated parts of the world and as a result the pressures on the countryside are enormous. Urban development, agricultural intensification, pollution and the spread of invasive introductions have had an inevitable effect on the abundance of a large number of species, about 20 of which have actually become extinct in the last 100 years. In addition, climate change is affecting both the abundance and distribution of many species, threatening some while favouring the spread of others.

When visiting the countryside and studying plants, great care should always be taken not to trample and compact the soil around species. In addition, botanists should avoid drawing attention to uncommon species. It is important that the local Wildlife Trust or BSBI County Recorder is told of the discovery of any rare or interesting species so that appropriate steps can be taken for its protection and the record properly noted.

The most recent edition of the British Red Data List for plants, *The Vascular Plant Red Data List for Great Britain* (Cheffings & Farrell, 2005), lists all British species along with the threat level of the most endangered, using the standard IUCN (International Union for Conservation of Nature) categories: EX, extinct (in British Isles); EW, extinct in the wild; CR, critically endangered; EN, endangered; VU, vulnerable; and NT, near threatened. These categories, except NT, are identified in the individual species accounts in the *Flower Guide* (*see* 'Symbols and Abbreviations' below).

The legislation relating to the protection of wild plants is complex and the following notes are not a definitive statement of the law but intended only as guidance . Under the Wildlife and Countryside Act 1981 (WCA), which covers Great Britain, it is illegal to uproot any wild plant without the permission of the landowner or occupier. It should be remembered that all wild plants belong to someone, and that under the Theft Act 1968 it is an offence to uproot plants for commercial purposes without authorisation.

Schedule 8 of the Wildlife and Countryside Act 1981 gives special protection to a list of 112 particularly rare and endangered plants that it is illegal to pick, uproot, destroy or offer for sale. The equivalent legislation in Northern Ireland, the Wildlife (Northern Ireland) Order 1985, lists 56 such species. In the Republic of Ireland, the Flora Protection Order 1987 lists 68 specially protected species. These species are all identified in the relevant species accounts in this guide (*see* 'Symbols and Abbreviations' below). Two species, the Bluebell in Britain and the Primrose in Northern Ireland, are protected against being offered for sale only. By-laws prohibiting the uprooting or picking of plants are also in operation on most statutory national and local nature reserves and National Trust properties.

In addition to the above, nine internationally rare British species are listed under the 1992 EEC Habitats Directive as being legally protected throughout the European Community: Creeping Marshwort *Apium repens*, Early Gentian *Gentianella anglica*, Fen Orchid *Liparis loeselii*, Floating Water-plantain *Luronium natans*, Killarney Fern *Trichomanes speciosum*, Lady's-slipper *Cypripedium calceolus*, Marsh Saxifrage *Saxifraga hirculus*, Shore Dock *Rumex rupestris* and Slender Naiad *Najas flexilis*.

One of the biggest threats to our native flora comes from the spread of invasive introductions, especially aquatic species. Recent examples are New Zealand Pigmyweed *Crassula helmsii*, Parrot's-feather *Myriophyllum aquaticum* and Floating Pennywort *Hydrocotyle ranunculoides*. Water Primrose *Ludwigia* *grandiflora* is spreading rapidly northwards through western Europe and has already been recorded in a few localities in England. Great care should be taken to avoid releasing such plants into the countryside as throw-outs, and if any are found in the wild they should be reported to the local Wildlife Trust.

Recording

It is important that the local Wildlife Trust, Biological Record Centre or BSBI County Recorder is told of the discovery of rare or interesting species so that appropriate steps can be taken for its protection and the find properly recorded.

Making records, whether they be of individual species or lists from specific sites, contributes significantly to our knowledge of our wild plants as well as aids their conservation. They can be sent to one of the organisations listed above together with all the relevant information, which should include your name, the date and details of the locality. The locality should include the Ordnance Survey grid reference. Since the C19th, biological recording has also been based on a system of vice-counties, the continued use of which enables us to track changes in distribution over the last 150 years. A map of the vice-counties together with the vice-county numbers can be found on page 4.

Collecting

If possible, it is generally better to try to identify an unfamiliar plant by taking the book to the plant rather than to pick the plant and take it to the book. However, there are occasions when certain identification will require a more detailed examination, and in these cases only as much of the plant as is needed should be removed. That said, an appreciation of wild plants can be fostered by the moderate collection of common species for detailed examination and appreciation, and little harm is done providing that common sense is exercised. The encouragement of a responsible familiarity with, and an interest in, the detailed structure of plants can only benefit conservation.

The Botanical Society of the British Isles (BSBI) published a *Code of Conduct for the Conservation and Enjoyment of Wild Plants* that can also be accessed on its website (www.bsbi.org.uk).

Photography

Nature photography is increasingly becoming an important and popular aspect of all areas of natural history, partly fuelled by the availability of ever more sophisticated digital technology. When photographing a particular species, the area around it should not be 'gardened' as this may unnaturally expose it or remove the support of neighbouring plants. Care should also be taken not to damage surrounding vegetation or draw attention to rare species. The well-being of the subject should always take precedence over the quality of the photograph. If the photograph is intended to aid identification, it should be remembered that several shots might be needed to illustrate all the important diagnostic characters.

How to Get Involved and Find Out More

Joining a botanical society or conservation organisation

Botanical Society of the British Isles (BSBI)
The BSBI is the leading scientific society in Britain and Ireland for the study of plant distribution and taxonomy. It publishes handbooks on identification, runs national surveys, publishes the journal *Watsonia* and newsletter *BSBI News*, and holds field meetings and conferences. www.bsbi.org.uk

Botanical Society of the **British Isles**

Plantlife
Plantlife is the conservation charity working to protect Britain's wild flowers, plants and fungi. It publishes the magazine *Plantlife*, owns and manages nature reserves, runs the 'Back from the Brink' conservation programme and involves its members in its practical conservation work. www.plantlife.org.uk

PLANTLIFE
our plants **our** planet **our** future

The Wildlife Trusts
The UK's 47 Wildlife Trusts together form the largest voluntary organisation concerned with all aspects of wildlife and the countryside. The trusts are mostly county-based, with separate bodies in the Isle of Man

THE **wildlife TRUSTS**

and Alderney. The trusts are all members of the Royal Society of Wildlife Trusts (RSWT) and between them manage 2200 nature reserves, run courses and involve members in practical conservation work. The junior branch, Wildlife Watch, has 108,000 members. www.wildlifetrusts.org

Attending courses

Field Studies Council (FSC)
The FSC runs a comprehensive series of courses on plant identification and habitats at their 13 resi-

FSC
BRINGING ENVIRONMENTAL UNDERSTANDING TO ALL

dential centres throughout the UK. These include such subjects as grasses, composites, orchids, water plants, alpines, coastal plants and how to use a key, as well as courses on painting and photography and a whole range of other natural history subjects. www.field-studies-council.org

Further reading
The standard work on the British flora is the second edition of *New Flora of the British Isles* by Clive Stace (1997), which is the most up-to-date and comprehensive account of all British species.

The BSBI publishes a series of illustrated handbooks on particular groups of plants. To date these include grasses, roses, pondweeds, umbellifers, crucifers, willows and poplars, docks and knotweeds, sedges, dandelions, starworts, fumitories and alien grasses. *Plant Crib 1998* by Tim Rich and Clive Jermy, published by the BSBI, is an indispensable aid to the identification of the more difficult plant groups.

The *New Atlas of the British and Irish Flora* by C.D. Preston, D.A. Pearman and T.D. Dines (2002) is a monumental work containing not only distribution maps of all British plants but also habitat and historical notes. Fortunately, it comes with an interactive CD that can be uploaded onto your computer.

A number of good general books on British plant life are available, but one of the best is still *Wild Flowers* by John Gilmour and Max Walters, one of the early classic volumes in the Collins New Naturalist series (No. 4), now republished as a facsimile.

See also the titles listed in the Bibliography (p.9).

Symbols and Abbreviations
Red Data Book categories:
EX = extinct (in British Isles)
EW = extinct in the wild
CR = critically endangered
EN = endangered
VU = vulnerable

* = specially protected by law:
*B = in Britain
*NI = in Northern Ireland
*R = in the Republic of Ireland
DIST. = distribution
FLS = flowering time

BI = British Isles
sp. (plural spp.) = species
ssp. (plural sspp.) = subspecies
× (as in 2×) = times (twice)
× (as in *Mentha* × *piperita*) indicates that the plant is a hybrid
N, E, S, W = points of the compass
c. (*circa*) = about
± = more or less
> = more than
< = less than
≥ = equal to or more than
≤ = equal to or less than
• = (in a key) indicates a non-British species

BIBLIOGRAPHY

Cheffings, C.M. & Farrell, L. (eds) (2005). *The Vascular Plant Red Data List for Great Britain*. Joint Nature Conservation Committee, Peterborough.

Clapham, A.R., Tutin, T.G. & Warburg, E.F. (1962). *Flora of the British Isles*. CUP, Cambridge.

Cope, T. & Gray, A. (2009) *Grasses of the British Isles*. BSBI, London.

Dony, J.G., Perring, F.H. & Rob, C.M. (1974). *English Names of Wild Flowers*. BSBI, London.

Foley, M. & Clarke, S. (2005). *Orchids of the British Isles*. Griffin Press, Maidenhead.

Fournier, P. (1977). *Les Quatre Flores de la France*. Éditions Lechevalier, Paris.

Garrard, I. & Streeter, D. (1998). *The Wild Flowers of the British Isles*. Midsummer Books, London.

Gilmour, J. & Walters, M. (2008). *Wild Flowers*. New Naturalist No. 5, facsimile edition. HarperCollins, London.

Graham, G.G. & Primavesi, A.L. (1993). *Roses of Great Britain and Ireland*. BSBI, London.

Haslam, S., Sinker, C. & Wolseley, P. (1975). British water plants. *Field Studies* **4**, 243.

Hickey, M. & King, C. (1997). *Common Families of Flowering Plants*. CUP, Cambridge.

Hubbard, C.E. (1984). *Grasses*. Penguin, Harmondsworth.

Jalas, J. & Suominen, J. (eds) (1972–2007). *Atlas Florae Europaeae*. Finnish Museum of Natural History, Helsinki.

Jermy, A.C. & Camus, J. (1991). *The Illustrated Field Guide to Ferns and Allied Plants of the British Isles*. Natural History Museum, London.

Jermy, A.C., Simpson, D.A., Foley, M.J.Y. & Porter, M.S. (2007). *Sedges of the British Isles*. BSBI, London.

Kent, D.H. (1992). *List of Vascular Plants of the British Isles*. BSBI, London.

Lambinon, J., Delvosalle, L. & Duvigneaud, J. (2004). *Nouvelle Flore de la Belgique, du Grand-Duché de Luxembourg, du Nord de la France et des Régions voisines*. Jardin botanique national de Belgique, Brussels.

Lansdown, R.V. (2008). *Water-starworts* Callitriche *of Europe*. BSBI, London.

Lousley, J.E. & Kent, D.H. (1981). *Docks and Knotweeds of the British Isles*. BSBI, London.

Meikle, R.D. (1984). *Willows and Poplars of Great Britain and Ireland*. BSBI, London.

Murphy, R.J. (2009). *Fumitories of Britain and Ireland*. BSBI, London.

Pearman, D.A. & Corner, R.W.M. (2003). *Altitudinal Limits of British and Irish Vascular Plants*. BSBI, London.

Poland, J. & Clement, E. (2009). *The Vegetative Key to the British Flora*. BSBI, London.

Preston, C.D. (1995). *Pondweeds of Great Britain and Ireland*. BSBI, London.

Preston, C.D. & Croft, J.M. (1997). *Aquatic Plants in Britain and Ireland*. Harley Books, Colchester.

Preston, C.D., Pearman, D.A. & Dines, T.D. (eds) (2002). *New Atlas of the British and Irish Flora*. OUP, Oxford.

Rich, T.C.G. (1999). List of plants endemic to the British Isles. *BSBI News* **80**, 23.

Rich, T.C.G. (2001). 'Flowering Plants' in Hawksworth, D.L. (ed.). *The Changing Wildlife of Great Britain and Ireland*. Taylor & Francis, London.

Rich, T.C.G. & Jermy, A.C. (1998). *Plant Crib 1998*. BSBI, London.

Rose, F. (1989). *Colour Identification Guide to the Grasses, Sedges, Rushes and Ferns of the British Isles and north-western Europe*. Viking, London.

Rose, F. & O'Reilly, C. (2006). *The Wild Flower Key*. Warne, London.

Sell, P. & Murrell, G. (1996–2006). *Flora of Great Britain and Ireland*. CUP, Cambridge.

Stace, C. (1997). *New Flora of the British Isles*. CUP, Cambridge.

Tutin, T.G., Heywood, V.H., Burges, N.A., Valentine, D.H., Walters, S.M. & Webb, D.A. (eds) (1964–1980). *Flora Europaea. Vols 1–5*. CUP, Cambridge.

Wigginton, M.J. (ed.) (1999). *British Red Data Books. 1. Vascular Plants*. 3rd ed. Joint Nature Conservation Committee, Peterborough.

SEEDLESS PLANTS

The horsetails, clubmosses and ferns are seedless flowerless plants that reproduce by spores. The microscopic spores are produced in tiny sacs, the *sporangia*, which are borne on fertile leaves, the *sporophylls*, which may or may not differ from the vegetative leaves. The sporophylls may be arranged in special cone-like structures.

Aerial stems jointed, hollow, longitudinally ridged. Branches whorled, ridged. Leaves small, scale-like. Sporangia arranged in apical spore-bearing cones.

Horsetails *Equisetum*

Stems branched, clothed in small simple leaves with single vein. Leaves spirally arranged or in 4 ranks. Sporangia in distinct terminal cones or in zones along stem.

Clubmosses

Submerged evergreen aquatics. Leaves smooth cylindrical, sheathing, in dense rosettes. Sporangia embedded in inner face of leaf sheaths.

Quillworts *Isoetes*

Leaves usually branched and frond-like with branched system of veins. Sporangia grouped into *sori* on underside of leaves.

Ferns

EQUISETACEAE Horsetails

Horsetails (*see* key on p.14) are perennial herbaceous plants with a branched underground rhizome that gives rise to clumps of stems. The aerial parts of the plants have a highly distinctive appearance. The stems are jointed, hollow and longitudinally ridged. Branches, if present, are whorled and ridged. The leaves, which are arranged in whorls, are small and scale-like, and are fused into sheaths that encircle the stem at the nodes. The tips of the sheaths bear a ring of apical teeth. Fertile stems, which in some species appear in spring before the vegetative stems, have apical spore-bearing cones. The number of stem ridges, the width of the central canal of the stem and details of the stem sheath teeth are important in identification. Hybrids between some species are widespread.

Great Horsetail
Equisetum telmateia

Robust deciduous perennial to 1.5 m, forming dense colonies. STEMS *c.10 mm diam. at base, whitish, with 20–40 fine ridges*. Richly branched to top of stem. Stem sheath teeth dark, fine-pointed, to 10 mm. Fertile stems separate in spring, to 25 cm, soon dying down. CONES 4–8 cm long. HABITAT Shaded hedge banks, base of sea and river cliffs, and open habitats, especially on seepage lines on damp soils. DIST. Native. Local throughout BI, rare in Scotland; lowland to 365 m. (All Europe except Scandinavia.)

Rough Horsetail, Dutch Rush
Equisetum hyemale

Evergreen perennial to 1 m, forming dense colonies. STEMS *Blue-green, rough, unbranched, with 10–30 ridges, sheaths pale with black band at top and bottom*, teeth soon withering to leave wavy upper edge to sheath. HABITAT Shaded stream and river banks, open woodland, dune slacks on damp mineral-rich soils. DIST. Native. Scattered throughout BI; to 610 m. (Most of Europe.)

Water Horsetail
Equisetum fluviatile

Deciduous perennial to 1.5 m. STEMS *Smooth, unbranched or sparsely and irregularly branched, with 10–30 obscure ridges*. Stem sheath teeth small, *black-tipped*, lacking pale margins. HABITAT Shallow waters of ponds, lakes and ditches, wet meadows on a wide variety of soils. DIST. Native. Frequent throughout BI; to 915 m. (All Europe, but rare in S.)

Branched Horsetail
Equisetum ramosissimum

Evergreen perennial to 1 m. Most branches from middle of stem, sometimes unbranched. STEMS *Slightly rough, with 8–20 ridges*. Stem sheath teeth *narrow, long, black, with narrow or absent pale border*. HABITAT Rough grassland near the sea. DIST. Probably introduced. Known in BI from 2 sites only: Lincolnshire and Somerset. (S and central Europe.)

Variegated Horsetail
Equisetum variegatum

Evergreen perennial to 60 cm. STEMS Rough, with 4–10 ridges, *prostrate to erect*, branched at base or with few single branches at each node further up stem. Sometimes unbranched. *Stem sheath with black band at base, teeth with broad pale border and black midrib*. HABITAT Open, gravelly, calcareous flushes, lake shores, dune slacks. DIST. Native. Local in N and W Britain, Ireland; to 1040 m. (N, W and central Europe.) SIMILAR SPP. Can be confused with prostrate forms of *E. palustre* (p.12), which has smooth stems and lacks black band at base of teeth.

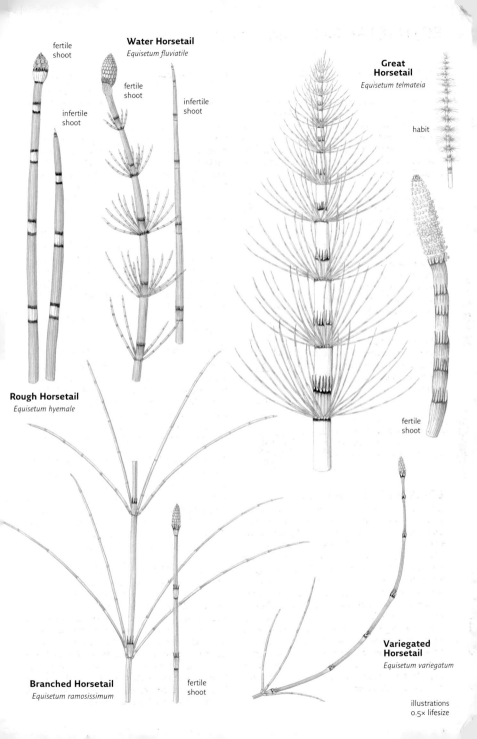

fertile
shoot

Water Horsetail
Equisetum fluviatile

**Great
Horsetail**
Equisetum telmateia

habit

fertile
shoot

infertile
shoot

infertile
shoot

infertile
shoot

Rough Horsetail
Equisetum hyemale

fertile
shoot

Branched Horsetail
Equisetum ramosissimum

fertile
shoot

**Variegated
Horsetail**
Equisetum variegatum

illustrations
0.5× lifesize

Field Horsetail   *Equisetum arvense*

Deciduous erect or prostrate perennial to 80 cm. STEMS Smooth, with 8-20 ridges. *Lowest internode of branches as long as, or longer than, adjacent stem sheath. Branches 4-angled. Stem sheath teeth with black tips, but without pale margins.* Fertile stems separate in spring, to 25 cm. CONES 1-4 cm long. HABITAT Arable land, roadsides, railway sidings, waste ground, gardens; also river banks, dune slacks, cliffs, upland flushes. DIST. Native. Common throughout BI; to 1005 m. (All Europe.) SIMILAR SPP. Can be confused with *E. palustre*, which has lowest branch internode shorter than adjacent stem sheath; and with *E. pratense*, which has rough stem and distinctive habit with drooping tips to branches.

Shady Horsetail   *Equisetum pratense*

Deciduous or evergreen erect perennial to 50 cm. STEMS *Pale green, rough, with 8-20 ridges, profusely branched, branches mostly 3-angled, drooping. Stem sheath teeth with conspicuous pale border.* HABITAT Shady stream banks and grassy slopes, usually on calcareous soils. DIST. Native. Local in Scotland, N Ireland, N England; to 915 m. (N, E and central Europe.) SIMILAR SPP. Can be confused with *E. arvense* (*see* above).

Wood Horsetail   *Equisetum sylvaticum*

Deciduous erect perennial to 80 cm, often forming large stands. STEMS Slightly rough, with 10-18 ridges. Branches pale green, drooping, *primary branches secondarily branched (the only horsetail with branched branches).* Stem sheath teeth joined along their margins into 3-6 lobes. HABITAT Open woodland, stream banks, lake margins, ditches on flushed, permanently wet, acid soils. DIST. Native. Widespread in uplands to 850 m, rare in lowlands. (All Europe except S.)

Marsh Horsetail   *Equisetum palustre*

Deciduous erect perennial to 50 cm. STEMS *Smooth, with 5-9 ridges.* Branching often irregular, branches upcurved. *Stem sheath teeth black with conspicuous pale border.* HABITAT Marshes, fens, wet meadows, dune slacks, stream and river banks, mountain flushes. DIST. Native. Throughout BI; to 945 m. (All Europe.) SIMILAR SPP. May be confused with *E. arvense* (*see* above), and with *E. variegatum* when growing in upland flushes (*see* p.10).

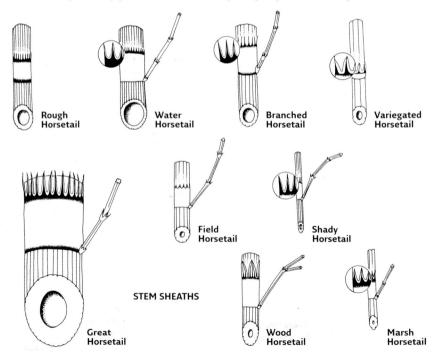

Rough Horsetail

Water Horsetail

Branched Horsetail

Variegated Horsetail

Great Horsetail

STEM SHEATHS

Field Horsetail

Shady Horsetail

Wood Horsetail

Marsh Horsetail

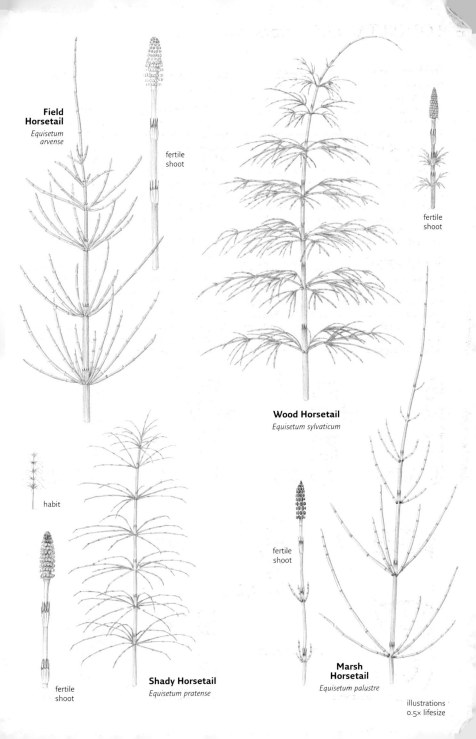

Field Horsetail
Equisetum arvense

fertile shoot

Wood Horsetail

Equisetum sylvaticum

fertile shoot

habit

fertile shoot

Shady Horsetail

Equisetum pratense

fertile shoot

Marsh Horsetail

Equisetum palustre

illustrations
0.5× lifesize

if	then
1 ▷ Stems green, branched or unbranched, with or without a cone at the tip. If stem whitish, then without a cone at the tip (summer)	Go to ▷ **2**
▷ Stems unbranched, whitish with a cone at the tip (spring)	Go to ▷ **11**
2 ▷ Stem branched	Go to ▷ **3**
▷ Stem unbranched	Go to ▷ **10**
3 ▷ Main branches with whorls of secondary branches, teeth of stem sheaths 3–6, broad and blunt	*Equisetum sylvaticum* (p.12)
▷ Main branches not secondarily branched	Go to ▷ **4**
4 ▷ Plant robust to 1.5 m, stem whitish, *c*.10 mm diam. at base, with 20–40 fine grooves.	*Equisetum telmateia* (p.10)
▷ Stem green, ≤7 mm diam.	Go to ▷ **5**
5 ▷ Stem smooth, finely ribbed, ridges not prominent, Central hollow large so stem 'gives' when squeezed	*Equisetum fluviatile* (p.10)
▷ Stem prominently ridged, stem firm when squeezed	Go to ▷ **6**
6 ▷ Lowest internode of branches as long as or longer than adjacent stem sheath	Go to ▷ **7**
▷ Lowest internode of branches shorter than adjacent stem sheath	Go to ▷ **8**
7 ▷ Branches spreading, usually 4-angled, teeth of stem sheath without pale border	*Equisetum arvense* (p.12)
▷ Branches usually drooping at tip, most 3-angled, teeth of stem sheath with pale border	*Equisetum pratense* (p.12)
8 ▷ Stem with 4–10 grooves, teeth of stem sheaths with distinct pale border	Go to ▷ **9**
▷ Stem with 8–20 grooves, pale border of stem sheath teeth narrow or absent	*Equisetum ramosissimum* (p.10)
9 ▷ Stem smooth, branched throughout its length, ridges rounded (note detail of sheath teeth)	*Equisetum palustre* (p.12)
▷ Stem rough, branched at base or with single branches at each node (note detail of sheath teeth)	*Equisetum variegatum* (p.10)
10 ▷ Stems hard, rough, glaucous; sheath with black band at top and bottom, teeth withering as stems mature	*Equisetum hyemale* (p.10)
▷ Stems smooth, green; sheaths without black bands, teeth sharply pointed	*Equisetum fluviatile* (p.10)

node and internode

if	**then**
11 ▷ Leaf sheaths with 20–30 teeth, cones 4–8 cm	*Equisetum telmateia* (p.10)
▷ Leaf sheaths with <20 teeth, cones 1–4 cm	*Equisetum arvense* (p.012)

Key to Lycopodiaceae and Selaginellaceae
Clubmosses and Lesser Clubmoss

if	**then**
1 ▷ Stems ± erect, branched, branches ± of equal length; no separate cones, sporophylls in distinct zones on main stem	*Huperzia selago* (p.16)
▷ Stems prostrate and rooting	Go to ▷ **2**
2 ▷ Leaves spirally arranged, all similar	Go to ▷ **3**
▷ Leaves in 4 ranks, of 2 kinds	*Diphasiastrum alpinum*, *Diphasiastrum complanatum* (p.16)
3 ▷ Sporophylls in distinct cones at apex of stems	Go to ▷ **4**
▷ Sporophylls not forming distinct cones, but in zones along stem	Go to ▷ **5**
4 ▷ Cones stalked, stalks often branched; leaves with long white hair points	*Lycopodium clavatum* (p.16)
▷ Cones sessile; leaves acute, without long white hair points	*Lycopodium annotinum* (p.16)
5 ▷ Fertile shoots erect in ill-defined cones; leaves green, without teeth	*Lycopodiella inundata* (p.16)
▷ Plant delicate; leaves yellow-green, toothed (very moss-like)	*Selaginella selaginoides* (p.16)

LYCOPODIACEAE Clubmosses

The clubmosses (*see* key on p.15) are herbaceous spore-producing plants, with branching stems clothed in small, simple leaves that have a single midrib. The leaves are either spirally arranged or in 4 ranks. The sporangia are borne at the base of fertile leaves (sporophylls), which may be similar to or different from the sterile leaves and arranged either in distinct terminal cones or in zones on the stems.

The clubmosses are the survivors of an ancient group of plants, some of which formed trees 35 m tall during the Carboniferous period 320 million years ago, when they dominated the coal-forming swamps.

Fir Clubmoss   *Huperzia selago*

Erect evergreen perennial to 25 cm. STEMS *Forked to give branches of ± equal length*, densely clothed with spirally arranged leaves. LEAVES Dark green, minutely toothed. Small bud-like plantlets sometimes form in axils. CONES *No separate cones*; yellow sporangia borne in axils of leaves in distinct zones on stem. HABITAT Montane rocky habitats, upland grassland, moors and bogs. DIST. Native. Widespread in uplands; to 1310 m. (All Europe except Mediterranean.)

Stag's-horn Clubmoss   *Lycopodium clavatum*

Much-branched creeping evergreen perennial, rooting at nodes. STEMS Up to 100 cm long, with dense, spirally arranged leaves. LEAVES *3–7 mm long, with long, white hair points*. CONES Number 1–3, 20–50 mm long on long stalks, stalks with scale-like leaves. HABITAT Heaths, moors and mountain grassland on acid or base-rich soils. DIST. Native. Widespread in Scotland, Wales; rare and local elsewhere. To 840 m. (All Europe except Mediterranean.)

Interrupted Clubmoss   *Lycopodium annotinum*

Branched creeping evergreen perennial to 100 cm. STEMS Branches widely spaced, *branch leaves produced at end of season shorter, giving 'interrupted' appearance*. LEAVES *4–6 mm long, sharply pointed*, denser on branches than on main stem. CONES 15–30 mm long, sessile, solitary. HABITAT Mountain moorland and old pine forest among heather and bilberry. DIST. Native. Scottish Highlands; to 1000 m. (N, E and central Europe.)

Marsh Clubmoss   *Lycopodiella inundata* EN. *(NI)

Sparsely branched, creeping evergreen perennial to 5–20 cm. STEMS *Erect fertile branches to 10 cm.* LEAVES 4–6 mm long, spirally arranged but tips curving upwards. CONES 10–30 mm long, *solitary, sporophylls similar to foliage leaves.* HABITAT Open, wet, peaty or sandy lake and pond margins, wet heaths, peat cuttings, tracksides. DIST. Native. Very local in S and E Britain, especially Dorset and New Forest. (W Europe, S Scandinavia.)

Alpine Clubmoss   *Diphasiastrum alpinum*

Creeping, much-branched evergreen perennial to 100 cm. STEMS *Main stem buried in surface litter.* Branches densely tufted, sub-erect to 10 cm. Main branches slightly flattened, divided repeatedly. LEAVES *Glaucous, 2–4 mm long, strongly 4-ranked.* Ventral leaves with short stalks. CONES 1–2 cm long, solitary, sessile at ends of branches. HABITAT Mountain moorland, grassland on shallow, acid, moist peaty soils. DIST. Native. N Wales, Scotland; rare in N England, Ireland. (Arctic and alpine Europe.)

Issler's Clubmoss   *Diphasiastrum complanatum*

Similar to *D. alpinum* (*see* above), *but main stem above ground, foliage yellow-green not glaucous*, upright shoots more flattened and fan-like, ventral leaves without a petiole, and cones stalked. HABITAT Dwarf shrub heath and old pine forest. DIST. Native. British plant is probably ssp. *issleri*. Very rare, at a few isolated sites in Scottish Highlands; to 960 m. (N and central Europe.)

SELAGINELLACEAE Lesser Clubmoss

See key on p.15.

Lesser Clubmoss   *Selaginella selaginoides*

Small, prostrate, evergreen *moss-like perennial*. STEMS Fertile shoots erect, 20–60 mm long. LEAVES *Small, thin*, acute, 2–3 mm, *margins with spiny teeth.* CONES Sessile, 15–20 mm, solitary. HABITAT Short vegetation of moist, open, base-rich fens, mires, wet upland grassland, mountain flushes and dune slacks. DIST. Native. N England, Scotland, N Wales, Ireland; to 1065 m. (N and alpine Europe.)

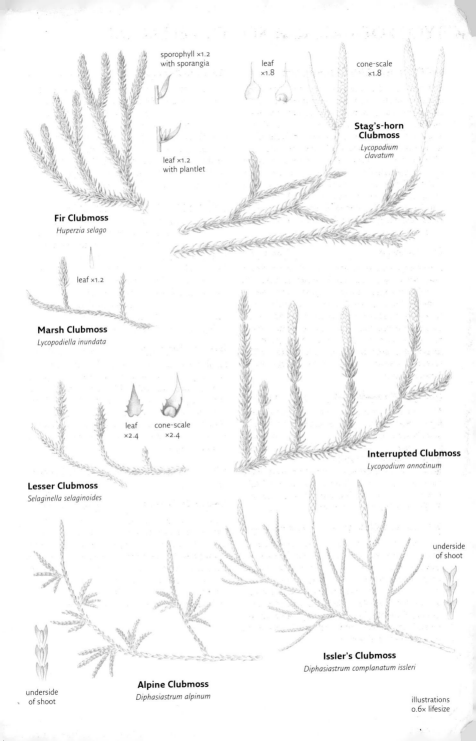

sporophyll ×1.2
with sporangia

leaf
×1.8

cone-scale
×1.8

**Stag's-horn
Clubmoss**
*Lycopodium
clavatum*

leaf ×1.2
with plantlet

Fir Clubmoss
Huperzia selago

leaf ×1.2

Marsh Clubmoss
Lycopodiella inundata

leaf
×2.4

cone-scale
×2.4

Lesser Clubmoss
Selaginella selaginoides

Interrupted Clubmoss
Lycopodium annotinum

underside
of shoot

underside
of shoot

Issler's Clubmoss
Diphasiastrum complanatum issleri

Alpine Clubmoss
Diphasiastrum alpinum

illustrations
0.6× lifesize

ISOETACEAE Quillworts

The quillworts, *Isoetes*, are submerged evergreen aquatics or plants of seasonally wet habitats, with a dense rosette of smooth, cylindrical, sheathing leaves that have 4 longitudinal air canals that can be seen in a cut section. Although closely related to the clubmosses, they bear no superficial resemblance to them, but their spores, which are of 2 kinds, are embedded on the inner face of the leaf sheath.

Quillwort
Isoetes lacustris

Submerged evergreen aquatic. LEAVES *Rosette of smooth, cylindrical, sheathing leaves, rather rigid, erect, remaining stiff when taken out of water*, 10-25 cm long × 2-5 mm wide, *parallel-sided for much of their length before finally tapering to asymmetric point*; with 4 longitudinal air canals visible in section. HABITAT Clear, nutrient-poor upland lakes, tarns; often forms extensive lawns. Usually recorded washed up on shore. DIST. Native. Widespread in Scotland to 850 m, also NW England, N Wales; scattered in Ireland. (Scandinavia, scattered in W Europe.)

Spring Quillwort
Isoetes echinospora

Similar to *I. lacustris*, but *leaves not so rigidly erect, rather spreading, giving plant a starfish-like appearance, and tapering from base to tip*. Only certain way to distinguish them is on character of megaspores, which are embedded in inner face of leaf sheath: *megaspores of* I. lacustris *have short, blunt tubercles; those of* I. echinospora *are spiny* (a ×20 lens is needed for this). HABITAT Similar to *I. lacustris* but usually in shallower water. DIST. Native. Similar to *I. lacustris* but much scarcer. (Scandinavia, scattered in W Europe.)

Land Quillwort
Isoetes histrix VU.

Terrestrial rosette-forming plant. LEAVES *Develop very early in year, Feb-Mar, and wither by end of Apr; leaf bases persistent, blackish; leaves short*, 2-10 cm long, keeled, with single longitudinal air canal. HABITAT Seasonally wet patches of bare acid soils, footpaths. DIST. Native. Very rare. SW Cornwall, Channel Is. (SW Europe, Mediterranean.)

FERNS

Herbaceous, spore-producing plants, which differ from the horsetails and clubmosses in having usually branched, frond-like leaves with a branched system of veins (*see key on p.20-23*). The spores are produced in microscopic spherical sacs (sporangia), which are borne in groups (sori, singular sorus), usually on the underside of the leaf. The sori may or may not have a protective covering, the indusium. Details

of the sori and the indusium are often essential to identification, but these can usually be seen with the naked eye or at least with a ×10 lens. Also important are the degree of branching and lobing of the leaves, and whether the fertile leaves (sporophylls) are different from the vegetative leaves. In some ferns the leaves are produced as a tuft at the apex of a short rhizome; in others, the leaves arise singly from an elongated underground rhizome.

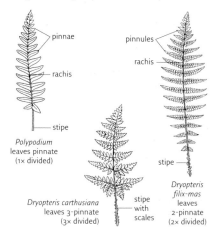

Polypodium leaves pinnate (1× divided)

Dryopteris carthusiana leaves 3-pinnate (3× divided)

stipe with scales

Dryopteris filix-mas leaves 2-pinnate (2× divided)

OPHIOGLOSSACEAE
Adder's-tongues

Adder's-tongue
Ophioglossum vulgatum

Rhizomatous deciduous *fern to 30 cm.* LEAVES Appear in spring, borne singly, each *with erect petiole and a simple unbranched flat blade*, 4-12 cm; *fertile leaves an unbranched bladeless spike with 10-40 sporangia*, ripening May-Aug. DIST. Native. Throughout BI but scarce in N Scotland, Ireland; to 660 m. HABITAT Old meadows, pastures, fens, open woods, dunes and dune slacks, on mildly acid to calcareous soils. (W and central Europe, scattered elsewhere.)

Small Adder's-tongue
Ophioglossum azoricum

Similar to *O. vulgatum* but smaller, to 8 cm. LEAVES *Usually arise in pairs*, blade slightly convex and becoming reflexed, almost horizontal, 3-3.5 cm; *fertile spikes with 4-13 sporangia*. HABITAT Short, grazed, cliff-top grassland, dune slacks; damp, grazed grassland in New Forest. DIST. Native. Very local, scattered around S and W coast of Britain and NW Ireland. (W Europe, scattered.)

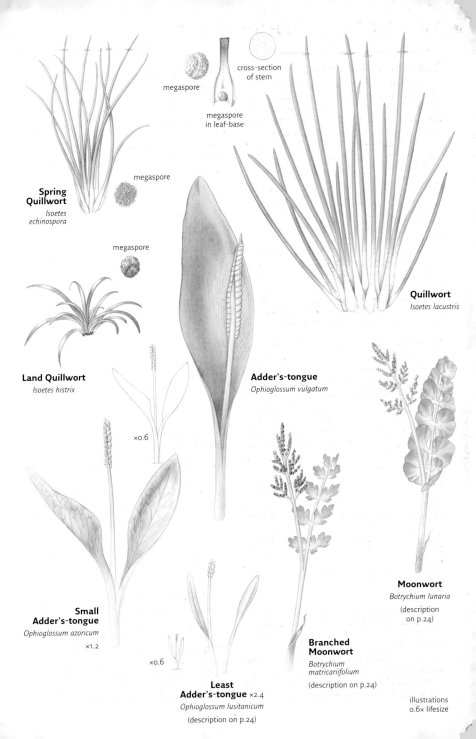

megaspore

cross-section
of stem

megaspore
in leaf-base

**Spring
Quillwort**
*Isoetes
echinospora*

megaspore

megaspore

Quillwort
Isoetes lacustris

Land Quillwort
Isoetes histrix

×0.6

Adder's-tongue
Ophioglossum vulgatum

Moonwort
Botrychium lunaria
(description
on p.24)

**Small
Adder's-tongue**
Ophioglossum azoricum
×1.2

×0.6

**Branched
Moonwort**
*Botrychium
matricariifolium*
(description on p.24)

**Least
Adder's-tongue** ×2.4
Ophioglossum lusitanicum
(description on p.24)

illustrations
0.6× lifesize

if	then

Un-fernlike ferns

A few ferns do not look like ferns at all and can easily be mistaken for some other kind of plant.

Aquatic plants or plants growing rooted in water

1
▷ Plant free-floating; leaves very small, to 2.5 mm, in 2 rows on upperside of much-branched stem, turning red at end of season — ***Azolla filiculoides*** (p.10)
▷ Plant rooted in shallow water, sometimes submerged — Go to ▷ **2**

2
▷ Leaves smooth, tubular, filiform, rather rush-like but with the coiled tip typical of young fern leaves — ***Pilularia globulifera*** (p.24)
▷ Leaves with 4 terminal leaflets in the form of a cross (quadrifoliate) — ***Marsilia quadrifolia*** • (p.24)

Terrestrial plants
▷ Small ferns; leaves in 2 parts, with a sterile blade at the base attached to a terminal fertile portion

▷ Leaf blade ovate to lanceolate, undivided (looks like leaf of a flowering plant), fertile portion unbranched — ***Ophioglossum vulgatum*** (p.18)
▷ Leaf blade pinnate, pinnae fan-shaped, fertile portion branched — ***Botrychium*** (p.18)

Typical ferns

1
▷ Leaves thin, translucent (1 cell thick), arising singly from thin, wiry rhizomes; indusia flask-like from edge of pinnules — ***Hymenophyllum, Trichomanes*** (p.26)
▷ Plant not like this — Go to ▷ **2**

2
▷ Large, robust, tufted fern; leaves to 300 cm, 2-pinnate; outer leaves sterile; inner leaves with sterile pinnae at base, upper pinnae fertile, producing brown plume-like heads when mature — ***Osmunda regalis*** (p.24)
▷ Plant not like this — Go to ▷ **3**

3
▷ Leaves simple, undivided, 10–60 cm; sori linear — ***Phyllitis scolopendrium*** (p.28)
▷ Leaves irregularly, sparsely forked into narrow, linear segments — ***Asplenium septentrionale*** (p.30)
▷ Leaves divided, 1-, 2- or 3-pinnate — Go to ▷ **4**

4
▷ Leaves pinnate (once divided) — Go to ▷ **5**
▷ Leaves 2–3-pinnate (more than once divided) — Go to ▷ **9**

Phyllitis scolopendrium leaves simple (undivided)

	if	**then**
5	▷ Undersurface of leaf covered by rust-brown scales (silvery when young)	*Ceterach officinarum* (p.30)
	▷ Undersurface of leaf not covered by rust-coloured scales	Go to ▷ **6**
6	▷ Leaves thick, rigid; margins of pinnules with sharp, spiny teeth	*Polystichum lonchitis* (p.40)
	▷ Pinnules without spiny teeth	Go to ▷ **7**
7	▷ Leaves arising at intervals from creeping rhizome	*Polypodium* (p.26)
	▷ Leaves clustered, tuft-forming	Go to ▷ **8**
8	▷ Leaf blade narrowly lanceolate, 10–75 cm; leaves of 2 kinds; pinnae of fertile leaves narrower than those of vegetative leaves; sori in linear row on either side of midrib	*Blechnum spicant* (p.40)
	▷ Vegetative and fertile leaves similar; sori not forming a continuous linear row on either side of midrib	*Asplenium* (p.30)
9	▷ Leaves 2-pinnate, in dense, shuttlecock-like tufts, of 2 kinds; vegetative leaves up to 140 cm long; fertile leaves shorter, pinnae narrow and covered by sori	*Matteuccia struthiopteris* (p.34)
	▷ Plant not like this	Go to ▷ **10**
10	▷ Sori on margin of undersurface of leaf and covered by indusium-like inrolled margin of the leaf	Go to ▷ **11**
	▷ Sori on lower surface of leaf but not covered by inrolled margin of leaf	Go to ▷ **12**
11	▷ Leaves arising individually from underground rhizome, large, to 3 m (including petiole), 3-pinnate, blade triangular in outline; sori continuous around underside of leaf margin	*Pteridium aquilinum* (p.28)
	▷ Plant tufted, to 30 cm; leaves distinctly parsley-like, of 2 sorts; fertile leaves longer and with narrower lobes than vegetative leaves	*Cryptogramma crispa* (p.24)
	▷ Vegetative and fertile leaves similar, petiole and rachis shining black, lobes fan- or wedge-shaped	*Adiantum capillus-veneris* (p.24)
12	▷ Slender annual fern; leaves soft-textured, usually <10 cm; fertile leaves longer than vegetative leaves; sporangia along veins of leaf lobes, indusium absent (Jersey only)	*Anogramma leptophylla* (p.24)
	▷ Plant not like this, perennial	Go to ▷ **13**
13	▷ Sori linear or oblong	Go to ▷ **14**
	▷ Sori ± round	Go to ▷ **15**

CONTINUED OVERLEAF

if	then

14
▷ Sori linear to oblong, lower margin of indusium straight; plant usually winter-green — ***Asplenium*** (p.30)
▷ Sori oblong, lower margin of indusium bent in middle (J-shaped); leaves dying back in winter — ***Athyrium filix-femina*** (p.32)

15
▷ Leaves appearing singly from creeping underground rhizome — Go to ▷ **16**
▷ Plant tufted; leaves in a crown — Go to ▷ **19**

16
▷ Leaves 2-pinnate (twice divided) — Go to ▷ **17**
▷ Leaves 3-pinnate — Go to ▷ **18**

17
▷ Lowest pair of pinnae deflexed, bent back out of plane of rest of leaf, lowest 2 pairs the longest; indusium absent — ***Phegopteris connectilis*** (p.28)
▷ Lowest pair of pinnae not bent back, longest pair towards middle of leaf; indusium present — ***Thelypteris palustris*** (p.28)

18
▷ Indusium absent — ***Gymnocarpium*** (p.34)
▷ Indusium present — ***Cystopteris montana*** (p.34)

19
▷ Teeth of pinnules spine-tipped; indusium peltate (round and stalked from middle) — ***Polystichum*** (p.40)
▷ Teeth of pinnules not spine-tipped; indusium not peltate — Go to ▷ **20**

20
▷ Small, rare alpine ferns; leaves ≥10 cm, petiole with joint close to base; indusium consisting of ring of hairs or narrow scales — ***Woodsia*** (p.34)
▷ Petiole without a joint; indusium not consisting of ring of hairs — Go to ▷ **21**

21
▷ Small ferns; leaves ≤25 cm, petiole ± without scales; indusium ovoid, flap-like — ***Cystopteris*** (p.34)
▷ Robust ferns; petioles usually with numerous scales; indusium kidney-shaped or absent — Go to ▷ **22**

22
▷ Indusium absent or vestigial — Go to ▷ **23**
▷ Indusium kidney-shaped, clearly visible — ***Dryopteris*** (p.36–38)

23
▷ Petiole very short, pinnae decreasing markedly in length to base of blade, pinnules ± entire; plant with lemon-like smell when crushed — ***Oreopteris limbosperma*** (p.28)
▷ Plant not like this; pinnules deeply toothed; plant not lemon-scented (Scottish mountains) — ***Athyrium*** (p.32)

Key to Male-ferns and Buckler-ferns *Dryopteris*

kidney-shaped indusium

pinnule
sorus without indusium

fern sori

		if	**then**
1	▷	Leaves ± 2-pinnate (1-pinnate with deeply lobed pinnae)	Go to ▷ **2**
	▷	Leaves 3-pinnate (2-pinnate with deeply lobed pinnae or 3-pinnate)	Go to ▷ **6**
2	▷	Leaves of 2 sorts, fertile leaves longer and more erect, held ± at 90° to plane of leaf (very rare, fens)	*D. cristata* (p.38)
	▷	Leaves green, not glandular (except on indusium)	Go to ▷ **4**
3	▷	Leaves dull green, covered by minute yellow glands on both surfaces	*D. submontana* (p.36)
	▷	Leaves green, not glandular (except on indusium)	Go to ▷ **4**
4	▷	Junction of pinnae and rachis with dark blotch below; base of stipe with dense golden-brown scales	*D. affinis* (p.36)
	▷	Junction of pinnae and rachis without dark blotch	Go to ▷ **5**
5	▷	Margins of pinnules flat, teeth pointing forward; indusium without glands, edges spreading and not tucked under	*D. filix-mas* (p.36)
	▷	Margins of pinnules turned up, giving a 'crisped' appearance, teeth blunt, divergent; indusium glandular, edges tucked under (mountains)	*D. oreades* (p.36)
6	▷	Leaves dull green, both surfaces densely covered by yellow glands	*D. submontana* (p.36)
	▷	Leaves not dull green, not glandular or if glandular only minutely so	Go to ▷ **7**
7	▷	Edges of pinnules turned up, giving leaf a 'crisped' parsley-like appearance, with minute glands producing hay-like scent when crushed; stipe dark purplish, scales pale brown	*D. aemula* (p.38)
	▷	Tips of pinnules flat or convex from above	Go to ▷ **8**
8	▷	Leaves ± triangular in outline, lower part of leaf 3-pinnate; scales at base of stipe pale with dark centre or mid-brown with faint darker central stripe	Go to ▷ **9**
	▷	Leaves narrowly lanceolate in outline, lower part of leaf 2-pinnate with deeply lobed pinnae; scales at base of stipe uniformly pale brown	*D. carthusiana* (p.38)
9	▷	Edges of pinnules turning down; stipe *c.⅓* length of leaf (common)	*D. dilatata* (p.38)
	▷	Pinnules flat; stipe *c.¼* length of leaf (mountains)	*D. expansa* (p.38)

(See main text for detailed differences between these two species.)

Least Adder's-tongue
Ophioglossum lusitanicum VU. *(B)

[*See* illustration p.20.] Similar to *O. vulgatum* but tiny, *1–1.5 cm tall*. LEAVES *Usually 2, appearing in autumn and dying back in spring, blade to 4 mm long, reflexed, often pressed* to ground; *fertile spike with 3–8 pairs sporangia*, ripening Jan–Mar. HABITAT Exposed, open, peaty or sandy acid grassland on S- and SW-facing coastal cliffs or rocks. DIST. Native. Very rare. Scilly Is (St Agnes), Channel Is (Guernsey). (SW Europe, Mediterranean.)

Moonwort
Botrychium lunaria

[*See* illustration p.20.] Rhizomatous deciduous fern to 25 cm. LEAVES *Sterile leaves borne singly, erect, pinnate, with 4–8 pairs opposite, fan-shaped, bluntly toothed leaflets*; *fertile blade branched*, 1–5 cm, longer than sterile blade. HABITAT Dry calcareous grassland, sand-dunes, rock ledges. DIST. Native. Throughout BI, but rare in E and SE Britain and in Ireland; to 1065 m. Declining. (Most of Europe except SW.)

Branched Moonwort
Botrychium matricariifolium

[*See* illustration p.20.] Similar to *B. lunaria*, but *blade bi-pinnate*, and leaflets with midrib. HABITAT Sandy grasslands. DIST. *Not BI*. (N and central Europe.)

MARSILEACEAE Pillwort family

Pillwort
Pilularia globulifera *(NI, R)

Very unfern-like fern that superficially might easily be mistaken for a rush. Small, *aquatic*, with long, creeping rhizomes. LEAVES *Smooth, erect, slender, cylindrical, unbranched*, 3–15 cm, tips spirally coiled in normal fern-like manner; produced singly by rhizomes but close together, so plants often form extensive 'lawns'. Sporangia borne in short-stalked, hairy, spherical structures (the 'pills'), *c*.3 mm across, at base of leaves. HABITAT Shallow margins of acid pools, lakes, reservoirs, slow-flowing rivers; often poached by animals. DIST. Native. Throughout BI, but rare and declining; to 450 m. (W Europe.)

Clover Fern
Marsilea quadrifolia

Aquatic fern with same habit as *Pilularia*. LEAVES *Long-stalked*, 7–20 cm, *with 4 apical wedge-shaped leaflets*, 1–2 cm. HABITAT Periodically flooded shallow habitats, muddy pools, water meadows. DIST. *Not BI*. (S, W and central Europe; rare.)

OSMUNDACEAE Royal ferns

Royal Fern
Osmunda regalis

Tall, handsome, robust, clump-forming rhizomatous fern, dying down in winter. LEAVES To 300 cm, outer sterile, inner fertile; sterile leaves 2-pinnate, pinnae with 5–13 pairs of pinnules, 2–6.5 cm; fertile leaves with pinnules at base, without pinnules above, plume-like, sporangia massed along frond branches. HABITAT Wet woodlands, fen carr, lake shores, riverbanks. Formerly much collected for gardens, so sometimes occurs as garden escape. DIST. Native. Throughout BI but mostly in W. (W and S Europe.)

ADIANTACEAE Maidenhair ferns

Maidenhair Fern
Adiantum capillus-veneris

Delicate fern with creeping rhizomes. LEAVES Fronds erect or pendulous, all alike, 6–30 cm, 2–3-pinnate, *petiole shining black, pinnules wide-spaced on slender black stalks, 5–15 mm, fan-shaped, without midrib*; sori borne on reflexed margins of fertile pinnules. HABITAT Damp, sheltered crevices on calcareous coastal cliffs; grikes in limestone pavements (W Ireland). Naturalised as an escape from cultivation in warm, damp, sheltered sites inland. DIST. Native. Rare. SW England, S Wales, W Ireland. (SW and S Europe.)

Jersey Fern
Anogramma leptophylla

Small annual fern with short rhizome. LEAVES Few, yellow-green; outer sterile leaves to 15 cm including petiole, pinnate, pinnae *c*.1 cm long, deeply and repeatedly lobed; *inner leaves fertile but not very different from sterile ones*; sori linear, along marginal veins, coalescing at maturity. HABITAT Well-drained, steep lanesides, hedge banks. DIST. Very rare. Channel Is (Jersey). (SW Europe, Mediterranean.)

Parsley Fern
Cryptogramma crispa *(R)

Densely tufted *'parsley-like' fern* with short rhizome. LEAVES *Sterile and fertile leaves differ*: sterile leaves 2–3-pinnate, to 20 cm, ultimate segments wedge-shaped; fertile leaves longer, 10–30 cm, 3–4-pinnate, ultimate segments linear, margins rolled under to protect sori. HABITAT Steep, well-drained scree on acid soils. DIST. Native. Widely distributed in N England, Wales, Scotland; rare in Ireland. To 1280 m. (Scandinavia, mts of S Europe.)

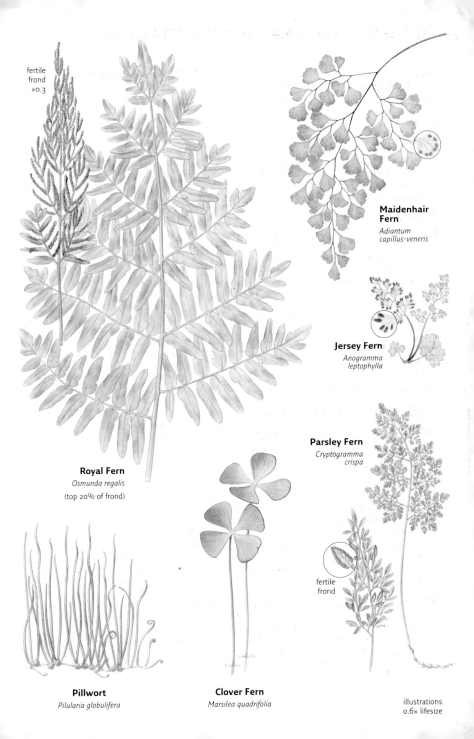

fertile
frond
×0.3

**Maidenhair
Fern**

*Adiantum
capillus-veneris*

Jersey Fern

*Anogramma
leptophylla*

Parsley Fern

*Cryptogramma
crispa*

Royal Fern

Osmunda regalis

(top 20% of frond)

fertile
frond

Pillwort

Pilularia globulifera

Clover Fern

Marsilea quadrifolia

illustrations
0.6× lifesize

HYMENOPHYLLACEAE Filmy-ferns

Small to medium-sized evergreen ferns with thin (only 1 cell thick) dark green translucent leaves produced at intervals on long, thin, creeping, wiry rhizomes. Grow in large colonies in damp, shaded, mossy stream ravines and on rocks and tree boles where humidity is constantly high, and are characteristic of oceanic climate of W Britain and Ireland. Sori are produced in flask-like or 2-valved indusium at tips of frond.

Killarney Fern — *Trichomanes speciosum* *(B, NI, R)

Rhizome covered with blackish hairs. LEAVES Dark green, 7–35 cm, irregularly 2–3-pinnately branched, petiole *c.⅓* length of leaf, upper part and rachis winged; *indusium flask-like without free lobes and with receptacle protruding as a bristle as sporangia mature.* HABITAT Damp, shaded, acid rocks, ravines with constantly running water. DIST. Native. Extreme W Britain, W Ireland. Very rare. (Brittany, N Spain, Madeira, Azores.) COMMENTS Uniquely, gametophyte sexual generation has more extensive range than sporophyte fern plant in N and W Britain and the Weald of SE England, where it grows in similar places and reproduces vegetatively. It resembles a filamentous green alga but needs microscopic examination for identification.

Tunbridge Filmy-fern — *Hymenophyllum tunbrigense*

Small moss-like fern, forming extensive colonies. LEAVES 2.5–8 cm, ± evenly divided on each side of rachis, main pinnae with 5–11 segments, ultimate segments flat, *vein ceasing just below tip; indusium not projecting from plane of leaf, mouth* (rim) *toothed.* HABITAT Damp, shaded stream ravines, mossy rocks, tree boles. DIST. Native. Very rare. Extreme W Britain, W Ireland; also in suitable habitats in the Weald of SE England. To 760 m. (W France, N Spain, Madeira, Azores.)

Wilson's Filmy-fern — *Hymenophyllum wilsonii*

Similar to *H. tunbrigense*. LEAVES Narrower than *H. tunbrigense*, more divided on 1 side, main pinnae with 3–5 segments, ultimate segments recurved, *vein reaching tip; indusium projecting somewhat from plane of leaf, mouth* (rim) *not toothed.* HABITAT Similar to *H. tunbrigense*. DIST. Native. Similar to *H. tunbrigense* but more frequent, especially in W Scotland; absent SE England. To 1005 m. (Norway, Brittany, Madeira, Azores.)

POLYPODIACEAE Polypodies

Evergreen ferns, usually forming large colonies on hedge banks, cliffs, old walls and dunes, and as epiphytes on trees. Distinguished by usually ± pinnate leaves, produced singly on creeping rhizomes. There are 3 closely related species in the BI and certain identification is not really possible without microscopic examination of the sporangia. The situation is made more complicated by the fact that all 3 hybridise with each other. However, they do differ in more observable field characters, summarised below.

Polypody — *Polypodium vulgare*

LEAVES Frond rather narrow, ± parallel-sided, pinnae on main part of frond ± same length, margins of pinnae not, or hardly, toothed, rounded at tip, lowest pair not inflexed (bent inwards towards rachis), young fronds produced in early summer; rhizome scales acute but without long tip; sori round when young, spores ripening (i.e. sori appear mature) in summer. HABITAT Hedge banks, walls, rock outcrops, on well-drained acid soils; also occurs as an epiphyte in W Britain. DIST. Native. Common throughout BI. (All Europe.)

Intermediate Polypody — *Polypodium interjectum*

LEAVES Frond ovate-lanceolate, longest pinnae ⅓–½ distance from base, rounded or tapered to tip, and obscurely to deeply toothed, lowest pair slightly inflexed, young fronds produced in late summer and autumn; rhizome scales acute and long-pointed; sori oval when young, spores ripening summer-autumn. DIST. Native. Throughout BI but scarce in NE England and N Scotland. HABITAT Similar to *P. vulgare* but prefers less acid conditions; also on coastal dunes.

Southern Polypody — *Polypodium cambricum*

LEAVES Frond almost triangular, with lowest pinnae hardly shorter than those above, usually distinctly inflexed, longest pinnae usually tapered to tip, toothed, young fronds produced in autumn to winter; rhizome scales with long, pointed, flexuous tip; sori oval, produced on upper ⅔ of leaf, spores ripening early spring. HABITAT Well-drained base-rich rocks, limestone cliffs, old mortared walls, quarries. DIST. Native. W Britain, Ireland; scattered in S England. Rather local. (W and S Europe.)

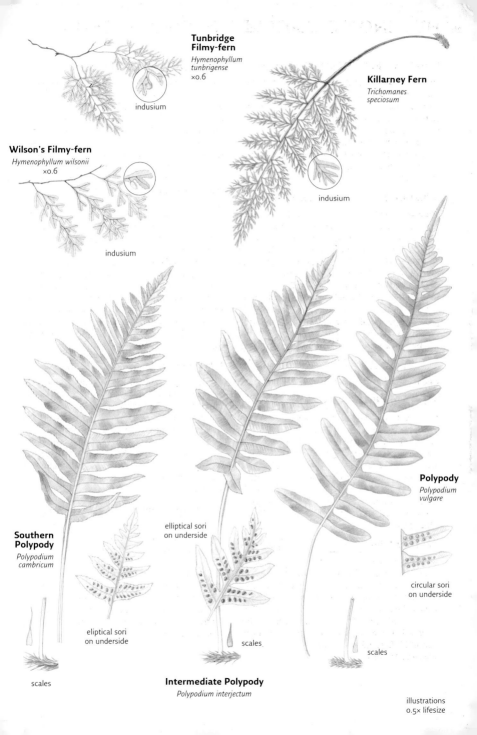

Tunbridge Filmy-fern
Hymenophyllum tunbrigense
×0.6

indusium

Killarney Fern
Trichomanes speciosum

indusium

Wilson's Filmy-fern
Hymenophyllum wilsonii
×0.6

indusium

indusium

Polypody
Polypodium vulgare

elliptical sori
on underside

circular sori
on underside

Southern Polypody
Polypodium cambricum

eliptical sori
on underside

scales

scales

Intermediate Polypody
Polypodium interjectum

scales

illustrations
0.5× lifesize

DENNSTAEDTIACEAE Bracken family

Bracken
Pteridium aquilinum

Vigorous, robust, long-lived rhizomatous fern, forming extensive stands. LEAVES Fronds deciduous, produced singly, tall, 1–2.5 m or more long, 2–3-pinnate, tough, leathery in exposed situations, pinnules linear-lanceolate, ultimate segments to 15 mm long, margins inrolled, densely hairy beneath; sori marginal and continuous round whole pinnule. HABITAT Moorland, hill pasture, heathlands, deciduous woodland, on well-drained acid (rarely basic) soils. Particularly dominant and aggressive on deep loams and abandoned agricultural land. DIST. Native. Ubiquitous throughout BI; to 585 m. (All Europe except extreme N.)

THELYPTERIDACEAE Marsh fern family

Marsh Fern
Thelypteris palustris

LEAVES *Produced singly on long, creeping rhizome,* well spaced, dying down in winter; pale green, rather thin-textured, *twice divided* (pinnate, pinnae divided almost to rachis); sterile leaves (appearing in spring) to 80 cm, fertile leaves (appearing early summer) to 150 cm; margins of pinnules rolled under, pinnules not toothed; indusium small, round or kidney-shaped. HABITAT Base-rich fens, fen carr, fen woodland. DIST. Native. Throughout BI except Scotland; to 335 m. Very local; scattered and declining. (W, E and central Europe.)

Lemon-scented Fern
Oreopteris limbosperma

LEAVES *Produced in a crown at apex of short rhizome,* dying down in winter, to 120 cm; *yellowish green,* lemon-scented when crushed, twice divided (pinnate, pinnae divided almost to rachis), lower surface covered by numerous small brownish-yellow glands, *pinnae decreasing in length towards base, basal pinnae very short* and reaching close to base of leaf, pinnules not toothed; sori without indusium. HABITAT Open acid woodland, stream sides, upland grassland, damp rock ledges. DIST. Native. Widespread in upland Britain to 1010 m, but scarce in S and SE; scarce also in Ireland. (NW, W and central Europe.)

Beech Fern
Phegopteris connectilis

LEAVES To 50 cm, *produced singly on long, creeping rhizome,* dying down in winter; petiole erect, up to 2× as long as *blade, blade twice divided* (pinnate, pinnae almost divided to rachis), *blade triangular-ovate, bent back from petiole, lowest pair of pinnae bent back away from others,* pinnules not toothed; sori without indusium. HABITAT Damp, shaded woodland banks, stream sides, wet rocks, cliff ledges. DIST. Native. N England, Wales, Scotland to 1120 m; scarce in Ireland. (N, NW and central Europe.)

ASPLENIACEAE Spleenworts

Hart's-tongue
Phyllitis scolopendrium

LEAVES Produced in a crown, 10–75 cm long, *blade undivided, strap-shaped,* lobed at base, evergreen; stipe blackish purple; sori in pairs, linear along veins. HABITAT Damp, shaded habitats: hedge banks, woods, shaded stream sides on base-rich soils, grikes in limestone pavement. DIST. Native. Throughout BI but scarce in N Scotland; to 700 m. (W, E and central Europe; rare in S.)

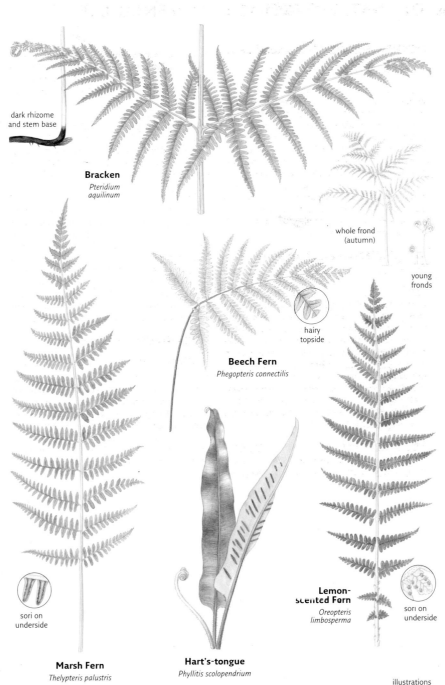

dark rhizome
and stem base

Bracken
*Pteridium
aquilinum*

whole frond
(autumn)

young
fronds

hairy
topside

Beech Fern
Phegopteris connectilis

sori on
underside

**Lemon-
scented Fern**
*Oreopteris
limbosperma*

sori on
underside

Marsh Fern
Thelypteris palustris

Hart's-tongue
Phyllitis scolopendrium

illustrations
0.1× lifesize

Asplenium

See key to *Asplenium* on p.32.

Maidenhair Spleenwort   *Asplenium trichomanes*

Small, tufted, evergreen fern. LEAVES 4-20 cm, *simply pinnate, petiole and rachis blackish*, blade linear, dark green, *pinnae 3-8 mm*; sori 1-2 mm, borne directly on veins, indusium narrow, whitish. HABITAT Rocks, cliffs, scree, walls, mine wastes, usually on calcareous substrates. DIST. Native. Widespread throughout BI; to 870 m. (Most of Europe except extreme N.)

Green Spleenwort   *Asplenium viride*

Similar to *A. trichomanes*, but *petiole and rachis green*. HABITAT Crevices in calcareous rocks, scree, limestone pavement. DIST. Native. N England, Wales, Scotland, W Ireland; to 975 m. Rather local. (N Europe, mts of central and S Europe.)

Sea Spleenwort   *Asplenium marinum*

Tufted evergreen fern. LEAVES *Simply pinnate*, lanceolate, rather thick, glossy green above; petiole brown, ⅛-½ as long as blade; *rachis winged, wings green*; *pinnae 1.5-4 cm*; sori 3-4 mm, linear. HABITAT Crevices of sea cliffs, often in range of salt spray. DIST. Native. All round coasts of BI except E and SE England. (Coasts of S Europe and W Europe from central Norway S.)

Forked Spleenwort   *Asplenium septentrionale* *(R)

Small, tufted, clump-forming evergreen fern. LEAVES *Irregularly forked 1-2(-3) times*, segments 2-4 mm wide, long, linear; petiole longer than blade; sori 3-4 mm, linear. HABITAT Well-drained exposed acid rocks and metalliferous mine spoil. DIST. Native. N England, Wales, Scotland; to 715 m. Rare. (Most of Europe except extreme S, N and much of E.)

Black Spleenwort   *Asplenium adiantum-nigrum*

Loosely tufted evergreen fern. LEAVES 10-25(-50) cm, 2-3-pinnate, dark, shining green; petiole blackish, about as long as, or longer than, blade; rachis winged, blackish below; *blade triangular to triangular ovate,* acute, *basal pinnae longest, decreasing in size upwards*; sori linear, 1-3 mm. HABITAT Steep, shaded lane banks, walls, cliffs, scree, usually on basic soils. DIST. Native. Throughout BI; to 575 m. (W, central and S Europe.)

Irish Spleenwort   *Asplenium onopteris*

Very similar to *A. adiantum-nigrum*, but *blade and pinnae tapering much longer*; spores are also smaller, but this requires microscopic examination. HABITAT Warm, shaded banks, rock faces, scree, in deciduous woodland on basic soils. DIST. Native. Very rare. Central and S Ireland. (SW and S Europe.)

Lanceolate Spleenwort   *Asplenium obovatum* *(R)

Similar to *A. adiantum-nigrum*, but leaf blade lanceolate, *longest pinnae in middle of blade*, basal pinnae slightly inflexed, and petioles usually much shorter than blade. HABITAT Acid rock crevices and outcrops, lane banks close to sea. DIST. Native. SW England, W Wales, S Ireland (very rare), Scilly Is, Channel Is. Very local. (W and SW Europe, W Mediterranean.)

Wall Rue   *Asplenium ruta-muraria*

Small, tufted evergreen fern. LEAVES 3-12 cm, 2(-3)-pinnate, rather thick, bluish green, *ultimate segments 2-8 mm, fan-shaped*. HABITAT Crevices in calcareous rocks, scree, limestone pavement; old mortared walls in lowlands. DIST. Native. Common throughout most of BI; to 625 m. (Most of Europe, but scarce in SW.)

Rustyback   *Ceterach officinarum*

Densely tufted evergreen fern. LEAVES 3-20 cm, *simply pinnate*, dull green and rather thick above, *underside densely covered by oval, light brown overlapping scales*, pinnae ovate to oblong, to 2 cm, rounded at tip; sori *c.*2 mm, linear, indusium absent. HABITAT Basic rocks, limestone pavement, mortared walls. DIST. Native. Widespread in W and SW England, Wales and Ireland; scattered elsewhere. To 550 m. (W and S Europe.)

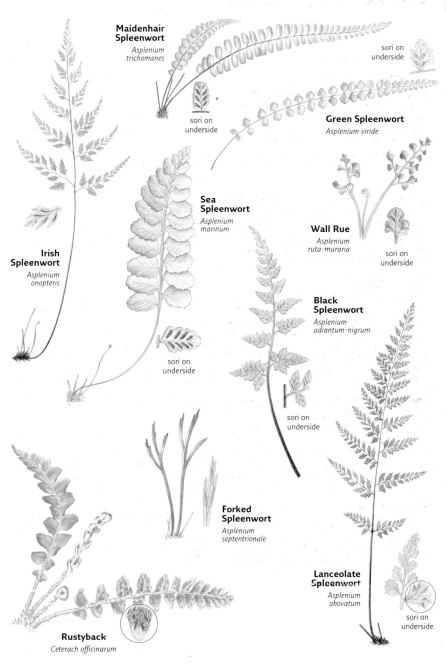

Maidenhair Spleenwort
Asplenium trichomanes

sori on underside

sori on underside

Green Spleenwort
Asplenium viride

Irish Spleenwort
Asplenium onopteris

Sea Spleenwort
Asplenium marinum

Wall Rue
Asplenium ruta-muraria

sori on underside

Black Spleenwort
Asplenium adiantum-nigrum

sori on underside

sori on underside

Forked Spleenwort
Asplenium septentrionale

Lanceolate Spleenwort
Asplenium obovatum

sori on underside

Rustyback
Ceterach officinarum

illustrations
0.5× lifesize

Key to Spleenworts *Asplenium*

	if	then
1	▷ Leaves irregularly and sparsely forked into narrow linear segments	*A. septentrionale* (p.30)
	▷ Leaves 1–3-pinnate, lobes not linear	Go to ▷ 2
2	▷ Leaves pinnate	Go to ▷ 3
	▷ Leaves 2–3-pinnate	Go to ▷ 5
3	▷ Upper part of rachis with green wing, leaf thick and glossy, pinnae ≥15 mm (sea cliffs, caves)	*A. marinum* (p.30)
	▷ Rachis not winged, pinnae <12 mm	Go to ▷ 4
4	▷ Rachis black	*A. trichomanes* (p.30)
	▷ Rachis green	*A. viride* (p.30)
5	▷ Leaves oblong-lanceolate in outline, longest pair of pinnae towards middle of leaf	*A. obovatum* (p.30)
	▷ Leaves triangular-ovate in outline, basal pair of pinnae the longest	Go to ▷ 6
6	▷ Petioles green, leaf blade irregularly 2–3-pinnate or ± trifoliate, pinnules rhomboid or fan-shaped	*A. ruta-muraria* (p.30)
	▷ Petioles blackish, leaf blade 3-pinnate	Go to ▷ 7
7	▷ Widespread	*A. adiantum-nigrum* (p.30)
	▷ Rare, SW Ireland	*A. onopteris* (p.30)

(See main text for characters separating these two species.)

WOODSIACEAE Lady-fern family

Lady-fern
Athyrium filix-femina

Tufted fern, dying down in autumn. LEAVES 20–120 cm, 2-pinnate; petiole ¼–⅓ as long as blade, pinkish when exposed; blade lanceolate, rather thin, rather bluish green when mature, rachis pinkish; *pinnules 3–20 mm, deeply lobed, lobes toothed; sori oblong, c.1 mm, indusium well developed*, oblong or j-shaped, toothed. HABITAT Damp woods, stream sides, ditches, damp rocky habitats, on well-drained acid soils. DIST. Native. Widespread throughout BI; to 1005 m. (Most of Europe; scarce in S and E.)

Alpine Lady-fern
Athyrium distentifolium

Very similar to *A. filix-femina*; distinguished with certainty only by *round, not oblong, sori and absence* of indusium. Tends to produce clumps of several crowns and leaves are usually pale yellow-green. HABITAT Acid rock ledges, gullies, block scree, especially N-facing corries in areas of late snow-lie. DIST. Native. Mts of central and NW Scotland; to 1220 m. (Scandinavia, mts of central Europe.)

Newman's Lady-fern
Athyrium distentifolium var. *flexile*

A form of *A. distentifolium*, with a narrower oblong-elliptic blade, spreading leaves, and shorter petiole, ≤⅙ as long as blade. HABITAT Acid N-facing block scree in areas of late snow-lie. DIST. Endemic. Very rare. Mts of central Scotland; to 1140 m. COMMENTS Sometimes regarded as a separate species but not genetically distinct.

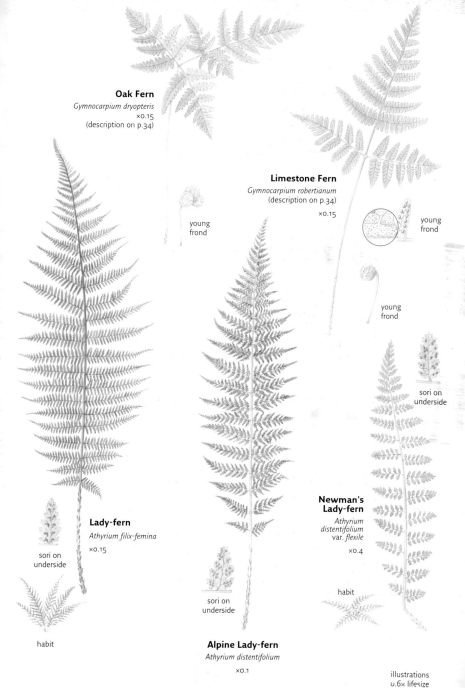

Oak Fern
Gymnocarpium dryopteris
×0.15
(description on p.34)

young
frond

Limestone Fern
Gymnocarpium robertianum
(description on p.34)
×0.15

young
frond

young
frond

sori on
underside

sori on
underside

Lady-fern
Athyrium filix-femina
×0.15

**Newman's
Lady-fern**
*Athyrium
distentifolium*
var. *flexile*
×0.4

habit

habit

sori on
underside

Alpine Lady-fern
Athyrium distentifolium
×0.1

illustrations
0.6× lifesize

Oak Fern
Gymnocarpium dryopteris *(NI)

[See illustration previous page.] Deciduous fern, dying down in autumn. LEAVES To 40 cm, *bright green*, arising singly from much-branched creeping subterranean rhizome and forming extensive colonies; petiole erect, long, slender, 1½-3× as long as blade; *blade broadly triangular, bent back at junction with petiole to almost 90°, not glandular*, 3-pinnate; lowest pinnae large, almost as large as rest of blade; sori round, 1-2 mm, indusium absent. HABITAT Damp open woods, upland stream sides, peaty banks. DIST. Native. Widespread in N England, Wales, Scotland; to 915 m. (Most of Europe except S.)

Limestone Fern
Gymnocarpium robertianum *(R)

[See illustration previous page.] Similar to *G. dryopteris*, but *leaves dull green*, top of petiole, rachis and *blade covered by small glands*, lowest pinnae not as large as rest of blade. HABITAT Cracks and fissures in rocky limestone habitats, limestone pavement, scree, usually in exposed situations; rarely on chalk. DIST. Native. Scattered throughout England and Wales; very rare in Scotland and Ireland; to 585 m. (N, W and central Europe.)

Brittle Bladder-fern
Cystopteris fragilis

Evergreen fern. LEAVES Tufted, dying back in autumn, 5-35 cm, 2(-3)-pinnate; petiole *c.⅓* as long as blade, slender and brittle; blade lanceolate, *pinnae widely spaced; pinnules 4-10 mm, not overlapping*, toothed to deeply lobed, *veins ending in tips of pinnule teeth*; sori round, on a vein running into segment tip; indusium oval or pear-shaped. HABITAT Damp, shaded, usually calcareous rock crevices, walls and cliffs. DIST. Native. Widely distributed in N England, Wales, Scotland; rather scattered in Ireland; to 1220 m. (Most of Europe; the most cosmopolitan of all ferns.)

Diaphanous Bladder-fern
Cystopteris diaphana VU.

Very similar to *C. fragilis*, differing in that most *veins end in notches between pinnule teeth*. Ornamentation of spores is also different, but this needs microscopic examination. HABITAT Steep, shaded banks. DIST. Probably native. Discovered new to BI in 2000 along R. Camel, Cornwall. (SW Europe.)

Dickie's Bladder-fern
Cystopteris dickieana VU. *(B)

Similar to *C. fragilis*, but *pinnae and pinnules strongly overlapping*; and sori usually on a vein that runs into sinus. Spores are wrinkled while those of *C. fragilis* are spiny, but this requires microscopic examination. HABITAT Basic rock crevices, overhangs, sea caves. DIST. Native. Very rare. N Scotland; to 380 m. (Scattered in arctic Europe, mts of S Europe.)

Mountain Bladder-fern
Cystopteris montana

Fern with long, creeping rhizome. LEAVES Solitary, widely spaced, 10-30 cm, *3-pinnate*, dying back in autumn; petiole longer than blade, scales fringed with glands; *blade as wide as long, triangular, lower pinnae much longer than rest*; sori small, widely separated, indusium oval-round, toothed. HABITAT Damp, dripping basic rocks, ledges, gullies, scree. DIST. Native. Rare. Mts of central Scotland; to 1125 m. (Mts of Scandinavia, S Europe.)

Alpine Woodsia
Woodsia alpina *(B)

Small, tufted alpine fern. LEAVES Spreading, 2-10 cm, pinnate to almost 2-pinnate; *petiole ¼-⅓ as long as blade, with visible joint c. halfway up*, sparsely scaly; rachis sparsely scaly; blade sparsely hairy below, upper surface glabrous, pinnae with 3-7 lobes; sori round, 2-5 towards tips of segments, indusium with fringe of long, jointed hairs arching over sporangia. HABITAT Steep, bare faces, crevices on well-drained base-rich rocks. DIST. Native. Rare in mts of central Scotland, very rare in Snowdonia; to 975 m. (Mts of Scandinavia, S Europe.)

Oblong Woodsia
Woodsia ilvensis EN. *(B)

Similar to *W. alpina, but petiole and rachis densely scaly*, leaves 5-10 cm, densely covered with jointed hairs on both surfaces, and pinnae with 7-13 lobes. HABITAT Rock crevices in well-drained alpine cliffs. DIST. Native. Very rare. Few scattered localities in N Wales, Lake District, Scotland; to 760 m. (Scandinavia, mts of central Europe.)

Ostrich Fern
Matteuccia struthiopteris

Robust, tufted, deciduous fern to 1.5 m. LEAVES 2 *kinds*: sterile leaves 2-pinnate, pinnae reducing in length to base, lowest very short; fertile leaves shorter, to 60 cm, not green, pinnae very narrow, inrolling. HABITAT Stream sides, lake shores, damp woodlands, on heavy soils. DIST. Introduced. Scattered throughout BI as naturalised garden escape. (N, central and E Europe.)

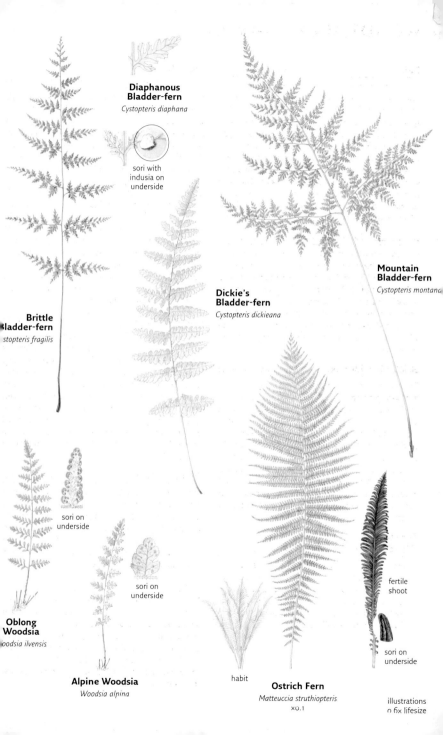

Diaphanous Bladder-fern
Cystopteris diaphana

sori with indusia on underside

Mountain Bladder-fern
Cystopteris montana

Dickie's Bladder-fern
Cystopteris dickieana

Brittle Bladder-fern
Cystopteris fragilis

sori on underside

Oblong Woodsia
Woodsia ilvensis

sori on underside

Alpine Woodsia
Woodsia alpina

habit

fertile shoot

sori on underside

Ostrich Fern
Matteuccia struthiopteris
×0.1

illustrations
0.6x lifesize

DRYOPTERIDACEAE Male-ferns and buckler-ferns

Male-ferns and buckler-ferns *Dryopteris*

Most of our familiar woodland ferns are male-ferns and buckler-ferns (*see* key on pp.20-23). They have short, densely scaly rhizomes, with leaves in a shuttlecock-like tuft when rhizome is erect, or fewer and less tufted when it is horizontal. Leaves are 2-3-pinnate, and indusium is kidney-shaped.

Male-fern   *Dryopteris filix-mas*

LEAVES To 150 cm, mostly dying down in autumn, 2-pinnate; petiole ¼-⅓ as long as blade, with sparse to moderately dense pale brown to straw-coloured scales; blade not glandular, *base of pinnae at junction with rachis lacking dark pigmentation*; pinnules ± flat, obtuse, ± equally toothed all round margin, *teeth acute, pointing forwards towards tip of pinnule*; sori *c*.1 mm, *indusium flattened*, not glandular, margins spreading. HABITAT Woods, hedge banks, ditches, stream banks, rocky hillsides, scree; also walls and gardens. DIST. Native. Common throughout BI; to 960 m. (All Europe, but scarce in SW.)

Scaly Male-fern   *Dryopteris affinis*

Complex species with a number of named forms, similar to *D. filix-mas*. LEAVES To 100 cm, evergreen, thicker in texture than *D. filix-mas*; petiole usually <¼ as long as blade, *densely covered with orange-brown scales; base of pinnae at junction with rachis has dark pigmentation*; pinnules flat, rather truncate, ± parallel-sided, toothed at tip; edges of indusium tucked under, lifting as sporangia ripen. HABITAT Woods, plantations, shaded banks. DIST. Native. Throughout BI, but commoner in N and W; to 705 m. (W and central Europe.)

Mountain Male-fern   *Dryopteris oreades*

Similar to *D. filix-mas* but smaller and with several crowns. LEAVES Usually 30-50 cm, dying back in autumn; blade with glands beneath; pinnules rather concave, giving frond a rather 'crisped' appearance, teeth blunt, not pointing forwards towards tip of pinnule; sori few on lower part of each pinnule, *indusium glandular, convex with edges tucked under*. HABITAT Well-drained inaccessible mountain ledges, steep scree slopes. DIST. Native. Wales, N England, Scotland; to 850 m. (Scattered throughout Europe, except S.)

Rigid Buckler-fern   *Dryopteris submontana*

LEAVES In loose tufts, to 60 cm, dying back in autumn, 2-pinnate, rather stiff; petiole about as long as blade, densely scaly, scales shiny, pale brown; *blade dull grey-green, densely glandular on both surfaces, with yellow glands*; sori crowded in 2 rows, surface and margin of *indusium glandular*. HABITAT Scree, rock crevices, grikes in limestone pavement. DIST. Native. Very rare, on Carboniferous limestone of N England; to 465 m. (Mts of S Europe.)

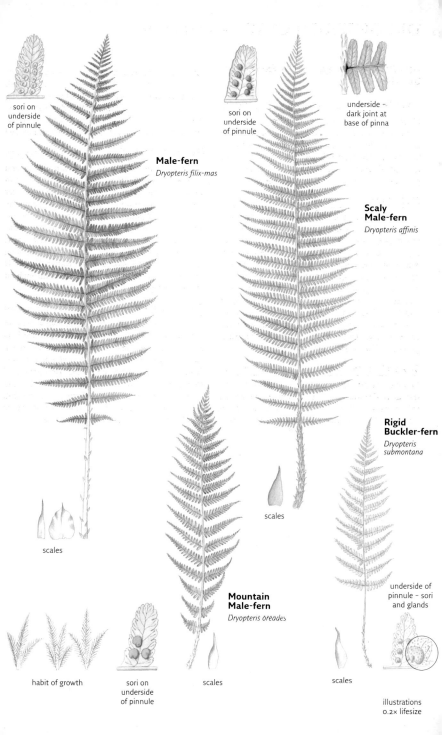

sori on
underside
of pinnule

Male-fern
Dryopteris filix-mas

sori on
underside
of pinnule

underside –
dark joint at
base of pinna

**Scaly
Male-fern**
Dryopteris affinis

**Rigid
Buckler-fern**
*Dryopteris
submontana*

scales

scales

**Mountain
Male-fern**
Dryopteris oreades

underside of
pinnule – sori
and glands

habit of growth

sori on
underside
of pinnule

scales

scales

illustrations
0.2× lifesize

Broad Buckler-fern   *Dryopteris dilatata*

LEAVES Clustered in a 'shuttlecock', remaining green for most of winter, 3-pinnate, broadly ovate, to 150 cm; *petiole c.⅓ length of leaf, densely scaly at base, scales dark brown in centre, paler on edges*; blade dark green, margins of pinnules usually turning under, segments not cut to midrib. HABITAT Woods, hedge banks, rocky slopes, scree, on neutral to acidic moist or well-drained soils. DIST. Native. Common throughout BI; to 1125 m. (Most of Europe except N and extreme S.)

Northern Buckler-fern   *Dryopteris expansa*

Very similar to *D. dilatata*. LEAVES 10–25 cm in open habitats, to 80 cm in woodland, mid-pale green; petiole up to ⅓ length of leaf, scales usually uniform brown with, occasionally, darker central stripe; edges of pinnules flat, *pinnule lobes more obviously toothed than* D. dilatata *and more deeply cut to midrib, giving frond a much more dissected appearance.* HABITAT Mountain scree, rock ledges; also, rarely, lowland woods. DIST. Native. Widespread but local in central and N Scotland; rare and scattered in N England, Wales. To 945 m. (N Europe, mts of central and S Europe.)

Narrow Buckler-fern   *Dryopteris carthusiana*

Rather similar to *D. dilatata* but dying down in autumn. LEAVES Narrower than *D. dilatata*, lanceolate to ovate-lanceolate, pinnae more equally spaced; *petiole c.⅓ leaf length, scales sparse, pale brown without dark centre*; tips of pinnules flat, margins of segments with sharp-tipped incurving teeth. HABITAT Wet woods, fen carr, fens, wet heaths. Often found with *D. dilatata*, but more restricted to wet habitats. DIST. Native. Throughout BI; to 730 m. (Most of Europe except S.)

Hay-scented Buckler-fern   *Dryopteris aemula*

Rather similar to *D. dilatata* but evergreen. LEAVES To 60 cm, 3–4-pinnate, *petiole dark shiny purplish-brown*, scales narrow, reddish brown without dark centre; blade bright green, triangular, *tips of pinnules turned up, giving whole frond a distinctive 'crisped' appearance*, minute glands on both surfaces giving smell of new-mown hay when crushed. HABITAT Banks, shady rocks, sea cliffs, acid wooded stream ravines. DIST. Native. Markedly oceanic distribution: SW England, W Wales, W Scotland, W and SW Ireland; also in the Weald of SE England. To 640 m. (Brittany, N Spain, Madeira, Azores.)

Crested Buckler-fern   *Dryopteris cristata* CR.

LEAVES Relatively few on creeping, branching rhizome, dying back in autumn; petiole leaves to 100 cm, 1–2-pinnate, *of 2 kinds*: outer sterile leaves ± spreading, shorter than sub-erect inner ones, pinnae flat in plane of blade; inner fertile leaves lanceolate, ± parallel-sided, pinnae twisted so as to be almost horizontal, *pinnule segments with incurved sharp-tipped teeth*. HABITAT *Sphagnum*-dominated 'floating' fens, fen carr. DIST. Native. Norfolk. Very rare. (W, central and E Europe.)

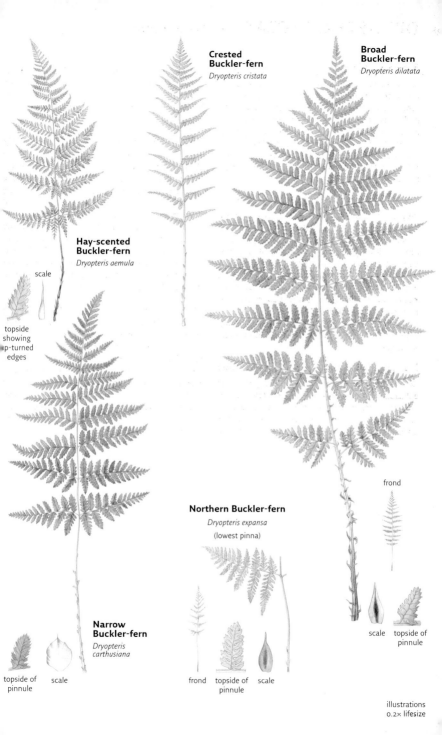

Crested Buckler-fern
Dryopteris cristata

Broad Buckler-fern
Dryopteris dilatata

Hay-scented Buckler-fern
Dryopteris aemula

scale

topside
showing
up-turned
edges

Narrow Buckler-fern
Dryopteris carthusiana

topside of
pinnule

scale

Northern Buckler-fern
Dryopteris expansa
(lowest pinna)

frond

topside of
pinnule

scale

frond

scale

topside of
pinnule

illustrations
0.2× lifesize

Shield-ferns *Polystichum*

Differ from *Dryopteris* in that pinnule teeth have fine spiny tips and indusium is peltate (umbrella-shaped, with attachment at centre).

Soft Shield-fern *Polystichum setiferum*

LEAVES Form a 'shuttlecock', ± evergreen, soft, arching or drooping, to 150 cm, 2-pinnate; *petiole* c.¼–½ *as long as blade*, very scaly; pinnae well spaced, *lowest pinna* c. *as long as middle pinna; pinnules ± stalked*, angle formed between basal margins obtuse; indusium round. HABITAT Shaded woodland banks, lanesides, hedgerows and stream sides on base-rich soils; grikes in limestone pavement. DIST. Native. Throughout most of BI, becoming scarcer to N and E; absent from Scotland. Lowland to 305 m. (W and SE Europe.)

Hard shield-fern *Polystichum aculeatum*

Evergreen fern similar to *P. setiferum*. LEAVES Darker green than *P. setiferum*, rather glossy, rigid to 90 cm, *petiole* c.⅙ *as long as blade*; pinnae not overlapping, *lowest pinna* c.½ *as long as middle pinna; pinnules sessile*, angles formed between basal margins acute. HABITAT Wooded valleys, rocky hillsides, walls, hedge banks, limestone pavement, on mildly acid to calcareous soils. DIST. Native. Throughout BI, becoming commoner to N; to 760 m. (Most of Europe except N and extreme S.)

Holly-fern *Polystichum lonchitis* VU. *(NI)

Tufted evergreen fern. LEAVES 10–50 cm long, linear-lanceolate, *1-pinnate*, dark glossy green, rather stiff; pinnae close-set or overlapping, *lowest pinna* <½ *as long as middle pinna, margins with stiff spines*. HABITAT Limestone rock ledges, cliffs, scree, grikes in limestone pavement. DIST. Native. Local in central and N Scotland to 1150 m; rare and scattered in N England, N Wales, W Ireland. (Scandinavia, mts of central and S Europe.)

BLECHNACEAE Hard-ferns

Hard-fern *Blechnum spicant*

LEAVES Produced in dense clusters from erect branching rhizome; 2 *kinds*: sterile leaves spreading, *1-pinnate*, 10–60 cm, glossy, glabrous, *blade lanceolate, pinnae numerous, close together, linear*, 1–2 cm; fertile leaves erect, taller, 15–75 cm, rachis blackish, pinnae linear, separated; sori forming continuous line down whole length of pinna. HABITAT Deciduous and coniferous acid woods, heaths, moorland, upland stream sides. DIST. Native. Widespread and common throughout most of BI, but scarce in E England; to 1065 m. (Most of Europe except extreme S and N.)

AZOLLACEAE Water ferns

Water Fern *Azolla filiculoides*

Small, free-floating unfern-like fern, with a much-branched horizontal stem and numerous tiny overlapping leaves. LEAVES Sessile; lobes ovate, rounded, *c.*2.5 mm, alternate in 2 rows; upper surface covered by hairs, making it non-wettable; green at beginning of season, turning rusty red at end of summer, when plant forms dense duckweed-like mats. HABITAT Calcareous waters of dykes, ponds, canals, sheltered lakes, rivers, especially near sea. DIST. Introduced (native of W North America). Naturalised throughout England and Wales; rare in Scotland and Ireland. Lowland to 450 m. Spreading.

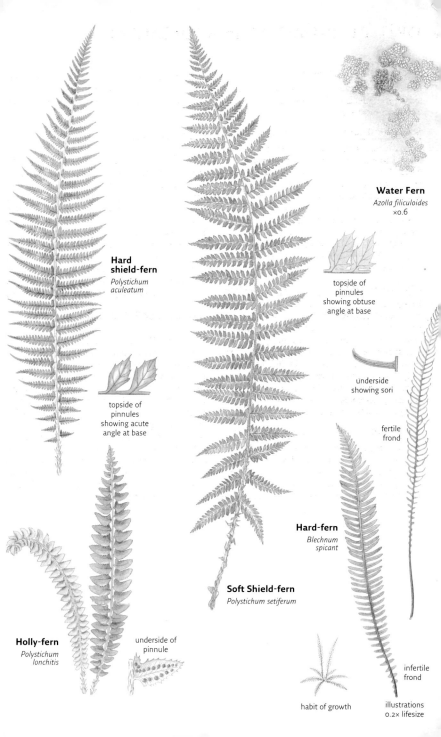

Hard shield-fern
Polystichum aculeatum

topside of
pinnules
showing acute
angle at base

Holly-fern
Polystichum lonchitis

underside of
pinnule

Soft Shield-fern
Polystichum setiferum

Water Fern
Azolla filiculoides
×0.6

topside of
pinnules
showing obtuse
angle at base

underside
showing sori

fertile
frond

Hard-fern
Blechnum spicant

habit of growth

infertile
frond

illustrations
0.2× lifesize

CONIFERS

There are only three native conifers in Britain; Scots Pine, Yew and Juniper. However, a number of species are regularly grown in forestry plantations and even more have been planted as specimen trees in parks and large gardens. Only those introduced species that regularly self-seed in the countryside have been included here. Conifers (*see* key on p.46.) differ from flowering plants in that the seeds are borne externally on the upper surface of the scales of the female cones, the 'fir cones'. Female cones are an important aid to identification, and if they either cannot be seen or reached, then searching the litter beneath the trees will usually prove successful (except in the case of *Abies*, the silver-firs, whose cones disintegrate on the tree). The male cones, which produce the wind-blown pollen, are usually smaller and don't vary much between species. The largest, tallest and oldest plants on the planet are conifers.

PINACEAE Pines, spruces, firs and larches

European Larch   *Larix decidua*

Deciduous tree to 45 m. LEAVES Needles to 30 mm long, <1 mm wide, in dense clusters of up to 50 on short lateral shoots. Underside with pale greenish (not whitish) stripes on either side of midrib. CONES *Mature female cones oval*, 20-40 mm long × 20-25 mm wide, *bracts not recurved at tip*. HABITAT Widely grown in parks, plantations and shelter belts. DIST. Introduced in early C17th. Frequently self-seeds; known in wild since end of C19th. (Native of mts of central Europe, E to the Tatras and Poland.)

Japanese Larch   *Larix kaempferi*

Deciduous tree to 35 m. LEAVES Needles as in *L. decidua*, but undersides with conspicuous whitish (not pale greenish) lines on either side of midrib. CONES Mature *female cones more spherical than L. decidua*, *c.*30 mm long × *c.*25 mm wide, *bracts recurved at tips*. HABITAT Widely planted as a forestry crop for timber; also in parks and large gardens in open situations. DIST. Introduced from Japan in 1861. Frequently self-seeds. (NW Europe) SIMILAR SPP. The hybrid between *L. decidua* and *L. kaempferi*, *L. × marschlinsii*, is a vigorous tree now more often grown for forestry than either parent. It is fertile, can backcross with the parents and is intermediate in characters between them. It occasionally occurs in the wild.

European Silver-fir   *Abies alba*

Tall evergreen tree, to >50 m, with *hairy twigs*. LEAVES Dark green needles, 20-30 mm long, those on lower branches spreading in 2 ranks on either side of twigs; underside with white band on either side of midrib. CONES *Female cones erect, 10-15 cm, bracts protruding and downcurved, disintegrating while still on tree.* HABITAT Favours fertile soils. DIST. Introduced in 1603. Regenerates freely from seed. (Native to mts of central Europe from Pyrenees to Balkans.)

Giant Fir   *Abies grandis*

Tall evergreen tree, to >60 m, with *sparsely hairy twigs*. LEAVES 25-60 mm (longer than *A. alba*), spreading in 2 ranks on either side of twigs; underside with white band on either side of midrib. CONES Female cones erect, *5-10 cm (smaller than A. alba), bracts not protruding*, breaking up while still on tree. HABITAT Increasingly grown for forestry and planted in parks and large gardens. DIST. Introduced in 1831 (native of W coast of North America from Vancouver to California). COMMENTS Together with *Pseudotsuga menziesii*, the tallest species of tree in Britain.

Douglas Fir   *Pseudotsuga menziesii*

Tall evergreen tree to >60 m. LEAVES 20-30 mm, underside with 2 whitish stripes on either side of midrib. CONES *Female cones distinctive*, 6-10 cm, pendulous, falling when ripe, *bracts protruding and 3-lobed*. HABITAT Widely grown in plantations on sheltered sites and as specimens in parks and gardens. DIST. Introduced in 1826 (native of W coast of North America). COMMENTS The tallest tree in Britain may be a 63 m specimen at Dunkeld, Perthshire.

Sitka Spruce   *Picea sitchensis*

Evergreen tree to 60 m. LEAVES 15-30 mm, stiff and spiny, *flattened, with 2 conspicuous whitish lines beneath; persistent peg-like base on twigs* left by fallen leaves. CONES *Female cones* to 10 cm (smaller than *P. abies*), *pendulous*. HABITAT The most commonly planted forestry conifer, especially in high-rainfall areas of the N and W. DIST. Introduced in 1831 (native of W coast of North America from Alaska to N California).

Norway Spruce   *Picea abies*

Evergreen tree to 50 m; the traditional 'Christmas tree'. LEAVES 10-25 mm, *4-angled, pale lines indistinct*; persistent peg-like base on twigs left by fallen leaves. CONES *Female cones 10-20 cm (longer than P. sitchensis), pendulous*. HABITAT Widely planted in forestry plantations and shelter belts, mostly in lowlands. DIST. Cultivated in Britain since C10th; regenerates freely in felled sites. (Scandinavia and central Europe, E into Russia.)

Douglas Fir
Pseudotsuga menziesii

European Silver-fir
Abies alba

Giant Fir
Abies grandis

Sitka Spruce
Picea sitchensis

young ♀ cone

Norway Spruce
Picea abies

European Larch
Larix decidua

young ♀ cone

Japanese Larch
Larix kaempferi

young ♀ cone

illustrations
0.6× lifesize

Scots Pine
Pinus sylvestris

Evergreen tree to 40 m; one of only 3 conifers native to Britain. Bark Distinctive orange-brown on upper trunk, shed in peeling scales. Leaves *Needles in pairs, 4–8 cm*, twisted and rather blue-green (glaucous). Cones Female cones 3–7 cm, cone-scales not spine-tipped. Habitat In native range found on acid sandy soils and peat; elsewhere commonly planted in woods and shelter belts. Dist. Native in Scottish Highlands (ssp. *scotica*); naturalised throughout rest of BI. (Central Europe, S Spain, Scandinavia, N Greece; E to temperate Asia.)

Corsican Pine
Pinus nigra ssp. *laricio*

Evergreen tree to 50 m. Bark Dark grey and deeply fissured on upper trunk. Leaves *Needles in pairs, 10–18 cm (distinctly longer than* P. sylvestris*)*, pale green. Cones Female cones 5–9 cm, cone-scales not spine-tipped. Habitat Widely grown in plantations, shelter belts, parks and large gardens. Dist. Introduced in the C19th. (Corsica, Sicily, S Italy.)

Austrian Pine
Pinus nigra ssp. *nigra*

Similar to *P. nigra* ssp. *laricio*, but leaves 8–12 cm, dark green. Habitat Widely planted as for *P. nigra* ssp. *laricio*. Dist. Introduced C19th. (SE Europe.)

Lodgepole Pine
Pinus contorta

Evergreen tree to 25 m. Bark Dark red-brown on upper trunk. Leaves *Needles in pairs, 3–10 cm*, twisted, broad. Cones *Female cones small, 2–5 cm, with small prickle at end of cone-scales* (these eventually wear off). Habitat Widely planted for forestry in the N and W in similar conditions to *Picea sitchensis (see* p.42*)*; regenerates freely from seed. Dist. Introduced in 1851 (native of W North America, mts from Alaska to Colorado).

CUPRESSACEAE Cypresses and junipers

Lawson's Cypress
Chamaecyparis lawsoniana

Evergreen tree to 40 m, with numerous cultivars. Crown narrow, *leading shoot drooping*, densely branched from base. Leaves Small and scale-like, up to 3 mm long, in opposite pairs that cover the young twigs. *Median leaf on upper side of twigs with pale oval gland. Crushed foliage has parsley-like smell.* Cones *Female cones small, globular, to 8 mm.* Habitat Widely planted in parks, gardens and cemeteries in churchyards. Dist. Introduced in 1854 (native of W North America from California to Oregon). Regenerates freely from seed.

Leyland Cypress
× *Cupressocyparis leylandii*

Superficially similar to *C. lawsoniana*. Dist. Widely planted as hedging and shelter belts; doesn't set viable seed so is seldom seen in the wild. Comments Notoriously vigorous tree that developed spontaneously in 1888 near Welshpool as a result of hybridisation between Monterey Cypress *Cupressus macrocarpa* and Nootka Cypress *Chamaecyparis nootkatensis*.

Western Red-cedar
Thuja plicata

Evergreen tree to >40 m, superficially resembling *Chamaecyparis lawsoniana* but *leading shoot not drooping*. Leaves To 6 mm; *foliage with sweet pineapple-like smell; median leaves without oval glands*. Cones *Female cones elongate, urn-shaped, c.*10 mm. Habitat Grown under hardwoods and larches in forestry plantations, and as hedging. Dist. Introduced in 1853 (native of W North America from Alaska to California). Frequently self-seeds.

Common Juniper
Juniperus communis

Evergreen tree or shrub to *c.*10 m. Dioecious. Leaves *In 3s*, 5–15 mm, narrow, stiff, sharp-pointed; *smell apple-like*. Cones *Female cones fleshy and berry-like, green when young, blue-black when mature; smell of gin*. Habitat Chalk downland in S England; heather moors, oak, pine and birch woodland in N Britain; rocky slopes and coastal heaths. Dist. Local and declining in many areas of BI; to 975 m. (Wide native geographical distribution in arctic and north temperate zones; Europe S to N Africa.) Comments Has 2 subspecies: ssp. *nana* and ssp. *communis*. Ssp. *nana* is a dwarf, prostrate shrub with shorter (5–10 mm) and blunter leaves, so foliage is hardly prickly to touch, and is found on exposed coastal heaths, upland moorland and rock ledges.

TAXACEAE Yews

Yew
Taxus baccata

Evergreen tree or shrub to 25 m, often branching from base of massive trunk. Dioecious. Bark Reddish brown and scaly. Twigs green. Leaves Pale green below, *midrib prominent on both surfaces*. Cone *Female 'cone' berry-like*; single seed surrounded by fleshy red 'aril'. Habitat Woods and scrub, on well-drained, usually (but not exclusively) calcareous soils, especially chalk areas of S England. Dist. Native. Throughout most of BI to 470 m, scarce in Scotland, but widely planted obscuring native distribution. (Europe from S Scandinavia to mts of N Africa, E to Caucasus and W Himalaya.)

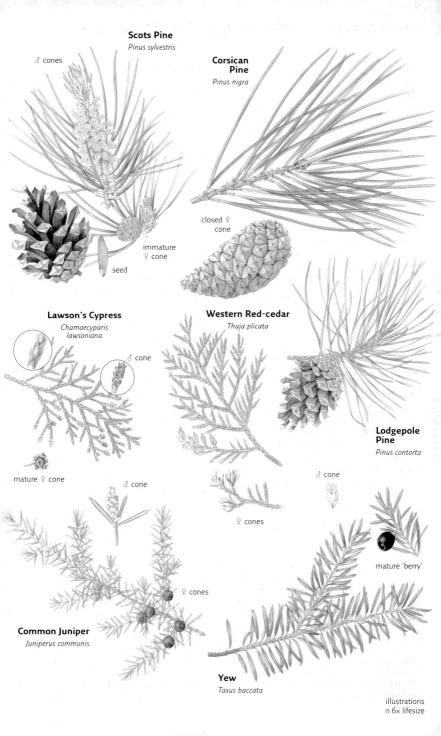

Scots Pine
Pinus sylvestris

♂ cones

immature ♀ cone

seed

Corsican Pine
Pinus nigra

closed ♀ cone

Lawson's Cypress
Chamaecyparis lawsoniana

♂ cone

mature ♀ cone

Western Red-cedar
Thuja plicata

Lodgepole Pine
Pinus contorta

♂ cone

♀ cones

♂ cone

mature 'berry'

Common Juniper
Juniperus communis

♀ cones

Yew
Taxus baccata

illustrations
0.6× lifesize

if	then
▷ Leaves small and scale-like, up to 5 mm long, in opposite pairs that completely cover young twigs; leafy shoots flattened and frond-like	*Chamaecyparis, Thuja* (p.44)
▷ Needles short, 10–15 mm long, in whorls of 3. Cone a 'berry'	*Juniperus* (p.44)
▷ Leaves up to 30 mm long, in dense clusters of up to 50 on short lateral shoots. Tree deciduous	*Larix* (p.42)
▷ Needles in groups of 2–5 on short lateral shoots on twigs	*Pinus* (p.44)
▷ Needles arranged singly on twigs:	
▷ Leaves spreading on either side of twigs, pale green beneath on either side of midrib. Female cone a red 'berry'	*Taxus* (p.44)
▷ Leaves spreading on either side of twigs, white stripes beneath, leaf scars smooth, cones erect and disintegrating on tree	*Abies* (p.42)
▷ Leaves not obviously spreading on either side of twigs:	
▷ Fallen leaves leaving peg-like projections on twigs. Cones pendulous, bracts not protruding	*Picea* (p.42)
▷ Leaf scars smooth on twigs. Cones pendulous, with protruding 3-lobed bracts	*Pseudotsuga* (p.42)
▷ Leaf scars smooth on twigs. Cones ≥50 mm, erect and breaking up on twigs, bracts protruding or not, not 3-lobed	*Abies* (p.42

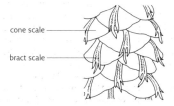

cone scale

bract scale

part of female cone of Douglas Fir showing bract and cone scales

FLOWERING PLANTS

Flowering plants have dominated life on Earth for the last 100 million years and more than 250,000 have so far been described in about 500 families. They differ from the conifers in the unique structure of their flowers, and in particular in that the *seed*, the fertilised *ovule*, is wholly enclosed within the *ovary* (*see* 'The Fruit' below). With the exception of the grasses, sedges and most temperate trees, the majority of flowering plants are pollinated by animals (in Britain predominantly by insects), while conifers are all wind pollinated. The *fruit* of flowering plants consists of the mature ovary together with its enclosed seeds.

Flowering plants are traditionally divided into two main groups: the dicotyledons and the monocotyledons. The names refer to the number of seed leaves, *cotyledons*, that appear when the plant first germinates; the dicotyledons have two, while the monocotyledons have just one. Modern classifications based on molecular data now recognise about six separate groups of flowering plants, but more than 90 per cent of species still fall within the two traditional groups. These can usually be separated as follows:

- DICOTYLEDONS Leaves usually 'net-veined', with a single midrib and numerous branching lateral veins; basic number of flower parts usually four or five.
- MONOCOTYLEDONS Leaves usually narrow and strap-like, with a single midrib with parallel lateral veins arising at the base of the leaf blade and converging towards the tip; basic number of flower parts usually three or six.

The Flower

The most obvious feature that distinguishes flowering plants is the flower. A typical flower consists of two sets of sterile organs and two sets of fertile organs arranged sequentially in a series of whorls. They are attached to the *receptacle*, the swollen tip of the flower stalk, or *pedicel*.

The outer whorl of *sepals*, comprising the *calyx*, are typically green, but may be coloured, and protect the flower while it is in bud. The inner whorl of *petals*, comprising the *corolla*, are usually brightly coloured and help attract pollinators. The calyx and corolla together comprise the *perianth*. In some flowers the sepals and petals are similar and indistinguishable, or there may be only a single whorl; in these cases the individual parts are usually termed *tepals*.

The sepals and petals may be separate and free from each other right to their point of attachment, or

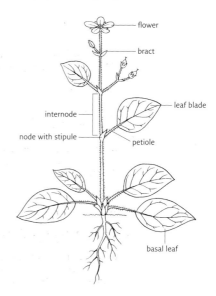

Fig. 1 Parts of a flowering plant.

the lower part may be joined to form a tube, the *calyx tube* or *corolla tube*.

The fertile parts of the flower consist of the male *stamens* and the female *carpels*. The stamens consist of the *anthers*, which contain the pollen, and which are attached to the tips of slender stalks, the *filaments*.

The female organs, the *carpels*, consist of three parts. At the base is the *ovary*, which encloses the *ovules* that after fertilisation develop into the *seeds*. Surmounting the ovary is a stalk, the *style*, the tip of which is a swollen or branched *stigma* that forms the receptive surface for the pollen.

Most plants have several carpels (*see* Fig. 2). If the individual carpels are separate, as in a buttercup, the flower is *apocarpous*. If the carpels are fused together into a single structure the flower in *syncarpous* and the whole structure is the ovary.

The receptacle to which the parts of the flower are attached may be swollen and convex, or concave and saucer- or cup-shaped (*see* Fig. 3). In the first case the sepals and petals are inserted around the base of the ovary, while in the latter they will be attached to the rim of the receptacle. In both cases the ovary is termed *superior*. In some flowers the receptacle completely encloses the ovary and is fused to it; in this case the insertion of the sepals and petals will be at the top of the ovary and the ovary is *inferior* (think of an apple).

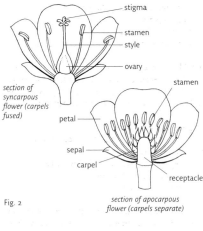

section of syncarpous flower (carpels fused)

Fig. 2

section of apocarpous flower (carpels separate)

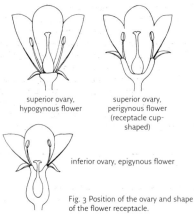

superior ovary, hypogynous flower

superior ovary, perigynous flower (receptacle cup-shaped)

inferior ovary, epigynous flower

Fig. 3 Position of the ovary and shape of the flower receptacle.

Some flowers are unisexual, possessing only stamens or carpels. In these cases the male and female flowers may be on the same plant, as in an oak tree, in which case the plant is termed *monoecious*, or on separate male and female plants, as in a Holly bush, in which case the plant is *dioecious*.

Flowers vary greatly in shape and size. If the petals and sepals are all of the same shape and size and the flowers are radially symmetrical, the flowers are described as *regular*, e.g. a Primrose. If the petals and sepals are not all of the same shape and size and it is possible to divide the flower only in one plane to produce two identical halves, then the flowers are *irregular*, e.g. a Sweet Pea.

In classifying plants into their separate families the important characters include:

- The numbers of sepals, petals, stamens and carpels.
- Whether flowers are apocarpous or syncarpous.
- Whether the ovary is superior or inferior.
- Whether the flowers are regular or irregular.
- Whether the sepals and petals are free or whether the lower parts are joined to form a tube.

The Inflorescence

The flowers are either *solitary*, borne singly on the plant, as in a Primrose or dandelion, or grouped together in an *inflorescence*. The stem of a solitary flower is termed the *scape*.

Inflorescences take many forms; the more common types are illustrated below in Fig. 4.

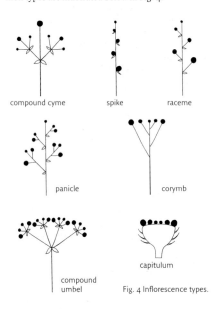

compound cyme

spike

raceme

panicle

corymb

compound umbel

capitulum

Fig. 4 Inflorescence types.

The Fruit

The fruit in flowering plants consists of the mature ovary together with the enclosed seeds. Fruits are either dry, like a nut, or fleshy, like a berry. Dry fruits are either *dehiscent* like a pod, splitting open to release the seeds, or are *indehiscent* like a nut. Fleshy fruits are either fleshy throughout with many seeds as in a tomato – known as a *berry* – or the innermost layer of the fruit is woody and contains a single seed like a plum, known as a *drupe*.

THE BRITISH FLORA

Excluding brambles, dandelions and hawkweeds (the large apomictic genera), there are about 2500 species of flowering plants in the British Isles distributed among about 120 families. However, about 70 per cent of these species belong to just 20 large families. Thus, becoming familiar with these '**top 20**' families is an obvious first step towards identifying individual species of flowering plants.

Top 20 families (in order of numbers of native species)

1 Poaceae (Gramineae): Grasses
2 Asteraceae (Compositae): Composites
3 Cyperaceae: Sedges
4 Rosaceae: Rose family
5 Caryophyllaceae: Chickweeds, pinks, campions
6 Fabaceae (Leguminosae): Vetches, peas, clovers
7 Scrophulariaceae: Figworts, mulleins, foxgloves, speedwells
8 Brassicaceae (Cruciferae): Crucifers
9 Orchidaceae: Orchids
10 Apiaceae (Umbelliferae): Umbellifers
11 Lamiaceae (Labiatae): Labiates
12 Ranunculaceae: Buttercups, crowfoots, hellebores, anemones
13 Liliaceae: Lily family
14 Juncaceae: Rushes, wood-rushes
15 Polygonaceae: Docks, sorrels, knotweeds
16 Chenopodiaceae: Oraches, goosefoots
17 Boraginaceae: Borage family
18 Potamogetonaceae: Pondweeds
19 Ericaceae: Heath family
20 Geraniaceae: Crane's-bills, stork's-bills

In addition, there are five families or genera (called here the '**typical 5**') that, although not so large, are nevertheless very distinctive and easily recognised, and contain many common and widespread species.

Typical 5 families

1 Clusiaceae (Hypericaceae): St John's-worts
2 Violaceae: Violets, pansies
3 Onagraceae (*Epilobium*): Willowherbs
4 Euphorbiaceae: Spurges
5 Rubiaceae: Bedstraws

The family key below first describes the 'top 20 families' and then the 'typical 5'. The remaining 95 families are divided first into 'Trees and shrubs' and 'Submerged and floating water plants'. As trees and shrubs are often not flowering when met in the field, the key has been designed without the use of flowering characters. Both vegetative and flowering characters are used in the aquatics key.

The family key then divides into 'Emergent monocotyledons', 'Climbers', 'Insectivorous plants' and saprophytic or parasitic 'Plants without chlorophyll'. This leaves 'The rest', which are subdivided into five further groups on the basis of flower structure.

THE FAMILY KEY

First, become familiar with the '**top 20**' and the '**typical 5**' families, then, if your plant is not in one of those 25, place it in one of the following 11 main groups by following through the groups sequentially and then proceeding to the appropriate key (*see* pp.52–71).

Top 20 families

A DICOTYLEDONS (p.47)

Cirsium Asteraceae

Aster Asteraceae

	if	then
1	▷ Herbs	Go to ▷ **2**
	▷ Woody plants	Go to ▷ **13**
2	▷ *Flowers (florets) very small, in daisy-, dandelion- or thistle-like heads*; individual flowers either ray florets with corolla a petal-like *ligule*, or disc florets with a 5-lobed corolla; calyx usually reduced to a plume of hairs, the *pappus*; 5 stamens, anthers united into a tube surrounding style; ovary inferior	**Asteraceae** (Compositae) (p.460)
	▷ Plants not like this (not Asteraceae)	Go to ▷ **3**

Smyrnium
Apiaceae

Rumex
Polygonaceae

Chenopodium
Chenopodiaceae

Echium
Boraginaceae

Ranunculus
Ranunculaceae

Potentilla Rosaceae

Geranium
Geraniaceae

Cardamine
Brassicaceae

Silene
Caryophyllaceae

Lathyrus
Fabaceae

	if	**then**
3	▷ Flowers small, white or yellow; *inflorescence an umbel*; 5 sepals; 5 petals; 5 stamens; ovary inferior	**Apiaceae** (Umbelliferae) (p.338)
	▷ Plant not like this (not Apiaceae)	Go to ▷ **4**
4	▷ Flowers small and inconspicuous	Go to ▷ **5**
	▷ Flowers not small and inconspicuous	Go to ▷ **6**
5	▷ Leaves with fused stipules sheathing the stem; flowers greenish, brown, white or pink; 3–6 tepals in 1–2 whorls	**Polygonaceae** (p.142)
	▷ Leaves without stipules; flowers greenish; 3–5 tepals in a single whorl; plants often succulent	**Chenopodiaceae** (p.102)
6	▷ Flowers regular	Go to ▷ **7**
	▷ Flowers irregular	Go to ▷ **11**
7	▷ Petals and sepals free	Go to ▷ **8**
	▷ Petals and sepals joined; plants usually roughly hairy; *leaves alternate*; calyx and corolla 5-lobed; 5 stamens; *ovary deeply 4-lobed* (flowers of *Echium* are slightly irregular)	**Boraginaceae** (with Hydrophyllaceae) (p.372)
8	▷ Stamens numerous (usually >2× the number of sepals)	Go to ▷ **9**
	▷ Stamens ≤2× the number of sepals	Go to ▷ **10**
9	▷ Mostly herbs; *leaves spirally arranged, without stipules*; flowers variable	**Ranunculaceae** (p.78)
	▷ Herbs, shrubs and trees; *leaves alternate, usually with stipules*; petals and sepals equal in number	**Rosaceae** (p.240)
10	▷ 5 sepals; 5 petals; 10 stamens; flowers pink, blue or purple; leaves palmate or pinnate	**Geraniaceae** (p.330)
	▷ 4 sepals; 4 petals; 4 (or 6) stamens; *leaves alternate*	**Brassicaceae** (Cruciferae) (p.186)
	▷ 4 or 5 sepals and petals; 5 or 10 stamens; *leaves opposite*; inflorescence usually a cyme	**Caryophyllaceae** (p.130)
	▷ Flowers blue (pink or white) (1 petal slightly larger than other 3); 4 petals; 2 stamens. *Veronica*	**Scrophulariaceae** (p.40)
11	▷ Flowers typically shaped like those of a Sweet Pea; 5 sepals, united; *5 petals, with a large standard petal, 2 wing petals and a lower keel of 2 united petals; 10 stamens, united into a tube*	**Fabaceae** (Leguminosae) (p.274)

Lamiastrum
Lamiaceae

Rhinanthus
Scrophulariaceae

Erica
Ericaceae

	if	then
	▷ Flowers not shaped like those of a Sweet Pea; <10 stamens	Go to ▷ **12**
12	▷ *Stems 4-angled*; leaves opposite; calyx with 5 teeth; corolla 5-lobed, often appearing 2-lipped; *4 stamens; ovary deeply 4-lobed* (looks like a hot cross bun at base of calyx when corolla removed and viewed from above); plants often aromatic	**Lamiaceae** (Labiatae) (p.384)
	▷ Leaves alternate or opposite; 2, 4 or 5 stamens; *ovary not 5-lobed* (some species resemble the Lamiaceae, but the lack of the 4-lobed ovary will distinguish them)	**Scrophulariaceae** (with Acanthaceae) (p.406)
13	▷ Plants usually evergreen; leaves simple, often leathery or needle-like; *flowers often urn-shaped*, sepals and petals joined at base (except *Ledum*); 4 or 5 sepals; 4 or 5 petals; 8 or 10 stamens	**Ericaceae** (p.212)

MONOCOTYLEDONS (p.47)

Potamogeton
tamogetonaceae

Orchis
Orchidaceae

Scilla
Liliaceae

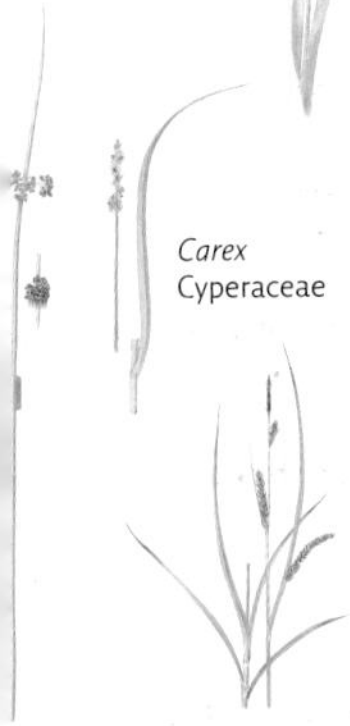

Carex
Cyperaceae

cus
caceae

Carex
Cyperaceae

	if	then
1	▷ Aquatic plants, either entirely submerged or with floating leaves	**Potamogetonaceae** (p.526)
	▷ Plants not entirely submerged or with floating leaves	Go to ▷ **2**
2	▷ Flowers conspicuous and colourful	Go to ▷ **3**
	▷ Flowers small and inconspicuous, or perianth absent	Go to ▷ **5**
3	▷ Flowers regular	Go to ▷ **4**
	▷ Flowers irregular	**Orchidaceae** (p.665)
4	▷ 6 stamens	**Liliaceae** (p.646)
	▷ 3 stamens	**Iridaceae** (p.660)
5	▷ Perianth with 6 small brownish or yellowish tepals; flowers hermaphrodite; leaves often cylindrical in section	**Juncaceae** (rushes) (p.542)
	▷ Perianth absent	Go to ▷ **6**
6	▷ Stem cylindrical in section, hollow; leaves alternate; flowers hermaphrodite, enclosed between 2 bracts	**Poaceae** (grasses) (p.586)
	▷ Stem often 3-angled, solid; leaves 3-ranked; flowers hermaphrodite or unisexual, subtended by a single bract	**Cyperaceae** (sedges) (p.550)

Typical 5 families

CLUSIACEAE (Hypericaceae; St John's-worts) (p.156, key on p.160)
Herbs or small shrubs with entire, opposite leaves and yellow flowers;
5 petals, free; sepals and petals often fringed with black glands; stamens
numerous and joined together in bundles

Hypericum
Clusiaceae

RUBIACEAE (bedstraws) (p.446, key on p.448)
Recognised by the narrow, sessile leaves in whorls of ≥4 (actually 2
opposite leaves plus ≥2 leaf-like stipules); flowers small, white or yellow,
regular in compound inflorescences; sepals minute or absent; 4–5 petals,
joined into a tube at base

Asperula
Rubiaceae

VIOLACEAE (violets and pansies) (p.166, key on p.170)
Flowers strongly irregular, blue, yellow or white; 5 sepals with short
appendage below point of attachment; 5 petals, free, the lowest with a
backward-pointing spur; violets with heart-shaped leaves and narrow
stipules; pansies with lobed leaf-like stipules

Viola
Violaceae

ONAGRACEAE (*Epilobium*; willowherbs) (p.306, key on p.308)
Flowers pink, regular; 4 petals, free; 8 stamens; ovary inferior; fruit an
elongated capsule dehiscing to expose seeds, which have a plume of
hairs; at least lower leaves opposite. The Onagraceae is a rather variable
family and members other than the willowherbs will key out under the
key 'Flowers regular, petals free' (p.68)

Epilobium
Onagraceae

EUPHORBIACEAE (spurges) (p.316, key on p.318)
The strange green or reddish-tinged 'flowers' of spurges appear to be
borne in umbels. In fact, the 'flowers' are condensed inflorescences
consisting of 4 fused bracts forming a corolla-like cup on the inside of
which several male flowers consisting of a single stamen, and a single
female flower. The leaves are usually alternate and the stems contain a
poisonous milky latex

Euphorbia
Euphorbiaceae

**If your plant is neither in the top 20 families nor one of the typical
5, then follow the rest of the family key (continued below)
sequentially.**

if	then
▷ **Trees and shrubs** Deciduous or evergreen woody plants growing to >c.50 cm tall	(p.54)
▷ **Submerged and floating aquatics** Water plants that are free-floating or with leafy stems entirely submerged, with or without floating leaves; flowering stems may be emergent	(p.58)
▷ **Emergent monocotyledons** Marginal monocotyledons rooted in the water but with most of the stem emergent and above the water level	(p.62)
▷ **Climbers** Climbing plants with or without woody stems	(p.64)
▷ **Insectivorous plants** Plants with insect-trapping adaptations such as sticky glands or water-filled traps	(p.64)
▷ **Plants without chlorophyll** Saprophytic or parasitic plants lacking chlorophyll	(p.65)
▷ If none of these, then go to 'The rest'	

Key to the rest

1 ▷ Much-branched woody evergreen plant, parasitic on branches of trees; leaves opposite; flowers inconspicuous; berries white. *Viscum*   **Viscaceae** (p.314)
    ▷ Plant not like this   Go to ▷ **2**

2 ▷ Flowers small, without perianth, unisexual, crowded at the base of a terminal club-shaped column, the *spadix*, male above, female below; the whole enclosed within a cowl-like sheath, the *spathe*; leaves hastate. *Arum*   **Araceae** (p.534)
    ▷ Plant not like this   Go to ▷ **3**

3 ▷ **Flowers small and inconspicuous**.
Flowers usually pale, greenish or brownish, <c.3 mm across. Some composites (Asteraceae) may apparently key out here, but these will have small heads of florets rather than individual flowers (*see* 'Top 20 families' key)   (p.65)
    ▷ Flowers not small and inconspicuous   Go to ▷ **4**

	if	then
4	▷ **Flowers in dense heads**. Some of these may resemble composites (Asteraceae), but if they do they will have projecting stamens with free anthers, whereas the anthers of composites are joined to form a tube that surrounds the style (*see* 'Top 20 families' key)	(p.67)
	▷ Flowers not in dense heads	Go to ▷ **5**
5	▷ **Flowers irregular** (zygomorphic)	(p.68)
	▷ Flowers regular (actinomorphic)	Go to ▷ **6**
6	▷ **Flowers regular, petals free** to point of insertion	(p.68)
	▷ **Flowers regular, petals united** at least at the base	(p.70)

TREES AND SHRUBS

Deciduous	A (below)
Evergreen	B (p.57)

A DECIDUOUS

	if	then
1	▷ Leaves compound	Go to ▷ **2**
	▷ Leaves simple	Go to ▷ **6**
2	▷ Leaves palmate; flowers in large terminal panicles. *Aesculus*	**Hippocastanaceae** (p.326)
	▷ Leaves pinnate	Go to ▷ **3**
3	▷ Leaves alternate	Go to ▷ **4**
	▷ Leaves opposite	Go to ▷ **5**
4	▷ Shrub; stem with prickles. *Rosa*	**Rosaceae** (p.258)
	▷ Small tree; stem without prickles. *Sorbus aucuparia*	**Rosaceae** (p.266)
5	▷ Tree to 25 m; bark smooth, becoming fissured with age; twigs without prominent lenticels; buds black. *Fraxinus*	**Oleaceae** (p.406)
	▷ Shrub or small tree to 10 m; bark deeply furrowed, corky; twigs with prominent lenticels; buds pale. *Sambucus*	**Caprifoliaceae** (p.452)
6	▷ Leaves opposite	Go to ▷ **7**
	▷ Leaves alternate	Go to ▷ **15**
7	▷ Leaves lobed; shrubs or trees	Go to ▷ **8**
	▷ Leaves not lobed; shrubs	Go to ▷ **9**

if	**then**
8 ▷ Petioles with narrow stipules and concave circular glands; flowers white, inflorescence conspicuous, umbel-like; fruit a red berry. *Viburnum opulus*	**Caprifoliaceae** (p.452)
▷ Petioles without stipules or glands; flowers green; fruit dry, double, winged. *Acer*	**Aceraceae** (p.326)
9 ▷ Leaves pubescent	Go to ▷ **10**
▷ Leaves glabrous	Go to ▷ **12**
10 ▷ Twigs red, especially on exposed side; leaves entire, thinly pubescent. *Cornus*	**Cornaceae** (p.314)
▷ Twigs not red; leaf margins toothed, densely pubescent beneath	Go to ▷ **11**
11 ▷ Leaves ovate-lanceolate, not cordate at base, 10–25 cm. *Buddleja*	**Buddlejaceae** (p.404)
▷ Leaves oval, cordate at base, 5–10 cm. *Viburnum lantana*	**Caprifoliaceae** (p.452)
12 ▷ Twigs green; fruit 4-lobed, bright pink with orange centre. *Euonymus*	**Celastraceae** (p.314)
▷ Twigs not green; fruit not as above	Go to ▷ **13**
13 ▷ Leaves toothed (often not quite opposite), twigs becoming thorny. *Rhamnus*	**Rhamnaceae** (p.322)
▷ Leaves entire	Go to ▷ **14**
14 ▷ Leaves of sucker shoots and some lower branches conspicuously lobed; flowers pink; berries white. *Symphoricarpos*	**Caprifoliaceae** (p.452)
▷ No leaves lobed. *Syringa, Ligustrum*	**Oleaceae** (p.406)
15 ▷ Leaves small, scale-like, ≤1 mm, acute; feathery shrub to 3 m. *Tamarix*	**Tamaricaceae** (p.174)
▷ Plant not like this	Go to ▷ **16**
16 ▷ Leaves lobed	Go to ▷ **17**
▷ Leaves not lobed	Go to ▷ **21**
17 ▷ Small shrubs, 1–2 m; leaves palmately lobed. *Ribes*	**Grossulariaceae** (p.226)
▷ Shrubs or trees; if shrubs then >5 m at maturity	Go to ▷ **18**
18 ▷ Leaves densely white-felted beneath. *Populus*	**Salicaceae** (p.174)
▷ Leaves not densely white-felted beneath	Go to ▷ **19**
19 ▷ Thorny shrubs or small tree. *Crataegus*	**Rosaceae** (p.272)
▷ Tree, not thorny	Go to ▷ **20**

if	then
20 ▷ Leaves entire, oblong or obovate in outline, lobes rounded or pointed. *Quercus*	**Fagaceae** (p.98)
▷ Leaves toothed, broadly ovate; lobes acute. *Sorbus torminalis*	**Rosaceae** (p.270)
21 ▷ Thorny or spiny shrubs	Go to ▷ **22**
▷ Trees or shrubs; not thorny or spiny	Go to ▷ **25**
22 ▷ Stems with branched spines; leaf margins with spiny teeth. *Berberis*	**Berberidaceae** (p.88)
▷ Twigs thorny; leaves entire or margins with blunt teeth	Go to ▷ **23**
23 ▷ Leaves entire, greyish	Go to ▷ **24**
▷ Leaves green, margins toothed. *Prunus*	**Rosaceae** (p.262)
24 ▷ Dense, much-branched, erect shrub; leaves linear-lanceolate, covered by silvery scales; berries orange. *Hippophae*	**Eleagnaceae** (p.304)
▷ Scrambling shrub; leaves ovate-elliptic, not covered by silvery scales; berries red. *Lycium*	**Solanaceae** (p.366)

if	then
25 ▷ Buds with a single bud scale, flattened on inner side and closely appressed to twigs; leaves elliptic-ovate or lanceolate, >5× as long as broad. *Salix*	**Salicaceae** (p.176)
▷ Buds not like this	Go to ▷ **26**
26 ▷ Twigs and short shoots with crowded concentric wrinkles of old leaf scars; at least some leaves with stipules	**Rosaceae** (p.240)
▷ Twigs without concentric wrinkles; stipules falling early	Go to ▷ **27**
27 ▷ Leaves entire	Go to ▷ **28**
▷ Leaf margins toothed	Go to ▷ **30**
28 ▷ Large tree; buds long, spindle-shaped, with bud scales; leaves ovate, acute. *Fagus*	**Fagaceae** (p.98)
▷ Shrub	Go to ▷ **29**
29 ▷ Shrub to 5 m; buds without bud scales; leaves broadly obovate, rounded at tip with short, blunt point, glossy (widespread). *Frangula*	**Rhamnaceae** (p.322)
▷ Small, little-branched shrub, to 1 m; leaves oblanceolate, acute, not glossy (very rare). *Daphne mezereon*	**Thymelaeaceae** (p.306)

if	then
30 ▷ Small aromatic shrub to 2.5 m; leaves oblanceolate, toothed towards tips and covered on both surfaces by shining yellow glands. *Myrica*	**Myricaceae** (p.98)
▷ Shrub or tree; if shrub then >4 m at maturity; leaves equally toothed all round, neither glandular nor aromatic	Go to ▷ **31**
31 ▷ Shrub or small tree; upper pair of large lateral veins curving upwards and converging towards tip; twigs becoming spiny (leaves may be almost opposite). *Rhamnus*	**Rhamnaceae** (p.322)
▷ Trees; upper pair of lateral veins not converging towards tip; twigs not spiny	Go to ▷ **32**
32 ▷ Leaf strongly asymmetrical, 2 sides of leaf meeting petiole at different points at base. *Ulmus*	**Ulmaceae** (p.96)
▷ Base of leaf not asymmetrical in that way	Go to ▷ **33**
33 ▷ Leaf base oblique and/or cordate; toothing regular, teeth sharp-pointed. *Tilia*	**Tiliaceae** (p.164)
▷ Leaf base not oblique-cordate, or if cordate, then leaf pubescent	Go to ▷ **34**
34 ▷ At least some petioles > ¼ as long as blade; petioles flatted towards tip. *Populus*	**Salicaceae** (p.174)
▷ Petiole ≤ ¼ as long as blade; petioles not distinctly flattened	Go to ▷ **35**
35 ▷ Leaves oblong-lanceolate, 10–25 cm, coarsely toothed with bristle-tipped teeth; catkins erect; fruit covered by long, branched spines. *Castanea*	**Fagaceae** (p.98)
▷ Leaves ovate to sub-orbicular; male catkins pendulous	**Betulaceae** (p.100)

EVERGREEN

if	then
1 ▷ Small shrub to 1 m, with stiff, spine-tipped, flattened, leaf-like shoots and green twigs. *Ruscus*	**Liliaceae** (p.660)
▷ Plant not like this	Go to ▷ **2**
2 ▷ Densely spiny shrub to 2 m, spines branched; leaves on mature plants absent. *Ulex*	**Fabaceae** (p.274)
▷ Plant not like this	Go to ▷ **3**

	if	then
3	▷ Leaves pinnate, leaflets with spiny teeth along margins; shrub ≤1.5 m. *Mahonia*	**Berberidaceae** (p.88)
	▷ Leaves simple	Go to ▷ **4**
4	▷ Leaves opposite, entire, small, 1–2.5 cm, oblong, leathery; shrub or small tree	Go to ▷ **5**
	▷ Leaves alternate or whorled	Go to ▷ **6**
5	▷ Young twigs green. *Buxus*	**Buxaceae** (p.314)
	▷ Young twigs not green, leaves small 6–18 mm, distinctly glossy above. *Lonicera*	**Caprifoliaceae** (p.452)
	▷ Young twigs not green, leaves 30–50 mm, not distinctly glossy above. *Ligustrum*	**Oleaceae** (p.406)
6	▷ Leaves needle-like, in whorls of 3–5; shrubs to 2 m. *Erica*	**Ericaceae** (p.215)
	▷ Leaves alternate	Go to ▷ **7**
7	▷ Leaves succulent, ± round in section, 5–18 × *c*.1 mm, blunt-tipped; small coastal shrub to 1.5 m. *Suaeda vera*	**Chenopodiaceae** (p.112)
	▷ Plant not like this	Go to ▷ **8**
8	▷ Small heath-like shrub, <50 cm; leaves dense, 4–6 mm. *Empetrum*	**Empetraceae** (p.212)
	▷ Plant not a small heath-like shrub	Go to ▷ **9**
9	▷ Leaves spiny, glossy, leathery in texture. *Ilex*	**Aquifoliaceae** (p.314)
	▷ Leaves not spiny	Go to ▷ **10**
10	▷ Tree to 30 m; leaves densely hairy beneath, entire or with sharp teeth. *Quercus ilex*	**Fagaceae** (p.98)
	▷ Shrubs or small trees; leaves ± glabrous	Go to ▷ **11**
11	▷ Leaves entire	Go to ▷ **12**
	▷ Leaves toothed	Go to ▷ **13**
12	▷ Little-branched, small shrub ≤ 1 m; leaves to 12 cm, often crowded towards top of ± leafless stems. *Daphne laureola*	**Thymelaeaceae** (p.306)
	▷ Densely branched shrub to 5 m; leaves elliptic to 16 cm. *Rhododendron*	**Ericaceae** (p.212)
13	▷ Leaves elliptic-obovate, 4–10 cm, distinctly but bluntly toothed, bright green beneath; shrub or small tree to 12 m. *Arbutus*	**Ericaceae** (p.216)
	▷ Leaves oblong-obovate, 5–18 cm, teeth small, sharp, well-separated, very glossy above, rather glaucous beneath; shrub or small tree to 5 m. *Prunus laurocerasus*	**Rosaceae** (p.262)

Note Evergreen prostrate or dwarf shrubs, rarely >50 cm tall, belonging to the Ericaceae would also key out here. Most have small ovate or elliptic, toothed or entire leaves (*see* 'Top 20 families' key).

Plants free-floating at or just below water surface   A (below)
Plants rooted, with floating leaves   B (p.59)
Plants rooted, floating leaves absent, leaves all submerged   C (p.60)

A PLANTS FREE-FLOATING AT OR JUST BELOW WATER SURFACE

if	then
▷ Individual plants consisting of single small, leaf-like thallus, <10 mm across:	
▷ Plant stalkless, floating on surface	**Lemnaceae** (p.534)
▷ Individual plants joined by their stalks in groups of 3, floating beneath surface	**Lemnaceae** (p.534)
▷ Individual plants consisting of a lobed thallus ≤20 mm across:	
▷ Thallus ≤15 mm across; lobes broad, ≤4 mm wide; scales on underside of thallus conspicuous. *Ricciocarpos natans*	**Aquatic liverworts**
▷ Thallus ≤20 mm across; lobes long, narrow, ≤1 mm wide; scales on underside of thallus inconspicuous or absent. *Riccia fluitans*	**Aquatic liverworts**
▷ Individual plants 1–5 cm across, much branched; leaves very small, ≤2 mm, in 2 rows on upper side of stem, turning red in summer. *Azolla* (fern)	**Azollaceae** (p.40)
▷ Leaves ± circular, *c.*3 cm across; flowers 2 cm across; 3 petals, white. *Hydrocharis*	**Hydrocharitaceae** (p.520)
▷ Leaves lanceolate, in large, tight rosettes, stiff, to 50 cm long, margins serrated; flowers 3–4 cm across; 3 petals, white. *Stratiotes*	**Hydrocharitaceae** (p.520)

B PLANTS ROOTED, WITH FLOATING LEAVES

	if	then
1	▷ Floating leaves distinctly lobed; submerged leaves much branched, with thread-like segments; flowers white; 5 petals, free. *Ranunculus* (water-crowfoots)	**Ranunculaceae** (p.84)
	▷ Floating leaves not lobed; submerged leaves, if present, not much branched, with thread-like segments	Go to ▷ **2**
2	▷ Floating leaves broad, rounded at tip, <1½× as long as broad, deeply cordate at base	Go to ▷ **3**
	▷ Floating leaves >2× as long as broad	Go to ▷ **4**

	if	then
3	▷ Leaf margins entire; flowers solitary, terminal. Water-lilies	**Nymphaeaceae** (p.72)
	▷ Leaf margins wavy; flowers yellow, in small axillary groups. *Nymphoides*	**Menyanthaceae** (p.370)
4	▷ Submerged leaves opposite; floating leaves obovate, in rosettes	**Callitrichaceae** (p.402)
	▷ Submerged leaves alternate or basal	Go to ▷ **5**
5	▷ Floating leaves strap-shaped or grass-like	Go to ▷ **6**
	▷ Floating leaves not grass-like, blades ovate-elliptic	Go to ▷ **7**
6	▷ Leaves consisting of basal sheath and free blade with ligule at junction. Grasses, e.g. *Glyceria*	**Poaceae** (p.586)
	▷ Leaves without sheath, ligule absent; flowers unisexual, in spherical head	**Sparganiaceae** (p.644)
7	▷ Floating leaves with a single midrib and branching lateral veins; flowers pink, in spikes. *Persicaria amphibia*	**Polygonaceae** (p.142)
	▷ Floating leaves with several ± parallel veins converging at tip	Go to ▷ **8**
8	▷ Submerged leaves alternate, with stipule at junction with stem	**Potamogetonaceae** (p.526)
	▷ All leaves basal without stipules	Go to ▷ **9**
9	▷ Flowers in racemes or whorled panicles; 3 sepals; 3 petals, lilac or white	**Alismataceae** (p.518)
	▷ Flowers in 2 spikes; 1 tepal, white. *Aponogeton*	**Aponogetonaceae** (p.520)

C PLANTS ROOTED, FLOATING LEAVES ABSENT, LEAVES ALL SUBMERGED

	if	then
1	▷ Plants leafless, with whorls of branches arranged along stem; stems may appear striated when examined with a lens and fresh plants may have a strong, distinctive smell of stale vegetables. Stoneworts (green algae); may be confused with *Ceratophyllum*, which has whorls of forked leaves resembling the branches of stoneworts	**Charophyta**
	▷ Plants leafy	Go to ▷ **2**
2	▷ Leaves simple	Go to ▷ **3**
	▷ Leaves compound	Go to ▷ **24**

	if	then
3	▷ Submerged stems leafy	Go to ▷ **4**
	▷ Submerged leaves all basal	Go to ▷ **18**
4	▷ Leaves in whorls	Go to ▷ **5**
	▷ Leaves not in whorls	Go to ▷ **6**
5	▷ Leaves in whorls of 6–12. *Hippuris*	**Hippuridaceae** (p.402)
	▷ Leaves in whorls of 3–5. *Elodea*	**Hydrocharitaceae** (p.520)
6	▷ Plant free-floating; leaves lanceolate, in large, tight rosettes, stiff, to 50 cm long, margins serrated; flowers 3–4 cm across; 3 petals, white. *Stratiotes*	**Hydrocharitaceae** (p.520)
	▷ Plant not like this	Go to ▷ **7**
7	▷ Leaves very narrow, filiform, ≤1 mm wide	Go to ▷ **8**
	▷ Leaves linear-ovate, >1 mm wide	Go to ▷ **13**
8	▷ Leaves with ligule	**Potamogetonaceae** (p.526)
	▷ Leaves without a ligule	Go to ▷ **9**
9	▷ Stem leaves arising in clusters along stem; stems often reddish. *Juncus bulbosus*	**Juncaceae** (p.542)
	▷ Stem leaves not in clusters	Go to ▷ **10**
10	▷ Apex of leaves minutely toothed (use a lens)	Go to ▷ **11**
	▷ Apex of leaves not toothed	Go to ▷ **12**
11	▷ Most leaves alternate; flowers small, in umbel-like groups on end of long peduncle	**Ruppiaceae** (p.532)
	▷ Most leaves opposite or whorled; very small, sessile, in leaf axils	**Najadaceae** (p.532)
12	▷ Leaves opposite. *Zannichellia*	**Zannichelliacae** (p.532)
	▷ Leaves alternate. *Eleogiton*	**Cyperaceae** (p.554)
13	▷ Leaves opposite	Go to ▷ **14**
	▷ Leaves alternate or spirally arranged	Go to ▷ **17**
14	▷ Stems procumbent, rooting at nodes; flowers small, in axils of leaves	Go to ▷ **15**
	▷ Stems not procumbent and rooting at nodes	Go to ▷ **16**
15	▷ Stems and leaves usually distinctly reddish purple; leaves at stem tips sometimes floating; 4 sepals; petals absent. *Ludwigia*	**Onagraceae** (p.310)
	▷ Slender annuals; stems and leaves not reddish purple; 3 or 4 petals and sepals. *Elatine*	**Elatinaceae** (p.156)

if	then
16 ▷ Leaves lanceolate-ovate, ± clasping at base, translucent, midrib conspicuous; inflorescence a stalked 2-flowered head. *Groenlandia*	**Potamogetonaceae** (p.526)
▷ Leaves linear or elliptic, not clasping, midrib obscure; flowers sessile, solitary or in pairs in leaf axils; perianth absent. *Callitriche*	**Callitrichaceae** (p.402)
17 ▷ Leaves alternate, with basal sheath; blades long, grass-like	**Potamogetonaceae** (p.526)
▷ Leaves spirally arranged, without basal sheath, densely crowded, recurved. *Lagarosiphon*	**Hydrocharitaceae** (p.520)
18 ▷ Leaves thread-like, <1.5 mm wide	Go to ▷ **19**
▷ Leaves in rosettes, succulent or translucent, >2 mm wide	Go to ▷ **21**
19 ▷ Leaves arising singly from slender rhizome, slender, coiled at tip when young. *Pilularia* (fern)	**Marsileaceae** (p.24)
▷ Leaves and stems arising in tufts from slender rhizomes	Go to ▷ **20**
20 ▷ Leaves cylindrical, with 2 hollow tubes; stems often reddish, limp. *Juncus bulbosus*	**Juncaceae** (p.542)
▷ Leaf-like stems 4-angled, stiff. *Eleocharis acicularis*	**Cyperaceae** (p.552)
21 ▷ Plant with distinctive white, segmented, 'worm-like' roots; leaves numerous, finely pointed; flowers dark greyish, in tight heads; 2+2 tepals. *Eriocaulon*	**Eriocaulaceae** (p.534)
▷ Plant not like this	Go to ▷ **22**
22 ▷ Plant stoloniferous; leaves cylindrical; flowers unisexual, male flowers on long stalks. *Littorella*	**Plantaginaceae** (p.404)
▷ Plants not stoloniferous	Go to ▷ **23**
23 ▷ Leaves with 4 longitudinal hollow tubes, base flattened and expanded; flowerless. *Isoetes* (quillworts)	**Isoetaceae** (p.18)
▷ Leaves compressed, with 2 longitudinal hollow tubes, flattened at tip, recurved; flowers pale lilac. *Lobelia*	**Campanulaceae** (p.444)
▷ Leaves solid, expanded at base and tapering to fine point; flowers submerged, small; petals white or absent. *Subularia*	**Brassicaceae** (p.206)
24 ▷ Leaves pinnate	Go to ▷ **25**
▷ Leaves not pinnate, repeatedly branched	Go to ▷ **27**

if	then
25 ▷ Leaves whorled, segments very fine, cylindrical, not crowded at top of stem or forming rosette-like cluster just beneath surface. *Myriophyllum*	**Haloragaceae** (p.304)
▷ Leaves alternate but closely arranged on stem, so appearing whorled, segments flat, crowded at top of stem to form rosette-like cluster just beneath surface. *Hottonia*	**Primulaceae** (p.222)
▷ Leaves clearly alternate, not crowded into rosette-like cluster at stem apex	Go to ▷ **26**
26 ▷ Stems striate; basal leaf segments narrow, flat; plant robust. *Oenanthe*	**Apiaceae** (p.346)
▷ Stems smooth; all submerged leaf segments linear; plant small, slender. *Apium inundatum*	**Apiaceae** (p.352)
27 ▷ Leaves whorled. *Ceratophyllum*	**Ceratophyllaceae** (p.72)
▷ Leaves alternate	Go to ▷ **28**
28 ▷ Leaves with small, distinct bladders on some segments. *Utricularia*	**Lentibulariaceae** (p.436)
▷ Leaves without bladders. *Ranunculus* (water-crowfoots)	**Ranunculaceae** (p.84)

EMERGENT MONOCOTYLEDONS

if	then
1 ▷ Perianth absent; individual flowers enclosed between 2 bracts or subtended by a single bract; leaves linear, with sheathing base	Go to ▷ **2**
▷ Perianth present or, if small or absent, individual flowers not enclosed by 1 or 2 bracts; leaves various	Go to ▷ **3**
2 ▷ Stem cylindrical in section, hollow; leaves alternate; flowers hermaphrodite, enclosed between 2 bracts	**Poaceae** (*see* 'Top 20 families' key) (p.586)
▷ Stem often 3-angled, solid; leaves 3-ranked; flowers hermaphrodite or unisexual; subtended by a single bract	**Cyperaceae** (*see* 'Top 20 families' key) (p.171)
3 ▷ Flowers large, conspicuous, white or pink	Go to ▷ **4**
▷ Flowers small, inconspicuous, in spikes, racemes or heads	Go to ▷ **5**

	if	then
4	▷ Leaves long, narrow, keeled; flowers in terminal umbels, 25–30 mm across; 3 sepals and petals, both pink. *Butomus*	**Butomaceae** (p.518)
	▷ Leaves ovate or sagittate, long-stalked, sometimes floating; 3 sepals, green; 3 petals, white, pale lilac or pink	**Alismataceae** (p.518)
5	▷ Flowers unisexual; male and female flowers in separate inflorescences on same plant or in separate parts of same inflorescence	Go to ▷ **6**
	▷ Flowers hermaphrodite	Go to ▷ **7**
6	▷ Flowers in globular heads; male heads above, female below. *Sparganium*	**Sparganiaceae** (p.644)
	▷ Flowers in dense cylindrical spikes; male above, female below. *Typha*	**Typhaceae** (p.644)
7	▷ Flowers in dense cylindrical and tapering spikes borne laterally on leaf-like stems; leaves transversely wrinkled, smelling of tangerines when crushed. *Acorus*	**Araceae** (p.534)
	▷ Plant not like this	Go to ▷ **8**
8	▷ Flowers in branched cymes; leaves mostly cylindrical. *Juncus*	**Juncaceae** (*see* 'Top 20 families' (p.544)
	▷ Flowers in terminal racemes	Go to ▷ **9**
9	▷ Stems leafy; flowers in racemes, with leaf-like bracts (central Scotland). *Scheuchzeria*	**Scheuchzeriaceae** (p.520)
	▷ Leaves all basal, half-cylindrical; flowers in plantain-like racemes without bracts. *Triglochin*	**Juncaginaceae** (p.526)

CLIMBERS

	if	then
1	▷ Stems woody	Go to ▷ **2**
	▷ Stems not woody	Go to ▷ **5**
2	▷ Leaves evergreen, 3–5-lobed to entire; flowers in ball-shaped umbels; flowers regular, small, yellow-green; fruit a black berry. *Hedera*	**Araliaceae** (p.352)
	▷ Leaves not evergreen	Go to ▷ **3**
3	▷ Leaves entire	Go to ▷ **4**
	▷ Leaves pinnate; flowers regular; 4 tepals. *Clematis*	**Ranunculaceae** (p.80)

	if	then
4	Leaves opposite, petiole <10 mm; flowers irregular, 2-lipped. *Lonicera*	**Caprifoliaceae** (p.454)
	Leaves alternate, petiole long; flowers white, regular in branched inflorescence. *Fallopia*	**Polygonaceae** (p.146)
5	▷ Slender, much-branched, leafless parasite scrambling over host; stems reddish; flowers small, <5 mm across, funnel-shaped. *Cuscuta*	**Cuscutaceae** (p.370)
	▷ Plant not like this	Go to ▷ **6**
6	▷ Leaves with 2 basal lobes; flowers large, >20 mm across, funnel-shaped, white or pink, 5-lobed; fruit a capsule	**Convolvulaceae** (p.368)
	▷ Flowers small, <20 mm across, not funnel-shaped	Go to ▷ **7**
7	▷ Plant glabrous; leaves ovate, entire, deeply cordate; flowers in axillary inflorescences; 6 tepals; fruit a glistening red berry. *Tamus*	**Dioscoreaceae** (p.662)
	▷ Plant roughly hairy; leaves lobed	Go to ▷ **8**
8	▷ Leaves opposite, 3–5-lobed; flowers small *c*.5 mm across; female flowers in cone-like spike that enlarges after flowering. *Humulus*	**Cannabiaceae** (p.96)
	▷ Leaves spirally arranged, 5-lobed; flowers 12–18 mm across; 5 petals, greenish yellow; fruit a red berry. *Bryonia*	**Cucurbitaceae** (p.174)

INSECTIVOROUS PLANTS

	if	then
1	▷ Flowers regular	Go to ▷ **2**
	▷ Flowers irregular; leaves entire, in basal rosette; plant covered by sticky insect-trapping glands; flowers 2-lipped and with a spur. *Pinguicula* (*see also* 'Submerged and floating aquatics' key for *Utricularia*)	**Lentibulariaceae** (p.436)
	if	**then**
2	▷ Leaves ± circular to obovate, densely covered by sticky red glandular hairs; flowers small, white. *Drosera*	**Droseraceae** (p.164)
	▷ Leaves modified into large pitchers; flowers purple; stigma very large, umbrella-shaped (peat bogs; rare). *Sarracenia*	**Sarraceniaceae** (p.164)

if	then
1 ▷ Flowers regular	Go to ▷ **2**
▷ Flowers irregular	Go to ▷ **3**
2 ▷ Erect yellowish saprophytes. *Monotropa*	**Monotropaceae** (p.222)
▷ Slender, much-branched parasite scrambling over host; stems reddish, thread-like; flowers small, funnel-shaped. *Cuscuta*	**Cuscutaceae** (p.370)
3 ▷ Perianth segments free	**Orchidaceae** (p.665)
▷ Perianth segments united into tubular 2-lipped corolla. *Orobanche, Lathraea*	**Orobanchaceae** (p.432)

FLOWERS SMALL AND INCONSPICUOUS

if	then
1 ▷ Leaves all basal; flowers in spikes	Go to ▷ **2**
▷ Stems leafy	Go to ▷ **3**
2 ▷ Leaves in basal rosette; 4 tepals, green to colourless, filaments of stamens conspicuously long. *Plantago*	**Plantaginaceae** (p.404)
▷ Leaves sheathing with a ligule; 6 tepals, filaments of stamens very short. *Triglochin* (marshes and salt marshes)	**Juncaginaceae** (p.526)
3 ▷ Plant with stinging hairs; flowers in catkin-like spikes. *Urtica*	**Urticaceae** (p.96)
▷ Plants without stinging hairs	Go to ▷ **4**
4 ▷ Flowers irregular. *Reseda*	**Resedaceae** (p.212)
▷ Flowers regular	Go to ▷ **5**
5 ▷ Leaves compound	Go to ▷ **6**
▷ Leaves simple	Go to ▷ **8**
6 ▷ Leaves ternate; 5 flowers in cube-shaped heads. *Adoxa*	**Adoxaceae** (p.452)
▷ At least upper stem leaves pinnate, or 2–3-pinnate; flowers not in heads of 5	Go to ▷ **7**
7 ▷ At least upper stem leaves pinnate; ovary inferior. *Valeriana*	**Valerianaceae** (p.458)
▷ Leaves 2–3-pinnate; ovary superior. *Actaea*	**Ranunculaceae** (p.80)
8 ▷ Leaves orbicular, bluntly toothed, sparsely hairy; flowers 3-6 mm across; sepals green, petals absent. *Chrysosplenium*	**Saxifragaceae** (p.240)
▷ Leaves not orbicular	Go to ▷ **9**

	if	then
9	▷ Leaves opposite	Go to ▷ **10**
	▷ Leaves alternate	Go to ▷ **17**
10	▷ Plant erect, ≥15 cm; leaves stalked, toothed	Go to **11**
	▷ Plant usually <10 cm; leaves sessile, entire	Go to **12**
11	▷ Flowers in long axillary spikes or clusters; 3 tepals, green, sepal-like. *Mercurialis*	**Euphorbiaceae** (p.316)
	▷ Flowers in racemes; 2 sepals; 2 petals, pinkish white. *Circaea*	**Onagraceae** (p.312)
12	▷ Plant often tufted, with prostrate or erect flowering shoots; leaves linear, joined at base; flowers in cymes or solitary; 4–5 sepals; petals white, minute or absent. *Sagina*	**Caryophyllaceae** (p.130)
	▷ Plants not tufted, with linear leaves	Go to ▷ **13**
13	▷ Flowers solitary, in axils of leaves	Go to ▷ **14**
	▷ Flowers in groups or terminal inflorescences	Go to ▷ **15**
14	▷ Sepals and petals absent; 1 stamen (wet mud). *Callitriche*	**Callitrichaceae** (p.402)
	▷ 3–4 sepals and petals. *Crassula*	**Crassulaceae** (p.228)
	▷ 5 sepals, pink; petals absent (upper parts of salt marshes). *Glaux*	**Primulaceae** (p.226)
	▷ 5 sepals and petals. *Herniaria, Illecebrum*	**Caryophyllaceae** (p.132)
	▷ 6 sepals; 6 petals (soon withering); 6 stamens (wet places). *Lythrum portula*	**Lythraceae** (p.304)
15	▷ Flowers in small, terminal, axillary groups that may appear lateral; 2 sepals; 5 petals; 3 stamens. *Montia*	**Portulacaceae** (p.112)
	▷ Flowers in terminal cyme-like inflorescences	Go to ▷ **16**
16	▷ Leaves small, ≤3 mm; 3 sepals; 4 petals. *Radiola*	**Linaceae** (p.322)
	▷ Leaves 2–7 cm; sepals ± absent; 5 petals. *Valerianella*	**Valerianaceae** (p.454)
17	▷ Plants robust, to *c.*100 cm; inflorescence dense, spike-like; flowers reddish or brownish. *Amaranthus*	**Amaranthaceae** (p.112)
	▷ Plant not like this	Go to ▷ **18**
18	▷ Plant glabrous	Go to ▷ **19**
	▷ Plant pubescent	Go to ▷ **21**
19	▷ Plant erect; flowers solitary or in racemes. *Samolus, Anagallis minima*	**Primulaceae** (p.224, 226)
	▷ Plant prostrate	Go to ▷ **20**

if	then
20 ▷ Stems reddish; leaves linear-lanceolate; flowers in dense axillary and terminal heads; 5 sepals; 5 petals, white (S Devon; very rare). *Corrigiola*	**Caryophyllaceae** (p.132)
▷ Plant yellowish green; leaves linear; flowers greenish; perianth in 1 whorl, 5 lobes. *Thesium*	**Santalaceae** (p.314)
21 ▷ Plant prostrate to erect; leaves ovate, >10 mm, stalked. *Parietaria*	**Urticaceae** (p.96)
▷ Stems prostrate, rooting, mat-forming; leaves small, 2–6 mm, sessile. *Soleirolia*	**Urticaceae** (p.96)

FLOWERS IN DENSE HEADS

if	then
1 ▷ Leaves spiny; heads spherical, dense-flowered, surrounded by ring of leaf-like spiny bracts. *Eryngium*	**Apiaceae** (Umbelliferae; *see also* 'Top 20 families' key) (p.338)
▷ Plants not like this	Go to ▷ **2**
2 ▷ Leaves linear, all basal, in tight cushions or rosettes; flowers pink. *Armeria*	**Plumbaginaceae** (p.154)
▷ Plants not like this	Go to ▷ **3**
3 ▷ Individual flowers (florets) either ray florets with corolla a petal-like ligule, or disc florets with a 5-lobed corolla; calyx absent or reduced to a plume of hairs (pappus); 5 stamens; ovary inferior	**Asteraceae** (*see also* 'Top 20 families' key) (p.460)
▷ Plants not like this	Go to ▷ **4**
4 ▷ Stem leaves opposite	**Dipsacaceae** (p.456)
▷ Stem leaves alternate	Go to ▷ **5**
5 ▷ Base of flower heads not surrounded by a ring of bracts; 5 stamens; ovary inferior	**Campanulaceae** (p.438)
▷ Base of flower heads surrounded by ring of leafy bracts; 4 stamens; ovary superior. *Globularia*	**Globulariaceae** ● (p.456)

FLOWERS IRREGULAR

if	then
1 ▷ Leaves deeply cordate; flowers in clusters in axils of leaves; each consisting of a single yellowish-brown perianth lobe and a narrow tube with swollen base. *Aristolochia*	**Aristolochiaceae** (p.72)
▷ Plant not like this	Go to ▷ **2**

	if	then
2	▷ Petals free	Go to ▷ **3**
	▷ Petals united	Go to ▷ **6**
3	▷ Flowers with a spur	Go to ▷ **4**
	▷ Flowers not spurred	Go to ▷ **5**
4	▷ Leaves much divided; flowers laterally compressed; 2 stamens, branched	**Fumariaceae** (p.92)
	▷ Leaves simple; flowers not laterally compressed; 5 stamens. *Impatiens*	**Balsaminaceae** (p.336)
5	▷ 5 sepals, 2 inner sepals large and petal-like; 3 petals; 8 stamens, united into a tube. *Polygala*	**Polygalaceae** (p.326)
	▷ 5 stamens, free; flowers small, yellow, green or white. *Reseda*	**Resedaceae** (p.212)
6	▷ Plant tall, robust; corolla 1-lipped, 3-lobed, white with purple veins; bracts spiny. *Acanthus*	**Acanthaceae** (p.444)
	▷ Plant not like this	Go to ▷ **7**
7	▷ Leaves alternate, toothed; corolla 10–15 mm; ovary inferior. *Lobelia* (*see also* 'Submerged and floating aquatics' key)	**Campanulaceae** (p.444)
	▷ Leaves opposite	Go to ▷ **8**
8	▷ Leaves pinnately lobed; corolla 3.5–5 mm, not spurred or pouched at base; ovary superior. *Verbena*	**Verbenaceae** (p.400)
	▷ Leaves simple or lobed; flowers small; corolla pouched or spurred at base; ovary inferior	**Valerianaceae** (p.454)

LOWERS REGULAR, PETALS FREE

	if	then
1	▷ Carpels free	Go to ▷ **2**
	▷ Carpels fused; ovary syncarpous	Go to ▷ **3**
2	▷ Plants succulent; leaves simple; flowers ≤3 cm across; 2× as many stamens as petals	**Crassulaceae** (p.230)
	▷ Plant not succulent; leaves compound; flowers c.10 cm across, red; stamens numerous. *Paeonia*	**Paeoniaceae** (p.156)
3	▷ Leaves very succulent; petals and stamens numerous	**Aizoaceae** (p.100)
	▷ Leaves not succulent; ≤5 petals	Go to ▷ **4**
4	▷ Leaves trifoliate (like a clover). *Oxalis*	**Oxalidaceae** (p.328)
	▷ Leaves not trifoliate	Go to ▷ **5**

	if	then
5	▷ Plant prostrate; leaves linear, heath-like; flowers pink; 5 sepals and petals; 6 stamens (upper parts of salt marshes). *Frankenia*	**Frankeniaceae** (p.174)
	▷ Plant not heath-like or prostrate	Go to ▷ **6**
6	▷ >2× as many stamens as petals	Go to ▷ **7**
	▷ Stamens ≤ petals	Go to ▷ **9**
	▷ 10 stamens or 5 + 5 staminodes; 5 petals	**Saxifragaceae** (p.234)
7	▷ Lower part of stamens joined to form tube; leaves usually palmately lobed; flowers pink or purple	**Malvaceae** (p.162)
	▷ Stamens free; leaves never palmately lobed	Go to ▷ **8**
8	▷ 2 sepals; 4 petals; leaves lobed or toothed	**Papaveraceae** (p.90)
	▷ 5 sepals and petals; leaves entire	**Cistaceae** (p.166)
9	▷ 2 sepals; 5 petals	**Portulacaceae** (p.112)
	▷ >2 sepals	Go to ▷ **10**
10	▷ Ovary superior	Go to ▷ **11**
	▷ Ovary inferior or partly so	Go to ▷ **14**
11	▷ Receptacle long, tubular; 12 (6+6) calyx teeth; 6 petals; flowers pink	**Lythraceae** (p.304)
	▷ Plant not like this	Go to ▷ **12**
12	▷ Flowers with a single style	**Pyrolaceae** (p.220)
	▷ Flowers with >1 style	Go to ▷ **13**
13	▷ Stems leafy; flowers in cymes. *Linum*	**Linaceae** (p.322)
	▷ Leaves all basal; flowers in heads or panicles	**Plumbaginaceae** (p.154)
14	▷ Flowers small, dark purple, in umbels, surrounded by 4 white petal-like bracts	**Cornaceae** (p.314)
	▷ Plant not like this	Go to ▷ **15**
15	▷ 5 petals; 10 stamens; 2 styles	**Saxifragaceae** (p.234)
	▷ 2, 4 (or 5) petals; 2, 4, 8 (or 10) stamens; 1 style	**Onagraceae** (p.308)

FLOWERS REGULAR, PETALS UNITED

	if	then
1	▷ Leaves peltate; 2× as many stamens as corolla lobes. *Umbilicus*	**Crassulaceae** (p.228)
	▷ Leaves not peltate	Go to ▷ **2**
2	▷ Flowers brownish, solitary; perianth in a single whorl, 3-lobed; 12 stamens. *Asarum*	**Aristolochiaceae** (p.72)
	▷ Plant not like this	Go to ▷ **3**

	if	then
3	▷ 2 sepals; 5 petals	**Portulacaceae** (p.112)
	▷ >2 sepals	Go to ▷ **4**
4	▷ Stamens opposite corolla lobes	Go to ▷ **5**
	▷ Stamens alternating with corolla lobes	Go to ▷ **6**
5	▷ 1 style and stigma; leaves all basal or stems leafy	**Primulaceae** (p.222)
	▷ >1 stigma; flowers in globular heads or terminal panicles; leaves all basal	**Plumbaginaceae** (p.154)
6	▷ Cushion-forming evergreen alpine; flowers solitary, white (W Scotland; rare). *Diapensia*	**Diapensiaceae** (p.222)
	▷ Plants not cushion-forming alpines	Go to ▷ **7**
7	▷ Leaves opposite	Go to ▷ **8**
	▷ Leaves alternate or basal	Go to ▷ **10**
8	▷ 2 carpels, free	Go to ▷ **9**
	▷ Carpels fused, ovary syncarpous	**Gentianaceae** (p.362)
9	▷ Flowers in axillary groups, white or yellow; base of corolla with corona consisting of ring of short lobes. *Vincetoxicum*	**Asclepiadaceae** • (p.366)
	▷ Plant trailing or scrambling; leaves ovate, evergreen; flowers solitary, blue; corolla lacking corona. *Vinca*	**Apocyanaceae** (p.366)
10	▷ Leaves ternate; flowers white or pink, inner side of corolla lobes fringed (aquatic or bog plants). *Menyanthes*	**Menyanthaceae** (p.370)
	▷ Plant not like this	Go to ▷ **11**
11	▷ Ovary inferior; corolla usually bell-shaped, blue (or white)	**Campanulaceae** (p.438)
	▷ Ovary superior	Go to ▷ **12**
12	▷ Leaves cordate or spear-shaped at base; corolla trumpet-shaped, white or pink, lobes shallow; plant prostrate, twining or climbing	**Convolvulaceae** (p.368)
	▷ Plants erect; leaves not cordate or spear-shaped	Go to ▷ **13**
13	▷ Leaves regularly pinnate, with 6-15 pairs of entire leaflets; flowers blue (or white); 1 style with 3 stigmas. *Polemonium*	**Polemoniaceae** (p.370)
	▷ Leaves various, if pinnate then not regularly so or with leaflets lobed or toothed; 2 (or 1) stigmas	**Solanaceae** (p.366)

ARISTOLOCHIACEAE Birthwort family

Asarabacca   *Asarum europaeum*

Perennial evergreen herb with creeping rhizome. Stem, leaves and flowers pubescent. STEM Short, to 5 cm. LEAVES 2, *petiole longer than blade*. FLOWERS *3 petals, 12 stamens*. HABITAT Shaded places. DIST. Introduced as medicinal plant in Middle Ages; naturalised since C17th. Rare and scattered in lowlands; declining. (Central and E Europe.) FLS May-Aug.

Birthwort   *Aristolochia clematitis*

Perennial glabrous herb to 80 cm with a strong, unpleasant smell. LEAVES Petiole about ½ as long as blade. FLOWERS *In axillary bunches, 2-3 cm, perianth tube with bulbous base and single 'petal', 6 stamens*. DIST. Introduced as medicinal plant in Middle Ages; naturalised as escape from cultivation since C17th. Rare and scattered in lowlands; declining. (SE Europe, Asia Minor.) FLS Jun-Sep.

NYMPHAEACEAE Water-lilies

White Water-lily   *Nyphaea alba*

Perennial aquatic. LEAVES Large, 5-30 cm diam., ± circular, floating, with *veins radiating from petiole insertion*. FLOWERS *Large, 10-20 cm diam.*, floating; 4 green sepals; *petals numerous, outermost ones longer than sepals*. HABITAT Lowland ponds, lakes, drainage dykes, canals. DIST. Native throughout BI. (Europe.) FLS Jul-Aug. COMMENTS Two subspecies are recognised in Britain: ssp. *occidentalis* and ssp. *alba*. Ssp. *occidentalis* has smaller leaves (9-13 cm diam.) and flowers (5-12 cm diam.), and is restricted to W Ireland and N and W Scotland.

Yellow Water-lily   *Nuphar lutea*

Perennial aquatic. LEAVES *Large*, up to 30 cm long, ovate-oblong, floating and submerged, *with up to 28 veins in herringbone arrangement*. FLOWERS 4-6 cm diam., *long-stalked above the water*; sepals yellow inside, longer than petals. *Top of ovary not lobed*. HABITAT Rivers, canals, lakes, ponds. DIST. Native throughout most of BI except N Scotland. (Europe.) FLS Jun-Aug.

Least Water-lily   *Nuphar pumila*

Differs from *N. lutea* in being smaller in all parts. LEAVES *Up to 13 cm, with up to 18 lateral veins*. FLOWERS *1.5-3.5 cm diam. Top of ovary deeply lobed*. HABITAT Lochs and lochans in Highlands, meres in Shropshire. DIST. Scottish Highlands and Shropshire. Rare. (Central and N Europe.) FLS Jul-Aug. COMMENTS In some localities, hybrid between *N. lutea* and *N. pumila* occurs in absence of *N. pumila*.

CERATOPHYLLACEAE Hornworts

Submerged aquatic herbs. Leaves whorled, divided into fine segments. Flowers minute, unisexual, in axils of leaves. Not to be confused with milfoils (*Myriophyllum*), which have pinnate leaves (p.304).

Rigid Hornwort   *Ceratophyllum demersum*

Dark green, rather stiff aquatic perennial. STEMS Up to 1 m long. LEAVES *Once or twice forked*, segments finely toothed, 1-2 cm. HABITAT Eutrophic lowland lakes, ponds, ditches, canals. Tolerant of mildly brackish conditions. DIST. Widespread and often abundant in England; scarce in rest of BI. (Most of Europe.) FLS Jul-Sep.

Soft Hornwort   *Ceratophyllum submersum*

Differs from *C. demersum* in having *soft, bright green leaves*, 3-4 cm long, *thrice forked*. HABITAT Similar to *C. demersum*; especially near coasts. DIST. Infrequent in England; absent from rest of Britain; very rare in Ireland. (Europe except extreme N.) FLS Jul-Sep.

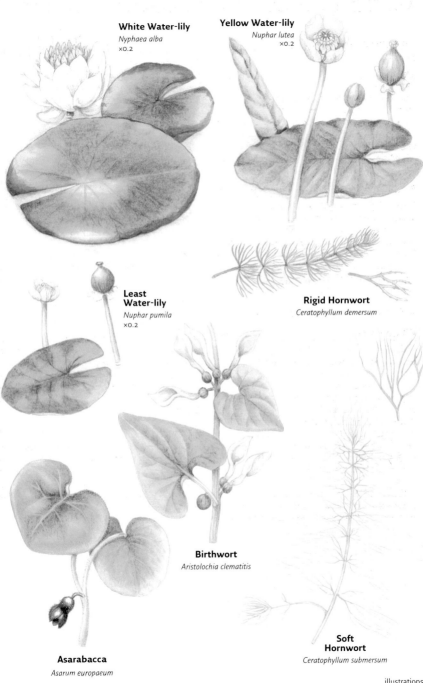

White Water-lily
Nyphaea alba
×0.2

Yellow Water-lily
Nuphar lutea
×0.2

**Least
Water-lily**
Nuphar pumila
×0.2

Rigid Hornwort
Ceratophyllum demersum

Birthwort
Aristolochia clematitis

Asarabacca
Asarum europaeum

**Soft
Hornwort**
Ceratophyllum submersum

illustrations
0.6× lifesize

Key to **Ranunculaceae** Hellebores, Anemones, Buttercups and Crowfoots

	if	**then**
1	▷ Woody climber; leaves opposite	**Clematis** (p.80)
	▷ Not a climber; leaves not opposite	Go to ▷ **2**
2	▷ Flowering stems with whorl of 3 leaves	Go to ▷ **3**
	▷ Flowering stems without whorl of 3 leaves	Go to ▷ **5**
3	▷ Stem leaves forming involucre-like ring immediately beneath flowers	Go to ▷ **4**
	▷ Stem leaves inserted some distance below flowers	**Anemone, Pulsatilla** (p.80)
4	▷ Plant glabrous; flowers yellow	**Eranthis** (p.78)
	▷ Leaves and petioles hairy; flowers purple, pink or white	**Pulsatilla** (p.80)
5	▷ Flowers solitary, terminal on leafless stem; receptacle elongating in fruit	**Myosurus** (p.88)
	▷ Flowers green	**Helleborus** (p.78)
	▷ Flowers red	**Adonis** (p.88)
	▷ Flowers yellow	Go to ▷ **7**
	▷ Flowers blue	Go to ▷ **9**
	▷ Flowers white or cream	Go to ▷ **6**
6	▷ Flowers small, <10 mm diam., in many-flowered inflorescence	Go to ▷ **12**
	▷ Flowers >10 mm diam., solitary (aquatic or wet places)	**Ranunculus, crowfoots** (p.75)
7	▷ Sepals and petals distinct	**Ranunculus** (p.75)
	▷ Perianth segments all petal-like	Go to ▷ **8**
8	▷ Leaves rounded	**Caltha** (p.78)
	▷ Leaves palmately lobed	**Trollius** (p.78)
9	▷ Flowers regular	Go to ▷ **10**
	▷ Flowers zygomorphic	Go to ▷ **11**
10	▷ 5 sepals; 5 petals, each one spurred 5 petal-like sepals, not spurred	**Aquilegia** (p.88) **Nigella** (p.78)
	▷ 3 sepals; 6–10 petals; leaves all basal, 3-lobed	**Hepatica** (p.80)
11	▷ Sepals petal-like, rear sepal spurred	**Delphinium**
	▷ Sepals petal-like, rear sepal forming large, helmet-shaped hood	**Aconitum** (p.78)
12	▷ Leaflets toothed; fruit a black berry	**Actaea** (p.80)
	▷ Leaflets not toothed; fruit a cluster of achenes	**Thalictrum** (p.88)

Ranunculus

Key to Buttercups *Ranunculus*

	if	**then**
1	▷ Leaves cordate; 3 sepals, 7–12 petals	*R. ficaria* (p.84)
	▷ 5 sepals, ≤5 petals	Go to ▷ **2**
2	▷ Leaves distinctly lobed or deeply divided	Go to ▷ **3**
	▷ Leaves not lobed	Go to ▷ **13**
3	▷ Sepals reflexed at flowering	Go to ▷ **4**
	▷ Sepals not reflexed, appressed to petals at flowering	Go to ▷ **8**
4	▷ Base of stem swollen and corm-like	*R. bulbosus* (p.82)
	▷ Base of stem not swollen	Go to ▷ **5**
5	▷ Plant prostrate; flowers small, 3–6 mm diam.; receptacle glabrous	*R. parviflorus* (p.82)
	▷ Plant erect; flowers >6 mm diam.; receptacle hairy	Go to ▷ **6**
6	▷ Lobes of basal leaves stalked; whole plant very hairy	*R. sardous* (p.82)
	▷ Lobes of basal leaves not stalked; plant sparsely hairy to glabrous	Go to ▷ **7**
7	▷ Flowers 6–15 mm diam.; achenes 7 mm, spiny	*R. muricatus* (p.82)
	▷ Flowers 15–25 mm diam.; achenes 3–5 mm, with tubercles	*R. marginatus* (p.82)
8	▷ Stems with leafy stolons, rooting at nodes	*R. repens* (p.82)
	▷ Stems without stolons	Go to ▷ **9**
9	▷ Stems and leaves distinctly hairy	Go to ▷ **10**
	▷ Stems and leaves glabrous, shiny	Go to ▷ **12**
10	▷ Achenes spiny	*R. arvensis* (p.82)
	▷ Achenes without spines	Go to ▷ **11**
11	▷ Plant with root tubers at base of stem; 1 stem leaf (Jersey)	*R. paludosus* (p.82)
	▷ Plant without root tubers; usually >2 stem leaves	*R. acris* (p.82)
12	▷ Flowers 5–10 mm diam.; receptacle elongated (wet places)	*R. sceleratus* (p.84)
	▷ Flowers 15–25 mm diam., 0–5 petals; receptacle not elongated	*R. auricomus* (p.84)
13	▷ Plant ≤*c.*1 m tall; flowers 2–4 cm diam.	*R. lingua* (p.84)
	▷ Plant ≤60 cm tall; flowers <2 cm diam.	Go to ▷ **14**

CONTINUED OVERLEAF

	if	then
14	▷ Plant erect; petals not overlapping	*R. ophioglossifolius* (p.84)
	▷ Plant usually prostrate; petals overlapping at base	Go to ▷ **15**
15	▷ Plant usually smaller in all its parts to *R. flammula*, with slender, creeping stolons, rooting at each node;	*R. reptans* (p.84)
	▷ If creeping, rooting at lower nodes only; 1 to several flowers	*R. flammula* (p.84)

Key to Water-crowfoots *Ranunculus*

	if	then
1	▷ Plant with finely divided submerged leaves	Go to ▷ **2**
	▷ Plant without finely divided submerged leaves	Go to ▷ **9**
2	▷ Plant with both finely divided submerged leaves and lobed rounded leaves	Go to ▷ **3**
	▷ Plant with finely divided submerged leaves only	Go to ▷ **6**
3	▷ Receptacle elongate, nectar pits crescent-shaped, sepals often blue-tipped	*R. baudotii* (p.86)
	▷ Receptacle globular, nectar pits rounded or pear-shaped, sepals not blue-tipped	Go to ▷ **4**
4	▷ Submerged leaves longer than internodes, segments ± parallel	*R. penicillatus penicillatus* (p.86)
	▷ Submerged leaves shorter than internodes, segments divergent	Go to ▷ **5**
5	▷ Petals <10 mm, nectaries circular	*R. aquatilis* (p.86)
	▷ Petals >10 mm, nectaries pear-shaped	*R. peltatus* (p.86)
6	▷ Leaves circular in outline, rigid, segments all in one plane	*R. circinatus* (p.86)
	▷ Leaves not circular in outline with segments all in one plane	Go to ▷ **7**
7	▷ Petals usually <5 mm long, nectaries crescent-shaped	*R. trichophyllus* (p.86)
	▷ Petals >5 mm long, nectaries pear-shaped	Go to ▷ **8**

if		then
8	▷ Leaves 4× divided; receptacle sparsely hairy	*R. fluitans* (p.86)
	▷ Leaves usually ≥6× divided; receptacle densely hairy	*R. penicillatus pseudofluitans* (p.86)
9	▷ Leaves lobed >¼ halfway into 3 main lobes; petals ≤4.5 mm	*R. tripartitus* (p.86)
	▷ Leaves lobed <¼ halfway into 3–5 main lobes	Go to ▷ **10**
10	▷ Leaf lobes broadest at base; petals <4.5 mm	*R. hederaceus* (p.84)
	▷ Leaf lobes broadest in the middle; petals >4.5 mm	*R. omiophyllus* (p.86)

RANUNCULACEAE Hellebores, anemones, buttercups and crowfoots

Annual or perennial herbs or woody climbers (*see* key on p. 74). Leaves are usually spirally arranged and lack stipules (except for the water-crowfoots and *Thalictrum*). Flowers have distinct sepals and petals, or perianth is undifferentiated; numerous stamens; 1 to numerous carpels, usually free; 1 to numerous ovules. Fruit is a cluster of achenes or of 1 to several follicles. Most members of the family are very poisonous.

Hellebores *Helleborus*

Perennial herbs. Leaves palmate with toothed margins. Flowers with 5 greenish sepals; petals reduced to nectaries.

Stinking Hellebore   *Helleborus foetidus*

Perennial with strong, unpleasant smell. STEMS *Leafy, evergreen*, to 80 cm. LEAVES Basal leaves absent. FLOWERS Numerous, *drooping, bowl-shaped*, 1–3 cm across, greenish edged with purple. *Bracts ovate, entire*. HABITAT Woodlands and scrub on shallow calcareous soils. DIST. Native as far N as Wales; often occurring as garden escape. Rare. (SW and W Europe.) FLS Jan–Apr.

Green Hellebore   *Helleborus viridis*

STEMS To 40 cm. LEAVES 2, *both basal, not evergreen*. FLOWERS 2–4, *flat*, 3–5 cm diam. *Bracts divided*. HABITAT Woodlands and scrub on damp calcareous soils. DIST. Native as far N as N England; often occurring as garden escape. Scarce. (W and central Europe.) FLS Mar–Apr.

Marsh-marigold   *Caltha palustris*

Perennial glabrous herb with creeping rhizomes. FLOWERS *15–50 mm diam.; 5–8 petal-like sepals*. HABITAT Marshes, fens, wet meadows, ditches, wet woodlands, river and lake margins, mountain flushes. DIST. Native throughout BI; to 1100 m. FLS Mar–Jul.

Globeflower   *Trollius europaeus* *(NI, R)

Tall, glabrous perennial to 60 cm. LEAVES *Palmate*. FLOWERS 2.5–3.0 cm, *usually single, cup-shaped; usually 10 sepals, petal-like*. HABITAT Hay meadows, alpine pastures, fens, damp woodland, banks of streams and rivers. DIST. Native. N Britain, Wales; to 1005 m. Declining. (Europe.) FLS Jun–Aug.

Winter Aconite   *Eranthis hyemalis*

Erect, glabrous perennial herb to 15 cm. LEAVES Basal leaves palmately lobed, deeply divided. FLOWERS Single, 2–3 cm diam.; 6 petal-like sepals; *3 deeply divided leaf-like bracts form whorl beneath each flower*. HABITAT Parks and woodland. DIST. Introduced as garden plant in C16th; now naturalised, especially in E England. (S Europe and Turkey.) FLS Jan–Mar.

Love-in-a-mist   *Nigella damascena*

Glabrous annual herb to 50 cm. LEAVES Pinnate with finely divided linear segments. FLOWERS *Solitary, regular*; 5 petal-like sepals; *whorl of leaf-like bracts beneath each flower*. HABITAT Occasional coloniser of waste ground and rubbish tips. DIST. Introduced, cultivated since C16th. (Mediterranean.)

Larkspur   *Consolida ajacis*

Pubescent annual herb to 60 cm. LEAVES Palmate, divided into linear segments. FLOWERS *4–16* form an inflorescence; *zygomorphic*; 5 petal-like sepals with a single 15 mm spur. HABITAT Waste ground or on well-drained soils. DIST. Introduced. Cultivated since C16th; occasional garden escape or arable weed, especially in E England. (S Europe.) FLS Jun–Jul

Monk's-hood   *Aconitum napellus*

Tall perennial herb to 1.5 m. LEAVES *Deeply palmately lobed*. FLOWERS Form a raceme; *zygomorphic; 5 petal-like sepals, rear sepal forming large helmet-shaped hood*. HABITAT Damp open woodlands, shady stream banks, damp meadows; also waste ground, roadsides. DIST. Native in SW England and S Wales as ssp. *napellus*, but commonly cultivated forms that occur widely as garden escapes are not native plants (W and central Europe). FLS (Ssp. *napellus*) May–Jun.

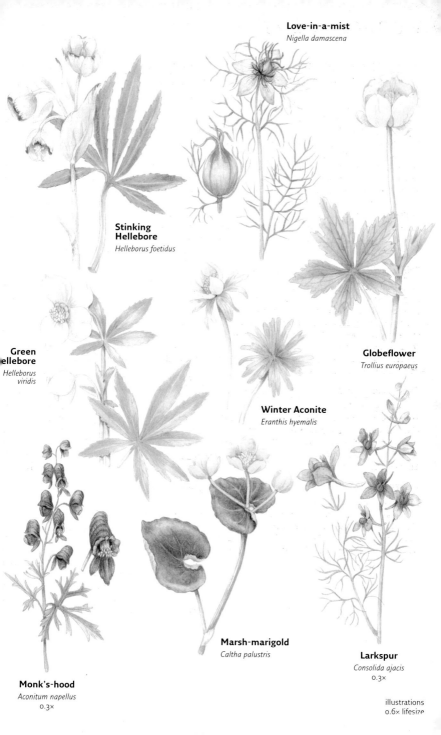

Love-in-a-mist
Nigella damascena

Stinking Hellebore
Helleborus foetidus

Green Hellebore
Helleborus viridis

Globeflower
Trollius europaeus

Winter Aconite
Eranthis hyemalis

Monk's-hood
Aconitum napellus
0.3×

Marsh-marigold
Caltha palustris

Larkspur
Consolida ajacis
0.3×

illustrations
0.6× lifesize

Wood Anemone
Anemone nemorosa

Glabrous to sparsely hairy perennial, to 30 cm. LEAVES 1–2 basal leaves; 3 stem leaves, stalked, borne about ⅔ up stem, divided into 3 lobes. FLOWERS Comprise 6–7 white sepals, sometimes tinged pink. HABITAT Abundant in woodlands, especially coppice, and on acid or waterlogged soils; also hedge banks, grassy heathland, limestone pavement. DIST. Native. Throughout BI; to 1190 m. (Most of Europe, rare in S.) FLS Mar–May.

Blue Anemone
Anemone apennina

Similar in habit to *A. nemorosa*. LEAVES Stem leaves stalked, pubescent below. FLOWERS Comprise 10–15 sepals, pubescent below. HABITAT Occasionally naturalised near habitation, woods and churchyards. DIST. Introduced. Much cultivated, and established in wild since C18th. (S Europe.) FLS Apr. SIMILAR SPP. Balkan Anemone *Anemone blanda,* from SE Europe and SW Asia, occasionally occurs as a relic of cultivation or as a garden throw-out. Easily confused with *A. apennina,* but has up to 20 sepals and glabrous leaves and sepals.

Yellow Anemone
Anemone ranunculoides

Similar in habit to *A. nemorosa*, but 0–1 basal leaves, stem leaves with short stalks, and usually 5 sepals. HABITAT Naturalised in few scattered localities in woodland near habitation. DIST. Introduced. Cultivated since C16th. (Most of Europe except W; W Asia.) FLS Apr.

Pasqueflower
Pulsatilla vulgaris VU.

Hairy perennial. STEM To 12 cm when in flower. LEAVES Basal leaves long-stalked, stem leaves sessile just below single flowers. FLOWERS *Erect, becoming drooping, bell-shaped, 5.5–8.5 cm diam.* FRUITS Achene with long silky plume. HABITAT Shallow calcareous grasslands. DIST. Native. England N of Thames. Rare and declining. (N and central Europe, E to Ukraine.) FLS Apr–May.

Small Pasqueflower
Pulsatilla pratensis

Similar to *P. vulgaris*, but smaller, stem to 10 cm when in flower; and flowers nodding, more bell-shaped, *3–4 cm diam.* HABITAT Dry acid grasslands. DIST. *Not BI,* to 2100 m. (Central and E Europe to SE Norway and W Denmark.) FLS Apr–Jun.

Pale Pasqueflower
Pulsatilla vernalis

Similar to *P. vulgaris*, but stem to 15 cm when in flower; basal leaves evergreen, 1-pinnate; and flowers, 4–6 cm diam., nodding, becoming erect, *outer perianth segments violet-pink, inner white.* HABITAT Dry grasslands. DIST. *Not BI.* (Central Europe from Scandinavia to S Spain.) FLS Apr–Jun.

Hepatica
Hepatica nobilis

Evergreen glabrous perennial to 15 cm. LEAVES *Basal, 3-lobed, purplish beneath.* FLOWERS 15–25 mm diam.; apparently in 2 whorls, outer whorl consisting of 3 sepal-like bracts; 6–10 sepals. HABITAT Cultivated in British gardens. Woods on calcareous soils. DIST. *Not BI.* (Most of Continental Europe except extreme N and S.) FLS Mar–May.

Baneberry
Actaea spicata

Perennial with an unpleasant smell. STEM To 60 cm, glabrous. LEAVES Basal leaves large, leaflets coarsely toothed, hairy beneath. FLOWERS *Small, in dense inflorescence; 4 sepals; 0–6 petals.* FRUITS *Berry,* green turning shiny black. HABITAT Open or light woodland. DIST. Native. Rare and local, confined to limestone of N England; to 450 m. (Throughout Europe, N to Norway, E to China.) FLS May–Jun.

Traveller's-joy, Old Man's Beard
Clematis vitalba

Perennial woody climber, to 30 m. FLOWERS Fragrant, 2 cm diam.; sepals greenish white, hairy beneath. FRUITS Achenes with long silky plumes (hence alternative common name). HABITAT Scrub, hedgerows, wood margins, railway embankments, on calcareous soils. DIST. Native. Widespread in lowland England and Wales, introduced further N. (Europe S to N Africa, E to Caucasus.) FLS Jul–Aug.

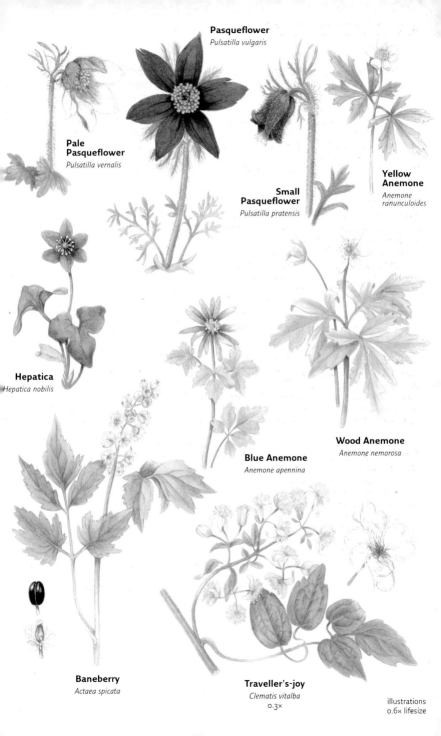

Pasqueflower
Pulsatilla vulgaris

Pale Pasqueflower
Pulsatilla vernalis

Small Pasqueflower
Pulsatilla pratensis

Yellow Anemone
Anemone ranunculoides

Hepatica
Hepatica nobilis

Blue Anemone
Anemone apennina

Wood Anemone
Anemone nemorosa

Baneberry
Actaea spicata

Traveller's-joy
Clematis vitalba
0.3×

illustrations
0.6× lifesize

Buttercups *Ranunculus*

See key to *Ranunculus* on p.75.

Meadow Buttercup
Ranunculus acris

Hairy perennial to 100 cm. STEM Not stoloniferous. LEAVES *Terminal lobe of leaf sessile.* FLOWERS 18–25 mm diam., stalks not furrowed, *sepals erect.* FRUITS Glabrous achenes. DIST. Native. Common throughout BI; to 1220 m. (Europe.) HABITAT Damp pastures and meadows, road verges, upland rock ledges. FLS May–Aug.

Creeping Buttercup
Ranunculus repens

Hairy perennial to 60 cm. STEM Long leafy stolons, rooting at nodes. LEAVES *Leaf lobes stalked.* FLOWERS 20–30 mm diam., stalks furrowed, *sepals erect.* FRUITS Glabrous achenes. HABITAT Damp grassland, marshes, fens, woodland clearings and rides, pond and lake margins, and as arable weed. DIST. Native. Common throughout BI; to 1035 m. (Europe.) FLS May–Aug.

Bulbous Buttercup
Ranunculus bulbosus

Hairy perennial to 40 cm. STEM Base swollen to form rounded corm-like tuber. LEAVES *Lobes stalked.* FLOWERS 15–30 mm diam., stalks furrowed, *sepals strongly reflexed.* HABITAT Grasslands on dry, well-drained soils. DIST. Native. Common throughout most of BI; lowland to 580 m. (Most of Europe.) FLS Apr to Jun (earlier than *R. acris* and *R. repens*).

Hairy Buttercup
Ranunculus sardous

Hairy annual to 45 cm. Similar to *R. bulbosus*, but without swollen stem base and *with whole plant covered by spreading hairs;* basal leaves rather glossy, leaflets stalked; and flowers 12–25 mm, *sepals reflexed.* HABITAT Damp grazed pastures, pond margins. DIST. Common near coast in E and S England; rare inland. Rare in Scotland. Absent from Ireland. (Central and S Europe.) FLS Jun–Oct.

Rough-fruited Buttercup
Ranunculus muricatus

Annual to 40 cm. LEAVES Basal leaves shallowly lobed, *leaflets not stalked,* glabrous to sparsely hairy. FLOWERS *Small, 6–15 mm diam.;* sepals reflexed. FRUITS *Large achenes (5–8 mm) with short spines.* HABITAT Arable land. DIST. Introduced. Casual as arable weed in SW England, especially on bulb fields in Scilly Is. (Native of SW Europe, Mediterranean.) FLS May–Aug.

St Martin's Buttercup
Ranunculus marginatus

Small erect annual to 40 cm. *Similar to* R. murica-tus, *but flowers larger, 15–25 mm diam.;* sepals reflexed; and *achenes 3–5 mm, covered by small tubercles.* HABITAT Arable land. DIST. Naturalised weed of bulb fields in Scilly Is. (Native of E Mediterranean, SW Asia.) FLS May–Jul.

Small-flowered Buttercup
Ranunculus parviflorus

Small, prostrate, hairy annual herb. LEAVES *Distinct yellowish green.* FLOWERS *Small, 3–6 mm diam., often buried among leaves;* stalks short, furrowed, opposite leaves; sepals reflexed. HABITAT Broken ground, cliff edges, grassy banks, usually near coast. DIST. Native. England, Wales. Scarce and decreasing. (S and SW Europe.) FLS Apr–Jun.

Corn Buttercup
Ranunculus arvensis CR

Erect annual to 60 cm. LEAVES *Lower leaves shallowly lobed, upper deeply divided.* FLOWERS 4–12 mm diam., sepals not reflexed. FRUITS *Achenes with prominent spines, >1 mm.* HABITAT Arable weed of wide range of soils. DIST. Long-established alien. England. Scarce and in rapid decline. (All Europe.) FLS Jun–Jul.

Jersey Buttercup
Ranunculus paludosus

Erect, hairy, stoloniferous perennial to 30 cm. *Base of plant with cluster of fleshy root tubers* as well as fibrous roots. LEAVES Mostly basal, lowest 3-lobed, rest deeply divided. FLOWERS 25–30 mm diam., sepals not reflexed. HABITAT Seasonally water-logged grassland that dries out in summer. DIST. Confined to Jersey in Channel Is. (W and S Europe.) FLS May.

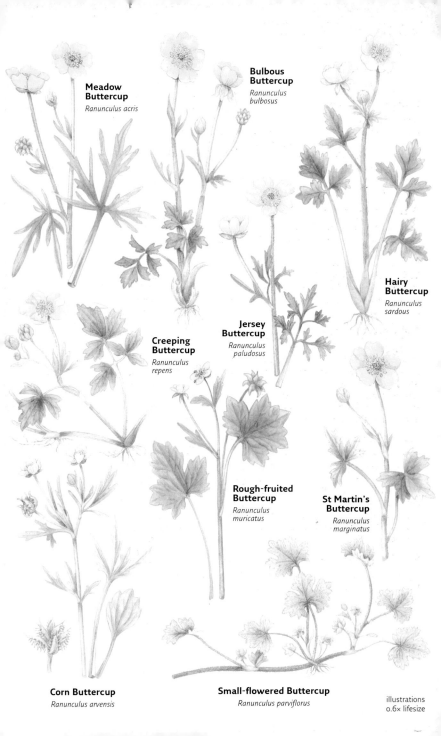

Meadow Buttercup
Ranunculus acris

Bulbous Buttercup
Ranunculus bulbosus

Hairy Buttercup
Ranunculus sardous

Creeping Buttercup
Ranunculus repens

Jersey Buttercup
Ranunculus paludosus

Rough-fruited Buttercup
Ranunculus muricatus

St Martin's Buttercup
Ranunculus marginatus

Corn Buttercup
Ranunculus arvensis

Small-flowered Buttercup
Ranunculus parviflorus

illustrations
0.6× lifesize

Goldilocks Buttercup — *Ranunculus auricomus*

Erect, sparsely hairy perennial to 40 cm. LEAVES *Very variable: lowest leaves long-stalked, rounded, hardly lobed; upper leaves deeply divided.* FLOWERS 15–25 mm diam.; sepals erect; *0–5 petals, variable in number on same plant.* HABITAT Deciduous woodland, especially on heavy basic soils. DIST. Native. Throughout BI; lowland to 1090 m. (All Europe.) FLS Apr–May.

Celery-leaved Buttercup — *Ranunculus sceleratus*

Erect annual to 60 cm. LEAVES Lower *leaves deeply 3-lobed, glabrous, shiny.* FLOWERS 5–10 mm diam., sepals reflexed. FRUITS Achenes, *receptacle elongating when ripe.* HABITAT Marshes, muddy margins of ponds, ditches and dykes; especially coastal and tolerant of brackish conditions. DIST. Native. Throughout BI; lowland. (N and central Europe.) FLS May–Sep.

Greater Spearwort — *Ranunculus lingua*

Tall stoloniferous perennial to 120 cm. LEAVES *Stem leaves to 25 cm, entire* or obscurely toothed. FLOWERS 2–5 *cm diam.* HABITAT Marshes, fens, ditch and pond margins. Frequently planted and establishing in wild. DIST. Native. Local throughout BI except N Scotland; lowland. (All Europe.) FLS Jun–Sep.

Lesser Spearwort — *Ranunculus flammula*

Prostrate or erect perennial to 50 cm, often rooting at lower nodes. Very variable. LEAVES *Typically lanceolate to linear, tapering to base.* FLOWERS 8–20 mm diam. HABITAT Marshes, fens, woodland flushes, stream sides, pond margins, lake shores. DIST. Native. Common throughout BI. (Most of Europe.) FLS May–Sep.

Creeping Spearwort — *Ranunculus reptans* VU.

Creeping, stoloniferous perennial. *Resembles slender forms of* R. flammula, *but roots at each node,* has *arching internodes,* and flowers 5–10mm diam. HABITAT Lake margins. DIST. Native. Rare. Lake District and Scotland. (N and central Europe.) FLS Jun–Aug. COMMENTS All British populations are probably hybrids with *R. flammula*, and characters distinguishing the 2 species overlap.

Adder's-tongue Spearwort — *Ranunculus ophioglossifolius* VU. *(B)

Erect annual to 40 cm. LEAVES Basal leaves long-stalked, ovate, cordate. FLOWERS *Distinguished from* R. flammula *by paler petals that don't overlap;* 6–9 mm diam. HABITAT Marshes with little competition and bare mud for germination. DIST. Native. Very rare, confined to 2 sites in Gloucestershire. (France, S Europe.) FLS Jun–Jul.

Lesser Celandine — *Ranunculus ficaria*

Glabrous perennial to 25 cm. Roots with numerous spindle-shaped tubers. LEAVES *Basal leaves 1–4 cm,* stem leaves smaller. FLOWERS 2–4 cm diam., *3 sepals, 7–12 petals.* HABITAT Woods, hedgerows, damp pastures, road verges, river and stream sides. DIST. Native. Throughout BI; to 750 m. (All Europe.) COMMENTS Ssp. *bulbilifer* has bulbils developing in leaf axils after flowering; ssp. *ficaria* has no bulbils and is more characteristic of disturbed ground and gardens. FLS Mar–May.

Water-crowfoots *Ranunculus*

Water-crowfoots are not always easy to identify and can only be named with certainty when in flower (*see* key on p.76). They show great morphological variation and frequently hybridise. Two kinds of leaves can be produced: finely divided submerged leaves; and rounded, lobed floating or terrestrial leaves. The shape of the nectaries at the base of the petals is important (remove the petals and examine with a lens). Characters of the receptacle are also important.

Ivy-leaved Crowfoot — *Ranunculus hederaceus*

Prostrate annual or perennial, growing on mud or floating in shallow water. LEAVES *1–3 cm wide,* shallowly lobed, *lobes broadest at base.* No finely divided leaves. FLOWERS *3–6 mm diam., petals hardly longer than sepals.* HABITAT Mud and shallow water of pond edges, ditches, streams, wet paths, cattle tracks. DIST. Native. Throughout BI; to 770 m. (W Europe.) FLS Jun–Sep.

Adder's-tongue Spearwort
Ranunculus ophioglossifolius

×0.15

Greater Spearwort
Ranunculus lingua

Celery-leaved Buttercup
Ranunculus sceleratus

Lesser Spearwort
Ranunculus flammula

Goldilocks Buttercup
Ranunculus auricomus

Lesser Celandine
Ranunculus ficaria

Ivy-leaved Crowfoot
Ranunculus hederaceus

Creeping Spearwort
Ranunculus reptans

illustrations
0.6× lifesize

Round-leaved Crowfoot   *Ranunculus omiophyllus*

Prostrate annual or perennial, growing on mud or in shallow water. LEAVES *8-30 mm wide*, shallowly lobed, *lobes narrowest at base*. No finely divided leaves. FLOWERS 8-12 mm diam., petals c.2× as long as sepals. HABITAT Small, slow-moving streams, ditches, pools, damp depressions in pastures and heathland, on acid, nutrient-poor soils. DIST. Native. Wales, W England, SW Scotland, S Ireland; to 1005 m. (W Europe.) FLS Jun–Aug.

Three-lobed Crowfoot   *Ranunculus tripartitus* EN. *(R)

Prostrate annual or perennial, growing on mud or in water. LEAVES *5-20 mm wide, deeply 3-lobed* to *>halfway, lobes widest above base*. Finely divided submerged leaves few or absent. FLOWERS 3-10 mm diam., *sepals with blue tip, petals ≤4.5 mm*. HABITAT Wet mud, temporary ponds, pools and ditches, on acid soils. DIST. Native. Rare and declining. SE and SW England, W Wales, Ireland (1 site). (W Europe.) FLS Apr–Jun. COMMENTS The hybrid with *R. omiophyllus* occurs in the New Forest.

Brackish Water-crowfoot   *Ranunculus baudotii*

Annual or perennial aquatic. LEAVES Finely divided leaves always present, segments rigid, spreading; floating leaves (sometimes absent) deeply lobed, usually with 3 lobes. FLOWERS *12-18 mm diam. Receptacle pubescent, nectaries crescent-shaped*. Sepals usually blue-tipped. FRUITS With elongated receptacle. HABITAT Brackish coastal lagoons, ditches, dykes, pools. DIST. Native. Local, all round British coasts. (Most European coasts.) FLS May–Sep.

Thread-leaved Water-crowfoot   *Ranunculus trichophyllus*

Annual or perennial aquatic. LEAVES Finely divided submerged leaves rigid or soft; *floating leaves absent*. FLOWERS *Small, 8-10 mm diam.*; petals usually <5 mm; *nectaries crescent-shaped*. HABITAT Wide range of shallow aquatic habitats, including ponds, drainage ditches, temporary water bodies. DIST. Native. Local throughout BI; most frequent in S and E. To 550 m. (All Europe.) FLS May–Jun.

Common Water-crowfoot   *Ranunculus aquatilis*

Annual or perennial aquatic with *both floating and finely divided submerged leaves*. LEAVES Submerged leaves shorter than internodes, segments spreading; floating leaves deeply lobed. FLOWERS *12-18 mm diam., petals <10 mm, nectaries circular*. HABITAT Shallow ponds, drainage dykes, small streams. DIST. Native. Throughout most of BI, but scarce in Scotland; lowland to 445 m. (All Europe.) FLS May–Sep.

Pond Water-crowfoot   *Ranunculus peltatus*

Annual or perennial aquatic with both floating and finely divided leaves. LEAVES Like *R. aquatilis* but floating leaves less deeply lobed. FLOWERS *15-22 mm diam., petals >10 mm, nectaries pear-shaped*. HABITAT Wide range of shallow waters, from small pools and drainage dykes to small lakes and streams. DIST. Native. Throughout BI, but scarce in Scotland; lowland to 500 m. (Most of Europe.) FLS May–Aug.

Stream Water-crowfoot   *Ranunculus penicillatus*

Very variable aquatic perennial. LEAVES Ssp. *penicillatus* has floating leaves similar to those of *R. aquatilis* and *R. peltatus*. Ssp. *pseudofluitans* similar to *R. fluitans*, with submerged leaves only (for differences, *see* key on p.76). HABITAT Ssp. *penicillatus* forms dense stands in fast-flowing rivers; ssp. *pseudofluitans* found in rivers and streams. DIST. Native. Ssp. *penicillatus* scarce in SW England, Wales, Ireland. Ssp. *pseudofluitans* frequent in England and Wales; rare in Scotland and Ireland. (Most of Europe.) FLS May–Aug.

River Water-crowfoot   *Ranunculus fluitans* *(NI)

Large aquatic perennial, *stems to 6 m*. LEAVES *Submerged leaves to 30 cm, longer than internodes, divided 4×; floating leaves absent*. FLOWERS 20-30 mm diam., petals 7-13 mm, nectaries pear-shaped. HABITAT Medium- to fast-flowing rivers with hard beds. DIST. Native. Scattered throughout BI; very rare in Ireland. (Most of Europe.) FLS Jun–Aug.

Fan-leaved Water-crowfoot   *Ranunculus circinatus*

Submerged aquatic with ± erect stems. LEAVES *Submerged leaves distinctly rounded in outline, segments rigid, all lying in 1 plane*; floating leaves absent. FLOWERS 8-18 mm diam., petals up to 10 mm, *nectaries crescent-shaped*. HABITAT Deep water in lakes, slow streams, canals, ditches. DIST. Native. Widespread in England, Wales; rare in Scotland, Ireland. Lowland to 310 m. (Most of Europe.) FLS Jun–Aug.

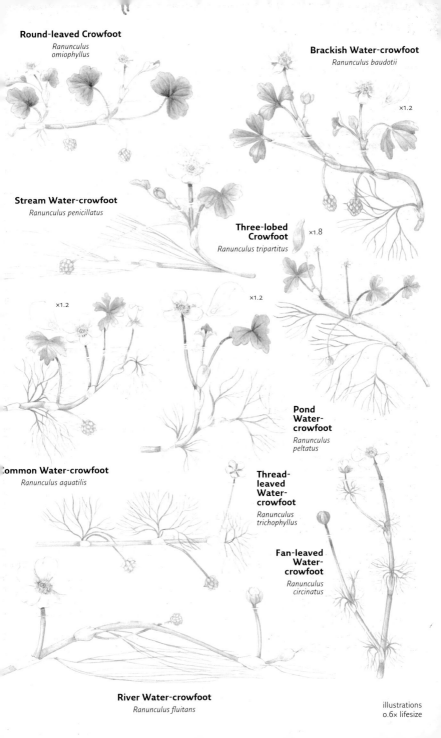

Round-leaved Crowfoot
Ranunculus omiophyllus

Brackish Water-crowfoot
Ranunculus baudotii

×1.2

Stream Water-crowfoot
Ranunculus penicillatus

Three-lobed Crowfoot
Ranunculus tripartitus

×1.8

×1.2

×1.2

Pond Water-crowfoot
Ranunculus peltatus

Common Water-crowfoot
Ranunculus aquatilis

Thread-leaved Water-crowfoot
Ranunculus trichophyllus

Fan-leaved Water-crowfoot
Ranunculus circinatus

River Water-crowfoot
Ranunculus fluitans

illustrations
0.6× lifesize

Pheasant's-eye
Adonis annua EN.

Glabrous annual to 40 cm. Leaves *Much divided into narrow segments.* Flowers 15-25 mm diam.; 5 sepals; 5-8 petals, *bright red with black basal spot.* Habitat Calcareous soils. Dist. Introduced as arable weed in antiquity. Occasionally occurs as escape from cultivation in S England. Rare and declining. (S Europe, SW Asia.) Fls Midsummer.

Mousetail
Myosurus minimus VU.

Small, inconspicuous annual to 10 cm. Leaves *Linear, in basal rosette.* Flowers Solitary, 5 sepals, 5 petals. Fruits *With elongated receptacle (the 'mousetail').* Habitat Bare patches on damp arable soils, such as pathsides and cattle troughs. Dist. Native. Scattered throughout lowland England; local and declining. (Central and S Europe.) Fls Midsummer.

Columbine
Aquilegia vulgaris

Glabrous or finely hairy perennial to 100 cm. Leaves Basal leaves long-stalked. Flowers 3-5 cm diam., *sepals petal-like, petals each with curved spur with swollen tip.* Habitat Damp woodland glades, marshes, fens, especially on calcareous soils. Often occurs as garden escape. (S and central Europe.) Dist. Native. Local throughout BI; to 470 m. Fls May-Jun.

Meadow-rue *Thalictrum*

Plant small, to 15 cm, stem leaves absent, inflorescence unbranched   *T. alpinum*

Plant >15 cm, stem leafy, inflorescence branched

   Leaflets longer than wide, inflorescence dense, stamens erect   *T. flavum*

   Leaflets about as long as wide, inflorescence diffuse, stamens drooping   *T. minus*

Common Meadow-rue
Thalictrum flavu

Erect rhizomatous *perennial to 120 cm.* Leaves Ultimate *leaflets distinctly longer than broad.* Flowers dense clusters, *stamens erect.* Habitat Marshes, fens, wet meadows, stream sides, on base-rich soils. Dist. Native. Locally abundant in lowland England (All Europe.) Fls Jul-Aug.

Lesser Meadow-rue
Thalictrum minu

Erect perennial to 120 cm. Leaves *Ultimate leaflet about as long as broad.* Flowers In loose clusters *stamens drooping.* Habitat Very variable: calcareous grassland, limestone pavement, sand-dunes, lak and stream margins. Dist. Native throughout B except for much of S, where it is naturalised; t 855 m. (All Europe.) Fls Jun-Aug.

Alpine Meadow-rue
Thalictrum alpinu

Small, erect, stoloniferous *perennial to 15 cm.* Leaves *Stem leaves absent.* Flowers Form *unbranched inflo rescence*, purplish, stamens drooping. Habitat Mountain grassland, rock ledges, stream sides, o base-rich soils. (Arctic and alpine Europe.) Dist Native. Widespread in Scottish Highlands, also mts c N Wales and N England; to 1190 m. Fls Midsumme

BERBERIDACEAE Barberry family

Barberry
Berberis vulgar

Deciduous spiny shrub to 3 m. Leaves *Have spin marginal teeth.* Flowers 6-8 mm diam. Fruits *Re berries.* Habitat Scattered in hedgerows, copses waste ground. (All Europe except N.) Dist. Probabl native throughout BI; lowland to 380 m. Cultivate since Middle Ages. Fls May-Jun.

Oregon-grape
Mahonia aquifoliu

Evergreen stoloniferous *shrub to 1.5 m.* Leaves *Pin nate*, leaflets with spiny marginal teeth. Fruits *Blac berries.* Habitat Hedgerows and woodlands. Dist Introduced in 1823 (native of W North America widely cultivated and planted as game cover. Natu ralised throughout BI, but rare or absent in N Scot land and Ireland. (Naturalised in most of Europe Fls Dec-May.

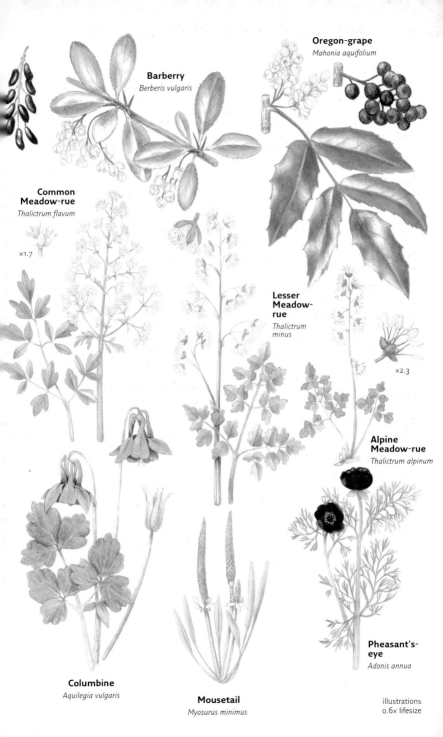

Oregon-grape
Mahonia aquifolium

Barberry
Berberis vulgaris

**Common
Meadow-rue**
Thalictrum flavum

×1.7

**Lesser
Meadow-
rue**
*Thalictrum
minus*

×2.3

**Alpine
Meadow-rue**
Thalictrum alpinum

**Pheasant's-
eye**
Adonis annua

Columbine
Aquilegia vulgaris

Mousetail
Myosurus minimus

illustrations
0.6× lifesize

PAPAVERACEAE Poppies

A distinctive family of herbaceous annuals and perennials, with 2 sepals (which fall early) and 4 showy petals (in the garden plume poppies *Macleaya*, the petals are absent), and a milky or yellow latex. Leaves are spirally arranged, often deeply lobed and lack stipules. Flowers are regular; 2 sepals; 2+2 petals (or absent); numerous stamens; ovary superior. Fruit is usually a capsule.

1	Flowers red, lilac or white	2 *Papaver*
	Flowers yellow	6
2	Flowers usually lilac; leaves glaucous, clasping stem, lobed but not deeply divided	*P. somniferum*
	Flowers red; leaves green, not clasping stem, deeply divided	3
3	Capsule glabrous	4
	Capsule with long, stiff hairs	5
4	Capsule a little longer than wide	*P. rhoeas*
	Capsule ≥2× as long as wide	*P. dubium*
5	Capsule almost spherical	*P. hybridum*
	Capsule ≥2× as long as wide	*P. argemone*
6	Capsule >10× as long as wide	7
	Capsule <6× as long as wide	*Meconopsis*
7	Flowers >5 cm diam.; capsule an elongated curved pod, 15-30 cm	*Glaucium*
	Flowers <3 cm diam., borne in umbels; capsule 3-5 cm	*Chelidonium*

Common Poppy
Papaver rhoeas

Annual branched herb to 20 cm. LEAVES Hairy, deeply lobed, lowest stalked, upper sessile. FLOWERS 7-10 cm diam., petals often with black blotch at base. FRUITS *Globose capsule, slightly longer than wide, glabrous.* HABITAT Arable fields, disturbed ground, roadside verges, especially on calcareous soils. DIST. Introduced in antiquity. Common on lowland throughout BI, but rare in Scotland and N Ireland. (Europe N to S Sweden.) FLS Jun-Sep.

Long-headed Poppy
Papaver dubium

Annual herb. Similar to *P. rhoeas*, but leaves glaucous; flowers smaller, 3-7 cm diam., paler; and *capsule ≥2× as long as wide, glabrous.* HABITAT Similar to *P. rhoeas* and sometimes mixed with it, but less frequent. DIST. Introduced in antiquity. Throughout BI but scarcer in N; lowland to 450 m. (Europe N to S Sweden.) FLS Jun-Jul. COMMENTS There are 2 subspecies: ssp. *dubium*, with colourless latex and over-

lapping petals, extending further N in Scotland tha *P. rhoeas*; and ssp. *lecoqii*, with latex turning yellow on exposure to air, base of petals not overlapping, less common and ± restricted to England and Ireland.

Prickly Poppy
Papaver argemone VU

Annual herb to 45 cm. Similar to *P. rhoeas*, but *flowers* smaller, 2-6 cm diam., petals not overlapping an with black spot at base; *capsule elongated, ribbed an bristly.* HABITAT Arable fields on light sandy or chalk soils. DIST. Introduced with agriculture. Widespread but scattered in lowland England; rare elsewhere (Europe N to S Sweden.) FLS Jun-Jul.

Rough Poppy
Papaver hybridum *(F

Annual herb to 50 cm. Similar to *P. rhoeas*, but *flowers* much smaller, 2-5 cm diam., petals not overlapping and with black spot at base; *capsule almost spherical with dense yellowish bristles.* HABITAT Arable fields on light calcareous soils. DIST. Introduced with agriculture. Lowland S and E England Rarer than *P. rhoeas*, *P. dubium* and *P. argemone* (SW and S Europe.) FLS Jun-Jul.

Opium Poppy
Papaver somniferum

Tall, glabrous, glaucous or sparsely hairy annual to 100 cm. LEAVES Shallowly lobed, upper ones clasping stem. FLOWERS *To 18 cm diam., petals white to lilac* (sometimes red) without basal blotch. FRUIT Large ± spherical capsule. HABITAT Casual and frequent escape from cultivation, on waste ground DIST. Introduced and cultivated in antiquity. Lowland throughout BI, but scarce in Scotland and Ireland. (All Europe as an archaeophyte.) COMMENT Common form is ssp. *somniferum*. FLS Jul-Aug.

Welsh Poppy
Meconopsis cambrica

Branched, glabrous perennial to 60 cm. FLOWERS 5-7.5 cm diam., solitary in leaf axils. FRUITS Ribbed capsule, 2.5-3 cm. HABITAT Damp rocky woodland in native range; also hedge banks, walls, waste ground. DIST. Native in Wales, SW England, Ireland to 640 m. Naturalised throughout rest of BI, especially in N. (W Europe: N Spain, Pyrenees, S France. FLS Jun-Sep.

Greater Celandine
Chelidonium maju

Erect perennial to 90 cm. STEM Sparsely hairy, *producing bright orange latex when cut.* FLOWERS *In umbels* 2-2.5 cm diam., 2 sepals (soon falling), 4 petals. FRUITS Capsule, 3-5 cm. HABITAT Hedge banks, hedgerows walls, especially near buildings. DIST. Introduced and originally cultivated for medicinal purposes, but whole

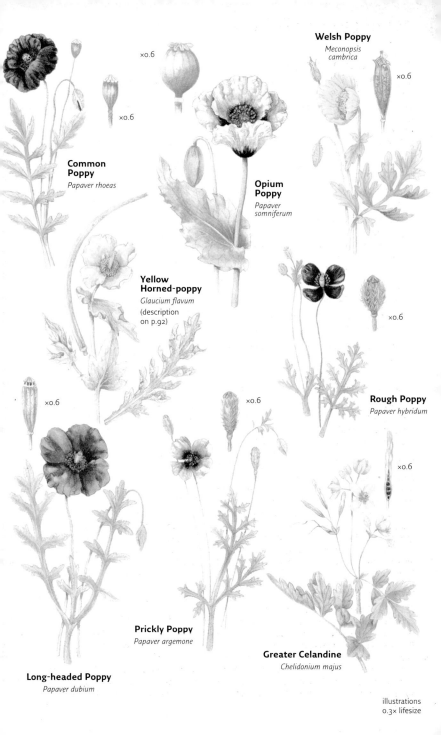

Welsh Poppy
Meconopsis cambrica

×0.6

×0.6

×0.6

Common Poppy
Papaver rhoeas

Opium Poppy
Papaver somniferum

Yellow Horned-poppy
Glaucium flavum
(description on p.92)

×0.6

Rough Poppy
Papaver hybridum

×0.6

×0.6

×0.6

Prickly Poppy
Papaver argemone

Greater Celandine
Chelidonium majus

Long-headed Poppy
Papaver dubium

illustrations
0.3× lifesize

plant is very poisonous. Naturalised throughout BI but rare in Scotland and W Ireland. (All Europe except far N.) FLS May–Aug.

Yellow Horned-poppy *Glaucium flavum*

[*See* illustration previous page.] *Extremely glaucous*, branched, short-lived perennial to 90 cm. STEM Glabrous. LEAVES Much lobed and divided, roughly hairy. FLOWERS *6–9 cm diam.* FRUITS *Distinctive long, curved, rough pod, 15–30 cm.* HABITAT Characteristic plant of shingle beaches; also less commonly on cliffs, sand-dunes, waste ground close to sea. DIST. Native. All round coast of Britain as far N as Solway; also S Ireland. (Coasts of S and W Europe.) FLS Jun–Sep.

FUMARIACEAE Fumitories

Annuals or perennials, often climbing or scrambling, with much-divided leaves (*see* key on p.94). Inflorescence usually a raceme, flowers zygomorphic, 2 sepals, 4 petals with 1 or 2 spurs, 2 stamens. The fumitories are not easy to identify. Details of the flowers and fruits are important, including colour and petal shape; sepals and fruits are illustrated within each species description.

Flowers are measured from the tip of the spur to the tip of the longest petal. Petal colour excludes the dark tips. Some species are highly variable, with several subspecies and varieties.

pedicel   upper petal

sepal   lower petal

bract   *Fumaria flower*

Common Fumitory *Fumaria officinalis*

Commonest small-flowered *Fumaria*. Variable species with several named varieties. LEAVES *Lobes flat, narrow.* FLOWERS ≥6 mm, lower petal paddle-shaped; inflorescence longer than peduncle; *bracts shorter than flower stalks.* FRUITS Rough, tip truncate or slightly notched. HABITAT Arable fields, gardens on light sandy or calcareous soils. DIST. Archaeophyte. Throughout BI; to 305 m. (All Europe.) FLS May–Oct.

Dense-flowered Fumitory *Fumaria densiflora*

LEAVES *Lobes channelled*, narrow. FLOWERS 6–7 mm, lower petal paddle-shaped; inflorescence longer than peduncle. FRUITS Rough, tip rounded; *bracts longer than pedicels.* HABITAT Arable fields, gardens, usually on dry calcareous soils. DIST. Archaeophyte. SE England, E Scotland; rare and declining. (S and W Europe.) FLS Jun–Oct.

Few-flowered Fumitory *Fumaria vaillantii* V

LEAVES *Lobes flat*, narrow. FLOWERS 5–6 mm, lower lip paddle-shaped; *sepals small, 1 × 0.5 mm; inflorescence longer than short peduncle.* FRUITS Rounded, obscurely keeled; *bracts shorter than pedicel.* HABITAT Arable fields on chalk. DIST. Archaeophyte. SE England; rare. (W and central Europe.) FLS Jun–Sep.

Fine-leaved Fumitory *Fumaria parviflora* VU

LEAVES *Lobes channelled*, very narrow. FLOWERS Pale 5–6 mm, lower petal paddle-shaped; *inflorescence almost sessile.* FRUITS Rounded or with short beak, distinctly keeled; *bracts equalling or longer than pedicels.* HABITAT Arable fields on chalk. DIST. Archaeophyte. SE England, NE Yorkshire; rare. (W, central and S Europe.) FLS Jun–Sep.

Common Ramping-fumitory *Fumaria muralis*

Commonest large-flowered *Fumaria*. Very variable species whose commonest form is ssp. *boraei*. LEAVES Lobes flat, wedge-shaped. FLOWERS 9–12 mm, *lower petal not paddle-shaped and with erect margins.* FRUITS Smooth, bracts >⅓ as long as pedicels. HABITAT Arable fields, waste ground, hedge banks, walls. DIST. Native. Throughout BI. (W Europe.) FLS May–Oct.

Tall Ramping-fumitory *Fumaria bastardii*

LEAVES Lobes flat, oblong. FLOWERS *9–11 mm*, lower petal not paddle-shaped and with narrow, spreading margins; sepals toothed. FRUITS *Rough, bracts <⅓ as long as pedicels.* HABITAT Arable fields, waste ground, hedge banks, on dry acid soils. DIST. Native. S and W BI; scarce. (S and W Europe.) FLS Apr–Oct.

Martin's Ramping-fumitory *Fumaria reuteri* *(EN)

LEAVES Lobes flat, small, wedge-shaped. FLOWERS *11–13 mm*, lower petal not paddle-shaped and with narrow, spreading margins; sepals not toothed. FRUITS Smooth, bracts >⅓ as long as pedicels. HABITAT Allotments, gardens, potato fields. DIST. Introduced. Very rare: only in 2 sites in S England. (Spain, Portugal.) FLS May–Oct.

Purple Ramping-fumitory *Fumaria purpurea*

LEAVES Lobes flat, oblong or wedge-shaped. FLOWERS *10–13 mm, pale purple, upper petal not laterally compressed, wings concealing keel;* inflorescence about as

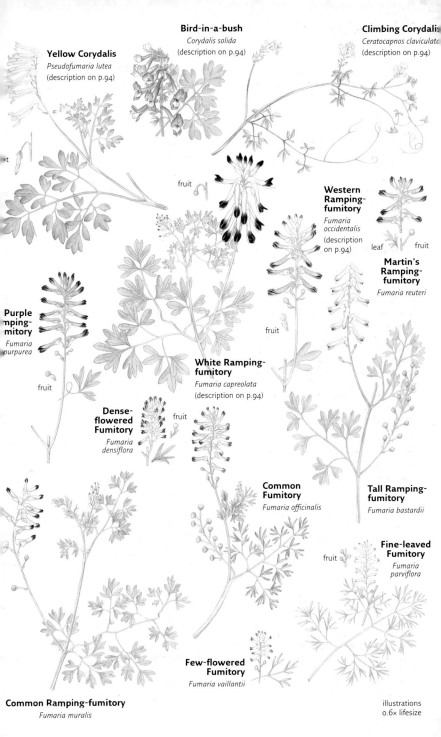

Yellow Corydalis
Pseudofumaria lutea
(description on p.94)

fruit

Bird-in-a-bush
Corydalis solida
(description on p.94)

Climbing Corydalis
Ceratocapnos claviculata
(description on p.94)

fruit

Western Ramping-fumitory
Fumaria occidentalis
(description on p.94)

leaf   fruit

Martin's Ramping-fumitory
Fumaria reuteri

Purple Ramping-fumitory
Fumaria purpurea

fruit

White Ramping-fumitory
Fumaria capreolata
(description on p.94)

fruit

Dense-flowered Fumitory
Fumaria densiflora

fruit

Common Fumitory
Fumaria officinalis

Tall Ramping-fumitory
Fumaria bastardii

Fine-leaved Fumitory
Fumaria parviflora

fruit

Common Ramping-fumitory
Fumaria muralis

Few-flowered Fumitory
Fumaria vaillantii

illustrations
0.6× lifesize

long as peduncle. FRUITS Pedicels slightly recurved; bracts broad, about as long as pedicels. HABITAT Hedge banks, arable land, gardens, on dry acid soils. DIST. Endemic. Local and scattered, mostly in W. FLS Jul-Oct.

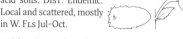

White Ramping-fumitory — *Fumaria capreolata*

[*See* illustration previous page.] LEAVES Lobes flat, oblong or wedge-shaped. FLOWERS *10-12 mm, cream, upper petal strongly laterally compressed, wings not concealing keel;* inflorescence shorter than peduncle. FRUITS Pedicels strongly recurved; bracts narrow, equalling or shorter than pedicels. HABITAT Hedge banks, scrub, cliffs. DIST. Native, scattered throughout BI. (S and W Europe.) Fls May-Sep.

Western Ramping-fumitory — *Fumaria occidentalis*

[*See* illustration previous page.] Robust plant. LEAVES Lobes flat, oblong. FLOWERS 12-14 mm; white turning pink, wings dark red with white border; upper *petal dorsally compressed, lower petal with broad, spreading margin*; inflorescence about equal in length to peduncle. FRUITS c. *3mm* Bracts about equal in length to pedicels. HABITAT Hedge banks, waste ground, bulb fields on light sandy soils. DIST. Endemic. Scilly Is, Cornwall. FLS May-Oct.

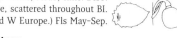

Climbing Corydalis — *Ceratocapnos claviculat*

[*See* illustration previous page.] *Much-branche scrambling annual* to 80 cm. LEAVES *Pinnate, endin in a branched tendril.* FLOWERS *Cream*, 5-6 mm; c. forming inflorescence arising opposite leaves. HABI TAT Acid woodlands, shaded rocky hillsides; als heathy ground, peat. DIST. Native. Throughout BI but rare in Ireland; lowland to 430 m. (W Europe. FLS Jun-Sep.

Bird-in-a-bush — *Corydalis solid*

[*See* illustration previous page.] Erect perennial t 20 cm. LEAVES *Lobes wedge-shaped.* FLOWERS Uni formly purple; *15-22 mm with long spur;* in solitary ter minal inflorescence. DIST. Introduced; cultivate since C16th. Scattered throughout England as garder escape. (Native throughout most of Europe except N FLS Spring.

Yellow Corydalis — *Pseudofumaria lute*

[*See* illustration previous page.] Much-branched erec perennial to 30 cm. LEAVES *Pinnate, ending in a leaflet* FLOWERS *Yellow,* 12-18 mm; 5-10 forming inflores cence arising opposite leaves. HABITAT Found espe cially on old mortared walls. DIST. Introduced commonly cultivated since C16th. Widely naturalise throughout BI, but rare in Scotland and Ireland. (Nativ of Italian Alps.) FLS May-Aug.

Key to Fumariaceae Fumatories

	if	then
1	▷ Flowers yellow or cream	Go to ▷ **2**
	▷ At least tips of petals red or purple	Go to ▷ **3**
2	▷ Flowers cream; leaves ending in tendrils	***Ceratocapnos claviculata*** (p.94)
	▷ Flowers yellow; leaves ending in a leaflet	***Pseudofumaria lutea*** (p.94)
3	▷ Flowers uniformly purple, 15-22 mm, spur *c.⅓* length of flower	***Corydalis solida*** (p.94)
	▷ Lateral petals with dark tips, flowers 5-14 mm, spur <⅓ length of flower	Go to ▷ **4** *Fumaria* (p.92)

if	**then**
4 ▷ Leaflets narrow, linear-lanceolate; flowers 5–8 mm, lower petal paddle-shaped	Go to ▷ **5**
▷ Leaflets oblong or wedge-shaped; flowers 9–14 mm, lower petal not paddle-shaped	Go to ▷ **8**
5 ▷ Sepals ≥1.5 × 1.0 mm, flowers ≥6 mm	Go to ▷ **6**
▷ Sepals ≤1.2 x 1.0 mm, flowers 5–6 mm	Go to ▷ **7**
6 ▷ Leaf lobes flat; bracts shorter than pedicels; fruits truncate at the tip	***F. officinalis*** (p.92)
▷ Leaf lobes channelled; bracts longer than pedicels; fruits rounded at tip	***F. densiflora*** (p.92)
7 ▷ Leaf lobes flat; inflorescence with short peduncle, flowers pink; bracts shorter than pedicels in fruit	***F. vaillantii*** (p.92)
▷ Leaf lobes channelled; inflorescence almost sessile, flowers white; bracts longer than or equal to pedicels in fruit	***F. parviflora*** (p.92)
8 ▷ Lower petal with broad, spreading margins, wing of upper petal with white margin; fruit *c.*3 mm (Cornwall, Scilly Is only)	***F. occidentalis*** (p.94)
▷ Lower petal with narrow margins; fruit <3 mm	Go to ▷ **9**
9 ▷ Peduncles shorter than inflorescence or flowers few, *c.*12; sepals 3–5 mm; pedicels not rigidly recurved in fruit	Go to ▷ **10**
▷ Peduncles longer than or equal to inflorescence, ≥20 flowers; sepals 4–6 mm; pedicels rigidly recurved in fruit, with a distinct collar when fresh	Go to ▷ **12**
10 ▷ Inflorescence shorter than or equal to peduncle; lower petal with erect margins; flowers few, *c.*12; fruit smooth when dry	***F. muralis*** (p.92)
▷ Inflorescence longer than peduncle; lower petal with spreading margins; flowers numerous, *c.*15–25	Go to ▷ **11**
11 ▷ Flowers 9–11 mm; sepals 2–3.5 mm, toothed; bracts <¼ as long as pedicel; fruits rough when dry	***F. bastardii*** (p.92)
▷ Flowers 11–13 mm; sepals 3–5 mm, untoothed; bracts >¼ as long as pedicel; fruits smooth when dry (very rare)	***F. reuteri*** (p.92)
12 ▷ Flowers white-cream, upper petal laterally compressed, wings not concealing keel	***F. capreolata*** (p.94)
▷ Flowers purple, upper petal not laterally compressed, wings concealing keel	***F. purpurea*** (p.92)

ULMACEAE Elms

Deciduous trees. Leaves asymmetrical at the base. Flowers borne in clusters and produced before leaves; perianth inconspicuous, 4–5-lobed; 4–5 stamens. Fruit a broad-winged achene. Elms are very difficult to identify. Opinions differ as to the number of species and their origins in Britain. There is also much geographical variation and many hybrid combinations are described. Only the 3 most widespread species are included here. Identification should be attempted only on mature leaves on short shoots in mid-season. Leaves are measured from the tip to the base of the longer side of the blade. The Dutch elm disease outbreak, which first appeared in Britain in 1965, has virtually eliminated elms from large parts of the country.

Wych Elm   *Ulmus glabra*

Crown broadly rounded, irregular; to 38 m. Rarely suckering. BUDS Dense reddish hairs. LEAVES *Large, 8–16 cm, 12–18 pairs of lateral veins*, upper surface rough, base asymmetric, *long side with rounded lobe that overlaps and almost hides short petiole*. HABITAT Mixed woodlands on limestone and base-rich soils, hedgerows, stream sides; to 530 m. DIST. Native. Throughout BI, but commoner in N and W. (Most of Europe except extreme N and S.) FLS Feb–Mar.

English Elm   *Ulmus procera*

Main trunk persisting more than halfway through crown; height to 36 m. Suckers and epicormic growth frequent. BRANCHES Main branches strong, forming lobed canopy. Young shoots densely hairy; buds small, slightly hairy. LEAVES *Rounded, base unequal, rough above, uniformly hairy below, 10–12 pairs of lateral veins*. HABITAT Hedges, field borders. DIST. Archaeophyte, introduced by Romans. England, Wales; rare in Scotland and Ireland. FLS Feb–Mar but does not set seed.

Small-leaved Elm   *Ulmus minor*

Extremely variable tree with several well-marked, named regional populations; very susceptible to Dutch elm disease. Height to 30 m. LEAVES *Usually 4–10 cm, smooth and shining on upper surface, base ± symmetrical to strongly unequal*. HABITAT Hedgerows, field borders, copses. (All Europe except N.) DIST. Archaeophyte. English lowlands. FLS Feb–Mar.

CANNABACEAE Hops and hemp

Hop   *Humulus lupulus*

Perennial, dioecious *evergreen climber*. LEAVES *Opposite, 3–5-lobed, toothed*. FLOWERS Male inflorescence branched, flowers small, 5 stamens; *female inflorescence a stalked cone-like spike with broad, overlapping membranous bracts, persisting in fruit*. HABITAT Hedgerows, fen carr, woodland edges, on moist soils; often occurring as relic of cultivation. DIST. Native to England, Wales; introduced to Scotland, Ireland. Cultivated since C16th. (All Europe except extreme N.) FLS Jul–Aug.

URTICACEAE Nettles

Common Nettle   *Urtica dioica*

Erect, dioecious perennial to 150 cm. STEMS With stinging hairs. LEAVES *Cordate*, with stinging hairs, *lower leaves longer than petioles*. FLOWERS Small, perianth with 4 segments; in elongated spike-like inflorescence. HABITAT Woodlands, fens, ditches, riverbanks, stream sides, areas associated with habitation on fertile or enriched soils; to 850 m. DIST. Native. Common throughout BI. (All Europe.) FLS Jun–Aug. NOTE Plants growing in wet fen woodland at Wicken Fen, Cambridgeshire, without stinging hairs and with narrower, more elongated leaves, densely hairy on the underside, have been named as *Urtica galeopsifolia*, but they need further study.

Small Nettle   *Urtica urens*

Erect, monoecious annual to 60 cm. Similar to *U. dioica, but lower leaves shorter than petioles and not cordate*. HABITAT Arable fields, gardens, waste ground on fertile, well-drained sandy soils; to 500 m. DIST. Archaeophyte. Throughout lowland BI. (All Europe.) FLS Jun–Sep.

Pellitory-of-the-wall   *Parietaria judaica*

Much-branched, softly hairy perennial to c.50 cm. LEAVES *Alternate*. FLOWERS Unisexual, perianth with 4 segments. HABITAT Crevices in old mortared walls, cliffs, steep-sided hedge banks, on dry, well-drained soils. DIST. Native. Throughout England, Wales; rare in Scotland, N Ireland. (W, central and S Europe.) FLS Jun–Oct.

Mind-your-own-business   *Soleirolia soleirolii*

Small, creeping, mat-forming evergreen perennial. STEMS Slender, rooting at nodes. LEAVES *2–6 mm alternate*. FLOWERS Unisexual, perianth 4-lobed. HABITAT Damp walls, banks, pathsides, gardens. (Endemic to islands of W Mediterranean.) DIST. Introduced; cultivated since 1905. Throughout BI, spreading from SW, but rare in Scotland and most of Ireland. FLS Jun–Oct.

♂ flower

fruit

English Elm
Ulmus procera

flower

Common Nettle
Urtica dioica

Wych Elm
Ulmus glabra

♂ ♀

♂

**Small-
leaved Elm**
Ulmus minor

**Pellitory-of-
the-wall**
Parietaria judaica

♀ ♂

Mind-your-own-business
Soleirolia soleirolii

ower

Small Nettle
Urtica urens

Hop
Humulus lupulus

ssp. *galeopsifolia*

illustrations
0.5× lifesize

MYRICACEAE Bog-myrtle family
Bog-myrtle
Myrica gale

Suckering deciduous shrub to 2 m. Usually dioecious, occasionally monoecious or hermaphrodite. LEAVES *Grey-green*, glabrous above, downy beneath, *toothed towards apex, strongly aromatic* when crushed. FLOWERS *In catkins, perianth absent.* HABITAT Abundant in wetter parts of acid bogs and fens, especially where there is moving ground water; lowland to 520 m. DIST. Native. Widespread in N and W BI, and on heaths in S. (NW Europe.) FLS Apr–May.

FAGACEAE Oaks, chestnut and beech

A family of predominantly long-lived forest trees. Leaves are deciduous or evergreen, alternate, with stipules that fall early. Flowers are unisexual, usually borne in different inflorescences on the same tree (monoecious), small and inconspicuous, regular; perianth 4–6-lobed; male flowers in catkins or tassel-like heads; female flowers in groups of 1–3, surrounded by small scales. Fruit is a 1-seeded nut in groups of 1–3, surrounded by a scaly or spiny 'cup' formed from the enlarged scales.

Oaks *Quercus*
Monoecious deciduous or evergreen trees. Buds clustered towards tips of twigs. Male flowers in long, drooping catkins; female flowers solitary or in clusters of 2–3. Fruit (acorn) large, surrounded by cup-like cupule. There are two native species of deciduous oak in Britain, Pedunculate and Sessile Oak. Both species occur throughout BI. Identification is sometimes difficult as intermediates are frequent, arising from different degrees of hybridisation.

Pedunculate Oak	*Sessile Oak*
Acorns stalked, 2–8 cm	Acorns sessile
Petioles short or absent, base of leaf blade with small lobes (auricles) where joins petiole	Petioles >1 cm, base of leaf blade ± tapers into petiole
Underside of leaf glabrous	Underside of leaf finely pubescent along midrib
Leaf lobes 3–5 pairs, rather unequal	Leaf lobes 4–6 pairs, rather equal

Pedunculate Oak
Quercus robur

Long-lived deciduous tree to 37 m. Many ancient specimens are old pollards and can achieve girths to *c*.17 m. HABITAT The dominant forest tree throughout English lowlands, especially on fertile clays but also on light acid soils. High forest, wood pasture, coppice. To 450 m. DIST. Native. Throughout BI. (S Scandinavia to Mediterranean.) FLS Apr–May.

Sessile Oak
Quercus petraea

Long-lived deciduous tree to 40 m. HABITAT Well-drained siliceous soils; also characteristic species of upland oak woods in W Britain. Grows mixed with *Q. robur* on acid sands but unable to tolerate heavy soils. High forest and coppice. To 450 m. DIST. Native. Throughout BI. (S Scandinavia to Mediterranean.) FLS Apr–May.

Turkey Oak
Quercus cerris

Long-lived deciduous tree to 39 m. Similar to *Q. robur* and *Q. petraea*, but has *more deeply divided leaves with 7–8 pairs of lobes, rough above, downy beneath;* BUDS *Surrounded by long, narrow scales* (persistent stipules); and *acorn cup covered by long, spreading, narrow scales.* HABITAT Parks, railway embankments, roadsides calcareous grassland, heathland. DIST. Introduced in 1735. Naturalised; reproduces freely from seed. Throughout BI, but rare in Scotland and Ireland. (Native of E Mediterranean.) FLS May.

Evergreen Oak
Quercus ilex

Evergreen tree to 30 m. LEAVES *Dark green above when mature, densely hairy beneath, entire or sparsely toothed, teeth sharp-pointed.* HABITAT Widely planted in parks, large gardens, churchyards, especially close to sea. DIST. Introduced in C16th; reproduces freely by seed, especially in SE England. (Native of S Europe.) FLS May.

Sweet Chestnut
Castanea sativa

Deciduous tree to 30 m. LEAVES *10–25 cm, coarsely toothed, glabrous when mature.* FLOWERS Male catkins large, conspicuous, 12–20 cm, ± erect. FRUITS 2–3.5 cm, dark shining brown, surrounded by densely spiny green 'cupule'. HABITAT Woodland, parks, large gardens; major coppice crop in SE England. DIST. Introduced by Romans. Throughout BI but rare in N Scotland and Ireland. Seedling regeneration rare. (Native of E Mediterranean.) FLS Jul.

Beech
Fagus sylvatica

Large, long-lived deciduous tree to 40 m. BUDS *Spindle-shaped, 1–2 cm, evenly spaced along twigs.* LEAVES *Glabrous except for long silky hairs on margins and on veins beneath.* FLOWERS Male flowers clustered on long peduncles. FRUITS 12–18 mm, glossy brown, enclosed in 'cupule' covered by stiff narrow scales. HABITATS Woodlands on well-drained sandy or calcareous soils. DIST. Native of S England, S Wales; widely planted throughout rest of BI. (All Europe except N and SW.) FLS Apr–May.

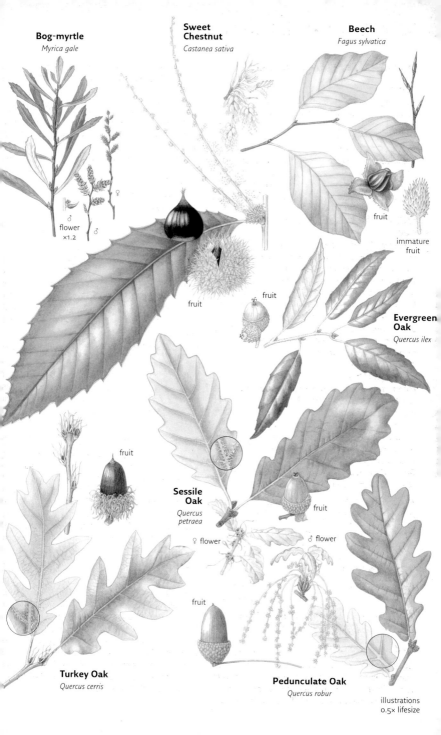

Bog-myrtle
Myrica gale

flower
×1.2

♀ ♂

Sweet Chestnut
Castanea sativa

fruit

Beech
Fagus sylvatica

fruit

immature fruit

fruit

Evergreen Oak
Quercus ilex

fruit

fruit

Sessile Oak
Quercus petraea

♀ flower

♂ flower

Turkey Oak
Quercus cerris

fruit

Pedunculate Oak
Quercus robur

illustrations 0.5× lifesize

BETULACEAE Birches, alders and hazels

Deciduous trees or shrubs with alternate simple leaves. Monoecious. Flowers very small; male catkins long, pendulous; female flowers few, clustered, with 2 styles.

Birches *Betula*

Trees or shrubs. Male catkins with 2 stamens, flowering with leaves. Fruiting catkins falling with the small winged fruits. Hybrids intermediate between the 2 species of tree birch are frequent.

Tree to 20-30 m; leaves >2 cm, ± ovate, pointed at tip	B. pubescens, B. pendula
Shrub to 1 m; leaves <2 cm, ± orbicular, rounded at tip	B. nana

Silver Birch — *Betula pendula*

Deciduous tree to 30 m. HABITAT Common in mixed woodland on well-drained acid soils; vigorous coloniser of open ground and heathland. Also widely planted. DIST. Native. Throughout BI. (All Europe except extreme N and Mediterranean.) FLS Apr-May.

Downy Birch — *Betula pubescens*

Deciduous tree to 25 m. HABITAT Common in mixed woodland or pure stands and on heathland, preferring damp, acid, peaty soils. Also widely planted. To 685 m. DIST. Native. Throughout BI. (All Europe except Mediterranean.) FLS Apr-May.

Silver Birch	Downy Birch
Young twigs glossy, glabrous, with small white warts	Young twigs downy, without small white warts
Bark white above, with irregular black diamond-shaped fissures on lower part of trunk	Bark without black fissures on lower part of trunk
Teeth on leaf margin irregular with both primary and secondary teeth giving jagged appearance	Teeth on leaf margin more even-sized
Leaf tip usually acuminate (drawn out)	Leaf tip acute, not drawn out
Branches often ± pendulous	Branches usually spreading or ascending

Dwarf Birch — *Betula nana*

Small deciduous shrub to 1 m. BRANCHES *Prostrate to ascending.* Twigs pubescent. LEAVES *Small, <2 cm,* *coarsely toothed, rounded at tip.* HABITAT Upland moorland and blanket bogs on acid peat; to 860 m. DIST. Native. Scotland; very rare in N England. (N Europe, Alps.) FLS May.

Alder — *Alnus glutinosa*

Deciduous tree to 30 m. BARK Fissured. BRANCHES Twigs glabrous; BUDS *Stalked, purple.* LEAVES *3-9 cm,* truncate at apex, glabrous except for tufts in axils of veins beneath. FLOWERS Appear before leaves. FRUITS *Fruiting catkins woody, cone-like, persistent.* HABITAT Wet woodland, banks of rivers, streams and lakes, fens and bogs; to 470 m. DIST. Native. Common throughout BI. (All Europe except extreme N.) FLS Feb-Mar.

Grey Alder — *Alnus incana*

Deciduous tree to 20 m. BARK Smooth. BRANCHES Twigs pubescent. LEAVES *3-10 cm, apex acute,* green above, grey-green and pubescent below. HABITAT Riverbanks, lake sides, reclaimed land, roadsides. Naturalises by seed and suckering. DIST. Introduced in 1780. Widely planted throughout BI. (N, central and E Europe.) FLS Feb-Mar.

Hornbeam — *Carpinus betulus*

Deciduous tree to 30 m. BARK *Smooth, grey.* BRANCHES Twigs sparsely hairy. BUDS *5-10 mm, narrow, pointed.* LEAVES *Glabrous, veins pubescent beneath.* FRUIT *Small nut with large 3-lobed bract.* HABITAT Mixed woodlands on sands, loams, and clay with flints; frequently grown as coppice. DIST. Native of SE England; extensively planted as far N as central Scotland. (Central and E Europe.) FLS Apr-May.

Hazel — *Corylus avellana*

Deciduous shrub or small tree to 6 m, usually grown as coppice. BARK Smooth. BRANCHES *Twigs with dense reddish hairs.* BUDS *Oval.* LEAVES *5-12 cm, cordate at base, sparsely hairy.* FLOWERS Appear before leaves. Male catkins 2-8 cm, conspicuous; female flowers small, stigmas red. FRUITS Brown nut, 1.5-2 cm, surrounded by lobed involucre. HABITAT Woodlands, especially with moist, fertile soils, hedgerows, scrub, cliffs; to 640 m. DIST. Native. Common throughout BI. (All Europe except extreme N.) FLS Jan-Apr.

AIZOACEAE Hottentot-fig family

Hottentot-fig — *Carpobrotus edulis*

Succulent, mat-forming perennial. LEAVES *7-10 cm,* triangular in section. FLOWERS *Yellow or purple.* HABITAT Sea cliffs, rocks, walls, sand-dunes. DIST. Introduced in 1690 (native of S Africa). Abundant in coastal SW England, where it is a serious threat to native vegetation. (S and SW Europe.) FLS May-Jul.

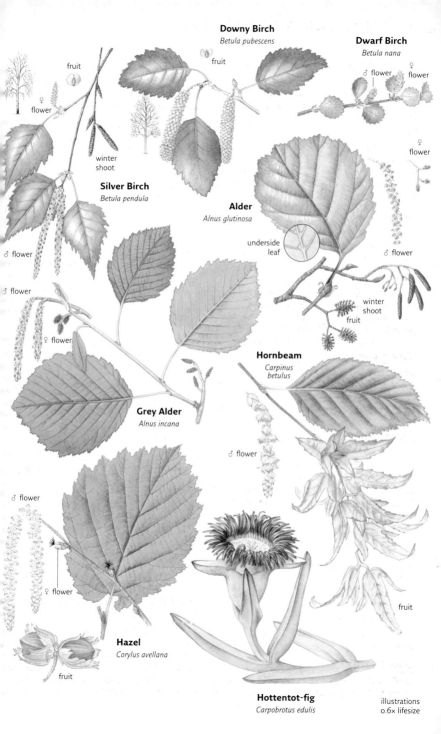

Downy Birch
Betula pubescens

fruit

Dwarf Birch
Betula nana

♂ flower   ♀ flower

fruit

♀ flower

winter shoot

Silver Birch
Betula pendula

♀ flower

Alder
Alnus glutinosa

underside leaf

♂ flower

♂ flower

winter shoot

fruit

♂ flower

♀ flower

Hornbeam
Carpinus betulus

Grey Alder
Alnus incana

♂ flower

♂ flower

♀ flower

fruit

Hazel
Corylus avellana

fruit

Hottentot-fig
Carpobrotus edulis

illustrations
0.6× lifesize

CHENOPODIACEAE Goosefoots and oraches

A family of annual or perennial, often succulent herbs or shrubs with small, inconspicuous flowers. Leaves are alternate, simple, without stipules, and often 'mealy' with a whitish bloom. Flowers are greenish, regular, hermaphrodite or unisexual; 3-5 tepals in 1 whorl; as many or fewer stamens as tepals; ovary superior or half-inferior, 2-3 stigmas. Fruit is an achene.

1 Plant obviously leafy 2
  Plant with no apparent leaves;
  stems succulent *Salicornia, Sarcocornia*

2 Leaf blades flattened in the usual way 3
  Leaves round or half-round in section 5

3 Flowers hermaphrodite; fruit
  surrounded by persistent tepals 4
  Flowers unisexual; fruit enclosed
  between 2 enlarged bracteoles *Atriplex*

4 Flowers (receptacle + tepals)
  swelling in fruit, giving inflorescence a 'knobbly' appearance *Beta*
  Tepals not conspicuously swelling
  in fruit, inflorescence not 'knobbly'
  looking *Chenopodium*

5 Plant not spiny; leaves without
  a spiny tip *Suaeda*
  Plant spiny; leaves with a spiny tip *Salsola*

Goosefoots *Chenopodium*

The goosefoots are a difficult group, and certain identification is often possible only by examining the sculpturing of the seed coat. The key on p.104 uses more accessible characters, but a number of rare casuals closely related to *C. album* have been omitted.

Good-King-Henry   *Chenopodium bonus-henricus*

Erect perennial to 50 cm. LEAVES To 10 cm, *dull green, broadly spear-shaped, margins wavy, untoothed.* FLOWERS Stigmas long, exserted. HABITAT Enriched soil around farmyards, hedge banks, near old buildings. DIST. Archaeophyte. Widely distributed as relic of cultivation; rare in Scotland, Ireland. (All Europe except N and SW.) FLS May-Jul.

Oak-leaved Goosefoot   *Chenopodium glaucum*

Branched, *prostrate* to erect annual, to 50 cm. LEAVES *Narrow, green above, glaucous and mealy below.* HABITAT Waste ground, gardens, refuse tips on fertile soils. DIST. Archaeophyte. Rare, with scattered localities in England. (W, central and E Europe.) FLS Jun-Sep.

Red Goosefoot   *Chenopodium rubrum*

Prostrate to erect, *glabrous, often reddish annual, to* 70 cm. Vegetative plants superficially similar to *Atriplex prostrata* (p.106), and prostrate coastal forms very similar to *C. chenopodioides*. LEAVES *Glossy, triangular, coarsely and irregularly toothed.* HABITAT Farmyards, manure heaps, exposed mud of lake and pond margins, brackish marshes, dune slacks. DIST. Native. Throughout BI; lowland, coastal in N and W. (W, central and E Europe.) FLS Jun-Sep.

Saltmarsh Goosefoot   *Chenopodium chenopodioides*

Prostrate to erect, *glabrous, distinctly reddish annual to 30 cm.* Very similar to small coastal forms of *C. rubrum*, the only certain distinction being in the form of the perianth (*see* key on p.104). LEAVES Triangular, scarcely toothed, deeply reddish below. HABITAT Mud, muddy shingle close to sea. DIST. Native. Very rare. E and SE coast of England. (Europe, coasts S from Denmark.) FLS Jul-Sep.

Many-seeded Goosefoot, All-seed   *Chenopodium polyspermum*

Erect, glabrous annual to 1 m. LEAVES *Unlobed, almost untoothed, often with purplish tinge.* HABITAT Weed of arable crops, gardens, waste ground. DIST. Archaeophyte. Common but local in England and Wales; rare in Scotland and Ireland. (All Europe except N and SW.) FLS Jul-Aug.

Stinking Goosefoot   *Chenopodium vulvaria* EN. *(E)*

Prostrate to erect, *mealy annual, to 35 cm, smelling strongly of rotten fish.* LEAVES *Small, 1-2.5 cm, triangular, untoothed.* HABITAT Waste ground near sea, upper levels of salt marshes and shingle beaches, cliffs with bird colonies. DIST. Archaeophyte. Very rare. England, Scotland. (All Europe except N.) FLS Jul-Sep.

Maple-leaved Goosefoot, Sowbane   *Chenopodium hybridum*

Erect, glabrous annual to 1 m. LEAVES *Large, to 15 cm, broadly triangular with cordate base*, few large teeth. HABITAT Waste ground, arable soils. DIST. Archaeophyte. Rare and local in lowland England, especially East Anglian fens. (W, central and E Europe.) FLS Aug-Oct.

Upright Goosefoot   *Chenopodium urbicum* CR.

Erect, glabrous annual to 70 cm. LEAVES *To 9 cm*, teeth long, hooked. HABITAT Rich arable soils, farmyards, manure heaps, waste ground. DIST. Archaeophyte. Lowland. Rare. (Native of W, central and E Europe.) FLS Aug-Sep.

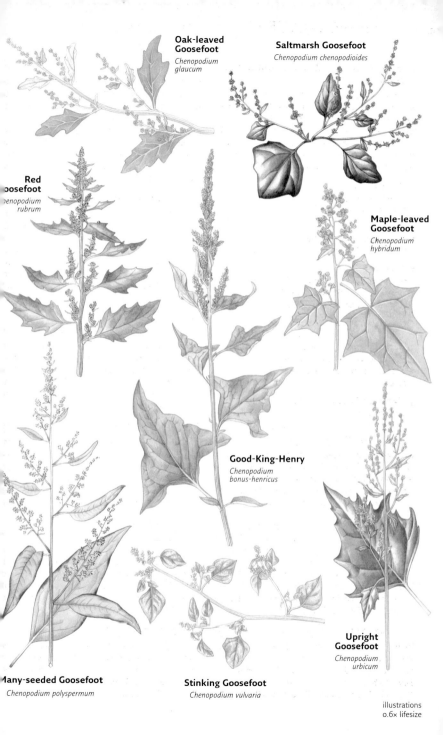

Oak-leaved Goosefoot
Chenopodium glaucum

Saltmarsh Goosefoot
Chenopodium chenopodioides

Red Goosefoot
Chenopodium rubrum

Maple-leaved Goosefoot
Chenopodium hybridum

Good-King-Henry
Chenopodium bonus-henricus

Many-seeded Goosefoot
Chenopodium polyspermum

Stinking Goosefoot
Chenopodium vulvaria

Upright Goosefoot
Chenopodium urbicum

illustrations
0.6× lifesize

Chenopodium
flower

	if	**then**
1	▷ Perennial; leaves broadly triangular; stigmas long, 0.8-1.5 mm, projecting beyond perianth	*C. bonus-henricus* (p.102)
	▷ Annual; stigmas short, <0.8 mm	Go to ▷ **2**
2	▷ At least some leaf blades weakly cordate at base and with few large teeth	*C. hybridum* (p.102)
	▷ Leaves tapering at base	Go to ▷ **3**
3	▷ At least lower leaves distinctly lobed or toothed	Go to ▷ **4**
	▷ Leaves entire, or with single tooth or lobe at base	Go to ▷ **11**
4	▷ Inflorescence and perianth mealy, at least when young	Go to ▷ **5**
	▷ Inflorescence and perianth glabrous	Go to ▷ **8**
5	▷ Leaves toothed, but not distinctly 3-lobed	Go to ▷ **6**
	▷ At least some leaves 3-lobed	Go to ▷ **7**
6	▷ Teeth on leaves blunt; inflorescence leafless above, with long, erect branches; tepals without fine teeth	*C. album* (p.106)
	▷ Leaves coarsely and irregularly toothed with acute teeth; inflorescence leafy almost to top, with short, spreading branches; margins of tepals with fine teeth	*C. murale* (p.106)
7	▷ Leaves distinctly longer than broad, middle lobe longer than laterals and ± parallel-sided	*C. ficifolium* (p.106)
	▷ Leaves broader than or as broad as long, grey-green, glaucous; inflorescence densely mealy	*C. opulifolium* (p.106)
8	▷ All flowers with 5 tepals, 5 stamens; seeds black	*C. urbicum* (p.102)
	▷ Flowers with 2-4 tepals and stamens; seeds red-brown	Go to ▷ **9**
9	▷ Leaves green above, mealy, glaucous beneath	*C. glaucum* (p.102)
	▷ Leaves green or reddish beneath	Go to ▷ **10**
10	▷ Leaves ± triangular-diamond shaped, thick, glossy, coarsely toothed, often tinged reddish; tepals not joined above middle	*C. rubrum* (p.102)
	▷ Leaves ± triangular, scarcely toothed, deep purplish red beneath; tepals red, joined almost to tip	*C. chenopodioides* (p.102)
11	▷ Stem square in section; leaves greenish or purplish on both surfaces, not mealy; plant not evil-smelling	*C. polyspermum* (p.102)
	▷ Stem not ridged; leaves greyish and mealy beneath; plant smelling strongly of rotten fish	*C. vulvaria* (p.102)

bracteole

Atriplex fruit

	if	**then**
1	Shrubs	Go to ▷ **2**
	Annual herbs	Go to ▷ **3**
2	Lower leaves opposite	***A. portulacoides*** (p.108)
	All leaves alternate	***A. halimus*** (p.108)
3	Bracteoles markedly long-stalked, 3-lobed, the outer much longer than the middle (salt marshes, very rare)	***A. pedunculata*** (p.108)
	Bracteoles not like this	Go to ▷ **4**
4	Lower leaves linear-lanceolate, toothed or not, without basal lobes	***A. littoralis*** (p.108)
	Leaves triangular or rhomboidal	Go to ▷ **5**
5	Bracteoles fused at base only (for <¼ of their length)	Go to ▷ **6**
	Bracteoles fused for ¼–½ of their length	Go to ▷ **8**
6	Bracteoles <10 mm long, ± sessile	Go to ▷ **7**
	Largest bracteoles >15 mm, stalks >10 mm	***A. longipes*** (p.106)
7	Lower leaves triangular, truncate at base (widespread, both inland and coastal)	***A. prostrata*** (p.106)
	Lower leaves rhomboidal, scarcely lobed (Scottish coasts, rare)	***A. praecox*** (p.106)
8	Plant distinctly silvery; lower part of bracteoles hardened in fruit (sandy, shingly beaches)	***A. laciniata*** (p.108)
	Plant green, sometimes mealy; bracteoles not hardened in fruit	Go to ▷ **9**
9	Leaves lanceolate to rhomboidal with forward-pointing basal lobes; bracteoles not thickened at base (widespread, both inland and coastal)	***A. patula*** (p.108)
	Leaves triangular to rhomboidal; base of bracteoles thickened and spongy (sandy and shingly beaches)	***A. glabriuscula*** (p.106)

Grey Goosefoot
Chenopodium opulifolium

Prostrate to erect, *densely mealy annual*, to 80 cm. LEAVES 2–3 cm, *rhomboidal, often broader than long, weakly 3-lobed, strongly glaucous-mealy beneath.* HABITAT Rare casual of waste ground and rubbish tips. DIST. Introduced. (Native of central, E and S Europe.) FLS Aug–Oct.

Nettle-leaved Goosefoot
Chenopodium murale

Erect, slightly mealy annual to 70 cm. LEAVES 1.5–6 cm, *coarsely and irregularly sharp-toothed (hence 'nettle-leaved')*. HABITAT Dunes, disturbed ground, waste places, on light soils especially near the sea. DIST. Archaeophyte. Infrequent casual in lowland England, Wales. (Europe, except Scandinavia.) FLS Jul–Oct.

Fig-leaved Goosefoot
Chenopodium ficifolium

Erect, slightly mealy annual to 90 cm. LEAVES To 8 cm, *3-lobed; middle lobe long, ± parallel-sided; lateral lobes short*, usually with 1 tooth on lower margin. HABITAT Arable weed of rich fertile soils, manure heaps, farmyards. DIST. Archaeophyte. Frequent in lowland central and S England, S Wales. (W, central and E Europe.) FLS Jul–Sep.

Fat-hen
Chenopodium album

Erect, usually mealy annual. STEM Often red-tinged. BRANCHES Usually short, stiffly erect. LEAVES *Toothed, variable in shape*. SIMILAR SPP. Several other closely related species occur less commonly in similar habitats, but can only be reliably distinguished from *C. album* by details of seed coat. HABITAT Abundant weed of arable crops, waste ground, gardens, manure heaps, roadsides; lowland to 435 m. DIST. Native. Common throughout BI. (All Europe.) FLS Jul–Oct.

Oraches and sea-purslanes *Atriplex*
The oraches are superficially very similar to the goosefoots and they often grow together on disturbed and enriched ground (*see* key on p.105). They differ in having unisexual flowers and fruits that are enclosed between a pair of enlarged bracteoles (note that these only develop as the seeds ripen and are scarcely evident during flowering).

Spear-leaved Orache
Atriplex prostrata

Erect or decumbent, glabrous to slightly mealy annual, to 100 cm. LEAVES *Broadly triangular, upper leaves narrower, joined only in basal ¼.* HABITAT Brackish marshes, dykes, shingle (where it needs to be distinguished carefully from *A. glabriuscula*); weed of disturbed soils, gardens, arable land and roadsides inland. Lowland to 415 m. DIST. Native. Throughout BI, but mainly coastal in N and W. (All Europe.) FLS Jul–Sep.

Babington's Orache
Atriplex glabriuscula

Prostrate, mealy annual. Very similar to prostrate forms of *A. prostrata*, but with larger *bracteoles, 4–10 mm, joined for c.½ their length, and swollen and slightly 'knobbly' at base.* HABITAT *Characteristic plant of shingle and, less often, sandy beaches* close to strand line. DIST. Native. Local. All round British coasts (NW coasts of Europe.) FLS Jul–Sep.

Long-stalked Orache
Atriplex longipes

Erect to prostrate annual, to 90 cm. Similar to *A. prostrata*, but leaves narrower, not mealy; *some bracteoles large, to 25 mm, leafy towards tips, with long stalks to 25 mm.* HABITAT Tall vegetation in upper parts of estuarine salt marshes. DIST. Native. Scattered around coasts of Britain; absent from Ireland. (S Scandinavia.) FLS Jul–Sep. NOTE The hybrid with *A. prostrata, A. × gustafssoniana*, occurs in the absence of the parents and is commoner than *A. longipes*.

Early Orache
Atriplex praecox

Small, erect to prostrate annual, to 10 cm. LEAVES *Narrowly rhomboidal, unlobed*, not mealy, *often tinged red*. FLOWERS *Bracteoles 3–5 mm, sessile, joined only at base*. HABITAT Low down on sand and shingle beaches around margins of sheltered sea lochs, just above zone of brown seaweeds. DIST. Native. W coast of Scotland, Shetland. (Coasts of Iceland, Scandinavia.) FLS Jun–Jul.

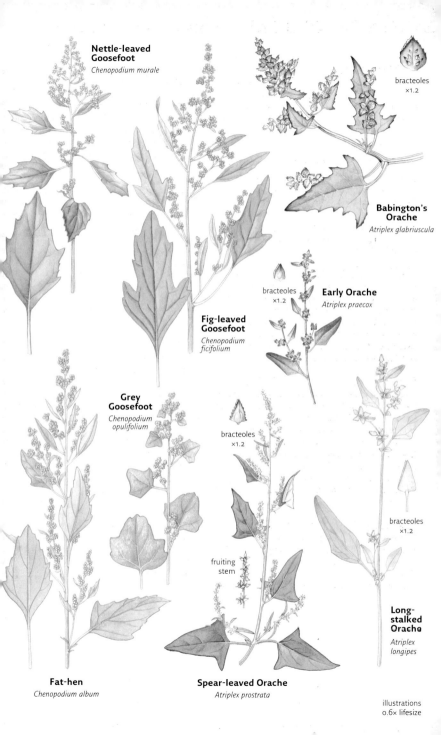

Nettle-leaved Goosefoot
Chenopodium murale

bracteoles
×1.2

Babington's Orache
Atriplex glabriuscula

bracteoles
×1.2

Early Orache
Atriplex praecox

Fig-leaved Goosefoot
Chenopodium ficifolium

Grey Goosefoot
Chenopodium opulifolium

bracteoles
×1.2

bracteoles
×1.2

fruiting stem

Long-stalked Orache
Atriplex longipes

Fat-hen
Chenopodium album

Spear-leaved Orache
Atriplex prostrata

illustrations
0.6× lifesize

Grass-leaved Orache
Atriplex littoralis

Much-branched, ± mealy annual to 100 cm. Leaves *Narrow, remotely toothed or entire.* Fruits Fruiting bracteoles triangular, rough. Habitat Upper part of salt marshes, drift lines, brackish grassland, sea walls, waste ground close to sea; sometimes forms dense stands. Spreading inland along salted road verges. Dist. Native. All round coasts of BI, except NW Scotland, W Ireland. (Coasts of Europe, except SE Mediterranean.) Fls Jul–Aug.

Common Orache
Atriplex patula

Prostrate to erect annual, to 100 cm. Similar to *A. prostrata, but leaves narrowly rhomboidal and tapering into petiole; and fruiting bracteoles triangular, fused to c.⅓ their length.* Habitat Annual weed of arable land, gardens, open ground near sea; lowland to 435 m. Dist. Native. Common throughout most BI, but rare in N Scotland. (All Europe.) Fls Jul–Sep.

Frosted Orache
Atriplex laciniata

Mealy white or silvery, prostrate annual to 30 cm. Stems Yellow or reddish. Leaves Small, 1.5–2 cm. Fruits *Fruiting bracteoles broader than long, warty on back and hardened at base.* Habitat Drift line on fine shingle and sandy shores, foot of sand-dunes, often with *Salsola kali.* Dist. Native. All round coasts of BI. (Coasts of W Europe, SW Spain.) Fls Aug–Sep.

Shrubby Orache
Atriplex halimus

Much-branched, erect, mealy shrub to 2.5 m. Leaves Ovate, entire. Fruits Fruiting bracteoles small, 1.5–3 mm, fused only at base. Dist. Introduced in 1640. Planted as windbreak by sea in scattered localities in S England. Naturalised in Channel Is. (Native of Mediterranean.) Fls Aug–Sep.

Sea-purslane
Atriplex portulacoides

Much-branched, sprawling, mealy shrub, to 100 cm. Leaves *Grey-green, entire, lower leaves opposite.* Fruits Fruiting bracteoles triangular, fused to >halfway from base, apex 3-lobed. Habitat Forms zone along upper levels of salt marshes and banks of salt-marsh creeks and pools. Dist. Native. Coasts of BI, N to Scotland. (European coasts N to Denmark.) Fls Jul–Sep.

Pedunculate Sea-purslane
Atriplex pedunculata CR. *(B)

Small, erect, mealy annual to 30 cm. Leaves *All alternate.* Fruits *With long stalks (to 12 mm) when mature.* Bracteoles fused almost to tip, with 3 apical lobes. Habitat Open patches of bare mud, upper levels of salt marshes. Dist. Native. Very rare; thought extinct until refound in S Essex in 1987. (E North Sea, Baltic coasts.) Fls Aug–Sep.

Sea Beet
Beta vulgaris ssp. *maritima*

Much-branched, straggling perennial, usually with red pigmentation in stems and leaves. Leaves To 10 cm, usually thick, glossy. Flowers *In large, branched inflorescence.* Fruits *Bracteoles absent; perianth and receptacle swelling.* Habitat Drift line on salt marshes, sand and shingle beaches, sea walls, cliffs and waste ground near sea, especially where nutrient-enriched. Dist. Native. All round coasts of BI, but rare in Scotland. (Coasts of Europe, N to Denmark.) Fls Jul–Sep. Similar spp. Beetroot, Sugar Beet and Mangel-wurzel, cultivated annuals with swollen roots, are forms of *B. vulgaris* ssp. *vulgaris* and sometimes occur as casuals.

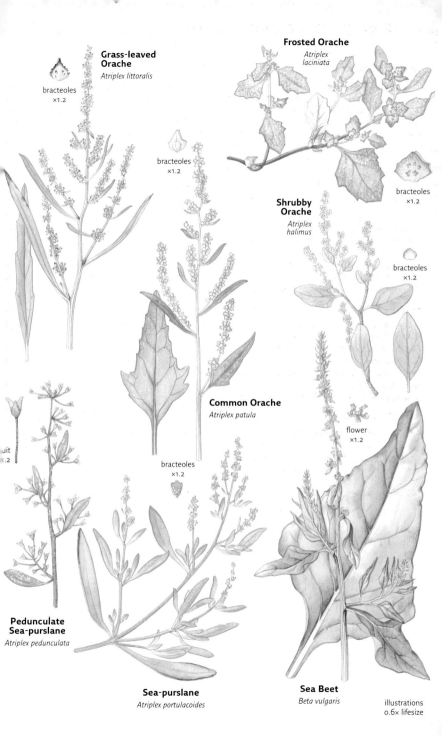

Grass-leaved Orache
Atriplex littoralis

bracteoles
×1.2

Frosted Orache
Atriplex laciniata

bracteoles
×1.2

bracteoles
×1.2

Shrubby Orache
Atriplex halimus

bracteoles
×1.2

Common Orache
Atriplex patula

flower
×1.2

bracteoles
×1.2

fruit
×1.2

Pedunculate Sea-purslane
Atriplex pedunculata

Sea-purslane
Atriplex portulacoides

Sea Beet
Beta vulgaris

illustrations
0.6× lifesize

Glassworts *Sarcocornia, Salicornia*

Glassworts (*see* key on p.114) are distinctive-looking succulent plants, with no apparent leaves and with the stems appearing jointed. In fact, the succulent sheath is composed of opposite pairs of fused leaves that surround the stem. The small flowers, which are embedded in the succulent tissue, develop in groups of three (except for *Salicornia pusilla*, where the flowers are solitary). All are plants of salt marshes and intertidal mud flats, and are physiologically adapted to growing in saline conditions (halophytes).

    Glassworts are extremely variable and very difficult to identify as the distinction between species is not clear. Four taxa are reasonably distinctive. *Sarcocornia perennis* is perennial, while *Salicornia* species are annual. Of these, *S. pusilla* is distinguished by its solitary flowers while the rest can be divided into two aggregate species, *S. europaea* and *S. procumbens*. The last two have been further subdivided into a variable number of ill-defined species. Six of the most widely accepted are included here. Identification should only be attempted on groups of well-developed plants in late summer when the plants are in flower or fruiting and they develop their characteristic late-season coloration. Many populations will be found that cannot be named with confidence as they do not fit any of the descriptions precisely.

Perennial Glasswort   *Sarcocornia perennis* *(R)

Prostrate to erect *perennial*, somewhat woody at base, to 30 cm. Rhizomes often forming mats up to 1 m diam. STEMS Both fertile and non-fertile, becoming orange in colour. FLOWERS ± *equal in size, in ± transverse row.* HABITAT Firm gravelly mud on middle levels of salt marshes. DIST. Native. Local on SE coasts from Norfolk to Devon; rare elsewhere. (European coasts from BI to E Mediterranean.) FLS Aug–Sep.

One-flowered Glasswort   *Salicornia pusilla*

Erect or sometimes decumbent annual to 25 cm. Usually much branched and rather bushy in appearance. *Distinguished from other annual species by its 1-flowered inflorescences.* STEMS Short, rather stubby; terminal segment <10 mm. Becoming yellowish or reddish when mature. HABITAT Upper parts of salt marshes. DIST. Native. S coast from Humber to S Wales; SE Ireland. (NW France.) FLS Aug–Sep.

Salicornia europaea agg.

Common Glasswort   *Salicornia europaea*

Much-branched, erect or sometimes prostrate annual to 30 cm. STEMS Lowest branches about as long as main stem. *Light green, hardly glossy, becoming yellowish orange to red.* Fertile segments swollen but not 'beaded' or 'waisted'; pale margin of segment tip narrow and inconspicuous, ≤0.1 mm broad, internal angle of tip *c.*90°. FLOWERS Central flower much larger than laterals. HABITAT Upper and middle levels of salt marshes. DIST. Native. All round British coast. (All Europe coasts.) FLS Aug–Sep.

Purple Glasswort   *Salicornia ramosissima*

Very variable erect or prostrate annual; commonest member of genus. STEMS Branching very variable. *Dark glossy green, becoming dark glossy purplish red, especially in prostrate forms.* Fertile segments conspicuously swollen, giving 'beaded' or 'waisted' appearance. Pale margin of segment tip conspicuous, >0.1 mm broad, internal angle of apex >90°. FLOWERS Central flower much larger than laterals. HABITAT Upper and middle levels of marshes, creek sides, muddy shingle. DIST. Native. British coasts except NW Scotland. FLS Aug–Sep.

Glaucous Glasswort   *Salicornia obscura*

Erect annual to 40 cm. STEMS Branches short, lowest not more than ⅛ length of main stem. *Dull, glaucous green becoming yellowish green, not reddening.* Pale margin of segment apex inconspicuous, *internal angle of apex markedly obtuse, >140°.* FLOWERS Central flower not much larger than laterals. DIST. Native. Rare. FLS Aug–Sep.

Salicornia procumbens agg.

Yellow Glasswort   *Salicornia fragilis*

Erect annual to 40 cm. STEMS Usually with primary branches only. Green, becoming yellowish green to yellow. Fertile segments cylindrical, *terminal spikes with 8–16 fertile segments.* FLOWERS Central flower hardly larger than laterals. HABITAT *Often forming dense stands* on bare mud on lower parts of salt marshes. DIST. Native. British coasts N to S Scotland; absent from SW. FLS Aug–Sep.

Long-spiked Glasswort   *Salicornia dolichostachya*

Often prostrate or collapsed, much-branched, bushy annual. STEMS *Lower branches about as long as main stem.* Dark green becoming yellowish then brownish. Fertile segments cylindrical, branches tapering, *terminal spike distinctly elongated, 12–30 fertile segments.* FLOWERS Central flower hardly larger than laterals. HABITAT Lower parts of salt marshes, intertidal mud flats. DIST. Native. All British coasts, SE Ireland. FLS Jul–Aug.

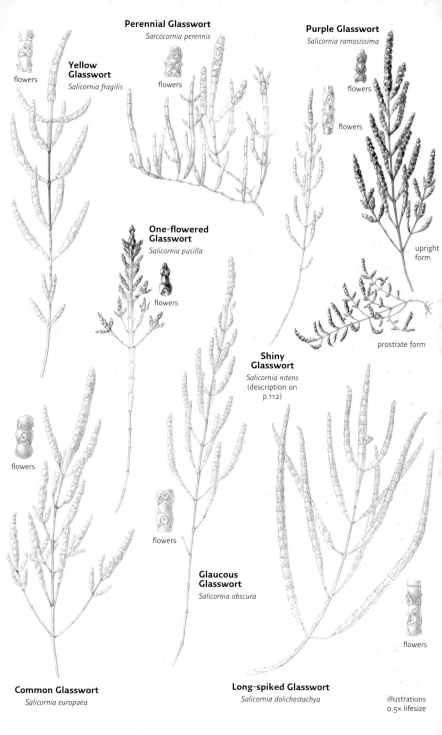

Yellow Glasswort
Salicornia fragilis

flowers

Perennial Glasswort
Sarcocornia perennis

flowers

Purple Glasswort
Salicornia ramosissima

flowers

flowers

upright form

prostrate form

One-flowered Glasswort
Salicornia pusilla

flowers

Shiny Glasswort
Salicornia nitens
(description on p.112)

flowers

flowers

Glaucous Glasswort
Salicornia obscura

flowers

Common Glasswort
Salicornia europaea

Long-spiked Glasswort
Salicornia dolichostachya

illustrations
0.5× lifesize

Shiny Glasswort
Salicornia nitens

[*See* illustration previous page.] Erect annual to 25 cm. STEMS Primary branches only, lower branches usually <¼ length of main stem. Green to yellowish *green, smooth, shining, becoming brownish purple to brownish orange.* FLOWERS Central flower hardly larger than laterals. HABITAT Bare mud, middle and upper levels of salt marshes. DIST. Native. Rare. FLS Sep.

Shrubby Sea-blite
Suaeda vera

Small, much-branched evergreen shrub to 120 cm. STEMS Twigs densely leafy. LEAVES Glabrous, 5–18 × 1 mm, smooth, ± rounded in section, tip blunt. FLOWERS In groups of 1–3; 3 stigmas. HABITAT Distinct zone along drift line of sand and shingle beaches, landward end of salt marshes. DIST. Native. Very local. Coast of East Anglia, isolated occurrences elsewhere in S. (SW Europe, Mediterranean.) FLS Jul–Oct.

Annual Sea-blite
Suaeda maritima

Erect to prostrate annual, to *c.*30 cm. Very variable, with several named forms. STEMS Glaucous, becoming purplish. LEAVES Colour as stems, glabrous, 3–25 × 1–2 mm, ± *half-round in section*, tip acute. FLOWERS In groups of 1–3; 2 stigmas. HABITAT Middle and lower levels of salt marshes, creeks, muddy shingle, dune slacks, often with *Salicornia*. DIST. Native. All round British coasts. (Coasts of Europe except extreme N.) FLS Jul–Aug.

Prickly Saltwort
Salsola kali VU.

Prostrate prickly, usually rough annual to 60 cm. STEMS Much branched, with reddish stripes. LEAVES Succulent, 1–4 cm, ± *half-round in section, with spiny tip.* FLOWERS Solitary, tepals spine-tipped. FRUITS Tepals winged. HABITAT Drift line of sandy shores, foot of sand-dunes, often with *Atriplex laciniata* and *Cakile maritima.* DIST. Native. All round British coasts, except extreme N. (Coasts of Europe N to latitude of N Scotland.) FLS Jul–Sep.

AMARANTHACEAE Pigweeds
Similar to the Chenopodiaceae, but perianth brownish or coloured, with thin papery tepals. Mainly tropical or warm temperate family. Several species occur as casuals in BI, all of which are difficult to identify, the commonest being *A. retroflexus.*

Common Amaranth
Amaranthus retroflexus

Tall, erect, pubescent annual to 90 cm. LEAVES To 15 cm, petioles long. FLOWERS Unisexual, with 5 tepals. *In dense, much-branched inflorescence*, upper part leafless. HABITAT Casual on waste land,

cultivated ground, rubbish tips. DIST. Introduced in 1759 (native of tropical and temperate America). Throughout BI, but rare in N. (All Europe except Scandinavia.) FLS Jul–Sep.

PORTULACACEAE Purslanes
Similar to Caryophyllaceae, but *calyx has only 2 sepals.* Annual or perennial glabrous herbs. Flowers hermaphrodite, actinomorphic, with 2 sepals, 2–6 petals (sometimes absent), 3–20 stamens, ovary superior.

Blinks
Montia fontana

Annual to perennial; erect, prostrate or floating. STEMS Branched, 1–20 cm. LEAVES Opposite, 2–20 × 1.5–6 mm. FLOWERS *Tiny, inconspicuous, 2–3 mm diam.; 5 white petals; 3–5 stamens.* HABITAT Springs, flushes, stream sides, wet rocks, marshes, damp meadows, trackways, on acid soils; to 945 m. DIST. Native. Widespread throughout BI. (All Europe, but rare in S.) FLS May–Oct. NOTE Usually divided into 4 subspecies, separable only by sculpturing of seed coat. Non-flowering plants can look similar to starworts or water-purslanes.

Springbeauty
Claytonia perfoliata

Erect, glabrous annual to 30 cm. LEAVES Basal leaves long-stalked; *2 stem leaves, opposite, fused across stem.* FLOWERS 5–8 mm diam., 5 petals white, 5 stamens. HABITAT Well established on dunes, wasteland, disturbed ground, gardens on light sandy soils. DIST. Introduced in 1794 (native of W North America). (W Europe.) FLS May–Jul.

Pink Purslane
Claytonia sibirica

Erect, glabrous annual to perennial, to 40 cm. LEAVES Basal leaves long-stalked; *2 stem leaves, opposite, sessile but not fused across stem.* FLOWERS 15–20 mm diam.; 5 petals pink, deeply notched; 5 stamens. HABITAT Damp woodland, shaded stream banks on sandy soils. DIST. Introduced in 1768 (native of Siberia and W North America). Well established throughout BI; rare in Ireland. (NW Europe.) FLS Apr–Jul.

Common Purslane
Portulaca oleracea

Prostrate to erect, succulent, glabrous annual, to 50 cm. LEAVES 1–2 cm with bristle-like stipules. FLOWERS In groups of 1–3, 8–12 mm diam., *surrounded by group of leaves, petals yellow.* DIST. Introduced, cultivated since Middle Ages. Native area uncertain. Arable weed, especially in Scilly Is, Channel Is; rare casual elsewhere. (All Europe except N.) FLS Jun–Sep.

Annual Sea-blite
Suaeda maritima

flower ×2.4

Prickly Saltwort
Salsola kali

**Shrubby
Sea-blite**
Suaeda vera

Springbeauty
Claytonia perfoliata

Common Purslane
Portulaca oleracea

flower ×2.4

**Common
Amaranth**
*Amaranthus
retroflexus*

**Pink
Purslane**
*Claytonia
sibirica*

Blinks
Montia fontana

illustrations
0.6× lifesize

Key to Glassworts *Sarcocornia* and *Salicornia*

	if	then
 section of stem and flowers of *Salicornia* **1**	▷ Rhizomatous perennial forming spreading mats; shoots both fertile and vegetative, becoming orange in colour; flowers ± equal in size, in transverse rows	***Sarcocornia perennis*** (p.110)
	▷ Annuals; flowers in triangular groups or solitary	Go to ▷ **2**
2	▷ Flowers solitary	***Salicornia pusilla*** (p.110)
	▷ Flowers in groups of 3	Go to ▷ **3**
3	▷ Fertile segments distinctly convex in outline; central flowers distinctly larger than 2 laterals; 1 stamen	***S. europaea* agg.** (p.110)
	▷ Fertile segments ± cylindrical in outline; flowers all ± same size; 2 stamens	***S. procumbens* agg.** (p.110)

Key to Caryophyllaceae Chickweeds, Pinks and Campions

	if	then
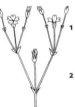 typical inflorescence (dichasial cyme) **1**	▷ Leaves in opposite pairs	Go to ▷ **2**
	▷ Leaves alternate; small, prostrate plant of lake margins (very rare; Devon)	***Corrigiola litoralis*** (p.132)
2	▷ Leaves without stipules	Go to ▷ **3**
	▷ Leaves with stipules	Go to ▷ **16**
3	▷ Petals absent, 2 styles; fruit a 1-seeded achene; small herbs with opposite awl-shaped leaves joined across stem	***Scleranthus*** (p.130)
	▷ >2 styles; fruit with many seeds; plant not as above	Go to ▷ **4**
4	▷ Sepals free	Go to ▷ **5**
	▷ Sepals joined at their edges, forming calyx tube	Go to ▷ **10**
 Cerastium flower **5**	▷ Petals present	Go to ▷ **6**
	▷ Petals absent	***Sagina, Stellaria, Minuartia*** (p.116)
6	▷ Petals deeply bifid (>¾)	**Chickweeds, stitchworts, mou ears** (p.117)
	▷ Petals entire, notched or toothed at tip	Go to ▷ **7**

if	**then**
7 ▷ Flowers in umbels, petals toothed at tip	*Holosteum* (p.126)
▷ Flowers not in umbels, petals entire or shallowly notched	Go to ▷ **8**
8 ▷ 2–3 styles	*Sandworts* (p.116)
▷ 4–5 styles	Go to ▷ **9**
9 ▷ Plant glaucous; leaves lanceolate	*Moenchia* (p.128)
▷ Plant green; leaves linear	*Sagina* (p.119)
10 ▷ 2 styles	Go to ▷ **11**
▷ 3–5 styles (or flowers with stamens only)	Go to ▷ **13**
11 ▷ Calyx tube with white scarious seams between sepals	*Petrorhagia* (p.138)
▷ Calyx tube without seams	Go to ▷ **12**
12 ▷ Base of calyx with epicalyx of 1–3 pairs of bracteoles	*Dianthus* (p.121)
▷ Epicalyx absent	*Saponaria* (p.138)
13 ▷ Plant scrambling; fruit a black berry	*Cucubalus* (p.134)
▷ Plant not scrambling; fruit a capsule	Go to ▷ **14**
14 ▷ Calyx teeth long, narrow, much longer than petals	*Agrostemma* (p.134)
▷ Calyx teeth not longer than sepals	Go to ▷ **15**
15 ▷ 3 styles, or 5 in flowers without stamens, or flowers with stamens only	*Silene* (p.120)
▷ 5 styles, flowers always with both styles and stamens	*Lychnis* (p.134)
16 ▷ Petals as long as or longer than sepals	Go to ▷ **17**
▷ Petals minute or absent	Go to ▷ **18**
17 ▷ 3 styles, petals pink	*Spergularia* (p.119)
▷ 5 styles, petals white	*Spergula* (p.119)
18 ▷ Lower pairs of leaves closely adjacent, resembling whorls of 4; 3 stigmas	*Polycarpon* (p.132)
▷ At least lower leaves in separate opposite pairs; 2 stigmas	Go to ▷ **19**
19 ▷ Flowers white, in axillary clusters; sepals conspicuous, hooded	*Illecebrum* (p.132)
▷ Flowers greenish or brownish, in lateral clusters; sepals inconspicuous, not hooded	*Herniaria* (p.132)

	if	**then**
1	▷ Petals present	Go to ▷ **2**
	▷ Petals minute or absent	**Minuartia sedoides** (p.124)
2	▷ Succulent maritime plant; flowers greenish; fruits globular	**Honckenya peploides** (p.122)
	▷ Plant not like this	Go to ▷ **3**
3	▷ Leaves linear	Go to ▷ **4 Minuartia** (p.122–124)
	▷ Leaves not linear	Go to ▷ **8**
4	▷ Annual; stems erect; non-flowering shoots absent	**M. hybrida** (p.124)
	▷ Cushion- or tuft-forming perennial; non-flowering shoots present	Go to ▷ **5**
5	▷ Petals minute or absent	**M. sedoides** (p.124)
	▷ Petals ≥½ as long as sepals	Go to ▷ **6**
6	▷ Leaves distinctly 3-veined; flower stalks glandular-hairy	Go to ▷ **7**
	▷ Leaves 1-veined; flower stalks glabrous	**M. rubella** (p.122)
7	▷ Sepals 3-veined, tufts lax	**M. verna** (p.122)
	▷ Sepals 5-veined, densely tufted (SW Ireland)	**Mi. recurva** (p.122)
8	▷ Leaves 1–2.5 cm, conspicuously 3-veined beneath	**Moehringia trinervia** (p.122)
	▷ Leaves ≤1 cm, not conspicuously 3-veined	Go to ▷ **9 Arenaria** (p.122)
9	▷ Petals shorter than sepals	**A. serpyllifolia** (p.122)
	▷ Petals longer than sepals	Go to ▷ **10**
10	▷ Leaf margins hairy almost to tip, midrib prominent	**A. ciliata** (p.122)
	▷ Leaf margins hairy at base only, midrib obscure	**A. norvegica** (p.122)

Key to Stitchworts, Chickweeds and Mouse-ears

if	then
▷ 3 styles	**Stellaria** (below for key)
▷ 5 styles, petals split almost to base	**Myosoton aquaticum** (p.128)
▷ 5 styles, petals split to less than halfway	**Cerastium** (below for key)

Stitchworts and chickweeds *Stellaria*

1
▷ Leaves ovate or cordate, at least lower leaves stalked — Go to ▷ **2**
▷ Leaves narrow, linear to oblong, sessile — Go to ▷ **6**

2
▷ Petals >1.5× as long as sepals; stems ± equally hairy all round — *S. nemorum* (p.124)
▷ Petals not as long as or only slightly longer than sepals or absent — Go to ▷ **3**

3
▷ Stems glabrous, square in section — *S. uliginosa* (p.126)
▷ Stems with a line of hairs down each internode, ± smooth in section — Go to ▷ **4**

4
▷ Sepals 2–5 mm, <8 stamens — Go to ▷ **5**
▷ Sepals 5–6.5 mm, 10 stamens — *S. neglecta* (p.124)

5
▷ Sepals >4 mm, petals present, 3–8 stamens, anthers red-violet — *S. media* (p.124)
▷ Sepals ≤3 mm, petals absent, 1–3 stamens, anthers grey-violet — *S. pallida* (p.124)

6
▷ Mat-forming alpine perennial (rare, Scottish mountains) — *Cerastium cerastoides* (p.126)
▷ Not as above — Go to ▷ **7**

7
▷ Petals distinctly shorter than sepals — *S. uliginosa* (p.126)
▷ Petals as long as or longer than sepals — Go to ▷ **8**

8
▷ Bracts wholly green; flowers 20–30 mm across, petals notched to about halfway to base — *S. holostea* (p.124)
▷ Bracts with pale margins; flowers 5–18 mm across, petals divided almost to base — Go to ▷ **9**

9
▷ Margins of bracts hairy; plant not glaucous; flowers 5–12 mm across — *S. graminea* (p.126)
▷ Bracts glabrous; plant glaucous; flowers 12–18 mm across — *S. palustris* (p.126)

Mouse-ears *Cerastium*

1
▷ Usually 3 (varying 3–6) styles; 6 capsule teeth (Scottish alpine) — *C. cerastoides* (p.126)
▷ 4–5 styles; 10 capsule teeth — Go to ▷ **2**

CONTINUED OVERLEAF

	if	**then**
2	▷ Perennials with ± prostrate non-flowering shoots	Go to ▷ **3**
	▷ Annuals with all shoots flowering	Go to ▷ **8**
3	▷ Petals ≤2× as long as sepals	*C. fontanum* (p.128)
	▷ Petals >2× as long as sepals	Go to ▷ **4**
4	▷ Leaves linear-lanceolate to narrowly oblong, lower leaves often with axillary leaf clusters (mostly lowland)	Go to ▷ **5**
	▷ Leaves elliptical to almost circular, lower leaves without axillary leaf clusters (mostly alpine)	Go to ▷ **6**
5	▷ Stem and leaves covered by dense white hairs	*C. tomentosum* (p.126)
	▷ Stem and leaves almost glabrous or sparsely hairy	*C. arvense* (p.126)
6	▷ Whole plant densely covered by long white hairs	*C. alpinum* (p.126)
	▷ Plant with short white and glandular hairs	Go to ▷ **7**
7	▷ Leaves almost circular, dark and tinged purple, densely glandular-pubescent (Shetland)	*C. nigrescens* (p.128)
	▷ Leaves elliptical, not dark and purplish, sparsely pubescent (not Shetland)	*C. arcticum* (p.126)
8	▷ Sepals with long hairs projecting beyond tips	Go to ▷ **9**
	▷ Sepals without long hairs projecting beyond tips	Go to ▷ **10**
9	▷ Inflorescence compact at fruiting; fruiting pedicels shorter than sepals; sepals glandular	*C. glomeratum* (p.128)
	▷ Inflorescence lax at fruiting; fruiting pedicels longer than sepals; sepals without glandular hairs	*C. brachypetalum*
10	▷ Bracts wholly green; 4 petals and stamens	*C. diffusum* (p.128)
	▷ Bracts with pale tips; usually 5 petals and sepals	Go to ▷ **11**
11	▷ Upper ⅙–⅓ of bracts pale-tipped; petals distinctly shorter than sepals	*C. semidecandrum* (p.128)
	▷ Upper ¼ of bracts pale-tipped; petals as long as sepals	*C. pumilum* (p.128)

Key to Pearlworts *Sagina*

	if	then
1	▷ 4 sepals, 4 petals (if present), 4 stamens	Go to ▷ **2**
	▷ 5 sepals and petals, 10 stamens	Go to ▷ **4**
2	▷ Perennial with long, rooting branches from a basal rosette; main stem not flowering	*S. procumbens* (p.130)
	▷ Annual; main stem flowering	Go to ▷ **3**
3	▷ Leaves blunt or minutely mucronate	*S. maritima* (p.130)
	▷ Leaves with a fine point	*S. apetala* (p.130)
4	▷ Petals 2× long as sepals	*S. nodosa* (p.130)
	▷ Petals scarcely longer than sepals	Go to ▷ **5**
5	▷ Sepals with glandular hairs	*S. subulata* (p.130)
	▷ Sepals glabrous	Go to ▷ **6**
6	▷ Plant forming compact tufts; basal leaf rosettes persisting only for 1st year; ripe capsule 2.5–3 mm (very rare, Scottish mountains)	*S. nivalis* (p.130)
	▷ Plant forming tufts or mats, with conspicuous basal rosette; leafy shoots 2–7 cm high; ripe capsule 3.5–4 mm (rare, Scottish alpine)	*S. saginoides* (p.130)

Key to Spurreys *Spergula* and *Spergularia*

	if	then
1	▷ Stem leaves with axillary clusters of leaves; flowers white, 5 styles	***Spergula arvensis*** (p.132)
	▷ Stem leaves without conspicuous axillary clusters of leaves; flowers pink(-white), 3 styles	Go to ▷ **2 *Spergularia***
2	▷ Seeds all broadly winged	***Spergularia media*** (p.132)
	▷ Seeds not winged	Go to ▷ **3**
3	▷ Flowers 8–10 mm across; whole plant covered with glandular hairs	***Spergularia rupicola*** (p.132)
	▷ Flowers ≤8 mm across; plant glabrous or with few glandular hairs on inflorescence	Go to ▷ **4**

if	then
4 ▷ Leaves yellowish green, blunt or shortly mucronate; flowers 6–8 mm across; seeds ≥0.6 mm	***Spergularia marina*** (p.134)
▷ Leaves grey-green, finely pointed; flowers 2–5 mm across; seeds <6 mm	Go to ▷ **5**
5 ▷ Stipules silvery; flowers 3–5 mm across, stalks longer than sepals	***Spergularia rubra*** (p.134)
▷ Stipules dull; flowers *c.*2 mm across, stalks shorter than sepals (very rare)	***Spergularia bocconei*** (p.134)

Key to Campions and Catchflies *Silene*

if	then
1 ▷ Inflorescence of numerous flowers in whorl-like groups; calyx 3–6 mm	***S. otites*** (p.136)
▷ Inflorescence not of whorl-like groups of flowers; calyx 5–30 mm	Go to ▷ **2**
2 ▷ 5 styles; plants dioecious	Go to ▷ **3**
▷ Usually 3 styles, plant usually bisexual	Go to ▷ **4**
3 ▷ Flowers red	***S. dioica*** (p.136)
▷ Flowers white	***S. latifolia*** (p.136)
4 ▷ Fruiting calyx strongly inflated, with 20–30 veins	Go to ▷ **5**
▷ Fruiting calyx not strongly inflated, with 10 veins	Go to ▷ **7**
5 ▷ Fruiting calyx usually glabrous, almost globular, conspicuously net-veined	Go to ▷ **6**
▷ Fruiting calyx pubescent, strongly ribbed but not net-veined	***S. conica*** (p.138)
6 ▷ Plant without non-flowering shoots; capsule teeth erect	***S. vulgaris*** (p.136)
▷ Plant with prostrate non-flowering shoots; capsule teeth spreading or recurved	***S. uniflora*** (p.136)
7 ▷ Perennial plants with non-flowering shoots	Go to ▷ **8**
▷ Annual plants without non-flowering shoots	Go to ▷ **9**

if	then
8 ▷ Densely tufted cushion-forming alpine or cliff plant; flowers pink	*S. acaulis* (p.136)
▷ Plant erect, glandular-pubescent; flowers drooping, cream, petals inrolled	*S. nutans* (p.136)
9 ▷ Calyx >20 mm; petals yellowish below, pink above, inrolled during day	*S. noctiflora* (p.136)
▷ Calyx <15 mm; petals white to pale pink, sometimes with basal red blotch, expanded during day	*S. gallica* (p.136)

Key to Pinks *Dianthus*

if	then
1 ▷ Flowers in ± head-like clusters surrounded by involucre of leaf-like bracts	Go to ▷ **2**
▷ Flowers solitary, or 2–5 in lax inflorescence, not surrounded by involucre of bracts	Go to ▷ **3**
2 ▷ Involucral bracts and epicalyx hairy	*D. armeria* (p.138)
▷ Involucral bracts and epicalyx glabrous	*D. carthusianorum* ● (p.138)
3 ▷ Petals deeply cut into long, narrow segments ⅓–½ length of limb	Go to ▷ **4**
▷ Petals toothed	Go to ▷ **5**
4 ▷ Leaves on sterile shoots >2 cm; margins of calyx teeth hairy; petals cut to middle	*D. plumarius* (p.138)
▷ Leaves on sterile shoots <1.5 cm; margins of calyx teeth glabrous; petals cut to ⅓ their length	*D. gallicus* (p.138)
5 ▷ Stem downy below; inner epicalyx bracts with long, fine point; flowers not fragrant	*D. deltoides* (p.138)
▷ Stem glabrous; inner epicalyx bracts mucronate; flowers fragrant	*D. gratianopolitanus* (p.138)

CARYOPHYLLACEAE Chickweeds, pinks and campions

A large but distinctive family of annuals and perennials (*see* key on p.114 for Caryophyllaceae and on p.116 for *Arenaria*, *Moehringia*, *Honckenya* and *Minuartia*), including the pinks, campions, chickweeds and stitchworts. Leaves are usually in opposite and alternating pairs, narrow, simple and entire, and mostly without stipules. Inflorescence is usually a characteristic *dichasial cyme* (*see* Introduction). Flowers are normally hermaphrodite (occasionally dioecious), regular; 4-5 sepals, free or joined below; 4-5 petals (rarely absent), often notched or bifid; 8 or 10 stamens; ovary superior; 2-5 styles. Fruit is a capsule or, rarely, a berry or 1-seeded nutlet (achene).

Thyme-leaved Sandwort   *Arenaria serpyllifolia*

Slender, erect to ascending annual or biennial herb, to 25 cm. LEAVES Hairy, to 6 mm. FLOWERS *5-8 mm diam., petals shorter than sepals, 10 stamens, 3 styles.* HABITAT Common on bare ground in rough grassland, grassy heaths, field margins, walls, on dry, well-drained soils. The 2 subspecies (*see* 'Note') occur in similar habitats, sometimes together. DIST. Native. Throughout BI. (Most of Europe; ssp. *leptoclados* absent from Scandinavia.) FLS Jun-Aug. NOTE There are 2 subspecies: ssp. *serpyllifolia*, with 3-4 mm sepals and flask-shaped capsule; and ssp. *leptoclados*, with 2.5-3.1 mm sepals and ± straight-sided capsule.

English Sandwort

Arenaria norvegica ssp. *anglica* *(B)

Slender annual to biennial with *few non-flowering* shoots, to 6 cm. LEAVES 4.5-5 mm. FLOWERS 11-13 mm diam., sepals *slightly hairy at base.* HABITAT Bare peaty depressions in limestone pavement, mossy flushes. DIST. Endemic. Very rare, found on single area of Carboniferous limestone in Ribblesdale, W Yorkshire. FLS Jun-Sep.

Arctic Sandwort

Arenaria norvegica ssp. *norvegica* VU. *(B)

Slender perennial with many *non-flowering shoots*, to 6 cm. LEAVES 3-4.5 mm. FLOWERS 9-10 mm diam., sepals glabrous. HABITAT Scree, river gravels over basic rocks. DIST. Native. Very rare. Isolated sites in NW Scotland, Shetland. (W Scandinavia, Iceland.) FLS Jun-Sep.

Fringed Sandwort   *Arenaria ciliata* ssp. *hibernica* *(R)

Low, prostrate perennial with hairy non-flowering shoots, to 5 cm. LEAVES 4-6 mm, prominently veined, *margins hairy to tip.* FLOWERS 12-16 mm diam., *sepals conspicuously hairy.* DIST. Native. An endemic subspecies is confined to Carboniferous limestone cliffs in Co. Sligo between 365 and 600 m (Species has arctic-alpine distribution in Europe.) FLS Jun-Jul.

Three-nerved Sandwort   *Moehringia trinervia*

Slender, branched, prostrate to ascending pubescent annual. LEAVES 6-25 mm, *conspicuously 3-veined below.* FLOWERS *c.*6 mm diam., petals shorter than sepals, 10 stamens, 3 styles. HABITAT Deciduous woodland, on fertile, well-drained soils; lowland to 425 m. DIST. Native. Throughout BI except extreme N. (Most of Europe.) FLS May-Jun.

Sea Sandwort   *Honckenya peploides*

Succulent maritime, dioecious *perennial.* Flowering and non-flowering shoots arising from long, creeping stolons. LEAVES *Glabrous, fleshy*, 6-18 mm. FLOWERS 6-10 mm diam., *petals greenish*, 10 stamens. FRUITS Globular, 8 mm diam., longer than sepals. HABITAT Sand and sand-shingle shores. DIST. Native. Common all round British coasts. (W and NW Europe.) FLS May-Aug.

Recurved Sandwort   *Minuartia recurva* *(R

Short, densely tufted, cushion-forming perennial, to 5 cm. LEAVES Recurved, 3-veined, 4-8 mm. FLOWERS Stalks glandular-hairy, *sepals 5-veined, petals longer than sepals*, 3 styles. HABITAT Thin humus in dry cracks of acid siliceous rocks; 510-610 m. DIST. Native; discovered in 1964. Very rare, found only in 2 sites in *W Ireland* (S Kerry, W Cork). (Alpine and S Europe.) FLS Jun-Oct.

Spring Sandwort   *Minuartia verna*

Cushion-forming perennial with flowering and non-flowering shoots, to 15 cm. LEAVES 3-veined 6-15 mm. FLOWERS Stalks glandular-hairy, *sepals 3 veined, petals longer than sepals*, 3 styles. HABITAT Open rocky habitats, scree, spoil heaps of old lead mines; to 875 m. DIST. Native. Local. Carboniferous limestone in N England, scattered elsewhere. (Montane Europe, except Scandinavia.) FLS May-Sep.

Mountain Sandwort   *Minuartia rubella* VU

Low, tufted, cushion-forming alpine perennial with flowering and non-flowering shoots, to 6 cm. LEAVES 3-veined, 4-8 mm. FLOWERS Stalks glandular, *sepals 3-veined, petals shorter than sepals*, 3-styles. HABITAT Rock ledges, detritus on base-rich rocks; to 1180 m. DIST. Native. Rare. Scottish Highlands. (W Scandinavia, Iceland.) FLS Jun-Aug.

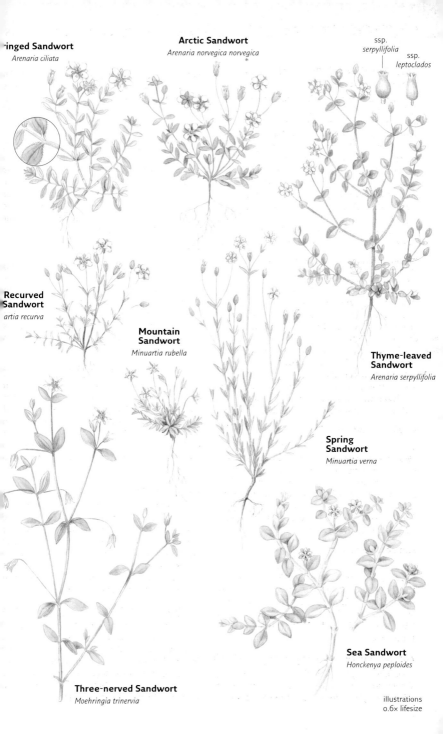

Fringed Sandwort
Arenaria ciliata

Arctic Sandwort
Arenaria norvegica norvegica

ssp.
serpyllifolia

ssp.
leptoclados

**Recurved
Sandwort**
Minuartia recurva

**Mountain
Sandwort**
Minuartia rubella

**Thyme-leaved
Sandwort**
Arenaria serpyllifolia

**Spring
Sandwort**
Minuartia verna

Sea Sandwort
Honckenya peploides

Three-nerved Sandwort
Moehringia trinervia

illustrations
0.6× lifesize

Teesdale Sandwort
Minuartia stricta VU. *(B)

Loosely tufted, glabrous perennial with non-flowering and flowering shoots, to 10 cm. LEAVES *Obscurely 1-veined or apparently veinless*, 6-12 mm. FLOWERS *Stalks glabrous*, flowers 5-8 mm diam., petals ± equalling sepals. HABITAT Calcareous flushes; 490-510 m. DIST. Native. Very rare: found only in 2 areas of Widdybank Fell, Upper Teesdale, Co. Durham. (Arctic and alpine Europe.) FLS Jun-Jul.

Fine-leaved Sandwort
Minuartia hybrida EN.

Slender, erect annual *without non-flowering shoots*, to 20 cm. LEAVES 3-veined at base, 5-15 mm. FLOWERS Stalks glabrous or glandular, flowers 6 mm diam., sepals 3-veined, petals distinctly shorter than sepals. HABITAT Dry calcareous grassland, disturbed ground, arable fields, road verges, waste ground, old walls. DIST. Native. Local, declining; introduced in Ireland. (W and S Europe.) FLS May-Jun.

Cyphel
Minuartia sedoides VU.

Yellow-green mossy cushion-forming alpine perennial with densely leafy flowering and non-flowering shoots. LEAVES Crowded, channelled above, 5-15 mm. FLOWERS *Greenish*, 4-5 mm diam., sepals 3-veined, *petals absent*. HABITAT Bare open mountain ledges, flushed grassland on base-rich soils; to 1190 m. DIST. Native. Scottish Highlands, Inner Hebrides. (Alpine Europe.) FLS Jun-Aug.

Stitchworts and chickweeds *Stellaria*, and *Myosoton*, mouse-ears *Cerastium*
See key to stitchworts, chickweeds and mouse-ears on p.117.

Wood Stitchwort
Stellaria nemorum

Prostrate to erect, stoloniferous perennial, to 60 cm. STEMS Pubescent. LEAVES *Lower leaves long-stalked*. FLOWERS 13-18 mm diam., *petals c.2× as long as sepals*. HABITAT Damp deciduous woodland, stream sides, on base-rich soils; lowland to 915 m. DIST. Native. N England, S Scotland, Wales; absent from Ireland. (Europe, except extreme SW.) FLS May-Jun. NOTE There are 2 subspecies in Britain: ssp. *montana*, with bracts decreasing abruptly in size after 1st branching of inflorescence, confined to Wales; and ssp. *nemorum*, with bracts decreasing gradually in size with each successive inflorescence branch.

Common Chickweed
Stellaria media

Very variable prostrate to erect, much-branched annual, to 40 cm. STEM With single line of hairs down length. LEAVES Lower leaves long-stalked, 3-20 mm. FLOWERS *Sepals 4.5-5 mm*; petals deeply bifid, ≤sepals, sometimes absent; *3-8 stamens; red-violet anthers*. HABITAT Persistent weed of arable crops, gardens, roadsides, waste ground, on fertile soils; also coastal seabird and seal colonies, shore drift lines. DIST. Native. Abundant throughout BI. (All Europe.) FLS Year-round.

Lesser Chickweed
Stellaria pallida

Much-branched, prostrate annual to 40 cm. Similar to *S. media*, but more slender; leaves all short stalked, <7 mm; *sepals 2-3.5 mm*, petals minute or absent, *1-2 stamens, and grey-violet anthers*. HABITAT Coastal sand-dunes, waste ground, arable land, heath grassland, woodland rides, on light, sandy soils. DIST. Native. Local throughout BI, rare in NW Scotland, Ireland. (Europe, except Scandinavia.) FLS May-Aug.

Greater Chickweed
Stellaria neglecta

Prostrate to erect annual or perennial, to 90 cm. Similar to *S. media*, but larger in all parts, flowers *c.10 mm diam.*, sepals 5-6.5 mm, petals ≥sepals, and 10 stamens. HABITAT Wet woodlands, shady stream sides; lowland to 440 m. DIST. Native. Local in England, Wales; rare in Scotland; absent from Ireland. (W, central and S Europe.) FLS Apr-Jul.

Greater Stitchwort
Stellaria holostea

Ascending to erect perennial, to 60 cm. STEMS *4 angled, rough*, glabrous below, hairy above. LEAVES 4-8 cm. FLOWERS *20-30 mm diam., petals much longer than sepals*, 10 stamens. HABITAT Hedgerows, open woodland, roadsides, on well-drained soils. DIST. Native. Common throughout BI. (All Europe except Scandinavia and extreme SW.) FLS Apr-Jun.

Teesdale Sandwort
Minuartia stricta

Fine-leaved Sandwort
Minuartia hybrida

Wood Stitchwort
Stellaria nemorum

Lesser Chickweed
Stellaria pallida

Cyphel
Minuartia sedoides

Greater Stitchwort
Stellaria holostea

Common Chickweed
Stellaria media

Greater Chickweed
Stellaria neglecta

illustrations
0.6× lifesize

Marsh Stitchwort
Stellaria palustris VU.

Erect, glaucous, glabrous perennial to 60 cm. STEMS *4-angled, smooth.* LEAVES 1.5-5 cm, linear-lanceolate, sessile; *bracts narrow, margins hairy, with central green stripe and broad pale edges.* FLOWERS 12-18 mm diam., petals 2× as long as sepals; 10 stamens. HABITAT Marshes, fens, wet pastures, dyke margins, on base-rich soils; to 360 m. DIST. Scattered and local throughout BI, except N Scotland, SW England. (Central and W Europe.) FLS May-Jul.

Lesser Stitchwort
Stellaria graminea

Prostrate to erect perennial, to 75 cm. STEMS 4-angled, smooth, glabrous. LEAVES 1.5-4 cm, linear-lanceolate, sessile; *bracts pale, without central green stripe, margins hairy.* FLOWERS 5-12 mm diam.; sepals 3-veined; *petals as long as or longer than sepals, split to >halfway;* 10 stamens. HABITAT Rough grassland, permanent pasture, woodland rides, roadsides, on well-drained acid soils; to 740 m. DIST. Common throughout BI. (All Europe except Mediterranean.) FLS May-Aug.

Bog Stitchwort
Stellaria uliginosa

Prostrate to erect perennial, to 30 cm. STEMS 4-angled, smooth, glabrous. LEAVES 5-10 mm, sessile, narrowly ovate; *bracts pale with central green stripe.* FLOWERS 6 mm across; sepals 3-veined; *petals shorter than sepals, split almost to base;* 10 stamens. HABITAT Wet woodland, stream sides, marshes, spring lines, on acid soils; to 1005 m. DIST. Widely distributed throughout BI. (Central and W Europe.) FLS May-Jun.

Jagged Chickweed
Holosteum umbellatum

Erect, glaucous annual to 20 cm. STEMS Hairy below, sticky above. LEAVES Lower leaves short-stalked, 10-25 mm; stem leaves sessile. FLOWERS White or pale pink, 4-5 mm diam., *long-stalked, in umbel-like heads; petals* longer than sepals, *irregularly toothed;* 3-5 stamens. HABITAT Old walls, banks, arable fields. DIST. Introduced; first recorded in BI in 1765 but extinct here since 1930. (W, central and S Europe.) FLS Apr-May. *Not illustrated.*

Starwort Mouse-ear
Cerastium cerastoides

Prostrate, mat-forming alpine perennial to 15 cm. Almost glabrous except for line of short hairs down stems. LEAVES 6-12 mm, oblong to lanceolate. FLOWERS 9-12 mm diam.; stalks glandular, to 8 cm; petals deeply split, *c.*2× as long as sepals; 10 stamens;

3 styles. HABITAT Scree and grassy slopes on acid rocks, often where late snow lies; mostly 750-1220 m. DIST. Native. Very local. Scottish Highlands. (Arctic and alpine Europe.) FLS Jul-Aug.

Field Mouse-ear
Cerastium arvense

Pubescent, glandular perennial with prostrate and erect non-flowering and flowering shoots to 30 cm. LEAVES 5-20 mm, *lower leaves with axillary bunches of small leaves.* FLOWERS 12-20 mm diam., petals about 2× as long as sepals, 10 stamens, 5 styles. HABITAT Well-drained permanent grassland, hedge banks, road verges, sand-dunes, on calcareous to slightly acid sandy soils; lowland to 300 m. DIST. Native. Local throughout BI but rare in W. (Most of Europe; introduced in Scandinavia.) FLS Apr-Aug.

Snow-in-summer
Cerastium tomentosum

Mat-forming perennial with prostrate and erect *densely white-hairy stems and leaves,* to 30 cm. LEAVES *Lower leaves with axillary bunches of small leaves.* FLOWERS 12-18 mm diam., petals 2× as long as sepals, 10 stamens, 5 styles. HABITAT Roadsides, waste ground, dunes, coastal shingle. DIST. Introduced in 1648. Naturalised throughout BI. (Italy; endemic to Europe.) FLS May-Aug.

Alpine Mouse-ear
Cerastium alpinum

Mat-forming alpine perennial with prostrate non-flowering shoots and flowering shoots to 15 cm, and *long, soft white hairs densely covering stems and leaves.* LEAVES *Bracts with pale narrow margins.* FLOWERS 18-25 mm diam.; sepals usually violet-tipped; petals 2× as long as sepals, notched. HABITAT Mica-schist alpine rock ledges; to 1220 m. DIST. Native. Local but widespread in Scottish Highlands. (Arctic and alpine Europe.) FLS Jun-Aug.

Arctic Mouse-ear
Cerastium arcticum VU

Mat-forming alpine perennial with erect non-flowering and flowering shoots to 15 cm. Similar to *C. alpinum* but hairs shorter, stiffer and less dense. LEAVES *Narrower than C. alpinum; bracts and bracteoles without pale margins.* FLOWERS 18-30 mm diam with stalks extending 1-3 cm beyond bracteole; petals ≥2× as long as sepals, notched; 10 stamens; styles. HABITAT Rock ledges, wet crevices, on acid or calcareous rocks; 700-1200 m. DIST. Native. Local in Snowdonia, Scottish Highlands. (Arctic Europe.) FLS Jun-Aug.

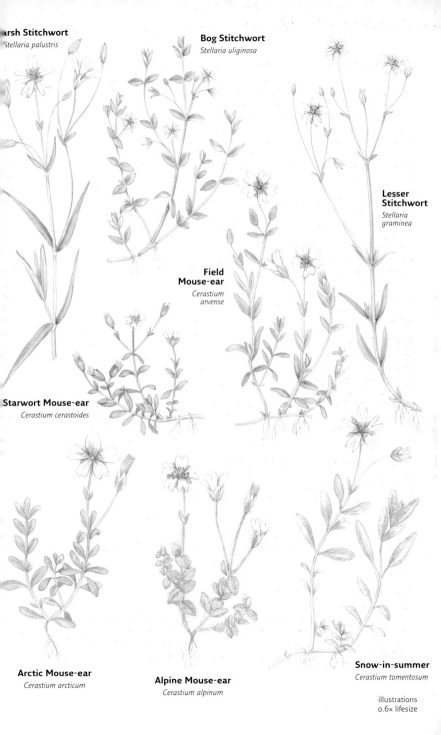

arsh Stitchwort
Stellaria palustris

Bog Stitchwort
Stellaria uliginosa

Lesser Stitchwort
Stellaria graminea

Field Mouse-ear
Cerastium arvense

Starwort Mouse-ear
Cerastium cerastoides

Arctic Mouse-ear
Cerastium arcticum

Alpine Mouse-ear
Cerastium alpinum

Snow-in-summer
Cerastium tomentosum

illustrations
0.6× lifesize

Shetland Mouse-ear
Cerastium nigrescens EN.

Dwarf, tufted purplish perennial to only *c.*5 cm. LEAVES 4–7 mm, almost circular, *dark purple, densely covered with glandular hairs*. FLOWERS Similar to *C. arcticum* (p.124). HABITAT Confined to an area of serpentine debris at *c.*15 m. DIST. Endemic. Uist, Shetland. FLS Jun–Aug.

Common Mouse-ear
Cerastium fontanum

Pubescent, mat-forming perennial *with prostrate non-flowering shoots* and erect flowering shoots to *c.*40 cm. LEAVES Dark green, covered with white hairs. FLOWERS *Petals as long as or slightly longer than sepals*, deeply split; 10 stamens; *5 styles*. HABITAT Meadows, pastures, montane grassland, cultivated soils, road verges, sand-dunes, shingle; to 1220 m. DIST. Native. Common throughout BI. (All Europe.) FLS Apr–Sep. NOTE Very variable species with a number of named subspecies; the common British plant is ssp. *vulgare*.

Sticky Mouse-ear
Cerastium glomeratum

Erect, pubescent, glandular annual. LEAVES *Yellow-green, broader than* C. fontanum. FLOWERS Clustered into compact heads, flower stalks very short; *sepals glandular with long white hairs extending beyond tips*; petals about equalling sepals, split to *c.*¼ of their length; 10 stamens; 5 styles. HABITAT Arable weed, improved grassland, walls, roadsides, sand-dunes; lowland to 610 m. DIST. Native. Common throughout BI. (Most of Europe except extreme N.) FLS Apr–Sep.

Sea Mouse-ear
Cerastium diffusum

Slender, prostrate to erect, branched, glandular annual, to 30 cm. LEAVES *Bracts and bracteoles wholly green without pale margins*. FLOWERS 3–6 mm diam.; *usually 4 sepals and petals*, sepals glandular-hairy but hairs not projecting beyond tips, petals shorter than sepals; *4 stamens; 4 styles*. HABITAT Sand-dunes, open grassland, sandy and gravelly habitats, close to sea; lowland and coastal. DIST. Native. Throughout BI. (W Europe.) FLS May–Jul.

Dwarf Mouse-ear
Cerastium pumilum

Erect, pubescent, glandular, branched annual to 12 cm. LEAVES *Lower leaves often reddish; upper bracts with narrow pale margins at tips*. FLOWERS 6–7 mm diam.; petals about as long as sepals, notched to *c.*⅓ of their length; 5 stamens; 5 styles. FRUITS Stalk downcurved at first then ± erect. HABITAT Short, open calcareous grassland, limestone quarries. DIST. Native. Rare and local in S England. (Central W and S Europe.) FLS Apr–May.

Little Mouse-ear
Cerastium semidecandrum

Slender, erect, pubescent, glandular, branched annual to 20 cm. LEAVES *Upper bracts almost wholly pale with narrow green central strip*. FLOWERS 5–7 mm diam. petals *c.*⅔ length of sepals, slightly notched; *5 stamens*; 5 styles. HABITAT Short, open, broken turf, sand-dunes, walls, waste ground, on dry, well-drained soils; lowland to 485 m. DIST. Native. Frequent throughout BI, but more coastal in N. (All Europe except extreme N.) FLS Apr–May.

Water Chickweed
Myosoton aquaticum

Prostrate to erect, somewhat trailing or scrambling perennial, to 100 cm. STEMS Glabrous below, hairy and glandular above. LEAVES 2–5 cm; base cordate, often with wavy margin. FLOWERS *12–15 cm diam.*, stalks glandular; *petals longer than sepals, split almost to base*. HABITAT Marshes, wet meadows, river banks, sides of ponds, streams and ditches. DIST. Native. Lowland England, W Wales. (W, central and E Europe.) FLS Jul–Aug.

Upright Chickweed
Moenchia erecta

Slender, erect, little-branched, *glaucous annual*, to 10 cm, whose flowers remain closed in dull weather. LEAVES 6–20 mm, sessile, erect, rigid, glabrous. FLOWERS *c.*8 mm diam.; *sepals acute, with broad white margins; petals shorter than sepals*; 4 stamens, 4 styles. HABITAT Sandy heaths, short, rough grassland on banks, maritime cliffs, sand-dunes, on well-drained acid soils; lowland to 410 m. DIST. Native. Local and scattered in England, Wales. (W and SW Europe.) FLS May–Jun.

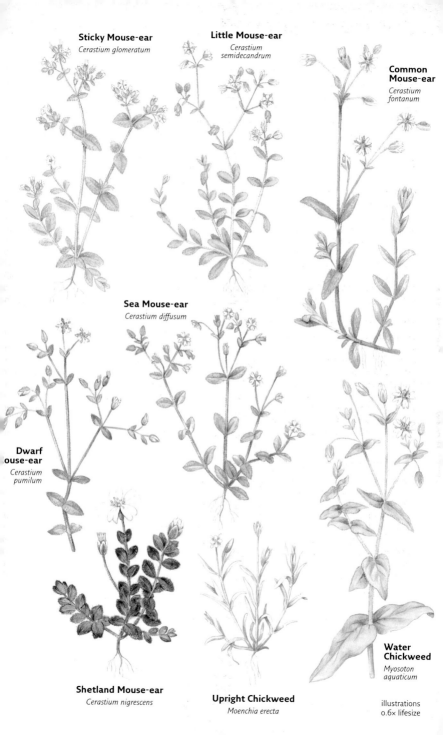

Sticky Mouse-ear
Cerastium glomeratum

Little Mouse-ear
Cerastium semidecandrum

Common Mouse-ear
Cerastium fontanum

Sea Mouse-ear
Cerastium diffusum

Dwarf Mouse-ear
Cerastium pumilum

Shetland Mouse-ear
Cerastium nigrescens

Upright Chickweed
Moenchia erecta

Water Chickweed
Myosoton aquaticum

illustrations
0.6× lifesize

Pearlworts *Sagina*

See key to *Sagina* on p.119.

Knotted Pearlwort *Sagina nodosa*

Tufted, procumbent to erect, glabrous or glandular-hairy perennial, to 15 cm, with basal leaf rosettes. LEAVES Linear; *upper leaves with bunches of short leaves in their axils*, giving characteristic 'knotted' appearance. FLOWERS 0.5–1.0 cm diam.; *5 petals, 2× as long as sepals*; sepals glandular; 10 stamens; 5 styles. HABITAT Short, wet, broken turf on calcareous or peaty soils, mires, dune slacks; lowland to 850 m. DIST. Native. Throughout BI, but rare and declining in S. (All Europe except S.) FLS Jul–Sep.

Snow Pearlwort *Sagina nivalis* VU.

Small, tufted, cushion-forming alpine perennial to 3 cm. STEMS Glabrous. LEAVES Glabrous. FLOWERS 3–4 mm diam.; stalks short, to 5 mm; 4–5 glabrous sepals; petals shorter than sepals; 8–10 stamens. FRUITS Greenish-yellow *capsule, longer than sepals, 2.5–3 mm*. HABITAT Broken open rocky ground, scree, on gravelly mica-schist; 840–1190 m. DIST. Native. Very rare. Central Scottish Highlands. (Arctic Europe.) FLS Jun–Aug.

Heath Pearlwort *Sagina subulata*

Mat-forming perennial with rosettes of linear leaves, to 15 cm. STEMS Flowering shoots erect, to 7.5 cm, glandular-hairy. LEAVES With a short-pointed tip. FLOWERS *Sepals glandular-hairy*; 5 petals, as long as or shorter than sepals; 10 stamens. FRUITS Capsule, longer than sepals. HABITAT Open areas on rocky or gravelly soils, sandy heaths; often close to sea. DIST. Native. Local in Scotland, W and S Britain. (Most of Europe except N Scandinavia.) FLS Jun–Aug.

Alpine Pearlwort *Sagina saginoides* EN.

Mat-forming alpine perennial to 7 cm. LEAVES Rosette leaves to 2 cm, with pointed tip. FLOWERS *c*.4 mm diam., solitary, stalks slender; sepals glabrous; 5 petals, as long as or shorter than sepals; 10 stamens; 5 styles. FRUITS *Capsule, 3.5–4 mm*. HABITAT Bare rocky ground, wet rock ledges, gullies in areas of late snow-lie; to 1190 m. DIST. Native. Very rare. Scottish Highlands. (Arctic and alpine Europe.) FLS Jun–Aug.

Procumbent Pearlwort *Sagina procumbens*

Tufted, mat-forming perennial with a tight rosette of leaves and long, prostrate side-shoots that root at nodes. FLOWERS Stalks glabrous; 4–5 sepals, blunt-tipped, hooded, spreading in fruit; *petals minute or absent.* HABITAT Paths, banks, wall tops, grass verges, waste ground; to 1150 m. DIST. Native. Abundant throughout BI. (All Europe.) FLS May–Sep.

Annual Pearlwort *Sagina apetala*

Erect, branching annual to 15 cm, with 2 subspecies: ssp. *erecta* and ssp. *apetala*. STEMS Main stem flowering. LEAVES *Tapering to a fine point.* FLOWERS 4 sepals, petals minute or absent; in ssp. *erecta* sepals spread in fruit and all 4 are blunt; in ssp. *apetala* sepals are erect in fruit, the outer acute and the inner blunt. HABITAT Walls, paths, bare ground, on dry sandy or gravelly soils. DIST. Native. Throughout BI. (All Europe except Scandinavia.) FLS May–Aug.

Sea Pearlwort *Sagina maritima*

Erect, branching annual to 15 cm. Similar *S. apetala*, but *leaves are blunt with a short point (<0.1 mm), not tapering to a fine point.* HABITAT Bare patches in dune slacks, cliff tops, fine shingle, roadsides. DIST. Native. All round British coasts. (All European coasts.) FLS May–Sep.

Knawels *Scleranthus*

Much-branched annuals or perennials, with opposite pairs of linear leaves that meet across the stem. Flowers inconspicuous, greenish white, in dense inflorescences; 5 sepals, petals absent.

Annual; sepals acute, pale margin narrow, ± erect in fruit	*S. annuus*
Perennial; sepals blunt, with broad pale margins, incurved in fruit	*S. perennis*
Stems ± erect; fruit 3.5–4.5 mm	ssp. *perennis*
Stems ± prostrate; fruit 2–3 mm	ssp. *prostratus*

Annual Knawel *Scleranthus annuus*

Erect, branched annual to 20 cm. LEAVES 5–15 mm. FLOWERS *c*.4 mm diam., *calyx glabrous*. HABITAT Open, disturbed ground of grassy heaths, arable land on dry sandy soils; lowland to 365 m. DIST. Native. Scattered and local throughout BI; rare in N and Ireland. (All Europe except extreme N.) FLS Jun–Aug.

Perennial Knawel *Scleranthus perennis* CR. *(E)

Perennial with 2 subspecies: ssp. *perennis* and ssp. *prostratus*. Similar to *S. annuus*, but more robust and slightly glaucous, and *base of calyx hairy (see also key above)*. HABITAT/DIST. Very rare: ssp. *perennis* native, occurring in single locality in central Powys; ssp. *prostratus* endemic, limited to 3 localities on dry sandy, abandoned arable land in Suffolk. (Ssp. *perennis* in most of Europe except extreme N and SW.) FLS Jun–Aug.

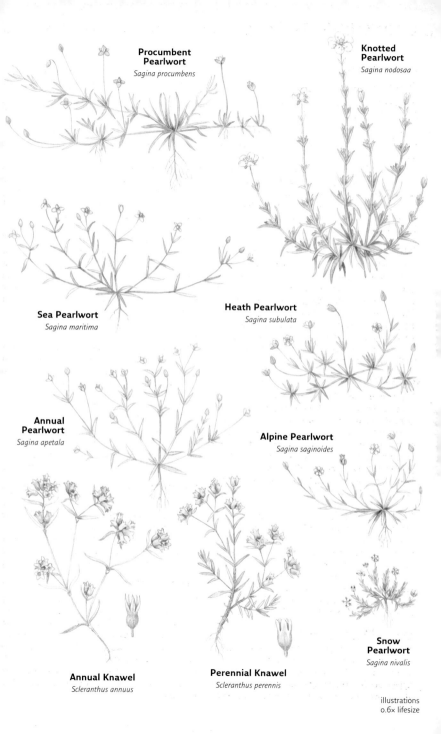

Procumbent Pearlwort
Sagina procumbens

Knotted Pearlwort
Sagina nodosaa

Sea Pearlwort
Sagina maritima

Heath Pearlwort
Sagina subulata

Annual Pearlwort
Sagina apetala

Alpine Pearlwort
Sagina saginoides

Annual Knawel
Scleranthus annuus

Perennial Knawel
Scleranthus perennis

Snow Pearlwort
Sagina nivalis

illustrations
0.6× lifesize

Strapwort
Corrigiola litoralis CR. *(B)

Prostrate, slightly glaucous glabrous annual. LEAVES *Alternate, narrow, strap-shaped, with stipules*. FLOWERS Very small, crowded in small heads; sepals with broad white margins; petals white or red-tipped, about as long as sepals. HABITAT Exposed gravelly shores. DIST. Native. Very rare: found only on Slapton Ley, S Devon. (W Europe S from Denmark; scattered elsewhere.) FLS Jul–Aug.

Smooth Rupturewort
Herniaria glabra

Prostrate, mat-forming annual or biennial. STEMS Glabrous or slightly hairy. LEAVES Upper leaves alternate; *stipules small, greenish*. FLOWERS Small, to 2 mm diam., greenish, *in dense clusters that tend to converge; sepals blunt, glabrous*; petals minute. FRUITS Longer than sepals. HABITAT Road verges, wheel ruts, footpaths, on sandy or gravelly compacted soils. DIST. Native. Very rare. East Anglia. (All Europe except NW and N.) FLS Jul.

Fringed Rupturewort
Herniaria ciliolata VU.

Prostrate, woody evergreen perennial to 20 cm. STEMS Hairy on upper side only. LEAVES *Stipules conspicuous, silvery, fringed at tip*. FLOWERS *c*.2 mm across; greenish, *in roundish clusters that remain distinct; sepals with short bristle at tip*; petals minute. FRUITS Hardly longer than sepals. HABITAT Cliff-top grassland, sandy turf, footpaths. DIST. British plant is ssp. *ciliolata*; endemic and very rare. Lizard Peninsula, Cornwall, and Guernsey, Jersey. (Ssp. *robusta* on coasts of France, Portugal.) FLS Jul.

Coral-necklace
Illecebrum verticillatum VU.

Prostrate, glabrous annual. STEMS Often reddish. LEAVES Rounded, stipules pale. FLOWERS 4–5 mm diam., *in dense clusters; sepals white, hooded, with fine point on back behind tip*; petals narrow, shorter than sepals. HABITAT Damp, sandy ground, path edges, pond margins. DIST. Native. Very rare. New Forest and Cornwall. (W Europe, N to Denmark.) FLS Jul–Sep.

Four-leaved Allseed
Polycarpon tetraphyllum

Much-branched, glabrous annual to 15 cm. LEAVES 8–13 mm, the *lower pairs apparently in whorls of 4*; stipules small. FLOWERS Small, 2–3 mm diam., in much-branched inflorescence; sepals with broad pale margins; petals white. HABITAT Warm, dry sandy soils, sand-dunes, bulb fields, walls. DIST. Native. Rare. Devon, Cornwall, Scilly Is, Channel Is. (S and SW Europe.) FLS Jun–Jul.

Spurreys *Spergula* and *Spergularia*
See key to Spergula *and* Spergularia *on p.119.*

Corn Spurrey
Spergula arvensis VU.

Very variable weak-stemmed, rather scrambling, glandular annual to 40 cm. LEAVES Linear, channelled beneath, 1–3 cm; stipules deciduous. FLOWERS 4–7 mm diam., petals slightly longer than sepals, 10 stamens, *5 stigmas*. HABITAT Arable weed of light, sandy, acid soils; lowland to 450 m. DIST. Archaeophyte. Common throughout BI. (All Europe.) FLS Jun–Sep.

Rock Sea-spurrey
Spergularia rupicola

Densely glandular, hairy perennial to 15 cm. STEMS Not ridged, often purplish. LEAVES Fleshy, slightly flattened, 5–15 mm; stipules silvery. FLOWERS 8–10 mm diam.; petals as long as or slightly longer than sepals, deep pink. HABITAT Short turf and broken ground on cliffs, scree, rocks, walls and bird colonies close to sea. DIST. Native. Local. S and W coasts of BI as far N as N Uist. (W coast of Europe.) FLS Jun–Sep.

Greater Sea-spurrey
Spergularia media

Prostrate to ascending, glabrous perennial, to 30 cm. LEAVES Linear, fleshy, 1–2.5 cm; stipules triangular, pale but not silvery. FLOWERS 7.5–12 mm diam. *petals slightly longer than sepals, pale pink.* FRUITS *Seeds pale yellowish brown, winged, with broad pale border.* HABITAT Salt and brackish marshes on sandy and muddy shores; also occasionally on salt-treated roadsides. DIST. Native. Common all round coasts of BI. (All round coasts of Europe; inland in E.) FLS Jun–Sep.

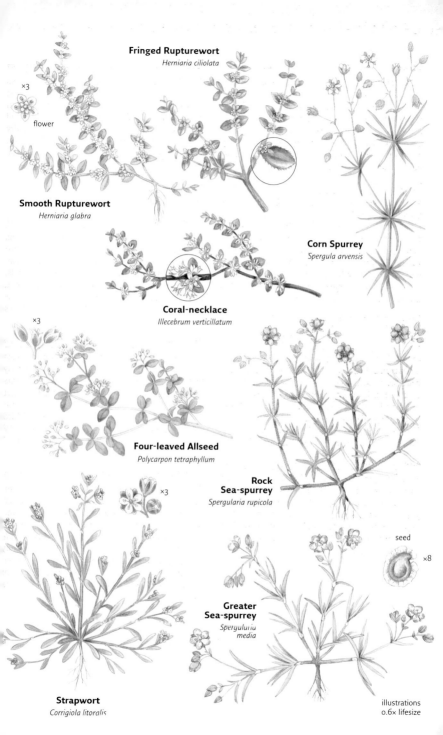

Fringed Rupturewort
Herniaria ciliolata

×3

flower

Smooth Rupturewort
Herniaria glabra

Corn Spurrey
Spergula arvensis

Coral-necklace
Illecebrum verticillatum

×3

Four-leaved Allseed
Polycarpon tetraphyllum

**Rock
Sea-spurrey**
Spergularia rupicola

×3

seed

×8

**Greater
Sea-spurrey**
*Spergularia
media*

Strapwort
Corrigiola litoralis

illustrations
0.6× lifesize

Lesser Sea-spurrey
Spergularia marina

Prostrate, glabrous or slightly glandular-hairy annual to 20 cm. LEAVES Yellowish green. FLOWERS Similar to *S. media* (p.132), but smaller, 6-8 mm diam., *petals shorter than sepals, deep pink*. FRUITS *Seeds mostly without a border*. HABITAT Drier parts of salt and brackish marshes on sandy and muddy shores, often with *S. media*; also saline lagoons inland, and spreading along salt-treated road verges. DIST. Native. All round coasts of BI. (All coasts of Europe; also saline soils inland.) FLS Jun-Aug.

Sand Spurrey
Spergularia rubra

Prostrate, glandular-hairy annual or biennial to 25 cm. LEAVES Not fleshy, tapering to a fine point, 4-25 mm; *stipules conspicuous, silvery,* narrow, torn at tip. FLOWERS 3-5 mm diam., *stalk longer than sepals; petals deep pink,* pale at base, shorter than sepals. HABITAT Open ground on heathland, cliff tops, dunes, tracks, quarries, waste ground, on dry, acid, sandy soils; lowland to 560 m. DIST. Native. Throughout BI, but rare in Ireland. (All Europe except extreme N.) FLS May-Sep.

Greek Sea-spurrey
Spergularia bocconei

Prostrate, glandular annual or biennial. Similar to *S. rubra*, but leaves with shorter point; *stipules triangular, not silvery; flowers* paler and smaller, *c.2 mm diam.,* stalks shorter than sepals. HABITAT Dry sandy waste ground near sea. DIST. Introduced; first recorded in 1901. Very rare. E Kent, Cornwall, Channel Is. (Mediterranean.) FLS May-Sep.

Ragged-robin
Lychnis flos-cuculi

Erect, glabrous or sparsely hairy perennial to *c.*70 cm. FLOWERS 3-4 cm diam.; calyx tube reddish, strongly 10-veined; *petals deeply divided into 4 narrow lobes*; 10 stamens; 5 styles. HABITAT Marshes, fens, wet meadows, woodlands, avoiding acid soils; to 750 m. DIST. Native. Common throughout BI. (All Europe, except extreme S.) FLS May-Jun.

Sticky Catchfly
Lychnis viscaria

Erect, densely tufted evergreen perennial with leafy non-flowering and flowering shoots to 60 cm. STEMS *Covered by sticky glands beneath each node.* FLOWERS *18-20 mm diam.,* with short stalks, in interrupted spike-like inflorescence. HABITAT Cliffs, rocks, rock debris, on mildly acid soils; to 425 m. DIST. Native. Very rare. In a few scattered localities in Scotland Wales. (Central, N and E Europe.) FLS Jun-Aug.

Alpine Catchfly
Lychnis alpina VU. *(B)

Tufted, glabrous alpine perennial with leafy non-flowering rosettes and erect, leafy flowering stems to 15 cm. FLOWERS *6-12 mm diam., in crowded heads* calyx faintly veined; petals deeply lobed to about halfway. HABITAT Serpentine debris and other metal-rich rocks; 600-870 m. DIST. Native. Very rare. In only 2 localities in Lake District and central Scottish Highlands. (Arctic and alpine Europe.) FLS Jun-Jul.

Corncockle
Agrostemma githago

Erect, pubescent annual to 100 cm. FLOWERS Large conspicuous, 3-5 cm diam.; *calyx tube 10-ribbed with long, narrow, spreading teeth, 3-5 cm, longer than petals*. DIST. Archaeophyte, introduced with agriculture in Iron Age. Originally most of BI but now extinct as an arable weed. Frequently introduced in wildflower mixes. (Native in most of Europe except extreme N.) FLS Jun-Aug.

Berry Catchfly
Cucubalus baccifer

Large, *scrambling, pubescent perennial* to 100 cm. FLOWERS Drooping, *c.*18 mm diam.; *petals greenish white,* spreading, deeply lobed. FRUITS *Black, berry like,* 6-8 mm diam. HABITAT Roadsides, hedge banks. DIST. Neophyte. Naturalised in Kent; rare birdseed casual. (W, central and E Europe.) FLS Jul-Sep.

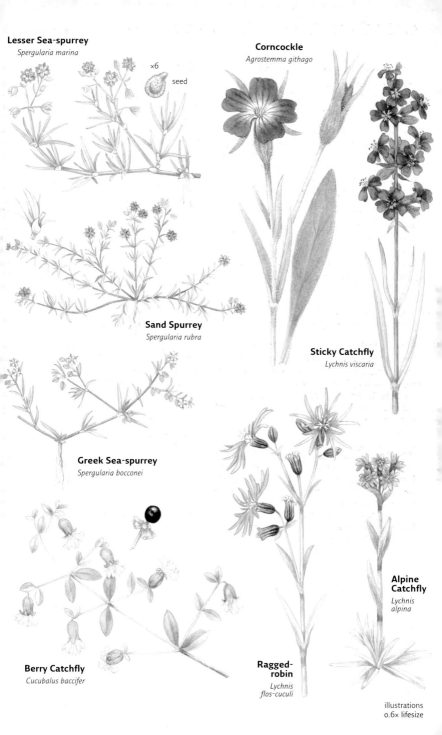

Lesser Sea-spurrey
Spergularia marina

×6
seed

Corncockle
Agrostemma githago

Sand Spurrey
Spergularia rubra

Sticky Catchfly
Lychnis viscaria

Greek Sea-spurrey
Spergularia bocconei

Alpine Catchfly
Lychnis alpina

Berry Catchfly
Cucubalus baccifer

Ragged-robin
Lychnis flos-cuculi

illustrations
0.6× lifesize

Campions and catchflies *Silene*

See key to Silene on p.120.

Nottingham Catchfly   *Silene nutans*

Erect, *pubescent, glandular perennial* to 80 cm. FLOWERS Hermaphrodite or unisexual, drooping, 18 mm diam., *c.*12 mm long; stalks short; calyx with 10 purplish veins, all glandular-pubescent; petals deeply lobed, lobes inrolled. HABITAT Short broken turf of calcareous grassland, coastal cliff tops and shingle. DIST. Native. Rare and local. Scattered throughout Britain; absent from Ireland. (Most of Europe except extreme N.) FLS May–Jul.

Spanish Catchfly   *Silene otites* EN.

Erect, glandular, and perennial with non-flowering rosettes and flowering stems to 90 cm. FLOWERS 3–4 mm diam., 4–5 mm long, mostly dioecious, *in crowded, long, narrow, ± interrupted inflorescence;* calyx faintly 10-veined, glabrous. HABITAT Bare patches in short calcareous turf and road verges. DIST. Native. Very rare. Found only in Breckland, East Anglia. (Central and E Europe.) FLS Jun.

Bladder Campion   *Silene vulgaris*

Erect, usually glabrous but sometimes pubescent, rather glaucous perennial to 90 cm. FLOWERS Male, female or hermaphrodite, drooping, *c.*18 mm diam.; calyx strongly inflated, narrowed at apex, pale or pinkish, net-veined with 20 main veins; petals deeply notched. FRUITS *Teeth of capsule erect.* HABITAT Permanent grassland, arable fields, hedge banks, roadsides, disturbed ground on dry calcareous soils; to 350 m. DIST. Native. All BI except for Northern Isles. (All Europe.) FLS Jun–Aug.

Sea Campion   *Silene uniflora*

Prostrate maritime perennial *with cushion of non-flowering shoots,* to 25 cm. LEAVES Similar to *S. vulgaris.* FLOWERS Similar to *S. vulgaris,* but larger, 20–25 mm diam.; *calyx not narrowed at apex and calyx teeth recurved.* HABITAT Sea cliffs, bird colonies, rocky ground, shingle beaches; also grows as an alpine plant of cliff ledges and lake margins to 970 m in Scotland. DIST. Native. Common all round coasts of BI. (Coasts of W Europe.) FLS Jun–Aug.

Moss Campion   *Silene acaulis* *(NI)

Densely tufted, cushion-forming alpine perennial to 10 cm. LEAVES In tight rosettes, linear, fringed with stiff hairs. FLOWERS 9–12 mm diam., solitary; calyx glabrous, faintly 10-veined, reddish. HABITAT Rock ledges, scree, crevices, mountain-top detritus, on basic soils; to 1305 m. DIST. Native. Widespread in Scottish Highlands; scattered in N Wales, Lake District. (Arctic and alpine Europe.) FLS Jul–Aug.

Night-flowering Catchfly   *Silene noctiflora* VU.

Erect, glandular, hairy annual to 60 cm. FLOWERS *c.*18 mm diam., *night-scented;* calyx ± cylindrical, hairy with sticky glands, pale with 10 greenish veins; *petals yellowish below, pink above, inrolled during day.* HABITAT Arable fields on well-drained sandy or, rarely, calcareous soils. DIST. Archaeophyte. Local and declining. Lowland England. (W, central and E Europe.) FLS Jul–Sep.

White Campion   *Silene latifolia*

Erect, hairy, slightly glandular, dioecious perennial to 100 cm. FLOWERS 25–30 mm diam., unisexual; calyx tube hairy, glandular, 10- or 20-veined, 18–25 mm long; *5 styles.* FRUITS Capsule teeth ± erect. HABITAT Cultivated ground, waste places, roadsides, on dry, especially calcareous soils; lowland to 425 m. DIST. Archaeophyte. Throughout BI. (All Europe except extreme N.) FLS May–Sep.

Red Campion   *Silene dioica*

Erect, hairy, dioecious biennial or perennial to 90 cm, with numerous prostrate non-flowering shoots. FLOWERS 18–25 mm diam., unisexual; calyx tube hairy, glandular, 10- or 20-veined, 10–15 mm long; *5 styles.* FRUITS Capsule teeth recurved. HABITAT Deciduous woodland, hedgerows, hedge banks, on fertile, base-rich soils; also cliffs (including bird cliffs), scree. To 1065 m. DIST. Native. Common throughout BI. (Most of Europe except extreme SW.) FLS May–Jun. NOTE Hybrids between *S. dioica* and *S. latifolia*, *S.* × *hampeana*, with pink flowers and intermediate characters, are common where the parents grow together.

Small-flowered Catchfly   *Silene gallica* EN.

Erect, pubescent, glandular annual to 45 cm. FLOWERS Short-stalked, alternate, erect, in little-branched inflorescence, 10–12 mm diam.; calyx ± cylindrical, sticky, hairy, 10-veined, 7–10 mm long; *base of petals sometimes with dark red blotch* (var. *quinquevulnera*). HABITAT Sandy arable fields, old walls, waste places; lowland. DIST. Archaeophyte. Rare and declining throughout BI. (S and SW Europe.) FLS Jun–Oct.

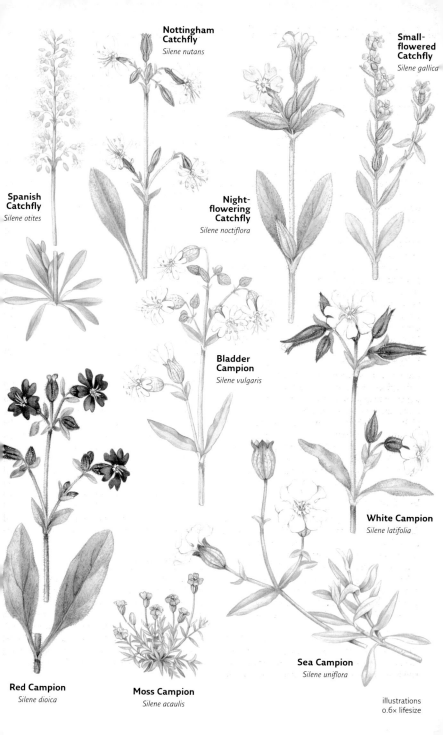

Nottingham Catchfly
Silene nutans

Small-flowered Catchfly
Silene gallica

Spanish Catchfly
Silene otites

Night-flowering Catchfly
Silene noctiflora

Bladder Campion
Silene vulgaris

White Campion
Silene latifolia

Red Campion
Silene dioica

Moss Campion
Silene acaulis

Sea Campion
Silene uniflora

illustrations
0.6× lifesize

Sand Catchfly
Silene conica VU.

Erect, glandular, sticky annual to 35 cm. Leaves Narrow, hairy. Flowers Small, 4–5 mm diam., short-stalked, erect; *calyx swollen, with 30 prominent veins, densely glandular with long, fine teeth*; 3 styles. Habitat Open, disturbed ground on sandy soils, grassland, roadsides, trackways, stabilised coastal dunes. Dist. Native. Very local. Scattered localities in East Anglia, S and E coasts, Channel Is. (Most of Europe except N.) Fls Jun–Aug.

Soapwort
Saponaria officinalis

Erect, stoloniferous, *glabrous perennial to 90 cm*. Flowers 2.5 *cm diam.*; sepals joined at base; calyx tube glabrous, 18–20 mm, reddish; 2 styles. Fruits Capsule with 4 unequal teeth. Habitat Hedge banks, roadsides, damp, shady habitats, usually near habitation. Dist. Archaeophyte. Naturalised throughout BI except extreme NW. (Native throughout Europe except Scandinavia.) Fls Jul–Sep.

Childing Pink
Petrorhagia nanteuilii VU. *(B)

Erect, shortly pubescent annual to 50 cm. Flowers *In compact heads; individual flowers enclosed in involucre of broad, shining brown bracts* below calyx; sepals joined at base, the seams between them whitish; 2 styles. Habitat/Dist. Native. Very rare. Only coastal shingle in W Sussex and stabilised dunes in Jersey. (SW Europe.) Fls Jul.

Pinks *Dianthus*
See key to *Dianthus* on p.121.

Cheddar Pink
Dianthus gratianopolitanus VU. *(B)

Densely tufted, glabrous, glaucous perennial to 20 cm, with long, prostrate non-flowering shoots. Flowers Solitary, 25 mm diam., *strongly fragrant*; epicalyx ≤¼ length of calyx, *epicalyx bracts blunt with short point*; tips of petals toothed. Habitat Limestone cliffs. Dist. Native. Very rare. Only N Somerset. (Central Europe.) Fls Jun–Jul.

Pink
Dianthus plumarius

Tufted, glabrous, glaucous perennial to 30 cm, with prostrate, rooting non-flowering shoots. Flowers 25–35 mm diam., strongly fragrant; epicalyx ¼–⅓ as long as calyx; *margins of sepals hairy; petals deeply divided to middle into narrow lobes.* Habitat Occasional casual escape from gardens on old walls. Dist. Introduced. Cultivated since 1629. (Mts of E-central Europe.) Fls Jun–Aug.

Jersey Pink
Dianthus gallicus

Tufted, glaucous perennial to 25 cm. Stems Base downy. Leaves On non-flowering shoots <1.5 cm. Flowers Fragrant, 15–25 mm across; epicalyx ¼ as long as calyx; *sepals without hairs; petals lobed to ⅙ of their length.* Habitat Grassy sand-dunes. Dist. Introduced. Naturalised in Jersey. (Native of W coast of Europe from S Brittany to N Spain.) Fls Jun–Aug.

Maiden Pink
Dianthus deltoides

Loosely tufted, green-glaucous perennial to 45 cm. Stems Flowering stems with short, prostrate non-flowering shoots. Flowers *Scentless, c.*18 mm across; epicalyx *c.*½ as long as calyx; petals with pale spots and dark band at base, tips irregularly toothed. Habitat Rough grassland, grassy banks, hill pastures, on dry, well-drained soils. Dist. Native. Very local. Scattered throughout Britain; absent from Ireland. (Most of Europe.) Fls Jun–Sep.

Deptford Pink
Dianthus armeria EN. *(B)

Erect green, not glaucous, shortly hairy annual to 60 cm. Flowers *8–13 mm across, in short-stalked clusters; bracts hairy*, as long as flower clusters; epicalyx hairy, as long as calyx; petals with pale dots, tips irregularly toothed. Habitat Dry grassland, hedge banks, roadsides, on dry, well-drained soils. Dist. Native. Rare and very local. Scattered in England, Wales, Ireland. (Most of Europe except N.) Fls Jul–Aug.

Carthusian Pink
Dianthus carthusianorum

Stiffly erect, glabrous perennial to 50 cm. Leaves Narrow, with sheathing bases to 15 mm. Flowers 20 mm across, *sessile, in dense, compact heads*; epicalyx *c.*½ as long as calyx; *petals with dark spots.* Habitat Dry grassland, open woodland, hedge banks Dist. *Not BI.* (Central and E Europe from S Denmark to N Spain.) Fls May–Aug.

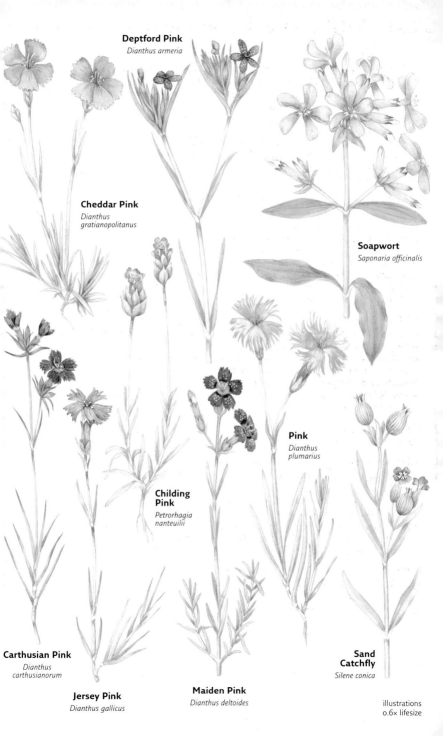

Deptford Pink
Dianthus armeria

Cheddar Pink
Dianthus gratianopolitanus

Soapwort
Saponaria officinalis

Pink
Dianthus plumarius

Childing Pink
Petrorhagia nanteuilii

Carthusian Pink
Dianthus carthusianorum

Jersey Pink
Dianthus gallicus

Maiden Pink
Dianthus deltoides

Sand Catchfly
Silene conica

illustrations
0.6× lifesize

	if	then
1	▷ Leaves alternate; ≥4 tepals	Go to ▷ **2**
	▷ Tiny alpine annual; leaves ± opposite; 3 tepals (very rare, Skye, Mull)	*Koenigia* (p.144)
2	▷ Leaves kidney-shaped; 4 tepals	*Oxyria* (p.144)
	▷ Leaves not kidney-shaped; 5 or 6 tepals	Go to ▷ **3**
3	▷ 6 tepals	*Rumex* (p.148)
	▷ 5 tepals	Go to ▷ **4**
4	▷ Outer tepals keeled or winged; woody climbers, scrambling annuals or tall, thicket-forming perennials	*Fallopia* (p.146)
	▷ Outer tepals neither winged nor keeled	Go to ▷ **5**
5	▷ Leaves triangular, cordate or hastate, about as wide as long; fruit >2× as long as perianth	*Fagopyrum* (p.144)
	▷ Leaves not shaped as above; fruit <2× as long as perianth	Go to ▷ **6**
6	▷ Inflorescences ≤6-flowered, all axillary	*Polygonum* (p.141)
	▷ Inflorescences usually ≥6-flowered, some or all terminal	*Persicaria* (below)

Rumex: section of stem showing stipules

Key to Knotweeds and Bistorts *Persicaria*

	if	then
1	▷ Stems branched	Go to ▷ **2**
	▷ Stems unbranched	Go to ▷ **8**
2	▷ Leaf base cordate; stamens protruding	*P. amphibia* (p.142)
	▷ Leaves narrowed to base; stamens not protruding	Go to ▷ **3**
3	▷ Tall, robust perennials to 180 cm; inflorescence a diffuse terminal panicle, 3 stigmas	*P. wallichii* (p.142)
	▷ Plants rarely taller than 75 cm; flowers in spikes, 2 stigmas	Go to ▷ **4**
4	▷ Tepals or peduncles glandular	Go to ▷ **5**
	▷ Inflorescence wholly without glands	Go to ▷ **6**
5	▷ Inflorescence slender, nodding, flowers separated; tepals with yellow glands; peduncles without glands	*P. hydropiper* (p.142)
	▷ Inflorescence erect, flowers crowded; tepals sparsely glandular; peduncles glandular	*P. lapathifolia* (p.142)

	if	then
6	▷ Inflorescence dense, flowers crowded; leaves usually with dark blotch	*P. maculosa* (p.142)
	▷ Inflorescence slender, few-flowered; leaves never blotched	Go to ▷ 7
7	▷ Leaves linear-lanceolate, usually >5× as long as wide; tepals deep pink; fruit 2–2.5 mm long	*P. minor* (p.142)
	▷ Leaves <5× as long as wide; tepals greenish, tinged pink; fruit 2.5–3.5 mm long	*P. mitis* (p.142)
8	▷ Lower leaves tapering at base; inflorescence slender, lower flowers replaced by bulbils	*P. vivipara* (p.144)
	▷ Lower leaves truncate to cordate at base; inflorescence dense, bulbils absent	*P. bistorta* (p.142)

Key to Knotgrasses *Polygonum*

	if	then
1	▷ Plant glaucous; base of stems woody; stipules at least as long as upper internodes, with 6–12 branched veins (very rare, S and SW coasts)	*P. maritimum* (p.144)
	▷ Base of stem hardly woody; upper stipules much shorter than internodes, with unbranched veins	Go to ▷ 2
2	▷ Leaves glaucous; fruit shiny, usually much longer than perianth	*P. oxyspermum* (p.144)
	▷ Leaves green; fruit dull, striate, shorter than to slightly longer than perianth	Go to ▷ 3
3	▷ Branch leaves much smaller than stem leaves; tepals fused only near base (for <¼ of their length); fruit with 3 concave sides	Go to ▷ 4
	▷ Branch and stem leaves ± the same size; tepals fused for c.½ their length; fruit with 2 convex and 1 concave side; forms dense mats	*P. arenastrum* (p.144)
4	▷ Stem leaves >5 mm wide; tepals obovate, overlapping almost to tip	Go to ▷ 5
	▷ Stem leaves 1–4 mm wide; tepals narrowly oblong, separated at tip to expose fruit	*P. rurivagum* (p.144)
5	▷ Stem leaves ovate-lanceolate; petiole short, to 2 mm, included in stipules; fruit 2.5–3.5 mm	*P. aviculare* (p.144)
	▷ Stem leaves obovate; petiole 4–8 mm, projecting from stipules; fruit 3.5–4.5 mm	*P. boreale* (p.144)

POLYGONACEAE Knotweeds, sorrels and docks

A family of herbs, shrubs and climbers, usually with rather small, inconspicuous flowers (*see* key on p.140). Leaves are alternate, simple and usually entire, with characteristic sheathing stipules that surround the stem above the petiole. Flowers are regular, and hermaphrodite or unisexual; 3-6 greenish, brownish, white or pink tepals in 2 whorls; 6-9 stamens; ovary superior, 2-3 stigmas. Fruit is an achene.

Himalayan Knotweed
Persicaria wallichii

Tall, erect perennial to 180 cm. STEMS Glabrous. LEAVES 8-20 cm, varyingly hairy beneath, veins often reddish; stipules crowded, sometimes exceeding internodes. FLOWERS *In lax, leafy inflorescence*; tepals ≥3 mm, unequal; *3 stigmas.* HABITAT Waste ground, hedge banks, roadsides, railways, stream banks; lowland to 330 m. DIST. Introduced *c.*1900 (native of Himalayas). Scattered throughout BI. (Central and NW Europe.) FLS Aug-Sep.

Common Bistort
Persicaria bistorta

Erect, almost glabrous, *unbranched perennial to 50 cm.* LEAVES *Petiole of basal leaves winged*, stem leaves sessile. FLOWERS In a dense terminal spike; tepals 4-5 mm, pink. HABITAT Wet meadows, pastures, damp roadsides, alder carr; to 430 m. Often occurs as garden escape. DIST. Native. Throughout BI, but rare in Ireland. (Most of Europe except Scandinavia and Mediterranean.) FLS Jun-Aug.

Amphibious Bistort
Persicaria amphibia *(R)

Creeping, rhizomatous perennial. Occurs in both terrestrial and aquatic forms. STEMS Erect in terrestrial plant, rooting at nodes. LEAVES *Rounded or cordate at base*; ± sessile and pubescent in terrestrial plant; floating and glabrous with long petiole in aquatic. FLOWERS In dense inflorescence; tepals 3.5 mm, pink; *stamens protruding*; 2 styles. HABITAT Terrestrial form on margins of dykes, lakes and ponds and as arable weed; aquatic form in ponds, lakes, canals, dykes, streams; to 570 m. DIST. Native. Throughout BI. (All Europe.) FLS Jul-Sep.

Redshank
Persicaria maculosa

Prostrate to erect, ± glabrous annual, to 75 cm. LEAVES 3-11 cm, *often with large black blotch*. FLOWERS *In dense inflorescence; peduncle and flowers without glands*, glabrous; tepals bright pink, sometimes whitish. HABITAT Weed of cultivated land, gardens, waste ground, roadsides; also banks of ponds, rivers, streams. Lowland to 450 m. DIST. Native. Common throughout BI. (All Europe except extreme N.) FLS Jun-Oct.

Pale Persicaria
Persicaria lapathifolia

Prostrate to erect, often pubescent annual, to 60 cm. LEAVES 5-15 cm, often with large black blotch. FLOWERS In dense inflorescence; *peduncle and flowers with numerous yellow glands*; tepals dull pink to white or greenish (but note that colour of flower is not a reliable difference from *P. maculosa*). HABITAT Similar to *P. maculosa*, with which it sometimes grows; lowland to 450 m. DIST. Native. Throughout BI, but scarce in extreme N. (All Europe.) FLS Jun-Aug.

Water-pepper
Persicaria hydropiper

Erect, glabrous annual, with stems rooting at nodes. LEAVES Mid-stem stipule teeth *c.*0.3 mm; *with burning, acrid taste* (hence 'pepper'). FLOWERS Glandular, ≥4 mm, pale pink to greenish white, *in long, slender, interrupted, nodding inflorescence*. FRUITS Dull nuts. HABITAT Margins of ponds, lakes, rivers, streams and dykes, woodland rides where water stands in winter. DIST. Native. Common throughout BI, but rare in extreme N. (All Europe except extreme N.) FLS Jul-Sep.

Tasteless Water-pepper
Persicaria mitis VU.

Erect, glabrous annual to 60 cm. Very similar to *P. hydropiper* and easily confused with it. STEMS Mid-stem stipule teeth *c.*1.7 mm. LEAVES *Tasteless.* FLOWERS Less glandular than *P. hydropiper*, *c.*3.7 mm, *pale to purplish pink*, in long, slender, interrupted, slightly nodding inflorescence. FRUITS Very shiny nuts. HABITAT Wet meadows, margins of ponds, lakes, ditches, dykes and rivers; lowland. DIST. Native. *Not Scotland.* Rare and declining. (W, central and E Europe.) FLS Jul-Sep.

Small Water-pepper
Persicaria minor VU.

Prostrate to erect, ± glabrous annual, to 30 cm. STEMS Mid-stem stipule teeth *c.*1.7 mm. LEAVES *Narrow, ± parallel-sided.* FLOWERS *Without glands, c.*2.5 mm, deep pink, in slender, erect, ± interrupted inflorescence. FRUITS Slightly shiny nuts. HABITAT Marshy ground around ponds, lakes, ditches, dykes; to 315 m. DIST. Native. Rare and scattered throughout BI except N Scotland. (W, central and E Europe.) FLS Jul-Oct.

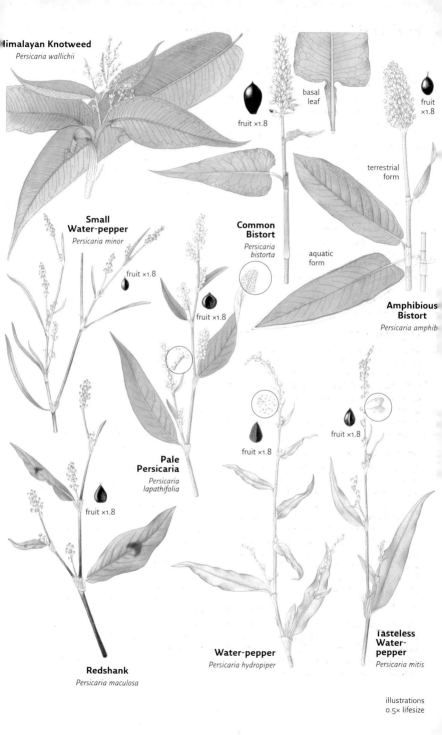

Himalayan Knotweed
Persicaria wallichii

fruit ×1.8

basal
leaf

fruit
×1.8

terrestrial
form

**Small
Water-pepper**
Persicaria minor

fruit ×1.8

**Common
Bistort**
*Persicaria
bistorta*

fruit ×1.8

aquatic
form

**Amphibious
Bistort**
Persicaria amphib

**Pale
Persicaria**
*Persicaria
lapathifolia*

fruit ×1.8

fruit ×1.8

fruit ×1.8

Redshank
Persicaria maculosa

Water-pepper
Persicaria hydropiper

**Tasteless
Water-
pepper**
Persicaria mitis

illustrations
0.5× lifesize

Alpine Bistort
Persicaria vivipara *(R)

Slender, erect, unbranched, glabrous perennial to 30 cm. Leaves *Basal leaves stalked, unwinged; upper leaves sessile.* Flowers In slender *inflorescence spike, flowers in upper part only, lower part consisting of purple bulbils;* tepals 3–4 mm, pink-white. Habitat Mountain grassland and pastures, scree, wet rocks; uplands to 1210 m. Dist. Native. N England, Scotland. (N and alpine Europe.) Fls Jun–Aug.

Iceland-purslane
Koenigia islandica

Small, erect, glabrous, usually reddish annual to 5 cm. Leaves ± opposite, 4–8 mm. Flowers Small, inconspicuous; 3 tepals, *c*.1 mm; 3 stamens; 2 styles. Habitat Bare, stony ground and fine, damp gravel at foot of cliffs; 300–725 m. Dist. Native. Very rare. Skye and Mull. (Arctic Europe, Norway, Iceland.) Fls Jun–Aug.

Buckwheat
Fagopyrum esculentum

Erect, thinly pubescent, little-branched annual to 60 cm. Leaves *Triangular, cordate.* Flowers *Inflorescence of compact clusters at ends of long peduncles;* 5 tepals, 3–4 mm, white to pale pink. Fruits Tepals neither keeled nor winged. Habitat Casual of waste ground, rubbish tips, field borders; also a relic of cultivation. Dist. Introduced (native of SW China). (W, central and E Europe.) Fls Jul–Aug.

Knotgrasses *Polygonum*
See key to *Polygonum* on p.141.

Sea Knotgrass
Polygonum maritimum VU. *(B, R)

Prostrate, glabrous, glaucous, much-branched *perennial,* woody at base, to 50 cm long. Leaves Greyish green with revolute margins; *stipules conspicuous, silvery, with 6–12 branched veins, upper at least as long as internodes.* Flowers Tepals pink-white, 2–2.5 mm. Fruits Shiny nut, as long as or slightly longer than perianth. Habitat Sand, fine shingle beaches. Dist. Native. Very rare. Scattered localities along S and SW coast, Channel Is, S Ireland. (Mediterranean coasts N to Brittany.) Fls Jul–Oct.

Ray's Knotgrass
Polygonum oxyspermum

Prostrate, glabrous, slightly glaucous annual to 100 cm long. Leaves Flat; *stipules silvery, with 4–6 unbranched veins, much shorter than upper internodes.* Flowers Tepals pink-white, *c*.3 mm. Fruits Large, shining nut, distinctly longer than perianth. Habitat Sand, shingle, shell-gravel at level of extreme high-water spring tides. Dist. Native. Rare and scattered on S and W coasts; very rare on N and E coasts. Fls Jul–Oct. Note The W European plant is ssp. *raii*.

Equal-leaved Knotgrass
Polygonum arenastrum

Much-branched, prostrate, mat-forming annual to 30 cm. Leaves *All ± same size, crowded and overlapping.* Flowers *Tepals* greenish white to pinkish, *c*.1.5 mm, *fused for ⅓–⅔ of their length.* Fruits Nut, about as long as perianth. Habitat Compacted sandy, gravelly soils of tracks, footpaths, gateways, waste ground. Dist. Archaeophyte. Common throughout BI. (All Europe except extreme N.) Fls Jul–Nov.

Knotgrass
Polygonum aviculare

Much-branched, prostrate to erect annual, to 200 cm. Leaves *Of markedly different sizes,* those on main stem much larger, >5 mm wide, than those on branches and flowering stems; petioles enclosed within stipules. Flowers *Tepals c*.2 mm, *fused for up to ⅓ of their length,* overlapping almost to tip. Fruits Nut, 2.5–3.5 mm. Habitat Waste and disturbed ground, roadsides, seashores; also garden and arable weed. To 550 m. Dist. Native. Common throughout BI (except Shetland). (All Europe.) Fls Jul–Nov.

Northern Knotgrass
Polygonum boreale

Prostrate to erect, scrambling annual, to 100 cm. Similar to *P. aviculare, but petioles longer than stipules and nut larger, 3.5–4.5 mm.* Habitat Similar to *P. aviculare.* Dist. Native. N Scotland, Outer Hebrides, Orkney, Shetland (where it replaces *P. aviculare*). (N Scandinavia, Iceland, Faeroes.) Fls Jun–Oct.

Cornfield Knotgrass
Polygonum rurivagum

Slender, erect annual to 30 cm. Leaves *Narrow, 0.5–3.5 mm wide,* ± sessile, those on main stem 2–3× as long as those on flowering branches. Flowers *Tepals red, c*.2 mm, narrow, joined only at base, *separated and not overlapping near tip.* Fruits *Nut, slightly longer than perianth,* 2.5–3.5 mm. Habitat Arable weed on light, well-drained, usually calcareous soils. Dist. Archaeophyte. S England; rare elsewhere and absent from Ireland. (W Europe, Scandinavia.) Fls Aug–Nov.

Mountain Sorrel
Oxyria digyna

Tufted, glabrous, dioecious perennial to 30 cm. Leaves *Basal, kidney-shaped, acid to the taste,* becoming reddish in late summer. Flowers In branched inflorescence. Fruits Broadly winged nut, 3–4 mm. Habitat Wet rock ledges, damp rocks by streams, river shingle; to 1190 m. Dist. Native. Locally common in mts of N Wales, Lake District, Scotland, Ireland. (Arctic and alpine Europe.) Fls Jul–Aug.

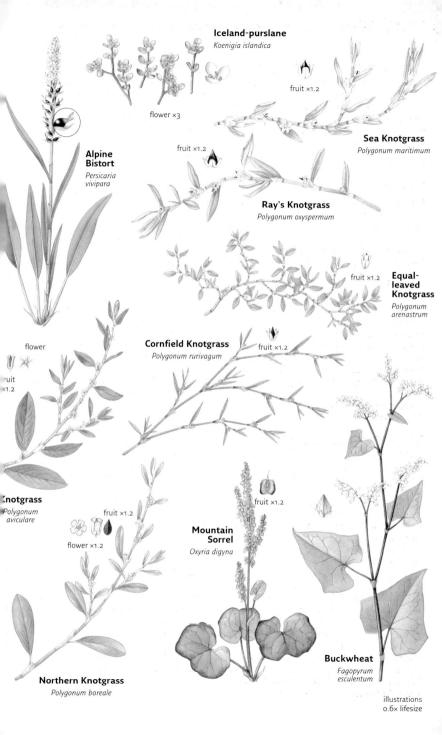

Iceland-purslane
Koenigia islandica

flower ×3

fruit ×1.2

Alpine Bistort
Persicaria vivipara

Sea Knotgrass
Polygonum maritimum

fruit ×1.2

Ray's Knotgrass
Polygonum oxyspermum

fruit ×1.2

Equal-leaved Knotgrass
Polygonum arenastrum

flower

fruit ×1.2

Cornfield Knotgrass
Polygonum rurivagum

fruit ×1.2

Knotgrass
Polygonum aviculare

fruit ×1.2

flower ×1.2

fruit ×1.2

Mountain Sorrel
Oxyria digyna

Buckwheat
Fagopyrum esculentum

Northern Knotgrass
Polygonum boreale

illustrations 0.6× lifesize

Bindweeds *Fallopia*

Japanese Knotweed
Fallopia japonica

Tall, erect, clump- or thicket-forming perennial to 200 cm. STEMS Annual, glaucous to reddish. LEAVES *Truncate at base*, 6–12 cm, *glabrous*. FLOWERS Inflorescence branches slender, shorter than leaves. HABITAT Roadsides, railways, riverbanks, waste ground. DIST. Introduced as a garden plant from Japan in 1825. Established and persistent throughout BI. (Established in W, central and E Europe.) FLS Aug–Oct.

Giant Knotweed
Fallopia sachalinensis

Similar to *F. japonica*, but taller, to 400 cm; LEAVES *larger, 15–40 cm, cordate at base, undersides sparsely pubescent*. HABITAT Forms extensive thickets on roadsides, waste ground, riverbanks, and lake and loch shores. DIST. Introduced as a garden plant in 1869 from Sakhalin I. Established throughout BI, but less common than *F. japonica*. (Established in W and central Europe.) FLS Aug–Sep.

Russian-vine
Fallopia baldschuanica

Vigorous, twining, scrambling woody perennial climber to >10 m. LEAVES With long petioles. FLOWERS 5 mm across in much-branched, showy inflorescence. HABITAT Casual as garden throw-out close to habitation; hedges, scrub, waste ground. DIST. Introduced to British gardens from central Asia at end of C19th. FLS Aug–Oct.

Black-bindweed
Fallopia convolvulus

Scrambling or climbing, slightly mealy annual to 120 cm. FRUITS *Dull* black nut, 4–5 mm; *fruiting pedicels 1–3 mm, jointed above middle; outer tepals narrowly winged in fruit.* HABITAT Weed of arable land, gardens, rubbish tips, waste ground, roadsides; to 450 m. DIST. Archaeophyte. Common throughout BI. (All Europe.) FLS Jul–Oct.

Copse-bindweed
Fallopia dumetorum VU

Similar to *F. convolvulus*, but more robust, to 300 cm; *fruit a glossy black nut, 2.5–3 mm; fruiting pedicels 3–8 mm, jointed at or below middle, deflexed; outer tepals broadly winged in fruit.* HABITAT Makes erratic appearances in wood margins, hedgerows, copses, often following coppicing. DIST. Native. Rare and local. SE England. (W, central and E Europe.) FLS Jul–Oct.

Key to Bindweeds *Fallopia*

	if	then
1	▷ Tall, erect, thicket-forming, rhizomatous perennials to 2–3 m tall	Go to ▷ **2**
	▷ Scrambling, twining annuals or woody climbers	Go to ▷ **3**
2	▷ Leaves to 12 cm long, truncate at base, cuspidate	***F. japonica*** (above)
	▷ Leaves usually >15 cm long, weakly cordate, acute	***F. sachalinensis*** (above)
3	▷ Vigorous woody climber; inflorescence richly branched	***F. baldschuanica*** (above)
	▷ Scrambling or twining annual; inflorescence scarcely branched	Go to ▷ **4**
4	▷ Fruiting pedicels 1–3 mm, fruit 4–5 mm, dull black	***F. convolvulus*** (above)
	▷ Fruiting pedicels 5–8 mm, fruit 2.5–3 mm, shining black	***F. dumetorum*** (above)

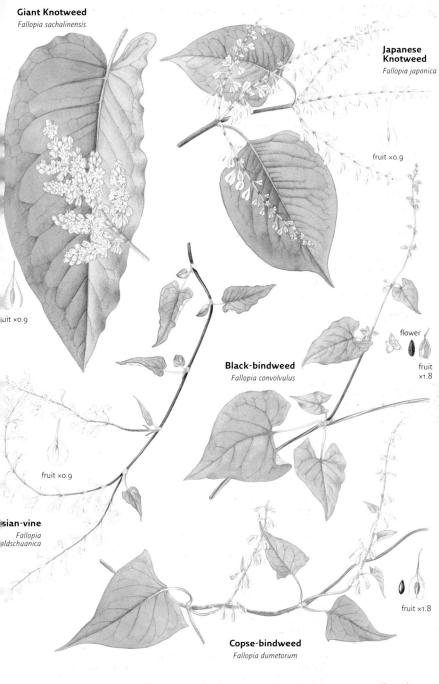

Giant Knotweed
Fallopia sachalinensis

Japanese Knotweed
Fallopia japonica

fruit ×0.9

uit ×0.9

flower

fruit
×1.8

Black-bindweed
Fallopia convolvulus

fruit ×0.9

sian-vine
Fallopia
aldschuanica

fruit ×1.8

Copse-bindweed
Fallopia dumetorum

illustrations
0.6× lifesize

if	**then**
1 ▷ Basal leaves spear-shaped (with single lobe at each side at base), acid-tasting (sorrels)	Go to ▷ **2**
▷ Basal leaves not spear-shaped, not acid-tasting (docks)	Go to ▷ **3**
2 ▷ Lobes of leaves downward-pointing, upper leaves clasping stem	*R. acetosa* (p.150)
▷ Lobes of leaves spreading or forward-pointing, upper leaves not clasping	*R. acetosella* (p.150)
3 ▷ At least 1 tepal with a distinct swollen tubercle at fruiting	Go to ▷ **4**
▷ All tepals without tubercles	Go to ▷ **16**
4 ▷ Fruiting tepals distinctly toothed	Go to ▷ **5**
▷ Fruiting tepals without teeth	Go to ▷ **9**
5 ▷ Branches spreading, making wide angle with stem and a tangled mass in fruit; leaves with lower half of blade distinctly constricted	*R. pulcher* (p.152)
▷ Branches not wide-spreading and tangled in fruit; leaf blades not constricted	Go to ▷ **6**
6 ▷ Fruiting tepals ≥4 mm, reddish brown	Go to ▷ **7**
▷ Fruiting tepals <4 mm, golden or yellow	Go to ▷ **8**
7 ▷ Tepals triangular, <4 mm wide (excluding teeth)	*R. obtusifolius* (p.152)
▷ Tepals broadly ovate, cordate, ≥6 mm wide	*R. cristatus* (p.150)
8 ▷ Tepals mostly <3 mm long, with some teeth as long	*R. maritimus* (p.152)
▷ Tepals mostly >3 mm long, with all teeth shorter	*R. palustris* (p.152)
9 ▷ Inflorescence dense, whorls crowded and converging; tepals mostly >5 mm	Go to ▷ **10**
▷ Inflorescence not dense, with whorls separated; tepals <5 mm (except for *R. pulcher*)	Go to ▷ **13**
10 ▷ Leaves lanceolate, narrow, with undulate crisped margins	*R. crispus* (p.152)
▷ Leaves ovate or oblong-lanceolate, margins not crisped	Go to ▷ **11**

	if	then
11	▷ Tepals triangular, ± truncate at base (robust waterside plant)	*R. hydrolapathum* (p.150)
	▷ Tepals broadly ovate to roundish, cordate at base	Go to ▷ **12**
12	▷ Leaf base cuneate, veins in middle of leaf making angle of ≤60° with midrib	*R. patientia* (p.150)
	▷ Leaf base cordate, veins in middle of leaf making angle of ≥60° with midrib	*R. cristatus* (p.150)
13	▷ Branches spreading, making wide angle with stem and a tangled mass in fruit; leaves rarely >10 cm, with lower half of blade distinctly constricted; tepals >5 mm	*R. pulcher* (p.152)
	▷ Branching not as in *R. pulcher*; basal leaves usually >10 cm long, blade not constricted; tepals ≤4 mm	Go to ▷ **14**
14	▷ Leaves slightly glaucous; tepals c.4 mm, all with large (*c.*2.5 mm) tubercles	*R. rupestris* (p.152)
	▷ Leaves green; tepals ≤3 mm	Go to ▷ **15**
15	▷ Inflorescence branches leafy for *c.*⅔ their length; all 3 tepals with well-developed oblong tubercle	*R. conglomeratus* (p.152)
	▷ Inflorescence branches leafy at base; 1 tepal with well-developed globular tubercle (other 2 may have very small tubercles or tubercles absent)	*R. sanguineus* (p.152)
16	▷ Tepals distinctly longer than wide	*R. aquaticus* (p.150)
	▷ Tepals about as long as wide	Go to ▷ **17**
17	▷ Rhizomatous; leaves about as long as broad; base of tepals truncate	*R. pseudoalpinus* (p.150)
	▷ Not rhizomatous; leaves distinctly longer than broad; base of tepals cordate	*R. longifolius* (p.150)

Rumex fruit

Sorels and docks *Rumex*

See key to *Rumex* on p.148.

Sheep's Sorrel
Rumex acetosella

Slender, erect, glabrous, dioecious perennial to 30 cm. Leaves To 4 cm, with *narrow, spreading basal lobes*; upper leaves distinctly stalked. Flowers Outer tepals remain appressed to inner. Fruits Glossy nut, 1.3–1.5 mm. Habitat Acid grassland, heaths, commons, on well-drained sandy soils; to 1050 m. Dist. Native. Common throughout BI. (All Europe.) Fls May–Sep.

Common Sorrel
Rumex acetosa

Erect, glabrous, tufted, dioecious perennial to 50(-100) cm. Leaves *4–7 cm; basal lobes pointing downwards or slightly convergent*; upper leaves sessile, clasping stem. Flowers Outer tepals reflexed after flowering. Fruits Glossy nut, 2–2.5 mm. Habitat Grassland, woodland rides, roadside verges, riverbanks, coastal shingle, mountain ledges; to 1215 m. Dist. Native. Common throughout BI. (All Europe.) Fls May–Jun.

Monk's-rhubarb
Rumex pseudoalpinus

Robust perennial to 80 cm, rhizome extensively creeping to form large patches. Leaves *Large, orbicular*, to 40 cm. Flowers In dense spindle-shaped inflorescence. Fruits Nut, *c.*3 mm; *fruiting tepals c.6 mm, entire, without tubercles*. Habitat Relic of cultivation near farms, streams, roadsides; lowland to 375 m. Dist. Archaeophyte. N England, Scotland. (Native of mts of central and S Europe.) Fls Jun–Aug.

Scottish Dock
Rumex aquaticus VU.

Robust perennial to 200 cm. Leaves Basal leaves to 45 cm, triangular, cordate. Fruits *Fruiting tepals longer than wide, without teeth or tubercles*. Habitat Sides of lochs, rivers and ditches, sand banks, alder carr. Dist. Native. Very rare. SE and W banks of Loch Lomond, Scotland. (N, central and E Europe.) Fls Jul–Aug. Note Hybridises freely with *R. obtusifolius* (p.152).

Northern Dock
Rumex longifolius

Robust perennial to 120 cm. Similar to *R. aquaticus*, but *basal leaves to 60 cm, broadly lanceolate*, margins undulate; *fruiting tepals kidney-shaped, about as long as wide, without teeth or tubercles*. Habitat Wet meadows, banks of rivers, streams and lakes, farmland; to 520 m. Dist. Native. Widespread in N England, Scotland. (NW Europe, Pyrenees.) Fls Jun–Aug.

Water Dock
Rumex hydrolapathum

Tall, robust, erect, much-branched, tufted perennial to 200 cm. Leaves *Basal leaves to 110 cm*. Flowers In dense inflorescence. Fruits *Fruiting tepals ± triangular, without teeth, each with elongated tubercle*. Habitat Margins of lakes, ponds, rivers, ditches, dykes and canal, fens, marshes; lowland. Dist. Native. Widespread in England, rare in rest of BI. (W, central and E Europe.) Fls Jul–Sep.

Greek Dock
Rumex cristatus

Tall, erect perennial to 200 cm. Leaves *Basal leaves to 35 cm, cordate*, margins somewhat undulate, *veins in middle of leaf at angle of 60-90° to midrib*. Flowers In dense inflorescence. Fruits Fruiting tepals with short teeth and 1 round, smooth tubercle. Habitat Waste ground, riverbanks. Dist. Introduced. Casual; especially London, Thames estuary. (Greece, Sicily.) Fls Jun–Jul.

Patience Dock
Rumex patientia

Tall, erect perennial to 200 cm. Similar to *R. cristatus*, but *basal leaves* to 45 cm, *not cordate, veins in middle of leaf at angle of 40-60° to midrib*; fruiting tepals broad, hardly toothed, with 1 small tubercle. Habitat Docks, wharves, riverbanks, breweries. Dist. Introduced in 1573 as a vegetable. Especially London, Bristol. (E and SE Europe.) Fls May–Jun.

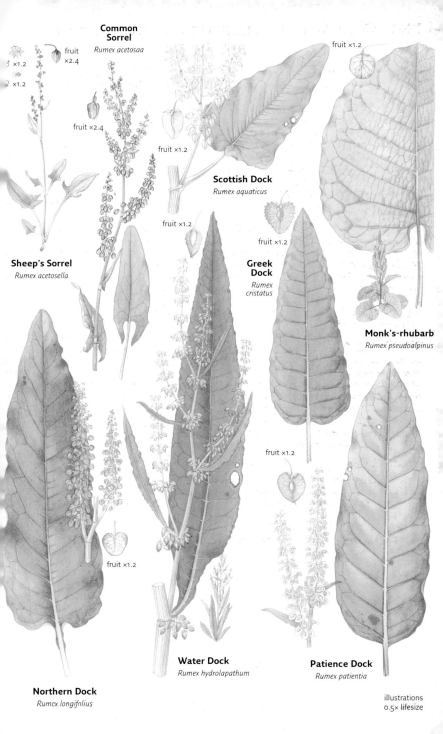

Common Sorrel
Rumex acetosaa

fruit ×2.4

×1.2

×1.2

fruit ×2.4

fruit ×1.2

fruit ×1.2

Scottish Dock
Rumex aquaticus

fruit ×1.2

fruit ×1.2

Greek Dock
Rumex cristatus

Sheep's Sorrel
Rumex acetosella

Monk's-rhubarb
Rumex pseudoalpinus

fruit ×1.2

fruit ×1.2

Northern Dock
Rumex longifolius

Water Dock
Rumex hydrolapathum

Patience Dock
Rumex patientia

illustrations
0.5× lifesize

Curled Dock
Rumex crispus

Tall, erect perennial to 100 cm. The commonest British dock, with 2 or 3 subspecies. LEAVES *Basal leaves narrow, almost parallel-sided, edges strongly undulate or crisped*, to 35 cm. FLOWERS In open inflorescence in ssp. *crispus*; in dense inflorescence in ssp. *littoreus*. FRUITS *Fruiting tepals triangular, without teeth*, variously 1–3 tubercles, unequal or subequal in size. In ssp. *crispus*, tubercles on fruiting tepals unequal or only 1, nuts ≤2.5 mm; in ssp. *littoreus*, usually 3 tubercles, ± equal, nuts ≥2.5 mm. HABITAT Cultivated soils, waste places, roadsides, hedge banks, water margins; ssp. *littoreus* found on coastal shingle, sand-dunes. To 845 m. DIST. Native. Throughout BI. (All Europe except extreme N.) FLS Jun–Oct.

Clustered Dock
Rumex conglomeratus

Erect, branched perennial to 60 cm. LEAVES To 30 cm, petiole often as long as leaf blade. FLOWERS In whorls, forming much-branched, *leafy inflorescence*, branches making wide angle of ≥30° with main stem. FRUITS *Fruiting tepals narrow, without teeth, each with oblong tubercle* (perianth with 3 tubercles). HABITAT Banks of ponds, ditches, streams and rivers, marshes, wet places where water stands in winter. DIST. Native. Common throughout BI except N Scotland. (Most of Europe except Scandinavia.) FLS Jul–Oct.

Wood Dock
Rumex sanguineus

Erect, sparsely branched perennial to 60 cm. Similar to *R. conglomeratus*, but *inflorescence* branches less wide-spreading (angle ≤30° to main stem), *not leafy to top*; fruiting tepals narrow, without teeth, *perianth with 1 tubercle*, rounded. HABITAT Woodland rides, clearings, roadside verges, hedgerows, waste ground; lowland to 350 m. DIST. Native. Common throughout BI except extreme N Scotland. (Most of Europe except Spain and Scandinavia.) FLS Jun–Jul.

Shore Dock
Rumex rupestris EN. *(B)

Erect, branched perennial to 70 cm. LEAVES Glaucous, oblong; blade longer than petiole. FLOWERS In whorls, forming inflorescence with long, erect branches that make acute angle with stem. FRUITS *Fruiting tepals oblong, without teeth, each with a large tubercle* (perianth with 3 tubercles). HABITAT Dune slacks, sandy shores, seepage lines on cliffs. DIST. Native. Very rare. SW England, Channel Is, Scilly Is. (W France, N Spain.) FLS Jun–Jul.

Fiddle Dock
Rumex pulche

Much-branched, spreading biennial or perennial to 40 cm. STEMS *Branches tangled, making wide angle with stem*. LEAVES To 10 cm, *distinctly constricted above base*. FLOWERS In whorls; inflorescence a tangle of wide-spreading branches. FRUITS *Fruiting tepals toothed, each with rough tubercle (perianth with 3 tubercles)*. HABITAT Well-drained, short coastal grassland, village greens, churchyards, roadsides. DIST. Native. S and SE England. (S and SW Europe.) FLS Jun–Jul.

Broad-leaved Dock
Rumex obtusifolius

Tall, robust perennial to 100 cm. LEAVES *Basal leaves* to 100 cm, broad, *strongly cordate at base, glabrous above, hairy below*. FLOWERS In open inflorescence leafy below. FRUITS *Fruiting tepals* triangular, *with prominent teeth, 1 with a tubercle (perianth with 1 tubercle)*. HABITAT Waste places, hedge banks, pastures, roadsides, water margins, disturbed ground. DIST. Native. Abundant throughout BI. (Most Europe except N Scandinavia.) FLS Jun–Oct.

Marsh Dock
Rumex palustris

Tall biennial or perennial to 60–100 cm. Whole plant turns yellowish brown at fruiting. LEAVES *Basal leaves narrow*, to 35 cm. FLOWERS In tight whorled clusters, forming inflorescence with long, spreading, incurved branches. FRUITS *Fruiting tepals >3 mm, teeth prominent, shorter than tepals*, all with tubercle (perianth with 3 tubercles). HABITAT Bare muddy margins of ponds, lakes, reservoirs and gravel pits that are dry in summer, wet in winter. DIST. Native. Local in E and S England. (W, central and E Europe.) FLS Jun–Aug.

Golden Dock
Rumex maritimus

Erect annual to perennial, to 40–100 cm. Very similar to *R. palustris*, but whole plant turning golden yellow at fruiting; branches shorter; *fruiting tepals shorter, <3 mm, teeth longer, finer, some longer than tepals*. HABITAT Margins of pools, meres, pits, ditches, marshy fields, where water stands in winter. (In spite of its specific name, it has no special preference for coastal sites.) DIST. Native. Local and scattered N to S Scotland. (W, central and E Europe.) FLS Jul–Sep.

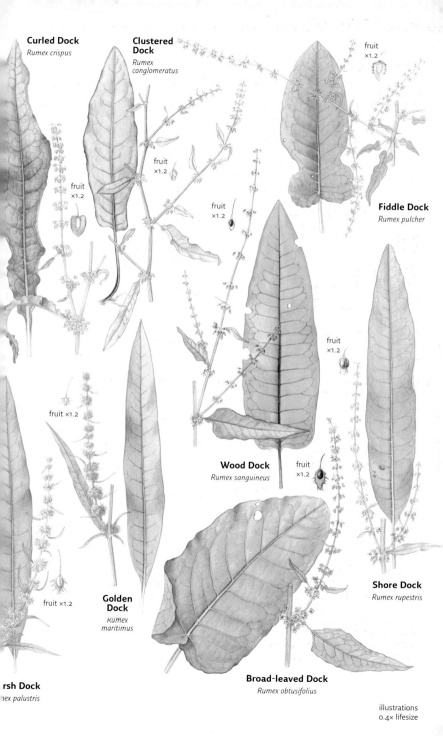

Curled Dock
Rumex crispus

Clustered Dock
Rumex conglomeratus

fruit
×1.2

fruit
×1.2

fruit
×1.2

Fiddle Dock
Rumex pulcher

fruit ×1.2

fruit ×1.2

Wood Dock
Rumex sanguineus

fruit
×1.2

Golden Dock
Rumex maritimus

fruit ×1.2

Shore Dock
Rumex rupestris

Broad-leaved Dock
Rumex obtusifolius

rsh Dock
nex palustris

illustrations
0.4× lifesize

PLUMBAGINACEAE Sea-lavenders and thrifts

Characteristic and unmistakable plants of coastal habitats, with purple or pink flowers. Leaves are all basal. Flowers are regular; 5 petals and sepals, fused below; 5 stamens; ovary superior.

Sea-lavenders *Limonium*

The small flowers of the sea-lavenders (*see* key on p.160) are arranged in 1–5-flowered spikelets, each of which has 3 scale-like bracts; the spikelets are further grouped together into spikes at the end of the branches of the inflorescence.

Common Sea-lavender   *Limonium vulgare*

Erect perennial to 40 cm. LEAVES Pinnately veined, tip with short recurved spine. FLOWERS In dense, rather flat-topped inflorescence, *branching from above middle of stem*; outer bract of flower clusters ≤3 mm, rounded on back; *anthers yellow*. HABITAT Intermediate zone of inter-tidal salt marsh. DIST. Native. Abundant on coasts of BI except extreme SW Wales, Scotland, Ireland. (W and S Europe.) FLS Jun–Oct.

Lax-flowered Sea-lavender   *Limonium humile*

Erect perennial to 40 cm. Similar to *L. vulgare* (with which it frequently hybridises, giving rise to intermediate individuals), but inflorescence more open, *branching from below middle of stem*; outer bract of flower clusters ≥3 mm, usually keeled; *anthers reddish. In cases of doubt, certain identification is possible only by microscopic examination of the pollen.* HABITAT Intermediate zone of inter-tidal salt marsh. DIST. Native. Coasts of BI as for *L. vulgare*, but also including SW Wales, Ireland. (W Europe.) FLS Jun–Oct.

Matted Sea-lavender   *Limonium bellidifolium*

Much-branched, prostrate to erect perennial, to 30 cm. STEMS *Flowering stems much branched, spreading, with numerous interwoven flowerless branches.* FLOWERS In dense, spreading inflorescence. HABITAT Sandy margins on upper levels of salt marshes. DIST. Native. Very local, on coasts of N Norfolk only. (Mediterranean.) FLS Jul–Aug.

Broad-leaved Sea-lavender   *Limonium auriculae-ursifolium*

Robust, erect perennial to 45 cm. LEAVES To 12 cm, broad, evergreen, glaucous, *with 5–7 veins*. FLOWERS In dense inflorescence, *outer bract ≤2.5 mm*, calyx 4–4.5 mm. HABITAT Coastal granite crevices. DIST. Native. Very rare, in a single locality on Jersey, Channel Is. (SW France, W Mediterranean.) FLS Jun–Sep.

Alderney Sea-lavender   *Limonium normannicum*

Erect evergreen perennial to 20 cm. Similar to *L. auriculae-ursifolium*, but inflorescence more dense, *outer bract 3–4 mm*. HABITAT Stabilised sand-dunes, coastal rocks. DIST. Native. Very rare, in single localities on Jersey and Alderney, Channel Is. (W France.) FLS Jun–Sep.

Rock Sea-lavender   *Limonium binervosum* *(N...)

Erect evergreen perennial to 30 cm. LEAVES *Narrowly obovate, with 1–3 veins*. FLOWERS In variable inflorescence. HABITAT Dry maritime cliffs, rocks, consolidated shingle. DIST. Native. Local on coasts of BI except NE England, Scotland. (Coasts of SW Europe.) FLS Jul–Sep. NOTE Extremely variable species; in the past it has been divided into several separate species and subspecies, but more recent work now considers this unjustified.

Thrift   *Armeria maritima*

Dense mat- or cushion-forming perennial with 2 subspecies: ssp. *maritima* and ssp. *elongata*. STEMS Flowering stems erect, unbranched, to 30 cm. Stems hairy in ssp. *maritima*, glabrous in ssp. *elongata*. LEAVES Linear, narrow, <2 mm wide, with 1 vein. FLOWERS In heads, 15–25 mm across; in ssp. *maritima*, sheath surrounding bracts ≤15 mm, outer bracts shorter than inner; in ssp. *elongata*, sheath surrounding bracts 12–25 mm, outer bracts as long as inner. HABITAT Ssp. *maritima* in middle zone of salt marshes, maritime rocks, cliffs; alpine habitats inland on mountain rocks, cliffs, moss heaths; metal-rich waste, salted road verges; to 1270 m. Ssp. *elongata* on sandy soil. DIST. Native. Ssp. *maritima* common on all coasts of BI and inland; ssp. *elongata* CR. in only 2 localities in Lincolnshire. (W Europe.) FLS Apr–Oct.

Jersey Thrift   *Armeria arenaria*

More robust than *A. maritima*. STEMS *Flowering stems to 60 cm, glabrous*. LEAVES ≥3 mm wide, 3-veined. FLOWERS In heads 20–30 mm across, sheath surrounding bracts 20–40 mm. HABITAT Stable coastal sand-dunes. DIST. Native. Jersey, Channel Is. (Central and S Europe.) FLS Jun–Sep.

Broad-leaved Sea-lavender
nium auriculae-ursifolium

Alderney Sea-lavender
Limonium normannicum

Matted Sea-lavender
Limonium bellidifolium

Rock Sea-lavender
Limonium binervosum

flowers ×1.2

flowers ×1.2

Thrift
Armeria maritima

Jersey Thrift
Armeria arenaria

Lax-flowered Sea-lavender
Limonium humile

anthers ×2.4

bracts ×1.2

L. vulgare

L. humile

flowers ×1.2

spikes ×0.6

Common Sea-lavender
Limonium vulgare

illustrations
0.6× lifesize

PAEONIACEAE Peonies

Peony
Paeonia mascula

Erect, clump-forming perennial to 60 cm. STEMS Unbranched. LEAVES Large, biternate, glabrous above, glaucous and finely pubescent beneath. FLOWERS 1 per stem, *c.*10 cm across; 5 sepals; 5–8 petals; stamens with red filaments, yellow anthers. HABITAT Limestone cliffs. DIST. Introduced. Naturalised on Steep Holm island, Bristol Channel, where it has been known since 1803. (Native of S Europe.) FLS Apr–May.

ELATINACEAE Waterworts

Small, submerged, glabrous aquatic annuals. Leaves opposite, entire. Flowers small, single, in axils of leaves; 3 or 4 sepals and petals; 6 or 8 stamens.

Petiole shorter than leaf blade; flowers stalked, 3 sepals and petals, 6 stamens   *Elatine hexandra*

Petiole longer than leaf blade; flowers ± sessile, 4 sepals and petals, 8 stamens   *Elatine hydropiper*

Six-stamened Waterwort
Elatine hexandra

HABITAT On bare mud or submerged in shallow margins of ponds or small lakes with infertile or nutrient-rich water; to 440 m. DIST. Native. Rare. Scattered throughout BI. (W Europe.) FLS Jul–Sep.

Eight-stamened Waterwort
Elatine hydropiper *(NI)

HABITAT Similar to *E. hexandra*, but more often confined to nutrient-rich waters; lowland. DIST. Native. Very rare. (Most of Europe.) FLS Jul–Aug.

CLUSIACEAE (HYPERICACEAE) St John's-worts

An easily recognised family of annuals or perennials or small shrubs with opposite leaves without stipules and yellow flowers. Leaves sessile, often with translucent or colourless glands; flowers regular; sepals and petals 5, often glandular; stamens numerous and grouped in bundles; ovary superior; fruit a capsule or berry-like. *See* key to *Hypericum* on p.160.

Rose-of-Sharon
Hypericum calycinum

Creeping, rhizomatous *evergreen shrub* to 60 cm. FLOWERS Single, on unbranched stems, *large, 7–8 cm across*; stamens shorter than petals; 5 *styles*, shorter than stamens. HABITAT Parks, roadsides, railway embankments; shade-tolerant. DIST. Introduced in 1676. Widely planted and naturalised throughout BI. (Native of Turkey, SE Bulgaria.) FLS Jun–Sep.

Tutsan
Hypericum androsaemum

Erect, branched, half-evergreen, shrubby, mildly aromatic perennial to 100 cm. STEMS With 2 raised lines. LEAVES Glabrous, to 10 cm. FLOWERS *c.*2 cm across, in few-flowered inflorescence; *sepals unequal; stamens as long as petals*; styles shorter than stamens. FRUITS Red, turning black. HABITAT Damp deciduous woodland, hedge banks, grikes in limestone pavement. DIST. Native. Widely distributed throughout W and S BI; frequently naturalised outside native range. (W and S Europe.) FLS Jun–Aug.

Stinking Tutsan
Hypericum hircinum

Bushy shrub. Similar to *H. androsaemum*, but stems with 4 ridges; *leaves* to 6 cm and *smelling strongly of goats when crushed; flowers* c.3 cm across, sepals shorter than petals, *stamens longer than petals*, styles longer than stamens. DIST. Introduced *c.*1640. Sometimes planted in woodland and naturalised in a few localities. (C and E Mediterranean.) FLS May–Aug.

Perforate St John's-wort
Hypericum perforatum

Erect, glabrous, rhizomatous perennial to 90 cm. STEMS With 2 raised lines. LEAVES To 2 cm, with abundant small yellowish translucent glandular dots (visible when held up to light). FLOWERS c.2 cm across; *sepals glandular, shorter than petals*. HABITAT Rough grassland, meadows, road verges, hedge banks, open woodland. DIST. Native. Common throughout BI except extreme N Scotland. (All Europe except extreme N.) FLS Jun–Sep.

Imperforate St John's-wort
Hypericum maculatum

Erect, glabrous, rhizomatous perennial to 60 cm. STEMS With 4 raised lines. LEAVES Narrowed to base, not clasping stem. FLOWERS Bright yellow, *c.*2 cm across, *petals* ≥2× *as long as sepals*, sepals and petals with black glands. HABITAT Damp wood margins, rough grassland, hedge banks, roadsides; lowland to 320 m. DIST. Native. Ssp. *maculatum* rare, in scattered localities in Scotland only; ssp. *obtusiusculum* local throughout most of BI. (Central and N Europe.) FLS Jun–Aug.

Ssp. *maculatum* sparsely branched, branches making angle of 30° with stem; leaves without transparent glands; sepals 2–3 mm wide, tip entire.

Ssp. *obtusiusculum* more branched, branches making angle of *c.*50° with main stem; leaves usually with transparent glands; sepals 1.2–2 mm wide, tip toothed.

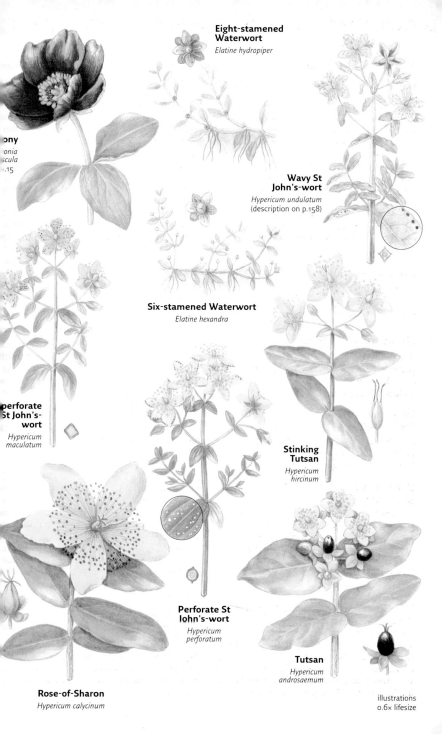

Eight-stamened Waterwort
Elatine hydropiper

Wavy St John's-wort
Hypericum undulatum
(description on p.158)

ony
onia
scula
.15

Six-stamened Waterwort
Elatine hexandra

perforate St John's-wort
Hypericum maculatum

Stinking Tutsan
Hypericum hircinum

Perforate St John's-wort
Hypericum perforatum

Tutsan
Hypericum androsaemum

Rose-of-Sharon
Hypericum calycinum

illustrations
0.6× lifesize

Wavy St John's-wort
Hypericum undulatum

[*See* illustration previous page.] Erect, glabrous, stoloniferous or rhizomatous perennial to 60 cm. STEMS Square in section, narrowly winged. LEAVES To 2 cm, bases partly clasping stem, with distinctly wavy edges and numerous translucent glandular dots. FLOWERS *c*.2 cm across, petals markedly longer than sepals. HABITAT Boggy and marshy patches along stream sides on acid soils. DIST. Native. Very local. SW England, W Wales. (SW Europe.) FLS Aug–Sep.

Square-stalked St John's-wort
Hypericum tetrapterum

Erect stoloniferous glabrous perennial to 70 cm. STEMS *Square in section, angles winged.* LEAVES To 2 cm, half-clasping stem, with small translucent glands. FLOWERS *Pale yellow, c.1 cm across; sepals c.⅔ length of petals.* HABITAT Damp grassland, woodland clearings, road verges, pond and stream margins; lowland to 380 m. DIST. Native. Frequent throughout BI except extreme N Scotland. (All Europe.) FLS Jun–Sep.

Trailing St John's-wort
Hypericum humifusum

Slender, prostrate, glabrous perennial to 20 cm. STEMS With 2 raised lines. LEAVES Elliptic, to 1 cm, with translucent glands. FLOWERS *c*.1 cm across; *petals ≤2× as long as sepals*; sepals unequal, glandular. HABITAT Open patches in woodland paths and clearings, heaths, moors, on acid soils; lowland to 530 m. DIST. Native. Most of BI. (W and central Europe.) FLS Jun–Sep.

Toadflax-leaved St John's-wort
Hypericum linariifolium

Prostrate to erect glabrous perennial, to 50 cm. STEMS Without lines, often reddish. LEAVES *Linear, to 2.5 cm, margins revolute*, hardly glandular. FLOWERS *c*.1 cm across; petals ≥2× as long as sepals; *sepals ± equal, fringed with stalked black glands.* HABITAT Sparse vegetation on steep, rocky, warm, SW-facing slopes on acid soils. DIST. Native. Very rare. S Devon, W Wales, Channel Is. (SW Europe.) FLS Jun–Jul.

Slender St John's-wort
Hypericum pulchrum

Erect, glabrous perennial to 60 cm. STEMS *Without raised lines.* LEAVES To 1 cm, with transparent glands, *broadly cordate, their bases clasping and meeting across*

stem. FLOWERS 1.5 cm across, petals red-tinged, sepals fringed with stalked black glands. HABITAT Grassy heaths, commons, woodland clearings, rides, on well-drained acid soils; to 820 m. DIST. Native. Throughout BI. (W and central Europe.) FLS Jun–Aug.

Hairy St John's-wort
Hypericum hirsutum *(●)

Erect, pubescent, little-branched perennial to 100 cm. STEMS *Without raised lines.* FLOWERS *c*.1.5 cm across, in many-flowered inflorescence; petals pale yellow, sepals ⅓ length of petals, fringed with stalked black glands. HABITAT Rough grassland, scrub, open woodland, chiefly on calcareous soils. DIST. Native. Most of BI, but rare or absent in N Scotland and W. (N and central Europe.) FLS Jul–Aug.

Pale St John's-wort
Hypericum montanum

Erect, ± glabrous, usually unbranched perennial to 80 cm. STEM *Without raised lines.* LEAVES Ovate, clasping, *thinly hairy and with fringe of black glands beneath.* FLOWERS 1–1.5 cm across, in dense inflorescence; petals pale yellow; *sepals with numerous black-stalked glands.* HABITAT Woodlands, scrub, hedge banks, rough grassland, on calcareous soils to 330 m. DIST. Native. Local and declining. Scattered throughout England, Wales. (Most of Europe except N.) FLS Jun–Aug.

Marsh St John's-wort
Hypericum elodes

Prostrate to erect, *stoloniferous, densely hairy perennial*, to 30 cm. STEMS *Without raised lines*, rooting at nodes. LEAVES *Rounded, ± clasping.* FLOWERS *c*.1.5 cm across, in few-flowered inflorescence; *sepals with stalked red glandular teeth.* HABITAT Margins of acid pools, streams, flushes on heaths, bogs. DIST. Native. Local and declining. W BI, S England; scattered elsewhere. (W Europe.) FLS Jun–Sep.

Irish St John's-wort
Hypericum canadense *(●)

Slender, erect, glabrous annual or perennial to 20 cm. STEMS *Square in section.* LEAVES To 8 mm, with translucent glands. FLOWERS *Small, <10 mm across; petals deep yellow, widely separated; sepals without black glands.* HABITAT Wet peaty, acid grazed grassland, flushes, stream sides. DIST. Introduced (native of North America; it is not known how it reached W Europe). In only 2 sites in W Ireland (W Galway, W Cork). (France.) FLS Jul–Aug.

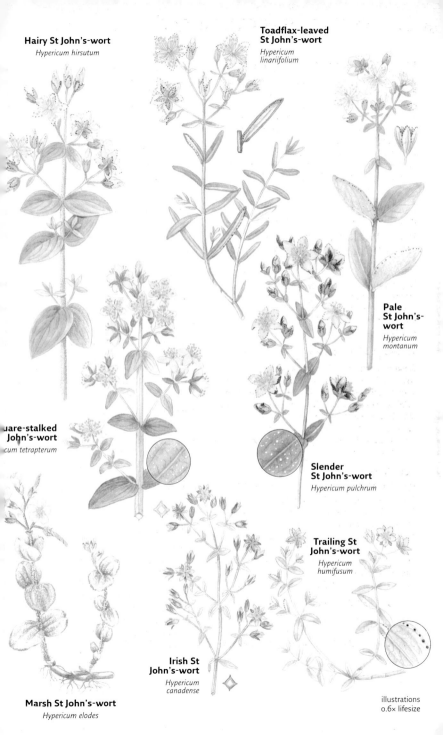

Hairy St John's-wort
Hypericum hirsutum

Toadflax-leaved St John's-wort
Hypericum linariifolium

Pale St John's-wort
Hypericum montanum

uare-stalked John's-wort
cum tetrapterum

Slender St John's-wort
Hypericum pulchrum

Trailing St John's-wort
Hypericum humifusum

Irish St John's-wort
Hypericum canadense

Marsh St John's-wort
Hypericum elodes

illustrations
0.6× lifesize

	if	then
1	▷ Leaves pinnately veined	*L. vulgare*, *L. humile* (p.154)
	▷ Leaves not pinnately veined, veins (1–7) arising separately from petiole	Go to ▷ **2**
2	▷ Inflorescence with numerous bare, zigzag, flowerless branches	*L. bellidifolium* (p.154)
	▷ Inflorescence without bare, flowerless branches	Go to ▷ **3**
3	▷ Leaves linear-oblong with 1–3 obvious veins	*L. binervosum* (p.154)
	▷ Leaves broadly obovate with 5–7 obvious veins	*L. auriculae-ursifolium*, *L. normannicum* (p.154)

(illustrations: spikelet with 3 bracts, spike)

Key to St John's-wort *Hypericum*

	if	then
1	▷ Plant ± shrubby; stems woody	Go to ▷ **10**
	▷ Plant not shrubby; stems not woody or only at base	Go to ▷ **2**
2	▷ Stems glabrous; leaves glabrous or sparingly hairy beneath	Go to ▷ **3**
	▷ Stems and leaves conspicuously hairy	Go to ▷ **9**
3	▷ Stems with 2 ridges	Go to ▷ **4**
	▷ Stems with 4 ridges, square in section	Go to ▷ **5**
	▷ Stems smooth, with no ridges	Go to ▷ **8**
4	▷ Stems slender, prostrate; petals <2× as long as sepals	*H. humifusum* (p.158)
	▷ Flowering stems erect; petals ≥2× as long as sepals:	
	▷ Sepals entire (common)	*H. perforatum* (p.156)
	▷ Sepals fringed with black glands (rare, Wales, SW)	*H. linariifolium* (p.158)
5	▷ Petals <2× as long as sepals	Go to ▷ **6**
	▷ Petals >2–3× as long as sepals	Go to ▷ **7**
6	▷ Stems 30–70 cm, firm; leaves with black glandular dots; petals pale yellow, flowers ≥10 mm across	*H. tetrapterum* (p.158)
	▷ Stems ≤20 cm, slender; leaves without black glandular dots; petals bright yellow, flowers <10 mm across	*H. canadense* (p.158)

flower

	if	then
7	▷ Leaves narrowed to base, translucent glands few or absent; sepals blunt	*H. maculatum* (p.156)
	▷ Leaves ± clasping stem, translucent glands abundant, margins of leaves wavy; sepals acute	*H. undulatum* (p.156)
8	▷ Leaves 0.5–1 cm, glabrous beneath	*H. pulchrum* (p.158)
	▷ Leaves 3–5 cm, sparsely hairy and with marginal row of black glands beneath	*H. montanum* (p.158)
9	▷ Plant erect; leaves ovate, downy; edge of sepals with black glands (dry grassland, scrub)	*H. hirsutum* (p.158)
	▷ Bog plant, rooting at nodes; leaves rounded, woolly; edge of sepals with red glands	*H. elodes* (p.158)
10	▷ Plant rhizomatous; 5 styles, petals >20 mm	*H. calycinum* (p.156)
	▷ Plant not rhizomatous; 3 styles, petals <20 mm:	
	▷ Petals >15 mm, leaves smelling of goats when crushed	*H. hircinum* (p.156)
	▷ Petals <15 mm; leaves not smelling of goats	*H. androsaemum* (p.156)

Key to Malvaceae Mallows

	if	then
1	▷ Epicalyx of 3 segments	Go to ▷ **2**
	▷ Epicalyx of 6–9 segments	*Althaea* (p.162)
2	▷ Epicalyx segments free to base	Go to ▷ **3** *Malva*
	▷ Epicalyx segments joined below	*Lavatera* (p.162)
3	▷ Stem leaves deeply divided into narrow lobes	*M. moschata* (p.162)
	▷ Stem leaves ± circular, palmately lobed or bluntly toothed	Go to ▷ **4**
4	▷ Petals 20–45 mm, 2–4× as long as sepals	*M. sylvestris* (p.162)
	▷ Petals 4–13 mm, ≤2× as long as sepals	Go to ▷ **5**
5	▷ Flowers 1.8–2.5 cm across, epicalyx ≤⅔ as long as calyx, petals ≥2× as long as sepals	*M. neglecta* (p.162)
	▷ Flowers *c.*0.5 cm across, epicalyx about as long as calyx, petals hardly longer than sepals	*M. pusilla* (p.162)

MALVACEAE Mallows

Herbs or shrubs, usually with showy pink or purplish flowers (*see* key on p.161). Leaves are alternate, often palmately lobed. Flowers are in racemes or solitary in axils of leaves, regular and with an epicalyx of 3 to several sepal-like segments below calyx (looks like an outer ring of sepals); 5 sepals; 5 petals; free; numerous stamens, the filaments joined below into a tube that divides above into branches; ovary superior. Fruit is a capsule or consists of a group of nutlets.

Musk-mallow   *Malva moschata*

Erect, branched, sparsely hairy perennial to 80 cm. LEAVES Basal leaves kidney-shaped, 3-lobed; *stem leaves deeply divided, with narrow linear lobes.* FLOWERS 3–6 cm across; epicalyx ⅙ as long as calyx; petals 3× as long as sepals. HABITAT Roadsides, hedge banks, pastures, field borders, on well-drained soils; lowland to 305 m. DIST. Native in England, Wales; introduced in Scotland, Ireland. (Most of Europe.) FLS Jul–Aug.

Common Mallow   *Malva sylvestris*

Prostrate to erect, sparsely hairy perennial, to 100 cm. LEAVES Basal leaves 5–10 cm across. FLOWERS 2.5–4 cm across; epicalyx ⅓ as long as calyx; *petals 2–4× as long as sepals.* HABITAT Roadsides, banks, waste ground, on well-drained soils. DIST. Archaeophyte. Common in most of BI except N Scotland. (All Europe.) FLS Jun–Sep.

Small Mallow   *Malva pusilla*

Prostrate to erect annual herb. Similar to *M. neglecta*, but flowers only *c.5 mm across, epicalyx about as long as calyx, petals hardly longer than sepals.* HABITAT Casual of waste ground, rubbish tips, coastal habitats. DIST. Introduced. Rare. Scattered throughout BI. (N and central Europe.) FLS Jun–Sep.

Dwarf Mallow   *Malva neglecta*

Prostrate to erect, densely hairy annual or biennial, to 60 cm. LEAVES Basal leaves 4–7 cm across. FLOWERS 1.8–2.5 cm across, epicalyx ≤⅓ as long as calyx, *petals ≥2× as long as sepals.* HABITAT Grassy banks, roadsides, rough ground, coastal drift lines, on dry soils. DIST. Archaeophyte. Throughout BI, but rare in Scotland, Ireland. (Most of Europe.) FLS Jun–Sep.

Tree-mallow   *Lavatera arborea*

Tall, hairy shrub- or tree-like biennial to 300 cm. LEAVES To 20 cm across. FLOWERS 3–4 cm across; *epicalyx joined to about halfway, longer than calyx,* enlarging in fruit; petals overlapping, 2–3× as long as sepals. HABITAT Cliffs, rocks, waste ground, close to sea. DIST. Native in Ireland and W coast of BI from N Wales to I of Wight; introduced elsewhere except N Scotland. (Mediterranean, SW Europe.) FLS Jul–Sep.

Smaller Tree-mallow   *Lavatera cretica*

Prostrate to erect, pubescent annual or biennial, to 150 cm. FLOWERS *Epicalyx slightly shorter than calyx* not enlarging in fruit; petals 2–3× as long as sepals, not overlapping. HABITAT Disturbed ground, old quarries, roadsides, hedge banks. DIST. Introduced. Very rare. Scilly Is, W Cornwall, Kent, Channel Is (SW Europe, Mediterranean.) FLS Jun–Jul.

Marsh-mallow   *Althaea officinalis*

Erect, softly downy, velvety perennial to 120 cm. LEAVES Lower leaves 3–8 cm across. FLOWERS 2.5–4 cm across, stalks shorter than leaves; 6–9 epicalyx lobes; petals 2–3× as long as sepals. HABITAT Brackish marshes, banks of coastal drainage dykes, ditches. DIST. Native. Local, declining. S England from Wash to S Wales. (Central and S Europe.) FLS Aug–Sep.

Rough Marsh-mallow   *Althaea hirsuta* *(B

Prostrate to ascending, roughly hairy annual or biennial, to 60 cm. LEAVES Lower leaves 2–4 cm across. FLOWERS 2.5 cm across, stalks longer than leaves; petals 12–16 mm, longer than sepals. HABITAT Field borders, scrub, wood margins. DIST. Introduced. Very rare. Scattered in lowland England. (All Europe except N.) FLS Jun–Jul.

Common Mallow
Malva sylvestris

Musk-mallow
Malva moschata

Small Mallow
Malva pusilla

Dwarf Mallow
Malva neglecta

Rough Marsh-mallow
Althaea hirsuta

Tree-mallow
Lavatera arborea

Marsh-mallow
Althaea officinalis

Smaller Tree-mallow
Lavatera cretica

illustrations
0.6× lifesize

TILIACEAE Limes

Limes are large deciduous trees with fragrant, actinomorphic (star-shaped), bisexual insect-pollinated flowers. Inflorescence stalk is fused for about ⅓ its length to a large, thin, oblong bract that is shed with fruit. Flowers have 5 free sepals and petals, and numerous stamens in 5 bundles. Fruits are ovoid and nut-like.

The 2 native British species are variable and their widely planted hybrid is also very variable. Identification should be made only on mature shoots from the exposed outside of canopy. Hairiness of leaves, form of inflorescence and details of fruit are all important.

Leaves 60–120 mm across, upper surface usually sparsely hairy, lower surface green, at least main veins hairy, lateral veins prominent, petiole <⅓ length of lamina; inflorescence with 1–5 flowers, hanging below leaves; fruits 5-ribbed   *Tilia platyphyllos*

Leaves 35–70 mm across, cordate, upper surface glabrous, lower surface glaucous and glabrous except for patches of rust-coloured hairs in axils of main veins, lateral veins obscure, petiole ⅔ length of lamina; inflorescence with 4–10 flowers, held above leaves; fruit not, or obscurely, ribbed   *T. cordata*

Leaves 60–100 mm across, glabrous except for tufts of pale hairs in axils of main veins beneath, lateral veins prominent; inflorescence with 4–10 flowers, hanging below leaves; fruits slightly ribbed   *T. × vulgaris*

Large-leaved Lime   *Tilia platyphyllos*

Large tree to 40 m. HABITAT Old mixed deciduous woodland, often as coppice stools, usually on calcareous soils; to 400 m. Widely planted in parks, gardens, roadsides. DIST. Native. Local in England, Wales. (Central and SE Europe.) FLS Jun.

Small-leaved Lime   *Tilia cordata*

Large tree to 35 m. HABITAT Mixed deciduous woodland, wooded cliffs, on a range of fertile soils; often occurs as ancient coppice stools. Lowland to 600 m. Widely planted as amenity tree. DIST. Native. Local throughout BI, but rare in Scotland, Ireland. (Central and E Europe.) FLS Jul.

Lime   *Tilia × vulgaris*

Tall tree to 45 m. Lower part of trunk with large bosses and epicormic growth. HABITAT Woods, parks, roadsides, along urban streets. DIST. Very rare as a native tree alongside both parents. Widely and commonly planted throughout BI. (All Europe.) FLS Jul.

SARRACENIACEAE Pitcherplants

Pitcherplant   *Sarracenia purpurea*

Distinctive low-growing, insectivorous perennial. LEAVES Lower leaves modified into pitchers, 10–15 cm. FLOWERS Solitary, actinomorphic, bisexual, *c*.5 cm across; stalk to 40 cm; 5 sepals and petals. DIST. Introduced (native of North America). First planted in bogs in central Ireland in 1906, now locally abundant in Roscommon, W Meath; scattered elsewhere in BI. FLS Jun.

DROSERACEAE Sundews

Slender, insectivorous perennial bog plants. Leaves in a basal rosette, densely glandular and fringed with long glandular hairs. Flowers actinomorphic, bisexual; 4–8 sepals and petals; as many stamens as petals. Flowers of British species frequently don't open, but self-pollinate in bud.

Leaves rounded, shaped like a table-tennis bat
          D. rotundifolia

Leaves distinctly longer than broad

  Flower stalk straight, much
  longer than leaves, apparently
  arising from centre of rosette   *D. anglica*

  Flower stalk curved at base,
  slightly longer than leaves, arising
  laterally from below rosette   *D. intermedia*

Round-leaved Sundew   *Drosera rotundifolia*

HABITAT Bare acid peat, among *Sphagnum*, wet heaths, bogs, moors, especially margins of bog pools; to 700 m. DIST. Native. Throughout BI where suitable habitats occur. (All Europe except Mediterranean.) FLS Jun–Aug.

Great Sundew   *Drosera anglica*

HABITAT Wetter parts of acid *Sphagnum* bogs, stony lakeshores; lowland. DIST. Native. Widespread in W and NW Scotland, W Ireland; rare, scattered, declining elsewhere. (All Europe except Mediterranean.)

Oblong-leaved Sundew   *Drosera intermedia*

HABITAT Wet heaths, bogs; drier habitats than *D. rotundifolia* and *D. anglica*, most often on bare peat. Lowland to 335 m. DIST. Native. Local and declining. Scattered throughout BI in suitable habitats. (W and central Europe.) FLS Jun–Aug.

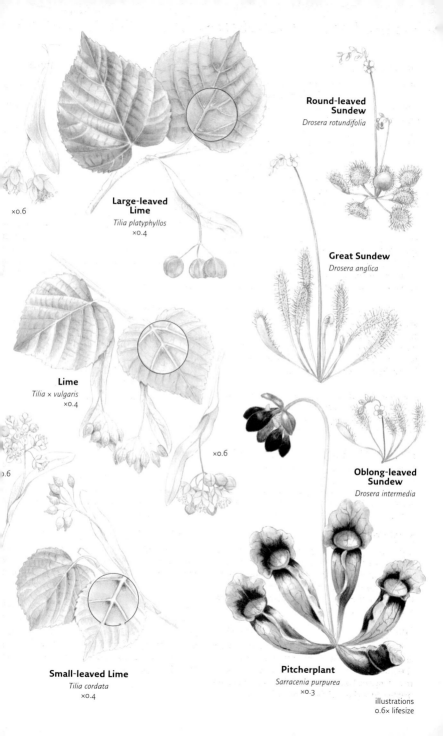

×0.6

Large-leaved Lime
Tilia platyphyllos
×0.4

Round-leaved Sundew
Drosera rotundifolia

Great Sundew
Drosera anglica

Lime
Tilia × vulgaris
×0.4

×0.6

×0.6

Oblong-leaved Sundew
Drosera intermedia

Small-leaved Lime
Tilia cordata
×0.4

Pitcherplant
Sarracenia purpurea
×0.3

illustrations
0.6× lifesize

CISTACEAE Rock-roses

Shrubs or herbs. Leaves simple, usually opposite. Flowers bisexual, actinomorphic; 5 sepals and petals, numerous stamens, ovary superior, 3 or 5 stigmas.

Spotted Rock-rose   *Tuberaria guttata* *

Erect, simple or branched, hairy *annual* to 30 cm. LEAVES Basal leaves in a rosette, upper stem leaves with narrow stipules. FLOWERS 8–12 mm across, sepals unequal, petals pale yellow with red spot at base. HABITAT Bare patches among gorse, heather on exposed maritime heath, rocky moorland near sea. DIST. Native. Very rare. Anglesey, Lleyn Peninsula, W Ireland, Channel Is. (SW Europe, Mediterranean.) FLS May–Aug.

Common Rock-rose   *Helianthemum nummularium* *(R)

Creeping woody *perennial* to 30 cm. LEAVES Sparsely hairy above, densely white-pubescent beneath; stipules narrow, 2× as long as petiole. FLOWERS 2–2.5 cm across; sepals unequal, petals *bright yellow*; style ± straight. HABITAT Short, grazed calcareous grassland, cliffs, rocks, scree; to 640 m. DIST. Native. Throughout most of BI except extreme SW England, NW Scotland; very rare in Ireland. (Most of Europe.) FLS Jun–Sep.

White Rock-rose   *Helianthemum apenninum* VU.

Creeping woody *perennial* to 30 cm. LEAVES With dense grey hairs; stipules scarcely longer than petiole. FLOWERS *White*. HABITAT Dry calcareous cliff grassland on S- and SW-facing slopes. DIST. Native. Very rare. Only on Brean Down (N Somerset) and Berry Head (S Devon). (S and W Europe.) FLS May–Jul.

Hoary Rock-rose   *Helianthemum oelandicum*

Creeping woody *perennial* to 20 cm. LEAVES 2–12 mm, green, with dense grey-white felt beneath; stipules absent. FLOWERS *Bright yellow* 1–1.5 cm across, style bent in middle. HABITAT Thin, dry, open limestone turf, rocks, cliffs. DIST. Native (ssp. *levigatum* VU. is endemic). Rare, very local. Wales, NW England (ssp. *incanum*), W Ireland (ssp. *piloselloides*), Cronkley Fell (NW Yorkshire; ssp. *levigatum*). (W, central and S Europe.) FLS May–Jul.

VIOLACEAE Violets and pansies

Annuals or perennials with alternate stalked leaves that have stipules (*see* key on p.170). Flowers solitary, irregular; 5 sepals with short, backward-pointing lobes; 5 petals, the lower with a backward-pointing spur. Fruits are a 3-valved capsule.

Sweet Violet   *Viola odorata*

Perennial with long, creeping stolons, rooting at ends. Leaves and flower stalks emerge from basal tuft. LEAVES Broadly ovate, deeply cordate, rounded at tip, blades thinly hairy, petioles with short reflexed hairs. FLOWERS *c.*15 mm, *sweet-scented; sepals blunt; petals rich violet or white, with lilac spur.* HABITAT Wood margins, scrub, shady hedge banks, chiefly on calcareous soils. DIST. Native in England, Wales, SE Ireland; naturalised elsewhere. (Most of Europe.) FLS Feb–Apr. NOTE Our only fragrant violet, with many garden cultivars, including ones with pink and apricot flowers.

Hairy Violet   *Viola hirta* *(R)

Perennial. Similar to *V. odorata*, but *without stolons*; leaves narrower, tips not rounded, hairs on petioles spreading; *flowers pale blue-violet, not fragrant.* HABITAT Open woodland, wood margins, scrub, grassland on calcareous soils. DIST. Native. N to central Scotland; rare in Ireland. (W, central and E Europe.) FLS Apr–May. NOTE Small plants with narrow petals and short spurs are sometimes separated as ssp. *calcarea* and are confined to calcareous grassland.

Teesdale Violet   *Viola rupestris*

Small, pubescent, tufted perennial, to 4 cm when in flower, with a central non-flowering rosette and leafy flowering stems. LEAVES Blades 5–10 mm, kidney-shaped; petioles pubescent. FLOWERS Pale blue-violet, spur stout. *Sepals* acute. FRUITS Pubescent capsule. HABITAT Open, mossy, sheep-grazed calcareous turf and bare ground; to 600 m. DIST. Native. Very rare. Yorkshire, Durham, Cumbria. (N and alpine Europe.) FLS May.

Common Dog-violet   *Viola riviniana*

Glabrous or slightly pubescent perennial, to 20 cm when in flower, *with a central non-flowering rosette and leafy flowering shoots.* Our commonest violet. LEAVES Cordate; stipules narrow, fringed, shorter than glabrous petiole. FLOWERS 14–22 mm; *spur white or yellowish, paler than petals, notched at tip; sepals 7–12 mm, lobes >1.5 mm.* FRUITS Glabrous capsule. HABITAT Woodland, hedge banks, downland, grass heaths, old pasture, mountain grassland to 1020 m. DIST. Native. Common throughout BI (All Europe.) FLS Apr–Jun.

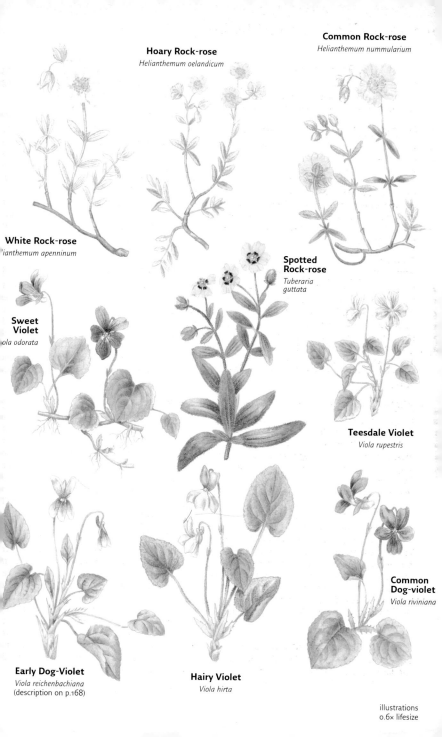

Common Rock-rose
Helianthemum nummularium

Hoary Rock-rose
Helianthemum oelandicum

White Rock-rose
ianthemum apenninum

Spotted Rock-rose
Tuberaria guttata

Sweet Violet
ola odorata

Teesdale Violet
Viola rupestris

Early Dog-Violet
Viola reichenbachiana
(description on p.168)

Hairy Violet
Viola hirta

Common Dog-violet
Viola riviniana

illustrations
0.6× lifesize

Early Dog-Violet
Viola reichenbachiana

[*See* illustration previous page.] Similar to *V. riviniana*, but *sepal lobes smaller, <1.5 mm; spur darker than petals, not notched at tip.* HABITAT Hedge banks, deciduous woodland, avoiding acid soils. DIST. Native. Locally abundant as far N as S Scotland. (All Europe except N.) FLS Mar–May.

Heath Dog-violet
Viola canina

Glabrous or sparsely pubescent perennial to 30 cm. STEMS Prostrate to erect; *no central non-flowering rosette.* LEAVES *Ovate,* truncate or shallowly cordate at base; stipules to ≤⅓ length of glabrous petiole, teeth triangular. FLOWERS 7–18 mm, *blue;* spur yellowish, >2× as long as sepal lobes. FRUITS Glabrous capsule. HABITAT Grassy heaths, commons, coastal dunes, fens; to 370 m. DIST. Native. Local and scattered throughout BI. (All Europe except Mediterranean.) FLS Apr–Jun. NOTE Ssp. *montana* EN., with stipules of middle leaves ≤⅓ as long as petiole, is a very rare plant of East Anglian fens.

Pale Dog-Violet
Viola lactea VU. *(R)

Almost glabrous perennial to 20 cm. STEMS Prostrate to erect; no central non-flowering rosette. LEAVES *Narrowly ovate to lanceolate,* middle stipules *c.⅓* as long as petioles, upper stipules coarsely toothed, longer than or as long as petioles. FLOWERS 12–20 mm, pale *greyish violet;* spur *c.*2× as long as sepal lobes. FRUITS Glabrous capsule. HABITAT Short grassy turf of dry acid heaths. DIST. Native. Local, declining. S and SW England; scattered in Ireland. (SW Europe.) FLS May–Jun.

Fen Violet
Viola persicifolia EN. *(B, NI)

Almost glabrous perennial to 25 cm, with long, creeping rhizomes. STEMS *Produced at intervals from rhizomes;* no non-flowering central rosettes. LEAVES 2–4 cm, *broadly lanceolate,* truncate or shallowly cordate at base; stipules *c.⅓* as long as petiole, weakly toothed. FLOWERS 10–15 mm, *bluish white, spur shorter than or equal to sepal lobes.* FRUITS Glabrous capsule. HABITAT Fresh peat cuttings in East Anglia; wet, grassy limestone hollows at edge of turloughs in Ireland. DIST. Native. Very rare. East Anglian fens and W Ireland only. (Central and E Europe.) FLS May–Jun.

Marsh Violet
Viola palustris

Perennial with long, creeping rhizomes that produce leaves and flowers at nodes. STEMS No aerial stems. LEAVES *1–4 cm wide, rounded or kidney-shaped, cordate.* FLOWERS 10–15 mm, sepals blunt, petals lilac with dark veins. FRUITS Glabrous capsule. HABITAT Acid bogs, marshes, wet woods, woodland flushes. DIST. Native. Throughout BI. (All Europe except Mediterranean.) FLS Apr–Jul. NOTE Ssp. *juressii,* with narrower leaves and hairy petioles, occurs in similar habitats in SW England and W Wales.

Mountain Pansy
Viola lutea

Perennial with creeping rhizomes. STEMS Aerial stems to 20 cm. LEAVES Stipules palmately lobed, terminal segment scarcely wider than others. FLOWERS *Large, 2–3.5 cm;* bright yellow or violet, or a combination of both; spur 2–3× *as long as sepal lobes;* stalks long, to 9 cm. HABITAT Short montane grassland, often on leached soils overlying limestone; to 1050 m. DIST. Native. Widespread in upland Britain; very rare in Ireland. (W and central Europe.) FLS May–Aug.

Wild Pansy
Viola tricolor

Much-branched, glabrous annual (ssp. *tricolor*) or tufted perennial (ssp. *curtisii*). LEAVES *Stipules ± palmately lobed, middle lobe lanceolate, entire, not leaf-like.* FLOWERS 1.5–2.5 cm (<2 cm in ssp. *curtisii*) flat; *petals longer than sepals,* yellow (ssp. *curtisii*), or blue-violet or a combination of both (ssp. *tricolor*) *spur longer than or as long as sepal lobes;* stalks 2–8 cm. HABITAT Ssp. *tricolor* on arable land, rough grassland, waste ground; ssp. *curtisii* on sand-dunes and coastal grassland. DIST. Native. Ssp. *tricolor* throughout BI; ssp. *curtisii* on N and W coasts, inland East Anglia. (Ssp. *tricolor* throughout Europe; ssp. *curtisii* on Baltic and North Sea coasts.) FLS Apr–Sep.

Field Pansy
Viola arvensis

Much-branched annual. Similar to *V. tricolor,* but *mid-lobe of stipules ovate, toothed and leaf-like;* flowers smaller, 8–20 mm, flat, *petals shorter than sepals,* usually yellow-cream. HABITAT Arable fields, waste ground, on neutral and calcareous soils. DIST. Archaeophyte. Common throughout most of BI but rare in N Scotland, W Ireland. (Most of Europe except E Mediterranean.) FLS Apr–Oct.

Dwarf Pansy
Viola kitaibeliana

Small, pubescent, little-branched annual to 10 cm. LEAVES Lower stipules with few lateral lobes and large, broad, toothed mid-lobes. FLOWERS Concave *very small, c.5 mm; petals c.⅓ length of sepals.* HABITAT Disturbed ground on sand-dunes, dune turf; weed of sandy arable fields. DIST. Native. Very rare, in Scilly Is and Channel Is only. (W France.) FLS Apr–Jul.

Fen Violet
Viola persicifolia

Pale Dog-violet
Viola lactea

Heath Dog-violet
Viola canina

Marsh Violet
Viola palustris

Dwarf Pansy
Viola kitaibeliana

Wild Pansy
Viola tricolor

Mountain Pansy
Viola lutea

Field Pansy
Viola arvensis

illustrations
0.6× lifesize

		if	**then**
1	▷	Stipules entire, finely toothed; 2 lateral petals spreading horizontally; tip of style not thickened, often hooked (violets)	Go to ▷ **2**
	▷	Stipules leaf-like, deeply lobed; lateral petals erect; tip of style swollen, globose (pansies)	Go to ▷ **10**
2	▷	Leaves orbicular, rounded at tip; style straight, with oblique tip	*Viola palustris* (p.168)
	▷	Leaves acute to blunt at tip; style hooked or beaked at tip	Go to ▷ **3**
3	▷	Leaves and capsules glabrous	Go to ▷ **4**
	▷	Leaves and capsules hairy	Go to ▷ **8**
4	▷	Plants with basal rosette of leaves; leaves ovate	Go to ▷ **5**
	▷	Plants without basal leaf rosette; leaves ovate to lanceolate	Go to ▷ **6**
5	▷	Sepal appendages >1.5 mm; corolla spur paler than petals	*V. riviniana* (p.166)
	▷	Sepal appendages < 1.5 mm; corolla spur as dark as or darker than petals	*V. reichenbachiana* (p.168)
6	▷	Petals clear blue; leaves ovate	*V. canina* (p.168)
	▷	Petals pale blue to whitish; leaves lanceolate	Go to ▷ **7**
7	▷	Corolla spur short, not or scarcely longer than sepal appendages; roots creeping, sending up shoots at intervals	*V. persicifolia* (p.168)
	▷	Corolla spur >2× as long as sepal appendages; plant not creeping	*V. lactea* (p.168)
8	▷	Sepals acute	*V. rupestris* (p.166)
	▷	Sepals obtuse or rounded	Go to ▷ **9**
9	▷	Plant with long stolons; flowers rich dark violet (or white); hairs on petioles deflexed; sweet-scented	*V. odorata* (p.166)
	▷	Plants not stoloniferous; flowers blue-violet; hairs on petioles spreading; not scented	*V. hirta* (p.166)
10	▷	Spur usually 2× as long as sepal appendages; petals much longer than sepals	Go to ▷ **11**
	▷	Spur usually <2× as long as sepal appendages; petals shorter or longer than sepals	Go to ▷ **12**
11	▷	Corolla large (2–3.5 cm vertically) on long (5–9 cm) pedicels; plant rhizomatous	*V. lutea* (p.168)
	▷	Corolla 1.5–2.5 cm vertically; plant tufted	*V. tricolor* (p.168)

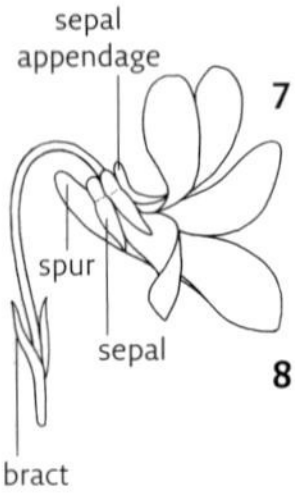

sepal
appendage

spur

sepal

bract

Viola flower

if	then
12 ▷ Corolla small, 4–8 mm vertically, concave (Scilly Is, Channel Is only)	**V. kitaibeliana** (p.168)
▷ Corolla ≥8 mm vertically, ± flat	Go to ▷ **13**
13 ▷ Corolla 15–25 mm vertically, with some blue or violet; petals longer than calyx; mid-lobe of stipules lanceolate, entire, not leaf-like	**V. tricolor** (p.168)
▷ Corolla 8–20 mm vertically, yellow or cream; petals shorter than calyx; mid-lobe of stipules bluntly toothed, leaf-like	**V. arvensis** (p.168)

Key to Salicaceae Willows and Poplars

Flowers with cup-like disc; bracts with long fine teeth; winter buds with several bud scales	**Populus**
Flowers without cup-like disc; bracts entire; winter buds with only 1 bud scale	**Salix**

Poplars Populus

1 ▷ Bark smooth; leaves blunt, coarsely toothed or lobed; catkin scales with long hairs	Go to ▷ **2**
▷ Bark deeply fissured; leaves acute, finely and regularly toothed; catkin scales glabrous	Go to ▷ **4**
2 ▷ Leaves of long shoots densely hairy beneath	Go to ▷ **3**
▷ Leaves glabrous, ± orbicular, margins crinkled with blunt teeth	**P. tremula** (p.174)
3 ▷ Leaves of long shoots palmately 5-lobed	**P. alba** (p.174)
▷ Leaves of long shoots coarsely and bluntly toothed	**P. × canescens** (p.174)
4 ▷ Trunk dark, deeply fissured, with large swollen bosses; crown spreading, branches arching downwards	**P. nigra** (p.174)
▷ Trunk without bosses; main branches ascending and curving upwards, not arching downwards	**P. × canadensis** (p.174)

CONTINUED OVERLEAF

Willows *Salix*

Identification of willows is made difficult by the large number and frequency of hybrids, including triple hybrids. The key is based mainly on vegetative characters. Leaf characters are those of mature leaves and should preferably be examined from midsummer, while twig characters refer to the previous two seasons' growth, not the current growth. Hybrids generally have characters intermediate between those of the parents but are not described separately here.

	if	**then**
1	▷ Trees and shrubs more than 1 m high	Go to ▷ **2**
	▷ Shrubs no more than 1 m high	Go to ▷ **13**
2	▷ Leaves linear, lanceolate, narrowly elliptic, >3× as long as wide	Go to ▷ **3**
	▷ Leaves ovate to almost rounded, <3× as long as wide	Go to ▷ **7**
3	▷ Most leaves virtually opposite, bluish green	*S. purpurea* (p.176)
	▷ All leaves clearly alternate	Go to ▷ **4**
4	▷ Leaves ± glabrous	Go to ▷ **5**
	▷ Leaves hairy at least beneath	Go to ▷ **6**
5	▷ Bark rough, fissured; stipules small, falling early	*S. fragilis* (p.176)
	▷ Bark smooth, peeling in patches; stipules broad, persistent	*S. triandra* (p.176)
6	▷ Leaves with silky hairs on both surfaces, margins finely toothed	*S. alba* (p.176)
	▷ Leaves dark green above, silvery hairy beneath, margins untoothed, recurved	*S. viminalis* (p.176)
7	▷ Leaves ± glabrous	Go to ▷ **8**
	▷ Leaves hairy at least beneath	Go to ▷ **10**
8	▷ Leaves glossy green above, pale green below, margins with fine, regular glandular teeth; junction of petiole and leaf blade with glands	*S. pentandra* (p.176)
	▷ Leaves usually somewhat glaucous below, margins entire or with obscure uneven teeth; no glands at junction of petiole and leaf blade	Go to ▷ **9**
9	▷ Stipules mostly small, soon falling; leaves not blackening when dried; twigs usually ± glabrous	*S. phylicifolia* (p.178)
	▷ Stipules mostly large, persistent; leaves blackening when dried; twigs usually pubescent	*S. myrsinifolia* (p.178)

(These 2 species can be difficult to separate with certainty; see main text.)

if		then
10	▷ Underside of leaves with dense white silky appressed hairs	***S. repens*** (p.178)
	▷ Hairs on underside of leaves not dense or closely appressed	Go to ▷ **11**
11	▷ Leaves wrinkled above, margins undulate; stipules conspicuous, persistent; branches slender and spreading	***S. aurita*** (p.176)
	▷ Upper surface of leaves smooth, margins ± flat; stipules conspicuous and persistent or not	Go to ▷ **12**
12	▷ Leaves broadly ovate, softly hairy beneath with prominent veins; stipules soon disappearing; wood of peeled 2nd-year twigs without raised striations	***S. caprea*** (p.176)
	▷ Leaves usually obovate, sparsely hairy beneath, veins not particularly prominent; stipules sometimes persistent; wood of peeled 2nd-year twigs with scattered, raised striations	***S. cinerea*** (p.176)
13	▷ Shrubs 10–100 cm tall	Go to ▷ **14**
	▷ Mat-forming, dwarf alpine shrubs <10 cm high; leaves ± rounded	Go to ▷ **18**
14	▷ Leaves broadly ovate to almost rounded; stipules large, persistent; upper surface of leaves with woolly hairs (Scottish mountains)	***S. lanata*** (p.178)
	▷ Leaves generally ovate	Go to ▷ **15**
15	▷ Leaf margins entire	Go to ▷ **16**
	▷ Leaf margins finely toothed (Scottish mountains)	Go to ▷ **17**
16	▷ Leaves densely silky beneath	***S. repens*** (p.178)
	▷ Leaves with dense, matted woolly hairs beneath (Scottish mountains)	***S. lapponum*** (p.178)
17	▷ Leaves bright glossy green on both surfaces; stipules conspicuous, persistent	***S. myrsinites*** (p.178)
	▷ Leaves ± glaucous beneath; stipules absent or falling early	***S. arbuscula*** (p.178)
18	▷ Leaves becoming shining green; margins toothed	***S. herbacea*** (p.178)
	▷ Leaves glaucous beneath, prominently net-veined, upper surface becoming dull green, margins entire (rare, Scottish mountains)	***S. reticulata*** (p.178)

TAMARICACEAE Tamarisks

Tamarisk
Tamarix gallica

Deciduous or semi-evergreen shrub to 3 m. Leaves Small, 1.5–3 mm, scale-like, alternate, simple, entire. Flowers In long catkin-like racemes, bisexual, actinomorphic; 5 sepals, petals and stamens; 3 styles; ovary superior. Habitat Widely planted as windbreak on sandy soils in coastal areas. Dist. Introduced England, Wales. (SW Europe, N Africa.) Fls Jul–Sep.

FRANKENIACEAE Sea-heath family

Sea-heath
Frankenia laevis

Prostrate, mat-forming, evergreen woody perennial. Leaves Small, opposite, heather-like. Flowers Small, *c.*5 mm across, sessile, bisexual, actinomorphic; 5 sepals and petals; 6 stamens; 1 style. Habitat Sand, sandy mud on upper levels of salt marshes, stable shingle, edge of dune slacks. Dist. Native. Very local, declining. Coasts of E and SE England, Channel Is. (SW Europe, W Mediterranean.) Fls Jun–Sep.

CUCURBITACEAE Cucurbits

White Bryony
Bryonia cretica

Tendril-climbing, dioecious perennial to *c.*4 m. Leaves Palmately lobed. Flowers Actinomorphic; male flowers stalked, 12–18 mm across; female flowers sessile, 10–12 mm across; 5 sepals and petals; 5 stamens. Fruits Red berry. Habitat Hedgerows, scrub, wood margins, on well-drained calcareous or base-rich soils. Dist. Native. Widespread and frequent in lowland England. (W, central and S Europe.) Fls May–Sep. Note All parts of plant are poisonous.

SALICACEAE Willows and poplars

Deciduous trees or shrubs with alternate leaves (rarely ± opposite) that have stipules (*see* key on p.171). Flowers are dioecious and borne singly in catkins, each with a bract (catkin scale). There is no real perianth but flowers may have a cup-like disc; 2 to many stamens; 2 stigmas. Fruit a capsule surrounded at base by long, silky hairs.

female   male
Salix flowers

White Poplar
Populus alba

Suckering deciduous tree to 25 m, with wide-spreading crown. Trees are mostly female. Bark Smooth, grey. Leaves Those of long shoots palmately lobed, with dense felt of white hairs beneath when young. Flowers Catkins, scales with ciliate teeth. Habitat Amenity tree in parks, roadsides, windbreaks, coastal dunes. Dist. Introduced. Widely planted throughout BI except extreme N. (Native of S, central and E Europe; planted and naturalised in W Europe.) Fls Mar.

Grey Poplar
Populus × canescens

Large tree to 40 m, crown with multiple domes. The hybrid of *P. alba* and *P. tremula*. Bark Base of mature trunk dark brown with ridges, upper bole pale with horizontal lines of diamond-shaped pits. Branches Outer branches somewhat pendulous. Leaves Those of long shoots coarsely, bluntly toothed, not or hardly palmately lobed, with persistent grey or white felted hairs beneath. Flowers Catkins, scales coarsely, irregularly toothed, with long ciliate hairs. Habitat Damp woods, stream sides; widely planted as amenity tree. Dist. Introduced. Throughout BI except N Scotland. (Native of central and E Europe.) Fls Feb–Mar.

Aspen
Populus tremula

Small, slender, suckering tree to 25 m. Will sucker to produce thickets. Bark Pale, smooth, with horizontal bands of small pits, grey and ridged at base. Leaves Almost orbicular, margin crinkled with blunt curved teeth, glabrous when mature; petiole 40–60 mm, very flattened, causing leaves to 'tremble' in breeze. Flowers Catkins, scales with long silky hairs. Habitat Mixed broadleaved woodland, hedgerows, heathland, disused pits; also cliffs, riverbanks in uplands. To 640 m. Dist. Native. Throughout BI. (All Europe except extreme SW.) Fls Feb–Mar.

Black-poplar
Populus nigra

Large tree to 35 m, with massive, spreading crown when mature. Bark *Trunk* dark, deeply fissured, *with large, swollen bosses.* Branches *Large, arching.* Leaves 5–10 cm, usually longer than wide, tip elongated, margins bluntly toothed. Habitat River valleys, floodplains, pond and lake margins, hedgerows (rarely); lowland. Dist. Native. Uncommon. Scattered throughout BI except Scotland. (All Europe except Scandinavia and extreme SW.) Fls Apr.

Hybrid Black-poplar
Populus × canadensis

Tall, fast-growing tree to 40 m. The hybrid between *P. nigra* and the American Eastern Cottonwood *P. deltoides*. Occurs as a large number of unisexual cultivars. Similar to *P. nigra*, but bark greyer and more regularly fissured; trunk lacks bosses; main branches ascending and curving upwards, not arching downwards; canopy more open; and usually 1–3 small glands at base of leaf blade at junction with petiole. Habitat Roadsides, parks, plantations, shelter belts. Dist. Introduced *c.*1770. (All Europe.) Fls Apr.

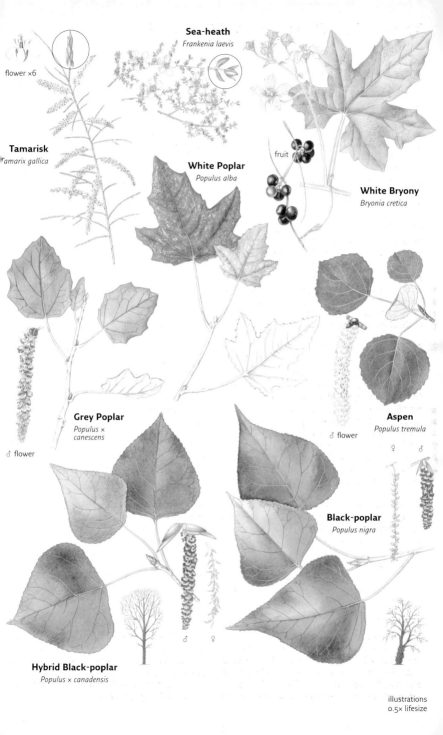

Sea-heath
Frankenia laevis

flower ×6

Tamarisk
Tamarix gallica

White Poplar
Populus alba

fruit

White Bryony
Bryonia cretica

Grey Poplar
*Populus ×
canescens*

♂ flower

Aspen
Populus tremula

♂ flower

♀   ♂

Black-poplar
Populus nigra

Hybrid Black-poplar
Populus × canadensis

♂   ♀

illustrations
0.5× lifesize

Bay Willow · Salix pentandra

Shrub or small tree to 7 m. BRANCHES Twigs glossy. LEAVES 5–12 cm, 2–4× as long as broad; *glabrous; dark glossy green above, paler beneath; margin with closely set glandular teeth*; stipules, if present, soon falling. FLOWERS Catkins, appearing with or slightly later than leaves. HABITAT Wet woods, fens, marshes, stream sides, wet dune slacks; to 410 m. DIST. Native. N from N Wales and central England. Frequently planted outside native range. (Most of Europe except S and SW.) FLS May-Jun.

Crack-willow · Salix fragilis

Tree to 25 m. Crown broad, spreading; canopy appearing green in leaf. Often pollarded. Very variable, with several named varieties. BARK Deeply fissured, not peeling. BRANCHES Twigs brittle. LEAVES *Lanceolate, 6–16 cm, 4.5–9× as long as broad; green above, paler beneath; with sparse silky hairs when young, becoming glabrous; margins rather coarsely toothed*. FLOWERS Catkins, appearing with leaves. HABITAT Banks of streams and rivers, marshes, fens, wet woods; to 410 m. DIST. Archaeophyte. Common throughout BI. (W, central and E Europe.) FLS Apr.

White Willow · Salix alba

Tree to 25 m. Crown narrow; canopy appearing distinctly silvery in leaf. Has several named varieties. BARK Deeply fissured, not peeling. BRANCHES Ascending. LEAVES Lanceolate, 5–10 cm, 5.5–7.5× as long as broad, covered with *white silky hairs on both surfaces, margins finely toothed*. FLOWERS Catkins, appearing with leaves. HABITAT Banks of streams and rivers, marshes, wet woods; lowland to 350 m. Commonly planted. DIST. Archaeophyte. Throughout BI. (All Europe except Scandinavia.) FLS Apr-May.

Almond Willow · Salix triandra

Very variable shrub or small tree to 10 m, much planted for basket-making. BARK Smooth, *peeling off in patches*. BRANCHES *Young twigs taste of rose-water when chewed*. LEAVES Variable, 5–10 cm, 3.5–7.7× as long as broad; glabrous; dark and rather shining green above, paler beneath; *stipules usually large and conspicuous*, 5–10 mm, persistent. FLOWERS Catkins, appearing with leaves. HABITAT Banks of rivers and streams, marshes, osier beds; lowland. DIST. Archaeophyte. Mostly S and E of line from Humber to Severn. (Most of Europe except extreme N.) FLS Mar-May.

Purple Willow · Salix purpurea

Shrub to 5 m. BARK Smooth, greyish, with bitter taste. LEAVES Variable, 4–10 cm, 3.5–10× as long as broad, glabrous, *rather blue-green above, almost opposite*; stipules small, soon falling. FLOWERS Catkins, appearing before leaves. HABITAT Marshes, fens, river banks, osier beds; to 410 m. DIST. Native. Throughout BI except extreme N. (All Europe except Scandinavia.) FLS Mar-Apr.

Osier · Salix viminalis

Shrub to 5 m, much planted for basketry. BRANCHES Long, straight, flexible; young twigs hairy, becoming glabrous later. LEAVES *Long, narrow*, 10–25 cm, 7–18× as long as broad; dark green and glabrous above, *covered by white silky hairs beneath; margins undulate, revolute when young*; stipules small, soon falling. FLOWERS Catkins, appearing before leaves. HABITAT Stream and pond margins, marshes, fens, osier beds; to 410 m. DIST. Archaeophyte. Throughout BI. (W, central and E Europe.) FLS Apr-May.

Goat Willow · Salix caprea

Shrub or small tree to 10 m. BARK Greyish brown, fissured. BRANCHES *Twigs* pubescent when young, becoming glabrous, *without striations beneath bark of* 2-year-old shoots. LEAVES *Broadly ovate to oval*, 5–10 cm, 1.2–2× as long as broad; *dark green above, densely hairy beneath with prominent reticulate veins*; stipules ear-shaped, toothed, but falling early in season. FLOWERS Catkins, appearing before leaves. HABITAT Open woodland, scrub, hedgerows, waste ground, lake and stream margins; to 760 m. DIST. Native. Common throughout BI. (Most of Europe.) FLS Mar-Apr.

Grey Willow, Common Sallow · Salix cinerea

Shrub or small tree to 10 m. BRANCHES *Young twigs hairy, with raised striations on wood beneath bark of* 2-year-old shoots. LEAVES Obovate, 2.5–7 cm, 2–4× as long as wide; thinly hairy above when young, persistently hairy beneath; stipules usually persistent. FLOWERS Catkins, appearing before leaves. HABITAT Marshes, fens, bogs, wet woodland, hedgerows, waste ground. DIST. Native. Common throughout BI. (Most of Europe except extreme N.) FLS Mar-Apr. NOTE The common and widespread plant throughout most of BI is ssp. *oleifolia*.

Eared Willow · Salix aurita

Twiggy shrub to 2 m. BRANCHES Slender, spreading, with raised striations on wood beneath bark. LEAVES Obovate, 2–3 cm, 1.5–2.5× as long as broad; dull grey-green; *thinly pubescent above, densely hairy beneath; surface distinctly wrinkled; stipules large, conspicuous*, persistent, with toothed margins. FLOWERS Catkins, appearing before leaves. HABITAT Damp heathland, moorland, scrub, upland stream sides, on acid soils; to 790 m. DIST. Native. Declining in lowlands. In suitable habitats throughout BI. (All Europe except Mediterranean and extreme N.) FLS Apr.

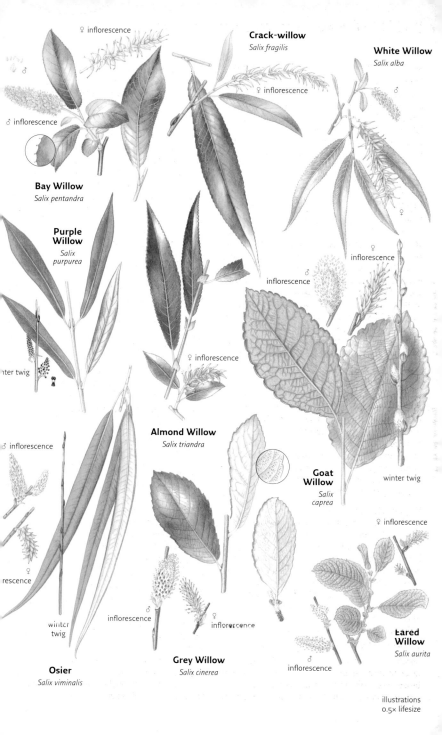

♀ inflorescence

Crack-willow
Salix fragilis

♀ inflorescence

White Willow
Salix alba

♂

♂ inflorescence

♀

Bay Willow
Salix pentandra

Purple Willow
Salix purpurea

♂ inflorescence

inflorescence

♂

♀

winter twig

♀ inflorescence

winter twig

♂ inflorescence

♀ inflorescence

Almond Willow
Salix triandra

Goat Willow
Salix caprea

winter twig

♂ inflorescence

♀ inflorescence

♀ inflorescence

winter twig

♂
inflorescence

♀
inflorescence

Grey Willow
Salix cinerea

Eared Willow
Salix aurita

♂
inflorescence

Osier
Salix viminalis

illustrations
0.5× lifesize

Dark-leaved Willow
Salix myrsinifolia

Spreading shrub to 4 m. BRANCHES Twigs dull, usually pubescent. LEAVES Variable, 2–7 cm, 1.5–3× as long as broad, *rather thin; dark green above, paler below*; thinly pubescent when young, midrib remaining hairy below, *turning black when dried; stipules usually well developed and persisting.* FLOWERS Catkins, appearing with leaves; ovaries usually glabrous. HABITAT Gravelly riverbanks, lake shores, stream sides, wet rock ledges; to 940 m. DIST. Native. N England, Scotland; rare in Ireland. (N Europe and mts of central Europe.) FLS Apr–May.

Tea-leaved Willow
Salix phylicifolia

Shrub to 4 m. BRANCHES *Twigs* glossy brown, usually *glabrous at maturity.* LEAVES 2–8 cm, 1.7–2.5× as long as broad; *glabrous; shining green above, rather glaucous beneath*, not turn and papery, and not turning black on drying; *stipules usually absent* or small and soon falling. FLOWERS Catkins, appearing with leaves; ovaries usually hairy. HABITAT Fens, lakes, streams, rivers, wet rocks, usually on calcareous soils; to 685 m. DIST. Native. N England, Scotland. (N Europe.) FLS Apr–May. NOTE Can be difficult to distinguish with certainty from *S. myrsinifolia*, but the thin papery leaves turning black on drying is a distinctive character of *S. myrsinifolia*.

Creeping Willow
Salix repens

Prostrate to erect, slender, rhizomatous *dwarf shrub, to 1.5 m.* The only lowland dwarf willow. BRANCHES Twigs densely pubescent when young. LEAVES Very variable in shape, 0.5–4.5 cm, 1.5–3.5× as long as broad; *long silky hairs on both surfaces when young, usually becoming glabrous above and remaining pubescent beneath; margins somewhat revolute;* stipules soon falling or absent. FLOWERS Catkins, appearing before leaves, very variable. HABITAT Heaths, moors, dune slacks, fens; to 855 m. DIST. Native. Throughout BI. (W Europe to S Scandinavia.) FLS Apr–May.

Downy Willow
Salix lapponum VU.

Much-branched dwarf shrub to 1 m. BRANCHES *Twigs* pubescent, becoming glabrous, glossy *brown with prominent bud scars.* LEAVES 1.5–7 cm, 2–4× *as long as broad; grey-green with silky hairs above, grey and densely silky beneath.* FLOWERS Catkins, appearing with or before leaves. HABITAT Wet rocks on mountain slopes, cliffs; 210–1000 m. DIST. Native. Scottish Highlands. (Mts of N and E Europe.) FLS May–Jul.

Woolly Willow
Salix lanata VU.

Very distinctive low-growing, much-branched dwarf shrub to 1 m. BRANCHES Twigs pubescent when young, becoming glabrous and glossy with prominent leaf scars. LEAVES *Broad*, 2.5–6.5 cm, *1.2–2× as long as broad*; with long silky hairs above when young, persistently woolly beneath. FLOWERS Catkins, appearing with leaves. HABITAT Damp, base-rich mountain ledges, often in areas of late snow-lie; 620–1035 m. DIST. Native. Very rare. Scottish Highlands. (Arctic and sub-arctic Europe.) FLS May–Jul.

Mountain Willow
Salix arbuscula

Prostrate, much-branched dwarf shrub to 70 cm. BRANCHES Twigs glabrous, becoming dark brown, glossy. LEAVES 0.5–2 cm, *1.5–3× as long as broad; glabrous and glossy above, densely pubescent below when young and becoming ± glabrous*; stipules soon falling or absent. FLOWERS Catkins, appearing with leaves. HABITAT Base-rich or calcareous flushes, gravelly stream sides, wet rock ledges; to 870 m. DIST. Native. Very local. Scottish Highlands. (Arctic and sub-arctic Europe.) FLS May–Jun.

Whortle-leaved Willow
Salix myrsinites EN.

Low, spreading dwarf shrub to 40 cm. BRANCHES Twigs pubescent when young, becoming glabrous; dark, shining reddish brown. LEAVES 1.5–3 cm, 1.5–2.5× as long as broad; *bright, shining green on both surfaces*, becoming glabrous; *stipules usually prominent and persistent.* FLOWERS Female catkins conspicuously large, appearing with leaves. HABITAT Wet basic or calcareous rocks; to 915 m. DIST. Native. Very local. Scottish mts. (N Europe.) FLS May–Jun.

Dwarf Willow
Salix herbacea

Prostrate, rhizomatous, mat-forming dwarf shrub to 5 cm. LEAVES *Rounded, 0.6–2 cm*; sparsely pubescent at first, becoming glabrous, bright green, shining, veins prominent; stipules small or absent, soon falling. FLOWERS Catkins, appearing after leaves. HABITAT Areas of extreme exposure on mountain tops, ridges, screes, corries, often in areas of late snow-lie; to 1310 m, but down to near sea-level in Shetland. DIST. Native. Lake District, N Scotland, scattered mt areas elsewhere. (Mts of arctic and central Europe.) FLS Jun–Jul.

Net-leaved Willow
Salix reticulata

Prostrate, rhizomatous, mat-forming dwarf shrub to 15 cm. LEAVES *Orbicular, 1–3 cm*, <2× as long as broad, with long silky hairs when young, becoming dark green, glabrous and *strongly wrinkled above; glaucous and thinly hairy with prominent reticulate veins below*; stipules absent. FLOWERS Catkins, appearing after leaves. HABITAT Moist, base-rich mountain rock ledges; to 1125 m. DIST. Native. Very local. Scottish Highlands. (Mts of central and N Europe.) FLS Jun–Jul

Dark-leaved Willow
Salix myrsinifolia

♂

♀

dried leaf

Tea-leaved Willow
Salix phylicifolia

♂

♀

Creeping Willow
Salix repens

var. *fusca* (fens)

♂

Downy Willow
Salix lapponum

♂

♀

scale ×0.9

Mountain Willow
Salix arbuscula

♂

♀

♂

Woolly Willow
Salix lanata

♂ ♀

Whortle-leaved Willow
Salix mysinites

♂

♀

Net-leaved Willow
Salix reticulata

♀

♂

Dwarf Willow
Salix herbacea

illustrations
0.6× lifesize

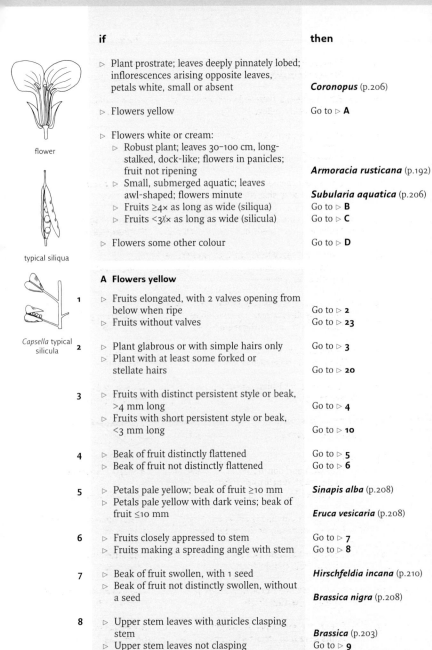

flower

typical siliqua

Capsella typical silicula

	if	**then**
	▷ Plant prostrate; leaves deeply pinnately lobed; inflorescences arising opposite leaves, petals white, small or absent	*Coronopus* (p.206)
	▷ Flowers yellow	Go to ▷ **A**
	▷ Flowers white or cream:	
	▷ Robust plant; leaves 30–100 cm, long-stalked, dock-like; flowers in panicles; fruit not ripening	*Armoracia rusticana* (p.192)
	▷ Small, submerged aquatic; leaves awl-shaped; flowers minute	*Subularia aquatica* (p.206)
	▷ Fruits ≥4× as long as wide (siliqua)	Go to ▷ **B**
	▷ Fruits <3½× as long as wide (silicula)	Go to ▷ **C**
	▷ Flowers some other colour	Go to ▷ **D**

A Flowers yellow

1	▷ Fruits elongated, with 2 valves opening from below when ripe	Go to ▷ **2**
	▷ Fruits without valves	Go to ▷ **23**
2	▷ Plant glabrous or with simple hairs only	Go to ▷ **3**
	▷ Plant with at least some forked or stellate hairs	Go to ▷ **20**
3	▷ Fruits with distinct persistent style or beak, >4 mm long	Go to ▷ **4**
	▷ Fruits with short persistent style or beak, <3 mm long	Go to ▷ **10**
4	▷ Beak of fruit distinctly flattened	Go to ▷ **5**
	▷ Beak of fruit not distinctly flattened	Go to ▷ **6**
5	▷ Petals pale yellow; beak of fruit ≥10 mm	*Sinapis alba* (p.208)
	▷ Petals pale yellow with dark veins; beak of fruit ≤10 mm	*Eruca vesicaria* (p.208)
6	▷ Fruits closely appressed to stem	Go to ▷ **7**
	▷ Fruits making a spreading angle with stem	Go to ▷ **8**
7	▷ Beak of fruit swollen, with 1 seed	*Hirschfeldia incana* (p.210)
	▷ Beak of fruit not distinctly swollen, without a seed	*Brassica nigra* (p.208)
8	▷ Upper stem leaves with auricles clasping stem	*Brassica* (p.203)
	▷ Upper stem leaves not clasping	Go to ▷ **9**

	if	then
9	▷ Flowers with spreading or reflexed sepals ▷ Flowers with erect sepals	*Sinapis* (p.203) *Coincya* (p.203)
10	▷ Fruits pendent, flattened with a broad wing ▷ Fruits erect to reflexed	*Isatis* (p.186) Go to ▷ **11**
11	▷ Upper stem leaves with auricles clasping stem ▷ Upper stem leaves without auricles	Go to ▷ **12** Go to ▷ **14**
12	▷ Fruits pear-shaped ▷ Fruits not pear-shaped	*Camelina sativa* (p.200) Go to ▷ **13**
13	▷ Fruits 4–12 mm, seeds in 2 rows in each cell ▷ Fruits >12 mm, seeds in 1 row in each cell	*Rorippa* (p.194) *Barbarea* (p.188)
14	▷ Tufted perennial to 10 cm; leaves in dense rosettes; stems leafless (very rare, S Wales) ▷ Plant not as above	*Draba aizoides* (p.198) Go to ▷ **15**
15	▷ Flowers in lower part of inflorescence with pinnately divided leaf-like bracteoles ▷ Flowers without leaf-like bracteoles	*Erucastrum gallicum* (p.208) Go to ▷ **16**
16	▷ Seeds in 2 rows in each cell ▷ Seeds in 1 row in each cell	Go to ▷ **17** Go to ▷ **18**
17	▷ At least larger fruits >23 mm ▷ Fruits ≤23 mm	*Diplotaxis* (p.206) *Rorippa* (p.194)
18	▷ Petals 6–17 mm ▷ Petals 1–6 mm	*Sisymbrium* (p.184) Go to ▷ **19**
19	▷ Rhizomatous perennial with creeping rhizomes and non-flowering rosettes ▷ Annual without rhizomes and non-flowering rosettes	*Rorippa sylvestris* (p.190) *Sisymbrium* (p.184)
20	▷ Beak of fruit distinctly flattened ▷ Leaves not deeply or finely divided	*Descurainia sophia* (p.186) Go to ▷ **21**
21	▷ Beak of fruit ≥4 mm long ▷ Beak of fruit <3 mm long	*Erysimum* (p.188) Go to ▷ **22**
22	▷ Fruits 2–8 mm, + orbicular ▷ Fruits 30–70 mm; linear	*Alyssum alyssoides* (p.196) *Arabis* (p.185)
23	▷ Fruits 15–90 mm, petals ≥11 mm ▷ Fruits 5–12 mm, petals ≤11 mm	*Raphanus* (p.210) Go to ▷ **24**

CONTINUED OVERLEAF

	if	then
24	▷ Fruit and pedicels with large glands, fruit with 1 segment	***Bunias orientalis*** (p.188)
	▷ Fruit and pedicels without glands, fruit with 2 segments	***Rapistrum rugosum*** (p.210)

B Flowers white or cream; fruits ≥4× as long as wide

	if	then
1	▷ Stems leafy	Go to ▷ **2**
	▷ Stem leaves absent; petals deeply notched	***Erophila*** (p.198)
2	▷ Fruits without valves, indehiscent, constricted between segments	***Raphanus*** (p.210)
	▷ Fruits with valves opening from below	Go to ▷ **3**
3	▷ Stem leaves pinnate	Go to ▷ **4**
	▷ Stem leaves not pinnate	Go to ▷ **5**
4	▷ At least some lobes of leaves stalked; fruits ± flattened	***Cardamine*** (p.192)
	▷ Lobes of leaves sessile; fruits not flattened	***Rorippa*** (p.195)
5	▷ Stem leaves distinctly stalked	***Alliaria petiolata*** (p.186)
	▷ Stem leaves sessile	Go to ▷ **6**
6	▷ Stem leaves with auricles	***Arabis*** (p.185)
	▷ Stem leaves without auricles	Go to ▷ **7**
7	▷ Petals 2.5–4.5 mm	Go to ▷ **8**
	▷ Petals ≥4.5 mm	***Arabis*** (p.185)
8	▷ Fruits linear, straight	***Arabidopsis thaliana*** (p.186)
	▷ Fruits flattened, lanceolate, twisted	***Draba incana*** (p.198)

C Flowers white or cream; fruits <3½× as long as wide

	if	then
1	▷ Large, glaucous, cabbage-like shingle-beach plant; inflorescence much branched; flowers white; fruits in 2 parts, the upper almost spherical and indehiscent	***Crambe maritima*** (p.210)
	▷ Plant not like this	Go to ▷ **2**
2	▷ Outer petals larger than inner ones	Go to ▷ **3**
	▷ Petals of ± equal size	Go to ▷ **4**
3	▷ Outer petals 3–16 mm, style as long as or longer than apical notch of fruit	***Iberis amara*** (p.204)
	▷ Outer petals <2 mm, style shorter than apical notch of fruit	***Teesdalia nudicaulis*** (p.200)

if	**then**

4
▷ Petals notched to about halfway — Go to ▷ **5**
▷ Petals not deeply notched — Go to ▷ **6**

5
▷ Stem leafless, 2–20 cm — *Erophila* (p.198)
▷ Stem leafy, 20–60 cm — *Bertoroa incana* (p.198)

6
▷ Fruit rounded — *Cochlearia* (p.195)
▷ Fruit flattened — Go to ▷ **7**

7
▷ Cells of fruit 1-seeded — *Lepidium* (p.202)
▷ Cells of fruit 2-seeded — Go to ▷ **8**

8
▷ Fruit winged — *Thlaspi* (p.202)
▷ Fruit not winged — Go to ▷ **9**

9
▷ Fruit the shape of an inverted triangle — *Capsella bursa-pastoris* (p.200)
▷ Fruit oval or elliptical — Go to ▷ **10**

10
▷ Leaves deeply pinnately divided — *Hornungia petraea* (p.200)
▷ Leaves simple, entire or toothed — *Draba* (p.195)

D Flowers blue, lilac, pink, orange or red

1
▷ Maritime plant of sandy or shingly shores; leaves fleshy, pinnately lobed; flowers pale violet-purple; fruits in 2 segments — *Cakile maritima* (p.210)
▷ Plant not like this — Go to ▷ **2**

2
▷ Plant with at least some forked or stellate (branched) hairs — Go to ▷ **3**
▷ Plant glabrous or with simple hairs only — Go to ▷ **7**

3
▷ Upper stem leaves with auricles clasping stem — *Arabis* (p.185)
▷ Upper stem leaves without auricles — Go to ▷ **4**

4
▷ Petals 4–9 mm — *Arabis* (p.185)
▷ Petals 15–30 mm — Go to ▷ **5**

5
▷ Flowers yellow, red or orange — *Erysimum* (p.188)
▷ Flowers pink or purple — Go to ▷ **6**

6
▷ Plant densely hairy with stellate hairs, grey or grey-green — *Matthiola* (p.188)
▷ Plant sparsely hairy, dark green — *Hesperis matronalis* (p.188)

7
▷ Plant hairy — Go to ▷ **8**
▷ Plant glabrous — Go to ▷ **9**

CONTINUED OVERLEAF

if	then
8 ▷ Fruits broadly ovate, flat, 15–35 mm wide	*Lunaria annua* (p.192)
▷ Fruits ≤15 mm wide, winged	*Lepidium sativum* (p.204)
9 ▷ Stem leaves pinnate; fruits linear, ≥4× as long as wide	*Cardamine* (p.192)
▷ Stem leaves simple or shallowly lobed; fruits elliptic	*Cochlearia danica* (p.200)

Key to Rockets and Hedge Mustard *Sisymbrium*

if	then
1 ▷ Fruits 10–20 mm, appressed to stem	*S. officinale* (p.186)
▷ Fruits 20–120 mm, erect or recurved	Go to ▷ **2**
2 ▷ Upper stem leaves sessile, pinnate, with linear lobes	*S. altissimum* (p.186)
▷ Upper stem leaves stalked, if divided then lobes not linear	Go to ▷ **3**
3 ▷ Fruits 50–120 mm, pubescent when young	*S. orientale* (p.186)
▷ Fruits 10–50 mm, glabrous	Go to ▷ **4**
4 ▷ Petals 2.5–4 mm, young fruits overtopping open flowers	*S. irio* (p.186)
▷ Petals 4.5–7 mm, young fruits not overtopping open flowers	*S. loeselii* (p.186)

Key to Rock-cresses *Arabis*

	if	**then**
1	▷ Stem leaves strongly clasping stem, auricles longer than width of stem	Go to ▷ **2**
	▷ Stem leaves not or scarcely clasping stem, auricles absent or shorter than width of stem	Go to ▷ **6**
2	▷ Petals yellowish	Go to ▷ **3**
	▷ Petals white	Go to ▷ **4**
3	▷ Fruits long, >7 cm, spreading and curved downwards when ripe	**A. turrita** (p.196)
	▷ Fruits erect	**A. glabra** (p.196)
4	▷ Non-flowering shoots absent or forming rosettes	**A. hirsuta** (p.196)
	▷ Non-flowering shoots elongating and mat-forming	Go to ▷ **5**
5	▷ Lowest leaves with petiole about as long as blade; petals 10–15 mm	**A. caucasica** (p.196)
	▷ Lowest leaves with petiole much shorter than blade; petals ≤10 mm (very rare alpine, Skye)	**A. alpina** (p.196)
6	▷ Basal leaves deeply lobed, with long petioles	Go to ▷ **7**
	▷ Basal leaves ± entire or shallowly lobed, with short petioles	Go to ▷ **8**
7	▷ Flowers *c.*6 mm across (mountains of N and W Britain)	**A. petraea** (p.196)
	▷ Flowers *c.*8 mm across (not BI)	**A. arenosa** ● (p.196)
8	▷ Basal leaves entire; petals white	**A. hirsuta** (p.196)
	▷ Basal leaves lobed; petals pale yellow (very rare, Avon Gorge)	**A. scabra** (p.196)

BRASSICACEAE (CRUCIFERAE)
Crucifers

Annual or perennial herbs with alternate leaves that lack stipules, and with distinctive regular flowers that have 4 sepals in opposite pairs, 4 petals alternating with the sepals and 6 stamens (sometimes 4) (*see* key on p.180). The ovary is superior, usually with 2 cells and a single style with 2 stigmas. The fruit is usually a capsule opening from below by 2 valves or sometimes breaking transversely into 1-seeded segments.

Identification often depends on details of the ripe fruits, and a lens may be needed to examine the hairs on the stems and leaves. Many species are annuals of open habitats or weeds of cultivation.

Rockets and Hedge Mustard *Sisymbrium*
See key to *Sisymbrium* on p.184.

London-rocket
Sisymbrium irio

Erect, much-branched, glabrous or sparsely hairy annual to 60 cm. FLOWERS 3-4 mm across. FRUITS *25-55 mm, glabrous*, valves 3-veined; *overtopping flowers when young*. HABITAT Waste ground. DIST. Introduced. Rare. Around London, spread after Great Fire in 1666; casual elsewhere. (S and SW Europe.) FLS Jun-Aug.

False London-rocket
Sisymbrium loeselii

Erect, branched, sparsely hairy annual to 150 cm. FRUITS *10-30 mm, glabrous*, valves 3-veined; *not overtopping open flowers when young*. HABITAT Casual of waste ground, railways, docks. DIST. Introduced. May be spreading. (E Europe.) FLS Jun-Aug.

Tall Rocket
Sisymbrium altissimum

Erect, branched annual, hairy below, glabrous above, to 100 cm. LEAVES Upper *stem leaves sessile* finely divided, *with 2-5 pairs of linear lateral lobes*. FLOWERS *c*.12 mm across, petals 2× as long as sepals. FRUITS 40-90 mm, ± glabrous when young, veins obscure; stalks about as wide as fruits. HABITAT Waste ground, railways, rubbish tips. DIST. Introduced; birdseed contaminant. Occasional casual throughout BI. (Central and E Europe.) FLS Jun-Aug.

Eastern Rocket
Sisymbrium orientale

Erect, branched, pubescent annual to 80 cm. LEAVES Upper stem leaves with narrow terminal lobe and 0-1 pairs of lateral lobes. FLOWERS *c*.7 mm across, petals 1.5-2× as long as sepals. FRUITS *50-120 mm, pubescent when young*. HABITAT Waste ground, roadsides, railways. DIST. Introduced. Casual and locally common throughout most of BI. (S Europe.) FLS Jun-Aug.

Hedge Mustard
Sisymbrium officinale

Erect, glabrous or sparsely hairy annual or biennial to 100 cm. LEAVES Deeply divided, basal leaves in a rosette. FLOWERS 3 mm across, petals 1.5× as long as sepals. FRUITS *10-20 mm, held stiffly erect and closely appressed to stem*. HABITAT Hedgerows, roadsides, cultivated ground, waste places, usually close to habitation. DIST. Archaeophyte. Throughout BI, but rare in extreme N. (All Europe except N.) FLS Jun-Jul.

Flixweed
Descurainia sophia

Erect, little-branched, pubescent annual to 90 cm. LEAVES *Greyish green, deeply divided, with branched hairs*. FLOWERS 3 mm across, petals about as long as sepals. FRUITS 15-25 mm, stalks *c*.10 mm. HABITAT Cultivated land, road verges, waste ground, on sandy soils. DIST. Archaeophyte. E England; scattered throughout rest of BI. (All Europe except extreme N.) FLS Jun-Aug.

Garlic Mustard
Alliaria petiolata

Erect, unbranched biennial to 120 cm. Sparsely hairy below, glabrous above. *Roots and leaves smelling of garlic when crushed*. LEAVES *Basal leaves in a rosette, stem leaves stalked*. FLOWERS 6 mm across, petals *c*.2× as long as sepals. FRUITS 35-60 mm, 4-angled glabrous, standing ± erect. HABITAT Wood margins hedgerows, roadsides, shady places, gardens, on fertile soils. DIST. Native. Common throughout BI except extreme N. (All Europe except N.) FLS Apr-Jun.

Thale Cress
Arabidopsis thaliana

Erect, sparsely hairy annual to 50 cm. LEAVES Basal leaves hairy, in a rosette. FLOWERS *3 mm across* petals *c*.2× as long as sepals. FRUITS *10-18 mm glabrous, on slender, spreading stalks*. HABITAT Dry open stony ground, walls, waste places; common garden weed. DIST. Native. Throughout BI. (All Europe except extreme N.) FLS Apr-May, Sep-Oct

Woad
Isatis tinctoria

Erect, sparsely hairy, glaucous biennial or perennial LEAVES Basal leaves in a rosette, to 30 cm; stem leaves glabrous, glaucous, with clasping auricles FLOWERS 4 mm across, in much-branched inflorescence, petals 2× as long as sepals. FRUITS 11-20 mm *flattened, glabrous, pendulous*. HABITAT Rare casual of quarries, arable fields, waste ground. DIST. Archaeophyte. Cultivated for blue dye since antiquity. (Most of Europe.) FLS Jul-Aug.

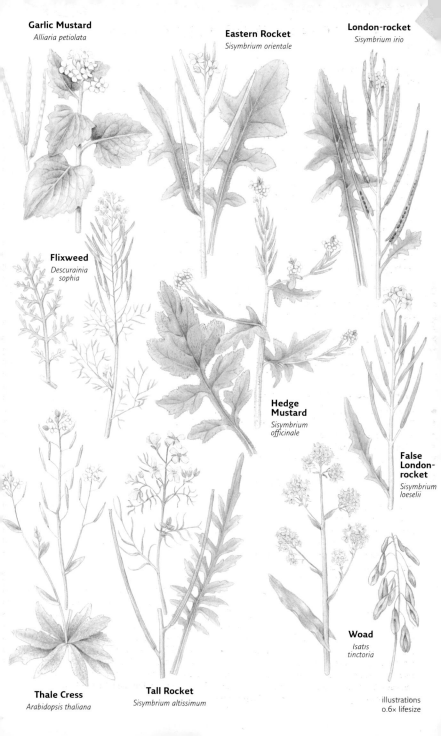

Garlic Mustard
Alliaria petiolata

Eastern Rocket
Sisymbrium orientale

London-rocket
Sisymbrium irio

Flixweed
Descurainia sophia

Hedge Mustard
Sisymbrium officinale

False London-rocket
Sisymbrium loeselii

Thale Cress
Arabidopsis thaliana

Tall Rocket
Sisymbrium altissimum

Woad
Isatis tinctoria

illustrations
0.6× lifesize

Warty-cabbage
Bunias orientalis

Erect, much-branched, sparsely hairy perennial to 120 cm. LEAVES Rosette leaves to 45 cm. FLOWERS In crowded inflorescence; flower stalks with large, conspicuous yellow to black glands; petals *c.*2× as long as sepals. FRUITS 6-8 mm, asymmetrical, ovoid, *without valves; covered by large, irregular warts*. HABITAT Persistent casual of waste ground, roadsides, railways, docks. DIST. Introduced. Around London; scattered elsewhere. (E Europe.) FLS May-Aug.

Treacle Mustard
Erysimum cheiranthoides

Erect, branched annual to 90 cm, with *appressed, branched hairs*. LEAVES Narrow, to 10 cm. FLOWERS *Small, 6 mm across*, in crowded inflorescence; petals 2× as long as sepals. FRUITS 12-25 mm, 4-angled, conspicuously 1-veined. HABITAT Weed of arable fields, waste ground, road verges, on light soils. DIST. Archaeophyte. Throughout BI, rare in N. (All Europe except S.) FLS Jun-Aug.

Wall-flower
Erysimum cheiri

Erect, branched, pubescent perennial to 60 cm. LEAVES Rosette leaves to 10 cm. FLOWERS *c.*2.5 *cm across*, petals ≥2× as long as sepals. FRUITS 25-70 mm, hairy, ± erect, flattened, conspicuously 1-veined. HABITAT Walls, cliffs, rocks. DIST. Archaeophyte. Cultivated since Middle Ages. Naturalised throughout BI except extreme N. (SE Europe.) FLS Apr-Jun.

Dame's-violet
Hesperis matronalis

Erect, *sparsely hairy*, branched perennial to 80 cm. STEMS Very leafy. FLOWERS *Showy, pink, purple or white*, in crowded inflorescence; petals 15-30 mm, 2-3× as long as sepals. FRUITS *Long, narrow, 50-115 mm, 'beaded'*. HABITAT Hedgerows, roadsides, verges, usually near habitation. DIST. Introduced. Cultivated since Middle Ages. Naturalised throughout BI. (S and E Europe.) FLS May-Jul.

Hoary Stock
Matthiola incana

Densely hairy, erect grey-green perennial to 80 cm. STEMS Woody, leafless below. LEAVES *In rosettes, narrow, entire*, covered by short greyish hairs (hoary). FLOWERS 2.5-5 *cm across*, purple, red or white. FRUITS 45-130 mm, erect; valves downy, with distinct central vein. HABITAT Sea cliffs. DIST. Introduced. Cultivated since C16th. Rare. S and SW England; scattered in suitable habitats elsewhere. (Central Mediterranean.) FLS May-Jul.

Sea Stock
Matthiola sinuata VU.

Prostrate to erect, densely hairy biennial, with conspicuous yellow to black glands, to 100 cm. LEAVES *Basal leaves lobed, upper stem leaves entire, all densely hairy and glandular*. FLOWERS Fragrant, 2-2.5 cm *across*, petals *c.*2× as long as sepals. FRUITS 70-120 mm, erect; valves downy and glandular, with distinct central vein. HABITAT Sea cliffs, sand-dunes. DIST. Native. Very rare. N Devon, S Wales, Channel Is. (SW Europe, Mediterranean.) FLS Jun-Aug.

Winter-cresses *Barbarea*

Upper stem leaves simple, toothed or shallowly lobed; seeds 1-1.8 mm

Flower buds glabrous; persistent style 2-3.5 mm	*B. vulgaris*
Flower buds hairy at tip; persistent style 0.5-1.8 mm	*B. stricta*

Upper stem leaves deeply lobed to >halfway to midrib; seeds 1.6-2.4 mm

Petals ≤5.6 mm; fruits <40 mm	*B. intermedia*
Petals >5.6 mm; some fruits >40 mm	*B. verna*

Winter-cress
Barbarea vulgaris

Erect, branched, glabrous biennial or perennial to 90 cm. LEAVES Rosette leaves pinnate, with clasping auricles; *upper stem leaves clasping, ovate, ± simple*; all a deep, shining green. FLOWERS 7-9 mm across, *buds glabrous*, petals 2× as long as sepals. FRUITS ± erect, 15-32 mm, *persistent style 2-3.5 mm*. HABITAT Stream banks, ditches, roadsides, hedgerows; lowland to 380 m. DIST. Native. Throughout BI except extreme N. (All Europe except extreme SW.) FLS May-Aug.

Small-flowered Winter-cress
Barbarea stricta

Erect, branched, glabrous biennial or perennial to 100 cm. Similar to *B. vulgaris*, but upper stem leaves clasping, ± entire to remotely shallowly lobed, yellowish green, shining; flowers smaller, 5-6 mm across, *buds hairy*; fruits 13-28 mm, *persistent style short, 0.5-1.8 mm*. HABITAT Damp habitats, including rivers, ditches, canals, marshes, waste places DIST. Introduced. Rare and scattered throughout England. (Central, N and E Europe.) FLS May-Aug

ame's-violet
Hesperis matronalis

Wall-flower
Erysimum cheiri

Warty-cabbage
Bunias orientalis

Treacle Mustard
Erysimum cheiranthoides

Sea Stock
Matthiola sinuata

Hoary Stock
Matthiola incana

Small-flowered Winter-cress
Barbarea stricta

Winter-cress
Barbarea vulgaris

illustrations
0.6× lifesize

Medium-flowered
Winter-cress
Barbarea intermedia

Erect, ± glabrous, branched biennial to 60 cm. LEAVES Dark, glossy green; basal leaves with 2–5 pairs of lateral lobes; *upper stem leaves clasping, deeply lobed.* FLOWERS c.6 mm across, petals c.2× as long as sepals. FRUITS *Straight, 15–35 mm.* HABITAT Occasional casual of waysides, waste ground, stream banks, arable fields; lowland to 340 m. DIST. Introduced. Probably increasing. Whole of BI. (W, S and central Europe.) FLS May–Aug.

American Winter-cress,
Land-cress
Barbarea verna

Erect, ± glabrous, branched biennial to 70 cm. Similar to *B. intermedia*, but basal leaves with 4–10 pairs of lateral lobes; *flowers 7–10 mm across*, petals >2× as long as sepals; *fruits curved, >40 mm long.* HABITAT Roadsides, waste ground. DIST. Introduced. Cultivated as alternative to Water-cress *Rorippa nasturtium-aquaticum* (*see* below). Scattered throughout BI, usually as garden escape. (S France, Italy.) FLS May–Jul.

Water-cresses and yellow-cresses
Rorippa
See key to *Rorippa* on p.194.

Water-cress
Rorippa nasturtium-aquaticum

Prostrate to erect, glabrous aquatic perennial, to 60 cm, rooting at nodes. LEAVES Evergreen and remaining green in autumn, leaflets entire or with remote rounded teeth. FLOWERS 4–6 mm across, petals c.2× as long as sepals. FRUITS 13–18 mm; *seeds in 2 distinct rows in each cell, with c.25–50 depressions on each face.* HABITAT Shallow, clear, unpolluted streams, ditches, spring-heads, ponds, marshes. DIST. Native. Common throughout BI. (Most of Europe except Scandinavia and NE.) FLS May–Oct.

Narrow-fruited
Water-cress
Rorippa microphylla

Very similar to *R. nasturtium-aquaticum*, but *leaves tend to turn purplish in autumn*; fruits 16–23 mm, *seeds in middle and upper part in 1 row in each cell, with c.100 depressions on each face.* HABITAT Similar to *R. nasturtium-aquaticum*, but tolerant of slightly more acid conditions. DIST. Native. Throughout BI. (W Europe.) FLS May–Oct, about 2 weeks later than *R. nasturtium-aquaticum*. NOTE The hybrid between *R.*

nasturtium-aquaticum and *R. microphylla*, *R. × ste ilis*, is quite common; its fruits are usually sterile an deformed.

Marsh Yellow-cress
Rorippa palustr

Erect, glabrous annual to 60 cm. LEAVES Stem leave with 2–6 pairs of lateral lobes, leaflets entire or coarse toothed. FLOWERS *Sepals ≥1.6 mm, petals about as lon as sepals.* FRUITS 5–10 mm, *1–2× as long as stalks*, usu ally arising from all round stem. HABITAT Bare mud o lake, reservoir and pond margins that dry out in sum mer. DIST. Native. Throughout BI except N Scotlan (All Europe except S and SW.) FLS Jun–Sep.

Northern Yellow-cress
Rorippa islandic

Prostrate to erect, glabrous annual, to 30 cm. Ver similar to *R. palustris*, but stem leaves with 2–5 pair of lobes, leaflets entire or coarsely toothed; *sepa <1.6 mm, petals about as long as sepals*; fruits 6 12 mm, c.2–3× *as long as stalks*, often mostly arisin from one side of stem. HABITAT Muddy lake, pon and ditch margins that dry out in summer. DIST Native. Very local. Scattered N from Wales, mostly i W. (Norway, Iceland, mts of S Europe.) FLS Jul–Oc

Creeping Yellow-cress
Rorippa sylvestr

Prostrate to erect, stoloniferous, ± glabrous peren nial, to 60 cm. LEAVES *Stem leaves deeply divide with 3–6 pairs of narrow lateral lobes, these withou auricles.* FLOWERS 5 mm across, *petals 1.5–2× a long as sepals.* FRUITS 9–22 mm, 2× as long as stall persistent style 0.5–2 mm. HABITAT Margins o ponds, dykes, rivers and streams where water stand in winter; also garden weed on wet soils. DIST Native. Throughout BI except extreme N Scotlan (All Europe except Scandinavia and extreme SW.) FLS Jun–Aug.

Great Yellow-cress
Rorippa amphib

Tall, erect, ± glabrous, stoloniferous, branche perennial to 120 cm. LEAVES *Stem leaves yellowis green, simple, toothed or lobed.* FLOWERS *c.6 m across, petals 1.5–2× as long as sepals.* FRUITS 4.5–7. mm, *shorter than stalk*, persistent style 0.8–1.8 mm HABITAT Marshy ground, marginal vegetation o rivers, lakes, ponds, streams. DIST. Native. Englan Ireland; absent from Wales, Scotland, SW. (A Europe except Scandinavia and SW.) FLS Jun–Aug

edium-flowered Winter-cress
Barbarea intermedia

American Winter-cress
Barbarea verna

Creeping Yellow-cress
Rorippa sylvestris

Great Yellow-cress
Rorippa amphibia

Northern ow-cress
pa islandica

Narrow-fruited Water-cress
Rorippa microphylla

Water-cress
Rorippa nasturtium-aquaticum

Marsh Yellow-cress
Rorippa palustris

illustrations
0.6x lifesize

Horse-radish
Armoracia rusticana

Tall, robust, spreading, glabrous perennial to 125 cm. Leaves *Basal leaves large, to 100 cm*, dock-like. Flowers 8-9 mm across, in much-branched inflorescence; petals 2-3× as long as sepals. Fruits Mature fruits not known in Britain. Habitat Relic of cultivation or casual of waste ground, roadsides, railway embankments, sandy seashores. Dist. Archaeophyte (native of central Asia). Throughout BI, but rare in N and W. (Most of Europe.) Fls May–Jun.

Honesty
Lunaria annua

Tall, pubescent biennial to 100 cm. Leaves Basal leaves long-stalked, stem leaves ± sessile. Flowers *c.30 mm across, deep purple*, sometimes white; petals about 2× as long as sepals. Fruits *Flattened, broadly ovate to almost circular*, rounded at apex. Habitat Naturalised in hedgerows, pathsides, waste ground, near habitation. Dist. Introduced. Cultivated since C16th. Throughout BI, but rare in Scotland and Ireland. (Italy, SE Europe.) Fls Apr–Jun.

Bitter-cresses *Cardamine*

Stem leaves ternate and/or simple, with dark purple-brown bulbils in axils   *C. bulbifera*

Stem leaves not ternate, without bulbils

    Petals >5 mm, purple, pink or white:
       Petals pale to dark pink,
       anthers yellow   *C. pratensis*
       Petals almost white, anthers
       dark violet   *C. amara*

    Petals <5 mm, white:
       Stem leaves with narrow
       basal lobes clasping stem   *C. impatiens*
       Stem leaves without clasping
       basal lobes:
          6 stamens   *C. flexuosa*
          4 stamens   *C. hirsuta*

Coral-root
Cardamine bulbifera

Erect, ± glabrous, rhizomatous, unbranched perennial to 70 cm. Rhizome whitish, with small triangular scale leaves. Leaves Basal leaves pinnate, *mid-stem leaves ternate*, upper stem leaves simple; leaflets narrow, acute, usually with remote teeth, sometimes sparsely hairy; *stem leaves with glossy purple-brown bulbils in axils.* Flowers 12-18 mm across. Fruits Rare. Habitat Beechwoods on chalk; damp loamy soils by woodland streams on sands and clay. Dist. Native. Very local. Chilterns, the Weald (SE England). (Central and E Europe.) Fls Apr–Jun.

Cuckooflower, Lady's-smock
Cardamine pratensis

Erect, ± glabrous, unbranched perennial to 60 cm. Extremely variable. Leaves Rosette leaves pinnate, leaflets rounded, coarsely toothed, *terminal leaflet larger than laterals*; upper stem leaves with narrower entire leaflets. Flowers 12-18 mm across, petals *c.3× as long as sepals, lilac; anthers yellow.* Fruits 25-40 mm, valves without veins. Habitat Damp grassland, marshes, roadsides, hedgerows, stream sides; to 1080 m. Dist. Native. Common throughout BI. (All Europe except Mediterranean.) Fls Apr–Jun.

Large Bitter-cress
Cardamine amara

Prostrate to erect, glabrous winter-green perennial to 60 cm. Leaves Pale green, with no basal rosette. Flowers 12-15 mm across; *petals c.2× as long as sepals, white; anthers dark violet.* Fruits 15-40 mm. Habitat Stream sides, marshes, fens, wet woodlands, on acid soils; shade-tolerant. To 640 m. Dist. Native. Most of BI, but absent from SW England, most of Wales and Ireland, N Scotland. (All Europe except Mediterranean and extreme N.) Fls Apr–Jun.

Wavy Bitter-cress
Cardamine flexuosa

Erect, sparsely hairy annual to perennial, to 50 cm. Leaves Basal leaves in a loose rosette. Flowers Petals white, narrow, *c.2× as long as sepals; 6 stamens.* Fruits 12-25 mm, valves without veins. Habitat Damp, shaded places, including woodland, stream sides, marshes, gardens; to 830 m. Dist. Native. Common throughout BI. (Most of Europe except extreme N.) Fls Apr–Sep.

Hairy Bitter-cress
Cardamine hirsuta

Erect, sparsely hairy annual to 30 cm. Leaves Basal leaves in compact rosette. Flowers Petals white, narrow, *c.2× as long as sepals; 4 stamens.* Fruits 10-25 mm, valves without veins. Habitat Garden weed; rocks and scree, especially on limestone. To 1190 m. Dist. Native. Common throughout BI. (W, central and S Europe.) Fls Most of year.

Narrow-leaved Bitter-cress
Cardamine impatiens *(I)

Erect, glabrous biennial to 60 cm. Leaves No basal rosette; stem *leaves with conspicuous sharp-pointed clasping auricles.* Flowers *c.6 mm across, petals* scarcely longer than sepals. Fruits 15-30 mm. Habitat Shaded, damp rocks and scree on limestones. Dist. Native. Local and scattered throughout England, Wales. (W, central and E Europe.) Fls May–Aug.

Horse-radish
Armoracia rusticana

Cuckooflower
Cardamine pratensis

Coral-root
Cardamine bulbifera

Narrow-leaved Bitter-cress
Cardamine impatiens

Large Bitter-cress
Cardamine amara

Hairy Bitter-cress
Cardamine hirsuta

Wavy Bitter-cress
Cardamine flexuosa

Honesty
Lunaria annua

illustrations
0.6× lifesize

if	then
Flowers white	
▷ Valves of fruit with seeds in 2 rows; face of seeds with 25–50 depressions	*R. nasturtium-aquaticum* (p.190
▷ Middle and upper part of valves of fruit with seeds in 1 row; face of seeds with *c*.100 depressions	*R. microphylla* (p.190)
Flowers yellow	
▷ Petals about as long as sepals:	
Sepals ≥1.6 mm; fruit 0.8–2× as long as stalk	*R. palustris* (p.190)
Sepals <1.6 mm; fruit 2–3× as long as stalk	*R. islandica* (p.190)
▷ Petals ≥1.5× as long as sepals:	
Upper stem leaves lobed; fruit 2× as long as stalk	*R. sylvestris* (p.190)
Upper stem leaves toothed not lobed; fruit shorter than stalk	*R. amphibia* (p.190)

Key to Whitlowgrasses *Draba*

	if	then
1	▷ Flowers yellow; leaves glabrous except for marginal hairs (very rare, S Wales)	*D. aizoides* (p.198)
	▷ Flowers white; leaves pubescent	Go to ▷ **2**
2	▷ Flowering stems ± leafless (v. rare; Scottish mountains)	*D. norvegica* (p.198)
	▷ Flowering stems leafy	Go to ▷ **3**
3	▷ Stem leaves narrowly ovate; flowers 3–5 mm across, 6 stamens	*D. incana* (p.198)
	▷ Stem leaves broadly ovate; flowers 2.5–3 mm across, 4 stamens	*D. muralis* (p.198)

Key to Scurvygrasses *Cochlearia*

if	then
1 ▷ Blades of basal leaves tapering to petiole (cuneate)	*C. anglica* (p.200)
▷ Basal leaves cordate	Go to ▷ **2**
2 ▷ Stem leaves stalked; flowers ≤5 mm across	*C. danica* (p.200)
▷ Stem leaves sessile; flowers mostly >5 mm across	Go to ▷ **3**
3 ▷ Lower leaf blades ≥2 cm long; fruits ± globose, valves strongly veined (coastal)	*C. officinalis* (p.200)
▷ Lower leaf blades <2 cm long; fruits ovoid, valves weakly veined (mostly inland)	Go to ▷ **4**
4 ▷ Basal leaves mid-green; fruit valves mostly symmetrical	*C. pyrenaica* (p.200)
▷ Basal leaves dark glossy green; fruit valves mostly asymmetrical (very rare alpine; Scottish mountains)	*C. micacea* (p.200)

Key to Penny-cresses *Thlaspi*

if	then
1 ▷ Fruit almost circular, 10–20 mm across	*T. arvense* (p.204)
▷ Fruit ovate, <10 mm across	Go to ▷ **2**
2 ▷ Plant with non-flowering leaf rosettes; style as long as or longer than apical notch of fruit	*T. caerulescens* (p.204)
▷ Plant without non-flowering leaf rosettes; style *c.*½ as long as apical notch of fruit	Go to ▷ **3**
3 ▷ Plant glabrous; stem leaves glaucous with rounded auricles, not smelling of garlic	*T. perfoliatum* (p.204)
▷ Base of plant sparsely hairy; stem leaves with acute auricles, smelling of garlic when crushed	*T. alliaceum* (p.204)

Rock-cresses and relatives *Arabis*

See key to *Arabis* on p.185.

Northern Rock-cress — *Arabis petraea* VU. *(R)

Sparsely hairy rosette-forming rhizomatous perennial to 25 cm. LEAVES Basal leaves lobed, long-stalked, paddle-shaped, with simple or branched hairs. FLOWERS *c.6 mm across*, in few-flowered inflorescence; *petals pale mauve or white*, 2× as long as sepals. FRUITS 12–30 mm, valves 3-veined. HABITAT Alpine rocks, scree, usually on basic soils; to 1220 m and down to sea-level on serpentine rock in Shetland. DIST. Native. Very local. N Wales, Scottish Highlands, Shetland; very rare in Ireland. (N Europe, mts of central Europe.) FLS Jun–Aug.

Sand Rock-cress — *Arabis arenosa*

Erect, tufted annual to perennial, without rhizomes, to 40 cm. LEAVES Basal leaves lobed, long-stalked. FLOWERS *c.8 mm across*, petals mauve or white. FRUITS 12–30 mm. HABITAT Chalk and limestone rocks. DIST. *Not BI*, although has been recorded here as rare casual. (W, central and E Europe; naturalised in Scandinavia.) FLS May–Jun.

Tower Mustard — *Arabis glabra* EN.

Tall, erect, pubescent, glaucous, branched biennial to 100 cm. LEAVES Rosette leaves to 15 cm, stalked; stem leaves glabrous, with clasping auricles. FLOWERS *c.6 mm across; petals yellowish white*, <2× as long as sepals. FRUITS *Long, 40–70 mm, held erect close to stem*. HABITAT Dry heaths, banks, roadsides, disturbed ground. DIST. Native. Very local. Scattered throughout lowland England. (Most of Europe except extreme N.) FLS May–Jul.

Tower Cress — *Arabis turrita*

Pubescent biennial or perennial to 70 cm, with non-flowering rosettes and erect flowering stems to 70 cm. LEAVES Stem leaves densely hairy, sessile, bases clasping stem. FLOWERS *Petals pale yellow*, 2× as long as sepals. FRUITS *Very long*, 80–120 mm, *twisted and hanging to one side*. HABITAT/DIST. Introduced. Very rare. Found only on walls of St John's College, Cambridge. (Central and S Europe.) FLS May–Aug.

Alpine Rock-cress — *Arabis alpina* EN. *(B)

Pubescent, stoloniferous, mat-forming alpine perennial to 40 cm. LEAVES Stem leaves coarsely toothed, with broad, rounded basal lobes clasping stem. FLOWERS *Petals 5–8 mm*, 2× as long as sepals. FRUITS 17–30 mm, valves veinless. HABITAT Wet rock ledges at *c*.820 m. DIST. Native. Very rare. Found only in Cuillins, Skye. (Mts of S Europe, Arctic Europe.) FLS Jun–Aug.

Garden Arabis — *Arabis caucasica*

Pubescent, mat-forming alpine perennial. Very similar to *A. alpina*, but leaves more densely hairy with greyish pubescence, basal lobes of stem leaves narrower; flowers much larger, *petals 9.5–16 mm*. HABITAT Rocks, walls, usually close to habitation. DIST. Introduced. Commonly grown as a garden rock plant and naturalised throughout BI. (E Mediterranean.) FLS Mar–May.

Hairy Rock-cress — *Arabis hirsuta*

Erect, unbranched, pubescent biennial or perennial to 60 cm. LEAVES *Basal leaves entire or obscurely toothed*; stem leaves numerous, erect, scarcely clasping at base. FLOWERS In dense inflorescence; petals 4–6 mm, 2× as long as sepals. FRUITS Strictly erect, 18–45 mm, valves with single faint vein. HABITAT Dry chalk and limestone grassland, banks, limestone rocks, walls; to 1005 m. DIST. Native. Local and scattered throughout BI. (Most of N, W and Europe except extreme SW.) FLS Jun–Aug.

Bristol Rock-cress — *Arabis scabra* VU. *(E)

Erect, ± unbranched, pubescent perennial to 25 cm. LEAVES *Basal leaves lobed*, stem leaves not clasping at base. FLOWERS *Petals pale yellow*, 5.5–8 mm, 2× as long as sepals. FRUITS 15–50 mm, valves with veins. HABITAT Crevices in S-facing rocky slopes, limestone spoil. DIST. Native. Very rare. Avon Gorge near Bristol. (Pyrenees, SE France.) FLS Mar–May. NOTE Rather similar to *A. hirsuta*, but distinguished by lobed basal leaves and larger flowers.

Small Alison — *Alyssum alyssoides* *(E)

Much-branched, erect annual to 25 cm. *Whole plant hoary, grey-green, with dense covering of star-shaped hairs*. LEAVES To 2.5 cm. FLOWERS Small, *c*.3 mm across; petals pale yellow, longer than sepals. FRUITS 3–4 mm, *almost circular*. HABITAT Arable fields, tracks, waste ground, on sandy soils. DIST. Introduced. Very rare. East Anglia. (Most of Europe except Scandinavia.) FLS May–Jun.

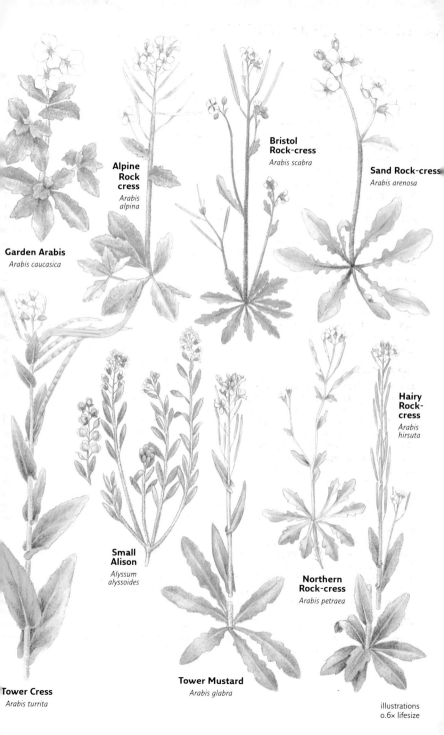

Garden Arabis
Arabis caucasica

Alpine Rock cress
Arabis alpina

Bristol Rock-cress
Arabis scabra

Sand Rock-cress
Arabis arenosa

Hairy Rock-cress
Arabis hirsuta

Tower Cress
Arabis turrita

Small Alison
Alyssum alyssoides

Tower Mustard
Arabis glabra

Northern Rock-cress
Arabis petraea

illustrations
0.6× lifesize

Hoary Alison
Berteroa incana

Erect, branching annual to 60 cm. *Whole plant densely covered by stellate (star-shaped) hairs.* STEMS Very leafy. FLOWERS In dense inflorescence; *petals deeply lobed*, >2× as long as sepals. FRUITS 4–10 mm, *oval, flattened*; valves without veins. HABITAT Waste places, cultivated ground, on sandy soils. DIST. Introduced. Rare casual in lowland England. (Central and E Europe.) FLS Jun–Sep.

Whitlowgrasses *Draba*
See key to Draba on p.194.

Yellow Whitlowgrass
Draba aizoides

Tufted, cushion-forming perennial, with numerous basal leaf rosettes and erect, leafless, glabrous flowering stems to 15 cm. LEAVES Stiff, narrow, margins fringed with stiff hairs. FLOWERS *Yellow*, 8–9 mm across, petals *c*.2× as long as sepals. FRUITS 6–10 mm, flattened; valves without veins. HABITAT Crevices on dry, open limestone cliffs. DIST. Native. Very rare. S coast of Gower, S Wales. (Mts of S Europe.) FLS Mar–May.

Rock Whitlowgrass
Draba norvegica

Densely tufted, pubescent perennial, with flowering stems to 5 cm. LEAVES Rosette leaves entire, to 1.5 cm; *stem leaves few or absent*. FLOWERS 4–5 mm across, in few-flowered inflorescence; petals *c*.1.5× as long as sepals; 6 stamens. FRUITS Erect, flattened, 4–7 mm. HABITAT Base-rich rock ledges, scree, cliffs; to 1160 m. DIST. Native. Very rare. Scottish Highlands. (Arctic Europe.) FLS Jul–Aug.

Hoary Whitlowgrass
Draba incana

Erect, pubescent biennial or perennial to 50 cm, with loose basal rosette and *leafy flowering stems*. LEAVES *Narrowly ovate*, rounded at base, densely hairy, usually coarsely toothed. FLOWERS 3–5 mm across, petals 1.5–2× as long as sepals, *6 stamens*. FRUITS Erect, flattened, twisted, 7–9 mm. HABITAT Limestone pavement, rocks and scree; other base-rich rocks, calcareous sand-dunes. To 1080 m. DIST. Native. Very local. N Britain. (Arctic Europe, Alps, Pyrenees.) FLS Jun–Jul.

Wall Whitlowgrass
Draba muralis

Erect, pubescent annual to 30 cm. Basal rosette soon dying; flowering stems leafy. LEAVES *Stem leaves broadly ovate*, cordate at base, ± clasping stem. FLOWERS 2.5–3 mm across, petals *c*.2× as long as sepals, *4* stamens. FRUITS Wide-spreading, flattened, 3–6 mm. HABITAT S-facing bare limestone rocks, walls, scree. DIST. Native. Rare. N and W England. (Most of Europe except N Scandinavia.) FLS Apr–May.

Whitlowgrasses *Erophila*

Small, delicate, early-flowering annuals to 20 cm. Leaves are small, in a basal rosette; *stem leaves are absent*. Flowers are 3–6 mm across, *the petals deeply notched*. Fruits are 1.5–9 mm; *stalks are slender, longer than fruits*. Native. Throughout Europe except extreme N. Flowering occurs Mar–Jun. This is a complicated genus, now regarded as comprising 3 separate species in BI:

Lower part of stem almost glabrous; leaves moderately hairy to glabrous, appearing green, stalks ≥⅓ as long as blades

Stems and leaves moderately hairy; petals notched ≥⅓ their length	*E. verna*
Stems and leaves almost glabrous, petals notched ≤⅓ their length	*E. glabrescens*

Lower part of stem and leaves densely hairy, appearing greyish; leaf stalks ≤⅓ as long as blades

	E. majuscula

Common Whitlowgrass
Erophila verna

The commonest *Erophila*. HABITAT Bare, open sandy areas, dunes, sandy heaths, rocks, walls, waste ground; also limestone rocks and pavement. DIST. Widespread and common throughout BI.

Glabrous Whitlowgrass
Erophila glabrescens

Less common than *E. verna*. HABITAT Similar to *E. verna*. DIST. Scattered throughout BI.

Hairy Whitlowgrass
Erophila majuscula

HABITAT Dry, open calcareous or sandy or gravelly habitats. DIST. Very scattered in England, Wales; rare in Scotland, Ireland.

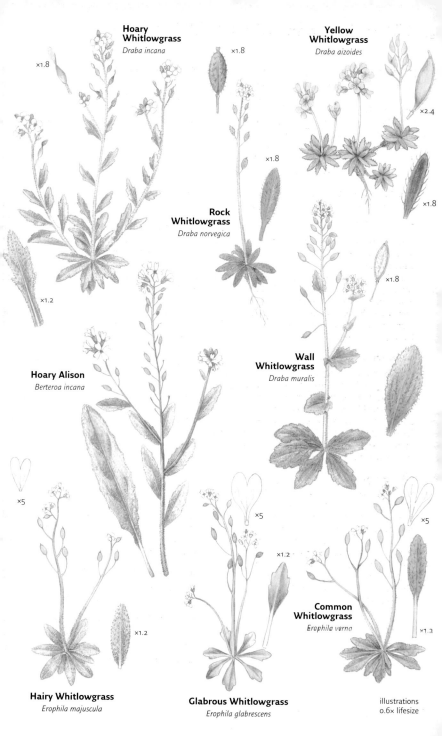

Hoary Whitlowgrass
Draba incana

×1.8

×1.8

Yellow Whitlowgrass
Draba aizoides

×2.4

×1.8

×1.8

Rock Whitlowgrass
Draba norvegica

×1.8

×1.2

×1.8

Wall Whitlowgrass
Draba muralis

Hoary Alison
Berteroa incana

×5

×5

×1.2

×5

Common Whitlowgrass
Erophila verna

×1.2

Hairy Whitlowgrass
Erophila majuscula

×1.2

Glabrous Whitlowgrass
Erophila glabrescens

illustrations
0.6× lifesize

Scurvygrass *Cochlearia*

See key to Cochlearia *on p.195.*

English Scurvygrass
Cochlearia anglica

Erect, glabrous perennial to 35 cm. LEAVES *Basal leaves in a rosette, leaf base tapering to long stalk; upper leaves sessile, usually clasping stem.* FLOWERS White or pale lilac, 10–14 mm across, petals 2–3× as long as sepals. FRUITS 8–15 mm, rounded, flattened. HABITAT Upper levels of salt marshes, muddy shores, tidal estuaries, brackish marshes. DIST. Native. Coasts of Britain and Ireland as far N as S Scotland. (Coast of Europe from S Sweden to S France.) FLS Apr–Jul.

Common Scurvygrass
Cochlearia officinalis

Prostrate to erect, glabrous biennial or perennial, to 40 cm. LEAVES Fleshy; basal leaves in loose rosette, long-stalked, rounded and cordate at base, blades ≥2 cm; *upper stem leaves sessile and clasping stem.* FLOWERS *8–10 mm across,* usually white; petals 2–3× as long as sepals. FRUITS *Globose,* 3–6 mm, *valves prominently veined.* HABITAT Upper parts of salt marshes, sea cliffs, sea walls, brackish marshes; occasional along salted roadsides inland. DIST. Native. All round coasts of BI, but rare in S and E. (Coasts of N Europe S to Brittany.) FLS May–Aug.

Pyrenean Scurvygrass
Cochlearia pyrenaica

Prostrate to erect, glabrous biennial or perennial, to 30 cm. Similar to Common Scurvygrass, but leaves not markedly fleshy, basal leaves smaller, blades usually <2 cm; flowers smaller, 5–8 mm across; *fruits ovoid rather than globose,* usually narrowed at apex and base, *with weakly veined valves.* HABITAT Fens, stream sides, wet cliffs, spoil tips, wet upland habitats; to 960 m. DIST. Native. N England, Scotland. (Central Europe.) FLS Midsummer.

Mountain Scurvygrass
Cochlearia micacea

Prostrate to erect, glabrous alpine biennial or perennial, to 10 cm. Similar to some forms of *C. pyrenaica,* but with smaller (leaf blades to 1 cm), *darker green glossy leaves;* narrower, almost veinless fruits *with mostly asymmetrical valves.* HABITAT Basic mountain ledges, flushes, springs, stream sides; to 1155 m. DIST. Native. Very rare. Scottish Highlands. (N Scandinavia.) FLS Midsummer.

Danish Scurvygrass
Cochlearia danica

Mat-forming, prostrate to erect, glabrous annual, to 20 cm. LEAVES Basal leaves long-stalked, shallowly lobed, cordate at base, often purplish; stem leaves distinctly lobed, *upper sessile but not clasping.* FLOWERS *Pale mauve, 4–5 mm across.* FRUITS Ovoid, 3–5.5 mm, tapering at both ends; valves finely net-veined. HABITAT Upper parts of sandy and shingly shores, cliffs, banks, walls. DIST. Native. Common all round coasts of BI; also rapidly spreading inland along salted road verges. (W coast of Europe N to S Finland.) FLS Jan–Jun.

Gold-of-pleasure
Camelina sativa

Erect, sparsely hairy or glabrous, branched annual to 80 cm. STEMS Leafy. LEAVES Narrow, sessile, ± *clasping.* FLOWERS 3 mm across, petals 1.5× as long as sepals. FRUITS *Inverted pear-shape,* narrowly winged, with prominent midrib. HABITAT Relic of cultivation, weed of flaxes and lucerne. DIST. Archaeophyte. Scattered throughout England; rare elsewhere. (Native of E Europe.) FLS Jun–Jul.

Shepherd's-purse
Capsella bursa-pastoris

Erect, glabrous or sparsely hairy annual to 40 cm. LEAVES Rosette leaves lobed; *stem leaves sessile, clasping.* FLOWERS 2.5 mm across, petals 2× as long as sepals. FRUITS *Inverted triangle, notched at the top* (the 'shepherd's purse'), 6–9 mm. HABITAT Gardens, arable fields, open areas, disturbed ground everywhere. DIST. Archaeophyte. Abundant throughout BI. (All Europe.) FLS Year-round.

Hutchinsia
Hornungia petraea

Erect, branched, glabrous, sometimes purplish annual to 15 cm. STEMS Flowering stems very leafy. LEAVES *Rosette leaves deeply pinnately divided, soon withering.* FLOWERS *Small, 1.5 mm across;* petals slightly longer than sepals. FRUITS 2–5 mm, flattened, stalks spreading. HABITAT/DIST. Native. Rare. Dry, open limestone rocks in N England; calcareous sand-dunes in S Wales. (S Europe; scattered N to S Scandinavia.) FLS Mar–May.

Shepherd's Cress
Teesdalia nudicaulis *(N)

Erect, ± glabrous or sparsely pubescent, branched annual to 45 cm. LEAVES *Rosette leaves deeply lobed,* stem leaves few. FLOWERS Small, 2 mm across, *petals unequal,* inner petals distinctly shorter than outer. FRUITS 3–4 mm, narrowly orbicular, notched at tip, flattened on one side; stalks spreading. HABITAT Open heaths, disturbed ground, on acid sandy or gravelly soils, coastal sand, fine shingle; lowland to 455 m. DIST. Native. Scattered and declining throughout BI; very rare in Ireland. (W and central Europe.) FLS Apr–Jun.

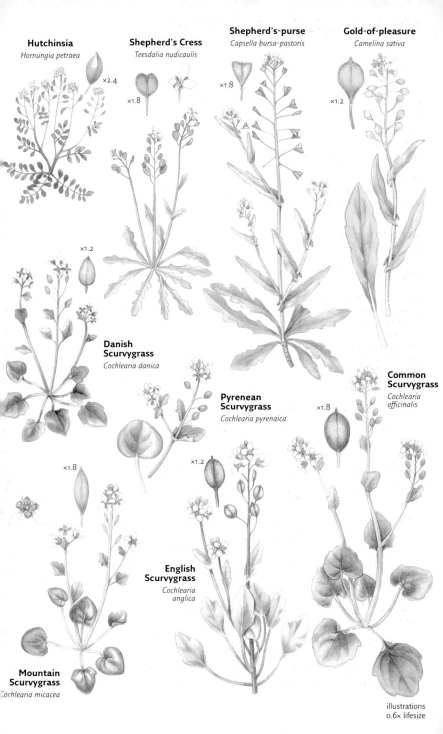

Hutchinsia
Hornungia petraea

×2.4

Shepherd's Cress
Teesdalia nudicaulis

×1.8

Shepherd's-purse
Capsella bursa-pastoris

×1.8

Gold-of-pleasure
Camelina sativa

×1.2

×1.2

Danish Scurvygrass
Cochlearia danica

Pyrenean Scurvygrass
Cochlearia pyrenaica

×1.8

Common Scurvygrass
Cochlearia officinalis

×1.2

×1.8

English Scurvygrass
Cochlearia anglica

Mountain Scurvygrass
Cochlearia micacea

illustrations
0.6× lifesize

	if	then
1	▷ Upper stem leaves with auricles clasping stem	Go to ▷ **2**
	▷ Upper stem leaves without auricles clasping stem	Go to ▷ **4**
2	▷ Upper part of fruit broadly winged	Go to ▷ **3**
	▷ Upper part of fruit not winged	**L. draba** (p.206)
3	▷ Style not or only just projecting beyond apical notch of fruit	**L. campestre** (p.204)
	▷ Style projecting well beyond apical notch of fruit	**L. heterophyllum** (p.204)
4	▷ Fruits 5–7 mm, as long as or longer than pedicels	**L. sativum** (p.204)
	▷ Fruits 1.5–4 mm, shorter than pedicels	Go to ▷ **5**
5	▷ Petals 1.5× as long as sepals	**L. latifolium** (p.206)
	▷ Petals absent or shorter than sepals	**L. ruderale** (p.206)

Key to Cabbage, Rape, Turnip, Mustard and Charlock
Brassica, Sinapis, Coincya and *Hirschfeldia*

	if	then
1	▷ At least some flowers with reflexed and inrolled sepals	Go to ▷ **2**
	▷ Sepals erect to spreading	Go to ▷ **3**
2	▷ Stem leaves sessile; beak of fruit *c*.1½ as long as valves	***S. arvensis*** (p.208)
	▷ Stem leaves stalked; beak of fruit flat, as long as valves	***S. alba*** (p.208)
3	▷ Fruit held at angle to stem, not closely appressed	Go to ▷ **4**
	▷ Fruit erect, closely appressed to stem	Go to ▷ **9**
4	▷ Valve of fruit with 1 prominent vein; beak conical	Go to ▷ **5**
	▷ Valve of fruit with 3 prominent veins; beak flat, sword-like	Go to ▷ **8**
5	▷ Upper stem leaves stalked	***B. nigra*** (p.208)
	▷ Base of upper stem leaves rounded or cordate, partly clasping	Go to ▷ **6**
6	▷ Base of stem woody; all leaves glabrous; petals 18-30 mm, buds overtopping open flowers	***B. oleracea*** (p.208)
	▷ Basal leaves ± bristly; petals 6-18 mm	Go to ▷ **7**
7	▷ Basal leaves glaucous; buds slightly overtopping open flowers	***B. napus*** (p.208)
	▷ Basal leaves green; open flowers overtopping buds	***B. rapa*** (p.208)
8	▷ Stems ± glabrous; young fruits glabrous	***C. monensis*** (p.210)
	▷ Stems densely hairy; young fruits hairy	***C. wrightii*** (p.210)
9	▷ Fruits 8-25 mm, beak seedless	***B. nigra*** (p.208)
	▷ Fruits 7-15 mm, beak swollen with 1 seed	***H. incana*** (p.210)

Penny-cresses *Thlaspi*

See key to *Thlaspi* on p.195.

Field Penny-cress
Thlaspi arvense

Erect, glabrous annual to 60 cm, with strong foetid smell when crushed. Stems Very leafy. Leaves No basal rosette; stem leaves oblong, sessile, with clasping, pointed basal lobes. Flowers 4–6 mm across, petals *c*.2× as long as sepals. Fruits *Almost circular, 10–20 mm across, flattened, with very broad wings and deep apical notch*; stalks curving upwards. Habitat Weed of arable fields, gardens, disturbed ground, on heavy, fertile soils. Dist. Archaeophyte. Throughout BI, but rare in N Scotland, N Ireland. (All Europe, but rare in S.) Fls May–Jul.

Perfoliate Penny-cress
Thlaspi perfoliatum VU. *(B)

Erect, *glabrous, slightly glaucous* annual to 20 cm. Leaves Rosette leaves soon withering; *stem leaves few (2–4), with* clasping, *rounded basal lobes, ±* meeting across stem. Flowers 2–2.5 mm across, petals *c*.2× as long as sepals. Fruits Broadly ovate, 3–6 mm, flattened, with narrow wings; persistent *style shorter than broad apical notch*; stalks spreading, ± at 90°. Habitat Quarries, spoil, open grassland, screes, on oolitic limestone. Dist. Native. Very rare. Cotswolds. (In Europe S from N Germany.) Fls Mar–May.

Alpine Penny-cress
Thlaspi caerulescens

Erect, glabrous, slightly glaucous or purplish perennial to 40 cm *with non-flowering leafy rosettes*. Leaves Rosette leaves paddle-shaped, persistent; 3–8 stem leaves, with clasping basal lobes. Flowers Petals 1.5–2× as long as sepals. Fruits Ovate, 5–9 mm, flattened, winged; *persistent style longer than or as long as apical notch*; stalks spreading, ± at 90°. Habitat Rock faces, scree, mine wastes, on soils rich in zinc or lead; also limestone outcrops. Upland to 940 m. Dist. Native. Very local. Scattered throughout Britain, but rare in alpine Scotland; absent from Ireland. (W and central Europe.) Fls Apr–Aug.

Garlic Penny-cress
Thlaspi alliaceum

Erect, *pubescent* annual to 60 cm. *Whole plant smells of garlic*. Stems Grooved. Leaves *Stem leaves* oblong, *with acute basal lobes*. Fruits Ovate, narrowly winged, 5–10 mm, swollen; persistent style shorter than apical notch. Habitat Rare casual or established weed of arable fields. Dist. Introduced. Scattered throughout E and SE England. (S and E Europe.) Fls May–Jun.

Wild Candytuft
Iberis amara VU.

Erect, sparsely hairy, branched annual to 30 cm. Stems Very leafy. Leaves No basal rosette. Flowers 6–8 mm across, in dense inflorescence; *petals white or mauve, 2–4× as long as sepals, outer 2 much larger than inner*. Fruits Rounded, flattened, winged, 4–6 mm across. Habitat Dry, bare calcareous hillsides, edge of arable fields, around rabbit burrows. Dist. Native. Rare. Virtually confined to Chilterns. (W Europe.) Fls Jul–Aug.

Pepperworts *Lepidium*

See key to *Lepidium* on p.202.

Field Pepperwort
Lepidium campestre

Erect, pubescent annual to 50 cm. Stems Flowering stem very leafy, branching above. Leaves Basal rosettes soon withering; *upper stem leaves narrow*, softly hairy, *basal lobes acute, clasping*. Flowers Small, 2–2.5 mm across, petals 1.5–2× as long as sepals; *anthers yellow*. Fruits Ovate, flattened, winged, 4.5–6.5 mm; *valves covered by small white vesicles (use lens); persistent style shorter than or just as long as notch*. Habitat Dry, open habitats, walls, waste ground, arable land. Dist. Archaeophyte. Throughout BI, but very rare in Scotland, Ireland. (In Europe S from S Sweden.) Fls May–Aug.

Smith's Pepperwort
Lepidium heterophyllum

Prostrate to erect, pubescent perennial, to 45 cm, branching from base as well as above. Similar to *L. campestre*, but flowers larger, 3–3.5 mm across, petals *c*.1.5× as long as sepals, *anthers reddish; valves of fruits without vesicles, persistent style distinctly longer than apical notch*. Habitat Dry, open heathy areas, banks, shingle, arable land. Dist. Native. Throughout BI, but rare in N Scotland. (W and SW Europe.) Fls May–Aug.

Garden Cress
Lepidium sativum

Erect, glabrous or sparsely hairy, branched annual to 100 cm. Leaves Lower stem leaves deeply divided; upper stem leaves sessile, not clasping. Flowers Petals white to pink, *c*.2× as long as sepals; anthers blue. Fruits Winged, *5–7 mm*; persistent style shorter than apical notch. Dist. Introduced (probably native of Egypt, W Asia). Scattered throughout BI as escape from cultivation or via birdseed. Fls Jun–Jul.

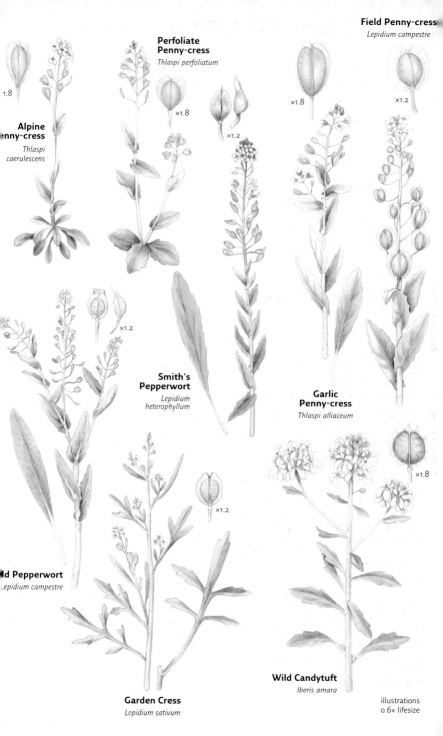

Field Penny-cress
Lepidium campestre

×1.8   ×1.2

Perfoliate Penny-cress
Thlaspi perfoliatum

×1.8

×1.2

×1.8

Alpine Penny-cress
Thlaspi caerulescens

×1.2

Smith's Pepperwort
Lepidium heterophyllum

Garlic Penny-cress
Thlaspi alliaceum

×1.8

Field Pepperwort
Lepidium campestre

×1.2

Garden Cress
Lepidium sativum

Wild Candytuft
Iberis amara

illustrations
0.6× lifesize

Narrow-leaved Pepperwort · *Lepidium ruderale*

Erect, ± glabrous, much-branched annual to 40 cm. Whole plant has a foetid smell. LEAVES Basal leaves deeply pinnate, with narrow lobes. FLOWERS Inconspicuous, greenish; *petals tiny or absent*; 2 stamens. FRUITS 2-2.5 mm, flattened; persistent style shorter than apical notch. HABITAT Dry upper end of salt marshes, sea walls, waste ground near sea; also waste places and salted road verges inland. DIST. Archaeophyte. Throughout BI, but rare in Scotland, Ireland. (W, central and E Europe.) FLS May-Jul.

Dittander · *Lepidium latifolium*

Tall, erect, glabrous perennial to 130 cm. LEAVES *Basal leaves to 30 cm, long-stalked, with toothed margin.* FLOWERS *2.5 mm across, in large, dense-flowered inflorescence*; sepals with broad white margins; petals 2× as long as sepals. FRUITS 1.5-2.5 mm, rounded, flattened, without apical notch. HABITAT Creeks, ditches, brackish grassland, estuarine salt marshes; waste ground inland. DIST. Native. E coast of England; also scattered inland as relic of cultivation. (Coasts of NW Europe; inland SW and E Europe.) FLS Jun-Jul.

Hoary Cress · *Lepidium draba*

Erect, glabrous or pubescent, branched perennial to 60 cm. Often forms extensive patches. LEAVES Basal leaves soon withering; *stem leaves with basal lobes clasping stem*. FLOWERS 5-6 mm across; in dense inflorescence, petals 1.5-2× as long as sepals. FRUITS 4-6 mm, cordate, flattened, *unwinged*; prominent persistent style to >1.5 mm. HABITAT Roadsides, railways, arable land, waste ground, especially near sea. DIST. Introduced. Common and increasing throughout most of BI, but rare in N Scotland, Ireland. (S and E Europe.) FLS May-Jun.

Swine-cresses *Coronopus*

Distinguished from all other white-flowered crucifers by inflorescences that arise opposite stem leaves (leaf-opposed) rather than in their axils.

Swine-cress · *Coronopus squamatus*

Prostrate, much-branched, glabrous annual. LEAVES Rosette and stem leaves deeply divided. FLOWERS *c*.2.5 mm across, in dense inflorescences arising opposite stem leaves; *petals longer than sepals*. FRUITS 2.5-3.5 mm, *longer than stalks*, kidney-shaped, tapering to short persistent style, *valves coarsely and irregularly ridged*. HABITAT Fertile trampled soil of paths, gateways, pastures, waste ground. DIST. Archaeophyte. Common in lowland England; scattered elsewhere throughout BI. (All Europe except N.) FLS Jun-Sep.

Lesser Swine-cress · *Coronopus didymus*

Prostrate, much-branched, ± glabrous annual to 30 cm. Similar to *C. squamatus*, but *petals tiny or absent*; Fruits smaller, 1.3-1.7 mm, *shorter than stalks*, notched at both base and apex, *valves smooth* (without ridges). HABITAT Weed of cultivated and waste ground, paths, roadsides. DIST. Introduced (native of South America). Widespread in England, Wales; spreading to N. (W, central and S Europe) FLS Jul-Sep.

Awlwort · *Subularia aquatica*

Dwarf aquatic annual to 10 cm. The only aquatic crucifer with awl-shaped leaves and tiny white flowers. LEAVES Glabrous, awl-shaped, in a basal rosette. FLOWERS In few-flowered inflorescence, *often submerged*; petals white, 2× as long as sepals. FRUITS 2-5 mm, slightly compressed. HABITAT Clear shallow margins of acidic upland pools, lakes; to 825 m. DIST. Native. Scotland, N England, W Wales, W Ireland. (N Europe, Pyrenees.) FLS Jun-Aug.

Wall-rockets *Diplotaxis*

Distinguished from other yellow-flowered crucifers with elongated fruits by having slightly compressed fruits, their valves with a single prominent vein and seeds in 2 rows in each cell.

Perennial Wall-rocket · *Diplotaxis tenuifolia*

Erect, much-branched, glabrous, glaucous perennial to 80 cm. STEMS Very leafy. LEAVES *Foetid when crushed, rosette leaves absent.* FLOWERS *Petals pale yellow*, 8-15 mm, 2× as long as sepals. FRUITS 20-50 mm, *with a distinct stalk above sepal scars*, valves with 1 distinct vein. HABITAT Waste ground, especially around ports, industrial areas. DIST. Archaeophyte. Throughout BI, especially SE England, but very rare in Scotland, Ireland. (W, S and E Europe.) FLS May-Sep.

Annual Wall-rocket · *Diplotaxis muralis*

Erect, sparsely pubescent annual to 60 cm, branched from base. Similar to *D. tenuifolia*, but *basal leaves in a rosette*, stem leaves few; *petals deep yellow*, ≤8 mm, *c*.1.5× as long as sepals; fruits 20-40 mm, *without stalk above sepal scars*. HABITAT Dry, open areas, waste ground, especially on calcareous soils. DIST. Introduced. Scattered throughout BI but rare in Scotland, Ireland. (Most of Europe except Scandinavia.) FLS Jun-Sep.

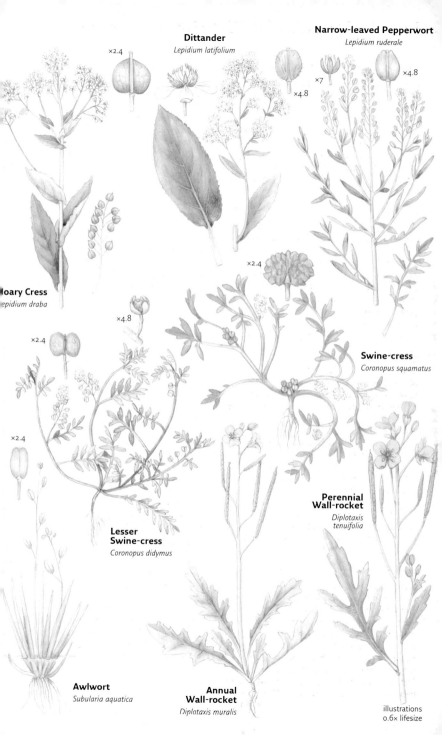

Dittander
Lepidium latifolium

×2.4

Narrow-leaved Pepperwort
Lepidium ruderale

×7

×4.8

×4.8

Hoary Cress
Lepidium draba

×2.4

×2.4

×4.8

×2.4

Swine-cress
Coronopus squamatus

**Lesser
Swine-cress**
Coronopus didymus

**Perennial
Wall-rocket**
*Diplotaxis
tenuifolia*

Awlwort
Subularia aquatica

**Annual
Wall-rocket**
Diplotaxis muralis

illustrations
0.6× lifesize

Spanish

Cabbage, Rape, Turnip, Mustard and Charlock *Brassica, Sinapis, Coincya, Hirschfeldia*

See key on p.203.

Cabbage
Brassica oleracea

Robust, *glabrous, glaucous perennial to 60 cm.* STEMS Base woody, covered by numerous conspicuous leaf scars. LEAVES Basal leaves stalked; stem leaves sessile, with rounded basal lobes partly clasping stem. FLOWERS In open inflorescence, this elongating so that *buds overtop open flowers;* sepals erect; *petals pale yellow, 15–30 mm, c.2× as long as sepals.* FRUITS 40–85 mm, beak short, usually 1-seeded. HABITAT Steep chalk and limestone cliffs. DIST. Doubtfully native. Very local all round British coasts, chiefly in SW; also casual as relic of cultivation inland. (NW France, N Spain.) FLS Apr–Jun. NOTE Wild plants are var. *oleracea.*

Rape
Brassica napus

Erect, glaucous annual or biennial to 100 cm, *sparsely pubescent below.* LEAVES Basal leaves long-stalked, glaucous; upper stem leaves sessile, simple, with rounded basal lobes clasping stem. FLOWERS In dense inflorescence, *buds overtopping open flowers;* sepals erect; *petals 11–15 mm, c.2× as long as sepals.* FRUITS 35–95 mm, beak with 0–1 seeds. HABITAT Common as weed of arable land, roadsides, disturbed ground. DIST. Introduced. Casual or naturalised throughout BI, but rare in NW Scotland, N Ireland. (Naturalised throughout Europe.) FLS Mar–Aug. NOTE Oil-seed Rape is ssp. *oleifera.*

Turnip
Brassica rapa

Erect annual or biennial to 100 cm. LEAVES *Basal leaves coarsely hairy,* stalked, pinnate, *green;* upper stem leaves glabrous, sessile, basal lobes ± completely clasping stem. FLOWERS In dense inflorescence, *flowers overtopping buds;* petals 6–13 mm, 1.5–2× as long as sepals. FRUITS 30–65 mm, beak without seed. HABITAT Weed of cultivation, waste ground, roadsides, banks of streams and rivers. DIST. Archaeophyte. Established throughout BI, but rare in N Scotland. (All Europe, but rare in SW.) FLS May–Aug.

Black Mustard
Brassica nigra

Tall, much-branched annual to 200 cm, *bristly below, glabrous above.* STEMS Wide-spreading. LEAVES *All leaves stalked,* upper leaves rather glaucous. FLOWERS Petals 8–12 mm, 2× as long as sepals. FRUITS 8–25 mm, *erect and held closely appressed to stem;* valves strongly keeled with fine lateral veins; beak seedless. HABITAT Sea cliffs, shingle, riverbanks; also

casual of waste ground and roadsides inland. Lowland to 380 m. DIST. Probably native. Widespread in England, Wales; rare in Scotland, Ireland. (Most of Europe except Scandinavia.) FLS May–Sep. SIMILAR SPP. Often confused with *Sinapis arvensis* (below) or *Hirschfeldia incana* (see p.210).

Charlock
Sinapis arvensis

Erect, branched or unbranched, sparsely hairy annual to 100 cm. LEAVES Lower leaves stalked, with a large terminal lobe and few small laterals; *upper leaves sessile.* FLOWERS In dense inflorescence; *sepals narrow, inrolled, wide-spreading or reflexed;* petals 8–15 mm, *c.2× as long as sepals.* FRUITS 25–50 mm; valves with 3–7 distinct veins; beak 7–16 mm, *c.½ as long as valves;* usually 1-seeded. HABITAT Common arable weed of roadsides, waste ground; lowland to 450 m. DIST. Archaeophyte. Abundant throughout BI. (All Europe except NE.) FLS May–Jul.

White Mustard
Sinapis alba

Erect, branched or unbranched, sparsely hairy annual to 100 cm. Similar to *S. arvensis, but stem leaves stalked,* pinnate; FRUITS 20–40 mm, *with distinctive flat, often upward-curving beak, 10–24 mm, as long as valves.* HABITAT Persistent arable weed, casual on waste ground, roadsides, usually on calcareous soils. DIST. Archaeophyte (origins unknown). Throughout BI, but rare and scattered outside England. FLS Jun–Aug. NOTE The original mustard of 'mustard and cress', now often replaced for this use by *Brassica napus.*

Garden Rocket
Eruca vesicaria

Erect, sparsely hairy or glabrous, branched or unbranched annual to 80 cm. LEAVES Variable. FLOWERS Sepals erect, soon falling; *petals cream to pale yellow with violet veins,* 2× as long as sepals. FRUITS 15–30 mm; 2 rows of seeds in each cell; *beak c.½ as long as valves, flat, 5–11 mm.* HABITAT Casual of waste ground and escape from cultivation. DIST. Introduced. Scattered throughout England. (Native of S Europe.) FLS May–Aug. NOTE The cultivated and casual plant is ssp. *sativa.*

Hairy Rocket
Erucastrum gallicum

Erect, densely pubescent annual or biennial to 60 cm. LEAVES Stem leaves deeply divided. FLOWERS *In inflorescence, lower part with leaf-like bracteoles;* petals 6–10 mm, 2× as long as sepals. FRUITS 20–45 mm, valves with 1 central vein. HABITAT Quarries, roadsides, waste ground, on calcareous soils. DIST. Introduced. Casual, scattered throughout BI, but rare in Scotland. (Central Europe, Pyrenees.) FLS May–Sep

Black Mustard
Brassica nigra

Rape
Brassica napus

arden Rocket
Eruca vesicaria

Cabbage
Brassica oleracea

Turnip
Brassica rapa

Charlock
Sinapis arvensis

White Mustard
Sinapis alba

Hairy Rocket
Erucastrum gallicum

illustrations
0.6× lifesize

Isle of Man Cabbage
Coincya monensis ssp. *monensis*

Prostrate to ascending, *almost glabrous biennial* to 50 cm. Leaves Rosette and stem leaves long-stalked, deeply pinnate, glabrous. Flowers Sepals erect; petals 15-20 mm, *c.*2× as long as sepals; ovaries glabrous. Fruits *Glabrous when young*; mature fruits 35-70 mm; *valves with 3-5 veins; beak flattened*, 7-25 mm; seeds 1.3-2 mm. Habitat Sand-dunes, strand lines. Dist. Endemic. Very local. W coast from Lancashire to Ayrshire, I of Man, S Wales. Fls May-Sep.

Wallflower Cabbage
Coincya m. ssp. *cheiranthos*

Similar to ssp. *monensis*, but *stems erect, pubescent;* leaves pubescent; seeds 0.8-1.6 mm. Habitat Docks, waste ground, roadsides, railways. Dist. Introduced. Casual in suitable habitats, especially S Wales. (S and SW Europe.) Fls May-Oct. *Not illustrated.*

Lundy Cabbage
Coincya wrightii VU. *(B)

Erect pubescent, rather glaucous *perennial* to 90 cm. Stems Branched, woody below. Flowers Sepals erect; petals 15-20 mm, *c.*2× as long as sepals; ovaries pubescent. Fruits *Pubescent when young*; mature fruits 30-65 mm; valves with 3 veins; beak flattened, 8-15 mm. Habitat S-facing cliffs, open ground. Dist. Endemic (discovered in 1936). Lundy I, Bristol Channel. Fls May-Aug.

Hoary Mustard
Hirschfeldia incana

Erect, branched annual (or rarely perennial) to 120 cm. Stems *Lower part usually densely pubescent, with short, stiff white hairs.* Leaves *Densely pubescent*, as lower stems. Flowers Petals 5.5-10 mm, *c.*2× as long as sepals. Fruits *Erect, closely appressed to stem, 7-15 mm; beak* 3-6.5 mm, *c.⅓ as long as valves; 1(-2)-seeded.* Habitat Naturalised or casual of waste ground, roadsides, railways, docks, on well-drained soils. Dist. Introduced. Increasing. Widely distributed in England, Wales; rare further N. (S and SW Europe.) Fls May-Oct. Similar to *Brassica nigra* (p.208), from which it differs in shorter fruits, 1-seeded beak, and more hairy leaves and stems.

Sea Rocket
Cakile maritima

Prostrate to erect, *glabrous, succulent annual*, to 50 cm. Leaves Simple to pinnate. Flowers Sepals erect; Petals 6-10 mm, *mauve, pink or white*, 2× as long as sepals. Fruits *10-25 mm; comprising 2 unequal, 1-seeded joints that separate on ripening.* Habitat Fore dunes and drift line on sandy shores. Dist. Native. Frequent all round coasts of BI. (All round coasts of Europe.) Fls Jun-Aug.

Bastard Cabbage
Rapistrum rugosum

Erect annual to 100 cm. Stems Stiffly hairy, rather glaucous. Leaves Pinnate, stiffly hairy, dark green. Flowers Petals 2× as long as sepals. Fruits 3-10 mm, *comprising 2 unequal joints, the lower cylindrical and usually seedless, the upper 1-seeded, strongly ribbed and wrinkled.* Habitat Casual of waste ground, sometimes naturalised. Dist. Introduced with grain and birdseed. Occasional in lowland England; rare elsewhere. (S and SW Europe.) Fls May-Sep.

Sea-kale
Crambe maritima

Large, glaucous, glabrous, much-branched *cabbage-like perennial* to 75 cm. Shoots and leaves dying back in winter. Leaves Lower leaves large, to 30 cm, ± lobed, with wavy margins. Flowers 10-15 mm across; petals white, green at base. Fruits *Large*, 10-14 mm; 2-jointed, the lower stalk-like, the terminal 1-seeded, ± spherical. Habitat *Undisturbed shingle beaches*; rarely on cliffs and dunes. Dist. Native. Local, possibly declining. Coasts of BI N to Clyde. (Coasts of NW Europe to S Finland, Black Sea.) Fls Jun-Aug.

Wild Radish
Raphanus raphanistrum ssp. *raphanistrum*

Erect, roughly hairy or bristly annual to 60 cm. Leaves ± pinnate, with a large, rounded terminal lobe and 1-4 pairs of separated lateral lobes. Flowers *Petals yellow, lilac or white, usually with dark veins*, 12-20 mm, 2× as long as sepals. Fruits *25-90 mm, constricted between the 3-8 seeds into ± oblong segments that separate on ripening.* Habitat Casual or persistent weed of cultivation, waste ground. Dist. Archaeophyte. Common throughout BI. (All Europe except extreme N.) Fls May-Sep.

Sea Radish
Raphanus raphanistrum ssp. *maritimus*

Tall, much-branched, roughly hairy or bristly biennial or perennial to 80 cm. Similar to ssp. *raphanistrum*, but basal leaves ± pinnate, with large *terminal lobe and 4-8 pairs of contiguous or overlapping lateral lobes*; petals yellow, sometimes white; Fruits 15-55 mm, *deeply constricted between the 1-5 seeds into ± spherical segments*. Habitat Open areas, rough maritime grassland, disturbed ground, cliffs, drift line on sand or shingle. Dist. Native. S and W coasts of BI; rare elsewhere. (Coasts of W and S Europe.) Fls Jun-Aug. Note Intermediates between the 2 subspecies occur in some parts of their ranges. The Garden Radish *R. sativus* also occasionally occurs as a casual; its origins are unknown and it does not occur as a wild plant.

undy Cabbage
Coincya wrightii

Sea Rocket
Cakile maritima

Sea-kale
Crambe maritima

×1.8

×1.8

Bastard Cabbage
Rapistrum rugosum

Hoary Mustard
Hirschfeldia incana

Isle of Man Cabbage
Coincya monensis

Wild Radish
Raphanus raphanistrum

Sea Radish
Raphanus raphanistrum ssp. maritimus

illustrations
0.6× lifesize

RESEDACEAE Mignonettes

Annuals, biennials or perennials. Leaves simple or pinnate, with glandular stipules. Flowers irregular, small, in spike-like racemes; 4-7 sepals and petals; 7-40 stamens. Fruits are a capsule.

Flowers yellowish; capsule with 3 apical lobes

Leaves simple, entire; 4 petals and sepals	*R. luteola*
Leaves pinnate; 6 petals and sepals	*R. lutea*

Flowers white; capsule with 4 apical lobes   *R. alba*

Weld   *Reseda luteola*

Robust, erect, little-branched, glabrous biennial to 150 cm. LEAVES *Rosette and stem leaves simple, entire, margins wavy*, midrib pale. FLOWERS 4-5 mm across; 4 sepals and petals; back and side petals lobed, front entire; *20-25 stamens*. FRUITS Almost spherical capsule, 5-6 mm, with 3 apical lobes. HABITAT Disturbed and waste ground on calcareous soils, roadsides, field margins, abandoned quarries; lowland. DIST. Archaeophyte. Throughout BI, but rare in N Scotland, W Ireland. (Central and S Europe.) FLS Jun-Aug.

Wild Mignonette   *Reseda lutea*

Erect, much-branched, ± glabrous biennial or perennial to 75 cm. LEAVES *Rosette leaves soon withering; stem leaves deeply lobed, with narrow segments*. FLOWERS 6 mm across; 6 sepals and petals; back and side petals lobed, front entire; *12-20 stamens*. FRUITS Oblong capsule, 10-18 mm, with 3 apical lobes. HABITAT Disturbed ground on calcareous soils, road verges, field margins; lowland. DIST. Native. Throughout BI, but rare in Scotland; introduced in Ireland. (Central and S Europe.) FLS Jun-Aug.

White Mignonette   *Reseda alba*

Erect, glabrous, branched annual to perennial, to 75 cm. LEAVES Deeply divided, segments narrow. FLOWERS *c.*9 mm across, *white*; 5 sepals and petals; 11-14 stamens. FRUITS Oblong capsule, 6-15 mm, with 4 apical lobes. HABITAT Casual on waste ground, old walls, around ports. DIST. Introduced. Local and scattered throughout England, Wales; very rare in Scotland, Ireland. (S and E Europe.) FLS Jun-Aug.

EMPETRACEAE Crowberries

Crowberry   *Empetrum nigrum*

Low evergreen, heather-like shrub to 45 cm. LEAVES *Alternate, entire, with revolute margins*. FLOWERS Pink, bisexual or dioecious; *3 sepals; 3 petals, free* (heathers have 4-5 fused petals); *3 stamens*. FRUITS Black berry-like drupe. HABITAT Mountains, moorlands, blanket bog on dry, acid peat in exposed places; open birch, pine woodland. To 1270 m. DIST. Native. Common in upland Britain. (N Europe, mts of central and S Europe.) FLS May-Jun. NOTE Ssp. *nigrum* has prostrate, rooting stems, ± parallel-sided leaves, 3-4× as long as broad, and dioecious flowers, and is found throughout species' range. Ssp. *hermaphroditum* has ± erect stems, not rooting, leaves 2-3× as long as broad, with ± convex margins, and bisexual flowers, and is confined to exposed sites at higher altitudes in N Scotland, Lake District (rare), Snowdonia.

ERICACEAE Heaths and rhododendron family

A family of trees or dwarf shrubs with simple, usually evergreen, whorled, opposite or alternate leaves (*see* key on p.214). Flowers are regular or slightly irregular; 4 or 5 sepals and petals, petals usually fused; as many as, or 2× as many, stamens as petals; ovary superior to inferior, 1 style. Fruit is a capsule or berry. Almost all members of the Ericaceae, except for *Arbutus*, are plants of acid soils.

Rhododendron   *Rhododendron ponticum*

Evergreen glabrous shrub to 3 m. Can form extensive thickets. LEAVES 6-12 cm. FLOWERS *Campanulate* (bell- or funnel-shaped), *c.*50 mm across, slightly zygomorphic; sepals small; 10 stamens. HABITAT Woods, heaths, rocky hillsides, on acid sandy or peaty soils; to 600 m. DIST. Introduced 1763. Naturalised throughout BI. (SW Europe to Asia Minor.) FLS May-Jun.

Labrador-tea   *Ledum palustre*

Much-branched evergreen shrub to 1 m. LEAVES 1-4.5 cm, margins revolute, dark green above, *with dense covering of rusty hairs beneath*. FLOWERS 10-15 mm across, *petals free*, 6-8 stamens. FRUITS Oblong capsule, 4-5 mm. HABITAT Bogs. DIST. Introduced in 1762 (British plant is ssp. *groenlandicum*, a native of North America). Naturalised near Bridge of Allan, Perthshire; sporadic elsewhere. (N Europe and N America.) FLS Jun-Jul.

Trailing Azalea   *Loiseleuria procumbens*

Dwarf, glabrous, much-branched *evergreen alpine shrub* to 25 cm. LEAVES 3-8 mm, *opposite*. FLOWERS Bell-shaped, 3-5 mm across; 5 stamens. FRUITS Capsule, 3-4 mm. HABITAT Exposed ridges, plateaux, moorland, on acid soil; to 900 m. DIST. Native. Scottish Highlands. (N Europe.) FLS May-Jul.

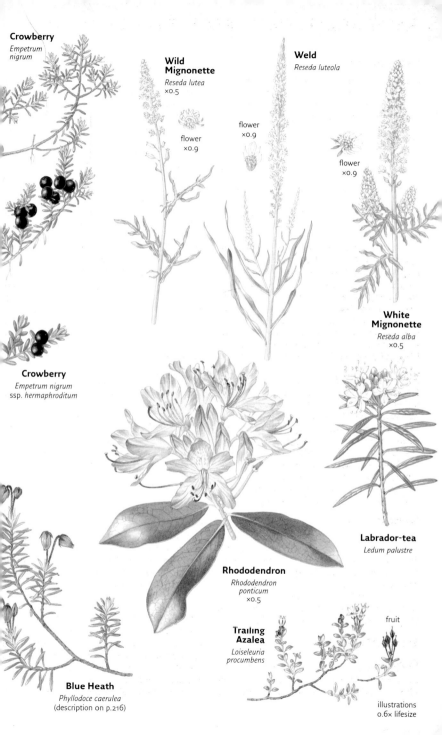

Crowberry
Empetrum nigrum

Wild Mignonette
Reseda lutea
×0.5

flower
×0.9

flower
×0.9

Weld
Reseda luteola

flower
×0.9

White Mignonette
Reseda alba
×0.5

Crowberry
Empetrum nigrum
ssp. *hermaphroditum*

Labrador-tea
Ledum palustre

Rhododendron
Rhododendron ponticum
×0.5

Blue Heath
Phyllodoce caerulea
(description on p.216)

Trailing Azalea
Loiseleuria procumbens

fruit

illustrations
0.6× lifesize

	if	**then**
1	▷ Leaves opposite or in whorls	Go to ▷ **2**
	▷ Leaves alternate	Go to ▷ **4**
2	▷ Leaves in whorls	*Erica* (p.215)
	▷ Leaves opposite	Go to ▷ **3**
3	▷ 4 sepals and petals, corolla shorter than calyx; leaves small (1–2 mm), in 4 rows and overlapping on young shoots	*Calluna vulgaris* (p.216)
	▷ 5 sepals and petals, corolla 2× length of calyx; leaves 3–8 mm (low alpine shrubs)	*Loiseleuria procumbens* (p.212)
4	▷ Petals united	Go to ▷ **5**
	▷ Petals free; leaves with rust-coloured hairs beneath	*Ledum palustre* (p.212)
5	▷ Ovary inferior; fruit a berry	*Vaccinium* (p.215)
	▷ Ovary superior	Go to ▷ **6**
6	▷ Flowers ≥15 mm, slightly zygomorphic, campanulate	*Rhododendron* (p.212)
	▷ Flowers ≤15 mm, regular urceolate (contracted at mouth)	Go to ▷ **7**
7	▷ Evergreen tree or shrub; fruit orange-red and warty	*Arbutus unedo* (p.216)
	▷ Dwarf shrub	Go to ▷ **8**
8	▷ 4 petals and sepals	*Daboecia cantabrica* (p.216)
	▷ 5 petals and sepals	Go to ▷ **9**
9	▷ Leaves linear, <5 mm broad	Go to ▷ **10**
	▷ Leaves ovate, >5 mm broad	Go to ▷ **11**
10	▷ Calyx and pedicels glabrous, flowers pink (bogs)	*Andromeda polifolia* (p.216)
	▷ Calyx and pedicels with glandular hairs, flowers purple (rare, mountains)	*Phyllodoce caerulea* (p.216)
11	▷ Leaves >5 mm; flowers in panicles; calyx enlarging and becoming fleshy in fruit	*Gaultheria shallon* (p.216)
	▷ Leaves ≤3 mm; flowers in racemes or solitary; calyx not enlarging in fruit	*Arctostaphylos* (p.216)

Keys to Heaths *Erica*; Cranberries and Bilberries *Vaccinium*

	if	then
	Heaths *Erica*	
1	▷ Stamens not protruding from mouth of corolla	Go to ▷ **2**
	▷ Stamens protruding from mouth of corolla	Go to ▷ **6**
2	▷ Leaves and sepals glabrous	Go to ▷ **3**
	▷ Leaves and sepals with long, usually glandular hairs	Go to ▷ **4**
3	▷ Dwarf shrub to 60 cm; stems with bunches of short, leafy shoots in leaf axils; flowers dark reddish purple	*E. cinerea* (p.218)
	▷ Shrub to 2 m; flowers pink in bud, white when open	*E. lusitanica* (p.218)
4	▷ Flowers in umbel-like clusters, anthers with awn-like appendage	Go to ▷ **5**
	▷ Flowers in racemes, anthers without appendage	*E. ciliaris* (p.218)
5	▷ Sepals and upper side of leaves with short, dense hairs as well as glandular hairs; leaves revolute, obscuring most of lower side	*E. tetralix* (p.218)
	▷ Leaves and sepals glabrous except for long hairs; leaves revolute but most of underside exposed (W Ireland)	*E. mackaiana* (p.218)
6	▷ Pedicels longer than flowers; flowers bell-shaped	*E. vagans* (p.216)
	▷ Pedicels shorter than flowers; flowers ± tubular (W Ireland)	*E. erigena* (p.218)
	Cranberries and Bilberries *Vaccinium*	
1	▷ Dwarf shrubs; stems not creeping and thread-like; corolla bell-shaped or constricted at mouth	Go to ▷ **2**
	▷ Plant creeping; stems thread-like; corolla divided almost to base, petals reflexed	Go to ▷ **4**
2	▷ Leaves evergreen, dark green, glossy; flowers in racemes, corolla bell-shape	*V. vitis-idaea* (p.218)
	▷ Leaves deciduous; 1–4 flowers in axillary groups, mouth of corolla constricted	Go to ▷ **3**
3	▷ Leaves toothed, bright green; twigs ridged	*V. myrtillus* (p.220)
	▷ Leaves entire, blue-green; twigs smooth	*V. uliginosum* (p.218)
4	▷ Leaves ± oblong; flower stalks minutely hairy	*V. oxycoccos* (p.218)
	▷ Leaves widest at base; flower stalks glabrous	*V. microcarpum* (p.218)

Blue heath
Phyllodoce caerulea VU. *(B)

[*See* illustration p.212.] Dwarf evergreen shrub to 20 cm. LEAVES Dense, *alternate*, <10 mm, *linear, strongly revolute*, minutely toothed. FLOWERS *On long, slender reddish glandular stalks*, 7–8 mm across; 5 petals; 10 stamens. HABITAT Steep N- or E-facing rocky slopes in areas of late snow-lie; 670–800 m. DIST. Native. Very rare. Only in about three localities in Scottish Highlands. (N Europe, mts of S Europe.) FLS Jun–Jul.

St Dabeoc's Heath
Daboecia cantabrica

Low, straggling, glandular-hairy evergreen shrub to 50 cm. LEAVES *Alternate*, 5–10 mm, revolute, glandular, dark green above, dense white hairs beneath. FLOWERS 8–12 mm across, *4 sepals and petals*. HABITAT Exposed heathland on thin, rocky acid soils, avoiding peat; to 580 m. DIST. Native. W Ireland (W Galway, Mayo). (SW Europe.) FLS Jul–Sep.

Bog-rosemary
Andromeda polifolia *(NI)

Low, straggling, glabrous, dwarf evergreen shrub to 35 cm. LEAVES 15–35 mm, *alternate*, linear, revolute, *green above, glaucous beneath*. FLOWERS 5–7 mm across, *5 sepals and petals*, 10 stamens. HABITAT Acid *Sphagnum* peat of raised and blanket bogs; to 735 m. DIST. Native. Local in upland Britain; common in central Ireland. (N and central Europe.) FLS May–Sep.

Shallon
Gaultheria shallon

Low evergreen shrub to 150 cm, forming dense patches. LEAVES 5–10 cm, *glabrous, broadly ovate, alternate*, margins finely toothed. FLOWERS *c.*10 mm across, *in a panicle*; 5 petals. FRUITS *c.*10 mm, *calyx enlarging and becoming fleshy*. HABITAT Open woodland on acid sands. DIST. Introduced as game cover in 1826 (native of W North America). Naturalised throughout BI, but rare in Ireland. (NW Europe.) FLS May–Jun.

Strawberry-tree
Arbutus unedo

Small, erect evergreen tree or shrub to 12 m. BARK Thin, reddish brown. LEAVES 4–10 cm, alternate, glabrous, margins finely toothed. FLOWERS In panicles, corolla *c.*7 mm across, 5 petals, 10 stamens. FRUITS 15–20 mm, *an orange-red warty berry* (the 'strawberry'). HABITAT Scrub, open woodland, on rocky lake shores. DIST. Native. SW Ireland. Scattered elsewhere as relic of cultivation. (SW Europe, Mediterranean.) FLS Sep–Dec with previous year's fruits.

Bearberry
Arctostaphylos uva-ursi

Dwarf, mat-forming evergreen shrub to 150 cm with prostrate rooting branches. LEAVES 1–2.5 cm, alternate, rather leathery, *glabrous, entire, conspicuously net-veined beneath*. FLOWERS Corolla 4–6 mm across; 5 sepals and petals; 10 stamens. FRUITS *Red* berry-like drupe. HABITAT Exposed moorland on thin, stony or peaty soil; to 915 m. DIST. Native. Common in Scottish Highlands; scattered in W Ireland, N England. (N Europe, mts of S Europe.) FLS May–Jul.

Mountain Bearberry
Arctostaphylos alpinus

Prostrate, much-branched, dwarf deciduous shrub to 60 cm. LEAVES 1–2.5 cm, alternate, rather thin, glabrous, *margins finely toothed, conspicuously net-veined above and below*. FLOWERS Corolla *c.*4 mm across. FRUITS *Black*. HABITAT Exposed alpine heathland, peaty moorland, on acid soils; to 915 m. DIST. Native. Very local. Mts of N and NW Scotland. (N Europe, mts of S Europe.) FLS May–Aug.

Heather, Ling
Calluna vulgaris

Much-branched, prostrate to erect, dwarf evergreen shrub, to *c.*60 cm. LEAVES *Small*, 1–3 mm, *opposite*, overlapping on young shoots, linear, margins revolute. FLOWERS In raceme-like inflorescence, 3–15 cm; corolla 3–4.5 mm; 4 petals, fused at base only; *calyx same colour as, and larger than, corolla*; 8 stamens. HABITAT Abundant and often dominant on heaths, moors, bogs, and open birch, pine and oak woodland on acid soils and peat; to 1040 m. DIST. Native. Throughout BI. (Most of Europe, decreasing to E.) FLS Jul–Sep.

Heaths *Erica*
See key to *Erica* on p.215.

Cornish Heath
Erica vagans *(NI)

Much-branched, erect, glabrous dwarf shrub to 80 cm. LEAVES In whorls of 4–5, 5–10 mm, linear, bright green, strongly revolute. FLOWERS In dense leafy racemes; *stalks 3–4× as long as flowers*; corolla 2.5–4 mm; *stamens protruding*, anthers purple. HABITAT/DIST. Native. W Cornwall; locally abundant in mixed heath on ultra-basic serpentine rocks around Lizard Peninsula. Also at one site in Fermanagh, Ireland. (SW Europe.) FLS Jul–Aug.

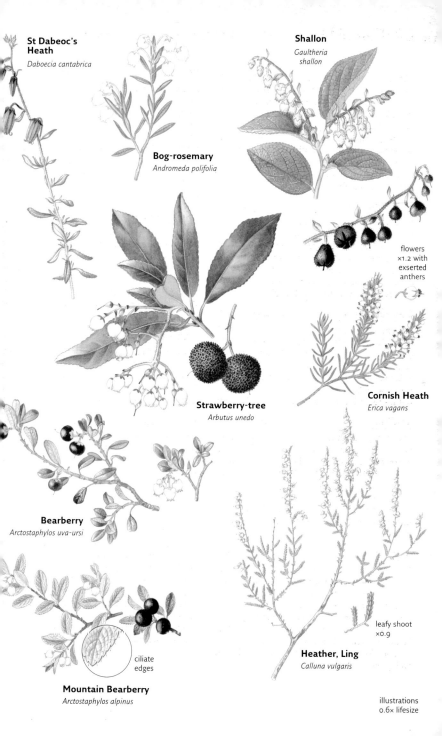

St Dabeoc's Heath
Daboecia cantabrica

Shallon
Gaultheria shallon

Bog-rosemary
Andromeda polifolia

flowers
×1.2 with
exserted
anthers

Strawberry-tree
Arbutus unedo

Cornish Heath
Erica vagans

Bearberry
Arctostaphylos uva-ursi

ciliate
edges

Mountain Bearberry
Arctostaphylos alpinus

Heather, Ling
Calluna vulgaris

leafy shoot
×0.9

illustrations
0.6× lifesize

Cross-leaved Heath
Erica tetralix

Erect, much-branched, evergreen dwarf shrub to 60 cm. STEMS Rooting at base, twigs pubescent. LEAVES 2-4 mm, *in whorls of 4; grey-green with dense, short hairs and long glandular hairs*; margins revolute, obscuring most of lower side of leaf. FLOWERS In umbel-like clusters; *sepals shortly pubescent and with long glandular hairs*; corolla 6-7 mm, pale pink; stamens not projecting, *anthers with an appendage*. HABITAT Acid bogs, wet heaths, moorland; to 670 m. DIST. Native. Throughout BI, abundant in N and W. (W Europe.) FLS Jul-Sep.

Mackay's Heath
Erica mackaiana

Similar to *E. tetralix*, but more densely branched; *leaves green and glabrous on upper surface except for long hairs*, margins revolute but leaving most of undersurface of leaf exposed; *sepals glabrous except for long hairs*. HABITAT Blanket bog and wet heath. DIST. Native. Rare, very local. W Galway, W Donegal only. (NW Spain.) FLS Aug-Sep.

Dorset Heath
Erica ciliaris *(R)

Erect, much-branched, evergreen dwarf shrub to 60 cm. STEMS Rooting at base, twigs pubescent. LEAVES 1-3 mm, *in whorls of 3*, with long glandular hairs. FLOWERS *In racemes*; sepals with long glandular hairs; corolla 8-10 mm, deep pink; stamens not projecting, *anthers without an appendage*. HABITAT Valley bogs, damp heaths. DIST. Native. Very local. Hampshire to Cornwall; also two sites in W Ireland. (SW Europe.) FLS Jun-Sep.

Bell Heather
Erica cinerea

Erect, much-branched, evergreen dwarf shrub to 60 cm. STEMS *With bunches of short leafy shoots in leaf axils*. LEAVES 5-7 mm, in whorls of 3, linear, *glabrous*; dark, shining green. FLOWERS In short racemes; corolla 4-6 mm, dark reddish purple; stamens not projecting. HABITAT Dry heathland, open woodland, maritime heaths, on acid, well-drained soils; to 930 m. DIST. Native. Throughout BI. (W Europe.) FLS Jul-Sep.

Irish Heath
Erica erigena

Erect, *glabrous* evergreen shrub to 2 m. LEAVES 5-10 mm, *in whorls of 4*, linear, bright green. FLOWERS In racemes, *stalks much shorter than flowers*; corolla 5-7 mm; *stamens projecting beyond corolla*. HABITAT Acid peat bogs around margins of lakes, streams. DIST. Native. Rare, very local. W Mayo, W Galway. (SW Europe.) FLS Mar-May.

Portuguese Heath
Erica lusitanica

Erect evergreen shrub to 2 m. LEAVES 5-7 mm, glabrous, in whorls of 3-4. FLOWERS In long panicles; corolla 4-5 mm, *pink in bud, white when open*; stamens not projecting. HABITAT Heathland, railway banks, roadsides. DIST. Introduced *c.*1800. Naturalised in Cornwall, Dorset. (SW Europe.) FLS Mar-May.

Cranberries and bilberries *Vaccinium*
See key to *Vaccinium* on p.215.

Cranberry
Vaccinium oxycoccos

Prostrate, trailing, creeping perennial, with long, wiry stems. LEAVES *Small, 4-8 mm*, alternate, widely spaced, ± oblong, green above, pale beneath, margins revolute. FLOWERS In groups of 1-4, *stalks minutely hairy; corolla lobed nearly to base, lobes strongly revolute*. FRUITS 6-8 mm, spherical to pear-shaped. HABITAT Wet acid bogs and heaths, open boggy woodland, often creeping over *Sphagnum* moss; to 760 m. DIST. Native. Widespread in N and W Britain; very rare elsewhere (N, central and E Europe.) FLS Jun-Aug.

Small Cranberry
Vaccinium microcarpum

Similar to *V. oxycoccos*, but *leaves 3-5 mm*, widest at base; flowers in groups of 1-2, *stalks glabrous*; fruits 5-8 mm, elliptical or pear-shaped. HABITAT Hummocks in acid *Sphagnum* bogs; to 850 m. DIST. Native. Very local. N Scotland. (N Europe.) FLS Jul.

Cowberry
Vaccinium vitis-idaea

[*See* illustration on following page.] *Dwarf evergreen shrub* to 30 cm, with numerous erect, much-branched stems. STEMS Twigs smooth. LEAVES 1-3 cm, glabrous; dark green and glossy above, paler below, margin entire, or obscurely and bluntly toothed. FLOWERS Corolla *c.*6 mm, *bell-shaped*. FRUITS Red, 6-10 mm across, spherical. HABITAT Moors, open woodland on acid soils; to 1095 m. DIST. Native. Common in upland and N Britain, Ireland. (N Europe, mts of central Europe.) FLS Jun-Aug.

Bog Bilberry
Vaccinium uliginosum

[*See* illustration on following page.] *Dwarf deciduous shrub* to 50 cm. STEMS *Twigs smooth*, brownish. LEAVES 1-2.5 cm, *blue-green, entire*, conspicuously net-veined, glabrous or minutely hairy. FLOWERS Corolla *c.*4 mm. FRUITS Black, with a bloom, *c.*6 mm across, spherical. HABITAT Damp dwarf shrub heaths, moorland, blanket bog; to 1130 m. DIST. Native. Very rare. Scottish Highlands, N England. (N Europe.) FLS May-Jun.

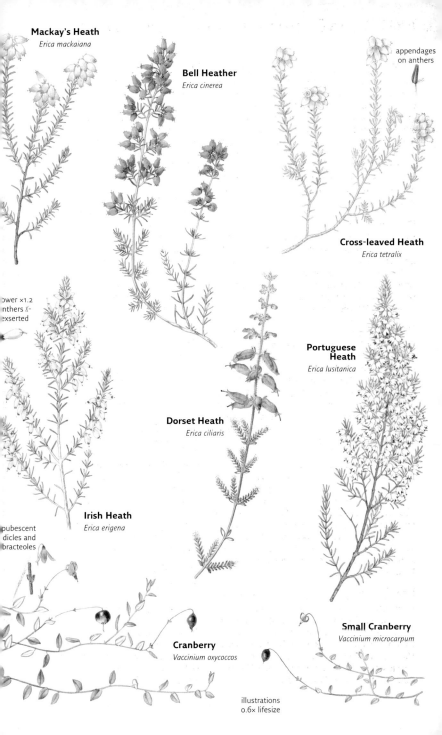

Mackay's Heath
Erica mackaiana

Bell Heather
Erica cinerea

appendages on anthers

Cross-leaved Heath
Erica tetralix

ower ×1.2
nthers ½-
exserted

Portuguese Heath
Erica lusitanica

Dorset Heath
Erica ciliaris

Irish Heath
Erica erigena

pubescent
dicles and
bracteoles

Cranberry
Vaccinium oxycoccos

Small Cranberry
Vaccinium microcarpum

illustrations
0.6× lifesize

Bilberry
Vaccinium myrtillus

Dwarf deciduous shrub to 60 cm, with numerous erect stems. STEMS *Twigs conspicuously ridged*, green. LEAVES 1–3 cm, *bright green, conspicuously net-veined, margin toothed*. FLOWERS Corolla 4–6 mm. FRUITS Black, with a bloom, *c.*8 mm across, spherical. HABITAT Moors, heathland, open acid woodlands, drier parts of peat bogs; to 1300 m. DIST. Native. Common in N and W BI; local on heaths of S England. (Most of Europe.) FLS Apr–Jun.

PYROLACEAE Wintergreens

Closely related to the Ericaceae, from which they differ in herbaceous habit. Evergreen perennials with a creeping rhizome. Flowers bisexual, regular, 5 petals and sepals, petals free.

Flowers in umbels, most leaves on flowering stem	*Chimaphila umbellata*
Flowers solitary, leaves mostly basal	*Moneses uniflora*
Flowers in racemes, leaves mostly basal	
Flowers all turned to one side of inflorescence	*Orthilia secunda*
Inflorescence not one-sided	*Pyrola*

Pyrola

Style straight, flowers globose	
Style 1–2 mm, not projecting beyond corolla	*P. minor*
Style 4–6 mm, projecting beyond corolla	*P. media*
Style curved, flowers saucer-shaped	
Flowers white	*P. rotundifolia*
Flowers yellow	*P. chlorantha*

Common Wintergreen
Pyrola minor

Erect evergreen perennial, flowering stem to 30 cm. LEAVES 2.5–4 cm, oval, light green, petiole shorter than blade. FLOWERS *c.*6 mm, globose; *style straight*, 1–2 mm, *shorter than stamens, not projecting beyond corolla*, without a ring below stigma. HABITAT Moorland, damp rock ledges in N; calcareous woodland in S. To 1130 m. DIST. Native. Scattered throughout BI, but absent in SW. (N and central Europe.) FLS Jun–Aug.

Intermediate Wintergreen
Pyrola media VU.

Similar to *P. minor*, but leaves more rounded, dark green, petiole as long as or longer than blade; flowers *c.*10 mm across; *style straight*, 4–6 mm, *longer than stamens and projecting beyond corolla*, with a ring below

stigma. HABITAT Scottish pine woods, dwarf-shrub moorland; to 550 m. DIST. Native. Local and declining. N Scotland, N Ireland; very scattered elsewhere (N Europe, mts of S and SE Europe.) FLS Jun–Aug.

Round-leaved Wintergreen
Pyrola rotundifolia *(R)

Similar to *P. minor*, but leaves more rounded, dark green, glossy; petiole 3–7 cm, longer than blade; ssp *rotundifolia* with 1–2 scale leaves on inflorescence stalk, ssp. *maritima* with 2–5; flower stalks 4–8 mm in ssp. *rotundifolia*, 2–5 mm in ssp. *maritima*; flower saucer-shaped, *c.*12 mm across; petals white; *style long*, 6–10 mm in ssp. *rotundifolia* and 4–6 mm in ssp *maritima*, hanging downwards, *strongly curved, longer than petals*. HABITAT Ssp. *rotundifolia* on damp mountain rock ledges, acid woodland, bogs, fens; to 760 m. Ssp. *maritima* on calcareous dune slacks. DIST. Native Very scarce, local. Ssp. *rotundifolia* declining; Scotland, scattered and rare elsewhere. (N Europe, mts of S and E Europe.) Ssp. *maritima* rare; W coast of England Wales. (W coast of Europe from Germany to NW France.) FLS Jul–Sep.

Yellow Wintergreen
Pyrola chlorantha

Similar to *P. rotundifolia*, but leaves rounded 0.5–2 cm, pale green above, darker below, petiole longer than blade; flowers saucer-shaped, 8–12 mm across; *petals yellowish green; style* 6–7 mm, hanging downwards, *strongly curved, longer than petals*. HABITAT Coniferous woodlands. DIST. *Not BI.* (Most of Europe except extreme W.) FLS Jul–Sep.

Serrated Wintergreen
Orthilia secunda *(N

STEMS Flowering stems to 12 cm. LEAVES 2–4 cm ovate, acute, finely toothed; petioles *c.*1 cm, shorter than blade. FLOWERS 4–5 mm across, *all turned to one side of inflorescence*; petals greenish white; style straight, 4.5–6 mm, projecting beyond corolla HABITAT Montane *Calluna-Vaccinium* woodland rock ledges, open moorland; to 690 m. DIST. Native Very scattered in Scottish Highlands; very rare elsewhere in N Britain. (N Europe.) FLS Jul–Aug.

One-flowered Wintergreen
Moneses uniflora VU

STEMS Flowering stems to 15 cm. LEAVES Opposite 1–2.5 cm, rounded, finely toothed, light green. FLOWERS Solitary, white, 12–20 mm across, *wide open*; styl 5–7 mm. HABITAT Mossy pine woods; lowland to 300 m. DIST. Native. Very rare and declining. NE Scotland. (N Europe, mts of S Europe.) FLS Jun–Aug.

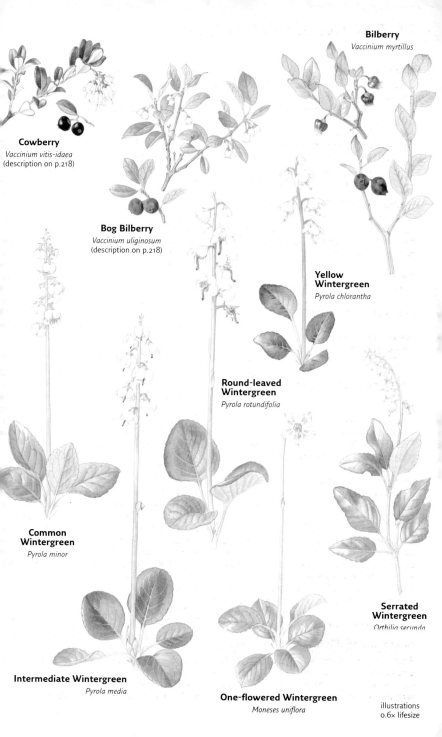

Bilberry
Vaccinium myrtillus

Cowberry
Vaccinium vitis-idaea
(description on p.218)

Bog Bilberry
Vaccinium uliginosum
(description on p.218)

Yellow Wintergreen
Pyrola chlorantha

Round-leaved Wintergreen
Pyrola rotundifolia

Common Wintergreen
Pyrola minor

Serrated Wintergreen
Orthilia secunda

Intermediate Wintergreen
Pyrola media

One-flowered Wintergreen
Moneses uniflora

illustrations
0.6× lifesize

Umbellate Wintergreen   *Chimaphila umbellata*

LEAVES *Most cauline, alternate or appearing whorled*, lanceolate, margins toothed, 4–7 cm; petiole short, 3–5 mm. FLOWERS Pinkish, 7–12 mm across, *in umbels* of 3–7; style short. DIST. *Not BI.* HABITAT Coniferous woods. (N, central and E Europe.) FLS Jul–Sep.

MONOTROPACEAE Bird's-nests

Yellow Bird's-nest   *Monotropa hypopitys* EN. *(NI)

Erect saprophytic perennial to 30 cm. *Whole plant white to yellowish, without chlorophyll.* Has 2 subspecies that are genetically different but difficult to separate on morphological characters. LEAVES Scale-like. FLOWERS Regular, in racemes; 4–5 sepals and petals; 8–10 stamens. In ssp. *hypopitys*, inside of petals, stamens and carpels is pubescent; in ssp. *hypophegea*, it is usually glabrous. SIMILAR SPP. Unlikely to be confused with any other plant, except for the saprophytic *Neottia nidus-avis* (p.672) and the broomrapes (p.432), although these have quite different flowers. HABITAT On leaf litter, usually in pine, Beech or Hazel woods. DIST. Native. Scattered, declining and very local throughout BI; very rare in Scotland, Ireland. (All Europe.) FLS Jun–Aug.

DIAPENSIACEAE Diapensia family

Diapensia   *Diapensia lapponica* VU. *(B)

Cushion-forming, evergreen dwarf shrub to *c*.6 cm. LEAVES 5–10 mm. FLOWERS Solitary, regular, 1–2 cm across; 5 sepals, petals and stamens; ovary 3-celled. HABITAT/DIST. Native. Very rare. Only on one site, in W Inverness on an exposed mountain ridge at 760 m. (Arctic Europe.) FLS May–Jun.

PRIMULACEAE Primrose family

Superficially a very variable family of annuals and herbaceous perennials with a single-celled superior ovary (*see* key on p.230). Leaves are simple or pinnate, without stipules. Flowers are regular; 5 sepals; 5 petals (absent in *Glaux*), united at least at base; 5 stamens; numerous ovules. Fruit is a capsule.

Primrose   *Primula vulgaris* *(NI, against sale only)

Perennial. LEAVES 8–15 cm, in a basal rosette, sparsely hairy above, pubescent below, tapering gradually to base (cf. Cowslip). FLOWERS *c*.30 mm across, *arising singly from base of plant*; stalks to *c*.10 cm, with long, shaggy hairs. HABITAT Woodland clearings, coppice, hedge banks, old grassland, especially on heavy soils. DIST. Native. Throughout BI. (W, S and SE Europe.) FLS Dec–May.

Cowslip   *Primula veris* *(N

Glandular-pubescent perennial. LEAVES 5–15 cm, in a basal rosette, finely pubescent on both surfaces, abruptly contracted towards base (cf. Primrose). FLOWERS *c*.10–15 mm across, *in umbels on scape* (stalk to 30 cm; distinct *orange spots at base of petals; corolla with folds in throat; calyx uniformly green.* FRUITS Capsule enclosed by enlarged calyx. HABITAT Old meadows, grassland, hedge banks, woodland clearings, motorway verges, usually on calcareous soils. DIST. Native. Throughout BI, but very rare in N Scotland, N Ireland. (All Europe except extreme N.) FLS Apr–May.

Oxlip   *Primula elatio

Pubescent perennial. LEAVES In a basal rosette; similar to *P. veris*. FLOWERS 15–18 mm across, *in umbels* scape to 30 cm; paler than *P. veris*, nodding and all turned to one side; *corolla without folds in throat; calyx with dark green midribs.* FRUITS Capsule as long as calyx. HABITAT Old coppice woodlands on chalky boulder clay. DIST. Native. Very local. E England (Cambridgeshire, Essex, Suffolk). (Central Europe.) FLS Apr–May.

Bird's-eye Primrose   *Primula farinosa* VU

Perennial. LEAVES 1–5 cm, in a basal rosette, *edge crinkly*, undersides mealy white. FLOWERS *c*.1 cm across; scape to 15 cm, mealy; *petals separated from each other.* FRUITS Capsule much longer than calyx. HABITAT Damp, grazed calcareous grassland, calcareous mires. DIST. Native. Very local. Carboniferous limestone areas of N England. (All Europe except SE) FLS May–Jun.

Scottish Primrose   *Primula scotic

Biennial or perennial. Similar to *P. farinosa*, but *leave broader, without crinkly edges*; scape to 10 cm; flower darker, *petals contiguous*, notched; capsule slightly longer than calyx. HABITAT Coastal cliff pastures, dun slacks, grass heaths, on calcareous soils. DIST. Endemic. N coast of Scotland, Orkney. FLS May–Aug.

Water-violet   *Hottonia palustris* *(N

Floating and rooting aquatic perennial. LEAVES *Submerged, whorled, pinnate with narrow lobes.* FLOWERS whorled, 20–25 mm across, *lilac with yellow throa* in emergent inflorescence; scape erect, to 40 cm calyx divided to base. FRUITS Spherical capsule HABITAT Shallow, clear, unpolluted, still or slow moving base-rich water, ditches, dykes, ponds; low land. DIST. Native. Declining. Scattered throughou England; rare in Wales, Ireland; absent from Sco land. (N and central Europe.) FLS May–Jun.

Umbellate Wintergreen
Chimaphila umbellata

Yellow Bird's-nest
Monotropa hypopitys

Diapensia
Diapensia lapponica

Scottish Primrose
Primula scotica

Water-violet
Hottonia palustris

Cowslip
Primula veris

Bird's-eye Primrose
Primula farinosa

Oxlip
Primula elatior

Primrose
Primula vulgaris

illustrations
0.6× lifesize

Sowbread
Cyclamen hederifolium

Perennial with *large underground corms*, from which leaves and flowers arise. Plants ± glabrous; corms 2–10 m across. LEAVES 3–8 cm, appearing in autumn after flowers. FLOWERS *Petals 12–20 mm, reflexed*. FRUITS Flower stalks spiralled in fruit. HABITAT Woods, hedgerows, near habitation. DIST. Introduced. Rare. Naturalised in S England as relic of cultivation; scattered elsewhere. (S Europe.) FLS Aug–Sep.

Yellow loosestrifes *Lysimachia*

Plant prostrate

    Leaves with acute apex;
    calyx lobes linear   *L. nemorum*

    Leaves with rounded apex;
    calyx lobes ovate   *L. nummularia*

Plant erect

    Flowers >15 mm across, not in axillary racemes:

        Petals not fringed, sepals with
        orange margin   *L. vulgaris*

        Petals fringed with glandular
        hairs, sepals all green   *L. punctata*

    Flowers <10 mm across, in
    dense axillary racemes   *L. thyrsiflora*

Yellow Pimpernel
Lysimachia nemorum

Slender, *evergreen, glabrous, prostrate* perennial to 40 cm. LEAVES 1–3 cm, opposite, ovate, *acute*. FLOWERS In axils of leaves, 5–10 mm across, on slender stalks; *sepals narrow*. HABITAT Damp woodland rides, woodland flushes, hedge banks, ditch sides, marshes, on acid soils. DIST. Native. Throughout BI. (W and central Europe.) FLS May–Sep.

Creeping-Jenny
Lysimachia nummularia

Creeping, evergreen, glabrous perennial to 60 cm. LEAVES 1.5–3 cm, opposite, broadly ovate, *rounded at tip*. FLOWERS In axils of leaves, 15–25 mm across; *sepals ovate*; petals dotted with black glands, shortly fringed. HABITAT Shaded river and stream margins, damp hedgerows, ditches, grassland. DIST. Native. Most of England, Wales, Ireland; introduced in SW England, Scotland. (Most of Europe.) FLS Jun–Aug.

Yellow Loosestrife
Lysimachia vulgaris

Tall, erect, pubescent, rhizomatous perennial to 150 cm, often forming large clumps. LEAVES Opposite or in whorls, 3–10 cm, dotted with orange or black glands. FLOWERS In panicles, 8–15 mm across; *margins of sepals orange, hairy; margins of petals glabrous*. HABITAT Marshes, fens, margins of rivers, lakes and ponds, on fertile soils. DIST. Native. Throughout B except N Scotland. (All Europe.) FLS Jul–Aug.

Dotted Loosestrife
Lysimachia punctata

Tall, erect, pubescent perennial to 120 cm, often forming dense patches. LEAVES Opposite o whorled, 4–12 cm, glandular-pubescent. FLOWER In axils of leaves, *c*.25 mm across; stalks shorte than leaves; *calyx teeth glandular-pubescent; margin of petals with dense glandular hairs*. HABITAT Wood land stream sides, rough grassland, roadsides, waste ground. DIST. Introduced. Naturalised throughou BI. (SE Europe.) FLS Jun–Sep.

Tufted Loosestrife
Lysimachia thyrsiflor

Erect, glabrous perennial to 70 cm. LEAVES Opposite, 5–10 cm, *densely covered by black glands*. FLOW ERS *c*.5 mm across, in dense axillary racemes; petal narrow, with black glands; stamens projectin beyond corolla. HABITAT Shallow water at margin of lakes, ditches, canals, fens, wet marshes. DIST Native. Rare and local. Yorkshire, S Scotland. (W central and E Europe.) FLS Jun–Jul.

Chickweed-wintergreen
Trientalis europae

Erect, unbranched, glabrous, rhizomatous, decidu ous perennial to 25 cm. LEAVES Shining, with o without fine teeth, ± sessile, *in a whorl of 5–6 at to of stem*. FLOWERS *Solitary*, 15–18 mm across; stalk long, 2–7 cm; *usually 7 sepals and petals*. DIST Native. Local in N England, E and N Scotland. HABI TAT Mossy pine, birch and oak woods, moorland, o damp acid soil; to 1100 m. (N Europe.) FLS Jun–Ju.

Brookweed
Samolus valeran

Glabrous, little-branched, deciduous perennial t 45 cm. LEAVES Basal and cauline, alternate. FLOW ERS *White, 2–4 mm across, in a leafy raceme*; 5 sepals petals and stamens. HABITAT Spring lines on se cliffs, and open, seasonally wet ditches, lagoon an lake shores, on calcareous or brackish soils. DIST Native. Local. Predominantly coastal, all round E except N and NE Scotland; also inland East Angli Somerset, Ireland. (All Europe.) FLS Jun–Aug.

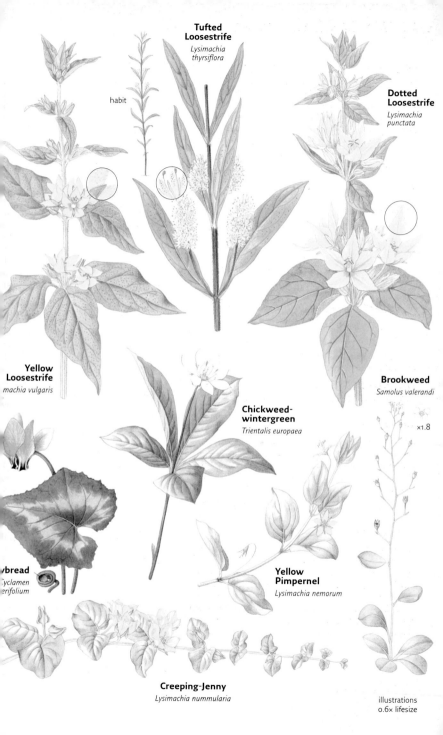

Tufted Loosestrife
Lysimachia thyrsiflora

habit

Dotted Loosestrife
Lysimachia punctata

Yellow Loosestrife
machia vulgaris

Chickweed-wintergreen
Trientalis europaea

Brookweed
Samolus valerandi

×1.8

bread
yclamen
erifolium

Yellow Pimpernel
Lysimachia nemorum

Creeping-Jenny
Lysimachia nummularia

illustrations
0.6× lifesize

Bog Pimpernel
Anagallis tenella

Slender, creeping, glabrous, evergreen perennial to 15 cm, *rooting at nodes*. LEAVES Opposite, entire, *c*.5 mm. FLOWERS *c*.10 mm across; stalks slender, much longer than leaves; *petals ≥×2 longer than sepals*. HABITAT Mossy spring mires, edges of acid pools, woodland rides and wet pastures on acid soils, dune slacks; to 610 m. DIST. Native. Throughout BI. (W Europe.) FLS Jun-Aug.

Scarlet Pimpernel
Anagallis arvensis

Prostrate, glabrous annual or perennial to 30 cm. STEMS *Square in section*, with glandular dots, *not rooting at nodes*. LEAVES Opposite, entire, 15–28 mm, with black glandular dots beneath. FLOWERS 5–7 mm across; stalks slender; *sepals not much shorter than petals*. Ssp. *arvensis* flowers red or pink, rarely blue or violet; petals densely fringed with glandular hairs (seen to consist of 3 cells under microscope). Ssp. *foemina*, Blue Pimpernel, flowers blue; petals sparsely fringed with glandular hairs (seen to consist of 4 cells under microscope). HABITAT Ssp. *arvensis* common weed of arable crops, gardens, dunes, waste ground; ssp. *foemina* weed of arable land. DIST. Cosmopolitan. Ssp. *arvensis* native; throughout BI, but rare in Scotland. Ssp. *foemina* archaeophyte; local and scattered in lowland England. FLS Jun-Sep. NOTE Blue-flowered pimpernels are difficult to identify without examining the petal hairs under a microscope.

Chaffweed
Anagallis minima

Small, erect, glabrous annual to 5 cm. LEAVES Upper leaves alternate, 3–5 mm. FLOWERS Sessile, in axils of leaves; *tiny, c.1 mm across, petals much shorter than sepals*. HABITAT Bare, damp, open ground on acid soils, heaths, woodland rides, dune slacks, sea cliffs. DIST. Native. Scattered throughout BI, mostly in S and W. (Most of Europe.) FLS Jun-Jul. SIMILAR SPP. Sometimes confused with *Radiola linoides* (p.322) of similar stature, with which it often grows, but that species is more branched, and has opposite leaves, flowers in a branched inflorescence and 4 petals.

Sea-milkwort
Glaux maritima

Small, prostrate or sub-erect, glabrous, *succulent* perennial to 30 cm. LEAVES *Opposite, in 4 rows*, 4–12 mm. FLOWERS Sessile, in axils of leaves, *c*.5 mm across; *sepals white or pink; petals absent*. HABITAT Drier parts of salt marshes, dune slacks, brackish grassland, rock crevices. DIST. Native. All round British coasts. (Coasts of N and W Europe.) FLS Jun-Aug.

GROSSULARIACEAE Currants

Shrubs with alternate, simple, often lobed leaves that lack stipules. Flowers solitary or in racemes, regular; 5 sepals, petals and stamens; ovary inferior; fruit a berry or capsule.

Leaves deciduous, lobed; petals shorter than sepals; fruit a berry	*Ribes*
Leaves evergreen, not lobed; petals longer than sepals; fruit a capsule	*Escallonia*

Red Currant
Ribes rubrum

Deciduous shrub to 2 m. LEAVES Blades 3–10 cm *deeply cordate at base with narrow sinus, ± glabrous without glands and not smelling when crushed*. FLOWERS Bisexual, greenish or tinged with purple; in racemes of 6–20 flowers, drooping or curving downwards at flowering; *receptacle saucer-shaped with raised rim*. FRUITS *Red berry*. HABITAT Wet woodland, fen carr, shaded stream sides; to 460 m. DIST. Native or introduced in Britain; introduced in Ireland. Throughout BI except extreme N Scotland. Widely naturalised as escape from cultivation. (W Europe.) FLS Apr-May.

Downy Currant
Ribes spicatum

Deciduous shrub to 2 m. Similar to *R. rubrum*, but *leaves truncate at base or shallowly cordate with wide sinus*, thinly pubescent beneath; flowers green tinged with brownish purple, inflorescence not drooping downwards at flowering, *receptacle cup-shaped without a rim*. HABITAT Woodland, stream sides, grikes in limestone pavement; to 425 m. DIST. Native. Limestone areas of N England, Scotland. (N Europe.) FLS Apr-May.

Black Currant
Ribes nigrum

Deciduous shrub to 2 m. LEAVES Blades 3–10 cm cordate at base, lobes more pointed than in *R. rubrum*, glabrous above, *hairy on veins beneath and with scattered brownish glands, smelling strongly of black currants when crushed!* FLOWERS Greenish tinged purplish; in drooping inflorescence of 5–10 flowers; receptacle cup-shaped, hairy. FRUITS *Black berry*. HABITAT Damp woodland, fen carr. DIST. Introduced. Naturalised as escape from cultivation throughout BI. (N, central and E Europe.) FLS Apr-May.

Bog Pimpernel
Anagallis tenella

leaves ×1.2
glandular edge)

flowers ×1.8

Scarlet Pimpernel
Anagallis arvensis

blue form

purple form

×1.8

ssp. *arvensis*
(margin densely
fringed)

ssp. *foemina*

Chaffweed
Anagallis minin

ea-milkwort
Glaux maritima

flower
×1.2

glands on
underside

Red Currant
Ribes rubrum

Black Currant
Ribes nigrum

Downy Currant
Ribes spicatum

ower
×1.2

♀ flower
raceme

♂ flower
raceme

Gooseberry
Ribes uva-crispa
(description on
p.228)

flower
×1.2

♂   ♀

flower
×1.2

Mountain Currant
Ribes alpinum
(description on p.228)

illustrations
0.6× lifesize

Mountain Currant *Ribes alpinum*

[*See* illustration previous page.] Deciduous shrub to 3 m. LEAVES Blades 3–5 cm, deeply lobed, truncate or shallowly cordate at base, sparsely hairy, not scented. FLOWERS Dioecious, greenish yellow, *in erect inflorescence; bracts narrow, longer than flower stalks.* FRUITS Red berry. HABITAT Ash woodland on sides of limestone cliffs. DIST. Native. Carboniferous limestone areas of N England; widely cultivated and naturalised as relic of cultivation throughout lowland Britain. (Mts of Europe.) FLS Apr–May.

Gooseberry *Ribes uva-crispa*

[*See* illustration previous page.] Deciduous, *spiny*, much-branched shrub to c.1 m. LEAVES Blades 2–5 cm, lobes coarsely toothed, glabrous or pubescent. FLOWERS Greenish, tinged purplish, in drooping inflorescence of 1–2 flowers. FRUITS *Yellowish-green to reddish-purple* berry, 10–20 mm, *often bristly.* HABITAT Hedgerows, woodland, shaded stream sides. DIST. Introduced. Naturalised as garden escape and relic of cultivation throughout BI. (Most of Europe.) FLS Mar–May.

Escallonia *Escallonia macrantha*

Evergreen shrub to 3 m. BRANCHES *Young twigs pubescent, sticky.* LEAVES 2–8 cm, dark glossy green, unlobed, margin toothed, glandular beneath. FLOWERS c.15 mm, *in racemes, pink to dark red.* FRUITS Capsule. HABITAT Cliffs, banks, roadsides. DIST. Introduced (native of Chiloe I, Chile). Widely planted for hedging, especially near sea. Naturalised as a relic of cultivation throughout BI, especially in SW. FLS Jun–Sep.

CRASSULACEAE Stonecrops

Easily recognised family (*see* key on p.230), with usually succulent, simple and entire leaves. Flowers are regular, bisexual; usually 5 petals and sepals; as many as or 2× as many stamens as petals; as many carpels as petals, free.

Mossy Stonecrop *Crassula tillaea*

Small, ± prostrate reddish annual to 5 cm. STEMS *Densely clothed with small, succulent, overlapping leaves.* LEAVES 1–2 mm, opposite, sessile, meeting across stem. FLOWERS Small, solitary, sessile, in axils of leaves; *3 petals*, shorter than sepals. HABITAT Bare compacted sandy or gravelly ground, tracks, paths. DIST. Native. Very local. East Anglia, S England, Channel Is. (Mediterranean, W Europe.) FLS Jun–Jul.

Pigmyweed *Crassula aquatica* VU. *(B)

Small, slender, prostrate, glabrous annual to 5 cm. LEAVES 3–5 mm, opposite, meeting across stem pairs well separated. FLOWERS *Small, solitary, ± sessile*, in axils of leaves; 4 petals, longer than sepals. HABITAT Shallow water, bare exposed mud. DIST. Probably native. Very rare. In one site only: R Shiel, W Scotland. (N and central Europe.) FLS Jun–Jul.

New Zealand Pigmyweed *Crassula helmsii*

Trailing or prostrate, glabrous perennial to 30 cm. LEAVES 4–15 mm, in well-separated opposite pairs. FLOWERS 1–2 mm across, *on long stalks in axils of leaves*; 4 petals, longer than sepals. HABITAT Forms extensive mats in shallow water at edge of ponds, dykes, reservoirs. Competes aggressively with native vegetation. DIST. Introduced (native of Australia and New Zealand). Rapidly spreading, but still scarce in Scotland, Ireland. FLS Jun–Aug.

Navelwort, Pennywort *Umbilicus rupestris*

Erect, glabrous, unbranched perennial to 40 cm. LEAVES *Mostly basal, stalked, circular, peltate*, 1.5–7 cm across. FLOWERS *Drooping*, 8–10 mm, tubular, *in many-flowered spike*; 5 petals; 10 stamens. HABITAT Cliffs, rock crevices, walls, dry sandy hedge banks; to 550 m. DIST. Native. Common in W BI. (Mediterranean, W Europe.) FLS Jun–Sep.

House-leek *Sempervivum tectorum*

Succulent, long-lived *evergreen perennial.* STEMS Flowering stems branched, glandular-pubescent, to 50 cm. LEAVES Alternate, 2.5–6 cm, *reddish above*, crowded into dense basal rosette. FLOWERS 1.5–3 cm across, c.13 petals. HABITAT Widely planted on old roofs, walls, porches, churchyards, rockeries. Rarely truly naturalised. DIST. Introduced (origins obscure). (Mountains of central and S Europe) FLS Jun–Jul.

Aeonium *Aeonium cuneatum*

Large, glabrous perennial, woody at base. STEMS *Flowering stems leafy, to 100 cm.* LEAVES Basal leaves large, succulent, in saucer-shaped rosette up to 50 cm across; stem leaves alternate, entire. FLOWERS 10–20 mm across, *densely crowded at top of stem.* HABITAT/DIST. Introduced. Planted on old walls, naturalised in Cornwall and I of Man, and characteristic feature of Isles of Scilly.

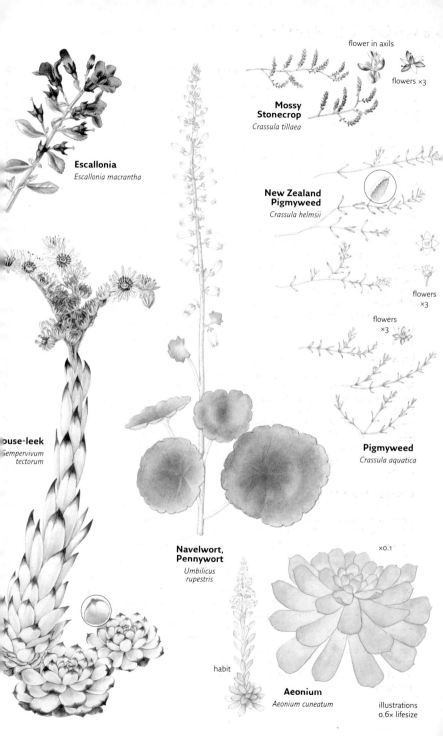

Escallonia
Escallonia macrantha

flower in axils

Mossy Stonecrop
Crassula tillaea

flowers ×3

New Zealand Pigmyweed
Crassula helmsii

flowers ×3

flowers ×3

Pigmyweed
Crassula aquatica

House-leek
Sempervivum tectorum

Navelwort, Pennywort
Umbilicus rupestris

habit

×0.1

Aeonium
Aeonium cuneatum

illustrations 0.6× lifesize

if	then
1 ▷ Leaves all basal	Go to ▷ **2**
▷ Stem leaves present	Go to ▷ **3**
2 ▷ Leaves ovate or obovate; flowers yellow or pink, petals flat	***Primula*** (p.222)
▷ Leaves cordate, 5–9-angled; flowers pink, petals reflexed	***Cyclamen*** (p.224)
3 ▷ Submerged water plant; leaves pinnate; flowers lilac	***Hottonia*** (p.222)
▷ Land plant; leaves not pinnate; flowers not lilac	Go to ▷ **4**
4 ▷ Flowers yellow	***Lysimachia*** (p.224)
▷ Flowers not yellow	Go to ▷ **5**
5 ▷ Flowers white; stems erect	Go to ▷ **6**
▷ Flowers not white; stems creeping	Go to ▷ **7**
6 ▷ Small annual; leaves alternate; flowers solitary in leaf axils, <1 mm across	***Anagallis minima*** (p.226)
▷ Leaves whorled at top of stem; flowers solitary	***Trientalis*** (p.224)
▷ Leaves not whorled; flowers in leafy raceme	***Samolus*** (p.224)
7 ▷ Leaves opposite, in 4 rows; flowers sessile in leaf axils, petals absent	***Glaux*** (p.226)
▷ Leaves not in 4 rows; flowers on long slender stalks, petals present	***Anagallis*** (p.226)

Key to Crassulaceae Stonecrops

Sedum flower

if	then
1 ▷ Leaves peltate; petals yellowish green, united into a tube	***Umbilicus rupestris*** (p.228)
▷ Leaves not peltate; petals free or joined only at base	Go to ▷ **2**
2 ▷ As many stamens as petals; small annuals	***Crassula*** (p.228)
▷ Stamens twice as many as petals	Go to ▷ **3**
3 ▷ 4–5 sepals and petals, or if >5 then leaves ± cylindrical	***Sedum*** (p.231)
▷ >6 sepals and petals; leaves broad	Go to ▷ **4**

if	**then**
4 ▷ Petals dark pink	***Sempervivum tectorum*** (p.228)
▷ Petals yellow	***Aeonium cuneatum*** (p.228)

Sedum

	if	**then**
1	▷ Leaves broad, flat, toothed	Go to ▷ **2**
	▷ Leaves ± cylindrical, smooth, rounded or semicircular in section	Go to ▷ **4**
2	▷ Stems prostrate, rooting along their length	***S. spurium*** (p.232)
	▷ Stems erect	Go to ▷ **3**
3	▷ Flowers red, 5 sepals and petals, bisexual	***S. telephium*** (p.234)
	▷ Flowers greenish, 4 sepals and petals, dioecious	***S. rosea*** (p.232)
4	▷ Flowers pink; leaves glandular-pubescent	***S. villosum*** (p.234)
	▷ Flowers yellow	Go to ▷ **5**
	▷ Flowers white	Go to ▷ **8**

Flowers yellow

	if	**then**
5	▷ Leaves small, ≤7 mm, egg-shaped or cylindrical, blunt	Go to ▷ **6**
	▷ Leaves >8 mm, linear, acute	Go to ▷ **7**
6	▷ Leaves egg-shaped, overlapping, with acrid taste	***S. acre*** (p.232)
	▷ Leaves cylindrical, spreading, without acrid taste	***S. sexangulare*** (p.232)
7	▷ Non-flowering shoots with leaves clustered towards tip and persistent dead leaves below; leaves flattened, abruptly contracted to pointed tip	***S. forsterianum*** (p.232)
	▷ Leaves on non-flowering shoots ± evenly spaced, dead leaves not persisting; leaves rounded in section, evenly tapered at tip	***S. rupestre*** (p.232)

Flowers white

	if	**then**
8	▷ Leaves opposite, with glandular hairs	***S. dasyphyllum*** (p.234)
	▷ Leaves alternate, glabrous	Go to ▷ **9**
9	▷ Leaves 3–5 mm; inflorescence with 2 main branches	***S. anglicum*** (p.232)
	▷ Leaves 6–12 mm; inflorescence with several branches	***S. album*** (p.232)

Roseroot
Sedum rosea

Erect, glabrous, glaucous perennial to 30 cm. RHIZOMES Thick, fleshy. STEMS Several. LEAVES *Flat*, 1–4 cm, alternate, dense, increasing in size up stem. FLOWERS Dioecious, 4 *petals, greenish yellow*. HABITAT Mountain rock ledges, crevices, usually on base-rich soils; to 1160 m. DIST. Native. Upland Britain, sea cliffs in W and N. (Arctic Europe.) FLS May–Aug.

Caucasian-stonecrop
Sedum spurium

Glabrous, *mat-forming*, much-branched, *creeping perennial*. STEMS Flowering stems to 15 cm. LEAVES Flat, 1.5–3 cm, opposite. FLOWERS *Pink*, in dense, flat-topped inflorescence; 5 petals, 8–10 mm. HABITAT Walls, rocks, banks. DIST. Introduced. Widely cultivated and naturalised throughout BI. (Native of Caucasus; naturalised throughout much of Europe.) FLS Jul–Aug.

Rock Stonecrop
Sedum forsterianum

Glabrous, evergreen, mat-forming perennial to 30 cm. LEAVES Alternate, *linear*, 10–20 mm, upper surface flat, *tips abruptly pointed; in dense, rosette-like clusters at tips of sterile branches*, with persistent dead leaves below. FLOWERS *Yellow*, *c.*12 mm across, in umbel-like inflorescence; 6–8 petals. HABITAT Rocks, scree, rocky hillsides; to 365 m. DIST. Native. Wales, SW England. Widely cultivated and naturalised outside native range. (W and SW Europe.) FLS Jun–Jul.

Reflexed Stonecrop
Sedum rupestre

Similar to *S. forsterianum*, but more robust, *leaves on sterile shoots ± evenly spaced, not clustered at tip*, dead leaves not persisting; leaves *±* rounded in section, not flat-topped, *tapering to fine point*; some leaves on flowering stems reflexed. HABITAT Old walls, banks, rock outcrops, waste ground. DIST. Introduced. Widely cultivated and naturalised throughout BI, especially England, Wales. (Most of Europe.) FLS Jun–Aug.

Biting Stonecrop
Sedum acre

Glabrous, mat-forming, evergreen perennial to 10 cm. LEAVES Alternate, *overlapping*, broadest near base, rounded in section, 3–5 mm; *hot and acrid to taste*. FLOWERS *Yellow*, *c.*12 mm across, in few-flowered inflorescence; 5 petals, 6–8 mm. HABITAT Sand-dunes, shingle beaches, cliff tops, heaths, walls, motorway reservations, dry, open grassland. DIST. Native. Throughout BI, but scarce in N Scotland. (All Europe.) FLS Jun–Jul.

Tasteless Stonecrop
Sedum sexangulare

Similar to *S. acre*, but taller, to 25 cm; *leaves* cylindrical, parallel-sided, *not overlapping, not hot to taste*; petals 4–6 mm. HABITAT Cliffs, old walls, churchyards. DIST. Introduced. Rare and very scattered as escape from cultivation in England, Wales; absent from Scotland, Ireland. (Central Europe.) FLS Jul–Aug.

English Stonecrop
Sedum anglicum

Creeping, mat-forming, glabrous, glaucous, evergreen perennial to 5 cm. LEAVES *Alternate*, 3–5 mm, egg-shaped, spreading and *clasping stem at base*. FLOWERS *White*, *c.*12 mm across, in *few-flowered inflorescence with 2 main branches*; scales at base of petals red. HABITAT Rocks, dunes, shingle beaches; also rocky woodlands, walls, mine spoil, on acid soils. To 1080 m. DIST. Native. W Britain, Ireland, scattered elsewhere. (W Europe.) FLS Jun–Sep.

White Stonecrop
Sedum album

Creeping, mat-forming, glabrous, bright green perennial to 15 cm. LEAVES *Alternate*, 6–12 mm, *not clasping at base*. FLOWERS *White*, 6–9 mm across, in *dense-flowered inflorescence with several branches*; scales at base of petals yellow. HABITAT Rocks and old walls, shingle, churchyards; to 570 m. DIST. Archaeophyte, although may be native on limestone rocks in S Devon, Mendips. Throughout BI, but rare in N Scotland. (All Europe.) FLS Jun to Aug.

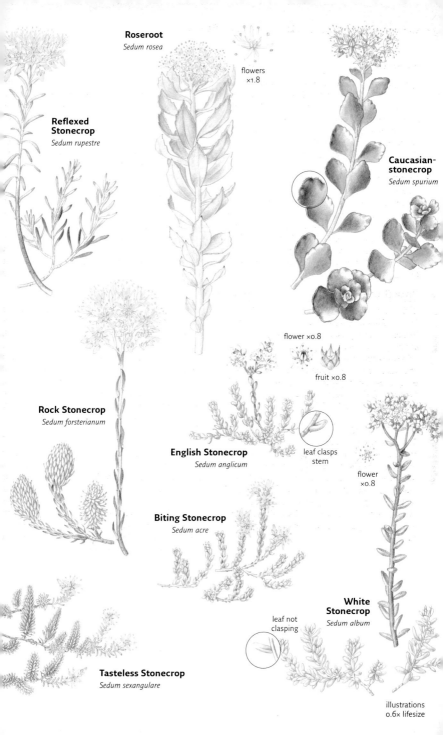

Roseroot
Sedum rosea

flowers
×1.8

Reflexed Stonecrop
Sedum rupestre

Caucasian-stonecrop
Sedum spurium

Rock Stonecrop
Sedum forsterianum

flower ×0.8

fruit ×0.8

English Stonecrop
Sedum anglicum

leaf clasps
stem

flower
×0.8

Biting Stonecrop
Sedum acre

White Stonecrop
Sedum album

leaf not
clasping

Tasteless Stonecrop
Sedum sexangulare

illustrations
0.6× lifesize

Orpine
Sedum telephium

Erect, glabrous, slightly glaucous perennial to 60 cm, with carrot-shaped root tubers. LEAVES *Flat*, 2–8 cm, alternate, numerous. FLOWERS *Red, 5 petals*, 3–5 mm. HABITAT Hedge banks, lanesides, woodland clearings, field borders, limestone pavement; to 455 m. DIST. Native; introduced in Ireland. Throughout BI except N Scotland. Native distribution obscured by frequent escapes from cultivation. (N, W and central Europe.) FLS Jul–Sep.

Hairy Stonecrop
Sedum villosum

Small, erect, *glandular-pubescent* reddish biennial or perennial to 15 cm, often with short non-flowering shoots. LEAVES 6–12 mm, alternate, *linear*, flat above. FLOWERS *Pink, c.6 mm across, in few-flowered inflorescence; stalks long. HABITAT Alpine of usually calcareous wet pastures, stream sides, stony ground, mossy flushes; to 1100 m. DIST. Native. Local in N England, Scotland. (N Europe, mts of central and S Europe.) FLS Jun–Jul.

Thick-leaved Stonecrop
Sedum dasyphyllum

Small, tufted, glaucous perennial to 10 cm, often tinged reddish. LEAVES 3–6 mm, egg-shaped, *glandular-pubescent, mostly opposite*. FLOWERS *White, c.6 mm across*, in few-flowered inflorescence. HABITAT Old walls, quarries, limestone rocks. DIST. Introduced. Scattered in lowland Britain. Naturalised as escape from cultivation. (S Europe.) FLS Jun–Jul.

SAXIFRAGACEAE Saxifrages

See key on p.236. Leaves are usually alternate or all basal. Flowers are bisexual, regular; usually 5 sepals and petals; 10 stamens; receptacle characteristically cup-shaped or flat; 2 carpels, fused at base. Fruit is a capsule. *Saxifraga* includes a number of cushion-forming alpines.

Marsh Saxifrage
Saxifraga hirculus VU. *(B, NI, R)

Erect perennial to 20 cm, with short, prostrate non-flowering shoots. STEMS Flowering stems reddish, with long hairs. LEAVES *Lower leaves lanceolate*, 1–3 cm, tapering into long petiole. FLOWERS *Yellow. Usually solitary*, petals 10–13 mm, ovary superior. HABITAT Wet, base-rich upland hollows, flushes,

mires; to 750 m. DIST. Very rare. N England, Scotland, Ireland. (Arctic and N Europe.) FLS Aug.

Alpine Saxifrage
Saxifraga nivalis *(R)

Erect, rhizomatous alpine perennial with basal leaf rosettes. STEMS *Flowering stems leafless*, with glandular hairs, 15 cm. LEAVES Blades 1–2 cm, *purplish beneath*, with marginal glandular hairs. FLOWERS In dense inflorescence, *petals 2–3 mm*. HABITAT Damp, shaded, base-rich rock ledges; 365–1300 m. DIST. Native. Rare. Scottish Highlands; also isolated localities in N England, N Wales, W Ireland. (Arctic Europe.) FLS Jul–Aug.

Starry Saxifrage
Saxifraga stellaris

Erect, stoloniferous perennial with basal leaf rosettes. STEMS *Flowering stems leafless*, hairy, glandular, to 20 cm. LEAVES 0.5–3 cm, ± *sessile*. FLOWERS *In open inflorescence; petals 4–6 mm, with 2 yellow spots near base*. HABITAT Stream sides, springs, flushes, wet rock ledges, wet stony ground; to 1340 m. DIST. Native. Widespread in uplands. (N Europe, mts of central and S Europe.) FLS Jun–Aug.

St Patrick's-cabbage
Saxifraga spathularis

Erect, stoloniferous perennial with basal leaf rosettes. STEMS Flowering stems leafless, to 40 cm, glandular, hairy. LEAVES *Glabrous; 9–15 marginal teeth, acute; petiole long, flattened*, ± glabrous to sparsely pubescent at base. FLOWERS *Petals 3–5 mm, with yellow and red spots at base*. HABITAT Damp rocky woods, stream sides, exposed slopes; to 1040 m. DIST. Native. Confined to high-rainfall upland areas in W Ireland, where it is widespread. (Mts of SW Europe.) FLS Jun–Aug.

Londonpride
Saxifraga × urbium

Hybrid between *S. umbrosa* (see 'Similar spp.') and *S. spathularis*. Similar to *S. spathularis*, but leaves larger, *with 19–25 ± blunt teeth; petioles hairy along margins*; petals 4–5 mm, *with red spots at base*. HABITAT Damp woods, stream sides, banks, walls. DIST. Introduced; hybrid of garden origin. Widely naturalised as garden escape throughout most of BI. FLS Jun–Aug. SIMILAR SPP. **Pyrenean Saxifrage** *S. umbrosa* is an endemic of the Pyrenees and has been established at one locality in Yorkshire since the C18th.

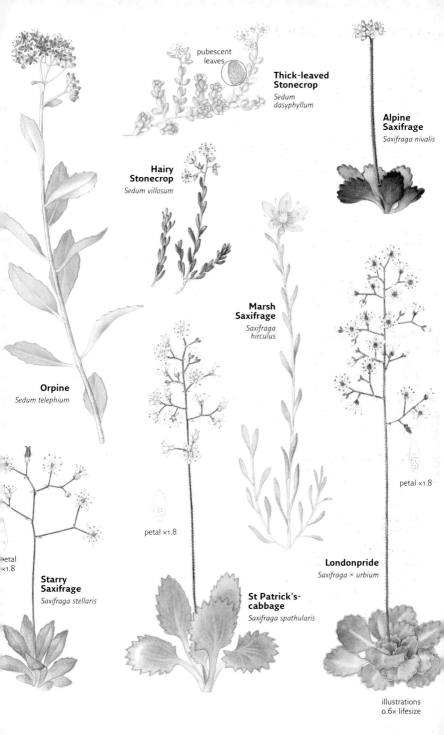

Thick-leaved Stonecrop
Sedum dasyphyllum

pubescent leaves

Alpine Saxifrage
Saxifraga nivalis

Hairy Stonecrop
Sedum villosum

Marsh Saxifrage
Saxifraga hirculus

Orpine
Sedum telephium

petal ×1.8

Starry Saxifrage
Saxifraga stellaris

etal ×1.8

petal ×1.8

St Patrick's-cabbage
Saxifraga spathularis

Londonpride
Saxifraga × urbium

illustrations
0.6× lifesize

	if	**then**
	▷ 5 sepals and petals	*Saxifraga* (below)
	▷ 4 sepals, petals absent	*Chrysosplenium* (p.240)
	▷ Flowering stems with a single leaf and single flower; flowers with 5 staminodes (sterile stamens)	*Parnassia* (p.240)

Saxifraga flower

Saxifraga

	▷ Most or all flowers replaced by reddish bulbils (very rare Scottish alpine)	*S. cernua* (p.238)
	▷ Leaves opposite; flowers purple	*S. oppositifolia* (p.238)
	▷ Leaves alternate; flowers white or yellow	*see* **below**

Leaves alternate; flowers white

1	▷ Flowering stems leafless	Go to ▷ **2**
	▷ Flowering stems leafy	Go to ▷ **6**
2	▷ Leaves sessile	*S. stellaris* (p.234)
	▷ Leaves stalked	Go to ▷ **3**
3	▷ Petals with small red dots	Go to ▷ **4**
	▷ Petals without small red dots	*S. nivalis* (p.234)
4	▷ Petiole round in section; leaves cordate, pubescent on both surfaces (W Ireland)	*S. hirsuta* (p.238)
	▷ Petiole flattened; leaves not cordate, ± glabrous	Go to ▷ **5**
5	▷ Leaf blade with 9–15 acute teeth, petiole ± glabrous (W Ireland)	*S. spathularis* (p.234)
	▷ Leaf blade with 19–25 blunt teeth, petiole pubescent on margins (escape from cultivation)	*S.* × *urbium* (p.234)
6	▷ Plants with numerous dense, prostrate rosettes of non-flowering shoots	Go to ▷ **7**
	▷ Plants without rosettes on non-flowering shoots	Go to ▷ **9**
7	▷ Lobes of leaves linear, tips with short, stiff point	*S. hypnoides* (p.238)
	▷ Lobes of leaves oblong, tips without short point	Go to ▷ **8**
8	▷ Leaves covered by long non-glandular hairs (W Ireland)	*S. rosacea* (p.238)
	▷ Leaves covered by short glandular hairs	*S. cespitosa* (p.238)

	if	**then**
9	▷ Perennial; leaves cordate; plant with basal bulbils	Go to ▷ **10**
	▷ Annual; base of leaf blades tapering to petiole; plant without bulbils	*S. tridactylites* (p.240)
10	▷ Basal leaves with ≥7 lobes; petals >9 mm (lowland)	*S. granulata* (p.238)
	▷ Basal leaves with 3–7 lobes; petals <6 mm (Scottish alpine)	*S. rivularis* (p.238)

Leaves alternate; flowers yellow

	if	**then**
1	▷ Annual; leaves rounded, cordate, shallowly lobed (escape from cultivation; *not illustrated*)	*S. cymbalaria* (p.240)
	▷ Perennial; leaves linear, lanceolate	Go to ▷ **2**
2	▷ Flowers solitary; leaves with petiole	*S. hirculus* (p.234)
	▷ Flowers not solitary, usually >3 per stem; leaves sessile	*S. aizoides* (p.238)

Kidney Saxifrage
Saxifraga hirsuta

Erect, stoloniferous perennial with basal leaf rosettes. STEMS Flowering stem to 30 cm, leafless, glandular-hairy. LEAVES *Densely hairy*; blades 1–4 cm, thin, *rounded to kidney-shaped, cordate at base*; 15–25 blunt marginal teeth; *petioles long, not flattened*. FLOWERS Petals 3–5 mm, with red spots and yellow blotch near base. HABITAT Shaded stream sides, damp woods, mountain rocks; to 915 m. DIST. Native. SW Ireland. (Pyrenees, N Spain.) FLS May–Jul. NOTE Often grows with *S. spathularis* (p.234) in SW Ireland, where their hybrid, False Londonpride *S. × polita*, may become more abundant than *S. hirsuta* or occur in the absence of one or both parents.

Purple Saxifrage
Saxifraga oppositifolia *(NI)

Densely tufted, cushion- or mat-forming alpine perennial. LEAVES Opposite, in 4 rows, overlapping, 2–6 mm, with marginal hairs. FLOWERS Purple, solitary, petals 5–10 mm. HABITAT Damp rocks, ledges, stony ground, scree, steep slopes, on calcareous or basic rocks; to 1210 m. DIST. Native. Locally common in mts of N and W Britain. (Arctic Europe, mts of central and S Europe.) FLS Feb–May.

Yellow Saxifrage
Saxifraga aizoides *(NI)

Erect alpine perennial to 20 cm. STEMS Non-flowering stems prostrate, densely leafy. LEAVES 1–2 cm, narrow with fringe of marginal hairs. FLOWERS *Yellow, in open inflorescence of 1–10 flowers*; petals 4–7 mm with red dots. HABITAT Rocks, boulders, in mountain streams; wet gravelly, stony ground. To 1175 m. DIST. Native. Locally common in mts of N England, Scotland, NW Ireland. (Arctic Europe, mts of central and S Europe.) FLS Jun–Sep.

Highland Saxifrage
Saxifraga rivularis

Stoloniferous *alpine* perennial to 8 cm. STEMS *Base often with bulbils among leaves.* LEAVES *Basal leaves 5–20 mm, cordate, 3–7-lobed*; petioles much longer than blade. FLOWERS In few-flowered inflorescence, sepals erect, *petals 3–5 mm*. HABITAT Wet acid mountain rocks, mossy flushes; to 1200 m. DIST. Native. Very rare. Scottish Highlands. (Arctic Europe.) FLS Jul–Aug.

Drooping Saxifrage
Saxifraga cernua VU. *(B)

Erect alpine perennial to *c*.10 cm. *Rarely flowers*. STEMS Flowering stems solitary. LEAVES Bulbils produced in axils of basal leaves, leaf blades 5–18 mm. FLOWERS *Solitary or absent, inflorescence with numerous red bulbils in axils of bracts*. HABITAT Basic rocks and crevices; 915–1170 m. DIST. Native. Very rare: in only 3 localities in central Scottish Highlands. (Arctic Europe, mts of central and S Europe.)

Mossy Saxifrage
Saxifraga hypnoides VU.

Mat-forming, stoloniferous perennial to 20 cm. STEMS Non-flowering shoots numerous, prostrate; flowering stems ± glabrous. LEAVES *c*.1 cm, with long non-glandular hairs, *lobes linear, terminal lobe with short hair point*. FLOWERS Petals 4–10 mm. HABITAT Sides of mountain streams, cliffs, screes, rocky slopes; rarely on sand-dunes. To 1215 m. DIST. Native. Widespread throughout British uplands. (NW Europe.) FLS May–Jul.

Irish Saxifrage
Saxifraga rosacea EN.

Very variable mat-forming, loosely tufted, stoloniferous perennial to 20 cm. STEMS *Non-flowering* shoots ascending, *often with characteristic pinkish colour*; flowering stems glandular. LEAVES Similar to *S. hypnoides*, but *lobes oblong, tip of terminal leaf lobe acute or obtuse, and without a short hair point*. FLOWERS Petals 6–8 mm. HABITAT Banks of mountain streams; damp cliff ledges, scree, rocky gullies, sea cliffs. To 960 m. DIST. Native. W Ireland only. (Arctic Europe, mts of central and S Europe.) FLS Jun–Aug. NOTE Ssp. *hartii* *(R) is endemic to sea cliffs on Aranmore I, Donegal.

Tufted Saxifrage
Saxifraga cespitosa EN. *(B)

Cushion-forming alpine perennial to 10 cm. STEMS Non-flowering shoots forming densely leafy rosettes; flowering stems glandular. LEAVES To 1 cm, *covered by short glandular hairs, terminal lobe blunt*. FLOWERS Petals 4–5 mm, dirty white. HABITAT Inaccessible mossy ledges, scree, crevices; to 1180 m. DIST. Native. Very rare. N Wales (one locality), Scottish Highlands. (Arctic Europe.) FLS May–Jul.

Meadow Saxifrage
Saxifraga granulata *(R)

[*See* illustration following page.] Erect, pubescent, glandular perennial to 50 cm, *with brown bulbils in axils of basal rosette leaves*. STEMS Flowering stems, solitary, unbranched. LEAVES *Blades* 0.5–3 cm, *with lobes* long glandular and non-glandular hairs; petiole much longer than blade. FLOWERS White, pedicels 5–20 mm, densely glandular; *petals 10–17 mm*. HABITAT Well-drained neutral or basic rough pastures, meadows, grassy banks, churchyards. DIST. Native. Local throughout most of BI except SW England, N Scotland, Ireland. (Most of Europe.) FLS Jun–Aug.

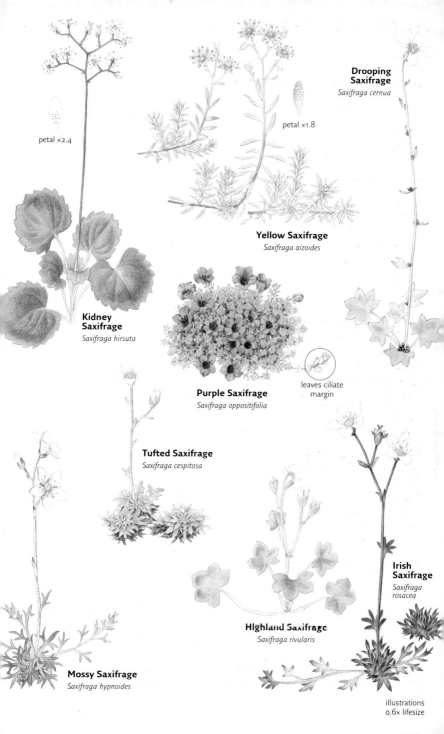

petal ×2.4

Drooping Saxifrage
Saxifraga cernua

petal ×1.8

Yellow Saxifrage
Saxifraga aizoides

Kidney Saxifrage
Saxifraga hirsuta

Purple Saxifrage
Saxifraga oppositifolia

leaves ciliate margin

Tufted Saxifrage
Saxifraga cespitosa

Irish Saxifrage
Saxifraga rosacea

Highland Saxifrage
Saxifraga rivularis

Mossy Saxifrage
Saxifraga hypnoides

illustrations
0.6× lifesize

Rue-leaved Saxifrage   *Saxifraga tridactylites*

Erect, glandular-hairy, sparsely branched, often red-dish *annual to c.10 cm*. LEAVES *Basal leaves lobed, bulbils absent*. FLOWERS White, in sparse inflorescence, pedicels much longer than flowers, petals 2–3 mm. HABITAT Dry, open areas, wall tops, sand-dunes, heath grassland, waste ground, limestone rocks; to 595 m. DIST. Native. Widespread in lowland S Britain; rare in Scotland. (Most of Europe.) FLS Apr–Jun.

Celandine Saxifrage   *Saxifraga cymbalaria*

Creeping annual to 20 cm. LEAVES *Glossy, rounded, cordate, shallowly lobed*. FLOWERS *Yellow*, petioles long, petals 3–5 mm. HABITAT Damp, shaded old walls, rockeries. DIST. Introduced (native of SW Asia). Garden escape, thinly scattered but increasing throughout BI. (Rare in Romania.) FLS Jun–Jul. *Not illustrated.*

Opposite-leaved Golden Saxifrage   *Chrysosplenium oppositifolium*

Sparsely hairy, stoloniferous perennial to 15cm. STEMS Leafy; non-flowering shoots prostrate, flowering stems erect. LEAVES *Opposite, not cordate, petiole as long as or shorter than blade*. FLOWERS 3–4 mm across; 4–5 sepals; petals absent. HABITAT Woodland flushes, stream sides, springs, wet rocks, on acid soils; to 1100 m. DIST. Native. Common throughout BI. (W and central Europe.) FLS Apr–Jun.

Alternate-leaved Golden Saxifrage   *Chrysosplenium alternifolium*

Similar to *C. oppositifolium*, but more robust, stolons leafless; *basal leaves cordate, pedicels much longer than blade*; flowering stems taller, and with only 1 leaf; flowers 5–6 mm across. HABITAT Similar to *C. oppositifolium*, with which it often grows, but more local, ± restricted to base-rich moving ground water; also upland mossy flushes. To 915 m. DIST. Native. Widespread in N and W; rare in E and SW England; absent from Ireland. (Most of Europe except S.) FLS Apr–Jun.

Grass-of-Parnassus   *Parnassia palustris*

Distinctive, erect, glabrous perennial. STEMS *Flowering stems* to 30 cm, *with single leaf near base*. LEAVES Basal leaves cordate, 1–5 cm; petioles long. FLOWERS *Solitary*, with 5 large yellowish staminodes (sterile stamens); petals 7–12 mm. HABITAT Base-rich fens, mires, wet grassland; machair, dune slacks. To 1005 m. DIST. Native. Widespread in N Britain, East Anglia; declining in S. (All Europe except extreme N.) FLS Jul–Oct.

ROSACEAE Rose family

A large, diverse family of trees, shrubs and herbs with alternate leaves that almost always have stipules (*see* key on p.242). Flowers are regular, sometimes with an epicalyx beneath the calyx looking like a second ring of sepals; usually 5 sepals and petals, petals free, sometimes absent; stamens numerous, usually 2–4× as many as petals; 1 to many carpels, usually free, or ovary inferior with carpels united and enclosed by the receptacle. Fruits vary, usually an achene or follicle or, in trees and shrubs, a drupe. Flowers with numerous stamens and free carpels are sometimes mistaken for the Ranunculaceae, but the alternate leaves with stipules should almost always avoid confusion (although note that the water-crowfoots do have stipules).

Bridewort   *Spiraea* spp.

Deciduous shrubs to 2 m with numerous erect branches, sometimes forming large thickets. LEAVES 3–7 cm, glabrous or pubescent. FLOWERS *Usually pink, sometimes white, in dense, narrow terminal panicles*. HABITAT Roadsides, hedgerows, riverbanks. DIST. Introduced. Several species have been introduced into gardens and become naturalised throughout BI. Most are hybrids or varieties of *S. douglasii* and *S. alba* (N America), or *S. salicifolia* (central and E Europe). *S. salicifolia* itself is now very rare as an escape. FLS Jun–Sep.

Meadowsweet   *Filipendula ulmaria*

Tall perennial to 120 cm, sometimes forming dense stands. LEAVES Basal ones 30–60 cm, with up to 5 large leaflets. FLOWERS *In dense inflorescence; 5 sepals; 5 petals*, 2–5 mm. HABITAT Marshes, fens, wet woods, ditches; river, stream and lake margins; wet alpine meadows, rock ledges. To 880 m. DIST. Native. Common throughout BI. (All Europe except Mediterranean.) FLS Jun–Sep.

Dropwort   *Filipendula vulgaris*

Erect, ± glabrous perennial to 80 cm. STEMS *Flowering stems ± unbranched*. LEAVES Basal ones numerous, 2–25 cm, with 8–20 pairs of leaflets; stem leaves few. FLOWERS *6 sepals; 6 petals*, 5–9 mm. HABITAT Dry calcareous grassland; to 365 m. DIST. Native. Lowland England; scattered elsewhere. Planted in N Wales. (Most of Europe.) FLS May–Aug.

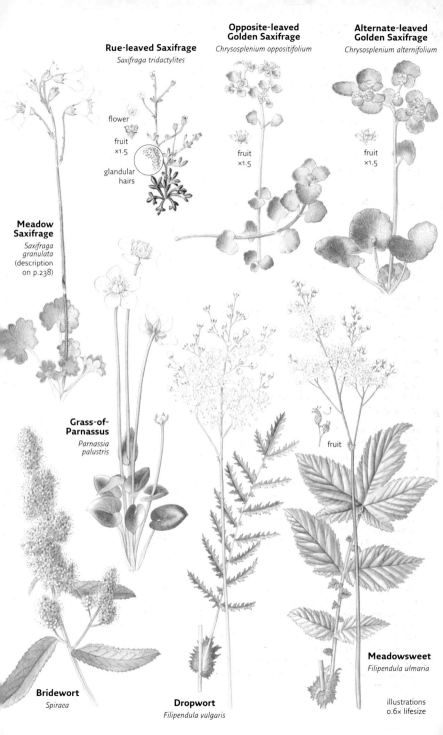

Rue-leaved Saxifrage
Saxifraga tridactylites

flower

fruit
×1.5

glandular
hairs

**Opposite-leaved
Golden Saxifrage**
Chrysosplenium oppositifolium

fruit
×1.5

**Alternate-leaved
Golden Saxifrage**
Chrysosplenium alternifolium

fruit
×1.5

**Meadow
Saxifrage**
*Saxifraga
granulata*
(description
on p.238)

**Grass-of-
Parnassus**
*Parnassia
palustris*

fruit

Bridewort
Spiraea

Dropwort
Filipendula vulgaris

Meadowsweet
Filipendula ulmaria

illustrations
0.6× lifesize

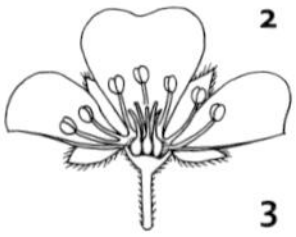

	if	then
	Trees and Shrubs	
1	▷ Flowers yellow	**Potentilla** (p.244)
	▷ Flowers pink or white	Go to ▷ **2**
2	▷ Flowers pink, numerous, *c*.8 mm across, in dense panicles	**Spiraea** (p.240)
	▷ Plant not like this	Go to ▷ **3**
3	▷ Plant spiny; receptacle strongly convex; leaves compound	**Rubus** (p.246)
	▷ Receptacle cup-shaped or completely enclosing carpels and ovary inferior	Go to ▷ **4**
4	▷ Numerous carpels and styles; plant prickly and spiny; leaves pinnate	**Rosa** (p.245)
	▷ 1–5 carpels and styles	Go to ▷ **5**
5	▷ Receptacle cup-shaped; 1 carpel, free of receptacle	**Prunus** (p.262)
	▷ 1–5 carpels; receptacle completely enclosing carpels and ovary inferior	Go to ▷ **6**
6	▷ Plant thorny	Go to ▷ **7**
	▷ Plant not thorny	Go to ▷ **8**
7	▷ Leaves deciduous, lobed; stipules persistent	**Crataegus** (p.272)
	▷ Leaves evergreen, toothed; stipules small, soon falling	**Pyracantha** (p.272)
8	▷ Flowers solitary, sepals leaf-like; fruit crowned by calyx	**Mespilus** (p.272)
	▷ Flowers in racemes	**Amelanchier** (p.270)
	▷ Flowers in few-flowered, simple umbels or corymbs	Go to ▷ **9**
	▷ Flowers in branched corymbs	Go to ▷ **11**
9	▷ Flowers ≥3 cm across	Go to ▷ **10**
	▷ Flowers <1 cm across	**Cotoneaster** (p.272)
10	▷ Anthers yellow, styles fused at base	**Malus** (p.266)
	▷ Anthers purple, styles free	**Pyrus** (p.266)
11	▷ Leaves toothed, lobed or pinnate	**Sorbus** (p.266)
	▷ Leaves entire	**Cotoneaster** (p.272)
	Herbs	
1	▷ Flowers with petals	Go to ▷ **2**
	▷ Flowers without petals	Go to ▷ **11**

Potentilla flower

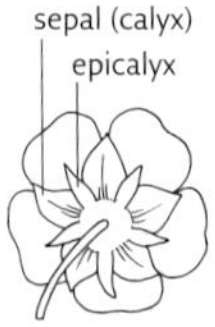

sepal (calyx)
epicalyx

Potentilla

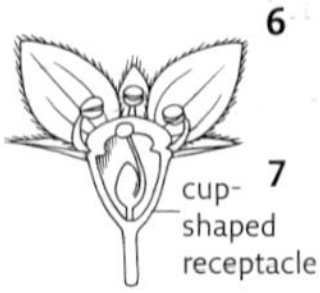

cup-
shaped
receptacle

Alchemilla flower

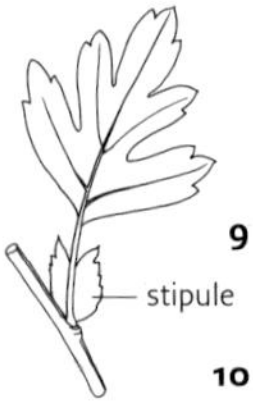

stipule

Craetagus twig,
stipule and leaf

	if	then
2	▷ 4–6 petals	Go to ▷ **3**
	▷ >6 petals	*Dryas* (p.250)
3	▷ Flowers with epicalyx (looks like another ring of sepals beneath calyx)	Go to ▷ **4**
	▷ Flowers without epicalyx	Go to ▷ **9**
4	▷ Leaves palmate or ternate	Go to ▷ **5**
	▷ At least basal leaves pinnate	Go to ▷ **7**
5	▷ Receptacle becoming red and fleshy in fruit (strawberries)	*Fragaria* (p.250)
	▷ Receptacle remaining dry in fruit	Go to ▷ **6**
6	▷ Petals conspicuous, >2 mm long; upper part of leaflets toothed all round margins	*Potentilla* (p.244)
	▷ Petals tiny, inconspicuous; tips of leaflets with 3 teeth (alpine)	*Sibbaldia* (p.250)
7	▷ Each flower surrounded by involucre of 6–10 fused, sepal-like bracts	*Aremonia* (p.252)
	▷ Flowers not surrounded by involucre	Go to ▷ **8**
8	▷ Style strongly hooked, elongating in fruit; basal leaves with terminal leaflet much larger than lateral ones	*Geum* (p.252)
	▷ Style not hooked, falling before fruiting; terminal leaflet of basal leaves not much larger than laterals	*Potentilla* (p.244)
9	▷ Flowers yellow	*Agrimonia* (p.252)
	▷ Flowers white	Go to ▷ **10**
10	▷ Leaves pinnate; flowers small, in dense, many-flowered panicles	*Filipendula* (p.240)
	▷ Leaves not pinnate; inflorescence of 1–6 flowers	*Rubus* (p.246)
11	▷ Leaves pinnate	Go to ▷ **12**
	▷ Leaves palmate or palmately or deeply 3-lobed	Go to ▷ **13**
12	▷ Plant erect; receptacle not spiny in fruit	*Sanguisorba* (p.252)
	▷ Plant prostrate; receptacle not spiny	*Acaena* (p.252)
13	▷ Small annuals; flowers tiny, in dense, leaf-opposed clusters	*Aphanes* (p.254)
	▷ Perennials; flowers in terminal inflorescences	Go to ▷ **14**
14	▷ Leaves palmate or palmately lobed	*Alchemilla* (p.254-6)
	▷ Leaves deeply 3-lobed, tips of leaflets with 3 teeth	*Sibbaldia* (p.250)

	if	then
1	▷ Shrub; leaves pinnate, leaflets entire	*P. fruticosa* (p.246)
	▷ Herb	Go to ▷ **2**
2	▷ Leaves ternate (3 leaflets) or palmate (≥5 leaflets)	Go to ▷ **3**
	▷ Leaves pinnate	Go to ▷ **12**
3	▷ Flowers white	Go to ▷ **4**
	▷ Flowers yellow	Go to ▷ **5**
4	▷ Leaflets toothed to base; petals *c.*5 mm	*P. sterilis* (p.250)
	▷ Leaflets toothed towards apex only; petals 6–9 mm	*P. montana* ● (p.250)
5	▷ Leaves densely white-felted beneath	*P. argentea* (p.248)
	▷ Leaves green beneath	Go to ▷ **6**
6	▷ Flowers solitary or, if forming an inflorescence, then all or some flowers with 4 petals	Go to ▷ **7**
	▷ Flowers in few to several-flowered terminal cymes	Go to ▷ **9**
7	▷ Stems prostrate, rooting at nodes; leaves palmate; all flowers with 5 petals	*P. reptans* (p.250)
	▷ Stems prostrate or erect; at least some flowers with 4 petals	Go to ▷ **8**
8	▷ Stem leaves sessile, most leaves ternate (exclude stipules); stems not rooting at nodes; all flowers with 4 petals	*P. erecta* (p.248)
	▷ Lower stem leaves stalked, some leaves with 4–5 leaflets; stems rooting at nodes late in season; some flowers with 5 petals	*P. anglica* (p.248)
9	▷ Flowering stems terminal, erect; some leaves with 7 leaflets	*P. recta* (p.248)
	▷ Flowering stems prostrate to erect; leaves with 3 or 5 leaflets	Go to ▷ **10**
10	▷ Petals as long as or shorter than sepals; flowering stems terminal	*P. norvegica* (p.248)
	▷ Petals longer than sepals; flowering stems axillary from basal rosette	Go to ▷ **11**
11	▷ Basal rosettes with short, non-rooting branches; flowers 15–25 mm across	*P. crantzii* (p.248)
	▷ Basal rosette with long, prostrate, rooting branches; flowers 10–15 mm across	*P. neumanniana* (p.248)
12	▷ Flowers yellow	*P. anserina* (p.246)
	▷ Flowers white (very rare)	*P. rupestris* (p.248)
	▷ Flowers purple (wet habitats)	*P. palustris* (p.246)

Key to Roses *Rosa*

	if	**then**
1	▷ Leaves glabrous	Go to ▷ **2**
	▷ Leaves hairy, at least on veins beneath	Go to ▷ **5**
2	▷ Styles united into column at least as long as shorter stamens	*R. arvensis* (p.258)
	▷ Styles free and not united into column	Go to ▷ **3**
3	▷ Low shrub, to 50 cm; sepals entire; flowers solitary	*R. pimpinellifolia* (p.258)
	▷ Taller shrub, to 3 m; sepals lobed; flowers not solitary	Go to ▷ **4**
4	▷ Pedicels not hidden by bracts; sepals reflexed in fruit, soon falling	*R. canina* (p.258)
	▷ Pedicels short, hidden by bracts; sepals erect, persistent	*R. caesia* ssp. *glauca* (p.258)
5	▷ Disc strongly conical; styles united into short column, free later	*R. stylosa* (p.258)
	▷ Disc not conical; styles in domed head	Go to ▷ **6**
6	▷ Underside of leaves with numerous conspicuous sticky glands, with fruity or apple smell when rubbed	Go to ▷ **7**
	▷ Leaves without glands, or if with glands lacking fruity smell	Go to ▷ **9**
7	▷ Base of leaflets rounded; pedicels glandular	Go to ▷ **8**
	▷ Base of leaflets cuneate; pedicels not glandular	*R. agrestis* (p.260)
8	▷ Prickles unequal in size, mixed with stout bristles; sepals persistent, erect or spreading	*R. rubiginosa* (p.260)
	▷ Prickles equal in size, no stout bristles; sepals reflexed, soon falling	*R. micrantha* (p.260)
9	▷ Stems covered by dense cottony hairs; hips large, ≥2 cm	*R. rugosa* (p.258)
	▷ Stems not covered by cottony hairs; hips <2 cm	Go to ▷ **10**
10	▷ Pedicels smooth; leaflets hairy but not densely pubescent	Go to ▷ **11**
	▷ Pedicels glandular; leaflets densely pubescent	Go to ▷ **12**
11	▷ Pedicels short, concealed by bracts; sepals erect, persistent	*R. caesia* ssp. *caesia* (p.258)
	▷ Pedicels long or short, not concealed by bracts; sepals strongly reflexed	*R. obtusifolia* (p.260)
12	▷ Scrambling shrub with arching branches; pedicels 2–3.5 cm	*R. tomentosa* (p.260)
	▷ Erect shrub; pedicels ≤1.5 cm	Go to ▷ **13**
13	▷ Sepals erect, simple or with few lobes, persistent until fruit decays	*R. mollis* (p.260)
	▷ Sepals erect, lobed, persistent until fruit ripens and then falling	*R. sherardii* (p.260)

Rose flower shoot

Rose hip with lobed sepals

Cloudberry
Rubus chamaemorus *(NI)

Low, dioecious, *non-spiny*, rhizomatous perennial, with annual shoots. STEMS Flowering stems erect, to 20 cm. FLOWERS *Solitary*; 5 sepals; 5 petals, 8-12 mm. FRUITS *Orange when ripe*, with 4-20 drupelets. HABITAT Hummocks in blanket bogs, upland moorland; to 1160 m. DIST. Native. Locally abundant in upland Britain N from Pennines; very rare in Wales, Ireland. (N Europe, mts of S and E Europe.) FLS Jun-Aug.

Stone Bramble
Rubus saxatilis

Stoloniferous, deciduous perennial to 40 cm, pubescent and with weak prickles. STEMS Flowering stems arising from base of plant. LEAVES *With 3 leaflets*; stipules attached to stem, not petiole. FLOWERS *8-15 mm across, in few-flowered inflorescence*. FRUITS *Red*. HABITAT Open, damp rocky woodland, shaded rocks, scree, on calcareous or base-rich soils; to 975 m. DIST. Native. Widespread, but local in uplands. (N Europe, mts of S Europe.) FLS Jun-Aug.

Raspberry
Rubus idaeus

Erect shrub to 160 cm. STEMS Usually biennial, with weak prickles. LEAVES *Pinnate*; 3-7 leaflets, *white beneath*. FLOWERS *c*.10 mm across, in few-flowered cyme; petals as long as sepals. FRUITS *Red*. HABITAT Open woodland, heaths, commons, downland; also as an escape from cultivation. To 745 m. DIST. Native. Throughout BI. (Most of Europe.) FLS Jun-Aug.

Dewberry
Rubus caesius

Deciduous shrub. STEMS *Prostrate*, rooting at tip, *glabrous, with bluish bloom*; prickles weak. LEAVES *With 3 overlapping leaflets*. FLOWERS Large, 2-3 cm across. FRUITS *Large, black; few drupelets, these with bluish bloom*. HABITAT Hedges, scrub, rough, dry grassland, on basic soils; fen carr, dune slacks. DIST. Native. Widespread in England, Wales; rare in Ireland; ± absent from Scotland. (Most of Europe.) FLS Jun-Sep.

Bramble, Blackberry
Rubus 'fruticosus'

Deciduous or semi-evergreen, intensely prickly shrub, often forming dense patches. STEMS Rooting at tips. LEAVES *Palmate*. FRUITS *Black, hardly pruinose* (with a bloom). DIST. Native. Common throughout BI. HABITAT Woodlands, hedgerows, scrub, commons, heaths, cliffs. (All Europe.) FLS May-Sep. NOTE *Rubus 'fruticosus'* is an aggregate name for a large number of 'apomictic' (producing viable seed without fertilisation) 'microspecies'. Over 320 different 'microspecies' have been named from the BI; no attempt is made to deal with these individually here.

Cinquefoils *Potentilla*
See key to *Potentilla* on p.244.

Shrubby Cinquefoil
Potentilla fruticosa

Deciduous, much-branched, *dioecious shrub* to *c*.1 m. LEAVES *Pinnate, with 5 leaflets*. FLOWERS Solitary or in few-flowered inflorescence; 5 sepals; 5 petals, 8-12 mm. HABITAT River and lake margins, rock ledges, on calcareous soils. DIST. Native. Very rare. Restricted as a native to Upper Teesdale, Lake District, W Ireland. Widely established as garden escape elsewhere. (S Sweden, Estonia, Latvia, Pyrenees.) FLS Jun-Jul.

Marsh Cinquefoil
Potentilla palustris

Rhizomatous, ascending perennial to 45 cm. LEAVES With 5 or 7 leaflets, these 3-6 cm. FLOWERS In few-flowered inflorescence, *all parts of flowers purple, sepals enlarging after flowering, petals shorter than sepals*. HABITAT Fens, marshes, flushed bogs, lake and pool margins; to 800 m. DIST. Native. Common and widespread in N and W Britain; local in S, East Anglia. (All Europe except S and SW.) FLS May-Jul.

Silverweed
Potentilla anserina

Stoloniferous perennial. LEAVES *In basal rosettes, pinnate, with 7-12 pairs of main leaflets, densely silvery-silky beneath*. FLOWERS Solitary, on long stalks, 5 sepals; 5 petals, *c*.10 mm. HABITAT Roadsides, farm tracks, gateways, waste ground, abandoned arable land, dunes, upper levels of salt marshes. DIST. Native. Common throughout BI. (All Europe except S and SW.) FLS Jun-Aug.

Cloudberry
Rubus chamaemorus

Stone Bramble
Rubus saxatilis

Raspberry
Rubus idaeus

Dewberry
Rubus caesius

Bramble
Rubus 'fruticosus'

Shrubby Cinquefoil
Potentilla fruticosa

Silverweed
Potentilla anserina

Marsh Cinquefoil
Potentilla palustris

illustrations
0.5× lifesize

Rock Cinquefoil   *Potentilla rupestris* EN. *(B)

Erect, pubescent perennial to 60 cm. STEMS Flowering stems leafy. LEAVES *Pinnate*. Basal leaves in a rosette. FLOWERS *White*, petals 5–7 mm, longer than sepals. HABITAT Thin soils over basic rock on open cliffs and rocky places. DIST. Native. Very rare: in only 4 localities in Wales, Scotland. (SW, central and SE Europe.) FLS May–Jun.

Hoary Cinquefoil   *Potentilla argentea*

Prostrate to ascending, pubescent perennial to 50 cm. LEAVES *Basal leaves palmate, lobes narrow, densely covered by felt of short white hairs beneath.* FLOWERS 10–15 mm across, sepals pubescent, petals about as long as sepals. HABITAT Short open turf, dry sandy soils, old arable land, tracks, verges, coastal habitats. DIST. Native. Very local. S and E Britain, especially East Anglia; absent from Ireland. (Most of Europe except SW.) FLS Jun–Sep.

Sulphur Cinquefoil   *Potentilla recta*

Erect, pubescent perennial to 70 cm. STEMS *Flowering stems leafy, arising from centre of basal rosette.* LEAVES *Palmate, up to 7 leaflets.* FLOWERS 20–25 mm across; sepals densely glandular, hairy; petals 6–12 mm, deeply notched, longer than sepals. HABITAT Roadsides, waste ground, grassy places. DIST. Introduced. Naturalised as garden escape. Scattered throughout England, Wales, Scotland. (SW, S and E Europe.) FLS Jun–Jul.

Ternate-leaved Cinquefoil   *Potentilla norvegica*

Erect, ± pubescent annual to perennial to 50 cm. LEAVES *All ternate.* FLOWERS Sepals with long hairs; *petals 4–5 mm, as long as or shorter than sepals.* FRUITS Calyx enlarging. HABITAT Waste ground, roadsides, quarries. DIST. Introduced. Casual, originating from cultivation or birdseed. Thinly scattered throughout BI. (E Europe.) FLS Jun–Sep.

Alpine Cinquefoil   *Potentilla crantzii*

Perennial to 25 cm, *with basal leaf rosettes and short, non-rooting branches.* STEMS Flowering stems arising from sides of leaf rosettes (axillary). LEAVES Stipule lobes of basal leaves ovate. FLOWERS 15–25 mm across; petals often with orange spot at base, deeply notched, longer than sepals. HABITAT Rock ledges, crevices, calcareous grassland, on base-rich rock; to 1065 m. DIST. Native. Very local. N Wales, N England, Scotland. (Arctic Europe, mts of central and S Europe.) FLS Jun–Jul.

Spring Cinquefoil   *Potentilla neumanniana*

Mat-forming, pubescent perennial to 20 cm, *with long, prostrate, rooting branches.* STEMS Flowering stems arising from sides of leaf rosettes (axillary). LEAVES Stipule lobes of basal leaves linear-lanceolate. FLOWERS *10–15 mm across*; petals deeply notched, longer than sepals. HABITAT Warm, dry calcareous grassland, scree, rock outcrops. DIST. Native. Local, scattered throughout Britain; absent from Ireland. (S Scandinavia, W and central Europe.) FLS Apr–Jun.

Tormentil   *Potentilla erecta*

Perennial to 30 cm, with basal rosette of leaves that withers before flowering. STEMS Not rooting. LEAVES *Ternate*, basal leaves with long stalks, *stem leaves sessile*, stipules leaflet-like. FLOWERS 7–15 mm across, 4 petals; ≤20 carpels. HABITAT Grassland, heaths, moors, bogs, fens, open woodland, hedgebanks, usually on mildly acid soils; to 1040 m. DIST. Native. Common throughout BI. (All Europe except extreme S.) FLS Jun–Sep.

Trailing Tormentil   *Potentilla anglica*

Perennial to 80 cm, with rooting prostrate stems and persistent basal rosette. LEAVES *Basal leaves with leaflets*, long-stalked; stem leaves ternate; stipules entire. FLOWERS *Solitary, 14–18 mm across, 4 or 5 petals; 20–50 carpels.* HABITAT Field borders, woodland clearings, hedge banks, grass heaths, on well-drained acid soils. DIST. Native. Throughout BI except N Scotland; commoner in W. (Central and W Europe.) FLS Jun–Sep.

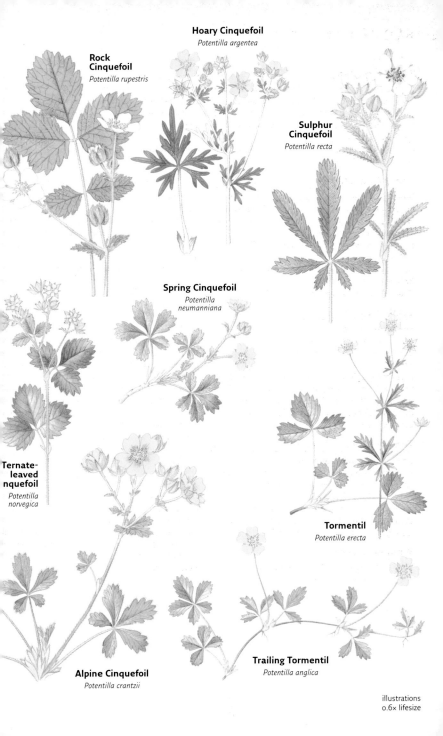

Rock Cinquefoil
Potentilla rupestris

Hoary Cinquefoil
Potentilla argentea

Sulphur Cinquefoil
Potentilla recta

Spring Cinquefoil
Potentilla neumanniana

Ternate-leaved Cinquefoil
Potentilla norvegica

Tormentil
Potentilla erecta

Alpine Cinquefoil
Potentilla crantzii

Trailing Tormentil
Potentilla anglica

illustrations
0.6× lifesize

Creeping Cinquefoil
Potentilla reptans

Prostrate, stoloniferous perennial to 100 cm, with *persistent basal rosette*. Leaves *Palmate*, petioles long. Flowers Solitary; 5 sepals; *5 petals, 15-25 mm across*, 2× as long as sepals; *60-120 carpels*. Habitat Grazed grassland, road verges, tracks, hedge banks, waste ground; lowland to 415 m. Dist. Native. BI as far N as Clyde. (Most of Europe.) Fls Jun-Sep.

Hybrids between *P. anglica*, *P. erecta* and *P. reptans* are common and identification of intermediate plants can be very difficult. The hybrids are always sterile so the only reliable character for good *P. anglica* is the presence of viable seeds, which can be checked by examining the fruiting heads to see whether the carpels are swollen.

White Cinquefoil
Potentilla montana

Pubescent, stoloniferous perennial to 20 cm. Leaves Ternate; *leaflets narrow, silvery-hairy beneath*, toothed towards apex only. Flowers *White*, 15-20 mm across, petals 6-9 mm, longer than sepals. Habitat Grass heaths, rocks, field verges, open woods; to 1000 m. Dist. Not BI. (W France, Pyrenees.) Fls Apr-Jun.

Barren Strawberry
Potentilla sterilis

Pubescent, stoloniferous perennial to 15 cm. Leaves *Ternate, dull bluish green*; leaflets broadly obovate, toothed to base, apical tooth shorter than its neighbours. Flowers *White*, 10-15 mm across; *petals c.5 mm, not contiguous, about as long as sepals*. Habitat Hedge banks, dry grassland, walls, scrub, woodland clearings, on well-drained soils; to 790 m. Dist. Throughout BI except extreme N Scotland. (W and central Europe.) Fls Feb-May.

Wild Strawberry
Fragaria vesca

Pubescent, stoloniferous perennial to 30 cm. Leaves Ternate, bright green; leaflets sessile, apical tooth as long as or longer than its neighbours (cf. *P. sterilis*). Flowers 12-18 mm across; *petals contiguous or overlapping, longer than sepals*. Habitat Woodlands, scrub, hedge banks, rough grassland, on base-rich soils; to 640 m. Dist. Throughout BI. (Most of Europe.) Fls Apr-Jul.

Hautbois Strawberry
Fragaria moschata

Larger than *F. vesca*. Leaves Upper side dull green, leaflets stalked. Flowers 15-30 mm across, hairs on fruiting stalks spreading. Habitat Roadsides, woodland hedgerows. Dist. Introduced. Naturalised and thinly scattered throughout BI. (Central Europe.) Fls Apr-Jul.

Fragaria viridis

Similar to *F. vesca*. Leaves Upper surface pubescent. Flowers Creamy-white, sepals appressed to fruit after flowering, base of fruiting receptacle without achenes. Habitat Woods, rocky places, calcareous grasslands. Dist. Not BI. (Europe except extreme N, SW, W.) Fls May-Jun.

Garden Strawberry
Fragaria × ananassa, frequently becomes naturalised as an escape from cultivation. It is larger than *F. vesca* and has more and longer stolons; the upper surface of the leaflets are glabrous, terminal leaflet rounded at base; flowers 20-35 mm across; fruiting receptacle large, *c.* 3 cm; achenes buried in flesh and not projecting. *Not illustrated.*

Sibbaldia
Sibbaldia procumbens VU.

Short, tufted, pubescent alpine perennial, with basal rosette of leaves. Leaves *Ternate, apical tooth of leaflets smaller than its neighbours*. Flowers About 5 mm across, in compact heads; *petals tiny or absent*. Habitat Areas of late snow-lie, exposed ridges, summit detritus; to 1310 m. Dist. Native. Local and widespread in Scottish Highlands. (Arctic Europe, mts of central and S Europe.) Fls Jul-Aug.

Mountain Avens
Dryas octopetala *(NI)

Much-branched, prostrate, evergreen perennial, with woody base. Leaves 0.5-2.5 cm, *densely white-felted beneath*. Flowers *Solitary*, 2.5-4 cm across; stalks 2-8 cm; *usually 8 petals*; numerous carpels. Fruits Style persistent, covered by long, feathery hairs. Habitat Rock ledges, steep cliffs, calcareous grassland, limestone pavement (Ireland), on calcareous soils; coastal shell-sand (N Scotland). To 1035 m. Dist. Native. Very local in upland Britain. (Arctic Europe, mts of central and S Europe.) Fls Jun-Jul.

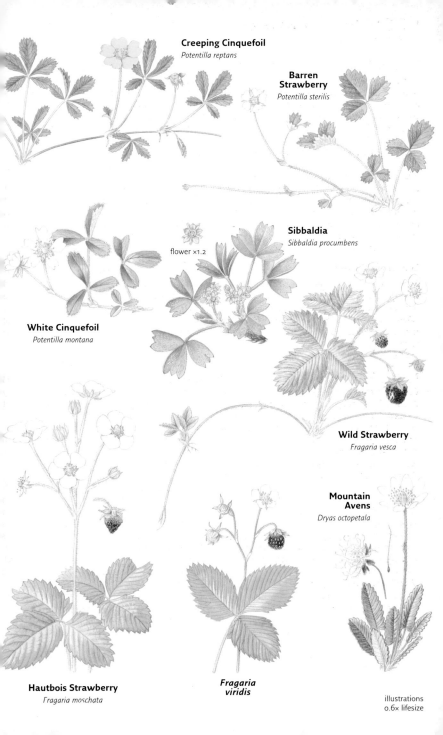

Creeping Cinquefoil
Potentilla reptans

Barren Strawberry
Potentilla sterilis

flower ×1.2

Sibbaldia
Sibbaldia procumbens

White Cinquefoil
Potentilla montana

Wild Strawberry
Fragaria vesca

Mountain Avens
Dryas octopetala

Hautbois Strawberry
Fragaria moschata

Fragaria viridis

illustrations
0.6× lifesize

Water Avens
Geum rivale

Erect, pubescent perennial to 60 cm. Leaves Basal leaves with 3-6 pairs of lateral leaflets, *terminal leaflet rounded, 2-5 cm across; stipules small, c.5 mm.* Flowers *Nodding; petals purple* about as long as sepals, 10-15 mm, *with long, narrow basal segment (clawed), tip notched;* stamens and carpels numerous. Fruits Style persistent as awn on fruit tip. Habitat Wet meadows, marshes, fens, damp woodlands, stream sides, rock ledges, on base-rich soils; prefers shade. To 975 m. Dist. Native. Throughout BI but commoner in N. (Most of Europe except extreme N.) Fls May-Sep.

Wood Avens
Geum urbanum

Erect, pubescent perennial to 60 cm. Leaves Basal leaves with 2-3 pairs of lateral leaflets, *terminal leaflet large, 3-lobed; stipules large, leaf-like.* Flowers *Erect; petals yellow* about as long as sepals, 5-9 mm, *neither clawed nor notched at tip.* Habitat Shaded areas, woodlands, scrub, hedgerows, roadsides, gardens, on base-rich soils; lowland to 450 m. Dist. Native. Common throughout BI except extreme N. (All Europe except extreme N.) Fls Jun-Aug.

Agrimony
Agrimonia eupatoria

Erect, pubescent, sparsely branched perennial to 100 cm. Leaves *Densely hairy but not glandular.* Flowers 5-8 mm across, in spike-like inflorescence; epicalyx absent; petals not notched. Fruits *Receptacle grooved throughout its length, lowest spines spreading horizontally or ascending.* Habitat Rough grassland, field borders, scrub, hedge banks, roadsides, woodland clearings; lowland to 365 m. Dist. Native. Common throughout BI except N Scotland. (All Europe except extreme N.) Fls Jun-Aug.

Fragrant Agrimony
Agrimonia procera

Similar to *A. eupatoria*, but more robust; stems more leafy; *leaves sweet-smelling when crushed and with numerous small, shining glands beneath;* petals notched; *fruiting receptacle without grooves at base, and lowest spines reflexed.* Habitat Similar to *A. eupatoria*; lowland to 335 m. Dist. Native. Local throughout BI. (Central, E and W Europe.) Fls Jun-Aug.

Bastard Agrimony
Aremonia agrimonioides

Prostrate to ascending perennial. Stems *To 40 cm, not much longer than basal leaves.* Flowers 7-10 mm across, in small cymes; *surrounded by involucre of fused bracts;* epicalyx absent. Fruits Receptacle without spines. Habitat Woods. Dist. Introduced.

Naturalised in a few places in central Scotland. (Italy SE Europe.) Fls Jun-Jul.

Great Burnet
Sanguisorba officinalis *(R

Tall, erect, glabrous *perennial to 100 cm.* Leaves *Leaflets to 2-4 cm, stalked, cordate at base.* Flowers 10-20 mm, crimson, in oblong heads; 4 stamens. Habitat Wet meadows, pastures, marshes, lake shores; to 460 m. Dist. Native. Central, N and SW England Wales. (W, central and E Europe.) Fls Jun-Sep.

Salad Burnet
Sanguisorba minor ssp. *mino*

Erect, glabrous, rather glaucous perennial to 50 cm smelling of cucumber when crushed. Leaves *Leaflets 0.5-2 cm, rounded at base, with short stalk;* few stem leaves or these absent. Flowers 7-12 mm, *green, in globular heads;* lower flowers male, middle bisexual, upper female; numerous stamens. Fruits *Receptacle ridged but not winged, faces reticulate.* Habitat Dry calcareous grassland; to 500 m. Dist. Native. Common in Britain as far N as S Scotland; rare in Ireland (W, central and E Europe.) Fls May-Aug.

Fodder Burnet
Sanguisorba minor ssp. *muricata*

Similar to Salad Burnet, but more robust and taller to 80 cm; *stem leaves always present; fruiting receptacle ridged and winged, faces smooth or wrinkled.* Habitat Found scattered throughout a range of species. Dist. Introduced. Formerly grown as fodder, now naturalised. (S and SW Europe.)

Bronze Pirri-pirri-bur
Acaena anserinifolia

Prostrate, mat-forming, much-branched woody perennial. Stems To 15 cm, erect, densely hairy. Leaves *Matt, distinctively tinted bronze; terminal leaflets ≤2× as long as wide.* Flowers Greenish, in solitary head on long stalks; epicalyx absent; 3-4 sepals; petals absent. Fruits *Receptacle with 4 spines, 3.5-6 mm.* Habitat Naturalised on banks, roadsides waste ground. Dist. Introduced (native of Australia and New Zealand). Very scattered. Fls Jun-Jul. *No illustrated.*

Pirri-pirri-bur
Acaena novae-zelandiae

Similar to Bronze Pirri-pirri-bur, but with *glossy, green, not bronze-tinted, leaves and terminal leaflets ≥2× as long as wide; receptacle spines 6-10 mm.* Habitat Bare, disturbed sandy habitats, waste ground. Dist. Introduced (native of Australia and New Zealand). Naturalised and persistent in scattered localities throughout BI except N Scotland. Fls Jun-Jul.

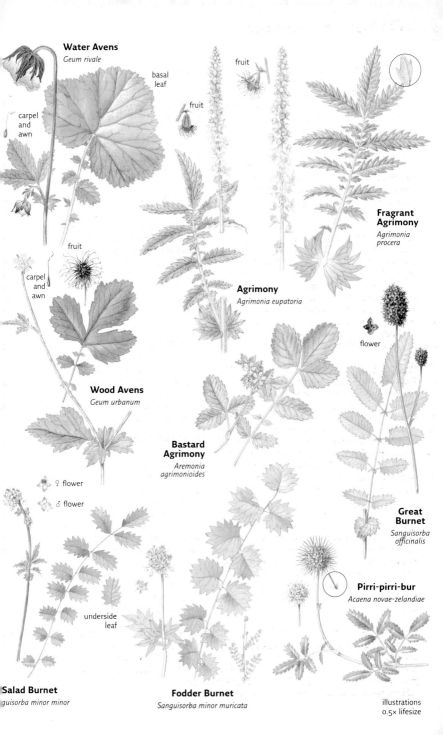

Water Avens
Geum rivale

basal
leaf

carpel
and
awn

fruit

fruit

fruit

**Fragrant
Agrimony**

*Agrimonia
procera*

fruit

carpel
and
awn

Agrimony
Agrimonia eupatoria

flower

Wood Avens
Geum urbanum

**Bastard
Agrimony**
*Aremonia
agrimonioides*

**Great
Burnet**
*Sanguisorba
officinalis*

♀ flower

♂ flower

underside
leaf

Pirri-pirri-bur
Acaena novae-zelandiae

Salad Burnet
Sanguisorba minor minor

Fodder Burnet
Sanguisorba minor muricata

illustrations
0.5× lifesize

Parsley-piert
Aphanes arvensis

Small, inconspicuous, prostrate to erect, pubescent annual, to *c*.10 cm. Flowers Small, in dense clusters opposite leaves; stipules fused into a lobed leaf-like cup; fruiting inflorescence partly enclosed by stipular cup; *stipule lobes triangular, c.⅓ length of entire portion, as long as or shorter than calyx; receptacle constricted below sepals; sepals erect.* Habitat Arable fields, bare patches in permanent grassland, woodland rides, waste places. Dist. Native. Throughout BI. (Most of Europe except N and SW.) Fls Apr–Oct. Note The 2 species of *Aphanes* can be difficult to separate. Stipule lobes and receptacle must be examined when plant is in fruit; sterile plants can't be distinguished.

Slender Parsley-piert
Aphanes australis

Similar to *A. arvensis*, but more slender; *stipule lobes ovate-oblong, about as long as entire portion, longer than calyx; outline of calyx and receptacle ± continuous; sepals convergent.* Habitat Woodland rides, tracks, roadsides, bare sandy places; less often on arable land than *A. arvensis.* Dist. Native. Throughout BI. (Most of Europe except N.) Fls Apr–Oct.

Lady's-mantles *Alchemilla*

Nearly all the British species of *Alchemilla* reproduce apomictically, that is they produce viable seeds without fertilisation. As a result, with the exception of *A. alpina* and *A. conjuncta*, they are all very difficult to identify. The most important characters are shape of leaves and leaf lobes, details of marginal teeth and width of sinus between lobes, and distribution and nature of pubescence. Summer basal leaves attached to flowering stem should be examined. Some species are very rare and confined to restricted areas of limestone in N Pennines or other parts of N Britain. Three species are more widespread and common in N Britain; these are keyed below. Identification of the rare species should always be checked by an expert. The common garden *A. mollis* is spreading as a naturalised plant in the wild and care needs to be taken to ensure that it can be recognised; this is also keyed below.

1 Leaves lobed to >⅓ way, densely silvery
   and silky beneath 2
   Leaves lobed to <⅓ way, not densely
   silvery and silky beneath 3

2 Leaves divided almost to base,
   lobes ≤ 6mm broad .... *A. alpina*
   Leaves divided ⅔–⅘, lobes
   ≥ 6 mm broad .... *A. conjuncta*

3 Epicalyx lobes as long as sepals
   giving flowers the appearance of
   an 8-pointed star (garden escape) *A. mollis*
   Epicalyx lobes distinctly shorter
   than sepals 4

4 Almost completely glabrous,
   some scattered appressed hairs on
   petiole and lower part of stem *A. glabra*
   At least petioles and lower part
   of stem with spreading hairs 5

5 Leaves glabrous above, thinly
   hairy below; flowers and pedicels
   ± glabrous .... *A. xanthochlora*
   Both surfaces of leaves hairy 6

6 Pedicels and inflorescence hairy;
   base of plant tinged wine-red *A. filicaulis*
   Pedicels glabrous, or if hairy
   then base of plant not tinged
   wine-red .... Other rarer
                                      species

Pale Lady's-mantle
Alchemilla xanthochlora

One of the 3 commonest species of genus. Habitat Herb-rich meadows, pastures, roadside verges; to 885 m. Dist. Native. Common in N Britain, Wales, N Ireland. (Most of Europe except extreme N.) Fls Jun–Sep.

Hairy Lady's-mantle
Alchemilla filicaulis ssp. *vestita*

Stems Upper part hairy. Flowers Inflorescence hairy. Habitat Rough pasture, mountain flushes, woodland rides, roadside verges; to 915 m. Dist. Native. Widespread throughout BI except for SE. (Most of Europe except S.) Fls Jun–Sep.

Slender Lady's-mantle
Alchemilla filicaulis ssp. *filicaulis*

Stems Upper part glabrous. Flowers Inflorescence glabrous. Habitat Lowland pasture, mountain grassland, rock outcrops, mountain ledges; to 975 m. Dist. N Scotland; scattered elsewhere in N Britain; absent from Ireland. (Most of Europe except S.) Fls Jun–Sep. *Not illustrated.*

Smooth Lady's-mantle
Alchemilla glabra

Commonest species of genus. Habitat Damp meadows, pastures, roadside verges, open woodland, rock ledges; to 1215 m. Dist. Native. Widespread in N England, N Wales, Scotland, N Ireland. (Most of Europe except S.) Fls Jun–Sep.

Pale Lady's-mantle
Alchemilla xanthochlora

Hairy Lady's-mantle
Alchemilla filicaulis
ssp. *vestita*

Alchemilla minima
(description on p.256)

underside

Clustered Lady's-mantle
Alchemilla glomerulans
(description on p.256)

Rock Lady's-mantle
Alchemilla wichurae
(description on p.256)

Parsley-piert
Aphanes arvensis

flower ×1.2

Smooth Lady's-mantle
Alchemilla glabra

Slender Parsley-piert
Aphanes australis

Soft Lady's-mantle
Alchemilla mollis

illustrations
0.6× lifesize

Soft Lady's-mantle
Alchemilla mollis

[*See* illustration previous page.] Large plant covered by soft, spreading hairs. HABITAT Roadsides, riverbanks, rough ground; lowland to 520 m. DIST. Introduced. Increasing throughout BI as a garden escape. (SE Europe.) FLS Jun–Sep. NOTE Care should be taken not to confuse it with other pubescent native species (*see* key above).

Alchemilla minima
*

[*See* illustration previous page.] HABITAT Limestone pasture; 210–610 m. DIST. Endemic. N Pennines (Ingleborough). FLS Jun–Sep.

Clustered Lady's-mantle
Alchemilla glomerulans VU.

[*See* illustration previous page.] HABITAT Herb-rich meadows, stream sides, roadside verges, rock ledges; to 1030 m. DIST. Native. Very scattered, local. N Pennines (Teesdale), Scottish Highlands. (Arctic and N Europe, mts of S and central Europe.) FLS Jun–Sep.

Rock Lady's-mantle
Alchemilla wichurae EN.

[*See* illustration previous page.] HABITAT Damp, herb-rich meadows, pastures, open woodland, calcareous grassland, rock ledges; to 990 m. DIST. Native. N Pennines (Upper Teesdale, Craven), Lake District, central and NW Scottish Highlands. (N Europe.) FLS Jun–Sep.

Silky Lady's-mantle
Alchemilla glaucescens *

HABITAT Limestone grassland, riverbanks, roadsides. DIST. Native. Very rare. N Pennines (Craven), NW Scotland, Co. Leitrim, W Ireland. (Scandinavia, mts of S Europe.) FLS Jun–Sep.

Velvet Lady's-mantle
Alchemilla monticola EN.

HABITAT Hay meadows, herb-rich pastures, roadside verges; 150–450 m. DIST. Native. Very rare. Teesdale, N Pennines. (Scandinavia, Alps, SE Europe.) FLS Jun–Sep.

Large-toothed Lady's-mantle
Alchemilla subcrenata EN

HABITAT Pastures, herb-rich meadows, roadside verges; 270–320 m. DIST. Native. First reported in 1951; very rare. Only 2 localities: Teesdale and Weardale, N Pennines. FLS Jun–Sep.

Starry Lady's-mantle
Alchemilla acutiloba VU

HABITAT Hay meadows, roadside verges, railway banks; 140–450 m. DIST. Native. Very rare. Teesdale and Weardale, N Pennines. (N Europe, Alps.) FLS Jun–Sep.

Shining Lady's-mantle
Alchemilla micans EN

HABITAT Species-rich grazed limestone pasture, hay meadows, roadside verges. DIST. Native. First recorded in 1976; very rare. Only 3 localities in Northumberland. FLS Jun–Sep.

Crimean Lady's-mantle
Alchemilla tytthantha

HABITAT Naturalised garden escape, on tracksides, waste ground, rough grassland. DIST. Introduced. Very rare. Lowland Scotland. (Crimea.) FLS Jun–Sep.

Alpine Lady's-mantle
Alchemilla alpina

Perennial alpine to 20 cm. LEAVES Most basal, 2.5–3.5 mm across, *palmately divided to base; green glabrous above, densely silvery-silky beneath*. FLOWERS *c.3 mm across*. HABITAT Mountain grassland, scree, rock ledges, summit detritus; to 1270 m. Down to sea-level on W coast of Scotland. DIST. Native. Locally common in Lake District and Scottish Highlands. (N Europe, Alps, Pyrenees.) FLS Jun–Aug.

Silver Lady's-mantle
Alchemilla conjuncta

Similar to *A. alpina*, but more robust, to 30 cm; *basal leaves divided to base or less so*; and *flowers larger c.4 mm across*. HABITAT Montane grassland, stream sides, lowland roadsides, riverbanks. DIST. Introduced; widely cultivated as rockery plant. Naturalised in scattered localities throughout England and Wales. (Alps, Jura Mts.) FLS Jun–Jul.

Alpine Lady's-mantle
Alchemilla alpina

flower ×1.8

flower ×1.8

Silver Lady's-mantle
Alchemilla conjuncta

Silky Lady's-mantle
Alchemilla glaucescens

flower ×1.8

flower ×1.8

Crimean Lady's-mantle
Alchemilla tytthantha

Velvet Lady's-mantle
Alchemilla monticola

flower ×1.8

flower ×1.8

Starry Lady's-mantle
Alchemilla acutiloba

flower ×1.8

Large-toothed Lady's-mantle
Alchemilla subcrenata

Shining Lady's-mantle
Alchemilla micans

illustrations
0.6× lifesize

Roses *Rosa*

Some 12 species of native rose are usually recognised in the British Isles, but the picture is complicated by the large number and frequency of hybrids and the variability shown by the different species (*see* key on p.245). For this reason naming is not always easy and there will always be individuals that defy certain identification. The leaves and the ripe hips provide the most useful characters, but the habit of the plant, the details of the prickles and bristles on the stems, and the lobing of the sepals are also important. The colour of the flowers is more variable. The receptacle is deeply concave and flask-like, and the apex has a thickened rim, the *disc*, in the middle of which is an opening, the *orifice*, through which the styles project. The width of the orifice in relation to the width of the disc is another important identification character.

Burnet Rose
Rosa pimpinellifolia

Low, erect, suckering deciduous *shrub* to 50 cm, *forming large patches.* STEMS *Densely covered by slender prickles and stiff bristles* (acicles). LEAVES *Glabrous*, leaflets small, 0.5–1.5 cm. FLOWERS 2–4 cm across, solitary; pedicels 1.5–2.5 cm, glandular or smooth, sepals entire. FRUITS ± spherical, 1–1.5 cm, *purplish black*. HABITAT Sand-dunes, dune slacks, sea cliffs, rough chalk grassland, limestone pavement; to 520 m. DIST. Native. Throughout BI, especially coastal; scattered inland. (W, central and E Europe.) FLS May–Jul.

Field Rose
Rosa arvensis

Glabrous deciduous shrub with weak trailing or scrambling stems, often climbing over other shrubs. STEMS Prickles hooked, ± equal. FLOWERS White, 3–5 cm across; *pedicels 2–4 cm with stalked glands; sepals short, ovate, lobes few or absent; styles united into column as long as shorter stamens.* HABITAT Scrub, hedgerows, wood margins; to 410 m. DIST. Native. Frequent in England, Wales, E Ireland; absent from Scotland. (W, central and SE Europe.) FLS Jun–Jul.

Japanese Rose
Rosa rugosa

Erect, *densely prickly, bristly, suckering* deciduous *shrub* to 1.5 m. LEAVES Leaflets dark green, wrinkled above, pubescent beneath. FLOWERS 6–8 cm across, *bright pink* (or white). FRUITS *Large*, 2–2.5 cm, *sepals persistent, erect*. HABITAT Sand-dunes, sea cliffs, road verges, waste ground. DIST. Introduced (native of N China and Japan). Commonly cultivated and naturalised throughout BI. (N, W and central Europe) FLS Jun–Jul.

Short-styled Field-rose
Rosa stylosa

Shrub with arching stems, to 4 m. STEMS Prickles hooked. LEAVES *Leaflets 1.5–5 cm, narrowly ovate, well separated, without glands.* FLOWERS 3–5 cm across; *pedicels long*, 2–4 cm, *glandular;* sepals reflexed after flowering, falling before fruit ripe; *disc conical, prominent; stylar column glabrous, shorter than stamens.* FRUITS 1–1.5 cm, smooth. HABITAT Hedgerows, open woodlands, scrub, on calcareous clay soils. DIST. Native. S and SW England; scattered in S Wales, Ireland. (France, Pyrenees.) FLS Jun–Jul.

Dog-rose
Rosa canina

Deciduous shrub with arching stems, to 3 m. The commonest British rose. STEMS Prickles strongly hooked. LEAVES *Leaflets 1.5–4 cm, glabrous, eglandular or with a few glands on main veins beneath* FLOWERS 4–6 cm across. Pedicels 0.5–2 cm, glabrous or sparsely glandular-pubescent; *sepals reflexed after flowering, falling before fruit reddens lobes ± entire; stigmas in conical head that is narrower than disc.* FRUITS 1.5–2 cm, smooth. HABITAT Hedgerows, scrub, thickets, cliffs, wood margins, waste ground; to 550 m. DIST. Native. Throughout BI, becoming less common in Scotland. (Most of Europe except N Scandinavia, W France.) FLS Jun–Jul.

Hairy Dog-rose
Rosa caesia ssp. *caesia*

Deciduous shrub with arching stems, to 2 m. STEMS Prickles strongly hooked. LEAVES *Leaflets wrinkled, pubescent beneath.* FLOWERS *Pedicels short* 0.5–1.5 cm, *often hidden by bracts; sepals persistent, becoming erect after flowering;* stigmas in flat head concealing disc. HABITAT Hedgerows, scrub, wood margins, cliffs, rock outcrops, riverbanks, waste ground. DIST. Native. N England, Scotland; scattered in Wales; rare in Ireland. (W, central and E Europe.) FLS Jun–Jul.

Glaucous Dog-rose
Rosa caesia ssp. *glauca*

Similar to ssp. *caesia*, but bushes appear more open, less dense; stems often reddish; *leaflets hardly wrinkled, glabrous,* glaucous, usually folded down midrib. HABITAT Hedgerows, scrub, wood margins, cliffs, rock outcrops, riverbanks, waste ground. DIST. Native. More widespread in central England and Wales than ssp. *caesia*; tends to replace *R. canina* in N Scotland. FLS Jun–Jul.

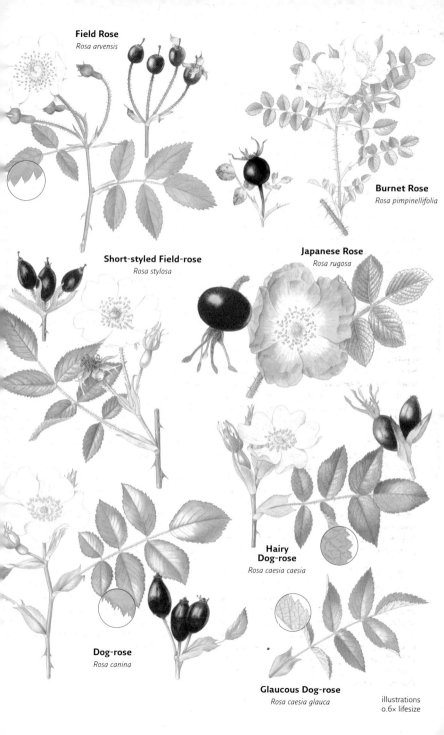

Field Rose
Rosa arvensis

Burnet Rose
Rosa pimpinellifolia

Short-styled Field-rose
Rosa stylosa

Japanese Rose
Rosa rugosa

Hairy Dog-rose
Rosa caesia caesia

Dog-rose
Rosa canina

Glaucous Dog-rose
Rosa caesia glauca

illustrations
0.6× lifesize

Round-leaved Dog-rose
Rosa obtusifolia

Deciduous shrub with arching branches, to 2 m. STEMS Prickles strongly hooked. LEAVES *Leaflets 1.5–3.5 cm, broader and more rounded than* R. canina *(p.258), pubescent and often glandular beneath*, sometimes pubescent above, margins biserrate with glandular teeth. FLOWERS Usually white; pedicels 0.5–1.5 cm, glabrous; *sepals lobed, reflexed after flowering, falling before fruit ripens.* HABITAT Scrub, hedgerows, wood margins, road verges, on well-drained soils. DIST. Native. Central and S England; rare in Wales, Ireland. (Scattered throughout Europe except N and SW.) FLS Jun–Jul.

Harsh Downy-rose
Rosa tomentosa

Scrambling deciduous shrub with arching branches, to 2 m. STEMS Prickles stout, curved to nearly straight. LEAVES *Leaflets 1.5–4 cm, densely pubescent on both surfaces, glandular beneath.* FLOWERS *Pedicels long, 2–3.5 cm, glandular-hispid; sepals falling before fruit ripens*, constricted at attachment, *lobes pinnate.* FRUITS Glandular-hispid or smooth; stylar orifice 0.2× diam. of disc. HABITAT Hedgerows, wood margins, scrub, rough grassland. DIST. Native. Widespread in central and S England, Wales; rare in Ireland. (W, central and E Europe.) FLS Jun–Jul.

Soft Downy-rose
Rosa mollis

Erect deciduous shrub to 1.5 m. STEMS *Branches straight; prickles slender, straight.* LEAVES *Leaflets* green, 2–4 cm, *densely pubescent on both surfaces*, usually glandular beneath. FLOWERS *Deep pink*, 3–4.5 cm across; *pedicels short, 0.5–1.0 cm, glandular-hispid; sepals erect, persistent until fruit decays, simple to slightly lobed.* FRUITS Glandular-hispid, stylar orifice ≥⅔ diam. of disc. HABITAT Woodland, hedges, scrub, cliffs, sand-dunes, waste ground; to 450 m. DIST. Native. Widespread in N England, Scotland; local in Wales. (NW, W, central and E Europe.) FLS Jun–Jul.

Sherard's Downy-rose
Rosa sherardi

Erect deciduous shrub to 1.5 m. Similar to *R. mollis* but *branches crooked; some prickles curved; leaves* bluish green; flowers 2.5–4 cm across; *sepals lobed, sub-erect, persistent until fruit ripens but then falling*, fruit usually glandular-hispid, stylar orifice *c.⅓ diam.* of disc. HABITAT Wood margins, hedges, scrub cliffs, rough grassland, heathland. DIST. Native. Most of BI except S and E. (NW and N-central Europe.) FLS Jun–Jul.

Sweet-briar
Rosa rubiginosa

Erect deciduous shrub to 2 m. STEMS *Prickles hooked, unequal in size, mixed with stout bristles.* LEAVES *Leaflets oval, rounded at base; covered beneath with sweet-scented glands, smelling of apples when crushed.* FLOWERS *Bright pink*, 2.5–4 cm across; *pedicels c.1 cm, glandular-hispid; sepals persistent, erect or spreading.* FRUITS 1–1.5 cm, *glandular-hispid at base.* HABITAT Calcareous grassland, scrub, hedges, quarries, waste ground. DIST. Native. Throughout most of BI. (W, central and E Europe.) FLS Jun–Jul.

Small-flowered Sweet-briar
Rosa micrantha

Scrambling deciduous shrub *with arching branches, to* 2 m. STEMS *Prickles hooked, all ± equal in size*, without stout bristles. LEAVES *Leaflets rounded at base*, glandular beneath. FLOWERS Pink (paler than *R. rubiginosa*) 2–3.5 cm across; *pedicels 1–2 cm, glandular-hispid sepals reflexed, falling early.* FRUITS *Glandular-hispid* HABITAT Woodlands, scrub, hedgerows, grassland heathland, cliffs, quarries, usually on calcareous soil. DIST. Native. S England, Wales, S Ireland. (Most of Europe except N and E.) FLS Jun–Jul.

Small-leaved Sweet-briar
Rosa agrestis

Erect deciduous shrub to 1.5 m. STEMS Prickles ± equal. LEAVES *Leaflets cuneate at base.* FLOWERS 2–4 cm across, pale pink-white; *pedicels glabrous sepals reflexed, falling before fruit ripens.* FRUIT *Glabrous.* HABITAT Open scrub, chalk, limestone grassland. DIST. Native. Rare. A few scattered localities in S England, more frequent in central Ireland. (Most of Europe except N and E.) FLS Jun–Jul.

Harsh Downy-rose
Rosa tomentosa

Round-leaved Dog-rose
Rosa obtusifolia

underside

Soft Downy-rose
Rosa mollis

underside

topside

Sherard's Downy-rose
Rosa sherardii

topside

Sweet-briar
Rosa rubiginosa

nderside

Small-flowered Sweet-briar
Rosa micrantha

Small-leaved Sweet-briar
Rosa agrestis

underside

illustrations
0.6x lifesize

Plums and cherries *Prunus*

See key to Prunus on p.264.

Blackthorn
Prunus spinosa

Dense, thicket-forming, much-branched, spiny, suckering deciduous shrub to 4 m. Branches Young twigs pubescent, becoming black or dark grey; *short lateral shoots thorny* (i.e. thorns have lateral buds on them). Leaves 1–4 cm, ± pubescent. Flowers *Appear before leaves. Petals 5–8 mm.* Fruits 10–15 mm, globose, pruinose (with a bloom), *flesh adhering to stone, stone globose.* Habitat Hedgerows, scrub, wood margins, cliff tops, shingle beaches (prostrate form). Dist. Native. Common throughout BI except extreme N Scotland. (Most of Europe except extreme N.) Fls Mar–May, before leaves.

Wild Plum
Prunus domestica

Often suckering, deciduous shrub or small tree to 8 m. Branches Twigs often ± pubescent when young, becoming grey or brown, rarely thorny. Leaves 4–10 cm, ± pubescent when young, becoming glabrous. Flowers *Appearing with leaves. Petals 7–12 mm.* Fruits *Globose-oblong, 2–4 cm (larger in cultivated varieties); stone flattened.* Habitat Naturalised in hedgerows, scrub, wood margins, waste places. Dist. Introduced. Throughout BI, but rare in N Scotland. Fls Apr–May, with leaves. (*See also note on p.264.*)

Cherry Plum, Myrobalan
Prunus cerasifera

Sometimes thorny, deciduous shrub or small tree to 8 m. Branches *Young twigs glabrous, green* (or reddish). Leaves 3–7 cm, glabrous, rather glossy above. Flowers *Appearing with leaves.* Usually solitary, *petals 7–11 mm.* Fruits *2–2.5 cm, yellow or reddish, stone flattened,* smooth. Habitat Hedgerows, copses, wood edges, roadsides. Dist. Introduced. Throughout BI, but rare in Scotland, Ireland. (Native of Balkan Peninsula, central Asia.) Fls Mar–Apr, with leaves (the earliest plum to flower).

Wild Cherry, Gean
Prunus avium

Suckering deciduous tree to 25 m. Bark Smooth, reddish brown, peeling. Leaves 6–15 cm, glabrous above, thinly pubescent beneath; *petioles with pair of reddish glands towards apex.* Flowers Bowl-shaped, in umbels of 2–6; persistent bud scales not leaf-like; *pedicels 2–4 cm; receptacle constricted at apex;* petals 8–15 mm. Fruits *c.*1 cm, red, glabrous. Habitat Woodland, hedges, roadside verges; to 400 m. Dist. Native. Throughout BI except extreme N Scotland. Widely planted. (Most of Europe.) Fls Apr–May.

Dwarf Cherry
Prunus cerasus

Freely suckering, deciduous shrub or small tree to 7 m. Similar to *P. avium,* but leaves darker green, 5–8 cm, glabrous; *flowers saucer-shaped,* fewer, 2–4, some inner bud scales green and leaf-like, *pedicels shorter* 1–2.5 cm, *receptacle not constricted at apex.* Habitat Hedgerows, copses, wood margins, sometimes forming dense suckering thickets. Dist. Archaeophyte (native of SW Asia). Scattered throughout BI, but rare in N Scotland. (Most of Europe) Fls Apr–May.

Bird Cherry
Prunus padus

Deciduous suckering tree to 19 m. Bark Brown, peeling, strong-smelling. Leaves 5–10 cm, glabrous o with tufts of hairs in axils of main veins beneath. Flowers *In long, ± erect or drooping racemes; pedicel. 8–15 mm; petals 5–9 mm;* sepals falling before fruit ripe. Fruits Black, 6–8 mm. Habitat Damp woodland scrub, stream sides, fen carr (East Anglia); to 650 m. Dist. Native. N England, East Anglia, N Wales, Scotland, N Ireland. Widely planted outside natural range (N Europe, mts of S and E Europe.) Fls May.

Rum Cherry
Prunus serotin

Deciduous tree to 30 m. Similar to *P. padus,* bu leaves glabrous or with rows of hairs along lower side midrib when mature; *inflorescence more closel packed, pedicels 3–7 mm, petals smaller, 3–4.5 mm* sepals persistent until fruit ripe; fruits 8–10 mm Habitat Woods, commons, hedgerows, roa verges. Dist. Introduced (native of E North America Widely planted; naturalised in scattered localities i England (especially SE), Wales. Fls May.

St Lucie Cherry
Prunus mahale

Deciduous shrub or small tree to 6 m. Leaves 3–7 cm glabrous, glossy above, rounded or cordate at base Flowers 12–20 mm across, 6–10 *in short raceme with green bracts at base;* pedicels to 15 mm. Fruit ≤1 cm, black. Habitat Woodland, rough grassland railway embankments. Dist. Introduced. Planted i gardens and naturalised in a few scattered localities i lowland Britain. (S and central Europe.) Fls May.

Cherry Laurel
Prunus laurocerasu

Glossy-leaved evergreen shrub or small tree to 10 n Leaves *Large, 5–18 cm,* glossy, dark green; petiole green. Flowers 7–13 cm, crowded in erect raceme petals *c.*4 mm. Fruits 10–12 mm, purplish black Habitat Woods and scrub, forming dense thicket by layering. Dist. Introduced. Commonly plante and naturalised throughout BI. (Balkan Peninsula Fls Apr–Jun.

Cherry Plum
Prunus cerasifera

Blackthorn
Prunus spinosa

Wild Plum
Prunus domestica ssp. *insititia* Bullace

Wild Cherry
Prunus avium

Dwarf Cherry
Prunus cerasus

Bird Cherry
Prunus padus

Cherry Laurel
Prunus laurocerasus

St Lucie Cherry
Prunus mahaleb

Rum Cherry
Prunus serotina

illustrations
0.6× lifesize

	if	then
1	▷ Flowers solitary or in 2-10-flowered clusters or umbels	Go to ▷ **2**
	▷ Flowers in many-flowered elongated racemes	Go to ▷ **7**
2	▷ Flowers solitary or in umbels	Go to ▷ **3**
	▷ Flowers in short racemes with green bracts towards base of inflorescence	***P. mahaleb*** (p.262)
3	▷ Flowers solitary or in groups of 2-3; persistent bud scales at base of cluster absent or very small	Go to ▷ **4**
	▷ Flowers in few-flowered umbels; base of inflorescence with large, persistent green or reddish bud scales	Go to ▷ **6**
4	▷ 1st-year twigs green, shiny, glabrous	***P. cerasifera*** (p.262)
	▷ 1st-year twigs brown to dark grey, dull, often pubescent	Go to ▷ **5**
5	▷ Flowers appearing before leaves; petals 5-8 mm; twigs very spiny; fruit 1-1.5 cm, blue-black	***P. spinosa*** (p.262)
	▷ Flowers appearing with leaves; petals 7-12 mm; twigs not or scarcely spiny; fruit 2-4 cm, blue-black, red or yellow-green	***P. domestica*** (p.262)
6	▷ Persistent bud scales not leaf-like (but some with green lobe at tip); pedicels 2-4 cm; receptacle constricted at apex; usually a tree	***P. avium*** (p.262)
	▷ At least some bud-scales leaf-like; pedicels 1-2.5 cm; receptacle not constricted at apex; usually a shrub	***P. cerasus*** (p.262)
7	▷ Leaves evergreen, glossy, leathery	***P. laurocerasus*** (p.262)
	▷ Leaves deciduous	Go to ▷ **8**
8	▷ Petals >5 mm; sepals falling before fruit ripe	***P. padus*** (p.262)
	▷ Petals <5 mm; sepals persistent until fruit ripe	***P. serotina*** (p.262)

NOTE TO WILD PLUM *Prunus domestica* (see p.262) Very variable and probably not truly wild anywhere. Three ssp. are usually recognised but with much intergrading. They can be safely identified only with fruits: **Bullace**, ssp. *insititia*, slightly thorny, twigs usually densely pubescent, fruit 2-3 cm, globose, blue-black, stone bluntly angled, flesh adherent to stone; **Greengage**, ssp. *italica*, not thorny, fruit 3-5 cm, usually green, stone bluntly or sharply angled, flesh adherent; **Plum**, ssp. *domestica*, twigs sparsely pubescent, spineless, fruits large, 4-8 cm, oblong ovoid, variously coloured, stone very flattened sharply angled, flesh separating from stone.

Because *P. domestica* is so variable, it is easily confused with *P. spinosa* and *P. cerasifera*. The best strategy is to assume that if a plant is clearly neither *P. spinosa* nor *P. cerasifera*, then it must be a form of *P. domestica*.

Key to Rowan, Whitebeam and Wild Service-tree *Sorbus*

	if	**then**
1	▷ Leaves pinnate, with 6–7 pairs of leaflets, terminal leaflet the same size as the laterals	Go to ▷ **2**
	▷ Leaves simple, or if pinnate having terminal lobe larger than laterals	Go to ▷ **3**
2	▷ Buds ± glabrous, dark brown-purplish, 2–5 bud scales	*S. aucuparia* (p.266)
	▷ Buds densely hairy, shining green to pale brown, 4–9 bud scales	*S. domestica* (p.266)
3	▷ Leaves ± glabrous, deeply lobed, lobes triangular, acute	*S. torminalis* (p.270)
	▷ Leaves densely hairy beneath	Go to ▷ **4**
4	▷ Underside of leaves with dense white pubescence	*S. aria* and *S. aria* group (p.268)
	▷ Underside of leaves with yellow-grey pubescence	Go to ▷ **5**
5	▷ Fruit red	*S. intermedia* group (p.266)
	▷ Fruit orange-brown	*S. latifolia* group (p.270)

Key to Cotoneasters *Cotoneaster*

	if	**then**
1	▷ Flowers white, petals spreading	Go to ▷ **2**
	▷ Flowers red or pink, petals erect	Go to ▷ **3**
2	▷ Shrub to 5 m; leaves narrow, 30–100 mm	*C. salicifolius* (p.272)
	▷ Shrub to 1 m; leaves ovate, 7–15 mm	*C. integrifolius* (p.272)
3	▷ Leaves densely pubescent beneath	*C. cambricus* (p.272)
	▷ Leaves thinly pubescent beneath	Go to ▷ **4**
4	▷ Erect shrub to 4 m; fruits 8–11 mm	*C. simonsii* (p.272)
	▷ Prostrate shrub to 1 m, branches flattened; fruits 4–6 mm	*C. horizontalis* (p.272)

Wild Pear
Pyrus pyraster

Shrub or small tree to 15 m, usually ± thorny. BARK Deeply fissured, *scaly*. LEAVES 2.5–7 cm, glossy, glabrous above when mature; *petiole about as long as blade*. FLOWERS Petals 10–15 mm, *anthers purple*. FRUITS 1.5–4 cm, globose, *not pear-shaped*; calyx persistent. HABITAT Hedges, wood margins, waste ground. DIST. Archaeophyte. Local in England, Wales. (Most of Europe.) FLS Apr–May. SIMILAR SPP. The **Cultivated Pear** *Pyrus communis* is a taller, thornless tree and differs from *P. pyraster* in its larger, sweet-tasting, pear-shaped fruit. It occurs naturalised in similar places as an escape from cultivation.

Plymouth Pear
Pyrus cordata VU. *(B)

Thorny, suckering shrub or small tree to 8 m. LEAVES 1–4.5 cm. FLOWERS Petals 6–10 mm. FRUITS *1–2 cm, spherical*, calyx falling early. HABITAT Hedgerows. DIST. Probably native. Very rare. S Devon, Cornwall. (W France.) FLS Apr–May.

Crab Apple
Malus sylvestris

Shrub or small tree to 10 m, often thorny. LEAVES 3–5 cm, *glabrous when mature*. FLOWERS Pedicels and outside of calyx glabrous, petals 13–28 mm, *anthers yellow*. FRUITS 2–3 cm, apple-shaped. HABITAT Woodland, scrub, hedgerows; to 380 m. DIST. Native. Throughout BI, but rare in N Scotland. (Most of Europe.) FLS May.

Apple
Malus domestica

Similar to *M. sylvestris*, but larger in all its parts; *underside of leaves, pedicels, outside of calyx pubescent*; fruits to 12 cm. DIST. Introduced. Occurs commonly as an escape from cultivation. FLS May. NOTE Probably not a close relative of *M. sylvestris*.

Rowan, Whitebeam and Wild Service-tree *Sorbus*
A very difficult genus of trees and shrubs, consisting of 3 well-defined and widespread species – Rowan, Whitebeam and Wild Service-tree – together with a large number of apomictic (producing viable seed without fertilisation) 'micro-species' of hybrid origin (*see* key on p.265). Many of these are endemic to BI, are very rare and restricted to specific areas, and consist of small populations, sometimes of <10 individuals. Identification is dependent upon details of both the leaves and the fruit. The apomictic species mostly fall within 3 groups: *see* key on p.265.

Rowan, Mountain Ash
Sorbus aucuparia

Small to medium-sized tree, to 18 m. BRANCHES *Smooth, pale grey*. LEAVES 10–25 cm; *pinnate, with 5–7 pairs of toothed leaflets*. FLOWERS In many-flowered inflorescence. FRUITS 6–9 mm, *red*. HABITAT Open woodland, scrub, mountain rocks, cliffs, rocky riverbanks, on acid soils; commonly planted; waste ground, railway embankments (bird-sown). To 870 m. DIST. Native. Throughout BI; common in N and W. (N Europe, mts of S and central Europe.) FLS May–Jun.

Service-tree
Sorbus domestica CR.

Similar to *S. aucuparia*. Tree to 23 m. LEAVES Pinnate with 6–8 pairs leaflets. BUDS Glabrous, sticky, green to pale brown, bud scales 4–9. FRUITS 20–25 mm, pear-shaped, greenish brown, with numerous large lenticels. HABITAT Coastal cliffs, scrub on limestone. Also occasionally cultivated in parks and gardens. DIST. Native, very rare. S Wales (Glamorgan). (S, C Europe.) *Not illustrated.*

Sorbus intermedia group
Hairs on underside of leaves grey-yellowish; fruit red.

Sorbus pseudofennica
VU.

Small tree to 7 m. LEAVES *Partially pinnate, with 1 pair of free lobes at base*. FRUITS Red. HABITAT Rocky granite stream ravines. DIST. Endemic. Single location on I of Arran.

Sorbus arranensis
VU.

Small tree to 7.5 m. LEAVES Lobed to ½–¾ way to midrib. FRUITS 8–10 mm. HABITAT Rocky granite outcrops. DIST. Endemic. I of Arran.

Sorbus pseudomeinichii
*

Small tree to 4 m. LEAVES Pinnate, with 4–5 pairs leaflets, terminal leaflet larger than laterals. FRUITS Red. HABITAT Stream-sides 150–200 m. DIST. Native, endemic, Isle of Arran. New species recently described by Dr A. Robertson and C. Sydes. *Not illustrated.*

Sorbus leyana
CR.

Shrub to *c*.2 m. LEAVES Lobed to ½–¾ way to midrib. FRUITS *c*.10 mm. HABITAT Open woodland on limestone cliffs; 300 m. DIST. Endemic. S Powys.

Sorbus minima
VU.

Shrub to 3 m. LEAVES Narrow, 1.8–2.2 × as long as wide, lobed ½–⅓ way to midrib. FRUITS 6–9 mm. HABITAT Limestone crags; 360–480 m. DIST. Endemic. S Powys.

Plymouth Pear
Pyrus cordata

Wild Pear
Pyrus pyraster

Crab Apple
Malus sylvestris

Sorbus pseudofennica

leaf of apple

Sorbus minima

Rowan
Sorbus aucuparia

Sorbus leyana

Sorbus arranensis

illustrations
0.6× lifesize

Sorbus anglica

Shrub to 3 m. LEAVES Lobed ¼ way to midrib. FRUITS 7-12 mm. HABITAT Rocky woods, cliffs, on limestone; to 395 m. DIST. Endemic. Very local. SW England, Wales, SW Ireland.

Sorbus intermedia

Tree to 10 m. LEAVES 1.6-1.8× as long as broad; lobed ⅓-½ way to midrib. FRUITS 12-15 mm, oblong, much longer than broad. DIST. Introduced. Commonly planted as ornamental tree. Self-sown in wild throughout BI, but rare N Scotland, Ireland. (N Europe.)

Sorbus aria group

Hairs on underside of leaf white; fruit red.

Whitebeam   Sorbus aria

Tree to 15 m. One of the 3 widespread, sexually reproducing species. LEAVES *10-14 pairs of veins*, teeth not markedly uneven *underside with dense white pubescence*. FRUITS *Longer than broad, 8-15 mm*. DIST. Native of S England; widely planted and established outside natural range. HABITAT Scrub, open woodlands, on well-drained, usually calcareous soils. (Central and S Europe.) FLS May-Jun.

Sorbus leptophylla   EN.

Shrub to 3 m. LEAVES Similar to *S. aria*, but with 11 pairs of veins and teeth markedly uneven. FRUITS *c.*20 mm, longer than broad. HABITAT Vertical limestone cliffs. DIST. Endemic. Very rare. Wales.

Sorbus wilmottiana   CR.

Shrub or small tree to 6 m. LEAVES 8-9 pairs of veins, teeth ± even. FRUITS 8-12 mm, longer than broad. HABITAT Steep, rocky limestone slopes. DIST. Endemic. Very rare. Avon Gorge.

Sorbus eminens   EN.

Shrub or small tree to 6 m. LEAVES Obovate, with 10-12 pairs of veins. FRUITS *c.*20 mm, slightly longer than broad, with a few large lenticels towards base. HABITAT Limestone grassland, scrub, open woodland. DIST. Endemic. Very rare. Wye Valley, Avon Gorge.

Sorbus hibernica   *

Small tree to 6 m. LEAVES Ovate, with 9-11 pairs of veins. FRUITS 15 mm, broader than long, with a few large lenticels towards base. HABITAT Rocky calcareous grassland, scrub, open woodland. DIST. Endemic. Very local. Scattered throughout most of Ireland.

Sorbus porrigentiformis

Shrub or small tree to 5 m. LEAVES 1.3-1.7× as long as broad, with 8-10 pairs of veins, teeth markedly uneven. FRUITS 8-12 mm, ± spherical or broader than long. HABITAT Rocky limestone scrub, woodland. DIST. Endemic. Very rare. Avon Gorge.

Sorbus whiteana   *

Shrub or small tree to 10 m. LEAVES Obovate, 8.5-11.5 pairs of veins, 1.4-1.9 times as long as broad, underside of leaf greyish green. FRUITS 10-13.5 mm, slightly longer than wide. HABITAT Cliffs, scree, scrub. DIST. Native, endemic, very rare. Avon Gorge, Wye Valley. New species recently described by Dr T.C.G. Rich and Dr L. Houston. *Not illustrated.*

Summary of the localities of *Sorbus* species

Wye Valley	**Avon Gorge**	**Brecon Beacons**
Sorbus anglica	*Sorbus bristoliensis*	*Sorbus anglica*
Sorbus domestica	*Sorbus porrigentiformis*	*Sorbus leptophylla*
Sorbus eminens	*Sorbus willmottiana*	*Sorbus leyana*
Sorbus porrigentiformis		*Sorbus minima*
Sorbus rupicola		*Sorbus porrigentiformis*
Sorbus whiteana		*Sorbus rupicola*

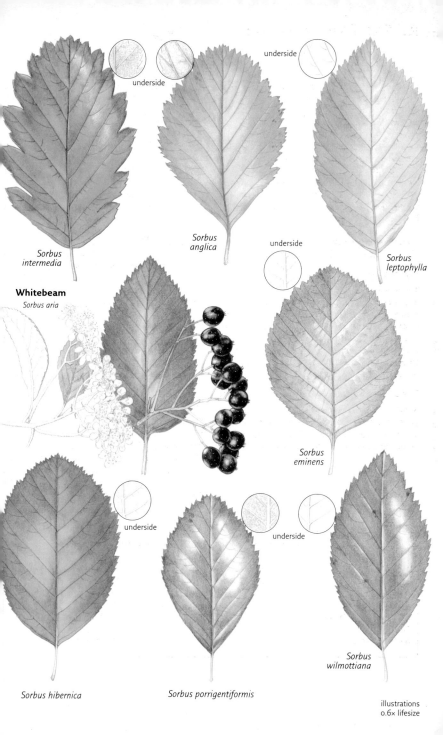

Sorbus
intermedia

underside

Sorbus
anglica

underside

Sorbus
leptophylla

Whitebeam
Sorbus aria

underside

Sorbus
eminens

Sorbus
hibernica

underside

Sorbus porrigentiformis

underside

Sorbus
wilmottiana

illustrations
0.6× lifesize

Sorbus rupicola

Shrub or small tree to 5 m. The most widespread species of apomictic *Sorbus* in BI. LEAVES 1.6-2.5× as long as broad, with 7-9 pairs of veins. FRUITS 12-15 mm, broader than long. HABITAT Limestone, rocks, cliffs, pavement; to 500 m. DIST. Native. Scattered throughout BI. (Scandinavia.)

Sorbus lancastriensis

Shrub or small tree to 5 m. Similar to *S. rupicola*, but leaves 1.3-1.8× as long as broad, with 8-10 pairs of veins; fruits ± spherical or broader than long. HABITAT Limestone cliffs, rocky outcrops, open woodland. DIST. Endemic. Very rare. Near Morecombe Bay.

Sorbus vexans   EN.

Small tree to 6 m. LEAVES 1.5-1.9× as long as broad, with 8-9 pairs of veins. FRUITS 12-15 mm, longer than broad. HABITAT Rocky woodland on Old Red Sandstone close to coast. DIST. Endemic. Very rare. N Devon.

Sorbus latifolia group

Hairs on underside of leaves grey-yellowish; fruits orange to brown.

Sorbus subcuneata   VU.

Tree to 10 m. Leaves 1.1-1.3× as long as broad, base cuneate to narrowly rounded, with 8-9 pairs of veins. FRUITS Brownish orange, 10-13 mm. HABITAT Open, rocky oak woodland on Old Red Sandstone. DIST. Endemic. Very rare. N Devon.

Sorbus devoniensis

Tree to 15 m. LEAVES 1.2-1.7× as long as broad, base rounded, with 7-9 pairs of veins. FRUITS Brownish orange, 10-15 mm. HABITAT Hedgerows, rocky woodland. DIST. Endemic. Local. N Devon, SE Ireland.

Sorbus bristoliensis   EN.

Tree to 10 m. LEAVES Obovate, 1.4-1.7× as long as broad; cuneate to narrowly rounded at base; with 8-9 pairs of veins. FRUITS 9-11 mm, longer than broad, orange. HABITAT Rocky woodland on limestone. DIST. Endemic. Very rare. Avon Gorge.

Sorbus latifolia

Tree to 20 m. LEAVES 1.1-1.3× as long as broad, rounded at base, with 7-9 pairs of veins. FRUITS 14-17 mm, yellowish orange. HABITAT Planted in parks, gardens; naturalised in woodland, scrub, on riverbanks. DIST. Introduced. Scattered throughout BI. (W and SW Europe.)

Wild Service Tree   *Sorbus torminalis*

Deciduous tree to 25 m. LEAVES 7-10 cm, *deeply lobed with triangular acute lobes, glabrous* to sparsely pubescent beneath. FRUITS 12-16 mm, longer than broad, *brown*. HABITAT Old woods, hedges, on clay or limestone. DIST. Native. Rather scattered and local. England, Wales. (Most of Europe except N.) FLS May-Jun.

Juneberry   *Amelanchier lamarkii*

[*See* illustration on following page.] Deciduous shrub or small tree to 10 m. LEAVES Blades 3-7 cm. FLOWERS *In racemes; petals 10-22 mm, narrow, separated;* 10-20 stamens; *ovary inferior*. FRUITS Blackish purple (rarely formed). HABITAT Open woodland, scrub, heathland. DIST. Introduced (native of North America). Naturalised, especially in S. (W Europe) FLS Apr-May.

Summary of the localities of *Sorbus* species

N. Devon; Somerset	I of Arran, Scotland	Morecombe Bay	Ireland
Sorbus anglica	Sorbus arranensis	Sorbus lancastriensis	Sorbus hibernica
Sorbus devoniensis	Sorbus pseudofennica	Sorbus rupicola	(scattered throughout)
Sorbus porrigentiformis	Sorbus pseudomeinichii		Sorbus devoniensis (SE)
Sorbus subcuneata			Sorbus rupicola (v. rare)
			Sorbus anglica (v. rare)

Sorbus rupicola is scattered on hard limestones throughout the north and west of the BI.

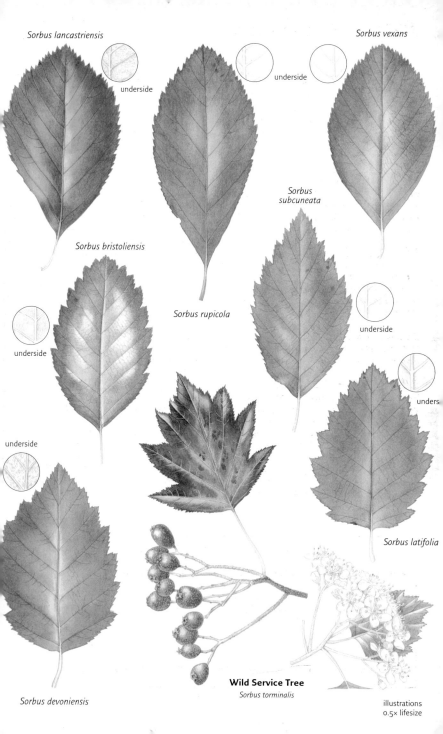

Sorbus lancastriensis

underside

Sorbus vexans

underside

Sorbus subcuneata

Sorbus bristoliensis

underside

Sorbus rupicola

underside

underside

unders

underside

Sorbus latifolia

Sorbus devoniensis

Wild Service Tree
Sorbus torminalis

illustrations
0.5× lifesize

Cotoneasters *Cotoneaster*

See key to *Cotoneaster* on p.265.

Willow-leaved Cotoneaster
Cotoneaster salicifolius

Large, arching evergreen shrub to 5 m. LEAVES *Narrow*, 3–10 cm, *shiny on upper side, densely hairy beneath*. FLOWERS Receptacle and calyx pubescent; *petals white, spreading*. FRUITS Red, 4–5 mm. HABITAT Woodland, scrub, hedgerows, rough grassland, waste ground as garden escape. DIST. Introduced (native of W China). Scattered throughout BI. FLS May-Jun.

Entire-leaved Cotoneaster
Cotoneaster integrifolius

Procumbent to arching evergreen shrub, to 1 m. The most widespread of 12 closely related species that are very difficult to separate. LEAVES *Ovate*, 7–15 mm, *shiny above, pubescent beneath*. FLOWERS *White, 11 mm across, petals spreading*. FRUITS Red, 8–10 mm. DIST. Introduced (native of Himalayas, W China). Naturalised over much of BI, especially in W. FLS May-Jun.

Wall Cotoneaster
Cotoneaster horizontalis

Arching or prostrate deciduous shrub to 1 m. BRANCHES *Flattened in a herringbone pattern*. LEAVES *Small*, 0.6–1.2 cm, shiny above. FLOWERS *2–3 together; petals red, erect*. FRUITS Orange-red, *4–6 mm*. HABITAT Vigorous coloniser of cliffs, walls, roadside and railway embankments, quarries, rocky grassland. DIST. Introduced (native of W China). Throughout BI; very common in S. FLS May-Jun.

Himalayan Cotoneaster
Cotoneaster simonsii

Erect deciduous shrub to 4 m. BRANCHES *Twigs pubescent*. LEAVES *Ovate*, 1–3 cm; *deep green above; paler below, with stiff, appressed hairs*. FLOWERS 2–4 in short inflorescence; *petals erect, pink*. FRUITS *8–11 mm*, orange-red. HABITAT Woods, scrub, hedges, rocky grassland, walls, quarries, waste ground. DIST. Introduced (native of Himalayas). Throughout BI, especially in SW. FLS May-Jul.

Wild Cotoneaster
Cotoneaster cambricus CR. *(B)

Spreading deciduous shrub to 1.5 m. LEAVES *Ovate* to ± spherical, 1.5–4 cm, *green above, grey-pubescent beneath*. FLOWERS 1–4 in short inflorescence; *petals red, erect*. FRUITS 7–11 mm, red. HABITAT Limestone rocks. DIST. Originally thought to be endemic, but probably introduced or of garden origin. Great Orme, Conwy. FLS May-Jun.

Firethorn
Pyracantha coccinea

Spiny evergreen shrub to 2 m. LEAVES 2–7 cm, *toothed*. FLOWERS *c.*8 mm across, in corymbs; 20 stamens; 5 carpels. FRUITS 5–6 mm, orange or scarlet. HABITAT Waste ground, roadsides, hedgerows. DIST. Introduced. Scattered throughout England as garden escape. (S Europe.) FLS May-Jun. *Not illustrated.*

Medlar
Mespilus germanica

Shrub or small tree to 9 m, sometimes thorny. BRANCHES *Young twigs densely pubescent*. LEAVES *Large*, 5–12 cm. FLOWERS *3–5 cm across; sepals longer than petals; pedicels, receptacle and calyx densely pubescent*; anthers red. FRUITS 2–3 cm, *crowned by persistent sepals*. HABITAT Hedges, woods. DIST. Archaeophyte. Occasional as escape or relic of cultivation in England, Wales. (SE Europe.) FLS May-Jun.

Hawthorns *Crataegus*

The 2 native British species are closely related and hybrids are common. The main problem is separating pure *C. laevigata* from the hybrid; leaves (which should be taken from short lateral shoots on outside of crown) are the most useful character, but fruits should also be examined if possible. The hybrid, *C. × media*, is common throughout the range of *C. laevigata* and is intermediate in all characters.

Hawthorn
Crataegus monogyna

Thorny tree or shrub to 10 m. LEAVES *Lobes longer than broad, sinuses reaching more than halfway to midrib, lower margin of lowest lobe without teeth*. FLOWERS ≤15 mm across, *1 style*. FRUITS *Have 1 stone*. HABITAT Hedges, scrub, open woodland; to 610 m. DIST. Native. Common throughout BI. (All Europe.) FLS May-Jun.

Midland Hawthorn
Crataegus laevigata

Similar to *C. monogyna*, but branches more spreading; *leaves shallowly lobed, lobes extending less than halfway to midrib* (leaf shape rather similar to that of a plum), *lower margin of lower lobe toothed almost to base*; flowers ≥15 mm across, *2 styles; 2 stones in fruit* (tend to adhere together so need to be prised apart). HABITAT Ancient woodlands, old hedgerows, on clay soils. DIST. Native. Central, E and SE England; widely established in rest of England, Wales; rare in Scotland, Ireland. (All Europe except for N.) FLS May-Jun 1–2 weeks earlier than *C. monogyna*.

Entire-leaved Cotoneaster
Cotoneaster integrifolius

Willow-leaved Cotoneaster
Cotoneaster salicifolius

Juneberry
Amelanchier lamarkii
(description on p.270)

Wild Cotoneaster
Cotoneaster cambricus

Himalayan Cotoneaster
Cotoneaster simonsii

Wall Cotoneaster
Cotoneaster horizontalis

Hawthorn
Crataegus monogyna

Midland Hawthorn
Crataegus laevigata

Medlar
Mespilus germanica

illustrations
0.6× lifesize

	if	**then**
1	▷ Trees or shrubs	Go to ▷ **18**
	▷ Herbs	Go to ▷ **2**
2	▷ Leaves trifoliate (clover-like)	Go to ▷ **3**
	▷ Leaves not trifoliate	Go to ▷ **6**
3	▷ Flowers in dense heads or racemes	Go to ▷ **4**
	▷ Flowers solitary	Go to ▷ **5**
4	▷ Inflorescence a many-flowered raceme (flowers yellow or white)	*Melilotus* (p.290)
	▷ Inflorescence in dense heads or few-flowered	*Trifolium* (p.292), *Medicago* (p.2
5	▷ Flowers pink or yellow, in axils of leaves	*Ononis* (p.288)
	▷ Flowers yellow, peduncle much longer than adjacent leaf	*Tetragonolobus maritimus* (p.27
6	▷ Leaves pinnate	Go to ▷ **7**
	▷ Leaves not pinnate	Go to ▷ **17**
7	▷ Leaves with a terminal leaflet	Go to ▷ **8**
	▷ Leaves without a terminal leaflet, usually with a tendril	*Vicia, Lathyrus* (p.280)
8	▷ Flowers in umbels	Go to ▷ **9**
	▷ Flowers in racemes	Go to ▷ **13**
9	▷ Flowers pink	*Securigera varia* (p.280)
	▷ Flowers not pink	Go to ▷ **10**
10	▷ 5 leaflets	*Lotus* (p.278)
	▷ >5 leaflets	Go to ▷ **11**
11	▷ Umbels in pairs, calyx inflated and woolly	*Anthyllis vulneraria* (p.278)
	▷ Umbels not in pairs, calyx not inflated or woolly	Go to ▷ **12**
12	▷ Flowers yellow, peduncles longer than adjacent leaves	*Hippocrepis comosa* (p.280)
	▷ Flowers whitish or yellow, peduncles shorter than adjacent leaves	*Ornithopus* (p.280)
13	▷ Flowers bright pink	*Onobrychis viciifolia* (p.278)
	▷ Flowers not bright pink (but may be purple)	Go to ▷ **14**
14	▷ Plant hairy	Go to ▷ **15**
	▷ Plant glabrous	Go to ▷ **16**

if	**then**

15
▷ Tip of lower petal (keel) blunt — ***Astragalus*** (p.276)
▷ Tip of lower petal pointed — ***Oxytropis*** (p.276)

16
▷ Flowers purple, inflorescence at least as long as adjacent leaf — ***Galega officinalis*** (p.276)
▷ Flowers cream, inflorescence shorter than adjacent leaf — ***Astragalus glyphyllos*** (p.276)

17
▷ Leaves grass-like; flowers pink — ***Lathyrus nissolia*** (p.288)
▷ Leaves reduced to a tendril, stipules large; flowers yellow — ***Lathyrus aphaca*** (p.288)

18
▷ Tree; flowers white in pendulous raceme — ***Robinia pseudoacacia*** (p.276)
▷ Shrub; flowers yellow — Go to ▷ **19**

19
▷ Leaves palmate — ***Lupinus arboreus*** (p.300)
▷ Leaves not palmate — Go to ▷ **20**

20
▷ Densely spiny shrub, leaves reduced to green branched spines — ***Ulex*** (p.300)
▷ Leaves not reduced to spines, stems with or without brown spines — Go to ▷ **21**

21
▷ Leaves pinnate; pod greatly inflated — ***Colutea arborescens*** (p.276)
▷ Leaves simple or trifoliate — Go to ▷ **22**

22
▷ Stems with broad wings — ***Chamaespartium sagittale*** (p.302)
▷ Stems unwinged — Go to ▷ **23**

23
▷ Twigs green, deeply grooved; some leaves trifoliate — ***Cytisus scoparius*** (p.302)
▷ Twigs not deeply grooved; all leaves simple — ***Genista, Spartium*** (p.302)

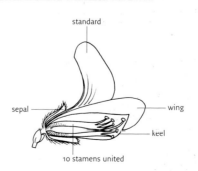

legume flower

FABACEAE Peas, vetches and clovers (legumes)

One of the largest families of flowering plants, with characteristic flowers like that of a Sweet Pea (*see* key on p.274). Trees, shrubs or (in British Isles usually) herbs. Leaves are simple or, more usually, compound, often pinnate or trifoliate, alternate and usually with stipules. Flowers are strongly irregular; 5 sepals, joined into a tube at the base; 5 petals, consisting of an upper standard, 2 lateral wings, and a lower lip (keel) comprised of the 2 fused lower petals; 10 stamens, all united into a tube, or with 9 joined and 1 free and contained within the keel; ovary superior, 1 style. Fruit is basically a dehiscent pod (legume) with large seeds.

False-acacia   *Robinia pseudoacacia*

Suckering deciduous tree to 29 m. BARK Coarsely fissured. LEAVES Glabrous, *stipules developing spines.* FLOWERS *White, in pendulous racemes.* FRUITS Pods, 5-10 cm. HABITAT Woods, roadsides, waste ground. DIST. Introduced in the 1630s (native of E North America). Widely planted and naturalised throughout England, Wales. (S, W, central and E Europe). FLS Jun.

Goat's-rue   *Galega officinalis*

Robust, glabrous, erect perennial to 150 cm. FLOWERS Purple, 12-15 mm, *inflorescence equalling or exceeding length of leaves.* FRUITS Pod, 2-3 cm, smooth. HABITAT Roadsides, waste ground, railway banks. DIST. Introduced. Cultivated since C16th, now naturalised. (E Europe.) FLS Jun-Jul.

Bladder-senna   *Colutea arborescens*

Small, deciduous, sparsely pubescent shrub to 4 m. FLOWERS In racemes of 2-8 flowers. FRUITS *Pods, 5-7 cm, much inflated, walls thin.* HABITAT Railway banks, waste ground, rough grassland. DIST. Introduced. Cultivated since C16th, now naturalised. (S Europe.) FLS May-Jul.

Wild Liquorice   *Astragalus glycyphyllos*

Robust, *glabrous*, sprawling perennial to 100 cm. LEAVES 10-20 cm; stipules *c.*2 cm, free. FLOWERS *Cream, inflorescence shorter that adjacent leaf.* 10-15 mm. FRUITS Curved pod, 25-35 mm. HABITAT Roadsides, scrub, rough grassland, cliffs, on calcareous soils; to 365 m. DIST. Native. Very local in lowland Britain; absent from W and Ireland. (Most of Europe except extreme N and S.) FLS Jul-Aug.

Purple Milk-vetch   *Astragalus danicus* EN. *(R)

Ascending, *pubescent* perennial to 35 cm. LEAVES 3-7 cm, *stipules joined at base.* FLOWERS 15-18 mm, *blue-purple,* erect, tip of lower petal blunt, *peduncle longer than adjacent leaf.* FRUITS Pod, 7-10 mm, with white appressed hairs. HABITAT/DIST. Native. Very local. Old calcareous grassland in E England, Wiltshire; calcareous sand-dunes on E coast of Scotland. (Central and E Europe.) FLS May-Jul.

Alpine Milk-vetch   *Astragalus alpinus* VU.

Similar to *A. danicus,* but more slender; *stipules not joined at base; flowers* 10-14 mm, *pale blue with darker tips,* spreading or deflexed, tip of lower petal blunt, *peduncle about as long as adjacent leaf;* pod *c.*10 mm, with dark appressed hairs. HABITAT Damp calcareous grassland, ledges, rocky outcrops; 650-770 m. DIST. Native. Very rare: in 4 localities only in Scottish Highlands. (Mountains of N Europe, Alps, Pyrenees.) FLS Jul.

Purple Oxytropis   *Oxytropis halleri*

Pubescent perennial. LEAVES *c.*10 cm, leaflets 5-8 mm. FLOWERS 15-20 mm, *pale purple, dark-tipped, lower petal ending in sharp point;* in inflorescence of 6-10 flowers; peduncle arising from dense tuft of leaves, leafless, stout, longer than leaves. FRUITS Pod, 15-20 mm. HABITAT Mountain rock ledges, sea cliffs, calcareous sand-dunes. DIST. Native. Very rare. Highlands and N coast of Scotland. (Alpine Europe.) FLS Jun-Jul.

Yellow Oxytropis   *Oxytropis campestris* VU.

Similar to *O. halleri,* but larger; leaves to 15 cm, leaflets 10-20 mm; *flowers yellow, tinged purple*; pod 14-18 mm. HABITAT Basic rock ledges, scree; 500-640 m. DIST. Native. Very rare; in 3 sites only in Scottish Highlands and on sea cliffs on W coast. (Arctic Europe, mts of S Europe.) FLS Jun-Jul.

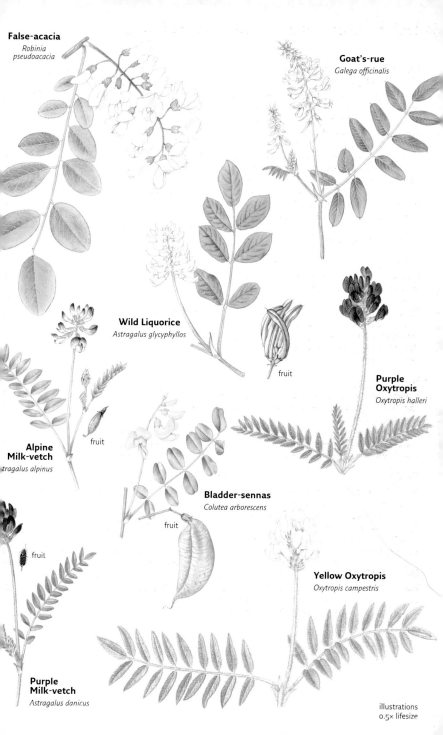

False-acacia
Robinia pseudoacacia

Goat's-rue
Galega officinalis

Wild Liquorice
Astragalus glycyphyllos

fruit

Purple Oxytropis
Oxytropis halleri

Alpine Milk-vetch
Astragalus alpinus

fruit

Bladder-sennas
Colutea arborescens

fruit

Yellow Oxytropis
Oxytropis campestris

fruit

Purple Milk-vetch
Astragalus danicus

illustrations
0.5× lifesize

Sainfoin   *Onobrychis viciifolia*

Erect, *pubescent* perennial to 60 cm. LEAVES *Leaflets* 1–3 mm, *6–12 pairs*. FLOWERS *Pink*, 10–12 mm, peduncle longer than leaves. FRUITS Pubescent pod, 6–8 mm, with reticulated ridges. HABITAT Unimproved chalk grassland, tracksides, road verges; to 335 m. DIST. Alien or native. Widely cultivated for fodder until C19th, natural distribution obscured by relic of cultivation. Locally frequent in lowland England; rare elsewhere. (Most of Europe except N.) FLS Jun–Aug.

Kidney Vetch   *Anthyllis vulneraria*

Prostrate to erect, pubescent perennial, to 60 cm. Very variable, with a number of named forms. LEAVES To 14 cm, *pinnate, without tendrils*, lower leaves often reduced to single large terminal leaflet. FLOWERS 12–15 mm, *in paired umbels surrounded by leaf-like bracts; calyx inflated and covered by white woolly hairs*. FRUITS Glabrous pod, *c.*3mm. HABITAT Calcareous grassland, sea cliffs, rock ledges, maritime heath; to 945 m. DIST. Native. Common throughout BI. (All Europe.) FLS Jun–Sep.

Dragon's-teeth   *Tetragonolobus maritimus*

Thinly pubescent perennial to 25 cm. LEAVES *Trifoliate*. FLOWERS *Yellow, solitary*, 25–30 mm, with a single leaf-like bract, *peduncle much longer than adjacent leaf*. FRUITS Pod, 25–50 mm, with 4-winged ridges. HABITAT Waste ground, rough chalk grassland. DIST. Introduced. Naturalised in scattered localities in S England. (Central and S Europe.) FLS Jun–Jul.

Bird's-foot-trefoils *Lotus*

1	Perennial; flowers ≥10 mm	**2**
	Annual or perennial; flowers <10 mm	**4**
2	Stem solid; calyx teeth erect in bud	**3**
	Stem hollow; calyx teeth spreading in bud	*L. pedunculatus*
3	Leaflets of upper leaves <3× as long as wide; 2 rear calyx teeth not converging	*L. corniculatus*
	Leaflets of upper leaves >4× as long as wide; 2 rear calyx teeth converging	*L. glaber*
4	Plant covered by long, spreading hairs (annual)	**5**
	Plant ± glabrous (perennial)	*L. glaber*
5	Pods 12–30 mm, ≥3× as long as calyx	*L. angustissimus*
	Pods 5–15 mm, ≤3× as long as calyx	*L. subbiflorus*

Common Bird's-foot-trefoil   *Lotus corniculatus*

Prostrate, ± glabrous perennial to 40 cm. STEMS *Solid*. LEAVES Leaflets 3–10 mm, *<3 × as long as wide*. FLOWERS 10–15 mm; calyx teeth erect in bud, sinus between upper 2 calyx teeth obtuse. FRUITS Pod, 15–30 mm. HABITAT Calcareous grassland, meadows, hill pastures, grass heaths, cliffs, shingle, sanddunes; to 915 m. DIST. Native. Throughout BI. (All Europe.) FLS Jun–Sep.

Greater Bird's-foot-trefoil   *Lotus pedunculatus*

Erect, *usually pubescent perennial* to 75 cm. STEMS *Hollow*. LEAVES Leaflets 15–20 mm, those of upper leaves <3× as long as broad. FLOWERS 10–18 mm, calyx teeth spreading in bud. FRUITS Pods, 15–35 mm. HABITAT Marshes, wet pastures, ditches, woodland paths, pond and river margins; lowland to 390 m. DIST. Native. Most of BI. (Most of Europe except extreme N and S.) FLS Jun–Aug.

Narrow-leaved Bird's-foot-trefoil   *Lotus glaber*

Similar to *L. corniculatus*, but more slender; *leaflets narrower, those of upper leaves >4× as long as broad; flowers 6–12 mm, 2 upper calyx teeth converging; pod* 15–30 mm. HABITAT Coastal grazing marshes, sea walls; inland rough grassland, pits, road verges. DIST. Native. Local in England S of line from Humber to Severn. (All Europe except N.) FLS Jun–Aug.

Hairy Bird's-foot-trefoil   *Lotus subbiflorus* *(R

Much-branched, *densely pubescent* prostrate annual to 30 cm. FLOWERS 5–10 mm, *in heads of 3–4 flowers*; lower edge of lower petal (keel) with obtuse-angled bend. FRUITS *Pod 5–15 mm, <3× as long as calyx*. HABITAT Coastal cliff-top grassland, path verges. DIST. Native. Very local. S and SW England. (W Europe, W Mediterranean.) FLS Jul–Aug.

Slender Bird's-foot-trefoil   *Lotus angustissimus*

Similar to *L. subbiflorus*, but flowers 5–12 mm, in *heads of 1–2 flowers*, lower edge of lower petal (keel) with right-angled bend; *pod 12–30 mm, ≥3× as long as calyx*. HABITAT Similar to *L. subbiflorus*, with which it often grows; also sand and gravel workings inland. DIST. Native. Very local. S and SW England. Channel Is. (W and S Europe.) FLS Jul–Aug.

Kidney Vetch
Anthyllis vulneraria

Common Bird's-foot-trefoil
Lotus corniculatus

Narrow-leaved Bird's-foot-trefoil
Lotus glaber

fruit

Sainfoin
Onobrychis viciifolia

fruit

Slender Bird's-foot-trefoil
Lotus angustissimus

Greater Bird's-foot-trefoil
Lotus pedunculatus

Hairy Bird's-foot-trefoil
Lotus subbiflorus

fruit

fruit

Dragon's-teeth
Tetragonolobus maritimus

illustrations
0.6× lifesize

Bird's-foot
Ornithopus perpusillus *(R)

Tiny, prostrate, *pubescent annual* to 30 cm. LEAVES 15–30 mm, *with 4–10 pairs of leaflets plus a terminal leaflet*. FLOWERS *White*, 3–4 mm, *in 3–6-flowered umbels, with pinnate bracts*. FRUITS Curved pod, 10–20 mm, constricted between seeds. HABITAT Short turf: grass heaths, dunes, lawns, road verges, on dry sandy soils. Lowland to 380 m. DIST. Native. Throughout most of BI except N Scotland; rare in Ireland. (Most of Europe except extreme N and S.) FLS Apr–Aug.

Orange Bird's-foot
Ornithopus pinnatus

Similar to *O. perpusillus*, but ± *glabrous*; 2–4 pairs of leaflets; *flowers* 6–8 mm, *yellow with red veins*, in 1–2-flowered heads, *without bracts*; pods 20–35 mm, only slightly constricted between seeds. HABITAT Short turf, dry heath, dunes, sandy fields. DIST. Native. Rare. Channel Is, Scilly Is. (W and S Europe) FLS Apr–Aug.

Horseshoe Vetch
Hippocrepis comosa

Almost *glabrous*, prostrate perennial to 45 cm. LEAVES 30–50 mm, *with 4–5 pairs leaflets plus a terminal leaflet*. FLOWERS *Yellow*, 5–10 mm, *in 5–8-flowered umbels*, peduncles longer than adjacent leaf. FRUITS *Pods*, 10–30 mm, *constricted into horseshoe-shaped segments*. HABITAT Short, dry turf, warm slopes, chalk and limestone grassland. DIST. Native. Local in England N to N Yorkshire. (S and SW Europe.) FLS May–Jul.

Crown Vetch
Securigera varia

Straggling, glabrous perennial to 100 cm. LEAVES *With 5–12 pairs of leaflets plus a terminal leaflet*. FLOWERS *White, purple or pink*, 8–15 mm, in *10–20-flowered umbels*, peduncles longer than leaves. FRUITS Pods, 20–60 mm, straight-curved, hardly constricted between seeds. HABITAT Grassy roadsides, banks, quarries, waste ground. DIST. Introduced. Escape from cultivation, now naturalised. Scattered throughout most of BI except N Scotland, Ireland. (S and central Europe.) FLS Jun.

Vetches, peas and vetchlings
Vicia and *Lathyrus*

The vetches, *Vicia*, and peas and vetchlings, *Lathyrus*, are very similar, the technical difference between them relying on details of the stamen tube and stigmas, which are not easy to see (*see key on p.282*). For the sake of simplicity and to avoid confusion, the two are treated together in the following key. In general, *Lathyrus* species have angled, flat-

tened or winged stems with 0–2 pairs of leaflets with or without tendrils, whilst the stems of *Vicia* species are round in section and have 2 to many pairs o leaflets with tendrils. Exceptions include *V. bithyn ica*, which has winged stems and only 1–2 pairs o leaflets, and *V. orobus*, which has no tendrils. *See key on p.282*.

Tufted Vetch
Vicia cracc

Tall, straggling, pubescent perennial to 200 cm LEAVES With 5–12 pairs of lanceolate leaflets, tendril branched, stipules entire. FLOWERS 10–12 mm, 10–4(*forming 2–10 cm inflorescence; peduncles long*, 2–10 cm FRUITS *Glabrous*, pod, 10–25 mm. HABITAT Rough grassland, old pasture, hedge banks, scrub, woodlan(edges, coastal shingle; to 550 m. DIST. Native. Com mon throughout BI. (All Europe.) FLS Jun–Aug.

Bush Vetch
Vicia sepiur

Tall, scrambling ± glabrous perennial to 100 cm LEAVES With *5–9 pairs* of ovate leaflets, tendril branched; stipules not, or only slightly, toothed FLOWERS 12–15 mm, 2–6 forming *1–2 cm inflores cence*, ± sessile. FRUITS Glabrous pod, 20–25 mm HABITAT Hedge banks, woodland clearings, scrub rough grassland; to 820 m. DIST. Native. Commo throughout BI. (All Europe, but rare in Mediter ranean.) FLS May–Aug.

Wood Bitter-vetch
Vicia orobus *(I

Erect, branched, ± pubescent perennial to 60 cm LEAVES With *6–10 pairs of leaflets, tendrils absen* stipules slightly toothed. FLOWERS *White, with pur ple veins*, 12–15 mm, drooping; 6–20 forming 1–3 cn inflorescence; peduncles about as long as leaves FRUITS Glabrous pod, 20–30 mm. HABITAT Rock woodlands, cliffs, shaded rocks; coastal in N Scot land. To 455 m. DIST. Native. Scattered, loca declining. W Britain, especially Wales. (W Europe FLS Jun–Sep.

Wood Vetch
Vicia sylvatic

Scrambling, glabrous perennial to 130 cm. LEAVE *With 5–12 pairs of leaflets*, tendrils much branche(lobes of stipules with fine teeth at base. FLOWEF *White with blue veins*, 15–20 mm, 5–15 formin 1–7 cm inflorescence; peduncles long, to 10 cn FRUITS Glabrous pods, 25–30 mm. HABITAT Rock woodland, scrub, wood margins, shaded maritim and inland cliffs, shingle beaches (var. *condensata* to 675 m. DIST. Native. Rare and very loca Throughout most of BI, but absent from E and S (All Europe except N and extreme S.) FLS Jun–Au

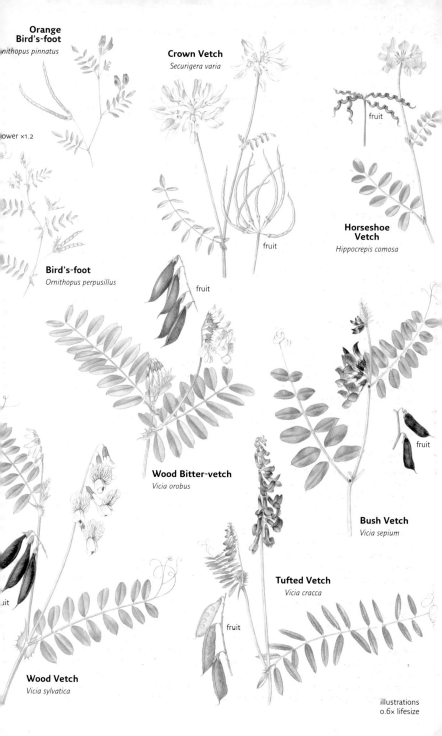

Orange Bird's-foot
Ornithopus pinnatus

flower ×1.2

Crown Vetch
Securigera varia

fruit

fruit

Horseshoe Vetch
Hippocrepis comosa

fruit

Bird's-foot
Ornithopus perpusillus

fruit

Wood Bitter-vetch
Vicia orobus

fruit

Bush Vetch
Vicia sepium

Tufted Vetch
Vicia cracca

fruit

fruit

Wood Vetch
Vicia sylvatica

illustrations
0.6× lifesize

	if	then
1	▷ Leaflets present	Go to ▷ **2**
	▷ Leaflets absent	Go to ▷ **5**
2	▷ ≥2 pairs of leaflets	Go to ▷ **3**
	▷ 1 pair of leaflets	Go to ▷ **D**
3	▷ Tendrils present	Go to ▷ **4**
	▷ Tendrils absent	Go to ▷ **C**
4	▷ Stem round	Go to ▷ **A**
	▷ Stem angled, flattened or winged	Go to ▷ **B**
5	▷ Leaves grass-like; flowers pink	*L. nissolia* (p.288)
	▷ Leaves reduced to a tendril, stipules large; flowers yellow	*L. aphaca* (p.288)

A ≥2 pairs of leaflets; tendrils present; stems round

1	▷ Flowers in stalked racemes, peduncles longer than flowers	Go to ▷ **2**
	▷ Flowers ± sessile, borne singly or in small groups in axils of leaves	Go to ▷ **6**
2	▷ Flowers 8–20 mm, >8 per raceme	Go to ▷ **3**
	▷ Flowers 2–8 mm, 1–8 per raceme	Go to ▷ **5**
3	▷ Leaves thinly pubescent; flowers ≤12 mm	*V. cracca* (p.280)
	▷ Leaves glabrous; flowers ≥12 mm	Go to ▷ **4**
4	▷ 5–12 pairs of leaflets; flowers white with blue or purple veins	*V. sylvatica* (p.280)
	▷ 3–5 pairs of leaflets; flowers blue or purple	*V. dumetorum* ● (p.284)
5	▷ Pods pubescent, 2-seeded; flowers 3–5 mm; tendrils branched	*V. hirsuta* (p.284)
	▷ Pods glabrous, 4-seeded; flowers 4–8 mm; tendrils unbranched	*V. tetrasperma* (p.284)
	▷ Pods glabrous, 4–8-seeded; flowers 6–9 mm	*V. parviflora* (p.284)
6	▷ Flowers dirty yellow; pods densely pubescent	*V. lutea* (p.284)
	▷ Flowers bluish or purple; pods glabrous or thinly pubescent	Go to ▷ **7**
7	▷ Flowers ≤9 mm long	*V. lathyroides* (p.284)
	▷ Flowers >9 mm long	Go to ▷ **8**
8	▷ 2 pairs of leaflets; standard purple, wings white	*V. bithynica* (p.284)
	▷ ≥4 pairs of leaflets; standard and wings purplish	Go to ▷ **9**

	if	**then**
9	▷ Calyx teeth ± equal, as long as calyx tube	*V. sativa* (p.284)
	▷ Calyx teeth unequal, the shorter ones shorter than calyx tube	*V. sepium* (p.280)

B ≥2 pairs of leaflets; tendrils present; stems angled

1	▷ 1–2 pairs of leaflets; standard purple, wings white; pods pubescent	*V. bithynica* (p.284)
	▷ 2–5 pairs of leaflets; all petals pinkish purplish; pods glabrous	Go to ▷ **2**
2	▷ Stem winged, pods flattened; rare, fens	*L. palustris* (p.286)
	▷ Stem not winged, pods not flattened; prostrate mats on coastal shingle	*L. japonicus* (p.286)

C ≥2 pairs of leaflets; tendrils absent

1	▷ Flowers ≤9 mm	*V. lathyroides* (p.284)
	▷ Flowers >9 mm	Go to ▷ **2**
2	▷ Stems round in section; 6–10 pairs of leaflets; flowers white with purple veins	*V. orobus* (p.280)
	▷ Stems winged or 4-angled; 2–6 pairs of leaflets; flowers purple to deep pink	Go to ▷ **3**
3	▷ Stem winged	*L. linifolius* (p.286)
	▷ Stem 4-angled, not winged	Go to ▷ **4**
4	▷ Peduncles glabrous	*L. vernus* • (p.286)
	▷ Peduncles pubescent	*L. niger* (p.286)

D 1 pair of leaflets

1	▷ Stem 4-angled, not winged	Go to ▷ **2**
	▷ Stem winged	Go to ▷ **3**
2	▷ Flowers yellow; pod flattened	*L. pratensis* (p.288)
	▷ Flowers deep pink; pod cylindrical	*L. tuberosus* (p.286)
3	▷ Pod pubescent; 1–3 flowers, standard purple, wings white	*V. bithynica* (p.284)
	▷ Pod glabrous; 3–15 flowers, all petals same colour	Go to ▷ **4**
4	▷ Flowers bright pink, 20–30 mm; stipules >½ as wide as stem	*L. latifolius* (p.286)
	▷ Flowers pale pink, 15–17 mm; stipules <½ as wide as stem	*L. sylvestris* (p.286)

Hairy Tare
Vicia hirsuta

Slender, scrambling, glabrous annual to 30 cm. LEAVES With 4-10 pairs of narrow leaflets, *tendrils branched*, stipules 4-lobed. FLOWERS *3-5 mm, in 1-9-flowered inflorescence*, peduncles 1-3 cm. FRUITS *Pubescent pod*, 6-11 mm, *2-seeded*. HABITAT Rough grassland, pastures, scrub, sea cliffs, shingle beaches, roadside verges; to 335 m. DIST. Native. Common throughout most of BI, but rare in NW Scotland, W Ireland. (All Europe.) FLS May-Aug.

Smooth Tare
Vicia tetrasperma

Slender, scrambling, ± glabrous annual to 60 cm. LEAVES With 4-6 pairs of narrow leaflets, these 10-20 mm; tendrils usually unbranched. FLOWERS *4-8 mm, in 1-2-flowered inflorescence*; peduncle equalling or shorter than leaves. FRUITS *Glabrous pod*, 10-15 mm, *4-seeded, hilum of seed oblong*. HABITAT Rough grassland, old pastures, scrub, roadsides, arable fields. DIST. Native. England, Wales, N to Yorkshire; casual further N. (All Europe except N.) FLS May-Aug.

Slender Tare
Vicia parviflora VU.

Similar to *V. tetrasperma*, but leaves with *2-4 pairs of leaflets*, these to 25 mm; flowers 6-9 mm, in 1-4-flowered inflorescence; pods 12-17 mm, *4-8-seeded, hilum of seed almost circular*. HABITAT Hedgerows, verges, rough grassland, arable fields, coastal cliffs. DIST. Native. Very local, declining. S England. (S and W Europe.) FLS Jun-Aug.

Common Vetch
Vicia sativa

Sparsely hairy, scrambling annual to 120 cm. Very variable; 3 ssp. usually recognised (*see* key below). LEAVES With 4-8 pairs of leaflets, these 10-20 mm; tendrils branched; *stipules often with black blotch*. FLOWERS *1-2, ± sessile*, 10-30 mm. FRUITS Glabrous to sparsely pubescent pods, 25-80 mm, 4-12-seeded, seeds smooth. HABITAT Ssp. *nigra* on dry grassland, dunes, shingle, sea cliffs; ssp. *segetalis* and ssp. *sativa* on field borders, roadside verges, waste and cultivated ground. DIST. Ssp. *nigra* native throughout BI, but rare in N Scotland, Ireland; ssp. *segetalis* archaeophyte, originally a fodder crop and now naturalised, common throughout BI N to S Scotland, but rare in Ireland; ssp. *sativa* originally a fodder crop, now local, declining, throughout BI. (All Europe.) FLS May-Sep.

Leaflets of upper leaves markedly narrower than lower flowers uniformly bright pink ssp. *nigra*

Leaflets of upper leaves only slightly narrower than lower; standard paler than wings

Pods not constricted between seeds, glabrous, brown-black ssp. *segetalis*

Pods constricted between seeds, pubescent, pale brown ssp. *sativa*

Spring Vetch
Vicia lathyroide

Prostrate, pubescent annual to 20 cm, more slender than *V. sativa* ssp. *nigra*. LEAVES With 2-3 pairs of leaflets, those of upper leaves distinctly narrower than lower ones; tendrils unbranched or absent. FLOWERS 6-9 mm, solitary. FRUITS Glabrous pods, 15-30 mm 6-12-seeded, seeds rough. HABITAT Sand-dunes coastal grassland, sandy heaths, old walls. DIST Native. Throughout Britain, mainly in coastal areas especially East Anglia; very rare in Ireland. (Al Europe except N.) FLS May-Jun.

Yellow-vetch
Vicia lute

Prostrate, ± glabrous annual to 60 cm. LEAVES With 3-8 pairs of leaflets, tendrils branched, stipules small FLOWERS Solitary, dirty yellow, 15-25 mm. FRUIT Pubescent pods, 20-40 mm, 4-8-seeded. HABITA Short coastal grassland, cliffs, consolidated shingle DIST. Native. Rare. S and E coasts, SW Scotland; occa sional as casual inland. (Mediterranean.) FLS Jun-Aug

Bithynian Vetch
Vicia bithynica VU

Scrambling, ± glabrous annual to 60 cm. STEM Angled. LEAVES With 1-2 pairs of leaflets; tendril branched; stipules large (to 1 cm), broad, strongl toothed. FLOWERS 1-2, standard purple, wings white 16-20 mm. FRUITS Pods, 25-50 mm, 4-8-seeded HABITAT Rough coastal grassland, cliffs; inlane rough grassland, railway banks and as a casual DIST. Native. Rare, declining. S England; rare else where. (S and W Europe.) FLS May-Jun.

Vicia dumetorum

Scrambling, ± glabrous perennial to 150 cm, similar t *V. sylvatica* (p.280). LEAVES With 3-5 pairs of leaflets tendrils branched; stipules crescent-shaped, toothed FLOWERS Blue or purple, 12-20 mm, in 2-14-flowere inflorescence. FRUITS Pods, 20-40 mm, 6-10-seeded HABITAT Open woods, hedgerows. DIST. *Not BI*. (E an central Europe to France, Denmark.) FLS Jul-Aug.

Slender Tare
Vicia parviflora

Smooth Tare
Vicia tetrasperma

Hairy Tare
Vicia hirsuta

Common Vetch
Vicia sativa

Bithynian Vetch
Vicia bithynica

Yellow-vetch
Vicia lutea

Vicia dumetorum

Spring Vetch
Vicia lathyroides

illustrations
0.6x lifesize

NOTE The **Broad Bean**, *Vicia faba*, commonly occurs as a casual or relic of cultivation. An erect annual to 1 m, with 2-3 pairs of leaflets, *no tendrils and white flowers with a black blotch*; 4-8-seeded pods to 30 cm. *Not illustrated.*

Sea Pea
Lathyrus japonicus *(R)

Prostrate, glabrous, glaucous perennial to 90 cm. STEMS *Angled, not winged.* LEAVES *With 3-5 pairs of leaflets*, these 20-40 mm; *tendrils simple or branched*; stipules ovate. FLOWERS 15-25 mm, in 2-10-flowered inflorescence, peduncles shorter than leaves. FRUITS Glabrous pod, 3-5 cm. HABITAT Forms conspicuous patches on *shingle beaches*. DIST. Native. Very local. Scattered around coasts of BI, principally in East Anglia and SE. (W and N Europe.) FLS Jun-Aug.

Black Pea
Lathyrus niger

Erect, ± glabrous perennial to 60 cm. STEMS *Angled, not winged.* LEAVES *With 3-6 pairs of leaflets*, these 10-30 mm; *tendrils absent*; stipules linear-lanceolate. FLOWERS 10-15 mm; *peduncles pubescent*, with 2-8 flowers. FRUITS Black pod, *c.* 5 cm, surface wrinkled. DIST. Introduced. Very rare as naturalised garden escape. (All Europe except extreme S.) FLS Jun-Jul.

Bitter-vetch
Lathyrus linifolius

Erect, glabrous perennial to 40 cm. STEMS *Winged.* LEAVES *With 2-4 pairs of leaflets*, these 10-30 mm; *tendrils absent*; stipules linear, entire. FLOWERS 10-15 mm; *peduncles glabrous*, with 2-6 flowers. FRUITS Glabrous pod, 3-4 cm. HABITAT Hill grassland, hedge banks, rocky woodlands, wood borders, on dry acid soils; to 760 m. DIST. Native. Throughout BI except East Anglia. (S, W and central Europe.) FLS Apr-Jul.

Marsh Pea
Lathyrus palustris *(NI)

Scrambling, glabrous perennial to 120 cm. STEMS *Winged.* LEAVES *With 2-3 pairs of leaflets*, these 35-70 mm; *tendrils branched*; stipules narrow. FLOWERS 12-20 mm; peduncles longer than leaves, with 2-6 flowers. FRUITS Glabrous, *compressed pod*, 3-5 cm. HABITAT Fens rich in tall herbs, fen meadows, reed-beds, on calcareous peats. DIST. Native. Rare, declining. Norfolk Broads, central Ireland; very scattered elsewhere. (Most of Europe except Mediterranean.) FLS May-Jul.

Tuberous Pea
Lathyrus tuberosus

Glabrous, scrambling perennial to 120 cm. STEM *Angled but not winged.* LEAVES *With 1 pair of leaflets*, these 15-30 mm; tendrils branched; stipules narrow. FLOWERS 12-20 mm; peduncles longer than leaves, with 2-7 flowers. FRUITS Glabrous pods, 25 mm. HABITAT Hedgerows, rough scrub; weed of cereal crops. DIST. Introduced. Naturalised, scattered throughout England; rare in Scotland, Wales; absent from Ireland. (Most of Europe except N and extreme S.) FLS Jul.

Spring Pea
Lathyrus vernus

Erect, glabrous to sparsely pubescent perennial, to 40 cm. STEMS *Not winged.* LEAVES *With 2-4 pairs of leaflets*, these 30-70 mm; *tendrils absent.* FLOWERS 13-20 mm, in 3-10-flowered inflorescence, *peduncles glabrous.* FRUITS Glabrous brown pods, 40-60 mm. HABITAT Upland woodlands on calcareous soils. DIST. *Not BI.* (Most of Europe except parts of W and S.) FLS Apr-Jun.

Narrow-leaved Everlasting-pea
Lathyrus sylvestris

Glabrous, scrambling perennial to 200 cm. STEM *Broadly winged.* LEAVES *With 1 pair of leaflets*, these 70-150 mm; *tendrils much branched; stipules <½ as wide as stem.* FLOWERS *15-17 mm, pale pink*, in 3-8-flowered inflorescence, calyx teeth shorter than tube. FRUITS Glabrous pod, 5-7 cm. HABITAT Wood margins, scrub, hedgerows, sea cliffs. DIST. Native. Local in England, Wales; scattered and naturalised elsewhere, but absent from Ireland. (Most of Europe except extreme N and S.) FLS Jun-Aug.

Broad-leaved Everlasting-pea
Lathyrus latifolius

Vigorous, scrambling perennial. Similar to *L. sylvestris*, but more robust, to 3 m; leaflets broader, *stipules >½ as wide as stem; flowers* larger, 20-30 mm *brighter coloured*, in 5-15-flowered inflorescence, lowest calyx tooth as long as or longer than tube; pod 5-11 cm. HABITAT Persistent escape from cultivation on roadside and railway banks, sea cliffs, waste ground. DIST. Introduced. Naturalised and common throughout England; scattered elsewhere. (S and central Europe.) FLS Jun-Aug.

NOTE The garden **Sweet Pea** is *L. odoratus* while the **Garden Pea** is *Pisum sativum* (*Pisum* differs from *Lathyrus* in having smooth, not angled, stems).

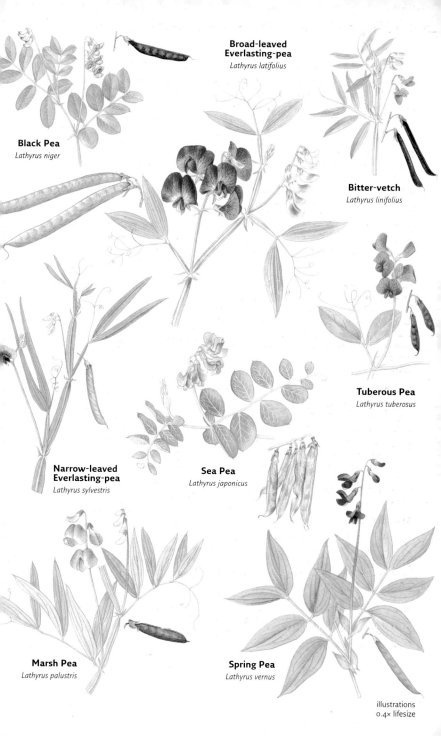

Black Pea
Lathyrus niger

Broad-leaved Everlasting-pea
Lathyrus latifolius

Bitter-vetch
Lathyrus linifolius

Tuberous Pea
Lathyrus tuberosus

Narrow-leaved Everlasting-pea
Lathyrus sylvestris

Sea Pea
Lathyrus japonicus

Marsh Pea
Lathyrus palustris

Spring Pea
Lathyrus vernus

illustrations
0.4× lifesize

Meadow Vetchling
Lathyrus pratensis

Sparsely pubescent, scrambling perennial to 120 cm. STEMS *Angled, not winged.* LEAVES *With 1 pair of leaflets*, these 10-30 mm; tendrils simple or branched. FLOWERS *Yellow*, 10-18 mm; peduncles longer than leaves, with 5-12 flowers. FRUITS Glabrous or sparsely pubescent, *flattened pod*, 25-35 mm. HABITAT Rough grassland, meadows, hedge banks, rough ground close to sea; lowland to 450 m. DIST. Native. Common throughout BI. (All Europe.) FLS May-Aug.

Grass Vetchling
Lathyrus nissolia

Erect, ± glabrous annual to 90 cm. LEAVES *Grass-like*, to 15 cm; *tendrils absent.* FLOWERS *Pink*, 8-18 mm; peduncles equalling or shorter than leaves, with 1-2 flowers. FRUITS Pod, 30-60 mm. HABITAT Rough grassland, roadside verges, woodland rides, coastal grassland, shingle. DIST. Native. Local in central and S England, E Wales; scattered casual further N; absent from Ireland. (W, central and S Europe.) FLS May-Jul.

Yellow Vetchling
Lathyrus aphaca VU.

Glabrous, scrambling annual to 100 cm. STEMS Angled, not winged. LEAVES *Reduced to simple tendrils with large, broad, triangular stipules*, 10-40 mm. FLOWERS *Yellow, solitary,* 10-12 mm, peduncles equalling or exceeding stipules. FRUITS Pod, 20-30 mm. HABITAT Short, dry calcareous grassland, especially near coast. DIST. Probably native in S England, casual elsewhere. Very local. (W, central and S Europe.) FLS Jun-Aug.

Restharrows *Ononis*

1	Flowers pink	2
	Flowers yellow	4
2	Stems woody; flowers ≥10 mm; pods erect	3
	Stems not woody; flowers ≤10 mm; pods drooping	*O. reclinata*
3	Stems hairy all round; wings as long as keel	*O. repens*
	Stems with single line of hairs; wings shorter than keel	*O. spinosa*
4	Flowers 6-20 mm, with red veins	*O. natrix*
	Flowers 5-12 mm, without red veins	*O. pusilla* ●

Common Restharrow
Ononis repen

Prostrate, glandular-pubescent, *woody perennial t* 60 cm. STEMS Rooting at base, green, sometime tinged red, *equally hairy all round.* LEAVES Stipule clasping stem, toothed; leaflets <2.5× as long a wide, blunt. FLOWERS 10-20 mm, *wings as long a keel.* FRUITS Pod, 5-8 mm, shorter than calyx. HAB TAT Well-drained, usually calcareous soils; roug grassland, tracksides, roadside verges, sand-dunes shingle. Lowland to 365 m. DIST. Native. Most of F except N Scotland, W Ireland. (W and centra Europe.) FLS Jun-Sep.

Spiny Restharrow
Ononis spinos

Erect perennial, superficially similar to *O. repen* but *stems with 1(-2) rows of hairs*, red, *often with pa spines* and not rooting at base; leaflets ≥2.5× as lon as wide; *wings shorter than keel*; pods longer tha calyx. SIMILAR SPP. Beware confusion with spin forms of *O. repens.* HABITAT Rough grassland, pe manent pasture, on dry calcareous soils; coast grazing marshes. DIST. Native. Local and declining Most of England SE of a line from Humber to Severn not SW. (W, central and S Europe.) FLS Jun-Sep.

Small Restharrow
Ononis reclinata *(●

Small, erect, sticky *pubescent annual* to 10 cm. FLOW ERS *5-7 mm; stalks strongly recurved after flowerin* sepals as long as, or longer than, petals. FRUITS Po 12-25 mm, about as long as calyx. HABITAT Calcare ous coastal cliffs, dune grassland. DIST. Native. Ve rare. S Devon, S Wales, SW Scotland, Channel Is. and W Europe.) FLS Jun-Jul.

Yellow Restharrow
Ononis natr

Erect, much-branched, glandular-pubescent, dwa shrub to 60 cm, not spiny. FLOWERS *6-20 mm* petals longer than calyx, *yellow with red veins.* FRUIT Pod, 10-25 mm, longer than calyx. HABITAT Dry ca careous grasslands, dunes. DIST. *Not BI.* (S and \ Europe, N to N France.) FLS Jun-Jul.

Ononis pusilla

Pubescent, woody perennial to 25 cm. FLOWEF *Smaller than* O. natrix, *5-12 mm*; calyx as long a petals; *petals yellow, without red veins.* FRUITS Po 6-8 mm, as long as calyx. HABITAT Calcareou grasslands, waste ground. DIST. *Not BI.* (S Europ N to N France.) FLS Jun-Aug.

Common Restharrow
Ononis repens

Small Restharrow
Ononis reclinata

Meadow Vetchling
Lathyrus pratensis

Spiny Restharrow
Ononis spinosa

Grass Vetchling
Lathyrus nissolia

Yellow Restharrow
Ononis natrix

Ononis pusilla

Yellow Vetchling
Lathyrus aphaca

illustrations
0.6× lifesize

Melilots *Melilotus*

1 Flowers white	*M. albus*
Flowers yellow	2
2 Flowers ≥5 mm	3
Flowers ≤3.5 mm	4
3 Petals all same length; pod black, pubescent	*M. altissimus*
Keel shorter than wings and standard; pod brown, glabrous	*M. officinalis*
4 Wings as long as keel; pod <4 mm, olive-green when ripe	*M. indica*
Wings longer than keel; pod >4 mm, blackish brown	*M. dentata* ●

Tall Melilot
Melilotus altissimus

Erect, branched biennial to perennial to 150 cm. FLOWERS 5–6 mm, in rather compact racemes, 20–50 mm; *petals all ± same length*. FRUITS Pod, 5–6 mm, *black and pubescent when ripe*. HABITAT Roadsides, waste ground, field borders, coastal habitats. DIST. Archaeophyte. Widespread SE of a line from Tyne to Severn; scattered elsewhere; rare in Ireland. (Most of Europe.) FLS Jun–Aug.

Ribbed Melilot, Common Melilot
Melilotus officinalis

Erect biennial to 150 cm. Similar to, and confused with, *M. altissimus*, but flowers 5–6 mm, in less compact racemes, *keel shorter than wings and standard; pod 3–5 mm, transversely wrinkled, glabrous*, brown when ripe. HABITAT Waste ground, roadsides, coastal habitats. DIST. Introduced. Widespread SE of a line from Tyne to Severn; scattered elsewhere; rare in Ireland, N Scotland. (Central and S Europe). FLS Jul–Sep.

White Melilot
Melilotus albus

Erect, branched annual or biennial to 150 cm. FLOWERS *White*, 4–5 mm. FRUITS Ridged, glabrous pod, 4–5 mm, brown when ripe. HABITAT Weed of arable land, waste ground, roadsides. DIST. Introduced. Casual or naturalised, N to central Scotland; commonest in SE. (Most of Europe.) FLS Jul–Aug.

Small Melilot
Melilotus indicus

Erect, branched annual to 40 cm, smaller than *M. altissimus*. FLOWERS 2–3.5 mm, in dense inflorescence; *wings and keel equal, shorter than standard*. FRUITS *Glabrous pod, 1.5–3 mm*, strongly wrinkled, *olive-green when ripe*. HABITAT Casual of waste ground, roadsides. DIST. Introduced. Declining. Scattered throughout BI; very rare in N and W, and in Ireland. (Mediterranean, SW Europe.) FLS Jun–Oct.

Melilotus dentata

Erect, branched biennial to 150 cm. LEAVES Stipules toothed. FLOWERS 3–3.5 mm; *wings shorter than standard, longer than keel*. FRUITS Glabrous pod, 4.5–5.5 mm, faintly ridged, *blackish brown* when ripe. HABITAT Coastal brackish grassland, riverbanks. DIST. Not BI. (E and central Europe, W to Denmark.)

Medicks *Medicago*

Leaves of medicks can usually be distinguished from those of clovers (*Trifolium*; pp.292–300) by the tooth in the apical notch of the middle leaflet.

1 Flowers purple	*M. sativa sativa*
Flowers yellow	2
2 Leaflets with dark spot	*M. arabica*
Leaflets not spotted	3
3 Flowers ≥6 mm	*M. sativa falcate*
Flowers <5 mm	4
4 Heads with >10 flowers; pods black, without spines	*M. lupulina*
Heads with ≤8 flowers; pods spiny	5
5 Plant glabrous; pods glabrous	*M. polymorpha*
Plant densely pubescent; pods pubescent	*M. minima*

Lucerne, Alfalfa
Medicago sativa sativa

Erect, pubescent perennial to 90 cm. LEAVES Leaflet narrow. FLOWERS *Purple*, 8–11 mm, in compact racemes to 40 mm. FRUITS Pubescent or glabrous pod, spiralled 2–3 turns. HABITAT Field borders, roadsides, waste ground. DIST. Introduced (origin obscure, probably SW Asia). First cultivated as fodder crop in C17th. Widely naturalised SE of a line from Tyne to Severn; scattered elsewhere; very rare in N Scotland, Ireland. (Throughout Europe.) FLS Aug–Sep.

Sickle Medick
Medicago sativa falcata

Prostrate to erect perennial, to 60 cm. LEAVES Leaflet narrow, to 15 mm. FLOWERS *Yellow, 6–9 mm*, in racemes to 25 mm. FRUITS Thinly pubescent pod sickle-shaped to almost straight, 8–11 mm. HABITAT Dry, open grassland, roadside verges, grassy banks secure from grazing. DIST. Native. Rare in East Anglia, casual elsewhere. (Most of Europe.) FLS Jun–Jul.

White Melilot
Melilotus albus

Ribbed Melilot
Melilotus ufficinalis

Tall Melilot
Melilotus tissimus

fruit

fruit

fruit

Small Melilot
Melilotus indicus

fruit

Lucerne
Medicago sativa sativa

fruit

Melilotus dentata

fruit

Black Medick
Medicago lupulina
(description on p.292)

Sickle Medick
Medicago sativa falcata

fruit

illustrations
0.6× lifesize

Black Medick   *Medicago lupulina*

[*See* illustration previous page.] Prostrate or ascending, pubescent annual or perennial to 50 cm. LEAVES Leaflets 3–20 mm. FLOWERS *2–3 mm*, in compact 3–8 mm inflorescence. FRUITS *Spineless pod*, 1.5–3 mm, *black when ripe*. HABITAT Short calcareous grassland, well-drained soils, road verges, lawns; lowland to 440 m. DIST. Native. Common throughout BI except for N Scotland. (All Europe except extreme N.) FLS May–Sep.

Bur Medick   *Medicago minima* VU.

Prostrate to erect, *densely pubescent annual*, to 20 cm. LEAVES Leaflets 3–6 mm, stipules almost entire. FLOWERS 2.5–4.5 mm, *in 1–5-flowered inflorescence*. FRUITS *Spiny, pubescent pods*, 4–5 mm across, with 4–5 coils. HABITAT Dry, open areas, heath tracks, road verges, mature coastal sand-dunes. DIST. Native. Very local. East Anglia, SE, Channel Is; occasional casual elsewhere. (Most of Europe.) FLS Jun–Aug.

Toothed Medick   *Medicago polymorpha*

Prostrate, ± *glabrous annual* to 60 cm, larger than *M. minima*. LEAVES Leaflets to 25 mm; stipules with long, fine teeth. FLOWERS 3–4.5 mm, in 1–8-flowered inflorescence. FRUITS *Spiny, glabrous, flat, ridged pods*, 4–6 mm across, with 1.5–6 coils. HABITAT Dry, open sandy habitats, grassland close to sea. DIST. Native. Very local. SW, S and E coast, N to Wash; casual inland. (S Europe N to latitude of BI.) FLS Jun–Sep.

Spotted Medick   *Medicago arabica*

Prostrate, ± glabrous annual to 60 cm. LEAVES *Leaflets to 25 mm, each with black blotch* (may fade); stipules toothed. FLOWERS 4–6 mm, in 1–5-flowered inflorescence. FRUITS *Spiny, glabrous pods*, 4–6 mm across, with 3–5 coils. HABITAT Light soils; grassy habitats, lawns, waste ground, especially near coast. DIST. Native. SE of a line from Wash to Severn; casual elsewhere. (S Europe, NW to Netherlands.) FLS May–Sep.

Clovers and trefoils *Trifolium*
See key to *Trifolium* on p.294.

Bird's-foot Clover, Fenugreek   *Trifolium ornithopodioides*

Slender, ± *glabrous*, prostrate annual to 20 cm. LEAVES *Petioles to 25 mm, >2× as long as leaflet*; stipules with long, fine points. FLOWERS *Pink*, 6–8 mm, in 1–4-flowered inflorescence; peduncles shorter than petioles. FRUITS Slightly curved pod, 5–7 mm, *longer than calyx*. HABITAT Short, compacted sandy turf close to sea. DIST. Native. Coastal areas of England, Wales, N to Lancashire, I of Man; very rare in W Ireland. (W Europe.) FLS May–Sep.

White Clover, Dutch Clover   *Trifolium repens*

Creeping, *glabrous* perennial to 50 cm, *rooting at nodes*. Extremely variable species with many cultivated varieties. LEAVES *Leaflets 10–25 mm, usually with inverted white V-shaped mark*, lateral veins straight; *stipules green*, sometimes with red veins. FLOWERS 7–12 mm, *white* (to pale pink), standards with rounded tip; in 15–20-flowered inflorescence; peduncles erect, glabrous, to 20 cm; *calyx green with white veins*. HABITAT Meadows, pastures, calcareous grassland, lawns, tracks; to 800 m. DIST. Abundant throughout BI. (All Europe.) FLS Jun–Sep.

Western Clover   *Trifolium occidentale*

Similar to *T. repens*, but *leaflets thicker, more rounded, 6–8 mm, unmarked; petiole pubescent; stipules deep red*; tip of standard notched; upper part of calyx becoming red. HABITAT Short turf close to sea, cliff and dune grassland. DIST. Native. Very local. Cornwall, Channel Is, Scilly Is; scattered localities in W Wales, E Ireland. (NW France.) FLS Apr–Jul (earlier than *T. repens*).

Alsike Clover   *Trifolium hybridum*

Erect to ± prostrate, almost glabrous perennial to 60 cm. LEAVES Stipules entire, tapering to fine point. FLOWERS 7–10 mm, *white and pink, in axillary inflorescence; peduncles to 15 cm*. HABITAT Meadows, pastures, roadside verges. DIST. Introduced. Formerly much cultivated as a forage crop. Widely distributed throughout BI, but scarce in most of Scotland, Ireland. (Most of Europe.) FLS Jun–Sep.

Clustered Clover   *Trifolium glomeratum* *(F

Prostrate, glabrous annual to 25 cm. LEAVES Petioles to 20 mm; stipules with long, fine points. FLOWERS *Purplish*, 4–5 mm; in terminal, axillary, sessile heads, *corolla longer than calyx*. FRUITS Pod enclosed in calyx. HABITAT Short coastal turf, sand dunes, wall tops, old quarries close to sea. DIST. Native. Local. East Anglia, S and SW. (S and W Europe.) FLS Jun–Aug.

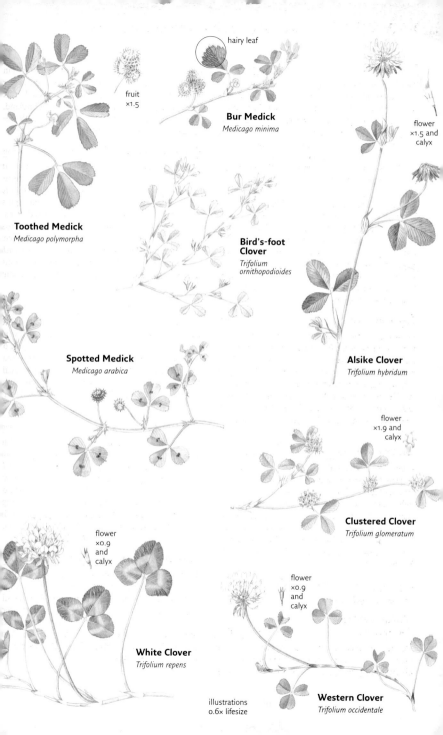

Toothed Medick
Medicago polymorpha

fruit
×1.5

hairy leaf

Bur Medick
Medicago minima

**Bird's-foot
Clover**

*Trifolium
ornithopodioides*

flower
×1.5 and
calyx

Spotted Medick
Medicago arabica

Alsike Clover
Trifolium hybridum

flower
×1.9 and
calyx

Clustered Clover
Trifolium glomeratum

flower
×0.9
and
calyx

White Clover
Trifolium repens

flower
×0.9
and
calyx

illustrations
0.6× lifesize

Western Clover
Trifolium occidentale

	if	**then**
	Flowers red, pink or white	
1	▷ Stems with runners, rooting at nodes; flowers all axillary	Go to ▷ **2**
	▷ Stems without runners	Go to ▷ **4**
2	▷ Lateral veins straight and not thickened towards margins of leaf; calyx glabrous, not inflated in fruit	Go to ▷ **3**
	▷ Lateral veins recurved and thickened towards margins of leaf; calyx inflated and pubescent in fruit	*T. fragiferum* (p.296)
3	▷ Leaflets >10 mm, with white inverted 'V'; petioles glabrous; stipules green or red-veined; tip of standard rounded	*T. repens* (p.292)
	▷ Leaflets <10 mm, unmarked; petioles sparsely hairy; stipules red; tip of standard notched	*T. occidentale* (p.292)
4	▷ Numerous flowers, in dense heads	Go to ▷ **5**
	▷ ≤6 flowers, in lax heads	Go to ▷ **18**
5	▷ Flower heads all terminal	Go to ▷ **6**
	▷ Some flower heads axillary	Go to ▷ **11**
6	▷ Calyx tube with sparse, long hairs or ± glabrous	Go to ▷ **7**
	▷ Calyx tube densely pubescent with appressed brown hairs	Go to ▷ **9**
7	▷ Petals dark pink, much longer than calyx; flowers 12–20 mm	Go to ▷ **8**
	▷ Petals pale pink, scarcely longer than calyx; flowers 7–9 mm; calyx teeth spreading (maritime, rare)	*T. squamosum* (p.300)
8	▷ Stipules ovate, ± abruptly contracted to a short bristle; heads sessile	*T. pratense* (p.296)
	▷ Stipules narrow, tapered to long, fine point; heads distinctly short-stalked	*T. medium* (p.298)
9	▷ Flower heads spherical; stipules toothed	*T. stellatum* (p.298)
	▷ Flower heads cylindrical; stipules entire	Go to ▷ **10**
10	▷ Flowers crimson	*T. incarnatum incarnatum* (p.2
	▷ Flowers cream to pink	*T. incarnatum molinerii* (p.298
11	▷ Flower heads distinctly stalked	Go to ▷ **12**
	▷ Flower heads sessile	Go to ▷ **14**

if	then

12
▷ Flower heads softly downy, cylindrical — ***T. arvense*** (p.300)
▷ Flower heads not downy, ± spherical — Go to ▷ **13**

13
▷ Flowers ≥7 mm; stipules entire — ***T. hybridum*** (p.292)
▷ Flowers ≤7 mm; stipules toothed (rare, W Cornwall) — ***T. strictum*** (p.296)

14
▷ Leaflets pubescent, at least on veins beneath — Go to ▷ **15**
▷ Leaflets glabrous — Go to ▷ **17**

15
▷ Lateral veins thickened and recurved towards leaflet margins — ***T. scabrum*** (p.298)
▷ Lateral veins neither thickened nor recurved — Go to ▷ **16**

16
▷ Leaflets hairy above — ***T. striatum*** (p.298)
▷ Leaflets glabrous above (rare, W Cornwall) — ***T. bocconei*** (p.298)

17
▷ Corolla shorter than calyx, white; flower heads tightly clustered at base of plant — ***T. suffocatum*** (p.296)
▷ Corolla longer than calyx, purplish; flower heads separate, distributed along stems — ***T. glomeratum*** (p.292)

18
▷ Leaves glabrous; petals pink; pods longer than calyx — ***T. ornithopodioides*** (p.292)
▷ Leaves pubescent; petals white; pods hidden within enlarged calyces — ***T. subterraneum*** (p.300)

Flowers yellow

1
▷ Flowers whitish yellow, flower heads 20–30 mm — ***T. ochroleucon*** (p.298)
▷ Flowers yellow, flower heads ≤20 mm — Go to ▷ **2**

2
▷ Standard petal ± flat, flowers ≥4 mm — Go to ▷ **3**
▷ Standard petal folded along its length, flowers ≤4 mm — Go to ▷ **4**

3
▷ Stipules ovate; petals pale yellow — ***T. campestre*** (p.296)
▷ Stipules linear; petals deep yellow — ***T. aureum*** (p.296)

4
▷ Middle leaflet ± sessile; heads 2–6-flowered, standard notched — ***T. micranthum*** (p.296)
▷ Middle leaflet with stalk longer than that of lateral leaflets; heads 10–25-flowered, standard not notched — ***T. dubium*** (p.296)

Strawberry Clover
Trifolium fragiferum

Creeping, stoloniferous, ± glabrous perennial to 30 cm, *rooting at nodes*. LEAVES *Leaflets* 10–15 mm, *unmarked, lateral veins thickened, recurved at margin* (cf. *T. repens*, p.292). FLOWERS 5–7 mm; peduncles shorter than petioles; *calyx strongly inflated, densely hairy.* FRUITS Pod, enclosed in persistent calyx. HABITAT Old pasture, grazed commons, on heavy clay soils; brackish grazing marsh, sea walls near coast. DIST. Native. Widespread SE of a line from Humber to Severn; coastal further N to central Scotland, Ireland. (Most of Europe except extreme N.) FLS Jul–Sep.

Red Clover
Trifolium pratense

Prostrate to erect, *pubescent perennial*, to 60 cm. Very variable. LEAVES Leaflets 10–30 mm, often with inverted white V-shaped mark; free part of stipules ovate, with fine brown bristle-like point. FLOWERS *Red, in terminal, ± sessile inflorescence*; corolla 15–18 mm, longer than calyx. HABITAT Pastures, meadows, rough grassland, verges. DIST. Native. Abundant throughout BI. Widely cultivated. (All Europe.) FLS May–Sep.

Upright Clover
Trifolium strictum VU.

Erect, glabrous annual to 15 cm. LEAVES Leaflets narrow, 5–15 mm; *stipules toothed*. FLOWERS *Purplish, 5–7 mm*; in terminal, axillary inflorescence; *peduncles 10–20 mm*. HABITAT Short, grazed grassland, rock outcrops, on infertile mineral-rich soils. DIST. Native. Very rare. SW Cornwall (Lizard), central Wales, Channel Is (Jersey). (W and S Europe.) FLS May–Jul.

Suffocated Clover
Trifolium suffocatum

Small, prostrate, *glabrous annual* to 10 cm. LEAVES Leaflets triangular, 3–5 mm; stipules colourless; petioles long, >2× as long as leaflets. FLOWERS *3–4 mm; in terminal, axillary, sessile inflorescences, densely crowded at base of plant, corolla shorter than calyx, white.* HABITAT Short, dry, open turf, bare ground, on compacted sand or shingle near sea. DIST. Native. Very local. East Anglia, S, SW, Channel Is, Scilly Is. (S and W Europe.) FLS Apr–Aug.

Large Trefoil
Trifolium aureum

Erect, sparsely pubescent annual to 30 cm. LEAVES Leaflets to 15 mm, terminal leaflet ± sessile, *stipules linear*. FLOWERS *5–8 mm*; in terminal, axillary inflorescences; peduncles to 50 mm, as long as or longer than leaves. HABITAT Rough grassland, scrub, waste ground. DIST. Introduced. Rare casual, scattered throughout BI. (Central and E Europe.) FLS Jul–Aug.

Hop Trefoil
Trifolium campestre

Erect, ± pubescent annual to 30 cm. LEAVES Leaflets 8–10 mm, *stalk of terminal leaflet >5 mm*; stipules acute. FLOWERS 4–7 mm, *pale yellow, turning brownish*; in 10–26-flowered inflorescence; *standard rather broad, not folded, becoming pleated; pedicels* c.½ *as long as calyx tube*. HABITAT Rough grassland, road verges, sand-dunes, waste ground. DIST. Native. Frequent throughout BI, becoming rarer to N. (Most of Europe except extreme N.) FLS Jun–Sep.

Lesser Trefoil
Trifolium dubium

Slender, prostrate, sparsely pubescent annual to 25 cm. LEAVES Leaflets to 11 mm, *terminal leaflet with short stalk*; petiole <2× length of leaflet. FLOWERS 3–4 mm, in 10–26-flowered inflorescence; *standard folded; pedicels shorter than calyx tube*. HABITAT Short, open grassland, roadside verges, lawns, commons. DIST. Native. Common throughout BI. (Most of Europe except extreme N.) FLS May–Oct. NOTE Often grows with *T. micranthum* and *Medicago lupulina* (p.292), with which it is frequently confused.

Slender Trefoil
Trifolium micranthum

Slender, prostrate, sparsely pubescent annual to 10 cm. LEAVES Leaflets *c.*5 mm, *terminal leaflet sessile*. FLOWERS 2.5–3 mm, *in 2–6-flowered inflorescence*; peduncles as long as, or longer than, leaves; standard notched, folded; *pedicels about as long as calyx tube* (cf. *T. dubium*). HABITAT Short, open grassland, garden lawns, road verges, waste ground. DIST. Native. Widely distributed in England, Wales (more common in SE), coastal Ireland; scattered elsewhere; casual in Scotland. (W and S Europe.) FLS Jun–Jul.

lower ×1.2
and calyx

Strawberry Clover
Trifolium fragiferum

Red Clover
Trifolium pratense

flower
×1.2 and
calyx

flower
×1.2

Slender Trefoil
*Trifolium
micranthum*

Upright Clover
Trifolium strictum

Suffocated Clover
Trifolium suffocatum

flower
×1.2 and
calyx

Lesser Trefoil
Trifolium dubium

Hop Trefoil
Trifolium campestre

flower
×1.2 and
calyx

Large Trefoil
Trifolium aureum

illustrations
0.6× lifesize

Zigzag Clover
Trifolium medium

Straggling, prostrate to erect, thinly pubescent, rhizomatous perennial to 50 cm. LEAVES Leaflets narrow, 10-15 mm; *free part of stipules awl-shaped, green*. FLOWERS *Pink*, in terminal inflorescence, *with pair of leaves beneath*; corolla 12-20 mm, 2-3× as long as calyx. HABITAT Meadows, pastures, roadsides, on heavy soils; upland grasslands rich in tall herbs. To 610 m. DIST. Native. Local throughout BI, but scarce in N Scotland, Ireland. (All Europe except extreme N and S.) FLS Jun-Sep.

Sulphur Clover
Trifolium ochroleucon

Erect, ± pubescent perennial to 50 cm. LEAVES Leaflets 15-30 mm, lanceolate; free part of stipules filiform. FLOWERS 15-20 mm, *whitish yellow, in terminal heads with pair of sessile leaves beneath*. HABITAT Pastures, grassy roadside verges, on chalky boulder-clay. DIST. Native. Very local, declining. East Anglia. (W, central and S Europe.) FLS Jun-Jul.

Crimson Clover
Trifolium incarnatum spp. *incarnatum*

Erect, pubescent annual to 50 cm, hairs on stem and petiole usually spreading. LEAVES Leaflets broad, widest above middle, 5-30 mm; stipules broad, blunt, bluntly toothed. FLOWERS 9-15 mm, *crimson; in cylindrical, terminal heads*, 15-50 mm; *calyx tube densely pubescent*. HABITAT Field margins, waste ground. DIST. Introduced. Formerly cultivated as a forage crop. Infrequent casual, scattered in England, Wales. (S Europe, Mediterranean.) FLS May-Sep.

Long-headed Clover
Trifolium incarnatum spp. *molinerii* VU.

Similar to T. i. incarnatum, but prostrate to erect, to *c.*20 cm; hairs on stems and petioles usually appressed; *flowers cream to pink*. HABITAT Short, cliff-top grassland. DIST. Native. Very rare. Cornwall (Lizard), Channel Is (Jersey). (W and S Europe.) FLS May-Jun.

Starry Clover
Trifolium stellatum

Erect, pubescent annual to 20 cm, *hairs on stems spreading*. LEAVES Leaflets 8-12 mm; *stipules broad, blunt, sharply toothed*, veins green. FLOWERS Pink, 12-18 mm; in spherical, terminal heads, 15-25 mm; calyx teeth long, narrow, pointed. FRUITS *Calyx teeth spreading to give star-like appearance*. HABITAT Coastal shingle. (Mediterranean.) DIST. Introduced. Very rare. W Sussex, Hampshire. FLS May-Jul.

Knotted Clover
Trifolium striatum

Prostrate to erect, *softly pubescent annual*, to 30 cm. LEAVES Leaflets 5-15 mm, *lateral veins straight*; stipules triangular, finely pointed, with red or green veins. FLOWERS Pink, 4-7 mm; *in terminal and axillary, sessile heads, ± enclosed in enlarged stipule of adjacent leaf*. HABITAT Grassy banks, heath grassland, dune turf, on dry sandy soils. DIST. Native. Local. Scattered throughout BI N to central Scotland; very rare in Ireland. (W Europe, Mediterranean.) FLS May-Jul.

Twin-headed Clover
Trifolium bocconei VU

Small, erect, ± pubescent annual to 20 cm. LEAVES *Leaflets 5-15 mm, glabrous above*, sparsely pubescent beneath, lateral veins straight; stipules with long, fine points. FLOWERS White, turning pink 4-6 mm; *in terminal and axillary, sessile heads, usually in pairs*, to 10 mm; calyx strongly ribbed. HABITAT Short, open, grazed turf over serpentine near sea. DIST. Native. Very rare. Only on Lizard Peninsula (Cornwall). (SW Europe, Mediterranean.) FLS May-Jun.

Rough Clover
Trifolium scabrum

Prostrate or erect, *pubescent annual* to 25 cm. LEAVES *Leaflets 5-8 mm, pubescent on both surfaces, lateral veins curving backwards and thickened towards margins* (visible when held up to light). FLOWERS *White* 4-7 mm; in *mostly axillary, sessile heads*, 5-12 mm. HABITAT Similar to T. striatum: open dune turf, banks, tracksides, on dry sandy or gravelly soils. DIST. Native. Local and predominantly coastal throughout BI to central Scotland; inland East Anglia; very rare in Ireland. (S and W Europe.) FLS May-Jul.

Sulphur Clover
Trifolium ochroleucon

Starry Clover
Trifolium stellatum

calyx ×1.2

fruit

Zigzag Clover
Trifolium medium

Long-headed Clover

Trifolium incarnatum molinerii

Rough Clover
Trifolium scabrum

flower
×1.2

fruit
×1.2

Crimson Clover
Trifolium incarnatum incarnatum

lower and
calyx ×1.2

Twin-headed Clover

Trifolium bocconei

fruit

Knotted Clover
Trifolium striatum

illustrations
0.6× lifesize

Hare's-foot Clover
Trifolium arvense

Softly pubescent, rather *grey-green erect*, branched annual to 20 cm. LEAVES *Leaflets* 10-15 mm, *narrow*, oblong, terminal leaflet longer than petiole; stipules with long, fine points. FLOWERS White or pink, 3-6 mm; *in terminal, axillary, softly downy, cylindrical heads*, to 20 mm; corolla much shorter than calyx. HABITAT Sand-dunes, sea cliffs, road verges, grassy heaths, waste ground, on dry sandy soils. DIST. Native. Local throughout BI except N Scotland and most of Ireland. (Most of Europe except extreme N.) FLS Jun-Sep.

Sea Clover
Trifolium squamosum

Erect, ± *sparsely pubescent annual* to 40 cm. LEAVES *Leaflets* 10-20 mm, *linear-oblong*, terminal leaflet as long as or shorter than petiole; stipules with long, fine points. FLOWERS White, 7-9 mm; *in terminal, short-stalked heads*, 10-20 mm, *with a pair of leaves at base*; calyx strongly ribbed, teeth triangular. FRUITS *Calyx spreading*. HABITAT Upper edge of salt marshes, brackish meadows, tidal drainage dykes, sea walls. DIST. Native. Rare, declining. E coast S from Essex, W coasts to S Wales. (W Europe, Mediterranean.) FLS Jun-Jul.

Subterranean Clover
Trifolium subterraneum *(R)

Pubescent, prostrate annual to 20 cm. LEAVES Leaflets 5-12 mm, cordate; petioles long, 2-5 cm; stipules ovate, acute. FLOWERS *In axillary heads with a mix of 2-5 fertile and several sterile flowers*; fertile flowers cream, 8-12 mm; *sterile flowers with lobed calyx teeth*. FRUITS *Spherical pod, 2.5 mm, becoming buried*. HABITAT Grassland on sandy soils, walls, cliff tops near coast; calcareous grassland inland. DIST. Native. Local and mostly coastal. S England, Wales. (S and W Europe.) FLS May-Jun.

Tree Lupin
Lupinus arboreus

Erect, sparsely pubescent, much-branched shrub to 3 m. LEAVES *Palmate*; 5-12 leaflets, glabrous above, silky below. FLOWERS *Yellow*, 14-17 mm; *in a raceme*, 10-30 cm; calyx bilobed. HABITAT Widely planted on sand-dunes; naturalised inland on waste ground, roadsides, railways. Vigorous; possible threat to native vegetation. DIST. Introduced in 1793 (native of California). Established throughout most of BI except NW Scotland and most of Ireland. FLS Jun-Sep.

Gorses *Ulex*

Densely spiny shrubs, with branched green spines. Mature plants lack leaves, young plants have trifoliate leaves.

Main spines very rigid, deeply furrowed; bracteoles 2-4.5 mm, ≥2× as wide as pedicels; flowers winter, spring   *U. europaeus*

Main spines faintly furrowed or striate; bracteoles c.0.5 mm, ≤2× as wide as pedicels; flowers late summer, autumn

Spines rigid; calyx teeth convergent; calyx 9-13 mm	*U. gallii*
Spines weak, calyx teeth divergent; calyx 5-9 mm	*U. minor*

Gorse, Furze
Ulex europaeus

Densely spiny, evergreen *shrub to 2 m*. STEMS Sparsely pubescent, hairs black; *main spines* 1.5-2.5 cm, *very rigid, deeply furrowed*. FLOWERS Smell of coconut; *bracteoles 2-4.5 mm, ≥2× as wide as pedicels*; calyx ⅔ length of corolla, with spreading hairs. HABITAT Heathland, commons, roadsides, sea cliffs, waste ground, on well-drained, usually acid soils, but also calcareous soils near coast; to 640 m. DIST. Native. Widespread and locally abundant throughout BI except Scottish islands. (W Europe.) FLS Dec-Jun.

Western Gorse
Ulex gallii

Similar to *U. europaeus*, but smaller in stature, 1.5-2 m; stems pubescent, hairs brown; *main spines rigid, faintly furrowed to striate*; bracteoles 0.5-0.8 mm; *calyx 9-13 mm, ⅔-¾ length of corolla*, with appressed hairs, *teeth convergent*; wings longer than keel. HABITAT Heaths, cliff tops, abandoned pasture, coastal shingle; to 670 m. DIST. Native. W Britain, N to Solway, E to Dorset; also East Anglia. (W Europe.) FLS Jul-Sep.

Dwarf Gorse
Ulex minor

Less robust than *U. gallii*, prostrate to erect, usually to c.1 m. STEMS Pubescent, hairs brown; *main spines weak*, 0.8-1.5 cm, striate or smooth, not furrowed, slightly curved. FLOWERS Bracteoles 0.6-0.8 mm; *calyx 5-9 mm*, almost as long as corolla, *teeth divergent*; wings about as long as keel. HABITAT Dry to damp acid sandy heaths. DIST. Native. Very local. SE England. (W Europe.) FLS Jul-Sep.

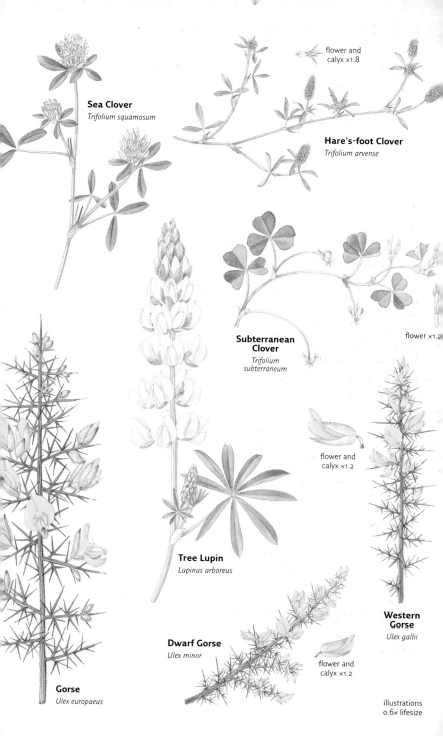

Sea Clover
Trifolium squamosum

flower and
calyx ×1.8

Hare's-foot Clover
Trifolium arvense

**Subterranean
Clover**
*Trifolium
subterraneum*

flower ×1.2

flower and
calyx ×1.2

Tree Lupin
Lupinus arboreus

**Western
Gorse**
Ulex gallii

Dwarf Gorse
Ulex minor

flower and
calyx ×1.2

Gorse
Ulex europaeus

illustrations
0.6× lifesize

Broom *Cytisus scoparius*

Erect, much-branched, non-spiny shrub to 2 m. Stems *Twigs green, deeply grooved, glabrous.* Leaves *Trifoliate.* Flowers 15–20 mm. Fruits Black pod, 2.5–4 cm, pubescent on margins. Habitat Heathlands, open woodland, roadside verges, railway embankments, on light sandy soils. Dist. Native. Widespread throughout BI except Scottish islands. (W, central and S Europe.) Fls May–Jun. Note Ssp. *maritimus* is a rare prostrate plant with silky twigs, found on sea cliffs in SW England, Wales, Channel Is.

Greenweeds and broom *Genista* and *Spartium*

1	Non-spiny shrub to 3 m; leaves sparse; pods 40–100 mm	*Spartium junceum*
	Spiny or non-spiny shrub to 1 m; leafiness normal; pods to 30 mm	2 *Genista*
2	Shrubs spiny	3
	Shrubs not spiny	5
3	Spines simple	*G. anglica*
	Spines branched	4
4	Flowers in dense heads, standard about as long as keel	*G. hispanica*
	Flowers in elongated racemes, standard ½–⅔ as long as keel	*G. germanica* •
5	Leaves lanceolate, margins hairy; flowers glabrous, on long branches	*G. tinctoria*
	Leaves ovate, densely pubescent beneath; flowers pubescent, on short lateral branches	*G. pilosa*

Dyer's Greenweed *Genista tinctoria*

Small, prostrate to erect, *spineless* shrub, to 70 cm. Leaves Simple, to 30 mm. Flowers 10–15 mm, *glabrous, on long branches.* Fruits Glabrous black pod, 25–30 mm. Habitat Old meadows, grassy commons, rough pasture, roadside verges, on heavy soils. Dist. Native. Widespread throughout England, Wales, N to S Scotland; absent from Ireland. (Most of Europe.) Fls Jul–Sep. Note Ssp. *littoralis*, with broader leaves and pubescent pods, is a prostrate plant of sea cliffs in Cornwall and N Devon.

Petty Whin, Needle Furze *Genista anglica*

Spiny, erect shrub to 100 cm. Stems Twigs brown; *spines curved, unbranched,* 1–2 cm. Leaves Simple, 2–8 mm, glabrous. Flowers 7–10 mm, glabrous. Fruits Glabrous pod, 12–15 mm, inflated. Habitat Heaths, moors; to 730 m. Dist. Native. Local, declining. Throughout Britain except extreme N Scotland; absent from Ireland. (W Europe.) Fls May–Jun.

Hairy Greenweed *Genista pilosa*

Prostrate, *pubescent,* much-branched, *spineless shrub* to 40 cm. Leaves Simple, 3–5 mm, pubescent beneath, glabrous above. Flowers 7–11 mm, *pubescent, on short lateral branches.* Fruits Pubescent pod, 14–20 mm, not inflated. Habitat Maritime heath, grassland, cliffs. Dist. Native. Very rare. W Cornwall, Wales (St David's Head, Cadair Idris, Brecon Beacons). (W and central Europe.) Fls May–Jun.

Spanish Gorse *Genista hispanica*

Erect, pubescent shrub to 70 cm. Stems *Spines branched.* Leaves Simple, pubescent, 6–10 mm. Flowers 8–14 mm, *in dense terminal racemes, standard about as long as keel.* Fruits Pod, 8–11 mm. Dist. Introduced. Common garden species, sometimes planted on roadsides and becoming naturalised. (N Spain, S France.) Fls Apr–Sep.

German Greenweed *Genista germanica*

Erect, pubescent shrub to 60 cm. Stems *Spines branched.* Leaves Simple, pubescent beneath, 8–20 mm. Flowers *In elongated racemes,* pubescent, *standard ½–⅔ as long as keel.* Fruits Pubescent pod. Habitat Sandy heaths, grassland. Dist. *Not BI.* (W, central and E Europe.) Fls May–Jun.

Winged Broom *Chamaespartium sagittale*

Prostrate to erect, mat-forming, dwarf shrub to 50 cm. Stems Distinctly winged, flattened. Leaves 5–20 mm, glabrous above, pubescent beneath. Flowers In dense terminal racemes, 10–12 mm. Fruits Pubescent pod, 14–20 mm. Habitat Calcareous grasslands. Dist. *Not BI.* (Central Europe to France, Belgium.) Fls May–Jun.

Spanish Broom *Spartium junceum*

Erect, non-spiny, glabrous shrub to 3 m. Stems Smooth. Leaves *Simple,* 10–30 mm, *sparse.* Flowers 20–28 mm. Fruits *Long pod, 4–10 cm,* compressed, pubescent. Habitat Widely planted on road verges; naturalised on light soils on roadsides, railways, coastal cliffs. Dist. Introduced. Cultivated since 1548. (SW Europe, Mediterranean.) Fls May–Sep. Note Differs from *Cytisus scoparius* in having smooth, not grooved twigs; simple, not trifoliate leaves; and larger flowers.

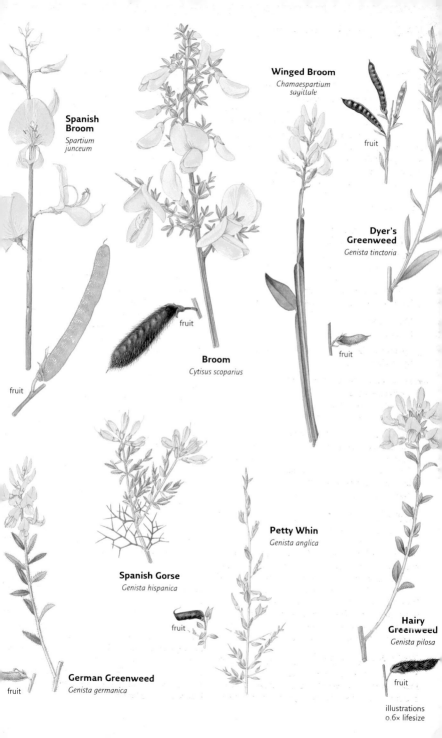

Spanish Broom
Spartium junceum

fruit

Winged Broom
Chamaespartium sagittale

fruit

Dyer's Greenweed
Genista tinctoria

fruit

fruit

Broom
Cytisus scoparius

fruit

Spanish Gorse
Genista hispanica

Petty Whin
Genista anglica

fruit

Hairy Greenweed
Genista pilosa

fruit

German Greenweed
Genista germanica

fruit

illustrations
0.6× lifesize

HALORAGACEAE Water-milfoils

Water-milfoils *Myriophyllum*

Submerged aquatic or sub-aquatic perennials. Leaves in whorls of 3–6, pinnate, with hair-like segments. Flowers tiny and inconspicuous, in terminal emergent spikes; 4 sepals and petals, or these absent; 8 stamens. Fruits separating into up to 4 nutlets. Identification of non-flowering shoots is not always possible with confidence, as some vegetative characters overlap.

Parrot's-feather   *Myriophyllum aquaticum*

Pale, slightly glaucous green *emergent, glandular aquatic* to 200 cm. Leaves 4–6 in a whorl. Flowers 4–6 in a whorl; dioecious, female only in Britain. Habitat Forms dense masses in eutrophic ponds, ditches, canals. Dist. Introduced (native of Central America). First recorded in wild in 1960, highly invasive. Lowland England, Wales.

Alternate Water-milfoil   *Myriophyllum alterniflorum*

Submerged aquatic to 120 cm. Leaves With 6–18 segments, usually 4 in a whorl, *about equalling internodes.* Flowers *Opposite or alternate. Flowering spike drooping in bud*; basal flowers female, with leaf-like bracts; upper flowers male, with small, entire bracts, petals yellow and red. Habitat Lakes, ponds, streams, dykes, in peaty, acid waters; to 780 m. Dist. Native. Widely distributed; common in N and W of BI, scarce in lowlands. (Most of Europe except extreme N.) Fls May–Aug.

Spiked Water-milfoil   *Myriophyllum spicatum*

Submerged aquatic to 250 cm, *with distinct reddish tinge.* Leaves *Rather rigid,* not collapsing when removed from water, usually *4 in a whorl,* 0.5–1.5× as long as internodes, with 13–35 segments. Flowers Flowering spikes erect in bud; flowers in whorls of 4, all but lowest bracts *entire and shorter than flowers*, petals red. Habitat Ponds, lakes, ditches, streams, in clear, eutrophic, usually calcareous waters; will tolerate brackish conditions. Dist. Native. Widespread throughout BI, but becoming scarcer in N and W. (All Europe.) Fls Jun–Jul.

Whorled Water-milfoil   *Myriophyllum verticillatum* VU.

Submerged aquatic to 300 cm, without reddish tinge. Stems *Base of stem with detachable overwintering buds* (turions) in late summer. Leaves Usually 5 in a whorl, with 25–35 segments, 1.5–4× *longer than internodes, collapsing when removed from water.* Flowers *In whorls of 5*; bracts pinnate, not entire, longer than flowers; petals greenish yellow. Habitat Clear calcareous water in lakes, canals, streams, dykes; tolerant of slightly brackish conditions. Dist. Native. Local and declining. Lowland England, central Ireland. (Most of Europe.) Fls Jul–Aug.

ELEAGNACEAE Sea-buckthorn family

Sea-buckthorn   *Hippophae rhamnoides*

Much-branched, thorny, suckering deciduous shrub to 3 m. Leaves Alternate, silvery, 1–8 cm. Flowers Dioecious, 2 sepals, petals absent. Fruits *Berry-like, bright orange*, 6–8 mm. Habitat Fixed coastal dunes, forming dense thickets. Dist. Native. E coast N to Scottish border; widely planted in coastal areas and along roadsides throughout BI. (W coast of Europe; inland central and E Europe.) Fls Mar–Apr, before leaves.

LYTHRACEAE Loosestrifes

Purple-loosestrife   *Lythrum salicaria*

Tall, pubescent perennial to 120 cm. Leaves 4–7 cm, opposite or in whorls of 3. Flowers Regular, 10–15 mm across with epicalyx, in dense, many-flowered inflorescence spike; 6 sepals and petals; 12 stamens. Habitat Tall fens, fen carr, reed swamp, marginal vegetation of lakes, rivers, ponds, canals. Dist. Native. Widespread and locally common throughout BI, but rare in N Scotland. (All Europe except extreme N.) Fls Jun–Aug.

Grass-poly   *Lythrum hyssopifolium* EN. *(B)

Glabrous, ± erect, much-branched annual to 25 cm. Leaves 1–1.5 cm, alternate. Flowers *c.5 mm across, solitary, sessile, in axils of leaves*; 6 petals; 6 stamens. Habitat Winter-flooded disturbed and open ground of arable fields, damp pastures. Dist. Archaeophyte. Very rare, declining. Lowland BI. (All Europe except N.) Fls Jun–Jul.

Water-purslane   *Lythrum portula*

Glabrous, creeping annual to 25 cm, *rooting at nodes.* Leaves *c.*1 cm, opposite. Flowers *Tiny, c.*1 mm *across, in axils of leaves*; 6 sepals and petals; 6 or 12 stamens. Habitat Seasonally flooded, open habitats, woodland rides, pool and reservoir margins, on acid soils. Dist. Native. Throughout BI, especially S and W; rare in N Scotland. (All Europe except extreme N.) Fls Jun–Oct.

Spiked Water-milfoil
Myriophyllum spicatum

Purple-loosestrife
Lythrum salicaria

Sea-buckthorn
Hippophae rhamnoides

Alternate Water-milfoil
Myriophyllum alterniflorum

Grass-poly
Lythrum hyssopifolium

Water-purslane
Lythrum portula

Whorled Water-milfoil
Myriophyllum verticillatum

Parrot's-feather
Myriophyllum aquaticum

illustrations
0.6× lifesize

THYMELAEACEAE Daphnes

Spurge-laurel
Daphne laureola

Small, glabrous evergreen shrub. LEAVES Dark, glossy green, 5–12 cm, crowded towards top of stem. FLOWERS 8–12 mm across, green, forming inflorescence of 5–10 flowers in axillary groups; 4 sepals; petals absent. FRUITS Black, berry-like. HABITAT Deciduous woodland on heavy and calcareous soils; shade-tolerant. DIST. Native in England, Wales, N to Scottish border; planted elsewhere as game cover. (W, S and S-central Europe.) FLS Feb–Mar.

Mezereon
Daphne mezereum VU.

Small, glabrous deciduous shrub to 100 cm. LEAVES 3–10 cm. FLOWERS 3–10 cm across, purple, in 2–4-flowered inflorescence, sessile, on bare twigs. FRUITS Scarlet, berry-like. HABITAT Calcareous woodlands. Commonly grown in gardens and an occasional escape from cultivation. DIST. Native or introduced. Rare, scattered in England, Wales. (Most of Europe except extreme N, W and S.) FLS Feb–Mar, before leaves.

ONAGRACEAE Willowherbs and Evening-primroses

A rather varied family (*see* key on p.308), characterised by the combination of regular flowers with an inferior ovary; 2 or 4(5) free sepals; 2 or 4(5) petals and 2, 4 or 8(10) stamens; fruit is a capsule or berry. Annuals or perennials with simple opposite or alternate leaves; flowers sometimes with a hypanthium (elongated part of flower between top of ovary and base of calyx, an extension of the receptacle).

Willowherbs *Epilobium*
See key to *Epilobium* on p.308.

Great Willowherb, Codlins and Cream
Epilobium hirsutum

Tall, erect, pubescent, rhizomatous perennial to 180 cm, with *dense glandular, spreading hairs*. LEAVES Sessile, *opposite, weakly clasping and decurrent*, 6–12 cm. FLOWERS *15–23 mm across, stigma 4-lobed*. FRUITS Capsule, 5–8 cm. HABITAT River, stream, lake and pond margins, fens, marshes, on fertile soils; to 665 m. DIST. Native. Common throughout BI N to central Scotland; rare further N. (All Europe except extreme N.) FLS Jul–Aug.

Hoary Willowherb
Epilobium parviflorum

Erect, *pubescent, stoloniferous perennial to 60 cm, with dense glandular, spreading hairs*. LEAVES *Sessile, opposite, not clasping or decurrent*, 3–7 cm. FLOWERS 6–9 mm across, pale pink; *stigma 4-lobed*. FRUITS Capsule, 3.5–6.5 cm. HABITAT Disturbed and waste ground, marshes, stream banks; to 365 m. DIST. Native. Common throughout BI, but becoming scarce in N Scotland. (All Europe except extreme N.) FLS Jul–Aug.

Broad-leaved Willowherb
Epilobium montanum

Erect, ± glabrous, stoloniferous perennial to 60 cm. STEMS Smooth. LEAVES *Ovate, opposite, 4–7 cm, rounded at base*; petiole short, 2–6 mm. FLOWERS 6–9 mm across, *stigma 4-lobed*. FRUITS Capsule, 4–8 cm. HABITAT Woodland, waste ground, walls, hedge banks, ditches; also a garden weed. To 845 m. DIST. Native. Common throughout BI. (All Europe.) FLS Jun–Aug.

Spear-leaved Willowherb
Epilobium lanceolatum

Erect, stoloniferous perennial to 60 cm. STEMS *With 4 faint lines*; ± glabrous below; sparse, short, crisped hairs above. LEAVES Lanceolate, mostly alternate, 2–5 cm, *narrowed to 3–10 mm petiole*. FLOWERS 6–7 mm across, *stigma 4-lobed*. FRUITS Capsule 5–7 mm. HABITAT Roadsides, waste ground, walls, dunes, gardens; to 400 m. DIST. Native. SW England; scattered elsewhere in lowland England, Wales. (W, central and S Europe.) FLS Jul–Sep.

Square-stalked Willowherb
Epilobium tetragonum

Erect, stoloniferous perennial to 60 cm, *producing overwintering leaf rosettes in autumn*. STEMS *4-angled*, glabrous below, pubescent above. LEAVES 2–7.5 cm, *narrow, strap-shaped*; lower leaves opposite, middle ones alternate. FLOWERS 6–8 mm across, *calyx tube without glandular hairs*, stigma entire. FRUITS *Long capsule, 6.5–10 cm*. HABITAT Cultivated and waste ground, roadsides, hedge banks, stream sides; lowland. DIST. Native. Widespread in England, Wales, N to Yorkshire. (All Europe except extreme N.) FLS Jul–Aug.

Short-fruited Willowherb
Epilobium obscurum

Erect perennial to 75 cm, *producing leafy stolons*. STEMS With 4 raised lines, glabrous below, pubescent above. LEAVES 3–7 cm, *ovate-lanceolate*, sessile, decurrent. FLOWERS 7–9 mm across; *calyx tube with sparse, spreading glandular hairs*; stigma entire. FRUITS *Capsule, 4–6 cm*. HABITAT Damp woodland, stream sides, ditches, marshes, cultivated ground; to 775 m. DIST. Native. Widespread throughout BI. (All Europe except extreme N and E.) FLS Jul–Aug.

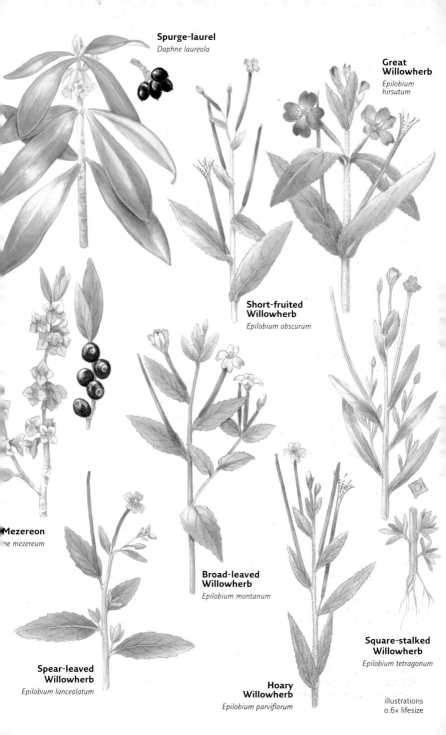

Spurge-laurel
Daphne laureola

Great Willowherb
Epilobium hirsutum

Short-fruited Willowherb
Epilobium obscurum

Mezereon
Daphne mezereum

Broad-leaved Willowherb
Epilobium montanum

Spear-leaved Willowherb
Epilobium lanceolatum

Hoary Willowherb
Epilobium parviflorum

Square-stalked Willowherb
Epilobium tetragonum

illustrations
0.6× lifesize

if	then
Herbs	
Flowers pink	
At least lower leaves in opposite pairs; flowers erect, regular	**Epilobium** (pp.306 and 310)
All leaves alternate; flowers slightly zygomorphic, held horizontally	**Chamerion** (p.310)
Flowers yellow	
4 petals, 8 stamens	**Oenothera** (p.309)
5 petals, 10 stamens	**Ludwigia** (p.310)
Flowers white	
2 petals, 2 stamens	**Circaea** (p.312)
Petals absent	
4 stamens; plant purplish, aquatic	**Ludwigia** (p.310)
Shrub	
Flowers pink, purple; 4 sepals; 4 petals; 8 stamens, projecting beyond corolla	**Fuchsia** (p.312)

Key to Willowherbs *Epilobium*

	if	then
1	▷ Plant wholly prostrate, rooting at nodes; leaves ± circular	*E. brunnescens* (p.310)
	▷ Plant nor wholly prostrate; leaves not ± circular	Go to ▷ **2**
2	▷ Stigma 4-lobed	Go to ▷ **3**
	▷ Stigma knob-shaped	Go to ▷ **6**
3	▷ Stem clothed with dense, spreading glandular and non-glandular hairs	Go to ▷ **4**
	▷ Stem glabrous or with appressed non-glandular hairs (spreading glandular hairs present or not)	Go to ▷ **5**
4	▷ Leaves 6–12 cm, slightly clasping stem; flowers 15–23 mm across, deep pink	*E. hirsutum* (p.306)
	▷ Leaves 3–7 cm, not clasping stem; flowers 6–9 mm across, pale pink	*E. parviflorum* (p.306)
5	▷ All leaves opposite, ovate, rounded at base; petiole short	*E. montanum* (p.306)
	▷ Most leaves alternate, only lower leaves opposite, lanceolate, tapering to petiole; petiole 3–10 mm	*E. lanceolatum* (p.306)

	if	then
6	▷ Upper part of stem with numerous spreading glandular hairs	*E. ciliatum* (p.310)
	▷ Glandular hairs absent, or sparse and confined to calyx tube; with or without appressed non-glandular hairs	Go to ▷ **7**
7	▷ Leaves distinctly stalked, stalks 4–15 mm	*E. roseum* (p.310)
	▷ Leaves ± sessile	Go to ▷ **8**
8	▷ Stems without ridges or raised lines (don't confuse these with lines of hairs)	*E. palustre* (p.310)
	▷ Stems with 2–4 ridges or raised lines	Go to ▷ **9**
9	▷ Stems erect, 25–75 cm; inflorescence and flower buds erect	Go to ▷ **10**
	▷ Small alpines; stems procumbent to ascending, to 25 cm; buds nodding	Go to ▷ **11**
10	▷ Glandular hairs absent; capsules long, 7–10 cm	*E. tetragonum* (p.306)
	▷ Calyx tube with sparse glandular hairs; capsules 4–6 cm	*E. obscurum* (p.306)
11	▷ Leaves lanceolate, 1–2 cm; stolons above ground, with small green leaves; flowers 4–5 mm across	*E. anagallidifolium* (p.310)
	▷ Leaves ovate, 1.5–4 cm; stolons below ground; flowers 8–9 mm across	*E. alsinifolium* (p.310)

Key to Evening-primroses *Oenothera*

	if	then
1	▷ Sepals red-striped	Go to ▷ **2**
	▷ Sepals green	Go to ▷ **4**
2	▷ Green parts of stem with long hairs that have red bulbous bases	Go to ▷ **3**
	▷ Green parts of stem without red-based hairs	*O. stricta* (p.312)
3	▷ Flowers large; petals 30–50 mm	*O. glazioviana* (p.312)
	▷ Petals 20–30 mm	*O. × fallax* (p.312)
4	▷ Petals 15–30 mm, wider than long; capsules 20–30 mm	*O. biennis* (p.312)
	▷ Petals 20–30 mm, as wide as long; capsules 30–40 mm	*O. cambrica* (p.312)

Pale Willowherb
Epilobium roseum

Erect, stoloniferous perennial to 75 cm, *producing overwintering leaf rosettes*. STEMS Glabrous below, with crisped non-glandular and spreading glandular hairs above. LEAVES 3–8 cm, mostly alternate; *distinctly stalked*, petiole 4–15 mm. FLOWERS 4–6 mm across, *petals pale pink*, stigma club-shaped. FRUITS Capsule, 4–7 cm. HABITAT Waste ground on damp soils, moist woodland, hedgerows, gardens; lowland to 560 m. DIST. Native. Scattered and local throughout BI, but rare in Scotland, Ireland. (Most of Europe except extreme N.) FLS Jul–Aug.

American Willowherb
Epilobium ciliatum

Tall, much-branched, often reddish *non-stoloniferous* perennial to 75 cm. STEMS With 4 raised lines; crisped hairs and *numerous spreading glandular hairs above*. LEAVES Opposite, ± glabrous, 3–10 cm. FLOWERS 4–6 mm across, *petals deeply notched*, stigma club-shaped. FRUITS Capsule, 4–6.5 cm, with glandular hairs. HABITAT Gardens, waste ground, roadsides, walls, stream sides, damp woodland. DIST. Introduced (native of North America); first recorded in BI in 1891. Common throughout much of lowland BI, still spreading N and W. (Most of Europe especially NW.) FLS Jun–Aug.

Marsh Willowherb
Epilobium palustre

Erect, sub-glabrous, stoloniferous perennial to 60 cm. STEMS *Stolons long and producing bulbil-like buds at tips in autumn; stems smooth, without raised lines.* LEAVES Lanceolate, rather glaucous, 0.5–1.0 cm, opposite, ± sessile. FLOWERS 4–6 mm across, petals pale pink, stigma club-shaped. FRUITS Capsule, 5–8 cm. HABITAT Fens, marshes, valley bogs, woodland flushes on mildly acid soils; to 845 m. DIST. Native. Frequent throughout BI. (All Europe except extreme S.) FLS Jul–Aug.

Alpine Willowherb
Epilobium anagallidifolium

Prostrate to erect, ± glabrous, stoloniferous alpine perennial to 20 cm. STEMS *Stolons above ground, with small, leafy rosettes and pairs of small green leaves.* LEAVES *Yellowish green, entire or faintly toothed*, opposite, 1–2 cm, lanceolate. FLOWERS 4–5 mm across, in drooping inflorescence. FRUITS Reddish capsule, 2.5–4 cm. HABITAT Mossy mountain flushes, springs, stream sides, on acid or basic soils; to 1190 m. DIST. Native. Scottish Highlands. (N Europe, mts of central and S Europe.) FLS Jul–Aug.

Chickweed Willowherb
Epilobium alsinifolium *(R)

Prostrate to erect, ± glabrous, stoloniferous alpine perennial to 20 cm. STEMS *Stolons below ground, with pairs of yellowish scale-leaves.* LEAVES *Rather glaucous, distinctly toothed*, opposite, 1.5–4 cm, ovate-lanceolate. FLOWERS 8–9 mm across. FRUITS Capsule, 3–5 cm. HABITAT Mossy mountain flushes, springs, stream sides, on acid or basic soils; to 1140 m. DIST. Native. N England, N Wales (rare), Scotland. (Arctic and montane Europe.) FLS Jul–Aug.

New Zealand Willowherb
Epilobium brunnescens

Prostrate, creeping, ± glabrous perennial to 20 cm, rooting at nodes. LEAVES *3–7 mm, orbicular, ± entire*, smooth above. FLOWERS *Solitary*, erect, 3–4 mm across. FRUITS Capsule, 2–4 cm, peduncle to 6 cm. HABITAT Open areas on grits, shales, gravel, shingle, walls, quarries. DIST. Introduced (native of New Zealand). Widespread in upland areas of N and W; spreading. FLS Jul–Aug.

Rosebay Willowherb
Chamerion angustifolium

Tall perennial to 150 cm. LEAVES *5–15 cm, all spirally arranged*. FLOWERS *2–3 cm across, slightly zygomorphic, held horizontally*; in long, spike-like inflorescence; stigma 4-lobed. FRUITS Capsule, 2.5–8 cm. HABITAT Forms dense stands on waste ground, roadsides, railways, heathland, woodland clearings, disturbed and burnt ground, upland scree; to 975 m. DIST. Native. Common throughout BI. (All Europe, but rare in S.) FLS Jul–Sep.

Hampshire-purslane
Ludwigia palustris

Prostrate to ascending, glabrous *reddish-purple* submerged to emergent aquatic perennial. LEAVES Reddish purple, 1.5–3 cm, in opposite pairs. FLOWERS *Tiny, 3 mm across*; 4 sepals; *petals absent*. HABITAT Shallow pools, streams, seasonally flooded patches in woodland glades. DIST. Native. Very rare; ± confined to New Forest. (W, central and S Europe.) FLS Jun.

Water Primrose
Ludwigia grandiflora

Vigorous, densely pubescent, prostrate to ascending aquatic perennial. *Free-floating, forming dense rafts, or rooted in mud.* STEMS Emergent stems to 150 cm. LEAVES 3–13 cm, alternate, lanceolate or suborbicular. FLOWERS *Axillary, large, showy, bright yellow*; 5 sepals; 5 petals, 12–30 mm; 10 stamens. HABITAT Margins of shallow water bodies, rivers, lakes. Highly invasive; spreads by seed and shoot fragments. DIST. Introduced (native of South and Central America). In a few sites in lowland England. (Spreading rapidly N in W Europe.) FLS Jul–Sep. *Not illustrated.*

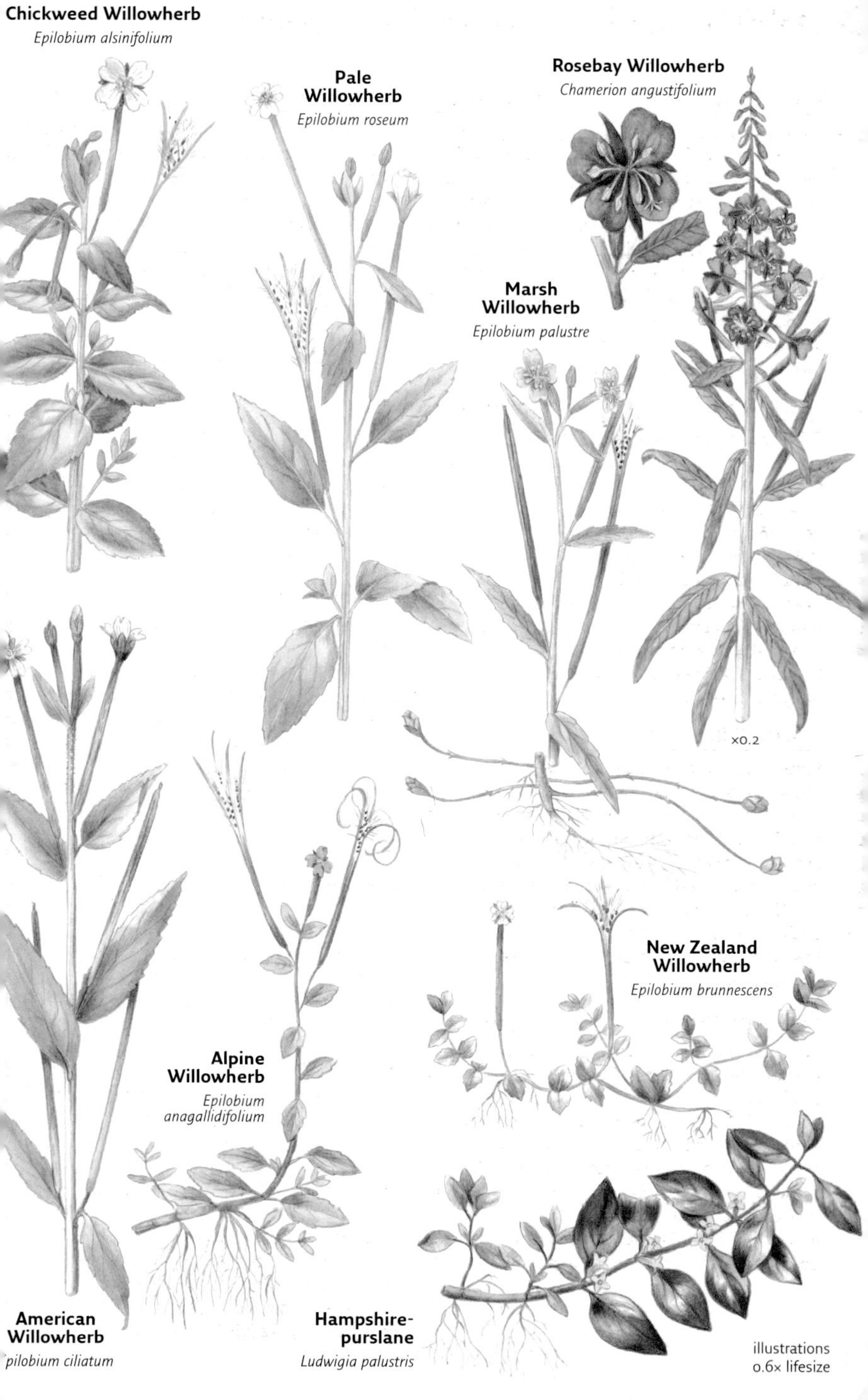

Chickweed Willowherb
Epilobium alsinifolium

Pale Willowherb
Epilobium roseum

Rosebay Willowherb
Chamerion angustifolium

Marsh Willowherb
Epilobium palustre

×0.2

American Willowherb
Epilobium ciliatum

Alpine Willowherb
Epilobium anagallidifolium

Hampshire-purslane
Ludwigia palustris

New Zealand Willowherb
Epilobium brunnescens

illustrations
0.6× lifesize

Evening-primroses *Oenothera*
See key to Oenothera on p.309.

Large-flowered Evening-primrose
Oenothera glazioviana

Tall, erect biennial to 180 cm, *densely covered by long hairs with red bulbous bases*. Our commonest evening-primrose. Flowers *Large*, in erect inflorescence; *sepals red-striped*, pubescent; petals 30-50 mm, wholly yellow; *style longer than stamens*. Fruits Capsule, widest near base. Habitat Roadside verges, railways, waste ground, coastal sand-dunes. Dist. Introduced (native of North America). Throughout England, Wales; rare in Scotland, Ireland. (Established in W and central Europe.) Fls Jun–Sep.

Common Evening-primrose
Oenothera biennis

Tall, erect biennial to 150 cm; *green parts of stems and capsules without red-based hairs*. Flowers In erect inflorescence; *sepals green; petals 15-30 mm, wider than long*. Fruits Capsule, 2-3 cm, *all glandular-hairy*. Habitat Waste ground, roadsides, railways, sand-dunes. Dist. Introduced (native of North America). Established throughout lowland England; rare elsewhere. (Most of Europe except extreme N and S.) Fls Jun–Sep.

Intermediate Evening-primrose
Oenothera × fallax

Tall, erect biennial to 150 cm; *green parts of stems and capsules with red-based, bulbous hairs*. Flowers *Sepals red-striped, petals 20-30 mm, style same length as stamens*. Fruits Capsule, 2-3 cm, wholly glandular-hairy. Habitat Waste ground, sandy places, dunes. Dist. Thinly scattered throughout England; rare elsewhere. Fls Jun–Sep. Note This is the hybrid between *O. glazioviana* and *O. biennis*, and is sometimes found in the absence of its parents.

Small-flowered Evening-primrose
Oenothera cambrica

Tall, erect biennial to 120 cm; green parts of stem and capsules with or without red-based hairs. Flowers *Sepals green, petals 20-30 mm*. Fruits Capsule, 3-4 cm, *only upper part glandular-hairy*. Habitat Coastal sand-dunes, waste places, docks, roadsides, riverbanks. Dist. Introduced (probably native of N America). Scattered throughout England, Wales; absent from Ireland. Fls Jun–Sep.

Fragrant Evening-primrose
Oenothera stricta

Tall, erect biennial to 100 cm; *green parts of stem without red-based hairs*. Flowers Sepals red-striped, petals 15-35 mm, yellow turning reddish when withering. Fruits Capsule, widest near apex. Habitat Open sandy ground, established coastal dunes casual inland. Dist. Introduced (native of Chile) Very scarce, scattered throughout England, Wales (W and central Europe.) Fls Jun–Sep.

Fuchsia
Fuchsia magellanica

Small shrub to 300 cm. Leaves Opposite, slightly pubescent. Flowers Solitary, pendulous; 4 sepals and petals; 8 stamens, longer than corolla. Fruits Black berry. Habitat Hedgerows, scrub, stream sides. Dist. Introduced (native of Chile, Argentina) Widely planted in hedges and now naturalised, especially in SW and Ireland. Fls Jun–Sep.

Enchanter's-nightshade
Circaea lutetiana

Erect, stoloniferous perennial to 70 cm. Leaves 4-10 cm, *obscurely toothed, rounded at base; petiole furrowed above*, pubescent. Flowers *Open flowers distributed along inflorescence; flower stalks and sepals (2) glandular-pubescent*; 2 petals, 2-4 mm, notched to at least halfway. Fruits *c*.3 mm, densely covered by stiff, hooked bristles. Habitat Woodlands hedgerows, stream banks; also a garden weed. Dist. Native. Common throughout BI N to central Scotland. (Most of Europe except NE.) Fls Jun–Aug.

Alpine Enchanter's-nightshade
Circaea alpina

Erect, stoloniferous perennial to 30 cm. Similar to *C. lutetiana*, but *leaves smaller, 2-6 cm, cordate at base strongly toothed; petiole winged, not furrowed glabrous; open flowers clustered at top of inflorescence flower stalks and sepals glabrous; petals 0.6-1.5 mm shallowly notched; fruit 1-1.5 mm, with soft bristles.* Habitat Upland woodland, shaded rocks, scree waterfalls, stream banks; to 755 m. Dist. Native Very rare. Lake District, N Wales, W Scotland. (N Europe, mts of central and S Europe.) Fls Jul–Aug Note The sterile hybrid between *C. lutetiana* and *C. alpina, C. × intermedia,* intermediate between the two parent species, is widespread in upland Britain often in the absence of one or both parents. It occur in similar habitats to *C. alpina*, but also occasionally on disturbed ground.

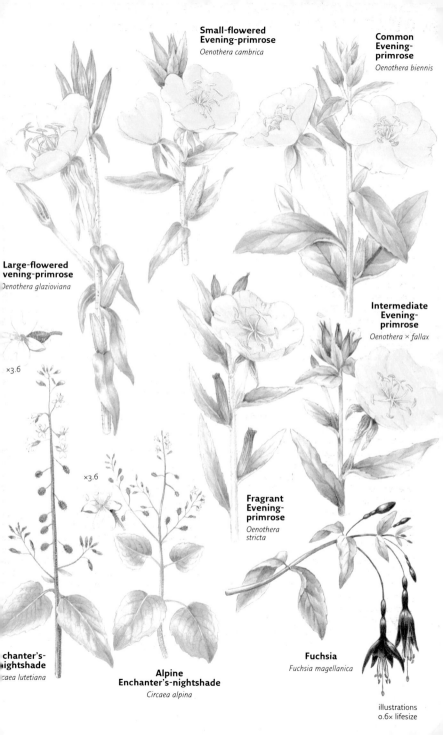

Small-flowered Evening-primrose
Oenothera cambrica

Common Evening-primrose
Oenothera biennis

Large-flowered Evening-primrose
Oenothera glazioviana

×3.6

Intermediate Evening-primrose
Oenothera × fallax

×3.6

Fragrant Evening-primrose
Oenothera stricta

Enchanter's-nightshade
Circaea lutetiana

Alpine Enchanter's-nightshade
Circaea alpina

Fuchsia
Fuchsia magellanica

illustrations
0.6× lifesize

CORNACEAE Dogwoods

A family of deciduous or evergreen trees and shrubs or perennial herbs. Leaves are opposite or alternate, simple and without stipules. Flowers are small, in panicles or umbel-like inflorescences; regular, hermaphrodite; 4 (or 5) free sepals and petals, sepals small, petals sometimes absent; 4 (or 5) stamens; ovary inferior, 1–3 styles. Fruit is a drupe.

Dogwood
Cornus sanguinea

Deciduous shrub to 4 m. TWIGS *purplish red*, buds naked (without bud scales). LEAVES Opposite, 4–8 cm, *with 3–4 pairs of lateral veins*, becoming deep purplish red in autumn. FLOWERS In umbel-like inflorescence; sepals tiny; 4 petals, 4–6 mm; ovary inferior. FRUITS Berry-like, *black*, 6–8 mm. HABITAT Scrub, hedgerows, wood margins, on calcareous soils. DIST. Native. Common in England, Wales, N to Yorkshire; rare in Ireland. (Most of Europe.) FLS Jun–Jul.

Red Osier Dogwood
Cornus sericea

Deciduous shrub to 3 m. TWIGS dark red or greenish yellow. LEAVES 4–10 cm, long and tapering, *with 6 pairs of lateral veins*. FLOWERS Petals 2–4 mm. FRUITS *White*, 4–7 mm, *rounded at base, stone spherical*. HABITAT Planted in parks, roadsides; naturalised in woodland, riverbanks. DIST. Introduced (native of E North America). Scattered throughout BI; increasing.

Cornelian Cherry
Cornus mas

Deciduous shrub or small tree to 8 m. TWIGS greenish grey. LEAVES 4–10 cm. FLOWERS *With 4 large yellow petal-like bracts*. FRUITS 12–15 mm, red. HABITAT Popular garden species, planted on roadside verges, hedgerows; rarely naturalised. DIST. (Central and SE Europe.) FLS *Appearing before leaves*.

Dwarf Cornel
Cornus suecica

Erect perennial to 20 cm. LEAVES 1–3 cm, pubescent above, glabrous beneath. FLOWERS *Inflorescence appearing flower-like, an umbel of 8–25 flowers surrounded by 4 white ovate bracts, 5–8 mm*. FRUITS Red, *c.*5 mm. HABITAT Among dwarf shrubs and mosses on acid mountain moorland; to 915 m. DIST. Native. Scottish Highlands; very rare in N England. (N Europe.) FLS Jul–Aug.

SANTALACEAE Bastard-toadflax and sandalwood family

Bastard-toadflax
Thesium humifusum

Prostrate, semi-parasitic yellowish-green perennial to 45 cm. LEAVES Alternate, 5–15 mm. FLOWERS *Small*, *c.*3 mm across; 5 *greenish* perianth segments. HABITAT Short turf on dry, thin calcareous soils on warm slopes. DIST. Native. Rare. Chalk areas of S England. (W Europe.) FLS Jun–Aug.

VISCACEAE Mistletoes

Mistletoe
Viscum album

Woody evergreen partial parasite on branches of trees. STEMS To 100 cm, green, much branched. LEAVES 5–8 cm. FLOWERS Dioecious, in compact 3–5-flowered inflorescence; sepals small or absent, 4 petals. FRUITS White berry, *c.*10 mm. HABITAT Orchards, hedgerows, parks, gardens, on apples, limes, hawthorn, poplars; also on maples, willows. DIST. Native. Local in England, Wales; rare in Scotland, Ireland. (Most of Europe.) FLS Feb–Mar.

CELASTRACEAE Spindles

Spindle
Euonymus europaeus

Much-branched deciduous shrub or small tree to 6 m. TWIGS *green*, angled. LEAVES Opposite, glabrous, 3–13 cm. FLOWERS 8–10 mm across, 4 sepals and petals. FRUITS *Bright pink*, 10–15 mm, *opening to expose fleshy orange arils enclosing the seeds*. HABITAT Hedges, scrub, wood margins, on calcareous, base-rich soils. Widely planted. DIST. Native. Widespread in Britain N to S Scotland, and in Ireland. (Most of Europe.) FLS May–Jun.

AQUIFOLIACEAE Hollies

Holly
Ilex aquifolium

Small, dioecious evergreen tree to 15 m. BARK Grey, smooth. TWIGS green. LEAVES Thick, glossy, glabrous, with spiny margins, or mostly entire on older trees. FLOWERS *c.*6 mm across, 4 sepals and petals. FRUITS Berry-like, red, 7–12 mm. HABITAT Deciduous woodland on acid soils, wood pasture, scrub, hedgerows; to 600 m. DIST. Native. Common throughout BI. (W and central Europe.) FLS May–Aug.

BUXACEAE Box

Box
Buxus sempervirens

Evergreen shrub or small tree to 5 m. BRANCHES Twigs green. LEAVES Opposite, entire, thick, glossy, 1–2.5 cm. FLOWERS Monoecious, borne in axillary clusters, whitish green; 4 or several sepals; petals absent. FRUITS Capsule, *c.*8 mm, valves 'horned'. HABITAT Scrub, open woodland, on steep chalk slopes in natural range; woodland in naturalised range. DIST. Native. Very local as a native in Kent, Surrey, Gloucestershire; widely planted and naturalised throughout BI, but rare in N Scotland, Ireland. (S Europe.) FLS Apr–May.

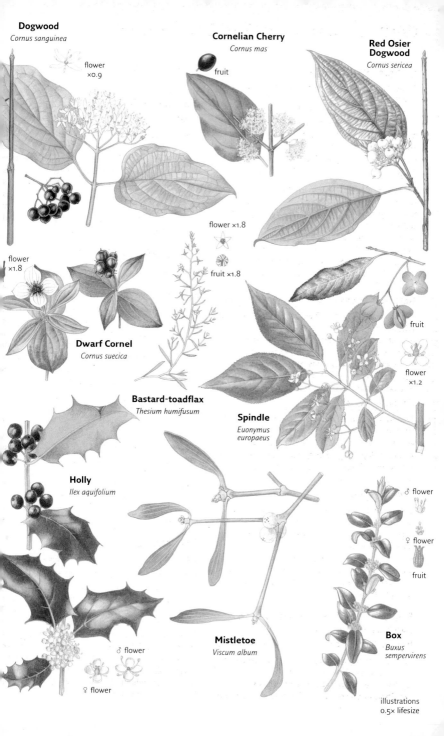

Dogwood
Cornus sanguinea

flower
×0.9

Cornelian Cherry
Cornus mas

fruit

Red Osier Dogwood
Cornus sericea

flower ×1.8

fruit ×1.8

flower
×1.8

Dwarf Cornel
Cornus suecica

fruit

flower
×1.2

Bastard-toadflax
Thesium humifusum

Spindle
Euonymus europaeus

Holly
Ilex aquifolium

♂ flower

♀ flower

fruit

Mistletoe
Viscum album

Box
Buxus sempervirens

♂ flower

♀ flower

illustrations
0.5× lifesize

EUPHORBIACEAE Spurges

A varied family consisting of 2 herbaceous genera in Britain: *Euphorbia*, the spurges; and *Mercurialis*, mercuries. Leaves are simple, alternate. Inflorescence is complex; flowers are unisexual, monoecious or dioecious; 3 or 5 sepals and petals, or these absent; 1 to many stamens; ovary superior. Fruit is a capsule separating into 3 parts.

Dog's Mercury   *Mercurialis perennis*

Erect, rhizomatous, pubescent, unbranched perennial to 40 cm. Dioecious. LEAVES 3–8 cm, opposite. FLOWERS 4–5 mm across; 3 tepals, sepal-like; *female flowers long-stalked*, in axillary clusters; male flowers on pendulous, catkin-like spikes. FRUITS Capsule, 6–8 mm. HABITAT Deciduous woodland, old hedgerows, hillside scree, limestone pavement, calcareous or base-rich soils; to 1005 m. DIST. Native. Common throughout Britain except N Scotland; very rare in Ireland (Burren only). (Most of Europe except extreme N.) FLS Feb–Apr.

Annual Mercury   *Mercurialis annua*

Erect, ± glabrous, branched annual to 50 cm. Dioecious. LEAVES 1.5–5 cm. FLOWERS *Female flowers axillary, sessile*. HABITAT Gardens, allotments, waste ground, on light, fertile soils. DIST. Archaeophyte. Common in S England, SE of line from Wash to Severn; scattered further N; absent from Scotland. (Most of Europe.) FLS Jul–Oct.

Spurges *Euphorbia*

See key and introduction to *Euphorbia* on p.318.

Purple Spurge   *Euphorbia peplis* EX.

Prostrate, glabrous, glaucous to purplish annual, to 6 cm. LEAVES 3–10 mm, *markedly unequal at base*; stipules linear. Bracts similar to leaves. HABITAT Sandy, shingly beaches. DIST. Extinct; last record in Channel Is (Alderney) in 1976. (S and W Europe.) FLS Jul–Sep.

Irish Spurge   *Euphorbia hyberna* VU.

Erect, rhizomatous perennial to 60 cm. LEAVES 5–10 cm, *glabrous above, thinly pubescent beneath*. Bracts rounded at base, yellowish; glands rounded, yellowish. FRUITS *Strongly warted capsule*, 5–6 mm. HABITAT Damp woodlands, shaded stream banks, hedge banks, on acid soils; to 500 m. DIST. Native. Locally common in SW Ireland; very rare in SW England. (W and S Europe.) FLS Apr–Jul.

Marsh Spurge   *Euphorbia palustris*

Tall, tufted, rhizomatous, glaucous, glabrous perennial to 150 cm, *with numerous non-flowering branches*. LEAVES 20–60 mm, turning reddish in autumn. Bracts yellowish, glands rounded; in umbel with >5 rays. FRUITS Capsule, 4.5–6 mm, covered by tubercles. HABITAT Wet woodlands, riverbanks, ditches, wet grassland near sea. DIST. *Not BI*. (Most of Europe except extreme N; rare in Mediterranean.) FLS May–Jun.

Sweet Spurge   *Euphorbia dulcis*

Erect, rhizomatous perennial to 50 cm. LEAVES 3–7 cm, sparsely pubescent to ± glabrous. Bracts green, *base truncate*; *glands rounded, green turning purple*; in 5-rayed umbel. FRUITS Capsule, 2–4 mm, deeply grooved, glabrous with prominent warts. HABITAT Woodland, scrub, roadsides, riverbanks. DIST. Introduced. Naturalised in scattered localities throughout Britain. (W and central Europe.) FLS May–Jul.

Broad-leaved Spurge   *Euphorbia platyphyllos*

Erect, unbranched, glabrous or pubescent annual to 80 cm. LEAVES 1–4.5 cm, *deeply cordate at base*; umbel with 5 branches, *bracts at base of umbel similar to leaves, but markedly different from bracts above*; glands rounded. FRUITS Capsule, 2–3 mm, with hemispherical tubercles. HABITAT Arable and waste ground on heavy soils. DIST. Archaeophyte. Very local, declining. S England. (S, W and central Europe.) FLS Jun–Oct.

Upright Spurge   *Euphorbia serrulata*

Erect, glabrous annual to 80 cm. Similar to *E. platyphyllos*, but leaves narrower; umbel with 2–5 rays, *bracts at base of umbel intermediate between leaves and bracts above*; capsule glabrous, with cylindrical tubercles. HABITAT Woodland clearings, recent coppice, on limestone. DIST. Native. Rare. Gloucestershire, Monmouthshire. Naturalised as garden escape in scattered localities in lowland England. (S, central and W Europe.) FLS Jun–Oct.

Sun Spurge   *Euphorbia helioscopia*

Erect, glabrous, unbranched annual to 50 cm. LEAVES 1.5–3 cm, *obovate*, toothed; umbel 5-rayed, *all bracts similar to leaves*; glands rounded, green. FRUITS Smooth, glabrous capsule, 3–5 mm. HABITAT Arable land, waste ground, roadsides, gardens; lowland to 450 m. DIST. Archaeophyte. Common throughout most of BI, but rare in N Scotland, W Ireland. (All Europe.) FLS May–Oct.

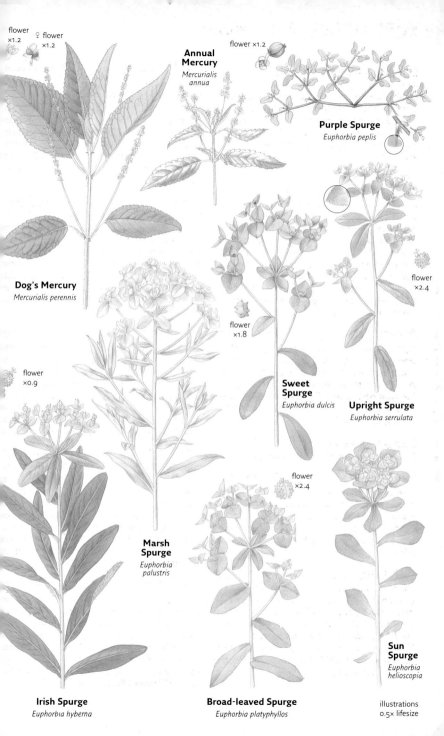

flower ×1.2 ♀ flower ×1.2

Annual Mercury
Mercurialis annua

flower ×1.2

Purple Spurge
Euphorbia peplis

Dog's Mercury
Mercurialis perennis

flower ×2.4

flower ×1.8

Sweet Spurge
Euphorbia dulcis

Upright Spurge
Euphorbia serrulata

flower ×0.9

Marsh Spurge
Euphorbia palustris

flower ×2.4

Broad-leaved Spurge
Euphorbia platyphyllos

Sun Spurge
Euphorbia helioscopia

Irish Spurge
Euphorbia hyberna

illustrations
0.5× lifesize

The 'flowers' of the spurges look a bit of a mystery. The individual flowers are arranged in a cup-like condensed inflorescence, the cyathium, the whole resembling a single conventional flower. The cup contains several male flowers, these each consisting of a single stamen, and a single female flower on a long stalk, and with 4–5 conspicuous glands arranged around the rim. The cyathia are borne on branches arising from the leaf axils, the primary branches, or rays, in the form of an umbel. The bracts are leafy but often different from the leaves. Spurges are poisonous and the milky latex can be a skin irritant.

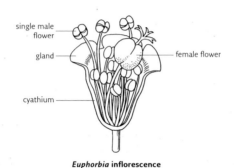

single male
flower

gland

female flower

cyathium

Euphorbia **inflorescence**

	if	then
1	▷ Prostrate purplish maritime annual; leaf bases very asymmetrical (extinct in BI)	*E. peplis* (p.316)
	▷ Not prostrate purplish marine annual; leaves symmetrical at base	Go to ▷ **2**
2	▷ Leaves opposite	*E. lathyris* (p.320)
	▷ Leaves alternate	Go to ▷ **3**
3	▷ Glands crescent-shaped, looking like horns of a cow	Go to ▷ **4**
	▷ Outside edge of glands rounded	Go to ▷ **11**
4	▷ Stem glabrous	Go to ▷ **5**
	▷ Stem pubescent; leaf rosette at apex of 1st year's shoot	*E. amygdaloides* (p.320)
5	▷ Annuals with single stems	Go to ▷ **6**
	▷ Biennial or perennial, with several stems	Go to ▷ **7**
6	▷ Leaves oval with short stalks	*E. peplus* (p.320)
	▷ Leaves linear, sessile	*E. exigua* (p.320)
7	▷ Leaves succulent, <2 cm long; without a rhizome; maritime plants	Go to ▷ **8**
	▷ Leaves not succulent, >2 cm long; rhizomatous; not maritime	Go to ▷ **9**

	if	then
8	▷ Leaves ovate-oblong; midrib obscure beneath	*E. paralias* (p.320)
	▷ Leaves obovate, broadest above middle; midrib prominent beneath	*E. portlandica* (p.320)
9	▷ Leaves ≤2 mm wide, linear	*E. cyparissias* (p.320)
	▷ Leaves ≥4 mm wide	Go to ▷ **10**
10	▷ Leaves widest above middle, tapering towards base	*E. esula* (p.320)
	▷ Leaves widest at or below middle, abruptly narrowed at base	*E. × pseudovirgata* (p.320)
11	▷ Unbranched annuals	Go to ▷ **12**
	▷ Rhizomatous perennials	Go to ▷ **13**
12	▷ All bracts similar to leaves; leaves not cordate	*E. helioscopia* (p.316)
	▷ Bracts at base of umbel similar to leaves but markedly different from bracts above; leaves cordate	*E. platyphyllos* (p.316)
	▷ Bracts at base of umbel intermediate between leaves and bracts above	*E. serrulata* (p.316)
13	▷ Tall plant with numerous non-flowering branches; leaves turning reddish in autumn	*E. palustris* • (p.316)
	▷ Without non-flowering branches; leaves not turning reddish	Go to ▷ **14**
14	▷ Leaves oblanceolate; umbel with 4–6 rays	Go to ▷ **15**
	▷ Leaves linear; umbel with ≤15 rays	*E. seguierana* • (p.320)
15	▷ Bracts rounded at base, yellowish; glands yellow	*E. hyberna* (p.316)
	▷ Bracts truncate at base, green; glands green turning purple	*E. dulcis* (p.316)

Caper Spurge
Euphorbia lathyris

Erect, glabrous, glaucous biennial to 200 cm in 2nd year. LEAVES *Opposite, in 4 rows*, 4-20 cm; umbel 2-6-rayed, bracts at base triangular-lanceolate; glands horned. FRUITS Smooth, glabrous capsule. HABITAT Waste places, old gardens, open woodland, close to habitation as escape from cultivation or casual. DIST. Archaeophyte. Throughout BI, but rare in N and W Britain, Ireland. (S, W and central Europe.) FLS Jun-Jul.

Dwarf Spurge
Euphorbia exigua

Erect, glabrous, glaucous *annual* to 20 cm. LEAVES *Linear, sessile*; umbel 3-rayed; *bracts similar to leaves, glands horned*. FRUITS Smooth, glabrous capsule, 2 mm. HABITAT Arable weed on light calcareous soils. DIST. Archaeophyte. Widespread but declining. Local SE of line from Humber to Wash; rare elsewhere; absent from Scotland, rare in Ireland. (Most of Europe except extreme N.) FLS Jun-Oct.

Petty Spurge
Euphorbia peplus

Erect, glabrous green annual to 30 cm. LEAVES *Ovate-obovate, short-stalked*; umbel 3-rayed; *bracts similar to leaves*, glands horned. FRUITS Glabrous, winged capsule, 2 mm. HABITAT Weed of gardens, cultivated land, waste ground, on fertile soils. DIST. Archaeophyte. Common throughout most of BI, but scarce in extreme N. (Most of Europe except extreme N.) FLS Apr-Nov.

Sea Spurge
Euphorbia paralias

Prostrate to erect, glabrous, glaucous perennial to 40 cm, with unbranched sterile and flowering stems. Bracts and leaves markedly different. LEAVES *Ovate-oblong*, sessile, fleshy, *blunt*, 0.5-2 cm, crowded and overlapping, *midrib obscure beneath*; umbel 3-6-rayed; glands horned. FRUITS Capsule, 4 mm, rough all over; *seeds smooth*. HABITAT Sandy shores, sand-dunes, fine shingle. DIST. Native. Local on coasts of Britain, Ireland, N to Solway. (Coasts of W and S Europe.) FLS Jul-Oct.

Portland Spurge
Euphorbia portlandica

Erect, glabrous biennial or perennial to 40 cm, most stems flowering. Bracts and leaves different. LEAVES *Obovate, widest above middle*, somewhat fleshy, *blunt with sharp point*, 0.5-2 cm, *midrib prominent beneath*; umbel 3-6-rayed; glands horned. FRUITS Capsule, 3 mm, rough near midline; *seeds pitted*. HABITAT Sandy shores, limestone cliffs. DIST. Native. W coast of BI, N to Clyde and E to I of Wight. (W Europe.) FLS May-Sep.

Wood Spurge
Euphorbia amygdaloide

Erect, *pubescent* perennial to 90 cm, *flowering in 2n year from top of previous year's stem*. LEAVES 3-8 cm umbel 5-10-rayed; *bracts yellow, fused at base*; gland horned. FRUITS Rough capsule, 4 mm. HABITAT Ol woods, coppice, hedge banks, on mildly acid soils DIST. Native. Local in lowland Britain, N to N Wale absent from Ireland. (NW, central and S Europe.) FL Mar-May. NOTE Ssp. *robbiae*, with shiny, glabrous dark green leaves, is widely cultivated and occasion ally becomes naturalised.

Leafy Spurge
Euphorbia esu

Erect, glabrous, rhizomatous perennial to 60 cm, wit numerous axillary non-flowering branches. LEAVE 20-45 mm × 5-10 mm, *oblanceolate, widest above mic dle, tapering to base*; umbel bracts markedly differer from those above; glands with short horns. FRUIT Deeply grooved capsule, 2.5-3 mm. HABITAT Wast ground, road verges. DIST. Introduced. Naturalised i scattered localities throughout Britain. (Most c Europe except N.) FLS May-Jul.

Twiggy Spurge
Euphorbia × pseudovirga
(*E. esula × E. waldstein*

Erect, glabrous, rhizomatous perennial to 100 cm Similar to *E. esula*, but leaves 4-5 mm wide, linear t lanceolate, widest at or below middle, or ± parallel sided, and abruptly narrowed at base. HABITAT Roa verges, waste ground, tracks, hedgerows. DIST Introduced. Naturalised in scattered localitie throughout Britain; local, but more frequent than *F esula*. (S, E and E-central Europe.) FLS May-Jul.

Cypress Spurge
Euphorbia cyparissia

Glabrous, rhizomatous perennial to 50 cm, wit numerous erect flowering and non-flowering stem LEAVES *Narrow, ≤2 mm wide, linear, numerous, thos on non-flowering shoots crowded;* umbel 9-15-rayec umbel bracts markedly different from those abov which become reddish; glands horned. HABITA Commonly cultivated, occurring as garden escape o roadsides, tracksides, banks, walls, calcareous grass land. DIST. Introduced. Naturalised throughout B but rare in Scotland, Ireland. (Most of Europe excep extreme N and S.) FLS May-Aug.

Séguier's Spurge
Euphorbia seguierar

Glabrous, glaucous, tufted perennial to 60 cr LEAVES 10-35 mm, linear, acute, erect; *umbel with u to 15 rays*; glands rounded. FRUITS Capsule, 2-3 mn HABITAT Dry calcareous grassland, riverbank DIST. *Not BI*. (Most of Europe except N and extrem S.) FLS Jun-Aug.

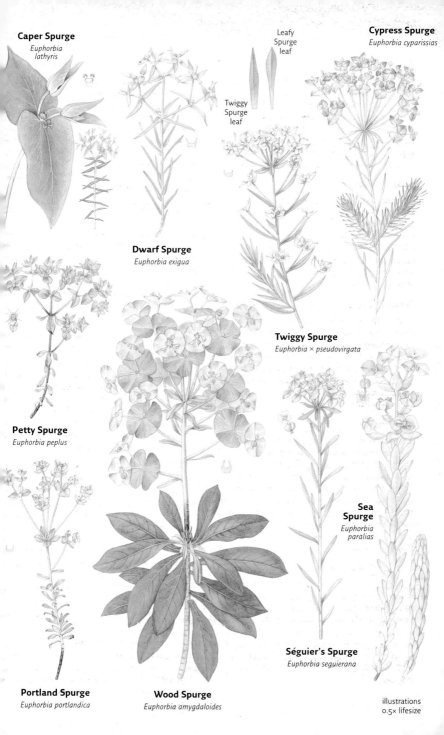

Caper Spurge
Euphorbia lathyris

Leafy Spurge leaf

Twiggy Spurge leaf

Cypress Spurge
Euphorbia cyparissias

Dwarf Spurge
Euphorbia exigua

Twiggy Spurge
Euphorbia × pseudovirgata

Petty Spurge
Euphorbia peplus

Sea Spurge
Euphorbia paralias

Portland Spurge
Euphorbia portlandica

Wood Spurge
Euphorbia amygdaloides

Séguier's Spurge
Euphorbia seguierana

illustrations
0.5× lifesize

RHAMNACEAE Buckthorns

Deciduous shrubs or small trees. Leaves simple, with stipules. Flowers small, solitary or in axillary clusters; 4-5 petals and sepals; receptacle cup-shaped; ovary superior. Fruits are a black berry.

Buckthorn   *Rhamnus cathartica*

Thorny deciduous shrub or small tree to 8 m. BARK Inner side of peeled bark orange. BUDS with scales. LEAVES 3-9 cm, margin toothed, with 2-4 pairs of lateral veins. FLOWERS 4 mm across, 4 sepals and petals. FRUITS Black berry, 6-10 mm. HABITAT Damp woodland, scrub, hedgerows, fen carr, on calcareous soils; lowland to 380 m. DIST. Native. SE of line from Humber to Severn; rare in Wales and SW; scattered in central Ireland. (Most of Europe except extreme N and S.) FLS May-Jun.

Alder Buckthorn   *Frangula alnus* *(NI)

Thornless deciduous shrub or small tree to 5 m. BARK Inner side of peeled bark yellow. BUDS without bud scales, pubescent. LEAVES 2-7 cm, shining green, entire, with 7 pairs of lateral veins. FLOWERS 3 mm across, 5 sepals and petals. FRUITS Black berry, 6-10 mm. HABITAT Heaths, valley mires, fen peat, scrub, hedgerows, woodland; lowland to 450 m. DIST. Native. Local throughout BI except Scotland. (Most of Europe except extreme N and S.) FLS May-Jun.

LINACEAE Flaxes

Annuals or perennials, with simple, entire leaves that lack stipules (*see* key on p.324). Flowers bisexual, regular; 4-5 sepals and petals, free; 4-5 stamens; ovary superior. Fruits are an 8-10-valved capsule.

Pale Flax   *Linum bienne*

Erect, glabrous annual or perennial, with several stems, to 60 cm. LEAVES Alternate, 10-25 mm × *0.5-1.5 mm*, with 1-3 veins. FLOWERS Pale blue; *sepals as long as capsule, tapering to tip*, inner ones with glandular hairs; petals 8-12 mm; *stigmas club-shaped*. FRUITS Capsule, 4-6 mm. HABITAT Dry, well-drained, permanent pastures near sea; lowland. DIST. Native. S and SW England, Wales, SE Ireland. (W and S Europe.) FLS May-Sep.

Flax   *Linum usitatissimum*

Similar to *L. bienne*, but larger and always annual; stems solitary, to 85 cm; *leaves 1.5-3 mm wide*, with 3 veins; sepals 6-9 mm; *petals 12-20 mm; capsule 6-9 mm*. HABITAT Casual on waste ground, roadsides. Not known in wild. DIST. Introduced. Formerly cultivated for fibre, now increasingly grown for linseed oil; also a birdseed alien. Throughout BI, but rare in Scotland, Ireland. FLS May-Sep.

Perennial Flax   *Linum perenne*

Glabrous, glaucous perennial, with several stems, to 60 cm. LEAVES Alternate, 10-20 mm × 1-3.5 mm *with 1 vein*. FLOWERS *Sky-blue*; sepals 3.5-6 mm, *c.* as long as capsule; *inner sepals rounded at tip, with pale border*; petals 13-20 mm; *stigmas spherical*. FRUITS Capsule, 5.5-7.5 mm. HABITAT Permanent well-drained calcareous grassland. DIST. Native (the British plant is ssp. *anglicum*, which is endemic). Very local, declining. Mostly E England. (Central and E Europe.) FLS Jun-Jul.

Narrow-leaved Flax   *Linum tenuifolium*

Prostrate to erect, glabrous perennial to 45 cm, with short non-flowering shoots. LEAVES 0.5-1 mm wide with 1 vein. FLOWERS Pink or white, sepals 5-8 mm, petals 2-2.5× as long as sepals, stigmas spherical. FRUITS Capsule, 2.7-3.5 mm. HABITAT Dry calcareous grassland. DIST. *Not BI*. (Central and S Europe, N to Belgium.) FLS May-Jul.

Fairy Flax   *Linum catharticum*

Slender, erect, unbranched, glabrous annual to 25 cm. LEAVES *Opposite*, ovate, 5-12 mm, with 1 vein. FLOWERS In loose, open cyme; *pedicels slender 5-10 mm; petals white, 4-6 mm*. HABITAT Grazed calcareous grassland, mires, flushes, limestone cliffs, calcareous dunes; to 840 m. DIST. Native. Common throughout BI. (Most of Europe except extreme N.) FLS Jun-Sep.

Allseed   *Radiola linoides*

Tiny, delicate annual to 8 cm. STEMS Usually branched. LEAVES Opposite, *c.* 3 mm, with 1 vein. FLOWERS Numerous, very small; 4 sepals and *petals c.1 mm*. FRUITS Capsule, *c.*1 mm. SIMILAR SPP. Sometimes confused with *Anagallis minima* (p.226), with which it often grows, but differs in its more branched habit, 4 not 5 petals, and opposite not alternate leaves. HABITAT Damp, open patches on sandy heaths, acid grassland, woodland rides, dune slacks, machair. DIST. Native. Very local, declining. S and W Britain, N Scotland, W Ireland. (Most of Europe except extreme N.) FLS Jul-Aug.

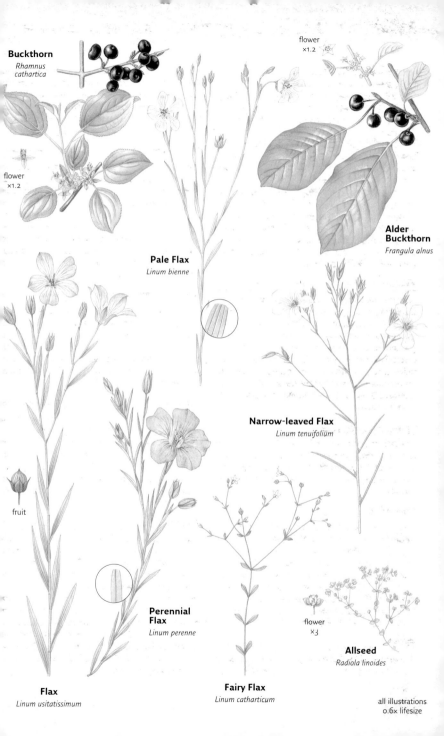

Buckthorn
Rhamnus cathartica

flower
×1.2

flower
×1.2

Alder Buckthorn
Frangula alnus

Pale Flax
Linum bienne

Narrow-leaved Flax
Linum tenuifolium

fruit

Flax
Linum usitatissimum

Perennial Flax
Linum perenne

Fairy Flax
Linum catharticum

flower
×3

Allseed
Radiola linoides

all illustrations
0.6x lifesize

	if	then
1	▷ 5 sepals, petals and stamens	Go to ▷ **2** *Linum*
	▷ 4 sepals, petals and stamens	*Radiola linoides* (p.322)
2	▷ Leaves opposite; petals white, <7 mm	*L. catharticum* (p.322)
	▷ Leaves alternate; petals, blue, pink or white, >7 mm	Go to ▷ **3**
3	▷ Petals pink or white; sepals longer than capsule	*L. tenuifolium* • (p.322)
	▷ Petals blue; sepals as long as or shorter than capsule	Go to ▷ **4**
4	▷ Inner sepals rounded at tip with pale border, shorter than capsule; leaves with 1 vein	*L. perenne* ssp. *anglicum* (p.322)
	▷ All sepals acute, about as long as capsule; leaves usually with 3 veins	Go to ▷ **5**
5	▷ Usually >1 stem; petals 8–12 mm; capsule 6 mm	*L. bienne* (p.322)
	▷ Single stem; petals *c*.15 mm; capsule 10 mm	*L. usitatissimum* (p.322)

Key to Aceraceae Maples

	if	then
1	▷ Leaves small, 4–7 cm, pubescent beneath, lobes blunt	*Acer campestre* (p.326)
	▷ Leaves large, 10–15 cm, glabrous, lobes acute	Go to ▷ **2**
2	▷ Leaf lobes irregularly, coarsely toothed; inflorescence pendulous	*A. pseudoplatanus* (p.326)
	▷ Tips of leaf lobes ending in sharp teeth; inflorescence erect	*A. platanoides* (p.326)

Key to Polygalaceae Milkworts

The flowers of milkworts are very unusual in being strongly irregular and consisting of 5 sepals, 3 petals and 8 stamens with a superior ovary. The 2 inner sepals are petal-like and much larger than the outer 3. The 3 petals are fused, the 2 upper being entire, but the tip of the lower petal deeply divided into narrow lobes (fimbriate). The filaments of the stamens are fused into a tube that is also fused to the petals.

	if	**then**
1	▷ Leaves near base of stem smaller than those above, not forming a loose rosette; veins of inner sepals much branched and joining at tips; lobes of lower petal not projecting beyond tip of inner sepals	Go to ▷ **2**
	▷ Leaves near base of stem larger than those above, forming a loose rosette; veins of inner sepals little branched and not joining at tips; lobes of lower petal projecting beyond tips of inner sepals	Go to ▷ **3**
2	▷ All leaves alternate; inflorescence 10–40-flowered, inner sepals *c*.6 mm	*Polygala vulgaris* (p.326)
	▷ At least some lower leaves opposite; inflorescence 3–10-flowered, inner sepals 4.5–5.5 mm	*P. serpyllifolia* (p.326)
3	▷ Lower part of stem beneath rosette leafless; flowers 6–7 mm	*P. calcarea* (p.326)
	▷ Rosette close to base of stem; flowers ≤5 mm	*P. amarella* (p.326)

Polygala flower

outer sepal — inner sepal — fimbriate tip of lower petal

POLYGALACEAE Milkworts

See key and introduction to Polygalaceae on p.325.

Common Milkwort
Polygala vulgaris

Prostrate to erect, much-branched perennial, to 30 cm. Very variable. LEAVES *All leaves alternate,* ± acute; lower leaves 5-10 mm, upper ones longer. FLOWERS *5-8 mm,* blue, pink or white, in inflorescence of >10 flowers; *inner sepals c.6 mm, veins much branched.* HABITAT Short calcareous grassland, heaths, commons, sand-dunes; to 730 m. DIST. Native. Frequent throughout BI. (Most of Europe.) FLS May-Sep.

Heath Milkwort
Polygala serpyllifolia

Similar to *P. vulgaris,* but smaller, ± prostrate, to 25 cm; *lower stem leaves opposite* (if withered, check leaf scars); *flowers 5-6 mm,* usually deep blue, rarely white or pink, in shorter *inflorescence of 3-8 flowers; inner sepals c.4.5-5.5 mm,* veins much branched. HABITAT Heaths, moors, acid and mountain grassland; to 1035 m. DIST. Native. Throughout BI, common in N and W. (W and central Europe.) FLS Apr-Aug.

Chalk Milkwort
Polygala calcarea

Prostrate to erect perennial, to 20 cm. LEAVES *Lower leaves 5-20 mm, obovate, pale green, crowded into loose rosette above base of stem, stem below rosette leafless;* upper leaves smaller, narrower. FLOWERS Bright blue or bluish white, 6-7 mm, in *dense 6-20-flowered inflorescence; inner sepals slightly shorter than petals, c.5 mm,* veins little branched. HABITAT Close-grazed calcareous grassland on warm slopes. DIST. Native. Very local on chalk areas of S England. (W Europe.) FLS May-Jul.

Dwarf Milkwort
Polygala amarella

Prostrate to erect perennial, to 10 cm. Similar to *P. calcarea,* but *basal leaf rosette close to base of stem;* flowers blue, pink or greyish white, *2-5 mm,* in dense lateral inflorescence of 7-30 flowers; *inner sepals longer than petals,* veins little branched. HABITAT/ DIST. Native. Very local. Damp limestone grassland, calcareous mires in N England; short chalk turf in E Kent. (Most of Europe except S.) FLS Jun-Aug.

HIPPOCASTANACEAE
Horse-chestnuts

Horse-chestnut
Aesculus hippocastanum

Large, wide-spreading deciduous tree to 35 m. BRANCHES *Winter buds large, red-brown, very sticky.* LEAVES *Palmate, opposite;* leaflets 10-25 cm. FLOWERS *In showy, erect, conical panicles,* irregular, *c.*2 cm across; 5 sepals; 4 petals; 5-8 stamens. FRUITS *Large spherical, prickly capsule,* 5-8 cm; 1-2 seeds, large, rich shining brown ('conkers'). HABITAT Widely planted in parks, large gardens, village greens. Sometimes self-sown in wild. DIST. Introduced in 1612. Throughout BI. (SE Europe.) FLS May-Jun.

ACERACEAE Maples

Deciduous trees (*see* key on p.324); leaves opposite, lobed or pinnate; flowers regular, ovary superior, 5 sepals, 5 or 0 petals; 8 stamens; fruit of paired winged seeds.

Maple
Acer campestre

Small deciduous tree to 15 m. BRANCHES Twigs pubescent. LEAVES *4-7 cm, lobes blunt, without marginal teeth,* pubescent beneath. FLOWERS *Few, c.*6 mm across, in erect inflorescence; 5 sepals and petals. FRUITS Pubescent, wings spreading horizontally. HABITAT Woodland, old hedgerows, on moist basic soils; to 380 m. DIST. Native. Frequent throughout England, Wales. Widely planted as amenity tree and established outside native area. (Most of Europe, but rare in Mediterranean.) FLS May-Jun, with leaves.

Sycamore
Acer pseudoplatanus

Large deciduous tree to 30 m. BRANCHES Twigs glabrous; *winter buds large, green.* LEAVES *10-15 cm,* glabrous except in vein axils beneath, *lobes irregularly toothed.* FLOWERS *Numerous, c.*6 mm across, in *pendulous inflorescence;* 5 sepals and petals. FRUITS Glabrous, wings spreading at acute angle. HABITAT Planted in parks, gardens, plantations, woods, roadsides, hedgerows; thoroughly naturalised in a wide range of habitats to 580 m. DIST. Introduced in C16th. Common throughout BI. (Mts of central and S Europe.) FLS Apr-Jun, with leaves.

Norway Maple
Acer platanoides

Large deciduous tree to 30 m. BRANCHES Twigs glabrous; winter buds green and brown. LEAVES *10-15 cm, glabrous* except in vein axils beneath, *lobes with few sharp teeth,* tips acute. FLOWERS 8 mm across, in erect inflorescence; 5 sepals and petals. FRUITS Wings widely divergent to horizontal, spreading. HABITAT Commonly planted in parks, gardens, roadsides; thoroughly naturalised in a wide range of habitats to 340 m. DIST. Introduced in C17th. Throughout BI, but rare in N Scotland, Ireland. (Most of Europe except extreme N and W.) FLS Apr-May, before leaves.

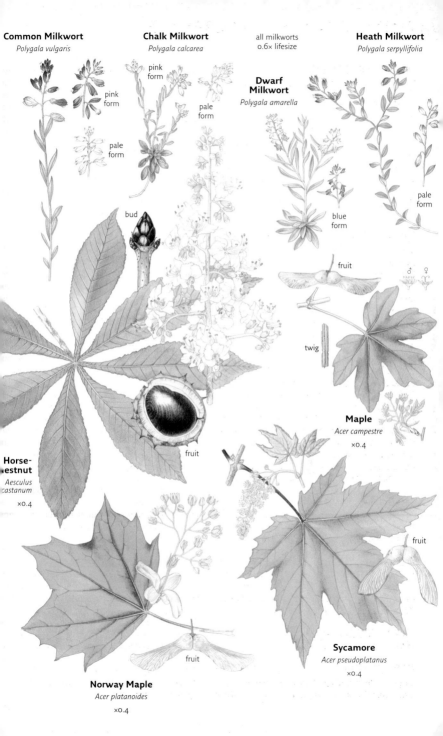

Common Milkwort
Polygala vulgaris

pink form

pale form

Chalk Milkwort
Polygala calcarea

pink form

pale form

all milkworts
0.6× lifesize

Dwarf Milkwort
Polygala amarella

blue form

Heath Milkwort
Polygala serpyllifolia

pale form

bud

fruit

twig

Maple
Acer campestre

×0.4

fruit

Horse-chestnut
Aesculus hippocastanum

×0.4

fruit

Norway Maple
Acer platanoides

×0.4

fruit

Sycamore
Acer pseudoplatanus

×0.4

OXALIDACEAE Wood-sorrels

Perennial herbs with trifoliate (or palmate) leaves. Flowers bisexual, regular, with 5 free petals and sepals, and 10 stamens; ovary superior; 5 styles. Fruit is a capsule. Most of the introduced *Oxalis* species occur as casuals or are naturalised as relics of cultivation. They rarely set seed, but spread by means of bulbils or stem fragments, frequently becoming weeds of gardens or nurseries, or establishing on waste ground or hedge banks near habitation.

Wood-sorrels *Oxalis*

Flowers white	O. acetosella
Flowers yellow	
1 Base of plant with bulbils; leaves all basal	O. pes-caprae
Bulbils absent; stems leafy	2
2 Stems ± erect, not rooting; leaves clustered	O. stricta
Stems creeping, rooting; leaves alternate	3
3 Inflorescence of 2–8 flowers; capsule 8–20 mm	O. corniculata
Flowers solitary; capsules 3–4.5 mm	O. exilis
Flowers pink	
1 Stems erect, leafy; flowers solitary	O. incarnata
Leaves and flowers all basal; flowers in umbels	2
2 Bulbs, bulbils absent; leaves arise from tip of rhizome	O. articulata
Leaves and inflorescences arise from bulb or bulbils	3
3 Leaves broadest near apex, ± glabrous, without dots	O. latifolia
Leaves broadest at about middle, pubescent with dark dots beneath	O. debilis

Wood-sorrel *Oxalis acetosella*

Slender, rhizomatous perennial. LEAVES Trifoliate, pubescent. FLOWERS Solitary; petals 8–15 mm, white with lilac veins. HABITAT Shaded woodlands, hedgerows, banks, rough upland grassland, grikes in limestone pavement; to 1160 m. DIST. Native. Common throughout BI. (Most of Europe, but rare in S.) FLS Apr–May.

Bermuda-buttercup *Oxalis pes-caprae*

HABITAT Weed of agricultural and bulb fields. DIST. Introduced in C18th (native of S Africa). Channel Is, Scilly Is. FLS Mar–Jun.

Procumbent Yellow-sorrel *Oxalis corniculata*

HABITAT Cosmopolitan weed, persistent in gardens and nurseries. DIST. Introduced in C17th (native distribution unknown). Most widely distributed of the introduced *Oxalis*. FLS Jun–Sep.

Least Yellow-sorrel *Oxalis exilis*

Smaller than *O. corniculata*. HABITAT Grown in gardens and rockeries, escaping as casual in similar habitats. DIST. Introduced (native of New Zealand and Tasmania). FLS Jun–Sep.

Upright Yellow-sorrel *Oxalis stricta*

HABITAT Usually annual garden weed on light soils. DIST. Introduced (native of North America); naturalised in most temperate parts of world. FLS Jun–Sep.

Pink-sorrel *Oxalis articulata*

Commonest pink sorrel in cultivation. HABITAT Waste ground, roadsides, seashore. DIST. Introduced (native of South America). Commonly naturalised in SW. FLS May–Oct.

Pale Pink-sorrel *Oxalis incarnata*

HABITAT Popular cottage garden plant; naturalised on hedge banks, stone walls. DIST. Introduced (native of S Africa). Mostly in SW. FLS May–Jul.

Garden Pink-sorrel *Oxalis latifolia*

HABITAT Old gardens, greenhouses. DIST. Introduced (native of West Indies, Central and South America). Formerly cultivated, now troublesome weed in SW, Channel Is. FLS May–Sep.

Large-flowered Pink-sorrel *Oxalis debilis*

HABITAT/DIST. Introduced (native of South America). Formerly widely grown as garden plant, now naturalised as relic of cultivation, spreading by detached bulbils, especially around London. FLS Jul–Sep.

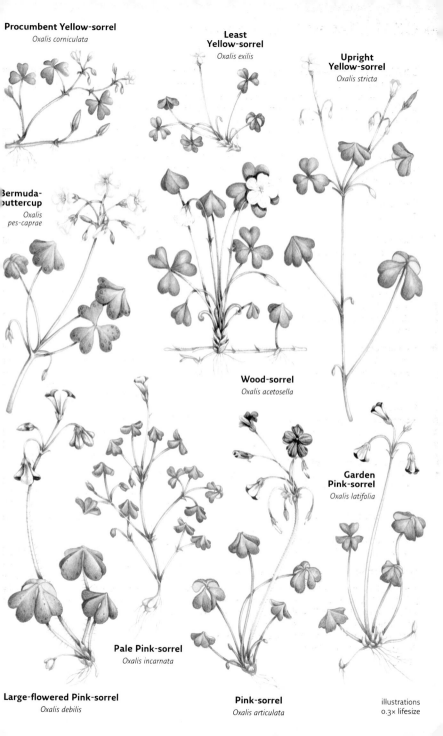

Procumbent Yellow-sorrel
Oxalis corniculata

**Least
Yellow-sorrel**
Oxalis exilis

**Upright
Yellow-sorrel**
Oxalis stricta

**Bermuda-
buttercup**
*Oxalis
pes-caprae*

Wood-sorrel
Oxalis acetosella

**Garden
Pink-sorrel**
Oxalis latifolia

Pale Pink-sorrel
Oxalis incarnata

Large-flowered Pink-sorrel
Oxalis debilis

Pink-sorrel
Oxalis articulata

illustrations
0.3× lifesize

if	then
Leaves palmate or palmately lobed	**Crane's-bills – *Geranium***
Leaves pinnate or pinnately lobed	**Stork's-bills – *Erodium***

Crane's-bills *Geranium*

Geranium flower

1
▷ Flowers large, petals usually ≥10 mm — Go to ▷ **2**
▷ Flowers small, petals ≤10 mm — Go to ▷ **10**

2
▷ Flowers blackish purple, petals apiculate — ***G. phaeum*** (p.334)
▷ Flowers not blackish purple, petals rounded or notched at tip — Go to ▷ **3**

3
▷ Petals rounded at tip — Go to ▷ **4**
▷ Petals notched at tip — Go to ▷ **7**

4
▷ Petals with a 'claw' about as long as limb — ***G. macrorrhizum*** (p.334)
▷ Petals without a claw — Go to ▷ **5**

5
▷ Upper part of stem and sepals with glandular hairs — Go to ▷ **6**
▷ Plant without glandular hairs — ***G. endressii*** (p.332)

6
▷ Flowers violet-blue; leaf lobes narrow (*see* illustration) — ***G. pratense*** (p.332)
▷ Flowers pinkish mauve; leaf lobes broader (*see* illustration) — ***G. sylvaticum*** (p.332)

7
▷ Flowers solitary, bright pinkish purple — ***G. sanguineum*** (p.334)
▷ Flowers in pairs — Go to ▷ **8**

8
▷ Petals ≥15 mm, petals with darker veins — Go to ▷ **9**
▷ Petals 7–10 mm, without darker veins — ***G. pyrenaicum*** (p.334)

9
▷ Stems with short, sparse, appressed hairs; leaf shape distinctive (*see* illustration) — ***G. nodosum*** (p.332)
▷ Stems with spreading hairs; leaf shape distinctive (*see* illustration) — ***G. versicolor*** (p.332)

10
▷ Sepals erect; leaves glossy green — Go to ▷ **11**
▷ Sepals spreading; leaves dull green — Go to ▷ **13**

11
▷ Leaves deeply divided almost to base — Go to ▷ **12**
▷ Leaves lobed to half way or less — ***G. lucidum*** (p.334)

12
▷ Petals ≥8 mm, anthers orange or purple — ***G. robertianum*** (p.334)
▷ Petals 6–9 mm, anthers yellow — ***G. purpureum*** (p.334)

if	**then**

13
▷ Leaves divided almost to base, lobes narrow — Go to ▷ **14**
▷ Leaves divided to ¾ or less, lobes widened towards tip — Go to ▷ **15**

14
▷ Pedicels ≥2 cm, carpels glabrous — *G. columbinum* (p.332)
▷ Pedicels ≤2 cm, carpels pubescent — *G. dissectum* (p.334)

15
▷ Petals notched at tip — Go to ▷ **16**
▷ Petals rounded at tip — *G. rotundifolium* (p.332)

16
▷ Petals 7-10 mm — *G. pyrenaicum* (p.334)
▷ Petals ≤7 mm — Go to ▷ **17**

17
▷ Leaves and pedicels with a mix of short glandular and short and long eglandular hairs; carpels glabrous, all stamens with anthers — *G. molle* (p.334)
▷ Leaves and pedicels with uniformly short eglandular hairs (glandular hairs present or not); carpels pubescent, 5 stamens without anthers — *G. pusillum* (p.334)

Stork's-bills *Erodium*

1
▷ Leaves simple, lobed; petals small or absent — *E. maritimum* (p.336)
▷ Leaves pinnate; petals ≥5 mm — Go to ▷ **2**

2
▷ Plant densely glandular, smelling of musk; primary leaflets divided to ≤¾ way to midrib; apical pits of carpels glandular — *E. moschatum* (p.336)
▷ Plant glandular or not, not smelling of musk; primary leaflets divided nearly to base; apical pits of carpels not glandular — Go to ▷ **3**

3
▷ Inflorescence of 3-7 flowers, flowers >10 mm across — *E. cicutarium* (p.336)
▷ Inflorescence of 2-4 flowers, flowers <10 mm across — *E. lebelii* (p.336)

GERANIACEAE Crane's-bills and stork's-bills

A distinctive family of annual and perennial herbs, often with large, showy flowers (*see* key on p.330). Leaves are alternate, usually palmate or pinnate, and with stipules. Flowers are regular or slightly irregular; 5 free petals and sepals; 5 or 10 stamens; ovary superior with 5 cells, each of which is elongated into a beak; 5 stigmas. Fruit is dry, with each cell containing 1 seed. The shape of the leaves, hairiness of the stems, leaves and carpels, and the shape of the petals are important identification characters. Garden ivy-leaved 'geraniums' belong to the genus *Pelargonium*.

French Crane's-bill   *Geranium endressii*

Erect, rhizomatous, pubescent perennial to 80 cm, without glandular hairs. LEAVES 5–8 cm across. FLOWERS In pairs; petals *c.*16 mm, *rounded at tip.* SIMILAR SPP. *Distinguished from* G. versicolor *and* G. nodosum *by rounded, not notched, tips to petals.* HABITAT Often found as a garden throw-out and naturalised on grassy roadsides. DIST. Introduced. Commonly grown in gardens. (Native of Pyrenees.) FLS Jun–Jul.

Pencilled Crane's-bill   *Geranium versicolor*

Erect, rhizomatous, pubescent perennial to 60 cm. LEAVES 4–8 cm across. FLOWERS In pairs; petals 15–18 mm, tip notched. HABITAT Hedgerows, shady hedge banks. DIST. Introduced. Widely cultivated and naturalised, especially in SW England. (Native of S Italy and Sicily, SE Europe, Caucasus.) FLS May–Sep. NOTE Forms of Druce's Crane's-bill, *Geranium × oxonianum*, the hybrid between *G. endressii* and *G. versicolor*, which are common in gardens and occasionally occur as escapes from cultivation, can be confused with the parents.

Knotted Crane's-bill   *Geranium nodosum*

Erect, ± glabrous, rhizomatous perennial to 60 cm. FLOWERS Petals 13–18 mm, tip notched. SIMILAR SPP. *Distinguished from* G. versicolor *by appressed, not spreading, hairs on stem, less prominent violet veins of petals, and characteristic leaf shape.* HABITAT Occasionally found as a garden escape on roadsides, hedgerows, rough grassland. DIST. Introduced; cultivated since C17th. (Native of mts of S Europe.) FLS Jun–Jul.

Meadow Crane's-bill   *Geranium pratense*

Tall, erect, rhizomatous, glandular-pubescent perennial to 80 cm. LEAVES 7–15 cm across. FLOWERS Axillary, in pairs; petals 15–18 mm, apex rounded. SIMILAR SPP. *Leaves are more deeply divided than those of* G. sylvaticum; *flowers are violet-blue, while those of* G. sylvaticum *are pinkish mauve.* HABITAT Lowland hay meadows, permanent pastures, roadsides, on base-rich or calcareous soils; to *c.*550 m. DIST. Native. Widespread throughout much of Britain, but scarce in Scotland, East Anglia, SW; absent from Ireland. Commonly cultivated, and widely naturalised outside its native range. (Most of Europe, but rare in N and Mediterranean.) FLS Jun–Sep.

Wood Crane's-bill   *Geranium sylvaticum* *(NI)

Erect, rhizomatous, glandular perennial to 80 cm. LEAVES 7–12 cm across. FLOWERS Axillary, in pairs; petals 12–18 mm across, apex rounded. SIMILAR SPP. For separation details from *G. pratense, see* that species. HABITAT Damp woodlands, hay meadows, permanent pastures, verges, stream banks, damp mountain rock ledges, on base-rich or calcareous soils; to *c.*1000 m. DIST. Native; also commonly cultivated. Widely distributed and often common in N Britain from S Yorkshire to central Scotland; very rare in Ireland. (Most of Europe; restricted to mts in S.) FLS Jun–Jul.

Round-leaved Crane's-bill   *Geranium rotundifolium*

Much-branched, trailing to erect, glandular-hairy annual, to 40 cm. LEAVES 3–6 cm across. FLOWERS Numerous; petals 5–7 mm, rounded to slightly emarginate. SIMILAR SPP. *Distinguished from similar species by rounded, not notched, tips to petals and relatively shallowly lobed leaves.* HABITAT Usually dry hedge banks, wall tops; occasionally an arable weed on both sandy and calcareous soils. DIST. Native. Local in S Britain, S Wales, S Ireland. (Most of Europe except extreme N.) FLS Apr–Sep.

Long-stalked Crane's-bill   *Geranium columbinum*

Erect or scrambling, sparsely hairy annual to 60 cm. LEAVES 2–5 cm across, deeply lobed. FLOWERS Stalks long, to 6 cm; petals 7–9 mm across. SIMILAR SPP. *The long flower stalks are characteristic and distinguish it from other small-flowered species with deeply divided leaves.* HABITAT Open grassland, field margins, scrub, rocky hillsides, sand-dunes, quarries, chiefly on dry calcareous or base-rich soils. Occasionally an arable weed. DIST. Native. Rather local, most frequent in S and SW England, becoming increasingly scarce to N. (All Europe except extreme N.) FLS Jun–Sep.

**French
Crane's-bill**
Geranium endressii

**Pencilled
Crane's-bill**
Geranium versicolor

**Knotted
Crane's-bill**
Geranium nodosum

fruit

**Round-leaved
Crane's-bill**
Geranium rotundifolium

**Long-stalked
Crane's-bill**
Geranium columbinum

**Meadow
Crane's-bill**
Geranium pratense

Bloody Crane's-bill
Geranium sanguineum
(description on p.334)

Wood Crane's-bill
Geranium sylvaticum

illustrations
0.5× lifesize

Bloody Crane's-bill   *Geranium sanguineum*

[*See* illustration previous page.] Much-branched perennial to 40 cm. LEAVES Deeply divided, 2–6 cm across. FLOWERS Solitary, peduncles long, petals 12–18 mm across. SIMILAR SPP. *Distinguished from other large-flowered species by solitary crimson flowers.* HABITAT Limestone rocks, coastal cliffs, open woodland, scree, grassland; also fixed calcareous coastal sand-dunes. To *c.*370 m. DIST. Native. Scattered throughout much of N and W Britain. (Most of Europe except extreme N.) FLS May–Aug.

Cut-leaved Crane's-bill   *Geranium dissectum*

Straggling, pubescent annual to 60 cm. LEAVES *Divided almost to base, 2–7 cm.* FLOWERS Stalks 0.5–1.5 cm, petals 4.5–6 mm across, carpels pubescent. HABITAT Waste ground, gardens, rough grassland, waysides, especially on fertile soils; to 380 m. DIST. Archaeophyte. Widespread and common throughout BI, becoming scarcer N from central Scotland. (Most of Europe except extreme N.) Fls May–Aug.

Hedgerow Crane's-bill   *Geranium pyrenaicum*

Erect, glandular-pubescent perennial to 60 cm. LEAVES 5–8 cm, lobes widened towards tip. FLOWERS In pairs; *petals 7–10 mm, deeply notched;* carpels pubescent. HABITAT Hedgerows, field margins, waste ground, on well-drained soils. DIST. Introduced. Frequent in S and E England; scarce elsewhere. (Native of the mts of S Europe and SW Asia.) FLS Jun–Aug.

Dove's-foot Crane's-bill   *Geranium molle*

Glandular-pubescent annual to 40 cm. LEAVES 1–5 cm across. FLOWERS Pedicels *with mix of long and short eglandular and short glandular hairs; petals 3–6 mm, deeply notched; all stamens with anthers; carpels glabrous.* HABITAT Dry grassland, lawns, arable, cultivated and waste ground, sand-dunes, on both calcareous and sandy soils. DIST. Native. Widespread and common throughout BI, but less frequent in Scotland and Ireland. (All Europe except extreme N.) FLS Apr–Oct.

Small-flowered Crane's-bill   *Geranium pusillum*

Pubescent annual to 40 cm. LEAVES 1–4 cm across. FLOWERS Pedicels *with uniformly short eglandular hairs (glandular hairs present or not); petals 2–4 mm,* deeply notched; *5 stamens without anthers; carpels pubescent.* SIMILAR SPP. Easily overlooked for *G. molle*, but the hairs on the stem are uniformly short; flowers are smaller (petals 2–4 mm) and a paler, dull pink; carpels are hairy; and only 5 stamens have anthers. HABITAT Short grassland, arable, cultivated and waste ground, roadsides, on dry, well-drained soils. DIST. Native. Widespread in England except SW; rare, scattered and usually coastal elsewhere. (Most of Europe except N.) FLS Jun–Sep.

Dusky Crane's-bill   *Geranium phaeum*

Erect, glandular-pubescent perennial to 60 cm. LEAVES Basal leaves 7–12 cm. FLOWERS *Blackish purple with apiculate petals.* HABITAT Frequently occurs as a garden escape in hedge banks and shady places near habitation on moist, fertile soils. DIST. Introduced. Widely grown in gardens; numerous cultivars. (Native of mts of central and S Europe.) FLS May–Jun.

Shining Crane's-bill   *Geranium lucidum*

Much-branched, leafy annual to 40 cm. LEAVES ± *glabrous, shallowly lobed, bright glossy green,* 2–6 cm across. FLOWERS Petals 8–9 mm; carpels reticulate, glabrous. HABITAT Shaded rocks, walls, hedge banks, waste ground, especially on calcareous soils. Occasionally as a garden weed. DIST. Native. Widespread throughout most of BI except N Scotland. (Most of Europe except NE.) FLS May–Aug.

Rock Crane's-bill   *Geranium macrorrhizum*

Pubescent, *aromatic* perennial to 30 cm. LEAVES Blades 5–10 cm across. FLOWERS *In pairs; petals clawed, rounded at tip.* HABITAT Occasionally escapes and establishes on hedge banks, old walls, roadsides, close to habitation. DIST. Introduced. Long grown in gardens, with numerous cultivars. (Native of mts of S Europe and Balkans.) FLS Jun–Aug.

Herb-Robert   *Geranium robertianum*

Much-branched, pubescent annual or biennial to 50 cm, with *distinctive unpleasant smell.* STEMS *Often reddish.* LEAVES *Bright dark green.* FLOWERS *Sepals erect, petals 9–14 mm, anthers orange or purple.* HABITAT Woodlands, hedge banks, scree, limestone pavement, old walls, coastal shingle, avoiding the most acid soils and preferring shaded habitats. DIST. Native. Widespread and common throughout BI. (All Europe except extreme N.) Fls May–Sep. NOTE The prostrate plant of coastal shingle, with small flowers and glabrous fruits, is spp. *maritimum*.

Little-Robin   *Geranium purpureum*

Much-branched, pubescent annual or biennial. *Very similar to* G. robertianum, *but flowers smaller, petals 6–9 mm, anthers yellow.* HABITAT Open rocky habitats, hedge banks, railway ballast, shingle beaches. DIST. Native. Very rare and local. S and SW England, S Ireland. (S and W Europe.) FLS May–Sep.

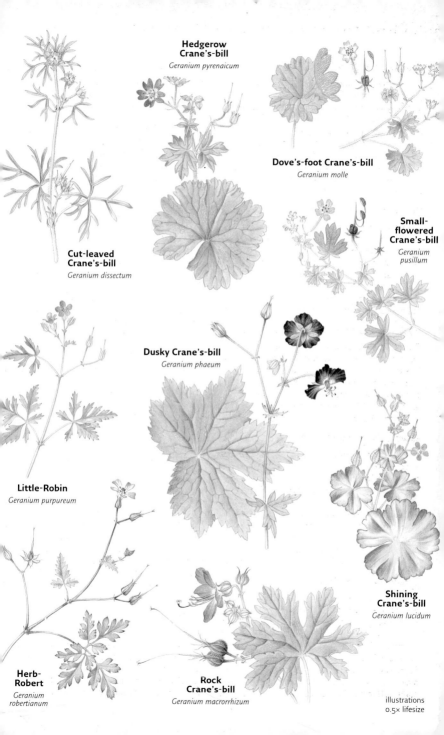

Hedgerow Crane's-bill
Geranium pyrenaicum

Dove's-foot Crane's-bill
Geranium molle

Small-flowered Crane's-bill
Geranium pusillum

Cut-leaved Crane's-bill
Geranium dissectum

Dusky Crane's-bill
Geranium phaeum

Little-Robin
Geranium purpureum

Shining Crane's-bill
Geranium lucidum

Herb-Robert
Geranium robertianum

Rock Crane's-bill
Geranium macrorrhizum

illustrations
0.5× lifesize

Common Stork's-bill
Erodium cicutarium

Much-branched, glandular or eglandular annual to 60 cm. FLOWERS 12–14 mm across, in 3–7-flowered inflorescence. FRUITS *carpels 5–6.5 mm, pit at apex not glandular, separated from rest of fruit by ridge and furrow* (need to use a lens). HABITAT Dry heaths, commons, sandy grassland, sand-dunes; to 420 m. DIST. Native. Throughout BI, mostly coastal in W, Ireland. (All Europe.) FLS Jun–Sep.

Sticky Stork's-bill
Erodium lebelii

Similar to *E. cicutarium*, but more slender, to 15 cm; densely glandular-pubescent, sticky; flowers paler, *c.*7 mm across, in 2–4-flowered inflorescence; *carpels ≤5 mm, apical pit without furrow.* HABITAT Bare patches on stabilised sand-dunes. DIST. Native. Very scarce. Mostly W coasts of England, Wales; E coast of Ireland. (W Europe.) FLS Jun–Sep.

Musk Stork's-bill
Erodium moschatum

Much-branched annual to 60 cm, *covered by long white hairs and stalked glands, smelling strongly of musk.* LEAVES 5–15 cm, primary leaflets divided to ≤¾ way to midrib. FLOWERS In 2–8-flowered inflorescence; *carpels with long white hairs, apical pits glandular* (need to use a lens). HABITAT Waste places, roadsides, field margins, sand-dunes. DIST. Archaeophyte. England (especially SW), Wales; Ireland; mostly coastal, casual inland. (S and W Europe.) FLS May–Jul.

Sea Stork's-bill
Erodium maritimum

Small, prostrate annual to 30 cm. LEAVES *5–15 mm, simple, pinnately lobed.* FLOWERS 1–2, peduncles about as long as leaves; sepals *c.*4 mm; *petals as long as sepals or absent*; carpels pubescent. HABITAT Open areas, cliff tops, mature dunes, walls, sea-bird colonies. DIST. Native. Coasts of SW England, Wales, N to Solway Firth; E Ireland, Channel Is, I of Man. (NW Europe.) FLS May–Jul.

BALSAMINACEAE Balsams

Glabrous, somewhat succulent annuals. Leaves simple, alternate, opposite or whorled. Flowers strongly irregular, ovary superior; 5 or 3 petal-like sepals, the lower large and spurred; 5 petals, the upper large, the lower united in pairs; 5 stamens. Fruit is a capsule.

Balsams *Impatiens*

Flowers pink	*I. glandulifera*
Flowers yellow, <1.5 cm; leaves with >20 teeth on each side	*I. parviflora*
Flowers yellow, >2 cm; leaves with <20 teeth on each side	*I. noli-tangere*
Flowers orange	*I. capensis*

Indian Balsam
Impatiens glandulifera

Tall, erect, glabrous annual to 200 cm. LEAVES Opposite or in whorls of 3, 6–15 cm. FLOWERS Large, 2.5–4 cm, deep or pale pink or white. HABITAT River sides, ditches, wet woodlands; very invasive, forming dense stands. DIST. Introduced in 1839 (native of Himalayas). Naturalised throughout BI. (Most of Europe.) FLS Jul–Oct.

Small Balsam
Impatiens parviflora

Erect, glabrous annual to 100 cm. LEAVES Alternate, 5–15 cm, with >20 teeth on each side. FLOWERS Small, 5–15 mm, pale yellow, 4–10 forming axillary inflorescence. HABITAT Woodland, parks, plantations, tracksides, shaded riverbanks. DIST. Introduced (native of Siberia, Turkestan). Naturalised throughout Britain, but rare in SW and Scotland. (Naturalised throughout Europe.) FLS Jul–Nov.

Touch-me-not Balsam
Impatiens noli-tangere

Erect, glabrous annual to 100 cm. LEAVES Alternate, 5–12 cm, with 10–15 teeth on each side. FLOWERS *c.*3.5 cm, yellow with brown spots, in few-flowered axillary inflorescence. HABITAT Wet woodlands, banks of rivers and streams. DIST. Native, very rare. Lake District, Yorkshire, N Wales; casual elsewhere. (SE Europe.) FLS Jul–Oct.

Orange Balsam
Impatiens capensis

Erect, glabrous annual to 150 cm. Vegetatively similar to *I. noli-tangere*, but leaves smaller, 3–8 cm, with <10 teeth on each side; flowers 2–3 cm, orange with brown spots inside. HABITAT Banks of rivers, canals, reservoirs. DIST. Introduced (native of E North America). Naturalised in scattered localities throughout England. (France.) FLS Jun–Aug.

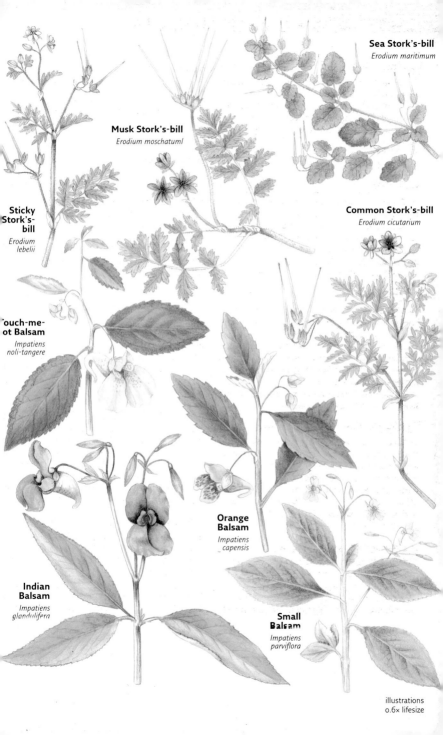

Sea Stork's-bill
Erodium maritimum

Musk Stork's-bill
Erodium moschatuml

Sticky Stork's-bill
Erodium lebelii

Common Stork's-bill
Erodium cicutarium

Touch-me-ot Balsam
Impatiens noli-tangere

Orange Balsam
Impatiens capensis

Indian Balsam
Impatiens glandulifera

Small Balsam
Impatiens parviflora

illustrations
0.6× lifesize

ARALIACEAE Ivies

Ivy
Hedera helix

Woody evergreen climber. STEMS Climbing stems densely clothed with adhesive roots, young twigs with branched hairs. LEAVES Alternate, simple, glabrous; those of creeping and climbing stems 4–10 cm, palmate with 3–5 lobes; those of flowering stems entire, ovate. FLOWERS In umbels, regular; calyx with 5 small teeth; 5 petals, 3–4 mm; 5 stamens; ovary inferior. FRUITS Berry-like, 6-8 mm, black. HABITAT Woods, hedgerows, scrub, walls, cliffs, rock outcrops; to 610 m. DIST. Native. Common throughout BI. (W, central and S Europe.) FLS Sep–Nov. NOTE Two genetically distinct ssp. are recognised: ssp. *helix* and ssp. *hibernica*. However, they are very difficult to separate, this depending on details of the branched hairs on the twigs. The commoner plant in W Britain seems to be ssp. *hibernica*.

APIACEAE (UMBELLIFERAE)
Umbellifers

See key on p.340. Most umbellifers are readily recognised when in flower by the characteristic umbel inflorescence, in which all the branches arise from the same point like the ribs of an umbrella. Umbellifers are annual or perennial herbs (rarely shrubs, none of which are native to BI); the leaves are alternate, without stipules (except for *Hydrocotyle*), and usually much divided with sheathing petioles. The umbels are usually compound with bracts and bracteoles; the flowers are regular (except that the outer petals of the outer flowers of the umbel may be enlarged); 5 small calyx teeth, or these absent; 5 petals; 5 stamens; ovary inferior, with 2 stigmas that usually have a swollen base (stylopodium). The fruit consists of 2, usually compressed, ribbed carpels separated by a septum. When ripe, the 2 carpels separate, held together by the split stalk, the carpophore.

Details of the fruit are very important in identification and should be checked with the illustrations and descriptions in the text. In addition, the leaves, degree of hairiness of the plant and numbers of bracts and bracteoles should be carefully examined.

Marsh Pennywort
Hydrocotyle vulgaris

Slender, creeping perennial, rooting at nodes. LEAVES *Peltate*, 1–5 cm across, circular, *shallowly lobed*; petioles 1–25 cm, erect. FLOWERS Tiny, about 1 mm across, in 2–5-flowered umbels; peduncles shorter than petioles. HABITAT Bogs, fens, marshes, wet meadows, dune slacks, pond and stream margins; to 530 m. DIST. Native. Throughout BI. (W, central and S Europe.) FLS Jun–Aug.

Floating Pennywort
Hydrocotyle ranunculoides

Rooted or free-floating perennial. Similar to *H. vulgaris*, but stems often floating; *leaves reniform not peltate*, up to 7 cm across, *lobed ± halfway to base, with deep basal sinus*; umbels of 5–10 flowers. HABITAT Lakes, ponds, rivers, streams, ditches, canals, forming dense colonies. DIST. Introduced (native of North America); first recorded in 1990. Scattered localities in lowland England; vigorous and invasive, spreading rapidly.

Sanicle
Sanicula europaea

Erect, glabrous perennial to 60 cm. LEAVES *Most basal, palmately lobed*, 2–6 cm across; petioles long, 5–25 cm. FLOWERS *In few simple umbels; bracts small*, 2–5, simple or branched; bracteoles several, simple. FRUITS *c.*3 mm, with hooked bristles. HABITAT Deciduous woodland, hedge banks, on calcareous or base-rich soils; lowland to 500 m. DIST. Native. Throughout BI. (Most of Europe except NE.) FLS May–Sep.

Astrantia
Astrantia major

Erect, glabrous perennial to 80 cm. LEAVES Palmately lobed, petioles long. FLOWERS In simple umbels; *bracts large, pale greenish purple above, 1–2 cm, as long as umbel, forming an involucre*. FRUITS 5–7 mm. HABITAT Popular garden plant, occurring as occasional escape from cultivation. DIST. Introduced. Scattered throughout Britain. (Central Europe.) FLS May–Jul.

Sea-holly
Eryngium maritimum

Intensely glaucous, spiny, glabrous perennial to 60 cm. LEAVES All spiny; *basal leaves 5–12 cm, suborbicular*; stem leaves palmate. FLOWERS 8 mm across, in 1.5–2.5 cm heads; bracts spiny; bracteoles longer than flowers. HABITAT Coastal sand-dunes, fine shingle. DIST. Native. All round coasts of BI except N and E Scotland, NE England. (Coasts of Europe to S Scandinavia.) FLS Jul–Aug.

Field Eryngo
Eryngium campestre CR. *(B)

Pale green spiny, glabrous, much-branched perennial to 75 cm. LEAVES Less spiny than *E. maritimum; basal leaves pinnate*; stem leaves sessile, clasping stem. FLOWERS In 1–1.5 cm heads; *bracteoles spiny, 2–3× as long as flowers*. HABITAT Old pastures, coastal grassland, on dry calcareous soils. DIST. Archaeophyte. Very rare. SW England; casual elsewhere. (Central and S Europe.) FLS Jul–Aug.

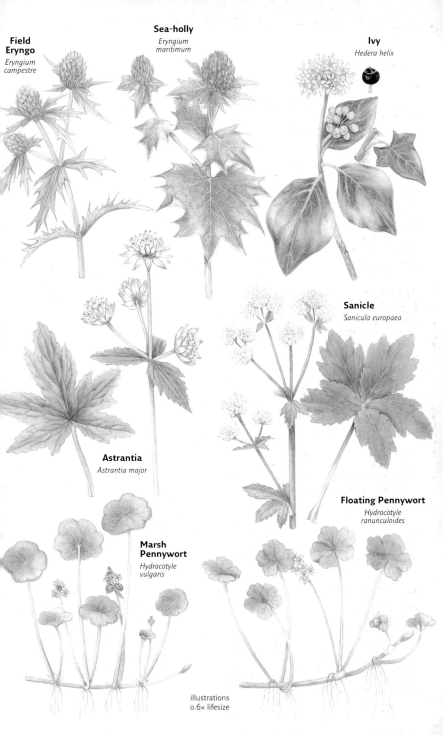

Field Eryngo
Eryngium campestre

Sea-holly
Eryngium maritimum

Ivy
Hedera helix

Astrantia
Astrantia major

Sanicle
Sanicula europaea

Floating Pennywort
Hydrocotyle ranunculoides

Marsh Pennywort
Hydrocotyle vulgaris

illustrations
0.6× lifesize

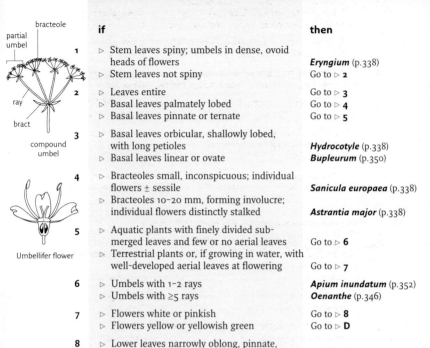

bracteole

partial umbel

ray

bract

compound umbel

Umbellifer flower

	if	**then**
1	▷ Stem leaves spiny; umbels in dense, ovoid heads of flowers	***Eryngium*** (p.338)
	▷ Stem leaves not spiny	Go to ▷ **2**
2	▷ Leaves entire	Go to ▷ **3**
	▷ Basal leaves palmately lobed	Go to ▷ **4**
	▷ Basal leaves pinnate or ternate	Go to ▷ **5**
3	▷ Basal leaves orbicular, shallowly lobed, with long petioles	***Hydrocotyle*** (p.338)
	▷ Basal leaves linear or ovate	***Bupleurum*** (p.350)
4	▷ Bracteoles small, inconspicuous; individual flowers ± sessile	***Sanicula europaea*** (p.338)
	▷ Bracteoles 10-20 mm, forming involucre; individual flowers distinctly stalked	***Astrantia major*** (p.338)
5	▷ Aquatic plants with finely divided sub-merged leaves and few or no aerial leaves	Go to ▷ **6**
	▷ Terrestrial plants or, if growing in water, with well-developed aerial leaves at flowering	Go to ▷ **7**
6	▷ Umbels with 1-2 rays	***Apium inundatum*** (p.352)
	▷ Umbels with ≥5 rays	***Oenanthe*** (p.346)
7	▷ Flowers white or pinkish	Go to ▷ **8**
	▷ Flowers yellow or yellowish green	Go to ▷ **D**
8	▷ Lower leaves narrowly oblong, pinnate, leaflets repeatedly lobed into filiform segments, appearing as if whorled	***Carum verticillatum*** (p.356)
	▷ Leaves not appearing as if consisting of numerous whorled filiform segments	Go to ▷ **9**
9	▷ Lower leaves simply pinnate or pinnately lobed	Go to ▷ **A**
	▷ Lower leaves 2-3-pinnate or ternate	Go to ▷ **10**
10	▷ Plant hairy, often minutely so (examine leaf veins and peduncles with lens)	Go to ▷ **B**
	▷ Plant glabrous	Go to ▷ **C**

A Lower leaves simply pinnate or pinnately lobed

1	▷ Plant ± hairy (check leaf veins and peduncles with lens)	Go to ▷ **2**
	▷ Plant quite glabrous	Go to ▷ **4**
2	▷ Calyx teeth conspicuous, about as long as petals (very rare, Thames estuary)	***Tordylium maximum*** (p.358)
	▷ Calyx teeth absent	Go to ▷ **3**
3	▷ Bracteoles absent	***Pimpinella*** (p.344)
	▷ Bracteoles present, narrow, reflexed	***Heracleum*** (p.358)

	if	**then**
4	▷ Petioles tubular, much longer than leaf blade; partial umbels distinctly convex	***Oenanthe*** (p.346)
	▷ Petioles not tubular; partial umbels ± flat	Go to ▷ **5**
5	▷ Longest bracts ≥¼ as long as shortest rays	Go to ▷ **6**
	▷ Bracts absent or <¼ as long as rays	Go to ▷ **8**
6	▷ Bracts narrow, ± linear; stems solid	***Petroselinum*** (p.354)
	▷ Bracts lanceolate, often lobed; stems hollow	Go to ▷ **7**
7	▷ 4–6 pairs of leaf segments	***Sium latifolium*** (p.352)
	▷ 7–10 pairs of leaf segments	***Berula erecta*** (p.352)
8	▷ Some umbels ± sessile and leaf-opposed	***Apium*** (p.352)
	▷ Umbels with long peduncles, not leaf-opposed	Go to ▷ **9**
9	▷ Bracts present	***Sison amomum*** (p.354)
	▷ Bracts absent	***Pimpinella*** (p.344)

B Lower leaves 2–3-pinnate or ternate; plant hairy

1	▷ Fruit with apical beak 3–4× as long as basal seed-bearing section (rare arable weed)	***Scandix pecten-veneris*** (p.348)
	▷ Beak shorter than seed-bearing section or absent	Go to ▷ **2**
2	▷ Stems hollow	Go to ▷ **3**
	▷ Stems solid	Go to ▷ **8**
3	▷ Lower leaves deeply and repeatedly lobed, lobes usually <3 cm	Go to ▷ **4**
	▷ Lower leaves 2–3-pinnate, not deeply and repeatedly lobed, lobes usually >3 cm	Go to ▷ **6**
4	▷ Fresh plant smelling strongly of aniseed	***Myrrhis odorata*** (p.348)
	▷ Fresh plant not smelling of aniseed	Go to ▷ **5**
5	▷ Bracts absent	***Anthriscus*** (p.344)
	▷ Bracts present	***Peucedanum palustre*** (p.356)
6	▷ Bracteoles absent	***Pimpinella*** (p.344)
	▷ Bracteoles present	Go to ▷ **7**
7	▷ Plant almost glabrous; stems smooth, striate; leaves 2–3-pinnate, primary divisions long-stalked	***Angelica*** (p.348)
	▷ Plant roughly hairy; stems ridged; leaves simply pinnate, most primary divisions sessile	***Heracleum*** (p.358)
8	▷ Stems and leaf sheaths glabrous; leaves sparsely hairy on margins and veins	***Physospermum cornubiense*** (p.350)
	▷ Stems hairy, at least on nodes	Go to ▷ **9**
9	▷ Bracts large, pinnately branched	***Daucus*** (p.358)
	▷ Bracts small, simple	Go to ▷ **10**
10	▷ Stems purple-spotted or ± wholly purple	***Chaerophyllum*** (p.344)
	▷ Stems not purple-spotted or purple at base only	Go to ▷ **11**

CONTINUED OVERLEAF

	if	**then**
11	▷ Stems with deflexed, appressed hairs	*Torilis* (p.358)
	▷ Stems with sparse, short, spreading hairs or ± glabrous	Go to ▷ **12**
12	▷ Bracts present; base of plant with persistent fibres	*Seseli* (p.348)
	▷ Bracts absent; base of plant without persistent fibres	*Pimpinella* (p.344)

C Lower leaves 2–3-pinnate or ternate; plant glabrous

1	▷ Stems with purple spots	*Conium maculatum* (p.348)
	▷ Stems not purple-spotted	Go to ▷ **2**
2	▷ Leaf lobes narrow, slightly falcate, up to 30 cm long, sharply toothed; 4–15 bracts and bracteoles, linear	*Falcaria vulgaris* (p.354)
	▷ Not as above	Go to ▷ **3**
3	▷ 0–1 bracteoles	Go to ▷ **4**
	▷ ≥2 bracteoles	Go to ▷ **6**
4	▷ Lower leaves 1–2-ternate, lobes ovate, toothed	*Aegopodium podagraria* (p.352)
	▷ Lower leaves deeply divided, lobes linear-lanceolate	Go to ▷ **5**
5	▷ Basal leaves soon withering, petioles long, slender; styles sub-erect in fruit	*Conopodium majus* (p.344)
	▷ Basal leaves persistent, petioles sheathing; styles recurved and appressed in fruit	*Carum* (p.356)
6	▷ Bracts >⅓ as long as rays, branched with linear segments	*Ammi majus* (p.354)
	▷ Bracts shorter or absent	Go to ▷ **7**
7	▷ 3–4 bracteoles on outside of each partial umbel, down-pointing, conspicuous	*Aethusa cynapium* (p.350)
	▷ Bracteoles not as above	Go to ▷ **8**
8	▷ Stem tapering from ground surface downwards to underground tuber; leaves soon withering	Go to ▷ **9**
	▷ Not as above; flowering stems arising at or close to ground surface	Go to ▷ **10**
9	▷ Stems hollow after flowering; styles sub-erect in fruit	*Conopodium majus* (p.344)
	▷ Stems solid; styles recurved in fruit (rare, chalk areas of E England)	*Bunium bulbocastanum* (p.344)
10	▷ Leaf lobes very narrow, filiform; base of stems surrounded by fibrous remains of old petioles	Go to ▷ **11**
	▷ At least lower leaves with broad leaf lobes; fibres absent	Go to ▷ **12**

if	**then**

11 ▷ Stem solid; plant glaucous, dioecious (rare, limestone grassland, SW England) — ***Trinia glauca*** (p.354)

▷ Stem hollow; plant neither glaucous nor dioecious (unimproved grassland, N Britain) — ***Meum athamanticum*** (p.350)

12 ▷ Lobes of lower leaves ovate to sub-orbicular, at least some ≥2 cm — Go to ▷ **13**

▷ Lobes of lower leaves narrower, often deeply divided — Go to ▷ **15**

13 ▷ Lower leaves 3–4-pinnate, lobes numerous — ***Oenanthe*** (p.346)

▷ Lower leaves 1–2-ternate or 2-pinnate, lobes few — Go to ▷ **14**

14 ▷ Leaves (1)–2-ternate, petioles not inflated — ***Ligusticum scoticum*** (p.356)

▷ Leaves 2-pinnate, upper petioles inflated — ***Laserpitium latifolium*** ● (p.356)

15 ▷ Leaf lobes linear-lanceolate, margins sharply toothed but not lobed — ***Cicuta virosa*** (p.354)

▷ Margins of leaf lobes not toothed — Go to ▷ **16**

16 ▷ Partial umbels often dense, pedicels longer than oblong fruits; some species aquatic, with much-divided submerged leaves — ***Oenanthe*** (p.346)

▷ Partial umbels not noticeably dense, pedicels longer than fruits — Go to ▷ **17**

17 ▷ Bracts usually absent — ***Selinum carvifolia*** (p.356)

▷ ≥4 bracts — Go to ▷ **18**

18 ▷ Stems hollow, strongly ridged — ***Peucedanum*** (p.356)

▷ Stems ± solid, smooth, striate — ***Physospermum cornubiense*** (p.350)

D Flowers yellow or yellowish green

1 ▷ Leaves all simple, entire — ***Bupleurum*** (p.350)

▷ Leaves compound — Go to ▷ **2**

2 ▷ Plant hairy — ***Pastinaca sativa*** (p.348)

▷ Not as above — Go to ▷ **3**

3 ▷ Leaf lobes linear, entire — Go to ▷ **4**

▷ Leaf lobes not linear — Go to ▷ **6**

4 ▷ Leaves fleshy; 5–10 bracts and bracteoles; plant 'bushy', to *c*.30 cm (coastal) — ***Crithmum maritimum*** (p.354)

▷ Leaf lobes not fleshy; plant erect, to 200 cm — Go to ▷ **5**

5 ▷ Lower leaves 3–6-ternate — ***Peucedanum officinale*** (p.356)

▷ Lower leaves pinnate — ***Foeniculum vulgare*** (p.350)

6 ▷ Lobes of lower leaves bluntly or sharply toothed, obtuse — ***Smyrnium olusatrum*** (p.346)

▷ Lobes of lower leaves deeply divided or lobed, acute — Go to ▷ **7**

7 ▷ Sheathing bases of petioles with broad, pale margins; leaf margins not finely toothed — ***Petroselinum crispum*** (p.354)

▷ Base of petioles without pale margins; leaf margins finely toothed — ***Silaum silaus*** (p.354)

Cow Parsley
Anthriscus sylvestris

Tall, erect, pubescent perennial to 150 cm. Commonest early flowering umbellifer. STEMS *Hollow*. LEAVES 3-pinnate. FLOWERS In umbels 2–6 cm across, terminal, rays glabrous; *bracts absent; several bracteoles*. FRUITS *6–10 mm, smooth*, with short beak. HABITAT Hedgerows, roadsides, railway banks, wood borders; to 760 m. DIST. Native. Throughout BI. (Most of Europe, but rare in Mediterranean.) FLS Apr–Jun.

Bur Parsley
Anthriscus caucalis

Spreading, sparsely pubescent annual to 70 cm. STEMS *Hollow, glabrous*. LEAVES 2–3-pinnate. FLOWERS In *umbels 2–4 cm across, leaf-opposed*, with short peduncle; 0–1 bracts; several bracteoles. FRUITS *3 mm, with hooked bristles*. SIMILAR SPP. **Garden Chervil** *Anthriscus cerefolium* is an erect, pubescent annual that occasionally occurs as a casual on waste ground. It has pubescent rays and, smooth fruits, 7–10 mm, with a long, slender beak. HABITAT Hedge banks, rough grassland, waste ground, sea walls, on sandy or gravelly soils. DIST. Native. Local, scattered throughout BI, especially East Anglia. (W, S and central Europe.) FLS May–Jun.

Rough Chervil
Chaerophyllum temulum

Tall, erect, pubescent biennial to 100 cm. STEMS *Solid, purple or purple-spotted*, with short, stiff hairs. LEAVES *2–3-pinnate, pubescent on both surfaces*. FLOWERS 0–2 bracts; 5–8 bracteoles, shorter than pedicels. FRUITS 4–6.5 mm. HABITAT Roadsides, hedge banks, rough grassland, woodland borders, usually on dry basic soils; lowland to 350 m. DIST. Native throughout Britain, but rare or absent in N Scotland; introduced and rare in Ireland. (Most of Europe, but rare in Mediterranean; absent from extreme N.) FLS Jun–Jul, after *Anthriscus sylvestris*.

Golden Chervil
Chaerophyllum aureum

Tall, erect, pubescent perennial to 120 cm. LEAVES *2–3-pinnate, yellow-green; segments acute, sparsely hairy below, ciliate on margins*. FLOWERS 0–3 bracts; 5–8 bracteoles, as long as or longer than pedicels. FRUITS 7–10 mm. DIST. Introduced. Popular garden plant, very rare as casual escape from cultivation. (Central and S Europe.) FLS Jul.

Pignut
Conopodium majus

Slender, erect, *glabrous perennial* to 50 cm. STEMS *Hollow*, with underground tuber. LEAVES *2–3-pinnate, lobes linear; basal leaves soon withering*, stem leaves with sheathing base. FLOWERS In umbels, nodding in bud; 0–2 bracts; several bracteoles. FRUITS 3–4.5 mm, *styles ± erect*. HABITAT Open woodlands, rough grassland, grass heaths, upland hay meadows, hedge banks, on mildly acid soils; to 700 m. DIST. Native. Throughout BI. (W Europe.) FLS May–Jun.

Great Pignut
Bunium bulbocastanum

Erect, glabrous perennial to 70 cm. STEMS Solid, with underground tuber. LEAVES *3-pinnate, lobes linear, withered by flowering*. FLOWERS Numerous bracts and bracteoles. FRUITS 3–4.5 mm, *styles recurved*. HABITAT Chalk downs, roadside verges, hedgerows arable fields. DIST. Native. Very local, in Chilterns (W, central and E Europe.) FLS Jun–Jul.

Burnet-saxifrage
Pimpinella saxifraga

Erect, thinly pubescent, slender perennial to 100 cm. STEMS Slightly ridged. LEAVES Very variable, *basal leaves simply pinnate, stem leaves 2-pinnate*. FLOWERS *Bracts and bracteoles absent*; sepals absent; *petals with long, incurved point*. FRUITS 2–3 mm. HABITAT Dry, rough or grazed grassland, woodland edges hedge banks, usually on base-rich or calcareous soils; to 810 m. DIST. Native. Throughout BI, but rare in N Scotland, N and W Ireland. (Most of Europe except extreme S.) FLS Jul–Aug.

Greater Burnet-saxifrage
Pimpinella major

Tall, erect, ± glabrous perennial to 120 cm. STEMS *Strongly ridged*. LEAVES *All simply pinnate*; segments of basal leaves shortly stalked, all coarsely toothed FLOWERS *Bracts and bracteoles absent*; sepals absent *petals with long, incurved points*. FRUITS 3–4 mm HABITAT Hedge banks, grassy roadsides, wood borders, on basic or calcareous soils; to 320 m. DIST Native. Lowland England, SW Ireland; ± absent from Wales, Scotland. (Most of Europe except extreme N S and SE.) FLS Jun–Jul.

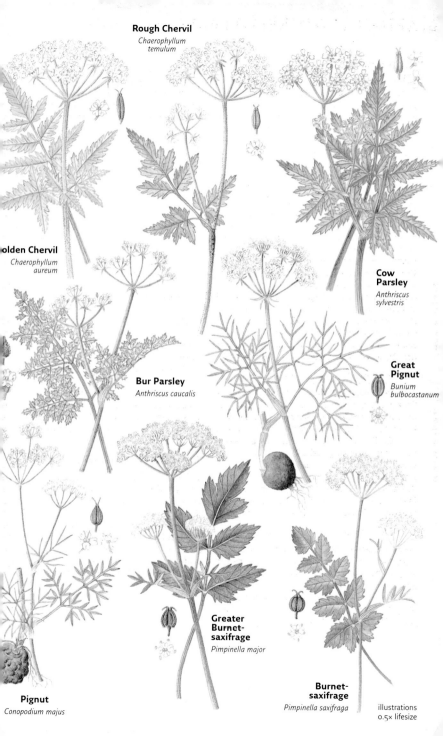

Rough Chervil
Chaerophyllum temulum

olden Chervil
Chaerophyllum aureum

Cow Parsley
Anthriscus sylvestris

Bur Parsley
Anthriscus caucalis

Great Pignut
Bunium bulbocastanum

Greater Burnet-saxifrage
Pimpinella major

Burnet-saxifrage
Pimpinella saxifraga

Pignut
Conopodium majus

illustrations
0.5× lifesize

Alexanders   *Smyrnium olusatrum*

Robust, glabrous biennial to 150 cm. STEMS Solid, becoming hollow. LEAVES Dark, glossy green, 2-3-pinnate or ternate, segments broad, petioles of stem leaves sheathing. FLOWERS Yellow-green; few bracts and bracteoles. FRUITS Broad, 6.5-8 mm, black. HABITAT Hedge banks, roadsides, cliffs, rough grassland, usually close to sea. DIST. Archaeophyte. Locally common in most of BI, but rare in N England, Scotland. (S and SW Europe.) FLS Mar-Jun.

Water-dropworts *Oenanthe*

1	Umbels terminal, peduncles longer than rays	2
	Umbels arising in leaf axils, peduncles short	6
2	Leaf segments broad, wedge-shaped	*O. crocata*
	Leaf segments of stem leaves linear	3
3	Pinnate part of stem leaves shorter than hollow petiole	*O. fistulosa*
	Pinnate part of stem leaves longer than petiole	4
4	Segments of basal leaves broad, toothed; umbels dense (partial umbels crowded), becoming flat-topped in fruit; styles as long as fruit	*O. pimpinelloides*
	Partial umbels remaining separate and rounded in fruit; styles shorter than fruit	5
5	0-1 bracts; lower leaves narrow, similar to stem leaves	*O. silaifolia*
	Several bracts; lower leaves broader than stem leaves, lobed, segments paddle-shaped	*O. lachenalii*
6	Stems erect; fruits 3.5-4.5 mm	*O. aquatica*
	Stems usually submerged, except for flowering stems; fruits 5.0-6.5 mm	*O. fluviatilis*

NOTE The basal leaves of *O. silaifolia*, *O. pimpinelloides* and *O. lachenalii* tend to wither at, or before, flowering, so are often of little help in identification.

Hemlock Water-dropwort   *Oenanthe crocata*

Tall, robust, erect perennial to 150 cm. LEAVES 3-4-pinnate; segments ovate, lobed or toothed; petioles sheathing. FLOWERS In terminal umbels, 5-10 cm across; several bracts and bracteoles. FRUITS 4.5-5 mm, styles *c.*⅓ as long as fruits. HABITAT Wet woodlands, ditches, and stream, river and lake margins, on acid soils; lowland to 320 m. DIST. Native. Throughout BI, but commonest in S and W. (W Mediterranean, W and SW Europe.) FLS Jun-Sep. NOTE *Whole plant is extremely toxic.*

Tubular Water-dropwort   *Oenanthe fistulosa* VU

Erect perennial to 60 cm. LEAVES 1-pinnate; petioles long, cylindrical, hollow, longer than pinnate part of leaf. FLOWERS 3-4 forming partial umbels; bracts absent, several bracteoles. FRUITS 3-4 mm, umbels becoming rounded, styles as long as fruit. HABITAT Wet meadows, pastures, margins of drainage ditches, dykes, ponds, canals, on fertile soils. DIST Native. Throughout lowland England, declining rare and local in rest of BI. (W, central and S Europe.) FLS Jul-Sep.

Parsley Water-dropwort   *Oenanthe lachenalii*

Erect perennial to 100 cm. STEMS Solid. LEAVES 2-pinnate; lobes paddle-shaped, blunt; lower leaves soon withering. FLOWERS Up to 10 forming partial umbels; 5 bracts, several bracteoles. FRUITS 2.5-3 mm, pedicels not thickening, styles shorter than fruit. HABITAT Grazing marshes, margins of brackish dykes, estuarine rivers, rough coastal grassland inland calcareous fens, marshes, wet meadows. DIST Native. Coastal areas of BI except N Scotland; very local inland. (W and central Europe.) FLS Jun-Sep.

Corky-fruited Water-dropwort   *Oenanthe pimpinelloides* *(F

Erect, branched perennial to 100 cm. STEMS Solid LEAVES 2-pinnate, segments of lower leaves wedge shaped. FLOWERS In crowded partial umbels; 1- bracts. FRUITS 3-3.5 mm, umbels becoming flat topped, pedicels and rays thickening, styles as long as fruit. HABITAT Old pastures, hay meadows, road side grassland. DIST. Native. Local in central-S England. (W and S Europe.) FLS Jun-Aug.

Narrow-leaved Water-dropwort   *Oenanthe silaifol.*

Erect, branched perennial to 100 cm. STEMS Hollow LEAVES Basal leaves 2-pinnate; segments narrow similar to upper leaves, soon withering. FLOWERS Bracts usually absent. FRUITS 2.5-3.5 mm, ray thickening, styles shorter than fruits. HABITAT Ol hay meadows, alluvial grassland, on floodplains calcareous rivers. DIST. Native. Very local in lowlan England. (Central, W and S Europe.) FLS May-Jun

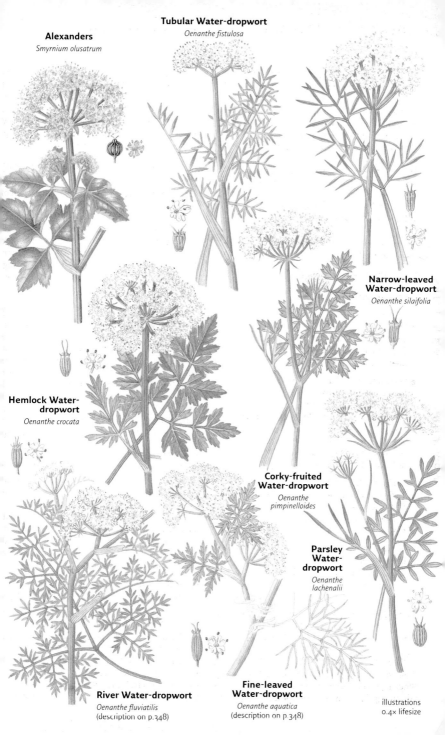

Alexanders
Smyrnium olusatrum

Tubular Water-dropwort
Oenanthe fistulosa

Narrow-leaved Water-dropwort
Oenanthe silaifolia

Hemlock Water-dropwort
Oenanthe crocata

Corky-fruited Water-dropwort
Oenanthe pimpinelloides

Parsley Water-dropwort
Oenanthe lachenalii

River Water-dropwort
Oenanthe fluviatilis
(description on p.348)

Fine-leaved Water-dropwort
Oenanthe aquatica
(description on p 348)

illustrations
0.4× lifesize

Fine-leaved Water-dropwort
Oenanthe aquatica

[*See* illustration previous page.] Robust, erect, stoloniferous annual or biennial to 150 cm. STEMS Hollow. LEAVES 3-pinnate; segments of aerial leaves lanceolate to ovate, acute; submerged leaves with fine, narrow segments. FLOWERS In umbels in axils of leaves, peduncles short. FRUITS 2.5–3.5 mm. HABITAT Ponds, slow-moving ditches, dykes, wet seasonal depressions, on fertile soils. DIST. Native. Local in lowland England, Wales, Ireland; absent from Scotland, SW England, W Wales. (Most of Europe except extreme N.) FLS Jun–Sep.

River Water-dropwort
Oenanthe fluviatilis

[*See* illustration previous page.] Aquatic perennial. Similar to *O. aquatica*, but stem procumbent, submerged except when flowering; submerged leaves 2-pinnate, deeply divided into narrow, wedge-shaped segments; aerial leaves broader, with blunt tips; fruits 5–6.5 mm. SIMILAR SPP. Can be distinguished from *O. aquatica* by habitat and larger fruits, but when not flowering and submerged it is easily overlooked. *O. aquatica* is a more delicate-looking plant and is more frequent. HABITAT Rivers, streams, with clear calcareous water. DIST. Native. Very local, declining. Lowland England, Ireland. (W Europe.) FLS Jul–Sep.

Hemlock
Conium maculatum

Tall, robust, much-branched, foetid, glabrous biennial to 250 cm. STEMS Hollow, smooth, *purple-spotted*, glaucous. LEAVES 2–3-pinnate; segments wedge-shaped, toothed. FLOWERS In terminal axillary umbels; *several bracts and bracteoles.* FRUITS 2–3.5 mm, rounded. HABITAT Riverbanks, ditches, roadsides, sea walls, waste ground; lowland to 305 m. DIST. Throughout BI, but rare in N Scotland. (All Europe except extreme N.) FLS Jun–Jul. NOTE *All parts of plant are poisonous.*

Wild Angelica
Angelica sylvestris

Tall, robust, ± *glabrous* perennial to 200 cm. STEMS Hollow. LEAVES 2–3-pinnate; *leaflets ovate, finely toothed; petioles strongly inflated.* FLOWERS Bracts absent, several bracteoles. FRUITS 4–5 mm. HABITAT Wet meadows, marshes, fens, wet woodlands, ditches; stream, river and lake margins. To 855 m. DIST. Native. Common throughout BI. (All Europe.) FLS Jul–Sep.

Wild Parsnip
Pastinaca sativa

Erect, thinly pubescent, *strong-smelling* biennial to 150 cm. STEMS Hollow. LEAVES 1-pinnate; leaflets large, ovate, toothed. FLOWERS Yellow; 0–2 bracts and bracteoles, soon falling. FRUITS 4–7 mm. HABITAT Rough grassland, roadside verges, hedge banks, waste ground, on calcareous soils. DIST. Native. England (common in S and SE), Wales; casual elsewhere. (Most of Europe except extreme N.) FLS Jul–Aug. NOTE The cultivated Parsnip, with its swollen root, is var. *hortensis* and occasionally occurs as a casual escape. *Juice of Parsnip can cause serious blisters in direct sunlight.*

Shepherd's-needle
Scandix pecten-veneris CR

Erect, branched, sparsely pubescent annual to 50 cm. STEMS Hollow. LEAVES 2–3-pinnate, segments narrow. FLOWERS *Umbels simple or with 2 rays only;* bracteoles lobed or entire. FRUITS 30–70 mm, *with very long beak (the 'needle').* HABITAT Arable weed of dry calcareous soils. DIST. Archaeophyte. Formerly throughout most of lowland Britain, now very local, declining. (W, central and S Europe.) FLS Apr–Jul.

Sweet Cicely
Myrrhis odorata

Robust, erect, sparsely pubescent perennial to 180 cm, *smelling strongly of aniseed.* STEMS Hollow. LEAVES 2–4-pinnate; lobes coarsely toothed, acute; *petioles of stem leaves sheathing.* FLOWERS *Bracts absent, c. 5 bracteoles.* FRUITS 15–25 mm, strongly ridged. HABITAT Road verges, hedge banks, riverbanks, wood margins, often near buildings. DIST. Introduced. Naturalised and common in N England, Wales, Scotland, N Ireland. (Mts of S Europe.) FLS May–Jun.

Moon Carrot
Seseli libanotis

Erect, *thinly pubescent* biennial or perennial to 60 cm. *Base of plant with fibrous remains of old petioles.* STEMS Ridged, solid. LEAVES 2–3-pinnate, *leaflets ovate.* FLOWERS Peduncles long; *bracts and bracteoles numerous,* narrow, entire; *petals pubescent on back.* FRUITS 2.5–3.5 mm, pubescent, strongly ridged. HABITAT Chalk grassland, roadside banks, abandoned quarries. DIST. Native. Very rare. East Anglia, Sussex. (Most of Europe except extreme N, W and S.) FLS Jul–Aug.

Mountain Seseli
Seseli montanum

Similar to *S. libanotis*, but erect, *glabrous* perennial to 80 cm; leaves 2–3-pinnate, *leaflets linear; bracts absent; petals glabrous;* fruit 2.5–4.5 mm, thinly pubescent, ridged. HABITAT Dry calcareous grassland. DIST. Not BI. (S Europe N to Somme Valley.) FLS Jul–Sep.

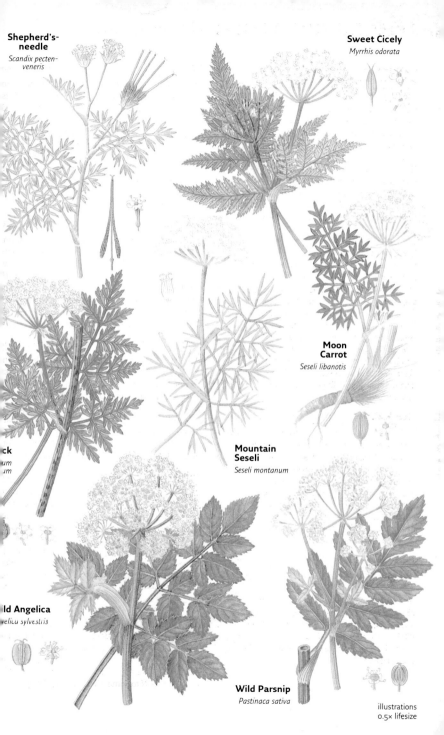

Shepherd's-needle
Scandix pecten-veneris

Sweet Cicely
Myrrhis odorata

Moon Carrot
Seseli libanotis

Mountain Seseli
Seseli montanum

...ck
...um
...um

...ld Angelica
...elica sylvestris

Wild Parsnip
Pastinaca sativa

illustrations
0.5× lifesize

Fool's Parsley
Aethusa cynapium

Branched, glabrous annual to 120 cm. STEMS Hollow. LEAVES 2-3-pinnate. FLOWERS In terminal, leaf-opposed umbels; bracts absent; *3-4 bracteoles, strongly reflexed, on outer side of partial umbels.* FRUITS 3-4 mm, glabrous, keeled. HABITAT Weed of waste ground, arable fields, gardens. DIST. Native in Britain, N to Solway Firth; naturalised in Ireland. (Most of Europe, but rare in Mediterranean.) FLS Jul-Aug.

Fennel
Foeniculum vulgare

Tall, glabrous, glaucous, perennial to 250 cm. LEAVES 3-4-pinnate; *segments long, filiform, not all in one plane.* FLOWERS *Yellow*; bracts and bracteoles absent. FRUITS 4-5 mm, glabrous, ribbed. HABITAT Cliffs, waste ground, rough grassland, roadsides, especially close to sea. DIST. Archaeophyte. Widely distributed in England, Wales; scarce elsewhere. (Most of Europe except N; native of S and SW.) FLS Jul-Oct.

Spignel
Meum athamanticum

Tufted, branched, glabrous, aromatic perennial to 60 cm. *Base of plant with fibrous remains of old petioles.* STEMS Hollow. LEAVES *Most basal, 3-4-pinnate; segments filiform, whorled.* FLOWERS 0-few bracts; several bracteoles, linear. FRUITS 5-7 mm, ridged. HABITAT Rough grassland, pastures, hay meadows, in upland areas; to 610 m. DIST. Native. N England, Scotland. (Mts of W and central Europe.) FLS Jun-Jul.

Bladderseed
Physospermum cornubiense

Erect, ± glabrous, rhizomatous perennial to 75 cm. STEMS Solid, ribbed. LEAVES *Most basal; petioles long, 2-ternate.* FLOWERS *With long pedicels, in umbels with long peduncles*; bracts and bracteoles lanceolate. FRUITS 2.5-4 mm, somewhat inflated. HABITAT Open woodland, scrub, heathland, rough grassland. DIST. Native. Very local. Devon, Cornwall. (S Europe.) FLS Jul-Aug.

Hare's-ears *Bupleurum*

Annuals or perennials. Leaves simple, entire. Sepals absent and petals yellow.

1	Leaves broad, upper fused across stem; bracts absent	*B. subovatum*
	Stem leaves narrow, not fused across stem; bracts present	2
2	Tall perennial to 100 cm; bracts shorter than rays	*B. falcatum*
	Annual; bracts longer than rays	3
3	Bracteoles narrow, not concealing flowers	*B. tenuissimum*
	Bracteoles ovate, concealing flowers	*B. baldense*

Slender Hare's-ear
Bupleurum tenuissimum Vt

Slender, erect, branched annual to 50 cm. STEM Wiry. LEAVES *Linear-lanceolate.* FLOWERS In axillar umbels up to 5 mm across; *1-3 rays, unequal; 3-bracts, longer than shorter rays.* HABITAT Rough grassland at upper levels of sa marshes, sea walls, banks of brackish dykes. DIST. Native. Very local. Coasts of England, especially Essex, Thames estuary. (S, W and central Europe FLS Jul-Sep.

Sickle-leaved Hare's-ear
Bupleurum falcatum *(

Erect biennial or perennial to 100 cm. LEAVE *3-8 cm, narrow.* FLOWERS 5-11 rays, unequal; *2-bracts, unequal; 4-5 bracteoles, shorter than pedicel* FRUITS 2.5-3.5 mm, ridged. HABITAT Hedge bank field borders, roadside verges. DIST. Introduced Widely grown in gardens, very rarely naturalised S Essex. (Central and E Europe.) FLS Jul-Oct.

Small Hare's-ear
Bupleurum baldense VU. *(

Small, slender erect annual to 10 cm. STEMS Soli LEAVES 1-1.5 cm. FLOWERS In umbels 5-10 mm across; *4 bracts, longer than rays; bracteoles ovat concealing flowers.* FRUITS 1.5-2.5 mm. HABITA Broken calcareous cliff-top turf, sand-dunes. DIST Native. Very rare. E Sussex, Devon, Channel Is. and W Europe.) FLS Jun-Jul.

False Thorow-wax
Bupleurum subovatu

Erect annual to 30 cm. LEAVES *Fused around ster >2× as long as wide.* FLOWERS Bracts absent; bract oles ovate, longer than flowers. FRUITS 3.5-5 mm *papillose between ridges.* HABITAT Casual of was ground, rubbish tips, garden weed. DIST. Introduce as birdseed alien. (S Europe.) FLS Jun-Jul. SIMILA SPP. **Thorow-wax** *Bupleurum rotundifolium*, fo merly a widespread arable weed, now occurs only a birdseed alien. It differs from *B. subovatum* in i broader leaves, <2× as long as wide, and fruits th are smooth between ridges.

False Thorow-wax
Bupleurum subovatum

Fennel
Foeniculum vulgare

Slender Hare's-ear
Bupleurum tenuissimum

Small Hare's-ear
Bupleurum baldense

l's Parsley
usa cynapium

Sickle-leaved Hare's-ear
Bupleurum falcatum

Spignel
Meum
manticum

Bladderseed
Physospermum cornubiense

illustrations
0.6× lifesize

Ground-elder
Aegopodium podagraria

Erect, glabrous, rhizomatous perennial to 100 cm, with *far-creeping rhizomes*. LEAVES *1-2-ternate; leaflets broad*, toothed. FLOWERS *Bracts and bracteoles absent.* FRUITS 3-4 mm, glabrous. HABITAT Hedgerows, road verges, wood margins; persistent and troublesome garden weed. To 450 m. DIST. Archaeophyte. Common throughout BI. (Most of Europe, but rare in S.) FLS May-Jul.

Greater Water-parsnip
Sium latifolium EN.

Robust, erect, glabrous perennial to 200 cm. LEAVES Simply pinnate; *3-6 pairs of leaflets*, large, to 15 cm, sessile, finely toothed. FLOWERS *In terminal umbels; several bracts and bracteoles*; sepals large, persistent. FRUITS 2.5-4 mm, prominently ridged, *longer than wide*. HABITAT Margins of dykes, ditches and drains in fenland and alluvial marshes with base-rich, calcareous water. DIST. Native. Very local and declining. England, central Ireland. (Most of Europe except parts of S and SW.) FLS Jul-Aug.

Lesser Water-parsnip
Berula erecta

Decumbent or erect, glabrous, submerged or emergent, stoloniferous aquatic perennial to 100 cm. LEAVES Simply pinnate; *5-10 pairs of leaflets*, 2-6 cm, sessile, coarsely toothed or slightly lobed; *lower petioles with ring-like mark towards base*. FLOWERS *In leaf-opposed umbels; several bracts and bracteoles.* FRUITS 1.5-2 mm, ridges not prominent, *almost circular*. HABITAT Margins of ponds, ditches, dykes, canals, slow-moving rivers and marshes with fertile, calcareous water. DIST. Native. Frequent throughout lowland BI, but rare in Scotland and SW. (All Europe except extreme N.) FLS Jul-Sep.

Marshworts *Apium*

1 Leaflets of lower leaves stalked; bracteoles absent; smelling of celery — *A. graveolens*
  Leaflets of lower leaves sessile; bracteoles present — 2

2 Lower leaves 2-3-pinnate, leaflets linear — *A. inundatum*
  Lower leaves pinnate, leaflets not linear — 3

3 Bracts absent; peduncles shorter than rays; fruits longer than wide — *A. nodiflorum*
  3-7 bracts; peduncles longer than rays; fruits slightly wider than long — *A. repens*

Fool's Water-cress
Apium nodiflorum

Prostrate to erect, glabrous perennial to 100 cm. STEMS Rooting at lower nodes. LEAVES Simply pinnate; *2-4 pairs of leaflets*, ovate, longer than wide, weakly toothed; *lower petioles without ring-like mark*. FLOWERS *In leaf-opposed umbels*; peduncles shorter than rays; *bracts absent*, bracteoles as long as flowers. FRUITS 1.5-2.5 mm, longer than wide, ridged. HABITAT Shallow water of dykes, ditches, streams, ponds, on fertile or calcareous soils. DIST. Native. Widespread and common in England, Wales, Ireland; rare in Scotland. (Most of Europe.) FLS Jul-Aug.

NOTE Often confused with *Berula erecta*, but distinguished from this in the vegetative state by absence of ring-like mark on petiole, and, when flowering, by absence of bracts. Also mistaken for *Rorippa nasturtium-aquaticum* (p.190).

Creeping Marshwort
Apium repens VU. *(®

Creeping perennial. Similar to small plants of *A. nodiflorum*, but prostrate stems rooting at all nodes; leaflets about as long as wide; peduncles longer than rays; 2-6 bracts; fruits ≤1 mm, slightly wider than long. HABITAT Damp, grazed meadows, ditches subject to winter flooding. DIST. Native. Very rare: one site only, in Oxfordshire. (Central and E Europe.) FLS Jun-Sep.

Wild Celery
Apium graveolens

Tall, erect, glabrous biennial to 100 cm, *smelling strongly of celery*. STEMS Solid, grooved. LEAVES *Basal leaves pinnate, basal leaflets stalked.* FLOWERS *Greenish white*; in terminal, axillary umbels; *bracts and bracteoles absent*. FRUITS 1-1.5 mm. HABITAT Usually in brackish water of river, stream, ditch and dyke margins, sea walls. DIST. Native. Coastal areas of BI N to Solway Firth; rare inland. (Coasts of Europe N to Denmark.) FLS Jun-Aug.

Lesser Marshwort
Apium inundatum

Prostrate, submerged or floating, slender perennial to 50 cm. STEMS Rooting at nodes. LEAVES *Lower leaves 2-3-pinnate; leaflets narrow*, those of upper leaves broader. FLOWERS *In leaf-opposed umbel; bracts absent*, 3-6 bracteoles. FRUITS 2.5-3 mm, ridged. HABITAT Shallow water of acid pools, ponds, lakes, ditches, streams; lowland to 500 m. DIST. Native. Local, declining. Scattered throughout BI. (W and central Europe.) FLS Jun-Aug.

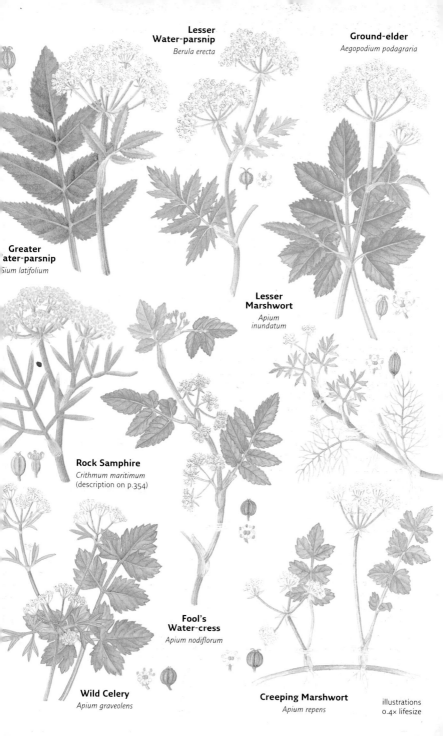

Lesser Water-parsnip
Berula erecta

Ground-elder
Aegopodium podagraria

Greater Water-parsnip
Sium latifolium

Lesser Marshwort
Apium inundatum

Rock Samphire
Crithmum maritimum
(description on p.354)

Fool's Water-cress
Apium nodiflorum

Wild Celery
Apium graveolens

Creeping Marshwort
Apium repens

illustrations
0.4× lifesize

Rock Samphire
Crithmum maritimum

[*See* illustration previous page.] Much-branched, *glabrous, fleshy perennial* to 30 cm. STEMS ± woody at base. LEAVES *Succulent, 2-3-pinnate*; leaflets smooth, rounded in section, acute; petioles sheathing. FLOWERS *Yellowish green*; several bracts and bracteoles. FRUITS 3.5-5 mm, glabrous, ridged. HABITAT Maritime rocks, cliffs, stabilised shingle, sea defences. DIST. Native. S and W coasts of Britain from Suffolk on E to Ayr on W; all round coasts of Ireland. (W and Mediterranean coasts of Europe.) FLS Jun-Aug.

Pepper-saxifrage
Silaum silaus

Erect, branched, glabrous perennial to 100 cm. LEAVES *2-3-pinnate; leaflets lanceolate, finely toothed.* FLOWERS *Yellowish*, in umbels with long peduncles; 0-3 bracts, several bracteoles. FRUITS 4-5 mm. HABITAT Old meadows and grassy commons, rough grassland, roadsides, on heavy soils. DIST. Native. Widely distributed S and E of line from Tees to Exe; absent from Ireland. (W, central and E Europe.) FLS Jun-Aug.

Honewort
Trinia glauca

Erect, rather glaucous, *dioecious biennial* or perennial to 20 cm. STEMS *Branching from base; base of stems with dense cluster of fibrous dead petioles.* LEAVES *1-3-pinnate, leaflets linear.* FLOWERS In umbels, female umbels larger and with more uneven rays than male umbels; 0-1 bracts, lobed; 2-3 bracteoles, simple. FRUITS 2.3-3 mm. HABITAT Short, dry limestone grassland. DIST. Native. Very rare. Devon, Gloucestershire, Somerset. (W, central and S Europe.) FLS May-Jun.

Corn Parsley
Petroselinum segetum

Erect, glabrous, *slightly glaucous* biennial to 100 cm. STEMS *Branching at wide angle.* LEAVES *Narrowly oblong*; lowest leaves simply pinnate, with *4-12 pairs of leaflets*; leaflets coarsely toothed, matt. FLOWERS *In uneven umbels;* 2-5 bracts and bracteoles, *longest bracts >½ as long as rays.* FRUITS 2.5-4 mm. HABITAT Brackish grassland, sea walls, riverbanks, roadsides, field margins, on fertile or calcareous soils. DIST. Native. Local. Widely distributed S and E of line from Humber to Severn. (W Europe.) FLS Aug-Sep.

Parsley
Petroselinum crispum

Erect, glabrous biennial with *characteristic parsley smell*. Similar to *P. segetum*, but stems branching at narrow angle; *leaves 3-pinnate*; leaflets often crisped,

shining; *flowers yellowish*. HABITAT Cliffs, banks, walls, waste ground, often in coastal areas. DIST. Archaeophyte (origins uncertain). Occasional casual and escape from cultivation throughout most of BI except N Scotland, sometimes persistent. (Naturalised in most of Europe.) FLS Jun-Aug.

Stone Parsley
Sison amomum

Erect, glabrous, branching biennial to 100 cm, with *characteristic unpleasant petrol-like smell*. LEAVES Lowest leaves simply pinnate, with *2-5 pairs of leaflets*; leaflets broad, coarsely toothed or lobed. FLOWERS In terminal, axillary umbels; 2-4 bracts and bracteoles, *bracts <⅛ as long as rays*. FRUITS 1.5-3 mm. HABITAT Hedgerows, grassy banks, roadside verges, on heavy soils. DIST. Locally frequent. Native. Widely distributed S and E of line from Humber to Severn, N Wales. (S and W Europe.) FLS Jul-Sep.

Cowbane
Cicuta virosa

Robust, erect, glabrous perennial to 150 cm. LEAVES *2-3-pinnate; leaflets linear-lanceolate, sharply toothed*; petioles hollow, base sheathing. FLOWERS In terminal, leaf-opposed, *dense-flowered* umbels; *bracts absent; several bracteoles, longer than pedicels.* FRUITS 1.2-2 mm. SIMILAR SPP. Only likely to be confused with *Sium latifolium* (p.352), but this has simply pinnate leaves. HABITAT Shallow water of marshes, pond margins, ditches, drainage dykes, carr woodland. DIST. Native. Very local. Norfolk Broads, Shropshire, Cheshire, central Ireland; scattered elsewhere. (Most of Europe, but rare in S.) FLS Jul-Aug.

Bullwort
Ammi majus

Erect, glabrous annual to 100 cm. LEAVES Lower leaves 1-2-pinnate; leaflets narrowly ovate, toothed. FLOWERS *Several bracts, pinnate, lobes linear; bracteoles narrow, as long as rays.* FRUITS 1.5-2 mm. HABITAT Waste places, parks, old gardens, roadsides. DIST. Introduced (birdseed and wool-shoddy alien). Infrequent casual throughout lowland Britain. (S Europe.) FLS Jun-Oct.

Longleaf
Falcaria vulgaris

Erect, much-branched, glabrous, glaucous, rhizomatous perennial to 90 cm. LEAVES *1-2-ternate; lobes to 30 cm, linear, sharply toothed, slightly falcate.* FLOWERS 4-15 bracts and bracteoles, linear. FRUITS 2.5-4 mm. HABITAT Arable fields, roadsides, waste ground, scrub, riverbanks. DIST. Introduced. Naturalised or casual, infrequent, in lowland England. (W, central and S Europe.) FLS Jul.

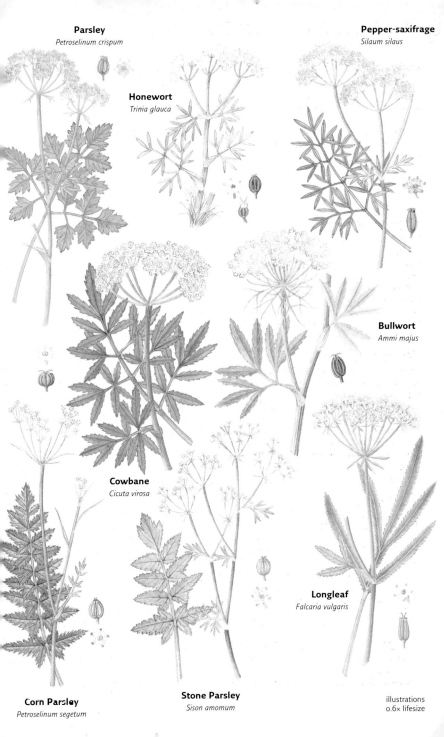

Parsley
Petroselinum crispum

Pepper-saxifrage
Silaum silaus

Honewort
Trinia glauca

Bullwort
Ammi majus

Cowbane
Cicuta virosa

Longleaf
Falcaria vulgaris

Corn Parsley
Petroselinum segetum

Stone Parsley
Sison amomum

illustrations
0.6× lifesize

Milk-parsley
Peucedanum palustre VU.

Erect, glabrous biennial to 150 cm. STEMS *Hollow.* LEAVES 2-4-pinnate; leaflets ovate-lanceolate, *acute but without short spiny tip*, margins finely toothed. FLOWERS White; *4 bracts; several bracteoles, reflexed.* FRUITS 4-5 mm. HABITAT Tall, herb-rich vegetation, calcareous fens and marshes. DIST. Native. Very local. East Anglian fens, Norfolk Broads. (Most of Europe except extreme S and SW.) FLS Jul-Sep. NOTE Food plant of Swallowtail butterfly.

Hog's Fennel
Peucedanum officinale

Erect, glabrous perennial to 120 cm. STEMS Solid. LEAVES *4-6-ternate; leaflets linear, entire.* FLOWERS *Yellow; 0-3 bracts*, narrow; several bracteoles. FRUITS *c.*7 mm. HABITAT Rough grassland, banks, grassy cliffs close to sea. DIST. Native. Rare, very local. Coastal areas of N Essex, N Kent. (Central and S Europe.) FLS Jul-Sep.

Cambridge Milk-parsley
Selinum carvifolia VU. *(B)

Erect, glabrous perennial to 100 cm. STEMS Solid. LEAVES 2-3-pinnate; *leaflets lanceolate-ovate with short spiny tip.* FLOWERS *Bracts usually absent; several bracteoles, erect or spreading.* FRUITS 3-4 mm. SIMI-LAR SPP. Confused with *Peucedanum palustre*, with which it grows, but distinguished by solid stem, short spiny tip to leaflets, bracts usually absent and bracteoles erect or spreading. HABITAT Tall, herb-rich vegetation, calcareous fens, marshes. DIST. Native. Very rare, in only *c.*3 localities in Cambridgeshire. (Most of Europe except Mediterranean.) FLS Jul-Oct.

Whorled Caraway
Carum verticillatum

Erect, glabrous perennial to 60 cm. STEMS Base with dense tuft of fibrous remains of old petioles. LEAVES *Mostly basal, narrow in outline, simply pinnate; each leaflet repeatedly lobed into fine segments, appearing as if whorled.* FLOWERS Several bracts and bracteoles. FRUITS 2-3 mm. HABITAT Damp marshes, rushy pastures, steam sides, on acid soils. DIST. Native. W England, Wales, Scotland, Ireland. (W Europe.) FLS Jul-Aug.

Caraway
Carum carvi EN.

Erect, much-branched, glabrous perennial to 60 cm. LEAVES *All basal, 2-pinnate; leaflets linear, deeply divided.* FLOWERS *Bracts and bracteoles absent or few.* FRUITS 3-4 mm, with *distinctive smell* when crushed, used for flavouring. HABITAT Naturalised or casual on meadows, roadsides, sand-dunes, waste places. DIST. Archaeophyte. Declining. Scattered throughout BI. (N and central Europe.) FLS Jun-Jul.

Scots Lovage
Ligusticum scoticum

Glabrous, *shiny, bright green perennial* to 90 cm. LEAVES 1-2-ternate; basal leaflets long-stalked, ovate. FLOWERS *Greenish white*; 1-5 bracts, *c.*7 bracteoles. FRUITS 4-7 mm. HABITAT Maritime cliffs, rocks, shingle, stabilised dunes, sea defences. DIST. Native. All round coasts of Scotland, N Ireland. (N Europe.) FLS Jul.

Lovage
Levisticum officinale

Tall, glabrous perennial to 250 cm, *smelling strongly of celery.* LEAVES *2-3-pinnate; leaflets broad, coarsely toothed.* FLOWERS *Yellowish*; numerous bracts and bracteoles. FRUITS 5-7 mm. SIMILAR SPP. Superficially similar to *Angelica* (p.348), but distinguished by leaf shape and yellowish flowers. HABITAT Occasionally occurs as relic of cultivation or naturalised on rough ground. DIST. Introduced (native of Iran and Afghanistan). FLS Jul-Aug.

Sermountain
Laserpitium latifolium

Tall, almost glabrous, *rather grey-green* perennial to 150 cm. LEAVES 2-pinnate; *leaflets ovate, cordate, toothed, slightly hairy beneath*; *petioles of stem leaves inflated*, sheathing. FLOWERS Numerous bracts, few bracteoles. FRUITS 5-10 mm. HABITAT Woodland margins, clearings, scrub, on calcareous soils. DIST. *Not BI.* (Most of Europe.) FLS Jul-Aug.

Sermountain
Laserpitium latifolium

Caraway
Carum carvi

Whorled Caraway
Carum verticillatum

Cambridge Milk-parsley
Selinum carvifolia

Scots Lovage
Ligusticum scoticum

Milk-parsley
Peucedanum palustre

Lovage
Levisticum officinale

Hog's Fennel
Peucedanum officinale

illustrations
0.4× lifesize

Hogweed
Heracleum sphondylium

Tall, robust, pubescent biennial to 200 cm. The commonest late-summer-flowering wayside umbellifer. STEMS Hollow. LEAVES *Simply pinnate, roughly hairy on both surfaces, leaflets lobed*. FLOWERS Bracts absent or few; several bracteoles, reflexed; *petals deeply notched*. FRUITS 7-8 mm. HABITAT Hedgerows, roadside verges, woodland clearings, rough grassland. DIST. Native. Common throughout BI. (All Europe except N Scandinavia.) FLS Jun-Sep.

Giant Hogweed
Heracleum mantegazzianum

Enormous pubescent biennial or perennial to 550 cm. STEMS Hollow, red-spotted. LEAVES Pinnate to ternate, up to 250 cm; *leaflets toothed or lobed, lobes acute.* FLOWERS In umbels to 50 cm across; several bracts and bracteoles. FRUITS 9-14 mm. HABITAT Banks of streams and rivers, waste ground, derelict gardens, roadsides. DIST. Introduced in 1820 (native of SW Asia). Naturalised, spreading throughout BI. (Most of Europe) FLS Jun-Jul. NOTE *Causes dermatitis on contact with skin in sunlight.*

Hartwort
Tordylium maximum

Erect, *coarsely hairy annual or biennial* to 130 cm. LEAVES Simply pinnate, roughly hairy on both surfaces; *leaflets of lower leaves almost orbicular*, those of upper leaves lanceolate. FLOWERS *In umbels with long peduncles*; several bracts and bracteoles. FRUITS 4.5-6 mm, roughly hairy. HABITAT Established on rough, scrubby grassland. DIST. Introduced. Very rare. S Essex. (S and S-central Europe.) FLS Jun-Jul.

Upright Hedge-parsley
Torilis japonica

Erect, roughly hairy annual to 120 cm. STEMS Solid. LEAVES 1-3-pinnate, *lanceolate in outline*. FLOWERS *In umbels with 5-12 rays; 4-6 bracts*; several bracteoles; petals hairy beneath. FRUITS 4-6 mm, with hooked spines. HABITAT Hedgerows, road verges, woodland margins, rough grassland; to 410 m. DIST. Native. Common throughout most of BI, but rare or absent in N Scotland. (Most of Europe.) FLS Jul-Aug, after *Chaerophyllum temulum* (p.344).

Spreading Hedge-parsley
Torilis arvensis EN

Erect annual to 50 cm. STEMS *Wide-spreading*. LEAVES 1-2-pinnate, lanceolate in outline. FLOWERS *In umbel with 3-5 rays; 0-1 bracts*; several bracteoles, with coarse hairs. FRUITS 4-6 mm, with long, tapering spines. HABITAT Arable weed of autumn-sown cereals. DIST. Archaeophyte. Very rare and declining. Lowland England. (W, central and S Europe.) FLS Jul-Sep.

Knotted Hedge-parsley
Torilis nodosa

Prostrate, sparsely pubescent annual to 35 cm. LEAVES 1-2-pinnate; leaflets lanceolate, deeply lobed. FLOWERS Pinkish, *in sessile, leaf-opposed umbels 0.5-1 cm across*; 2-3 rays, very short; bracts absent; bracteoles longer than flowers. FRUITS 2-3 mm, very spiny. HABITAT Dry, open areas, banks, sea walls, clifftops, arable fields, waste ground. DIST. Native. Locally declining. Scattered throughout lowland Britain; very rare and mostly coastal in Scotland, Ireland. (S and W Europe.) FLS May-Jul.

Wild Carrot
Daucus carota ssp. *carota*

Erect, thinly pubescent or hispid biennial with characteristic smell, to 100 cm. STEMS Solid. LEAVES 3-pinnate; leaflets branched, lobes lanceolate-ovate. FLOWERS White, in umbels with numerous glabrous or thinly pubescent rays, *central flower often dark purple; 7-13 bracts, branched, about as long as pedicels.* FRUITS 2.5-4 mm, spiny. HABITAT Broken turf, rough grassland, roadsides, waste ground, on dry calcareous soils. DIST. Native. Widespread throughout BI; mostly coastal in Scotland. (Most of Europe.) FLS Jun-Aug. NOTE The cultivated Carrot, with its fleshy orange taproot, is *D. carota* ssp. *sativus*; it occasionally occurs as a casual escape of cultivation.

Sea Carrot
Daucus carota ssp. *gummifer*

Similar to *Daucus carota* ssp. *carota*, but rays with spreading or reflexed hairs; umbels flat or convex in fruit. HABITAT Maritime grassland, cliffs, stable sand-dunes. DIST. Native. Local on coasts of S and SW England, Wales, SE Ireland, Channel Is, Scilly Is. (Coasts of France, N Spain.) FLS Jun-Aug.

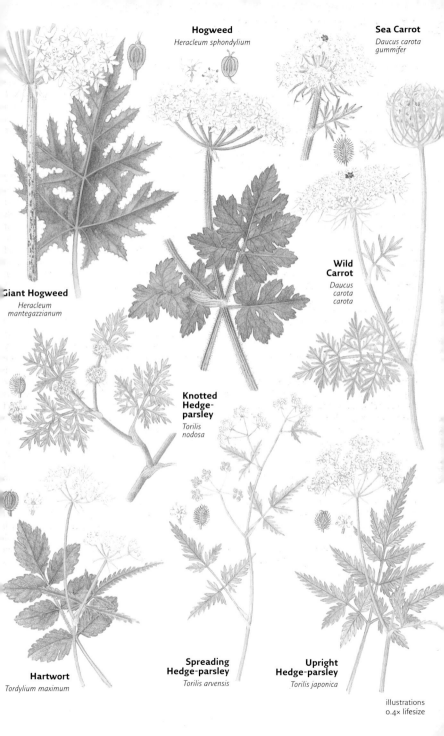

Hogweed
Heracleum sphondylium

Sea Carrot
Daucus carota gummifer

Giant Hogweed
Heracleum mantegazzianum

Wild Carrot
Daucus carota carota

Knotted Hedge-parsley
Torilis nodosa

Hartwort
Tordylium maximum

Spreading Hedge-parsley
Torilis arvensis

Upright Hedge-parsley
Torilis japonica

illustrations
0.4× lifesize

if		**then**
1	▷ Corolla blue or purple	Go to ▷ **2**
	▷ Corolla pink	Go to ▷ **3**
	▷ Corolla yellow	Go to ▷ **4**
2	▷ Corolla with small lobes between the large ones, without a fringe at mouth of corolla tube	*Gentiana* (p.362)
	▷ Corolla without small lobes between large ones, fringed at mouth of corolla tube	*Gentianella* (p.364)
3	▷ 5 corolla lobes, >2 mm	*Centaurium* (p.362)
	▷ 4 corolla lobes, <2 mm	*Exaculum* (Guernsey) (p.364)
4	▷ 6–8 petals; stem leaves broad, joined across stem; stems to 45 cm tall	*Blackstonia* (p.364)
	▷ 4 petals; stem leaves linear; small annual to 12 cm tall	*Cicendia* (p.364)

Centauries *Centaurium*

1	▷ Erect annuals or biennials without prostrate non-flowering shoots; corolla lobes ≤7 mm	Go to ▷ **2**
	▷ Perennial with prostrate non-flowering shoots; leaves rounded, shortly stalked; corolla lobes 8–9 mm	*C. scilloides* (p.362)
2	▷ Plants with basal leaf rosette at flowering; flowers ± sessile and clustered	Go to ▷ **3**
	▷ Plants without basal rosettes at flowering; flowers with 1–4 mm stalks, not clustered	Go to ▷ **4**
3	▷ Leaves ovate to oblong; calyx usually <¾ as long as corolla tube	*C. erythraea* (p.362)
	▷ Leaves linear, ± parallel-sided; calyx >¾ as long as corolla tube	*C. littorale* (p.362)
4	▷ Main stem with 2–4 internodes, branches spreading at wide angle; flowers bright pink	*C. pulchellum* (p.362)
	▷ Main stem with 5–9 internodes, branches spreading at narrow angle; flowers usually white	*C. tenuiflorum* (p.362)

if	then

Gentians *Gentianella*

Identification of species of *Gentianella* can be very difficult, as some are extremely variable and many hybridise freely. In addition, populations of some species can contain both annuals and biennials that may differ from one another.

1   ▷ Flowers blue with long fringes along sides of corolla lobes   ***G. ciliata*** (p.364)

     ▷ Flowers purple or bluish purple with narrow fringes at base of corolla lobes   Go to ▷ **2**

2   ▷ 4 calyx and corolla lobes, calyx with 2 large outer lobes that are several times wider and overlapping 2 smaller inner lobes   ***G. campestris*** (p.364)

     ▷ 4–5 calyx lobes, the widest <2× as wide as others   Go to ▷ **3**

3   ▷ Corolla 25–35 mm, ≥2× as long as calyx, with 9–15 internodes   ***G. germanica*** (p.364)

     ▷ Corolla 12–20 mm, ≤2× as long as calyx, with 2–11 internodes   Go to ▷ **4**

4   ▷ 4–9 internodes, uppermost internode and terminal pedicel together forming <⅕ total height of plant   ***G. amarella*** (p.364)

     ▷ 0–3 internodes; uppermost internode and terminal pedicel together forming >⅕ total height of plant   Go to ▷ **5**

5   ▷ Upper stem leaves lanceolate or linear-lanceolate; calyx lobes ± equal, appressed to corolla   ***G. anglica*** (p.364)

     ▷ Upper stem leaves ovate to ovate-lanceolate; calyx lobes usually unequal, not appressed to corolla   ***G. uliginosa*** (p.364)

GENTIANACEAE Gentians and centauries

Glabrous annuals or perennials with opposite, entire, sessile leaves (*see* key on p.360). Flowers are regular; 4–5 sepals, fused; 4–5 petals, fused into a corolla tube; 4–5 stamens; ovary superior; corolla persisting around the 2-valved capsule.

Marsh Gentian   *Gentiana pneumonanthe*

Erect glabrous perennial to 40 cm. Leaves *Stem leaves linear*, 1.5–4 cm. Flowers In 1–15-flowered inflorescence; *corolla tube 25–50 mm*, with 5 green lines on outside. Habitat Wet heaths, damp acidic grassland. Dist. Native. Very local, declining. Scattered throughout lowland England, N Wales, especially New Forest, Dorset. (Most of Europe except extreme N and S.) Fls Aug–Sep.

Spring Gentian   *Gentiana verna* *(B)

Erect perennial to 6 cm. Leaves 5–15 mm, ovate; *basal leaves in cushion-like rosette*. Flowers *Solitary, terminal; corolla tube 15–25 mm, corolla lobes spreading, 15–30 mm across*. Habitat Open limestone grassland, calcareous flushes, fixed calcareous dunes; to 730 m. Dist. Native. Rare, very local. Upper Teesdale, lowland W Ireland. (Mts of central and S Europe.) Fls Apr–Jun.

Alpine Gentian   *Gentiana nivalis* *(B)

Slender, erect annual to 15 cm. Leaves Lower leaves 2–10 mm, ovate. Flowers *1–10; corolla tube 10–15 mm, corolla lobes spreading, 7 10 mm across*. Habitat Grazed species-rich grassland, base-rich rocky slopes, scree; to 1095 m. Dist. Native. Very rare. Scottish Highlands. (N Europe, mts of S Europe.) Fls Jul–Sep.

Cross Gentian   *Gentiana cruciata*

Erect perennial to 40 cm. Stems Several arising from basal rosette. Leaves *Ovate, 3-veined, sheathing at base, stem leaves numerous*. Flowers In terminal, axillary clusters; corolla 20–25 mm. Habitat Dry calcareous grassland, woodland clearings. Dist. *Not BI*. (S, central and E Europe W to Netherlands.) Fls Jun–Sep.

Centauries *Centaurium*

See key to *Centaurium* on p.360.

Common Centaury   *Centaurium erythraea*

Erect, glabrous annual to 50 cm. Stems Usually solitary, branched. Leaves *Basal leaves 1–5 cm, in a rosette, ovate, prominently 3–7-veined beneath, apex acute*. Flowers *Sessile*, clustered; 1–2 bracts at base of calyx; corolla lobes 4.5–5.5 mm; *stigmas conical*. Habitat Permanent grassland, woodland rides, scrub, grassy heaths, dunes, road verges, on well-drained soils. Dist. Native. Throughout most of BI; rare, local and mostly coastal in Scotland. (Most of Europe except N Scandinavia.) Fls Jun–Oct.

Lesser Centaury   *Centaurium pulchellum* *(R)

Slender, erect annual to 15 cm. Stems Simple or much branched; *basal rosette absent; 2–4 stem internodes*. Leaves 2–15 mm, ovate. Flowers Deep pink; corolla lobes 2–4 mm; *bracts 1–4 mm below base of calyx; flower stalks 1–4 mm*. Habitat Dry, open areas, woodland rides, grassland, heaths, sand-dunes, on sandy or calcareous soils. Dist. Native. Widespread in S England; coastal further N; rare or absent in Scotland, Ireland. (Most of Europe except extreme N.) Fls Jun–Sep.

Seaside Centaury   *Centaurium littorale* *(NI)

Erect, slightly scabrid annual to 25 cm. Leaves *Basal leaves 1–2 cm, linear, 1-veined*, in a rosette; *stem leaves oblong, almost parallel-sided, rounded at apex*. Flowers Sessile, clustered; corolla lobes 5–6.5 mm long *stigma ± flat-topped*. Habitat Sand-dunes, short grazed maritime grassland. Dist. Native. Very local. Coasts of Wales, NW England, Scotland. (N Europe.) Fls Jul–Aug.

Slender Centaury   *Centaurium tenuiflorum* VU. *(B)

Glabrous, erect, much-branched annual to 35 cm. Stems *Basal rosette absent; branches erect, spreading at 20–30°; 5–9 stem internodes*. Leaves 10–25 mm. Flowers *Clustered, usually white*; corolla lobe 3–4 mm. Habitat Open, unstable, slumping coastal cliffs. Dist. Native. Very rare, in one site in Dorset only. (S and W Europe.) Fls Jul–Sep.

Perennial Centaury   *Centaurium scilloides* EN

Glabrous, *prostrate perennial* to 30 cm. Stems *Numerous sterile stems* and ascending flowering stems. Leaves *Basal leaves ± orbicular*, to 10 mm. Flowers 1–6 on pedicels; *corolla lobes 8–9 mm*. Habitat Coastal-cliff grassland, maritime heath. Dist. Native. Very rare. In a single site in W Wales; rare escape from cultivation elsewhere. (Atlantic coasts of Europe.) Fls Jul–Aug.

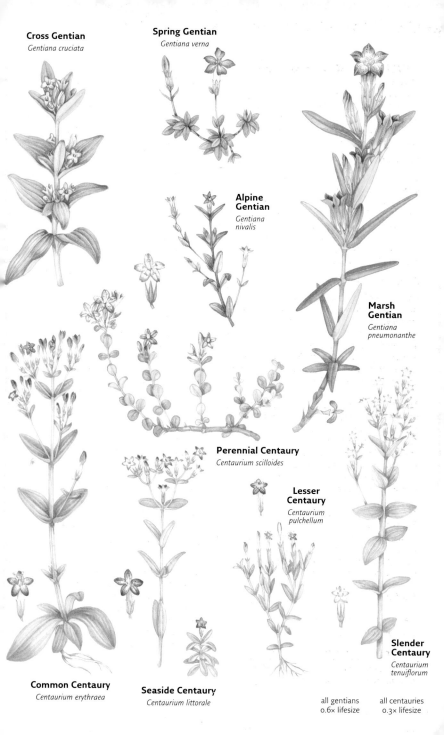

Cross Gentian
Gentiana cruciata

Spring Gentian
Gentiana verna

Alpine Gentian
Gentiana nivalis

Marsh Gentian
Gentiana pneumonanthe

Perennial Centaury
Centaurium scilloides

Lesser Centaury
Centaurium pulchellum

Common Centaury
Centaurium erythraea

Seaside Centaury
Centaurium littorale

Slender Centaury
Centaurium tenuiflorum

all gentians
0.6× lifesize

all centauries
0.3× lifesize

Gentians *Gentianella*
See key to *Gentianella* on p.361.

Autumn Gentian, Felwort   *Gentianella amarella*

Erect, branched biennial to 30 cm. STEMS 5-9 *internodes*, all ± equal or upper ones shorter. LEAVES Stem leaves 10-20 mm. FLOWERS *Calyx teeth ± equal*; corolla 14-20 mm, ≤2× as long as calyx. HABITAT Short calcareous grassland, calcareous dunes, dune slacks, machair; to 750 m. DIST. Native. Throughout BI. (N and central Europe.) FLS Aug-Oct.

Field Gentian   *Gentianella campestris* VU.

Erect annual or biennial to 30 cm. STEMS Simple or branched. LEAVES Stem leaves 20-30 mm. FLOWERS *4 calyx and corolla lobes; 2 outer calyx lobes much larger than, and hiding, 2 inner lobes*; corolla 15-25 mm, corolla tube as long as or longer than calyx. HABITAT Pastures, hill grassland, grass heaths, sand-dunes, machair, on acid soils; to 915 m. DIST. Native. Declining. Widely distributed in N and upland Britain; rare elsewhere. (N and central Europe.) FLS Jul-Oct.

Chiltern Gentian   *Gentianella germanica*

Erect annual or biennial to 35 cm. STEMS 9-15 *internodes*, all ± equal or upper ones shorter. LEAVES Basal leaves soon withering; stem leaves 1-2.5 cm. FLOWERS 5 calyx and corolla lobes; *corolla 25-35 mm, ≥2× as long as calyx*. HABITAT Rough chalk grassland, open scrub. DIST. Native. Very local. Chilterns. (W and central Europe.) FLS Sep-Oct.

Early Gentian   *Gentianella anglica* *(B)

Small, erect annual or biennial to 20 cm. STEMS *0-3 internodes; terminal internode ≥½ total height of plant*. LEAVES Stem leaves lanceolate-oblong. FLOWERS Calyx lobes ± equal, *appressed to corolla*; corolla 13-15 mm. HABITAT Short, grazed chalk grassland, cliff tops, sand-dunes. DIST. Endemic. Very local. S England. FLS Mar-Jul. NOTE Appears not to be genetically distinct from *G. amarella*, although flowering time and morphology differ.

Dune Gentian   *Gentianella uliginosa* VU. *(B)

Erect annual or biennial to 15 cm. STEMS *0-2 internodes; terminal internode >⅓ total height of plant*. LEAVES Stem leaves ovate. FLOWERS *Pedicels long; calyx lobes unequal, spreading*; corolla 9-22 mm. HABITAT Coastal dune slacks, machair. DIST. Native. Local, very rare. N Devon, S Wales, W Scotland. (N and N-central Europe.) FLS Aug-Nov.

Fringed Gentian   *Gentianella ciliata* CR. *(B)

Erect biennial to 30 cm. STEMS 4-6 internodes. LEAVES Stem leaves 1-3 cm, lanceolate. FLOWERS Calyx lobes equal; *corolla 25-50 mm, blue; corolla lobes with long fringes along margins*. HABITAT Short, grazed, herb-rich chalk grassland. DIST. Native. Very rare, at a single site in Chilterns. (Most of Europe except extreme N and W.) FLS Jun-Oct.

Yellow-wort   *Blackstonia perfoliata*

Erect, glaucous annual to 45 cm. LEAVES Basal leaves 1-2 cm, in a rosette, obovate, with strong midvein and weaker laterals beneath; *stem leaves broad, fused across stem at base*. FLOWERS Corolla 10-15 mm across; *6-8 petals, yellow*. HABITAT Herb-rich calcareous grassland, quarries, fixed coastal dunes. DIST. Native. Britain N to Humber; central and S Ireland. (W, S and central Europe.) FLS Jun-Oct.

Yellow Centaury   *Cicendia filiformis* VU.

Slender, erect annual to 12 cm. STEMS Simple or little branched. LEAVES 2-6 mm, linear. FLOWERS *Yellow, 3-5 mm across; 4 petals*. HABITAT Seasonally wet sandy patches in open heathland, woodland rides, dune slacks. DIST. Native. Very local. S and SW England, W Wales, SW Ireland. (S and W Europe.) FLS Jun-Oct.

Guernsey Centaury   *Exaculum pusillum*

Small, slender, prostrate to erect annual, to 10 cm. LEAVES Linear, 2-12 mm. FLOWERS *Pink; 4 calyx lobes, linear; corolla 3-6 mm; 4 petals, lobes spreading*. HABITAT Moist, open, short, rabbit-grazed turf of dune slacks. DIST. Native. Very rare. Guernsey (Channel Is). (SW Europe.) FLS Jul-Sep.

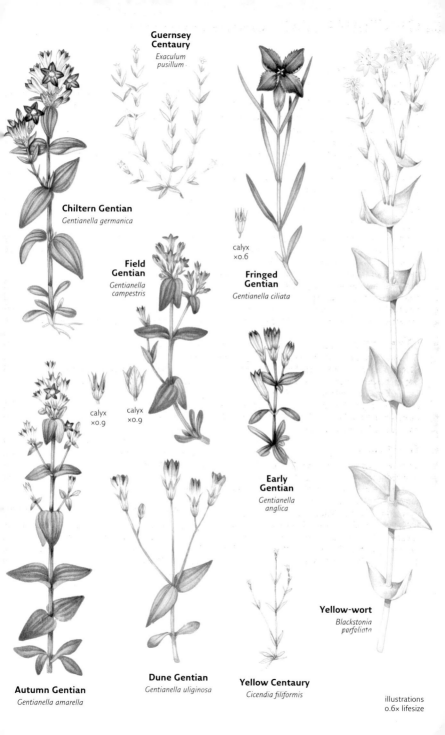

Guernsey Centaury
Exaculum pusillum

Chiltern Gentian
Gentianella germanica

calyx
×0.6

Field Gentian
Gentianella campestris

Fringed Gentian
Gentianella ciliata

calyx
×0.9

calyx
×0.9

Early Gentian
Gentianella anglica

Autumn Gentian
Gentianella amarella

Dune Gentian
Gentianella uliginosa

Yellow Centaury
Cicendia filiformis

Yellow-wort
Blackstonia perfoliata

illustrations
0.6× lifesize

ASCLEPIADACEAE Milkweeds

Vincetoxicum   *Vincetoxicum hirundinaria*

Erect, sparsely pubescent perennial to 120 cm. STEMS *Slightly twining.* LEAVES Opposite, 6-10 cm, thinly pubescent on veins and margins. FLOWERS In 6-7-flowered axillary inflorescence; 5 calyx lobes, linear; *5 corolla lobes, white or yellow, 3-10 mm across.* FRUITS *c.6 cm, spindle-shaped; seeds plumed.* HABITAT Wood margins, forest clearings, grasslands, rocky ground, on calcareous soils. DIST. *Not BI.* (Most of Europe except N Scandinavia.) FLS May-Aug.

APOCYANACEAE Periwinkles

Lesser Periwinkle   *Vinca minor*

Evergreen, glabrous, trailing, slightly woody perennial to 60 cm. STEMS Rooting. LEAVES Opposite, 25-40 mm, *short-stalked.* FLOWERS Solitary in axils of leaves, 25-30 mm across; *5 sepals, glabrous;* 5 petals. HABITAT Woodlands, roadside banks, waste ground; lowland to 380 m. DIST. Archaeophyte. Most of BI, but rare in N Scotland, Ireland. (S, W and central Europe.) FLS Mar-May.

Greater Periwinkle   *Vinca major*

Similar to *V. minor*, but stems ascending to 150 cm; leaves 20-70 mm, *leaf stalks c.10 mm*; flowers 40-50 mm across, *margins of sepals with fringe of hairs.* HABITAT Woodland, hedge banks, roadside verges, waste ground. DIST. Introduced. Naturalised throughout most of England, Wales; scattered in Scotland, Ireland. (W and central Mediterranean.) FLS May-Jun.

SOLANACEAE Nightshades

A rather varied family of herbs, shrubs and climbers often with large showy flowers. The leaves are almost always alternate and without stipules. The flowers are regular with a 5-lobed calyx and corolla; stamens 5; ovary superior with a single style with 1 or 2 stigmas. The fruit is a berry or capsule. Many members of the family contain poisonous alkaloids.

Deadly Nightshade   *Atropa belladonna*

Tall, much-branched, glabrous or pubescent, glandular perennial to 150 cm. *Poisonous.* LEAVES To 8-20 cm, alternate. FLOWERS *Solitary, axillary, pendulous, 25-30 mm*; 5 sepals and petals; *calyx deeply 5-lobed.* FRUITS *Black berry, 15-20 mm.* HABITAT Open woodland, scrub, hedgerows, disturbed ground, on calcareous soils. DIST. Native. Scattered throughout lowland England; rare and naturalised elsewhere. (S, W and central Europe.) FLS Jun-Aug.

Henbane   *Hyoscyamus niger* VU.

Tall, *sticky, pubescent, strong-smelling annual or biennial* to 80 cm. LEAVES 6-20 cm. FLOWERS Solitary, axillary; corolla 2-3 cm across. FRUITS *Capsule, enclosed within enlarged calyx.* HABITAT Disturbed ground, farmyards, sandy and calcareous soils, coastal dunes. DIST. Archaeophyte. Scarce and declining. Scattered throughout lowland England; rare and coastal elsewhere. (All Europe except extreme N.) FLS Jun-Aug.

Thorn-apple   *Datura stramonium*

Robust, erect, branched annual to 100 cm. *Poisonous.* LEAVES Coarsely toothed, to 20 cm. FLOWERS *6-8 cm, erect, solitary; calyx tubular, 5-angled; corolla trumpet-shaped.* FRUITS *Spiny capsule,* 3.5-7 cm. HABITAT Waste ground, rubbish tips, cultivated soils. DIST. Introduced (escape from cultivation or birdseed alien). Scarce casual throughout lowland England, Wales; rare in Scotland; absent from Ireland. (Naturalised in most of Europe; native range unknown.) FLS Jul-Oct.

Cock's-eggs   *Salpichroa origanifolia*

Much-branched, *sprawling, pubescent perennial* to 150 cm. STEMS Base woody. LEAVES Simple, entire, 15-25 mm. FLOWERS *Solitary, axillary; corolla 6-10 mm.* FRUITS *White berry,* 10-15 mm. HABITAT Rough ground, road verges, waste places, cliffs. DIST. Introduced (native of E South America). Rare casual. (Naturalised in S and SW Europe.) FLS Jul-Sep.

Duke of Argyll's Teaplant   *Lycium barbarum*

Suckering, scrambling, spiny deciduous shrub to 2.5 m. LEAVES Simple, entire, glabrous, widest at middle. FLOWERS Axillary; calyx and corolla 5-lobed; corolla <17 mm across, dark veins of corolla lobes mostly unbranched; stamens protruding. FRUITS Red berry. SIMILAR SPP. **Chinese Teaplant** *Lycium chinense* is similar, but leaves are widest below middle; corolla is >17 mm across, and dark veins of corolla lobes are branched. HABITAT Both species are used for hedging, particularly in coastal areas; also naturalised on hedge banks, walls, waste ground, shingle. DIST. Introduced (native of China). (Naturalised over much of Europe.) FLS Jun-Sep.

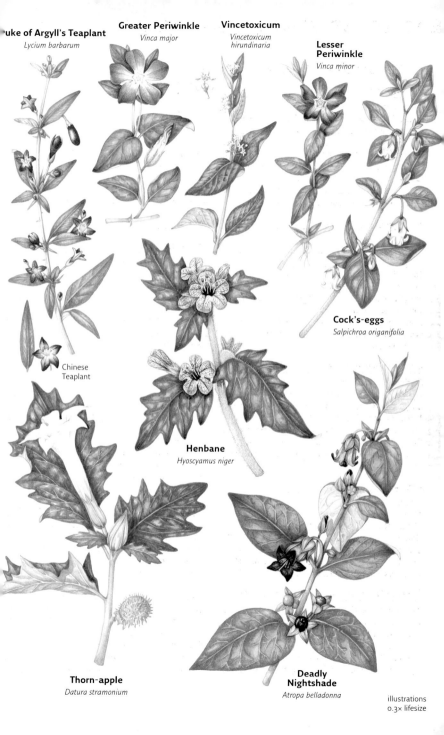

Duke of Argyll's Teaplant
Lycium barbarum

Greater Periwinkle
Vinca major

Vincetoxicum
Vincetoxicum hirundinaria

Lesser Periwinkle
Vinca minor

Chinese
Teaplant

Cock's-eggs
Salpichroa origanifolia

Henbane
Hyoscyamus niger

Thorn-apple
Datura stramonium

Deadly Nightshade
Atropa belladonna

illustrations
0.3× lifesize

Nightshades *Solanum*
Perennials

Scrambling woody perennial; flowers purple; berry red	*S. dulcamara*
Stems not woody; underground stems with root tubers; leaves irregularly pinnate; flowers purple or white	*S. tuberosum*

Annuals, flowers white

Leaves simple, entire or toothed; berry black	*S. nigrum*
Leaves deeply pinnate; berry mottled green and white	*S. triflorum*

Bittersweet, Woody Nightshade — Solanum dulcamara

Glabrous or pubescent, scrambling woody perennial to 300 cm. LEAVES To *c*.8 cm, simple, entire or lobed. FLOWERS *c*.10 mm across, in leaf-opposed inflorescence; petals purple. FRUITS Red berry, 8-12 mm. HABITAT Hedgerows, scrub, wood borders, tall-herb fens, fen carr, shingle beaches (var. *marinum*). DIST. Native. Common throughout BI, but rare in N Scotland. (Most of Europe except extreme N.) FLS Jun-Sep.

Black Nightshade — Solanum nigrum

Glabrous or pubescent, erect annual to 60 cm. LEAVES Ovate, entire or toothed. FLOWERS White, in 5-10-flowered inflorescence. FRUITS Black berry, 6-10 mm. HABITAT Common weed of cultivation and disturbed and waste ground, especially on fertile soils. DIST. Native and widespread in England, Wales; naturalised further N. (Most of Europe.) FLS Jul-Sep.

Small Nightshade — Solanum triflorum

Much-branched, sparsely pubescent annual to 60 cm. LEAVES Pinnate. FLOWERS White, in 2-3-flowered inflorescence. FRUITS Mottled green and white berry, 10-15 mm. HABITAT Arable fields, waste ground. DIST. Introduced (native of W North America and South America). Naturalised in a few scattered localities. (Naturalised in NW Europe.) FLS Jun-Sep.

Potato — Solanum tuberosum

Sparsely hairy, erect perennial to 100 cm, whose underground stems bear large tubers (potatoes!). LEAVES Irregularly pinnate. FLOWERS Purple, mauve or white, 25-35 mm across. FRUITS Greenish to purplish berry, 20-40 mm. HABITAT Occasional casual as relic of cultivation, fields, waste ground, rubbish tips, coastal sand, shingle. DIST. Introduced *c*.1590 (native of South America). Throughout BI. (Throughout Europe) FLS Jun-Aug.

CONVOLVULACEAE Bindweeds

Field Bindweed — Convolvulus arvensis

Trailing and climbing perennial to 75 cm. LEAVES 2-5 cm. FLOWERS 0-3, 10-30 mm across, white or pink; peduncles longer than leaves; pedicels with 2 narrow bracteoles below and not overlapping sepals. FRUITS Capsule, *c*.3 mm across. HABITAT Arable fields, roadsides, rough grassland, waste ground. DIST. Native. Common throughout BI, but scarce in N Scotland, W Ireland. (All Europe except extreme N.) FLS Jun-Sep.

Hedge Bindweed — Calystegia sepium

Climbing, rhizomatous perennial to 200 cm. FLOWERS Solitary, 3.5-7 cm across, white; bracteoles 10-18 mm wide, flattened against calyx, not or only slightly overlapping, not completely hiding sepals. HABITAT Hedgerows, scrub, wood margins, fen carr, riverbanks, waste ground, gardens. DIST. Native. Abundant throughout most of BI, but scarce in N Scotland. (Most of Europe except extreme N.) FLS Jul-Sep.

Large Bindweed — Calystegia silvatica

Similar to *C. sepium*, but flowers 6-9 cm across; bracteoles 18-45 mm wide, strongly inflated at base, strongly overlapping at edges, almost completely hiding sepals; pedicels glabrous. HABITAT Hedgerows, gardens, waste ground; less often in semi-natural habitats. DIST. Introduced. Established and common throughout BI, but scarce in N Scotland, Ireland. (S Europe.) FLS Jul-Sep.

Hairy Bindweed — Calystegia pulchra

Similar to *C. silvatica*, but stems, petioles, pedicels sparsely hairy; flowers pink or pink-striped, 5-7.5 cm; pedicels often narrowly winged. HABITAT Hedges, waste ground, usually close to gardens. DIST. Introduced (origins unknown). Naturalised and scattered throughout BI. (Naturalised in N and central Europe.) FLS Jul-Sep.

Sea Bindweed — Calystegia soldanella

Prostrate, rhizomatous, glabrous perennial to 60 cm, with far-creeping rhizomes. STEMS Not climbing. LEAVES 1-4 cm, kidney-shaped. FLOWERS Solitary, 2.5-4 cm across, pink with white stripes; bracteoles shorter than calyx. HABITAT Sand-dunes, sandy and fine shingly beaches. DIST. Native. All round coasts of BI except N Scotland. (Coasts of S and W Europe N to Denmark.) FLS Jun-Aug.

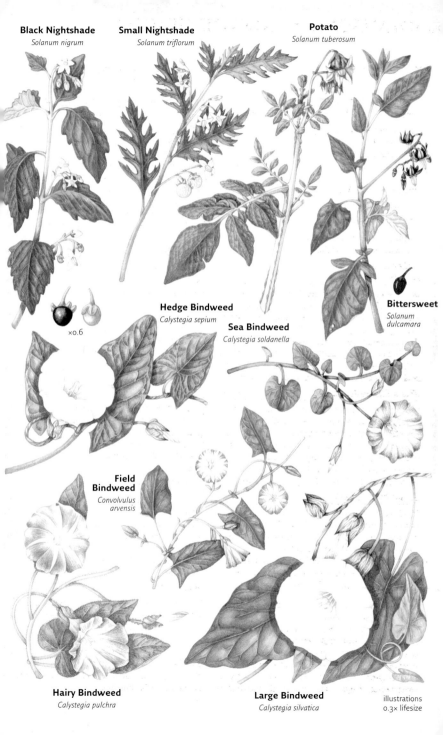

Black Nightshade
Solanum nigrum

Small Nightshade
Solanum triflorum

Potato
Solanum tuberosum

×0.6

Bittersweet
Solanum dulcamara

Hedge Bindweed
Calystegia sepium

Sea Bindweed
Calystegia soldanella

Field Bindweed
Convolvulus arvensis

Hairy Bindweed
Calystegia pulchra

Large Bindweed
Calystegia silvatica

illustrations
0.3× lifesize

CUSCUTACEAE Dodders

Rootless annual or perennial parasites without chlorophyll. Stems twining, attached to host plant by suckers. Leaves alternate, minute. Flowers in dense sessile heads; 4–5 calyx and corolla lobes; 4–5 stamens; corolla with ring of small scales below base of stamens; stigmas linear or capitate.

Dodder
Cuscuta epithymum

Annual. STEMS Red. FLOWERS 5 calyx and corolla lobes; sepals acute; *corolla scales not lobed, large, ± closing corolla tube; stamens longer than corolla*; styles longer than ovary, stigmas linear. HABITAT Heathlands, downland, dune grassland; parasitic on *gorses, heathers, Wild Thyme*; casual on crops further N. DIST. Native. Local in S and SW England; rare elsewhere; absent from Scotland. (All Europe except extreme N.) FLS Jul–Sep.

Greater Dodder
Cuscuta europaea

Annual or perennial. STEMS Red. FLOWERS 4–5 calyx and corolla lobes; *corolla scales deeply lobed; stamens shorter than corolla tube*; styles shorter than ovary, stigmas linear. HABITAT Damp, nutrient-rich habitats, riverbanks, hedges, ditches; parasitic on *nettles*, hops. DIST. Native. Scarce, local, declining. Central lowland England. (All Europe except extreme N.) FLS Aug–Sep.

Yellow Dodder
Cuscuta campestris

Annual. STEMS *Yellowish*. FLOWERS 5 calyx and corolla lobes; corolla scales lobed; stamens longer than corolla, *stigma capitate*. HABITAT Infrequent on a range of cultivated plants (e.g. Carrot, Beetroot, Lucerne, clovers). DIST. Introduced (native of North and South America). (Naturalised in S, central and W Europe.)

MENYANTHACEAE Bogbeans

Bogbean
Menyanthes trifoliata

Glabrous, aquatic, perennial, rhizomatous *bog plant*, with leaves and flowering stems raised above water. STEMS Flowering stems 12–30 cm. LEAVES Trifoliate. FLOWERS *White*, 15–20 mm across, *in 10–20-flowered inflorescence*; 5 sepals and petals, *inner surface of petals fringed*. HABITAT Shallow margins of acid pools, lakes dykes, streams, wet bogs, fens; to 1005 m. DIST. Native. Widely distributed throughout BI. (Most o Europe, but rare in Mediterranean.) FLS May–Jul.

Fringed Water-lily
Nymphoides peltate

Glabrous, aquatic perennial, with *floating leaves and flowers*. LEAVES *3–12 cm, orbicular, deeply cordate a base, margins sinuate. FLOWERS *Yellow, 3–4 cm across*, in 2–5-flowered inflorescence; calyx and corolla 5-lobed; *petals fringed*. HABITAT Shallow slow-moving water in drains, dykes, canals, lakes ponds. DIST. Native. ± restricted to East Anglian fens, but naturalised throughout most of rest of lowland Britain; rare in Scotland, Ireland. (Most o Europe.) FLS Jul–Aug.

POLEMONIACEAE Jacob's-ladder and phlox family

Jacob's-ladder
Polemonium caeruleum

Tall, erect, attractive rhizomatous perennial t 100 cm. LEAVES *10–40 cm, pinnate, alternate*. FLOWERS *2–3 cm across, blue*; 5 sepals and petals; 5 stamens, much longer than corolla. FRUITS Erec capsule. HABITAT Steep scree slopes in the open, and in light Ash woodland. DIST. Native. Rare. Carboniferous limestone areas of N England. Also widely naturalised as an escape from cultivation throughout BI (N and central Europe, mts of S Europe.) FLS Jun–Jul

HYDROPHYLLACEAE Phacelia family

Phacelia
Phacelia tanacetifoli

Erect, glandular-pubescent annual to 70 cm. LEAVES Alternate, pinnate. FLOWERS 6–10 mm across, blue mauve, *numerous, in spiralled terminal cymes*; 5 sepals and petals; 5 stamens, longer than corolla tube; *tip of style divided into 2*. FRUITS Capsule. HABITAT Cultivated ground, rubbish tips. DIST. Introduced (native of W North America). Commonly cultivated in gardens and for bees and green manure; occurs a casual throughout BI. (Naturalised over much o Europe.) FLS Jul–Sep.

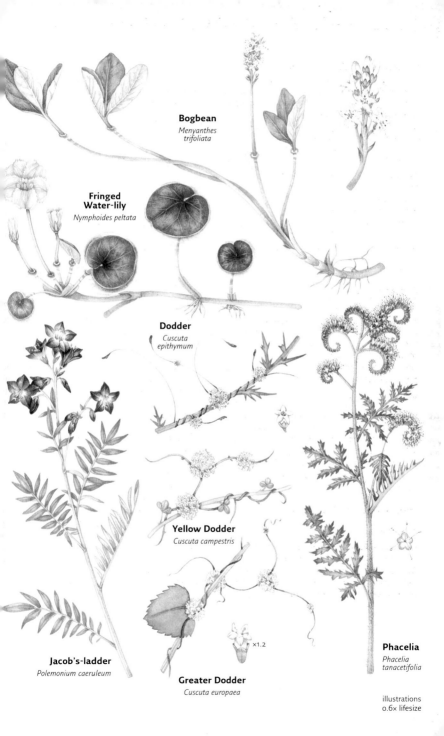

Bogbean
*Menyanthes
trifoliata*

**Fringed
Water-lily**
Nymphoides peltata

Dodder
*Cuscuta
epithymum*

Yellow Dodder
Cuscuta campestris

×1.2

Jacob's-ladder
Polemonium caeruleum

Greater Dodder
Cuscuta europaea

Phacelia
*Phacelia
tanacetifolia*

illustrations
0.6× lifesize

BORAGINACEAE Borage family

A distinctive family of usually roughly hairy annual or perennial herbs (*see* key on p.374). Leaves are alternate, entire, without stipules. FLOWERS are regular (except *Echium*); inflorescence is often a spiralled cyme; calyx is 5-toothed; corolla is often funnel-shaped, 5-lobed; 5 stamens; ovary is superior, 4-celled and deeply 4-lobed. Fruit is a cluster of 4 nutlets.

Purple Gromwell — *Lithospermum purpureocaeruleum*

Pubescent perennial to 60 cm. STEMS Creeping woody stems; long, prostrate sterile shoots; erect flowering stems. LEAVES To 7 cm, dark green above, light green below, lateral nerves not visible. FLOWERS Corolla 12–15 mm across, 2× as long as calyx, *reddish purple turning bright blue*. FRUITS Shining white nutlets. HABITAT Wood margins, lanesides, coastal scrub on limestone. DIST. Native. Very rare. SW England, S Wales. (S and central Europe.) FLS May–Jun.

Common Gromwell — *Lithospermum officinale*

Erect, much-branched, pubescent perennial to 80 cm. LEAVES To 7 cm, *lateral nerves conspicuous beneath*. FLOWERS Corolla 3–6 mm across, not much longer than calyx, *yellowish*. FRUITS Shining white nutlets. HABITAT Wood margins, scrub, hedgerows, on base-rich or calcareous soils. DIST. Native. Local. Throughout lowland England; rare elsewhere. (Most of Europe, but rare in N and W.) FLS Jun–Jul.

Field Gromwell — *Lithospermum arvense* EN.

Erect, pubescent annual to 50 cm. LEAVES *3–5 cm, lateral nerves not visible*. FLOWERS Corolla 5–9 mm across, not much longer than calyx, *white*. FRUITS Brown warty nutlets. DIST. Native. Very local, declining. Lowland England. HABITAT Arable fields on dry calcareous soils. (Most of Europe.) FLS May–Jul.

Viper's-bugloss — *Echium vulgare*

Erect, *very hispid* biennial to 90 cm. LEAVES Basal leaves to 15 cm, stalked, with prominent midrib and no apparent lateral veins. FLOWERS 10–18 mm, pink in bud turning bright blue; *corolla lobes unequal, uniformly pubescent on outside; 5 stamens, unequal, 4 longer than corolla*. FRUITS Ridged nutlets. HABITAT Open, disturbed ground, rough grassland, cliffs, dunes, shingle, waste ground, roadsides, on light calcareous or sandy soils; lowland to 365 m. DIST. Native. Widespread in Britain N to central Scotland; rare and coastal in Ireland. (All Europe.) FLS Jun–Sep.

Purple Viper's-bugloss — *Echium plantagineum*

Erect biennial to 75 cm. Similar to *E. vulgare*, but *softer; basal leaves with distinct lateral veins; flowers 20–30 mm; corolla lobes pubescent on veins and margins only; 2 stamens exserted, longer than corolla; nutlets warty*. HABITAT Arable weed, cliffs, sandy habitats close to sea. DIST. Introduced. Very local. Well established in SW England, Channel Is; absent from Ireland. (S and W Europe.) FLS Jun–Aug.

Lungwort — *Pulmonaria officinalis*

Pubescent, rhizomatous perennial to 30 cm. LEAVES *Basal leaves winter green, ovate, cordate; lamina longer than petiole, abruptly narrowed at base, with large white spots*. FLOWERS *In glandular inflorescence*; calyx lobes sub-acute; corolla *c.*10 mm across. HABITAT Woods, hedge banks, rough ground; lowland to 385 m. DIST. Introduced. Commonly grown in gardens, and naturalised throughout Britain; rare in Ireland. (Central and E Europe.) FLS Mar–May.

Suffolk Lungwort — *Pulmonaria obscura* EN

Similar to *P. officinalis*, but *leaves darker green unspotted and not persisting through winter; inflorescence sparsely glandular*. HABITAT Ancient coppice woods on chalky boulder clay. DIST. Native. Very rare, in only 3 localities in E Suffolk. (W, central and E Europe.) FLS Mar–May.

Narrow-leaved Lungwort — *Pulmonaria longifolia*

Erect, pubescent perennial to 40 cm. LEAVES *Basal leaves to 60 cm in autumn, lanceolate, gradually tapering into petiole, white-spotted*. FLOWERS Corolla 5–6 mm across, pink turning blue. HABITAT Coppice woodland, wood pasture, heathland. DIST. Native. Very local, in only a small area around Solent, S England. (W Europe.) FLS Apr–May.

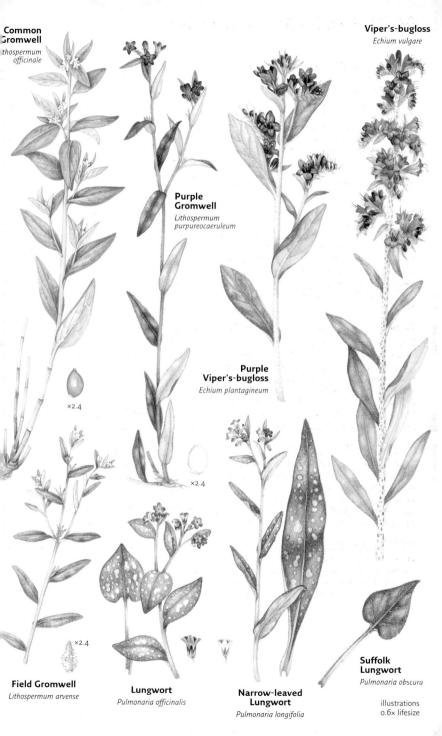

Common Gromwell
Lithospermum officinale

Purple Gromwell
Lithospermum purpureocaeruleum

Viper's-bugloss
Echium vulgare

Purple Viper's-bugloss
Echium plantagineum

×2.4

×2.4

Field Gromwell
Lithospermum arvense

×2.4

Lungwort
Pulmonaria officinalis

Narrow-leaved Lungwort
Pulmonaria longifolia

Suffolk Lungwort
Pulmonaria obscura

illustrations
0.6× lifesize

	if	**then**
1	▷ Flowers distinctly irregular, stamens of different lengths	*Echium* (p.372)
	▷ Flowers regular, all stamens same length	Go to ▷ **2**
2	▷ Stamens clearly protruding from corolla	Go to ▷ **3**
	▷ Stamens not or hardly protruding	Go to ▷ **4**
3	▷ Annual; anthers longer than filaments, filaments glabrous	*Borago* (p.380)
	▷ Perennial; anthers shorter than filaments, filaments pubescent	*Trachystemon* (p.380)
4	▷ Plant glabrous, glaucous (seashores in N)	*Mertensia* (p.380)
	▷ Plant hispid or pubescent	Go to ▷ **5**
5	▷ Nutlets covered by hooked bristles, calyx teeth spreading	*Cynoglossum* (below, p.380)
	▷ Nutlets without bristles, calyx ± obscuring fruit	Go to ▷ **6**
6	▷ Flowers nodding	*Symphytum* (below, p.376)
	▷ Flowers ± erect	Go to ▷ **7**
7	▷ Basal leaves long-stalked, deeply cordate at base	*Brunnera* (p.376)
	▷ Leaves tapering to base	Go to ▷ **8**
8	▷ Corolla with 5 short, glabrous, rounded, notched yellow scales closing mouth of corolla tube	*Myosotis* (opposite, p.378)
	▷ Corolla with hairy or papillose oblong scales or folds in throat	Go to ▷ **9**
9	▷ Leaves ovate	Go to ▷ **10**
	▷ Leaves lanceolate to linear-oblong	Go to ▷ **12**
10	▷ Calyx divided for ¼–⅓ of its length, corolla funnel-shaped	*Pulmonaria* (p.372)
	▷ Calyx divided almost to base	Go to ▷ **11**
11	▷ Inflorescence very hispid	*Pentaglottis* (p.376)
	▷ Inflorescence with appressed hairs	*Omphalodes* (p.380)
12	▷ Flowers yellow to orange	*Amsinckia* (p.380)
	▷ Flowers blue or bluish purple to white	Go to ▷ **13**
13	▷ Corolla with long, hairy folds in throat	*Lithospermum* (p.372)
	▷ Corolla with conspicuous scales in throat	*Anchusa* (p.376)

Comfrey *Symphytum*

1	▷ Stem leaves strongly decurrent, wings extending down stem for >1 internode; flowers purplish or creamy yellow	*S. officinale* (p.376)
	▷ Stems leaves not to slightly decurrent, not extending for more than ½ distance to leaf below	Go to ▷ **2**

	if	**then**
2	▷ Flowers pink, purple or blue	Go to ▷ **3**
	▷ Flowers cream or white	Go to ▷ **4**
3	▷ Upper stem leaves sessile, shortly decurrent or clasping; flowers pinkish blue, purplish or violet when open	***S. × uplandicum*** (p.376)
	▷ Upper stem leaves shortly stalked, not decurrent or clasping; flowers sky-blue when open	***S. asperum*** (p.376)
4	▷ Calyx divided <halfway to base; flowers white	***S. orientale*** (p.376)
	▷ Calyx divided >halfway to base; flowers pale yellow	***S. tuberosum*** (p.376)

Forget-me-nots *Myosotis*

1	▷ Hairs on calyx tube short, stiff, spreading, hooked	Go to ▷ **2**
	▷ Hairs on calyx tube appressed, not spreading or hooked	Go to ▷ **7**
2	▷ Style longer than calyx tube	Go to ▷ **3**
	▷ Style shorter than calyx tube	Go to ▷ **5**
3	▷ Flowers yellow or white at first, turning blue	***M. discolor*** (p.380)
	▷ Flowers blue from the start	Go to ▷ **4**
4	▷ Fruiting pedicels 1½–2× the length of calyx; nutlets acute at apex, dark brown	***M. sylvatica*** (p.378)
	▷ Fruiting pedicels about as long as calyx; nutlets rounded at apex, black (rare alpine)	***M. alpestris*** (p.378)
5	▷ Lower surface of leaves with hooked hairs	***M. stricta*** ● (p.380)
	▷ Lower surface of leaves without hooked hairs	Go to ▷ **6**
6	▷ Flower stalk at fruiting shorter than or as long as calyx	***M. ramosissima*** (p.378)
	▷ Flower stalk at fruiting ≤2× as long as calyx	***M. arvensis*** (p.378)
7	▷ Corolla 2.5–3 mm across; calyx lobed to <halfway to base; nutlets shining olive-brown (Jersey)	***M. sicula*** (p.378)
	▷ Corolla ≥3.5 mm across; nutlets mid-brown to black	Go to ▷ **8**
8	▷ Style longer than calyx tube, calyx with broad teeth forming equilateral triangle; flowers 4–8 mm across	***M. scorpioides*** (p.378)
	▷ Style shorter than calyx tube, calyx with teeth forming isosceles triangle (sides longer than base); flowers 3.5–6 mm across	Go to ▷ **9**
9	▷ Lower part of stem with spreading hairs	***M. secunda*** (p.378)
	▷ Lower part of stem with appressed hairs	Go to ▷ **10**
10	▷ Stolons absent; larger leaves >4× as long as wide; flowers sky-blue	***M. laxa*** (p.378)
	▷ Stolons produced from lower nodes; leaves rarely >3× as long as wide; flowers pale blue	***M. stolonifera*** (p.378)

Comfreys *Symphytum*
See key to *Symphytum* on p.374.

Common Comfrey · *Symphytum officinale*

Erect, hispid, branched perennial to 150 cm. STEMS With long, deflexed, conical hairs. LEAVES Strongly and broadly decurrent, wings longer than 1 internode; stem leaves sessile. FLOWERS Calyx 7-8 mm, teeth acute, 2-3× as long as tube; corolla 15-17 mm, yellowish white (to pinkish). HABITAT Fens, marshes, wet ditches, banks of rivers, streams and canals; lowland to 320 m. DIST. Native. Locally frequent throughout BI, but rare in W Wales, N Scotland. (Most of Europe, but rare in S.) FLS May-Jun.

Russian Comfrey · *Symphytum × uplandicum*

Tall, erect, branched perennial to 140 cm. Similar to *S. officinale*, but more hispid; upper stem leaves sessile and shortly decurrent, wings not extending >halfway to leaf below; calyx 5-7 mm; corolla pinkish blue, purplish or violet. HABITAT Roadsides, hedge banks, wood margins, waste ground; to 365 m. DIST. Introduced as forage plant in 1870. Frequent throughout most of BI, but rare in N Scotland, Ireland. (Naturalised in W and central Europe.) FLS Jun-Aug.

Rough Comfrey · *Symphytum asperum*

Much-branched, rough perennial to 180 cm. STEMS Covered in short hooked bristles. LEAVES Lower and middle stem leaves cordate; petioles long, unwinged. FLOWERS Calyx small in bud, 3-5 mm long, enlarging in fruit, teeth blunt; corolla 11-17 mm, pink in bud, turning sky-blue. HABITAT Waste ground. DIST. Introduced. Very rare. Naturalised in a few scattered localities. (Native of Turkey, Caucasus, Iran; naturalised in W and central Europe.) FLS Jun-Jul.

Tuberous Comfrey · *Symphytum tuberosum*

Erect, hispid, sparsely branched, rhizomatous perennial to 60 cm. STEMS Bristly. LEAVES Stem leaves sessile, middle leaves considerably larger than lower. FLOWERS Calyx 7-8 mm, divided almost to base; corolla 12-16 mm, pale yellow. HABITAT Damp woodland, hedge banks, margins of streams and rivers; to 335 m. DIST. Native in N England, Scotland; naturalised further S. Local. (W, central and S Europe.) FLS Jun-Jul.

White Comfrey · *Symphytum orientale*

Erect, little-branched, softly pubescent perennial to 70 cm. LEAVES Lower leaves to 14 cm, stalked, ovate cordate at base. FLOWERS Calyx 7-9 mm, teeth length of tube; corolla 15-17 mm, white. HABITAT Naturalised on hedge banks, lanesides, road verges, waste ground. DIST. Introduced. Frequent in SE England; scattered further N. (Native of Caucasus, S Russia, NW Turkey.) FLS Apr-May.

Great Forget-me-not · *Brunnera macrophylla*

Erect, pubescent, rhizomatous perennial to 50 cm. LEAVES Basal leaves 5-20 cm, cordate, with long petioles. FLOWERS In many-flowered inflorescence; calyx *c.*1 mm in flower; corolla 3-4 mm across, like a forget-me-not. HABITAT Rough grassland, rubbish tips. DIST. Introduced. Commonly cultivated and persists as a garden throw-out. (Native of Caucasus.) FLS Apr-May.

Bugloss · *Anchusa arvensis*

Erect, hispid annual to 50 cm. LEAVES To *c.*15 cm, linear-oblong, margins undulate, toothed. FLOWERS ± sessile; bracts leaf-like, 4-7 mm across; calyx deeply divided; corolla tube curved, lobes slightly unequal. HABITAT Arable weed on well-drained soils, sandy heaths, dunes near sea; to 420 m. DIST. Archaeophyte. Declining. Throughout BI, but rare in Ireland. (Most of Europe.) FLS Jun-Sep.

Alkanet · *Anchusa officinalis*

Erect, hispid perennial to 150 cm. LEAVES 5-12 cm. FLOWERS Calyx 5-7 mm in flower, divided halfway or almost to base; corolla 7-15 mm across, purplish violet. HABITAT Short-lived casual on waste ground, hedgerows, tips. DIST. Introduced; originating from gardens and birdseed. (Much of Europe except extreme N, parts of S and W.) FLS May-Oct. NOTE Garden Anchusa, with larger sky-blue flowers, is *Anchusa azurea*.

Green Alkanet · *Pentaglottis sempervirens*

Erect, branched, hispid perennial to 100 cm. LEAVES To 30 cm, ovate, lower leaves stalked. FLOWERS ± sessile, in terminal, axillary, long-stalked inflorescence; calyx divided >¾ way to base; corolla bright blue, 8-10 mm across. HABITAT Hedgerows, roadsides, woodland margins, usually near buildings; to 380 m. DIST. Introduced. Naturalised throughout BI, but rare in N Scotland, Ireland. (SW Europe.) FLS May-Jun.

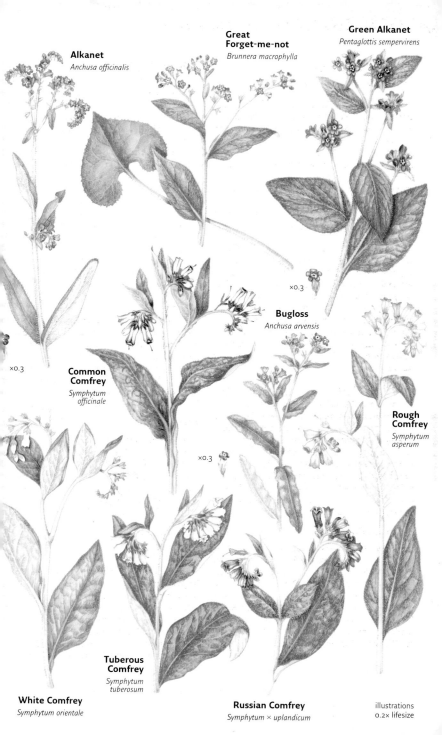

Alkanet
Anchusa officinalis

**Great
Forget-me-not**
Brunnera macrophylla

Green Alkanet
Pentaglottis sempervirens

×0.3

×0.3

Bugloss
Anchusa arvensis

**Common
Comfrey**
*Symphytum
officinale*

**Rough
Comfrey**
*Symphytum
asperum*

×0.3

**Tuberous
Comfrey**
*Symphytum
tuberosum*

White Comfrey
Symphytum orientale

Russian Comfrey
Symphytum × uplandicum

illustrations
0.2× lifesize

Forget-me-nots *Myosotis*

See key to *Myosotis* on p.375.

Water-forget-me-not
Myosotis scorpioides

Ascending to erect, pubescent, rhizomatous or stoloniferous perennial, to 45 cm. LEAVES Lower leaves to 7 cm. FLOWERS In inflorescence without bracts, *c.*20 cm long; calyx divided to <halfway, teeth forming an equal-sided triangle, hairs appressed; corolla to 8-13 mm across; tips of petals emarginate; style longer than calyx tube at flowering. HABITAT Margins of ponds, rivers, ditches, canals, streams; to 600 m. DIST. Native. Common throughout BI; introduced in Orkney, Shetland. (Central and N Europe.) FLS May-Sep.

Tufted Forget-me-not
Myosotis laxa

Ascending to erect, pubescent annual to biennial. Similar to *M. scorpioides*, with which it often grows, but without rhizomes or stolons. FLOWERS Inflorescence *c.*15 cm long; calyx divided to ≥halfway, teeth forming isosceles triangle (sides longer than base); corolla 3.5-4 mm across; tips of petals rounded; style shorter than calyx tube at flowering. HABITAT Marshes, fens, margins of streams, rivers, dykes, canals, ponds and pools; lowland to 550 m. DIST. Native. Frequent throughout BI. (Most of Europe, but rare in S.) FLS May-Aug.

Creeping Forget-me-not
Myosotis secunda

Decumbent to erect, pubescent, stoloniferous perennial to 60 cm. STEMS Lower part with spreading hairs. LEAVES Rather pale. FLOWERS Lower part of inflorescence with leafy bracts; fruiting pedicels 3-5× as long as calyx, reflexed; corolla 4-6 mm across; style shorter than calyx tube at flowering. HABITAT Streams, springs, pools, woodland flushes, wet pastures, in acid water; to 805 m. DIST. Native. Widespread in N, W and S BI. (W Europe.) FLS May-Aug.

Pale Forget-me-not
Myosotis stolonifera

Erect, pubescent perennial to 20 cm, with numerous leafy stolons. STEMS Lower part with appressed hairs. LEAVES Stem leaves short, ≤3× as long as wide. FLOWERS In inflorescence without bracts; calyx lobed to >halfway to base; corolla pale blue, to 5 mm across. HABITAT Calcareous upland springs, flushes, stream sides; to 820 m. DIST. Native. Very local. N England, S Scotland. (SW Europe.) FLS Jun-Aug.

Jersey Forget-me-not
Myosotis sicula

Prostrate to erect, pubescent annual, to 20 cm. STEMS Solitary or several, little branched, branches almost glabrous. LEAVES Lower leaves 2.5-3 cm, ± glabrous beneath. FLOWERS In elongated inflorescence; calyx lobed to <halfway to base; corolla 2.5-3 mm across, lobes concave. HABITAT/DIST. Very rare, in Jersey (Channel Is) only, on margins of a single pool near coast. (S and W Europe.) FLS Apr-Jun.

Early Forget-me-not
Myosotis ramosissima

Slender, often tiny, prostrate to erect annual, to 25 cm. LEAVES Lower ones ovate, forming rosette. FLOWERS Inflorescence without bracts, longer than leafy part of stem in fruit; pedicels shorter than or as long as calyx at fruiting; calyx with spreading hooked hairs; corolla blue, *c.*3 mm across; corolla tube shorter than calyx. HABITAT Open habitats on dry, infertile soils, heath, grassland, mature sand-dunes. DIST. Native. Frequent throughout most of BI, but rare and coastal in N Scotland, Ireland. (Most of Europe except extreme N.) FLS Apr-Jun.

Field Forget-me-not
Myosotis arvensis

Erect, pubescent annual to 30 cm. LEAVES Lower leaves broadly ovate, forming rosette. FLOWERS In inflorescence without bracts, about as long as leafy stem at fruiting; pedicels to 2× as long as calyx at fruiting; calyx with crisped hairs; corolla blue ≤5 mm across, lobes concave; corolla tube shorter than calyx. HABITAT Arable soils, roadsides, woodland rides, grassy heaths, disturbed ground; to 610 m. DIST. Archaeophyte. Common throughout BI. (All Europe.) FLS Apr-Sep.

Wood Forget-me-not
Myosotis sylvatica

Erect, pubescent perennial to 45 cm. STEMS With spreading hairs. FLOWERS In inflorescence without bracts, elongated after flowering; pedicels 1.5-2× as long as calyx at fruiting; calyx densely pubescent with both curved and hooked hairs; corolla 6-10 mm across, lobes flat. FRUITS Brown nutlet, acute at apex. HABITAT Damp woodlands on fertile soils, rocky grassland; to 485 m. DIST. Native. Rather local. Throughout BI, but rare in N Scotland, Ireland. (Most of Europe except SW and extreme N.) FLS May-Jun.

Alpine Forget-me-not
Myosotis alpestris

Erect, rhizomatous, tufted alpine perennial to 20 cm. STEMS With stiff, spreading hairs. FLOWERS In inflorescence without bracts, rather short; pedicels <2× as long as calyx at fruiting; calyx densely pubescent with curved hairs, and with or without hooked hairs; corolla 5-10 mm across, lobes flat. FRUITS Black nutlet, rounded at apex. HABITAT Grazed limestone grassland (N Pennines), ungrazed mica-schist rock ledges (Perthshire); to 1180 m. DIST. Native. Very rare. N England, Scottish Highlands. (Mts of Europe.) FLS Jul-Se

Pale Forget-me-not
Myosotis stolonifera

Jersey Forget-me-not
Myosotis sicula

Field Forget-me-not
Myosotis arvensis

calyx

nutlet

Alpine Forget-me-not
Myosotis alpestris

calyx

nutlet

Early Forget-me-not
Myosotis ramosissima

Creeping Forget-me-not
Myosotis secunda

calyx

nutlet

calyx

nutlet

calyx

nutlet

ater Forget-me-not
Myosotis scorpioides

Wood Forget-me-not
Myosotis sylvatica

Tufted Forget-me-not
Myosotis laxa

all plants 0.3× lifesize;
calyx and nutlets ×3

Changing Forget-me-not
Myosotis discolor

Erect, slender, pubescent annual to 26 cm. FLOWERS In inflorescence without bracts; calyx teeth oblong-lanceolate; corolla to 2 mm across, at first yellow then pink to blue; corolla tube longer than calyx. FRUITS Pedicels shorter than calyx. HABITAT Open and disturbed ground, grass heaths, arable land, woodland rides, road verges, banks, walls, on dry soils; to 610 m. DIST. Native. Throughout BI. (Most of Europe.) FLS May–Sep.

Upright Forget-me-not
Myosotis stricta

Erect, much-branched, pubescent annual, to 30 cm but usually less. LEAVES Basal leaves lanceolate, to 2.5 cm; lower surface of leaves with hooked hairs. FLOWERS Tiny, in inflorescence with spreading hairs; pedicels ≤1.5 mm; corolla scarcely longer than calyx, about 1.5 mm across. FRUITS Calyx 4 mm, divided to halfway. HABITAT Dry, open grassland, sandy places, rail tracks. DIST. *Not BI*. (Most of Europe.) FLS Apr–Jun.

Blue-eyed Mary
Omphalodes verna

Creeping, rhizomatous, stoloniferous, pubescent perennial to 25 cm. LEAVES Ovate, long-stalked. FLOWERS 10-15 mm across, in few-flowered inflorescence. FRUITS Smooth, pubescent nutlet. HABITAT Woodland, lanes, near habitation. DIST. Introduced. Casual as garden escape. (S Europe.) FLS Mar–May.

Borage
Borago officinalis

Robust, erect, hispid annual to 60 cm. LEAVES 10-20 cm; lower leaves stalked, upper ones sessile. FLOWERS 20 mm across, in few-flowered inflorescence with leaf-like bracts; pedicels 2-4 cm; calyx hispid, divided to base, lobes narrow; petals spreading; filaments glabrous, shorter than anthers; anthers united, dark purple, exserted. HABITAT Roadsides, waste ground, near habitation. DIST. Throughout BI as casual garden escape. (S Europe.) FLS Jun–Aug.

Abraham-Isaac-Jacob
Trachystemon orientalis

Hispid, rhizomatous perennial to 40 cm. LEAVES Basal leaves ovate, cordate, long-stalked. FLOWERS In dense inflorescence; calyx divided halfway to base; petals spreading, revolute; filaments pubescent, longer than anthers; anthers exserted. HABITAT Laneside banks, damp woods. DIST. Introduced. Throughout BI; occasional garden escape. (SE Europe.) FLS Apr–May.

Fiddleneck
Amsinckia micrantha

Erect, hispid annual to 70 cm. STEMS With spreading white bristles. LEAVES Narrow, sessile. FLOWERS In elongated, spiralled inflorescence; calyx divided to base; corolla yellow, 3–5 mm long. FRUITS Warty nutlet. SIMILAR SPP. The *Amsinckia* on the island of Inner Farne is the only European locality for the W North American species *A. lycopsoides*; it has larger flowers than *A. micrantha*, and scales in the apex of the corolla tube. HABITAT Arable land, waste ground, on light sandy soils. DIST. Introduced (native of W North America). Naturalised and spreading in E England, E Scotland. (Casual in N, W and E Europe.) FLS Jun–Jul.

Hound's-tongue
Cynoglossum officinale

Erect, softly pubescent grey-green biennial to 90 cm. LEAVES Basal leaves softly silky on both surfaces lanceolate-ovate, to c.30 cm. FLOWERS In elongated, spiralled, branched inflorescence; pedicels c.5 mm; calyx divided almost to base; corolla 6–10 mm across. FRUITS Large nutlet covered by hooked bristles, with distinct thickened border. HABITAT Wood margins, rough open grassland, on dry, well-drained soils, coastal dunes, shingle; to 400 m. DIST. Native. Scattered throughout most of lowland England, Wales; coastal in the SW, Scotland, Ireland. (Most of Europe except extreme N and S.) FLS Jun–Aug.

Green
Hound's-tongue
Cynoglossum germanicum CR. *(E)

Similar to *C. officinale*, but branches longer; leaves green, sparsely hispid not silky; pedicels >5 mm; corolla c.5 mm across; nutlets without thickened border, but bristles longer. HABITAT Margins, clearings, in calcareous woodland. DIST. Native. Very rare, declining. Chalk and limestone areas of S England. (W and central Europe.) FLS May–Jul.

Oysterplant
Mertensia maritima

A ± prostrate *glabrous, glaucous rather succulent* perennial to c.60 cm; LEAVES In 2 rows, 2-6 cm ovate, blunt, finely glandular on upper surface. FLOWERS Corolla c.6 mm across, blue and pink throat with 5 ridges. HABITAT Coastal shingle beaches. DIST. Native. Local, coasts of NW England, Scotland, NE Ireland. (Coasts of Europe from Denmark northwards.) FLS Jun–Aug.

Oysterplant
×0.1

×2   ×0.8

Blue-eyed Mary
Omphalodes verna

Abraham-Isaac-Jacob
Trachystemon orientalis

**Upright
Forget-me-not**
Myosotis stricta

**Changing
Forget-
me-not**
Myosotis discolor

**Hound's-
tongue**
*Cynoglossum
officinale*

nutlet
×1.2

nutlet
×1.2

Borage
Borago officinalis

Fiddleneck
Amsinckia micrantha

**Green
Hound's-tongue**
Cynoglossum germanicum

illustrations
0.6× lifesize

	if	**then**
1	▷ Corolla of 2 unequal toothed lobes or lips	Go to ▷ **2**
	▷ Corolla of 4 almost equal lobes	Go to ▷ **18**
	▷ Corolla with upper lip absent or consisting of 2 short teeth	Go to ▷ **19**
2	▷ Calyx with 5 distinct teeth	Go to ▷ **3**
	▷ Calyx with 10 teeth	*Marrubium* (p.388)
	▷ Calyx of 2 entire lips	*Scutellaria* (p.392)
3	▷ 2 stamens	*Salvia* (p.400)
	▷ 4 stamens	Go to ▷ **4**
4	▷ At least the longest pair of stamens protruding beyond corolla	Go to ▷ **5**
	▷ Stamens not protruding beyond corolla	Go to ▷ **6**
5	▷ Tall plant to ≥30 cm; leaves ≥1 cm wide; flowers pink, in rounded terminal and axillary heads	*Origanum* (p.400)
	▷ Plant prostrate and creeping; leaves small, ≤5 mm wide; flowers pink, in small rounded or oblong heads	*Thymus* (p.394)
6	▷ Evergreen shrub to ≥1 m; leaves densely hairy beneath; flowers yellow	*Phlomis* (p.400)
	▷ Herbs	Go to ▷ **7**
7	▷ Leaves deeply lobed	*Leonurus* (p.400)
	▷ Leaves not deeply lobed	Go to ▷ **8**
8	▷ Stems creeping, rooting; leaves kidney-shaped, petioles long	*Glechoma* (p.392)
	▷ Stems not creeping, rooting; leaves not kidney-shaped	Go to ▷ **9**
9	▷ Calyx of 5 equal teeth	Go to ▷ **10**
	▷ Calyx 2-lipped, the upper lip with 3 teeth, the lower with 2	Go to ▷ **15**
10	▷ Outer pair of stamens longer than the inner	Go to ▷ **11**
	▷ Outer pair of stamens shorter than the inner	*Nepeta* (p.392)
11	▷ Calyx funnel-shaped, calyx teeth short, broad	*Ballota* (p.388)
	▷ Calyx tubular or bell-shaped, calyx teeth longer	Go to ▷ **12**
12	▷ Lateral lobes of lower lip short, obscure; terminal lobe notched for ≥⅓ its length	*Lamium* (p.386)
	▷ Lateral lobes of lower lip well developed	Go to ▷ **13**
13	▷ Stoloniferous perennial; flowers deep yellow	*Lamiastrum* (p.386)
	▷ Perennials with purple flowers, or annuals with purple or pale yellow flowers	Go to ▷ **14**

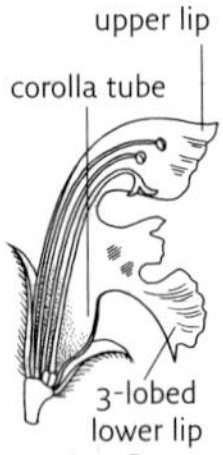

upper lip

corolla tube

3-lobed
lower lip
Lamium flower

	if	**then**
14	▷ Calyx teeth and bracteoles conspicuously spine-tipped; base of lower lip of corolla with 2 raised bosses	*Galeopsis* (p.388)
	▷ Calyx teeth not spine-tipped; lower lip without raised bosses	*Stachys* (*see* below)
15	▷ Flowers large, 25–40 mm, pink or white spotted with pink	*Melittis* (p.388)
	▷ Flowers ≤22 mm, yellow, violet, lavender, white or pinkish purple	Go to ▷ **16**
16	▷ Flowers yellow, plant strongly lemon-scented	*Melissa* (p.392)
	▷ Flowers neither yellow nor lemon-scented	Go to ▷ **17**
17	▷ Flowers in dense terminal heads; upper lip distinctly hooded	*Prunella* (p.392)
	▷ Most flowers in axillary whorls; upper lip ± flat	*Clinopodium* (p.394)
18	▷ 4 stamens; leaves entire or toothed	*Mentha* (p.398)
	▷ 2 stamens; leaves deeply lobed	*Lycopus* (p.400)
19	▷ Corolla of a single 5-lobed lower lip, upper lip absent	*Teucrium* (p.390)
	▷ Upper lip consisting of 2 short teeth, lower lip 3-lobed	*Ajuga* (p.390)

Woundworts *Stachys*

1	▷ Corolla purplish	Go to ▷ **2**
	▷ Corolla yellow or cream	Go to ▷ **7**
2	▷ Corolla small, <8 mm; annual	*S. arvensis* (p.384)
	▷ Corolla >10 mm; perennial	Go to ▷ **3**
3	▷ Basal rosette of leaves present; stem leaves few, 2–4 pairs	*S. officinalis* (p.384)
	▷ No basal rosette	Go to ▷ **4**
4	▷ Bracteoles very short or absent	Go to ▷ **5**
	▷ Bracteoles at least as long as calyx	Go to ▷ **6**
5	▷ Leaves ovate, stalked	*S. sylvatica* (p.384)
	▷ Leaves lanceolate, ± sessile	*S. palustris* (p.384)
6	▷ Stems and leaves densely clothed with long white hairs	*S. germanica* (p.384)
	▷ Leaves green	*S. alpina* (p.384)
7	▷ ≤6 flowers per node, corolla ≤15 mm; annual	*S. annua* (p.384)
	▷ ≥6 flowers per node, corolla ≥15 mm; perennial	*S. recta* (p.384)

LAMIACEAE (LABIATAE) Labiates

A distinctive family of annuals, perennials or dwarf shrubs with square stems and pairs of opposite leaves that lack stipules (*see* key on p.382). Inflorescences are often whorl-like or terminal and spike-or head-like; flowers are irregular; calyx 5-toothed, often 2-lipped; corolla with well-developed tube, and 5-lobed with the 2 upper lobes forming a distinct lip and the 3 others forming a 3-lobed lower lip; 4 stamens, 2 long and 2 short; ovary superior and deeply 4-lobed. Fruit is a cluster of 4 nutlets. Some members of the Scrophulariaceae, such as *Rhinanthus* (p.424), are similar to the labiates but these have a quite different ovary. The family contains many familiar culinary and aromatic herbs such as lavender, mint, thyme and rosemary.

Woundworts *Stachys*

See key to *Stachys* on p.383.

Betony
Stachys officinalis *(NI)

Sparsely pubescent, erect, rhizomatous perennial to 60 cm. Leaves Basal leaves long-stalked, forming persistent rosette; leaf blades 3–7 cm, cordate, crenate; few stem leaves. Flowers In inflorescence with bracteoles; corolla 12–18 mm, tube longer than calyx. Habitat Rough grassland, heaths, hedge banks, woodland clearings, cliff-top grassland, on dry, mildly acid soils; to 460 m. Dist. Native. Widespread in England, Wales; rare in Scotland, Ireland. (Most of Europe except N.) Fls Jun–Sep.

Hedge Woundwort
Stachys sylvatica

Erect, rhizomatous, roughly hairy, strong-smelling perennial to 100 cm. Leaves All leaves stalked, ovate, cordate; leaf blades 4–9 cm. Flowers In whorls in interrupted inflorescence; bracteoles very small; corolla reddish purple, 13–15 mm. Habitat Hedge banks, woodlands, shaded gardens; to 500 m. Dist. Native. Common throughout BI. (Most of Europe, but rare in S.) Fls Jul–Aug.

Marsh Woundwort
Stachys palustris

Erect, pubescent, rhizomatous perennial to 100 cm, slightly glandular above. Leaves Stem leaves sessile, oblong-lanceolate, 5–12 cm. Flowers In inflorescence, interrupted below; bracteoles very small; corolla pinkish purple, 12–15 mm. Habitat Pond, lake, river, stream, dyke and canal margins, fens, marshes; to 540 m. Dist. Native. Frequent throughout almost all BI. (Most of Europe, but rare in S.) Fl Jul–Sep. Note The hybrid between *S. sylvatica* and *palustris*, *S.* × *ambigua*, is not infrequent, occurring any of the parents' habitat.

Downy Woundwort
Stachys germanica VU. *(

Densely hairy, erect biennial to 80 cm. Whole plant appears white, covered by long, silky hairs. Leaves Blades 5–12 cm; lower leaves stalked, upper ones sessile. Flowers In inflorescence with bracteoles least as long as calyx; corolla 2× as long as calyx, pale purple. Habitat Calcareous grassland, hedge bank on oolitic limestone. Dist. Native. Very rare. Oxford shire. (W, central and S Europe.) Fls Jul–Aug.

Limestone Woundwort
Stachys alpina *

Erect, pubescent perennial to 100 cm. Leaves Blade 4–16 cm, petioles 3–10 cm. Flowers In inflorescence, whorls separated; bracteoles as long as sepal corolla 15–20 mm, reddish purple. Habitat Limestone woodland, hedge banks. Dist. Doubtful native. Very rare, in 2 sites only in Gloucestershire and N Wales. (W, central and S Europe.) Fls Jun–Au

Field Woundwort
Stachys arven

Slender, branched, ascending to erect, pubescent annual to 25 cm. Leaves Blades 15–30 mm, stalke Flowers Bracts leaf-like; bracteoles very small corolla 6–7 mm, pale purple. Habitat Arable field gardens, allotments, on light sandy soils. Dist Archaeophyte. Local and declining. Throughout B but rare in Scotland, Ireland. (S, W and centr Europe.) Fls Apr–Nov.

Annual Yellow-woundwort
Stachys ann

Erect, thinly pubescent annual to 30 cm. Leaves 20–60 mm. Flowers 3–6 per whorl; corol 10–16 mm, white to pale yellow. Habitat Arable fields, waste ground, usually on calcareous soil Dist. Introduced. Rare casual. (Most of Europe except N.) Fls Jun–Oct.

Perennial Yellow-woundwort
Stachys re

Erect to ascending, thinly pubescent perennial 70 cm. Leaves 10–80 mm. Flowers >6 per whorl corolla 15–20 mm, pale yellow, pubescent. Habitat Grassland, rocky places, scree, open woodland arable fields, on dry calcareous soils. Dist. Introduced. Very rare casual. Docks in S Wales. (Central and S Europe.) Fls Jun–Sep.

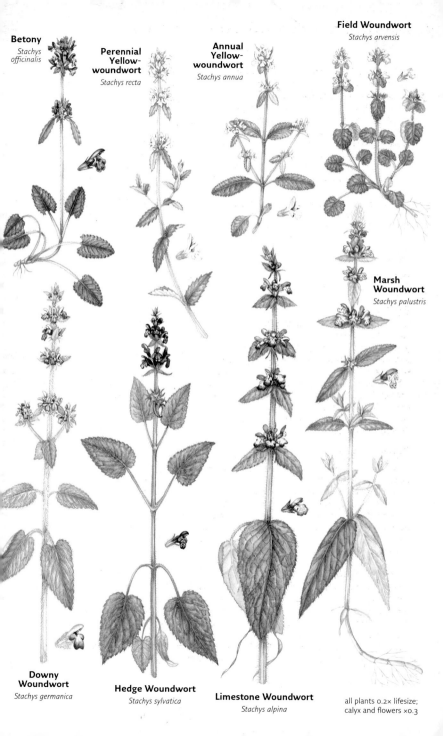

Betony
Stachys officinalis

Perennial Yellow-woundwort
Stachys recta

Annual Yellow-woundwort
Stachys annua

Field Woundwort
Stachys arvensis

Marsh Woundwort
Stachys palustris

Downy Woundwort
Stachys germanica

Hedge Woundwort
Stachys sylvatica

Limestone Woundwort
Stachys alpina

all plants 0.2× lifesize;
calyx and flowers ×0.3

Yellow Archangel
Lamiastrum galeobdolon

Erect, sparsely pubescent, stoloniferous perennial to 60 cm. STEMS Stolons long, leafy. LEAVES 40-70 mm, stalked. FLOWERS In dense axillary whorls; bracts leaf-like; corolla 2-lipped, *c.*20 cm, tube longer than calyx, yellow. HABITAT Woodlands on heavy, neutral or calcareous soils; to 425 m. DIST. Native. Frequent. Widespread in England, Wales; naturalised in Scotland, Ireland. (Most of Europe, but rare in N and S.) FLS May-Jun. NOTE The widespread British plant is ssp. *montanum*, with stems that are pubescent on faces as well as angles, and ≥10 flowers per whorl. Ssp. *galeobdolon*, with stems that are hairy on angles only, and ≤8 flowers per whorl, is a rare plant of a few Lincolnshire woods and hedgerows. Ssp. *argentatum* VU. has large, conspicuous white blotches on the leaves; it is much grown in gardens and is spreading rapidly in hedgerows, roadsides and woodland edges.

Dead-nettles *Lamium*

1	Corolla white	*L. album*
	Corolla pinkish purple	2
2	Corolla ≥20 mm; leaves usually with white blotches	*L. maculatum*
	Corolla ≤20 mm; leaves never with white blotches	3
3	Bracts stalked, resembling leaves	4
	Upper bracts sessile, differing from leaves	5
4	Leaves bluntly toothed, teeth <2 mm long	*L. purpureum*
	Leaves sharply, deeply toothed, at least some >2 mm	*L. hybridum*
5	Calyx ≤7 mm at flowering, densely clothed with spreading white hairs, teeth erect in fruit	*L. amplexicaule*
	Calyx ≥8 mm at flowering, hairs appressed, teeth spreading in fruit	*L. confertum*

White Dead-nettle
Lamium album

Erect, pubescent, rhizomatous or stoloniferous perennial to 60 cm. LEAVES Blades cordate, 30-70 mm, stalked. FLOWERS Bracts leaf-like; corolla 18-25 mm, white. HABITAT Hedgerows, roadsides, waste ground, gardens, farmyards, on fertile soils close to habitation; to 345 m. DIST. Archaeophyte. Common throughout BI except N and W Scotland, W Ireland. (Most of Europe, but rare in S.) FLS May-Dec.

Spotted Dead-nettle
Lamium maculatum

Similar to *L. album*, but leaf blades 20-50 mm, often with large white blotch. FLOWERS Pinkish purple; corolla 20-35 mm. HABITAT Waste ground, roadsides, rough ground, tips, close to habitation. DIST. Introduced. Commonly cultivated and naturalised. (Most of Europe N to N Germany.) FLS May-Oct.

Red Dead-nettle
Lamium purpureum

Erect, branched, pubescent annual to 45 cm. LEAVES Blades 10-50 mm; *all leaves and bracts stalked, regularly crenate-serrate.* FLOWERS Corolla 10-15 mm; corolla tube longer than calyx, with ring of hairs near base. HABITAT Gardens, arable fields, waste places, road verges, on fertile soils. DIST. Archaeophyte. Common throughout most of BI, but scarce in N Scotland, W Ireland. (Most of Europe.) FLS Mar-Oct.

Cut-leaved Dead-nettle
Lamium hybridum

Similar to *L. purpureum*, but *leaves and bracts deeply irregularly toothed*; corolla tube with or without faint ring of hairs towards base. HABITAT Similar to *L. purpureum*: arable weed on well-drained, fertilised soils, waste and disturbed ground. DIST. Archaeophyte. Throughout BI, but scarce in N and W. (Most of Europe except SE.) FLS Mar-Oct.

Henbit Dead-nettle
Lamium amplexicaule

Sparsely pubescent, branched annual to 25 cm. LEAVES Blades 10-25 mm, *orbicular, rounded or cordate at base, crenate or shallowly lobed, upper leaves sessile.* FLOWERS Sometimes not opening; *bracts sessile, clasping stem; calyx 5-7 mm at flowering, densely pubescent with spreading white hairs, teeth erect or connivent at fruiting; corolla with long, exserted tube, lower lip <3 mm.* HABITAT Weed of cultivation on light, dry soils. DIST. Archaeophyte. Most of BI, locally frequent in S and E, but rare or absent elsewhere. (All Europe.) FLS Apr-Aug.

Northern Dead-nettle
Lamium confertum

Similar to *L. amplexicaule*, but more robust; *bracts not clasping stem; calyx 8-12 mm at flowering, with appressed hairs, teeth divergent at fruiting; lower lip of corolla >3 mm.* HABITAT Weed of cultivation, waste ground. DIST. Archaeophyte. Coastal areas of Scotland, I of Man; rare elsewhere. (N Europe.) FLS May-Sep.

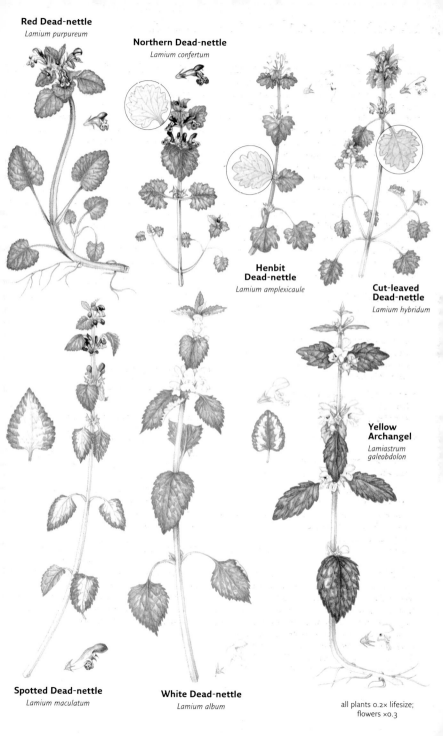

Red Dead-nettle
Lamium purpureum

Northern Dead-nettle
Lamium confertum

Henbit Dead-nettle
Lamium amplexicaule

Cut-leaved Dead-nettle
Lamium hybridum

Yellow Archangel
Lamiastrum galeobdolon

Spotted Dead-nettle
Lamium maculatum

White Dead-nettle
Lamium album

all plants 0.2× lifesize;
flowers ×0.3

Hemp-nettles *Galeopsis*
See key to *Galeopsis* on p.396.

Common Hemp-nettle
Galeopsis tetrahit

Erect, branched, hispid annual to 100 cm. STEMS With red-tipped glandular hairs below nodes. LEAVES 2.5–10 cm. FLOWERS Calyx with prominent veins; corolla 15–20 mm, tube not much longer than calyx, *lower lip ± flat, without notch at tip, dark markings restricted to centre and base of lip, leaving clear, unmarked border.* HABITAT Field borders, arable crops, fens, marshes, woodland clearings; to 450 m. DIST. Native. Throughout BI, but scarce in N Scotland, Ireland. (Most of Europe, but rare in SE.) FLS Jul–Sep.

Bifid Hemp-nettle
Galeopsis bifida

Similar to *G. tetrahit*, but corolla is slightly smaller, 13–16 mm, with *tip of lower lip distinctly notched, margins of lip turned under (revolute), and dark markings more extensive, almost covering lip.* Native. Distribution and ecology as for *G. tetrahit*, with which it sometimes grows, although it occurs more often on arable land.

Red Hemp-nettle
Galeopsis angustifolia CR. *(R)

Erect, branched, pubescent annual to 60 cm. STEMS Not swollen at nodes. LEAVES *1.5–8 cm, linear-lanceolate, <10 mm broad.* FLOWERS *Corolla 15–25 mm, reddish pink,* tube much longer than calyx. HABITAT Arable weed of cereals, open ground, on calcareous soils; also coastal shingle. DIST. Archaeophyte. Throughout lowland Britain, but now rare and declining; absent from Scotland. (W, central and S Europe.) FLS Jul–Oct.

Downy Hemp-nettle
Galeopsis segetum EX.

Softly downy, erect annual to 50 cm. STEMS Not swollen at nodes. LEAVES Lanceolate-ovate, *silky beneath.* FLOWERS Corolla large, 20–30 mm, pale yellow, c.4× as long as calyx. HABITAT Waste ground, arable land, on acid soils. DIST. Archaeophyte. Formerly rare casual, now extinct. (W and central Europe.) FLS Jul–Oct.

Large-flowered Hemp-nettle
Galeopsis speciosa VU.

Erect, hispid annual to 100 cm. STEMS Swollen at nodes. LEAVES Ovate. FLOWERS Calyx with prominent veins; *corolla large, 25–35 mm, pale yellow with purple spot on lower lip,* tube *c.*2× as long as calyx. HABITAT Weed of root crops, waste ground. DIST. Archaeophyte. Local and declining. N from central England and Wales, N Ireland. (Most of Europe except parts of S.) FLS Jul–Sep.

Bastard Balm
Melittis melissophyllum VU.

Erect, *strong-smelling* perennial to 70 cm. LEAVES Ovate, cordate, coarsely toothed, 5–10 cm. FLOWERS Calyx 2-lipped; *corolla large, 2.5–4 cm, pink, or white spotted with pink,* tube much longer than calyx. HABITAT Woodlands, hedge banks, scrub. DIST. Native. Very local, declining. New Forest, SW England, W Wales. (W, central and S Europe.) FLS May–Jul.

White Horehound
Marrubium vulgare

Erect or ascending, *densely white-pubescent*, much-branched perennial to 60 cm. LEAVES *Surface wrinkled*; blade 1.5–4 cm, broadly ovate. FLOWERS In inflorescence with dense-flowered whorls; *10 calyx teeth, hooked; corolla c.*15 mm, *white.* HABITAT Open calcareous grassland, sandy banks, shingle. DIST. Rare and local as native in E, S and SW England; usually coastal in S Wales. Scattered and declining as naturalised introduction elsewhere. (Most of Europe except N.) FLS Jun–Nov.

Black Horehound
Ballota nigra

Erect, branched, pubescent perennial to 100 cm, with unpleasant smell. LEAVES Stalked, leaf blades 2–5 cm. FLOWERS In many-flowered inflorescence with numerous whorls; bracts leaf-like; calyx funnel-shaped, with 5 broad, ± equal teeth; corolla reddish mauve, 10–15 mm, hairy. HABITAT Hedge banks, tracksides, waste places, on well-drained, usually calcareous soils, often near habitation; to 480 m. DIST. Archaeophyte. Widespread in England N to Humber; scarce or absent in much of Scotland, W Wales, Ireland. (Most of Europe except extreme N.) FLS Jun–Oct.

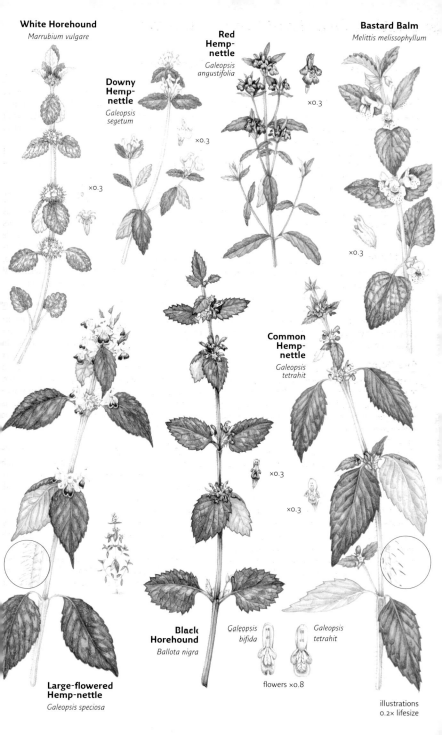

White Horehound
Marrubium vulgare

×0.3

Downy Hemp-nettle

Galeopsis segetum

×0.3

Red Hemp-nettle

Galeopsis angustifolia

×0.3

Bastard Balm
Melittis melissophyllum

×0.3

Common Hemp-nettle

Galeopsis tetrahit

×0.3

×0.3

Large-flowered Hemp-nettle

Galeopsis speciosa

Black Horehound

Ballota nigra

Galeopsis bifida

Galeopsis tetrahit

flowers ×0.8

illustrations
0.2× lifesize

Teucrium

1 Flowers in terminal racemes;
corolla pale yellowish green   *T. scorodonia*
Flowers in heads or axillary
whorls   2

2 Flowers purple, in axillary
whorls; leaves toothed or lobed   3
Flowers cream, in heads; leaves
entire   *T. montanum* ●

3 Leaves pinnately lobed   *T. botrys*
Leaves toothed   4

4 Whorls forming a terminal
inflorescence   *T. chamaedrys*
Whorls spaced down stem   *T. scordium*

Wood Sage   *Teucrium scorodonia*

Erect, pubescent, branched, rhizomatous perennial
to 30 cm. Leaves 30-70 mm, stalked, wrinkled.
Flowers *Pale yellowish green*; bracts shorter than
flowers. Habitat Woodlands, rough grassland,
hedgerows, scrub, heaths, rocky hillsides, limestone
pavement, sand-dunes, shingle; to 550 m. Dist.
Native. Widespread throughout almost all BI. (S, W
and central Europe.) Fls Jul-Sep.

Wall Germander   *Teucrium chamaedrys*

Low-growing perennial, *woody at base*, to 30 cm.
Stems Many ± erect, pubescent stems. Leaves
1-3 cm, short-stalked, *dark shining green above*,
deeply and bluntly toothed. Flowers *Inflorescence
whorls forming terminal head; bracts shorter than flowers*; corolla pinkish purple. Dist. Introduced, but may be
native on one site on chalk turf of South Downs, E
Sussex. Naturalised, scattered and declining elsewhere. (Most of Europe except N.) Fls Jul-Sep.

Water Germander   *Teucrium scordium* EN. *(B)

Softly hairy, rhizomatous or stoloniferous perennial
to 60 cm. Stems Rooting. Leaves 1-5 cm, ± sessile,
coarsely toothed. Flowers *Inflorescence whorls distant; bracts longer than flowers*; corolla 8-12 mm,
purple. Habitat Riverbanks, wet pits, fen ditches,
dune slacks. Dist. Native. Very rare. Central and W
Ireland, 2 sites in England. (Most of Europe except
extreme N.) Fls Jul-Oct.

Cut-leaved Germander   *Teucrium botrys* *(B

Softly hairy, erect annual to 30 cm. Leaves Stalked;
leaf blades 10-25 mm, *deeply divided, lobes narrow*.
Flowers Pinkish purple; bracts smaller than flowers. Habitat Open patches on chalk turf, arable
fields, bare ground on steep, warm chalk slopes.
Dist. Introduced. S England. Naturalised, very rare.
(S, W and central Europe.) Fls Jul-Sep.

Mountain Germander   *Teucrium montanum*

Decumbent, pubescent woody perennial or dwarf
shrub to 25 cm. Leaves 13-30 mm, *narrow, entire,
sessile, glabrous above, densely hairy below*. Flowers
Cream, in a terminal head; bracts leaf-like. Habitat
Dry, warm calcareous grassland, rocky and stony
ground. Dist. *Not BI*. (S and central Europe, N to
Netherlands.) Fls Jun-Aug.

Bugle   *Ajuga reptans*

Erect, slightly pubescent, *stoloniferous* perennial to
30 cm. Stems Simple, *upper part with 2 sides hairy*.
Leaves Basal leaves forming a rosette, stalked,
scarcely toothed, ± glabrous, blades 4-7 cm. Flowers Upper bracts shorter than flowers, tinged purple; corolla blue. Habitat Woodland clearings,
coppice, scrub, hedge banks, unimproved grassland
on damp, fertile, neutral to mildly acid soils; to
760 m. Dist. Native. Common throughout BI. (Most
of Europe except extreme N.) Fls May-Jul.

Pyramidal Bugle   *Ajuga pyramidalis* VU. *(N

Erect, pubescent perennial to 30 cm, *without stolons*.
Stems Simple, *hairy on all 4 sides*. Leaves Pubescent, *bluntly toothed*. Flowers Bracts much longer
than flowers; corolla pale violet-blue. Habitat Free
draining hillsides, bare rocky slopes, crevices, on
basic or acid soils; to 650 m. Dist. Native. Very local.
NW Scotland, W Ireland. (All Europe except S.) Fls
May-Jul.

Ground-pine   *Ajuga chamaepitys* EN. *(B

Short, pubescent, branched annual to 15 cm. Leaves
Deeply divided, lobes narrow, basal leaves soon withering. Flowers In axillary pairs, *yellow*. Habitat
Arable fields, tracks, on calcareous soil; also bare
patches on chalk turf. Dist. Native. Rare and declining. A few sites in S England. (Most of Europe except
N.) Fls May-Sep.

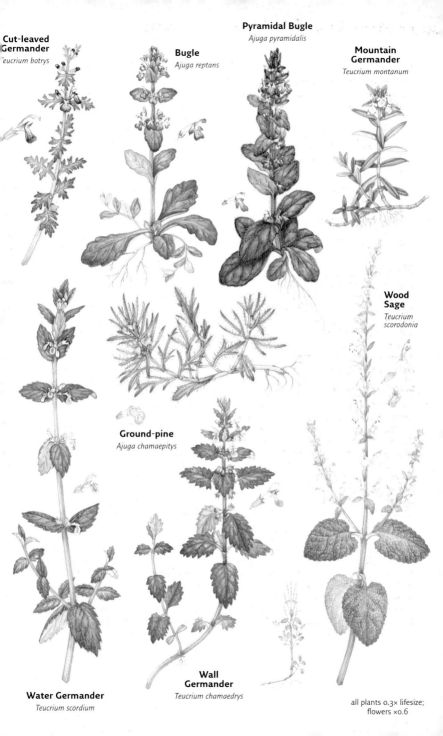

Cut-leaved Germander
Teucrium botrys

Bugle
Ajuga reptans

Pyramidal Bugle
Ajuga pyramidalis

Mountain Germander
Teucrium montanum

Wood Sage
Teucrium scorodonia

Ground-pine
Ajuga chamaepitys

Water Germander
Teucrium scordium

Wall Germander
Teucrium chamaedrys

all plants 0.3× lifesize; flowers ×0.6

Cat-mint
Nepeta cataria VU.

Erect, branched, densely *grey-white, pubescent, strongly scented* perennial to 100 cm. LEAVES 3–7 cm, *white-felted beneath*, coarsely toothed. FLOWERS Inflorescence whorls densely crowded; *corolla 7–10 mm, white with small purple spots.* HABITAT Hedge banks, roadsides, rough ground, on dry calcareous soils. DIST. Archaeophyte. Local and decreasing. Naturalised and scattered throughout England. (S, E and E-central Europe.) FLS Jul–Sep.

Ground-ivy
Glechoma hederacea

Trailing, stoloniferous perennial to 30 cm. STEMS Rooting at nodes, flowering branches ascending. LEAVES *Long-stalked, leaf blades kidney-shaped*, 10–30 mm across. FLOWERS Inflorescence whorls few-flowered; corolla 15–20 mm, blue. HABITAT Woodland rides, scrub, hedgerows, permanent grassland, waste ground, shaded gardens, on calcareous or heavy soils; to 465 m. DIST. Native. Common throughout BI, but rare in N Scotland, W Ireland. (All Europe.) FLS Mar–May.

Selfheal
Prunella vulgaris

Ascending to erect, sparsely pubescent perennial to 30 cm. LEAVES Stalked; leaf blades 20–50 mm, ± entire. FLOWERS In dense-flowered terminal head *with pair of leaves at base; bracts different from leaves, orbicular, with long white hairs*; calyx 2-lipped; *corolla 10–14 mm*, purple or, rarely, white. HABITAT Permanent grasslands, meadows, pastures, lawns, waste ground, on neutral or calcareous soils; to 845 m. DIST. Native. Ubiquitous throughout BI. (All Europe.) FLS Jun–Sep.

Large Selfheal
Prunella grandiflora

Similar to *P. vulgaris*, but stems to 60 cm; leaf blades 40–70 mm; *inflorescence without a pair of leaves at its base; corolla 25–30 mm*. HABITAT Calcareous grass-

land, dry banks. DIST. *Not BI*. (All Europe except for most of N.) FLS Jul–Sep.

Cut-leaved Selfheal
Prunella laciniata

Similar to *P. vulgaris*, but at least some of *upper leaves deeply divided; corolla* larger, 15–17 mm, *creamy white*. HABITAT Dry calcareous grassland, roadsides, waste ground. DIST. Introduced. Rare, declining. Naturalised in scattered sites in S England. (S, W, E and central Europe.) FLS Jun–Aug.

Balm
Melissa officinalis

Erect, much-branched, *lemon-scented*, sparsely pubescent perennial to 60 cm. LEAVES Stalked; leaf blades 30–70 mm, ovate. FLOWERS In axillary whorls; *calyx 2-lipped; corolla 2-lipped*, 8–15 mm, *pale yellow becoming pinkish*. HABITAT Road verges, banks, tips, close to habitation. DIST. Introduced. Widely naturalised in S Britain as garden escape. (S Europe.) FLS Aug–Sep.

Skullcap
Scutellaria galericulata

Erect, sparsely pubescent, rhizomatous perennial to 50 cm. LEAVES Ovate-lanceolate, 20–50 mm, *with 8–23 shallow teeth*. FLOWERS In axillary pairs; calyx 2-lipped; *corolla* 2-lipped, *10–20 mm, deep blue*. HABITAT Margins of ponds, lakes, rivers, streams, dykes and canals, fens, wet meadows, wet woods, dune slacks, avoiding acid soils; lowland to 365 m. DIST. Native. Throughout BI, but scarce in NW Scotland, Ireland. (All Europe.) FLS Jun–Sep.

Lesser Skullcap
Scutellaria minor

Similar to *S. galericulata*, but smaller, to 15 cm, ± glabrous; *leaves* 10–30 mm, *with 1–4 teeth; corolla* 6–10 mm, *pink with darker spots*. HABITAT Woodland rides, pond margins, acid flushes, wet heaths on acid soils; to 440 m. DIST. Native. Rather local. S and W Britain, SW Ireland. (W Europe.) FLS Jul–Oct

Cat-mint
Nepeta cataria

Selfheal
Prunella vulgaris

×0.6

**Cut-leaved
Selfheal**
Prunella laciniata

Balm
*Melissa
officinalis*

Skullcap
*Scutellaria
galericulata*

**Large
Selfheal**
*Prunella
grandiflora*

×1.2

Ground-ivy
Glechoma hederacea

Lesser Skullcap
Scutellaria minor

illustrations
0.3× lifesize

Calamint and Wild Basil *Clinopodium*
See key to Clinopodium on p.396.

Wild Basil
Clinopodium vulgare

Erect, pubescent, rhizomatous perennial to 80 cm. Leaves Stem leaves stalked, 1.5–5 cm. Flowers In *dense axillary whorls without a common stalk, whorls >8-flowered; bracts leaf-like; calyx 2-lipped, 2 teeth of lower lip longer than 3 teeth of upper lip;* upper lip of corolla flat; *stamens shorter than corolla.* Similar spp. Sometimes confused with *Origanum vulgare* (p.400), with which it often grows. Habitat Banks, hedgerows, scrub, rough grassland, on dry calcareous soils. Dist. Native. Widespread in S England, getting scarcer N to central Scotland; absent from Ireland. (Most of Europe except extreme N.) Fls Jul–Sep.

Basil Thyme
Clinopodium acinos VU. *(R)

Small, erect, pubescent annual to 20 cm. Leaves Stalked, 0.5–1.5 cm, ovate, obscurely toothed. Flowers Inflorescence whorls 3–8-flowered; calyx tube swollen near base; *corolla 7–10 mm, violet with white markings.* Habitat Dry calcareous grassland, arable land, stony waste ground. Dist. Native. Rather local in lowland England; introduced in Ireland. (Most of Europe except extreme N; rare in S.) Fls May–Sep.

Common Calamint
Clinopodium ascendens

Erect, little-branched, rhizomatous, pubescent perennial to 60 cm. Leaves Stalked; leaf blades 2–4 cm, *obscurely toothed.* Flowers *Stalks in upper inflorescence clusters usually unbranched, those of lower clusters branched once; lower 2 calyx teeth upward-curving and longer than upper 3 teeth; ring of hairs in calyx tube not protruding at fruiting;* corolla 10–15 mm, lilac with darker spots on lower lip. Habitat Hedgerows, banks, scrub, rough grassland, on dry calcareous or sandy soils. Dist. Native. Lowland England, W Wales, S Ireland. (W, S and S-central Europe.) Fls Jul–Sep.

Lesser Calamint
Clinopodium calamintha VU.

Similar to, and confused with, *C. ascendens*, but very aromatic; *leaves rather grey-green and pubescent;* leaf blades smaller, 1–2 cm, with 3–8 teeth on each side; *flower stalks of upper inflorescence clusters branched 2–3×; lower calyx teeth of upper flower clusters not much longer than upper 3 teeth; hairs in throat of calyx*

protruding at fruiting; corolla pale mauve, hardly spotted. Habitat Roadside banks, hedgerows, rough grassland, on dry calcareous soils. Dist. Native. Very local, declining. Parts of E England. (W, S and S-central Europe.) Fls Jul–Sep.

Wood Calamint
Clinopodium menthifolium CR. *(B)

Erect, little-branched, rhizomatous perennial to 60 cm. Leaves *3.5–7 cm, coarsely toothed with 3–8 teeth on each side.* Flowers Calyx 7–10 mm, lower calyx teeth upwards-curving, longer than wide-spreading upper 3 teeth; hairs in throat of calyx not protruding at fruiting; *corolla large, 17–22 mm, purplish pink with darker purple markings on lower lip.* Habitat Shaded wood borders, scrub on chalk. Dist. Native. Very rare, in one site on I of Wight only. (W, S and S-central Europe.) Fls Aug–Sep.

Wild Thyme
Thymus polytrichus

Mat-forming, aromatic woody perennial to *c.*7 cm. Stems Long, creeping, rooting branches; *stems below inflorescence 4-angled, with 2 opposite sides densely hairy and other 2 sides ± glabrous.* Leaves 4–8 mm held flat. Flowers *In rounded,* rarely somewhat elongated, *inflorescence.* Habitat Close-grazed permanent grassland, maritime and mountain heaths cliffs, limestone pavement, mature sand-dunes, or dry calcareous or acid soils. Dist. Native. Throughout BI, but ± confined to chalk areas in S England and coastal in Ireland. (W Europe.) Fls May–Aug.

Breckland Thyme
Thymus serpyllum

Similar to *T. polytrichus*, but smaller; *flowering stems scarcely angled, with short white hairs all round;* leaves 4–5 mm, held upright. Habitat Dry sandy heaths grasslands, especially where disturbed. Dist. Native. Rare. W Suffolk, W Norfolk (Breckland) (Central Europe.) Fls Jul–Aug.

Large Thyme
Thymus pulegioides

Tufted, strongly aromatic, prostrate woody perennial to 25 cm. Stems Ascending flowering branches and creeping stems; *stems below inflorescence sharply 4-sided, with long hairs on angles, 2 opposite faces narrow, shortly pubescent, the other 2 broader, glabrous.* Leaves 6–10 mm. Flowers *In elongated inflorescence.* Habitat Chalk grassland; occasionally also heaths, fixed dunes. Dist. Native. Local. S England (Most of Europe.) Fls Jul–Aug.

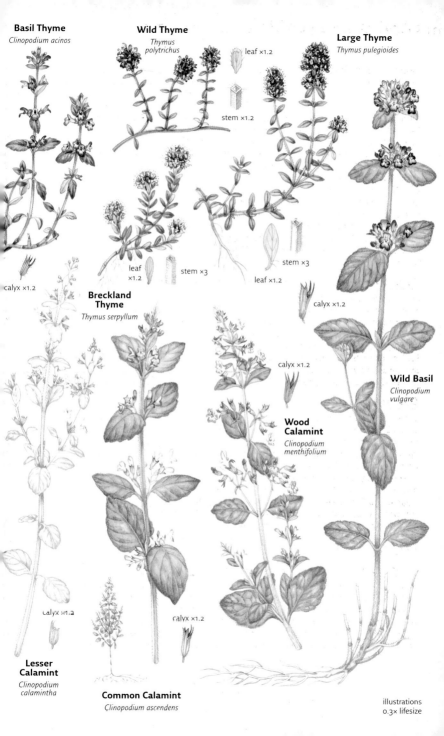

Basil Thyme
Clinopodium acinos

Wild Thyme
Thymus polytrichus

leaf ×1.2

stem ×1.2

Large Thyme
Thymus pulegioides

calyx ×1.2

leaf
×1.2

stem ×3

leaf ×1.2

stem ×3

calyx ×1.2

Breckland Thyme
Thymus serpyllum

calyx ×1.2

Wild Basil
Clinopodium vulgare

Wood Calamint
Clinopodium menthifolium

calyx ×1.2

calyx ×1.2

Lesser Calamint
Clinopodium calamintha

calyx ×1.2

Common Calamint
Clinopodium ascendens

illustrations
0.3× lifesize

	if	then
1	▷ Stem with bristly hairs, swollen at nodes	Go to ▷ **2**
	▷ Stem with soft hairs, not swollen at nodes	Go to ▷ **4**
2	▷ Corolla 13–20 mm, pink, purple or white; corolla tube rarely >1½× as long as calyx	Go to ▷ **3**
	▷ Corolla *c*.30 mm, pale yellow with violet spot on lower lip; corolla tube much longer than calyx	**G. speciosa** (p.388)
3	▷ Middle lobe of lower lip entire or slightly notched, ± flat	**G. tetrahit** (p.388)
	▷ Middle lobe of lower lip clearly notched, convex	**G. bifida** (p 388)
4	▷ Flowers purple	**G. angustifolia** (p.388)
	▷ Flowers pale yellow	**G. segetum** (p.388)

Key to Calamint and Wild Basil *Clinopodium*

	if	then
1	▷ Flowers in tight axillary whorls without a common stalk, purple or violet; calyx tube curved	Go to ▷ **2**
	▷ Flowers in short, opposite inflorescence clusters with common stalk, pale lilac; calyx tube straight	Go to ▷ **3**
2	▷ Whorls many-flowered, dense, rose-purple	**C. vulgare** (p.394)
	▷ Whorls 3–8-flowered, violet	**C. acinos** (p394)
3	▷ Corolla >15 mm (I of Wight)	**C. menthifolium** (p.394)
	▷ Corolla ≤15 mm	Go to ▷ **4**
4	▷ Flower stalks of upper inflorescence clusters branched 2–3×, hairs in throat of calyx protruding after flowering	**C. calamintha** (p.394)
	▷ Flower stalks of upper inflorescence clusters usually unbranched, hairs in throat of calyx not protruding after flowering	**C. ascendens** (p.394)

	if	**then**
1	▷ Stems erect or procumbent, if procumbent not rooting or mat-forming; leaves >5 mm; whorls >6-flowered	Go to ▷ **2**
	▷ Stems prostrate, mat-forming, with slender rooting branches; leaves small, ≤5 mm; whorls 2–6-flowered	**M. requienii** (p.398)
2	▷ Flowers usually all in axillary whorls; flowering stem terminated by leaves, sometimes with few small flowers in their axils	Go to ▷ **3**
	▷ Flowers in terminal spikes or heads	Go to ▷ **5**
3	▷ Calyx with hairs in throat; calyx teeth unequal, the lower 2 longer than upper 3	**M. pulegium** (p.398)
	▷ Calyx without hairs in throat; calyx teeth ± equal	Go to ▷ **4**
4	▷ Calyx bell-shaped, stamens protruding	**M. arvensis** (p.398)
	▷ Calyx tubular, stamens not protruding	**M. × verticillata** (p.398)
5	▷ Flowers in a head, often with axillary whorls below	**M. aquatica** (p.398)
	▷ Flowers in a spike	Go to ▷ **6**
6	▷ Leaves stalked	**M. × piperita** (p.398)
	▷ Leaves sessile	Go to ▷ **7**
7	▷ Leaves ovate to orbicular, wrinkled, teeth bent under and appearing blunt from above; flowers whitish, scent sickly	**M. suaveolens** (p.398)
	▷ Leaves lanceolate to ovate, teeth not bent under and appearing acute from above; plant with sweet smell	Go to ▷ **8**
8	▷ Leaves lanceolate to ovate, usually glabrous and not wrinkled, with spearmint scent	**M. spicata** (p.398)
	▷ Leaves ovate to suborbicular, usually both wrinkled and pubescent; flowers pinkish, with a sweet scent	**M. × villosa** (p.398)

Mint *Mentha*

The mints are not always easy to identify (*see* key on p.397). They are very variable and hybridise freely, and many forms are cultivated and frequently escape. Only 3 of the commonest hybrids are included here.

Corn Mint
Mentha arvensis

Erect, rhizomatous, pubescent perennial to 60 cm. Leaves Stalked, 2–6.5 cm. Flowers *In well-separated axillary whorls*; bracts leaf-like; calyx hairy all over, 1.5–2.5 mm, *teeth triangular, ≤0.5 mm*; corolla hairy on outside; *stamens protruding*. Habitat Woodland rides and clearings, roadsides, arable fields, damp pastures; to 390 m. Dist. Native. Frequent throughout BI. (Most of Europe.) Fls May–Oct.

Water Mint
Mentha aquatica

Erect, strongly aromatic, sparsely pubescent or glabrous perennial to 90 cm. Leaves Ovate, stalked, 2–6 cm. Flowers *In terminal head, c.*2 cm across, with 1–2 axillary whorls below; pedicels and calyx hairy; *stamens protruding*. Habitat Wet meadows, marshes, fens, damp woodlands, margins of dykes, ponds, streams and rivers; to 455 m. Dist. Native. Common throughout BI. (All Europe except extreme N.) Fls Jul–Oct.

Whorled Mint
Mentha × verticillata
(*Mentha aquatica × M. arvensis*)

Erect, sparsely pubescent, rhizomatous perennial to 90 cm. The commonest hybrid mint. Similar to *M. arvensis*, but more robust; leaves 2–6.5 cm; flowers in axillary whorls; *calyx 2–3.5 mm, teeth narrowly triangular, 0.5–1.5 mm, c.2× as long as broad; stamens not protruding*. Habitat Similar to parents, but usually in damp places; to 365 m. Dist. Native. Rather frequent throughout BI. (Most of Europe.) Fls Jul–Oct.

Spear Mint
Mentha spicata

Strongly aromatic, erect, usually glabrous, branched, rhizomatous perennial to 90 cm. The commonest cultivated pot-herb. Leaves Sessile, lanceolate, 4–9 cm, coarsely toothed, teeth pointing forward. Flowers *In terminal spike*, 3–6 cm. Habitat Damp roadsides, waste ground, as throw-out from cultivation. Dist. Archaeophyte (native origins unknown). Naturalised throughout BI, but scarce in N Scotland and rare in Ireland. (Naturalised throughout Europe.) Fls Aug–Sep.

Peppermint
Mentha × piperita
(*Mentha aquatica × M. spicata*)

Strongly aromatic, erect, glabrous or sparsely pubescent, rhizomatous perennial to 80 cm. Sterile.

Stems Branched, *often purple*. Leaves *Stalked, ovate-lanceolate, glabrous* or sparsely pubescent, 3.5–8.5 cm. Flowers In elongated, cylindrical, terminal head, 3.5–6 cm; corolla dark lilac-pink. Habitat Damp places, waste ground; to 450 m. Dist. Spontaneous hybrid or escape from cultivation; scattered and local throughout BI. (Most of Europe.) Fls Jul–Sep.

Round-leaved Mint
Mentha suaveolens

Erect, strongly aromatic, *densely pubescent*, rhizomatous perennial to 100 cm. Leaves Sessile, ovate to almost orbicular, apex rounded, surface wrinkled, *teeth bent under and appearing blunt from above*. Flowers In inflorescence of dense, branched, terminal spikes; *corolla whitish*; stamens protruding; *scent rather sickly*. Habitat Roadsides, hedge banks, waste ground. Dist. Native. SW England, Wales; scattered and declining as garden escape elsewhere. (N and central Europe.) Fls Aug–Sep.

Apple Mint
Mentha × villosa
(*Mentha spicata × M. suaveolens*)

Very variable rhizomatous perennial to 90 cm. Leaves Glabrous or pubescent, lanceolate to almost orbicular, *marginal teeth not curved under, so appearing acute from above*. Flowers *Pinkish*, with *sweet scent*. Habitat Damp waste ground, roadsides, tracksides. Dist. Introduced. Widely naturalised throughout BI, but scarce in N Scotland, Ireland. (Most of Europe). Fls Aug–Sep.

Pennyroyal
Mentha pulegium EN. *(B, NI, R)*

Prostrate to erect, sparsely pubescent perennial to 30 cm. Leaves *Oval, obscurely toothed, ≤10 mm broad, shortly stalked*. Flowers *Whorls separated*; bracts leaf-like; calyx 2–3 mm, lower 2 teeth slightly longer than 3 upper teeth; corolla hairy outside, glabrous within, lilac. Habitat Grazed village greens, coastal grassland. Dist. Native. Very rare. Scattered localities in S England, Wales, S Ireland, Channel Is. (S, W and central Europe.) Fls Aug–Oct.

Corsican Mint
Mentha requienii

Mat-forming, creeping perennial, rooting at nodes, glabrous or sparsely hairy. Plant has strong, pleasant smell. Stems Flowering stems to 12 cm. Leaves *Stalked, 3–5 mm, ovate-orbicular, entire*. Flowers 2–6, axillary. Habitat Cultivated ground, tracks, paths, tips. Dist. Introduced. Naturalised as infrequent garden escape. (Corsica, Sardinia.) Fls Jun–Aug.

Pennyroyal
Mentha pulegium

×1.2

×1.2

Peppermint
Mentha × piperita

×1.2

Corsican Mint
Mentha requienii

Water Mint
Mentha aquatica

Round-leaved Mint
Mentha suaveolens

Corn Mint
Mentha arvensis

Whorled Mint
Mentha × verticillata

Apple Mint
Mentha × villosa

Spear Mint
Mentha spicata

×1.2

illustrations
0.2× lifesize

Motherwort
Leonurus cardiaca

Tall, erect, branched, rhizomatous, pubescent perennial to 120 cm. LEAVES Lower leaves 6–12 cm, palmate, 5–7-lobed. FLOWERS Inflorescence whorls axillary, well separated; calyx equally 5-toothed; corolla *c*.12 mm, pubescent. HABITAT Hedgerows, walls, waste ground. DIST. Introduced. Rare casual, declining. Scattered localities. (Most of Europe except extreme N.) FLS Jul–Sep.

Jerusalem Sage
Phlomis fruticosa

Evergreen shrub to 130 cm. LEAVES Lower leaves absent; stem leaves 3–9 cm, densely white-felted beneath; leaf whorls many-flowered, axillary. FLOWERS Calyx 10–20 mm, equally 5-toothed; corolla 25–35 mm, upper lip strongly concave. HABITAT Coastal areas, waste ground. DIST. Introduced. Rare naturalised garden escape. (E Mediterranean.) FLS Jun–Jul.

Wild Marjoram
Origanum vulgare

Erect, sparsely pubescent, aromatic perennial to 80 cm. LEAVES Ovate, 1.5–4.5 cm. FLOWERS In dense terminal inflorescence; calyx ± equally 5-toothed; corolla 6–8 mm, stamens protruding. HABITAT Rough permanent grassland, hedge banks, scrub, roadsides, on dry calcareous soils; to 410 m. DIST. Native. Common throughout most of BI, but absent from N Scotland. (Most of Europe.) FLS Jul–Sep.

Gipsywort
Lycopus europaeus

Erect, sparsely pubescent, rhizomatous perennial to 100 cm. LEAVES To 10 cm, deeply lobed. FLOWERS Small, *c*.3 mm, in separated axillary inflorescence; bracts leaf-like; corolla of 4 ± equal lobes, white with purple dots; 2 stamens, protruding. HABITAT Marshes, fens, wet woodlands, margins of rivers, canals, dykes, ponds and lakes; to 485 m. DIST. Native. Common throughout BI, but rare in Scotland except W, and local in Ireland. (Most of Europe except extreme N.) FLS Jun–Sep.

Wild Clary
Salvia verbenaca

Erect, pubescent perennial to 80 cm. LEAVES Lower leaves 4–12 cm, distinctly lobed. FLOWERS In interrupted terminal spike; calyx 6–8 mm, glandular, with long white hairs; corolla eglandular, 6–10 mm, with 2 white spots at base of lower lip. HABITAT Rough grassland, old pastures, roadsides, churchyards, dunes, on well-drained calcareous or sandy soils. DIST. Native. Local in England SE of line from Wash to Severn; rare and coastal in Ireland. (S and W Europe.) FLS May–Aug.

Meadow Clary
Salvia pratensis *(B)

Erect, aromatic, pubescent, glandular perennial to 100 cm. Similar to *S. verbenaca*, but basal leaves ovate, 7–15 cm, deeply and bluntly toothed, surface wrinkled, not lobed; flowers larger, 15–25 mm, deep blue, glandular on outside, upper lip compressed, strongly curved (female flowers smaller, *c*.10 mm); calyx pubescent and glandular, but without long white hairs. HABITAT Rough grassland, roadsides, verges, on dry calcareous soils; also casual garden escape. DIST. Native and introduced. Rare. In scattered localities in S England. (Most of Europe except N.) FLS Jun–Jul.

VERBENACEAE Vervains

Vervain
Verbena officinalis

Erect, branched, roughly hairy, perennial to 75 cm. LEAVES Opposite; lower leaves stalked, deeply pinnately lobed. FLOWERS In elongated, slender terminal spikes, violet; 5 sepals; corolla 2-lipped with 5 lobes, 3.5–5 mm; 4 stamens. HABITAT Rough grassland, scrub, roadsides, bare ground, on well-drained calcareous soils. DIST. Archaeophyte. Declining. Widespread in S England, S Wales; rare further N and in Ireland. (Most of Europe except N.) FLS Jul–Sep.

Jerusalem Sage
Phlomis fruticosaa

Vervain
Verbena officinalis

Gipsywort
Lycopus europaeus

×0.6

×1.2

Motherwort
Leonurus cardiaca

×1.2

Meadow Clary
Salvia pratensis

×0.6

Wild Clary
Salvia verbenaca

×1.2

Wild Marjoram
Origanum vulgare

illustrations
0.6× lifesize

HIPPURIDACEAE Mare's-tail

Mare's-tail
Hippuris vulgaris

Rhizomatous, submerged or emergent aquatic perennial to 100 cm. STEMS Emergent, stiff, erect. LEAVES *6–12 in a whorl; linear, sessile, entire*, 1–7.5 cm; leaves of submerged shoots longer, more flaccid. FLOWERS Greenish, solitary in axils of shoots; *perianth absent; 1 stamen*. HABITAT Shallow, usually calcium-rich lakes, ponds, slow-moving streams, dykes; occasionally on mud, when smaller in all its parts. Usually lowland but to 900 m. DIST. Native. Throughout BI. (Most of Europe.) FLS Jun–Jul.

CALLITRICHACEAE Starworts

Aquatic or mud-growing annuals or perennials. Leaves opposite, entire, linear-ovate. Flowers monoecious, axillary, usually solitary; perianth absent; 1 stamen. A very difficult group to separate. Important differences are between submerged and floating rosette leaves, and fruit characters. In some cases, accurate identification is not possible without microscopic examination of pollen grains.

1 Upper leaves ovate, forming floating rosettes in summer; submerged leaves linear or narrowly elliptic; anthers yellow or whitish | 2
  All leaves linear, ± parallel-sided, submerged; plant without floating rosettes; anthers whitish | 4

2 Flowers submerged, anthers whitish, styles persistent and reflexed against sides of fruit; tips of submerged leaves abruptly expanded into wide, spanner-shaped tip | *C. brutia*
  Flowers not submerged, pollen yellow, styles, if present, erect or spreading; tips of submerged leaves notched but not expanded in spanner-shaped tip | 3

3 Fruits not winged | *C. obtusangula*
  Fruits winged (*see text*) | *C. stagnalis*, *C. platycarpa*

4 Fruit unwinged; leaves dark green, translucent | *C. truncata*
  Fruit with distinct wing | 5

5 Leaves broadest at base, tapering to notched tip | *C. hermaphro-ditica*
  Leaf tip expanded into broad, spanner-shaped notch | *C. brutia*

Common Water-starwort
Callitriche stagnalis

Aquatic or mud-growing annual or perennial. LEAVES *Submerged leaves narrowly ovate, never linear*; rosette and terrestrial leaves broadly ovate to sub-orbicular. FLOWERS Stamens 0.5–2 mm. FRUITS *Ripe fruits greyish with distinct wing* (>12% width of nutlet). HABITAT Shallow, still or fast-moving clear, often calcium-rich water; the common species of muddy woodland rides. To 610 m. DIST. Native. Common throughout BI. (Most of Europe except extreme N.) FLS May–Sep.

Various-leaved Water-starwort
Callitriche platycarpa

Similar to *C. stagnalis*, but *some submerged leaves usually linear*; rosette leaves narrower, elliptic; stamens *c.*4 mm; *ripe fruits pale brown*, wing narrower (<*c.*12% width of nutlet). HABITAT Similar to *C. stagnalis*, to 520 m. DIST. Native. Throughout BI. (W Europe from Denmark to Pyrenees.) FLS Apr–Oct. NOTE Often not distinguishable from *C. stagnalis* without microscopic examination of pollen grains.

Blunt-fruited Water-starwort
Callitriche obtusangula

Submerged, floating or terrestrial perennial. LEAVES *Submerged leaves linear, emarginate*; rosette leaves broadly rhomboidal, distinctly ridged along veins. FRUITS *Longer than wide, unwinged*. HABITAT Still, slow-flowing, nutrient-rich waters, including brackish dykes, wet mud. DIST. Native. Widespread in England, Wales, Ireland; very rare in Scotland. (Most of Europe except Scandinavia.) FLS May– Sep.

Intermediate Water-starwort
Callitriche brutia

Submerged or floating perennial or terrestrial annual. LEAVES *Tip of submerged leaves expanded to wide, spanner-shaped notch*; rosette leaves elliptic. FLOWERS Submerged, *styles* persistent, *reflexed against sides of fruit*. FRUITS Sessile. HABITAT Still and fast-flowing, usually acid water, bare wet mud, to 950 m. DIST. Native. Throughout BI. (Most of Europe E to Black Sea.) FLS Apr–Sep.

Autumnal Water-starwort
Callitriche hermaphroditica

Submerged pale green annual to 50 cm. LEAVES With 1 vein, 8–18 mm, widest near base, tapering to conspicuously notched tip. FRUITS *Broadly winged*, usually abundant. HABITAT Ponds, lakes, streams, canals, gravel pits, in moderately fertile water. DIST. Native. Widespread but scattered in N Britain, Ireland. (N and E Europe.) FLS May–Sep.

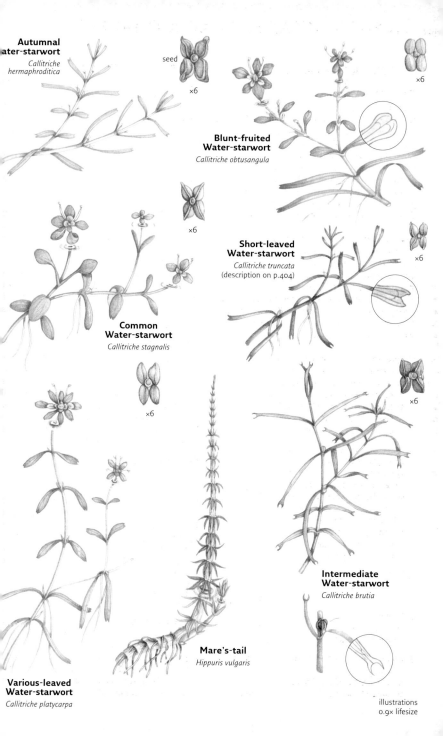

Autumnal Water-starwort
Callitriche hermaphroditica

seed

×6

Blunt-fruited Water-starwort
Callitriche obtusangula

×6

×6

Short-leaved Water-starwort
Callitriche truncata
(description on p.404)

×6

Common Water-starwort
Callitriche stagnalis

×6

×6

Intermediate Water-starwort
Callitriche brutia

Mare's-tail
Hippuris vulgaris

Various-leaved Water-starwort
Callitriche platycarpa

illustrations
0.9× lifesize

Short-leaved Water-starwort
Callitriche truncata

[*See* illustration previous page.] Submerged annual aquatic to 20 cm. STEMS Pale. LEAVES 2.5–11 mm, *translucent, dark blue-green*, parallel-sided, with 1 vein. FRUITS *Wider than long, unwinged*, rare. HABITAT Canals, ditches, lakes, gravel pits, in fertile calcium-rich waters. DIST. Native. Very local. Lincolnshire, Essex, Kent, the SW. (Coastal areas of SW Europe, W Mediterranean.)

Narrow-fruited Water-starwort
Callitriche palustris EN.

Discovered growing on the bed of a turlough in W Ireland in 1999, and since found in a number of sites in W Scotland. Similar to *C. stagnalis*, but *the ripe fruits are blackish, longer than wide and winged only towards apex of nutlets*. HABITAT Still, shallow water and temporary water bodies. DIST. Native. W Ireland, W Scotland. (All Europe except S.) *Not illustrated.*

PLANTAGINACEAE Plantains

Annual or perennials with leaves in a basal rosette. FLOWERS small, green or colourless, solitary or in dense spikes on leafless stalks; 4 sepals and petals.

Greater Plantain
Plantago major

Robust, glabrous or pubescent perennial. LEAVES In a single rosette, 10–15 cm, ovate, abruptly contracted into petiole, petiole about as long as blade. FLOWERS Inflorescence stalk 10–15 cm, not furrowed; flowers *c.*3 mm, yellowish white. HABITAT Common plant of disturbed ground, paths, tracks, gateways, gardens, cultivated ground generally; tolerant of trampling. To 625 m. DIST. Native. Ubiquitous throughout BI. (All Europe.) FLS May–Aug.

Ribwort Plantain
Plantago lanceolata

Glabrous or pubescent perennial. LEAVES 10–15 cm, narrowly ovate-lanceolate, entire or weakly toothed, gradually tapered into petiole. FLOWERS Inflorescence stalk deeply furrowed, to 45 cm; spikes to *c.*4 cm; flowers brownish, *c.*4 mm; corolla lobes with prominent brown midrib. HABITAT Common on meadows, pastures, grass heaths, verges, maritime and dune grassland, cliffs; to 790 m. DIST. Ubiquitous throughout BI. (All Europe except extreme N.) FLS Apr–Aug.

Hoary Plantain
Plantago media

Pubescent perennial. LEAVES 4–6 cm, ovate to elliptic, 5–9-ribbed, almost sessile or short-stalked. FLOWERS Inflorescence stalk much longer than leaves, to 30 cm, not furrowed; spike 2–6 cm; flowers whitish; filaments purple. HABITAT Permanent meadows, pastures,

rough grassland, on well-drained, usually calcareous soils; to 520 m. DIST. Native. Widespread in England, rare in the SW, Wales, Scotland; absent from Ireland as a native. (Most of Europe.) FLS May–Aug.

Buck's-horn Plantain
Plantago coronopus

Pubescent annual to perennial. LEAVES Very variable, linear, entire to toothed or deeply divided; in 1–many rosettes. FLOWERS Inflorescence stalk to 20 cm; spikes to 4 cm; flowers brown, *c.*3 mm; stamens yellow. HABITAT Heaths, cliffs, cliff tops, sand-dunes, waste ground, on dry sandy or gravelly soils; tolerant of trampling. DIST. Native. All round coasts of BI; also inland S and E England. (Coasts of Europe; also inland W Europe and Mediterranean.) FLS May–Jul.

Sea Plantain
Plantago maritima

Glabrous perennial. LEAVES Narrow, entire or sparsely toothed; inflorescence stalk to 30 cm; spike to 7 cm; in rosettes, 1–many rosettes, forming tight clump. FLOWERS Brownish, *c.*3 mm; corolla lobe with broad brown midrib. HABITAT Salt marshes, brackish grassland, sea cliffs; upland stream banks, rock ledges, scree. To 790 m. DIST. Native. All round coasts of BI; also inland NW Scotland, W Ireland. (Most of Europe, but rare in S.) FLS Jun–Aug.

Shoreweed
Littorella uniflora

Aquatic, turf-forming, stoloniferous perennial. STEMS Stolons far-creeping, producing rosettes at nodes. LEAVES 2–10 cm, linear, sheathing at base, cylindrical and solid in section (cf. *Lobelia dortmanna*, p.444, and *Isoetes* spp., p.18, of similar habitats). FLOWERS Unisexual; 2–4 sepals and petals; male flowers solitary, stalks as long as leaves; female flowers 1–few, sessile at base of male stalk; stamens long, 1–2 cm. HABITAT Shallow margins or exposed shores of acid or nutrient-deficient lakes, ponds, reservoirs, to depth of *c.*4 m; to 825 m. DIST. Native. Widespread in upland Britain; rare and declining in lowlands. (W and central Europe.) FLS Jun–Aug.

BUDDLEJACEAE Buddlejas

Butterfly-bush
Buddleja davidii

Evergreen shrub to 5 m. BRANCHES Twigs ridged, pubescent. LEAVES Opposite, 10–26 cm, ovate-lanceolate, finely toothed, green above, pale tomentose below. FLOWERS In dense, many-flowered inflorescence, 10–30 cm; corolla lilac-violet; 4 sepals and petals. HABITAT Waste ground, urban habitats. DIST. Introduced in 1890s (native of China). Popular garden plant; naturalised throughout BI. (Naturalised in W and central Europe.) FLS Jun–Oct.

Greater Plantain
Plantago major

Ribwort Plantain
Plantago lanceolata

Hoary Plantain
Plantago media

Buck's-horn Plantain
Plantago coronopus

Shoreweed
Littorella uniflora

Sea Plantain
Plantago maritima

Butterfly-bush
Buddleja davidii

illustrations
0.2× lifesize

OLEACEAE Ash, privet and olive

Trees or shrubs with opposite leaves that lack stipules. Inflorescence often dense; flowers regular; o or 4 small, fused sepals; o or 4 petals, united into tube at base; 2 stamens; ovary superior.

Lilac
Syringa vulgaris

Deciduous suckering shrub to 7 m. LEAVES Opposite, ovate, entire, 5–12 cm. FLOWERS Lilac or white, in pyramidal panicles, sweet-scented; 4 petals. FRUITS Capsule. HABITAT Hedges, waste ground, roadsides, railway banks. DIST. Introduced. Popular garden shrub, frequently naturalised as relic of cultivation. (Mts of SE Europe.) FLS May.

Wild Privet
Ligustrum vulgare

Semi-evergreen shrub to 5 m. BARK Smooth. BRANCHES Young twigs minutely pubescent (use a lens). LEAVES Lanceolate, 3–6 cm. FLOWERS 4–5 mm across, in thinly pubescent inflorescence, 3–6 cm; corolla tube about as long as lobes. FRUITS Black berry. HABITAT Old hedgerows, scrub, wood borders, on well-drained calcareous, base-rich soils; to 490 m. DIST. Native. Widespread in England, Wales to S Scotland; introduced further N, Ireland. (S, W and central Europe.) FLS Jun–Jul.

Garden Privet
Ligustrum ovalifolium

The most commonly planted garden hedge species. Similar to *L. vulgare*, but more evergreen; leaves broader, elliptic; young twigs and inflorescence glabrous (check with lens); corolla tube longer than lobes. HABITAT Waste ground, railway banks. DIST. Introduced (native of Japan). Naturalised throughout most of BI as garden relic or throw-out. FLS Jun–Jul.

Ash
Fraxinus excelsior

Deciduous tree to 25 m. BARK Grey, smooth becoming fissured. BUDS large, black. LEAVES Pinnate; 7–13 leaflets, toothed, *c.*7 cm. FLOWERS In dense axillary inflorescence, appearing before leaves; bisexual or unisexual; petals absent. FRUITS Achene with single wing. HABITAT Woodlands, scrub, hedgerows, cliffs, limestone pavement, on damp, base-rich soils; to 585 m. Also a coloniser of waste ground, railway banks. DIST. Native. Common throughout BI except extreme N Scotland. (Most of Europe except extreme N and S.) FLS Apr–May.

SCROPHULARIACEAE Figworts, mulleins, foxgloves and speedwells

A rather variable family of usually annuals or perennials (*see* key on p.408). Leaves are without stipules,

opposite or alternate, or rarely all basal. Flowers are irregular, sometimes weakly so, with basically 5 sepals, petals and stamens, but there are numerous variations on this theme; base of corolla is united into a tube; ovary superior and 2-celled. Fruit is a capsule. Plants with square stems and opposite leaves, such as *Rhinanthus*, look like members of the Lamiaceae, but the ovary is quite different and lacks the distinct 4-celled structure of members of that family.

Figworts *Scrophularia*
See key to Scrophularia *on p.409.*

Common Figwort
Scrophularia nodosa

Erect, glabrous perennial to 80 cm. STEMS Sharply 4-angled but not winged. LEAVES 6–13 cm, ovate, acute, coarsely toothed; petiole not winged. FLOWERS Calyx lobes with very narrow, pale border; staminode obovate, emarginate at tip. HABITAT Woodland clearings, hedgerows, stream sides, shaded places, on damp, fertile soils. DIST. Native. Frequent throughout BI. (Most of Europe.) FLS Jun–Sep.

Water Figwort
Scrophularia auriculata

Erect, glabrous perennial to 100 cm. STEMS Distinctly winged. LEAVES 6–12 cm, ovate, obtuse, bluntly toothed, sometimes with 1–2 small lobes at base; petiole winged. FLOWERS Calyx with broad, pale border; staminode ± orbicular, entire. HABITAT Margins of rivers, dykes, canals, lakes and ponds, marshes, fens, wet woods, on fertile, neutral soils. DIST. Native. Frequent and widespread N to S Scotland. (W Europe, N to Netherlands.) FLS Jun–Sep.

Green Figwort
Scrophularia umbrosa

Erect, glabrous perennial to 100 cm. Similar to *S. auriculata*, but stem more broadly winged; leaves sharply toothed, tip more acute, base rounded; staminode with 2 divergent lobes at apex. HABITAT Damp woodland, shaded marshes, fens, banks of streams and rivers, on fertile soils. DIST. Native. Very local, with widely scattered distribution throughout lowland BI. (Central and E Europe.) FLS Jul–Sep.

Balm-leaved Figwort
Scrophularia scorodonia

Erect, pubescent perennial to 100 cm. STEMS 4-angled but not winged. LEAVES 4–10 cm, ovate, cordate at base, margin with double sharp-pointed teeth, surface markedly wrinkled; petiole not winged. FLOWERS Staminode ± orbicular, entire. HABITAT Hedge banks, cliff tops, field borders. DIST. Introduced. Increasing. SW England, S Wales, Channel Is, Scilly Is. (W Europe.) FLS Jun–Aug.

Common Figwort
Scrophularia nodosa

Green Figwort
Scrophularia umbrosa

Water Figwort
Scrophularia auriculata

Balm-leaved Figwort
Scrophularia scorodonia

Garden Privet
Ligustrum ovalifolium

Wild Privet
Ligustrum vulgare

Ash
Fraxinus excelsior

×0.2

Lilac
Syringa vulgaris

illustrations
0.6× lifesize

	if	**then**
1	▷ 2 stamens; flowers blue, pink or white	**Veronica** (p.418)
	▷ 5 stamens; flowers yellow or white, in large terminal racemes or panicles	**Verbascum** (opposite, p.410)
	▷ 4 stamens	Go to ▷ **2**
2	▷ Base of corolla with conspicuous spur or pouch	Go to ▷ **3**
	▷ Corolla without spur or pouch	Go to ▷ **6**
3	▷ Leaves entire or toothed, with single midrib	Go to ▷ **4**
	▷ Leaves palmately lobed and veined	Go to ▷ **16**
4	▷ Base of corolla with broad, rounded pouch	**Antirrhinum, Misopates** (p.412)
	▷ Base of corolla with long, narrow spur	Go to ▷ **5**
5	▷ Leaves linear	**Chaenorhinum, Linaria** (p.412, p.414)
	▷ Leaves ovate to obovate	**Kickxia** (p.414)
6	▷ Leaves all in basal rosette (wet mud at edge of pools)	**Limosella** (p.410)
	▷ Plant with some stem leaves	Go to ▷ **7**
7	▷ Calyx 5-lobed, not inflated	Go to ▷ **8**
	▷ Calyx 4-lobed, or if 5-lobed then strongly inflated	Go to ▷ **10**
8	▷ Leaves alternate	**Digitalis, Erinus** (p.414, p.418)
	▷ Leaves opposite	Go to ▷ **9**
9	▷ Flowers purplish brown to yellowish green; corolla tube ± spherical	**Scrophularia** (opposite, p.406)
	▷ Flowers bright yellow, often with red spots or blotches; corolla tube much longer than wide	**Mimulus** (p.412)
10	▷ Calyx inflated	Go to ▷ **11**
	▷ Calyx not inflated	Go to ▷ **12**
11	▷ Flowers pink; leaves alternate	**Pedicularis** (p.430)
	▷ Flowers yellow; leaves opposite	**Rhinanthus** (p.424)
12	▷ Lower lip of corolla distinctly 3-lobed, tip of each lobe notched	**Euphrasia** (p.424)
	▷ Lower lip not distinctly 3-lobed	Go to ▷ **13**
13	▷ Mouth of corolla nearly closed by swellings on lower lip (flowers yellow)	**Melampyrum** (p.430)
	▷ Mouth of corolla open	Go to ▷ **14**
14	▷ Corolla yellow	**Parentucellia** (p.430)
	▷ Corolla pink	Go to ▷ **15**
15	▷ Flowers ≤10 mm, inflorescence 1-sided	**Odontites** (p.430)
	▷ Flowers ≥15 mm, inflorescence not 1-sided	**Bartsia** (p.430)
16	▷ Plant glabrous; flowers ≤25 mm, purple	**Cymbalaria** (p.412)
	▷ Plant glandular-pubescent; flowers ≥30 mm, yellow	**Asarina** (p.412)

Key to Figworts *Scrophularia*

	if	then
1	▷ Flowers greenish yellow; staminode (sterile stamen under upper lip of corolla) absent	*S. vernalis*
	▷ Flowers brownish purple; staminode present	Go to ▷ **2**
2	▷ Leaves and stems ± glabrous	Go to ▷ **3**
	▷ Leaves and stems pubescent	*S. scorodonia* (p.406)
3	▷ Stems 4-angled, not winged	*S. nodosa* (p.406)
	▷ Stems winged	Go to ▷ **4**
4	▷ Leaves bluntly toothed; staminode orbicular	*S. auriculata* (p.406)
	▷ Leaves sharply toothed; staminode 2-lobed	*S. umbrosa* (p.406)

Key to Mulleins *Verbascum*

	if	then
1	▷ Hairs on filaments of anthers white	Go to ▷ **2**
	▷ Hairs on filaments of anthers purple	Go to ▷ **4**
2	▷ Lower 2 filaments glabrous or much less hairy than upper	*V. thapsus* (p.410)
	▷ All 5 filaments equally hairy	Go to ▷ **3**
3	▷ Flowers usually white (rarely yellow); stem angled; leaves dark green above with dense white pubescence beneath	*V. lychnitis* (p.410)
	▷ Flowers yellow; stem not angled; both surfaces of leaves with dense white pubescence	*V. pulverulentum* (p.410)
4	▷ Leaves and stems hairy; anthers equal	*V. nigrum* (p.410)
	▷ Leaves and stems ± glabrous; lower 2 anthers larger than upper	Go to ▷ **5**
5	▷ Pedicels longer than calyx; flowers solitary	*V. blattaria* (p.410)
	▷ Pedicels shorter than calyx; 2-5 flowers per node	*V. virgatum* (p.410)

Mulleins *Verbascum*

See key on p.409. Hybrids between mulleins are frequent where the parents occur together. They are usually sterile and can be detected by rubbing the seed capsules between the fingers, which will break up into dust.

Great Mullein
Verbascum thapsus

Tall, erect biennial to 200 cm, densely clothed with soft whitish woolly hairs. LEAVES Ovate-lanceolate, basal leaves to 45 cm, stem leaves decurrent. FLOWERS Large, 1.5-3 cm across, in dense, spike-like inflorescence; hairs on 3 upper filaments yellowish white, 2 lower filaments ± glabrous; anthers attached obliquely. HABITAT Rough grassland, hedge banks, roadsides, waste ground, on dry sandy or calcareous soils. DIST. Native. Throughout almost all BI; absent from N Scotland. (All Europe except extreme N and SE.) FLS Jun-Aug.

White Mullein
Verbascum lychnitis

Tall, erect, pubescent biennial to 150 cm. STEMS Angled, covered with short white branched hairs. LEAVES Green, ± glabrous above, dense white-hairy beneath; basal leaves 10-30 cm; stem leaves not decurrent. FLOWERS Usually white, rarely yellow; 15-20 mm across; all filaments with white hairs; anthers transversely attached. HABITAT Rough grassland, cleared woodland, old quarries, roadsides, on dry calcareous soils. DIST. Native. Rare, very local. SE and SW England; naturalised elsewhere. (W, central and E Europe.) FLS Jul-Aug.

Hoary Mullein
Verbascum pulverulentum

Tall, erect perennial to 150 cm, thickly clothed with mealy white-woolly hairs, which eventually wear off. STEMS Not angled. FLOWERS <20 mm across, 4-10 in each bract; all filaments with white hairs; anthers transversely attached. HABITAT Roadside verges, quarries, coastal shingle. DIST. Native. Very local. East Anglia. (W, S and S-central Europe.) FLS Jul-Aug.

Dark Mullein
Verbascum nigrum

Tall, erect, pubescent biennial to 120 cm. STEMS Angled. LEAVES Dark green above, pale beneath; basal leaves long-stalked. FLOWERS 12-22 mm across, 5-10 in each bract; all filaments with purple hairs; anthers transversely attached. HABITAT Rough permanent grassland, road verges, banks, on dry calcareous soils. DIST. Native. Scattered throughout lowland England. (Most of Europe except N and extreme S.) FLS Jun-Oct.

Twiggy Mullein
Verbascum virgatum

Erect, + glabrous biennial to 100 cm, with stalked glands throughout. LEAVES Basal leaves 15-33 cm. FLOWERS 30-40 mm across, 2-5 per node in lower part of inflorescence; pedicels shorter than calyx; all filaments with purple hairs; lower 2 anthers attached obliquely and larger than upper 3. HABITAT Waste ground, banks, field margins, coastal cliffs, shingle. DIST. Probably introduced; naturalised or casual. Scarce; scattered throughout BI. (W Europe.) FLS Jun-Aug.

Moth Mullein
Verbascum blattaria

Similar to *V. virgatum*, but usually with stalked glands only on inflorescence; flowers 2-3 cm across, usually one per node; pedicels longer than calyx. HABITAT Rough grassland, field borders, waste ground. DIST. Introduced. Scattered, declining. Central and S England. (Central, E and S Europe, N to Netherlands.) FLS Jun-Oct.

Mudwort
Limosella aquatica *(N)

Small, glabrous, stoloniferous annual. LEAVES To 6 cm including blade, ± erect in basal rosettes; blade elliptical, 2 cm; petiole much longer than blade. FLOWERS Calyx longer than corolla tube; corolla 2-5 mm across, tube bell-shaped, *c*.1.5 mm. HABITAT Drying mud at edge of pools, ditches and lakes, cart ruts, limestone pavement; to 455 m. DIST. Native. Local, declining; scattered throughout BI. (Most of Europe except Mediterranean.) FLS Jun-Oct.

Welsh Mudwort
Limosella australis *(N)

Similar to *L. aquatica*, but leaves to 4 cm, awl-shaped, blade and petiole not differentiated; calyx shorter than corolla tube; corolla to 4 mm across. HABITAT Mud flats, salt-marsh pools. DIST. Probably introduced (native of S hemisphere, E North America). Very rare. N Wales. (Not Europe, apart from N Wales.) FLS Jun-Oct.

Dark Mullein
Verbascum nigrum

Moth Mullein
Verbascum blattaria

Great Mullein
Verbascum thapsus

Twiggy Mullein
Verbascum virgatum

Hoary Mullein
Verbascum pulverulentum

White Mullein
Verbascum lychnitis

Welsh Mudwort
Limosella australis

Mudwort
Limosella aquatica

illustrations
0.6× lifesize

Monkeyflower
Mimulus guttatus

Decumbent to erect perennial, to 75 cm. STEMS Glabrous below, glandular-pubescent above. LEAVES 1–7 cm, irregularly toothed. FLOWERS Pedicels 1.5–3 cm; calyx becoming inflated in fruit, upper tooth much longer than rest; corolla 2.5–4.5 cm, yellow with small red spots, base of lower lip with 2 swellings that almost close entrance to throat. HABITAT Wet marshy ground, edges of rivers, streams and lakes, open woods. DIST. Introduced (native of W North America). Naturalised throughout BI, but scarce in Ireland. (Naturalised throughout much of Europe.) FLS Jul–Sep.

Blood-drop-emlets
Mimulus luteus

Similar to *M. guttatus*, but glabrous all over, stem more decumbent; pedicels longer, 3.5–6 cm; corolla lobes with large red spots or variegated pinkish purple, throat open. HABITAT Similar to *M. guttatus*. DIST. Introduced (native of Chile). Naturalised throughout BI but rare and declining. (NW Europe; rare.) FLS Jun–Sep. NOTE The hybrid between *M. guttatus* and *M. luteus*, *M.* × *robertsii*, is frequent in N Britain and N Ireland and commoner than *M. luteus*, with which it is often mistaken.

Musk
Mimulus moschatus

Sticky-hairy, decumbent perennial to 40 cm. LEAVES 1–4 cm. FLOWERS Calyx teeth all ± equal; corolla 1–2 cm, pale yellow, neither spotted nor blotched. HABITAT Damp, shady places, ditches, woods, pond margins. DIST. Introduced (native of W North America). Naturalised or casual. Scattered throughout BI, but rare in Ireland. (Naturalised in N, W and central Europe.) FLS Jul–Aug.

Snapdragon
Antirrhinum majus

Erect, branched perennial to 80 cm. STEMS Glabrous below, pubescent above. LEAVES 3–5 cm, linear-lanceolate. FLOWERS In terminal raceme; corolla 4–5 cm, 3–4× as long as calyx, strongly 2-lipped, base of lower lip swollen and closing throat, without spur. HABITAT Old walls, stony waste ground. DIST.

Introduced. Popular garden plant; naturalised throughout BI, but rare in Scotland, Ireland. (SW Europe.) FLS Jul–Sep.

Weasel's-snout
Misopates orontium VU. *(R

Erect, glandular-pubescent annual to 50 cm. LEAVES 3–5 cm, linear, entire. FLOWERS Sessile, in axils of upper leaves; calyx lobes longer than or as long as corolla; corolla 10–15 mm. HABITAT Arable fields, cultivated ground, on light sandy soils. DIST. Archaeophyte. Becoming rare, declining. (S, W and central Europe.) FLS Jul–Oct.

Small Toadflax
Chaenorhinum minu

Erect, glandular-pubescent annual to 25 cm. LEAVES 1–2.5 cm, linear-lanceolate. FLOWERS Solitary, axillary; pedicels much longer than flowers; corolla 6–8 mm. HABITAT Waste ground, arable fields, old walls, railway lines, on well-drained, usually calcareous soils. DIST. Archaeophyte. Throughout BI, but rare in N Scotland and declining in Ireland. (Most of Europe.) FLS May–Oct.

Ivy-leaved Toadflax
Cymbalaria murali

Trailing, prostrate, glabrous perennial. STEMS To 60 cm. LEAVES 2.5 cm, purplish beneath; petiole longer than blade. FLOWERS Axillary; corolla 9–15 mm, including spur. HABITAT Old walls, stony waste ground, coastal shingle; to 450 m. DIST. Introduced. Naturalised throughout BI except N Scotland (S, central and SE Europe.) FLS May–Sep. NOTE Italian Toadflax *Cymbalaria pallida*, with densely pubescent stems, leaves and larger flowers, 15–25 mm, occasionally occurs in similar places.

Trailing Snapdragon
Asarina procumben

Procumbent, sticky-pubescent, stoloniferous perennial to 60 cm. LEAVES 2–7 cm, orbicular, shallowly lobed. FLOWERS 3–3.5 cm, pale yellow, solitary, axillary, without a spur. DIST. Introduced. Rarely naturalised in England, Wales. HABITAT Dry banks, walls, cliffs. (Mts of S France, NE Spain.)

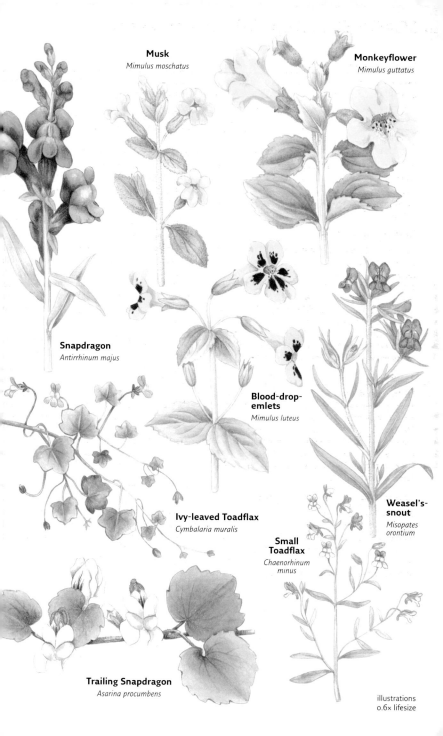

Musk
Mimulus moschatus

Monkeyflower
Mimulus guttatus

Snapdragon
Antirrhinum majus

Blood-drop-emlets
Mimulus luteus

Ivy-leaved Toadflax
Cymbalaria muralis

Weasel's-snout
Misopates orontium

Small Toadflax
Chaenorhinum minus

Trailing Snapdragon
Asarina procumbens

illustrations
0.6× lifesize

Foxglove
Digitalis purpurea

Tall, handsome, erect biennial to 150 cm, with softly hairy stems, leaves and flower stalks. Whole plant is poisonous. LEAVES To 30 cm. FLOWERS Pinkish purple, tubular, to 50 mm, in a raceme. DIST. Native. Common throughout BI. HABITAT Woodland clearings, hedge banks, open heathland, rocky hillsides, on acid, well-drained soils. (W Europe, N to central Norway.) FLS Jun–Sep.

Straw Foxglove
Digitalis lutea

Tall, erect, glabrous perennial to 1 m. FLOWERS Yellow, tubular, to 25 mm, in a raceme. HABITAT Open woodlands, scrub, grassland, on calcareous soils. DIST. Introduced. Occasionally naturalised in S England. (W Europe, N to Belgium, S to Spain and Italy.) FLS Jun–Aug.

Round-leaved Fluellen
Kickxia spuria

Prostrate, trailing, summer-germinating annual. Whole plant pubescent, with both glandular and non-glandular hairs. STEMS To 50 cm. LEAVES With short stalks, ovate *with rounded base*. FLOWERS To 11 mm, yellow, upper lip purple; *stalks with long hairs*. HABITAT Almost exclusively on late-summer stubble fields on light soils. DIST. Archaeophyte. Decreasing. Widely distributed in S Britain. (Most of Europe and Mediterranean.) FLS Jul–Oct.

Sharp-leaved Fluellen
Kickxia elatine *(R)

Prostrate, trailing, summer-germinating annual. Similar to *K. spuria*, but more slender, less hairy and hardly glandular. LEAVES Hastate. FLOWERS To 11 mm, yellow, upper lip purple; *stalks glabrous*. HABITAT Similar to *K. spuria*. DIST. Archaeophyte. Decreasing. Similar distribution to *K. spuria*. (Most of Europe and Mediterranean.) FLS Jul –Oct.

Toadflaxes *Linaria*
See key to *Linaria* on p.416

Common Toadflax
Linaria vulgaris

Erect, branched, glabrous grey-green perennial to 80 cm. LEAVES Linear-lanceolate, to 8 cm. FLOWERS To 25 mm, in a raceme; yellow, base of lower petal orange; spur almost as long as corolla. HABITAT Frequent plant of rough grassland, roadsides, hedge banks, waste ground, on well-drained calcareous or sandy soils. DIST. Native. Widely distributed in England, Wales; rare in Scotland, Ireland. (Most of Europe except extreme N and parts of Mediterranean.) FLS Jun–Oct.

Purple Toadflax
Linaria purpurea

Erect, branched, glabrous grey-green perennial to 90 cm. LEAVES Linear to linear-lanceolate, to 4.5 cm. FLOWERS To 8 mm, purple, in a raceme; spur curved >⅓ as long as corolla. HABITAT Old walls, dry hedge banks, stony waste ground. DIST. Introduced. Naturalised throughout BI. (Native to central and S Italy, Sicily.) FLS Jun–Aug.

Pale Toadflax
Linaria repens

Glabrous grey-green perennial, with numerous erect stems to 80 cm. LEAVES Linear, to 4 cm. FLOWERS To 14 mm, in a raceme; pale with purple stripes, lower petal with an orange spot at base; spur short, straight, about ⅛ as long as corolla. HABITAT Arable field, waste places, on dry, usually calcareous soils. DIST. Native. Local and scattered throughout England, Wales; rare in Scotland, Ireland. (France, Belgium, NW Germany to N Spain and NW Italy; widely naturalised elsewhere in central Europe.) FLS Jun–Sep.

Sand Toadflax
Linaria arenaria

Much-branched annual to 15 cm, covered by sticky glandular hairs. LEAVES To 10 mm, lanceolate. FLOWERS Small, to 6 mm, yellow, in a few-flowered raceme; spur shorter than corolla, violet. HABITAT/DIST. Introduced. Originally planted, now established on sand-dunes at Braunton Burrows in N Devon. (Native of W France, S to the Gironde.) FLS May–Sep.

Jersey Toadflax
Linaria pelisseriana

Erect, glabrous annual to 30 cm. LEAVES To 3 cm, linear. FLOWERS To 15 mm, in a few-flowered raceme, violet, with a white spot at base of lower petal; spur nearly as long as corolla, straight. HABITAT Dry cultivated ground, waste and heathy places. DIST. Introduced. Very rare, confined to Jersey (Channel Is). (W Europe, Mediterranean.) FLS May–Jul.

Prostrate Toadflax
Linaria supina

Prostrate annual to 20 cm. STEMS Glabrous below, pubescent above. FLOWERS Pale yellow, 15–25 mm including spur. HABITAT Sandy waste ground near sea. DIST. Introduced. Established in SW England. (SW Europe.) *Not illustrated.*

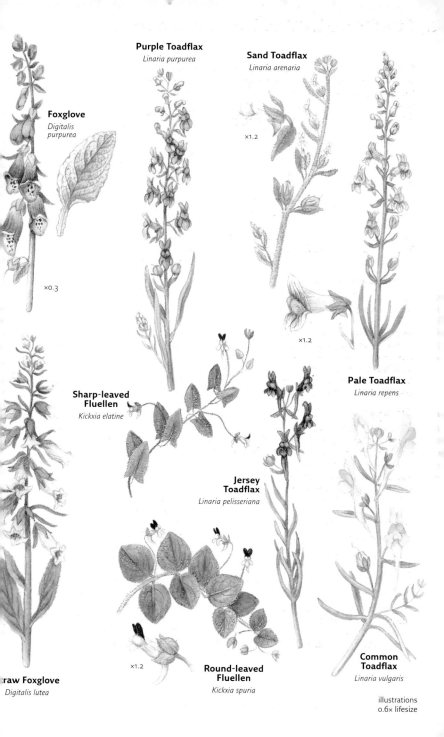

Foxglove
Digitalis purpurea

×0.3

Purple Toadflax
Linaria purpurea

Sand Toadflax
Linaria arenaria

×1.2

×1.2

Pale Toadflax
Linaria repens

Sharp-leaved Fluellen
Kickxia elatine

Jersey Toadflax
Linaria pelisseriana

×1.2

Round-leaved Fluellen
Kickxia spuria

raw Foxglove
Digitalis lutea

Common Toadflax
Linaria vulgaris

illustrations
0.6× lifesize

	if	then
1	▷ Flowers in terminal racemes	Go to ▷ **2**
	▷ Flowers axillary	***Chaenorhinum minus*** (p.412)
2	▷ Flowers yellow	Go to ▷ **3**
	▷ Flowers not yellow	Go to ▷ **5**
3	▷ Whole plant covered by sticky glandular hairs	***L. arenaria*** (p.414)
	▷ Plant glabrous	Go to ▷ **4**
4	▷ Erect perennial, sepals acute	***L. vulgaris*** (p.414)
	▷ Decumbent annual, sepals blunt	***L. supina*** (p.414)
5	▷ Perennial, spur distinctly shorter than rest of flower	Go to ▷ **6**
	▷ Annual, spur almost as long as rest of flower	***L. pelisseriana*** (p.414)
6	▷ Flowers purple	***L. purpurea*** (p.414)
	▷ Flowers pale, with purple stripes	***L. repens*** (p.414)

Key to Speedwells *Veronica*

	if	then
1	▷ Flowers in racemes arising from axils of leaves	Go to ▷ **2**
	▷ Flowers in terminal racemes or solitary	Go to ▷ **9**
2	▷ Stems and leaves hairy	Go to ▷ **3**
	▷ Stems and leaves glabrous (wet places)	Go to ▷ **6**
3	▷ Hairs on stems arranged in 2 opposite rows	***Veronica chamaedrys*** (p.418)
	▷ Stems hairy all round	Go to ▷ **4**
4	▷ Leaves distinctly stalked, stalks 5–15 mm	***Veronica montana*** (p.418)
	▷ Leaves sessile or stalks ≤5 mm	Go to ▷ **5**
5	▷ Lower leaves stalked, stalks 2–5 mm; 4 calyx teeth	***Veronica officinalis*** (p.418)
	▷ Leaves sessile; 5 calyx teeth, 1 very short	***Veronica austriaca*** (p.418)
6	▷ Leaves stalked, obtuse	***Veronica beccabunga*** (p.420)
	▷ Leaves sessile, acute	Go to ▷ **7**
7	▷ Single raceme from each pair of leaves; flowers white or pale blue	***Veronica scutellata*** (p.420)
	▷ Pair of racemes from each pair of leaves	Go to ▷ **8**

if	**then**
8 ▷ Flowers pale blue	*Veronica anagallis-aquatica* (p.420)
▷ Flowers pink	*Veronica catenata* (p.420)
9 ▷ Flowers solitary in axils of leaves	Go to ▷ **10**
▷ Flowers in terminal racemes	Go to ▷ **15**
10 ▷ Leaves with 5–7 large teeth or small lobes	*Veronica hederifolia* (p.422)
▷ Leaves regularly toothed	Go to ▷ **11**
11 ▷ Creeping perennial, rooting at nodes	*Veronica filiformis* (p.422)
▷ Annual, stems not rooting at nodes	Go to ▷ **12**
12 ▷ Flowers uniformly bright blue	Go to ▷ **13**
▷ At least lower petal pale blue or white	Go to ▷ **14**
13 ▷ Calyx lobes ovate, overlapping near base	*Veronica polita* (p.422)
▷ Calyx lobes oblong-lanceolate, not overlapping	*Veronica opaca* (p.422)
14 ▷ Lobes of fruit divergent; flowers 8–12 mm diam.	*Veronica persica* (p.422)
▷ Lobes of fruit erect; flowers 4–8 mm diam.	*Veronica agrestis* (p.422)
15 ▷ Leaves glabrous, ± entire	Go to ▷ **16**
▷ Leaves hairy, toothed or lobed	Go to ▷ **19**
16 ▷ Bracts shorter or scarcely longer than flowers	Go to ▷ **17**
▷ All bracts longer than flowers	*Veronica peregrina* (p.422)
17 ▷ Flowers pale blue to white	*Veronica serpyllifolia* (p.418)
▷ Flowers uniformly dull or bright blue (alpines)	Go to ▷ **18**
18 ▷ Stems woody at base; inflorescence with non-glandular hairs; flowers bright blue, >10 mm diam.	*Veronica fruticans* (p.418)
▷ Stems not woody at base; inflorescence with glandular hairs; flowers dull blue, <10 mm diam.	*Veronica alpina* (p.418)
19 ▷ Leaves regularly toothed	Go to ▷ **20**
▷ Leaves deeply lobed	Go to ▷ **22**
20 ▷ Inflorescence a dense, many-flowered, spike-like terminal raceme	*Veronica spicata* (p.422)
▷ Inflorescence not a dense, many-flowered raceme	Go to ▷ **21**
21 ▷ Pedicels much shorter than calyx	*Veronica arvensis* (p.420)
▷ Pedicels longer than calyx	*Veronica praecox* (p.420)
22 ▷ Pedicels longer than calyx	*Veronica triphyllos* (p.420)
▷ Pedicels shorter than calyx	*Veronica verna* (p.420)

Fairy Foxglove
Erinus alpinus

Small, tufted, semi-evergreen, pubescent perennial to 15 cm. LEAVES Alternate, *c*.1.5 cm, basal leaves forming rosette. FLOWERS Calyx deeply 5-lobed; corolla tube as long as calyx, 5 lobes, spreading, deeply notched; 4 stamens. HABITAT Old walls with calcareous substrate. DIST. Introduced. Naturalised throughout BI. (Mts of S Europe.) FLS May–Oct.

Speedwells *Veronica*

Large genus of annuals and perennials that can present identification problems (*see* key on p.416). Characterised by opposite leaves, and by blue flowers (rarely pink or white) with 4 sepals, 4 petals, 2 stamens; the upper petal is the largest, the lower the smallest.

Germander Speedwell
Veronica chamaedrys

Pubescent, stoloniferous perennial to 40 cm. STEMS Prostrate, rooting at nodes, with 2 lines of long white hairs on opposite sides. LEAVES 1–2.5 cm, ± sessile. FLOWERS In axillary, long-stalked, 10-20-flowered racemes; corolla *c*.10 mm across, sky-blue with white eye. FRUITS Capsule, shorter than calyx. HABITAT Familiar plant of hedge banks, verges, wood borders, rough grassland, upland scree, on well-drained or calcareous soils; to 750 m. DIST. Native. Throughout BI. (All Europe except extreme N.) FLS Mar–Jul.

Wood Speedwell
Veronica montana

Similar to *V. chamaedrys*, but stems hairy all round; leaves distinctly stalked, 5–15 mm; racemes 2-5-flowered; bracts much shorter than pedicels; corolla *c*.7 mm across, lilac-blue. HABITAT Well established in damp woodlands, coppice, hedge banks, on loamy, sandy soils; to 435 m. DIST. Native. Throughout BI, but rare in N Scotland. (W, central and S Europe.) FLS Apr–Jul.

Heath Speedwell
Veronica officinalis

Pubescent, mat-forming, creeping perennial to 40 cm. STEMS Rooting at nodes, hairy all round. LEAVES 2–3 cm, at least the lowest shortly stalked. FLOWERS In long-stalked, many-flowered racemes, usually emerging from both of a pair of leaves; bracts *c*.2× as long as pedicels; corolla *c*.6 mm across, lilac. FRUITS Capsule, longer than calyx. HABITAT Grass heaths, woodland clearings, commons, pastures, often on ant-hills; acid, well-drained soils. To 880

m. DIST. Native. Common throughout BI. (All Europe.) FLS May–Aug.

Large Speedwell
Veronica austriaca

Decumbent to erect, pubescent perennial, to 50 cm. STEMS Pubescent all round. LEAVES Almost sessile. FLOWERS 5 calyx lobes, one very short; corolla 10-15 mm across, bright blue. FRUITS Capsule, longer than wide. HABITAT Rough ground, sand-dunes. DIST. Introduced. Naturalised as a garden escape in a few scattered localities. (Most of Europe except Scandinavia.) FLS May–Jul.

Thyme-leaved Speedwell
Veronica serpyllifolia

Creeping perennial, rooting at nodes, to 30 cm. STEMS Flowering stems ascending. LEAVES 1–2 cm, ± entire, glabrous. FLOWERS In terminal, many-flowered racemes; bracts longer than pedicels; corolla 5-10 mm across, white or pale blue; style about as long as calyx. FRUITS Capsule, about as long as calyx. DIST. Native. Widespread and common throughout BI to 825 m. HABITAT Short grassland, commons, woodland rides, rock ledges, weed of gardens, on damp acid soils. (All Europe.) FLS Mar–Oct. NOTE The common plant is ssp. *serpyllifolia*. Ssp. *humifusa*, with more orbicular leaves, glandular-pubescent racemes and larger, bright blue flowers 7-10 mm across, is a local plant of montane rock ledges and flushes to 1160 m in the Scottish Highlands and, rarely, N England and N Wales.

Alpine Speedwell
Veronica alpina

Small, shortly creeping, glandular-pubescent alpine perennial to 15 cm. LEAVES Glabrous, ovate, entire. FLOWERS In dense, 4-12-flowered inflorescence; corolla dull blue, 5-10 mm across. HABITAT Damp rock ledges in areas of late snow-lie, on acid and basic mica-schist rocks; to 1190 m. DIST. Native. Rare. Scottish Highlands. (Arctic Europe, mts of central and S Europe.) FLS Jul–Aug.

Rock Speedwell
Veronica fruticans

Erect to ascending perennial, to 20 cm. STEMS Woody at base. LEAVES *c*.10 mm, glabrous. FLOWERS Inflorescence not glandular, up to 10-flowered; corolla a deep, bright blue, 10-15 mm across. DIST. Native. Rare. Scottish Highlands. HABITAT Base-rich, S-facing, dry, open slopes, alpine rock ledges to 1100 m. (NW Europe, mts of central and S Europe.) FLS Apr–May.

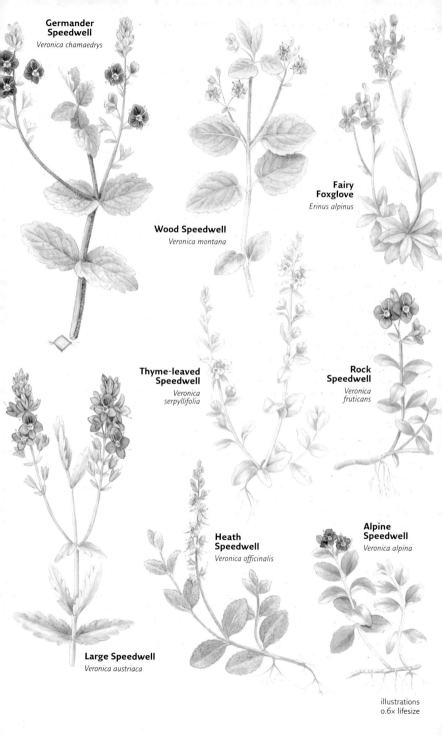

Germander Speedwell
Veronica chamaedrys

Wood Speedwell
Veronica montana

Fairy Foxglove
Erinus alpinus

Thyme-leaved Speedwell
Veronica serpyllifolia

Rock Speedwell
Veronica fruticans

Heath Speedwell
Veronica officinalis

Alpine Speedwell
Veronica alpina

Large Speedwell
Veronica austriaca

illustrations
0.6× lifesize

Brooklime
Veronica beccabunga

Creeping, ascending, glabrous perennial to 60 cm. Leaves Rather fleshy, ovate, short-stalked. Flowers In opposite, 10–20-flowered racemes; bracts as long as or shorter than pedicels; corolla 10 cm across, a deep, bright blue. Habitat Shallow margins of ponds, rivers, streams and dykes, wet meadows, marshes, woodland rides; to 845 m. Dist. Native. Frequent throughout BI. (Most of Europe except extreme N.) Fls May–Sep.

Blue Water-speedwell
Veronica anagallis-aquatica

Creeping, ascending, glabrous annual to 30 cm. Leaves Sessile, 5–12 cm, ovate-lanceolate. Flowers In opposite, 10–50-flowered racemes; bracts as long as or shorter than pedicels; corolla 5–6 mm across, pale blue; pedicels ascending after flowering. Habitat Shallow margins of pools, drainage ditches, rivers and streams, marshy meadows; lowland to 380 m. Dist. Native. Throughout BI; frequent in S, local further N. (Most of Europe except extreme N.) Fls Jun–Aug.

Pink Water-speedwell
Veronica catenata

Similar to *V. anagallis-aquatica*, but stems tinged purplish, leaves narrower, racemes more spreading, bracts longer than pedicels, corolla pink, pedicels spreading after flowering. Habitat Similar to *V. anagallis-aquatica*, with which it often grows and hybridises. Dist. Native. Throughout BI. Frequent in S Britain but rare and coastal in N and W; widespread in Ireland. (Most of Europe except N.) Fls Jun–Aug.

Marsh Speedwell
Veronica scutellata

Creeping, ascending, glabrous, sparsely branched perennial to 50 cm. Leaves Sessile, yellowish green, 2–4 cm, linear-lanceolate. Flowers In alternate, few-flowered racemes; corolla 5–8 mm across, whitish or lilac with dark lines. Habitat Shallow margins of ponds, pools, ditches and dykes, wet meadows, hillside flushes, on acid, calcium-poor soils; to 780 m.

Dist. Native. Throughout BI; commoner in N and W. (Most of Europe, but rare in S.) Fls Jun–Aug.

Wall Speedwell
Veronica arvensis

Small, erect, pubescent annual to 25 cm. Leaves To 15 mm, coarsely and bluntly toothed. Flowers ± sessile, small, 2–3 mm across, in long racemes; bracts entire, longer than flowers; corolla shorter than calyx, deep blue. Fruits Capsule, about as long as broad. Habitat Dry, open areas, including arable fields, open grassland (ant-hills), sand-dunes, walls, banks, paths; to 820 m. Dist. Native. Common throughout BI. (All Europe.) Fls Mar–Oct.

Spring Speedwell
Veronica verna EN.

Erect annual to 15 cm. Similar to *V. arvensis*, but leaves lobed with 3–7 lobes; raceme more dense, glandular; capsule broader than long. Habitat Short, grazed, open grassland on sandy soils. Dist. Native. Very rare, declining. East Anglia (Breckland). (Much of Europe except extreme N, parts of W and Mediterranean.) Fls May–Jun.

Fingered Speedwell
Veronica triphyllos EN. *(B)

Glandular-pubescent spreading to erect annual to 20 cm. Leaves 4–12 mm, 3–7-lobed, lobes oblong. Flowers Upper bracts entire, shorter than pedicels; pedicels longer than calyx; corolla deep blue, 3–4 mm across, shorter than calyx. Habitat Disturbed sandy field margins, banks, tracks. Dist. Archaeophyte. Very rare, declining. East Anglia (Breckland). (S, central and E Europe.) Fls Apr–Jun.

Breckland Speedwell
Veronica praecox

Erect, glandular-pubescent annual to 20 cm. Leaves Ovate, deeply toothed. Flowers Bracts slightly shorter than pedicels; pedicels longer than calyx; corolla blue, 2.5–4 mm across, longer than calyx. Habitat Disturbed sandy field margins, banks, tracks. (S, central and W Europe.) Dist. Introduced. Very rare. East Anglia (Breckland). Fls Mar–Jun.

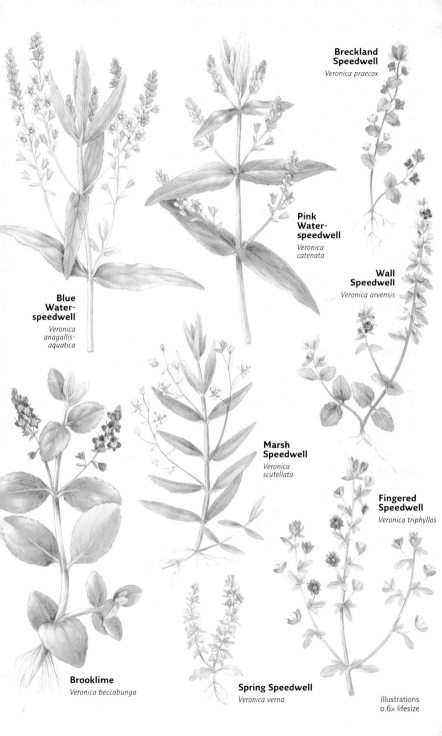

Breckland Speedwell
Veronica praecox

Pink Water-speedwell
Veronica catenata

Wall Speedwell
Veronica arvensis

Blue Water-speedwell
Veronica anagallis-aquatica

Marsh Speedwell
Veronica scutellata

Fingered Speedwell
Veronica triphyllos

Brooklime
Veronica beccabunga

Spring Speedwell
Veronica verna

illustrations
0.6× lifesize

Green Field-speedwell
Veronica agrestis

Prostrate to ascending, pubescent annual to 30 cm. LEAVES Ovate. FLOWERS Solitary, in leaf axils; *corolla 4-8 mm across, pale blue with lower petal white*. FRUITS Capsule, *with spreading glandular hairs only, lobes diverging at narrow angle*. HABITAT Arable fields, cultivated land, on well-drained sandy soils; to 410 m. DIST. Archaeophyte. Declining significantly. Throughout BI, but scarce in Scotland, Ireland. (Most of Europe except extreme N and SE.) FLS Year-round.

Grey Field-speedwell
Veronica polita

Branched, procumbent, pubescent annual to 40 cm. Similar to *V. agrestis*, but lower leaves broader than long; *calyx lobes ovate, overlapping near base; flowers bright blue; capsule with short, crisped, glandless hairs and few spreading, glandular hairs*. HABITAT Arable fields, cultivated ground, gardens, on light sandy or calcareous soils. DIST. Introduced. Throughout BI; frequent in central and S England, but scarce and declining elsewhere. (Most of Europe except extreme N.) FLS Year-round.

Veronica opaca

Procumbent, pubescent annual to 30 cm. LEAVES Shallowly toothed, lower leaves broader than long. FLOWERS *Deep blue; calyx lobes oblong-lanceolate, not overlapping*. FRUITS Capsule, *with crisped eglandular hairs and long glandular hairs*. HABITAT Arable fields, cultivated ground, waste places, on calcareous soils. DIST. *Not BI*. (Central Europe to E France.) FLS Apr-May, Aug-Oct.

Common Field-speedwell
Veronica persica

Branched, decumbent, pubescent annual to 40 cm. LEAVES 1-3 cm, ovate, strongly toothed. FLOWERS Solitary, axillary, *8-12 mm across, bright blue, lower petal almost white*; pedicels longer than leaves. FRUITS *Lobes of capsule divergent, c.2× as broad as long*. HABITAT Arable fields, gardens, waste ground, on fertile soils. DIST. Introduced. Common throughout BI, becoming scarce in N Scotland. (Native of Caucasus and Iran; naturalised throughout Europe.) FLS Year-round.

Slender Speedwell
Veronica filiformis

Mat-forming, pubescent perennial with numerous creeping stems, to 50 cm. LEAVES c.5 mm, orbicular to kidney-shaped, bluntly toothed, stalks short. FLOWERS *Pedicels slender, much longer than leaves, corolla 8-15 mm across, purplish blue*. FRUITS Rare. HABITAT Lawns, churchyards, parks, stream sides; lowland to 450 m. DIST. Introduced. Common, increasing. Throughout BI, but scarce in N Scotland, S Ireland. (Native of N Turkey and Caucasus; naturalised in N, W and central Europe.) FLS Apr-Jun.

Ivy-leaved Speedwell
Veronica hederifolia

Prostrate, pubescent annual to 60 cm. LEAVES *Kidney-shaped, with 1-3 large teeth or lobes*, light green, rather thick. FLOWERS Pedicels shorter than leaves sepals ovate, cordate at base; corolla shorter than calyx. FRUITS *Glabrous capsule*. HABITAT Weed of cultivation, arable fields, gardens, waste ground; to 380 m. DIST. Archaeophyte. Throughout BI, but rare in N Scotland, W Ireland. (Most of Europe except extreme N.) FLS Apr-May. NOTE Has 2 subspecies that are not always possible to separate. Ssp. *hederifolia* has apical leaf lobe that is wider than long; pedicel 3-4× as long as calyx; corolla mostly ≥6 mm across, whitish blue; and blue anthers. Ssp. *lucorum* has apical leaf lobe that is longer than wide; pedicel 3.5-7× as long as calyx; corolla ≤6 mm across whitish to pale lilac; and white to pale blue anthers It also occurs in more shaded habitats than ssp. *hederifolia*, including woodland rides and hedgerows

Spiked Speedwell
Veronica spicata *(B

Erect, rhizomatous, pubescent perennial to 60 cm LEAVES Oblong-elliptic, blunt-toothed. FLOWERS *In many-flowered, terminal, spike-like raceme*; pedicels short; corolla violet-blue. HABITAT Short, grazed turf on dry acidic to base-rich soils in East Anglia; elsewhere on thin base-rich soils over cliffs and rocks DIST. Native. Very rare. Scattered localities in England, Wales. (Most of Europe, but rare in W.) FLS Jul-Sep.

American Speedwell
Veronica peregrina

Erect, glabrous annual to 25 cm. LEAVES Ovate-oblong. FLOWERS *Upper bracts lanceolate, much longer than flowers*; pedicels short; corolla blue shorter than calyx. FRUITS Glabrous capsule. HABITAT Naturalised or casual weed of parks, gardens verges, stream sides. DIST. Introduced. Scattered and infrequent throughout BI. (Naturalised in W and central Europe.) FLS Apr-Jul.

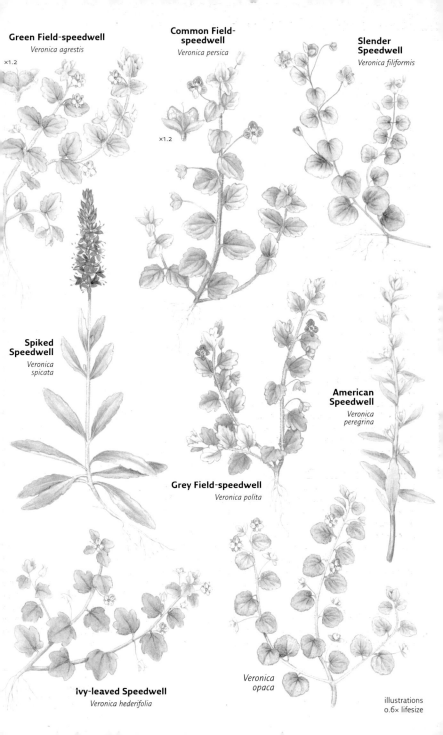

Green Field-speedwell
Veronica agrestis

×1.2

Common Field-speedwell
Veronica persica

×1.2

Slender Speedwell
Veronica filiformis

Spiked Speedwell
Veronica spicata

American Speedwell
Veronica peregrina

Grey Field-speedwell
Veronica polita

Veronica opaca

Ivy-leaved Speedwell
Veronica hederifolia

illustrations
0.6× lifesize

Cornish Moneywort
Sibthorpia europaea

Small, creeping, stoloniferous, pubescent perennial. LEAVES Orbicular, 0.5–2 cm across, 5–7-lobed; petiole long. FLOWERS axillary, inconspicuous; corolla 5-lobed, 1–2 mm across, lobes yellow and pink; 4 stamens. HABITAT Shaded stream banks, wet rocks and walls, ditches, wet heaths, on acid soils; to 515 m. DIST. Native. Local. SW England, SW Wales, SW Ireland, Channel Is, Scilly Is. (W Europe, mts of Greece.) FLS Jul–Oct.

Yellow-rattle
Rhinanthus minor

Erect, pubescent, simple or branched annual to 50 cm. FLOWERS In terminal leafy spike; calyx mid-green, strongly inflated in fruit; corolla 12–15 mm, dorsal edge of tube straight, lower lip turned down, teeth of upper lip violet, broader than long. HABITAT Partial parasite of nutrient-poor calcareous grassland, hay meadows, fens, montane grassland; to 1065 m. DIST. Native. Frequent throughout BI. (Most of Europe except Mediterranean.) FLS May–Sep. NOTE Extremely variable and variously divided into a number of subspecies based on branching, leaf arrangement and hairiness, and distinguished by habitat and flowering time.

Greater Yellow-rattle
Rhinanthus angustifolius *(B)

Similar to *R. minor*, but calyx paler green; corolla 17–20 mm, dorsal edge of corolla tube concave towards base, lower lip straight, teeth of upper lip longer than broad. HABITAT Formerly an arable weed, but now ± confined to chalk downland. DIST. Introduced. Very rare. Surrey. (Most of Europe except Mediterranean and SW.) FLS Jun–Sep.

Eyebrights *Euphrasia*

Eyebrights are all annual partial parasites on the roots of various grassland perennials. All species exhibit great variability and most hybridise freely. However, they do have distinct geographical distributions and habitat preferences, such as between acid and calcareous soils. Eyebrights are extremely difficult to identify and the treatment adopted here is based on the work of Dr P.F. Yeo. Identification should be based on several well-grown, undamaged plants with fruits as well as open flowers. Nodes are numbered from the base upwards (excluding seed leaves), and corolla length is measured from base of tube to tip of upper lip.

The following key is intended as a guide only to the commoner and more widespread species. The habitats and distributions of the rarer species are described under the individual species accounts.

1 Middle and upper stem leaves with stalked glands, stalks ≥10× as long as heads — 2
  Middle and upper stem leaves without stalked glands, or if glandular then stalks ≤6× as long as heads — 4

2 Capsule >2× as long as wide (widespread, N and W BI) — *E. arctica* ssp. *borealis*
  Capsule <2× as long as wide — 3

3 Corolla ≤7 mm — *E. anglica*
  Corolla >7 mm — *E. rostkoviana*

4 Corolla >7.5 mm — 5
  Corolla <7.5 mm — 7

5 Stems and branches flexuous; leaves near base of branches very small — *E. confusa*
  Stems and branches straight or gradually curved; leaves near base of branches not much smaller than rest — 6

6 Capsule usually slightly shorter than calyx (the commonest British species) — *E. nemorosa*
  Capsule much shorter than calyx (chalk, S England) — *E. pseudokerneri*

7 Stems and leaves purple-tinged; flowers violet or purple — *E. micrantha*
  Leaves usually green above; corolla predominantly white — 8

8 Leaves shorter than internodes — 9
  Lower leaves longer than internodes, upper leaves shorter than internodes (the commonest British species) — *E. nemorosa*
  All leaves longer than internodes, crowded; inflorescence rather 4-sided (predominantly coastal) — *E. tetraquetra*

9 Upper leaves elliptic-ovate, often purplish beneath — *E. scottica*
  Upper leaves broadly ovate to almost orbicular, not purplish beneath — *E. frigida*

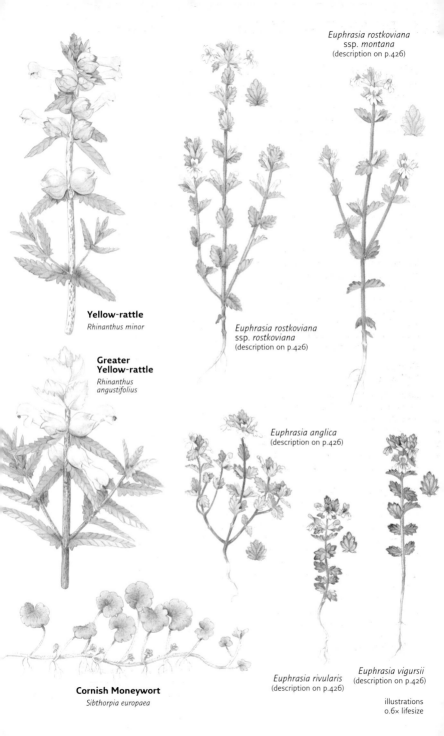

Yellow-rattle
Rhinanthus minor

**Greater
Yellow-rattle**
*Rhinanthus
angustifolius*

Cornish Moneywort
Sibthorpia europaea

Euphrasia rostkoviana
ssp. *montana*
(description on p.426)

Euphrasia rostkoviana
ssp. *rostkoviana*
(description on p.426)

Euphrasia anglica
(description on p.426)

Euphrasia rivularis
(description on p.426)

Euphrasia vigursii
(description on p.426)

illustrations
0.6× lifesize

Euphrasia rostkoviana   VU.

[*See* illustration previous page.] Tall, handsome plant to 35 cm; the largest-flowered British species. It has 2 subspecies: ssp. *rostkoviana* and ssp. *montana*. HABITAT Ssp. *rostkoviana* in damp pastures, hay meadows, roadsides; to 420 m. Ssp. *montana* in hay meadows, upland pastures, fens; 200-455 m. DIST. Ssp. *rostkoviana* in Wales, N England, S Scotland; widespread in Ireland. (Most of Europe except SE.) Ssp. *montana* very local in Lake District, N Pennines, S Scotland. FLS Jun-Aug, ssp. *montana* slightly earlier than ssp. *rostkoviana*.

Euphrasia anglica   EN.

[*See* illustration previous page.] HABITAT Grazed pastures, heathland, roadside verges; to 395 m. DIST. Possibly endemic. Widespread in S Britain (where it replaces *E. rostkoviana*), S Wales; scattered elsewhere. FLS May-Sep.

Euphrasia rivularis   VU.

[*See* illustration previous page.] Small, slender, typically unbranched plant to 15 cm, flowering early. HABITAT Damp mountain pastures, flushes, rocky stream banks; to 750 m. DIST. Endemic. Rare and local. Lake District, N Wales. FLS May-Jul.

Euphrasia vigursii   EN.

[*See* illustration previous page.] Distinctive, attractive species to 20 cm. LEAVES Tinged purple. FLOWERS Bright purple. HABITAT Grassy cliff tops, heaths, moorland characterised by Bristle Bent grass *Agrostis curtisii* (p.626). DIST. Rare, very local. Confined to Devon, Cornwall.

Euphrasia arctica ssp. borealis

Similar to *E. nemorosa* (*see* below), with which it freely hybridises, but lower branches are longer and more flexuous, and bracts are usually glandular. HABITAT Damp hay meadows, pastures, roadsides. DIST. Commonest eyebright in Scotland and parts of Wales and Ireland. (NW Europe.) FLS Jun-Aug. NOTE Ssp. *arctica* is a local plant of damp meadows in Orkney, Shetland. It is typically unbranched and ± glabrous, and has longer internodes and larger flowers than ssp. *borealis*.

Euphrasia nemorosa

Commonest British *Euphrasia*. Rather variable, 10-20 cm. HABITAT Grassy heaths, commons, chalk downs, dunes, woodland rides. DIST. Widespread throughout most of BI, but less frequent in N Scotland. (N, central and W Europe.) FLS Jul-Sep.

Euphrasia tetraquetra

Rather squat species, 5-15 cm tall. LEAVES Bluntly toothed, rather crowded. FLOWERS Small, in a 4-sided inflorescence. HABITAT Short turf of coastal cliffs, maritime dunes. DIST. All round BI coasts except E, SE and NW Scotland. (NW Europe.) FLS May-Aug.

Euphrasia pseudokerneri   EN.

Attractive, large-flowered species, to 10 mm, typically much branched and rather bushy. LEAVES Small, as long as internodes. HABITAT/DIST. Endemic. Rather local. Typical plant of short, grazed turf of chalk downs of S England and fens of Norfolk. FLS Aug-Sep.

Euphrasia confusa

Short, slender, rather bushy plant, to 20 cm, with numerous rather flexuous branches. Similar to *E. nemorosa*, with which it frequently hybridises. HABITAT Short, grazed turf of cliffs, moors, dunes; to 660 m. DIST. Predominantly N and W Britain; scarce in Ireland. (Faeroes.) FLS Jun-Sep.

Euphrasia frigida

Alpine species to 20 cm, branching from down low on stem. LEAVES Rather orbicular, with broad blunt teeth. FLOWERS Large upper bracts. HABITAT Damp basic cliff ledges; to 1190 m. DIST. Locally frequent in Scottish Highlands, Lake District, Ireland. (N Europe.) FLS Jun-Aug.

Euphrasia foulaensis

Dwarf, compact, rather dense plant. LEAVES Roundish, fleshy, bluntly toothed. FLOWERS Small, violet. HABITAT Exposed coastal grassland, upper parts of salt marshes, cliff tops. DIST. N Scotland, Hebrides, Orkney, Shetland. (Faeroes.) FLS Jun-Aug.

Euphrasia cambrica   VU.

Dwarf, compact plant, branching low down on stem. FLOWERS Small, pale. HABITAT Short, well-drained, sheep-grazed turf, rock ledges, cliffs. DIST. Endemic. Very rare. Confined to *c*.6 localities in mts of N Wales. FLS Jun-Jul.

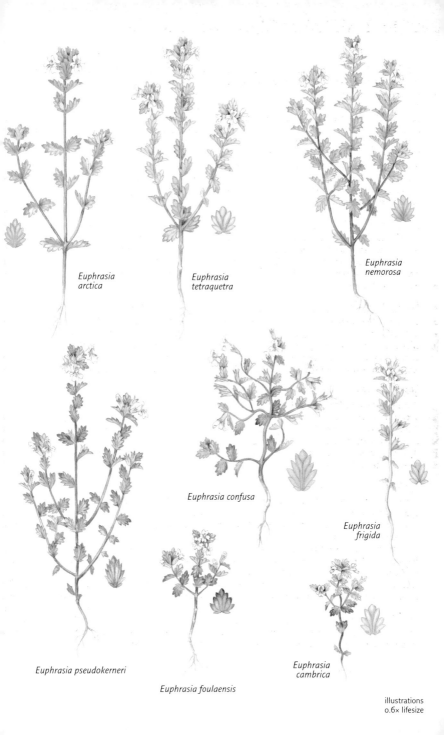

*Euphrasia
arctica*

*Euphrasia
tetraquetra*

*Euphrasia
nemorosa*

Euphrasia confusa

*Euphrasia
frigida*

Euphrasia pseudokerneri

Euphrasia foulaensis

*Euphrasia
cambrica*

illustrations
0.6× lifesize

Euphrasia ostenfeldii

Small, densely hairy plant to 12 cm. LEAVES Rather rounded. FLOWERS Tiny, white, hidden among foliage. HABITAT Sea cliffs, scree, serpentine debris, rocky and gravelly places, coastal grassland. DIST. Scattered in Orkney, Shetland, NW Scotland, Lake District, N Wales. (Faeroes, Iceland.) FLS Jun–Sep.

Euphrasia marshallii   EN.

Small, densely hairy greyish plant to 12 cm, with erect branches. FLOWERS In tight, rather 4-sided inflorescence; corolla 6-7 mm, conspicuously hairy, white, lower lip larger than upper. HABITAT Exposed rocky turf, foot of eroding sea cliffs. DIST. Endemic. Very local. NW coast of Scotland, Orkney, Shetland. FLS Jul–Aug.

Euphrasia rotundifolia   EN.

Similar to *E. marshallii*, but unbranched; leaves and bracts distinctly rounded, with blunt teeth; flowers smaller, 5-6 mm. HABITAT Flushed basic coastal turf. DIST. Endemic. Very rare. N coast of Scotland. FLS Aug–Sep.

Euphrasia cambelliae

Rather slender, erect, sparsely branched species. LEAVES Sparsely bristly. FLOWERS Calyx whitish; corolla 6-7 mm, upper lip lilac. HABITAT Grazed heathy turf close to sea. DIST. Endemic. Very rare. Confined to W coast of Lewis (Outer Hebrides). FLS Jul.

Euphrasia micrantha

Slender and erect, to 25 cm, with slender, erect branches. LEAVES Purplish. FLOWERS Small, 4.5-6.5 mm, purple-violet. HABITAT Dry acid heather moorland, heathland; to 530 m. DIST. Widespread in W and N BI. (N and central Europe.) FLS Jul–Sep.

Euphrasia scottica

Slender, erect, sparsely branched. LEAVES Small, shorter than internodes, green above, purplish beneath. FLOWERS Small, 4.5-6.5 mm, lower lip slightly longer than upper, white. HABITAT Wet upland moorland flushes; to 915 m. DIST. Widespread in Scotland, N England, Wales; scattered in Ireland. (N Europe.) FLS Jul–Aug.

Euphrasia heslop-harrisonii

Small to erect plant, to 15 cm, branching from near base. LEAVES Fleshy, glabrous; basal pair of teeth at mid-point along leaf margin, spreading; leaf margin below basal teeth convex. FLOWERS Small, 4-6 mm, white, lower lip scarcely longer than upper. FRUITS Capsule, to 5-7 mm. HABITAT Salt-marsh turf immediately above high-water mark. DIST. Endemic. Very local. W coast of Scotland. FLS Aug.

Euphrasia salisburgensis

Usually much branched, to 12 cm. LEAVES Narrow, with 3 pairs of separated spreading teeth, distinguishing it from all other British species. FRUITS Almost glabrous capsules. HABITAT Calcareous grassland, limestone cliffs, maritime dunes. DIST. Widespread in W Ireland. (Scandinavia, mts of central and S Europe.) FLS Jul–Aug.

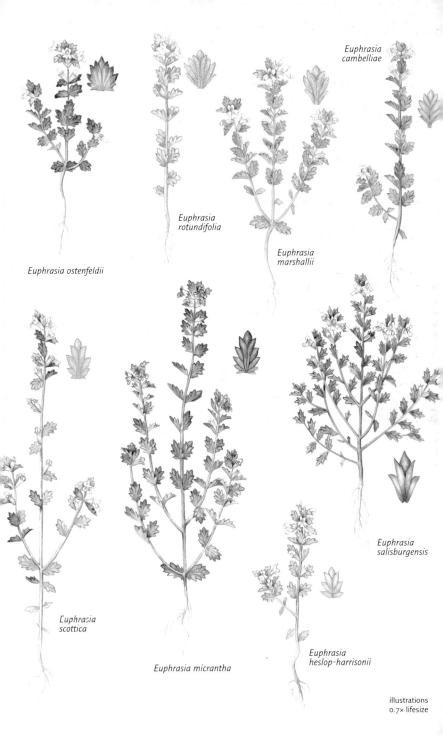

Euphrasia
cambelliae

Euphrasia
rotundifolia

Euphrasia
marshallii

Euphrasia ostenfeldii

Euphrasia salisburgensis

Euphrasia scottica

Euphrasia micrantha

Euphrasia heslop-harrisonii

illustrations
0.7× lifesize

Common Cow-wheat
Melampyrum pratense

Erect, usually glabrous, branched annual to 60 cm. LEAVES 1.5–10 cm, ± sessile, lanceolate. FLOWERS Axillary, in pairs, held horizontal; bracts leaf-like; corolla 11–17 mm, *lower lip straight, corolla tube longer than calyx.* HABITAT Heathy woodlands, moorlands, on acid soils; scrub, hedgerows, woodlands, on calcareous soils. DIST. Native. Widespread throughout most of BI, especially N and W. (Most of Europe.) FLS May–Oct.

Small Cow-wheat
Melampyrum sylvaticum EN. *(NI)

Erect, thinly pubescent annual to 35 cm. Similar to *M. pratense*, but smaller; flowers a deeper yellow; corolla 8–10 mm, *lower lip deflexed, corolla tube equalling or shorter than calyx.* HABITAT Damp woodlands, cliff ledges; to 760 m. DIST. Native. Very local, declining. Scotland, N Ireland. (N Europe, mts of central and S Europe.) FLS Jun–Aug.

Crested Cow-wheat
Melampyrum cristatum VU.

Thinly pubescent, sparsely branched annual to 50 cm. FLOWERS In dense 4-sided spike; *bracts overlapping, cordate, base bright purple, finely toothed, folded upwards longitudinally, strongly recurved, lower with long green leaf-like points;* corolla 12–16 mm, tube longer than calyx. HABITAT Margins and clearings of old woodlands, hedge banks. DIST. Native. Very local. Chalky boulder-clay areas in E England. (Most of Europe except extreme N and S.) FLS Jun–Sep.

Field Cow-wheat
Melampyrum arvense *(B)

Erect, pubescent annual with spreading branches, to 60 cm. FLOWERS In inflorescence, not markedly 4-sided; *bracts rounded at base, pink, with long, slender teeth, not recurved, not folded longitudinally;* corolla 20–24 mm, tube as long as calyx. HABITAT Field borders, hedge banks; formerly an arable weed. DIST. Introduced. Very rare, declining. S England. (W, central and E Europe.) FLS Jun–Sep.

Red Bartsia
Odontites vernus

Erect, pubescent, usually branched, purple-tinted annual to 50 cm. Very variable, with a number of

named subspecies. FLOWERS In terminal inflorescence; bracts leaf-like; calyx 4-toothed; corolla 8–10 mm, 2-lipped. HABITAT Rough grassland, tracksides, arable fields, waste ground, sandy shores, salt marshes. DIST. Native. Common throughout BI. (Most of Europe.) FLS Jun–Aug.

Alpine Bartsia
Bartsia alpina

Erect, pubescent, rhizomatous, unbranched perennial to 20 cm. LEAVES 1–2 cm. FLOWERS *In short, glandular inflorescence; bracts purplish; corolla 20 mm, upper lip much longer than lower.* HABITAT Damp upland pastures, seepage lines, rock ledges, on base-rich soils; calcareous mires. To 950 m. DIST. Native. Very rare. Central Scotland, N England. (N Europe, mts of S Europe.) FLS Jun–Aug.

Yellow Bartsia
Parentucellia viscosa

Erect, unbranched annual to 50 cm, *covered by sticky glandular hairs.* FLOWERS Axillary; bracts leaf-like; corolla 16–24 mm, lower lip much longer than upper. HABITAT Damp sandy grassland, dune slacks, heath pasture; casual elsewhere. DIST. Native. S and SW England, S Wales, N and S Ireland. (S and W Europe.) FLS Jun–Oct.

Lousewort
Pedicularis sylvatica

Decumbent to erect, ± glabrous, much-branched perennial to 25 cm. FLOWERS In terminal, 3–10-flowered inflorescence; bracts leaf-like; *calyx glabrous;* corolla 2–2.4 cm, *upper lip with 2 teeth,* one on each side near tip. HABITAT Damp acid grassland, heath, moors, drier parts of bogs; to 915 m. DIST. Native. Throughout BI, but rare in East Anglia. (W and central Europe.) FLS Apr–Sep.

Marsh Lousewort, Red-rattle
Pedicularis palustris

Erect, single-stemmed, branching, ± glabrous annual to 60 cm. Similar to *P. sylvatica,* but taller, *calyx pubescent, upper lip of corolla with 4 teeth.* HABITAT Fens, marshes, wet meadows, valley bogs, hillside flushes; to 550 m. DIST. Native. Widespread in W and N Britain, Ireland; rare elsewhere. (Most of Europe.) FLS May–Sep.

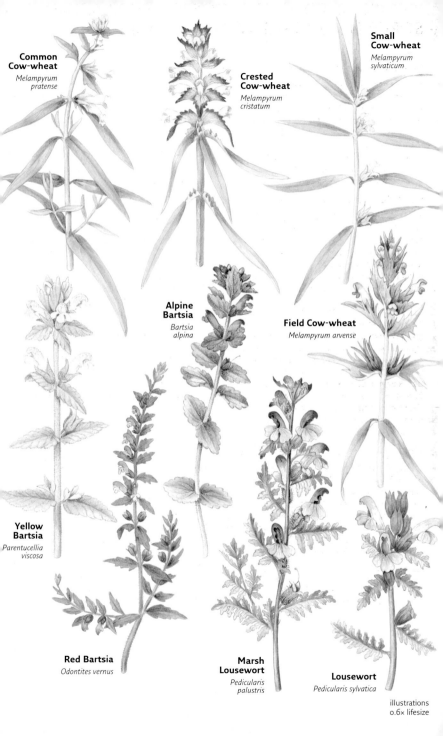

Common Cow-wheat
Melampyrum pratense

Crested Cow-wheat
Melampyrum cristatum

Small Cow-wheat
Melampyrum sylvaticum

Alpine Bartsia
Bartsia alpina

Field Cow-wheat
Melampyrum arvense

Yellow Bartsia
Parentucellia viscosa

Red Bartsia
Odontites vernus

Marsh Lousewort
Pedicularis palustris

Lousewort
Pedicularis sylvatica

illustrations
0.6× lifesize

OROBANCHACEAE Broomrapes

Root parasites related to the Scrophulariaceae but lacking chlorophyll. Erect perennials; leaves scale-like, alternate. Flowers zygomorphic, in racemes or spikes; calyx 4-lobed or 2-lipped; corolla 2-lipped; 4 stamens.

Plant without rhizome;
calyx with 2 lateral toothed
lips, most flowers sessile
Orobanche (*see* key on p.435)

Plant rhizomatous; calyx
equally 4-lobed, flowers stalked *Lathraea*

Knapweed Broomrape, Tall Broomrape *Orobanche elatior*

Parasitic on Greater Knapweed *Centaurea scabiosa* (p.480). STEMS Flowering stems to 70 cm. FLOWERS Numerous, in dense spikes; bracts as long as flowers; *calyx lobes fused beneath corolla; corolla* 18-25 mm, pale yellow, tinged purple, glandular-pubescent, *upper lip finely toothed; stamens attached well above base of corolla tube, lower part of filaments hairy; stigmas yellow.* HABITAT Chalk and limestone grassland, road verges. DIST. Native. Local, declining. S and E England. (All Europe except N and extreme S.) FLS Jun–Jul.

Ivy Broomrape *Orobanche hederae* *(NI)

Parasitic on Ivy *Hedera helix* (p.338). STEMS Flowering stems reddish or purple, to 60 cm. FLOWERS Rather few; bracts as long as or longer than flowers; *corolla constricted towards tip, 12-20 mm,* cream, veined purple, *lower lip with acute lobes;* stamens attached above base of corolla tube, *lower part of filaments almost glabrous; stigmas yellow.* HABITAT Coastal cliffs, rocky woodland, hedge banks. DIST. Native. Local. Coastal areas of S and SW England, Wales; scattered in Ireland. (W, S and SW Europe.) FLS Jun–Jul.

Common Broomrape *Orobanche minor*

Very variable on a wide variety of hosts, especially Fabaceae and Asteraceae; var. *maritima* parasitic on Sea Carrot *Daucus carota* ssp. *gummifer* (p.358). STEMS Flowering stems yellowish tinged with red, to 60 cm. FLOWERS Bracts about as long as flowers; corolla 10-16 mm, *upper edge of corolla tube slightly and ± regularly curved; stamens attached 2-3 mm above base of corolla tube, filaments ± glabrous throughout;* stigmas purple. HABITAT Rough grassland, cultivated land,

usually on dry soils; var. *maritima* on sand-dunes, cliffs, of S coast. DIST. Native. Frequent in England, Wales; casual elsewhere. (W, S and S-central Europe.) FLS Jun–Sep.

Greater Broomrape *Orobanche rapum-genistae*

Parasitic on gorses (*Ulex*; p.300) and Broom *Cytisus scoparius* (p.302). STEMS Flowering stems yellowish, glandular-hairy, to 80 cm. FLOWERS In long, compact spike; calyx bell-shaped; corolla 20-25 mm, yellow, tinged purple, *upper lip of corolla almost entire; stamens attached at base of corolla tube, lower ⅓ of filaments glabrous; stigmas yellow.* HABITAT Scrub, hedge banks. DIST. Native. Scarce and declining in England, Wales; rare in Scotland, Ireland. (W Europe.) FLS May–Jul.

Yarrow Broomrape *Orobanche purpurea* VU.

Parasitic on Yarrow *Achillea millefolium* (p.502). STEMS Flowering *stem bluish*, to 45 cm. FLOWERS In lax spike; *each flower with 2 bracteoles* similar to calyx teeth in axil of each bract; *corolla* 18-30 mm, *dull bluish purple*, upper lip with 2 acute lobes; filaments glabrous; *stigmas white.* HABITAT Dry cliff-top grassland, roadsides, walls near sea. DIST. Native. Very rare. Norfolk, I of Wight, Channel Is; scattered elsewhere. (Most of Europe except N.) FLS Jun–Jul.

Thistle Broomrape *Orobanche reticulata* *(B)

Parasitic on thistles. STEMS Flowering stem yellowish purplish. FLOWERS Numerous, in compact spike; *corolla* 15-22 mm, yellowish, tinged purple, *with sparse dark glands, upper edge strongly curved; stamens attached 3-4 mm above base of corolla,* filaments glabrous or sparsely hairy; *stigmas dark purple.* HABITAT Rough grassland, roadside verges, riverbanks. DIST. Native. Very local. Magnesian limestone areas of Yorkshire. (Central and S Europe.) FLS Jun–Aug.

Thyme Broomrape, Red broomrape *Orobanche alba*

Parasitic on Wild Thyme *Thymus polytrichus* (p.394). STEMS *Flowering stems purplish red*, to 25 cm. FLOWERS Few; bracts shorter than flowers; *corolla* 15 -20 mm, *dull purplish red;* stamens attached 1-2 mm above base of corolla tube; lower part of filaments slightly hairy; stigmas reddish. HABITAT Base-rich maritime cliffs, slopes, scree; limestone scree inland. DIST. Native. Very local. Coastal areas of NW Scotland, W Ireland, SW England; inland in N England (Yorkshire). (All Europe except N.) FLS Jun–Aug.

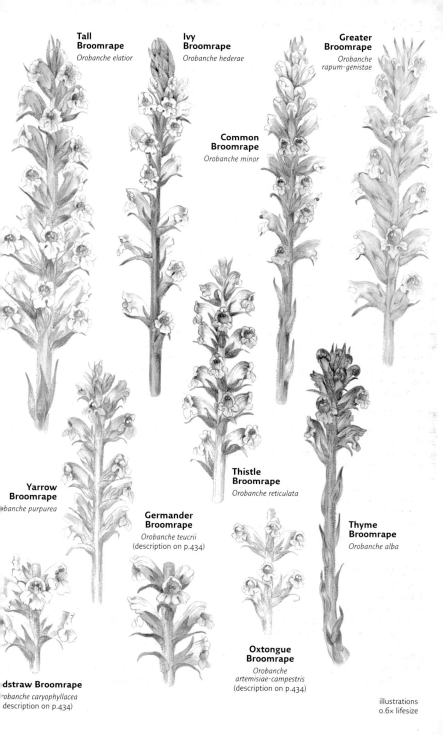

Tall Broomrape
Orobanche elatior

Ivy Broomrape
Orobanche hederae

Greater Broomrape
Orobanche rapum-genistae

Common Broomrape
Orobanche minor

Yarrow Broomrape
Orobanche purpurea

Germander Broomrape
Orobanche teucrii
(description on p.434)

Thistle Broomrape
Orobanche reticulata

Thyme Broomrape
Orobanche alba

Oxtongue Broomrape
Orobanche artemisiae-campestris
(description on p.434)

Bedstraw Broomrape
Orobanche caryophyllacea
(description on p.434)

illustrations
0.6× lifesize

Bedstraw Broomrape, Clove-scented Broomrape
Orobanche caryophyllacea *(B)

[*See* illustration previous page.] Parasitic on Hedge Bedstraw *Galium mollugo* (p.446). STEMS Flowering stems yellowish. FLOWERS Few, smelling of cloves, in lax spikes; bracts shorter than flowers, 17–25 mm; calyx 10–17 mm, teeth entire; *corolla large, 20–30 mm, yellowish*, margin of lobes of lower lip with fine teeth; stamens attached 1–3 mm above base of corolla, lower part of filaments hairy; *stigma lobes separate, dark red.* HABITAT Dune grassland, rough chalk grassland. DIST. Native. Very rare: E Kent only. (W, central and S Europe.) FLS Jun–Jul.

Germander Broomrape
Orobanche teucrii

[*See* illustration previous page.] Parasitic on Wall Germander *Teucrium chamaedrys* and Mountain Germander *T. montanum* (p.390). Similar to *O. caryophyllacea*, but bracts 12–20 mm; calyx ≤12 mm, teeth divided; stamens attached 3–5 mm above base of corolla. HABITAT Dry calcareous grasslands. DIST. *Not BI.* (W, central and E Europe.) FLS May–Jun.

Oxtongue Broomrape
Orobanche artemisiae-campestris EN. *(B)

[*See* illustration previous page.] Parasitic on Hawkweed Oxtongue *Picris hieracioides* (p.486). STEMS Flowering stems yellowish, tinged purple, to 60 cm. FLOWERS Bracts as long as or longer than flowers; *calyx teeth long, filiform*; corolla 15–20 mm, yellowish

white, tinged purple; *stamens attached ≥3 mm above base of corolla tube, lower part of filaments densely hairy*; stigma lobes dark purple. HABITAT Dry calcareous grassland, cliffs, chalk scree. DIST. Native. Very rare. Coasts of Kent, Sussex, I of Wight. (S, W and central Europe.) FLS Jun–Jul.

Toothwort
Lathraea squamaria

[*See* illustration following page.] Parasitic on a range of shrubs and trees, especially Hazel *Corylus avellana* (p.100), Ash *Fraxinus excelsior* (p.406) and Wych Elm *Ulmus glabra* (p.96). STEMS Flowering shoot erect, to 30 cm. FLOWERS With short stalks, in 1-sided raceme at first drooping then becoming erect; calyx glandular-hairy, 4 teeth; corolla white, tinged purple, slightly longer than calyx. HABITAT Woodlands, hedgerows on moist calcareous soils; lowland to 350 m. DIST. Native. Rather local, declining. Throughout most of BI N to S Scotland. (All Europe.) FLS Apr–May.

Purple Toothwort
Lathraea clandestina

[*See* illustration following page.] Striking-looking plant with no aerial shoot. Parasitic on Alder *Alnus glutinosa* (p.100), poplars (*Populus*; p.174) and willows (*Salix*; pp.176–179). FLOWERS Arising in clusters direct from rhizome just below soil surface, long-stalked; calyx glabrous; corolla bright purple, 40–50 mm, ≥2× as long as calyx. HABITAT Open woodland on damp soils, margins of streams, rivers. DIST. Introduced. Naturalised in scattered localities N to central Scotland. (W Europe.) FLS Apr–May.

Key to Broomrapes *Orobanche*

	if	**then**
1	▷ Flowers mauve; each flower with 1 bract and 2 bracteoles similar to the 4 calyx teeth (on *Achillea*, rare)	**O. purpurea** (p.432)
	▷ Flowers with 1 bract only	Go to ▷ **2**
2	▷ Stigma lobes purple, red or brown	Go to ▷ **3**
	▷ Stigma lobes yellowish, at least at first	Go to ▷ **8**
3	▷ Stem and flowers dark purplish red (on *Thymus*)	**O. alba** (p.432)
	▷ Stem and flowers not both dark purplish red	Go to ▷ **4**
4	▷ Corolla 10–22 mm	Go to ▷ **5**
	▷ Corolla 20–30 mm	Go to ▷ **7**
5	▷ Upper edge of corolla strongly curved, with sparse dark glands towards tip (on thistles, Yorkshire)	**O. reticulata** (p.432)
	▷ Upper edge of corolla almost straight to slightly curved, without dark glands towards tip	Go to ▷ **6**
6	▷ Flowers yellowish, tinged purple; filaments glabrous or sparsely hairy towards base; bract shorter than or as long as corolla; not all 4 calyx teeth long and filiform (widespread)	**O. minor** (p.432)
	▷ Flowers white; base of filaments with long white hairs; bract as long as or longer than corolla; all 4 calyx teeth long and filiform (on *Picris*, SE coasts England, very rare)	**O. artemisiae-campestris** (p.434)
7	▷ Stems and flowers yellowish; flowers few; calyx 10–17 mm, teeth entire (on *Galium mollugo*, E Kent, very rare)	**O. caryophyllacea** (p.434)
	▷ Calyx ≤12 mm, teeth divided (on *Teucrium chamaedrys*, *T. montanum*, not BI)	**O. teucrii** • (p.434)
8	▷ Corolla 18–25 mm	Go to ▷ **9**
	▷ Corolla 10–20 mm (on *Hedera*)	**O. hederae** (p.432)
9	▷ Upper lip of corolla almost entire; stamens inserted close to base of corolla tube, filaments glabrous (on *Ulex*, *Cytisus*)	**O. rapum-genistae** (p.432)
	▷ Upper lip of corolla finely toothed; stamens inserted 4–6 mm above base of corolla tube, base of filaments hairy (on *Centaurea scabiosa*)	**O. elatior** (p.432)

LENTIBULARIACEAE Bladderworts

Small family of insectivorous aquatic or bog plants related to Scrophulariaceae. Flowers solitary or in a raceme; calyx 5-lobed or 2-lipped; corolla 2-lipped and spurred; 2 stamens. Fruits are a capsule.

Leaves divided into fine filiform segments; insectivorous by bladder-like traps on leaves; submerged aquatics	*Utricularia*
Leaves entire, in basal rosette; insectivorous by sticky glands covering whole plant; bog plants	*Pinguicula*

Bladderworts *Utricularia*

Rootless aquatics, free-floating or with lower part of stems in bottom mud. Difficult to name; accurate identification often relies on microscopic examination of bladders, especially as some species rarely flower. The following notes rely on examination of fresh plants; the leaf characters need a strong lens.

Greater Bladderwort   *Utricularia vulgaris*

Free-floating, to 100 cm. STEMS and LEAVES All of one sort. FLOWERS Yellow, lower lip with strongly reflexed margins; flower stalks 8-15 mm, not elongating after flowering. HABITAT Ponds, ditches, lakes, grazing marshes, in rather infertile base-rich waters. DIST. Native. Very local, declining. Throughout BI, especially East Anglia, Somerset Levels, N Ireland. (Most of Europe, but rare in S.) FLS Jul-Aug.

Bladderwort   *Utricularia australis*

Similar to *U. vulgaris*, but stems to 60 cm; lower lip of flowers flat or with upturned margins; flower stalks 8-15 mm at flowering, elongating to 10-30 mm after. HABITAT Lakes, ponds, ditches, canals, in still, usually acid but also calcareous waters; lowland to 335 m. DIST. Native. Very local. Scattered throughout BI. (Most of Europe except extreme N.) FLS Jul-Aug.

Lesser Bladderwort   *Utricularia minor*

STEMS Slender, to 40 cm, of 2 kinds: free-floating with green leaves and few bladders; colourless, free-floating or ± buried in substratum, with bladders on reduced leaves. LEAVES Segments entire, without bristles. FLOWERS Flowering stems 4-15 cm, 2-6-flowered; corolla 6-8 mm, pale yellow; spur very short 1-2 mm, blunt. HABITAT Acid bog pools, peat cuttings ditches; to 650 m. DIST. Native. Throughout BI: widespread in N and W; rare and declining elsewhere. (Most of Europe, but rare in Mediterranean.) FLS Jun-Sep

Utricularia intermedia group

Group of 3 closely related species that rarely flower and whose distributions are incompletely known. Stems are of 2 kinds: free-floating with green leaves and no or few bladders; and attached to substratum, with reduced non-green leaves and numerous bladders

Intermediate Bladderwort   *Utricularia intermedia*

LEAVES Green leaves totally without bladders; apex of leaf segments blunt. FLOWERS Corolla yellow spur 8-10 mm, as long as lower lip. HABITAT Shallow acid, nutrient-deficient waters; to 650 m. DIST Mostly Scotland, but also Lake District, W Ireland (Most of Europe except S.) FLS Jul-Sep.

Nordic Bladderwort   *Utricularia stygia*

LEAVES Green leaves usually with some bladders; margins of leaf segments with 2-7 teeth, apex of segment fine-pointed. FLOWERS Corolla yellow with reddish tinge, lower lip flat or with slightly upturned margins spur 4-5 mm. HABITAT/DIST. As for *U. intermedia*

Pale Bladderwort   *Utricularia ochroleuca*

LEAVES Green leaves usually with some bladders margins of leaf segments with 0-5 teeth, apex of segments fine-pointed. FLOWERS Corolla pale yellow lower lip flat at first, margins becoming reflexed later spur *c*.3 mm. HABITAT/DIST. As for *U. intermedia*

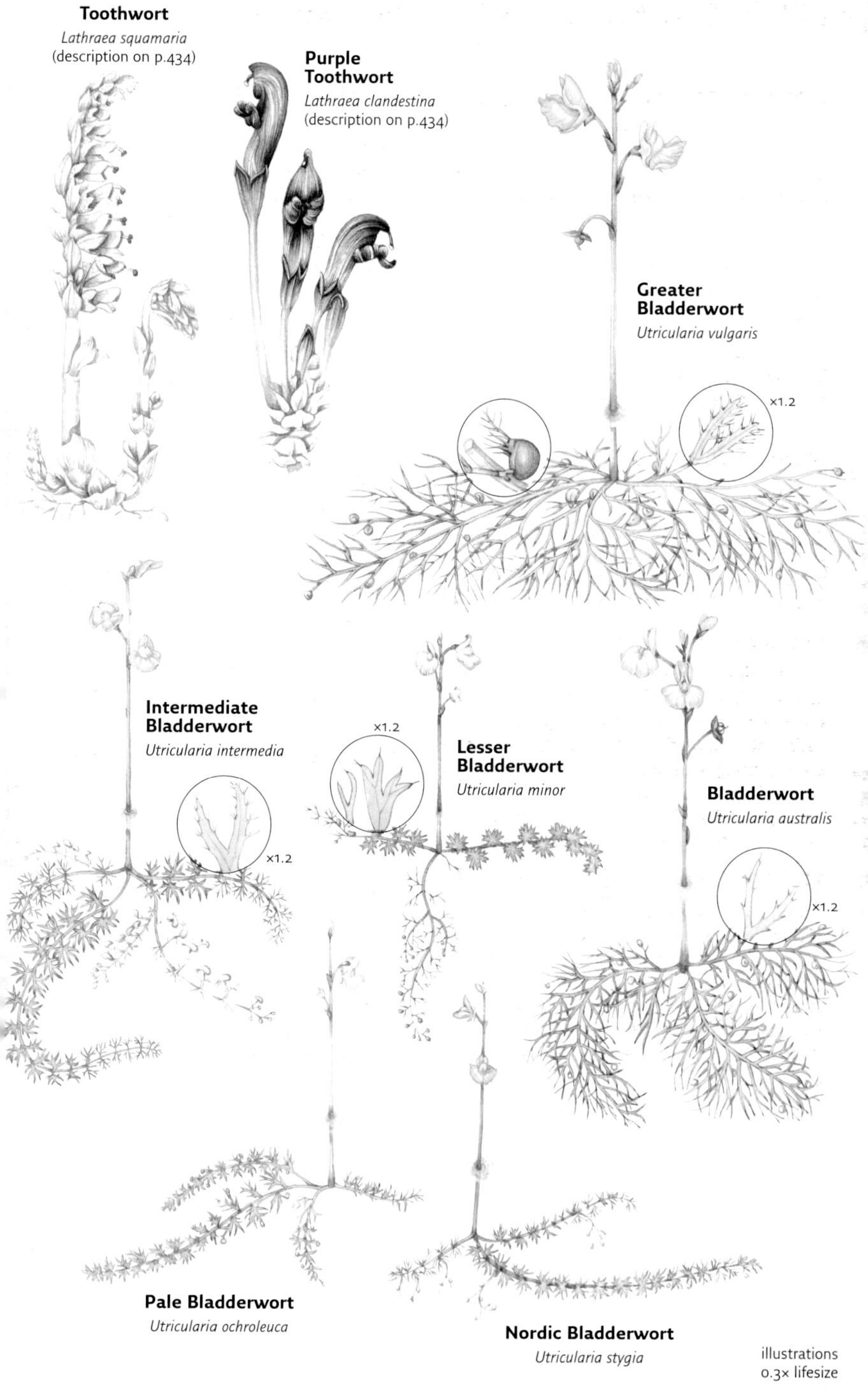

Toothwort
Lathraea squamaria
(description on p.434)

Purple Toothwort
Lathraea clandestina
(description on p.434)

Greater Bladderwort
Utricularia vulgaris

×1.2

Intermediate Bladderwort
Utricularia intermedia

×1.2

×1.2

Lesser Bladderwort
Utricularia minor

Bladderwort
Utricularia australis

×1.2

Pale Bladderwort
Utricularia ochroleuca

Nordic Bladderwort
Utricularia stygia

illustrations
0.3× lifesize

Butterworts *Pinguicula*

Perennial insectivorous plants. Whole plant covered by sticky glands. Leaves in basal rosette, entire, margins inrolled. Flowering stems leafless; flowers solitary; corolla 2-lipped, spurred.

Flowers bright violet; corolla ≥14 mm including spur

Corolla 14-22 mm including spur;
lobes of lower lip separated   *P. vulgaris*

Corolla 25-35 mm including spur;
lobes of lower lip overlapping
(SW Ireland)   *P. grandiflora*

Flower pale lilac; corolla ≤10 mm including spur
          P. lusitanica

Common Butterwort   *Pinguicula vulgaris*

LEAVES 2-8 cm, yellow-green. FLOWERS Flowering stems 5-15 cm; corolla 14-22 mm including spur, spur 4-7 mm, *lobes of lower lip longer than broad, divergent*. HABITAT Bare, wet acid peat, wet rocks, on wet heaths, moorland, acid bogs, flushes, moss-rich fens. DIST. Native. Widespread in N and W BI; rare and declining elsewhere. (N, W and central Europe.) FLS May-Jul.

Large-flowered Butterwort   *Pinguicula grandiflora*

Similar to *P. vulgaris*, but flowering stems 5-18 cm; corolla 25-35 mm including spur; spur 10-14 mm, *lobes of lower lip broader than long, overlapping*. HABITAT Wet rocks, damp moorland, bogs; to 855 m. DIST. Native. SW Ireland. (Mts of SW Europe.) FLS May-Jun.

Pale Butterwort   *Pinguicula lusitanica*

LEAVES 1-2 cm, yellowish purple. FLOWERS Flowering stems 3-15 cm; *flowers pale lilac*; corolla 7-11 mm including spur, spur 2-4 mm, lower lip notched. HABITAT Short, grazed turf, damp, bare peat, wet heaths, wet moorland flushes, drainage ditches. DIST. Native. Widespread in S and SW England, W Scotland, Ireland; rare in SW Wales. (W Europe.) FLS Jun-Oct.

CAMPANULACEAE Bellflowers

Annual or perennial plants, often showy and frequently with blue or purple flowers (*see* key on p.440). Leaves are alternate, simple and without stipules. Flowers are solitary, or arranged in open inflorescences, or in spherical heads or spikes; 5 sepals and petals, fused into a tube at the base; 5 stamens attached to the receptacle, and with their anthers often fused into a ring surrounding the style; ovary inferior. Fruit is usually a capsule.

Bellflowers *Campanula*

See key to Campanula *on p.440.*

Rampion Bellflower   *Campanula rapunculus* EN

Erect, coarsely pubescent perennial to 80 cm. LEAVES Basal leaves abruptly contracted at base, middle stem leaves linear-lanceolate. FLOWERS *In simple inflorescence; bracteoles at base of flower stalk*; corolla pale blue, 10-22 mm, lobes *c.⅓ as long as* tube. HABITAT Rough grassland, roadsides, hedge banks, as relic of cultivation. DIST. Archaeophyte. Once widely cultivated, now very rare, declining. (Most of Europe except N.) FLS Jul-Aug.

Peach-leaved Bellflower   *Campanula persicifolia*

Erect, *glabrous*, rhizomatous perennial to 80 cm. LEAVES Linear-lanceolate. FLOWERS Sub-erect, 25-50 mm, *in 1-8-flowered inflorescence*; corolla divided <¼ way to base. HABITAT Waysides, woods, hedgerows, waste ground. DIST. Introduced. Naturalised and scattered throughout Britain; absent from Ireland. (Most of Europe except extreme N.) FLS Jun-Aug.

Cornish Bellflower   *Campanula alliariifolia*

Erect, pubescent perennial to 70 cm. LEAVES Basal and lower stem leaves broad, cordate at base. FLOWERS *Calyx with sepal-like appendages alternating with* calyx lobes; corolla 20-40 mm, white, bell-shaped; 3 stigmas. HABITAT Railway banks, roadsides, waste ground. DIST. Introduced. Naturalised garden escape. Scattered localities in SW England. (Caucasus, Turkey.)

Creeping Bellflower   *Campanula rapunculoides*

Erect, thinly pubescent, *patch-forming perennial* to 80 cm; rhizomes and roots spreading and producing numerous buds. LEAVES Basal leaves long-stalked, 5-8 cm, broadly cordate; stem leaves sessile. FLOWERS Nodding; *calyx lobes spreading, reflexed*; corolla 20-30 mm, funnel-shaped; 3 stigmas. HABITAT Roadside verges, railway banks, rough ground. DIST. Introduced. Naturalised as a garden escape. Scattered throughout BI, but rare in Ireland. (Most of Europe except extreme N.) FLS Jul-Sep.

Canterbury-bells   *Campanula medium*

Erect, hispid biennial to 60 cm. FLOWERS Sub-erect short-stalked; *calyx with large, broad, reflexed appendages between calyx teeth*; corolla violet-blue 40-50 cm, *broadly bell-shaped; 5 stigmas*. HABITAT Road verges, waste ground. DIST. Introduced. Casual as a garden escape. Scattered throughout Britain, absent from Ireland. (Italy, France.) FLS May-Jun.

Large-flowered Butterwort
Pinguicula grandiflora

Common Butterwort
Pinguicula vulgaris

Pale Butterwort
Pinguicula lusitanica

Creeping Bellflower
Campanula rapunculoides

Peach-leaved Bellflower
Campanula persicifolia

Rampion Bellflower
Campanula rapunculus

Canterbury-bells
Campanula medium

Cornish Bellflower
Campanula alliariifolia

illustrations
0.3× lifesize

	if	then
1	▷ Flowers solitary or inflorescence a raceme or panicle; corolla lobes shorter than tube	Go to ▷ **2**
	▷ Flowers numerous, in dense heads or spikes; corolla deeply divided into linear lobes	Go to ▷ **5**
2	▷ Flowers distinctly zygomorphic	*Lobelia* (p.444)
	▷ Flowers regular	Go to ▷ **3**
3	▷ Stems creeping, slender; leaves with long petiole; flowers solitary, axillary	*Wahlenbergia* (p.444)
	▷ Stems erect; at least upper leaves sessile	Go to ▷ **4**
4	▷ Corolla shorter than calyx; ovary and capsule >3× as long as wide	*Legousia* (p.442)
	▷ Corolla longer than calyx; ovary and capsule <2× as long as wide	*Campanula* (*see* below)
5	▷ Plant glabrous; each flower with a bract; flower buds curved	*Phyteuma* (p.444)
	▷ Plant pubescent; flowers without a bract; flower buds straight	*Jasione* (p.444)

Bellflowers *Campanula*

1	▷ Calyx without reflexed sepal-like lobes between calyx teeth	Go to ▷ **2**
	▷ Calyx with reflexed sepal-like lobes between calyx teeth	Go to ▷ **10**
2	▷ Flowers distinctly stalked	Go to ▷ **3**
	▷ Flowers sessile	Go to ▷ **9**
3	▷ Middle stem leaves ovate	Go to ▷ **4**
	▷ Middle stem leaves linear or linear-lanceolate	Go to ▷ **6**
4	▷ Flowers erect or inclined, calyx teeth ± erect in flower	Go to ▷ **5**
	▷ Flowers nodding, calyx teeth spreading in flower	*C. rapunculoides* (p.438)
5	▷ Stem sharply angled; stem leaves stalked; corolla 25–35 mm; plant roughly hairy	*C. trachelium* (p.442)
	▷ Stem bluntly angled; stem leaves sessile; corolla 40–55 mm; plant softly hairy	*C. latifolia* (p.442)
6	▷ Flowers nodding; lower stem leaves stalked	*C. rotundifolia* (p.442)
	▷ Flowers ± erect; lower stem leaves sessile	Go to ▷ **7**

	if	**then**
7	▷ Plant glabrous, with non-flowering rosettes; corolla ≥30 mm	*C. persicifolia* (p.438)
	▷ Plant pubescent, without non-flowering rosettes; corolla ≤20 mm	Go to ▷ **8**
8	▷ Inflorescence wide-spreading, bracteoles at middle of flower stalks; basal leaves narrowed at base	*C. patula* (p.442)
	▷ Inflorescence narrow, bracteoles at base of flower stalks; basal leaves abruptly contracted to distinct petiole	*C. rapunculus* (p.438)
9	▷ Basal leaves cordate	*C. glomerata* (p.442)
	▷ Basal leaves narrowed to base	*C. cervicaria* • (p.442)
10	▷ Flowers dark violet-blue; basal leaves narrowed to base	*C. medium* (p.438)
	▷ Flowers white; basal leaves cordate	*C. alliariifolia* (p.438)

Spreading Bellflower · *Campanula patula* EN.

Erect, coarsely pubescent biennial to 60 cm. LEAVES Lower *leaf blades ovate, decurrent down petiole*; stem leaves narrow, sessile. FLOWERS Erect, *in much-branched inflorescence*, stalks slender; *bracteoles attached at middle of flower stalks; corolla* 15–20 mm, *broadly funnel-shaped,* lobed to halfway to base, *lobes spreading.* HABITAT Open woodland, rock outcrops, hedge banks, on well-drained sandy soils. DIST. Native. Local, declining. Welsh border counties. (Most of Europe except S.) FLS Jul–Sep.

Clustered Bellflower · *Campanula glomerata*

Erect, pubescent perennial to 20(–50) cm. LEAVES *Basal leaves long-stalked, blade 2–4 cm, ovate, rounded at base; stem leaves sessile, ± clasping stem.* FLOWERS *Erect, sessile, in a terminal head; corolla 15–20 mm,* bright purplish blue, lobes almost as long as tube. HABITAT Grazed or rough chalk grassland, open scrub, limestone cliffs, dunes; to 355 m. DIST. Native. Throughout England, local but widespread in S; rare in Wales, Scotland; absent from Ireland. (Most of Europe except extreme S and N.) FLS May–Sep.

Harebell · *Campanula rotundifolia*

Slender, glabrous, stoloniferous perennial to 40 cm. LEAVES *Basal leaves orbicular, long-stalked, cordate; stem leaves linear, sessile.* FLOWERS *Nodding,* in usually branched inflorescence, buds erect; calyx lobes linear, spreading; corolla *c.*12–20 mm, lobes *c.⅓* as long as tube; 3 stigmas. HABITAT Grassy hillsides, heaths, downs, dunes, cliffs, hedge banks, on dry acid or calcareous soils; to 1160 m. DIST. Native. Common throughout BI, but rare in SW England and in Ireland except for W. (Most of Europe, but rare in S.) FLS Jul–Sep.

Nettle-leaved Bellflower · *Campanula trachelium* *(R)

Tall, erect, unbranched, hispid perennial to 100 cm. STEMS *Sharply angled.* LEAVES *Basal leaves cordate; lower and middle stem leaves stalked,* blade *c.*10 cm, cordate, coarsely toothed. FLOWERS In leafy inflorescence with short branches; *corolla* blue-purple, 25–35 mm, lobes shorter than tube. HABITAT Wood margins, scrub, hedgerows, shaded banks, on dry calcareous soils; to 320 m. DIST. Native. England N to Humber; rare in SW England, Wales, Ireland. (Most of Europe except N.) FLS Jul–Sep.

Giant Bellflower · *Campanula latifolia*

Tall, handsome, softly pubescent perennial to 120 cm. STEMS *Bluntly angled.* LEAVES *Basal leaves narrowing to petiole; lower and middle stem leaves sessile.* FLOWERS *Corolla* blue-purple, *40–55 cm,* lobes shorter than tube. HABITAT Woods, shaded hedge banks, on moist calcareous or mildly acid soils; to 390 m. DIST. Native. Central England N to central Scotland; naturalised elsewhere. (Most of Europe except extreme N; rare in SW and Mediterranean.) FLS Jul–Aug.

Bristly Bellflower · *Campanula cervicaria*

Erect, hispid biennial to 70 cm. LEAVES Basal leaves soon withering; *stem leaves ovate-lanceolate, narrowing to petiole,* upper leaves sessile. FLOWERS *In a terminal head; corolla* pale blue, *13–16 mm,* hispid. HABITAT Warm, dry meadows, wood margins. DIST. *Not BI.* (Much of Europe except extreme N in Mediterranean.) FLS Jun–Aug.

Venus's-looking-glass · *Legousia hybrida*

Erect, hispid annual to 30 cm. LEAVES 10–30 mm, sessile, *oblong, margins undulate.* FLOWERS Erect, in terminal few-flowered inflorescence; *calyx teeth elliptic-lanceolate,* c.2× *as long as corolla;* c.⅓ *as long as ovary; corolla 8–15 mm across.* FRUITS *Capsule 15–30 mm.* HABITAT Arable fields on light sandy or calcareous soils. DIST. Archaeophyte. Local, declining. England, SE of line from Humber to Severn. (W and S Europe.) FLS May–Aug.

Large Venus's-looking-glass · *Legousia speculum-veneris*

Erect, thinly pubescent, much-branched annual to 40 cm. Similar to *L. hybrida,* but leaves scarcely undulate; flowers in terminal pyramidal inflorescence; *calyx teeth linear, slightly shorter than corolla, about as long as ovary; corolla 15–20 mm across; capsule 10–15 mm.* HABITAT Arable fields. DIST. Introduced. Naturalised in Hampshire. (SW and S-central Europe, N to Netherlands.) FLS May–Aug.

Venus's-looking-glass
Legousia speculum-veneris

Venus's-looking-glass
Legousia hybrida

Nettle-leaved Bellflower
Campanula trachelium

Harebell
Campanula rotundifolia

Clustered Bellflower
Campanula glomerata

Giant Bellflower
Campanula latifolia

Bristly Bellflower
Campanula cervicaria

Spreading Bellflower
Campanula patula

illustrations
0.2× lifesize

Ivy-leaved Bellflower
Wahlenbergia hederacea

Slender, glabrous, creeping perennial to 30 cm. LEAVES *All stalked*, blades 5-10 mm, ± *orbicular, angled, cordate*. FLOWERS Solitary, nodding; peduncles longer than petioles; corolla pale blue, 6-10 mm, bell-shaped. HABITAT Wet grassy flushes, margins of springs and streams, wet woodland rides, on acid soils; to 485 m. DIST. Native. SW England, Wales; rare elsewhere. (W Europe.) FLS Jul-Aug.

Round-headed Rampion
Phyteuma orbiculare

Erect, glabrous or sparsely pubescent perennial to 50 cm. LEAVES Basal leaves long-stalked, blade lanceolate to ovate; stem leaves few, sessile, narrow. FLOWERS In globose inflorescence, 1-2 cm across; corolla blue-violet, 5-8 mm, *curved in bud*. HABITAT Species-rich chalk grassland on warm, dry slopes. DIST. Native. Very local. S England. (W, central and E Europe.) FLS Jul-Aug.

Spiked Rampion
Phyteuma spicatum EN. *(B)

Tall, glabrous perennial to 80 cm. LEAVES Basal leaves long-stalked, blade ovate, deeply cordate; upper stem leaves linear-lanceolate. FLOWERS In cylindrical inflorescence, 3-8 cm; corolla yellowish white, 7-10 mm, curved in bud. HABITAT Hedge and roadside banks, coppice woodland, on acid sandy soils. DIST. Native. Very rare. E Sussex. (Central and S Europe except Mediterranean.) FLS Jul-Aug.

Blue Rampion
Phyteuma nigrum

Erect, glabrous perennial to 60 cm. LEAVES Middle and upper stem leaves with greatly reduced blade. FLOWERS In cylindrical inflorescence; corolla blackish violet, curved in bud. SIMILAR SPP. Note possible confusion with pale blue form of *P. spicatum* ssp. *caeruleum*. HABITAT Mountain meadows, damp woods, usually on acid soils. DIST. *Not BI*. (Central Europe: Austria to Belgium.) FLS May-Jun.

Sheep's-bit
Jasione montana

Decumbent, *pubescent*, simple or branched biennial to 50 cm. LEAVES Linear-oblong, undulate, basal leaves stalked, stem leaves sessile. FLOWERS In terminal globose head, 5-35 mm across; corolla blue, *c.*5 mm, *straight in bud, split nearly to base when open*; anthers fused; 2 stigmas, short. HABITAT Heaths, rough grassland, rocky hillsides, sea cliffs, dunes, walls, hedge banks, maritime heaths, on acid soils. DIST. Native. Widespread in W Britain except NW Scotland, scattered elsewhere; mostly coastal in Ireland. (Most of Europe except extreme N.) FLS May-Aug.

Heath Lobelia
Lobelia urens VU.

Erect, glabrous to thinly pubescent perennial, to 60 cm. STEMS Leafy. LEAVES To 7 cm, obovate-oblong, irregularly toothed. FLOWERS Erect or spreading, in inflorescence, *c.*20 cm; bracts narrower than leaves; corolla 10-15 mm, 2-lipped, purplish blue; filaments and anthers fused around style. HABITAT Grassy heaths, rough pastures, on damp acid, often seasonally waterlogged soils. DIST. Native. Very rare. In a few scattered localities along S coast. (W Europe.) FLS Aug-Sep.

Water Lobelia
Lobelia dortmanna

Glabrous, erect, aquatic perennial to 60 cm. STEMS Smooth, leafless. LEAVES In submerged basal rosette, 2-4 cm, linear, entire. FLOWERS 12-20 mm, 3-10 in lax, elongated inflorescence, nodding, pale lilac. HABITAT Shallow water of acid, nutrient-deficient mountain tarns, lakes; to 745 m. DIST. Native. Widespread and frequent in upland areas of Scotland, Lake District, Wales, W Ireland. (N and N-central Europe.) FLS Jul-Aug. NOTE Non-flowering plants can be distinguished from other smooth-leaved submerged aquatics of upland lakes by the compressed leaves, which have 2 hollow tubes in section. The familiar annual Garden Lobelia is *Lobelia erinus*.

ACANTHACEAE Acanthus family

Bear's-breech
Acanthus mollis

Robust, erect, clump-forming, glabrous perennial to 100 cm. LEAVES 25-60 cm, deeply pinnately lobed, in large basal rosette. FLOWERS In large, robust terminal spikes, each in axil of spiny purple-tinged bract; corolla with 3-lobed lower lip (upper lip absent), 3.5-5 cm, white with purple veins. HABITAT Roadsides, railway banks, waste ground. DIST. Introduced. Naturalised in scattered localities as garden escape, especially in the SW. (S Europe.) FLS Jun-Aug.

Ivy-leaved Bellflower
Wahlenbergia hederacea

×0.6

Round-headed Rampion
Phyteuma orbiculare

Blue Rampion
Phyteuma nigrum

Bear's-breech
Acanthus mollis

×0.6

flower
×0.6

flower
×0.6

flower
×0.6

Sheep's-bit
Jasione montana

flower
×0.6

Water Lobelia
Lobelia dortmanna

Heath Lobelia
Lobelia urens

Spiked Rampion
Phyteuma spicatum

illustrations
0.2× lifesize

RUBIACEAE Bedstraws

Distinctive family, easily recognised by whorls of 4 or more 'leaves' arranged regularly along stem (*see* key on p.448). In fact, only 2 are leaves, the rest leaf-like stipules. Annual, perennial or evergreen climbers, with small flowers in branched terminal or axillary inflorescences. Sepals minute or absent; 4–5 petals, united into tube at base; 4–5 stamens; ovary inferior. Fruits various, usually comprising 2 fused nutlets or a berry.

Field Madder   *Sherardia arvensis*

Prostrate, glabrous annual to 40 cm. STEMS Spreading. LEAVES 4–6 (including stipules) per whorl, margins with forward-pointing prickles. FLOWERS 3 mm across, in dense clusters with ring of 8–10 leaf-like bracts below; corolla 4–5 mm, mauve-lilac, funnel-shaped, tube *c.*2× as long as lobes. HABITAT Arable fields, pathsides, sand-dunes, waste ground, on well-drained acid or calcareous soils; to 365 m. Dist. Native. Throughout BI, becoming scarce in N Scotland. (All Europe.) Fls May–Oct.

Squinancywort   *Asperula cynanchica*

Slender, prostrate to ascending, much-branched, glabrous perennial to 40 cm. LEAVES Basal leaves soon withering; 4 upper leaves per whorl, linear, glabrous, unequal. FLOWERS 3–4 mm across, in few-flowered inflorescence; corolla pale pink, funnel-shaped, lobes shorter than tube. HABITAT Short, grazed turf, dry calcareous grassland, dunes; to 305 m. DIST. Native. Frequent on calcareous soils of lowland England N to Lake District, S Wales, W Ireland. (Most of Europe except N.) FLS Jun–Jul

Bedstraws *Galium*

See key to *Galium* on p.448.

Woodruff   *Galium odoratum*

Rhizomatous perennial to 45 cm, smelling of hay when dried. STEMS Erect, unbranched, ± glabrous. LEAVES Elliptical, 6–9 per whorl, upper leaves 2.5–4 cm. FLOWERS *c.*6 mm across, in umbel-like inflorescence; corolla pure white, funnel-shaped, tube about as long as lobes. FRUITS With hooked bristles. HABITAT Deciduous woodlands, coppice, hedge banks, on damp calcareous or base-rich soils; to 640 m. DIST. Native. Throughout BI. (Most of Europe, but rare in Mediterranean.) FLS May–Jun.

Northern Bedstraw   *Galium boreale*

Erect, rhizomatous perennial to 45 cm. STEMS Ascending. LEAVES Lanceolate-elliptic, 1–4 cm, 3-veined, 4 per whorl. FLOWERS 3 mm across, i pyramidal inflorescence. FRUITS With hooked bris tles. HABITAT Rough montane grassland, rock slopes, scree, cliffs, stream sides, on calcareous o base-rich soils; to 1065 m. Also river shingle, dunes DIST. Native. N Britain, Wales, Ireland. (Most o Europe, but rare in Mediterranean.) FLS Jul–Aug.

Fen Bedstraw   *Galium uliginosu*

Scrambling perennial to 60 cm. STEMS 4-angled angles rough, with downward-directed prickles LEAVES 5–10 mm, 6–8 per whorl, linear-lanceolate mucronate, margins with backward-directed prick les. FLOWERS 2.5–3 mm across, in narrow inflores cence. HABITAT Calcareous or base-rich marshes fens; to 750 m. DIST. Native. Throughout BI excep NW Scotland, S Ireland. (Most of Europe excep extreme N.) FLS Jul–Aug.

Common Marsh-bedstraw   *Galium palustr*

Ascending or scrambling perennial to 100 cm. Ver variable (*see* 'Note'). STEMS 4-angled. LEAVES 4–6 pe whorl, linear-oblong to elliptic; tip blunt, no mucronate. FLOWERS 3–4.5 mm across, in spreadin inflorescence; pedicels spreading after flowering FRUITS Smooth. HABITAT Marshes, fens, wet wood lands, edges of ponds, lakes, streams and ditches; t 825 m. DIST. Native. Common throughout BI. (Almos all Europe.) FLS Jun–Jul. NOTE The 2 most widesprea forms are ssp. *palustre*, with most leaves 4–10 mr flowers 2–3.5 mm across, fruits 1.2–1.5 mm long; an ssp. *elongatum*, with leaves 12–30 mm, flowers 3.5–5. mm across, fruits 2.5–3.5 mm long.

Slender Marsh-bedstraw   *Galium constrictu*

Prostrate to ascending, glabrous perennial to 40 cm STEMS Slender. LEAVES 5–10 mm, 4–6 per whorl, lin ear with acute but not mucronate tips. FLOWER 2.5 mm across, in inflorescence with ascendin branches; pedicels not spreading after flowering FRUITS With tubercles. SIMILAR SPP. Distinguishe from *G. palustre* by shape of inflorescence, narrowe leaves, pedicels not spreading after flowering, an tuberculate fruits. HABITAT Marshy pond edges, we depressions in grazed grassy commons. DIST Native. Very rare. Virtually confined to New Fores Channel Is. (S and W Europe.) FLS May–Jul.

Hedge Bedstraw   *Galium mollug*

Decumbent to erect, glabrous or pubescent, stoloni erous perennial to 120 cm. Very variable, with severa named subspecies. STEMS 4-angled. LEAVE

Field Madder
Sherardia arvensis

Slender Marsh-bedstraw
Galium constrictum

Squinancywort
Asperula cynanchica

Woodruff
Galium odoratum

Hedge Bedstraw
Galium mollugo

Lady's Bedstraw
Galium verum (description on p.448)

Common Marsh-bedstraw
Galium palustre

Fen Bedstraw
Galium uliginosum

Northern Bedstraw
Galium boreale

all plants 0.3× lifesize; stem details ×2.4

8-25 mm, 5-8 per whorl, linear-obovate with apical point, margins with forward-directed prickles. FLOWERS 2-5 mm across. FRUITS Smooth to wrinkled. HABITAT Hedgerows, scrub, wood margins, rough grassland, road verges, waste ground; to 845 m. DIST. Native. Common throughout BI, but scarce in N Scotland; introduced in Ireland. (All Europe.) FLS Jun-Jul.

Lady's Bedstraw　　　　　*Galium verum*

[*See* illustration previous page.] Decumbent to erect, sparsely pubescent, stoloniferous perennial to 100 cm. LEAVES 6-25 mm, linear, dark green, with revolute margins, 8-12 per whorl. FLOWERS 2-4 mm across, bright yellow. FRUITS Smooth. HABITAT Dry calcareous grassland, hay meadows, hedge banks, dunes, machair, cliff tops, verges; to 780 m. DIST. Native. Common throughout BI. (Most of Europe.) FLS Jul-Aug. NOTE Dwarf prostrate plants with leaves that are longer than internodes, frequent on dunes and cliff tops, are var. *maritimum*. The hybrid with *G. mollugo*, *G. × pomeranicum*, intermediate with pale yellow flowers, is frequent where the parents grow together.

Key to Rubiaceae Bedstraws

	if	then
1	▷ Evergreen scrambler; 4-6 leaves in a whorl; flowers yellowish green, 5 petals; fruit a berry	*Rubia* (p.450)
	▷ 4 petals; fruit a pair of 1-seeded nutlets	Go to ▷ **2**
2	▷ Calyx of 4 distinct teeth; flowers lilac	*Sherardia* (p.446)
	▷ Calyx absent	Go to ▷ **3**
3	▷ Stems and margins of leaves with long, spreading hairs; flowers yellow-green, in tight axillary whorls	*Cruciata* (p.450)
	▷ Plant ± glabrous, or if hairy, only sparsely so; flowers in axillary and terminal cymes	Go to ▷ **4**
4	▷ All leaves in a whorl, ± same length	*Galium* (*see* below)
	▷ Whorls on upper part of stem comprising 2 long and 2 short leaves	*Asperula* (p.446)

Bedstraws *Galium*

	if	then
1	▷ Flowers yellow	*G. verum* (p.448)
	▷ Flowers white	Go to ▷ **2**
2	▷ Leaves 3-veined, 4 in a whorl	*G. boreale* (p.446)
	▷ Leaves 1-veined, 4-8 in a whorl	Go to ▷ **3**
3	▷ Stems smooth or slightly rough on angles	Go to ▷ **4**
	▷ Stems distinctly rough, with recurved prickles on angles	Go to ▷ **9**

	if	then
4	▷ Leaves mucronate	Go to ▷ **5**
	▷ Leaves blunt or acute, not mucronate	Go to ▷ **8**
5	▷ Robust decumbent or erect plants; corolla lobes with fine points, flowers in large terminal inflorescences	*G. mollugo* (p.446)
	▷ Slender decumbent, prostrate or mat-forming plants; corolla lobes acute	Go to ▷ **6**
6	▷ Prickles on leaf margins pointing forwards	*G. saxatile* (p.450)
	▷ Prickles on leaf margins pointing backwards	Go to ▷ **7**
7	▷ Fruit covered with minute, sub-acute tubercles (NW of line from Severn to Humber)	*G. sterneri* (p.450)
	▷ Fruit covered with minute, low, dome-shaped tubercles (S of line Severn to Wash)	*G. pumilum* (p.450)
8	▷ Leaves linear-oblong to lanceolate; inflorescence widest below middle; pedicels spreading widely at fruiting (common)	*G. palustre* (p.446)
	▷ Leaves linear; inflorescence widest near top; pedicels not spreading widely at fruiting (rare)	*G. constrictum* (p.446)
9	▷ Prickles on leaf margins pointing forwards; corolla greenish inside, reddish outside; slender annual	*G. parisiense* (p.450)
	▷ Prickles on leaf margins pointing backwards	Go to ▷ **10**
10	▷ Fruits covered with hooked bristles; scrambling annual (common)	*G. aparine* (p.450)
	▷ Fruits rough or finely wrinkled, not bristly	Go to ▷ **11**
11	▷ Flowers white; perennial (fens, marshes)	*G. uliginosum* (p.446)
	▷ Flowers cream or greenish, not pure white; annuals (rare, arable weeds)	Go to ▷ **12**
12	▷ Flowers in 3-flowered axillary groups; fruit stalks strongly recurved	*G. tricornutum* (p.450)
	▷ Inflorescence 3-9-flowered; fruit stalks straight	*G. spurium* (p.450)

Heath Bedstraw
Galium saxatile

Prostrate, mat-forming perennial to 20 cm. STEMS Numerous non-flowering branches and much-branched ascending flowering shoots. LEAVES 7–10 mm, 6–8 per whorl, *obovate,* mucronate, *margins with forward-pointing prickles.* FLOWERS 3 mm across. FRUITS Glabrous, with pointed tubercles. HABITAT Heath, moorland, grassland, open rocky woodlands, on acid soils; to 1215 m. DIST. Native. Common throughout BI. (W and W-central Europe.) FLS Jun–Aug.

Limestone Bedstraw
Galium sterneri

Prostrate, mat-forming perennial. Similar to *G. saxatile,* but more non-flowering shoots; *leaves* narrower, *oblanceolate* and *prickles on the margins pointing backwards; fruits with high-domed acute tubercles.* HABITAT Short, grazed limestone grassland, scree, limestone pavement; to 975 m. DIST. Native. Restricted to areas of hard limestone upland or basic igneous rocks. S Wales to Orkney, W Ireland. (NW Europe.) FLS Jun–Jul. NOTE Grows together with *G. saxatile* in some upland grasslands, when it can be distinguished by the marginal leaf prickles.

Slender Bedstraw
Galium pumilum EN.

Decumbent perennial to 30 cm. STEMS Prostrate non-flowering and little-branched, erect flowering shoots. LEAVES 14–18 mm, 5–7 per whorl, linear-lanceolate, mucronate, with few backward-pointing prickles on margins. FLOWERS 4 mm across, in spreading inflorescence. FRUITS *With minute rounded tubercles.* HABITAT Short, species-rich chalk and limestone grassland. DIST. Native. Very scarce. S England. (W and central Europe.) FLS Jun–Jul.

Wall Bedstraw
Galium parisiense VU.

Slender, almost prostrate annual to 30 cm. STEMS Rough, with small, downward-directed prickles. LEAVES 3–12 mm, 5–7 per whorl, linear-oblong, *eventually reflexed, with forward-directed marginal prickles.* FLOWERS *Tiny, 0.5 mm across; corolla reddish* outside. FRUITS Glabrous, blackish. HABITAT Old walls, bare patches on dry, open calcareous grassland. DIST. Native. Rare, declining. Mostly East Anglia. (S, W and central Europe.) FLS Jun–Jul.

Cleavers, Goosegrass
Galium aparine

Prostrate, 'sticky', scrambling to erect annual, to 120 cm. STEMS *Very rough, with numerous backward-directed prickles.* LEAVES 12–50 mm, 6–8 per whorl, linear-oblanceolate, margins with backward-directed prickles. FLOWERS In 2–5-flowered axillary inflorescences. FRUITS *4–6 mm, covered with hooked white bristles.* HABITAT Hedgerows, cultivated ground, scrub, banks of streams and rivers, scree, shingle beaches, waste ground, on fertile soils. DIST. Native. Cosmopolitan weed. Abundant throughout BI. (All Europe.) FLS Jun–Aug.

False Cleavers
Galium spurium

Similar to *G. aparine,* but more slender; leaves narrower; *flowers c.1 mm across,* greenish, in 3–9-flowered inflorescence; *fruit smooth, 1.5–3 mm.* HABITAT Weed of arable land. DIST. Introduced. Very rare declining. E England. (Most of Europe.) FLS Jul.

Corn Cleavers
Galium tricornutum CR.

Scrambling annual to 60 cm. Similar to *G. aparine* but stems sharply 4-angled; *inflorescence 3-flowered; pedicels strongly recurved in fruit,* fruits 3–4 mm. papillose. HABITAT Arable weed of cereal crops or calcareous soils. DIST. Archaeophyte. Formerly widespread, now very rare. Lowland England. (S, W and central Europe.) FLS Jun–Sep.

Crosswort
Cruciata laevipes

Erect, *densely pubescent perennial* to 70 cm. LEAVES Pubescent, *yellow-green,* 10–20 mm, 4 per whorl, 3-veined. FLOWERS *In dense axillary clusters; corolla yellow,* 4-lobed. HABITAT Rough grassland, scrub, hedge banks, verges, wood borders, on well-drained neutral or calcareous soils; to 550 m. DIST. Native. Throughout Britain, N to central Scotland; absent from Ireland. (W, central and S Europe.) FLS May–Jun.

Wild Madder
Rubia peregrina

Robust, *scrambling evergreen* perennial to 120 cm. STEMS Glabrous, 4-angled, rough, with backward-directed prickles. LEAVES *Thick, shining, 4–6 per whorl,* 1.5–6 cm, 1-veined, margins with curved prickles. FLOWERS 5 mm across, *corolla* yellowish green 5-*lobed.* FRUITS Berry-like, black. HABITAT Coastal scrub, walls, cliffs, hedge banks. DIST. Native. SW England, Wales, S Ireland. (S and W Europe.) FLS Jun–Aug.

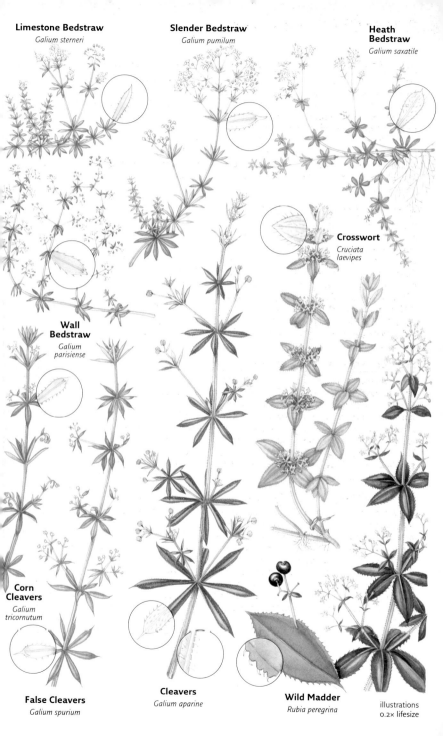

Limestone Bedstraw
Galium sterneri

Slender Bedstraw
Galium pumilum

Heath Bedstraw
Galium saxatile

Crosswort
Cruciata laevipes

Wall Bedstraw
Galium parisiense

Corn Cleavers
Galium tricornutum

False Cleavers
Galium spurium

Cleavers
Galium aparine

Wild Madder
Rubia peregrina

illustrations
0.2× lifesize

ADOXACEAE Moschatel family

Moschatel,
Townhall Clock
Adoxa moschatellina *(NI)

Rhizomatous perennial to 15 cm. STEMS Flowering stems erect, with 2 opposite leaves. LEAVES Ternate, long-stalked. FLOWERS Light green, in 5-flowered cube-shaped head, consisting of 1 terminal and 4 lateral flowers (the townhall clock); terminal flower with 4 corolla lobes, lateral flowers with 5; anthers yellow. HABITAT Woodlands, coppice, lanesides, hedge banks, shaded stream sides, on damp, fertile soils; to 1065 m. DIST. Native. Throughout Britain except NW Scotland; very rare in Ireland. (Most of Europe; restricted to mts in S.) FLS Apr–May.

CAPRIFOLIACEAE Honeysuckles, elders and viburnums

Deciduous or evergreen shrubs or woody climbers (*see* key on p.458). Leaves opposite, stipules usually absent. Flowers bisexual; 5 sepals, fused at base; 5 petals, fused at base, sometimes 2-lipped; 4–5 stamens; ovary inferior. Fruits berry-like, rarely an achene or capsule.

Elder
Sambucus nigra

Deciduous shrub or small tree to 10 m. BARK Deeply fissured, corky. BRANCHES With prominent lenticels. LEAVES With 5 leaflets, these 3–9 cm, ovate (deeply dissected in var. *laciniata*); *stipules absent*. FLOWERS In flat-topped inflorescence; corolla 5 mm across. FRUITS *Black*. HABITAT Woods, scrub, hedgerows, waste ground, roadsides, railway banks, sand-dunes, on fertile soils; to 470 m. DIST. Native. Common throughout BI except extreme N Scotland. (Most of Europe except extreme N.) FLS Aug–Sep.

Red-berried Elder
Sambucus racemosa

Deciduous shrub to 4 m. LEAVES With 5–7 leaflets, these 4–8 cm; *stipules represented by stalked glands*. FLOWERS In dense panicle. FRUITS *Red*. HABITAT Woodland, hedges, waste ground. DIST. Introduced. Naturalised as a garden escape, especially in Scotland. (W, central and E Europe.) FLS Jun–Jul.

Dwarf Elder
Sambucus ebulus

Tall, robust, glabrous, *rhizomatous perennial* to 120 cm. Whole plant has unpleasant smell. LEAVES With 7–13 leaflets, these 5–15 cm, oblong-lanceolate; *stipules large*, conspicuous. FLOWERS In inflorescence with 3 primary rays, *anthers purple*. FRUITS Black. HABITAT Hedgerows, roadsides, waste ground. DIST. Archaeophyte. Infrequent. Scattered throughout BI. (Most of Europe except N.) FLS Jul–Aug.

Guelder Rose
Viburnum opulus

Deciduous shrub to 4 m. STEMS Twigs glabrous buds with scales. LEAVES Blades 5–8 cm, irregularly 3-lobed, glabrous above, deep red in autumn. FLOWERS In inflorescence with *large outer sterile flowers* surrounding smaller fertile ones. FRUITS Red. HABITAT Woods, hedgerows, scrub, fen carr, on neutral and calcareous soils. DIST. Native. Throughout BI becoming scarcer to N. (All Europe except N and parts of Mediterranean.) FLS Jun–Jul.

Wayfaring-tree
Viburnum lantana

Deciduous shrub to 6 m. BRANCHES Twigs and *buds pubescent; buds naked*. LEAVES Blades 5–10 cm, regularly toothed, densely hairy beneath. FLOWERS All fertile. FRUITS Compressed, red becoming black. HABITAT Scrub, wood margins, hedgerows, on dry base-rich or calcareous soils. DIST. Native SE of line from Wash to Severn; naturalised further N. (Central and S Europe.) FLS May–Jun.

Snowberry
Symphoricarpos albus

Suckering, arching deciduous shrub to 3 m. LEAVES Glabrous, simple, entire or deeply lobed. FLOWERS 3–7 in dense terminal spikes; corolla 5–8 mm, pink. FRUIT White. HABITAT Woodland, scrub, hedgerows, waste ground; formerly planted as game cover. DIST. Introduced (native of W North America). Naturalised throughout BI except N Scotland. (Naturalised throughout much of Europe.) FLS Jun–Sep.

Twinflower
Linnaea borealis

Creeping, mat-forming woody perennial to 40 cm. STEMS Slender, pubescent. LEAVES Simple, broadly ovate, 4–16 mm. FLOWERS 2, each with 1 bract, bracteoles; peduncles 3–7 cm; corolla pink, *c*.8 mm, 4 stamens. FRUITS Achene. HABITAT Old pinewoods, pine plantations, creeping over mosses, litter; to 730 m. DIST. Native. Rare, local. NE Scotland. (N Europe.) FLS Jun–Aug.

Honeysuckle
Lonicera periclymenum

[*See* illustration following page.] Scrambling or twining, climbing deciduous shrub to 6 m. LEAVES Ovate, 30–70 mm, sessile or shortly stalked; leaves below inflorescence not fused at base. FLOWERS In terminal heads; corolla 40–50 mm, cream, yellowish purple, deeply 2-lipped, upper lip with 4 lobes, lower lip entire. FRUITS Red berry. HABITAT Woodland, scrub, hedgerows; to 610 m. DIST. Native. Common throughout BI. (W, central and S Europe.) FLS Jun–Sep.

Moschatel
Adoxa moschatellina

Red-berried Elder
Sambucus racemosa

Elder
Sambucus nigra

Dwarf Elder
Sambucus ebulus

Snowberry
Symphoricarpos albus

Twinflower
Linnaea borealis

Wayfaring-tree
Viburnum lantana

Guelder Rose
Viburnum opulus

illustrations
0.6× lifesize

Perfoliate Honeysuckle　　*Lonicera caprifolium*

Similar to *L. periclymenum*, but base of uppermost pairs of leaves below inflorescence fused around stem; berry orange. HABITAT Woods, scrub, hedgerows. DIST. Introduced. Declining. Naturalised in scattered localities throughout Britain. (E, central and S Europe.) FLS Aug–Sep.

Fly Honeysuckle　　*Lonicera xylosteum*

Deciduous bushy shrub to 2 m. BRANCHES Twigs pubescent. LEAVES 30–60 mm, ovate, pubescent, greyish green. FLOWERS In pairs, sessile; corolla 8–15 mm. FRUITS Red berry. HABITAT Naturalised in woods, hedgerows, scrub; possibly native on chalk woodland in W Sussex. DIST. Introduced. Scattered throughout BI. (Most of Europe except parts of extreme N and S.) FLS May–Jun.

Wilson's Honeysuckle　　*Lonicera nitida*

Erect or arching *evergreen* shrub to 1.8 m. LEAVES Small, 6–16 mm, ovate, rounded at base. FLOWERS In axillary pairs, ± regular, 5–7 mm, cream. FRUITS Violet berry. HABITAT Woodland, scrub, hedgerows, waste ground. DIST. Introduced (native of China). Much planted for hedging; naturalised as persistent garden escape, especially in S Britain, Ireland.

VALERIANACEAE Valerians

Annuals or perennials with opposite leaves that lack stipules (*see* key on p.458). Flowers small with inferior ovary; corolla tubular, funnel-shaped, 5-lobed, often spurred or pouched at base; calyx minute or absent, sometimes forming a feathery pappus at fruiting; 1 or 3 stamens.

Common Valerian　　*Valeriana officinalis*

Tall, erect, ± glabrous perennial to 150 cm. Very variable. LEAVES To *c*.20 cm, pinnate with terminal leaflet, leaflets entire or irregularly toothed. FLOWERS In dense terminal inflorescence; corolla *c*.5 mm across, pale pink. HABITAT Marshes, fens, alpine meadows, wet woods; also rough grassland on dry calcareous soils. DIST. Native. Frequent throughout BI. (Most of Europe except extreme S.) FLS Jun–Aug.

Marsh Valerian　　*Valeriana dioica*

Erect, ± glabrous, stoloniferous perennial to 30 cm. LEAVES Basal leaves entire, long-stalked, 2–3 cm; stem leaves sessile, pinnate. FLOWERS Pinkish, dioecious, male *c*.5 mm across, female 2 mm. HABITAT Marshes, fens, wet meadows, wet woodlands.

DIST. Native. Throughout Britain, N to S Scotland; absent from Ireland. (W and central Europe.) FLS May–Jun.

Red Valerian　　*Centranthus ruber*

Erect, glabrous, glaucous perennial to 80 cm. LEAVES Ovate, entire, lower leaves stalked, upper leaves sessile. FLOWERS Red or white, in dense terminal inflorescences; corolla tube 8–10 mm, spur long, 5–12 mm. HABITAT Sea cliffs, waste ground, old walls, buildings. DIST. Introduced. Popular garden plant, naturalised throughout most of BI except N Scotland; (Mediterranean.) FLS Jun–Aug.

Cornsalads *Valerianella*

Small annuals with characteristic repeatedly forked branching stems (*see* key on p.459). Leaves simple entire or sparsely toothed or lobed. Flowers in terminal open inflorescence; corolla neither pouched nor spurred; 3 stamens. Ripe fruits are essential to identify the 5 British species.

Common Cornsalad　　*Valerianella locusta*

HABITAT Disturbed ground, arable land, hedge banks, rocks, cliffs, walls, dunes, shingle. DIST. Native. Frequent throughout BI, but mostly coastal in N. (Most of Europe except N.) FLS Apr–Jun.

Keeled Cornsalad　　*Valerianella carinata*

HABITAT Walls, paths, railways, gardens. DIST. Archaeophyte. Throughout much of S Britain, Ireland, especially SW England. Increasing, more common in SW than *V. locusta*. (S, W and central Europe.) FLS Apr–Jun.

Broad-fruited Cornsalad　*Valerianella rimosa* EN

HABITAT Formerly widespread arable weed on dry sandy or calcareous soils. DIST. Archaeophyte. Rare and declining, now confined to scattered localities in S and E England. (W, central and S Europe.) FLS Jul–Aug.

Narrow-fruited Cornsalad　*Valerianella dentata* EN

HABITAT Arable weed of sandy and calcareous soils. DIST. Archaeophyte. Widespread throughout Britain, local, declining and very rare in Ireland. (Most of Europe except N.) FLS Jun–Jul.

Hairy-fruited Cornsalad　　*Valerianella eriocarpa*

HABITAT Dry, open areas, banks, cliff edges, walls, quarries. DIST. Introduced. Very rare. Dorset, I of Wight, Cornwall. (Mediterranean.) FLS Jun–Jul.

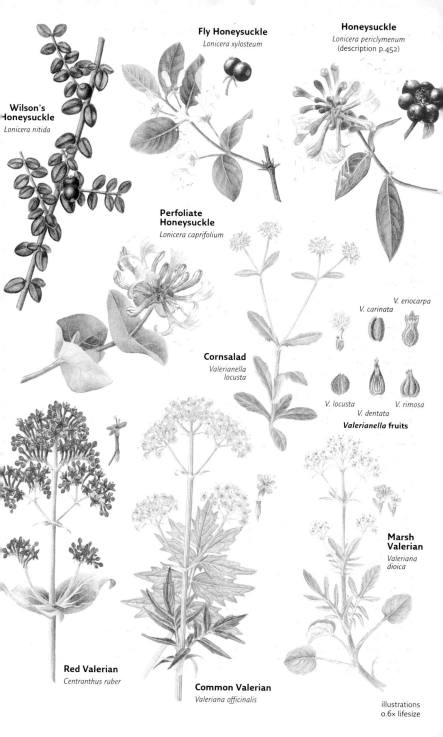

Fly Honeysuckle
Lonicera xylosteum

Honeysuckle
Lonicera periclymenum
(description p.452)

Wilson's Honeysuckle
Lonicera nitida

Perfoliate Honeysuckle
Lonicera caprifolium

Cornsalad
Valerianella locusta

V. eriocarpa

V. carinata

V. locusta

V. rimosa

V. dentata

***Valerianella* fruits**

Marsh Valerian
Valeriana dioica

Red Valerian
Centranthus ruber

Common Valerian
Valeriana officinalis

illustrations
0.6× lifesize

GLOBULARIACEAE & DIPSACACEAE

GLOBULARIACEAE

Globularia
Globularia vulgaris

Erect, glabrous, unbranched perennial to 20 cm.
LEAVES Basal leaves in a rosette, obovate, short-
stalked, simple, with 3 teeth at tip; *stem leaves alternate*, lanceolate, sessile. FLOWERS In tight scabious-
like heads with a whorl of leafy bracts at base; calyx
with 5 teeth; corolla tube 6-8 mm, 2-lipped, pale blue;
4 stamens, protruding; *ovary superior*. SIMILAR SPP.
Distinguished from scabiouses by its alternate leaves
and superior ovary. HABITAT Montane calcareous
grassland, rocks. DIST. *Not BI.* (W Europe, N to Belgium.) FLS Apr-Jul.

DIPSACACEAE Teasels

Herbs with erect stems and opposite leaves (*see* key on
p.459). Flowers in dense heads, surrounded by calyx-
like whorl of bracts (involucral bracts); with or without bracts mixed with flowers (receptacle bracts); each
flower surrounded by tubular epicalyx; calyx small,
cup-shaped or divided into 4-5 segments or with
numerous fine bristles; corolla with 4-5 lobes or 2-
lipped; 2 or 4 stamens, long-protruding; ovary inferior.

Wild Teasel
Dipsacus fullonum

Tall, erect biennial to 200 cm. STEMS Branched,
glabrous, spiny. LEAVES Basal leaves in rosette, withering in 2nd spring, with swollen-based prickles;
stem leaves lanceolate, fused across stem to form
water-collecting cup. FLOWERING HEADS In ovoid
heads; *involucral bracts curving upwards, often as long
as heads; receptacle bracts longer than flowers, spine on
tip straight.* HABITAT Rough grassland, roadsides,
banks of streams and rivers, waste ground. DIST.
Native. Throughout BI, but rare in N Scotland, Ireland. (S, W and central Europe.) FLS Jul-Aug.

Fuller's Teasel
Dipsacus sativus

Similar to *D. fullonum*, but *involucral bracts spreading; receptacle bracts* about as long as flowers, *spine
tip stiff, recurved.* DIST. Introduced (origin uncertain). Rare casual escape from cultivation (formerly
cultivated for use in fulling industry, for raising the
nap on cloth). (Naturalised in S, W and central
Europe.)

Small Teasel
Dipsacus pilosus

Erect, branched biennial to 150 cm. STEMS Angled,
with weak prickles. LEAVES Basal leaves in a rosette,
ovate, long-stalked; stem leaves short-stalked,
upper with pair of basal leaflets. FLOWERS *In spherical heads, 2-2.5 cm*; involucral bracts and bracts

among florets spine-tipped with long silky hairs;
corolla 6-9 mm, white. HABITAT Damp woods,
ditches, stream sides, hedge banks, especially on
calcareous soils. DIST. Native. Rather local, scattered throughout England. (W and central Europe.)
FLS Aug.

Field Scabious
Knautia arvensis

Erect, branched perennial to 100 cm. STEMS Roughly
hairy. LEAVES Basal leaves in overwintering rosette;
stem leaves deeply pinnate, with large terminal lobe.
FLOWERS In heads, 3-4 cm across; *involucral bracts
ovate-lanceolate*, hairy, in 2 rows, shorter than flowers; *outer flowers larger than inner*; calyx cup-shaped,
with 8 narrow teeth; corolla 4-lobed. HABITAT
Rough grassland, hedge banks, roadsides, wood
margins, on dry calcareous soils; to 365 m. DIST.
Native. Throughout BI except N Scotland, W Ireland.
(Most of Europe except Mediterranean.) FLS Jul-Sep.

Devil's-bit Scabious
Succisa pratensis

Erect, branched, sparsely hairy perennial to 100 cm.
LEAVES *Basal leaves ovate-lanceolate*, short-stalked;
stem leaves few, entire or sparsely toothed. FLOWERS
Bluish purple, ± equal in size, in heads, 1.5-2.5 mm
across; involucral bracts broadly lanceolate, in 2-3
rows; calyx cup-shaped, with 5 teeth; *corolla 4-lobed*,
4-7 mm. HABITAT Wet meadows, marshes, fens, wet
heathland, woodland rides, on mildly acid soils; also
chalk and limestone grassland. To 970 m. DIST.
Native. Common throughout BI. (Most of Europe
except extreme N and Mediterranean.) FLS Jun-Oct.

Small Scabious
Scabiosa columbaria

Slender, erect perennial to 70 cm. STEMS Branching,
sparsely hairy. LEAVES Basal leaves stalked, obovate,
variously lobed; stem leaves deeply pinnate, with narrow lobes. FLOWERS Bluish lilac, outer much larger
than inner, in heads, 1.5-3.5 cm across; c.10 involucral bracts, *almost linear*, in 1 row; calyx cup-shaped,
with 5 narrow, spreading teeth; *corolla 5-lobed.* DIST.
(All Europe except N.) HABITAT Common, well-
drained calcareous grassland to 610 m. DIST. Native.
Widespread N to S Scotland, absent Ireland FLS
Jul-Aug.

Scabiosa canescens

Erect, pubescent perennial to 60 cm. Similar to *S.
columbaria*, but *basal leaves grey-downy, lanceolate,
entire; involucral bracts ovate-lanceolate.* HABITAT
Grassy hillsides, rocky ground, scrub, open woodland, on warm calcareous soils. DIST. *Not BI.* (Central and W Europe; rare.) FLS Jul-Sep.

Small Scabious
Scabiosa columbaria

Scabiosa canescens

Devil's-bit Scabious
Succisa pratensis

Wild Teasel
Dipsacus fullonum

Fuller's Teasel
Dipsacus sativus

Globularia
Globularia vulgaris

Small Teasel
Dipsacus pilosus

illustrations
0.6× lifesize

Field Scabious
Knautia arvensis

	if	then
1	▷ Leaves pinnate	*Sambucus* (p.452)
	▷ Leaves simple	Go to ▷ **2**
2	▷ Stems prostrate; flowers in pairs on long pedicels	*Linnaea* (p.452)
	▷ Erect or climbing shrubs	Go to ▷ **3**
3	▷ Flowers numerous, in dense corymb-like inflorescence	*Viburnum* (p.452)
	▷ Inflorescence not corymb-like	Go to ▷ **4**
4	▷ Flowers strongly 2-lipped	*Lonicera* (p.454)
	▷ Flowers ± regular	Go to ▷ **5**
5	▷ Small evergreen shrub; flowers in axillary pairs	*Lonicera* (p.452)
	▷ Deciduous shrub; flowers in terminal spike-like inflorescence	*Symphoricarpos* (p.452)

Key to Valerianaceae Valerians

if	then
▷ Stems forking into 2 at each node; corolla neither spurred nor pouched; calyx not forming pappus; annuals	*Valerianella* (p.454)
▷ Base of corolla pouched; 3 stamens; calyx forming pappus; perennials	*Valeriana* (p.454)
▷ Base of corolla spurred; 1 stamens; calyx forming pappus; perennials	*Centranthus* (p.454)

Key to Cornsalads and Lamb's Lettuces *Valerianella*

	if	then
1	▷ Remains of calyx absent or inconspicuous at apex of fruit; flowers pale blue	Go to ▷ **2**
	▷ Remains of calyx conspicuous as teeth at apex of fruit; flower blue or white	Go to ▷ **3**
2	▷ Fruit compressed, scarcely longer than broad	*V. locusta* (p.454)
	▷ Fruit quadrangular in section, much longer than wide, deeply grooved	*V. carinata* (p.454)
3	▷ Calyx remains 5–6 teeth at apex of fruit; fruit hispid; flowers pale blue	*V. eriocarpa* (p.454)
	▷ Remains of calyx consisting of single main tooth; flowers white	Go to ▷ **4**
4	▷ Main calyx tooth itself distinctly toothed; fruit with 2 distinct ribs	*V. dentata* (p.454)
	▷ Main calyx tooth scarcely toothed; fruit smooth	*V. rimosa* (p.454)

Key to Dipsacaceae Teasels

	if	then
1	▷ Stems spiny; bracts spine-tipped	*Dipsacus* (p.456)
	▷ Stems not spiny; bracts not spine-tipped	Go to ▷ **2**
2	▷ Corolla 5-lobed	*Scabiosa* (p.456)
	▷ Corolla 4-lobed	Go to ▷ **3**
3	▷ Stem leaves entire or weakly toothed; flowers all ± equal in size	*Succisa* (p.456)
	▷ Stem leaves pinnate; outer flowers larger than inner	*Knautia* (p.456)

The largest family of flowering plants in the BI after the grasses (*see* key below and on following pages). The familiar daisy, dandelion- or thistle-like 'flowers' in fact consist of heads of a number of small individual flowers (*florets*).

Each individual floret consists of an inferior ovary with a single style that has a 2-lobed stigma. There are 5 stamens, their anthers joined to form a tube through which the style projects. There are 3 kinds of corolla: *discoid*, in which the corolla is regular and funnel-shaped, with 5 short, triangular corolla lobes; *tubular*, with a long, slender corolla tube that has 5 long, narrow lobes and with the style usually long and protruding; and *ray florets*, where the corolla is fused into a petal-like *ligule*, usually with 3 or 5 teeth at the tip. The calyx is absent or represented by a plume of silky hairs, the pappus. The fruit is a single-seeded *achene*.

The florets are clustered on the expanded tip of the flowering shoot, the *receptacle*, which may be flat or convex and is surrounded by a calyx-like involucre of bracts (*involucral bracts*), the whole head forming the *capitulum*. In addition, the receptacle may have small, inconspicuous, scale-like bracts mixed up among the florets (*receptacle scales*).

Flowering heads are of 3 basic kinds: *ligulate* (dandelion-like), consisting of ray florets only; *discoid* (thistle-like), consisting of disc or tubular florets only; and *radiate* (daisy-like), with disc florets in the middle and ray florets arranged around the periphery. The heads of some discoid species may be rather small and inconspicuous.

Identification depends primarily on a combination of the vegetative characters, the kind of flowering heads, details of the capitulum, the presence or absence of a pappus and details of the achenes.

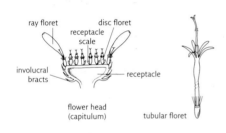

ray floret — disc floret — receptacle scale — involucral bracts — receptacle — flower head (capitulum)

tubular floret

ray floret

disc floret — pappus

if	**then**
▷ Flower heads ligulate, with ray florets only (dandelion-like)	Go to ▷ **A** (p.461)
▷ Flower heads discoid, with tubular florets only:	
▷ Florets in conspicuous thistle-like heads, often purplish or bluish; corolla lobes usually linear, much longer than wide; leaves and/or involucral bracts often spiny	Go to ▷ **B** (p.462)
▷ Leaves and stems with white cottony hairs; leaves simple, entire; flower heads yellowish to pale brown, often small and inconspicuous and aggregated into axillary or terminal heads	Go to ▷ **C** (p.463)
▷ Leaves and stems not covered by white cottony hairs or, if cottony, leaves much divided	Go to ▷ **D** (p.464)
▷ Flower heads radiate, with both ray florets and tubular florets (daisy-like):	
▷ Ray florets yellow	Go to ▷ **E** (p.465)
▷ Ray florets not yellow	Go to ▷ **F** (p.466)

	if	**then**

A. Flower heads ligulate, with ray florets only (dandelion-like)

1	▷ Flower heads yellow or orange	Go to ▷ **2**
	▷ Flower heads blue or purple	Go to ▷ **17**
2	▷ Florets without a pappus of hairs	Go to ▷ **3**
	▷ Florets with a pappus	Go to ▷ **4**
3	▷ Stems branched, leafy	*Lapsana* (p.484)
	▷ Leaves all basal; stems sparsely branched, conspicuously swollen beneath flower heads (extinct in BI)	*Arnoseris* (p.484)
4	▷ All leaves linear-lanceolate, entire	Go to ▷ **5**
	▷ Not all leaves linear-lanceolate or entire	Go to ▷ **6**
5	▷ Involucral bracts in 1 row	*Tragopogon* (p.486)
	▷ Involucral bracts in >1 row	*Scorzonera* (p.486)
6	▷ Flowering stems leafless or with few scale leaves (may have leafy runners)	Go to ▷ **7**
	▷ Flowering stems leafy	Go to ▷ **10**
7	▷ Flowering stems hollow, glabrous	*Taraxacum* (p.492)
	▷ Flowering stems sparsely or distinctly pubescent	Go to ▷ **8**
8	▷ Plant with leafy runners (stolons); underside of leaves white-felted	*Pilosella* (p.492)
	▷ Plant without runners; underside of leaves not white-felted	Go to ▷ **9**
9	▷ Receptacle with small, pale scales (receptacle scales) hidden among florets	*Hypochaeris* (p.484)
	▷ Receptacle without scales among florets	*Leontodon* (p.484)
10	▷ Achenes strongly compressed	Go to ▷ **11**
	▷ Achenes not strongly compressed	Go to ▷ **13**
11	▷ Achenes beaked or markedly narrowed towards apex	Go to ▷ **12**
	▷ Achenes neither beaked nor narrowed towards apex	*Sonchus* (p.488)
12	▷ Involucral bracts in 2 rows; flowering heads with 5 florets	*Mycelis* (p.492)
	▷ Involucral bracts in several rows; flowering heads with ≥6 florets	*Lactuca* (p.488)

CONTINUED OVERLEAF

	if	then
13	▷ Involucral bracts in 2 rows, outer shorter than inner	*Crepis* (p.490)
	▷ Involucral bracts in several rows	Go to ▷ **14**
14	▷ Plant bristly; outer involucral bracts either broad and cordate or narrow and spreading	*Picris* (p.486)
	▷ Plant hairy but not bristly; involucral bracts in irregular rows, outer bracts neither broadly cordate nor narrow and spreading	Go to ▷ **15**
15	▷ Basal leaves pinnately lobed	*Scorzonera* (p.486)
	▷ Basal leaves not pinnately lobed	Go to ▷ **16**
16	▷ Plant stoloniferous	*Pilosella* (p.492)
	▷ Plant not stoloniferous	*Hieracium* (p.490)
17	▷ Florets without a pappus of hairs	*Cichorium* (p.482)
	▷ Florets with a pappus of hairs	Go to ▷ **18**
18	▷ Stem leaves lanceolate, sheathing	*Tragopogon* (p.486)
	▷ Stem leaves lobed and toothed (rare Scottish alpine)	*Cicerbita* (p.486)

B. Flower heads discoid; florets in conspicuous thistle-like heads, often purplish or bluish; corolla lobes usually linear, much longer than wide; leaves and/or involucral bracts often spiny

1	▷ Heads red, purplish or blue	Go to ▷ **2**
	▷ Heads predominantly yellowish (note that the florets of *Carlina* are purple but the large yellow involucral bracts make the heads look straw-coloured and it keys out here)	Go to ▷ **11**
2	▷ Florets in tight spherical heads, 4–6 cm across, blue to grey-blue	*Echinops* (p.476)
	▷ Florets not in tight spherical heads	Go to ▷ **3**
3	▷ Basal leaves large, ovate, not spiny; heads globular; involucral bracts spreading, hook-tipped; fruiting heads forming a 'bur'	*Arctium* (p.476)
	▷ Plant not like this	Go to ▷ **4**
4	▷ Pappus hairs feathery, with slender branches from base (visible to naked eye or use lens)	Go to ▷ **5**
	▷ Pappus hairs unbranched (may be rough) or absent	Go to ▷ **7**
5	▷ Leaf margins spiny	*Cirsium* (p.478)
	▷ Leaf margins toothed but not spiny	Go to ▷ **6**

if	then

6   ▷ Flower heads clustered in groups of 4–10; leaves distantly toothed   *Saussurea* (p.476)

     ▷ Flowers usually solitary; leaves fringed with fine, sharp teeth   *Cirsium* (p.478)

7   ▷ Pappus absent or very short; involucral bracts with apical section fringed with teeth or spine-tipped and more or less distinct from basal portion   *Centaurea* (p.469)

     ▷ Pappus longer than achenes   Go to ▷ **8**

8   ▷ Leaves and involucral bracts spiny   Go to ▷ **9**

     ▷ Leaves and involucral bracts not spiny, leaves pinnately lobed   *Serratula* (p.480)

9   ▷ Leaves glabrous, conspicuously white-veined above; stem without spiny wings   *Silybum* (p.480)

     ▷ Leaves not conspicuously white-veined above; stem with spiny wings   Go to ▷ **10**

10   ▷ Leaves and stem covered with dense cottony white hairs   *Onopordum* (p.480)

     ▷ Leaves and stems not white   *Carduus* (p.476)

11   ▷ Leaves spiny; involucral bracts yellow, spreading   *Carlina* (p.476)

     ▷ Leaves not spiny; involucral bracts spine-tipped   Go to ▷ **12**

12   ▷ Pappus hairs feathery; involucral bracts ending in single spine   *Cirsium* (p.478)

     ▷ Pappus of hairs absent; involucral bracts ending in branched spine   *Centaurea* (p.480)

C. Flower heads discoid; leaves and stems with white cottony hairs; leaves simple, entire; flower heads yellowish to pale brown, often small and inconspicuous, and aggregated into axillary or terminal heads

1   ▷ Pappus absent (very rare, coast of SE Ireland only)   *Otanthus* (p.504)

     ▷ Florets with pappus   Go to ▷ **2**

2   ▷ Involucral bracts golden yellow, petal-like, curved back in fruit   *Helichrysum* (p.496)

     ▷ Involucral bracts not golden yellow, not curved back in fruit   Go to ▷ **3**

CONTINUED OVERLEAF

if	**then**

3   ▷ Plant with long, leafy stolons and basal rosette of obovate leaves; stem leaves erect; flowering heads in dense terminal cluster   *Antennaria* (p.492)

    ▷ Plant without long, leafy stolons and basal rosette of obovate leaves   Go to ▷ **4**

4   ▷ Erect perennial, 30–100 cm tall; heads in terminal clusters; involucral bracts shining white   *Anaphalis* (p.492)

    ▷ Annuals or perennials; heads in elongated panicles or axillary clusters; involucral bracts straw-coloured or brownish   *Filago, Gnaphalium* (p.494)

D. Flower heads discoid; leaves and stems not covered by white cottony hairs or, if cottony, leaves much divided

1   ▷ Leaves large, all basal, rounded to cordate, long-stalked   Go to ▷ **2**

    ▷ Leaves not all basal and cordate   Go to ▷ **3**

2   ▷ Leaves 10–90 cm across, often appearing after flowering; flower heads in racemes   *Petasites* (p.512)

    ▷ Leaves to 4 cm across; heads solitary (rare alpine)   *Homogyne* (p.514)

3   ▷ All leaves alternate   Go to ▷ **4**

    ▷ At least lower leaves opposite   Go to ▷ **11**

4   ▷ Leaves pinnate or pinnately divided; flowering heads small, inconspicuous, usually in long, loose inflorescences   *Artemisia, Seriphidium* (p.504)

    ▷ If flowering heads small and inconspicuous, then leaves not pinnately divided   Go to ▷ **5**

5   ▷ Leaves simple, entire or toothed   Go to ▷ **6**

    ▷ Leaves pinnately lobed or divided   Go to ▷ **8**

6   ▷ Leaves glabrous   *Aster* (p.500)

    ▷ Leaves not glabrous   Go to ▷ **7**

7   ▷ Heads ≥8 mm across, in corymb-like clusters; leaves ovate   *Inula* (p.496)

    ▷ Heads small, 3–5 mm across, in long panicles (minute, pale ray florets may be present); leaves linear-lanceolate   *Conyza* (p.498)

8   ▷ Florets with pappus of hairs   *Senecio* (p.508)

    ▷ Florets without pappus of hairs   Go to ▷ **9**

	if	**then**
9	▷ Leaves repeatedly divided into linear segments; receptacle conical	*Matricaria* (p.506)
	▷ Leaves not repeatedly divided into linear segments; receptacle ± flat	Go to ▷ **10**
10	▷ Flowering stems erect, >50 cm; leaves 15–25 cm, 1–2-pinnate	*Tanacetum* (p.502)
	▷ Stems procumbent, <30 cm; leaves 2–5 cm, deeply toothed or pinnately lobed, sheathing at base	*Cotula* (p.508)
11	▷ Male and female flowering heads separate on same plant, terminal heads male only, in elongated racemes; leaves deeply divided	*Ambrosia* (p.514)
	▷ Flowering heads hermaphrodite	Go to ▷ **12**
12	▷ Florets pale pink; pappus of hairs	*Eupatorium* (p.516)
	▷ Florets yellow; pappus of 2–4 stiff, barbed awns	*Bidens* (p.516)

E. Flower heads radiate, with both ray florets and tubular florets (daisy-like); ray florets yellow

1	▷ Flowering heads solitary, terminal, appearing before leaves; leaves large, circular, cordate; flowering stems with scale leaves	*Tussilago* (p.512)
	▷ Plant not as above	Go to ▷ **2**
2	▷ All leaves alternate	Go to ▷ **3**
	▷ At least lower leaves opposite	Go to ▷ **10**
3	▷ Florets with pappus of hairs	Go to ▷ **4**
	▷ Pappus absent	Go to ▷ **8**
4	▷ Involucral bracts in 2 or more overlapping rows, progressively shorter towards outside	Go to ▷ **5**
	▷ Involucral bracts in 1 or 2 rows, all of equal length or with a few much shorter bracts at base	Go to ▷ **7**
5	▷ Flowering heads 5–10 mm across, inflorescence usually elongated	*Solidago* (p.498)
	▷ Flowering heads ≥10 mm across, solitary or inflorescence not elongated	Go to ▷ **6**

CONTINUED OVERLEAF

	if	then
6	▷ Pappus of an inner row of hairs and outer row of scales	*Pulicaria* (p.498)
	▷ Pappus of 1 row of hairs	*Inula* (p.496)
7	▷ Heads ≥4 cm across, involucral bracts in 2 equal rows	*Doronicum* (p.512)
	▷ Heads ≤3.5 cm across, involucral bracts in 1 row or with a few much shorter basal bracts	*Senecio* (p.474) *Tephroseris* (p.510)
8	▷ Flowering heads ≥10 cm across, receptacle with small scales among florets	*Helianthus* (p.514)
	▷ Flowering heads <6 cm across	Go to ▷ **9**
9	▷ Leaves green, deeply divided into narrow, toothed lobes, densely hairy beneath; receptacle scales present	*Anthemis* (p.506)
	▷ Leaves glaucous, toothed or pinnately lobed, glabrous; receptacle scales absent	*Chrysanthemum* (p.502)
10	▷ Florets without a pappus of hairs	*Helianthus* (p.514)
	▷ Pappus of 1 row of hairs	*Arnica* (p.516)

F. Flower heads radiate, with both ray florets and tubular florets (daisy-like); ray florets not yellow

	if	then
1	▷ Leaves opposite	*Galinsoga* (p.516)
	▷ Leaves alternate or all basal	Go to ▷ **2**
2	▷ Florets with pappus of hairs	Go to ▷ **3**
	▷ Pappus of hairs absent	Go to ▷ **5**
3	▷ Ray florets in 1 row	*Aster* (p.500)
	▷ Ray florets in 2 or more rows	Go to ▷ **4**
4	▷ Flowering heads solitary or in lax inflorescences; ray florets conspicuous, spreading	*Erigeron* (p.498)
	▷ Flowering heads in elongated panicles; ray florets tiny, pale, inconspicuous, erect	*Conyza* (p.498)
5	▷ Leaves all basal; flowering heads solitary	*Bellis* (p.502)
	▷ Leaves not all basal	Go to ▷ **6**
6	▷ Leaves finely divided into narrow, linear segments	Go to ▷ **7**
	▷ Leaves not finely divided into narrow segments	Go to ▷ **8**

if	then
7 ▷ Flowering heads 4–6 mm across, 5 ray florets	***Achillea*** (p.502)
▷ Flowering heads ≥12 mm across, >10 ray florets	**Chamomile, Mayweeds** (p.506)
8 ▷ Stem leaves pinnately lobed	***Tanacetum*** (p.502)
▷ Stem leaves not pinnately lobed	Go to ▷ **9**
9 ▷ Basal leaves linear-lanceolate, margins toothed; flowering heads 12–18 mm across	***Achillea*** (p.502)
▷ Basal leaves rounded, long-stalked, shallowly lobed or toothed; heads ≥25 mm across	***Leucanthemum*** (p.502)

Key to Thistles *Carduus*

Thistles with simple (unbranched) pappus hairs and a bristly receptacle.

if	then
1 ▷ Heads ovoid or hemispherical; corolla 2-lipped	Go to ▷ **2**
▷ Heads oblong-cylindrical; corolla equally 5-lobed	Go to ▷ **3**
2 ▷ Heads 3–5 cm across, usually solitary, drooping; involucral bracts lanceolate, narrowed just above base; middle outer bracts strongly reflexed	***C. nutans*** (p.478)
▷ Heads 1–3 cm across, solitary or clustered, erect; involucral bracts not narrowed just above base; tips of outer bracts recurved	***C. crispus*** (p.478)
3 ▷ Stems continuously winged to just beneath heads; 2–10 heads in a cluster	***C. tenuiflorus*** (p.476)
▷ Stems bare beneath heads; heads solitary or 2–3 per cluster	***C. pycnocephalus*** (p.476)

Thistles with a pappus of feathery hairs.

	if	then
1	▷ Flowering heads purple	Go to ▷ **2**
	▷ Flowering heads yellow	**C. oleraceum** (p.478)
2	▷ Plant stemless; heads sessile in middle of leaf rosette	**C. acaule** (p.480)
	▷ Plant with elongated stems	Go to ▷ **3**
3	▷ Upper surface of leaves bristly, dull	Go to ▷ **4**
	▷ Upper surface of leaves not bristly, surface often shining	Go to ▷ **5**
4	▷ Stem with discontinuous spiny wings	**C. vulgare** (p.478)
	▷ Stem not winged	**C. eriophorum** (p.478)
5	▷ Stem with continuous spiny wings	**C. palustre** (p.480)
	▷ Stem not winged	Go to ▷ **6**
6	▷ Plant much branched; leaf lobes with strong spines; heads 1.5-2.5 cm	**C. arvense** (p.480)
	▷ Plant usually unbranched; leaves without strong spines; heads 2.5-5 cm	Go to ▷ **7**
7	▷ Leaves densely white-felted beneath; heads 3.5-5 cm	**C. heterophyllum** (p.478)
	▷ Leaves at most with white cottony hairs beneath; heads 2.5-3 cm	Go to ▷ **8**
8	▷ Basal leaves toothed, white cottony beneath	**C. dissectum** (p.478)
	▷ Basal leaves deeply pinnately lobed, green beneath	**C. tuberosum** (p.478)

Key to Knapweeds and Star-thistles *Centaurea*

	if	then
1	▷ Involucral bracts without strong spines	Go to ▷ **2**
	▷ Involucral bracts with strong spines	Go to ▷ **7**
2	▷ Flowers purple	Go to ▷ **3**
	▷ Flowers blue	Go to ▷ **6**
3	▷ Heads small, involucre 3–8 mm across	*C. paniculata* • (p.482)
	▷ Heads all ≥10 mm across at level of involucre	Go to ▷ **4**
4	▷ Apical portion of involucral bracts separated from basal portion by distinct constriction	Go to ▷ **5**
	▷ Apical portion of involucral bracts not separated from basal portion by distinct constriction	*C. scabiosa* (p.480)
5	▷ Apical portion of involucral bracts blackish, deeply and regularly toothed	*C. nigra* (p.482)
	▷ Apical portion of involucral bracts brown, thin, papery, jagged at tip	*C. jacea* • (p.482)
6	▷ Basal leaves absent at flowering; annual	*C. cyanus* (p.482)
	▷ Basal leaves simple, entire, present at flowering; perennial	*C. montana* (p.480)
7	▷ Flowers yellow; stems winged	*C. solstitialis* (p.482)
	▷ Flowers purple; stems not winged	Go to ▷ **8**
8	▷ Apical spine of bract >10 mm, much longer than laterals	*C. calcitrapa* (p.482)
	▷ Apical spine of bract <5 mm, spines ± same length	*C. aspera* (p.482)

Key to Sow-thistles *Sonchus*

1	▷ Involucre glabrous or with few sparse hairs; annual	Go to ▷ **2**
	▷ Involucre densely covered by yellow or blackish glandular hairs; perennial	Go to ▷ **3**
2	▷ Stem leaves with pointed, spreading auricles; achenes wrinkled between ribs	*S. oleraceus* (p.488)
	▷ Stem leaves with spiny, rounded auricles; achenes smooth between ribs	*S. asper* (p.488)
3	▷ Glands on involucre yellow	*S. arvensis* (p.488)
	▷ Glands on involucre blackish	*S. palustris* (p.488)

	if	then
1	▷ Flowering stems leafy	Go to ▷ **2**
	▷ Flowering stems leafless	**C. praemorsa** (p.490)
2	▷ Lower stem leaves deeply lobed	Go to ▷ **3**
	▷ Lower stem leaves entire or coarsely toothed, not deeply lobed	Go to ▷ **8**
3	▷ At least some achenes distinctly beaked (with stalk between seed and pappus) *at maturity*	Go to ▷ **4**
	▷ All achenes not beaked	Go to ▷ **6**
4	▷ Heads drooping in bud; inner achenes long-beaked, outer short-beaked or beak absent	**C. foetida** (p.490)
	▷ Heads not drooping in bud; all achenes with beaks same length	Go to ▷ **5**
5	▷ Basal lobes of stem leaves clasping stem; beak at least as long as basal part	**C. vesicaria** (p.490)
	▷ Base of stem leaves not clasping; beak short	**C. tectorum** (p.490)
6	▷ Inner surface of involucral bracts glabrous; heads 10-13 mm across	**C. capillaris** (p.490)
	▷ Inner surface of involucral bracts with white silky hairs; heads 15-45 mm across	Go to ▷ **7**
7	▷ Heads 30-45 mm across; achenes with 13-20 ribs	**C. biennis** (p.490)
	▷ Heads 15-20 mm across; achenes with 10 ribs	**C. tectorum** (p.490)
8	▷ Leaves strongly toothed; pappus yellow-white, stiff	**C. paludosa** (p.490)
	▷ Leaves entire or remotely toothed; pappus white, soft	**C. mollis** (p.490)

Key to Cudweeds *Filago* and *Gnaphalium*

if	then
Outer involucral bracts soft, greenish; ± woolly almost to tip	*Filago*
Outer involucral bracts thin, dry, brownish; glabrous or woolly at base only	*Gnaphalium*

	if	**then**

Filago

1 ▷ 2–8 heads in each cluster; tips of involucral bracts blunt — Go to ▷ **2**

▷ 8–40 heads in each cluster; tips of involucral bracts with long, fine points — Go to ▷ **4**

2 ▷ Leaves linear, uppermost much longer than clusters — *F. gallica* (p.494)

▷ Leaves lanceolate, uppermost not overtopping heads — Go to ▷ **3**

3 ▷ Leaves erect, appressed to stem; involucral bracts glabrous at tips — *F. minima* (p.494)

▷ Leaves erect but not closely appressed to stem; involucral bracts woolly to tips — *F. arvensis* • (p.494)

4 ▷ Leaves widest below middle, upper leaves not overtopping clusters — *F. vulgaris* (p.494)

▷ Leaves widest above middle, some leaves overtopping clusters — Go to ▷ **5**

5 ▷ Plant yellowish woolly, ± erect; tips of outer involucral bracts reddish purple when young; clusters overtopped by 1–2 leaves — *F. lutescens* (p.494)

▷ Plant white woolly; tips of outer involucral bracts recurved, yellowish; clusters overtopped by 2–4 leaves — *F. pyramidata* (p.494)

Gnaphalium

1 ▷ Heads in tight, globose terminal clusters — Go to ▷ **2**

▷ Heads in elongated, spike-like inflorescences — Go to ▷ **4**

2 ▷ Heads overtopped by upper leaves — *G. uliginosum* (p.496)

▷ Heads not overtopped by upper leaves — Go to ▷ **3**

3 ▷ Upper and lower surfaces of leaves white-woolly, leaves not decurrent — *G. luteoalbum* (p.496)

▷ Upper surface of leaves green, lower white-woolly, leaves decurrent — *G. undulatum* (p.496)

4 ▷ Short tufted alpine; 1–7 heads in short spike — *G. supinum* (p.494)

▷ Erect plant to >12 cm, >10 heads in elongated, spike-like inflorescence — Go to ▷ **5**

5 ▷ Leaves 1-veined; spike >½ length of stem — *G. sylvaticum* (p.494)

▷ Leaves 3-veined; spike *c.*¼ length of stem — *G. norvegicum* (p.494)

	if	**then**
1	▷ Ray florets absent	Go to ▷ **2**
	▷ Ray florets present	Go to ▷ **3**
2	▷ Leaves ovate; fleshy maritime plant	***A. tripolium* var. *flosculosus*** (p.500)
	▷ Leaves linear, numerous; not fleshy maritime plant	***A. linosyris*** (p.500)
3	▷ Glabrous fleshy maritime plant	***A. tripolium*** (p.500)
	▷ Plant neither glabrous nor fleshy	Go to ▷ **4**
4	▷ Upper part of stem and leaves densely glandular-hairy; heads reddish purple	***A. novae-angliae*** (p.500)
	▷ Stems and leaves without glandular hairs; heads blue, violet or whitish	Go to ▷ **5**
5	▷ Base of upper stem leaves more or less clasping stem	Go to ▷ **6**
	▷ Upper stem leaves not clasping stem; heads whitish	***A. lanceolatus*** (p.500)
6	▷ Involucral bracts whitish with green centre in upper half	***A. × versicolor*** (p.500)
	▷ Upper half of involucral bracts mainly greenish	Go to ▷ **7**
7	▷ Middle stem leaves 2.5–5× as long as wide; outer involucral bracts ≤¾ as long as inner	***A. × versicolor*** (p.500)
	▷ Middle stem leaves 4–10× as long as broad; outer involucral bracts about as long as inner	Go to ▷ **8**
8	▷ Outer involucral bracts widest at or just above middle, with conspicuously green apical half; heads 25–50 mm across	***A. novi-belgii*** (p.500)
	▷ Outer involucral bracts widest below middle; heads 15–25 mm across	***A. × salignus*** (p.500)

Key to Mugworts *Artemisia* and *Seriphidium*

	if	then
1	▷ Dwarf alpine, <10 cm tall; 1–2 heads (very rare, Scotland)	*A. norvegica* (p.504)
	▷ Not dwarf alpine; heads numerous	Go to ▷ **2**
2	▷ Upper surface of leaves glabrous, lower surface pubescent or not	Go to ▷ **3**
	▷ Upper surface of leaves densely white-pubescent	Go to ▷ **5**
3	▷ Leaf lobes >2 mm wide	Go to ▷ **4**
	▷ Leaf lobes *c.*1 mm wide	*A. campestris* (p.504)
4	▷ Tufted; stems becoming glabrous, branches erect; flowers Jul-Sep	*A. vulgare* (p.504)
	▷ Rhizomatous; stems borne singly, persistently hairy; branches arching; flowers Oct-Nov	*A. verlotiorum* (p.504)
5	▷ Leaf lobes ≤1 mm wide, strongly aromatic; heads 1–2 mm across	*S. maritimum* (p.504)
	▷ Leaf lobes ≥2 mm wide	Go to ▷ **6**
6	▷ Tufted, aromatic; heads 3–5 mm across	*A. absinthium* (p.504)
	▷ Rhizomatous, not aromatic; heads 4–10 mm across	*A. stelleriana* (p.504)

Key to Chamomile and Mayweeds *Chamaemelum*, *Matricaria*, *Anthemis* and *Tripleurospermum*

	if	then
1	▷ Flowering heads discoid, with disc florets only	*Matricaria discoidea* (p.506)
	▷ Flowering heads radiate, with both ray florets and disc florets	Go to ▷ **2**
2	▷ Ray florets yellow	*Anthemis tinctoria* (p.506)
	▷ Ray florets white	Go to ▷ **3**
3	▷ Receptacle scales present	Go to ▷ **4**
	▷ Receptacle scales absent	Go to ▷ **6**

CONTINUED OVERLEAF

	if	then
4	▷ Prostrate perennial; tube of disc florets not flattened or winged; achenes ribbed on only 1 face	***Chamaemelum*** (p.506)
	▷ Erect annuals; tube of disc florets flattened; achenes ribbed on both faces	Go to ▷ **5**
5	▷ Plant foetid, glabrous or sparsely hairy; receptacle scales linear-acute; involucral bracts whitish with green midrib	***Anthemis cotula*** (p.506)
	▷ Plant aromatic, pubescent or woolly; receptacle scales lanceolate; involucral bracts all green	***Anthemis arvensis*** (p.506)
6	▷ Heads with ray florets soon reflexed; receptacle conical from first, hollow	***Matricaria recutita*** (p.506)
	▷ Heads with ray florets spreading; receptacle solid, flat becoming conical in fruit	Go to ▷ **7**
7	▷ Erect annual; leaf segments not fleshy; achenes with ribs clearly separated, oil glands almost circular (lens required) (both inland and coastal)	***Tripleurospermum inodorum*** (p.506)
	▷ Prostrate perennial; leaf segments blunt, rather fleshy; achenes with ribs scarcely separated, oil glands >2× as long as wide (coastal only)	***Tripleurospermum maritimum*** (p.506)

Key to Ragworts *Senecio*

	if	then
1	▷ At least some leaves deeply lobed ≥halfway to midrib	Go to ▷ **2**
	▷ Leaves undivided, margins entire or remotely toothed	Go to ▷ **11**
2	▷ Leaves densely white-felted beneath or woolly	***S. cineraria*** (p.508)
	▷ Leaves glabrous or sparsely hairy beneath	Go to ▷ **3**
3	▷ Glandular hairs absent	Go to ▷ **4**
	▷ Inflorescence and usually leaves and stems with glandular hairs	Go to ▷ **10**

	if	**then**
4	▷ Heads with ray florets conspicuous, not revolute	Go to ▷ **5**
	▷ Heads with ray florets absent or short, ≤7 mm, revolute	Go to ▷ **9**
5	▷ Outer involucral bracts without black tips	Go to ▷ **6**
	▷ At least outer involucral bracts with black tips	Go to ▷ **8**
6	▷ Stem leaves deeply pinnately lobed, terminal lobe small, narrow, acute, margins revolute, whole surface grey-pubescent beneath	*S. erucifolius* (p.508)
	▷ Stem leaves irregularly lobed, glabrous or sparsely hairy on veins beneath, terminal lobe blunt	Go to ▷ **7**
7	▷ Stem leaves with terminal lobe not much broader than laterals; inflorescence dense so that neighbouring heads in contact or overlapping	*S. jacobaea* (p.508)
	▷ Stem leaves with large, broad terminal lobe and smaller laterals; inflorescence wide-spreading so that neighbouring heads not in contact	*S. aquaticus* (p.508)
8	▷ Leaves deeply lobed, flat, ± glabrous	*S. squalidus* (p.510)
	▷ Leaves shortly lobed, undulate, pubescent	*S. vernalis* (p.510)
9	▷ Heads 4–5 mm across; ray florets usually absent or, if present, ≤5 mm	*S. vulgaris* (p.510)
	▷ Heads to 15 mm across, radiate; ray florets 4–7 mm	*S. cambrensis* (p.510)
10	▷ Stem and leaves with sticky glands; heads 10–15 mm across; achenes glabrous	*S. viscosus* (p.510)
	▷ Stem and leaves sparsely glandular; heads 5–6 mm across; achenes pubescent	*S. sylvaticus* (p.510)
11	▷ 5–8 ray florets	Go to ▷ **12**
	▷ >8 ray florets	Go to ▷ **13**
12	▷ Plant stoloniferous; leaves glabrous; 6–8 ray florets	*S. fluviatilis* (p.508)
	▷ Stolons short or absent; leaves hairy beneath, 5–6 ray florets	*S. nemorensis* • (p.508)
13	▷ Leaves linear, <5 mm wide, glabrous; base of plant often woody	*S. inaequidens* (p.510)
	▷ Leaves elliptical, >5 mm wide, white cottony beneath	*S. paludosus* (p.508)

ASTERACEAE (COMPOSITAE)
Composites

Blue Globe-thistle
Echinops bannaticus

Tall, erect biennial or perennial to 1.25 m. STEMS *Pubescent, without glandular hairs.* LEAVES Pinnately lobed, with spiny teeth, upper side with glandular hairs. FLOWERING HEADS Spherical, comprising 1-flowered capitula aggregated together; *involucral bracts without glandular hairs; corolla blue.* HABITAT Roadsides, waste ground. DIST. Introduced. Popular garden plant occurring naturalised as escape. (SE Europe.) FLS Jul-Aug.

Glandular Globe-thistle
Echinops sphaerocephalus

Similar to *E. bannaticus*, but taller, to 2.5 m; *upper part of stems with glandular hairs; involucral bracts with dense, stalked glands; corolla greyish white.* HABITAT Roadsides, railway embankments, waste ground. DIST. Introduced. Naturalised as casual garden escape. (S and central Europe.) FLS Jul-Aug.

Carline Thistle
Carlina vulgaris

Erect, thistle-like biennial or monocarpic perennial to 60 cm. LEAVES Pinnately lobed, spiny; basal leaves cottony beneath. FLOWERING HEADS 2-4 cm across, 1-3 per inflorescence; *involucral bracts spiny, inner longer than outer, straw-coloured and stiffly spreading,* looking like ray florets. HABITAT Dry calcareous grassland, coastal cliffs, dunes; to 455 m. DIST. Native. Throughout BI, but mostly coastal in SW, Wales, Scotland. (Most of Europe except extreme N.) FLS Jul-Oct.

Burdocks *Arctium*
Robust biennials with erect, much-branched stems. Lower leaves are large, stalked, ovate, cordate, simple and untoothed. Flowering heads are globose, covered with numerous stiff, hooked involucral bracts (the burs); corolla is purple. Fruiting heads are dispersed by animals. Rather a difficult group, about which the experts differ!

Greater Burdock
Arctium lappa

Robust, much-branched, to 130 cm. LEAVES *Petioles solid.* FLOWERING HEADS 3-4 cm across, long-stalked, in corymb-like inflorescence. HABITAT Stream sides, roadsides, field borders, waste ground. DIST. Archaeophyte. Widespread in England N to Humber; rare Wales, SW England; absent from Scotland, Ireland. (Most of Europe except extreme N.) FLS Jul-Sep.

Lesser Burdock
Arctium minu[s]

LEAVES *Petioles hollow.* FLOWERING HEADS 15-32 ×
11-24 mm, those at ends of inflorescence sessile o[r]
short-stalked; middle involucral bracts ≤1.6 m[m]
wide; involucre shorter or longer than corolla[;]
corolla glandular-hairy or glabrous. HABITAT Woo[d]
margins, roadside verges, hedgerows, scrub, dunes[,]
waste ground; to 390 m. DIST. Native. Throughou[t]
BI. (Most of Europe except extreme N.) FLS Jul-Sep[.]

Wood Burdock
Arctium nemorosu[m]

Similar to, and confused with, *A. minus*, but flowerin[g]
heads larger, 27-40 × 19-29 mm; terminal heads o[f]
inflorescence sessile; middle involucral bracts 1.7[-]
2.5 mm wide; corolla glabrous, shorter than involucr[e.]
HABITAT Open woodlands, chiefly on calcareous soils[.]
DIST. Native. Distribution unclear, but probably rare o[r]
absent in SW England, Ireland. (Much of Europe, bu[t]
rare in S and N.) FLS Jul-Sep. *Not illustrated.*

Alpine Saw-wort
Saussurea alpina *(N[)]

Erect, stoloniferous perennial to 45 cm. LEAVES Ovate[-]
lanceolate, *sharply toothed*, with white cottony hair[s]
beneath, *not spiny.* FLOWERING HEADS ± sessile, 15[-]
20 mm, 4-10 forming inflorescence; *involucral bract[s]
not spiny*, purplish, inner with long hairs; florets longe[r]
than bracts, white below, purplish above; *pappus hair[s]
branched.* HABITAT Damp alpine and maritime cliff[s,]
ledges, scree, on calcareous or base-rich rocks; to 117[5]
m. DIST. Native. NW Scotland; rare elsewhere. (N[]
Europe, mts of central and S Europe.) FLS Aug-Sep[.]

Thistles *Carduus*
See key to *Carduus* on p.467.

Slender Thistle
Carduus tenuiflor[us]

Erect annual or biennial to 100 cm. STEMS *With con[-]
tinuous broad, spiny wings right up to heads.* LEAVE[S]
Cottony beneath. FLOWERING HEADS *Cylindrica[l],*
sessile, *3-10 forming tight clusters*; inner involucra[l]
bracts as long as or longer than florets. HABITA[T]
Roadsides, waste ground close to sea, coastal grass[-]
land, sea walls, sea-bird colonies. DIST. Nativ[e.]
Coastal areas of BI except W Scotland, W Irelan[d;]
casual inland. (W Europe.) FLS Jun-Aug.

Plymouth Thistle
Carduus pycnocephal[us]

Similar to *C. tenuiflorus*, but *spiny wings on stem di[s-]
continuous and not reaching as far as heads; heads soli[-]
tary or 2-3 per cluster*; inner involucral bracts shorte[r]
than florets. HABITAT/DIST. Introduced. Naturalise[d]
on open limestone cliff at Plymouth Hoe, Devon; rar[e]
casual elsewhere. (S and SE Europe.) FLS Jun-Aug[.]

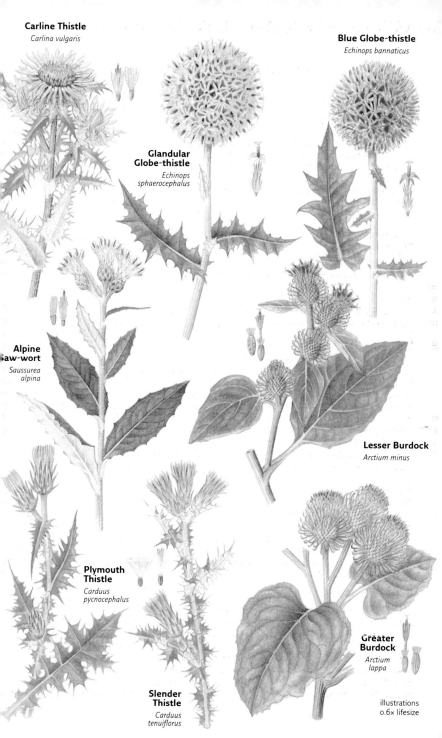

Carline Thistle
Carlina vulgaris

Blue Globe-thistle
Echinops bannaticus

Glandular Globe-thistle
Echinops sphaerocephalus

Alpine Saw-wort
Saussurea alpina

Lesser Burdock
Arctium minus

Plymouth Thistle
Carduus pycnocephalus

Greater Burdock
Arctium lappa

Slender Thistle
Carduus tenuiflorus

illustrations
0.6× lifesize

Welted Thistle
Carduus crispus

Tall, branched biennial thistle to 150 cm. STEMS Spiny, winged margin ceasing just below flowering heads. FLOWERING HEADS *15-25 mm across, erect, almost spherical, in dense clusters of 3-5; involucral bracts not narrowed just above base*, tips of outer bracts recurved; corolla 12-15 mm. HABITAT Roadsides, hedgerows, stream sides, rough grassland, waste ground, on fertile soils; lowland to 365 m. DIST. Native. Widely distributed as far N as central Scotland; local in E Ireland. (Most of Europe except parts of S.) FLS Jun-Aug.

Musk Thistle
Carduus nutans

Erect, usually branched biennial thistle to 100 cm. STEMS With white cottony hairs; spiny, winged margin ceasing some way below flowering heads. FLOWERING HEADS *Large, 30-60 mm across, spherical, drooping, usually solitary; outer involucral bracts strongly reflexed, lanceolate, contracted abruptly just above base*; corolla 15-25 mm. HABITAT Rough pastures, waste ground, roadsides, on calcareous soils. DIST. Native. Widely distributed as far N as central Scotland; casual in N Scotland, Ireland. (W and central Europe.) FLS May-Aug.

Thistles *Cirsium*
See key to *Cirsium* on p.468.

Spear Thistle
Cirsium vulgare

Tall, robust, branched biennial thistle to 150 cm. STEMS With discontinuous spiny wings. LEAVES *Upper surface bristly, dull, slightly glaucous; stem leaves decurrent, with* narrow, elongated terminal lobe. FLOWERING HEADS 2.5-5 cm, 2-3 per cluster, short-stalked. HABITAT Common weed of pastures, rough grassland, roadsides, waste ground, on fertile, base-rich soils; to 685 m. DIST. Ubiquitous throughout BI. (All Europe.) FLS Jul-Oct.

Woolly Thistle
Cirsium eriophorum

Tall, robust, branched biennial thistle to 150 cm. STEMS *Unwinged, not prickly, with cottony hairs.* LEAVES *Deeply pinnately lobed; upper surface bristly, dull*; tips of segments usually 2-lobed, one pointing up, the other down. FLOWERING HEADS *3-5 cm, solitary, erect; involucre with long white hairs (cottony).*

HABITAT Rough grasslands, scrub, railway banks roadsides, quarries, on dry calcareous soils; to 310 m. DIST. Native. Rather local. Central England N to Yorkshire. (W and central Europe.) FLS Jul-Sep

Meadow Thistle
Cirsium dissectum

Erect, stoloniferous perennial to 80 cm. STEM *Unwinged, cottony.* LEAVES *Stem leaves few; lower leaves elliptic-lanceolate, usually unlobed, 12-25 cm green and hairy above*, white-cottony beneath, margins with soft prickles. FLOWERING HEADS 1.5-3 cm usually solitary. HABITAT Fen meadows, wet pastures, flushes, wet heaths, on wet, mildly acid or calcareous peat; to 500 m. DIST. Native. Rather local England, Wales, N to Yorkshire; throughout Ireland (W Europe.) FLS Jun-Aug.

Tuberous Thistle
Cirsium tuberosum

Similar to *C. dissectum*, but *not stoloniferous; lower stem leaves deeply lobed, and green, not cottony beneath.* HABITAT N-facing old chalk and limestone grassland. DIST. Very rare. Wiltshire, Glamorgan (W and W-central Europe.) FLS Jun-Aug.

Melancholy Thistle
Cirsium heterophyllum *(N)

Tall, handsome perennial thistle to 120 cm. LEAVE Basal leaves elliptic-lanceolate, long-stalked; *middl stem leaves with broad auricled base clasping stem green above, white-felted beneath, margins with so teeth*; upper stem leaves few, small. FLOWERING HEADS *Large, 3.5-5 cm, usually solitary*; involucra bracts ± glabrous. HABITAT Hay meadows, road sides, open woodland; to 760 m. DIST. Native Widespread in N England, Scotland; very rare i Wales, Ireland. (N Europe.) FLS Jul-Aug.

Cabbage Thistle
Cirsium oleraceum

Tall, erect perennial to 150 cm. STEMS ± glabrous not winged, leafy throughout. LEAVES *Softly spiny middle and upper leaves unlobed, sessile, with large rounded basal auricles;* upper leaves bract-like, yel lowish, longer than flowering heads. FLOWERING HEADS 2.5-4 cm; *flowers yellow.* HABITAT Marshes streams, roadsides. DIST. Introduced. Naturalised i a few scattered localities, casual garden escape (Most of Europe.) FLS Jul-Sep.

Musk Thistle
Carduus nutans

Woolly Thistle
Cirsium eriophorum

Welted Thistle
Carduus crispus

Meadow Thistle
Cirsium dissectum

Spear Thistle
Cirsium vulgare

Tuberous Thistle
Cirsium tuberosum

Melancholy Thistle
Cirsium heterophyllum

Cabbage Thistle
Cirsium oleraceum

illustrations
0.5× lifesize

Dwarf Thistle
Cirsium acaule

Perennial. LEAVES Very spiny, forming basal rosette. FLOWERING HEADS 1–few, 3–4 cm, *sessile,* rarely with short stems. HABITAT Species-rich, short calcareous grassland; to 425 m. DIST. Native. Widespread in S Britain, SE of line from Humber to Severn. (Most of Europe except N and Mediterranean.) FLS Jul–Sep.

Marsh Thistle
Cirsium palustre

Tall biennial thistle to 200 cm. STEMS *Spiny-winged throughout, leafy to top.* LEAVES *Stem leaves sessile, decurrent,* hairy above, hairs blackish. FLOWERING HEADS 1.5–2 cm, short-stalked, in clusters at ends of often arching branches; flowers purple, sometimes white. HABITAT Marshes, fens, wet pastures, wet woodlands, upland flushes, communities of tall herbs; to 760 m. DIST. Native. Widespread throughout BI. (Most of Europe, but rare in Mediterranean.) FLS Jul–Sep.

Creeping Thistle
Cirsium arvense

Erect, branched, *rhizomatous* perennial to 120 cm. STEMS Unwinged, leafy to top. LEAVES Not forming basal rosette, very spiny, upper surface glabrous. FLOWERING HEADS 1.5–2.5 cm, short-stalked, solitary or in clusters of 2–4; florets dull purple, *upper part of corolla shorter than basal tube and divided almost to base into 5 segments.* HABITAT Pastures, meadows, rough grassland, roadsides, waste ground, on fertile soils; to 845 m. DIST. Native. Ubiquitous throughout BI. (All Europe.) FLS Jul–Sep.

Cotton Thistle
Onopordum acanthium

Tall, erect greyish-white biennial thistle to 250 cm. STEMS With continuous broad, spiny wings. LEAVES *With cottony hairs on both surfaces.* FLOWERING HEADS 3–5 cm, solitary; involucral bracts spreading or reflexed; florets pale purple; receptacle without hairs or bristles. HABITAT Field margins, hedgerows, waste ground, rubbish tips. DIST. Archaeophyte. Naturalised throughout lowland England; scarce elsewhere. (W, central and E Europe.) FLS Jul–Sep.

Milk Thistle
Silybum marianum

Erect annual or biennial to 100 cm. STEMS Neither winged nor spiny. LEAVES *Bright, shining green, variegated, veins white.* FLOWERING HEADS 4–5 cm, solitary; florets red-purple; involucral bracts broad, spiny, spreading or recurved, yellow-spine-tipped. FRUITS Pappus hairs rough but not branched. HABITAT Waste ground, rough pasture, hedgerows, especially close to sea. DIST. Archaeophyte. Naturalised or casual. Lowland England; scattered elsewhere (Mediterranean and SW Europe.) FLS Jun–Aug.

Saw-wort
Serratula tinctoria

Erect, slender, sparsely branched, glabrous, partially dioecious perennial to 90 cm. LEAVES *12–25 cm, lobed to pinnate, with bristle-tipped teeth.* FLOWERING HEADS 1.5–2 cm, in open inflorescence; receptacle with thin scales; *involucral bracts ovate, not spiny, appressed.* HABITAT Heathy and calcareous grassland, hay and fen meadows, commons, wood margins, cliff tops; to 560 m. DIST. Native. Throughout England (especially SW), Wales; absent from Ireland, most of Scotland. (Most of Europe except much of Scandinavia and Mediterranean.) FLS Jul–Sep.

Knapweeds and star-thistles *Centaurea*
See key to *Centaurea* on p.469.

Greater Knapweed
Centaurea scabiosa

Erect, branched, ± pubescent perennial to 90 cm. LEAVES *10–25 cm, usually deeply pinnately lobed.* FLOWERING HEADS 3–5 cm, solitary, long-stalked, partially radiate; *involucral bracts with blackish brown toothed, crescent-shaped apical portion decurrent down sides of basal section.* HABITAT Rough grassland, scrub, roadsides, hedge banks, cliffs, usually on calcareous soils; to 320 m. DIST. Native. Widespread in England; local and mostly coastal elsewhere. (Most of Europe except S.) FLS Jul–Sep.

Perennial Cornflower
Centaurea montana

Erect, rhizomatous perennial to 80 cm. LEAVES Simple, entire. FLOWERING HEADS Partially radiate; involucral bracts similar to *C. scabiosa,* florets blue. HABITAT Roadsides, railways, waste ground; to 380 m. DIST. Introduced. Widely cultivated and naturalised as garden escape throughout most of BI. (Mts of central and S Europe.) FLS May–Sep.

Dwarf Thistle
Cirsium acaule

Creeping Thistle
Cirsium arvense

Marsh Thistle
Cirsium palustre

Milk Thistle
Silybum marianum

Greater Knapweed
Centaurea scabiosa

Saw-wort
Serratula tinctoria

Cotton Thistle
Onopordum acanthium

Perennial Cornflower
Centaurea montana

illustrations
0.6× lifesize

Cornflower   *Centaurea cyanus*

Erect, branched annual to 90 cm. STEMS Slender, grooved, branching. LEAVES *Lower leaves stalked, pinnately branched*; upper leaves linear, simple, sessile; all leaves *greyish, pubescent*. FLOWERING HEADS 1.5–3 cm across, solitary, partially radiate; involucral bracts with decurrent apical portion, teeth of upper bracts silvery; *outer florets bright blue*. HABITAT Rubbish tips, waste places, roadsides. DIST. Archaeophyte. Formerly common arable weed, now casual garden escape. Throughout BI, but rare in Scotland, Ireland. (SE Europe.) FLS Jun–Aug.

Red Star-thistle   *Centaurea calcitrapa* CR.

Erect to spreading, ± glabrous, much-branched biennial to 60 cm. LEAVES Lower leaves deeply pinnately lobed, sparsely hairy, lobes bristle-tipped. FLOWERING HEADS 8–10 mm across, ± discoid; *involucral bracts with stout central spine, 20–25 mm, with shorter spines at base*; florets purple, glandular. HABITAT Dry calcareous sandy grasslands, tracksides, waste ground. DIST. Archaeophyte. Sometimes thought to be native in Sussex. Local, declining. Scattered throughout England. (S and S-central Europe.) FLS Jul–Sep.

Rough Star-thistle   *Centaurea aspera*

Similar to *C. calcitrapa*, but *involucral bracts with 3–5 ± equal spines, central spine <5 mm.* HABITAT Sand-dunes, sandy fields. DIST. Introduced. Naturalised in Channel Is (Guernsey). (SW Europe.) FLS Jul–Sep.

Yellow Star-thistle, St Barnaby's Thistle   *Centaurea solstitialis*

Erect to ascending, branched annual or biennial to 60 cm. STEMS *With broad and continuous wavy wings.* LEAVES Basal leaves deeply pinnately divided, *upper and lower surfaces with white cottony hairs*. FLOWERING HEADS *Involucral bracts with branched spines; florets pale yellow*. HABITAT Formerly frequent weed of Lucerne and Sainfoin, now rare casual of arable fields and waste ground. DIST. Introduced. (S Europe.) FLS Jul–Sep.

Common Knapweed   *Centaurea nigra*

Erect, branching, hairy perennial to 100 cm. LEAVES Entire to deeply lobed. FLOWERING HEADS 2–4 cm across, short-stalked, solitary, usually discoid but sometimes partially radiate; *apical portion of involucral bracts separated from basal portion by distinct constriction, apical portion dark brown-black, regularly toothed, teeth long*; florets reddish purple. HABITAT Rough grassland, meadows, pastures, roadsides, sea cliffs, waste ground; to 580 m. DIST. Native. Common throughout BI. (W and central Europe.) FLS Jun–Sep.

Brown Knapweed   *Centaurea jacea* EX.

Similar to *C. nigra*, but *apical portion of involucral bracts pale brown, thin and papery, with broad, pale margins, jagged tips, not regularly toothed*; pappus absent. HABITAT Rough grassland, roadsides, waste ground. DIST. Extinct in BI. Formerly naturalised in S England, Channel Is. (Most of Europe.) FLS Aug–Sep. NOTE Hybridises freely with *C. nigra* to produce *C. × monktonii*, which still persists.

Jersey Knapweed   *Centaurea paniculata* EX.

Similar to *C. nigra* and *C. jacea*, but *lower leaves pinnate, with narrow, linear lobes*; flowering heads smaller, 3–8 mm across; involucral bracts striate, with pale brown, regularly toothed apical portion. DIST. Extinct in BI. Formerly naturalised in Channel Is (Jersey). (SW Europe.) FLS Jul–Aug.

Chicory   *Cichorium intybus*

Erect to spreading, much-branched perennial, to 120 cm. STEMS Stiff, glabrous or pubescent. LEAVES Lower stem leaves lobed or toothed; upper stem leaves lanceolate, sessile, clasping stem with pointed auricles. FLOWERING HEADS Ligulate, 2.5–4 cm across; florets blue. FRUITS Pappus consisting of short scales. HABITAT Rough grassland, roadside verges, field margins, on dry soils; to 275 m. DIST. Archaeophyte. Declining. Throughout most of BI, but rare in Scotland, Ireland. (Most of Europe, but widely naturalised.) FLS Jul–Oct.

Cornflower
Centaurea cyanus

Red Star-thistle
Centaurea calcitrapa

Rough Star-thistle
Centaurea aspera

Yellow Star-thistle
Centaurea solstitialis

Common Knapweed
Centaurea nigra

Jersey Knapweed
Centaurea paniculata

Brown Knapweed
Centaurea jacea

illustrations
0.5× lifesize

Chicory
Cichorium intybus

Nipplewort
Lapsana communis

Erect, branched annual to 90 cm. STEMS Hairy below, glabrous above. LEAVES *Lower leaves lobed, terminal lobe much larger than laterals.* FLOWERING HEADS 1.5–2 cm across, 15–20 in open panicles; 8–10 involucral bracts, erect; *8–15 florets.* FRUITS *Pappus absent.* HABITAT Disturbed and shaded habitats, hedgerows, roadsides, walls, wood borders, gardens, waste ground. DIST. Native. Common throughout BI. (All Europe.) FLS Jul–Sep.

Lamb's Succory
Arnoseris minima EX.

Annual to 30 cm. STEMS *Flowering stems leafless, sparsely branched, markedly swollen beneath heads.* LEAVES In basal rosette. FLOWERING HEADS 7–11 mm across, solitary, terminal; receptacle bracts absent. FRUITS *Pappus absent.* HABITAT Arable weed on sandy soils. DIST. Extinct. Former archaeophyte, widespread in E England. (W and central Europe.) FLS Jun–Aug.

Cat's-ear
Hypochaeris radicata

Perennial to 60 cm. STEMS Flowering stems swollen below heads, *usually with few branches and several small, scale-like bracts.* LEAVES 7–25 cm, in basal rosette, roughly hairy, *hairs unbranched.* FLOWERING HEADS 2.5–4 cm across, ligules *c.*4× as long as wide, *receptacle scales present.* FRUITS Central achenes 8–17 mm. HABITAT Pastures, meadows, lawns, grass heaths, roadsides, dunes, on mildly acid soils. DIST. Native. Ubiquitous and common throughout BI except Shetland. (Most of Europe except NE.) FLS Jun–Sep.

Smooth Cat's-ear
Hypochaeris glabra VU. *(NI)

Annual to 40 cm (usually much less). LEAVES 1–20 cm, in basal rosette, glabrous. FLOWERING HEADS *Small, 1–1.5 cm across; florets about as long as involucre, opening only in bright sunlight*; ligules *c.*2× as long as wide. FRUITS *Central achenes 6–9 mm.* HABITAT Dry, open sandy or gravelly habitats, grass heaths, dunes, grassland; to 530 m. DIST. Native. Very local. East Anglia, scattered elsewhere; rare in Scotland, Ireland. (Most of Europe except N.) FLS Jun–Oct.

Spotted Cat's-ear
Hypochaeris maculata

Perennial to 60 cm. STEMS Flowering stems with few or 0 scale-like bracts. LEAVES 4–15 cm, in basal rosette, *with dark purple spots.* FLOWERING HEADS 3–4.5 cm across, *solitary* or in groups of 2–4; involucre black-green; outer involucral bracts pubescent; florets 2× as long as involucre. FRUITS Achenes, 5–7 mm. HABITAT Chalk and limestone grassland, serpentine cliffs, blown sand. DIST. Native. Very rare. East Anglia, Cornwall, Lancashire, Gwynedd, Channel Is (Jersey). (Most of Europe except extreme S and N.) FLS Jun–Aug.

Rough Hawkbit
Leontodon hispidus

Perennial to 60 cm. STEMS Flowering stems unbranched, usually densely hairy above. LEAVES With forked 'Y'-shaped hairs, in basal rosette. FLOWERING HEADS Solitary, 25–40 mm across; *involucral bracts conspicuously hairy*; outer ligules usually reddish beneath. FRUITS *All achenes with pappus of hairs.* HABITAT Hay meadows, pastures, rough grazing, roadside verges, on well-drained calcareous soils; to 575 m. DIST. Native. Throughout most of BI, N to S Scotland; local in Ireland, rare in SW. (Most of Europe.) FLS Jun–Sep.

Lesser Hawkbit
Leontodon saxatilis

Perennial to 30 cm. STEMS *Flowering stems* unbranched, *glabrous or sparsely hairy.* LEAVES With forked 'Y'-shaped hairs along margins, in basal rosette. FLOWERING HEADS Solitary, 12–20 mm across; *involucral bracts sparsely hairy*; outer ligules usually greyish beneath. FRUITS *Outer achenes with no pappus of hairs.* HABITAT Heaths, commons, grazed grassland, roadsides, dunes, on well-drained calcareous or sandy soils; to 500 m. DIST. Native. Throughout BI, N to central Scotland. (S, W and central Europe.) FLS Jun–Sep.

Autumn Hawkbit
Leontodon autumnalis

Perennial to 60 cm. STEMS Flowering stems glabrous, *usually with few branches, scale-like bracts beneath heads.* LEAVES Usually deeply lobed, with narrow segments; in basal rosette; glabrous or with sparse simple hairs. FLOWERING HEADS 12–35 mm across; outer ligules streaked reddish beneath. FRUITS *Pappus consisting of 1 row of feathery (branched) hairs.* HABITAT Meadows, pastures, grass heaths, commons, roadsides, scree, salt marshes, dunes; to 975 m. DIST. Native. Ubiquitous throughout BI. (Most of Europe, but local in S.) FLS Jun–Oct

Spotted Cat's-ear
Hypochaeris maculata

Lamb's Succory
Arnoseris minima

Lesser Hawkbit
Leontodon saxatilis

Rough Hawkbit
Leontodon hispidus

Autumn Hawkbit
Leontodon autumnalis

Nipplewort
Lapsana communis

Cat's-ear
Hypochaeris radicata

Smooth Cat's-ear
Hypochaeris glabra

illustrations
0.5× lifesize

Bristly Oxtongue
Picris echioides

Erect, branched, bristly annual or biennial 90 cm. LEAVES Stem leaves sessile, ± cordate, clasping, coarsely toothed, covered by rough bristles. FLOWERING HEADS 2–2.5 cm across, *3–5 outer involucral bracts, broad, leaf-like; beak as long as body*. FRUITS Pappus white. HABITAT Roadsides, rough ground, field margins, riverbanks, sea walls, on heavy calcareous soils. DIST. Archaeophyte. Widespread SE of line from Humber to Severn; scattered elsewhere. (S Europe.) FLS Jun–Oct.

Hawkweed Oxtongue
Picris hieracioides

Erect, branched, bristly biennial or perennial to 90 cm. LEAVES Stem leaves lanceolate, slightly clasping, margins undulate. FLOWERING HEADS 2–3.5 cm across; *inner and outer involucral bracts narrow, similar, outer ± spreading, recurved*. FRUITS *Short-beaked achenes*. HABITAT Chalk and limestone grassland, roadsides, railway banks, quarries, on calcareous soils. DIST. Native. Widespread SE of line from Humber to Severn, S Wales. (Most of Europe.) FLS Jul–Sep.

Viper's-grass
Scorzonera humilis VU. *(B)

Erect, usually unbranched perennial to 50 cm. STEMS *Woolly at first, becoming glabrous*. LEAVES As stems; *basal leaves 10–20 cm, narrowly lanceolate*; stem leaves smaller. FLOWERING HEADS 2.5–3 cm, solitary; outer ligules reddish beneath, 2× as long as involucral bracts; *involucral bracts in many overlapping rows*. FRUITS Achene, 7–9 mm, longitudinally ribbed. HABITAT Damp, unimproved grassland, fen meadows, on mildly acid soils. DIST. Native. Very rare, in 3 sites only in Dorset, Glamorgan. (Much of Europe except extreme N and S.) FLS May–Jul.

Podospermum laciniata

Similar to *S. humilis*, but annual or biennial; *basal leaves deeply pinnately divided; achenes with pale tubular base*, beak short. HABITAT Dry grassland, brackish meadows, limestone scree. DIST. *Not BI*. (Central, S and SE Europe, N to N France, Belgium.) FLS Jun–Jul.

Salsify
Tragopogon porrifolius

Erect, branching, glabrous, ± glaucous biennial to 120 cm. Vegetatively similar to *T. pratensis* (*see* below), but stem and branches conspicuously swollen beneath heads; *florets ¼ as long to as long as involucral bracts, violet*. HABITAT Rough grassland, roadside verges, cliffs, sea walls. DIST. Introduced. Cultivated as a vegetable and naturalised in SE England; casual

elsewhere. (Mediterranean; naturalised in N, W and central Europe.) FLS Jun–Aug.

Goat's-beard
Tragopogon pratensis

Erect annual to perennial, to 70 cm. Has 2 wide spread subspecies, ssp. *pratensis* and ssp. *minor*, which should be identified only when flowers are open on sunny mornings. LEAVES *Glabrous, linear lanceolate, long-pointed, entire, sheathing at base* with conspicuous white midrib. FLOWERING HEADS Large; involucral bracts in 1 row; ligules as long as involucral bracts in ssp. *pratensis*, c.½ as long in ssp. *minor*. FRUITS Pappus and fruiting heads very large. HABITAT Ssp. *pratensis* on dry grassland, roadsides, waste ground. Ssp. *minor* similar, but also rough grassland, sand-dunes; to 365 m. DIST. Ssp. *pratensis* introduced; casual in lowland England. Ssp. *minor* native; widespread N to central Scotland, scattered in Ireland. (Ssp. *pratensis* in most of Europe; ssp. *minor* in W and central Europe.) FLS Jun–Jul.

Alpine Blue-sow-thistle
Cicerbita alpina VU. *(B)

Tall, erect alpine perennial to 200 cm. STEM Branched, leafy, *bristly below, with dense reddish glandular hairs above*. LEAVES *Glabrous, with distinct triangular apical lobe*. FLOWERING HEADS 30 mm across, in open, elongated panicle, with glandular bristly branches; ligules pale blue. HABITAT Inaccessible N-facing acidic rocks in areas of late snow-lie to 1090 m. DIST. Native. Very rare, in only 4 sites in Scottish Highlands. (Scandinavia, mts of S and central Europe.) FLS Jul–Sep.

Common Blue-sow-thistle
Cicerbita macrophylla

Tall, erect, patch-forming, rhizomatous perennial to 200 cm. STEMS *Glabrous below*, glandular-hispid above. LEAVES *Underside of lower leaves pubescent on veins; apical lobe ovate, cordate*. FLOWERING HEADS 3 mm across, ± corymb-like inflorescence; florets lilac. HABITAT Roadsides, pond and riverbanks; to 320 m. DIST. Introduced. Widely naturalised throughout BI as garden escape. (Central and E Russia; widely naturalised throughout Europe.) FLS Jul–Sep.

Hairless Blue-sow-thistle
Cicerbita plumieri

Tall, erect, *glabrous* perennial to 130 cm. LEAVES *With triangular terminal lobe and several pairs of lateral lobes*. FLOWERING HEADS Ligules blue. HABITAT Hedgerows, sand-dunes, waste ground. DIST. Introduced. Naturalised as for *C. macrophylla*, but much rarer. (Mts of S and central Europe.) FLS Jul–Sep.

Hawkweed Oxtongue

Picris hieracioides

Viper's-grass

Scorzonera humilis

Alpine Blue-sow-thistle

Cicerbita alpina

Bristly Oxtongue

Picris echioides

Common Blue-sow-thistle

Cicerbita macrophylla

Podospermum laciniata

ssp. *pratensis*

Hairless Blue-sow-thistle

Cicerbita plumieri

ssp. *minor*

Goat's-beard

Tragopogon pratensis

Salsify

Tragopogon porrifolius

illustrations 0.5× lifesize

Sow-thistles *Sonchus*
See key to Sonchus on p.469.

Perennial Sow-thistle
Sonchus arvensis

Tall, erect, rhizomatous perennial to 150 cm. LEAVES Basal leaves ± pinnately lobed, lobes with spiny teeth; *stem leaves sessile with rounded auricles*. FLOWERING HEADS 4–5 cm across, deep yellow; *inflorescence branches and involucres densely covered by yellow glandular hairs*. FRUITS Dark brown achenes, 3–3.5 mm. HABITAT Banks of streams and rivers, arable land, road verges, sea walls, drift lines. DIST. Native. Widely distributed throughout BI, but scarce in N Scotland. (Most of Europe.) FLS Jul–Oct.

Marsh Sow-thistle
Sonchus palustris

Tall, erect perennial to 300 cm. STEMS 4-angled, glabrous below, glandular-hairy above. LEAVES Pinnately lobed; *sessile, with long, narrow, pointed auricles*. FLOWERING HEADS *c.*4 cm across, pale yellow; *inflorescence branches and involucres covered by blackish glandular hairs*. FRUITS Yellowish achenes, 3.5–4 mm. HABITAT Tall marginal vegetation on base-rich alluvial or peaty soils; tolerant of brackish conditions. DIST. Native. Very local. Norfolk Broads, E Suffolk, Medway estuary, Hampshire. Extinct in East Anglian fens, but now reintroduced. (Most of Europe except S.) FLS Jul–Sep.

Smooth Sow-thistle
Sonchus oleraceus

Erect, glabrous annual to 150 cm. LEAVES Variable, somewhat glaucous, not spinous, *with acute, spreading auricles*. FLOWERING HEADS 1.5–3.5 cm across, ligules yellow. FRUITS *Achenes, transversely wrinkled between ribs.* HABITAT Common weed of gardens, arable land, roadsides, disturbed ground, on fertile soils. DIST. Native. Widespread throughout lowland BI, but scarce in N Scotland. (Most of Europe.) FLS Jun–Aug.

Prickly Sow-thistle
Sonchus asper

Erect, glabrous annual to 120 cm. Very variable. Similar to *S. oleraceus*, but upper surface of leaves shining green, not glaucous; *stem leaves with rounded spinous auricles appressed to stem*; flowering heads 1.5–2.5 cm across; ligules deeper yellow; *achenes smooth between ribs*. In doubtful cases, the only certain way to distinguish it from *S. oleraceus* is on the sculpturing of the achenes. HABITAT Rough grassland, roadside verges, gardens, arable fields, coastal habitats, waste places.

DIST. Native. Common throughout BI. (All Europe except extreme N.) FLS Jun–Aug.

Prickly Lettuce
Lactuca serriola

Tall, erect annual or biennial to 200 cm. LEAVES Pinnately lobed to unlobed, *midribs whitish*, margins and underside of midrib sharply toothed, sessile with pointed auricles; *stem leaves held vertically in N-S plane*. FLOWERING HEADS 8–10 mm across, in elongated inflorescence; involucre cylindrical, glabrous. FRUITS Olive-grey *achenes, 3–4 mm (excluding beak)*. HABITAT Disturbed ground, roadsides, sea walls, coastal habitats; lowland. DIST. Archaeophyte. England N to Humber; rare in SW, Wales. (Most of Europe.) FLS Jul–Sep.

Great Lettuce
Lactuca virosa

Tall, erect annual or biennial to 200 cm. Similar to *L. serriola*, but *stems and midribs of leaves tinged brownish purple*; auricles rounded, appressed; stem leaves not usually held vertically in sun; flowering heads 17–20 mm across; *achenes >4 mm (excluding beak), purplish black*. HABITAT Disturbed ground, roadside banks, rough calcareous grassland, cliffs; lowland. DIST. Native. E England; rare in Scotland, Wales; absent from Ireland. (S, W and central Europe.) FLS Jul–Sep.

Least Lettuce
Lactuca saligna EN. *(B)

Erect annual to 100 cm. LEAVES *Stem leaves well separated, linear-lanceolate, base clasping with pointed lobes; basal leaves entire to pinnately lobed, all entire without spiny teeth, underside of midrib glabrous.* FLOWERING HEADS Solitary or in small clusters, forming narrow inflorescence; flowers closing before midday; outer ligules reddish beneath. FRUITS Pale brown achenes, 5–8 mm (excluding beak). HABITAT Old sea walls, sandy shingle. DIST. Native. Very rare, declining. Essex, Kent, E Sussex. (W, central and E Europe.) FLS Jul–Aug.

Blue Lettuce
Lactuca perennis

Erect, glabrous perennial to 80 cm. STEMS Branched above. LEAVES Pinnately lobed, grey-green. FLOWERING HEADS Few, on long branches, 30–40 mm across; ligules blue-lilac. FRUITS Black achenes, 10–14 mm. HABITAT Dry calcareous grasslands, roadsides, rocky places. DIST. *Not BI.* (Central Europe to Belgium, NW France.) FLS May–Aug.

Marsh Sow-thistle
Sonchus palustris

Perennial Sow-thistle
Sonchus arvensis

Prickly Sow-thistle
Sonchus asper

Smooth Sow-thistle
Sonchus oleraceus

Blue Lettuce
Lactuca perennis

Great Lettuce
Lactuca virosa

Least Lettuce
Lactuca saligna

Prickly Lettuce
Lactuca serriola

illustrations
0.4× lifesize

Hawk's-beards *Crepis*
See key to *Crepis* on p.470.

Marsh Hawk's-beard — *Crepis paludosa*

Erect, glabrous perennial to 90 cm. LEAVES *Stem leaves sharply toothed*, base sessile, clasping *with pointed auricles*. FLOWERING HEADS 15–25 mm across, few; involucre with numerous black glandular and non-glandular hairs. FRUITS Straw-coloured achenes 4–5 mm, not beaked; *pappus of stiff, brittle yellow-brown hairs*. HABITAT Wet meadows, pastures, stream sides, fens, marshes, wet woodland; to 915 m. DIST. Native. Widespread in N Britain, N Ireland. (N and central Europe.) FLS Jul-Sep.

Northern Hawk's-beard — *Crepis mollis* EN.

Erect, glabrous or sparsely pubescent, rhizomatous perennial to 60 cm. LEAVES *Stem leaves sparsely hairy, scarcely toothed, ± clasping with rounded auricles*. FLOWERING HEADS 20–30 mm across; involucre sparsely glandular-hairy. FRUITS Reddish-brown achenes, 4.5 mm; *pappus pure white, soft*. HABITAT Hilly stream sides, fens, wood pasture, on calcareous soils. DIST. Native. Very local, declining. N England, S Scotland. (Central and SE Europe.) FLS Jul-Aug.

Rough Hawk's-beard — *Crepis biennis*

Erect biennial to 120 cm. STEMS *Grooved, hispid*. LEAVES Irregularly lobed, ± clasping stem. FLOWERING HEADS 20–35 cm across; florets deep yellow, not reddish beneath; involucre sparsely glandular-hairy, bracts pubescent on inner surface, outer bracts spreading. FRUITS *Achenes, not beaked*, 4–7 mm, with 13–20 ribs. HABITAT Rough grassland, roadsides, waste ground, arable fields, on calcareous soils. DIST. Native in S England; introduced elsewhere, but absent from Scotland. Rather local. (Most of Europe except extreme S and N.) FLS Jun-Jul.

Smooth Hawk's-beard — *Crepis capillaris*

Erect, branched, ± *glabrous annual* to 75 cm. Very variable. LEAVES Lower leaves with toothed lobes; *stem leaves clasping, with long, arrow-shaped lobes*. FLOWERING HEADS 10–13 mm across, erect in bud; inner surface of inner bracts glabrous, outer bracts appressed. FRUITS Achenes, not beaked, 1.5–2.5 mm, with 10 ribs. HABITAT Grassland, roadsides, heaths, waste ground, old walls; to 445 m. DIST. Native. Common throughout BI. (W, central and S Europe.) FLS Jun-Sep.

Beaked Hawk's-beard — *Crepis vesicaria*

Erect, branched, *hispid biennial* to 80 cm. LEAVES Thinly pubescent; basal leaves stalked, variously lobed; stem leaves clasping. FLOWERING HEADS 15–25 mm across; *florets yellow, orange-striped beneath*, outer bracts spreading. FRUITS Achenes, 4–5 mm, with slender beak as long as achene when ripe. HABITAT Roadsides, rough grassland, waste ground. DIST. Introduced. Abundant and widespread as far N as Humber; absent from Scotland, N Ireland. (S, central and W Europe.) FLS May-Jul.

Stinking Hawk's-beard — *Crepis foetida* EW. *(B

Erect, pubescent, branched annual or biennial to 60 cm. *Whole plant smells strongly of bitter almonds when fresh*. LEAVES Densely hairy, in basal rosette; stem leaves few. FLOWERING HEADS 15–20 mm across *drooping in bud*, solitary on long stalks; involucral bracts with dense glandular and eglandular hairs florets pale yellow, purplish beneath. FRUITS *Achenes, 3–4 mm, outer short-beaked, inner long-beaked* inner bracts tightly enclose marginal achenes. HABITAT/DIST. Archaeophyte. Single locality on shingle at Dungeness, Kent; extinct 1980, reintroduced 1992. (Most of Europe except N.) FLS Jun-Aug.

Leafless Hawk's-beard — *Crepis praemorsa* EN

Erect, sparsely pubescent perennial to 75 cm LEAVES *Stem leaves absent*. FLOWERING HEADS 15–20 mm across; involucral bracts sparsely pubescent. FRUITS Pale brown achenes, 3–4 mm, no beaked. HABITAT/DIST. Native. Very rare. Single site on limestone grassland, Westmorland, discovered 1988. (Central and E Europe; absent from Mediterranean.) FLS Jun.

Narrow-leaved Hawk's-beard — *Crepis tectorum*

Erect annual to 60 cm. LEAVES *Stem leaves linear, sessile, clasping, with pointed lobes, glabrous, margins recurved*; involucral bracts pubescent on inner surface. FRUITS Dark purplish-brown achenes, 3–4 mm. HABITAT Cultivated land, grasslands on sandy soils dunes, old walls. DIST. *Not BI*. (Most of Europe except extreme S and W.) FLS May-Oct.

Hawkweeds — *Hieracium* spp

[*See* illustration following page.] Erect perennials exceedingly difficult to identify to species level as all are *apomictic*, i.e. producing seed without fertilisation Seedlings are thus genetically identical to the seed parent; in effect, 'cloning' by seed. This can give rise to large number of genetically invariable populations each of which can be recognised as separate species (sometimes referred to as '*micro-species*'). There are currently 412 species of *Hieracium* recognised in the BI many of which are rare endemics and a number of

**Rough
Hawk's-beard**
Crepis biennis

**Beaked
Hawk's-beard**
Crepis vesicaria

**Marsh
awk's-
beard**
*Crepis
paludosa*

**Narrow-leaved
Hawk's-beard**
Crepis tectorum

**Stinking
Hawk's-beard**
Crepis foetida

**Smooth
Hawk's-beard**
Crepis capillaris

**Leafless
Hawk's-beard**
Crepis praemorsa

**Northern
Hawk's-beard**
Crepis mollis

illustrations
0.5× lifesize

which are probably introduced. No attempt has been made to deal with these here. LEAVES Varying arrangement of basal and stem leaves. FLOWERING HEADS *Involucral bracts in several overlapping rows, absence of receptacle scales.* FRUITS *Pappus of 1 row of pale brown or dirty white simple hairs.* SIMILAR SPP. Often confused with species of hawk's-beards, especially *Crepis paludosa* and *C. mollis* (p.490), but these have the involucral bracts in 2 rows. HABITAT Found in a wide range of habitats, but prefer dry, open or rocky places, including cliffs, limestone pavement, hillside grassland, rock ledges, rocky stream sides, roadsides, walls and quarries; to 1220 m.

Mouse-ear-hawkweeds *Pilosella*

Stoloniferous perennials. *Flowering stem ± leafless (scapigerous). Leaves in a basal rosette, elliptical, without marginal teeth, the lower surface densely white-felted,* the upper surface with scattered long, stiff hairs. Involucre hairy; ligules red-streaked beneath.

Mouse-ear-hawkweed   *Pilosella officinarum*

Very variable, with 7 subspecies. STEMS *Stolons long, with small, well-spaced leaves,* not usually ending in rosettes; flowering stem 5–30 cm. FLOWERING HEADS Solitary, 15–25 mm across. HABITAT Short turf, grass heaths, dunes, banks, walls, cliffs, on dry sandy or calcareous soils; to 915 m. DIST. Native. Widely distributed throughout BI. (All Europe.) FLS May–Aug.

Shaggy Mouse-ear-hawkweed   *Pilosella peleteriana*

Very variable. Similar to *P. officinarum,* but *stolons short or absent*; stolon leaves of normal size, crowded; stolons usually ending in rosettes; *flowering heads larger, 25–45 mm across; involucre densely covered by long, shining whitish hairs.* DIST. Native. Very local. Dorset, I of Wight, Channel Is. HABITAT Short, open chalk and limestone grassland, quarries, dunes. (N, W and W-central Europe.) FLS May–Jul.

Fox-and-cubs   *Pilosella aurantiaca*

Erect, stoloniferous or rhizomatous perennial. STEMS Flowering stems to 40 cm, *branched, with 2–12 heads.* LEAVES Rosette leaves large, 6–20 cm. FLOWERING HEADS 10–20 mm across; *ligules orange-brown to red.* HABITAT Hedge banks, grassy roadsides, walls, churchyards; to 445 m. DIST. Introduced. Naturalised. Garden escape. (N and central Europe.) FLS May–Jul.

Wall Lettuce   *Mycelis muralis*

Erect, branched, *glabrous perennial* to 100 cm. LEAVES Lower leaves pinnately lobed, with large,

triangular terminal lobe; stem leaves sessile, clasping. FLOWERING HEADS 12–15 mm across, in large, open inflorescence; *5 florets per head.* HABITAT Shaded hedge banks, calcareous woods, rocks, walls, grikes in limestone pavement; to 500 m. DIST. Native. Throughout most of Britain, but rare in Scotland; introduced in Ireland. (All Europe except N.) FLS Jul–Sep.

Dandelions   *Taraxacum* spp.

Usually glabrous perennials. Like hawkweeds (*see* above), they are apomicts and pose the same problems of identification. There are currently 232 species recognised in the BI; as with the hawkweeds, no attempt is made to deal with these here. STEMS Leafless flowering stem arises from basal leaf rosette. LEAVES All in basal rosette. FLOWERING HEADS Solitary; involucral bracts in 2 different rows; receptacle bracts absent. FRUITS Pappus in several rows of simple white hairs (the dandelion 'clock'). HABITAT Native species occur in chalk grassland, fens, flushes, stream sides, sand-dunes, cliffs. Most introduced species are abundant plants of disturbed ground such as roadsides, pastures, gardens, waste ground. DIST. More than 40 species are endemic, 100-plus are probably introduced, and the remainder are native. Throughout BI. FLS Mar–Oct.

Mountain Everlasting   *Antennaria dioica*

Erect, stoloniferous, dioecious perennial to 20 cm. STEMS *Covered by whitish woolly hairs.* LEAVES *Mostly basal, 1–4 cm, white-woolly beneath.* FLOWERING HEADS *In tight clusters;* florets tubular, female 12 mm across, male c.6 mm; involucral bracts of male plants ovate, white; of female plants linear-lanceolate, pink. HABITAT Upland grassland, dwarf shrub heaths, stream sides, rock ledges; to 885 m. Also sand-dunes, machair, cliff tops, limestone grassland. DIST. Native. Declining. Widespread in upland Britain; rare and local in lowlands. (N and central Europe.) FLS Jun–Jul.

Pearly Everlasting   *Anaphalis margaritacea*

Erect, rhizomatous, ± dioecious perennial to 100 cm. STEMS *Covered by white-woolly hairs.* LEAVES *Basal rosette absent;* stem leaves white-woolly beneath. FLOWERING HEADS 9–12 mm across, in tight clusters; *involucral bracts in several rows, thin, shining white, papery.* HABITAT Rough grassland, waste ground, roadsides, railway banks. DIST. Introduced (native of North America, E Asia). Naturalised garden escape. (N and central Europe.) FLS Aug–Sep.

Pearly Everlasting
Anaphalis margaritacea

Dandelion
Taraxacum

Wall Lettuce
Mycelis muralis

Hawkweed
Hieracium
(description
p.490)

Mountain Everlasting
Antennaria dioica

Fox-and-cubs
Pilosella aurantiaca

Shaggy Mouse-ear-hawkweed
Pilosella peleteriana

Mouse-ear-hawkweed
Pilosella officinarum

illustrations
0.6× lifesize

Cudweeds *Filago* and *Gnaphalium*

Filago and *Gnaphalium* look very similar (*see* key on p.470); both are densely hairy or woolly annuals or perennials with heads of small yellowish or brownish florets, the heads in tight sessile clusters in the axils of leaves. The technical difference between them is that *Filago* has receptacle bracts mixed with the outer florets whilst there are no receptacle bracts in *Gnaphalium*. However, this character is often not easy to see. In practice, the two genera can usually be distinguished in the field. The stem and branches of *Filago* all end in axillary clusters, but the main stem is successively overtopped by the lower lateral branches, giving the whole plant a distinct 'jizz'. In addition, the leaves of most *Filago* are usually ± erect, whereas those of *Gnaphalium* are more spreading.

Common Cudweed   *Filago vulgaris*

Erect annual to 40 cm. STEMS Densely white-woolly, usually branched. LEAVES *Widest below middle*, erect, 1–2 cm, undulate, *upper leaves not overtopping clusters*. FLOWERING HEADS 20–40 in ± sessile clusters; involucral bracts in 5 rows, inner with pointed yellow tips. HABITAT Dry, open grassland, grass heaths, arable land, tracks on sandy soils, dunes. DIST. Native. Declining. Lowland Britain, especially East Anglia; rare in Scotland, Ireland. (Central and S Europe.) FLS Jul–Aug.

Red-tipped Cudweed   *Filago lutescens* EN. *(B)

Similar to *F. vulgaris*, but *yellowish woolly*, ± erect; stems more irregularly branched; *leaves widest above middle, 1–2 leaves overtopping clusters*; clusters with 10–20 heads; *outer involucral bracts with reddish-purple tips on young heads*. HABITAT Dry, open, disturbed sandy soils, heaths, tracks, commons, arable fields. DIST. Native. Rare, declining. E and SE England. (Much of Europe.) FLS Jul–Aug.

Broad-leaved Cudweed   *Filago pyramidata* EN. *(B)

Similar to *F. lutescens*, but plant white-woolly, prostrate or sprawling; *clusters of heads overtopped by 2–4 leaves; tips of outer involucral bracts yellowish, slightly recurved*. HABITAT Formerly frequent arable weed of dry, well-drained sandy or chalky soils. DIST. Archaeophyte. Rare, declining. E and SE England. (S and W Europe.) FLS Jul–Aug.

Small Cudweed   *Filago minima* *(R)

Slender, ± erect, branched annual to 25 cm. Plant covered by silky silvery hairs. STEMS Erect. LEAVES *Erect, closely appressed to stem, 4–10 mm*, linear-lanceolate, *apical leaves not overtopping clusters*. FLOWERING HEADS 3–6 forming clusters. HABITAT Grass heaths, commons, arable fields, pathsides, waste ground, pits, on dry, open sandy or gravelly soils; to 365 m. DIST. Native. Local, declining. Scattered throughout BI. (Much of Europe except N.) FLS Jun–Sep.

Narrow-leaved Cudweed   *Filago gallica* EW.

Similar to *F. minima*, but *leaves linear, 8–25 mm, apical leaves overtopping clusters*; clusters with 2–6 heads. HABITAT Well-drained, disturbed sandy or gravelly soils, arable fields, tracks, quarries. DIST. Archaeophyte. Reintroduced to Essex, Suffolk, Channel Is (Sark). (W and S Europe.) FLS Jul–Sep.

Field Cudweed   *Filago arvensis*

Similar to *F. minima*, but densely white-woolly, not greyish silky; stems erect, to 70 cm; leaves 10–20 mm, erect but not closely appressed to stem; flowering heads in clusters of 3–12, not overtopped by apical leaves. HABITAT Arable weed on dry sandy soils. DIST. *Not BI*. (Most of Europe except extreme N.) FLS Jul–Oct.

Heath Cudweed   *Gnaphalium sylvaticum* EN. *(R)

Erect perennial to 60 cm. STEMS Whitish woolly; short, leafy non-flowering shoots. LEAVES *Linear-lanceolate, 1-veined*, glabrous above, woolly beneath, *diminishing in size up stem*. FLOWERING HEADS 2–8 or solitary, in *elongated, spike-like inflorescence >⅓ length of stem*; involucral bracts with central green stripe and broad papery margins. HABITAT Open heathy woodlands, heaths, dunes; to 850 m. DIST. Native. Throughout BI but now local and seriously declining. (Most of Europe except extreme N.) FLS Jul–Sep.

Highland Cudweed   *Gnaphalium norvegicum*

Erect alpine perennial to 30 cm. Similar to *G. sylvaticum*, but *stem leaves 3-veined*, scarcely diminishing in size up stem near top; *spike more compact, ≤⅓ length of stem*; 2–3 flowering heads or solitary; involucral bracts with olive-green central stripe and papery dark brown margins. HABITAT Acidic rock ledges, gullies, gorges, scree; to 980 m. DIST. Native. Very rare. Central and NW Scotland. (Mts of Arctic, S and central Europe.) FLS Aug.

Dwarf Cudweed   *Gnaphalium supinum*

Densely tufted alpine perennial. STEMS *Leafy non-flowering shoots*; erect flowering stems, to 12 cm. LEAVES Stem leaves linear, woolly, 5–15 mm. FLOWERING HEADS 1–7, in short, compact, terminal spike; inner bracts almost as long as florets. HABITAT Mountain-top gravel, grassy slopes, cliffs, late snow patches; to 1305 m. DIST. Native. Widespread but local. Scottish Highlands. (Arctic Europe, mts of central Europe.) FLS Jul–Aug.

Common Cudweed
Filago vulgaris

Red-tipped Cudweed
Filago lutescens

Narrow-leaved Cudweed
Filago gallica

Broad-leaved Cudweed
Filago pyramidata

Small Cudweed
Filago minima

Field Cudweed
Filago arvensis

Dwarf Cudweed
Gnaphalium supinum

Heath Cudweed
Gnaphalium sylvaticum

Highland Cudweed
Gnaphalium norvegicum

illustrations
0.6× lifesize

Marsh Cudweed
Gnaphalium uliginosum

Much-branched decumbent to erect annual, to 20 cm, densely covered by woolly hairs. LEAVES Linear-lanceolate, 1–5 cm. FLOWERING HEADS *In dense, sessile, terminal clusters, 3–10 heads per cluster, overtopped by apical leaves*; involucral bracts brown. HABITAT Open trampled areas, pond margins, woodland rides, arable fields, heaths, gardens, on seasonally flooded clay or acid sandy soils. DIST. Native. Widely distributed throughout BI. (Most of Europe except extreme N.) FLS Jul–Aug.

Jersey Cudweed
Gnaphalium luteoalbum *(B)

Decumbent to erect annual, to 45 cm. STEMS Branched above, densely white-woolly. LEAVES *Oblong, 1.5–3 cm, ± undulate, not decurrent.* FLOWERING HEADS In dense, terminal, leafless clusters, 4–12 heads per cluster, not overtopped by leaves; *involucral bracts papery, straw-coloured.* HABITAT Sandy fields, dune slacks, waste ground. DIST. Native. Very rare. Norfolk, Kent, Channel Is (Jersey); rare casual elsewhere. (Most of Europe except N.) FLS Jun–Aug.

Cape Cudweed
Gnaphalium undulatum

Erect, bushy annual to 80 cm, with non-flowering shoots. LEAVES *Lanceolate, green on upper surface, white-woolly below, undulate, lower leaves decurrent.* FLOWERING HEADS In globose clusters, not overtopped by leaves; involucral bracts whitish, papery. HABITAT Cliffs, rough ground. DIST. Introduced (native of S Africa). Naturalised in Channel Is, W Cornwall. FLS Jun–Aug.

Immortelle
Helichrysum arenarium

Erect or ascending, branched, glandular-pubescent perennial to 30 cm, with non-flowering shoots. LEAVES Densely whitish woolly, 5–7 cm, upper leaves linear. FLOWERING HEADS *Involucre as long as florets, yellow-orange to reddish orange; florets bright yellow.* HABITAT Dry sandy grasslands, heaths. DIST. *Not BI.* (Most of Europe except N.) FLS Jul–Oct.

Helichrysum stoechas

Erect to ascending, *dwarf shrub,* to 50 cm. LEAVES *All linear, white-woolly, margins revolute.* FLOWERING HEADS In dense clusters, >5 heads per cluster; involucre as long as florets, bracts yellow. HABITAT Coastal sand-dunes. DIST. *Not BI.* (S and W Europe, N to NW France.) FLS May–Jun.

Ploughman's-spikenard
Inula conyzae

Erect, softly pubescent biennial or perennial to 130 cm. STEMS Simple or branched, often reddish. LEAVES *Basal leaves ovate*; stem leaves lanceolate, ± sessile, all toothed. FLOWERING HEADS *7–12 mm across, numerous, in terminal clusters; florets yellow, marginal ray florets absent*; involucral bracts in many rows, green with pale bases. SIMILAR SPP. The basal leaves closely resemble those of Foxglove *Digitalis purpurea* (p.414), but that invariably grows on acid soils. HABITAT Rough grassland, scrub, dunes, broken ground, quarries, roadsides, on dry calcareous soils. DIST. Native. Widespread in England, Wales, N to S Scotland. (Central and SE Europe, N to Denmark.) FLS Jul–Sep.

Irish Fleabane
Inula salicina *(R)

Erect, rhizomatous, ± glabrous perennial to 50 cm. STEMS Simple or branched. LEAVES *Stem leaves 2–6 cm, lanceolate, sessile, cordate, entire or remotely toothed,* sparsely pubescent beneath. FLOWERING HEADS *20–40 mm across*; solitary or 2–5 per inflorescence; ray florets golden yellow; disc florets brownish yellow. HABITAT/DIST. Native. Very rare, at a single site on the limestone shoreline of Lough Derg, Ireland. (Most of Europe.) FLS Jul–Aug.

Elecampane
Inula helenium

Tall, robust perennial to 150 cm. STEMS Downy, simple or branched. LEAVES *Basal leaves large, 25–40 cm,* elliptical; stem leaves sessile, ovate-cordate, glabrous above, softly hairy beneath. FLOWERING HEADS *6–8 cm across,* solitary or 2–3 per inflorescence; *outer bracts ovate, leaf-like*; florets bright yellow. HABITAT Verges of roads and lanes close to habitation. DIST. Archaeophyte. Widespread but scattered and declining throughout BI as persistent garden escape. (SE Europe.) FLS Jul–Aug.

Golden-samphire
Inula crithmoides

Erect, glabrous maritime perennial to 90 cm. STEMS *Fleshy,* branched. LEAVES 2.5–6 cm, *linear, fleshy, glabrous, simple or with 3 teeth at apex.* FLOWERING HEADS 23–28 mm across, few in corymb-like inflorescence; ray florets golden yellow. HABITAT Calcareous maritime cliffs, salt marshes. DIST. Native. Local. Coasts of S Britain from Suffolk to N Wales; SW and E Ireland. (Coasts of W and S Europe.) FLS Jul–Aug.

Jersey Cudweed
naphalium luteoalbum

Marsh Cudweed
Gnaphalium uliginosum

Ploughman's-spikenard
Inula conyzae

Golden-samphire
Inula crithmoides

ape Cudweed
Gnaphalium undulatum

Elecampane
Inula helenium

Helichrysum stoechas

Irish Fleabane
Inula salicina

Immortelle
Helichrysum arenarium

illustrations
0.6× lifesize

Common Fleabane
Pulicaria dysenterica

Erect, stoloniferous, sparsely hairy, clump-forming perennial to 60 cm. LEAVES 3–8 cm, densely, softly hairy; *stem leaves* oblong-lanceolate, *cordate, clasping*. FLOWERING HEADS 15–30 mm across, in loose inflorescence; *ray florets much longer than involucral bracts*. HABITAT Damp roadsides, ditches, banks of streams and rivers, marshes, fens, wet meadows, dune slacks. DIST. Native. Widespread and common in England, Wales; ± absent from Scotland; scattered in Ireland. (All Europe except N.) FLS Aug–Sep.

Small Fleabane
Pulicaria vulgaris CR. *(B)

Erect, much-branched, pubescent annual to 45 cm. LEAVES 2.5–4 cm, margins undulate, entire or distantly toothed, rounded at base, partially clasping. FLOWERING HEADS 6–12 mm across; ray florets in 1 row; *ligules short*, about as long as involucral bracts. HABITAT Winter-wet depressions, grazed acid grasslands of commons, village greens, cart ruts. DIST. Native. Very rare, declining. S England; now more or less confined to New Forest. (All Europe except N.) FLS Aug–Sep.

Goldenrod
Solidago virgaurea

Erect, simple or sparsely branched perennial. Very variable, with 2 subspecies. STEMS Smooth, leafy, glabrous or pubescent; much branched in ssp. *virgaurea*, to 100 cm; unbranched in ssp. *minuta*, to 20 cm. LEAVES Stem leaves oblong-lanceolate, entire or obscurely toothed; basal leaves ± acute in ssp. *virgaurea*, rounded in ssp. *minuta*. FLOWERING HEADS Numerous, *6–15 mm across*; in narrow, erect inflorescence, open in ssp. *virgaurea*, compact in ssp. *minuta*. HABITAT Ssp. *virgaurea* in acid woodlands, heathlands, hedge banks, dunes; ssp. *minuta* on stream sides, cliff ledges, montane heath, to 1095 m. DIST. Native. Throughout BI; ssp. *virgaurea* frequent in lowlands; ssp. *minuta* in mts. (Ssp. *virgaurea* in most of Europe; ssp. *minuta* in mts of N, central and E Europe.) FLS Ssp. *virgaurea* Jun–Jul; ssp. *minuta* Aug–Sep.

Canadian Goldenrod
Solidago canadensis

Tall, erect, *pubescent* perennial to 250 cm. LEAVES *Roughly hairy on both surfaces*, numerous, with 3 veins. FLOWERING HEADS Very numerous, *3–3.5 mm* across, in dense pyramidal inflorescence. DIST. Introduced (native of North America). Naturalised as persistent garden throw-out throughout most of BI. (Much of Europe) FLS Aug–Oct.

Early Goldenrod
Solidago gigantea

Similar to *S. canadensis*, but *stems and leaves ± glabrous*; heads 2–3 mm across. HABITAT Waste places, roadsides, riverbanks, rough grassland, dunes. DIST. Introduced (native of North America). Naturalised throughout England, Wales, but less frequent than *S. canadensis*. (Much of Europe) FLS Jul–Oct. *Not illustrated*.

Alpine Fleabane
Frigeron borealis VU. *(P

Erect, *unbranched, pubescent alpine* perennial to 20 cm. LEAVES 1.3–3 cm, *very hairy, mostly in basal rosette*. FLOWERING HEADS *Solitary*, 15–22 mm across; ligules purple; disc florets yellow. HABITAT Unstable, inaccessible mica-schist cliff ledges; to 1100 m. DIST. Native. Very rare. Scottish Highlands. (N and Arctic Europe.) FLS Jul–Aug.

Mexican Fleabane
Erigeron karvinskianu

Much-branched, slender perennial to 25 cm. STEM Leafy. LEAVES Lower leaves obovate, *coarsely toothed*, upper leaves linear, entire. FLOWERING HEADS 17–20 mm across, very 'daisy-like', in open, leafy inflorescence; *ligules white above*, pink beneath. HABITAT Old walls, rock outcrops, cliffs. DIST. Introduced (native of Mexico). Widely naturalised as garden escape. Common in S and SW England, Channel Is; scattered elsewhere. (S and W Europe) FLS Jul–Aug.

Blue Fleabane
Erigeron acer *(N

Slender, erect, branched annual or biennial to 60 cm. STEMS *Roughly hairy*, reddish. LEAVES Stem leaves numerous, lanceolate, *entire*. FLOWERING HEADS 12–18 mm across, 1–several per inflorescence; *ray florets purplish mauve, erect, not much longer than disc florets*. HABITAT Dry, open permanent grassland, mature sand-dunes, banks, old walls, on well drained calcareous soils. DIST. Native. Widespread in England SE of line from Humber to Severn; local and coastal in SW England, Wales; scarce in Ireland. (Most of Europe.) FLS Jul–Aug.

Canadian Fleabane
Conyza canadensis

Tall, erect, much-branched yellowish-green annual to 100 cm. LEAVES Stem leaves numerous, 3–12 cm, linear-lanceolate. FLOWERING HEADS 3–5 mm across, in elongated inflorescence; *involucral bracts glabrous*. HABITAT Increasingly common urban weed of waste ground, pavements, walls, railway ballast, cultivated ground. DIST. Introduced (native of North America). Spreading. Widespread in lowland England, but scarce in SW, Wales; rare in Ireland. (Throughout Europe) FLS Aug–Sep. NOTE *C. canadensis* is the commonest and most widespread of several species of North and South American *Conyza* that are well established in BI and appear to be spreading.

Canadian Goldenrod
Solidago canadensis

Small Fleabane
Pulicaria vulgaris

Canadian Fleabane
Conyza canadensis

Common Fleabane
Pulicaria dysenterica

Goldenrod
Solidago virgaurea

Mexican Fleabane
Erigeron karvinskianus

Blue Fleabane
Erigeron acer

Alpine Fleabane
Erigeron borealis

illustrations
0.8× lifesize

Guernsey Fleabane
Conyza sumatrensis

Similar to *C. canadensis*, but heads 5–8 mm across, *involucral bracts densely hairy.* HABITAT Similar to *C. canadensis.* DIST. Introduced (native of South America). Spreading in the London area, E England, Channel Is. (Throughout Europe) FLS Jul–Sep. *Not illustrated.*

Michaelmas-daisies *Aster*

See key on p.472. A number of North American Michaelmas-daisies have long been cultivated in British gardens, and several are commonly established on rough ground, waste places, roadsides and railway banks. The numerous cultivars and hybrids makes identification difficult; details of the involucral bracts are especially useful in this.

Hairy Michaelmas-daisy
Aster novae-angliae

Tall, erect, robust perennial to 220 cm. STEMS *Branched, with long, spreading hairs and shorter glandular hairs.* LEAVES Stem leaves with rounded auricles, *densely glandular-pubescent.* FLOWERING HEADS 20–40 mm across; involucral bracts green, glandular; *ligules reddish purple.* HABITAT *See* above. FLS Sep–Oct.

Confused Michaelmas-daisy
Aster novi-belgii

Tall, robust, ± glabrous, much-branched perennial to 150 cm. LEAVES Middle stem leaves lanceolate, *4–10× as long as wide, auricled, half-clasping.* FLOWERING HEADS 25–50 mm across; *outer involucral bracts not closely appressed, 5–8 mm, widest at or just above middle, green*; ligules violet-blue (violet, white or purple in cultivars). HABITAT *See* above. FLS Sep–Nov.

Late Michaelmas-daisy
Aster × versicolor
(*A. laevis × A. novi-belgii*)

Tall, robust, large-flowered, late-flowering Michaelmas-daisy, to 220 cm. LEAVES 2–15 cm, deep green, obtuse at apex; middle stem leaves 2.5–5× as long as broad, sessile, ± clasping. FLOWERING HEADS *30–50 mm across; involucral bracts appressed, 3.5–7 mm,* whitish with central green patch in upper half; ligules bluish purple. HABITAT *See* above. FLS Oct–Nov.

Narrow-leaved Michaelmas-daisy
Aster lanceolatus

Tall, glabrous or thinly pubescent perennial to 120 cm. LEAVES Upper leaves linear-lanceolate, tapering to base, not clasping, narrow, usually ≤10 mm wide. FLOWERING HEADS 13–25 mm across, in narrow inflorescence; *involucral bracts 3.5–5.5 mm, green with pale borders, red-tipped, appressed; ligules whitish.* HABITAT *See* above. FLS Sep–Jan.

Common Michaelmas-daisy
Aster × salignus
(*A. lanceolatus × A. novi-belgii*)

Commonest naturalised Michaelmas-daisy. Very similar to *A. lanceolatus*, but stems to 130 cm; leaves narrowed to semi-clasping base with short auricles; flowering heads 15–25 mm across; inflorescence wider than *A. lanceolatus; involucral bracts 5–7 mm, widest below middle, tips reddish; ligules whitish to pale blue.* HABITAT *See* above. FLS Sep–Nov.

Sea Aster
Aster tripolium

Erect, *glabrous*, short-lived *maritime* perennial to 100 cm. LEAVES Lanceolate, 7–12 cm, *fleshy, glabrous.* FLOWERING HEADS 8–30 mm across; involucral bracts few, blunt; ligules blue-purple or absent (var. *flosculosus*). HABITAT Salt marshes, creek sides, brackish ditches, tidal rivers, sea cliffs. DIST. Native. All round coasts of BI. (Most European coasts.) FLS Jul–Oct.

Goldilocks Aster
Aster linosyris

Erect, glabrous perennial to 50 cm. LEAVES 2–5 cm *very numerous, linear.* FLOWERING HEADS 12–18 mm across, in dense inflorescence; outer involucral bracts leaf-like, spreading; *ray florets absent;* disc florets longer than bracts, bright yellow. HABITAT Limestone sea cliffs, cliff-top grassland. DIST. Native. Very rare, in about 7 scattered localities in W England, Wales. (Most of Europe except N.) FLS Aug–Sep.

Hairy Michaelmas-daisy
Aster novae-angliae

Goldilocks Aster
Aster linosyris

**Common
Michaelmas-daisy**
Aster × salignus

**Late
Michaelmas-
daisy**
Aster × versicolor

**Sea
Aster**
*Aster
tripolium*

**Narrow-leaved
Michaelmas-daisy**
Aster lanceolatus

**Confused
Michaelmas-daisy**
Aster novi-belgii

illustrations
0.7× lifesize

Daisy
Bellis perennis

Perennial. STEMS Flowering stems to 12 cm, leafless, hairy. LEAVES 2-4 cm, all in basal rosette. FLOWERING HEADS 16-25 mm across, ray florets white, disc yellow. HABITAT Familiar plant of lawns, pastures, roadside verges; also characteristic of grazed, mown, trampled grasslands, dune slacks, stream sides, upland flushes. To 915 m. DIST. Native. Common throughout BI. (All Europe.) FLS Mar–Oct.

Feverfew
Tanacetum parthenium

Erect, branched, somewhat downy, strongly aromatic perennial to 70 cm. LEAVES *Yellowish green, deeply pinnately lobed.* FLOWERING HEADS Numerous, radiate, 15-25 mm across, in open corymb-like inflorescence; ray florets white, disc yellow. HABITAT Naturalised on old walls, gardens, tips, waste ground. DIST. Archaeophyte. Frequent throughout BI, but scarce in N Scotland, W Ireland. (SE Europe.) FLS Jul–Aug.

Tansy
Tanacetum vulgare

Tall, robust, rhizomatous, *aromatic* perennial to 120 cm. LEAVES 15-25 cm, oblong in outline, *pinnate.* FLOWERING HEADS *Discoid, yellow,* 7-12 mm across, in dense corymb-like inflorescence. DIST. Native throughout Britain, but scarce in N Scotland; introduced in Ireland. HABITAT Rough grassland, roadsides, riverbanks, waste ground; to 380 m. (Most of Europe.) FLS Jul–Sep.

Yarrow
Achillea millefolium

Stoloniferous, pubescent, aromatic perennial to 80 cm. LEAVES *Lanceolate, 5-15 cm, deeply dissected, 2-3-pinnate.* FLOWERING HEADS *Radiate,* 4-6 mm across, *in dense, terminal, corymb-like inflorescence*; ray florets white, disc cream. HABITAT All grassland habitats from sea-level to 1210 m, lawns, dunes, shingle, waste ground. DIST. Native. Common throughout BI. (All Europe.) FLS Jun–Sep.

Sneezewort
Achillea ptarmica

Erect perennial to 60 cm. STEMS Simple or branched, glabrous below, pubescent above. LEAVES *1.5-8 cm, linear-lanceolate, sharply toothed.* FLOWERING HEADS *Radiate, 12-18 mm* across, few in open inflorescence; ray florets white, disc cream. HABITAT Damp grasslands, meadows, grazed commons, marshes, wet heaths, stream sides, hillside flushes; to 770 m. DIST. Native. Throughout BI, but scarce in S Ireland and decreasing E and SE England. (All Europe except Mediterranean.) FLS Jul–Aug.

Corn Marigold
Chrysanthemum segetum VU.

Glabrous, glaucous annual to 50 cm. STEMS Simple or branched. LEAVES 2-8 cm, coarsely toothed or pinnately lobed. FLOWERING HEADS *Solitary,* long-stalked, 35-65 mm across, radiate; *ray florets golden yellow,* disc yellow. HABITAT Disturbed and waste ground, arable weed of light sandy soils; to 410 m. DIST. Archaeophyte. Declining. Throughout BI. (E Mediterranean.) FLS Jun–Aug.

Oxeye Daisy
Leucanthemum vulgare

Erect, branched, slender perennial with non-flowering rosettes and simple or branched flowering stems to 70 cm. LEAVES Basal leaves 1-8 cm, spathulate, long-stalked, bluntly toothed; upper stem leaves sessile. FLOWERING HEADS *Radiate, 25-60 mm across, solitary*; involucral bracts 6-8 mm. HABITAT Dry grasslands, coastal cliffs, dunes, waste ground, roadside verges, railway banks, on neutral or calcareous soils; to 845 m. DIST. Native. Common throughout most of BI. (All Europe.) FLS Jul–Sep.

Shasta Daisy
Leucanthemum × superbum
(*L. lacustre × L. maximum*)

Similar to *L. vulgare*, but much larger and more robust; stems to 120 cm; leaves to 15 cm; *flowering heads solitary, 60-100 mm across*; involucral bracts 11-15 mm. HABITAT Roadsides, railway banks, waste ground. DIST. Introduced. Popular garden perennial, naturalised throughout BI but infrequent in N Scotland, Ireland. FLS Jun–Aug.

Daisy
Bellis perennis

Feverfew
Tanacetum parthenium

Tansy
Tanacetum vulgare

Sneezewort
Achillea ptarmica

Yarrow
Achillea millefolium

Corn Marigold
Chrysanthemum segetum

Shasta Daisy
Leucanthemum × superbum

Oxeye Daisy
Leucanthemum vulgare

illustrations
0.6× lifesize

Mugworts *Artemisia* and *Seriphidium*
See key to *Seriphidium* and *Artemisia* on p.473.

Sea Wormwood
Seriphidium maritimum

Strongly aromatic, white-downy, rhizomatous perennial with non-flowering rosettes. STEMS Decumbent to erect flowering shoots, to 50 cm. LEAVES *White-woolly*, 2-5 cm, deeply pinnately divided, *ultimate segments linear, ≤1 mm wide*. FLOWERING HEADS Numerous, 1-2 mm across; florets all tubular. HABITAT Drier parts of salt marshes; also sea walls, shingle, cliffs, brackish dykes, rough ground near sea. DIST. Native. All round coast of Britain except W and N Scotland; rare in Ireland. (Atlantic and Mediterranean coasts of Europe; inland saline areas of E Europe.) FLS Aug-Sep.

Mugwort
Artemisia vulgaris

Tall, robust, tufted, aromatic perennial to 150 cm. STEMS *Becoming glabrous, central pith >¾ width of stem*. LEAVES 5-8 cm, deeply divided, dark green, glabrous above, whitish pubescent beneath, ultimate segments lanceolate, 3-6 mm wide. FLOWERING HEADS 3-4 mm across, numerous; in inflorescence, hardly leafy, *branches straight, erect*. HABITAT Roadsides, hedge banks, riverbanks, waste ground, on fertile soils; to 350 m. DIST. Archaeophyte. Common throughout most of BI, but sparse in N Scotland and most of Ireland. (All Europe except extreme N.) FLS Jul-Sep.

Chinese Mugwort
Artemisia verlotiorum

Strongly rhizomatous perennial. Similar to *A. vulgare*, but *stems persistently pubescent, central pith c.⅓ width of stem; ultimate segments of leaves linear-lanceolate*, more elongated; *inflorescence leafy, branches arching*. HABITAT Rough ground, roadsides. DIST. Introduced (native of SW China). Naturalised and locally common, especially in London area, scattered elsewhere. (Widely naturalised in W and central Europe.) FLS Oct-Dec.

Wormwood
Artemisia absinthium

Tufted, aromatic perennial to 90 cm, with *non-flowering rosettes*. STEMS *Erect, silky-hairy*. LEAVES Deeply pinnately divided, *greyish pubescent, lobes 2-4 mm* wide. FLOWERING HEADS Numerous, 3-5 mm, wider than long, drooping; *receptacle hairy*.

HABITAT Roadsides, waste ground, railway sidings to 370 m. DIST. Archaeophyte. Widely distributed in England, Wales; mostly coastal in E Scotland; rare in Ireland. (Most of Europe except extreme N and S.) FLS Jul-Aug.

Norwegian Mugwort
Artemisia norvegica VU

Dwarf, tufted, aromatic alpine perennial to 10 cm. LEAVES 1-2 cm, deeply lobed, with long, pale silky hairs. FLOWERING HEADS *Solitary*, 8-13 mm across nodding. DIST. Native (British plant is endemic ssp *scotica*). Very rare, in 3 localities only in former county of Ross-shire. HABITAT Bare stony mountain summits, 700-870 m. (Norway.) FLS Jul-Sep.

Field Wormwood
Artemisia campestris VU. *(B

Decumbent, ± glabrous, non-aromatic perennial STEMS *Tufts of non-flowering shoots*; ascending flowering shoots to 75 cm. LEAVES Deeply pinnately lobed, *glabrous when mature, ultimate segments linear, c.1 mm wide*. FLOWERING HEADS 3-4 mm across, numerous, in narrow, elongated inflorescence; florets yellow or reddish. HABITAT Short, dry open grassland, edges of arable fields, tracksides road verges. DIST. Native. Very rare, in 3 sites only in East Anglia (Breckland). (Most of Europe except extreme N.) FLS Aug-Sep.

Hoary Mugwort
Artemisia stelleriane

Non-aromatic, rhizomatous perennial. STEMS Non-flowering shoots; flowering stems, usually solitary to 60 cm. LEAVES Deeply pinnately lobed, ultimate segments 3-8 mm wide, *densely white-felted* on both surfaces. FLOWERING HEADS Numerous, 4-10 mm across, in dense spike-like inflorescence; receptacle glabrous. HABITAT Coastal sand-dunes in Scotland waste ground inland. DIST. Introduced (native of NE Asia). Naturalised in a few sites. FLS Jul-Sep.

Cottonweed
Otanthus maritimus EX. *(R

Much-branched, densely white-woolly, shrubby maritime perennial to 50 cm. LEAVES 5-20 mm, oblong, densely white-felted. FLOWERING HEADS 6-9 mm across, 3-10 in tight terminal corymbs; florets yellow. HABITAT Sand-dunes, stabilised shingle. DIST. Extinct in Britain; native in Ireland. Very rare, in 2 sites only in SE Ireland (Co. Wexford). (W Europe, Mediterranean.) FLS Aug-Sep.

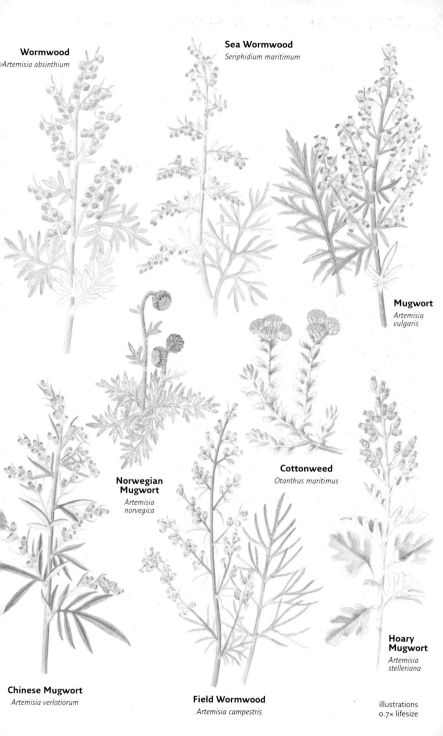

Wormwood
Artemisia absinthium

Sea Wormwood
Seriphidium maritimum

Mugwort
Artemisia vulgaris

Norwegian Mugwort
Artemisia norvegica

Cottonweed
Otanthus maritimus

Hoary Mugwort
Artemisia stelleriana

Chinese Mugwort
Artemisia verlotiorum

Field Wormwood
Artemisia campestris

illustrations
0.7× lifesize

Chamomile and Mayweeds
Chamaemelum, Matricaria, Anthemis and Tripleurospermum

A distinctive, similar-looking group of composites (*see* key on p.473), with radiate flower heads (occasionally discoid) comprising usually white ray florets (sometimes yellow) and yellow disc florets. The leaves are 1–3-pinnate and deeply dissected into narrow linear segments. Identification depends primarily on the presence of receptacle bracts and details of the achenes, as well as on whether the plants are hairy.

Chamomile
Chamaemelum nobile VU.

Pleasantly aromatic, prostrate to erect, branched, pubescent *perennial* to 30 cm. LEAVES 1.5–5 cm. FLOWERING HEADS 18–25 mm across, solitary, on long stalks; *receptacle scales oblong, blunt; base of corolla tube of disc florets enlarged and enclosing tip of achene*. Local, declining. HABITAT Seasonally wet, grazed, acid sandy grassland, village greens, commons, maritime grassland, cliffs; to 465 m. DIST. Native. S and SW Britain, SW Ireland. (W Europe.) FLS Jun–Jul. NOTE Non-flowering form cultivated as chamomile lawns is cultivar 'Treneague'.

Corn Chamomile
Anthemis arvensis EN.

Pleasantly aromatic, *densely pubescent*, decumbent to erect, branched annual to 50 cm. LEAVES *Leaf segments short, white-woolly beneath*. FLOWERING HEADS 20–40 mm across, solitary; *receptacle scales broad, with tapering point*, longer than disc florets. HABITAT Arable fields, disturbed ground, close to sea on light sandy or calcareous soils. DIST. Archaeophyte. Scattered, declining. Now mostly confined to East Anglia; rare or absent from most of Wales, Scotland, Ireland. (All Europe except N.) FLS Jun–Jul.

Stinking Chamomile
Anthemis cotula VU.

Sparsely pubescent annual *with unpleasant smell*, to 60 cm. STEMS Erect. LEAVES *Yellow-green*. FLOWERING HEADS 12–30 mm across, solitary, on long stalks; *receptacle scales narrow, bristle-like*. HABITAT Arable fields on heavy or calcareous soils. DIST. Archaeophyte. Lowland England; rare and declining elsewhere. (All Europe except N.) FLS Jul–Sep.

Yellow Chamomile
Anthemis tinctoria

Erect, pubescent biennial to perennial, to 60 cm. FLOWERING HEADS 25–40 mm across, solitary, on long stalks; *ray florets yellow*. HABITAT Waste ground on dry soils. DIST. Introduced. Scattered as rare casual escape from cultivation throughout BI. (S and central Europe.) FLS Jul–Aug.

Pineapple-weed
Matricaria discoidea

Much-branched, erect, glabrous annual to 30 cm. FLOWERING HEADS 5–8 mm across, solitary, on short stalks; *discoid; ray florets absent*. HABITAT Disturbed or trampled fertile ground, tracks, arable fields, gateways, roadsides; to 845 m. DIST. Introduced (native of NE Asia). Naturalised and common throughout BI. (Naturalised throughout Europe.) FLS Jun–Aug.

Scented Mayweed
Matricaria recutita

Pleasantly aromatic, erect, much-branched, glabrous annual to 60 cm. FLOWERING HEADS 12–22 mm across; *receptacle markedly conical, hollow, receptacle scales absent; ligules becoming reflexed soon after flowers open*. HABITAT Arable fields, waste ground, on light, fertile, mildly acid soils; to 365 m. DIST. Archaeophyte. Common throughout most of England, Wales; scarce in Scotland, Ireland. (Most of Europe.) FLS Jun–Aug.

Scentless Mayweed
Tripleurospermum inodorum

Non-aromatic, prostrate to erect, much-branched glabrous annual to 60 cm. LEAVES Leaflets not succulent. FLOWERING HEADS 15–40 mm across, solitary, on long stalks; *receptacle slightly convex, solid*. FRUITS Achenes, *with 2 dark brown, ± circular oil glands towards top of outer face; ribs separated*. HABITAT Common weed of arable fields, tracks, roadsides, waste ground, on disturbed, fertile soils; to 530 m. DIST. Archaeophyte. Throughout BI, but scarce in NW Scotland, W Ireland. (N and central Europe.) FLS Jul–Sep.

Sea Mayweed
Tripleurospermum maritimum

Perennial, similar to *T. inodorum*, but ± prostrate, mat-forming; *leaflets shorter, rather succulent; oil glands on achenes elongated, ribs almost touching*. HABITAT Shingle beaches, cliffs, sea walls, sand, waste ground close to sea. DIST. Native. Common around coasts of BI. (N Europe.) FLS Jul–Sep.

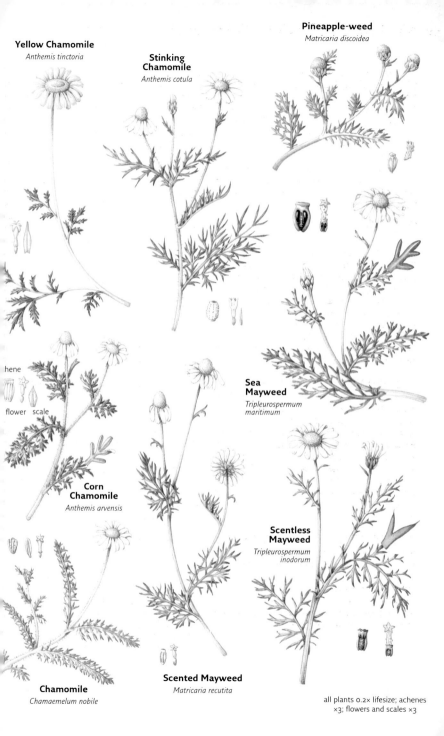

Yellow Chamomile
Anthemis tinctoria

Stinking Chamomile
Anthemis cotula

Pineapple-weed
Matricaria discoidea

hene

flower scale

Sea Mayweed
Tripleurospermum maritimum

Corn Chamomile
Anthemis arvensis

Scentless Mayweed
Tripleurospermum inodorum

Chamomile
Chamaemelum nobile

Scented Mayweed
Matricaria recutita

all plants 0.2× lifesize; achenes
×3; flowers and scales ×3

Buttonweed
Cotula coronopifolia

Procumbent, glabrous, succulent annual or perennial to 30 cm. LEAVES Entire or irregularly lobed. FLOWERING HEADS Solitary, discoid, 8–12 mm across, stalks longer than leaves, bright yellow. HABITAT Wet marshy places, bare mud at pond edges, bare, wet saline habitats. DIST. Introduced (native of S hemisphere). Infrequent, naturalised or casual in lowland England. (Cosmopolitan weed throughout Europe.) FLS Jul–Aug.

Ragworts *Senecio, Tephroseris*

Annuals or perennials with discoid or radiate flower heads (*see* key on p.474); the involucral bracts are mostly in 1 row or with a few short outer ones; disc florets and ray florets are both yellow. *Tephroseris* differs from *Senecio* in that the involucral bracts are all in 1 row with no shorter outer ones.

Silver Ragwort
Senecio cineraria

Densely white-woolly, erect, branching evergreen perennial to 100 cm. STEMS Base *woody*. LEAVES *Deeply pinnately divided,* white-felted beneath, green but pubescent above. FLOWERING HEADS Bright yellow, 10–15 mm across, in dense corymbs. HABITAT Waste ground, verges; also cliffs, shingle, rough ground near sea. DIST. Introduced. Naturalised or casual. Scattered in lowland England; mostly coastal elsewhere. (Mediterranean.) FLS Jun–Aug.

Marsh Fleawort
Senecio congestus

Tall, erect biennial to 200 cm. STEMS Flowering stems woolly, very leafy. LEAVES 7–12 cm, lanceolate, yellowish green, woolly. FLOWERING HEADS 20–30 cm across; involucral bracts glandular-woolly; *c*.20 ray florets, 7–10 mm. HABITAT Damp meadows, marshes, fens. DIST. Extinct in BI. (Central Europe.) FLS Jun–Jul. *Not illustrated.*

Broad-leaved Ragwort
Senecio fluviatilis

Tall, erect, *stoloniferous* perennial to 150 cm. LEAVES 4–20 cm, lanceolate, toothed, ± *glabrous*. FLOWERING HEADS Numerous, 15–30 mm across; outer involucral bracts *c*.⅓ as long as inner; 6–8 ray florets. HABITAT Stream banks, fens, wet woodlands, marshy places. DIST. Introduced. Naturalised in scattered localities throughout BI. (Central and S Europe.) FLS Jul–Sep.

Alpine Ragwort
Senecio nemorensis

Tall, erect, densely leafy perennial to 200 cm. Similar to *S. fluviatilis*, but stolons short or absent; *leaves glabrous above, hairy beneath*; flowering heads 20–35 mm across; 5–6 ray florets; outer involucral bracts about as long as inner. HABITAT Damp meadows, open woods; acid soils in upland areas. DIST. *Not BI*. (Most of Europe except N and Mediterranean.) FLS Jul–Sep.

Fen Ragwort
Senecio paludosus CR. *(B)

Tall, erect perennial to 200 cm. LEAVES 7–15 cm, *white-cottony pubescent beneath, narrowly elliptical,* sharply toothed, acute. FLOWERING HEADS 30–40 mm across, numerous, in corymbose inflorescence; 10–16 ray florets. HABITAT/DIST. Native. Very rare. Formerly found in fen ditches in East Anglia, rediscovered in 1972 in a ditch near Ely and now reintroduced to fen nature reserves. (Much of Europe except NW and Mediterranean.) FLS May–Jul.

Common Ragwort
Senecio jacobaea

Erect, branched, non-stoloniferous biennial or perennial to 100 cm. LEAVES Stem *leaves irregularly* lobed, glabrous above, *sparsely hairy on veins beneath*, several pairs of lateral lobes, terminal lobe not much broader than laterals. FLOWERING HEADS 15–25 mm across, *in dense inflorescence*, so that neighbouring heads in contact or overlapping; outer involucral bracts *c*.¼ as long as inner. HABITAT Rough grassland, rabbit-grazed pasture, scrub, woodland rides, waste ground, roadsides, sand dunes; to 670 m. DIST. Native. Common throughout BI. (Most of Europe, but rare in extreme N and S.) FLS Jun–Oct.

Hoary Ragwort
Senecio erucifolius

Tall, stiffly erect, stoloniferous perennial to 120 cm. LEAVES Stem *leaves deeply pinnately lobed, terminal lobe small, narrow, acute, margins revolute, whole surface grey-pubescent beneath*. FLOWERING HEADS 15–20 mm across; outer involucral bracts *c*.¼ as long as inner. HABITAT Rough grassland, roadsides, field borders, railway banks, on calcareous or clay soils; also waste ground, shingle, dunes. DIST. Native. Lowland England, Wales; absent from Scotland; rare in Ireland. (Most of Europe except N.) FLS Jul–Aug.

Marsh Ragwort
Senecio aquaticus

Erect, non-stoloniferous, glabrous or sparsely pubescent biennial to 80 cm. LEAVES Stem leaves with large, ovate terminal lobe and a few smaller lateral lobes. FLOWERING HEADS 25–30 mm across, *inflorescence spreading so that neighbouring heads not in contact*. HABITAT Wet meadows, marshes, by streams, ponds and ditches; to 460 m. DIST. Native. Throughout lowland BI, but declining in SE. (S, W and central Europe.) FLS Jul–Aug.

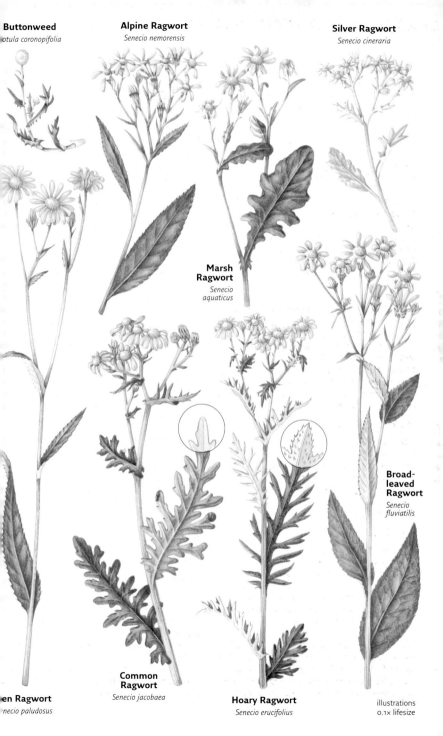

Buttonweed
Cotula coronopifolia

Alpine Ragwort
Senecio nemorensis

Silver Ragwort
Senecio cineraria

Marsh Ragwort
Senecio aquaticus

Broad-leaved Ragwort
Senecio fluviatilis

Common Ragwort
Senecio jacobaea

Hoary Ragwort
Senecio erucifolius

Fen Ragwort
Senecio paludosus

illustrations
0.1× lifesize

Oxford Ragwort
Senecio squalidus

Decumbent to erect, ± glabrous annual or short-lived perennial, to 30 cm. Very variable. LEAVES Deeply lobed. FLOWERING HEADS *16-20 mm across*, in open inflorescence; *involucral bracts all black-tipped; 12-15 ray florets*. HABITAT Naturalised on waste ground, walls, railways, roadsides. DIST. Introduced. Widespread throughout England, Wales; spreading in Scotland, Ireland. (Native of Sicily.) FLS May-Dec.

Groundsel
Senecio vulgaris

Erect, irregularly branched annual to 30 cm. LEAVES Pinnately lobed, glabrous or with cottony hairs. FLOWERING HEADS 4-5 mm across, *discoid; ray florets usually absent*, or ≤5 *mm if present; outer involucral bracts black-tipped*. FRUITS Achenes, ≤2.5 mm. HABITAT Ubiquitous weed of waste ground, gardens, arable fields; to 550 m. Also on dunes, shingle, cliffs. DIST. Native. Throughout BI. (All Europe except extreme N.) FLS Jan-Dec.

Welsh Groundsel
Senecio cambrensis

Erect, glabrous or sparsely pubescent annual to 30 cm. LEAVES Deeply pinnately lobed. FLOWERING HEADS *Radiate, to 15 mm across; 13 ray florets, 4-7 mm; involucral bracts black-tipped*. HABITAT Disturbed ground, waste places, walls, roadsides. DIST. Endemic. Very rare. N Wales, Scotland. FLS May-Oct. NOTE Hybrid in origin, from *S. vulgaris × S. squalidus*.

Eastern Groundsel
Senecio vernalis

Erect, cottony-pubescent annual to 50 cm. LEAVES *Yellowish green, shortly pinnately lobed*, pubescent. FLOWERING HEADS 20-30 mm across, in dense inflorescence; involucral bracts with black tips. HABITAT Landscaped areas, roadside verges. DIST. Introduced. In a few scattered localities in S England. (E and E-central Europe; spreading in W Europe.) FLS May-Nov.

Heath Groundsel
Senecio sylvaticus

Erect, pubescent annual to 70 cm. STEMS *Glandular but not sticky*. LEAVES *Yellow-green*, deeply pinnately lobed; pubescent, becoming glabrous. FLOWERING HEADS Numerous, 5-6 mm across; peduncles and involucral bracts with short glandular hairs; *8-14 ray*

florets, short, revolute. HABITAT Heaths, common open woodland, cliffs, on sandy soils; to 365 m DIST. Native. Rather local, throughout BI. (Centr Europe.) FLS Jul-Sep.

Sticky Groundsel
Senecio visco

Erect, branched, *sticky annual, with dense glandul hairs*, to 60 cm. LEAVES Dark green, deeply pinnate lobed, very sticky. FLOWERING HEADS 10-15 m across, long-stalked; 13 *ray florets, revolute*. HABIT Free-draining sands, gravels, on roadsides, railway banks, walls, waste ground, dunes, shingle; 430 m. DIST. Introduced. Naturalised througho most of BI, but rare in N Scotland, Ireland; sprea ing. (All Europe except extreme N.) FLS Jul-Sep.

Narrow-leaved Ragwort
Senecio inaequide

Rather *bushy, ± glabrous* perennial to 80 cm. STEM Base woody. LEAVES 2-6 cm, *linear, entire*. FLOWE ING HEADS 10-25 mm across; involucral brac black-tipped; 7-15 ray florets. HABITAT Was ground. DIST. Introduced (native of S Africa). Casu or naturalised in a few scattered localities throug out BI; spreading. (W Europe.) FLS Jun-Oct. N illustrated.

Field Fleawort
Tephroseris integrifolia E

Pubescent perennial with *white cottony* hairs. STEM Flowering stems to 30 cm. LEAVES *Basal leaves in rosette, ovate; stem leaves few*. FLOWERING HEA 3-12, 15-25 mm across, in branched inflorescenc ray florets 6-8.5 mm; involucral bracts in 1 ro HABITAT Short chalk and limestone grasslan earthworks, warm, S-facing slopes. DIST. Nativ Very local, declining. S England. (Central and Europe.) FLS May-Jul. NOTE Ssp. *maritima*, wi stems to 60 cm, toothed basal leaves, >6 heads a 8-12 mm ligules, is endemic to cliff slopes on Angl sey. VU *(B)

Swiss Fleawort
Tephroseris heleni

Similar to *T. integrifolia*, but basal leaves not rosette and withering by flowering; petiole long than leaf blade; several stem leaves. HABITAT Dan grassland, cool woods. DIST. *Not BI*. (Central Euro from NW France to E.) FLS Jun-Aug.

astern Groundsel
Senecio vernalis

Heath Groundsel
Senecio sylvaticus

Oxford Ragwort
Senecio squalidus

Groundsel
Senecio vulgaris

Swiss Fleawort
Tephroseris helenitis

Field Fleawort
Tephroseris integrifolia

Sticky Groundsel
Senecio viscosus

Welsh Groundsel
Senecio cambrensis

illustrations
0.2× lifesize

Leopard's-bane
Doronicum pardalianches

Rosette-forming, rhizomatous perennial to 90 cm. STEMS Flowering stems leafy. LEAVES *Rosette leaves long-stalked, ovate, cordate, pubescent.* FLOWERING HEADS *Radiate,* 40-60 mm across, several on long stalks; florets bright yellow. HABITAT Damp woods, stream sides, roadsides. DIST. Introduced. Naturalised throughout most of BI as escape from cultivation, but rare in Ireland. (W Europe.) FLS May-Jul.

Colt's-foot
Tussilago farfara

Rosette-forming, rhizomatous perennial. STEMS *Flowering stems erect, to 15 cm, appearing long before leaves.* LEAVES All basal, 20-30 cm across, densely white-felted beneath, cordate, shallowly lobed, *lobes with small blackish teeth.* FLOWERING HEADS Radiate, solitary, 15-35 mm across, yellow. HABITAT Disturbed ground, shingle, dunes, eroding cliffs, scree, riverbanks, waste ground, verges; to 1065 m. DIST. Native. Throughout BI. (All Europe except extreme N.) FLS Mar-Apr.

Butterburs *Petasites*

Dioecious, rhizomatous perennials with large, cordate basal leaves. Flowering stems are leafless but with few to several scale leaves. Flowering heads are in dense, spike-like terminal inflorescences. Stems and leaves are downy with white-cottony hairs.

1 Corolla of marginal florets
   ligulate   2
   Corolla of marginal florets
   tubular   3

2 Flowers lilac, appearing at same
   time as leaves, Nov-Feb; leaves
   orbicular, evenly toothed   *P. fragrans*
   Flowers yellowish; leaves
   triangular, with 2-3 lobes on
   each side at base   *P. spurius*

3 Leaves suborbicular, up to 30 cm
   across, with acute, toothed lobes,
   basal sinus with divergent or
   parallel sides; flowers pure white *P. albus*
   Leaves to 90 cm across, basal
   sinus with convergent sides;
   flowers cream or purplish   4

4 Leaves distinctly but shallowly
   lobed; bracts <1 cm wide;
   inflorescence ± cylindrical;
   flowers purplish white   *P. hybridus*

Leaves scarcely lobed; bracts >1 cm wide; inflorescence ± spherical; flowers cream *P. japonicus*

Butterbur
Petasites hybridu

FLOWERING STEMS Erect, to 40 cm, with man narrow *scale leaves, <10 mm wide.* LEAVES 10-90 cr across, long-stalked, shallowly lobed, margin. teeth uneven, *sides of basal sinus convergent.* FLOW ERING HEADS *Pale purplish, in ± cylindrical inflores cence,* appearing before leaves. HABITAT Dam woodlands, banks of rivers and streams, wet mead ows; to 380 m. DIST. Native. Throughout BI, bt scarce in N Scotland; female plants mostly in N an central England. (Most of Europe.) FLS Mar-Ma

Giant Butterbur
Petasites japonic

FLOWERING STEMS To 120 cm; with *numerous, ovat yellowish scale leaves, 5-12 cm.* LEAVES *Large, 30 100 cm across,* glabrous above, cottony hairy belov marginal teeth uneven. FLOWERING HEADS In hemispherical inflorescence; female flowers whit male cream. HABITAT Banks of streams and river DIST. Introduced (native of N Japan, Sakhalin). Mal plant naturalised as garden escape in scattered loca ities throughout BI except N Scotland, Ireland. Fr Mar-Apr, before leaves.

White Butterbur
Petasites alb

FLOWERING STEMS To 70 cm; scale leaves 2c 40 mm. LEAVES *15-30 cm across,* dark green abov white below, with large teeth or shallow lobes an smaller intervening teeth, *basal sinus with sides pa allel or divergent.* FLOWERING HEADS *Flowers pu white.* HABITAT Roadsides, waste ground, wood DIST. Introduced. Naturalised as garden escap especially in E Scotland; scattered elsewhere. (Mts Europe.) FLS Mar-May, before leaves.

Winter Heliotrope
Petasites fragra

FLOWERING STEMS To 25 cm; scale leaves 2-7 cr sometimes with fully developed blade. LEAVE *Persisting through winter,* 10-20 cm across, roundis green on both surfaces, slightly pubescent beneat marginal teeth all ± same size. FLOWERING HEA c.6-20, lilac, *marginal flowers ligulate,* vanilla-scente in rather loose inflorescence. HABITAT Hedge bank roadsides verges, stream sides, waste ground, form ing large, persistent colonies. DIST. Introduced (nati of N Africa). Naturalised throughout BI; common S, but rare in N Scotland. (Naturalised in central a S Europe.) FLS Dec-Mar, with leaves.

Winter Heliotrope
Petasites fragrans

Butterbur
Petasites hybridus

Leopard's-bane
Doronicum pardalianches

Colt's-foot
Tussilago farfara

White Butterbur
Petasites albus

illustrations 0.15× lifesize

Woolly Butterbur
Petasites spurius
(description on p.514)

Giant Butterbur
Petasites japonicus

Woolly Butterbur   *Petasites spurius*

[*See* illustration previous page.] LEAVES *Triangular, 2–3-lobed on each side at base*, margins evenly toothed. FLOWERING STEMS Scale leaves 5–10.5 cm. FLOWERING HEADS 10–45, yellowish, marginal florets ligulate. HABITAT Sandy seashores, dunes, riverbanks. DIST. *Not BI*. (E Europe, W to Denmark, N Germany.)

Purple Colt's-foot   *Homogyne alpina* EN. *(B)

Rhizomatous perennial. STEMS Flowering stems 10–40 cm. LEAVES All basal, orbicular, cordate, sparsely hairy beneath, 1.5–4.5 cm across. FLOWERING HEADS Solitary, discoid, 10–20 mm across; florets purple. HABITAT/DIST. Possibly native. Very rare, at a single site in Clova Mts, Angus, at 600 m. (Mts of central Europe.) FLS May–Aug.

Pot Marigold   *Calendula officinalis*

Procumbent to erect, glandular-pubescent annual to perennial, to 50 cm. STEMS Much branched, leafy. LEAVES 7–15 cm. FLOWERING HEADS *Radiate*, 20–70 mm across; ligules 2× as long as involucral bracts; florets yellow to orange, strong-smelling. HABITAT Waste ground, rubbish tips, near habitation. DIST. Introduced (origin unknown). Long cultivated as a pot-herb, now naturalised as garden throw-out throughout most of BI, but infrequent in Scotland, Ireland. FLS Jun–Aug.

Field Marigold   *Calendula arvensis*

Procumbent to erect annual, to 30 cm. STEMS Much branched, glandular-hairy. LEAVES 3–8 cm. FLOWERING HEADS *10–20 mm across*; ligules <2× as long as involucral bracts. FRUITS *Outer achenes 13–20 mm, incurved, beaked; inner achenes 6–10 mm, boat-shaped.* HABITAT Cultivated ground. DIST. Introduced. Naturalised in Channel Is, Scilly Is; rare casual elsewhere. (S and S-central Europe; naturalised further N.) FLS May–Aug.

Ragweed   *Ambrosia artemisiifolia*

Erect annual to 100 cm. Doesn't look like a composite; the rather umbellifer-like leaves and unusual structure of the distinctive inflorescence – with small, inconspicuous, single-sex heads – can prove a bit of a puzzle. LEAVES Opposite, deeply pinnately lobed, pubescent. FLOWERING HEADS Discoid, small, inconspicuous, male and female separate; male heads in elongated, drooping terminal spikes without bracts, corolla tubes greenish; female heads with only 1 flower in axils of leaf-like bracts at base of male spike, involucre with ring of 4–8 spines. HABITAT Rubbish tips, waste ground. DIST. Introduced (native of North America). Casual, scattered throughout Britain. (Widely naturalised Europe.) FLS Aug–Oct.

Sunflower   *Helianthus annuus*

Tall, erect, unbranched annual to 300 cm. LEAVES 10–40 cm, ovate, untoothed. FLOWERING HEADS Very large, 100–300 mm across, solitary, nodding. HABITAT Tips, waste places. DIST. Introduced (native of North America). Widely grown in gardens and as a field crop. Casual birdseed alien throughout BI. FLS Aug–Oct.

Jerusalem Artichoke   *Helianthus tuberosus*

Tall, erect, coarsely pubescent perennial to 300 cm with irregular tubers developing on rhizomes. LEAVES 10–25 cm. FLOWERING HEADS 1–several 40–80 mm across; involucral bracts linear-lanceolate, not appressed, 10–17 mm. HABITAT Rubbish tips, waste ground. DIST. Introduced (native of North America). Grown as crop and for game cover. Casual in S and E England. FLS Oct–Nov, but often frosted before flowering.

Perennial Sunflower   *Helianthus × laetiflorus* (*H. rigidus × H. tuberosus*)

Tall, erect, coarsely pubescent perennial to 150 cm. The commonest garden sunflower, sometimes double-flowered. LEAVES 4–30 cm. FLOWERING HEADS Usually solitary, 10–60 cm across; involucral bracts lax or loosely appressed, 8–15 mm. HABITAT Rubbish tips, waste places. DIST. Introduced. Naturalised o casual throughout Britain. (Much of Europe) FLS Sep–Oct.

Pot Marigold
Calendula officinalis

×0.15

flower

4–5mm fruit

×0.15

Field Marigold
Calendula arvensis

Purple Colt's-foot
Homogyne alpina

Ragweed
Ambrosia artemisiifolia

Sunflower
Helianthus annuus

Jerusalem Artichoke
Helianthus tuberosus

Perennial Sunflower
Helianthus × laetiflorus

illustrations 0.2× lifesize

Arnica
Arnica montana

Erect, rhizomatous perennial to 60 cm. LEAVES *Mostly basal*, 6–17 cm, ovate-lanceolate, acute, *densely glandular-pubescent, with strong parallel main veins*. FLOWERING HEADS 1–3, 40–80 mm across, *orange-yellow*. HABITAT Upland meadows, pastures, heaths, on acid soils. DIST. *Not BI*. (W, central and E Europe.) FLS Jun–Aug.

Gallant-soldier
Galinsoga parviflora

Erect, branched, *sparsely hairy* annual to 80 cm. LEAVES Opposite, simple, ovate, stalked. FLOWERING HEADS Radiate, 4–7 mm across; peduncles with short hairs, a few glandular; *receptacle scales distinctly 3-lobed*; 5 ray florets, white. FRUITS Pappus comprised of scales, these fringed with hairs and without terminal projection. HABITAT Arable fields, nurseries, urban weed. DIST. Introduced (native of South America). Naturalised or casual throughout England; rare elsewhere. (Cosmopolitan weed throughout Europe.) FLS May–Oct.

Shaggy-soldier
Galinsoga quadriradiata

Similar to *G. parviflora*, but stems more *densely pubescent*; peduncles with long glandular hairs and few simple hairs; *receptacle scales acute or weakly lobed*; pappus scales fringed with hairs and with terminal projection. HABITAT Similar to *G. parviflora*, with which it often grows. DIST. Introduced (native of Mexico). Naturalised or casual. Throughout BI, rare in Scotland and Ireland. FLS May–Oct.

Nodding Bur-marigold
Bidens cernua

Erect, branched annual to 75 cm. LEAVES *Unlobed*, strongly toothed, sessile, with long, drawn-out, acute apex. FLOWERING HEADS *Solitary*, discoid, 15–25 mm across, *drooping*; receptacle scales 6–8 mm, oblanceolate. FRUITS Achene, with 4 terminal barbed spines. HABITAT Wet meadows, sides of ditches, dykes, streams and ponds, especially where drying out in summer. DIST. Native. Throughout BI, but commoner in S and scarce in Scotland. (Most of Europe.) FLS Jul–Sep.

Trifid Bur-marigold
Bidens tripartita

Erect, branched annual to 75 cm. LEAVES Most 3-*lobed*, coarsely toothed; petioles winged. FLOWERING HEADS 15–25 mm across, solitary, ± *erect*; receptacle scales 8–10 mm, broadly linear, acute. FRUITS Achene, with 2–4 terminal, upwardly barbed spines. HABITAT Wet meadows, margins of streams, rivers, ditches, ponds and lakes. DIST. Native. Throughout most of BI, but scarce or absent in much of Scotland. (All Europe except extreme N.) FLS Jul–Sep.

Beggarticks
Bidens frondosa

Erect, branched annual to 120 cm. LEAVES *Lower leaves pinnate, with 1–2 pairs of lateral leaflets*, at least lower leaves with unwinged petioles. FLOWERING HEADS 8–20 mm across, solitary or few. FRUITS Achene, 6–10 mm; *barbs on margins backward-pointing, those on apical spines upward-pointing*. HABITAT Sides of rivers and canals, damp waste areas, ports. DIST. Introduced (native of North and South America). Naturalised in central England, S Wales. (W, S and central Europe) FLS Jul–Sep.

Hemp-agrimony
Eupatorium cannabinum

Tall, robust, clump-forming perennial to 150 cm. LEAVES *Basal leaves deeply 3(–5)-lobed*, lobe toothed. FLOWERING HEADS Discoid, 2–5 mm across, numerous, in dense terminal inflorescence; flower *pinkish purple*. HABITAT Tall herbaceous vegetation of fens, marshes, damp woods, sides of rivers and ponds, wet ditches; also calcareous scrub. DIST. Native. Throughout BI, but scarce and mostly coastal in Scotland. (Most of Europe.) FLS Jul–Sep.

Beggarticks
Bidens frondosa

Trifid Bur-marigold
Bidens tripartita

Nodding Bur-marigold
Bidens cernua

×0.9

×0.9

Arnica
Arnica montana

Hemp-agrimony
Eupatorium cannabinum

×1.8

Shaggy-soldier
Galinsoga quadriradiata

×0.9

Gallant-soldier
Galinsoga parviflora

×0.4

illustrations
0.15× lifesize

BUTOMACEAE Flowering Rushes

Flowering Rush
Butomus umbellatus

Tall, handsome, glabrous, erect perennial to 150 cm. STEMS Smooth. LEAVES Triangular in section. FLOWERS Forming an umbel, individual flower stalks up to 10 cm; 3 sepals and petals, pink; 9 stamens. HABITAT Shallow water of margins of ponds, slow-moving rivers, dykes and canals, on fertile soils. DIST. Native. Local throughout England; rare in Wales, Ireland; introduced in Scotland. (Most of Europe.) FLS Jul–Sep.

ALISMATACEAE Water-plantains

Glabrous aquatic or emergent annuals or perennials (*see* key on p.522). Leaves basal, entire, stalked. Flowers in simple umbels or whorls, regular; 3 sepals, green; 3 petals, white or mauve; ≥6 stamens; ovary superior. Fruits are usually a head of achenes.

Arrowhead
Sagittaria sagittifolia

Erect, glabrous, submerged or emergent aquatic perennial to *c*.90 cm. LEAVES Submerged leaves linear, grass-like; floating leaves narrowly ovate; erect leaves long-stalked, blade *sagittate*, to 20 cm. FLOWERS Monoecious, 3–5 in a whorl, 20–30 mm across; inflorescence stalk longer than leaves. HABITAT Characteristic of shallow, unpolluted waters of ponds, dykes, canals, slow-flowing rivers, on fertile soils. DIST. Native. Widespread in England; rare in Wales, Ireland. (Most of Europe.) FLS Jul–Aug.

Lesser Water-plantain
Baldellia ranunculoides

Erect or decumbent, glabrous, sometimes stoloniferous, perennial, to *c*.20 cm. LEAVES All basal, linear, acute, long-stalked. FLOWERS 10–15 mm across, pale mauve, forming an umbel or in 2–3 simple whorls; 6 sepals. HABITAT Wet ground or shallow water beside lowland slow-moving streams, dykes, ditches, ponds, on fertile soils. DIST. Native. Local and declining throughout BI. (Most of Europe N to S Norway.) FLS May–Aug.

Floating Water-plantain
Luronium natans *(B)

Slender, floating aquatic perennial to *c*.50 cm. LEAVES Submerged leaves without blades, 20–100 mm; floating leaves broad, blunt, 2–25 mm, with long stalks. FLOWERS Usually single, 12–18 cm across; 6 stamens. HABITAT Acid and infertile ponds, lakes and tarns, slow-moving canals. DIST. Native. Local and declining. Wales, W-central England. (W Europe to Bulgaria and S Norway.) FLS Jul–Aug.

Water-plantain
Alisma plantago-aquatica

Tall, robust, glabrous perennial to 1 m. LEAVES Emergent leaves long-stalked, blade to 20 cm, rounded to cordate at base; submerged leaves linear, 30–80 cm. FLOWERS 7–12 mm across, opening in the afternoon, in much-branched inflorescence, 20–100 cm; *inner petals blunt. Style arising from below middle of fruit.* HABITAT Shallow water or wet fertile mud of marginal vegetation of drainage dykes, slow-flowing rivers, canals, ponds, lakes. DIST. Native. Frequent throughout BI. (Most of Europe.) FLS Jun–Aug.

Narrow-leaved Water-plantain
Alisma lanceolatum

Tall, robust, glabrous perennial to 1 m. Similar to *A. plantago-aquatica*, but leaf blade tapers into petiole; flowers opening in morning; *inner petals pointed; style arising from above middle of fruit.* HABITAT Similar to *A. plantago-aquatica*, with which it may occur. DIST. Native. Scattered throughout England, Wales; rare in Scotland, Ireland. (Most of Europe.) FLS Jun–Aug.

Ribbon-leaved Water Plantain
Alisma gramineum CR. *(B

Glabrous perennial to *c*.40 cm. LEAVES Linear, none floating. FLOWERS Small, 3.5–8 mm across, in little branched inflorescence; 6 stamens; style coiled. HABITAT Shallow water of lakes, dykes, streams, or fertile muddy soils. DIST. Native. Very rare in BI, confined to 4 localities in England. (W and central Europe, N to Denmark.) FLS Jun–Aug.

Starfruit
Damasonium alisma CR. *(B

Aquatic annual. LEAVES Long-stalked, floating blade ovate, blunt, *cordate at base*, 1.5–7 cm, yellowish green. FLOWERS In simple whorls, 5–9 mm across; 6 stamens; *ripe carpels 5–14 mm, spread in 6 pointed star-like arrangement.* HABITAT Once characteristic of village and commons ponds subject to fluctuating water levels and stock grazing. Shallow water of acid ponds and ditches, usually on sand and gravelly soils. DIST. Native. Now very rare in BI, reduced to about 4 sites in SE England. (S and SW Europe.) FLS Jun–Aug.

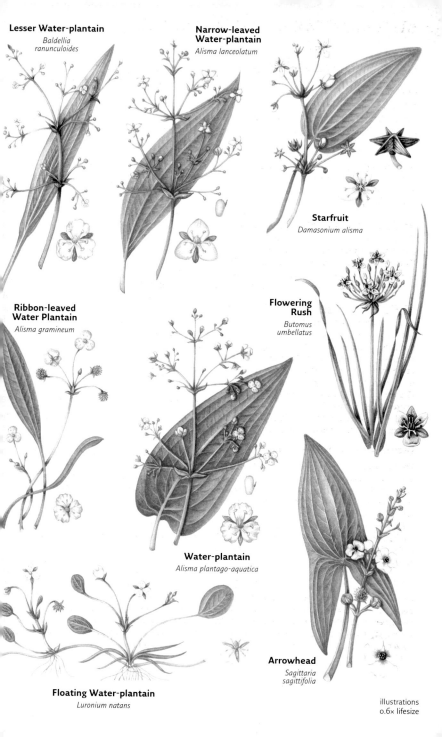

Lesser Water-plantain
*Baldellia
ranunculoides*

**Narrow-leaved
Water-plantain**
Alisma lanceolatum

Starfruit
Damasonium alisma

**Ribbon-leaved
Water Plantain**
Alisma gramineum

**Flowering
Rush**
*Butomus
umbellatus*

Water-plantain
Alisma plantago-aquatica

Arrowhead
*Sagittaria
sagittifolia*

Floating Water-plantain
Luronium natans

illustrations
0.6× lifesize

HYDROCHARITACEAE Frogbits and waterweeds

Frogbit
Hydrocharis morsus-ranae VU.

Free-floating, stoloniferous aquatic with roots hanging in water. Overwinters by means of perennating buds that sink to mud in autumn. LEAVES *In basal rosette, stalks long; blades orbicular, cordate, 1.5-5 cm across.* FLOWERS *Conspicuous,* unisexual, 20-30 mm across; 3 sepals, green; 3 petals, larger than sepals, white; 9-12 stamens. FRUITS Berry-like capsule (rarely formed). HABITAT Slow-flowing ditches, dykes, canals, pools, ponds, in calcareous or base-rich water. DIST. Native. Very local, declining. Throughout BI except Scotland. (Most of Europe.) FLS Jul-Aug.

Water-soldier
Stratiotes aloides

Free-floating, submerged perennial, rising to surface at flowering. British plants are all female. LEAVES *In large basal rosette, 40-60 cm long, sessile, linear, sword-like, with spiny marginal teeth.* FLOWERS Conspicuous, dioecious, 30-40 mm across; 3 sepals; 3 petals, larger than sepals, white. HABITAT Shallow water of calcareous ponds, lakes, dykes, ditches, canals, broads. DIST. Native or introduced. As a native, very local and ± confined to Norfolk Broads; short-lived populations widely established elsewhere throughout lowland England. (Most of Europe.) FLS Jun-Aug.

Waterweeds *Elodea*, *Hydrilla* and *Lagarosiphon*
See key to *Elodea*, *Hydrilla* and *Lagarosiphon* on p.525.

Canadian Waterweed
Elodea canadensis

Dioecious, submerged perennial, rooted in mud. All British plants are female. STEMS Long, to 3 m, branched. LEAVES *Upper leaves mostly in whorls of 3, not strongly recurved, 0.8-2.3 mm wide below tip, leaf tip blunt.* FLOWERS Inconspicuous, solitary, in axils of leaves; 3 sepals; 3 petals, 1.5-3 mm, narrower than sepals, white; female flowers reach surface by long, slender, stalk-like elongation of perianth tube; male flowers break off and float. HABITAT Most kinds of ponds, canals, dykes, slow-moving rivers, on fertile soils; to 440 m. DIST. Introduced (native of North America). Established throughout BI. Common, but now being replaced by *E. nuttallii* (*see* below). (Naturalised throughout much of Europe.) FLS May-Oct.

Nuttall's Waterweed
Elodea nuttallii

Submerged perennial. All British plants are female. Similar to *E. canadensis,* but upper leaves mostly in *whorls of 4, strongly recurved and twisted, narrower,*

0.2-0.7 mm wide below tip, margins minutely toothed in upper half, *leaf tip acute.* HABITAT Similar to *E. canadensis.* DIST. Introduced (native North America). First recorded in 1966 and spreading rapidly, in places replacing *E. canadensis.* Now common and widespread in England. (Spreading in Europe.)

Esthwaite Waterweed
Hydrilla verticillata VU. *(R)

Submerged perennial, similar to *Elodea nuttallii.* STEMS Long, branched. LEAVES Upper leaves in whorls of 3-6, margins minutely toothed through-out their length and with *2 minute fringed scales at base.* HABITAT Deep-water lakes. DIST. Native. Very rare, in 2 sites at Lough Rusheenduff (Galway) and Kirkcudbrightshire. (W Europe.)

Curly Waterweed
Lagarosiphon major

Submerged perennial, resembling a robust *Elodea.* Only female plants occur in Britain. LEAVES *Lower leaves spiralled around stem, not opposite or whorled, strongly recurved and with narrowly acute tips.* FLOWERS Petals reddish, as large as sepals. HABITAT Lakes, ponds, canals. DIST. Introduced (native of S Africa). Widely cultivated in garden ponds; now spreading vegetatively throughout most of lowland Britain, Ireland.

APONOGETONACEAE Cape-pondweed family

Cape-pondweed
Aponogeton distachyos

Glabrous aquatic perennial. LEAVES All basal, floating, long-stalked, blades oblong-elliptical, 6-25 cm. FLOWERS Pleasantly scented, 20-40 mm across, forming long-stalked inflorescence, forked at water surface, each fork with spike of *c.*10 flowers; 1(-2) perianth segments, white; 6-18 stamens. HABITAT Lakes, ponds, canals; persistent. DIST. Introduced (native of S Africa). Widely cultivated in ponds and water gardens; established in scattered localities mostly in S England. (France.)

SCHEUCHZERIACEAE Rannoch-rush

Rannoch-rush
Scheuchzeria palustris

Erect, glabrous, rhizomatous perennial to 20 cm. STEMS Leafy. LEAVES *Linear, alternate, 2-17 cm grooved, with conspicuous pore at tip.* FLOWERS *c.*4 mm across, in *3-10-flowered inflorescence, shorter than leaves;* 6 perianth segments, yellowish green; 6 stamens. HABITAT Acid *Sphagnum* bog pools. DIST. Native. Very rare, in only 2 sites on Rannoch Moor Scotland, at 300 m. (All Europe except S.) FLS Jun-Aug.

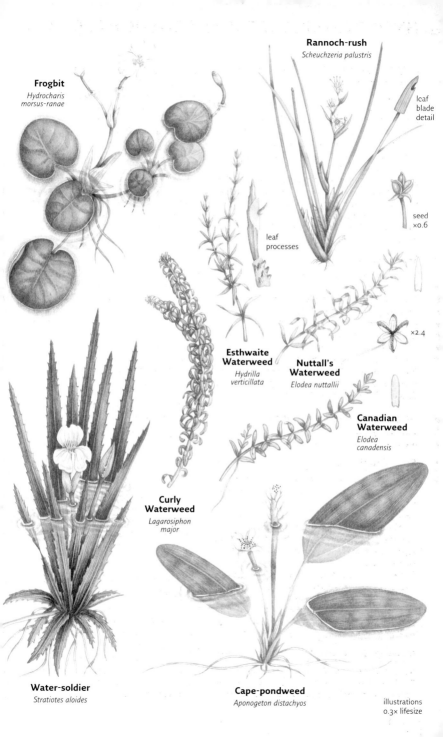

Frogbit
Hydrocharis morsus-ranae

Rannoch-rush
Scheuchzeria palustris

leaf blade detail

seed ×0.6

leaf processes

×2.4

Esthwaite Waterweed
Hydrilla verticillata

Nuttall's Waterweed
Elodea nuttallii

Canadian Waterweed
Elodea canadensis

Curly Waterweed
Lagarosiphon major

Water-soldier
Stratiotes aloides

Cape-pondweed
Aponogeton distachyos

illustrations 0.3× lifesize

	if	then
1	▷ Emergent leaves sagittate; flowers unisexual, >6 stamens	*Sagittaria* (p.518)
	▷ Leaves not sagittate; flowers bisexual, 6 stamens	Go to ▷ **2**
2	▷ Stems erect, flowering stems leafless; all leaves basal	Go to ▷ **3**
	▷ Stems procumbent or floating	Go to ▷ **5**
3	▷ Achenes in spherical head	*Baldellia* (p.518)
	▷ Achenes whorled	Go to ▷ **4**
4	▷ Leaves tapering or rounded at base; fruits incurving	*Alisma* (p.518)
	▷ Leaves cordate; fruits arranged in 6-pointed star	*Damasonium* (p.518)
5	▷ Stems and leaves not floating; leaves lanceolate	*Baldellia* (p.518)
	▷ Stems and leaves floating; leaves ovate	*Luronium* (p.518)

Key to Potamogetonaceae, Ruppiaceae, Najadaceae, Zannichelliaceae Pondweeds

if	then
Leaves mostly alternate (except *Groenlandia*); inflorescence a stalked axillary spike; flowers bisexual, 4 tepals, 4 stamens; fruits in groups of 1–4	**Potamogetonaceae** (*Potamogeton*, *Groenlandia*) (p.523)
Leaves mostly alternate; inflorescence submerged, a terminal umbel-like raceme of 2 to few flowers; flowers bisexual, perianth absent, 2 stamens but anthers 2-lobed so looking like 4; fruits long-stalked	**Ruppiaceae (*Ruppia*)** (p.532)
Leaves opposite or whorled, toothed or lobed; flowers unisexual, sessile in groups in leaf axils, perianth absent, 1 stamen	**Najadaceae (*Najas*)** (p.532)
Leaves mostly opposite; flowers unisexual, solitary in leaf axils, perianth absent; male flowers long-stalked; fruits in a group of 1–4 stalked, ± curved achenes	**Zannichellaceae** (*Zannichellia palustris*) (p.532)

if	then

Pondweeds *Potamogeton*, *Groenlandia*

All leaves in opposite pairs, stipules absent	***Groenlandia densa*** (p.530)
All leaves alternate, with stipules	***Potamogeton*** (below)

Potamogeton

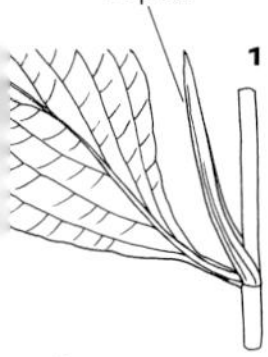

stipule

1

Potamogeton
leaf base
and stipule

Pondweeds with floating leaves
1 ▷ Floating leaves with flexible, hinge-like
   joint below junction of blade and petiole;
   submerged leaves (if present) all linear .... ***P. natans*** (p.526)
   ▷ Floating leaves without joint at upper end
   of petiole; at least some submerged leaves
   with narrow blade .... Go to ▷ **2**

2 ▷ Submerged leaves, if present, with distinct
   petiole >10 mm long .... Go to ▷ **3**
   ▷ Submerged leaves always present, ± sessile .... Go to ▷ **5**

3 ▷ Floating leaves thin, translucent, clearly
   net-veined (calcareous water) .... ***P. coloratus*** (p.526)
   ▷ Floating leaves opaque, not translucent,
   network of veins difficult to see .... Go to ▷ **4**

4 ▷ Most leaves floating in shallow water, at
   least some with rounded or cordate bases;
   fruits 1.9–2.6 mm (acid water) .... ***P. polygonifolius*** (p.526)
   ▷ Most leaves submerged, leaf bases tapering to
   petiole; not fruiting in BI (rare, lowland
   rivers) .... ***P. nodosus*** (p.526)

5 ▷ Stems flattened; all submerged leaves
   parallel-sided (very rare, Outer Hebrides) .... ***P. epihydrus*** (p.528)
   ▷ At least some leaves with convex sides .... Go to ▷ **6**

6 ▷ Submerged leaves with blunt or rounded
   tips .... ***P. alpinus*** (p.528)
   ▷ Submerged leaves acute .... ***P. gramineus*** (p.526)

*Pondweeds without floating leaves; submerged leaves not parallel-sided,
usually >10 mm wide*
1 ▷ Leaves ± parallel-sided, margins undulate
   and distinctly toothed (visible to naked eye) .... ***P. crispus*** (p.530)
   ▷ Leaves neither toothed nor undulate .... Go to ▷ **2**

2 ▷ At least some leaves with rounded bases,
   clasping or semi-clasping the stems .... Go to ▷ **3**
   ▷ Leaves tapering to base, not clasping stem .... Go to ▷ **4**

CONTINUED OVERLEAF

	if	then
3	▷ Leaves broadly clasping stem; stipules small, soon disappearing	*P. perfoliatus* (p.528)
	▷ Leaves semi-clasping, distinctly hooded at tip; stipules large, >10 mm, persistent	*P. praelongus* (p.528)
4	▷ Leaves blunt, often reddish	*P. alpinus* (p.528)
	▷ Leaves not blunt	Go to ▷ **5**
5	▷ Leaves ≤12 mm wide	*P. gramineus* (p.526)
	▷ Leaves ≥25 mm wide	*P. lucens* (p.526)

Pondweeds without floating leaves; submerged leaves parallel-sided, usually <6 mm wide (grass-leaved pondweeds)

	if	then
1	▷ Stipules fused to base of leaf to form sheathing leaf base around stem with free ligule at apex (similar to arrangement in a grass)	Go to ▷ **2**
	▷ Stipules not fused to leaf base, and forming outgrowths from node wholly or partially encircling stem	Go to ▷ **3**
2	▷ Leaves acute, sheathing leaf base not fused into tube around stem but margins overlapping; fruits ≥3.3 mm (lowland, tolerates brackish water)	*P. pectinatus* (p.530)
	▷ Leaves rounded at tip, sheathing leaf base fused into tube around stem; fruit ≤3.2 mm (Scotland, Ireland)	*P. filiformis* (p.530)
3	▷ Most leaves >2 mm wide, with 3–5(-many) veins	Go to ▷ **4**
	▷ Most leaves <2 mm wide, with 3(-5) veins	Go to ▷ **7**
4	▷ Stems strongly compressed; leaves with 3–5 main veins and many finer strands between them	Go to ▷ **5**
	▷ Stems not strongly compressed; leaves with 3 or 5 main veins only	Go to ▷ **6**
5	▷ Leaves finely acuminate, with 3 main veins; fruit usually with tooth near base (very rare, lowland grazing marshes)	*P. acutifolius* (p.530)
	▷ Leaves rounded and cuspidate at tip, with 5 main veins (2 near margins); fruit smooth	*P. compressus* (p.530)
6	▷ Stems much branched and fan-like; base of stipules not fused into tube	*P. obtusifolius* (p.528)
	▷ Branching of stems not fan-like; base of stipules fused into tube around stem when young (lowland, calcareous water)	*P. friesii* (p.528)

if	then
7 ▷ Base of stipules fused into tube around stem when young	Go to ▷ **8**
▷ Base of stipules not fused into tube around stem, but margins overlapping (this is a difficult character to see and may be best done by cutting the stem above the base of stipule and inserting the point of a pencil into the tip to see whether the edges move apart or the sheath splits)	Go to ▷ **9**
8 ▷ Leaves acute or obtuse and mucronate, not rigid (widespread)	*P. pusillus* (p.528)
▷ Leaf tips finely long-pointed (rare, N and W Scotland)	*P. rutilus* (p.528)
9 ▷ Leaves mostly >1 mm wide, leaf tip obtuse to sub-acute; fruit smooth, usually 4–5 per flower (widespread)	*P. berchtoldii* (p.530)
▷ Leaves mostly ≤1 mm wide, leaf tip finely pointed; fruits usually toothed at base, usually 1 per flower (lowland; scattered)	*P. trichoides* (p.530)

Key to Waterweeds *Elodea, Lagarosiphon* and *Hydrilla*

if	then
1 ▷ Leaves whorled	Go to ▷ **2**
▷ Leaves spiralled around stem, not opposite or whorled, strongly recurved	*L. major* (p.520)
2 ▷ Leaves in whorls of 3, not strongly recurved, tips blunt	*E. canadensis* (p.520)
▷ Leaves in whorls of 3–6, recurved, tips acute	Go to ▷ **3**
3 ▷ Leaves in whorls of 4, margins minutely toothed in upper half	*E. nuttallii* (p.520)
▷ Leaves in whorls of 3–6, margins minutely toothed throughout their length, with 2 minute fringed scales at base (very rare)	*H. verticillata* (p.520)

JUNCAGINACEAE Arrowgrasses

Glabrous, rhizomatous, 'plantain-like' perennials. Leaves all in a basal rosette, sessile, with sheathing base, linear, cylindrical, with ligule. Flowers inconspicuous, in a terminal spike; 6 tepals; 6 stamens. Fruits consisting of 3–6 separating carpels.

Sea Arrowgrass
Triglochin maritimum

Robust, rhizomatous perennial to 50 cm. LEAVES Half-cylindrical, not furrowed. FLOWERS Inflorescence not elongating after flowering. FRUITS 3–4 mm, not appressed to inflorescence axis. HABITAT Common plant of salt marshes, brackish grazing marshes. DIST. Native. All round coasts of BI. (All Europe except Mediterranean.) FLS Jul–Sep.

Marsh Arrowgrass
Triglochin palustre

Similar to *T. maritimum*, but more slender; leaves half-cylindrical, deeply furrowed on upper surface towards base; inflorescence elongating after flowering; fruits 7–10 mm, appressed to inflorescence axis. HABITAT Wet meadows, fens, marshes, spring flushes, on calcareous or mildly acid soils; to 970 m. DIST. Native. Throughout BI, but scarce in SE and SW. (All Europe except Mediterranean.) FLS Jun–Aug.

PONDWEEDS

There are four families of submerged or floating aquatic plants that look superficially similar (*see* key on p.522). All have leafy submerged flowering stems with opposite or alternate and submerged leaves, and/or floating linear or narrowly ovate leaves.

POTAMOGETONACEAE Pondweeds

Pondweeds *Potamogeton* and *Groenlandia*

Pondweeds can sometimes be difficult to identify (*see* key on p.523). It is important to look carefully at the leaf shape, the number of leaf veins, and details of the stipules and fruits (these are described under the individual species descriptions). Lengths of fruits include the beak. Numerous hybrids have been recorded, but these are not common and are usually sterile.

Broad-leaved Pondweed
Potamogeton natans

LEAVES Floating leaves stalked, blade 2.5–12.5 cm, thick and opaque, ovate-elliptic, *decurrent for short distance down stalk and therefore appearing jointed just below blade; submerged leaves linear, without expanded blade;* stipules 40–170 mm. FLOWERS In dense cylindrical inflorescence. FRUITS 4–5 mm. HABITAT Ponds, lakes, slow-moving streams, rivers, dykes and canals, in clear, mildly acid to calcareous water. DIST. Native. Common throughout BI. (All Europe.) FLS May–Sep.

Bog Pondweed
Potamogeton polygonifolius

LEAVES Floating leaves thick and opaque, secondary veins inconspicuous, similar in shape to *P. natans*, but *without 'joint' on petiole below blade; submerged leaves stalked, blade narrowly elliptic,* to 16 cm; stipules 10–15 mm. FRUITS 1.9–2.6 mm. HABITAT Small ponds, bog pools, wet *Sphagnum* lawns, spring heads, streams, in shallow acid, often peaty water; to 780 m. DIST. Native. Common in N and W Britain and parts of S. (W and central Europe.) FLS May–Oct.

Fen Pondweed
Potamogeton coloratus

LEAVES Floating leaves *translucent, secondary veins conspicuous,* broadly elliptic to ovate, 2.5–8.5 cm; submerged leaves narrowly elliptic; stipules 20–63 mm. FRUITS 1.5–1.9 mm. HABITAT Pools, ponds, dykes, streams, in calcareous fen peat, clay and marl pits. DIST. Native. Local, declining. East Anglia, central Ireland; scarce elsewhere. (W and central Europe.) FLS Jun–Jul.

Loddon Pondweed
Potamogeton nodosus

LEAVES Floating leaves elliptic, opaque, blade 70–130 mm, *petioles long,* 30–210 mm; submerged leaves elliptic, *margins toothed,* tapering to stalk, translucent; *petioles long,* 70–210 mm; stipules 45–125 mm. FRUITS Doesn't fruit in BI. HABITAT Calcareous shallow or deep water on gravelly bottom. DIST. Native. Rare. R. Avon (Bristol), R. Stour (Dorset), R. Loddon (Berkshire). (All Europe except N.) FLS May–Sep.

Shining Pondweed
Potamogeton lucens

LEAVES *Floating leaves absent*; submerged leaves large, 75–200 mm, *yellowish green,* translucent, elliptic, apex with short point, *margin finely toothed; petioles short,* to 10 mm, or leaves appearing ± sessile; *stipules 35–80 mm, winged.* FRUITS 3.2–4.5 mm. HABITAT Lakes, canals, rivers, fenland drains, in clear, calcium-rich water to depths of 4 m. DIST. Native. Widespread in England SE of line from Humber to Wash, central Ireland; scarce elsewhere. (Most of Europe.) FLS Jun–Sep.

Various-leaved Pondweed
Potamogeton gramineus

LEAVES Floating leaves elliptic, opaque, blade 19–70 mm; *submerged leaves translucent, narrowly elliptic, sessile, margins finely toothed, tip usually with short tooth,* 40–90 mm, 4.5–12× as long as wide; stipules 10–25 mm. FRUITS 2.4–3.1 mm. HABITAT Rivers, streams, canals, lakes, ditches, in acid to base-rich shallow water. DIST. Native. Widespread in N England, Scotland, Ireland; rare elsewhere. (Much of Europe, but rare in Mediterranean.) FLS Jun–Sep.

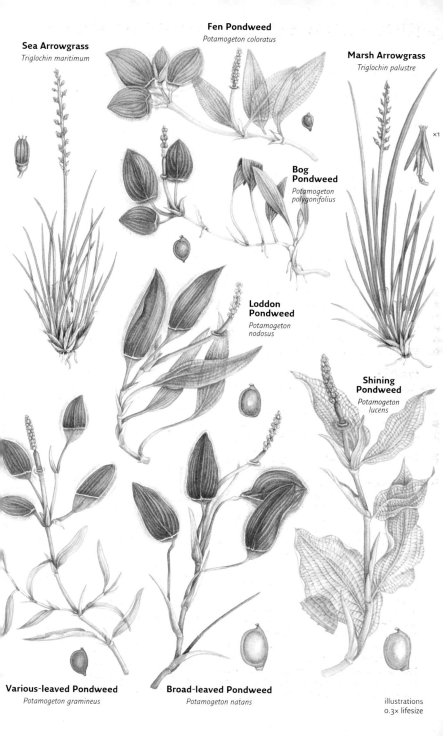

Sea Arrowgrass
Triglochin maritimum

Fen Pondweed
Potamogeton coloratus

Marsh Arrowgrass
Triglochin palustre

×1

Bog Pondweed
Potamogeton polygonifolius

Loddon Pondweed
Potamogeton nodosus

Shining Pondweed
Potamogeton lucens

Various-leaved Pondweed
Potamogeton gramineus

Broad-leaved Pondweed
Potamogeton natans

illustrations
0.3× lifesize

Red Pondweed
Potamogeton alpinus

LEAVES Floating leaves ovate-elliptic, 45–90 mm, narrowing to short stalk, blunt, entire; submerged *leaves often reddish, especially when dry*, 70–180 × 10–25 mm, narrowly oblong-elliptic, *sessile, blunt, entire*, with 7–11 longitudinal veins, *midrib bordered by broad band of lacunae at base*; stipules 20–60 mm, shorter than internodes. FRUITS 2.6–3.7 mm. HABITAT Lakes, canals, dykes, ponds, streams, in neutral to mildly acid water; to 945 m. DIST. Native. Widespread in N Britain, N Ireland; rare elsewhere. (Much of Europe, but rare in S.) FLS Jun–Sep.

Long-stalked Pondweed
Potamogeton praelongus

LEAVES Floating leaves absent; submerged leaves 60–150 mm, 3–6.5× as long as wide, lanceolate to oblong-lanceolate, *tip blunt and markedly hooded, entire, sessile and ± clasping*; stipules 10–80 mm. FLOWERS Peduncles long, 80–200 mm. FRUITS 4.5–5.5 mm. HABITAT Deep water of calcareous lakes, rivers, canals, fenland drains. DIST. Native. Locally frequent in Scotland, N Ireland; rare elsewhere. (N and central Europe.) FLS May–Aug.

Perfoliate Pondweed
Potamogeton perfoliatus

Robust aquatic plant. LEAVES Floating leaves absent; *submerged leaves* 20–115 mm, 1.3–10× as long as wide, lanceolate to ovate, thin, translucent, *sessile, cordate, ± completely clasping stem*; stipules 2.5–22 mm, soon disappearing. FRUITS 2.6–3.5 mm. HABITAT Mildly acid to neutral lakes, ponds, canals, slow-flowing streams; to 780 m. DIST. Native. Widespread throughout most of BI. (All Europe.) FLS Jun–Sep.

American Pondweed
Potamogeton epihydrus

STEMS *Markedly compressed*. LEAVES Floating leaves elliptic, 35–77 mm, opaque, petioles 20–60 mm, shorter than blade; *submerged leaves linear,* 65–240 × 2.5–10.5 mm, 18–30× as long as wide, midrib bordered by well-marked band of lacuna tissue, *sessile;* leaves of vegetative shoots sometimes distinctly arranged in 2 opposite rows; stipules 11–45 mm, open. FRUITS 2.5–3.1 mm. HABITAT Shallow water of peaty lochans; also established as introduction in a few canals in N England. DIST. Native. Very rare. Outer Hebrides (South Uist). FLS Jun–Aug.

Grass-leaved pondweeds

A group of 10 superficially similar-looking species, with narrow, linear, 'grass-like' submerged leaves. Identification can prove difficult. Leaf width, the numbers of longitudinal veins, the presence of a band of lacunae bordering the midrib and shape of the leaf tip are important. In addition, the stipules can be open with the edges free and overlapping, or fused into a tube surrounding the stem; this last character is particularly difficult to see.

Flat-stalked Pondweed
Potamogeton friesii

STEMS To 150 cm, strongly compressed, producing numerous short, leafy branches. LEAVES 1.5–3.5 mm wide, 5 *longitudinal veins; stipules* 9.5–25 mm, *base fused into tube round stem when young*, splitting later. FRUITS 2.4–3 mm. HABITAT Calcareous or base-rich lakes, ponds, drainage dykes, fenland lodes, canals. DIST. Native. Scattered throughout BI. (All Europe except extreme S.) FLS Jun–Aug.

Shetland Pondweed
Potamogeton rutilus

STEMS Very slender, to 45 cm, compressed. LEAVES *Submerged leaves 0.5–1.1 mm wide*, linear, *gradually tapering to fine, acute point;* 3 *longitudinal veins*, midrib prominent, not bordered by lacunae; *stipules* 15–19 mm, *tubular for basal 2–3 mm when young*, splitting later. FLOWERS In 6-flowered inflorescence, 3–7 mm, peduncles slender. FRUITS 2 mm. HABITAT Base-rich lowland lochs, streams. DIST. Native. Rare. Shetland, Outer Hebrides, NW Scotland. (N, central and E Europe.) FLS Aug.

Lesser Pondweed
Potamogeton pusillus

STEMS Slender, to 70 cm, compressed, richly branched in shallow water. LEAVES Submerged leaves 0.8–1.4 mm wide, linear, tapering or abruptly narrowing to acute tip; 3 *longitudinal veins, midrib prominent, not bordered by lacunae; stipules* 5–17 mm, *tubular for most of their length when young*, splitting later. FRUITS 1.8–2.3 mm. HABITAT Lakes, pools, canals, ditches, dykes, streams, in calcareous or brackish water. DIST. Native. Widely distributed throughout BI, but rather local. (Most of Europe.) FLS Jun–Sep.

Blunt-leaved Pondweed
Potamogeton obtusifolius

STEMS To 190 cm, compressed, richly branched. LEAVES Submerged leaves 2.5–3.6 mm wide, linear, *narrowed to sessile base, tip blunt;* 3(–5) longitudinal veins, without faint intermediate veins, midrib bordered by a band of lacunae, broad below, narrowed above; *stipules* 11–29 mm, *open.* FRUITS 2.6–3.2 mm. HABITAT Lakes, ponds, canals, in moderately fertile, mildly acid to neutral water; lowland to 480 m. DIST. Native. Throughout BI, but rather local; possibly declining in Britain. (All Europe except S.) FLS Jun–Sep

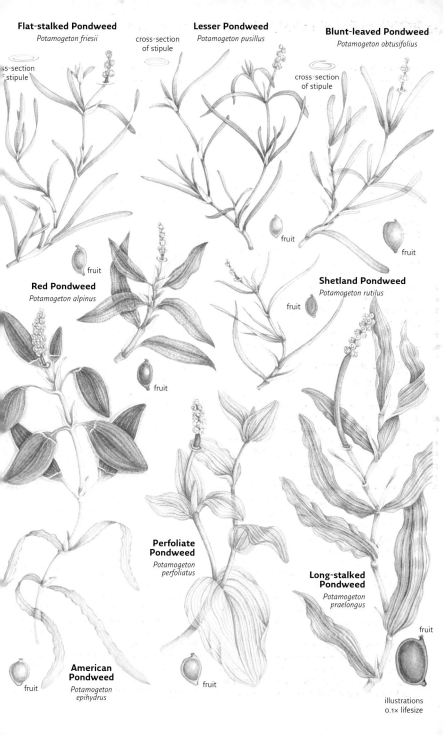

Flat-stalked Pondweed
Potamogeton friesii

cross-section
of stipule

cross-section
of stipule

Lesser Pondweed
Potamogeton pusillus

Blunt-leaved Pondweed
Potamogeton obtusifolius

cross-section
of stipule

fruit

fruit

fruit

Red Pondweed
Potamogeton alpinus

Shetland Pondweed
Potamogeton rutilus

fruit

fruit

**Perfoliate
Pondweed**
*Potamogeton
perfoliatus*

**Long-stalked
Pondweed**
*Potamogeton
praelongus*

fruit

**American
Pondweed**
*Potamogeton
epihydrus*

fruit

fruit

illustrations
0.1× lifesize

Small Pondweed
Potamogeton berchtoldii

STEMS To 60 cm, slender, only slightly compressed. LEAVES *Submerged leaves 0.8–1.8 mm wide, linear; 3 longitudinal veins,* without faint intermediate veins, midrib bordered by band of lacunae at least at base; *stipules 5–15 mm, open.* FRUITS 1.8–2.7 mm. SIMILAR SPP. Very similar to *P. pusillus* (p.528), but differing in the open stipules, which need to be examined carefully. HABITAT Occurring in almost the full range of aquatic habitats, but avoiding peaty water and, unlike *P. pusillus,* not tolerant of brackish conditions; to 500 m. DIST. Native. Throughout BI. (Most of Europe.) FLS Jun–Sep.

Hairlike Pondweed
Potamogeton trichoides

STEMS To 100 cm, very slender. LEAVES *Submerged leaves very narrow, 0.3–1 mm wide, linear, gradually tapering to fine point; 3 longitudinal veins, the lateral two indistinct;* stipules 5–30 mm, open. FRUITS 2.5–3.2 mm. HABITAT Still or slow-flowing lakes, ponds, rivers, canals and drainage dykes, often as an early colonist. DIST. Native. Very local in lowland England. (All Europe except N.) FLS Jun–Sep.

Grass-wrack Pondweed
Potamogeton compressus EN.

STEMS To 85 cm, *distinctly flattened.* LEAVES Submerged leaves 3–6.2 mm wide, *linear; 5 longitudinal veins, with many faint intermediate strands,* midrib bordered by band of lacunae at least at base; stipules 21–55 mm, open. FLOWERS *Inflorescences 11–25 mm, peduncles 28–95 mm.* FRUITS 3.4–4 mm, not toothed. HABITAT Still or slow-moving lakes, rivers, ditches and canals. DIST. Native. Very local, declining. Lowland central and E England. (Most of Europe except extreme N and Mediterranean.) FLS Jun–Sep.

Sharp-leaved Pondweed
Potamogeton acutifolius CR.

STEMS To 100 cm, *compressed.* LEAVES Submerged leaves 1.6–5.4 mm wide, linear, *tapering to fine point; 3 longitudinal veins, with many faint intermediate strands,* midrib bordered by band of lacunae at least at base; stipules 13–26 mm, open. FLOWERS *Inflorescences 2.5–5 mm, peduncles 5–20 mm.* FRUITS 3–4 mm, with single blunt tooth on lower side. HABITAT Calcareous grazing-marsh drainage dykes. DIST. Native. Very rare, declining. Norfolk Broads, Sussex. (Most of Europe except N and Mediterranean.) FLS Jun–Jul.

Curled Pondweed
Potamogeton crispus

STEMS Robust, compressed, to 150 cm. LEAVES *Submerged leaves 5–12 mm wide,* sessile, linear-oblong, tips usually blunt, *margins toothed, upper leaves strongly undulate;* 3–5 longitudinal veins, midrib bordered by band of lacunae; stipules 4–17 mm, open. FRUITS 4–6.2 mm. HABITAT Shallow lakes, ponds, streams, canals, drainage dykes; lowland to 350 m. DIST. Native. Frequent throughout BI, but rare in N Scotland. (Most of Europe.) FLS May–Oct.

Slender-leaved Pondweed
Potamogeton filiformis

STEMS To 30 cm, very slender, sparingly branched. LEAVES *Submerged leaves very narrow, 0.25–1.2 mm wide,* semicircular in cross section, midrib bordered on each side by longitudinal air channel; *stipules joined to leaf base, forming tubular leaf sheath, but free at apex, forming 5–15 mm ligule.* FRUITS 2.2–2.8 mm. HABITAT Shallow eutrophic or brackish water at edges of lakes, reservoirs; lowland to 390 m. DIST. Native. Scotland, NW Ireland; frequent in Orkney, Shetland. (N Europe, Alps.) FLS May–Aug.

Fennel Pondweed
Potamogeton pectinatus

STEMS *To 225 cm, richly branched.* LEAVES Submerged leaves 0.2–4 mm wide, midrib bordered on each side by longitudinal air channel; *leaf sheath open, ligule 5–15 mm.* FRUITS 3.3–4.7 mm. HABITAT Eutrophic or brackish water of ponds, lakes, canals, rivers, streams, drainage dykes. DIST. Native. Throughout lowland BI, but scarce in N Scotland. (Most of Europe.) FLS May–Sep.

Opposite-leaved Pondweed
Groenlandia densa VU. *(R)

STEMS To 65 cm. LEAVES *Submerged leaves opposite, 1.5–12.5 mm wide, lanceolate to ovate, often recurved, margins finely toothed, 3–5 longitudinal veins,* sessile, base clasping. FLOWERS In *2-flowered* inflorescence, 2–4.5 mm. FRUITS 3–4 mm. HABITAT Shallow, clear, base-rich water of dykes, streams, canals, lakes, rivers. DIST. Native. Local, declining. Lowland Britain, mostly SE of line from Humber to Severn; scarce in Ireland. (All Europe except N.) FLS May–Sep.

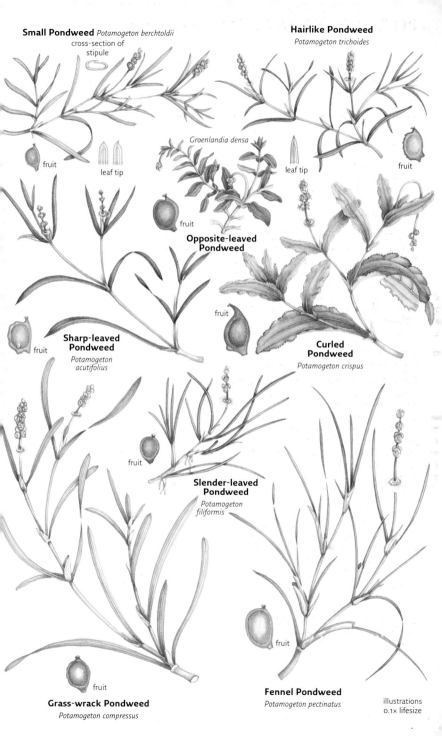

Small Pondweed *Potamogeton berchtoldii*
cross-section of stipule

fruit

leaf tip

Hairlike Pondweed
Potamogeton trichoides

fruit

Groenlandia densa

leaf tip

fruit

Opposite-leaved Pondweed

fruit

fruit

Sharp-leaved Pondweed

Potamogeton acutifolius

Curled Pondweed

Potamogeton crispus

fruit

fruit

Slender-leaved Pondweed

Potamogeton filiformis

fruit

Grass-wrack Pondweed

Potamogeton compressus

Fennel Pondweed

Potamogeton pectinatus

illustrations
0.1× lifesize

RUPPIACEAE Tasselweeds

Small family of submerged, brackish-water aquatic perennials. Leaves linear with sheathing bases, mostly alternate, but upper opposite. Inflorescence few-flowered, terminal, short and umbel-like; perianth absent; 2 stamens, but appearing as 4 as anthers widely bilobed. Superficially similar to grass-leaved pondweeds (p.528–531), but differ in the leaves (which have only a midrib), the terminal umbel-like inflorescence and the lack of perianth.

Beaked Tasselweed
Ruppia maritima

Slender aquatic perennial. STEMS Much branched, to 30 cm. LEAVES 0.4–0.9 mm wide. FLOWERS Peduncles ≤2.5 mm, straight or curved. FRUITS 2–2.8 mm. HABITAT Shallow water of brackish lagoons, creeks, drainage dykes. DIST. Native. All round coasts of BI, but declining in S. (Most of Europe.) FLS Jul–Sep.

Spiral Tasselweed
Ruppia cirrhosa

Similar to *R. maritima*, but leaves wider, 0.2–1.4 mm wide; peduncles spiralled, much longer, ≥4 cm; fruits larger, 2.7–3.4 mm. HABITAT Similar to *R. maritima*, but tolerant of deeper water and more brackish conditions. DIST. Native. Local. Scattered around coasts of BI, mostly in S and E. (Most of Europe except Arctic.) FLS Jul–Sep.

ZANNICHELLIACEAE
Horned pondweeds

Horned Pondweed
Zannichellia palustris

Submerged fresh- and brackish-water aquatic perennial. STEMS Slender, much branched, leafy, to 40 cm. LEAVES Linear, mostly opposite, 0.2–1.3 mm wide. FLOWERS Monoecious, in sessile axillary groups consisting of 1 male and 2–5 female flowers; perianth absent. FRUITS 2.6–5 mm, with distinct beak, 0.4–2.6 mm. SIMILAR SPP. Superficially similar to some grass-leaved pondweeds, especially *Potamogeton pectinatus* (p.530), but distinguished by opposite leaves and clusters of axillary flowers. HABITAT Shallow lakes, ponds, ditches, streams, brackish dykes and lagoons; lowland to 380 m. DIST. Native. Throughout BI; frequent in S, scarce in N and W. (All Europe.) FLS May–Aug.

NAJADACEAE Naiads

Glabrous, submerged aquatic perennials or annuals. Leaves opposite or whorled, linear, sessile, with toothed or lobed margins. Flowers monoecious, small, inconspicuous, 1–3, sessile in leaf axils, perianth absent.

Slender Naiad
Najas flexilis *(B, R)

Slender, brittle aquatic annual to 30 cm. LEAVES Linear, 2–3 together, 10–25 × 1 mm, margins minutely toothed. FRUITS 2.5–3.5 mm. DIST. Native. Very local. W Scotland, W Ireland. HABITAT Deep, clear calcareous lakes. (N and central Europe.) FLS Aug–Sep.

Holly-leaved Naiad
Najas marina VU. *(B)

Robust, submerged aquatic annual to 150 cm. STEMS With sparse spiny teeth. LEAVES 1–6 mm wide, margins strongly spiny. FRUITS 4–6 mm. HABITAT Shallow, slightly brackish water over peaty or silty mud. DIST. Native. Very rare. Norfolk Broads only. (All Europe except for extreme N.) FLS Jul–Aug.

ZOSTERACEAE Eelgrasses

Submerged, rhizomatous marine perennials, with alternate grass-like leaves in opposite ranks; leaves sheathing at base with ligule (*see* key on p.536). Flowers monoecious, small, inconspicuous, enclosed within leaf sheath, perianth absent.

Eelgrass
Zostera marina

STEMS Flowering stems much branched. LEAVES 5–10 mm wide, rounded, mucronate at tip, with 5–11 veins, sheaths tubular. FLOWERS Stigma 2× as long as style. FRUITS 3–3.5 mm. HABITAT In sub-tidal zone, from low-water springs to 4 m, on gravel, sand, sandy mud. DIST. Native. Declining owing to disease. All round coasts of BI, but rare in E. (All Europe except extreme N.) FLS Jun–Sep.

Narrow-leaved Eelgrass
Zostera angustifolia

LEAVES To 2 mm wide, rounded, notched at tip, with 3–5 veins, sheaths tubular. FLOWERS Style about as long as stigma. FRUITS 2.5–3 mm. HABITAT Intertidal mud flats, estuaries, from mid-tide level to low-water springs; coastal lagoons. DIST. Native. Very local. Scattered around coasts of BI. (NW Europe.) FLS Jun–Nov. NOTE Sometimes regarded as a sub-species of *Z. marina*.

Dwarf Eelgrass
Zostera noltii VU.

Slender, creeping, inter-tidal perennial. STEMS Flowering stems unbranched. LEAVES Very narrow, 0.5–1.5 mm wide, notched at tip, with 3 veins, sheaths open. FRUITS 1.5–2 mm. HABITAT Estuaries, mudflats, creeks, runnels, between mid-tide level and low-water springs. DIST. Native. Scattered all round coasts of BI. (All Europe except N.) FLS Jun–Oct.

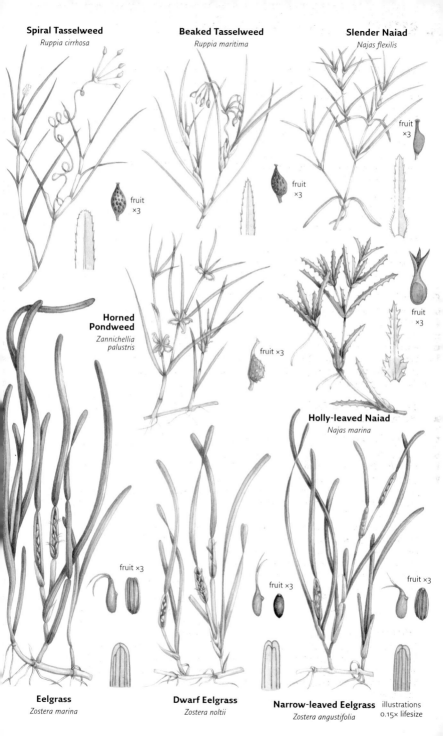

Spiral Tasselweed
Ruppia cirrhosa

Beaked Tasselweed
Ruppia maritima

Slender Naiad
Najas flexilis

fruit ×3

fruit ×3

fruit ×3

Horned Pondweed
Zannichellia palustris

fruit ×3

fruit ×3

Holly-leaved Naiad
Najas marina

fruit ×3

fruit ×3

fruit ×3

fruit ×3

Eelgrass
Zostera marina

Dwarf Eelgrass
Zostera noltii

Narrow-leaved Eelgrass
Zostera angustifolia

illustrations
0.15× lifesize

ARACEAE Arums

Large, essentially tropical family of mostly glabrous, rhizomatous or tuberous herbs, but also shrubs, climbers and epiphytes. Flowers commonly monoecious, small and packed together on a club-shaped spadix, this usually enclosed within a large leaf-like bract – the spathe. There are 2 native British species.

Lords-and-ladies, Cuckoo-pint *Arum maculatum*

Erect, glabrous perennial to 50 cm. LEAVES Appearing in spring; petioles long; blade 7–20 cm, often black-spotted, triangular-hastate, midrib dark green. FLOWERS Spathe 10–25 cm, erect, base completely enclosing flowers at base of spadix; *spadix 7–12 cm, c.½ as long as spathe, upper sterile portion dull purple (rarely yellow)*; flowers unisexual, in compact whorls, males above, females below. FRUITS Red, berry-like. HABITAT Hedgerows, woodlands, coppice, on moist, fertile soils; lowland to 425 m. DIST. Native. Common. England, Wales; introduced in Scotland. (W, central and S Europe.) FLS Apr–May.

Italian Lords-and-ladies *Arum italicum*

Similar to *A. maculatum* but leaves appearing in early winter; blade 15–35 cm, midrib paler than lamina; spathe 15–40 cm, tip drooping forward; *terminal portion of spadix yellow, c.½ as long as spathe*. FLS Apr–May. Ssp. *neglectum*: leaves with veins slightly paler than lamina, basal lobes not spreading. Ssp. *italicum*: leaves with distinct pale yellowish-green veins, basal lobes spreading. Ssp. *neglectum*: HABITAT Shaded hedge banks, scrub, field borders close to sea. DIST. Native. Very local; S, SW England, CI, Scilly. (SW Europe.) Ssp. *italicum*: DIST. Introduced. S Britain. (Naturalised as persistent garden throw-out W, S Europe.)

Sweet-flag *Acorus calamus*

Tall, rhizomatous perennial to 100 cm. LEAVES *Linear, rather sedge-like*, 50–125 × 0.7–2.5 cm, *transversely wrinkled; midrib prominent, with strong smell of tangerines* when crushed. FLOWERS *Spadix appearing lateral, without spathe, 5–9 cm, yellowish green*. HABITAT Shallow, nutrient-rich water at water's edge. DIST. Introduced (native of Asia and North America). Naturalised throughout BI, but rare in N and W. FLS May–Jul.

American Skunk-cabbage *Lysichiton americanus*

Robust, glabrous perennial, foul smelling when in flower. LEAVES Large, 30–150 cm, ovate-oblong, short-stalked. FLOWERS *Spathe 10–35 cm, yellow*; spadix 3.5–12 cm, greenish. FRUITS Green berry. DIST. Introduced (native of W North America). Widely grown in landscaped water gardens, beside lakes, streams; sometimes naturalised in marshy woodland. (Most of Europe except extreme N and Mediterranean.) FLS Apr.

LEMNACEAE Duckweeds

Small, floating aquatic plants that form a green carpet on the surface of stagnant water (*see key on p.536*). Each plant consists of a small, simple frond, with or without roots; the minute single-sex flowers are borne in hollows on the frond surface. Duckweeds include the smallest flowering plants known.

Common Duckweed *Lemna minor*

FRONDS 2–5 mm, with 3 veins, dark shining green, obovate, each with 1 root. HABITAT Stagnant or slow-moving nutrient-rich waters; damp exposed mud; lowland to 500 m. DIST. Native. Common throughout BI, but rare in NW Scotland. (All Europe.) FLS Jun–Jul.

Least Duckweed *Lemna minuta*

FRONDS 1–3 mm, with 0–1 veins, pale green, dull, elliptic, each with 1 root. FLOWERS Not known in BI. HABITAT Similar to *L. minor*, but more shade-tolerant. DIST. Introduced (native of N and S America). Lowland England; often abundant, spreading since 1970s. NOTE The vein character separating *L. minuta* and *L. minor* is not always easy to see: view leaves through transmitted light but at an angle to it. Also note that the frond on *L. minuta* has a faint, pale longitudinal ridge.

Ivy-leaved Duckweed *Lemna trisulca*

FRONDS 3–15 mm, with 3 veins, thin, tapering to short stalk, each with 1 root, cohering in branched groups, floating beneath surface. HABITAT Stagnant or slow-moving moderate to eutrophic water, ponds, ditches; lowland to 340 m. DIST. Native. Frequent throughout BI, N to central Scotland. (All Europe except extreme N.)

Fat Duckweed *Lemna gibba*

FRONDS 1–8 mm, with 4–5 veins, often turning very reddish purple, underside strongly swollen, each with 1 root. HABITAT Stagnant or slow-moving water in ditches, ponds, canals; tolerant of brackish water. DIST. Native. Rather local. Lowland England; scarce elsewhere. (Europe except N.) FLS Jun–Jul, rarely.

Greater Duckweed *Spirodela polyrhiza*

FRONDS 3–10 mm, with 5–15 veins, underside reddish, each with 5–15 roots. HABITAT Still or slow-moving base-rich ponds, drainage dykes, canals. DIST. Native. Local. Lowland England, Ireland. (All Europe except N and SW.) FLS Rarely.

Rootless Duckweed *Wolffia arrhiza* VU

Smallest British flowering plant. FRONDS 0.5–1.5 mm, ± spherical, swollen on both upper and lower surfaces; roots absent. HABITAT Ponds, ditches. DIST. Native. Rare. Somerset Levels, Kent, Sussex coastal levels. (W, central and E Europe.)

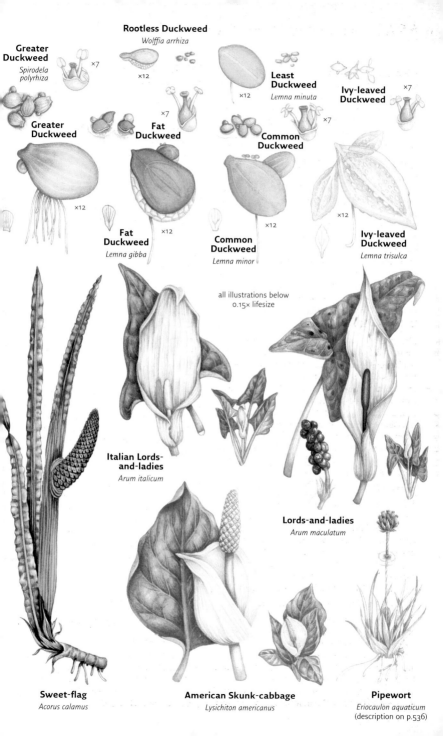

Greater Duckweed
Spirodela polyrhiza
×7

Rootless Duckweed
Wolffia arrhiza
×12

Least Duckweed
Lemna minuta

Ivy-leaved Duckweed
×7

Greater Duckweed
×12

Fat Duckweed
×7

Common Duckweed
×7

Fat Duckweed
Lemna gibba
×12

Common Duckweed
Lemna minor
×12

Ivy-leaved Duckweed
Lemna trisulca
×12

all illustrations below
0.15× lifesize

Italian Lords-and-ladies
Arum italicum

Lords-and-ladies
Arum maculatum

Sweet-flag
Acorus calamus

American Skunk-cabbage
Lysichiton americanus

Pipewort
Eriocaulon aquaticum
(description on p.536)

ERIOCAULACEAE Pipeworts

Pipewort   *Eriocaulon aquaticum*

[*See* illustration previous page.] Mat-forming aquatic perennial. STEMS Non-flowering stems short and densely leafy, so that leaves appear all in basal rosette; flowering stems leafless, 15-60 cm, furrowed, twisted. LEAVES 5-10 cm, narrow, flattened, septate. FLOWERS Small, unisexual, in terminal heads, 0.5-2 cm across, 4 perianth segments in 2 whorls of 2, greyish. HABITAT Shallow water, margins of acid peaty lochs, bare wet peat. DIST. Native. Locally common in W Ireland, rare in Inner Hebrides. (In Europe, restricted to BI.) FLS Jul-Sep.

Key to Zosteraceae Eelgrasses

	if	then
1	▷ Flowering stems branched, terminal; leaves 1-10 mm wide; leaf sheaths fused into tube around stem	Go to ▷ **2**
	▷ Flowering stems unbranched; leaves 0.5-1.5 mm wide, leaf sheaths split	**Z. noltii** (p.532)
2	▷ Leaves 5-10 mm wide; stigma 2× as long as wide	**Z. marina** (p.532)
	▷ Leaves 1-2 mm wide; style as long as stigma	**Z. angustifolia** (p.532)

Key to Lemnaceae Duckweeds

	if	then
1	▷ Fronds rootless, 0.5-1.5 mm, without veins, spherical	**Wolffia arrhiza** (p.534)
	▷ Fronds with roots, veins, ± flattened on upper surface	Go to ▷ **2**
2	▷ Each frond with 1 root, 1-5 veins	Go to ▷ **3**
	▷ Each frond with 5-15 roots and veins	**Spirodela polyrhiza** (p.534)
3	▷ Fronds narrowed to stalk-like base, coherent in groups, floating beneath surface	**Lemna trisulca** (p.534)
	▷ Fronds not narrowed to stalk-like base, not coherent, floating on surface	Go to ▷ **4**
4	▷ Underside of fronds strongly swollen, with 4-5 veins	**L. gibba** (p.534)
	▷ Fronds not swollen on underside	Go to ▷ **5**
5	▷ Fronds 2-5 mm long, usually obovate, with 3 veins	**L. minor** (p.534)
	▷ Fronds 0.8-3 mm long, elliptic, with 1 vein	**L. minuta** (p.534)

Key to **Juncaceae** Rushes and Wood-rushes

individual flower of
Juncaceae

if	then
Leaves usually cylindrical or channelled, glabrous	**Juncus (rushes)** (*see* below)
Leaves grass-like, hairy at base, at least when young	**Luzula (wood-rushes)** (p.539)

Rushes *Juncus*

1   ▷ Flowering stems apparently leafless; inflorescence appearing lateral, as overtopped by elongated stem-like bract   Go to ▷ **2**
       ▷ Flowering stems with leaves; inflorescence obviously terminal, or if apparently lateral, robust plants with sharp-pointed leaves   Go to ▷ **6**

2   ▷ Stems in dense clumps, usually >50 cm tall; inflorescence usually >20-flowered   Go to ▷ **3**
       ▷ Stems in straight lines or diffuse patches, usually <50 cm; inflorescence usually <20-flowered   Go to ▷ **5**

3   ▷ Stems glaucous, with 12–16 prominent ridges, pith in upper part interrupted   *J. inflexus* (p.544)
       ▷ Stems not glaucous, with >18 ridges or ± smooth, pith not interrupted   Go to ▷ **4**

4   ▷ Fresh stems dull, ridged in upper part   *J. conglomeratus* (p.544)
       ▷ Fresh stems glossy, smooth, faintly striate but not ridged   *J. effusus* (p.544)

5   ▷ Stem very slender, ≤1 mm diam.; inflorescence in lower ½ of apparent stem   *J. filiformis* (p.544)
       ▷ Stem ≥1 mm diam.; inflorescence in upper ½ of apparent stem   *J. balticus* (p.544)

6   ▷ Leaves and lowest bract ending in stiff, sharp points; inflorescence apparently lateral; robust coastal plants   Go to ▷ **7**
       ▷ Leaves and lowest bracts not sharp-pointed; inflorescence terminal   Go to ▷ **8**

7   ▷ Flowers straw-coloured; capsule about as long as tepals   *J. maritimus* (p.544)
       ▷ Flowers reddish brown; capsule clearly longer than tepals   *J. acutus* (p.544)

8   ▷ Leaves hollow, more or less cylindrical, with cross partitions (septate)   Go to ▷ **9**
       ▷ Leaves solid, flat or channelled   Go to ▷ **14**

CONTINUED OVERLEAF

		if	**then**
9	▷	Small, tufted plant to 25 cm; base of stem often swollen, creeping, reddish, sometimes floating; leaves bristle-like (setaceous), in section consisting of 2 tubes (use a lens)	*J. bulbosus* (p.542)
	▷	Plants usually >30 cm; leaves not setaceous	Go to ▷ **10**
10	▷	Leaves with longitudinal as well as transverse partitions; flowers pale brown or straw-coloured	*J. subnodulosus* (p.542)
	▷	Leaves with transverse partitions only; flowers dark brown to blackish	Go to ▷ **11**
11	▷	All tepals blunt, outer mucronate	Go to ▷ **12**
	▷	At least outer tepals acute	Go to ▷ **13**
12	▷	Anthers ⅓–⅔× as long as filaments; capsule blunt	*J. alpinoarticulatus* (p.542)
	▷	Anthers 1–1½× as long as filaments; capsule acute	*J. anceps* • (p.542)
13	▷	Plant prostrate to ascending; leaves strongly compressed; outer tepals with erect tips; fruit abruptly acuminate	*J. articulatus* (p.542)
	▷	Plant erect; leaves ± cylindrical; tips of outer tepals recurved; fruit acute	*J. acutiflorus* (p.542)
14	▷	Small alpine perennials; flowers solitary or in few-flowered terminal clusters; seeds with conspicuous white appendage	Go to ▷ **15**
	▷	Flowers neither solitary nor in few-flowered terminal clusters; seeds without appendages	Go to ▷ **18**
15	▷	Flower stems densely tufted; 1–3 flowers in axils of 2–3 long, bristle-like bracts	*J. trifidus* (p.540)
	▷	Flower stems solitary or in small clusters; bracts short and scale-like	Go to ▷ **16**
16	▷	Stems solitary; outer tepals acute; fruit ≥6 mm, longer than tepals	*J. castaneus* (p.544)
	▷	Stems in small tufts; outer tepals blunt; fruit <6 mm	Go to ▷ **17**
17	▷	(1–)2 flowers per inflorescence	*J. biglumis* (p.542)
	▷	(2–)3 flowers per inflorescence	*J. triglumis* (p.544)
18	▷	Perennials (difficult to uproot)	Go to ▷ **19**
	▷	Small annuals	Go to ▷ **23**
19	▷	Leaves all in basal rosette	Go to ▷ **20**
	▷	1–4 stem leaves	Go to ▷ **21**
20	▷	Leaves rounded beneath, channelled above; 6 stamens	*J. squarrosus* (p.540)
	▷	Leaves ± flat; 3 stamens	*J. planifolius* (p.540)

if		then
21	▷ Flowers greenish or straw-coloured, tepals acute	*J. tenuis* (p.540)
	▷ Flowers dark brown, tepals blunt	Go to ▷ **22**
22	▷ Lowest bract shorter than inflorescence, tepals ± as long as fruit (salt marshes)	*J. gerardii* (p.540)
	▷ Lowest bract longer than inflorescence, tepals shorter than fruit	*J. compressus* (p.540)
23	▷ Inflorescence a much-branched leafy panicle	Go to ▷ **24**
	▷ Inflorescence comprising head-like dense-flowered clusters	Go to ▷ **25**
24	▷ Inflorescence occupying ½ height of plant or more, bracts conspicuous	*J. bufonius* **group** (p.540)
	▷ Inflorescence occupying upper part of stem, bracts minute	*J. tenageia* • (p.540)
25	▷ Leaves all basal, without auricles; flower heads usually solitary, tips of tepals recurved	*J. capitatus* (p.542)
	▷ Stems with some leaves; leaves with pointed auricles; several flower heads per stem, tips of tepals erect (very rare, Cornwall)	*J. pygmaeus* (p.542)

Wood-rushes *Luzula*

	if	then
1	▷ Flowers borne singly in inflorescence, rarely in pairs	Go to ▷ **2**
	▷ Flowers borne in groups of 2 or more	Go to ▷ **3**
2	▷ Basal leaves usually >4 mm wide; inflorescence branches spreading	*L. pilosa* (p.546)
	▷ Basal leaves ≤4 mm wide; inflorescence branches drooping to one side	*L. forsteri* (p.546)
3	▷ Plant robust; basal leaves >8 mm wide	*L. sylvatica* (p.546)
	▷ All leaves <8 mm wide	Go to ▷ **4**
4	▷ Inflorescence drooping, spike-like (Scottish mountains)	*L. spicata* (p.546)
	▷ Inflorescence of stalked clusters	Go to ▷ **5**
5	▷ Dwarf alpine; leaves channelled, sparsely pubescent near base; flowers drooping in 2–5-flowered clusters (Scottish mountains)	*L. arcuata* (p.546)
	▷ Leaves flat, conspicuously pubescent	Go to ▷ **6**
6	▷ Plant with rhizomes or stolons; anthers 3–4× as long as filaments	*L. campestris* (p.546)
	▷ Plants without rhizomes or stolons; anthers shorter than to 2× as long as filaments	Go to ▷ **7**
7	▷ Flowers chestnut-brown, outer tepals 2.5–3.5 mm	*L. multiflora* (p.546)
	▷ Flowers pale yellowish brown, outer tepals 2–2.5 mm (very rare, fens, Huntingdonshire)	*L. pallidula* (p.546)

JUNCACEAE Rushes, Wood-rushes

Perennial or, less often, annual, wind-pollinated herbs with cylindrical, channelled or grass-like leaves (*see* key on p.537). Leaves are either alternate or, more usually, all basal. They are distinguished from other grass-like plants by the small, regular (lily-like) bisexual flowers, with 6 tepals (3+3), 6 stamens, 3 stigmas and the 1-3-celled superior ovary. Flowers are arranged in terminal inflorescences that often appear lateral, and the tepals are usually greenish or brownish. Many rushes are characteristic plants of wet habitats.

Heath Rush
Juncus squarrosus

Densely tufted, wiry perennial to 50 cm. Leaves *All basal*, 8-15 cm, *linear, stiff, reflexed, upper surface deeply channelled*. Flowers Inflorescence branches ± erect; lowest bract much shorter than inflorescence; tepals dark brown. Habitat Moorland, damp heaths, acid grassland, bogs, upland flushes; to 1040 m. Dist. Native. Common throughout BI, but scarce and declining in lowland England. (NW, W and central Europe.) Fls Jun-Jul.

Slender Rush
Juncus tenuis

Tufted perennial. Stems Flowering stems 15-35 cm, erect. Leaves Most basal, 10-25 cm, linear, yellowish green. Flowers *Lowest bracts much longer than inflorescence; inflorescence diffuse; tepals yellowish, lanceolate, acute*. Habitat Frequent on damp, open ground, paths, tracksides, heathland and woodland rides, lake margins. Dist. Introduced (native of North and South America). Widespread in S and W BI; scattered elsewhere. (N, W and central Europe.) Fls Jun-Sep.

Round-fruited Rush
Juncus compressus

Tufted perennial. Stems Flowering stems 10-50 cm. Leaves Linear, flattened. Flowers *Lowest bract usually longer than inflorescence*; inflorescence lax; perianth segments blunt; *anthers about as long as or slightly longer than filaments; style shorter than ovary*. Fruits ± globose, blunt, very glossy capsule, c.1⅓× as long as perianth. Habitat Grazed marshes, wet meadows, brackish grassland; often near sea and with *J. gerardii* (*see* below). Dist. Native. Local. Lowland central England; scarce elsewhere. (All Europe except extreme N.) Fls Jun-Jul.

Saltmarsh Rush
Juncus gerardii

Very similar to *J. compressus*, but *lowest bract usually shorter than inflorescence; anthers 2-3× as long as filaments; styles as long as or slightly longer than ovary; capsule about as long as perianth*, ovoid. Habitat Upper levels of salt marshes, wet brackish grassland, cliff-top turf. Dist. Native. Common all round coasts of BI. (All European coasts, saline habitats inland.) Fls Jun-Jul.

Three-leaved Rush
Juncus trifidus

Slender, densely tufted, patch-forming alpine perennial Stems Flowering stems to 30 cm, *with 1-2 leaves and leaf-like lower bract, all longer than inflorescence*. Flowers Sessile, 1-3 in tight cluster; tepals brown. Fruits Capsule, longer than perianth. Habitat Abundant on bare, exposed mountain plateaux, rock crevices, on acid or calcareous rock; to 1310 m. Dist. Native. Central and NW Scotland. (Arctic Europe, mts of central and S Europe.) Fls Jun-Aug.

Toad Rush
Juncus bufonius

Erect to procumbent tufted annual to 35 cm. Stems Simple or much branched. Leaves 0.5-2 cm × <1 mm, *bristle-like*, dark green. Flowers Inflorescence leafy, much branched; *tepals without dark lines, all acute*. Fruits Capsule, shorter than inner perianth segments. Habitat All kinds of seasonally wet, open habitats, dune slacks, estuarine mud. Dist. Native. Common throughout BI. (All Europe.) Fls Aug-Sep.

Leafy Rush
Juncus foliosus (J. bufonius group)

Similar to *J. bufonius*, but stems erect to ascending; leaves wider, 1.5-5 mm, pale green; *tepals with dark line on each side of midrib*; capsule about as long as inner perianth segments. Habitat Wet fields, marshes, muddy margins of ponds, lakes, streams and rivers; to 365 m. Dist. Native. Rather local. W and S Britain, Ireland. (S and W Europe.) Fls May-Sep.

Frog Rush
Juncus ambiguus (J. bufonius group)

Similar to *J. bufonius*, but *plant usually light brown; inner tepals blunt to notched and mucronate; capsule at least as long as inner tepals*. Habitat Bare, damp, brackish patches, sand and mud flats above high water mark. Dist. Native. Scattered all round coasts of BI. (Most of Europe.) Fls Aug-Sep.

Broad-leaved Rush
Juncus planifolius

Tufted perennial to 30 cm. Leaves *Basal, shorter than stems, 2-8 mm wide, inrolled*. Flowers Inflorescence with several unequal branches, much longer than lowest bract; 3 stamens. Fruits Capsule longer than perianth. Habitat Shallow running water, tracks, runnels; also acid peaty soils by streams, lake shores. Dist. Introduced (native of S hemisphere). Very rare. W Galway. Fls Jul-Aug.

Sand Rush
Juncus tenageia

Tufted erect annual to 35 cm. Leaves 0.5-1 mm wide, shorter than stems. Flowers Inflorescence <⅓ height of plant, rather dense. Fruits Globose capsule, as long as perianth. Habitat Damp, open habitats, woodland rides, on acid soils. Dist. *Not BI*. (Central and S Europe to Netherlands, N France.) Fls Jun-Sep.

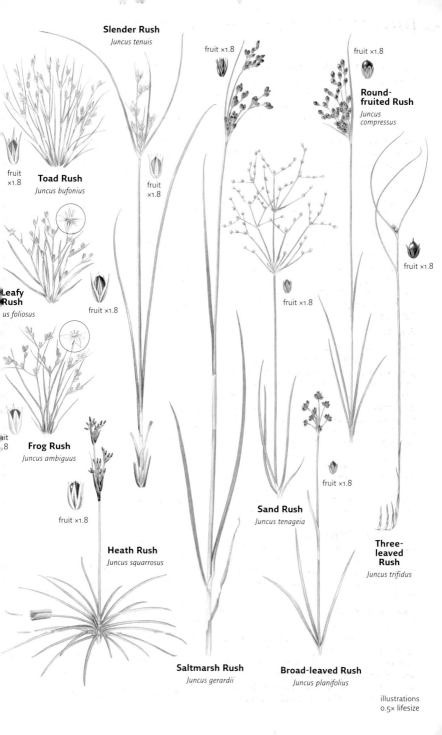

Slender Rush
Juncus tenuis

fruit ×1.8

fruit ×1.8

Round-fruited Rush
Juncus compressus

fruit
×1.8

Toad Rush
Juncus bufonius

fruit
×1.8

Leafy Rush
...us foliosus

fruit ×1.8

fruit ×1.8

fruit ×1.8

...it
.8

Frog Rush
Juncus ambiguus

fruit ×1.8

fruit ×1.8

Sand Rush
Juncus tenageia

Three-leaved Rush
Juncus trifidus

Heath Rush
Juncus squarrosus

Saltmarsh Rush
Juncus gerardii

Broad-leaved Rush
Juncus planifolius

illustrations
0.5× lifesize

Dwarf Rush *Juncus capitatus* VU.

Dwarf, tufted annual to 5 cm. LEAVES All basal, bristle-like, <1 mm wide. FLOWERS Inflorescence in compact terminal head; 1–2 bracts, longest much longer than inflorescence; outer tepals with fine recurved tips. FRUITS Capsule, shorter than perianth. HABITAT Bare patches on heaths where water stood in previous winter. DIST. Native. Very rare. SW Cornwall, Anglesey, Channel Is. (S and W Europe.) FLS Mar–Jun.

Blunt-flowered Rush *Juncus subnodulosus*

Tall, erect, rhizomatous perennial to 120 cm. STEMS and LEAVES Similar: *smooth, hollow, with longitudinal and transverse septa.* FLOWERS Inflorescence compound, not crowded, branches wide-spreading; *tepals straw-coloured, turning light reddish brown, incurved, blunt.* FRUITS *Light brown capsule, slightly longer than perianth.* HABITAT Forming extensive patches on base-rich or calcareous marshes, fens, wet meadows, dune slacks. DIST. Native. Throughout BI except Scotland, where very rare. (W, central and S Europe.) FLS Jul–Sep.

Alpine Rush *Juncus alpinoarticulatus*

Erect, rhizomatous perennial to 40 cm. LEAVES With distinct transverse septa, much shorter than inflorescence. FLOWERS Inflorescence branches erect, not wide-spreading, rather parallel to main axis; *tepals dark brown to blackish, inner tepals blunt.* FRUITS *Blunt capsules, as long as or longer than perianth.* HABITAT Base-rich calcareous mountain flushes, gravelly stream beds; to 880 m. DIST. Native. Very scarce, local. N England, Scotland. (Arctic Europe, mts of S Europe.) FLS Jul–Sep.

Jointed Rush *Juncus articulatus*

Prostrate to ascending, tufted, rhizomatous perennial to 80 cm. LEAVES *Curved, laterally compressed,* with inconspicuous transverse septa. FLOWERS Inflorescence repeatedly branched, branches diverging at acute angle; perianth dark brown to black; *inner and outer tepals same length, acute.* FRUITS *Shining black ovoid, mucronate capsule.* HABITAT Marshes, fens, dune slacks, damp woodland rides, margins of ponds, lakes and streams, on base-rich or calcareous soils; to 810 m. DIST. Native. Common throughout BI. (All Europe.) FLS Jun–Sep.

Sharp-flowered Rush *Juncus acutiflorus* VU.

Tall, stiffly erect, rhizomatous perennial to 100 cm. LEAVES *Straight, ± cylindrical in section,* with conspicuous transverse septa. FLOWERS Inflorescence repeatedly branched, branches diverging at acute angle; perianth brown; *tepals acute, tapering to fine points, the outer recurved at tip.* FRUITS *Brown capsule, evenly tapered to fine point.* HABITAT Wet pastures, marshes, wet heaths, bogs, pond sides, on acid soils; to 685 m. DIST. Native. Common throughout BI. (W, central and S Europe.) FLS Jul–Sep.

Bulbous Rush *Juncus bulbosus*

Small, slender perennial, greatly varying in habit and stature. STEMS *Tufted, procumbent, rooting at nodes, or free-floating,* often with *swollen base.* LEAVES Filiform, with numerous indistinct septa. FLOWERS Inflorescence diffuse, sparse, often proliferating into small, leafy non-flowering shoots; outer tepals acute, inner blunt. FRUITS Blunt capsule. HABITAT Frequent on bare mud or peat, woodland rides, wet heaths, mires, on acid soils; or free-floating. DIST. Native. Throughout BI, but scarce in English lowlands. (Most of Europe except SE.) FLS Jun–Sep.

Danish Sand Rush *Juncus ancep*

Erect, rhizomatous perennial to 60 cm. LEAVES With distinct transverse septa. FLOWERS Inflorescence lax or crowded; *tepals ovate-oblong, outer acute, inner blunt.* FRUITS Capsule, slightly longer than perianth, acute. HABITAT Wet dune slacks. DIST. *Not BI.* (W and S Europe.) FLS Jul–Sep.

Pygmy Rush *Juncus pygmaeus* EN.

Dwarf, tufted, often *purplish annual* to 8 cm. LEAVES Mostly basal, indistinctly septate. FLOWERS Inflorescence compact, with few heads; lowest bract longer than inflorescence; tepals narrow, acute to blunt, greenish or purplish. HABITAT Seasonally wet, compacted ground, damp hollows, on serpentine heathland. DIST. Native. Very rare. SW Cornwall only. (W Europe.) FLS May–Jun.

Two-flowered Rush *Juncus biglumis*

Small, erect, tufted, rhizomatous perennial to 12 cm. STEMS Channelled along one side. LEAVES All basal, curved. FLOWERS In 2-flowered inflorescence, one flower below other; bract longer than inflorescence; tepals purplish brown, obtuse. FRUITS Blunt capsule, much longer than perianth. HABITAT Base-rich flushes, wet rock faces, short, open, species-rich mires; to 1100 m. DIST. Native. Rare. Scottish mts. (N Europe.) FLS Jun–Jul.

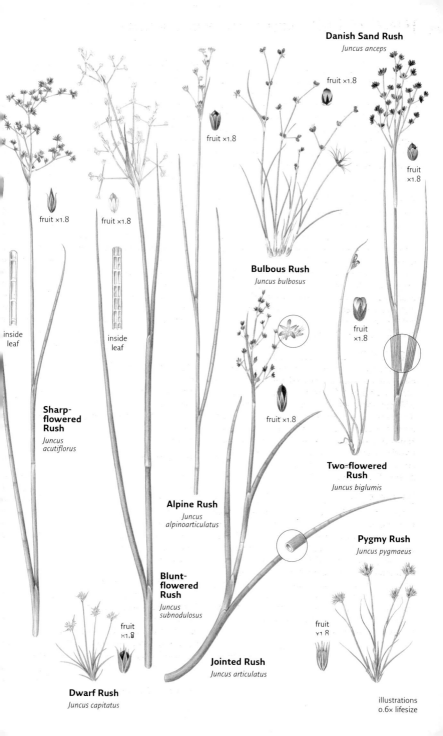

Danish Sand Rush
Juncus anceps

fruit ×1.8

fruit
×1.8

fruit ×1.8

fruit ×1.8

inside
leaf

inside
leaf

Bulbous Rush
Juncus bulbosus

fruit
×1.8

**Sharp-
flowered
Rush**
*Juncus
acutiflorus*

fruit ×1.8

**Two-flowered
Rush**
Juncus biglumis

Alpine Rush
*Juncus
alpinoarticulatus*

Pygmy Rush
Juncus pygmaeus

**Blunt-
flowered
Rush**
*Juncus
subnodulosus*

fruit
×1.8

Jointed Rush
Juncus articulatus

fruit
×1.8

Dwarf Rush
Juncus capitatus

illustrations
0.6× lifesize

Three-flowered Rush
Juncus triglumis

Stiffly erect, small, tufted perennial to 20 cm. LEAVES All basal, curved. FLOWERS *(2-)3 all at ± same level forming terminal cluster*; lowest bract shorter than inflorescence. FRUITS Blunt, mucronate capsule, 4-5.5 mm, slightly exceeding perianth. HABITAT Wet, gravelly base-rich flushes, rock ledges; to 1065 m. DIST. Native. Mts of N Wales and N England, Scottish Highlands. (N Europe, mts of S and E Europe.) FLS Jun-Jul.

Chestnut Rush
Juncus castaneus VU.

Erect, stoloniferous perennial to 30 cm. LEAVES 5-20 cm, channelled above. FLOWERS *Large, in 2-3 terminal clusters; tepals narrow, outer acute, inner blunt; lowest bract longer than inflorescence.* FRUITS *Blunt, mucronate capsule, 6-7.5 mm, much longer than perianth.* HABITAT Wet calcareous mountain flushes, springs; to 990 m. DIST. Native. Rare. Scottish Highlands. (Arctic and N Europe, mts of S Europe.) FLS Jun-Jul.

Sea Rush
Juncus maritimus

Erect, densely tufted, robust perennial to 100 cm. LEAVES *Sharply pointed.* FLOWERS In much-branched inflorescence, appearing lateral, shorter than sharply pointed bract; *tepals 3-4.5 mm, straw-coloured, inner blunt, outer acute.* FRUITS Ovoid, mucronate *capsule, about as long as perianth.* HABITAT Upper parts of salt marshes, dune slacks. DIST. Native. All round coasts of BI except NW Scotland. (All European coasts except extreme N; also inland E-central Europe.) FLS Jul-Aug.

Sharp Rush
Juncus acutus

Densely tussocky, prickly perennial to 150 cm, more robust than *J. maritimus.* LEAVES *Sharply pointed.* FLOWERS In rounded, compact inflorescence, shorter than bract; tepals 2.5-4 mm, reddish brown. FRUITS *Ovoid capsule, ≥2× as long as perianth.* HABITAT Saline dune slacks, drier parts of salt marshes. DIST. Native. Very local. Coasts of SW England, Wales, S Ireland, Channel Is; rare elsewhere. (SW Europe, Mediterranean.) FLS Jun.

Baltic Rush
Juncus balticus

Far-creeping, rhizomatous perennial. STEMS Erect, to 75 cm, smooth, glossy, pith continuous. FLOWERS *Inflorescence appearing lateral, in upper ¼ of apparent stem*, rather lax; tepals dark brown, acute. FRUITS Dark brown, glossy, ovoid, mucronate capsule. HABITAT Dune slacks. DIST. Native. Coasts of N and NE Scotland; occasional inland. (N Europe.) FLS Jun-Aug.

Thread Rush
Juncus filiform.

Slender, erect, rhizomatous perennial to 60 cm. STEMS *Filiform, faintly ridged.* FLOWERS *Inflorescence appearing lateral in lower ⅔ or ¼ of apparent stem*, forming compact head; tepals pale brown to straw-coloured. FRUITS Pale brown, ± spherical, shortly mucronate capsule, about as long as perianth. HABITAT Stony, silty shores of lakes and reservoirs. DIST. Native. Very local, possibly increasing. N England (especially Lake District), Scotland. (Much of Europe but rare in Mediterranean.) FLS Jun-Sep.

Hard Rush
Juncus inflexu

Densely tufted grey-green rhizomatous perennial to 120 cm. STEMS *Stiffly erect, dull, glaucous, prominently ridged, pith interrupted.* FLOWERS Inflorescence apparently lateral, diffuse; tepals narrow, unequal. FRUITS Dark brown, glossy capsule, as long as perianth. HABITAT Wet meadows, banks of ponds, lakes, dykes and rivers on base-rich soils, dune slacks. DIST. Native. Common throughout BI as far N as central Scotland. (All Europe except N.) FLS Jun-Aug.

Soft Rush
Juncus effusu

Densely tufted, stiffly erect perennial to 150 cm. STEMS *Bright green, smooth, glossy, pith continuous.* FLOWERS Inflorescence apparently lateral, diffuse or compacted into tight head (var. *subglomeratus*); tepals narrow, sharp-pointed. FRUITS Yellowish brown ovoid, blunt capsule, shorter than perianth. HABITAT Marshes, bogs, wet grassland, margins of streams, ponds, rivers and dykes, wet woods, usually on neutral or acid soils; to 845 m. DIST. Native. Common throughout BI. (All Europe except Arctic.) FLS Jun-Aug.

Compact Rush
Juncus conglomeratu

Densely tufted, erect perennial to 100 cm. Similar to *J. effusus*, but less robust, *stems rather greyish green, not glossy, with numerous fine ribs below inflorescence; inflorescence a tight head.* HABITAT Marshes, bogs, wet heaths, wet grassland, ditches, lakes, rivers, damp woods; more restricted to acid soils than *J. effusus.* To 840 m. DIST. Native. Throughout BI. (Most of Europe.) FLS May-Jul.

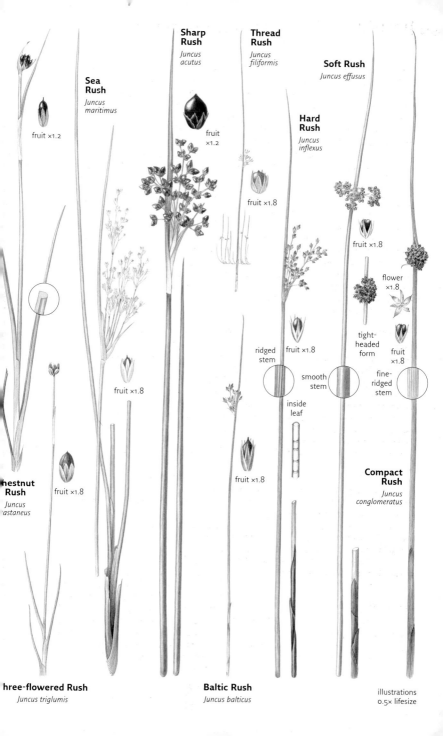

Sharp Rush
Juncus acutus

fruit ×1.2

Thread Rush
Juncus filiformis

Soft Rush
Juncus effusus

Sea Rush
Juncus maritimus

fruit ×1.2

Hard Rush
Juncus inflexus

fruit ×1.8

fruit ×1.8

fruit ×1.8

flower ×1.8

tight-headed form

ridged stem

fruit ×1.8

smooth stem

fine-ridged stem

inside leaf

fruit ×1.8

Compact Rush
Juncus conglomeratus

hestnut Rush

Juncus astaneus

fruit ×1.8

fruit ×1.8

hree-flowered Rush

Juncus triglumis

Baltic Rush
Juncus balticus

illustrations
0.5× lifesize

Wood-rushes *Luzula*
See key to *Luzula* on p.539.

Hairy Wood-rush
Luzula pilosa

Erect, tufted, grass-like perennial to 30 cm. LEAVES *Basal leaves 3–4 mm broad, sparsely hairy.* FLOWERS Single, dark brown, in lax inflorescence with *slender, spreading branches.* FRUITS Inflorescence branches reflexed; tepals shorter than or as long as capsule; seeds with hooked appendage, >½ as long as rest of seed. HABITAT Deciduous woodland, coppice, hedge banks, usually on acid soils; to 670 m. DIST. Native. Common throughout most of BI, but scarce in parts of Ireland. (Most of Europe except extreme S.) FLS Apr–Jun.

Southern Wood-rush
Luzula forsteri

Similar to *L. pilosa*, but *leaves narrower, 1.5–3 mm broad; inflorescence drooping to one side, remaining erect in fruit;* tepals longer than capsule; seeds with straight appendage ≤¼ as long as rest of seed. HABITAT Similar to *L. pilosa*, on mildly acid soils. DIST. Native. Rather local. S England, S Wales. (S, W and S-central Europe.) FLS Apr–Jun.

Great Wood-rush
Luzula sylvatica

Tall, erect, mat- or tussock-forming, robust, rhizomatous perennial to 80 cm. LEAVES *Basal leaves 8–12 mm wide*, glossy, sparsely hairy. FLOWERS Brown, in groups of 3–5 in lax terminal inflorescence. FRUITS Inflorescence branches spreading; tepals about as long as capsule. HABITAT Woodlands, shaded stream sides, heaths, moors, upland stream sides, on acid soils; to 1040 m. DIST. Native. Throughout BI, but scarce in E England. (S, W and central Europe.) FLS May–Jun.

Field Wood-rush
Luzula campestris

Erect, loosely tufted, *rhizomatous* perennial to 15 cm. LEAVES Grass-like, 2–4 mm broad, with long, colourless hairs. FLOWERS Inflorescence of 1 sessile and 3–6 stalked clusters of 3–12 flowers; tepals dark brown; *anthers 3–4× as long as filaments.* HABITAT Short, infertile, usually acid grassland; to 1005 m. DIST. Native. Common throughout BI. (Most of Europe except extreme N.) FLS Mar–Jun.

Heath Wood-rush
Luzula multiflora

Erect, densely tufted perennial *without rhizomes*, to 40 cm. Very variable, with a number of named subspecies based on characters of the seed, of which the 2 most widespread and equally common are ssp *congesta* and ssp. *multiflora*. LEAVES Grass-like, 3–4 mm broad, sparsely hairy. FLOWERS In sessile clusters in compact head (ssp. *congesta*), or in stalked clusters (ssp. *multiflora*); peduncles smooth; outer and inner tepals equal, outer tepals 2.6–3.3 mm; *anthers 0.8–2.2× as long as filaments*; style 0.4–0.9 mm. FRUITS Seeds 1.2–1.5 mm in ssp. *congesta* 0.8–1.2 mm in ssp. *multiflora*. HABITAT Acid grassland, open woods, heaths, moors, bogs; to 1020 m. DIST. Native. Common throughout BI. (Most of Europe.) FLS Apr–Jun.

Fen Wood-rush
Luzula pallidula CR

Similar to *L. multiflora* ssp. *multiflora*, but *flowers pale yellowish brown; peduncles densely minutely papillose; inner tepals shorter than outer*, outer tepal 2–2.6 mm; style 0.2–0.3 mm. HABITAT Damp peat woodland. DIST. Native. Very rare. Woodwalton and Holme fens, Cambridgeshire. (N and central Europe.) FLS May–Jun.

Curved Wood-rush
Luzula arcuata VU

Dwarf, tufted, stoloniferous alpine perennial to 10 cm. LEAVES *Basal leaves 1–3 mm wide, deeply channelled* ± glabrous. FLOWERS In inflorescence of several 2–5 flowered clusters, outer stalks curved downwards. HABITAT Bare, exposed plateaux and ridges; to 1290 m. DIST. Native. Very scarce. Scottish mts. (Arctic and N Europe.) FLS Jun–Jul.

Spiked Wood-rush
Luzula spicata

Small, tufted, stoloniferous alpine perennial to 30 cm. STEMS *Erect*. LEAVES Basal leaves 1–2 mm wide, recurved, slightly channelled. FLOWERS In *dense, drooping, spike-like inflorescence* of many several-flowered sessile clusters. FRUITS Blackish capsule 2.1–2.5 mm. HABITAT Open stony ground, ledges, scree, cliffs, on acid rocks; to 1220 m. DIST. Native. Widespread in Scottish mts. (Arctic and N Europe, mts of S Europe.) FLS Jun–Jul.

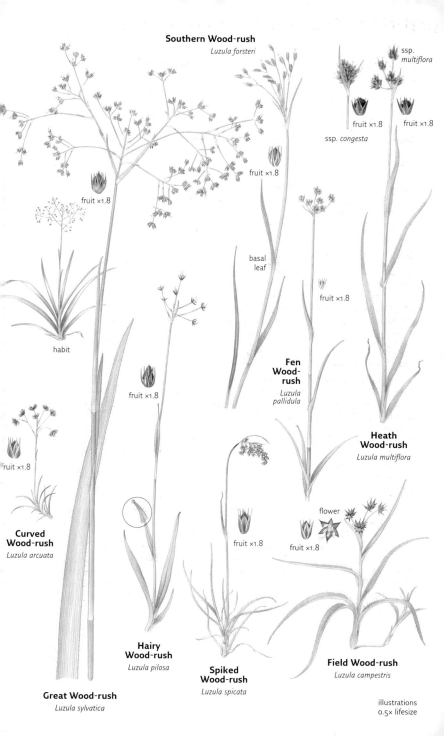

Southern Wood-rush
Luzula forsteri

ssp. *multiflora*

fruit ×1.8

fruit ×1.8

ssp. *congesta*

fruit ×1.8

fruit ×1.8

basal leaf

fruit ×1.8

habit

fruit ×1.8

Fen Wood-rush
Luzula pallidula

Heath Wood-rush
Luzula multiflora

fruit ×1.8

Curved Wood-rush
Luzula arcuata

flower

fruit ×1.8

fruit ×1.8

Hairy Wood-rush
Luzula pilosa

Spiked Wood-rush
Luzula spicata

Field Wood-rush
Luzula campestris

Great Wood-rush
Luzula sylvatica

illustrations
0.5× lifesize

	if	then
1	▷ Flowers all unisexual; male and female flowers in separate spikes or in separate parts of the same spike; female flowers (ovary and nut) wholly or partially enclosed in flask-like utricle (modified glume):	
	▷ Female flowers entirely enclosed within flask-like utricle	*Carex* (p.566)
	▷ Female flowers partially enclosed within extra folded glume	*Kobresia* (p.552)
	▷ Most flowers bisexual; female flowers not enclosed in a utricle	Go to ▷ **2**
2	▷ Stems hollow; leaf margins and keel with saw-like teeth sharp enough to cut skin	*Cladium* (p.556)
	▷ Stems solid; leaf margins without saw-like teeth	Go to ▷ **3**
3	▷ Perianth bristles long and silky, forming conspicuous cotton-like heads in fruit	*Eriophorum, Trichophorum* (p.5
	▷ Perianth bristles absent, or inconspicuous and shorter than glumes	Go to ▷ **4**
4	▷ Inflorescence a single terminal spike; lowest bract shorter than inflorescence	Go to ▷ **5**
	▷ Inflorescence comprising ≥2 spikelets; lowest bract leaf- or stem-like, as long as or longer than inflorescence	Go to ▷ **7**
5	▷ Floating aquatic; stems slender, much branched; leaf blades well developed	*Eleogiton* (p.554)
	▷ Not floating aquatic; stems unbranched; leaf blades short or absent	Go to ▷ **6**
6	▷ Leaf blades absent	*Eleocharis* (opposite and p.552)
	▷ Uppermost sheath with short green leaf blade, ≤10 mm	*Trichophorum* (p.550)
7	▷ Inflorescence with several flat or keeled leaf-like bracts clustered together at base	Go to ▷ **8**
	▷ Bracts not flat and leaf-like, or if leaf-like, then not clustered together at base of inflorescence	Go to ▷ **9**
8	▷ Spikelets rounded in section, glumes spirally arranged	*Scirpus, Bulboschoenus* (p.55(
	▷ Spikelets flattened, glumes in 2 opposite rows	*Cyperus* (p.556)
9	▷ Inflorescence a terminal flattened head, spikelets in 2 opposite rows	*Blysmus* (p.554)
	▷ Inflorescence not as above	Go to ▷ **10**

	if	then
10	▷ Spikelets distinctly flattened; glumes in 2 opposite rows	*Schoenus* (p.556)
	▷ Spikelets not flattened, glumes spirally arranged	Go to ▷ **11**
11	▷ Inflorescence a terminal head of spikelets, lowest bract leaf-like	*Rhynchospora* (p.556)
	▷ Bracts stem-like and inflorescence appearing lateral	Go to ▷ **12**
12	▷ Stems very slender, ≤1 mm wide; inflorescence of 1–3 spikelets	*Isolepis* (p.554)
	▷ Stems more robust, ≥2 mm wide; inflorescence of numerous spikelets	*Schoenoplectus* (p.554), *Scirpoides* (p.552)

Key to Spike-rushes *Eleocharis*

	if	then
1	▷ Lowest glume much less than ⅓ as long as spikelet	Go to ▷ **2**
	▷ Lowest glume at least ⅓ as long as spikelet	Go to ▷ **5**
2	▷ Plant densely tufted; 3 stigmas; nut triquetrous	*E. multicaulis* (p.552)
	▷ Pant not tufted; 2 stigmas; nut biconvex	Go to ▷ **3**
3	▷ Lowest glume not more than half-encircling base of spikelet	Go to ▷ **4**
	▷ Lowest glume ± completely encircling base of spikelet	*E. uniglumis* (p.552)
4	▷ Glumes 2–2.5 mm wide; 0–4 perianth bristles (common)	*E. palustris* (p.552)
	▷ Glumes 1–1.5 mm wide; 5 perianth bristles (rare, N England, S Scotland)	*E. austriaca* (p.552)
5	▷ Upper leaf sheath thin and inconspicuous; spikelet greenish (rare, estuarine mud)	*E. parvula* (p.552)
	▷ Upper leaf sheath conspicuous; spikelet brownish	Go to ▷ **6**
6	▷ Stems rounded in section; glumes 2.5–7 mm, ≤7 per spikelet	*E. quinqueflora* (p.552)
	▷ Stems 4-angled; glumes 1.5–3 mm, ≤15 per spikelet	*E. acicularis* (p.552)

CYPERACEAE Sedges

A large family of rhizomatous or tufted perennials (*see* key on p.548). Stems are usually solid, often 3-angled. Leaves are linear, often rather grass- or rush-like and consisting of a blade and basal sheath, but sometimes without a blade and reduced to the sheath. Flowers bisexual or unisexual, each arising in axil of a bract (glume) and arranged in 1- to many-flowered spikelets; spikelets solitary and terminal, or arranged in branched or spike-like inflorescences; perianth consists of 1 to many bristles or, more often, is absent; 2–3 stamens; 2–3 stigmas. Fruit is indehiscent. In the sedges, the female flowers are entirely enclosed within a flask-like extra glume, the utricle.

Common Cottongrass   *Eriophorum angustifolium*

Creeping, rhizomatous perennial to 75 cm. STEMS Erect, smooth, rounded to bluntly triangular in section. LEAVES 2–5 mm wide, channelled, narrowing to long, solid, triangular tip; dark green, tip turning characteristic rust colour. INFLORESCENCES 3–7 spikes, nodding, peduncles smooth; glumes 4–10 mm, 1-nerved; bristles to 5 cm. HABITAT Bog pools, *Sphagnum* bogs, acid flushes, wet heaths; to 1100 m. DIST. Native. Common in N and W BI; rare and declining in S and E. (Most of Europe except Mediterranean.) FLS May–Jun, fruits Jun–Sep.

Broad-leaved Cottongrass   *Eriophorum latifolium*

Tufted, rhizomatous perennial to 60 cm. Similar in general appearance to *E. angustifolium*, but stems bluntly triangular in section; leaves 3–8 mm wide, flat, with short, solid tip, rather yellowish green. INFLORESCENCES 2–12 spikes, nodding, peduncles rough with short, forward-directed hairs; glumes 5–6 mm, 1-nerved; bristles to 2.5 cm, pure white. HABITAT Base-rich fens, meadows, upland calcareous flushes; to 670 m. DIST. Native. Scattered throughout BI, but very local and declining. (Most of Europe.) FLS May–Jun, fruits Jun–Jul.

Slender Cottongrass   *Eriophorum gracile* *(B, R)

Slender, creeping, rhizomatous perennial to 60 cm. STEMS Solitary, smooth, triquetrous. LEAVES Narrow, 0.5–2 mm wide, 3-angled. INFLORESCENCES 3–6 spikes, nodding in fruit; peduncles densely but shortly hairy; glumes 4–5 mm, several-nerved; bristles 1.5–2 cm. HABITAT Wettest parts of bogs and fens. DIST. Native. Very rare, local, declining. S England, W Wales, W Ireland. (W, central and E Europe.) FLS Jun, fruits Jul–Aug.

Hare's-tail Cottongrass   *Eriophorum vaginatum*

Tussock-forming, rhizomatous perennial to 50 cm. Stems Smooth, bluntly triangular. LEAVES Narrow, bristle-like, 0.4–0.8 mm wide. INFLORESCENCES Solitary, erect spikes; glumes 6–7 mm, 1-nerved; bristles 2–2.5 cm. HABITAT Peaty moorland, peat bogs, wet heaths; to 945 m. DIST. Native. Upland areas of BI; often abundant. (N, NE and central Europe.) FLS Apr–May, fruits May–Jun.

Deergrass   *Trichophorum cespitosum*

Densely tufted perennial to 35 cm. Most British plants belong to ssp. *germanicum*. STEMS Smooth. LEAVES Basal leaves 5–18 mm long; lower stem leaf sheath without leaf blade; upper sheath with short blade to *c*.5 mm, fitting tightly round stem (opening *c*.1 mm) in ssp. *cespitosum*, loosely round stem (opening 2–3 mm) in ssp. *germanicum*. INFLORESCENCES Solitary terminal spikes, 3–8 mm, lowest bract glume-like; glumes 2.5–4 mm, 3-nerved, midrib yellowish brown in ssp. *cespitosum*, green in ssp. *germanicum*; bristles shorter than glumes, brownish. HABITAT Peaty moorland, acid bogs, wet heaths. DIST. Native. Common in upland areas of BI; scarce and local in S. (Most of Europe except S.) FLS May–Jun, fruits Jul–Aug.

Cotton Deergrass   *Trichophorum alpinum*

Slender, loosely tufted, creeping, rhizomatous perennial to 40 cm. STEMS Yellowish green, trigonous, rough. INFLORESCENCES Solitary terminal spikes 5–7 mm; glumes 3.5–4.5 mm; bristles to 2.5 cm, crinkled, in cottongrass-like head. HABITAT/DIST. Native but extinct. Known from a bog in Angus until 1813. (N Europe, mts of S Europe.) FLS Apr–May, fruits Jun.

Sea Club-rush   *Bolboschoenus maritimus*

Tall, robust, rhizomatous perennial to 100 cm. STEMS Triquetrous. LEAVES 5–7 mm wide, keeled, often longer than flowering stems. INFLORESCENCES Dense; lower bracts leaf-like, much longer than inflorescence; spikelets 10–20 mm, dark brown; glumes 3.5–4 mm. HABITAT Margins of brackish dykes, lagoons, borrow pits, tidal rivers, wet pastures; occasionally inland. DIST. Native. Frequent all round coasts of BI. (Most of Europe.) FLS Jul–Aug.

Wood Club-rush   *Scirpus sylvaticus*

Robust, rhizomatous perennial to 120 cm. STEMS Trigonous. LEAVES 5–20 mm wide, flat. INFLORESCENCES Wide-spreading; bracts leaf-like, lowest about as long as inflorescence; spikelets 3–4 mm, greenish brown; glumes 1.5–2.5 mm. HABITAT Forms extensive stands in wet woodlands, margins of rivers, ponds and lakes; to 300 m. DIST. Native. Rather local throughout most of BI; absent from Scotland; rare in Ireland. (Most of Europe except Mediterranean.) FLS Jun–Jul.

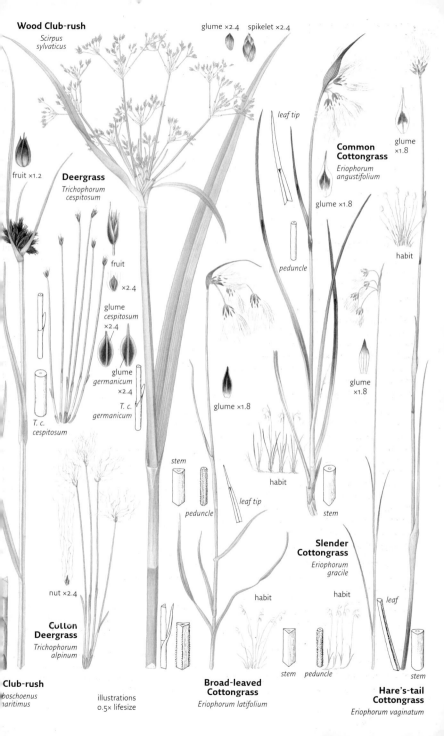

Wood Club-rush
Scirpus sylvaticus

glume ×2.4   spikelet ×2.4

fruit ×1.2

Deergrass
Trichophorum cespitosum

fruit

×2.4

glume
cespitosum
×2.4

glume
germanicum
×2.4

T. c. germanicum

T. c. cespitosum

nut ×2.4

Cotton Deergrass
Trichophorum alpinum

Club-rush
boschoenus maritimus

illustrations
0.5× lifesize

leaf tip

peduncle

glume ×1.8

stem

peduncle

leaf tip

glume ×1.8

habit

Broad-leaved Cottongrass
Eriophorum latifolium

Common Cottongrass
Eriophorum angustifolium

glume
×1.8

habit

glume
×1.8

habit

stem

Slender Cottongrass
Eriophorum gracile

habit

stem   peduncle

leaf

stem

Hare's-tail Cottongrass
Eriophorum vaginatum

Spike-rushes *Eleocharis*
See key to Eleocharis on p.549.

Common Spike-rush
Eleocharis palustris

Rhizomatous perennial to 75 cm. STEMS 1–4 mm diam., pliable; margin of upper stem sheath transverse, straight. INFLORESCENCES Spikelets 5–30 mm, many-flowered; *lowest glume much shorter than spikelet, not more than ⅓ encircling spikelet at base*; 2 stigmas; *4 bristles, base of style broad, obviously constricted at junction with nut.* HABITAT Margins of ponds, lakes, dykes and rivers, wet meadows, marshes, dune slacks; to 550 m. DIST. Native. Frequent throughout BI. (All Europe.) FLS May–Jul.

Northern Spike-rush
Eleocharis austriaca

Rhizomatous perennial to 60 cm. Similar to *E. palustris*, but stems rather brittle; spikelets 8–20 mm; *5 bristles, base of style narrow, not obviously constricted at junction with nut.* HABITAT Sheltered marshy margins of upland rivers and lakes; to 340 m. DIST. Native. Very local. N England, S Scotland. (Scattered throughout much of Europe.) FLS May–Jul.

Slender Spike-rush
Eleocharis uniglumis

Similar to *E. palustris*, but more slender; stems more shiny, to 1.5 mm diam.; spikelets 5–12 mm, often set at angle to stem; *lowest glume ± completely encircling base of spikelet; 2 stigmas.* HABITAT Wet brackish grassland, salt marshes, dune slacks; inland baserich fens, marshes. To 325 m. DIST. Native. Scattered all round coasts of BI; also inland. (Most of Europe, but rare in S.) FLS May–Jul.

Many-stalked Spike-rush
Eleocharis multicaulis

Densely tufted perennial to 30 cm. STEMS Slender, 1–1.5 mm diam., with longitudinal striations; *margin of upper stem sheath oblique, acute.* INFLORESCENCES Spikelets 5–15 mm; lowest glume ± completely encircling base of spikelet; *3 stigmas.* FRUITS 3-angled nut. HABITAT Acid bogs, wet heaths, bog pools; coastal dune slacks. To 610 m. DIST. Native. Widespread in uplands of N and W Britain, W Ireland; local and declining in lowland Britain, rest of Ireland. (W Europe.) FLS Jul–Aug.

Few-flowered Spike-rush
Eleocharis quinqueflora

Tufted, rhizomatous perennial to 30 cm. STEMS *Smooth, not angled*; margin of upper stem sheath oblique, blunt. INFLORESCENCES Spikelets 4–10 mm, 2–7-flowered; lowest glume 2.5–5 mm, >⅓ *as long as spikelet*; 3 stigmas. HABITAT Base-rich marshes, fens, calcareous flushes, coastal dune slacks; to 915 m. DIST. Native. Widespread in N and W Britain, Ireland; scattered and declining in lowlands. (Most of Europe, but rare in S.) FLS Jun–Jul.

Needle Spike-rush
Eleocharis acicularis

Slender, rhizomatous perennial to 10 cm. STEMS <0.5 mm diam., 4-angled; margin of upper stem sheath oblique. INFLORESCENCES Spikelets 2–5 mm, 3–11-flowered; lowest glume 1.5–2.5 mm, c.⅓ as long as spikelet, ± completely encircling its base. HABITAT Margins of lakes, ponds and rivers subject to seasonal flooding, often forming extensive lawns; also grows submerged in non-flowering state, with stems up to 50 cm long. DIST. Native. Scattered throughout BI except N Scotland. (Most of Europe, but rare in S.) FLS Aug–Oct.

Dwarf Spike-rush
Eleocharis parvula *(B, NI)

Small, slender, slightly tufted, rhizomatous perennial to 8 cm. LEAVES *Bristle-like, channelled; upper leaf sheath thin, inconspicuous.* INFLORESCENCES Spikelets 2–3 mm, 3–5-flowered, greenish; glumes 1.8–2 mm, lowest longer than or as long as spikelet, ± completely encircling its base. HABITAT Bare tidal mud of estuarine rivers. DIST. Native. Very rare. In a few scattered localities around coasts of BI. (W, central and E Europe.) FLS Aug–Sep.

Round-headed Club-rush
Scirpoides holoschoenus EN

Tall, densely tufted perennial to 150 cm. STEM Smooth, extended beyond inflorescence by smooth stem-like bract. INFLORESCENCE *Apparently lateral*, umbel-like; 2 bracts, long; *spikes dense globular heads* 5–10 mm diam. HABITAT Damp sandy places, dune slacks, near sea. DIST. Native. Very rare, in only 2 localities on coasts of N Devon, Somerset; rare introduction elsewhere. (All Europe except N.) FLS Aug–Sep.

False Sedge
Kobresia simpliciuscula

Densely tufted perennial to 20 cm. STEMS Erect, bluntly 3-angled. LEAVES Channelled, 0.5–1.5 mm wide. INFLORESCENCES *Terminal cluster of 3–10 spikes, each consisting of 1-flowered spikelets; flowers unisexual*, upper spikelets male and lower female on each spike; glumes 4–5 mm; 3 stamens; 3 stigmas. HABITAT Flushed calcareous hill and mountain grassland, base-rich mires; to 1065 m. DIST. Native. Very local. NW Yorkshire (Teesdale), central Scottish Highlands. (N Europe, mts of S Europe.) FLS Jun–Jul.

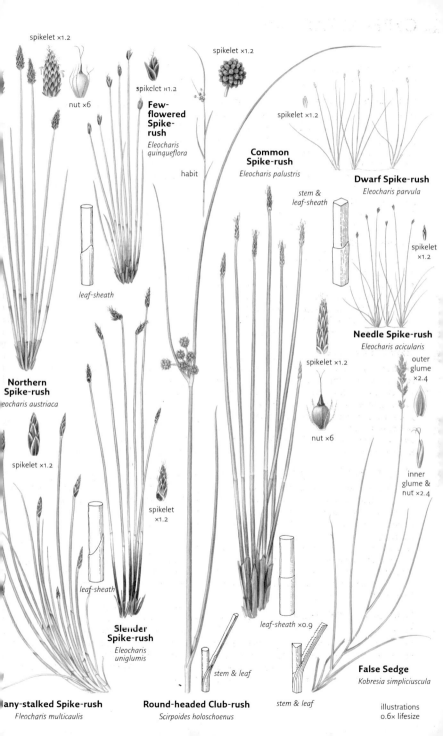

spikelet ×1.2

nut ×6

spikelet ×1.2

Few-flowered Spike-rush
Eleocharis quinqueflora

spikelet ×1.2

habit

spikelet ×1.2

Common Spike-rush
Eleocharis palustris

spikelet ×1.2

Dwarf Spike-rush
Eleocharis parvula

stem &
leaf-sheath

spikelet
×1.2

leaf-sheath

Needle Spike-rush
Eleocharis acicularis

spikelet ×1.2

outer
glume
×2.4

Northern Spike-rush
Eleocharis austriaca

spikelet ×1.2

nut ×6

spikelet
×1.2

inner
glume &
nut ×2.4

leaf-sheath

Slender Spike-rush
Eleocharis uniglumis

leaf-sheath ×0.9

Many-stalked Spike-rush
Eleocharis multicaulis

Round-headed Club-rush
Scirpoides holoschoenus

stem & leaf

stem & leaf

False Sedge
Kobresia simpliciuscula

illustrations
0.6× lifesize

Common Club-rush
Schoenoplectus lacustris

Tall, robust, rhizomatous perennial to 3 m. STEMS Smooth, round in section, up to 1.5 cm diam., green, leafless. INFLORESCENCES With numerous spikelets; lowest bract about as long as inflorescence; *glumes smooth; 3 stigmas.* FRUITS 3-angled nut, 2.5–3 mm. HABITAT Shallow water of slow-moving rivers, dykes, canals, lakes, ponds; lowland to 405 m. DIST. Native. Throughout BI. (All Europe.) FLS Jun–Jul, fruits Aug–Sep.

Grey Club-rush
Schoenoplectus tabernaemontani

Similar to *S. lacustris*, but *stems to* 1.5 m, *glaucous; centre of glumes with numerous reddish papillae (use a lens);* 2 *stigmas*; nut biconvex, 2–2.5 mm. HABITAT Similar to *S. lacustris*, but often in coastal or estuarine brackish waters. DIST. Native. Scattered throughout BI. (All Europe.) FLS Jun–Jul, fruits Aug–Sep.

Triangular Club-rush
Schoenoplectus triqueter CR. *(B, R)

Similar to *S. lacustris*, but *stems to* 1.5 m, *sharply 3-angled throughout length*, bright green; 2 stigmas; nut biconvex. HABITAT Banks of tidal rivers. DIST. Native. Very rare. R. Tamar (S Devon), R. Shannon (Co. Limerick). (W, central and S Europe.) FLS Aug–Sep, fruits Sep–Oct.

Bristle Club-rush
Isolepis setacea

Small, tufted annual or perennial to 15 cm, but usually much less. LEAVES Bristle-like, shorter than stems. INFLORESCENCES *Comprising 1–4 clustered, sessile spikelets; bract longer than inflorescence, ± stem-like.* FRUITS Longitudinally ridged, shiny nut. HABITAT Damp, open acidic habitats subject to seasonal flooding, tracks, sides of lakes, ponds and streams; occasionally on short coastal turf. DIST. Native. Throughout BI but rather local. (Most of Europe except NE.) FLS May–Jul.

Slender Club-rush
Isolepis cernua

Similar to *I. setacea*, but *bract shorter than inflorescence*, glume-like; nut smooth, not shiny. HABITAT Bare, wet, open coastal grassland, freshwater trickles from base of coastal cliffs; occasionally on flushed turf inland. DIST. Native. Coasts of Ireland, S and W Britain (also N Norfolk), Channel Is. (S and W Europe.) FLS Jun–Aug, fruits Jul–Sep.

Floating Club-rush
Eleogiton fluitans

Floating or submerged aquatic perennial. STEMS To 50 cm, light green, much branched, rooting at nodes. LEAVES Linear, to 2 mm wide. INFLORESCENCES *Solitary, terminal, 3–5-flowered; bract glume-like; glumes pale greenish.* SIMILAR SPP. Often confused with aquatic forms of *Juncus bulbosus* (p.542), with which it often grows, but the *Juncus* has untidy bunches of leaves at intervals along the often reddish stems. HABITAT Peaty pools, ditches, sheltered margins of lakes and tarns; lowland to 435 m. DIST. Native. Throughout BI; local and declining except in N and W. (W and W-central Europe.) FLS Jun–Sep.

Flat-sedge
Blysmus compressus VU

Erect, rhizomatous perennial to 45 cm. LEAVES Mostly basal, linear, 1–4 mm wide, *flat, keeled, rough.* INFLORESCENCES *Flattened* terminal spike; *10–25 spikelets on 2 opposite sides of axis*; lowest bract green, leaf-like; glumes yellowish brown; 3–6 perianth bristles, longer than nut. FRUITS Nut, 1.5–2 mm. HABITAT Short turf of damp grassland, marshes, fens, calcareous flushes. DIST. Native. Local and declining. Scattered throughout lowland England, N to Scottish border. (Most of Europe except SW.) FLS Jun–Jul, fruits Aug–Sep.

Saltmarsh Flat-sedge
Blysmus rufus

Similar to *B. compressus*, but *leaves inrolled, rush like*, smooth; *3–8 spikelets*; perianth bristles shorter than nut; nut 3–4 mm. HABITAT Brackish ditches, dune slacks, freshwater seepages on rocky shores, gravelly salt-marsh runnels. DIST. Native. Coasts of NW England, Scotland (especially W), N Ireland. (Coasts of N Europe.) FLS Jun–Jul, fruits Aug–Sep.

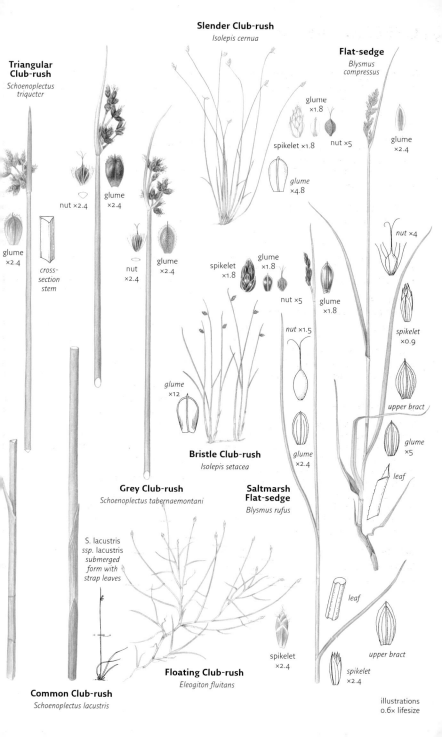

Triangular Club-rush
Schoenoplectus triqueter

nut ×2.4

glume ×2.4

glume ×2.4

cross-section stem

Slender Club-rush
Isolepis cernua

glume ×1.8

spikelet ×1.8   nut ×5

glume ×4.8

nut ×2.4

glume ×2.4

Flat-sedge
Blysmus compressus

glume ×2.4

nut ×4

spikelet ×1.8   glume ×1.8

nut ×5   glume ×1.8

nut ×1.5

spikelet ×0.9

glume ×12

upper bract

glume ×5

leaf

Bristle Club-rush
Isolepis setacea

glume ×2.4

Grey Club-rush
Schoenoplectus tabernaemontani

Saltmarsh Flat-sedge
Blysmus rufus

S. lacustris *ssp.* lacustris submerged form with strap leaves

leaf

spikelet ×2.4

upper bract

Floating Club-rush
Eleogiton fluitans

spikelet ×2.4

Common Club-rush
Schoenoplectus lacustris

illustrations 0.6× lifesize

Galingale
Cyperus longus

Tall, tufted, rhizomatous perennial to 150 cm. STEMS Erect, sharply 3-angled. LEAVES Linear, 3-10 mm wide. INFLORESCENCES *Diffuse compound umbel; 2-6 bracts, leafy, longer than inflorescence*; spikelets brown, numerous, narrow, 5-20 mm long, flattened; glumes 2-2.5 mm; 3 stamens. HABITAT Marshes, wet pastures, near coast; also extensively planted inland by ponds, lakes. DIST. Native. Very local. S England, Wales. (S, W and central Europe.) FLS Aug-Sep.

Brown Galingale
Cyperus fuscus VU. *(B)

Tufted annual to 25 cm. LEAVES Linear, 1.5-4 mm wide, shorter than inflorescence. INFLORESCENCES Compact; 3 bracts, leaf-like, longer than inflorescence; *spikelets purplish brown,* 2-5 mm long; glumes 1-1.5 mm; 2 stamens. HABITAT Damp, open ground of pond and ditch margins subject to seasonal flooding. DIST. Native. Very rare, in scattered localities in S England. (Most of Europe except N.) FLS Jul-Sep.

Yellow Galingale
Cyperus flavescens

Tufted annual to 50 cm. LEAVES 0.5-3 mm wide, shorter or longer than inflorescence. INFLORESCENCES 2-5 bracts, longer than inflorescence; *spikelets* 5-15 mm long, *yellowish*; glumes 1.5-2.2 mm; 2-3 stamens. HABITAT Damp, open habitats. DIST. *Not BI.* (Most of Europe except N.) FLS Jul-Oct.

Pale Galingale
Cyperus eragrostis

Erect, rhizomatous perennial to 60 cm. LEAVES 4-10 mm wide, shorter than or as long as stems. INFLORESCENCES *Comprising dense heads;* 5-11 bracts, longer than inflorescence; *spikelets* 8-13 mm long, flattened, *greenish to yellowish brown;* glumes 2-3 mm; 3 stamens. HABITAT Grown for ornament; casual or naturalised on roadsides, riverbanks, rough ground. DIST. Introduced (native of tropical America). Scattered localities in S Britain, Ireland. (Naturalised in SW Europe.) *Not illustrated.* FLS Aug-Oct.

Black Bog-rush
Schoenus nigricans

Densely tufted, tussock-forming perennial to 80 cm. STEMS Erect, wiry. LEAVES *All basal, at least ½ as long as stems*, linear, wiry, upper surface channelled. INFLORESCENCES *Dense, blackish;* 5-10 spikelets; *lowest bract much longer than inflorescence*; 3-4 perianth bristles. HABITAT Calcareous, base-rich fens, marshes, bogs, dune slacks, usually in areas subject to flushing or moving ground water; to 550 m. DIST. Native. Widespread in W Britain, Ireland; scarce and local elsewhere. (All Europe.) FLS May-Jun.

Brown Bog-rush
Schoenus ferrugineus

Tufted, erect perennial to 40 cm. LEAVES *All basal, up to ⅓ as long as stems*, linear, wiry, pale green. INFLORESCENCES Comprising 1-3 dark brown spikelets; *lowest bract shorter than or as long as inflorescence*; 6 perianth bristles. HABITAT Base-rich flushes in calcareous grassland. DIST. Native. Very rare. Perthshire (central Scotland). (Most of Europe except S and SW.) FLS Jun-Jul.

White Beak-sedge
Rhynchospora alba

Erect, tufted, rhizomatous perennial to 40 cm. STEMS Leafy. LEAVES Channelled, linear, pale yellowish green. INFLORESCENCES Terminal; *lowest bract not longer than inflorescence; spikelets* 4-5 mm, 2-flowered, *white* turning pale brown; 9-13 perianth bristles. HABITAT Open ground in acid bogs, wet heaths, with *Sphagnum* or on bare, wet peat. DIST. Native. Widespread in W Britain, Ireland; also local in S England. (Most of Europe except Mediterranean and SE.) FLS Jul-Aug.

Brown Beak-sedge
Rhynchospora fusca

Similar to *R. alba*, but leaves pale greyish green *bracts 2-4× as long as inflorescence*, spikelets dark reddish brown, 5-6 perianth bristles. HABITAT Similar to *R. alba*: bare peat, wet heaths, acid bogs. DIST. Native. Very local. S England, W Wales, W Scotland Ireland. (N, W and central Europe.) FLS May-Jun.

Great Fen-sedge, Sedge
Cladium mariscus

Tall, robust, tufted, rhizomatous perennial. STEMS Leafy, to 2 m. LEAVES To 2 m, channelled, *with vicious serrated, saw-like margins and keel.* INFLORESCENCES Much branched, with many compact heads; spikelets 1-3-flowered; inflorescence branches with long, leaflike bracts. HABITAT Tall-herb fens, fen carr, swampy margins of lakes, ponds and streams on calcareous (East Anglia) or acid (W Scotland, Ireland) peat. DIST. Native. Scattered throughout BI, but widespread in W Ireland. (Most of Europe except extreme N.) FLS Jul-Aug.

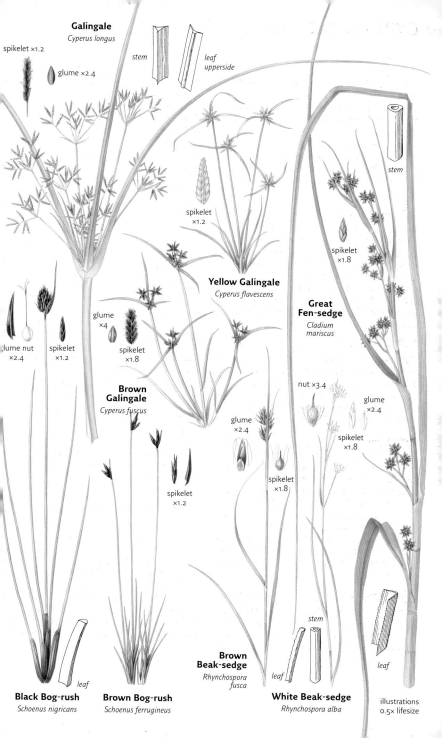

Galingale
Cyperus longus

spikelet ×1.2

glume ×2.4

stem

leaf upperside

spikelet ×1.2

Yellow Galingale
Cyperus flavescens

glume ×4

spikelet ×1.8

glume nut ×2.4

spikelet ×1.2

Brown Galingale
Cyperus fuscus

stem

spikelet ×1.8

Great Fen-sedge
Cladium mariscus

nut ×3.4

glume ×2.4

spikelet ×1.8

glume ×2.4

spikelet ×1.8

spikelet ×1.2

Brown Beak-sedge
Rhynchospora fusca

stem

leaf

leaf

leaf

Black Bog-rush
Schoenus nigricans

Brown Bog-rush
Schoenus ferrugineus

White Beak-sedge
Rhynchospora alba

illustrations
0.5× lifesize

The sedges are tufted or rhizomatous, often grass-like perennials, with solid, 3-angled, leafy stems. Leaves are linear, keeled, channelled or inrolled, usually with sheathing bases that have a *ligule* at the junction of the sheath and blade, which lies attached to the inner surface of the blade. Flowers are unisexual and arranged in spikes, each enclosed by a glume. Spikes may consist of a mixture of both male and female flowers, or may be entirely male or female, with the male spikes arranged above the female in a branched inflorescence. Alternatively, flowers may be arranged in a single unbranched spike. Flowers lack a perianth; male flowers have 2–3 stamens; female flowers entirely enclosed within an extra flask-shaped bract, the '*utricle*', the tip of which may or may not be narrowed into a '*beak*' and through which the stigmas protrude; ovary is either 3-angled with 3 stigmas, or biconvex with 2 stigmas. In the species descriptions, the utricle plus the ovary is referred to as the '*fruit*'.

Details of the ripe fruits and glumes are essential for accurate identification and are illustrated separately with each species. When not in flower, sedges can be distinguished from grasses by the solid (not hollow) 3-angled stem, with leaves in 3 ranks (rather than 2), and the attached (not free) ligule.

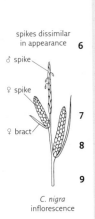

stigma
style
beak
♀ glume
utricle
ovary
female flower

spikes dissimilar in appearance
♂ spike
♀ spike
♀ bract

C. nigra inflorescence

if		then
1. Sedges with spikes dissimilar in appearance; male spikes at top, female spikes below		
1	▷ Fruits hairy or papillose	Go to ▷ **2**
	▷ Fruits glabrous	Go to ▷ **7**
2	▷ Flowering stems from lateral shoots, leafless	*C. digitata* (p.578), *C. ornithopoda* (p.580)
	▷ Flowering stems from centre of rosette, leafy	Go to ▷ **3**
3	▷ Plant short, tufted to 5 cm; leaves longer than stems; inflorescence ± hidden among leaves and bracts (chalk grassland)	*C. humilis* (p.580)
	▷ Plant not like this	Go to ▷ **4**
4	▷ Sheaths distinctly pubescent	*C. hirta* (p.572)
	▷ Sheaths glabrous	Go to ▷ **5**
5	▷ Leaves distinctly glaucous beneath; fruits papillose	*C. flacca* (p.576)
	▷ Leaves not or scarcely glaucous; fruits distinctly hairy	Go to ▷ **6**
6	▷ Plant to 50 cm; leaves ≥1.5 mm, ± flat; female spikes ovoid, usually ± contiguous	Go to ▷ **A**
	▷ Plant tall, to 120 cm; leaves very narrow, ≤1.5 mm wide, inrolled; female spikes cylindrical (swamps)	*C. lasiocarpa* (p.572)
7	▷ 2 stigmas	Go to ▷ **8**
	▷ 3 stigmas	Go to ▷ **9**
8	▷ Fruits flattened (bi-convex), green	Go to ▷ **B**
	▷ Fruits ± inflated, dark purple-green	*C. saxatilis* (p.574)
9	▷ Female spikes ± sessile and most clustered around base of male spike	Go to ▷ **10**
	▷ Female spikes mostly distant from each other, or if clustered, then nodding with long, slender stalks	Go to ▷ **12**

	if	**then**
10	▷ Leaf sheaths pubescent; base of lowest bract crinkled	*C. pallescens* (p.578)
	▷ Leaf sheaths glabrous	Go to ▷ **11**
11	▷ Leaves inrolled; stems bluntly angled (salt marshes)	*C. extensa* (p.578)
	▷ Leaves flat; stems sharply angled	Go to ▷ **C**
12	▷ Female spikes long, cylindrical, 7–16 cm × 5–7 mm, becoming pendulous; stalks enclosed in leaf sheath	*C. pendula* (p.574)
	▷ Female spikes shorter or narrower; if pendulous, stalks exserted (not wholly enclosed within leaf sheath)	Go to ▷ **13**
13	▷ Male spikes surrounded by or overtopped by female spikes; most or all female spikes at ± same level, ± nodding	Go to ▷ **14**
	▷ Female spikes distant, scarcely reaching beyond base of male spike	Go to ▷ **17**
14	▷ Female spikes ovoid; glumes blackish	*C. atrofusca* (p.580)
	▷ Female spikes cylindrical; glumes not blackish	Go to ▷ **15**
15	▷ Female spikes ≥5 mm across, not overtopping male spike	Go to ▷ **16**
	▷ Female spikes ≤ 3 mm across, overtopping male spike	*C. capillaris* (p.574)
16	▷ Lower sheaths pubescent; base of lowest bract crinkled; female spikes ovoid	*C. pallescens* (p.578)
	▷ Lower sheaths not pubescent; female spikes cylindrical	*C. pseudocyperus* (p.572)
17	▷ Lowest bract not sheathing	Go to ▷ **18**
	▷ At least lowest bract with entire cylindrical sheath	Go to ▷ **22**
18	▷ Female spikes nodding; peduncles slender, lowest as long as spike	Go to ▷ **19**
	▷ Female spikes ± erect; peduncles short or absent	Go to ▷ **21**
19	▷ Female spikes with 5–8 flowers	*C. rariflora* (p.582)
	▷ Female spikes with 7–20 flowers	Go to ▷ **20**
20	▷ Leaves 1–2 mm wide; female glumes slightly wider than fruits	*C. limosa* (p.582)
	▷ Leaves 2–4 mm wide; female glumes narrower than fruits	*C. magellanica* (p.582)
21	▷ Female spikes ovoid; glumes purple to dark red-brown; fruits dark purple-green	*C. saxatilis* (p.574)
	▷ Female spikes cylindrical; fruits not dark purple-green	Go to ▷ **D**

CONTINUED OVERLEAF

	if	**then**
22	▷ Female spikes with ≤6 flowers; fruit 8 mm (very rare)	*C. depauperata* (p.576)
	▷ Female spikes usually with >6 flowers; fruits smaller	Go to ▷ **23**
23	▷ Lower bracts with tight-fitting cylindrical sheaths, or if loose, plant glaucous	Go to ▷ **24**
	▷ Lower bracts with loose, narrowly funnel-shaped sheaths; plant green or yellowish green	*C. vaginata* (p.576)
24	▷ Beak ≤0.5 mm, not or hardly notched	Go to ▷ **25**
	▷ Beak >0.5 mm, distinctly notched	Go to ▷ **27**
25	▷ Leaves glaucous; female spikes 4–6 mm wide	Go to ▷ **26**
	▷ Leaves green; female spikes 2–3 mm wide	*C. strigosa* (p.574)
26	▷ 1 male spike; female spikes sparsely flowered; fruits 3.5–4 mm, smooth	*C. panicea* (p.576)
	▷ ≥2 male spikes; female spikes dense-flowered; fruits 2–2.5 mm, papillose	*C. flacca* (p.576)
27	▷ ≥2 male spikes, one of the lateral at least ½ length of terminal	Go to ▷ **D**
	▷ 1 male spikes or, if 2, lateral much smaller than terminal	Go to ▷ **28**
28	▷ Female spikes 3–5 mm wide, overlapping	*C. sylvatica* (p.574)
	▷ Female spikes 5–8 mm wide	Go to ▷ **E**

A

	if	**then**
1	▷ Stems tufted	Go to ▷ **2**
	▷ Stems not or scarcely tufted, often arising singly from long rhizome	Go to ▷ **5**
2	▷ Lowest bract green, leaf-like	Go to ▷ **3**
	▷ Lowest bract brown, glume- or bristle-like	Go to ▷ **4**
3	▷ Lowest bract with sheath; stems erect	*C. caryophyllea* (p.580)
	▷ Lowest bract without sheath; stems long, wiry, arching	*C. pilulifera* (p.580)
4	▷ Leaves mostly >2 mm wide, recurved; female glumes obtuse, margin pubescent	*C. ericetorum* (p.580)
	▷ Leaves mostly <2 mm wide, soft, erect; female glumes mucronate, margin glabrous	*C. montana* (p.580)
5	▷ Stems usually >20 cm; leaves somewhat glaucous, basal sheaths red-brown	*C. filiformis* (p.580)
	▷ Stems usually <20 cm; leaves not glaucous, basal sheaths brown	Go to ▷ **6**

if	then

6 ▷ Lowest bract green, leaf-like — ***C. caryophyllea*** (p.580)
   ▷ Lowest bract brown, glume-like — ***C. ericetorum*** (p.580)

B

1 ▷ Plant forming tussocks; lowest bract shorter
     than inflorescence — ***C. elata*** (p.584)
   ▷ Plant not forming tussocks — Go to ▷ **2**

2 ▷ Female glumes without awns — Go to ▷ **3**
   ▷ Female glumes of lower spikelets awned or
     aristate (coastal habitats) — Go to ▷ **7**

3 ▷ Utricles with 3 or more distinct nerves — ***C. trinervis*** • (p.584)
   ▷ Utricles without nerves or obscurely nerved — Go to ▷ **4**

4 ▷ Lowest bract much longer than
     inflorescence — Go to ▷ **5**
   ▷ Lowest bract as long as or shorter than
     inflorescence — Go to ▷ **6**

5 ▷ Leaves bright, shiny green beneath; stems
     brittle; 3–4 male spikes — ***C. aquatilis*** (p.582)
   ▷ Leaves dull green beneath; stems tough;
     2 male spikes — ***C. acuta*** (p.584)

6 ▷ Stems bluntly angled, usually >20 cm;
     lowest bract as long as inflorescence; basal
     sheaths brown or black — ***C. nigra*** (p.584)
   ▷ Stems sharply 3-angled, usually *c.*10 cm;
     lowest bract shorter than inflorescence;
     basal sheath reddish brown (mountains) — ***C. bigelowii*** (p.584)

7 ▷ Awns of lower female glumes of lower
     spikes up to 5 mm; leaves ± flat — ***C. recta*** (p.582)
   ▷ Awns of lower female glumes of lower
     spikes up to 1 mm; leaves inrolled or keeled — ***C. salina*** (p.582)

C Yellow sedges

1 ▷ Utricles 4.5–6.5 mm, beak curved, ≥2 mm
     long; leaves about as long as stems, ≤7 mm
     wide (very rare) — ***C. flava*** (p.578)
   ▷ Utricles 1.5–5.5 mm, <2 mm long; leaves
     shorter than stems, ≤5.5 mm wide — Go to ▷ **2**

CONTINUED OVERLEAF

	if	**then**
2	▷ Leaves ≤⅓ as long as stems; utricles curved, those in lower part of spike deflexed; male spike distinctly stalked (strongly calcicole)	***C. viridula* ssp. *brachyrrhyncha*** (p.578)
	▷ At least some leaves >⅓ as long as stems; utricles straight (some often deflexed)	Go to ▷ **3**
3	▷ Stems often curved; leaves ± flat, keeled; male spike stalked; lowest female spike usually distant from rest; beak usually ≥1 mm (usually calcifuge)	***C. viridula* ssp. *oedocarpa*** (p.578)
	▷ Stems straight; leaves usually channelled; male spike sessile; female spikes clustered at stem apex; beak usually <1 mm	***C. viridula* ssp. *viridula*** (p.578)

D

1	▷ Fruit longer than glume	Go to ▷ **2**
	▷ Fruit shorter than glume	Go to ▷ **3**
2	▷ Stem bluntly angled; leaves glaucous; fruit abruptly narrowed into beak	***C. rostrata*** (p.574)
	▷ Stem sharply angled; leaves yellowish green; fruit gradually narrowed into beak	***C. vesicaria*** (p.574)
3	▷ Male glumes blunt; fruit 3.5–5 mm, greyish green	***C. acutiformis*** (p.572)
	▷ Males glumes acute; fruit 5–8 mm, yellowish brown	***C. riparia*** (p.572)

E

1	▷ Leaves 5–12 mm wide; female spikes mostly ≥3 cm long	***C. laevigata*** (p.576)
	▷ Leaves 2–5 mm wide; female spikes usually <3 cm long	Go to ▷ **2**
2	▷ Leaves abruptly contracted below narrow linear tip; female glumes with broad silvery margins	***C. hostiana*** (p.578)
	▷ Leaf blade gradually narrowed to veined tip; female glumes without broad silvery margins	Go to ▷ **3**
3	▷ Female glumes dark reddish brown; utricles purple-brown with 2 prominent nerves	***C. binervis*** (p.576)
	▷ Female glumes pale brown; utricles usually green	Go to ▷ **4**

		if	then

| **4** | ▷ | Longest bract not longer than inflorescence; male glumes purple brown; utricles ± erect, without dark dots; beak rough | ***C. distans*** (p.576) |
| | ▷ | At least one bract longer than inflorescence; male glumes orange-brown; utricles spreading, shiny, with minute dark dots; beak smooth | ***C. punctata*** (p.576) |

2. Sedges with all spikes similar in appearance

all spikes similar in appearance

C. otrubae inflorescence

1	▷	Spikelets few, 3–5; glumes dark purple to black; 3 stigmas (rare Scottish alpines, mires)	Go to ▷ **18**
	▷	5–30 spikelets; glumes not dark purple or black; 2 stigmas	Go to ▷ **2**
2	▷	Plants tufted or forming dense tussocks; rhizomes short or absent	Go to ▷ **3**
	▷	Shoots appearing singly at intervals from long rhizomes; not tufted or tussock-forming	Go to ▷ **13**
3	▷	All spikes with female flowers at top	Go to ▷ **4**
	▷	At least one spike with male flowers at top	Go to ▷ **9**
4	▷	Lowest bract leaf-like, much longer than inflorescence; lower spikes widely separated	***C. remota*** (p.570)
	▷	Lowest bract not longer than inflorescence	Go to ▷ **5**
5	▷	Inflorescence ± spherical; fruits few, spreading, giving spikelets star-like appearance	***C. echinata*** (p.570)
	▷	Inflorescence oval to oblong	Go to ▷ **6**
6	▷	Inflorescence whitish or greenish, becoming brownish	***C. canescens*** (p.572)
	▷	Inflorescence pale to dark brown	Go to ▷ **7**
7	▷	Inflorescence a compact oval head; spikes overlapping	***C. leporina*** (p.570)
	▷	Spikes not overlapping to form a compact head	Go to ▷ **8**
8	▷	Stems >30 cm; 5–18 spikes, spreading, ± cylindrical (lowland, scattered)	***C. elongata*** (p.570)
	▷	Stems ≤20 cm; 2–5 spikes, forming a triangular group (wet alpine rock ledges, Scotland)	***C. lachenalii*** (p.570)
9	▷	Fruits weakly or strongly convex on inner face, strongly convex on outer face	Go to ▷ **10**
	▷	Fruits flat on inner face, convex on outer face	Go to ▷ **12**
10	▷	Upper half of fruits conspicuously winged, plant forming large tussocks	***C. paniculata*** (p.566)
	▷	Fruits not or scarcely winged; tussock-forming or not	Go to ▷ **11**

CONTINUED OVERLEAF

	if	then
11	▷ Tussock-forming; basal sheaths blackish, becoming fibrous when decaying (basal sheaths will break apart and become fibrous if rubbed between fingers, which can be done without uprooting or damaging the plant); inflorescence 4–8 cm (rare, fens)	**C. appropinquata** (p.566)
	▷ Not forming tussocks; basal sheaths pale brownish, not becoming fibrous; inflorescence 1–5 cm	**C. diandra** (p.566)
12	▷ Stems >2 mm wide; leaves mostly ≥4 mm wide; utricles with distinct veins	**C. otrubae, C. vulpina** (p.566)
	▷ Stems <2 mm wide; leaves mostly ≤4 mm wide; utricles obscurely veined	**C. muricata group** (*see* below)
13	▷ Terminal spike all male; rhizomes long (sandy places by sea, rarely inland)	**C. arenaria** (p.568)
	▷ Some flowers on terminal spike female	Go to ▷ **14**
14	▷ Inflorescence a small, 1–2 cm-long, ± globular head; bracts glume-like	Go to ▷ **15**
	▷ Inflorescence oval-oblong, 2–8 cm long, lobed; bracts leaf-like	Go to ▷ **16**
15	▷ Stems to 20 cm; leaves curved, as long as or almost as long as inflorescence; inflorescence ± globular (looks like rabbit droppings) (coastal, N Scotland)	**C. maritima** (p.568)
	▷ Stems to 40 cm; leaves straight, shorter than inflorescence; inflorescence ovoid (very rare, Scottish mires)	**C. chordorrhiza** (p.568)
16	▷ Fruit distinctly winged for part of its length; inflorescence 2–7 cm, brown	**C. disticha** (p.568)
	▷ Fruit unwinged	Go to ▷ **17**
17	▷ Lowest bract glume-like, shorter than inflorescence	**C. diandra** (p.566)
	▷ Lowest bract leaf-like, longer than inflorescence	**C. divisa** (p.568)
18	▷ Lowest spike erect, stalk short	Go to ▷ **19**
	▷ Lowest spike nodding, stalk pendulous	Go to ▷ **20**
19	▷ All spikes erect, clustered and overlapping; lowest bract longer than inflorescence	**C. norvegica** (p.582)
	▷ All spikes not clustered and overlapping, lowest distant from the one above	**C. buxbaumii** (p.582)
20	▷ Lowest bract shorter than its spike	**C. atrofusca** (p.580)
	▷ Lowest bract leaf-like, longer than inflorescence	**C. atrata** (p.582)

	if	then

3. Sedges with inflorescence consisting of single terminal spike

	if	then
1	▷ Spikes with male flowers at top, female flowers below	Go to ▷ **2**
	▷ Spikes either all male or all female, dioecious with separate male and female plants	Go to ▷ **5**
2	▷ Fruits deflexed when ripe; leaves *c.*1 mm wide	Go to ▷ **3**
	▷ Fruits not deflexed when ripe; leaves *c.*2 mm wide, usually much curled	*C. rupestris* (p.584)
3	▷ 2 stigmas; fruits dark brown	*C. pulicaris* (p.584)
	▷ 3 stigmas; fruits yellowish	Go to ▷ **4**
4	▷ Fruits 3.5–4.5 mm, with bristle arising from base of nut and protruding through beak of utricle together with stigmas	*C. microglochin* (p.584)
	▷ Fruits 5–7 mm, without a bristle	*C. pauciflora* (p.584)
5	▷ Plant rhizomatous, not densely tufted; stems smooth	*C. dioica* (p.570)
	▷ Plant densely tufted; stems rough	*C. davalliana* • (p.570)

inflorescence consisting of single spike

C. pulicaris inflorescence

Key to *Carex muricata* group

	if	then
1	▷ Ligule longer than wide; roots, base of stem and basal sheaths usually tinged purplish; utricles >4.5 mm	*C. spicata* (p.566)
	▷ Ligule not or only slightly longer than wide; base of plant without purplish tinge; utricles ≤4.5 mm	Go to ▷ **2**
2	▷ Inflorescences >4.5 cm long, interrupted; lowest 2 spikes 1–3 cm apart	Go to ▷ **3**
	▷ Inflorescences ≤4.5 cm long, spikes ± contiguous	Go to ▷ **4**
3	▷ Stems drooping; leaves as long as flowering stems; inflorescences to 10 cm, very interrupted; utricles 3.5–4 mm, not spreading	*C. divulsa* ssp. *divulsa* (p.566)
	▷ Stems erect; leaves shorter than flowering stems; inflorescences to 6 cm; utricles 4.0–4.5 mm, spreading	*C. divulsa* ssp. *leersii* (p.566)
4	▷ Flowering stems erect, rigid; glumes shorter than utricles, darker than unripe utricles	*C. muricata* ssp. *muricata* (p.566)
	▷ Flowering stems flexuous; glumes ± as long as utricles, yellowish brown, same colour as unripe utricles	*C. muricata* ssp. *pairae* (p.566)

Sedges *Carex*
See key to *Carex* on p.558.

Greater Tussock-sedge   *Carex paniculata*

Robust, densely tufted perennial, *forming large tussocks* up to 1 m across and 1.5 m tall. Leaves *4-7 mm wide*, with sharply toothed margins. Inflorescences Branched, 5-15 cm; spikelets 5-8 mm, male above, female below. Fruits 3-4 mm, not distinctly nerved, green to dark brown, beak winged. Habitat Fens, fen carr, swampy woodlands, margins of lakes, ponds and ditches, usually on base-rich soil. Dist. Native. Throughout BI. (All Europe except extreme N and S.) Fls May-Jun, fruits Jul.

Fibrous Tussock-sedge   *Carex appropinquata*

Similar to *C. paniculata*, but tussocks to 1 m tall; *leaves 1-3 mm wide, lower sheaths becoming fibrous with age, blackish brown*; inflorescences 4-8 cm, branched; 4-6 spikes; bracts bristle-like, shorter than spikes; *fruits 2.7-4 mm, distinctly 3-7-nerved*, beak not winged. Habitat Open calcareous fen; to 380 m. Dist. Native. Very local. East Anglia, central Ireland; rare elsewhere. (All Europe except S.) Fls May-Jun, fruits Jun-Jul.

Lesser Tussock-sedge   *Carex diandra*

Erect, rhizomatous perennial, sometimes forming loose tussocks. Stems Slender, to 60 cm. Leaves 1-2 mm wide, lower sheaths not becoming fibrous. Inflorescences 1-5 cm, similar in appearance to *C. appropinquata, but spikes all sessile in a compact cylindrical head.* Fruits 2.7-4 mm, *distinctly 2-5-nerved.* Habitat Swamps, fens, wet meadows, carr, on calcareous or acid peat; to 370 m. Dist. Native. Widely distributed in Scotland, Ireland; scarce and declining elsewhere. (Scattered throughout Europe except S.) Fls May-Jun, fruits Jun-Jul.

False Fox Sedge   *Carex otrubae*

Robust, tufted perennial to 100 cm. Stems Sharply 3-angled but not winged. Leaves 4-10 mm wide, bright green; *ligule 10-15 mm, longer than broad, acute, not overlapping leaf margin; face of leaf sheath opposite blade not wrinkled.* Inflorescences Dense spike, 8-14 mm. Fruits Shiny utricles, 5-6 mm, green turning brown. Habitat Sides of streams, ditches and ponds, wet meadows, pastures on heavy soils, upper end of salt marshes. Dist. Native. Throughout BI, but mostly coastal in N England, Scotland. (Most of Europe except extreme N.) Fls Jun-Jul, fruits Jul-Sep.

True Fox Sedge   *Carex vulpina* VU.

Very similar to *C. otrubae*, but very rare; *ligule 2-6 mm,*
broader than long, truncate, overlapping edges of leaf margin; face of leaf sheath opposite blade transversely wrinkled and glandular; bracts short, the auricles often with dark mark*; utricles 4-5 mm, not shiny. Habitat Drainage dykes, wet meadows, pastures, on heavy soils. Dist. Native. Very rare. Lowland England. (Much of Europe except W, S and extreme N.) Fls May-Jun, fruits Jun-Jul.

Carex muricata group
The next five sedges comprise a group of closely related species that are the most difficult to identify in the genus, so it will not always be easy to name every specimen with confidence (*see* key on p.565).

Spiked Sedge   *Carex spicata*

Densely tufted, rhizomatous perennial to 85 cm. Leaves 2-4 mm wide; *ligules 4-8 mm, acute.* Fruits *Base of utricles spongy*, thickened. Habitat Rough grassland, roadsides, hedge banks, woodland rides, on damp, heavy, base-rich soils. Dist. Native. Widely distributed throughout lowland England, Wales; scattered in Scotland, Ireland. (All Europe except extreme N and S.) Fls Jun-Jul, fruits Jul-Aug.

Grey Sedge   *Carex divulsa* ssp. *divulsa*

Densely tufted, rhizomatous perennial to 90 cm. Leaves 2-3 mm wide; ligules about as wide as long. Inflorescences *Lowest spikes ≥2 cm apart.* Fruits *Yellowish-brown utricles, ± erect.* Habitat Hedge banks, roadsides, rough grassland, woodland rides. Dist. Native. S England N to the Wash, SE Ireland; scattered elsewhere. (Most of Europe except extreme N.) Fls Jun-Oct, fruits Jul-Nov.

Leers' Sedge   *Carex divulsa* ssp. *leersii*

Similar to ssp. *divulsa*, but differs as in key; *lowest spikes <2 cm apart; utricles dark brown, spreading.* Habitat Hedge banks, roadsides, rough grassland, woodland rides, on dry calcareous soils. Dist. Native. Scattered throughout England, Wales; rare in Scotland; absent from Ireland. (Most of Europe except extreme N and SW.) Fls May-Jul, fruits Jul-Aug.

Prickly Sedge   *Carex muricata* ssp. *muricata*

Densely tufted, rhizomatous perennial to 85 cm. Leaves 2-4 mm wide; ligules 2-3.5 mm, rounded. Inflorescences 1-4 cm; spikes ± spherical; *female glumes 2.5-3.5 mm, dark reddish brown.* Fruits *Utricles, 4-4.5 mm.* Habitat Limestone grassland, pavement and scree; to 340 m. Dist. Native. Very rare, in a few scattered sites in England. (N and C Europe.) Fls May-Jun.

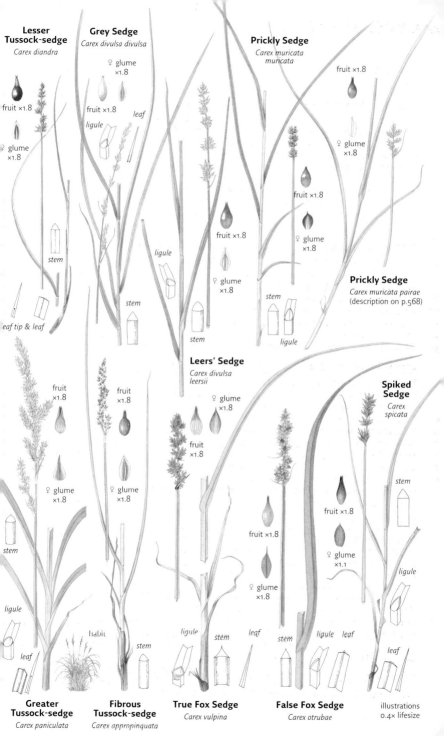

Lesser Tussock-sedge
Carex diandra

fruit ×1.8

♀ glume ×1.8

stem

leaf tip & leaf

Grey Sedge
Carex divulsa divulsa

♀ glume ×1.8

fruit ×1.8

ligule

leaf

stem

Prickly Sedge
Carex muricata muricata

fruit ×1.8

♀ glume ×1.8

fruit ×1.8

♀ glume ×1.8

stem

Prickly Sedge
Carex muricata pairae
(description on p.568)

ligule

stem

ligule

stem

Leers' Sedge
Carex divulsa leersii

♀ glume ×1.8

fruit ×1.8

fruit ×1.8

♀ glume ×1.8

Spiked Sedge
Carex spicata

fruit ×1.8

♀ glume ×1.8

stem

Greater Tussock-sedge
Carex paniculata

fruit ×1.8

♀ glume ×1.8

stem

ligule

leaf

habit

Fibrous Tussock-sedge
Carex appropinquata

fruit ×1.8

♀ glume ×1.8

stem

True Fox Sedge
Carex vulpina

ligule

stem

leaf

False Fox Sedge
Carex otrubae

fruit ×1.8

♀ glume ×1.1

stem

ligule

leaf

ligule

leaf

illustrations
0.4× lifesize

Prickly Sedge
Carex muricata ssp. pairae

[*See* illustration previous page.] Similar to ssp. *muricata*, but differs as in key; spikes ovoid; *female glumes 3–4.5 mm, pale brown; utricles 2.5–3.5 mm.* HABITAT Hedge banks, walls, roadsides, rough grassland, heathland, on light sandy soils. DIST. Native. Widely distributed throughout Britain N to central Scotland, S Ireland. (S and W Europe.) FLS Jun–Jul.

Sand Sedge
Carex arenaria

Perennial with *long, creeping rhizomes that produce shoots at regular intervals.* STEMS To 40 cm, sharply 3-angled. LEAVES 1.5–3.5 mm wide, flat, as long as stems. INFLORESCENCES Dense, to 8 cm, spikes contiguous; *terminal spikes male,* middle male at level of top female below, lower spikes all female; female glumes pale red-brown. FRUITS 4–5.5 mm, with many ribs, broadly winged, green-brown. HABITAT Sand-dunes, dune slacks, sandy tracks; also inland dunes, sands in East Anglia. DIST. Native. Common all round coasts of BI. (N, N-central and W Europe.) FLS Jun–Jul, fruits Jul–Aug.

Loire Sedge
Carex ligerica

Similar to *C. arenaria*, but smaller and more slender, to 30 cm; leaves 1–2 mm wide; inflorescences more compact, 2–3 cm; all spikes female above, male below; female glumes dark brown; fruit 3.5–5 mm. HABITAT Dunes, dry sandy grasslands. DIST. *Not BI.* (NW Europe, east to Poland.) FLS Apr–May.

Reichenbach's Sedge
Carex reichenbachii

Similar to *C. arenaria*, but leaves 2–3 mm wide, longer than stems; inflorescences 3–5 cm, lower spikes somewhat distant from rest, all with female flowers above and male below, or upper entirely male; female glumes pale yellowish brown; fruits 5 mm, conspicuously ribbed, pale greenish. HABITAT Dunes, dry sandy grassland, wood margins, roadsides. DIST. *Not BI.* (NW Europe, east to Poland.) FLS Apr–May.

Brown Sedge
Carex disticha

Perennial with *long, creeping rhizomes that produce erect shoots singly or in pairs.* STEMS To 100 cm, sharply 3-angled. LEAVES 2–4 mm wide. INFLORESCENCES Dense, rather untidy, 2–7 cm, spikes contiguous; *terminal spikes female,* intermediate male, lower female; female glumes 3.5–4.5 mm, red-brown. FRUITS 4–5 mm, red-brown, narrowly winged. HABITAT Wet meadows, marshes, fens, sides of lakes, dykes and streams, on base-rich, fertile soils. DIST. Native. Throughout most of BI, but rare in N Scotland, SW England. (Most of Europe except extreme N and Mediterranean.) FLS Jun–Jul, fruits Jul–Aug.

String Sedge
Carex chordorrhiza

Rhizomatous perennial, with *long runners that give off sterile lateral shoots.* STEMS *Solitary terminal flowering stem* to 40 cm. LEAVES 1–2 mm wide, stiff, erect, those on flowering shoots few and much shorter than stems. INFLORESCENCES *Small, compact, ovoid head, 7–15 mm;* 2–4 spikes, contiguous. FRUITS 3.5–4.5 mm, pale to dark brown. HABITAT Wet *Sphagnum* bogs. DIST. Native. Very rare. Sutherland, Easterness (Scotland). (N and central Europe.) FLS Jun–Jul, fruits Jul–Aug.

Divided Sedge
Carex divisa VU

Creeping, rhizomatous perennial. STEMS Slender, sharply 3-angled, to 80 cm. LEAVES *1.5–3 mm wide, stiff, channelled or inrolled.* INFLORESCENCES *1–3 cm,* lower bract shorter than or longer than inflorescence, 3–7 *spikes, contiguous or lower 2 slightly separate;* female glumes 3–4 mm, purplish brown. FRUITS 3.5–4 mm, unwinged, *pale brown.* HABITAT Brackish marshes, dune slacks, wet grassland, near sea. DIST. Native. E and S coasts of England; rare elsewhere. (S, S-central and W Europe.) FLS May–Jun, fruits Jul–Aug.

Early Sedge
Carex praecox

Similar to *C. divisa*, but stems more slender, to 30 cm; leaves 1–2 mm wide, much shorter than stems; inflorescence 1.5–2.5 cm; fruits 2–4 mm, reddish brown, obscurely veined. HABITAT Dry sandy grasslands, roadsides. DIST. *Not BI.* (Most of Europe except N.) FLS Apr–May.

Curved Sedge
Carex maritima EN

Extensively creeping, rhizomatous perennial. STEMS *Short, to 18 cm, strongly curved.* LEAVES 0.5–2 mm wide, stiff, curved, channelled or inrolled. INFLORESCENCES *Compact, ± spherical head, 0.5–1.5 cm,* comprising 4–8 spikes; bracts absent; female glumes 3–4 mm, red-brown. FRUITS 4–4.5 mm, brown turning black. HABITAT Wet sand by sea, dune slacks, freshwater seepages. DIST. Native. Rare. N and NE coasts of Scotland. (Coasts of Arctic and NW Europe, mts of Norway.) FLS Jun, fruits Jul.

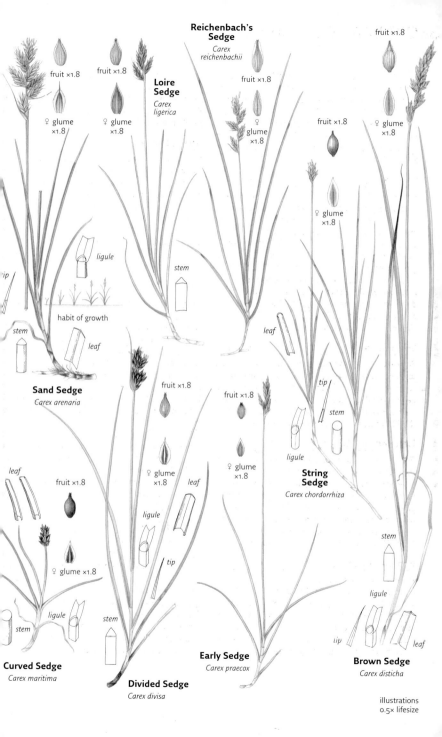

Reichenbach's Sedge
Carex reichenbachii

fruit ×1.8

♀ glume ×1.8

fruit ×1.8

Loire Sedge
Carex ligerica

fruit ×1.8

♀ glume ×1.8

fruit ×1.8

♀ glume ×1.8

fruit ×1.8

♀ glume ×1.8

fruit ×1.8

♀ glume ×1.8

ligule

stem

tip

habit of growth

stem

leaf

leaf

Sand Sedge
Carex arenaria

fruit ×1.8

♀ glume ×1.8

leaf

ligule

tip

stem

leaf

tip

stem

ligule

String Sedge
Carex chordorrhiza

leaf

fruit ×1.8

fruit ×1.8

♀ glume ×1.8

♀ glume ×1.8

ligule

tip

fruit ×1.8

Early Sedge
Carex praecox

stem

ligule

tip

leaf

Curved Sedge
Carex maritima

ligule

stem

stem

Divided Sedge
Carex divisa

stem

ligule

tip

leaf

Brown Sedge
Carex disticha

illustrations
0.5× lifesize

Remote Sedge
Carex remota

Densely tufted perennial to 60 cm. STEMS Bluntly 3-angled. LEAVES *Narrow*, 1.5-2 mm wide, pale bright green. INFLORESCENCES 4-7 spikes, the lower well separated; *lower bracts leaf-like, much longer than stem*; female glumes pale, with green midrib. FRUITS 2.5-3.5 mm, *green*. HABITAT Damp, shady habitats, wet woodlands, stream sides; lowland to 320 m. DIST. Native. Common throughout BI, but rare N Scotland. (Most of Europe except extreme N.) FLS Jun, fruits Jul-Aug.

Oval Sedge
Carex leporina (Carex ovalis)

Densely tufted perennial to 90 cm. STEMS Often curved or spreading. LEAVES 1-3 mm wide. INFLORESCENCES *Compact; 3-9 spikes, contiguous or overlapping, yellow-brown*; lower bracts bristle-like, longer than spike; female glumes 3-4.5 mm. FRUITS 4-5 mm, light brown. HABITAT All kinds of acid grassland, heather moors, lowland heaths, woodland rides; to 1005 m. DIST. Native. Common throughout BI. (Most of Europe, but rare in extreme N.) FLS Jun, fruits Jul-Aug.

Star Sedge
Carex echinata

Densely tufted perennial to 40 cm. STEMS Bluntly 3-angled, spreading. LEAVES 1-2.5 mm wide. INFLORESCENCES 1-3 cm; 2-5 spikes, separated; bracts glume-like, as long as or longer than inflorescence; female glumes 2-2.5 mm, pale brown. FRUITS *Spreading, giving characteristic star-like appearance, 3-4 mm, yellow-brown*. HABITAT Wide range of wet, usually acid, habitats: bogs, flushes, springs, wet meadows, pastures. DIST. Native. Common in N and W BI; local or scarce in lowlands. (Most of Europe except Mediterranean, NE and SE.) FLS May-Jun, fruits Jun-Jul.

Dioecious Sedge
Carex dioica

Slender, creeping, *dioecious*, tufted perennial to 30 cm. STEMS Smooth, erect. LEAVES Very narrow, 0.3-1 mm wide. INFLORESCENCES *Single terminal spike*; male spike 8-20 mm, dark brown; female spike 5-20 mm, broadly cylindric, 20-30-flowered. FRUITS 2.5-3.5 mm, reddish brown, broadly ovoid, spreading. HABITAT Wet, base-rich mires, calcareous springs, flushes. DIST. Native. Widespread in N England, Wales, Scotland, N Ireland; scarce and declining elsewhere. (Much of Europe except S.) FLS May, fruits Jul.

Davall's Sedge
Carex davalliana EX.

Similar to *C. dioica*, but leaves bristle-like, rough; female spike 15-20-flowered; fruits narrow, long-beaked. HABITAT Wet, base-rich or calcareous mires. DIST. Formerly in a calcareous mire near Bath, but extinct since *c*.1850. (W, central and E Europe.) FLS Apr-Jun.

Elongated Sedge
Carex elongata

Rhizomatous, densely tufted, tussock-forming perennial to 80 cm. STEMS Sharply 3-angled, rough. LEAVES 2-5 mm wide. INFLORESCENCES 3-7 cm, rather lax; *spikes long*, 5-15 mm, *spreading*; female glumes 2 mm, brownish with green midrib. FRUITS 3.5-4 mm, *curved, green, ribs reddish*. HABITAT Wet woodlands, ditches, lake and pond margins, wet meadows. DIST. Native. Very local. Scattered throughout BI. (Central and N Europe.) FLS May, fruits Jun.

Hare's-foot Sedge
Carex lachenalii

Tufted, rhizomatous perennial to 20 cm. STEMS Bluntly 3-angled, striate. LEAVES *Shorter than stems, 1-2 mm wide*. INFLORESCENCES Dense, 2-4 cm; 2-5 spikes, contiguous, reddish brown; *female glumes 2.5 mm, blunt, brown with broad, pale margins*. FRUITS 2.5-4 mm, narrowed at each end. HABITAT Wet acidic, N-facing slopes, rock ledges; 950-1150 m. DIST. Native. Rare. Scottish Highlands. (N Europe, mts of central and SW Europe.) FLS Jun-Jul, fruits Jul-Aug.

Peat Sedge
Carex heleonastes

Tufted perennial to 40 cm. Similar to *C. lachenalii* but *stems sharply 3-angled*, rough; *leaves 1-2 mm wide, bluish green*; inflorescence 1-2 cm, dense; 3-4 spikes, ovoid-spherical; female glumes pale brown with broad, pale margins; fruits 2.7-3.5 mm, brown ± spreading. HABITAT Peat bogs. DIST. *Not BI*. (N Europe.) FLS Jun, fruits Jul-Sep.

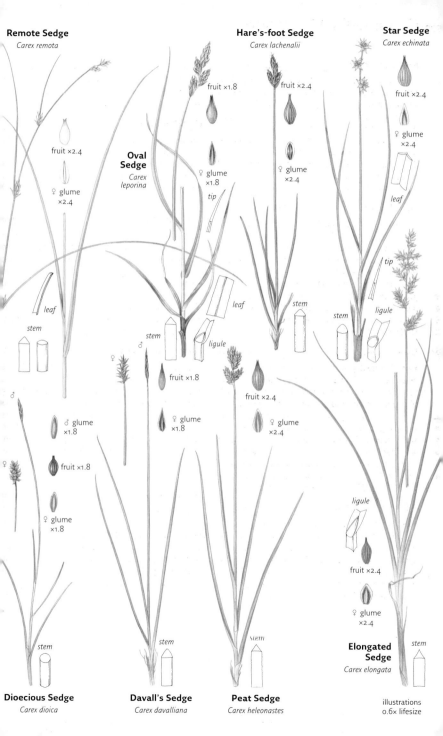

Remote Sedge
Carex remota

fruit ×2.4

♀ glume
×2.4

leaf

stem

**Oval
Sedge**
*Carex
leporina*

fruit ×1.8

♀ glume
×1.8

tip

leaf

ligule

stem

♂

Hare's-foot Sedge
Carex lachenalii

fruit ×2.4

♀ glume
×2.4

stem

Star Sedge
Carex echinata

fruit ×2.4

♀ glume
×2.4

leaf

tip

ligule

stem

♀

♂

♂ glume
×1.8

♀

fruit ×1.8

♀ glume
×1.8

Dioecious Sedge
Carex dioica

stem

♀

fruit ×1.8

♀ glume
×1.8

stem

Davall's Sedge
Carex davalliana

fruit ×2.4

♀ glume
×2.4

stem

Peat Sedge
Carex heleonastes

ligule

fruit ×2.4

♀ glume
×2.4

**Elongated
Sedge**
Carex elongata

stem

illustrations
0.6× lifesize

White Sedge
Carex canescens (Carex curta)

Tufted perennial to 80 cm. STEMS Sharply 3-angled, rough. LEAVES 2–3 mm wide, *pale green.* INFLORESCENCES 3–5 cm; 4–8 spikes, contiguous or separate; bracts glume-like; *female glumes pale, thin, with green midrib.* FRUITS 2–3 mm, pale. HABITAT Wide range of nutrient-poor upland mires, valley bogs, boggy woodlands. DIST. Native. Widespread in N England, Scotland, Wales, N Ireland; rare and local elsewhere. (All Europe except S.) FLS Jul-Aug, fruits Aug-Sep.

Quaking-grass Sedge
Carex brizoides

Creeping, rhizomatous perennial to 50 cm. LEAVES 1.3–3 mm wide, *longer than stems.* INFLORESCENCES 1.5–3 cm, narrow; 5–8 spikes, contiguous, lower separate, female above, male below; *female glumes pale brown to greenish.* FRUITS 3–4 mm, *greyish green.* HABITAT Damp woodlands. DIST. *Not BI.* (Central Europe, S from Belgium and Holland.) FLS Apr-May, fruits Jun-Jul.

Bohemian Sedge
Carex bohemica

Tufted perennial to 30 cm. LEAVES 1.5–2.5 mm wide. INFLORESCENCES ± *spherical head, 1.5–2.5 cm across, with 2–5 leaf-like bracts much longer than inflorescence; female glumes narrow, whitish, c.½ length of fruits.* FRUITS Narrow, 7–10 mm, pale green to yellow. HABITAT Damp, open sandy habitats, dried-up ponds. DIST. *Not BI.* (Central Europe to central France, Belgium.) FLS Fruits Jun-Sep.

Hairy Sedge
Carex hirta

Shortly creeping, tufted, rhizomatous perennial to 60 cm. LEAVES 2–5 mm wide, shorter than stems, *densely hairy.* INFLORESCENCES 2–3 male spikes; 2–3 female spikes, erect, distant, the lowest often near base of stem; lower bracts leaf-like, longer than spikes; *female glumes pale green.* FRUITS 5–7 mm, *greenish, hairy.* HABITAT Rough grassland, roadsides, hedge banks, on fertile soils; to 470 m. DIST. Native. Common throughout BI, N to central Scotland. (Most of Europe except extreme N and S.) FLS May-Jun, fruits Jun-Jul.

Slender Sedge
Carex lasiocarpa

Tall, rhizomatous perennial to 120 cm, sometimes forming dense stands. *Rhizome scales sometimes red.* STEMS Slender, bluntly 3-angled. LEAVES *Narrow, 1–2 mm wide.* INFLORESCENCES Bracts slender, leaf-like, lowest often longer than inflorescence; 1–3 male spikes, ± contiguous; 1–3 female spikes, usually separate, erect, 10–30 mm; female glumes 3.5–5 mm, dark brown with pale midrib. FRUITS *3.5–4.5 mm,*

grey-green, densely hairy. HABITAT Fens, reed swamps, marginal vegetation of lakes and rivers; to 650 m. DIST. Native. Rather local in N England, Scotland, Ireland; scarce elsewhere. (Most of Europe except S.) FLS Jun-Jul, but not often; fruits Jul-Aug.

Lesser Pond-sedge
Carex acutiformis

Tall, rhizomatous perennial to 150 cm, often forming dense stands. STEMS Sharply 3-angled. LEAVES 5–20 mm wide, slightly glaucous; *ligules acute, 5–15 mm.* INFLORESCENCES Bracts leaf-like, longer than inflorescence; *2–3 male spikes,* clustered, 10–40 mm, *glumes blunt;* 2–4 female spikes, 20–60 mm, glumes 4–5 mm, acute, apex toothed. FRUITS 3.5–5 mm, *beak shallow notched.* HABITAT Marginal vegetation of rivers, dykes, lakes, ponds, fens and carrs; to 370 m. DIST. Native. Most of BI, but rare in SW England, N Scotland. (Most of Europe except extreme N and S.) FLS Jun-Jul, fruits Jul-Aug. SIMILAR SPP. Along with *C. riparia* (see below), often grows together with *C. acuta* (p.584), which is superficially similar but has narrower leaves, 3–10 mm wide. In addition, the female glume is not toothed at the tip, and the fruits are flattened with 2, not 3, stigmas.

Greater Pond-sedge
Carex riparia

Tall, robust, rhizomatous perennial to 130 cm, often forming dense stands. STEMS Sharply 3-angled LEAVES 5–20 mm wide, *distinctly glaucous, ligules rounded,* 5–10 mm. INFLORESCENCES Lower bracts leaf-like, longer than inflorescence; 3–6 *male spikes* clustered, *glumes lanceolate;* 1–5 female spikes, contiguous, 3–10 cm, glumes 7–10 mm, lanceolate-ovate FRUITS 5–8 mm, *fat, yellowish brown, beak deeply notched.* HABITAT Similar to *C. acutiformis,* with which it often grows. DIST. Native. Widespread SE of line from Humber to Severn; scattered elsewhere. (Most of Europe except N.) FLS May-Jun, fruits Jul-Aug. SIMILAR SPP. Resembles *C. acuta* (p.584); see *C. acutiformis.* above for differences.

Cyperus Sedge
Carex pseudocyperus

Loosely tufted, rhizomatous perennial to 90 cm STEMS Sharply 3-angled. LEAVES 5–12 mm wide, *yellow-green, pleated.* INFLORESCENCES *Bracts leaf-like the lowest long, 3–4× as long as inflorescence;* 1 male spike; *3–5 female spikes, greenish, 2–10 cm, clustered on long, slender, pendent peduncles.* FRUITS 4–5 mm green, wider than glumes. HABITAT Reed swamp marginal vegetation of dykes, rivers, ponds and canals; shade-tolerant. DIST. Native. Lowland England; rare in Wales, Ireland; absent from Scotland (Most of Europe.) FLS May-Jun, fruits Jul-Aug.

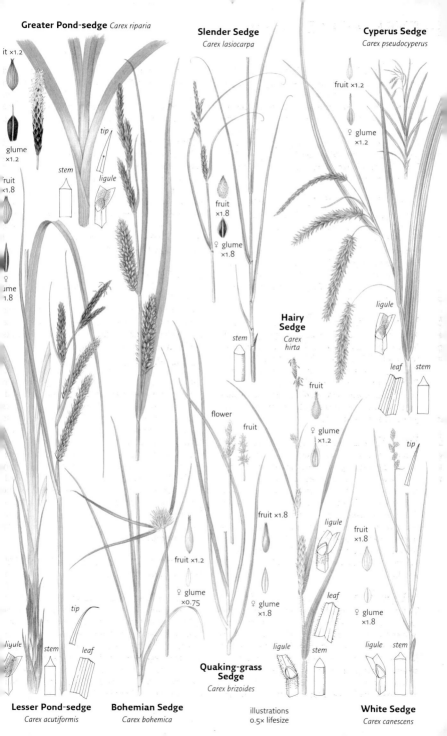

Greater Pond-sedge *Carex riparia*

it ×1.2

glume
×1.2

fruit
×1.8

stem

tip

ligule

♀
ume
1.8

Slender Sedge
Carex lasiocarpa

fruit
×1.8

♀ glume
×1.8

stem

Cyperus Sedge
Carex pseudocyperus

fruit ×1.2

♀ glume
×1.2

ligule

leaf   stem

**Hairy
Sedge**

*Carex
hirta*

fruit

♀ glume
×1.2

fruit ×1.8

♀ glume
×1.8

flower

fruit

tip

ligule

fruit
×1.8

leaf

♀ glume
×1.8

ligule   stem

fruit ×1.2

♀ glume
×0.75

tip

ligule

stem   leaf

**Quaking-grass
Sedge**

Carex brizoides

illustrations
0.5× lifesize

White Sedge

Carex canescens

ligule   stem

Lesser Pond-sedge

Carex acutiformis

Bohemian Sedge

Carex bohemica

Bottle Sedge
Carex rostrata

Rhizomatous, *glaucous*, erect perennial to 100 cm. STEMS *Bluntly 3-angled above.* LEAVES 3–7 mm wide, *longer than stems, keeled or inrolled.* INFLORESCENCES Bracts leaf-like, as long as or longer than inflorescence; 2–4 male spikes, 2–7 cm; 2–5 female spikes, contiguous or lowest separate; *glumes 3–5.5 mm, narrower than fruit.* FRUITS *3.5–6.5 mm, swollen, yellow-green, spreading.* HABITAT Shallow water of nutrient-poor, usually acid lakes, ponds, bog pools, rivers, dune slacks. DIST. Native. Common in N and W Britain, Ireland; local in lowland England. (Most of Europe, but rare in SE and SW.) FLS Jun–Jul, fruits Jul–Aug.

Bladder Sedge
Carex vesicaria

Erect, rhizomatous *green to yellow-green*, not glaucous, perennial to 120 cm. STEMS *Sharply 3-angled.* LEAVES 4–8 mm wide. INFLORESCENCES 2–4 male spikes, 10–40 mm; 2–3 female spikes, ± contiguous but separate from male spikes, glumes 4–6 mm, purplish brown with pale midrib. FRUITS *5–8 mm, swollen, much wider and longer than glumes, olive-green.* HABITAT Margins of rivers, dykes, lakes, ponds, marshes and wet meadows, on base-rich or peaty soils; lowland to 455 m. DIST. Native. Rather local throughout BI. (Most of Europe except extreme S.) FLS Jun, fruits Jul–Aug.

Russet Sedge
Carex saxatilis

Tufted, rhizomatous alpine perennial to 40 cm. STEMS Often curved. LEAVES Often curved, 2–4 mm wide. INFLORESCENCES Lower bracts leaf-like, as long as or longer than inflorescence; *1 male spike, glumes blackish* with pale border; *1–3 female spikes, ± contiguous, ovoid, erect, 5–20 mm, glumes dark purplish brown.* FRUITS 3–3.5 mm, swollen, shiny. HABITAT Mires, wet rock ledges, mountain tops, often in areas of late snow-lie and little water movement; to 1125 m. DIST. Native. Rather rare. Scottish mts. (N Europe.) FLS Jul, fruits Aug–Sep.

Pendulous Sedge
Carex pendula

Tall, handsome, tufted, rhizomatous perennial to 230 cm. STEMS Sharply 3-angled. LEAVES *12–20 mm wide; ligules long, 40–80 mm, acute.* INFLORESCENCES 1(-2) male spikes; *4–5 female spikes, narrowly cylindrical, long, 7–16 cm, becoming pendent.* FRUITS 3–3.5 mm, green becoming brown. HABITAT Damp woodlands on heavy soils, hedgerows, sides of ponds and stream. DIST. Native. Common throughout BI, N to central Scotland; spreading to N. (W, central and S Europe.) FLS May–Jun, fruits Jun–Jul.

Wood Sedge
Carex sylvatica

Tufted perennial to 60 cm. STEMS Slender, bluntly 3-angled, nodding. LEAVES 3–6 mm wide, rather yellow-green; *ligules 2–4 mm long, rounded.* INFLORESCENCES Lower bracts leaf-like; 1 male spike; *3–5 female spikes, 2–6.5 cm, well separated on long, slender pendent peduncles*; female glumes 3–5 mm straw-coloured, midrib green. FRUITS 3–5 mm green. HABITAT Woods, woodland rides, hedge banks, on damp, heavy or calcareous soils; to 565 m. DIST. Native. Frequent throughout BI, but rare in N Scotland. (Most of Europe except extreme N.) FLS May–Jul, fruits Jul–Sep.

Thin-spiked Wood Sedge
Carex strigosa

Tufted, rhizomatous perennial to 75 cm, often confused with *C. sylvatica*. STEMS Bluntly 3-angled spreading. LEAVES *6–10 mm wide; ligules 5–8 mm acute, markedly asymmetrical.* INFLORESCENCES Bracts leaf-like, longer than spikes; 1 male spike; *3–6 female spikes*, well separated, 2.5–8 cm, *± erect peduncles short,* enclosed within bract sheath; glumes 2.5 mm, green becoming brown. FRUITS 3–4 mm green. HABITAT Damp woods, clearings, stream sides, on heavy, base-rich soils. DIST. Native. Local in lowland England, Ireland; rare elsewhere; absent from Scotland. (S, central and W Europe.) FLS May–Jun, fruits Jun–Sep.

Hair Sedge
Carex capillaris

Slender, tufted perennial to 20 cm. STEMS Bluntly 3 angled. LEAVES Short, 1–2.5 mm wide. INFLORESCENCES *1 male spike, overtopped by female spikes; 2–4 female spikes, 5–25 mm, on long, hair-like, nodding peduncles, all appearing to arise from same bract* female glumes 2–3 mm, straw-coloured. FRUITS 3 mm, brown, shiny. HABITAT Short, open vegetation, wet base-rich upland grassland, calcareous flushes, ledges; to 1035 m. DIST. Native. Rather rare N England, N Wales, Scotland. (N Europe, mts of central and S Europe.) FLS Jun, fruits Jun–Aug.

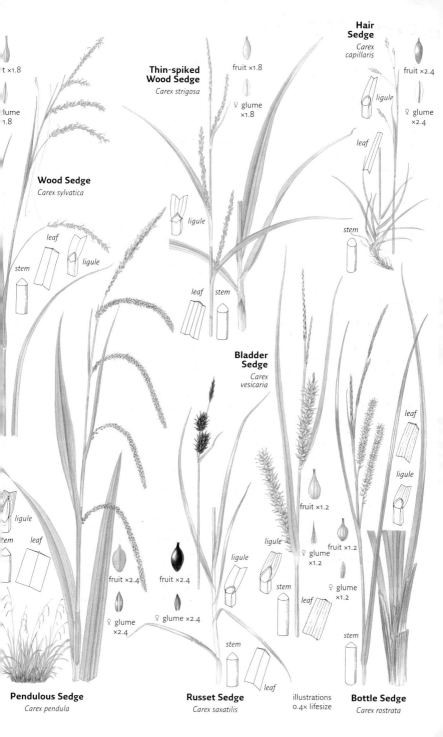

Hair Sedge
Carex capillaris

fruit ×2.4

♀ glume ×2.4

ligule

leaf

stem

t ×1.8

lume
1.8

Thin-spiked Wood Sedge
Carex strigosa

fruit ×1.8

♀ glume ×1.8

ligule

leaf *stem*

Wood Sedge
Carex sylvatica

leaf

ligule

stem

Bladder Sedge
Carex vesicaria

fruit ×1.2

♀ glume ×1.2

ligule

leaf

stem

leaf

ligule

fruit ×1.2

♀ glume ×1.2

stem

ligule

leaf

fruit ×2.4

♀ glume ×2.4

fruit ×2.4

♀ glume ×2.4

ligule

stem

leaf

Pendulous Sedge
Carex pendula

Russet Sedge
Carex saxatilis

illustrations
0.4× lifesize

Bottle Sedge
Carex rostrata

Glaucous Sedge
Carex flacca

Creeping, rhizomatous, tufted perennial to 60 cm. LEAVES 1.5–4 mm wide, distinctly glaucous beneath, tapering to fine, channelled point. INFLORESCENCES Bracts leaf-like, lowest about as long as inflorescence; 2–3 male spikes; 1–5 female spikes, 15–55 mm, upper erect, sessile, lower nodding; female glumes 2–3 mm, blackish with pale midrib. FRUITS 2–3 mm, green becoming black, minutely papillose. HABITAT All kinds of open neutral and calcareous grasslands, fens, dune slacks, upland flushes, rock ledges; to 790 m. DIST. Native. Common throughout BI. (Most of Europe except NE.) FLS May–Jun, fruits Jul–Aug.

Carnation Sedge
Carex panicea

Shortly creeping, rhizomatous, tufted perennial to 60 cm. LEAVES 1.5–5 mm wide, distinctly glaucous, tapering to solid 3-angled tip. INFLORESCENCES Bracts leaf-like, shorter than inflorescence; 1 male spike; 1–3 female spikes, 10–20 mm, few-flowered; female glumes 3–4 mm, red-brown, midrib pale green. FRUITS 3–4 mm, swollen, asymmetrical, olive-green to brownish, smooth, beak <0.5 mm. HABITAT All kinds of open, damp habitats on neutral to acid peaty soils, grassland, wet heaths, mires, flushed upland grassland, upper parts of salt marshes; to 1125 m. DIST. Native. Throughout BI, but declining in SE. (Most of Europe, but rare in S.) FLS May–Jun, fruits Jun–Jul. NOTE When growing with *C. flacca* and not flowering, can be distinguished by leaf tip.

Sheathed Sedge
Carex vaginata

Similar to *C. panicea*, but leaves yellow-green to bronze-green, those at base of flowering shoots very short, 1–3 cm long; *sheaths of bracts loose, funnel-shaped*; fruits apple-green, not swollen, beak *c*.1 mm. HABITAT Locally abundant on damp acid mountain grassland, flushed bogs, rock ledges; to 1150 m. DIST. Native. Scotland. (N Europe, mts of central and SW Europe.) FLS Jul, fruits Aug–Sep.

Starved Wood-sedge
Carex depauperata EN. *(B, R)

Shortly creeping, rhizomatous, loosely tufted perennial to 100 cm. LEAVES 2–4 mm wide, *sheaths purplish*. INFLORESCENCES Bracts leaf-like, longer than spikes; 1 male spike; 2–4 *female spikes*, well separated, *few-flowered*; female glumes 4.5–6 mm. FRUITS *Large, 7–9 mm*, brownish green. HABITAT Laneside banks, wood margins, on dry calcareous soils. DIST. Native. Very rare, at 3 sites only. (W and S Europe.) FLS May, fruits Jun–Oct.

Smooth-stalked Sedge
Carex laevigata

Densely tufted, rhizomatous perennial to 120 cm. STEMS Bluntly 3-angled. LEAVES *5–12 mm wide*. INFLORESCENCES Bracts leaf-like, longer than spikes; 1–2 male spikes, pale brown; *2–4 female spikes*, well separated, 2–5 cm, upper erect, lower pendent; *female glumes* 3–5 mm, *pale brown*, midrib green. FRUITS 4–6 mm, rather swollen, green. HABITAT Acid woodland flushes; to 410 m. DIST. Native. Rather local. Throughout BI, but commoner in S and W. (W Europe.) FLS Jun, fruits Jul–Aug.

Green-ribbed Sedge
Carex binervis

Tufted, rhizomatous perennial to 150 cm. STEMS Smooth to bluntly 3-angled. LEAVES *2–6 mm wide, dark green, persisting as rusty-brown litter*. INFLORESCENCES Lower bracts leaf-like, longer than spike; male spike; 2–4 female spikes, well separated, 15–34 mm, ± erect; *female glumes 3–4 mm, dark purple-brown with greenish midrib*. FRUITS 3.5–4.5 mm, green-purplish *with 2 prominent green nerves*. HABITAT Wet or dry acid heaths, moors, open woodland, upland grassland, rocky hillsides; to 975 m. DIST. Native. Frequent throughout BI, but rare in lowland England. (W Europe.) FLS Jun, fruits Jun–Aug.

Distant Sedge
Carex distans

Densely tufted, rhizomatous perennial to 100 cm. STEMS Smooth to bluntly 3-angled. LEAVES 2–6 mm wide, *becoming grey-green*, tapered to fine point. INFLORESCENCES *Bracts* leaf-like, *not longer than inflorescence*; *1 male spike, purplish brown*; 2–4 female spikes, 10–20 mm, ± sessile; female glumes 2.5–3.5 mm, pale brown with greenish midrib. FRUITS 3.5–4.5 mm, *greenish brown, ± erect*. HABITAT Brackish grassland, dyke and pool margins, upper levels of salt marshes, sea cliffs; also wet meadows, marshes and fens inland. DIST. Native. All round coasts of BI, inland lowland England. (Most of Europe except extreme N.) FLS May–Jun, fruits Jun–Jul.

Dotted Sedge
Carex punctata

Similar to *C. distans*, but *leaves broader, to 7 mm wide, more yellow-green*; ≥1 leaf-like bract longer than inflorescence; male glumes orange-brown; *fruits yellowish green*, speckled with fine red-brown dots (use lens), abruptly contracted into beak, *spreading or deflexed*. HABITAT Sandy salt marshes, dune slacks, freshwater seepage zones at foot of cliffs. DIST. Native. Very local. S and W coasts of Britain N to Solway Firth, SW Ireland. (W and S Europe.) FLS Jun–Jul, fruits Jul–Aug.

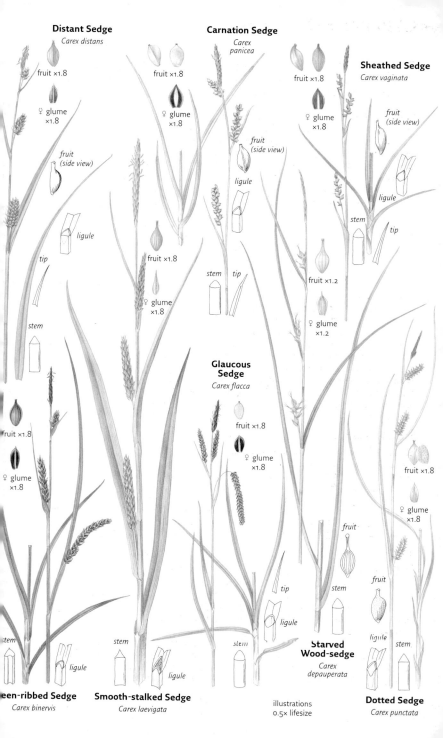

Distant Sedge
Carex distans

fruit ×1.8

♀ glume
×1.8

*fruit
(side view)*

ligule

tip

stem

Carnation Sedge
Carex panicea

fruit ×1.8

♀ glume
×1.8

*fruit
(side view)*

ligule

fruit ×1.8

♀ glume
×1.8

stem   tip

Sheathed Sedge
Carex vaginata

fruit ×1.8

♀ glume
×1.8

*fruit
(side view)*

ligule

stem   tip

fruit ×1.2

♀ glume
×1.2

fruit ×1.8

♀ glume
×1.8

**Glaucous
Sedge**
Carex flacca

fruit ×1.8

♀ glume
×1.8

fruit

stem

tip

ligule

stem

**Starved
Wood-sedge**
*Carex
depauperata*

fruit ×1.8

♀ glume
×1.8

fruit

ligule

stem

stem

ligule

een-ribbed Sedge
Carex binervis

Smooth-stalked Sedge
Carex laevigata

ligule

stem

illustrations
0.5× lifesize

Dotted Sedge
Carex punctata

Tawny Sedge
Carex hostiana

Shortly creeping, rhizomatous perennial to 60 cm. LEAVES 2–5 mm wide, light to yellowish green, keeled, *abruptly contracted to solid, parallel-sided, veinless tip, several mm behind apex*. INFLORESCENCES Bracts leaf-like, longer than spikes; 1–2 male spikes; 1–3 female spikes, well separated; *female glumes 2.5–3.5 mm, dark brown with conspicuous, broad silvery margin*, midrib green. FRUITS 4–5 mm, yellow-green. HABITAT Wet, base-rich or calcareous fens, marshes, mires, valley bogs. DIST. Native. Throughout BI, but rare in English lowlands. (Most of Europe, but rare in S and E.) FLS Jun, fruits Jul–Aug.

Long-bracted Sedge
Carex extensa

Tufted, rhizomatous perennial to 40 cm. LEAVES 2–3 mm wide, rigid, channelled or inrolled. INFLORESCENCES *Bracts leaf-like, much longer than inflorescence, spreading or deflexed*; 1 male spike; 2–4 female spikes, contiguous or lowest separated; female glumes 1.5–2 mm, pale brown with pale midrib. FRUITS 3–4 mm, greenish to brownish. HABITAT Upper parts of salt marshes, margins of brackish dykes and lagoons, wet rocks, cliffs. DIST. Native. All round coasts of BI, but rare in SE. (Coasts of Europe except extreme N.) FLS Jun–Jul, fruits Jul–Aug.

Yellow-sedges *Carex flava* and *C. viridula*
A complex group of related species, with frequent hybrids and characters that overlap. All are tufted, rhizomatous perennials with bright green leaves; long, leaf-like bracts; ± sessile, ovoid or shortly cylindrical female spikes; bright yellow or yellow-green fruits.

Large Yellow-sedge
Carex flava VU.

LEAVES 3–7 mm wide, about as long as stems; ligules 2–5 mm. INFLORESCENCES Bracts much longer than inflorescence, often deflexed; 2–3 female spikes, clustered around base of male spike. FRUITS *4.4–6.5 mm, gradually narrowed into beak, 2–2.8 mm*; lower fruits deflexed when ripe. HABITAT Shaded calcareous fen. DIST. Native. Very rare, in 2 sites only in N England. (Most of Europe except Mediterranean.) FLS Jun, fruits Jun–Aug.

Long-stalked Yellow-sedge
Carex viridula ssp. *brachyrrhyncha*

Similar to *C. flava*, but *leaves 1.2–3.5 mm wide, ≤⅔ as long as stem*; ligules 1 mm; bracts sometimes reflexed; female spikes clustered or lowest slightly distant; *fruits 3–5.5 mm, distinctly curved*, lower deflexed, *beak 1.5–2 mm, deflexed*. HABITAT Short, open vegetation of wet calcareous fens, mires, hillside flushes; to 775 m. DIST. Native. Throughout BI, but absent from SW England. (N, NW and central Europe.) FLS May–Jun, fruits Jul–Aug.

Common Yellow-sedge
Carex viridula ssp. *oedocarpa*

Similar to ssp. *brachyrrhyncha*, but stems often curved; leaves 1.5–5 mm wide, flat, recurved, at least some >⅔ as long as stem; bracts leaf-like, deflexed 2–4 female spikes, 7–13 mm, *lowest usually separate close to base of plant; fruits 3–4 mm*, not tapering gradually into beak, spreading or deflexed, beak *c.*1 mm. HABITAT Wet, usually acid heathland, sides of streams and ponds, woodland rides, rocky hillsides, upland flushes; to 930 m. DIST. Native. Throughout BI. (N, W and central Europe.) FLS Jun, fruits Jul–Sep.

Small-fruited Yellow-sedge
Carex viridula ssp. *viridula*

Similar to ssp. *oedocarpa*, but stems straight; leaves 0.8–3.4 mm wide, ± channelled, about as long as stems; 2–5 female spikes, 5–10 mm, all ± clustered at top of stem; *fruits 2–3 mm, beak ≤1 mm*. HABITAT Open, damp habitats with fluctuating water levels, dune slacks, pond and lake shores, sandy salt marshes. DIST. Native. Mostly coastal in N and W Britain, scattered inland; widespread but local in Ireland. (Most of Europe, but rare in Mediterranean.) FLS Jun–Aug, fruits Jul–Sep.

Pale Sedge
Carex pallescens

Densely tufted, rhizomatous perennial to 60 cm. STEMS Sharply 4-angled. LEAVES 2–5 mm wide, hairy beneath, *leaf sheaths hairy*. INFLORESCENCES Bracts leaf-like, lowest longer than inflorescence, *crimped at base*; 1 male spike, often hidden by female spikes; 2–3 female spikes, ovoid, clustered or lowest separate; female glumes 3–4 mm, pale brown. FRUITS 2.5–3.5 mm, *oblong, rounded, green, shiny*. HABITAT Woodland rides, clearings, coppice, damp hill grassland, stream banks, on mildly acid soils; to 790 m. DIST. Native. Throughout BI, but commoner in N and W, and rare in S Ireland. (Most of Europe except S and NE.) FLS May–Jun, fruits Jun–Jul.

Fingered Sedge
Carex digitata

Tufted, rhizomatous perennial to 25 cm. STEMS Slender, smooth to bluntly 3-angled. LEAVES 1.5–5 mm wide, sparsely hairy on upper surface, *sheaths red*. INFLORESCENCES Bracts to 10 mm, sheathing; male spike, overtopped by uppermost female spike; female spikes, separated; female glumes 3–4.5 mm, *purplish crimson, as long as fruits*. FRUITS 3–4.5 mm, greenish brown, hairy. HABITAT Limestone woodlands, scree, rock outcrops. DIST. Native. Rare. England. (Most of Europe except extreme W and Mediterranean.) FLS Apr–May, fruits Apr–Jun.

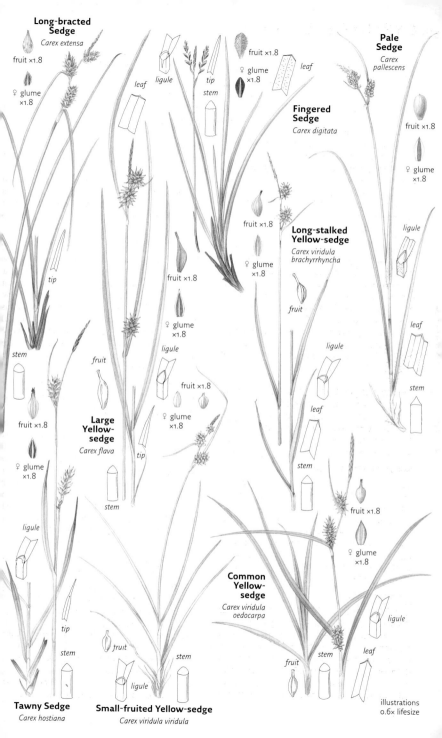

Long-bracted Sedge
Carex extensa

fruit ×1.8

♀ glume ×1.8

ligule

leaf

tip

stem

tip

stem

♀ glume ×1.8

fruit ×1.8

fruit ×1.8

Pale Sedge
Carex pallescens

fruit ×1.8

♀ glume ×1.8

ligule

leaf

stem

leaf

♀ glume ×1.8

fruit ×1.8

Fingered Sedge
Carex digitata

fruit ×1.8

♀ glume ×1.8

Long-stalked Yellow-sedge
Carex viridula brachyrrhyncha

fruit

ligule

leaf

stem

stem

♀ glume ×1.8

ligule

fruit ×1.8

♀ glume ×1.8

Large Yellow-sedge
Carex flava

fruit

tip

stem

fruit ×1.8

♀ glume ×1.8

Common Yellow-sedge
Carex viridula oedocarpa

fruit ×1.8

♀ glume ×1.8

ligule

tip

stem

ligule

stem

leaf

Tawny Sedge
Carex hostiana

fruit

ligule

Small-fruited Yellow-sedge
Carex viridula viridula

fruit

stem

fruit

stem

illustrations
0.6× lifesize

Bird's-foot Sedge
Carex ornithopoda

Slender, tufted perennial, similar to *C. digitata* (p.578). STEMS To 20 cm. LEAVES Sheaths orange to dark brown. INFLORESCENCES *Female spikes all arising from ± same point; female glumes pale orange-brown* with pale border. FRUITS 2-3 mm, longer than glumes. HABITAT Dry, well-drained limestone grassland, limestone pavement; to 600 m. DIST. Native. Rare. N England. (Most of Europe except SE and Mediterranean.) FLS May (later than *C. digitata*), fruits May-Jun.

Dwarf Sedge
Carex humilis

Dwarf, mat-forming, rhizomatous perennial, producing dense tufts of shoots at branch tips. STEMS Slender, to 10 cm, arching. LEAVES *Bristle-like (resembling* Festuca ovina *grass; p.606), dark green.* INFLORESCENCES *Often hidden among leaves;* 1 male spike; 2-4 female spikes, 2-4-flowered; female glumes red-brown with pale edges. FRUITS 2.5 mm, with short hairs. HABITAT Close-grazed, species-rich calcareous grassland, usually on chalk. DIST. Native. Very local. Central-S England (Wessex). (Central and S Europe.) FLS Early, Mar-May; fruits Apr-Sep.

Spring Sedge
Carex caryophyllea

Loosely tufted, rhizomatous perennial, to 30 cm but usually much less. STEMS *Erect, rigid.* LEAVES 1.5-3 mm wide, shiny, bright green. INFLORESCENCES 2-4 cm; *lowest bract sheathing* (look carefully); 1 male spike; female spikes clustered at base of male; *female glumes acute, brown, midrib green.* FRUITS 2-3 mm, green, with short hairs. HABITAT Dry calcareous and mildly acid grasslands, heaths; to 765 m. DIST. Native. Frequent throughout BI, but rare in N Scotland. (All Europe except extreme N.) FLS Apr-May, fruits May-Jul.

Downy-fruited Sedge
Carex filiformis

Creeping, rhizomatous perennial to 50 cm, sometimes forming patches. LEAVES 1.5-2 mm wide, ± glaucous, *sheaths red-purple becoming brown.* INFLORESCENCES *Lowest bract leaf-like, about as long as inflorescence;* 1-2 male spikes; 1-2 female spikes, contiguous; female glumes 2-3 mm, purplish to reddish brown with pale midrib. FRUITS 2-3 *mm, globose or pear-shaped,* green, *densely hairy.* HABITAT Dry calcareous grassland, damp meadows, roadside verges. DIST. Native. Very local. Central-S England. (Central Europe.) FLS May-Jun, fruits Jun-Jul.

Rare Spring Sedge
Carex ericetorum VU

Creeping, rhizomatous, often mat-forming perennial. Similar to *C. caryophyllea*, but *lowest bract without sheath or sheath to 2 mm; female glumes blunt purplish black with broad, pale border;* fruits 2-3 mm green, hairy. HABITAT Short, dry, grazed calcareous grassland. DIST. Native. Very local. In scattered localities in E England from East Anglia to Yorkshire. (Most of Europe except Mediterranean.) FLS Apr-May, fruits Apr-Jun.

Pill Sedge
Carex pilulifera

Densely tufted, rhizomatous perennial. STEMS *Wiry, long, arching,* to 30 cm. LEAVES 1.5-2 mm wide. INFLORESCENCES 1-4 mm, clustered; *lowest bract leaf-like, not sheathing;* 1 male spike; 2-4 female spikes, 4-8 mm, ovoid to sub-spherical, erect, sessile; *female glumes* 3-3.5 mm, *red-brown, apex acute.* FRUITS 2-3.5 mm, *ovoid,* hairy at tip, green. HABITAT Acid grassland, heaths, moorland, hill pasture to 1140 m. DIST. Native. Frequent throughout BI. (All Europe.) FLS May-Jun, fruits Jun-Jul.

Soft-leaved Sedge
Carex montana

Similar to *C. caryophyllea*, but mat-forming, often dying out in middle to produce characteristic ring of shoots; stems slender, to 40 cm; *leaves* 1.5-2 mm broad, *soft,* flat, sparsely hairy on upper surface becoming glabrous; inflorescence clustered; 1 male spike; 1-4 female spikes, 6-10 mm; *female glumes ovate, reddish black with pale midrib, apex blunt mucronate; fruits* 3.5-4 *mm, pear-shaped,* dense, with short hairs. HABITAT Short neutral to acidic grassland. DIST. Native. Very local in S England, S Wales, rare elsewhere. (Much of Europe except N and S.) FLS May, fruits May-Jun.

Scorched Alpine Sedge
Carex atrofusca VU

Loosely tufted, shortly creeping, rhizomatous perennial to 35 cm. LEAVES 2-5 mm wide. INFLORESCENCES Lower bracts leaf-like, shorter than spike with basal sheath; 1 male spike, broad, glumes dark reddish brown; 2-4 female spikes, clustered, 5-12 mm, ovoid, nodding; *female glumes purplish black.* FRUITS 4-4.5 mm, *purplish black.* HABITAT Stony mica-rich flushes; 680-1000 m. DIST. Native. Very rare, in 5 localities only in Scottish mts. (N Europe, Alps.) FLS Jul, fruits Jul-Sep.

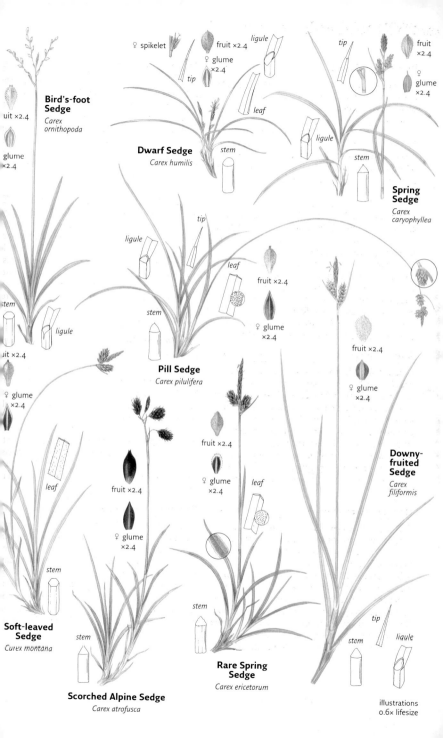

Bird's-foot Sedge
Carex ornithopoda

fruit ×2.4

glume ×2.4

♀ spikelet

tip

fruit ×2.4

♀ glume ×2.4

ligule

leaf

Dwarf Sedge
Carex humilis

stem

tip

fruit ×2.4

♀ glume ×2.4

ligule

stem

Spring Sedge
Carex caryophyllea

ligule

tip

leaf

fruit ×2.4

♀ glume ×2.4

stem

Pill Sedge
Carex pilulifera

stem

ligule

fruit ×2.4

♀ glume ×2.4

fruit ×2.4

♀ glume ×2.4

Downy-fruited Sedge
Carex filiformis

fruit ×2.4

♀ glume ×2.4

leaf

Soft-leaved Sedge
Carex montana

fruit ×2.4

♀ glume ×2.4

stem

Scorched Alpine Sedge
Carex atrofusca

stem

leaf

fruit ×2.4

♀ glume ×2.4

stem

Rare Spring Sedge
Carex ericetorum

stem

tip

ligule

illustrations 0.6× lifesize

Bog Sedge
Carex limosa

Loosely tufted, rhizomatous, creeping perennial to 40 cm. LEAVES 1–2 mm wide, folded or inrolled, pale bluish green; ligules 1–2 mm. INFLORESCENCES Bracts leaf-like, lowest about as long as spikes; 1 male spike; *1–3 female spikes, nodding, on slender peduncles, ≤20 flowers; female glumes 5–5.5 mm, slightly wider than fruits*, reddish brown, midrib green. FRUITS 3–3.5 mm, compressed, ribbed, *silvery grey*. HABITAT Wet acid *Sphagnum* bogs, bog pools; lowland to 830 m. DIST. Native. New Forest, N England, Scotland, Wales, Ireland. (N and central Europe.) FLS Fruits Jul–Aug.

Mountain Bog Sedge
Carex rariflora

Shortly creeping, rhizomatous, carpet-forming alpine perennial to *20 cm*. LEAVES 1–2 mm wide, grey-green. INFLORESCENCES *Lower bracts shorter than inflorescence, sheathed*; 1 male spike; *2 female spikes, each with ≤8 flowers*; female glumes 3–4 mm, dark purple-brown. FRUITS 3–4.5 mm, ribbed, narrower than glumes. HABITAT Wet acid peaty slopes, flushes; 790–1125 m. DIST. Native. Rare. Mts of central Scotland. (Arctic Europe.) FLS Jun, fruits Jul–Aug.

Tall Bog Sedge
Carex magellanica *(NI)

Tufted, rhizomatous perennial. Similar to *C. limosa*, but stems to 40 cm; leaves wider, to 4 mm, ligules longer, to 4.5 mm; *lowest bract leaf-like, longer than inflorescence*; 1 male spike; *2–4 female spikes, each with ≤10 flowers*, nodding; *female glumes 3–5 mm*, lanceolate, red-brown, *narrower than fruits*; fruits 3–3.5 mm, *pale green*. HABITAT Wet *Sphagnum* carpets, upland bogs, valley mires; to 685 m. DIST. Native. Scarce, local. Upland N England, N Wales, Scotland, N Ireland. (N and central Europe.) FLS May–Jun, fruits Jun–Jul.

Black Alpine Sedge
Carex atrata

Tufted, shortly rhizomatous alpine perennial to 55 cm. LEAVES 2–6 mm wide, green to glaucous. INFLORESCENCES *Lowest bract longer than inflorescence; 3–5 spikes, all similar*, clustered, becoming nodding; *glumes reddish black*, female glumes 3.5–4.5 mm. FRUITS 3–4 mm, green. HABITAT Steep, wet, ungrazed calcareous rock ledges; 700–1095 m. DIST. Native. Mts of central Scotland; very rare in N England, N Wales. (N Europe, mts of S Europe.) FLS Fruits Jul–Sep.

Club Sedge
Carex buxbaumii VU.

Shortly creeping, rhizomatous perennial to 70 cm. STEMS Sharply 3-angled. LEAVES Narrow, 1.5–2 mm wide, glaucous; ligules acute. INFLORESCENCES *Lowest bract ± as long as inflorescence; 2–5 spikes, all similar, erect; glumes reddish black with pale midrib*, female glumes 3–5 mm. FRUITS 3–4.5 mm, pale

green, slightly swollen. HABITAT Lake margins, mesotrophic fens. DIST. Native. Very rare, in 4 scattered sites only in Scotland. (N and central Europe.) FLS Jun–Jul, fruits Jul–Aug.

Close-headed Alpine Sedge
Carex norvegica

Tufted, rhizomatous alpine perennial to 30 cm. LEAVES 1.3–3 mm; ligules short, blunt, 0.5–1 mm. INFLORESCENCES *Compact terminal cluster; lower bracts leaf-like, longer than inflorescence*; 1–4 spikes, all similar, erect; *glumes dark red-brown and red-black with pale midrib*, female glumes 1.5–2 mm. FRUITS *2–2.5 mm, minutely papillose, greenish brown*. HABITAT Wet, stony base-rich slopes, ledges in areas of late snow-lie; 700–975 m. DIST. Native. Very rare. Mts of central Scotland. (N Europe, Alps.) FLS Fruits Jul–Aug.

Carex nigra group

The 8 species of closely related sedges belonging to this group show considerable variation and several hybridise freely. All have *flattened (biconvex) green fruits*, with the *beak very short or absent* and 2 stigmas; the female glumes are purplish brown to black with green midribs.

Estuarine Sedge
Carex recta VU

Tufted, rhizomatous perennial to 100 cm. STEMS Stiffly erect, bluntly 3-angled. INFLORESCENCES *Lowest bract longer than inflorescence, auricles purplish*; 1–6 male spikes; 2–6 female spikes, 2–8 cm; *female glumes 3–7 mm, those of lower florets with fine points to c.5mm*. HABITAT Brackish marshes along lower reaches of estuaries, often forming extensive colonies. DIST. Native. Rare. In a few scattered coastal localities in N Scotland. (Norway, Faeroes) FLS Jul, fruits Aug–Sep.

Saltmarsh Sedge
Carex salina

Similar to *C. recta*, but stems shorter, to 30 cm; female spikes shorter, 1–3 cm; *female glumes 4–5 mm, lower with fine points to c.1mm*. HABITAT Forms extensive patches near mean high-tide level at head of a sheltered sea loch. DIST. Native (discovered new to BI in 2004). Very rare, at a single site on W coast of Scotland. (Coasts of N Europe.) FLS May–Jun, fruits Jun–Jul.

Water Sedge
Carex aquatilis

Tall, tufted, rhizomatous perennial to 110 cm. STEMS Smooth to bluntly 3-angled, *brittle*. LEAVES 2.5–5 mm wide, green below, glaucous above, *sheaths wine-red*. INFLORESCENCES *Bracts leaf-like, lowest broad and sheathing at base, much longer than inflorescence*; 2–4 male spikes; 2–5 female spikes. FRUITS 2–3 mm. HABITAT Swamps beside lakes and rivers, mires; 0–975 m. DIST. Native. Widespread in Scotland; rare in N and W BI. (N Europe.) FLS Jul, fruits Jul–Sep.

fruit ×1.8

Bog Sedge
Carex limosa

fruit ×1.8

♀ glume ×1.8

Estuarine Sedge
Carex recta

♀ glume ×1.8

fruit ×1.8

Water Sedge
Carex aquatilis

fruit ×3

♀ glume ×3

♀ glume ×1.8

ligule

tip

ligule

ligule

leaf

fruit ×1.8

♀ glume ×1.8

ligule

Tall Bog Sedge
Carex nagellanica

leaf

stem

stem

fruit ×1.8

♀ glume ×1.8

leaf

stem

leaf

it ×1.8

ligule

ligule

stem

♀ glume ×1.8

ligule

Club Sedge
Carex buxbaumii

ligule

leaf

fruit ×1.8

♀ glume ×1.8

tip

leaf

stem

ume ×1.8

em

leaf

stem

Mountain Bog Sedge
Carex rariflora

Black Alpine Sedge
Carex atrata

fruit ×3

♀ glume ×3

Close-headed Alpine Sedge
Carex norvegica

stem

Saltmarsh Sedge
Carex salina

illustrations
0.5× lifesize

Slender Tufted-sedge
Carex acuta

Tall, tufted, rhizomatous perennial to 120 cm. STEMS Sharply 3-angled. LEAVES *Narrow 3-10 mm wide, green, glossy above, glaucous below, sheaths* brown to red-brown; *ligules 4-6 mm, truncate.* INFLORESCENCES *Bracts leaf-like, lowest longer than inflorescence*; 2-4 male spikes; 2-4 female spikes. FRUITS 2-3.5 mm, *faintly nerved.* HABITAT Marginal vegetation of rivers, streams, dykes, lakes, ponds, canals and marshes, wet woodlands. DIST. Native. Widespread but declining throughout lowland BI, N to S Scotland. (Most of Europe.) FLS May-Jun, fruits Jun-Jul. NOTE Often grows mixed with *C. riparia* and *C. acutiformis* (p.572); *C. acuta* has narrower leaves and more acute ligules.

Common Sedge
Carex nigra

Tufted, rhizomatous perennial to 70 cm. LEAVES *1-3 mm wide, glaucous*; ligules 1-3 mm, rounded. INFLORESCENCES *Bracts leaf-like, lowest ± as long as inflorescence*; 1-2 male spikes; 1-4 female spikes. FRUITS 2.5-3.5 mm, *faintly ribbed.* HABITAT Wide range of acidic to calcareous wetland habitats: marshes, fens, bogs, wet grassland, stream sides, dune slacks; 0-1005 m. DIST. Native. Widespread and frequent throughout BI. (Most of Europe, but rare in S.) FLS May-Jul, fruits Jun-Aug.

Three-nerved Sedge
Carex trinervis

Similar to *C. nigra*, but stems to 40 cm; *leaves stiffly erect, inrolled*; bracts stiff, channelled, lowest longer than inflorescence; *fruits larger, 3.5-5 mm*, broader, longer than glumes, *with ≥3 distinct veins.* HABITAT Upper parts of salt marshes, dune slacks, maritime heaths. DIST. *Not BI.* (W Europe.) FLS Fruits Jun-Aug.

Tufted Sedge
Carex elata

Densely tufted, tussock-forming perennial to 100 cm. STEMS Sharply 4-angled. LEAVES 3-6 mm wide, glaucous. INFLORESCENCES *Lower bracts leaf-like, < length of inflorescence*; 1-3 male spikes; 2-3 female spikes. FRUITS 3-4 mm. HABITAT Base-rich or calcareous marshes, fens, wet woodlands, margins of dykes, rivers, lakes and ponds. DIST. Native. Rather local. Widespread in East Anglia, Lake District, Ireland; scarce and declining elsewhere. (All Europe except extreme N and S.) FLS May-Jun, fruits Jun-Jul.

Stiff Sedge
Carex bigelowii

Shortly creeping, rhizomatous perennial to 25 cm. STEMS Sharply 4-angled. LEAVES 2-7 mm wide, *glaucous turning reddish brown, stiff, arching.* INFLORESCENCES *Bracts leaf-like, the lowest shorter than inflorescence*; 1 male spike, elliptic; 2-3 female spikes. FRUITS 2-3 mm, without veins. HABITAT Exposed, well-drained, montane acid grassland, sedge and lichen heath; to 1305 m. DIST. Native. N England, Scotland; rare in N Wales, Ireland. (N Europe, mts of central Europe.) FLS Jun-Jul, fruits Jul-Aug.

Bristle Sedge
Carex microglochin VU.

Slender, shortly creeping, rhizomatous perennial, producing single shoots to 12 cm. STEMS Stiffly erect. LEAVES *0.5-1 mm wide, stiff, erect, channelled.* INFLORESCENCES Single few-flowered terminal spike; female glumes *c.*2 mm; 3 stigmas. FRUITS *3.5-4.5 mm*, spreading or reflexed, *yellowish green; a stiff bristle arising from base of nut protrudes 1-2 mm through beak.* HABITAT Mica-rich alpine flushes; 610-975 m. DIST. Native. Very rare; only at one locality in Perthshire. (N Europe, Alps.) FLS Jul-Aug, fruits Jul-Sep.

Few-flowered Sedge
Carex pauciflora *(NI)

Shortly creeping, rhizomatous perennial to 25 cm. Similar to *C. microglochin*, but stems stiff, loosely tufted, forming open mat; leaves 1-2 mm wide; *female glumes 3.5-4.5 mm, lanceolate*; 3 stigmas; *fruits 5-7 mm, narrow, with persistent style* (not to be confused with bristle of *C. microglochin*). HABITAT Wet, *Sphagnum*-dominated, raised acidic blanket bogs; to 820 m. DIST. Native. Widespread in N Scotland; rare in N England, N Wales, N Ireland. (N and central Europe.) FLS May-Jun, fruits Jun-Jul.

Rock Sedge
Carex rupestris

Shortly creeping, rhizomatous, tufted perennial to 20 cm. LEAVES *1-1.5 mm wide, dark green, curled or twisted.* INFLORESCENCES 7-15 mm; female glumes 2.5-3.5 mm, ovate, dark purple-brown. FRUITS 2-3.5 mm, ovoid, grey-green to brown, ± erect at maturity. HABITAT Cliffs, ledges, crevices, on basic calcareous or mica-rich rocks; 600-935 m. DIST. Native. Very local. N Scotland. (N Europe, mts of S Europe.) FLS Jun-Jul, fruits Jul-Aug.

Flea Sedge
Carex pulicaris

Shortly creeping, rhizomatous perennial, forming dense patches. STEMS Slender, smooth, stiff, to 30 cm. LEAVES 0.5-1 mm wide. INFLORESCENCES Few-flowered terminal spike; female glumes *c.*3 mm, red-brown; 2 stigmas. FRUITS *Elliptic, dark brown, shiny* utricles, *4-6 mm*, deflexed at maturity, jumping off when touched! SIMILAR SPP. Superficially similar to *C. pauciflora*, but that species has narrower, paler fruits with a persistent style, and the ecology is quite different. HABITAT Base-rich sedge mires, damp meadows, pastures, calcareous grassland, springs, flushes, montane rock ledges; to 915 m. DIST. Native. Widespread in N and W Britain, Ireland; scarce and declining in lowland England. (N, central and W Europe.) FLS May-Jun, fruits Jun-Jul.

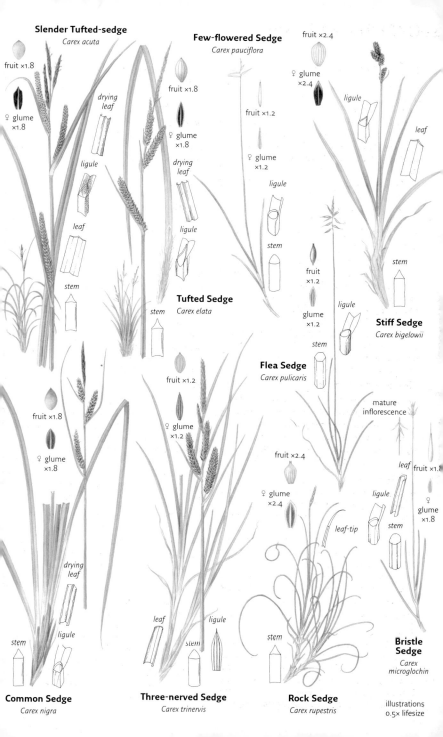

Slender Tufted-sedge
Carex acuta

fruit ×1.8

♀ glume ×1.8

drying leaf

ligule

leaf

stem

Few-flowered Sedge
Carex pauciflora

fruit ×1.8

♀ glume ×1.8

drying leaf

ligule

stem

fruit ×1.2

♀ glume ×1.2

ligule

stem

Tufted Sedge
Carex elata

fruit ×1.2

♀ glume ×1.2

leaf

stem

fruit ×2.4

♀ glume ×2.4

ligule

leaf

stem

fruit ×1.2

glume ×1.2

stem

ligule

Stiff Sedge
Carex bigelowii

Flea Sedge
Carex pulicaris

mature inflorescence

fruit ×1.8

♀ glume ×1.8

leaf

fruit ×2.4

♀ glume ×2.4

ligule

stem

leaf-tip

fruit ×1.8

♀ glume ×1.8

stem

drying leaf

ligule

stem

Common Sedge
Carex nigra

leaf

ligule

stem

Three-nerved Sedge
Carex trinervis

stem

Rock Sedge
Carex rupestris

Bristle Sedge
Carex microglochin

illustrations
0.5× lifesize

The largest family of flowering plants in Britain, with about 200 native and introduced species. Grasses are similar to the sedges, *Carex*, in that they both have long, narrow leaves that are divided into 2 parts: a basal *leaf sheath* that envelops the stem; and a free *leaf blade*. In addition, the flowers of both lack a perianth and are enclosed by 1 or 2 bracts.

Grasses	Sedges
Stems round or oval in section	Stems triangular in section
Stems hollow	Stems solid
Ligules free	Ligules fused to upper surface of leaf blade
Leaves opposite and alternate	Leaves in 3 ranks
Flowers enclosed between 2 bracts	Flowers subtended by a single bract

Grasses are annual or perennial herbs, often producing rhizomes or stolons and frequently sterile leafy shoots, *tillers*, which can produce the typical tight grass sward. The flowering stems, *culms*, are round or oval in section and hollow between the nodes (except in maize). On the inner side of the junction between the leaf sheath and leaf blade, facing the stem, is a small bract, the *ligule*, which is sometimes reduced to a ring of hairs.

The small flowers lack a perianth and consist of 3 stamens and a single 1-celled ovary with 2 feathery stigmas. The fruit is dry and 1-seeded, the typical cereal grain. The flowers are usually bisexual, each enclosed between 2 bracts, an upper *palea* and a lower *lemma*. The flower and 2 bracts together are referred as the *floret*. The florets are clustered together in *spikelets*, the whole enclosed between two sterile *glumes* at the base. Lemmas and glumes may or may not have a fine bristle, an *awn*, protruding from their tip, as in oats or barley. The number of florets in the spikelet is an important character and ranges from 1 to several. The number can usually be determined by counting the lemmas, making sure not to include the 2 glumes at the base of the spikelet.

The form of the inflorescence is extremely varied and an important character in identification. It ranges from a simple *spike*, with the unstalked spikelets attached directly to the inflorescence axis, to an open, much-branched *panicle*.

The ligules and lemmas of all the species are illustrated and should be carefully examined when identifying specimens. With experience, almost all grasses can be identified in the vegetative state without the inflorescence. Important characters include the habit of the plant; whether it is an annual or perennial, and, if perennial, whether it is tufted, tussock-forming, rhizomatous or stoloniferous; details of the ligule; hairiness of the leaf sheath and leaf blade; and whether the leaf blade is flat, channelled, rolled or bristle-like.

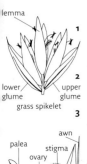

lemma

1

lower glume / upper glume

grass spikelet

awn

palea / stigma

ovary

stamen / lemma

grass floret

	if	then
1	▷ Stems woody; leaves with a distinct short petiole between sheath and the blade	**Bamboos** (p.602)
	▷ Not bamboos; stems not woody	Go to ▷ **2**
2	▷ Ligule consisting of a fringe of hairs	Go to ▷ **A**
	▷ Ligule membranous or absent	Go to ▷ **3**
3	▷ Inflorescence a single spike or a spike-like or cylindrical panicle with short pedicels, ≤2 mm:	
	▷ Spikelets in 2 rows on opposite sides of inflorescence axis	Go to ▷ **B**
	▷ Spikelets in ≥1 row on 1 side of inflorescence axis only	Go to ▷ **C**
	▷ Spikelets arranged all round inflorescence axis in a dense, cylindrical spike-like panicle	Go to ▷ **D**
	▷ Inflorescence consisting of 2 or more spikes arising close together towards top of flowering stem	Go to ▷ **E**

	if	then

> Inflorescence not spike-like, usually a branched panicle; pedicels >3 mm
  > Spikelets with only 1 fertile floret (sometimes with vestigial florets) — Go to ▷ **F**
  > Spikelets with ≥2 fertile florets — Go to ▷ **G**

A Ligule consisting of a fringe of hairs, not membranous

spike-like panicle **1**

> Inflorescence consisting of 2 or more spikes arising close together towards top of flowering stem; spikelets ± sessile — Go to ▷ **2**
> Inflorescence not like this — Go to ▷ **3**

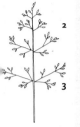

2

> Inflorescence umbel-like, all spikes arising from ± same point; plant very stoloniferous — ***Cynodon*** (p.642)
> Spikes arising from different points on upper part of stem (salt marshes) — ***Spartina*** (p.642)

3

> Large tussock-forming grass; leaves to >1 m long, with sharp, saw-like teeth along margins; Pampas-grass — ***Cortaderia*** (p.640)
> Plant not like this — Go to ▷ **4**

whorled panicle

grass inflorescences

4

> Very tall grass to 3.5 m; spikelets with tuft of long, silky hairs that become very conspicuous after flowering; Reed — ***Phragmites*** (p.640)
> Plant not reed-like — Go to ▷ **5**

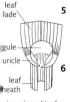

leaf blade

ligule

auricle

leaf sheath

junction of leaf blade and leaf sheath with ligule

5

> Inflorescence spike-like; pedicels with stiff, barbed bristles that project beyond spikelets (don't confuse with awns) — ***Setaria*** (p.642)
> Spikelets without barbed bristles — Go to ▷ **6**

6

> Spikelets with long, bent awns, spirally twisted in lower part — ***Stipa*** (p.602)
> Spikelets without awns — Go to ▷ **7**

7

> Tall annual; inflorescence a large, diffuse, drooping panicle; leaf sheaths densely hairy — ***Panicum*** (p.642)
> Tufted or tussock-forming perennials; leaf sheaths sparsely hairy — Go to ▷ **8**

8

> Glumes c.½ as long as spikelet — ***Molinia*** (p.640)
> Glumes about as long as spikelet — ***Danthonia*** (p.638)

B Inflorescence a single spike or a spike-like or cylindrical panicle with short pedicels, ≤2 mm; spikelets in 2 rows on opposite sides of inflorescence axis

1

> Each node on inflorescence with a single spikelet — Go to ▷ **2**
> Spikelets in groups of 2–3 at each node on inflorescence — Go to ▷ **8**

CONTINUED OVERLEAF

	if	then
2	▷ Spikelets 1-flowered, sunken in hollows in jointed inflorescence axis (salt marshes)	*Parapholis* (p.618)
	▷ Spikelets ≥2-flowered, appressed to or spreading from axis but not sunken in it	Go to ▷ **3**
3	▷ Spikelets short-stalked	*Brachypodium* (p.636)
	▷ Spikelets sessile	Go to ▷ **4**
4	▷ Spikelets with bent awn arising from back of lemma	*Gaudinia* (p.618)
	▷ Spikelets without awns or with straight awn from tip of lemma	Go to ▷ **5**
5	▷ Rhizomatous perennials	Go to ▷ **6**
	▷ Annuals without rhizomes or tillers (cereals)	Go to ▷ **7**
6	▷ Spikelets with their broader sides facing inflorescence axis; both glumes developed and lateral	*Elytrigia, Elymus* (p.636)
	▷ Spikelets laterally compressed with narrower edge facing inflorescence axis; only outside (upper) glume developed, lower glume absent	*Lolium* (p.606)
7	▷ Spikelets 3–6-flowered; glumes blunt	*Triticum* (p.638)
	▷ Spikelets 2-flowered; glumes acute	*Secale* (p.638)
8	▷ Lemmas with long awns	*Hordeum* (p.640), *Hordelymus* (p.638)
	▷ Lemmas not awned	*Leymus* (p.638)

C *Inflorescence a single spike or a spike-like or cylindrical panicle with short pedicels, ≤2 mm; spikelets in ≥1 row on 1 side of inflorescence axis only*

	if	then
1	▷ Spikelets in mixed dense clusters of 1 fertile and several sterile at each node; fertile spikelets 2–5-flowered	*Cynosurus* (p.608)
	▷ Spikelets not in mixed clusters	Go to ▷ **2**
2	▷ Densely tufted perennial; leaves tough, bristle-like; spikelets 1-flowered; lemmas with short awn (heaths, moors)	*Nardus* (p.602)
	▷ Annuals; leaves not tough or bristle-like	Go to ▷ **3**
3	▷ Lemmas awned	*Vulpia* (p.608)
	▷ Lemmas not awned	Go to ▷ **4**
4	▷ Stems slender, hair-like; spikelets 1-flowered (very rare, coastal dunes)	*Mibora* (p.628)
	▷ Stems stiff, rigid; spikelets 3–10-flowered	*Catapodium* (p.616)

	if	**then**

D Inflorescence a single spike or a spike-like or cylindrical panicle with short pedicels, ≤2 mm; spikelets arranged all round inflorescence axis in a dense, cylindrical spike-like panicle

1 ▷ Robust sand-binding grass; leaf blades tightly inrolled; inflorescence whitish; spikelets >10 mm — ***Ammophila*** (p.628)
▷ Plant not like this — Go to ▷ **2**

2 ▷ Inflorescence soft and woolly; lemma awned and with 2 apical bristles — ***Lagurus*** (p.624)
▷ Inflorescence not soft or woolly — Go to ▷ **3**

3 ▷ Pedicels with stiff, barbed bristles that project beyond spikelets (don't confuse with awns) — ***Setaria*** (p.642)
▷ Pedicels without stiff, barbed bristles — Go to ▷ **4**

4 ▷ Both glumes notched at tip, with long awns, 4–7 mm — ***Polypogon*** (p.630)
▷ Glumes without awns, or with short awns, ≤3 mm — Go to ▷ **5**

5 ▷ Glumes narrowly lanceolate; base of glumes swollen, hardened and shining — ***Gastridium*** (p.628)
▷ Base of glumes not swollen — Go to ▷ **6**

6 ▷ Lemmas blunt, with 3–5 apical teeth (limestone grassland) — ***Sesleria*** (p.616)
▷ Lemmas without 3–5 apical teeth — Go to ▷ **7**

7 ▷ Lemmas with wide, shiny edges, making inflorescence look silvery; inflorescence dense, ± parallel-sided — ***Koeleria*** (p.620)
▷ Plant not like this — Go to ▷ **8**

8 ▷ Leaf sheaths with long hairs (bearded) at junction with blade; glumes unequal, the lower shorter than spikelet — ***Anthoxanthum*** (p.624)
▷ Leaf sheaths glabrous; glumes ± equal, both about as long as spikelet — Go to ▷ **9**

9 ▷ Glumes conspicuously flattened, whitish with green keel, keel winged — ***Phalaris*** (p.624)
▷ Glumes not like this — Go to ▷ **10**

10 ▷ Lemmas awned from back, sometimes shortly so and then hardly projecting beyond tip of lemma; glumes without awns — ***Alopecurus*** (p.630)
▷ Lemmas not awned; glumes finely pointed or with short awns — ***Phleum*** (p.632)

CONTINUED OVERLEAF

if	then

E Inflorescence consisting of ≥2 spikes arising close together towards top of flowering stem

1 ▷ Spikes clustered at or near apex of flowering shoot in umbel-like inflorescence — Go to ▷ **2**

▷ Spikes arising at intervals along main axis of flowering shoot — Go to ▷ **3**

2 ▷ Ligule a fringe of hairs; stoloniferous perennials (coastal sands, SW England) — ***Cynodon*** (p.642)

▷ Ligule membranous; without stolons; annuals (arable and waste ground) — ***Digitaria*** (p.642)

3 ▷ Ligule a fringe of hairs; spikelets without awns; rhizomatous perennials (salt marshes, mud flats) — ***Spartina*** (p.642)

▷ Ligule absent; spikelets awned; annual (arable and waste ground) — ***Echinochloa*** (p.642)

F Inflorescence not spike-like, usually a branched panicle; spikelets with only 1 fertile floret (sometimes with vestigial florets)

1 ▷ Plant tall and reed-like; ligule long, 3–16 mm — ***Phalaris*** (p.624)

▷ Plant not tall or reed-like — Go to ▷ **2**

2 ▷ Glumes absent; inflorescence often remaining enclosed in upper leaf sheath; spikelets strongly flattened (very rare, wet places) — ***Leersia*** (p.602)

▷ Glumes present — Go to ▷ **3**

3 ▷ Spikelets with long, bent awns, spirally twisted in lower part — ***Stipa*** (p.602)

▷ Awns present or absent, if present then lower half not spirally twisted — Go to ▷ **4**

4 ▷ Glumes ovate, obtuse; lemma shiny, becoming much harder than glumes in fruit — ***Milium*** (p.602)

▷ Glumes lanceolate, acuminate; lemma not becoming hard in fruit — Go to ▷ **5**

5 ▷ Lemma with long, straight awns, 4–10 mm; annuals — ***Apera*** (p.630)

▷ Lemmas without awns or awns short, ≤2 mm; perennials — Go to ▷ **6**

6 ▷ Glumes *c.*½ as long as lemmas; leaf sheaths strongly compressed, leaf tip hooded — ***Catabrosa*** (p.614)

▷ Glumes about as long as lemmas; leaf sheaths rounded on back, leaf tips flat — Go to ▷ **7**

7 ▷ Glumes narrowly lanceolate, base of glumes swollen, hardened and shining — ***Gastridium*** (p.628)

▷ Base of glumes not hardened or shining — Go to ▷ **8**

	if	**then**
8	▷ Base of lemmas surrounded by a tuft of silky white hairs; hairs ⅓ as long to much longer than lemmas	*Calamagrostis* (p.628)
	▷ Lemmas minutely hairy at base or hairs absent	*Agrostis* (p.626), *Polypogon* (p.630)

G Inflorescence not spike-like, usually a branched panicle; spikelets with ≥2 florets

	if	**then**
1	▷ Spikelets not proliferating	Go to ▷ **2**
	▷ Spikelets proliferating with small plantlets	Go to ▷ **21**
2	▷ Lemmas without awns or with straight awn from tip	Go to ▷ **3**
	▷ Lemma awned from back, awn usually bent	Go to ▷ **14**
3	▷ Spikelets golden brown, broad uppermost leaf blades very short; margins of lemmas of 2 lowest florets fringed with hairs; vanilla-scented when crushed	*Hierochloe* (p.624)
	▷ Plant not like this	Go to ▷ **4**
4	▷ Spikelets crowded in dense 1-sided masses at ends of panicle branches; base of vegetative shoots markedly compressed	*Dactylis* (p.614)
	▷ Plant not like this	Go to ▷ **5**
5	▷ Spikelets compressed; lemmas keeled, not rounded on back	*Poa* (p.612)
	▷ Lemmas rounded on back	Go to ▷ **6**
6	▷ Lemmas awned or with pointed tips	Go to ▷ **7**
	▷ Lemmas not awned, with rounded tips	Go to ▷ **11**
7	▷ Basal leaves bristle-like, tightly inrolled, ± glabrous	*Festuca* (p.604)
	▷ Basal leaves flat or folded, not bristle-like	Go to ▷ **8**
8	▷ Leaf sheaths with spreading auricles at junction with blade	Go to ▷ **9**
	▷ Leaf sheaths without auricles	Go to ▷ **10**
9	▷ Leaf sheaths smooth, glabrous	*Festuca* (p.604)
	▷ Leaf sheaths softly hairy	**Bromes** (p.634)
10	▷ Lemmas pointed, without awns	*Festuca altissima* (p.604)
	▷ Lemmas awned	**Bromes** (p.634)
11	▷ Glumes almost as long as spikelets; spikelets few; leaf sheaths tubular, margins fused	*Melica* (p.618)
	▷ Glumes much shorter than spikelets; margins of leaf sheaths free	Go to ▷ **12**

CONTINUED OVERLEAF

	if	**then**
12	▷ Spikelets broadly ovate, laterally compressed, solitary, on long, slender pedicels; lemmas cordate at base	*Briza* (p.610)
	▷ Plant not like this	Go to ▷ **13**
13	▷ Leaf sheaths with margins fused; lemmas 7-nerved (wet places)	*Glyceria* (p.616)
	▷ Leaf sheaths not fused, overlapping; lemmas 5-nerved (salt marshes)	*Puccinellia* (p.610)
14	▷ Spikelets ≥10 mm long	Go to ▷ **15**
	▷ Spikelets ≤10 mm long	Go to ▷ **16**
15	▷ Awns 20-55 mm long; spikelets pendulous; annual	*Avena* (p.618)
	▷ Awns 12-22 mm long; spikelets erect or spreading; tufted perennial	*Helictotrichon* (p.618)
16	▷ Awns 10-17mm long, ovary pubescent	*Arrhenatherum* (p.618)
	▷ Awns ≤10 mm long; ovary glabrous	Go to ▷ **17**
17	▷ Small, easily uprooted annuals, 5-20 cm, without non-flowering vegetative shoots; leaves usually dead at flowering	*Aira* (p.622)
	▷ Perennials with non-flowering vegetative shoots; leaves green at flowering	Go to ▷ **18**
18	▷ Awns distinctly thickened towards tip; plant very glaucous; leaves bristle-like (rare, coastal dunes, E England)	*Corynephorus* (p.622)
	▷ Awns not thickened towards tip	Go to ▷ **19**
19	▷ Spikelets shiny; glumes glabrous	Go to ▷ **20**
	▷ Spikelets whitish or pinkish, not shiny; glumes pubescent	*Holcus* (p.622)
20	▷ Spikelets silvery to purplish; tip of lemma ± truncate, torn	*Deschampsia* (p.622)
	▷ Spikelets yellowish; tip of lemma acute, with 2 bristle points	*Trisetum* (p.620)
21	▷ Lemmas distinctly keeled on back; leaves flat	*Poa* (p.612)
	▷ Lemmas rounded on back; leaves inrolled or bristle-like	Go to ▷ **22**
22	▷ Awn arising from back of lemma; tuft of hairs at base of lemma	*Deschampsia* (p.622)
	▷ Awn absent or arising from tip of lemma; no tuft of hairs at base of lemma; leaves bristle-like	*Festuca* (p.604)

Key to Fescues *Festuca*

	if	**then**
1	▷ Leaves of vegetative shoots inrolled and bristle-like	Go to ▷ **2**
	▷ Leaves of vegetative shoots flat (or folded down middle when dry)	Go to ▷ **10**
2	▷ Leaves of flowering shoots flat, 2-4 mm wide, markedly different from inrolled leaves of vegetative shoots; awns 1.5-4.5 mm	*F. heterophylla* (p.604)
	▷ Leaves of flowering shoots inrolled or bristle-like	Go to ▷ **3**
3	▷ Young leaves with leaf sheaths fused almost to top	Go to ▷ **4**
	▷ Young leaves with leaf sheaths open for most of their length but with margins overlapping	Go to ▷ **5**, *F. ovina* group (p.606)
4	▷ Leaves stiff, inrolled (rush-like), ribs on upper surface prominent, densely and minutely hairy (coastal dunes)	*F. arenaria* (p.604)
	▷ Leaves not stiff, rush-like, ribs on upper surface not prominent (ubiquitous)	*F. rubra* (p.604)
5	▷ Inflorescence proliferating with small plantlets	*F. vivipara* (p.606)
	▷ Inflorescence not proliferating	Go to ▷ **6**
6	▷ Awns absent or <1.2 mm	Go to ▷ **7**
	▷ Awns usually >1.2 mm	Go to ▷ **9**
7	▷ Spikelets 4.7-7.2 mm; awns absent or ≤1 mm	Go to ▷ **8**
	▷ Spikelets 6-7 mm; awns 1.2-1.5 mm (rare, Channel Is)	*F. huonii* (p.606)
8	▷ Leaves usually hairy at base; spikelets ≥5.3 mm; awns 0.2-1.6 mm	*F. ovina* (p.606)
	▷ Leaves glabrous; spikelets to 5.2 mm; awns absent	*F. filiformis* (p.606)
9	▷ Leaves intensely glaucous, sheaths glabrous; awns 0.5-1.5 mm (rare)	*F. longifolia* (p.606)
	▷ Leaves not or only slightly glaucous, sheaths sparsely hairy; awns 1.2-2.5 mm	*F. brevipila* (p.606)
10	▷ Base of leaf blade with pointed auricles clasping stem at junction with leaf sheath	Go to ▷ **11**
	▷ Leaves without auricles	*F. altissima* (p.604)

CONTINUED OVERLEAF

	if	then
11	▷ Awns longer than lemmas; nodes of flowering stems dark purple	*F. gigantea* (p.604)
	▷ Awns absent or much shorter than lemmas; nodes usually green	Go to ▷ **12**
12	▷ Lowest 2 nodes of inflorescence with 2 branches, the shorter with 1–2 spikelets; auricles glabrous	*F. pratensis* (p.604)
	▷ Lowest 2 nodes of inflorescence with 2 branches; the shorter with ≥4 spikelets; margins of auricles with few scattered hairs (these soon rub off)	*F. arundinacea* (p.604)

Key to Squirrel-tail Fescues *Vulpia*

	if	then
1	▷ Inflorescence a 1-sided spike-like raceme; lemmas ≤4 mm	*V. unilateralis* (p.608)
	▷ Inflorescence a panicle, at least lower branches branched; lemmas ≥4 mm	Go to ▷ **2**
2	▷ Upper leaf sheath strongly inflated; lower glume absent or very small	*V. fasciculata* (p.608)
	▷ Upper leaf sheath not or only slightly inflated; lower glume at least ⅙ length of the upper	Go to ▷ **3**
3	▷ Lower glume ½–¾ length of upper glume; upper glume 3-nerved	*V. bromoides* (p.608)
	▷ Lower glume ⅙–⅓ length of upper glume; upper glume 1-nerved	Go to ▷ **4**
4	▷ Inflorescence curved, nodding; lemmas 5–7 mm	*V. myuros* (p.608)
	▷ Inflorescence stiffly erect; lemmas 4–5 mm	*V. ciliata* (p.608)

Key to Saltmarsh Grasses *Puccinellia*

	if	then
1	▷ Lemmas 2.8–5 mm	Go to ▷ **2**
	▷ Lemmas 1.5–2.5 mm	Go to ▷ **3**
2	▷ Perennial; plant stoloniferous, turf-forming; inflorescence rather contracted	***P. maritima*** (p.610)
	▷ Tufted, spreading or prostrate annual; inflorescence dense, branches spreading	***P. rupestris*** (p.610)
3	▷ Lower inflorescence branches deflexed; lower ¼ of basal inflorescence branches bare of spikelets	***P. distans*** (p.610)
	▷ Inflorescence branches ± erect; basal inflorescence branches with spikelets to base	***P. fasciculata*** (p.610)

Key to Meadow Grasses *Poa*

	if	then
1	▷ Plant large, densely tufted; leaves ≥5 mm wide	***P. chaixii*** (p.612)
	▷ Leaves ≤4 mm wide	Go to ▷ **2**
2	▷ Plant distinctly rhizomatous	Go to ▷ **3**
	▷ Plant without rhizomes	Go to ▷ **6**
3	▷ Flowering shoots strongly compressed, usually slightly bent at each node	***P. compressa*** (p.614)
	▷ Flowering shoots not strongly compressed, not bent except at base	Go to ▷ **4**
4	▷ Glumes distinctly unequal; sheaths glabrous at junction with blade	Go to ▷ **5**
	▷ Glumes ± equal; sheaths sparsely hairy at junction with blade; leaves bluish	***P. humilis*** (p.612)
5	▷ Flowering stems in loose or compact tufts; leaves 2–4 mm wide; spikelets 4–6 mm	***P. pratensis*** (p.612)
	▷ Flowering stems in stiff, erect, slender clusters; leaves long, narrow, 1.5–2 mm wide; spikelets 2.5–5 mm	***P. angustifolia*** (p.612)
6	▷ Base of flowering shoots swollen, bulb-like; spikelets sometimes proliferating (coastal, England)	***P. bulbosa*** (p.614)
	▷ Base of flowering shoots not swollen	Go to ▷ **7**

CONTINUED OVERLEAF

	if	then
7	▷ Base of flowering shoots surrounded by dense mass of dead, fibrous, persistent leaf sheaths (rare alpines)	Go to ▷ **8**
	▷ Base of flowering shoots not surrounded by dead leaf sheaths	Go to ▷ **9**
8	▷ Leaves 2–4.5 mm wide, tapering abruptly at tip; lower glume ⅔ length of upper; spikelets sometimes proliferating	*P. alpina* (p.614)
	▷ Leaves 1–2 mm wide, tapering gradually at tip; glumes ± equal; spikelets not proliferating	*P. flexuosa* (p.612)
9	▷ Annual (or perennial); anthers ≤1 mm; some leaves usually transversely wrinkled	Go to ▷ **10**
	▷ Perennial; anthers ≥1.3 mm; leaves not transversely wrinkled	Go to ▷ **11**
10	▷ Anthers 0.6–0.8 mm; inflorescence branches usually spreading or reflexed after flowering	*P. annua* (p.612)
	▷ Anthers 0.2–0.5 mm; inflorescence branches usually erect after flowering (coastal, S and SW England)	*P. infirma* (p.612)
11	▷ Ligule of uppermost leaf of flowering shoot 4–10 mm, acute; sheaths rough	*P. trivialis* (p.612)
	▷ Ligule of uppermost leaf ≤5 mm, blunt; sheaths smooth	Go to ▷ **12**
12	▷ Ligules 0.2–0.5 mm (shady places, lowland)	*P. nemoralis* (p.614)
	▷ Ligules 1–2.5 mm (alpine)	*P. glauca* (p.614)

Key to Sweet Grasses *Glyceria*

	if	then
1	▷ Large, erect, reed-like grass to 250 cm tall; ligule rounded, with central point; inflorescence compact, much branched; spikelets 5–12 mm	*G. maxima* (p.616)
	▷ Plant not erect or reed-like; ligule not rounded with central point; inflorescence not compact; spikelets 10–35 mm	Go to ▷ **2**

if	then
2 ▷ Tip of lemma with 3(–5) sharp teeth (don't confuse with 2 teeth at tip of palea, which project at ± same level)	***G. declinata*** (p.616)
▷ Tip of lemma not or only scarcely toothed	Go to ▷ **3**
3 ▷ Inflorescence sparsely branched, appearing whip-like; lemmas 5.5–6.5 mm	***G. fluitans*** (p.616)
▷ Inflorescence much branched, wide-spreading; lemmas 3.5–5 mm (*G. × pedicellata*, the hybrid between *G. fluitans* and *G. notata*, is intermediate between the parents, the spikelets remain intact after flowering, the anthers are indehiscent and the pollen grains are shrunken)	***G. notata*** (p.616)

Key to Canary-grasses *Phalaris*

if	then
1 ▷ Tall, rhizomatous perennials	Go to ▷ **2**
▷ Annuals; without rhizomes, not tall or reed-like	Go to ▷ **3**
2 ▷ Plant reed-like, inflorescence distinctly lobed and branched; keel on glumes not winged	***P. arundinacea*** (p.624)
▷ Inflorescence spike-like; keel on glumes distinctly winged	***P. aquatica*** (p.624)
3 ▷ Spikelets in groups of 3–7, 1 bisexual, the rest sterile	***P. paradoxa*** (p.624)
▷ Spikelets all bisexual	Go to ▷ **4**
4 ▷ Wings on keel of glumes not toothed	***P. canariensis*** (p.624)
▷ At least some glumes with minutely toothed wings on keel	***P. minor*** (p.624)

Key to Bent-grasses *Agrostis*

if	then
1 ▷ Densely tufted; basal leaves fine, bristle-like, <1 mm wide, blue-green; inflorescence narrow before and after flowering	***A. curtisii*** (p.626)
▷ Rhizomatous or stoloniferous; basal leaves flat or inrolled, >1 mm wide	Go to ▷ **2**

CONTINUED OVERLEAF

	if	then
2	▷ Palea tiny, <¼ as long as lemma	Go to ▷ **3**
	▷ Palea *c*.½ as long as lemma	Go to ▷ **4**
3	▷ Plant rhizomatous, stolons absent	*A. vinealis* (p.626)
	▷ Plant stoloniferous, with tufts of leaves at nodes	*A. canina* (p.626)
4	▷ Ligules of tillers shorter than wide; awns absent	*A. capillaris* (p.626)
	▷ Ligules of tillers as long as or longer than wide; awns absent or present	Go to ▷ **5**
5	▷ Plant stoloniferous, rhizomes absent; inflorescence contracted after flowering; awns absent	*A. stolonifera* (p.626)
	▷ Plant rhizomatous; inflorescence contracted or not after flowering; awns absent or present	Go to ▷ **6**
6	▷ Plant blue-green; inflorescence contracted after flowering; ligules ≤3 mm; with or without awns	*A. castellana* (p.626)
	▷ Plant not blue-green; inflorescence open at fruiting; ligules 1.5–12 mm; awns absent	*A. gigantea* (p.626)

Key to Small-reeds *Calamagrostis*

	if	then
1	▷ Hairs at base of lemma at least as long as lemma	Go to ▷ **2**
	▷ Hairs at base of lemma shorter than lemma	Go to ▷ **4**
2	▷ Flowering stems with 2–5 nodes; ligules 2–9 mm	Go to ▷ **3**
	▷ Flowering stems with 5–8 nodes; ligules 7–10 mm	*C. purpurea* (p.628)
3	▷ Upper surface of leaf not hairy, rough; ligules 4–9 mm; basal hairs of lemma >1½× as long as lemma	*C. epigejos* (p.628)
	▷ Upper surface of leaf hairy; ligules 2–6 mm; basal hairs of lemma ≤1½× as long as lemma	*C. canescens* (p.628)
4	▷ Glumes 3–4 mm	*C. stricta* (p.628)
	▷ Glumes 4.5–6 mm	*C. scotica* (p.628)

Key to Foxtails *Alopecurus*

	if	then
1	▷ Awns ≥2× as long as lemma	Go to ▷ **2**
	▷ Awns absent or scarcely longer than lemma	Go to ▷ **5**
2	▷ Annual; base of glumes fused for ⅓–½ their length (arable weed)	***A. myosuroides*** (p.632)
	▷ Perennial; glumes free almost to base	Go to ▷ **3**
3	▷ Base of stems swollen and bulbous (dry salt marshes)	***A. bulbosus*** (p.630)
	▷ Stems not swollen at base	Go to ▷ **4**
4	▷ Glumes acute	***A. pratensis*** (p.630)
	▷ Glumes obtuse (wet places)	***A. geniculatus*** (p.630)
5	▷ Inflorescence narrow, cylindrical, not silky-hairy (wet places)	***A. aequalis*** (p.632)
	▷ Inflorescence broadly cylindrical, silky-hairy (rare alpine)	***A. borealis*** (p.632)

Key to Cat's-tails *Phleum*

	if	then
1	▷ Small sand-dune annual; glumes gradually tapered to fine, sharp point	***P. arenarium*** (p.632)
	▷ Perennial; tip of glumes blunt, abruptly narrowed to the awn	Go to ▷ **2**
2	▷ Inflorescence narrowly cylindrical; awns of glumes ≤2 mm	Go to ▷ **3**
	▷ Inflorescence broadly cylindrical, 2–3× as long as wide; awns of glumes 2–3 mm (mountains, England and Scotland)	***P. alpinum*** (p.632)
3	▷ Tips of glumes truncate (and shortly awned); flowering stems usually swollen at base; ligules ≤6 mm (*see* main text)	***P. pratense, P. bertolonii*** (p.632)
	▷ Tips of glumes rounded (and shortly awned); flowering stems not swollen at base; ligules ≤2 mm (E England)	***P. phleoides*** (p.632)

	if	then
1	▷ Lower glume 3-5-nerved, upper glume 5-7-nerved	Go to ▷ **2**
	▷ Lower glume 1-nerved, upper glume 3-5-nerved	Go to ▷ **3**
2	▷ Annual; spikelets not strongly compressed, ± ovoid	Go to ▷ **4**, *Bromus*
	▷ Perennial; spikelets strongly compressed, lanceolate	*Ceratochloa carinata* (p.636)
3	▷ Annual; spikelets conspicuously wider towards top; awn longer than lemma	Go to ▷ **8**, *Anisantha*
	▷ Perennial; spikelets not conspicuously wider towards top; awn shorter than lemma or absent	Go to ▷ **11**, *Bromopsis*
4	▷ Lemmas wrapped tightly around seed so margins not overlapping those of lemma above; lower leaf sheaths ± glabrous	*Bromus secalinus* (p.634)
	▷ Lemmas not wrapped tightly around seed; lower leaf sheaths softly hairy	Go to ▷ **5**
5	▷ Inflorescence short, erect; at least some pedicels shorter than spikelet; ligules hairy	Go to ▷ **6**
	▷ Inflorescence long, nodding; most pedicels longer than spikelet; ligules glabrous	Go to ▷ **7**
6	▷ Lemma 8-11 mm, blunt	*Bromus hordeaceus* (p.634)
	▷ Lemma 5.5-6.5 mm, 2-toothed at tip	*Bromus lepidus* (p.634)
7	▷ Lemmas 6.5-8 mm; spikelets 10-16 mm	*Bromus racemosus* (p.634)
	▷ Lemmas 8-11 mm; spikelets 15-28 mm	*Bromus commutatus* (p.634)
8	▷ Lemmas 10-20 mm	Go to ▷ **9**
	▷ Lemmas 20-35 mm	Go to ▷ **10**
9	▷ Inflorescence branches spreading or pendent	*A. sterilis* (p.636)
	▷ Inflorescence branches stiffly erect	*A. madritensis* (p.636)
10	▷ Inflorescence branches spreading or pendent; spikelets 7-9 cm (including awns)	*A. diandra* (p.636)
	▷ Inflorescence branches erect; spikelets 2.5-3.5 cm	*A. rigida* (p.636)
11	▷ Leaf sheaths with pointed auricles at junction with blade; inflorescence branches pendent	Go to ▷ **12**
	▷ Leaf sheaths with or without short, rounded auricles; inflorescence branches ± erect	Go to ▷ **13**
12	▷ Lower inflorescence node with 2 branches, each with ≥5 spikelets; upper sheaths hairy	*Bromopsis ramosa* (p.634)
	▷ Lower inflorescence node with 3-5 branches, shortest with 1 spikelet; upper sheaths ± glabrous	*Bromopsis benekenii* (p.634)
13	▷ Leaves of vegetative shoots rolled, 2-3 mm wide, hairy; awns 3-8 mm	*Bromopsis erecta* (p.634)
	▷ Leaves of vegetative shoots flat, 9 mm wide, ± glabrous; awns absent or ≤3 mm	*Bromopsis inermis* (p.634)

Key to Barleys *Hordeum* and *Hordelymus*

	if	then
1	▷ Only central spikelet in each triplet bisexual, lateral spikelets either male or sterile	Go to ▷ **2, wild barleys**
	▷ All 3 spikelets in each triplet bisexual	Go to ▷ **5, cultivated barleys, Hordelymus**
2	▷ Glumes of lateral spikelets long, awn-like, >30 mm; awns of central lemmas >50 mm, purplish	*Hordeum jubatum* (p.640)
	▷ Glumes of lateral spikelets <30 mm; awns of central lemmas <50 mm	Go to ▷ **3**
3	▷ Perennial with tillers; sheath of upper leaf not inflated	*Hordeum secalinum* (p.640)
	▷ Non-tillering annuals; sheath of upper leaf ± inflated	Go to ▷ **4**
4	▷ Glumes of middle spikelets with marginal hairs	*Hordeum murinum* (p.640)
	▷ Glumes of middle spikelets rough, without marginal hairs	*Hordeum marinum* (p.640)
5	▷ Inflorescence not breaking up at maturity; awns usually 100-200 cm	*Hordeum distichon* (p.640)
	▷ Inflorescence breaking up at maturity; awns 15-25 mm	*Hordelymus europaeus* (p.638)

Key to Couch-grasses & Lyme-grass *Elymus, Elytrigia, Leymus*

	if	then
1	▷ Spikelets solitary at each node on inflorescence axis	Go to ▷ **2**
	▷ Spikelets in pairs at each node on inflorescence axis	*Leymus* (p.638)
2	▷ Plant tufted; some nodes on flowering stems finely pubescent; awns 7-20 mm, usually flexuous	*Elymus* (p.636)
	▷ Plants rhizomatous; nodes glabrous; awns, if present, <10 mm, stiff	Go to ▷ **3**
3	▷ Leaves flat, green, with scattered long hairs on upper surface, ribs obscure	*Elytrigia repens* (p.638)
	▷ Leaves inrolled when dry, blue-green, without scattered long hairs, ribs prominent	Go to ▷ **4**
4	▷ Spikelets closely overlapping; ribs on upper surface of leaves glabrous (coastal)	*Elytrigia atherica* (p.638)
	▷ Spikelets spaced ± their own length apart, not overlapping; ribs densely, shortly hairy (sandy shores)	*Elytrigia juncea* (p.638)

POACEAE (GRAMINEAE) Grasses

Broad-leaved Bamboo   *Sasa palmata*

Has the broadest leaves of our naturalised bamboos. STEMS 2–3 m, woody, smooth; mid-stem *nodes with 1 lateral branch*. LEAVES *12–30 × 3.5–9 cm, 5–13 veins on either side of midrib, sheaths glabrous*; bright shining green, midrib yellow, 'petioles' greenish yellow. INFLORESCENCES Panicle. HABITAT Damp woodlands, stream banks. DIST. Introduced (native of Japan). Widely cultivated and naturalised N to central Scotland.

Arrow Bamboo   *Pseudosasa japonica*

Clump-forming plant, the commonest bamboo grown in gardens. STEMS 2–5 m, woody, smooth; mid-stem nodes with 1 lateral branch. LEAVES *15–35 × 2–5 cm, 5–9 veins on either side of midrib; sheaths densely, roughly hairy*. INFLORESCENCES Panicle. HABITAT Old gardens, woodland stream sides. DIST. Introduced (native of Japan, Korea). Frequently naturalised in S England, SW Wales.

Cut-grass   *Leersia oryzoides* EN *(B)

Erect or ascending perennial to 120 cm. STEMS Nodes hairy. LEAVES *Yellowish green, flat, finely pointed, rough, margins minutely spiny, 8–30 × 5–10 mm,* spreading at ± 90° from stem; ligules 0.5–1.5 mm. INFLORESCENCES *Panicles, ± enclosed in upper leaf sheaths*, branches very fine, wavy when exserted; spikelets on 1 side of panicle branches, 1-flowered. HABITAT Margins of grazing-marsh dykes, lakes, ponds and rivers. DIST. Native. Very rare.4 sites only, W Sussex Levels, Surrey. (S and central Europe.) FLS Aug–Oct, but in many years inflorescence doesn't emerge from leaf sheath.

Mat Grass   *Nardus stricta*

Wiry, densely tufted perennial, with shoots closely packed at base. STEMS Erect, slender, to 40 cm. LEAVES Tightly rolled, bristle-like, stiff. INFLORESCENCES *1-sided spike*, green or purplish, 3–8 cm spikelets 1-flowered. HABITAT Acid, infertile peaty soils, moorland, hill grassland, lowland heaths mires; to 1250 m. Increases with overgrazing. DIST Native. Abundant throughout upland Britain; local in S and E Britain, Ireland. (All Europe.) FLS Jun–Aug

Common Feather-grass   *Stipa pennata*

Tufted perennial to 40 cm. LEAVES Channelled glabrous and smooth beneath, ribbed on upper surface. INFLORESCENCES Panicle, to 10 cm; *spikelets 1-flowered; lemmas 15–20 mm, with extremely long feathery awns, 20–28 cm.* HABITAT Dry calcareous grassland. DIST. *Not BI.* (S and central Europe.) FLS May–Jun.

Wood Millet   *Milium effusum*

Loosely tufted, glabrous perennial to 180 cm. LEAVES 5–15 mm wide, sheaths smooth; *ligules 3–10 mm* INFLORESCENCES *Open whorled panicle; spikelets 3–4 mm, pale green, 1-flowered; glumes ± equal, 3-veined* HABITAT Damp, shaded deciduous woodlands on calcareous to mildly acid clays and loams; lowland to 389 m. DIST. Native. Widespread in most of BI, but rare in N Scotland, Ireland. (Most of Europe.) FL May–Jul.

Early Millet   *Milium vernale*

Glabrous annual to 10 cm. STEMS Culms procumbent LEAVES Lower leaves 1.5–3 mm wide; sheaths purplish, margins rough; ligules 2–4 mm, acute. INFLORESCENCES *Narrow panicle,* 1–4 cm; spikelets 2.5–3.5 mm, pale green to purplish, 1-flowered. HABITAT Fixed sand-dunes, cliff turf. DIST. Native. Very rare Guernsey (Channel Is). (W and S Europe.) FL Apr–May.

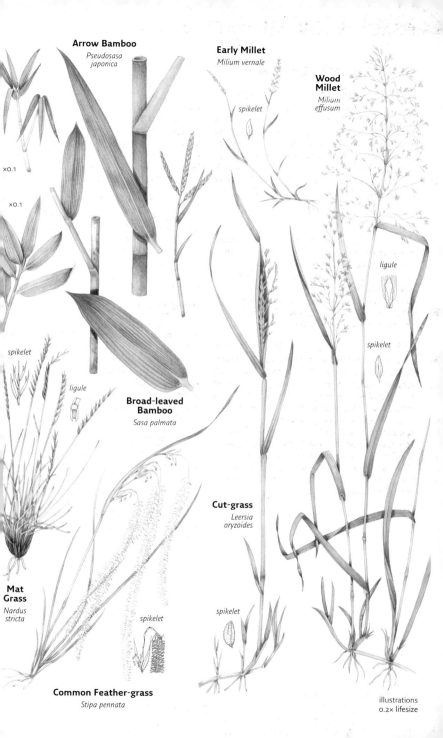

Arrow Bamboo
Pseudosasa japonica

Early Millet
Milium vernale

spikelet

Wood Millet
Milium effusum

×0.1

×0.1

ligule

spikelet

spikelet

Broad-leaved Bamboo
Sasa palmata

ligule

Cut-grass
Leersia oryzoides

Mat Grass
Nardus stricta

spikelet

Common Feather-grass
Stipa pennata

spikelet

illustrations
0.2× lifesize

Fescues *Festuca*

An important group of perennial grasses, some of which are the ecological dominants of some kinds of grassland (*see* key on p.593). The spikelets consist of 3 or more florets; glumes ± equal, shorter than the spikelet; lemmas 5–7-nerved, awned or with pointed tip. The ovary is glabrous or hairy at the top. Fescues of the *Festuca ovina* group are very difficult to differentiate and accurate identification sometimes requires microscopic examination of the leaf sections.

Meadow Fescue
Festuca pratensis

Erect, glabrous perennial to 80 cm. LEAVES 3–8 mm wide; auricles small, spreading, glabrous; ligules *c*.1 mm. INFLORESCENCES *Lowest panicle nodes with 2 branches, the shorter with 1–2 spikelets*; spikelets 10–11 mm, 5–14-flowered; lemmas 6–7 mm, *without awns*. HABITAT Meadows, pastures, water meadows, on fertile soils. DIST. Native. Throughout BI, but rare in N Scotland. May be decreasing. (Most of Europe.) FLS Jul–Aug.

Tall Fescue
Festuca arundinacea

Tall, robust, sometimes tussock-forming perennial to 200 cm. LEAVES Tough, 3–12 mm wide, sheaths whitish; *auricles large, with sparse hairs on margins* (often get rubbed off); ligules to 2 mm. INFLORESCENCES *Lowest panicle nodes with 2 branches, the shorter with ≥4 spikelets*; spikelets 10–18 mm, 3–10-flowered; lemmas 6–10 mm, awnless or with awns to 3.5 mm. HABITAT Rough grassland, hedge banks, roadsides, sea walls, brackish grassland, on fertile soils. DIST. Native. Throughout BI, but rare in N Scotland. (Most of Europe.) FLS Jun–Aug.

Giant Fescue
Festuca gigantea

Tall, robust, erect, *glabrous* perennial to 150 cm. STEMS *Nodes purple*. LEAVES 6–18 mm wide; *auricles large, strongly clasping, reddish*; ligules 2.5 mm. INFLORESCENCES Spikelets 8–20 mm, 3–10-flowered; lemmas 6–9 mm, with *long awns*, 10–18 mm. HABITAT Damp woodland, shaded stream sides, on neutral to base-rich soils; to 370 m. DIST. Native. Throughout BI, but rare in N Scotland. (Most of Europe except extreme N.) FLS Jul–Aug.

Wood Fescue
Festuca altissim

Tall, erect, glabrous, tufted perennial to 120 cm. STEMS *Bases clothed with pale, scale-like sheaths*. LEAVES 4–14 mm wide, *without auricles*; ligules t 5 mm. INFLORESCENCES Spikelets rather smal 5–8 mm, 2–5-flowered; lemmas 4–6 mm, *awnless*. HABITAT Damp, steep-sided wooded valleys, rock woodland, shaded stream sides. DIST. Native Rather local. Scattered throughout N and W Britain N Ireland. (N and central Europe.) FLS May–Jul.

Red Fescue
Festuca rubr

Densely tufted or rhizomatous perennial. Extremel variable, with 7 subspecies currently named. STEM Flowering stems erect, to 100 cm. LEAVES *Those non-flowering shoots bristle-like or tightly inrolled, lea sheaths fused almost to tip; culm leaves ± flat, 0.5* 3 mm wide; ligules very short; auricles absent. INFLO RESCENCES Spikelets 5–14 mm, 3–12-flowered; *lem mas 4–6 mm, awns 0.5–3 mm*. HABITAT All kinds grassy habitats; 0–1080 m. DIST. Native. Ubiquitou throughout BI. (All Europe.) FLS Jun–Aug.

Various-leaved Fescue
Festuca heterophyll

Tall, *densely tufted perennial*, without *rhizomes, t 100 cm*. LEAVES *Those of non-flowering shoots bristle like; culm leaves flat, 2–4 mm, with short hairs o nerves above*; ligules 0.3–0.5 mm, auricles absen INFLORESCENCES Spikelets 7–14 mm, 3–9-flowerec lemmas with shortly awns, 1.5–4.5 mm. HABITA Naturalised in woods, wood borders, on light soils DIST. Introduced. Very scattered throughout Britain rare in Ireland. (Central and S Europe.) FLS Jun–Ju

Rush-leaved Fescue
Festuca arenar

Extensively creeping, rhizomatous maritime perenni to 90 cm. LEAVES Stiff, flat or inrolled (rush-like); 5– *veins on upper surface, prominent, densely an minutely hairy*; auricles absent; sheaths fused almos to tip. INFLORESCENCES Spikelets 10–18 mm, 4–12 flowered; *lemmas 6–10 mm, softly and densely hair* awns short or absent. DIST. Native. Scattered aroun coast of BI except N Scotland, Ireland. HABITA Mobile sand-dunes, bare sandy shingle. (Coasts c W Europe, Baltic.) FLS Jun–Jul.

Tall Fescue
Festuca arundinacea

Meadow Fescue
Festuca pratensis

Rush-leaved Fescue
Festuca arenaria

Giant Fescue
Festuca gigantea

ligule

ligule

lemma

spikelet

spikelet

lemma

lemma

spikelet

spikelet

spikelet

ma

gule

spikelet

ligule

spikelet

kelet

Various-leaved Fescue

Festuca heterophylla

Wood Fescue
Festuca altissima

Red Fescue
Festuca rubra

illustrations
0.1× lifesize

The first 6 species below are all closely related and some are very variable. Certain identification sometimes has to rely on microscopic examination of leaf sections, so it is important that any of the less common species are checked by an expert.

Sheep's Fescue
Festuca ovina

Densely tufted perennial without rhizomes, to 60 cm. Extremely variable, with a number of subspecies and varieties characteristic of different habitats. LEAVES *All bristle-like, often hairy at base*, sheaths not fused; ligules very short. INFLORESCENCES Erect narrow, 1.5–8 cm; spikelets 5–7 mm, 2–9-flowered; lemmas >3.2 mm, with *short awns, 0.2–1.6 mm*. HABITAT Common and sometimes dominant on all kinds of short, well-drained calcareous or basic infertile grassland; 0–1305 m. DIST. Native. Throughout BI. (N and central Europe.) FLS May–Jul.

Viviparous Sheep's Fescue
Festuca vivipara

Similar to *F. ovina*, but *spikelets proliferating to produce* short, tufted, leafy shoots. HABITAT Wide range of rocky grassland habitats, mountain slopes, dry parts of bogs, on acid and base-rich soils; 0–1215 m. DIST. Native. Widespread in upland areas of BI; common in central and N Scotland. (Arctic and NE Europe.) FLS May–Jul.

Fine-leaved Sheep's Fescue
Festuca filiformis

Densely tufted perennial. Similar to *F. ovina*, but *leaves generally appear longer and finer, 4–10 cm long × 0.3–0.5 mm* wide, glabrous; lemmas <3.5 mm, *awnless*. HABITAT Grassy heaths, moors, on well-drained, sandy acid soils; to 1035 m. DIST. Native. Scattered throughout BI, but rare in central and S Ireland. (W and central Europe.) FLS May–Jun.

Huon's Fescue
Festuca huonii

Densely tufted perennial to 18 cm. Similar to *F. ovina*, but *leaves 0.4–0.7 mm wide*, slightly glaucous; inflorescence a dense panicle, 2.3–4.3 cm; *9–19 spikelets*, 6–7.5 mm, 3–5-flowered; *lemmas with awns, >1 mm*. HABITAT Grassy cliff tops on acid rocks. DIST. Native. Very rare, in Channel Is only. (Brittany.) FLS Jun–Aug. *Not illustrated.*

Blue Fescue
Festuca longifolia

Intensely glaucous, densely tufted, glabrous perennial to 30 cm. LEAVES 2–12 cm × 0.5–0.9 mm. INFLORESCENCES Erect, dense panicle, 2.5–8 cm; spikelets 5.4–7 mm, 3–6-flowered; *pedicels 0.5–1.8 mm; awns to 2.5 mm*. HABITAT/DIST. Native. Very local. Dry rabbit-grazed heath, sandy roadsides in E England, maritime-cliff grassland in S Devon, Channel Is. (W France.) FLS May–Jun.

Hard Fescue
Festuca brevipila

Erect, tufted perennial to 45 cm. LEAVES 0.6–1 mm wide, slightly glaucous. INFLORESCENCES 3.5–9.5 cm *pedicels 1.2–2.8 mm*, spikelets 6.1–8.5 mm, *awns 1.2–2.6 mm*. HABITAT Naturalised on roadsides, commons, amenity grasslands, on well-drained acid soils DIST. Introduced in grass-seed mixes. Scattered in lowland England. (Central Europe.) FLS May–Jun. *Not illustrated.*

Perennial Rye Grass
Lolium perenne

Loosely tufted, freely tillering perennial to 90 cm. The most valuable agricultural pasture grass. LEAVES 2–6 mm wide, folded when young; bright glossy green beneath, with prominent midrib; *base of sheaths red*; ligules to 2 mm, auricled. INFLORESCENCES *Spike*, to 30 cm; spikelets 7–20 mm, sessile 4–14-flowered; upper glume persistent, shorter than spikelet; *lemmas awnless*. HABITAT Improved lowland pasture, hay meadows, downland, amenity grassland, road verges, on fertile base-rich soils; to 570 m. DIST. Native. Ubiquitous throughout BI. (All Europe except Arctic.) FLS May–Aug.

Italian Rye Grass
Lolium multiflorum

Similar to *L. perenne*, but annual or biennial, without tillers at flowering; leaves rolled, not folded along long axis when young; *lemmas awned*. HABITAT Field margins, farm tracks, roadsides. Seldom persists DIST. Introduced. Scattered throughout BI, usually as casual escape from agriculture. (Possibly native to S Europe.) FLS Jun–Aug.

Blue Fescue
Festuca longifolia

Viviparous Sheep's Fescue
Festuca vivipara

×0.6

Italian Rye Grass
Lolium multiflorum

spikelet

lemma

spikelet

spikelet

Sheep's Fescue
Festuca ovina

auricle

Fine-leaved Sheep's Fescue
Festuca filiformis

Perennial Rye Grass
Lolium perenne

illustrations
0.3× lifesize

Squirrel-tail fescues *Vulpia*

Glabrous tufted or solitary annuals, with short, inrolled leaves when dry (*see* key on p.594). Slender, 1-sided inflorescences; spikelets with 2 to many flowers; glumes very unequal in length; lemmas 3-5-veined, with long, rough awns.

Dune Fescue   *Vulpia fasciculata*

STEMS Flowering stems to 20 cm. LEAVES *Upper leaf sheaths much inflated.* INFLORESCENCES 2-12 cm, stiff, erect, green-purplish, turning orange-brown; spikelets 12-16 mm, excluding awn; *glumes very unequal, lower minute, 0.2-1.6 mm, upper 10-14 mm*; lemmas long, 8-18 mm, 3-5-veined, awns 25 mm. HABITAT Sand-dunes, sandy shingle. DIST. Native. Coasts of England and Wales N to Norfolk and More-combe Bay, SE Ireland, Channel Is. (W Europe, Mediterranean.) FLS May-Jun.

Squirrel-tail Fescue   *Vulpia bromoides*

STEMS Flowering stems to 60 cm. LEAVES Upper sheath not inflated, ending well below inflorescence. INFLORESCENCES 1-10 cm, green-purplish, becoming straw-coloured; spikelets 7-14 mm; *upper glume, 6-10 mm, ≤2× as long as lower, 2.5-5 mm*; lemmas 5-7 mm, awns to 13 mm. HABITAT Open grassland, dunes, heaths, clifftops, on well-drained sandy soils. DIST. Native. Throughout BI, but commoner in S. (SW and central Europe.) FLS May-Jul.

Rat's-tail Fescue   *Vulpia myuros*

STEMS Flowering stems to 70 cm, densely tufted or solitary. LEAVES *Upper leaf sheath reaching base of inflorescence.* INFLORESCENCES 5-30 cm, *slender, interrupted, nodding*; spikelets 7-10 mm; *upper glume 3-8 mm, 3-4× as long as lower, 1-3.5 mm*; lemmas 5-7 mm, awns 15 mm. HABITAT Urban weed; also occasionally weed of cultivation. DIST. Native. Archaeophyte. Throughout BI, but frequent only in England, Wales. (W, central and S Europe.) FLS May-Jul.

Bearded Fescue   *Vulpia ciliata*

STEMS Flowering stems slender, to 30 cm. LEAVES Upper leaf sheath reaching base of inflorescence.

INFLORESCENCES 3-13 cm, purplish pink when mature, erect, narrow; spikelets 5-10.5 mm; *glumes very unequal, much shorter than lowest lemma; lower glume 0.2-1 mm, upper 2-3 mm; lemmas 4-8 mm*, awns to 10 mm. HABITAT Coastal dunes, sandy heaths, tracksides. DIST. Native. Very local. E, SE and S England; rare elsewhere. (Belgium, N France.) FLS May-Jun.

Mat-grass Fescue   *Vulpia unilateralis*

STEMS *Flowering stems slender*, to 40 cm. INFLORESCENCES *Spike-like*, 1-5 cm, green or purplish, *very 1-sided*; spikelets 4-7 mm, *compressed*; glumes unequal, upper 2× as long as lower, shorter than lemmas; lemmas 2.5-5 mm, awns 1-6 mm; 3 anthers protruding at flowering (other *Vulpia* have only 1 which remains enclosed). HABITAT Bare ground waste places, walls, banks, on calcareous soils. DIST. Introduced. Very scattered. Lowland England. (S and W Europe.) FLS May-Jul.

Crested Dog's-tail   *Cynosurus cristatus*

Tufted, erect, glabrous perennial to 75 cm. LEAVES 1-4 mm wide, bright glossy green with prominent midrib below, closely ribbed above, sheaths straw coloured (cf. *Lolium perenne*; p.606). INFLORESCENCES *Spike-like, stiff, 1-sided*, 1-14 cm; *spikelet sessile, of 2 kinds*, fertile and sterile mixed, sterile with rigid lemmas; lemmas with short awn. HABITAT All kinds of short or grazed grassland on neutral or base-rich soils; lowland to 660 m. DIST. Native. Common and widespread throughout BI. (All Europe except extreme N.) FLS Jun-Aug.

Rough Dog's-tail   *Cynosurus echinatus*

Tufted or solitary, glabrous annual to 100 cm. LEAVES 3-10 mm wide, upper sheaths inflated. INFLORESCENCES 1-8 cm, *dense, erect, ovoid, shining, prickly-looking*; sterile spikelets 7-13 mm, *with bristle-like glumes* and long, pointed lemmas; fertile spikelets with long, straight awns, 6-16 mm. HABITAT Open sandy ground. DIST. Introduced. Naturalised in S England, Channel Is, Scilly Is; rare casual elsewhere. (S Europe.) FLS Jun-Jul.

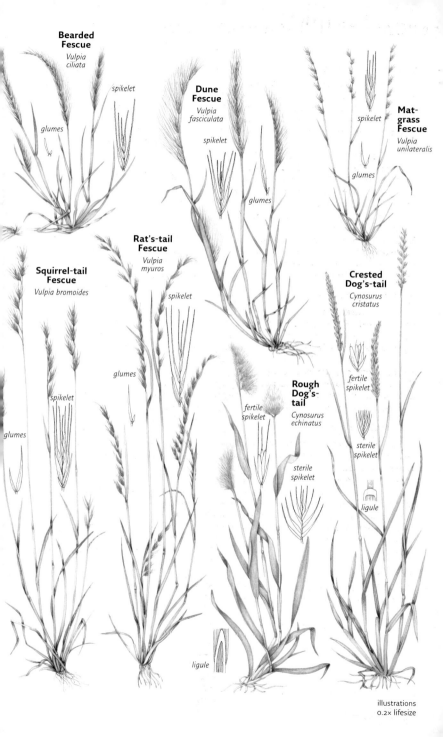

Bearded Fescue

Vulpia ciliata

spikelet

glumes

Dune Fescue

Vulpia fasciculata

spikelet

glumes

spikelet

Mat-grass Fescue

Vulpia unilateralis

glumes

Squirrel-tail Fescue

Vulpia bromoides

Rat's-tail Fescue

Vulpia myuros

spikelet

glumes

glumes

spikelet

Crested Dog's-tail

Cynosurus cristatus

fertile spikelet

sterile spikelet

ligule

fertile spikelet

Rough Dog's-tail

Cynosurus echinatus

sterile spikelet

ligule

illustrations 0.2× lifesize

Saltmarsh grasses *Puccinellia*

Annual or perennial maritime grasses, all without rhizomes but some with stolons (*see* key on p.595). Leaves glabrous, grey-green, folded in shoot, with hooded tips. Inflorescence a panicle; spikelets with 2 to many flowers; glumes unequal, shorter than 1st floret; lemmas rounded on back, 5-veined, without awns.

Common Saltmarsh Grass   *Puccinellia maritima*

Tufted, stoloniferous, turf-forming perennial to 40 cm, rooting at nodes. STEMS Prostrate to erect. LEAVES 1-3 mm wide, ligules 1-3 mm. INFLORESCENCES *Erect, branches contracted, 2-3 at each node; lemmas 2.8-5 mm, longer than glumes.* HABITAT Often the dominant plant of upper and middle levels of salt marshes, margins of tidal rivers. DIST. Native. All around coasts of BI. (Coasts of W Europe.) FLS Jun-Jul.

Reflexed Saltmarsh Grass   *Puccinellia distans*

Has 2 subspecies: ssp. *distans* and ssp. *borealis*. Similar to *P. maritima*, but not stoloniferous; flowering stems prostrate to erect, to 60 cm; leaves flat in ssp. *distans*, folded in ssp. *borealis; panicle branches long, 4-6 at each node, basal regions bare of spikelets,* erect before flowering, *becoming spreading or deflexed,* strongly reflexed at maturity in ssp. *distans,* panicles dense in ssp. *borealis;* spikelets 3-9 mm; lemmas 1.5-2.8 mm. HABITAT Ssp. *distans* on bare muddy areas close to sea, upper parts of salt marshes, sea walls, brackish grassland (especially where compacted); also spreading rapidly along salted roadsides inland. Ssp. *borealis* on rocks, boulders on rocky shores, sea walls. DIST. Native. Ssp. *distans* on most coasts of BI, especially E and S; rare in W Scotland, W Ireland. (Most of Europe.) Ssp. *borealis* on E coast of Scotland N to Shetland. (N and W Europe.) FLS Jun-Aug.

Borrer's Saltmarsh
Grass   *Puccinellia fasciculata* VU. *(R)

Tufted perennial. STEMS *Flowering stems erect or spreading,* to 60 cm. INFLORESCENCES Erect; *branches stiff, ascending, with numerous whitish-green spikelets to base; spikelets 3-6 mm, densely clustered; lemmas 1.7-2.3 mm.* HABITAT Bare, saline, compacted muddy places close to sea, brackish marshes, sea walls. DIST. Native. Rather local, possibly decreasing. E and S coasts of England; rare in E Ireland. (Coasts of W Europe.) FLS Jun-Sep.

Stiff Saltmarsh Grass   *Puccinellia rupestris*

Tufted, spreading or prostrate annual to 40 cm. LEAVES Hooded, sheaths inflated. INFLORESCENCES *2-8 cm, dense, branches stiff,* spreading, pedicels very short; spikelets 5-9 mm, crowded on one side of branches; lemmas 2.8-4 mm, longer than glumes. HABITAT Bare, compacted, saline mud, brackish marshes, tracks, muddy shingle, behind sea walls. DIST. Native. Local, declining. E, S and SW England. (Coasts of W Europe.) FLS May-Aug.

Quaking grasses *Briza*

Annual or perennial grasses. Inflorescence a panicle of characteristically flattened, oval, pendulous, many-flowered spikelets on long, slender stalks that 'quake' in the breeze.

Quaking Grass   *Briza media*

Loosely tufted, shortly rhizomatous, tillering perennial. STEMS Flowering stems erect, 15-75 cm. LEAVES 2-4 mm wide, glabrous; *ligules 0.5-1.5 mm.* INFLORESCENCES Spreading, pedicels 5-10 mm hair-like; *spikelets 4-7 × 4-7 mm, drooping, 4-12-flowered, purplish;* lemmas 3.5-4 mm, cordate at base, overlapping. HABITAT Characteristic species of unimproved, species-rich, grazed calcareous grassland; also fens, old meadows, pastures. DIST. Native. Throughout BI, but rare in N Scotland. (Most of Europe except Arctic.) FLS Jun-Aug.

Lesser Quaking Grass   *Briza minor*

Loosely tufted, non-tillering annual. Similar to *B. media,* but leaves 2-10 mm wide; *ligules longer 3-6 mm; spikelets smaller, 2.5-5 × 3-5 mm, pale green >20 per inflorescence.* HABITAT Arable weed of light sandy soils, including bulb fields. DIST. Archaeophyte. SW England, Channel Is, Scilly Is; casual elsewhere. (S and W Europe.) FLS Mar-Sep.

Greater Quaking Grass   *Briza maxima*

Loosely tufted, non-tillering annual to 60 cm. Similar to *B. media,* but leaves 3-8 mm wide; ligule 2-5 mm, with blunt, torn tip; *1-12 spikelets per inflorescence, 14-25 × 8-15 mm.* HABITAT Field margins, sand-dunes, bulb fields, waste ground, wall tops. DIST. Introduced. Commonly cultivated, and naturalised in SW England, Channel Is, Scilly Is; casual elsewhere. (Mediterranean.) FLS May-Jul.

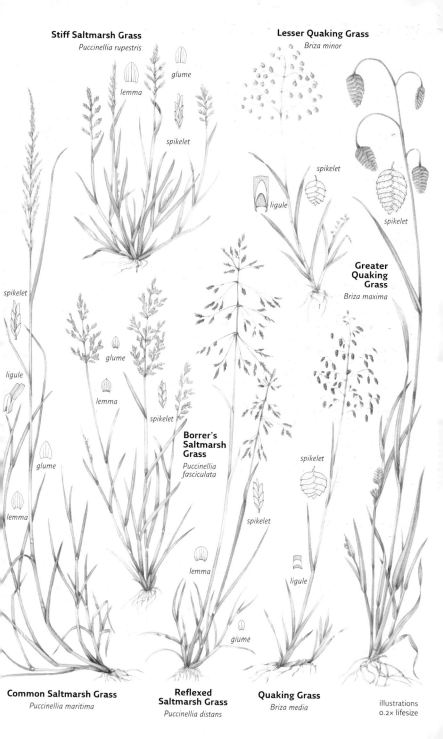

Stiff Saltmarsh Grass
Puccinellia rupestris

glume

lemma

spikelet

Lesser Quaking Grass
Briza minor

spikelet

ligule

Greater Quaking Grass
Briza maxima

spikelet

spikelet

ligule

glume

lemma

spikelet

Borrer's Saltmarsh Grass
Puccinellia fasciculata

spikelet

spikelet

lemma

glume

spikelet

ligule

glume

lemma

Common Saltmarsh Grass
Puccinellia maritima

Reflexed Saltmarsh Grass
Puccinellia distans

Quaking Grass
Briza media

illustrations
0.2× lifesize

Meadow grasses *Poa*

Glabrous annual or perennial grasses, with or without stolons or rhizomes (*see* key on p.595). Leaves mostly folded in the shoot. Inflorescence a whorled panicle; spikelets compressed, with ≥2 flowers; lemmas without awns.

Annual Meadow Grass   *Poa annua*

Tufted annual. STEMS Prostrate to erect, to 30 cm. LEAVES Pale green, 1–5 mm wide, hooded, often crinkled at edges; ligules 2–5 mm. INFLORESCENCES 1–12 cm, triangular, *1–2 branches at each node, branches becoming deflexed after flowering*; spikelets 3–5 mm; 3–5 florets; lemmas 2.5–3.8 mm, 5-veined; anthers 0.6–0.8 mm, 2–3× as long as wide. HABITAT Disturbed ground, bare or trampled patches in grassland, paths, arable fields, lawns, waste places, garden weed; to 1210 m. DIST. Native. Ubiquitous throughout BI. (All Europe.) FLS Year-round.

Early Meadow Grass   *Poa infirma*

Loosely tufted annual grass. Similar to *P. annua*, but smaller, more slender; flowering stems to 10 cm; *leaves yellowish green*, 1–4 mm wide; ligules to 3 mm; *inflorescence branches becoming erect after flowering; spikelets 2–4 mm; lemmas 2–2.5 mm; anthers 0.2–0.5 mm, 1–1.5× as long as wide*. HABITAT Rough sandy ground, trampled grassland, cliff-top paths, close to sea. DIST. Native. Very local. S and SW coast of England from W Sussex, Channel Is, Scilly Is. (SW Europe.) FLS Mar–May.

Rough Meadow Grass   *Poa trivialis*

Loosely tufted, *stoloniferous* grass. STEMS Flowering stems to 100 cm. LEAVES 1.5–6 mm wide, *sheaths rough; ligules long, pointed, 4–10 mm*. INFLORESCENCES To 20 cm, 3–7 branches from each node; spikelets 3–4 mm, 2–4-flowered; lemmas 2.5–3.8 mm, 5-veined. HABITAT Meadows, pastures, wood margins, roadsides, cultivated land, marshes, stream sides; to 1065 m. DIST. Native. Common throughout BI. (All Europe.) FLS Jun–Jul.

Spreading Meadow Grass   *Poa humilis*

Rhizomatous perennial grass to 25 cm, possibly often overlooked. Similar to *P. pratensis* (*see* below), but producing *scattered vegetative shoots and solitary flowering stems from the long, slender rhizomes*; leaves blue-grey to greenish white, 1.5–4 mm wide, hooded; ligules short, rounded, 0.5–2 mm; inflorescence 2–8 cm, 2–3 branches per node; spikelets 4–7 mm; *both glumes*

3-veined, fine-pointed; lemmas 2.5–4 mm. HABITAT Wide range of grasslands, meadows, roadsides, wall tops, sand-dunes, riverbanks, mountain grassland; to 670 m. DIST. Native. Throughout BI. (N and central Europe.) FLS Jun–Jul.

Smooth Meadow Grass   *Poa pratensis*

Tufted, rhizomatous grass to 190 cm. LEAVES 2–4 mm wide, hooded at apex, sheaths smooth; *ligules short, blunt*, to 3 mm. INFLORESCENCES 2–20 cm, 3–5 branches per node; spikelets 4–6 mm, 2–5-flowered; lemmas 3–4 mm. HABITAT All kinds of grassland; to 1065 m. DIST. Native. Common throughout BI. (All Europe.) FLS May–Jul.

Narrow-leaved Meadow Grass   *Poa angustifolia*

Tufted, rhizomatous grass to 70 cm. STEMS Flowering stems in stiff, erect, slender clusters. LEAVES *Long, narrow, 1.5–2 mm wide, inrolled or folded along midrib; basal leaves bristle-like*; basal ligules short, upper ligules to 2 mm. INFLORESCENCES Spikelets 2.5–5 mm, 2–5-flowered; lemmas 2–3.5 mm. HABITAT Dry grassland on infertile sandy or calcareous soils, wall tops, rough ground; shade-tolerant. DIST. Native. Widespread in lowland England; scarce and declining in Wales, Scotland; absent from Ireland (Most of Europe.) FLS Apr–Jul.

Broad-leaved Meadow Grass   *Poa chaixii*

Robust, densely tufted perennial grass to 130 cm. STEMS Vegetative shoots strongly flattened. LEAVES *Very broad, 4.5–12 mm wide*, sheaths compressed, sharply keeled, midrib prominent below; ligules short, 0.5–2 mm. INFLORESCENCES 10–25 cm long, up to 7 branches per node; spikelets 4–7 mm, crowded; lemmas 3.5–4 mm, 5-veined. HABITAT Woods, copses. DIST. Introduced. Grown in gardens for ornament and occasionally naturalised, especially in Scotland (Mts of central and S Europe.) FLS May–Jul.

Wavy Meadow Grass   *Poa flexuosa* VU

Tufted alpine perennial to 25 cm. LEAVES 2–6 cm × 1–2 mm, *gradually tapered to pointed tip, uppermost leaf arising >halfway up stem*; ligules 1–3 mm. INFLORESCENCES Narrowly ovate, 1–5 cm, branches in pairs; spikelets 3–5.5 mm, compressed, 2–4-flowered, variegated; lemmas 3–4 mm. HABITAT Screes, rocky ledges, summit plateaux; 760–1100 m. DIST. Native. Very rare. Scottish mts. (Mts of NW Europe.) FLS Jul–Aug.

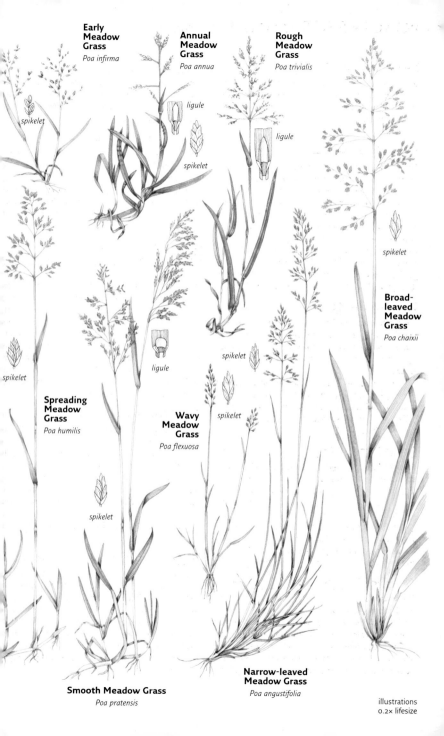

Early Meadow Grass
Poa infirma

spikelet

Annual Meadow Grass
Poa annua

ligule

spikelet

Rough Meadow Grass
Poa trivialis

ligule

spikelet

Broad-leaved Meadow Grass
Poa chaixii

spikelet

Spreading Meadow Grass
Poa humilis

spikelet

ligule

Wavy Meadow Grass
Poa flexuosa

spikelet

spikelet

spikelet

Smooth Meadow Grass
Poa pratensis

Narrow-leaved Meadow Grass
Poa angustifolia

illustrations
0.2× lifesize

Flattened Meadow Grass — *Poa compressa*

Stiff, rhizomatous perennial to 60 cm. STEMS Flowering stems tufted or scattered, *flattened*, wiry. LEAVES *Bluish green or greyish green*, 1–4 mm wide; ligules 0.5–3 mm, rounded at apex. INFLORESCENCES *Stiff, narrowly oblong*, 1.5–10 cm; *spikelets 3–8 mm, densely clustered*; lemmas 2.5–3 mm. HABITAT Dry grassy banks, wall tops, rough stony ground; lowland to 365 m. DIST. Native. Local throughout Britain to S Scotland; introduced in Ireland. (Most of Europe.) FLS Jun–Aug.

Glaucous Meadow Grass — *Poa glauca* VU.

Tufted *bluish-grey alpine perennial, with a covering of whitish wax*. STEMS Flowering stems to 25 cm, stiff, erect, slender. LEAVES 2–8 cm × 2–3 mm, with abruptly pointed, hooded tip; *ligules 1–2.5 mm*. INFLORESCENCES *Narrow*, stiff, erect, 2–6 cm, 2–3 branches per node; spikelets 3–4.5 mm; lemmas 3–4 mm, densely hairy on veins. HABITAT Damp calcareous rock ledges, crevices, slopes; 305–1110 m. DIST. Native. Very local. Mts of N England, N Wales, Scotland. (N Europe, mts of S Europe.) FLS Jul–Aug.

Wood Meadow Grass — *Poa nemoralis*

Loosely tufted perennial without rhizomes, to 90 cm. LEAVES *1–3 mm wide, fine-pointed, wide-spreading; ligules short*, 0.2–0.5 mm. INFLORESCENCES Lax, open, branches very fine, greenish purplish; *spikelets usually small*, 3–6 mm, 1–5-flowered; lemmas 2.5–3.5 mm. HABITAT Shaded places, woodlands, banks, hedgerows, walls, occasionally dry rocky ledges in mountains; to 915 m. DIST. Native. Common throughout Britain, but scarce in N Scotland; introduced in Ireland. (Most of Europe; restricted to mts in S.) FLS Jun–Jul.

Bulbous Meadow Grass — *Poa bulbosa*

Tufted perennial to 40 cm. STEMS *Base bulbous*. LEAVES Narrow, 0.5–2 mm wide, sheaths purplish or green; ligules to 4 mm. INFLORESCENCES Erect, contracted, dense, 2–6 cm; spikelets 3–5 mm, variegated, sometimes proliferous (var. *vivipara*); lemmas 2.5–3.5 mm. HABITAT Bare sandy, shingly grassland near sea. DIST. Native. Rather rare. S coasts of England, Wales, from the Wash to R. Severn. (All Europe except extreme W and N.) FLS Mar–May.

Alpine Meadow Grass — *Poa alpina*

Tufted alpine perennial to 40 cm, *without rhizomes*. STEMS *Thickened at base with old leaf sheaths*. LEAVES 2–5 mm wide, folded along midrib or flat, tips hooded; ligules 2–6 mm. INFLORESCENCES Moderately dense, 3–7 cm, purplish or green; *spikelets usually proliferous* (var. *vivipara*); lemmas 3.5–5 mm. HABITAT Damp calcareous rock faces, ledges; to 1190 m. DIST. Native. Very local in NW Scotland; very rare in N England, N Wales, W Ireland. (Arctic Europe.) FLS Jul–Aug.

Cock's-foot — *Dactylis glomerata*

Tall, tufted, robust perennial grass to 140 cm. STEMS *Base markedly compressed*. LEAVES Rather bluish green, keeled, folded in sheath, 2–14 mm wide, tip hooded; ligules 2–12 mm. INFLORESCENCES Branches erect, spreading or deflexed, spike-like, upper close together, lower distant, the *whole resembling a 'cock's foot'*; spikelets 5–9 mm, in dense masses at end of branches; lemmas 4–7 mm, fringed with hairs, awn to 2 mm. HABITAT All kinds of grassland on fertile base-rich or neutral soils; to 685 m. Also dunes, cliffs, waste ground. DIST. Native. Ubiquitous throughout BI. (All Europe.) FLS Jun–Sep.

Slender Cock's-foot — *Dactylis polygama* / *Dactylis glomerata* ssp. *aschersoniana*

Similar to *D. glomerata*, but more loosely tufted, leaves green; inflorescence slender, with small clusters of spikelets; lemmas hairless, awn very short or absent. HABITAT Woods. DIST. Introduced. Naturalised in a few scattered localities in S England. (W and central Europe.) FLS Jun–Sep.

Whorl Grass — *Catabrosa aquatica*

Creeping, stoloniferous perennial, rooting at nodes. STEMS Flowering stems erect or ascending, to 75 cm. LEAVES 2–10 mm wide, folded at first, parallel-sided, tip hooded, *sheaths purplish*; ligules 2–8 mm. INFLORESCENCES *Whorled panicle*, 5–30 cm; spikelets 3–5 mm, 1–3-flowered; lemmas 2.5–3.5 mm, prominently 3-nerved. HABITAT Muddy margins of ponds, ditches, dykes and streams, especially when poached by cattle; also wet, open sandy ground near sea. DIST. Native. Throughout lowland BI, but local and declining. (Most of Europe.) FLS May–Jul.

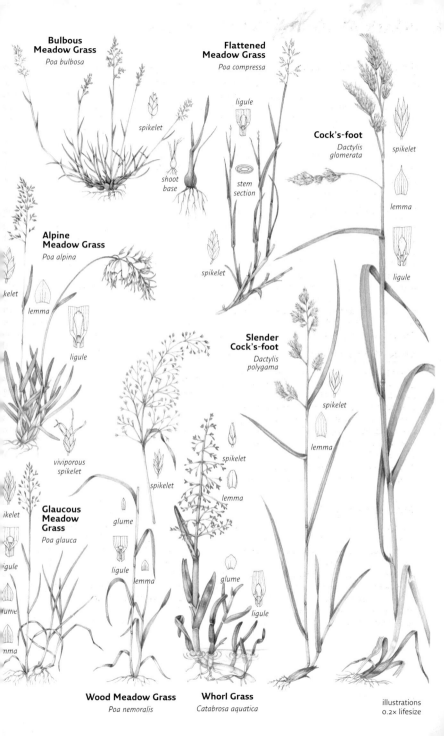

Bulbous Meadow Grass
Poa bulbosa

spikelet

shoot base

Flattened Meadow Grass
Poa compressa

ligule

stem section

spikelet

Cock's-foot
Dactylis glomerata

spikelet

lemma

ligule

Alpine Meadow Grass
Poa alpina

kelet

lemma

ligule

viviporous spikelet

Slender Cock's-foot
Dactylis polygama

spikelet

lemma

Glaucous Meadow Grass
Poa glauca

ikelet

igule

lume

nma

glume

ligule

lemma

spikelet

spikelet

lemma

glume

ligule

Wood Meadow Grass
Poa nemoralis

Whorl Grass
Catabrosa aquatica

illustrations
0.2× lifesize

Sea Fern Grass
Catapodium marinum

Slender, rigid, solitary or tufted annual to 20 cm. LEAVES Dark green, 1-3.5 mm wide, flat or rolled; ligules blunt, 0.5-3 mm. INFLORESCENCES 0.5-7 cm, stiff, *unbranched, spike-like*, axis flattened; spikelets sessile, 4-9 mm, in 2 rows; lemmas 2.5-3.8 mm, 5-veined. HABITAT Dry, bare ground near sea, sand-dunes, cliff tops, walls, stabilised shingle. DIST. Native. All round coasts of BI, but scarce in NE Scotland. (S and W Europe.) FLS May-Jul.

Fern Grass
Catapodium rigidum

Similar to *C. marinum*, but inflorescence 1-8 cm, branched in lower part with *at least some of spikelets distinctly stalked*, unbranched above, axis angled; spikelets 4-7 mm; lemmas 1.8-3 mm. HABITAT Bare, dry sandy or calcareous places, walls, banks, rock outcrops, stabilised shingle, quarries; to 355 m. DIST. Native. Throughout BI, N to central Scotland. (SW Europe.) FLS May-Jul.

Blue Moor Grass
Sesleria caerulea

Tufted, shortly rhizomatous perennial to 45 cm. LEAVES 2-6 mm wide, *bluish green, glabrous, keeled, tip hooded; ligules very short*. INFLORESCENCES 1-3 cm, a dense, cylindrical purplish-grey spike-like panicle; spikelets 4.5-7 mm, 2-3-flowered; lemmas 4-5 mm, 3-5-veined, tips broad, with 3-5 awn-like teeth. HABITAT/DIST. Native. Abundant plant of limestone grasslands in N England, W and NW Ireland; rare on mica-schists of central Scotland. To 1005 m. (Most of Europe.) FLS Early, Apr-Jun.

Sweet grasses *Glyceria*
See key on p.596. Glabrous perennial aquatic or marsh grasses, with rhizomes and/or stolons. Leaves flat, sheaths with cross-veins and air cavities between main veins. Panicle simple or much branched; spikelets 4-16-flowered; glumes hyaline, 1-nerved, shorter than 1st floret; lemmas with 7 prominent veins.

Reed Sweet Grass
Glyceria maxima

Tall, robust, rhizomatous, patch-forming perennial, with numerous leafy shoots. STEMS Flowering stems to 250 cm. LEAVES 30-60 cm × 7-20 mm wide, keeled; *ligules 3-6 mm, rounded, with central point*. INFLORESCENCES *Large, 15-45 cm, compact, much branched*; spikelets 5-12 mm, 4-10-flowered; lemmas 3-4 mm, 7-veined. HABITAT Margins of ditches, dykes, canals, rivers, ponds and lakes; lowland to 600 m. DIST. Native. Common throughout BI to central Scotland, but scarce in N England and Scotland, Wales, Ireland. (Most of Europe.) FLS Jun-Aug.

Floating Sweet Grass
Glyceria fluitans

Loosely tufted perennial, forming floating mats in shallow water. STEMS Flowering stems erect, or prostrate and floating, to 100 cm. LEAVES 3-10 mm wide, folded or flat; ligules 5-15 mm, lanceolate. INFLORESCENCES 10-54 cm, *narrow, sparingly branched*, appearing whip-like; spikelets 18-35 mm, 8-16-flowered; *lemmas 5.5-7 mm*, apex entire; anthers 1.5-2.5 mm. HABITAT Ditches, rivers, ponds, lakes, wet marshes, often where enriched by nutrients. DIST. Native. Common throughout BI. (Most of Europe.) FLS May-Aug.

Hybrid Sweet Grass
Glyceria × pedicellata (G. fluitans × G. notata)

Stoloniferous perennial growing in extensive floating mats and spreading vegetatively. STEMS Flowering stems to 100 cm. LEAVES 5-12 mm wide, folded or flat; ligules to 10 mm. INFLORESCENCES Loose, erect or spreading, 2-3 branches per node, or single above; *spikelets 10-35 mm, remaining intact and not breaking up at end of season; lemmas 4-6 mm; anthers remaining indehiscent, with shrunken pollen grains*. HABITAT Similar to parents, and often growing with them. DIST. Native. Scattered throughout range of parents. (W Europe.)

Plicate Sweet Grass
Glyceria notata

Tuft- or mat-forming perennial. STEMS Flowering stems prostrate to ascending, to 75 cm, branched below and rooting at nodes. LEAVES Long, 3-14 mm wide, green, folded or flat, tip hooded, sheaths keeled; ligules oval, 2-8 mm. INFLORESCENCES *Broad, loose, 10-45 cm, much branched*, 2-5 lower branches per node, with 1 branch longer than rest; spikelets 10-25 mm, 7-16-flowered; *lemmas 3.5-5 mm, tip blunt*. HABITAT Muddy margins of ditches, pools and streams, usually on calcareous soils; lowland to 380 m. DIST. Native. Throughout BI, N to central Scotland. (Most of Europe.) FLS Jun-Aug.

Small Sweet Grass
Glyceria declinata

Shortly tufted perennial to 45 cm. LEAVES *Greyish green or tinged purple*, rather short, tip hooded, 1.5-8 mm wide; ligules pointed, 4-9 mm. INFLORESCENCES 4-30 cm, slightly curved, 1-3 branches per node, rather appressed to axis; spikelets 13-25 mm, 8-15-flowered; *lemmas 3.5-5.5 mm, with 3-5-lobed or 3-toothed tip*, exceeded by 2 sharply pointed teeth of palea. HABITAT Muddy margins of ponds and ditches, marshy fields, especially where trampled by cattle. DIST. Native. Throughout BI, but scarce in N Scotland, Ireland. (W and central Europe.) FLS Jun-Sep.

Blue Moor Grass
Sesleria caerulea

ligule

spikelet

Fern Grass
Catapodium rigidum

spikelet

Sea Fern Grass
Catapodium marinum

spikelet

spikelet

lemma

ligule

lemma

spikelet

glume   *lemma*

spikelet

spikelet

lemma

ligule

Plicate Sweet Grass
Glyceria notata

Floating Sweet Grass
Glyceria fluitans

Hybrid Sweet Grass
*Glyceria ×
pedicellata*

Small Sweet Grass
*Glyceria
declinata*

Reed Sweet Grass
Glyceria maxima

illustrations
0.15× lifesize

Hard-grass
Parapholis strigosa

Slender, glabrous annual to 40 cm (usually much less). STEMS Stiff, solitary or tufted. LEAVES Greyish green, 1-2.5 mm wide, *sheaths rounded on back, not inflated*; ligules 0.3-1 mm. INFLORESCENCES *Slender, erect spike*, sometimes slightly curved, 2-20 cm long, stem jointed; *spikelets 3-7 mm, so embedded in hollows in stem that, except when flowering, they appear part of it*, alternating on opposite sides of stem, 1-flowered; glumes inserted side by side; *anthers 1.5-3 mm*. HABITAT Damp, bare sandy or muddy areas close to sea, upper levels of salt marshes, banks, sea walls, tracks. DIST. Native. Frequent all around coasts of BI, N to central Scotland. (Coastal W Europe, inland E Europe.) FLS Jun-Aug.

Curved Hard-grass
Parapholis incurva

Similar to *P. strigosa*, but smaller, 2-20 cm; stems spreading, curved, very slender; leaves short, to 3 cm, *uppermost sheaths inflated; inflorescence 1-8 cm, rigid, curved*; spikelets 4-6 mm; *anthers 0.5-1 mm*. HABITAT Upper parts of salt marshes, gravelly and muddy banks, sea walls, cliff tops, tracks. DIST. Native. Local on E and S coasts of England; rare elsewhere in Britain; very rare in E Ireland. (S and W Europe.) FLS Jun-Jul (earlier than *P. strigosa*).

Wood Melick
Melica uniflora

Rhizomatous, patch-forming perennial to 60 cm. LEAVES *Bright green*, 3-7 mm wide, flat, sparsely hairy above; *sheaths sparsely hairy, purple, apex of sheath on opposite side to blade with slender bristle*; ligules very short. INFLORESCENCES Sparingly branched, branches spreading, with few separated spikelets near tips; *spikelets erect, elliptic, 4-7 mm, with 1 fertile floret; glumes purplish or brownish*. HABITAT Deciduous woodlands, shaded hedge banks, rock ledges, on well-drained base-rich soils; to 485 m. DIST. Native. Common throughout BI, N to central Scotland. (Most of Europe.) FLS May-Jul.

Mountain Melick
Melica nutans

Similar to *M. uniflora*, but *leaf sheaths hairless, without apical bristles; inflorescence 1-sided, nodding*; spikelets larger, 6-8 mm, solitary or paired, eventually *nodding*, with *2-3 fertile flowers*. HABITAT Limestone woodland, grikes in limestone pavement, rock ledges; to 820 m. DIST. Native. N England, Scotland; scattered in Wales; absent from Ireland. (Most of Europe.) FLS May-Jul.

Oats and oat-like grasses *Helictotrichon, Gaudinia, Arrhenatherum, Avena* and *Trisetum*

Annual or perennial grasses with a characteristic appearance. Inflorescence is a loose panicle, with rather large, shiny, 2-6-flowered spikelets; glumes are often as long as spikelet; lemmas are narrow and translucent, with long, conspicuous, bent awns arising from back.

Meadow Oat-grass
Helictotrichon pratense

Densely tufted perennial to 80 cm. LEAVES *Bluish green, narrow, 1-5 mm wide, linear, stiff, often twisted, channelled and hooded*; ligules 2-5 mm. INFLORESCENCES 4-18 cm, narrow, erect, glossy, with 1-2 branches at lowest node; *spikelets 11-28 mm, 3-6-flowered*; lemmas 10-17 mm, awn arising from just above middle, bent, 12-22 mm. HABITAT Well-drained chalk and limestone grassland, sand-dunes montane grassland; to 835 m. DIST. Native. Most of England, Scotland; rare in SW England, Wales, N Scotland; absent from Ireland. (W and Europe.) FLS Jun-Jul.

Downy Oat-grass
Helictotrichon pubescens

Similar to *H. pratense*, but taller, to 100 cm; leaves 2-6 mm wide, green, *blades and sheaths softly hairy*; ligules to 8 mm; inflorescence 6-20 cm, with 3-4 branches at lowest node; *spikelets 10-17 mm, 2-3 flowered*; lemmas 9-14 mm, awn 12-22 mm. HABITAT Wide range of grasslands on moist or dry base-rich or calcareous soils: downland, meadows pastures, roadsides, cliffs, mature dunes. DIST. Native. Throughout BI. To 550 m. (Most of Europe except S.) FLS May-Jul.

French Oat-grass
Gaudinia fragilis

Erect, tufted annual to 120 cm. LEAVES 1-6.6 cm 0.6-4 mm, long, linear, flat, blades and sheaths downy; ligules very short. INFLORESCENCES *Spike with spikelets arranged in 2 opposite rows, to 35 cm* spikelets 7-20 mm, sessile, 3-11-flowered; lemmas 7-11 mm, awn bent, 5-13 mm. HABITAT Rough grassland, roadsides, on a range of soils, often calcareous. DIST. Probably introduced. S-central England; scattered elsewhere. (Mediterranean) FLS May-Jul.

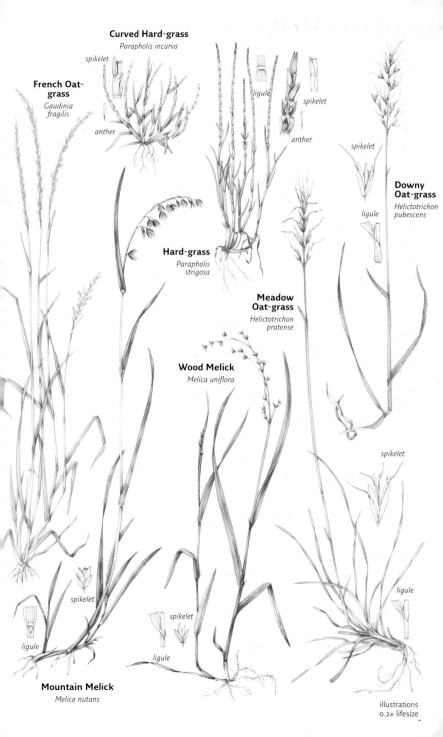

Curved Hard-grass
Parapholis incurva

spikelet

ligule

spikelet

anther

French Oat-grass
Gaudinia fragilis

anther

Downy Oat-grass
Helictotrichon pubescens

spikelet

ligule

Hard-grass
Parapholis strigosa

Meadow Oat-grass
Helictotrichon pratense

Wood Melick
Melica uniflora

spikelet

Mountain Melick
Melica nutans

spikelet

ligule

spikelet

ligule

ligule

illustrations
0.2× lifesize

False Oat-grass
Arrhenatherum elatius

Tall, erect, loosely tufted perennial to 180 cm. LEAVES 4–10 mm wide, long, flat, fine-pointed, usually sparsely hairy above; ligules 1–3 mm. INFLORESCENCES 10–30 cm long, green-purplish, shining, branches clustered; *spikelets 7–11 mm, 2-flowered*; lemmas 8–10 mm, *awn 10–20 mm, bent, arising c.⅓ way up lemma*. DIST. Native. Common throughout BI. HABITAT Rough grassland, roadsides, hedge banks, limestone scree, coastal shingle; to 550 m. (Most of Europe, but rare in S and SW.) FLS Jun–Sep. NOTE Ssp. *bulbosum* (Onion Couch) is frequent on roadsides and as an arable weed. It has 'bulb-like' swellings, 6–10 mm diam., on the basal internodes of the flowering stem.

Wild-oat
Avena fatua

Tall, erect annual to 150 cm. LEAVES 3–15 mm wide, flat, fine-pointed, basal sheaths hairy. INFLORESCENCES 10–40 cm long, nodding, branches clustered, wide-spreading; spikelets pendulous, narrowly oblong, 18–25 mm, 2–3-flowered; glumes 20–30 mm, as long as spikelet; lemmas 14–20 mm, with silky-brown hairs at base, awn 2.5–4 mm, bent; when mature, spikelets break up so that *individual florets separate from one another as well as from glumes at joints within spikelet*. HABITAT Weed of arable crops, roadsides, waste ground. DIST. Archaeophyte. Throughout BI, but chiefly lowland England. (Native of S Europe; naturalised throughout Europe.) FLS Jun–Sep.

Winter Wild-oat
Avena sterilis

Similar to *A. fatua*, but spikelets larger, 23–32 mm, and *breaking up at maturity at base of lower lemma only*, so that florets separate from glumes as a whole. HABITAT Arable weed of winter cereals on heavy soils. DIST. Introduced. Central England; scattered elsewhere. (S Europe.) FLS Jul–Aug.

Oat
Avena sativa

Similar to the wild-oats, but *spikelet not jointed between florets*, so not breaking up at maturity; spikelets 17–30 mm; base of *lemmas not hairy*; awns absent or on lowest lemma only, ± straight. HABITAT Field borders, roadsides, tips, waste ground. DIST.

Introduced. Formerly widespread arable crop, now casual relic of cultivation. FLS Jul–Sep.

Yellow Oat-grass
Trisetum flavescens

Loosely tufted, erect perennial to 80 cm. LEAVES 2–10 mm wide, flat, usually sparsely hairy above, fine-pointed; ligules 0.5–2 mm. INFLORESCENCES *Distinctly yellowish, shining*, 5–20 cm, loose or somewhat dense, branches clustered; *spikelets 5–7 mm, 2–4-flowered*, glumes shining; *lemmas 4–5.5 mm, tips with 2 teeth*, awn 2.5–9 mm, bent, twisted. HABITAT Well-drained neutral or calcareous grassland, lowland downland, pastures, hay meadows, roadsides. DIST. Native. Throughout BI, N to central Scotland. (Most of Europe.) FLS May–Jul.

Crested Hair-grass
Koeleria macrantha

Compact, tufted perennial to 60 cm. LEAVES Narrow, 1–2.5 mm wide, *blue-green, softly hairy, rolled, bristle-like*, finely ribbed on upper surface; ligules short, to 1 mm. INFLORESCENCES Cylindrical, *spike-like panicle*, 1–10 cm, silvery; spikelets 4–6 mm, densely clustered; lemmas 3.5–5.5 mm, pointed. HABITAT Dry calcareous or sandy base-rich grasslands, downs, dunes, cliff tops; to 680 m. DIST. Native Throughout BI, but mostly in N and W. (Most of Europe.) FLS Jun–Jul.

Somerset Hair-grass
Koeleria vallesiana VU

Similar to *K. macrantha*, but densely tufted, with *thickened base covered by dense, fibrous remains of old leaf sheaths*; leaves to 3 mm wide, grey-green, rolled or flat, margins rough; inflorescence shorter, 1.5–7 cm, silvery or tinged purplish. HABITAT S-facing sheep-grazed limestone grassland. DIST. Native Very rare. Mendips (Somerset). (W Europe.) FLS Jun–Aug.

Pyramidal Hair-grass
Koeleria pyramidata

Similar to *K. macrantha*, but more robust, taller, to 90 cm, with long, creeping rhizomes; inflorescence much longer, 10–22 cm; *spikelets 6–8 mm; glumes and lemmas glabrous*. HABITAT Calcareous grasslands, meadows, old quarries, wood margins. DIST. *Not BI*. (Most of Europe except N.) FLS Jun–Jul.

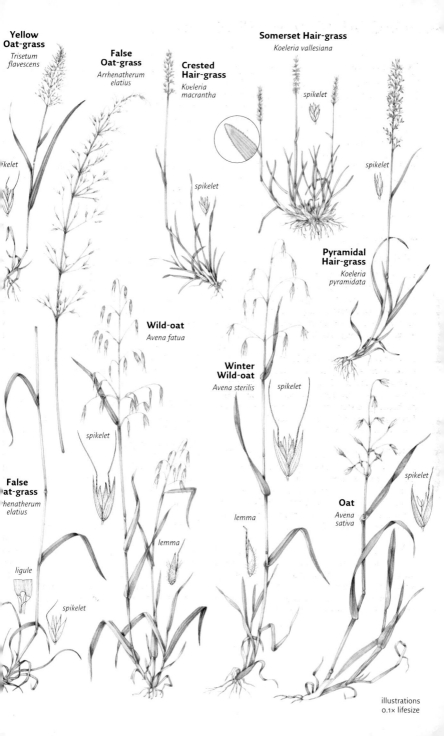

Yellow Oat-grass
Trisetum flavescens

False Oat-grass
Arrhenatherum elatius

Crested Hair-grass
Koeleria macrantha

Somerset Hair-grass
Koeleria vallesiana

spikelet

spikelet

spikelet

...kelet

spikelet

Pyramidal Hair-grass
Koeleria pyramidata

Wild-oat
Avena fatua

spikelet

Winter Wild-oat
Avena sterilis

spikelet

lemma

False ...at-grass
...henatherum elatius

ligule

spikelet

lemma

Oat
Avena sativa

spikelet

illustrations
0.1× lifesize

Tufted Hair-grass
Deschampsia cespitosa

Densely tufted, tussock-forming perennial to 200 cm. LEAVES Dark green, 2–5 mm wide, glabrous, *long-linear, flat or rolled, deeply ribbed above, margins very rough*; ligules to 15 mm. INFLORESCENCES *Whorled panicle to 50 cm long, green to silvery*; spikelets 2–6 mm, 2-flowered; lemmas 3–8 mm, enclosed within glumes, tips truncate, toothed, hairy at base, awn to 4 mm. HABITAT Woodland, rough grassland, marshes, fens, montane habitats, on damp, poorly drained, mildly acid to base-rich soils. DIST. Native. Common throughout BI. (Most of Europe.) FLS Jun–Aug. NOTE Ssp. *alpina* (Alpine Hair-grass) is small, with hooded leaf tips, reflexed branches and proliferating spikelets. It is a rare plant of mountain rock ledges and flushes in areas of late snow-lie at 800–1235 m in NW Scotland and W Ireland.

Wavy Hair-grass
Deschampsia flexuosa

Tufted perennial to 70 cm. LEAVES *Dark green, long, bristle-like*, 0.3–0.8 mm wide, glabrous, sheaths slightly rough; ligules 0.5–3 mm. INFLORESCENCES Open, loose, branches hair-like; spikelets 4–6 mm, with 2 flowers placed side by side; *glumes purplish brown, silvery; lemmas 3.5–5.5 mm, tips minutely toothed*, awn 4–7 mm. HABITAT Heaths, moors, upland grassland, open woodlands, on acid, well-drained sandy or peaty soils; to 1220 m. DIST. Native. Common throughout BI. (Most of Europe.) FLS Jun–Jul.

Bog Hair-grass
Deschampsia setacea *(R)

Similar to *D. flexuosa*, but leaf sheaths smooth; *ligules longer, 2–8 mm, finely pointed*; 2 florets in spikelets, one above the other; *lemmas blunt-tipped, with 4 unequal, jagged teeth.* HABITAT Wet peaty hollows in heaths and bogs, loch margins. DIST. Native. Very local. Central-S England, W Wales, W Ireland, N Scotland. (W Europe.) FLS Jul–Aug.

Yorkshire-fog
Holcus lanatus

Tufted, *softly hairy perennial* to 100 cm. LEAVES *Flat, grey-green, downy; sheaths usually striped purple*; ligules blunt, 1–4 mm. INFLORESCENCES Whorled panicle, whitish pinkish, 3–20 cm, dense to loose; spikelets 4–6 mm, 2-flowered; lemmas 2–2.5 mm, enclosed by glumes, upper with *short, recurved awn, 2 mm, enclosed within glumes.* HABITAT Wide range

of grasslands, meadows, pastures, downs, road-sides, hedge banks, open woodland; to 650m. DIST. Native. Ubiquitous throughout BI. (All Europe except Arctic.) FLS May–Sep.

Creeping Soft-grass
Holcus mollis

Similar to *H. lanatus*, but with *creeping rhizomes that form loose mats*; stems almost hairless, but with 'bearded' nodes; leaves sparsely hairy or glabrous; ligules 1–5 mm; upper lemma with straight *awn, 3.5–5 mm, protruding beyond glumes.* HABITAT Deciduous woodland, conifer plantations, hedge banks, heathland, on well-drained acidic soils. DIST. Native. Throughout BI. (All Europe.) FLS Jun–Aug.

Grey Hair-grass
Corynephorus canescens

Densely tufted perennial to 35 cm. LEAVES *Stiff, bristle-like*, to 6 cm, 0.3–0.5 mm wide, greyish, *sheaths pink or purplish*; ligules pointed, 2–4 mm. INFLORESCENCES Narrow, dense panicle, purplish, 1.5–8 cm; spikelets 3–4 mm, 2-flowered; lemmas 1.5–2 mm, enclosed by glumes, *awn orange-brown, twisted at base with club-shaped tip.* HABITAT Dunes, sandy shingle, dune heaths; also sandy heaths inland (Suffolk). DIST. Native. Very local. Coasts of Norfolk, Suffolk, Lancashire, Channel Is. (Central Europe.) FLS Jun–Jul.

Silver Hair-grass
Aira caryophyllea

Slender annual to 50 cm. STEMS Tufted or solitary. LEAVES Bristle-like, *c.*0.3 mm wide, greyish green, glabrous, soon withering; sheaths minutely rough; ligules to 5 mm, toothed. INFLORESCENCES *Loose panicle, branches wide-spreading*, hair-like, pedicels 1–10 mm; spikelets silvery, 2.2–3.5 mm, 2-flowered; lemmas enclosed by glumes, awns bent, projecting from tips of glumes. HABITAT Well-drained sandy places that dry out in summer, heaths, dunes, ant-hills, clifftops, wall tops; to 560 m. DIST. Native. Frequent throughout BI. (W and central Europe.) FLS May–Jul.

Early Hair-grass
Aira praecox

Similar to *A. caryophyllea*, but leaf sheaths smooth; ligules to 3 mm, blunt, not toothed; *inflorescence dense, spike-like*, pedicels shorter than spikelets. HABITAT Sandy, gravelly places on acid soils, heaths, rock outcrops, dunes, walls, cliff tops. DIST. Native. Common throughout BI. (W Europe.) FLS Apr–Jun

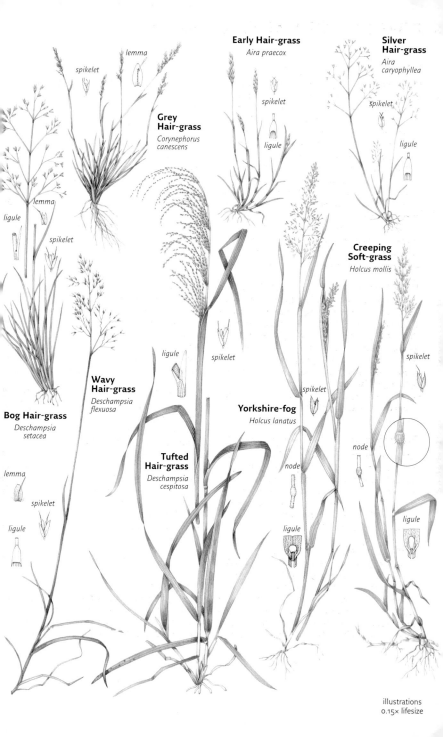

Early Hair-grass
Aira praecox

spikelet

ligule

Silver Hair-grass
Aira caryophyllea

spikelet

ligule

spikelet

lemma

Grey Hair-grass
Corynephorus canescens

lemma

ligule

spikelet

Creeping Soft-grass
Holcus mollis

spikelet

ligule

spikelet

Bog Hair-grass
Deschampsia setacea

lemma

spikelet

ligule

Wavy Hair-grass
Deschampsia flexuosa

Tufted Hair-grass
Deschampsia cespitosa

Yorkshire-fog
Holcus lanatus

spikelet

node

node

ligule

node

ligule

illustrations
0.15× lifesize

Holy-grass
Hierochloe odorata *(NI)

Aromatic, vanilla-scented perennial to 50 cm, with extensive, patch-forming rhizomes. LEAVES 1.5–5 mm wide, long-linear, finely pointed, glossy beneath, sparsely hairy or glabrous above; ligules 1.5–2 mm, pointed. INFLORESCENCES *Panicle with spreading branches; spikelets broadly oval, plump, 3.5–5 mm, golden brown,* 3-flowered; lemmas blunt, oval, margins minutely hairy. HABITAT Banks of lakes and rivers, reed-beds, wet meadows, spring lines at base of coastal cliffs. DIST. Native. In a few scattered localities in Scotland; very rare in Ireland (Lough Neagh). (N and central Europe.) FLS Mar–May.

Sweet Vernal-grass
Anthoxanthum odoratum

Erect, tufted, short-lived perennial to 50 cm, smelling of 'new-mown hay'. LEAVES 1.5–5 mm wide, flat, finely pointed, thinly hairy; *sheaths with conspicuous ring of hairs at junction with blade;* ligules 1–5 mm, blunt. INFLORESCENCES *Dense, spike-like panicle,* green; *spikelets* 6–10 mm, 3-*flowered, the lower 2 sterile;* sterile lemmas with awns, upper bent, lower straight. HABITAT Wide range of mildly acid grassland, meadows, pastures, hill grassland, dry parts of mires, dunes; to 1030 m. DIST. Native. Ubiquitous throughout BI. (Throughout Europe) FLS Apr–Jul.

Canary-grasses *Phalaris*
Annual or rhizomatous perennial grasses, with flat leaves (*see* key on p.596). Inflorescence a spike-like panicle, spikelets 1-flowered, lemma awnless, glumes longer than rest of spikelet.

Reed Canary-grass
Phalaris arundinacea

Tall, rhizomatous, reed-like perennial to 200 cm. LEAVES 10–35 cm, 6–18 mm wide, flat, fine-pointed, ligules 2.5–26 mm, becoming torn. INFLORESCENCES *Lobed, 5–25 cm; spikelets densely clustered,* 5–6.5 mm, greenish purple, 1-flowered; glumes keeled, 5–6.5 mm, as long as spikelet. SIMILAR SPP. Vegetatively, looks similar to *Phragmites australis* (p.640), but distinguished from that species by the ligules. HABITAT Margins of lakes, ponds, rivers, dykes and canals, carr woodland; to 475 m. DIST. Native. Common throughout BI. (Most of Europe.) FLS Jun–Aug.

Bulbous Canary-grass
Phalaris aquatica

Similar to *P. arundinacea,* but smaller; *stems* to 150 cm, *swollen at base;* inflorescence 3–12 cm, very dense, lanceolate, not lobed in outline, branches very short; glumes 4–5 mm, keeled, margins pale, *keel winged along its whole length.* HABITAT Woodlands, field borders, roadsides, waste ground. DIST. Introduced. Sown as game cover. Naturalised in scattered localities throughout England. (Mediterranean.) FLS Jun–Jul.

Canary-grass
Phalaris canariensis

Tufted annual to 120 cm. LEAVES 4–12 mm wide, green, glabrous; ligules 3–8 mm. INFLORESCENCES *Erect, spike-like, ovate, dense, whitish with green veins;* spikelets 6–10 mm, closely packed; glumes persistent, 6–10 mm, as long as spikelet, keel green. HABITAT Urban weed, waste ground, tips. DIST. Introduced with birdseed (native NW Africa, Canary Is). Casual throughout BI. FLS Jun–Sep.

Lesser Canary-grass
Phalaris minor

Similar to *P. canariensis,* but inflorescence narrower, cylindrical; spikelets shorter; glumes 4–6.5 mm, wing on keel toothed on at least 1 glume on some of spikelets. HABITAT/DIST. Introduced. Scattered throughout England, Channel Is as casual of rubbish tips, waste ground; weed of bulb fields in Scilly Is. (Mediterranean.) FLS Jun–Jul.

Awned Canary-grass
Phalaris paradoxa

Similar to *P. canariensis,* but spikelets in groups of 3–7, one fertile and the rest sterile, falling as a group when seeds ripe. HABITAT Casual arable weed, waste ground. DIST. Introduced as constituent of game-bird seed mixes. Scattered and increasing in lowland England. (Mediterranean.) FLS Jun–Aug.

Hare's-tail
Lagurus ovatus

Attractive, softly hairy annual to 60 cm. LEAVES Broad, 2–14 mm wide, flat, greyish green, densely hairy; upper sheaths inflated; ligules 3 mm, blunt. INFLORESCENCES *Pale, softly hairy (like a 'hare's tail')* spike-like, globose to ovoid, dense; spikelets 8–10 mm, densely overlapping, 1-flowered; glumes narrow, hairy, tapering into fine bristle; lemmas 4–5 mm, elliptic, tip with 2 long bristles, awn 8–18 mm, bent. HABITAT/DIST. Introduced. Naturalised on sand dunes in S England, Channel Is; elsewhere casual garden escape as urban weed. (Mediterranean.) FLS Jun–Aug.

Lesser Canary-grass
Phalaris minor

spikelet

Holy-grass
Hierochloe odorata

spikelet

ligule

Awned Canary-grass
Phalaris paradoxa

Bulbous Canary-grass
Phalaris aquatica

ligule

Hare's-tail
Lagurus ovatus

spikelet

spikelet

spikelet

spikelet

ligule

Reed Canary-grass
Phalaris arundinacea

Canary-grass
Phalaris canariensis

Sweet Vernal-grass
Anthoxanthum odoratum

illustrations
0.15× lifesize

Bent-grasses *Agrostis*

Erect, tufted perennial grasses, with or without rhizomes or stolons (*see* key on p.597). Inflorescence a whorled panicle; spikelets 1-flowered; glumes 1–3-veined, ± equal, longer than rest of spikelet; lemmas 3–5-veined, with or without an awn; palea very short or absent; anthers ≥1 mm. An important group, forming a dominant constituent of several kinds of grassland.

Common Bent
Agrostis capillaris

Tufted, rhizomatous, sometimes stoloniferous perennial to 50 cm. Leaves 1–5 mm wide, flat or inrolled, tapering to fine point; ligules short, ≤2 mm, blunt, wider than long. Inflorescences To 20 cm, open, branches clustered, spreading; spikelets 2–3.5 mm; lemmas ⅔ length of glumes, awnless. Habitat All kinds of poor, mildly acid grassland, meadows, pastures, heaths, upland hill pasture, dunes; to 1210 m. A common component of lawn seed, tolerant of soils contaminated with metal toxicity. Dist. Native. Abundant throughout BI. (All Europe.) Fls Jun–Aug.

Black Bent
Agrostis gigantea

Tall, tufted, erect, rhizomatous perennial. Similar to *A. capillaris*, but larger, flowering stems to 120 cm; leaves 2–8 mm wide; ligules longer than wide, 1.5–12 mm, tips torn; inflorescence 8–25 cm, very loose; spikelets 2–3 mm; lemmas usually awnless. Habitat Arable weed on light soils. Dist. Native. Archaeophyte. Throughout BI, but scarce in N Scotland, Ireland. (Most of Europe.) Fls Jun–Aug.

Highland Bent
Agrostis castellana

Rhizomatous, sometimes stoloniferous perennial to 80 cm. Probably under-recorded. Similar to *A. capillaris*, but leaves characteristically blue-green, long, narrow; upper ligules to 3 mm, tip jagged; spikelets 2.5–4 mm; lemmas sparsely pubescent, with 2 lateral tufts of white hairs on thickened base, awn, if present, arising from near base. Habitat Common constituent of amenity grassland seed mixes. Dist. Introduced. Scattered localities in lowland England, Scotland. (S Europe.) Fls Jul–Aug.

Creeping Bent
Agrostis stolonifera

Stoloniferous, turf-forming perennial to 40 cm, rooting at nodes. Stems Stolons often purplish. Leaves Greyish green, 1–10 cm long, 0.5–5 mm wide, rolled, becoming flat; ligules 1–6 mm, blunt. Inflorescences Spreading at flowering, contracting in fruit; spikelets 2–3 mm, densely clustered; lemmas awnless. Habitat Wide range of permanent wet or dry grassland habitats except the most acid, marshes, ditches, salt marshes, brackish grassland, dune slacks; to 945 m. Dist. Native. Abundant throughout BI. (All Europe.) Fls Jul–Aug.

Bristle Bent
Agrostis curtisii

Densely tufted, erect perennial to 60 cm. Leaves Greyish green, fine, bristle-like, 0.2–0.3 mm wide; ligules 2–4 mm, acute, torn. Inflorescences Narrow, spikelike, 3–10 cm, dense; spikelets 3–4 mm; lemmas *c.*⅔ length of glumes, awns arising from base, short, to 5 mm, bent. Habitat Dry and damp, poor, acid sandy or peaty heathland; to >610 m. Dist. Native. Restricted to S and SW England, S Wales. (SW Europe.) Fls Jun–Jul.

Velvet Bent
Agrostis canina

Stoloniferous, turf-forming perennial, rooting at nodes and producing tufts of leafy shoots. Stems Flowering stems erect from prostrate base, to 75 cm. Leaves 1–3 mm wide, bright green, long-linear, tapering to fine point; ligules >1.5× as long as wide, 2–4 mm, pointed. Inflorescences Diffuse, open, contracting in fruit, branches clustered; spikelets 1.5–4 mm; lemmas *c.*⅔ length of glumes, awns arising from near base or absent. Habitat Infertile, wet acidic grasslands, meadows, fens, marshes, heaths, springs, water margins; to 1035 m. Dist. Native. Common throughout BI. (All Europe.) Fls Jun–Aug.

Brown Bent
Agrostis vinealis

Densely tufted perennial to 60 cm. Similar to *A. canina*, but rhizomatous, without stolons; ligules 1–5 mm, <1.5× as long as wide; inflorescence strongly contracted in fruit; lemmas *c.*¾ length of glumes, awns 2–4.5 mm or absent. Habitat Dry, acid sandy or peaty grassland, heaths, open woodland; to 845 m. Dist. Native. Common throughout BI in suitable habitats. (N, W and central Europe.) Fls Jun–Aug.

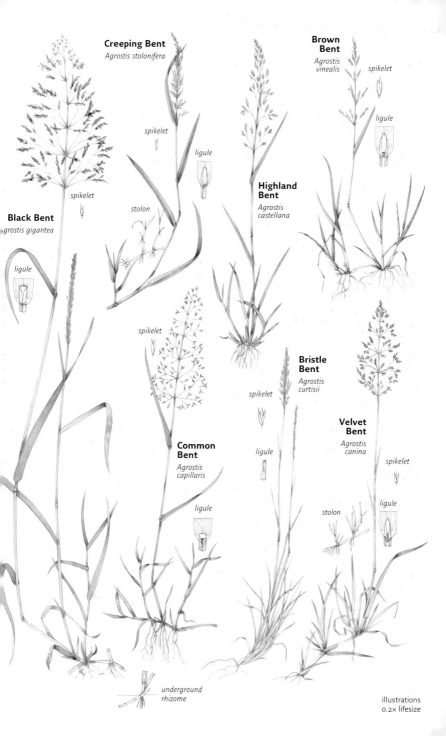

Creeping Bent
Agrostis stolonifera

spikelet

ligule

stolon

Brown Bent
Agrostis vinealis

spikelet

ligule

Highland Bent
Agrostis castellana

Black Bent
Agrostis gigantea

spikelet

ligule

Common Bent
Agrostis capillaris

spikelet

ligule

Bristle Bent
Agrostis curtisii

spikelet

ligule

Velvet Bent
Agrostis canina

spikelet

ligule

stolon

underground rhizome

illustrations
0.2× lifesize

Small-reeds *Calamagrostis*

Tall, rhizomatous, clump-forming reed-like grasses (*see* key on p.598). Inflorescence a 'bushy', much-branched panicle; spikelets 1-flowered, glumes ± equal, longer than rest of spikelet; lemmas awned, with a conspicuous tuft of long (>⅘ as long as lemma), silky white hairs at the base; palea *c.*⅘ as long as lemma. Plants of mostly wet habitats.

Wood Small-reed   *Calamagrostis epigejos*

Tall, robust, tussock-forming, rhizomatous perennial to 200 cm. LEAVES Long and linear, flat, finely pointed, 4–10 mm wide, glabrous, rough and prominently veined above; *ligules 4–9 mm*, blunt, torn. INFLORESCENCES Dense, 15–30 cm, purplish green or brownish; spikelets densely clustered, 5–7 mm; *lemmas 2.5–3 mm, 3-veined, awn arising from tip, hairs at base >1.5× as long as lemma.* HABITAT Wet woods, ditches, fens, dune slacks, old quarries. DIST. Native. Widespread throughout lowland England; scarce in rest of BI. (Most of Europe.) FLS Jun–Aug.

Purple Small-reed   *Calamagrostis canescens*

Similar to *C. epigejos*, but more slender, to 120 cm; leaves 3–6 mm wide, rough, upper surface sparsely hairy; *ligules 2–6 mm; lemmas 2–2.5 mm, 3–5-veined, basal hairs ≤1.5× as long as lemma.* HABITAT Fens, marshes, fen carr; to 335 m. DIST. Native. Rather local. E and central England N to S Scotland; scattered elsewhere; absent from Ireland. (Central and N Europe.) FLS Jun–Jul.

Scandinavian Small-reed   *Calamagrostis purpurea*

Tall, tufted, perennial with long rhizomes, to 200 cm. An apomictic species that was not recognised in Britain until 1980. STEMS Flowering stems with 5–8 nodes. LEAVES 5–10 mm wide, upper surface glabrous, rough or hairy; *ligules long, 7–10 mm.* INFLORESCENCES 5–35 cm, nodding; spikelets 4–7 mm, brownish green; *lemmas 2.5–3.5 mm, 5-veined, awn arising from apical third, basal hairs ≤1.5× as long as lemma; anthers without pollen.* HABITAT Wet willow carr, marshes, ditches. DIST. Native. Very rare. NW England, central Scotland. (N-central and E Europe.) FLS Jun–Aug.

Narrow-Small-reed   *Calamagrostis stricta* VU. *(NI)

Tufted, rhizomatous perennial. Similar to *C. canescens*, but flowering stems slender, erect, to 100 cm; *leaves 1.5–5 mm wide, glabrous or shortly hairy, smooth; ligules 1–3 mm*, rounded; inflorescence 7–20 cm; spikelets 3–4 mm, densely clustered; *glumes 3–4 mm*, lanceolate, tip acute; *lemmas 2.5–3.2 mm, 5-veined, tip toothed, ring of hairs ⅘ as long as lemma, awn arising ≤halfway from base, about as long as lemma.* HABITAT Fens, lake margins; to 340 m. DIST. Native. Very rare. In a few localities scattered throughout BI. (N and central Europe.) FLS Jun–Aug.

Scottish Small-reed   *Calamagrostis scotica* VU.

Very similar to *C. stricta*, but spikelets longer, 4.5–6 mm; *glumes 4.5–6 mm, narrowly lanceolate with acuminate tip.* HABITAT Rush-dominated pasture, willow carr. DIST. Endemic. At one locality only, in Caithness (NE Scotland). FLS Jun–Aug. NOTE May not be a distinct species from *C. stricta*.

Marram   *Ammophila arenaria*

Tall, tufted, rhizomatous, sand-binding perennial to 120 cm. LEAVES Greyish green, to 90 cm long × 6 mm wide, *stiff, tightly inrolled, sharp-pointed, prominently ribbed above*; ligules long, pointed. INFLORESCENCES *Spike-like, cylindrical, pale*, 7–22 cm long; spikelets 10–16 mm, compressed, 1-flowered; glumes longer than lemmas, narrow; lemmas 8–12 mm, blunt with short point, base with fine hairs. HABITAT Dominant plant of mobile dunes. DIST. Native all around coasts of BI. (Coasts of Europe except extreme N.) FLS Jun–Aug.

Nit Grass   *Gastridium ventricosum*

Loosely tufted or solitary, slender annual to 70 cm. LEAVES 2–4 mm wide, flat, glabrous, finely pointed; ligules 1–3 mm. INFLORESCENCES *Cylindrical, spike-like panicle*, 5–15 cm, pale green shining; spikelets 3–5 mm, 1-flowered; *glumes 3–5 mm, narrow, lanceolate, hard, shiny, with a swollen base*; lemmas rounded 0.8–1 mm, awned or awnless in same spikelet. HABITAT S-facing, open, broken limestone grassland; formerly an arable weed. DIST. Native. Rare, declining. S and SW England, S Wales. (S and W Europe.) FLS Jun–Aug.

Early Sand-grass   *Mibora minima*

Tiny, glabrous, tufted annual, 2–15 cm. STEMS *Numerous, slender*. LEAVES Mostly basal, bristle-like, inrolled, 0.5 mm wide. INFLORESCENCES *1-sided spike-like panicle*, 5–20 mm, *reddish purple* or green; spikelets 2–3 mm, 1-flowered; lemmas broad, hairy. HABITAT Moist coastal sand-dunes, gravelly cliff slopes. DIST. Native. Very rare. In a few localities in Anglesey, S Wales, Channel Is. (SW and S Europe.) FLS Apr–May, Aug–Sep.

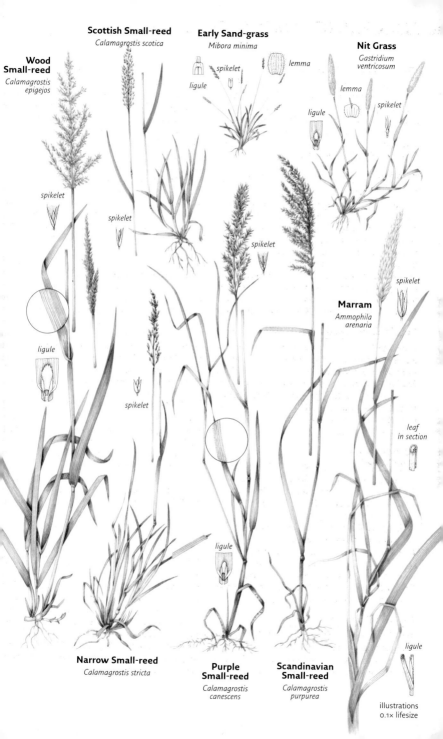

Scottish Small-reed
Calamagrostis scotica

Early Sand-grass
Mibora minima

spikelet

ligule

lemma

Nit Grass
Gastridium ventricosum

Wood Small-reed
Calamagrostis epigejos

lemma

ligule

spikelet

spikelet

spikelet

spikelet

ligule

Marram
Ammophila arenaria

spikelet

spikelet

ligule

spikelet

leaf in section

Narrow Small-reed
Calamagrostis stricta

Purple Small-reed
Calamagrostis canescens

Scandinavian Small-reed
Calamagrostis purpurea

ligule

illustrations 0.1× lifesize

Silky-bents *Apera*

Almost hairless annual grasses. Inflorescence a whorled panicle; spikelets 1-flowered; lower glume about as long as rest of spikelet; lemmas 5-veined, with long, straight awn arising from just below tip.

Loose Silky-bent   *Apera spica-venti*

Tall annual to 100 cm. LEAVES 3–10 mm wide, flat; *ligules 3–10 mm, torn.* INFLORESCENCES Diffuse whorled panicle; *spikelets small, 2.4–3 mm;* lemmas about as long as upper glumes; *awns straight, long, 5–10 mm; anthers 1–2 mm.* HABITAT Dry, sandy arable fields, tracks, roadsides. DIST. Archaeophyte. Scattered throughout lowland England, especially Thames Valley, East Anglia. (Most of Europe.) FLS Jun–Jul.

Dense Silky-bent   *Apera interrupta*

Similar to *A. spica-venti,* but smaller, to 60 cm; leaves shorter, 1–4 mm wide; ligules 2–5 mm, toothed; *inflorescence green or purplish, contracted and interrupted below;* spikelets 1.8–2.5 mm; *anthers 0.3–0.4 mm.* HABITAT Dry, sandy arable fields, road verges, heathy grassland. DIST. Introduced. Local in lowland England, especially East Anglia. (W and central Europe.) FLS Jun–Jul.

Annual Beard-grass   *Polypogon monspeliensis*

Erect, ± glabrous annual to 80 cm. LEAVES Flat, rough, 2–8 mm wide, upper sheaths somewhat inflated; ligules long, 3–15 mm, toothed. INFLORESCENCES *Cylindrical, dense, silky, yellowish green, 2–10 cm long;* spikelets 2–3 mm, 1-flowered, falling complete with glumes and pedicel at maturity; *glumes ± equal with awns, 3.5–7 mm;* lemmas c.¼ length of glumes, blunt, toothed, awnless or with short awn. HABITAT Upper levels of salt marshes, edges of brackish pools, ditches, bare trampled ground, near sea; casual inland. DIST. Native. Very local. Coasts of England from Norfolk to Dorset. (S and W Europe.) FLS Jun–Aug.

Southern Beard-grass   *Polypogon maritimus*

Similar to *P. monspeliensis,* but more slender, to 25 cm; glumes deeply divided at tip and more hairy; lemmas without awn. HABITAT Bare ground near sea. DIST. *Not BI.* (W Europe, Mediterranean.)

Water Bent   *Polypogon viridis*

Tufted annual or stoloniferous perennial to 60 cm. STEMS Ascending from prostrate base. LEAVES 2–10 mm wide, hairless; ligules 1.5–6 mm. INFLORESCENCES

Dense, lobed; spikelets 1-flowered; glumes without awns. SIMILAR SPP. *Looks like a bent-grass (p.626), but glumes falling with rest of spikelet when mature, lemma and palea ± equal in length, and anthers only c.0.5 mm long.* HABITAT Waste ground, nurseries, urban weed. DIST. Introduced. Naturalised in Channel Is; casual in lowland England. (S Europe.) FLS Jun–Aug.

Foxtails *Alopecurus*

See key on p.599. Inflorescence a cylindrical, spike-like panicle; spikelets 1-flowered, compressed, whole spikelet falling when mature; glumes ± equal, margins sometimes fused around spikelet; lemmas awned, palea absent.

Meadow Foxtail   *Alopecurus pratensis*

Tall, tufted, glabrous perennial to 120 cm. LEAVES 3–10 mm wide, flat; ligules 1–2.5 mm. INFLORESCENCES *Soft, 2–13 cm long, green or purplish;* spikelets 4–6 mm; glumes pointed, ± as long as spikelet, margins fused for c.¼ of their length from base; *lemma as long as glumes, awns projecting 3–5 mm from spikelet.* HABITAT Grasslands on damp, fertile soils; to 610 m. DIST. Native. Common throughout most of BI. (Most of Europe.) FLS Apr–Jul.

Marsh Foxtail   *Alopecurus geniculatus*

Creeping perennial, *rooting at nodes.* STEMS *Bent (kneed),* ascending. LEAVES 2–7 mm wide, green to greyish green, upper sheaths somewhat inflated; ligules 2–5 mm. INFLORESCENCES 1.5–7 cm long; spikelets 2–3.3 mm; *glumes obtuse,* margins free almost to base; lemmas about as long as glumes, *awns projecting 1.5–3 mm; anthers yellow or purple.* HABITAT Marshy fields, pond and ditch margins; lowland to 595 m. DIST. Native. Frequent throughout BI. (Most of Europe.) FLS Jun–Aug.

Bulbous Foxtail   *Alopecurus bulbosus*

Tufted perennial. Similar to *A. geniculatus,* but stem to 20 cm, *basal one or two joints swollen and bulb-like, not rooting at nodes;* leaves 1–3.5 mm wide, upper sheaths somewhat inflated; ligules 2–6 mm; spikelets 3–4 mm; glumes acute, margins free to base; lemmas shorter than glumes, awn projecting 3–4 mm. HABITAT Open, brackish, winter-wet habitats, trampled tracks, ditches, meadows. DIST. Native. Very local. S coast of England, Severn estuary, S Wales; rare elsewhere. (Coasts of N and W Europe.) FLS May–Aug

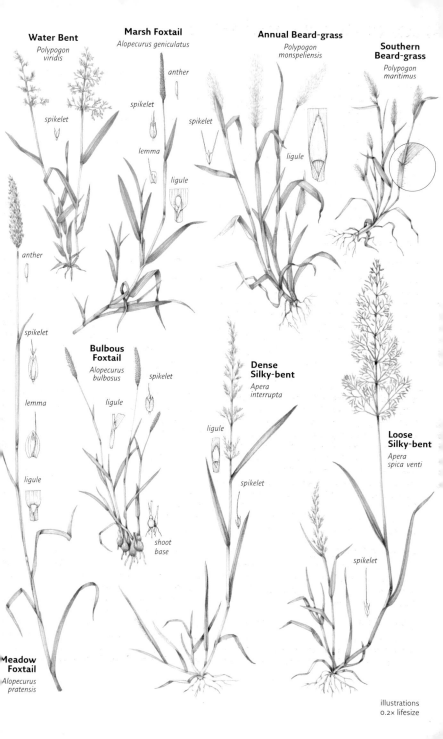

Water Bent
*Polypogon
viridis*

spikelet

Marsh Foxtail
Alopecurus geniculatus

anther

spikelet

lemma

ligule

Annual Beard-grass
*Polypogon
monspeliensis*

spikelet

ligule

**Southern
Beard-grass**
*Polypogon
maritimus*

anther

spikelet

lemma

ligule

**Bulbous
Foxtail**
*Alopecurus
bulbosus*

ligule

spikelet

*shoot
base*

**Dense
Silky-bent**
*Apera
interrupta*

ligule

spikelet

**Loose
Silky-bent**
*Apera
spica venti*

spikelet

**Meadow
Foxtail**
*Alopecurus
pratensis*

illustrations
0.2× lifesize

Orange Foxtail   *Alopecurus aequalis*

Annual or biennial, similar in habit to *A. geniculatus* (p.630). INFLORESCENCES *Lemmas with short awns, not or only just projecting beyond tips of glumes; anthers bright orange.* HABITAT Shallow water of ponds and ditches, wet meadows, especially on drying mud; lowland. DIST. Native. Local in England, Wales; very rare in Ireland. (Most of Europe.) FLS Jun-Sep.

Alpine Foxtail   *Alopecurus borealis*

Erect, tufted, rhizomatous *alpine perennial* to 40 cm. LEAVES 1.5-6 mm wide, upper sheaths somewhat inflated; ligules 1-2 mm. INFLORESCENCES *Broadly cylindrical*, very dense, 1-3 cm long, *silky*, greyish green or purplish; spikelets 2-2.5 mm; glumes hairy, margins joined at base; *lemmas very blunt, awn very short and not projecting or absent.* HABITAT Acid springs, flushes, often in areas of late snow-lie; 450-1220 m. DIST. Native. Rare. N England, Scotland. (Arctic Europe.) FLS Jul-Aug.

Black-grass, Twitch   *Alopecurus myosuroides*

Loosely tufted *annual* to 70 cm. LEAVES 2-8 mm wide, rough, hairless, *upper sheaths somewhat inflated*; ligules 2-5 mm, blunt. Spikelets *Very narrow*, 2-12 cm; spikelets 4.5-7 mm; *glumes pointed, margins united for ⅓-½ their length*; lemmas as long as or longer than glumes, blunt, *awn projecting 4-8 mm.* HABITAT Common and troublesome weed of cereal crops. DIST. Archaeophyte. Widely distributed SE of line from Humber to Severn; scattered elsewhere. (S and W Europe.) FLS May-Aug.

Cat's-tails *Phleum*

See key on p.599. Annual or perennial grasses with a spike-like inflorescence similar in appearance to *Alopecurus*, but *glumes with short, stiff awns and strongly keeled with short, stiff hairs; lemmas without awns.* Leaves flat, hairless; spikelets 1-flowered.

Timothy   *Phleum pratense*

Robust, tufted, erect perennial to 150 cm. STEMS Basal internodes usually swollen. LEAVES *4-8 mm wide*, rough; *ligules to 6 mm, blunt.* INFLORESCENCES 6-15 cm long, *6-10 mm wide; spikelets 4-5 mm*; glumes 3.5-5.5 mm, blunt, awn 1-2 mm; lemmas shorter than glumes, broad, blunt. HABITAT Rough

grassland, pastures, meadows, roadsides. DIST. Native. Widespread and common throughout most of BI, but scarce in N Scotland; introduced in outer isles of Orkney, Shetland. (Most of Europe.) FLS Jun-Aug.

Smaller Cat's-tail   *Phleum bertolonii*

Similar to *P. pratense*, and sometimes difficult to distinguish from that species, but smaller; flowering stems to 50 cm, basal internodes swollen and bulb-like; leaves 2-6 mm wide; *ligules 1-4 mm, acute; inflorescence 3-7.5 mm wide; spikelets 2-3.5 mm*, awns 0.2-1.2 mm. HABITAT Old pastures, meadows, downs, roadsides, often with *P. pratense* but also on poorer soils. DIST. Native. Throughout BI, but rare in N Scotland, Ireland. (Most of Europe.) FLS Jun-Aug.

Alpine Cat's-tail   *Phleum alpinum*

Loosely tufted, rhizomatous *alpine perennial* to 50 cm. LEAVES To 6 mm wide; ligules blunt, to 2 mm. INFLORESCENCES *Broadly cylindrical*, 1-5 cm long, 6-12 mm wide; *bristly*; spikelets 3-3.8 mm; glumes blunt, 5-8.5 mm including awns; *awns long 2-4 mm.* HABITAT Damp calcareous or base-rich cliffs, corries, grassy slopes; 610-1220 m. DIST. Native. Rare. N England, Scotland. (Arctic Europe mts of S Europe.) FLS Jul-Aug.

Purple-stem Cat's-tail   *Phleum phleoides*

Densely tufted perennial to 70 cm. STEMS *Often purplish*. LEAVES Greyish green, flat or rolled, 1-3.5 mm wide, rough; ligules blunt, to 2 mm. INFLORESCENCE 1.5-10 cm, very dense, tapered; spikelets 2.5-3 mm; glumes as long as spikelet, *abruptly narrowed to rough point to 0.5 mm long.* HABITAT Grazed grass heaths, tracksides, verges, disturbed ground, on dry sandy or calcareous soils. DIST. Native. Very local. East Anglia (especially Breckland). (Most of Europe.) FLS Jun-Aug.

Sand Cat's-tail   *Phleum arenarium*

Small, slender annual to 15 cm. LEAVES Pale green, flat to 4 mm wide, sheaths inflated; ligules to 7 mm. INFLORESCENCES 5-50 × 3-7 mm, narrowed at base, pale to whitish green, becoming straw-coloured spikelets 3-4 mm; *glumes gradually narrowed to sharp pointed tip.* HABITAT Coastal sand-dunes, sandy shingle; inland sandy heaths (Breckland, East Anglia). DIST. Native. All round coasts of BI except N and W Scotland, S Ireland. (S and W Europe.) FLS May-Jul.

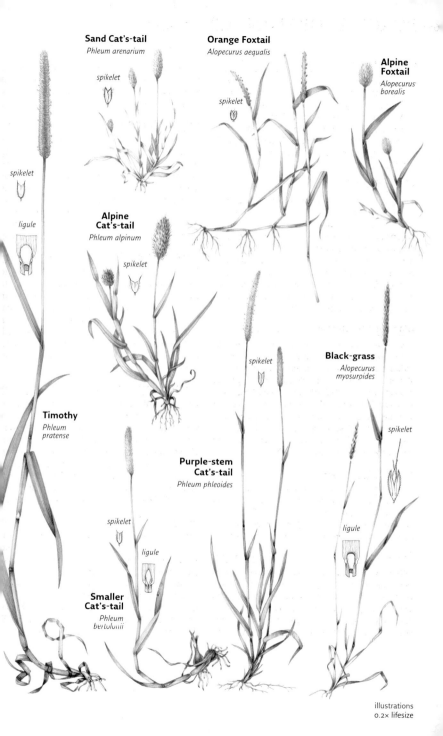

Sand Cat's-tail
Phleum arenarium

spikelet

Orange Foxtail
Alopecurus aequalis

spikelet

Alpine Foxtail
Alopecurus borealis

spikelet

ligule

Alpine Cat's-tail
Phleum alpinum

spikelet

Black-grass
Alopecurus myosuroides

spikelet

spikelet

Timothy
Phleum pratense

Purple-stem Cat's-tail
Phleum phleoides

spikelet

ligule

spikelet

ligule

Smaller Cat's-tail
Phleum bertolonii

illustrations
0.2× lifesize

Bromes *Bromus, Bromopsis, Anisantha* and *Ceratochloa*

Annual or perennial, usually pubescent, grasses without stolons (*see* key on p.600); spikelets with several to many florets; glumes unequal, much shorter than rest of spikelet; lemmas 5–11-veined, rounded or keeled on back, usually awned; tip of ovary with a hairy tuft.

Soft-brome
Bromus hordeaceus

Very variable with several ssp. Loosely tufted or solitary *annual* or biennial. STEMS Flowering stems 5–80 cm. LEAVES 2–7 mm wide, flat, softly hairy; ligules to 2.5 mm, blunt, toothed. INFLORESCENCES Greyish green or purplish; *spikelets 12–22 mm, narrowly ovate, softly hairy*; lower glume 3–7-veined, upper 5–7-veined; *lemmas 8–11 mm, with pale margin, overlapping, rounded on back*, 7–9-veined, awn 5–10 mm. HABITAT Pastures, meadows, cliffs, waste ground; to 550 m. DIST. Native. Widespread throughout BI, becoming scarce in N Scotland. (All Europe.) FLS May–Jul.

Meadow Brome
Bromus commutatus

Erect annual to 90 cm. LEAVES 3–9 mm wide, hairy; ligules 1–4 mm, toothed. INFLORESCENCES *Loose, open, eventually drooping, branches longer than spikelets*; spikelets 15–28 mm, 4–10-flowered; *lemmas 8–11 mm*, overlapping, awn 4–10 mm; anthers 1–1.5 mm. HABITAT Damp, unimproved meadows, old pastures, tracksides, field borders. DIST. Native. Declining. Mostly SE of line from Humber to Severn; scattered elsewhere. (Most of Europe except extreme N.) FLS May–Jul.

Smooth Brome
Bromus racemosus

Very similar to *B. commutatus*, but spikelets 10–16 mm; *lemmas 6.5–8 mm*, awn 5–9 mm; anthers 2–3 mm. HABITAT Hay fields, old pasture, water meadows, field margins. DIST. Native. Scattered; declining. England, Wales, Ireland. (Most of Europe.) FLS Jun–Jul.

Slender Soft-brome
Bromus lepidus

Loosely tufted annual or biennial to 90 cm. Similar to *B. hordeaceus*, but more slender; inflorescence more open; *spikelets 5–15 mm, almost hairless; lemmas 5.5–6.5 mm, with broad, pale, shiny margins*. HABITAT Improved and sown grassland, waste ground. DIST. Introduced. Scattered throughout BI but declining. (NW and N-central Europe.) FLS May–Jul.

Rye Brome
Bromus secalinus VU.

Loosely tufted, stiffly erect annual or biennial to 80 cm. LEAVES 4–12 mm wide, *sheaths glabrous*; ligules 1–2 mm. INFLORESCENCES Open or contracted; spikelets 12–24 mm, 4–11-flowered, breaking up below each lemma; *lemmas 6.5–9 mm, with inrolled margins tightly enclosing fruit* and so not overlapping each other, awn 4.5–9 mm. FRUITS Inrolled. HABITAT Arable weed of cereal fields, casual on waste ground. DIST. Archaeophyte. Throughout BI, but rare and declining. (S and S-central Europe.) FLS Jun–Jul.

Hairy-brome
Bromopsis ramosa

Tall, robust, loosely tufted perennial to 190 cm. LEAVES *6–16 mm wide, very hairy, dark green, flat, drooping; sheath with distinct auricles*, ligules to 6 mm. INFLORESCENCES 15–45 cm, loose, nodding; *branches drooping, in pairs*, each with up to 9 spikelets, *lowest branches with minute hairy scale at base*; spikelets 20–24 mm, pendulous, narrow, 4–11-flowered; lemmas 10–14 mm, awn straight, 4–8 mm. HABITAT Shaded woodlands, hedgerows, on moist, base-rich soils; lowland to 420 m. DIST. Native. Frequent throughout BI, but becoming scarce in N Scotland, W Ireland. (W, central and S Europe.) FLS Jul–Aug.

Lesser Hairy-brome
Bromopsis benekenii

Similar to *B. ramosa*, but leaves 4–12 mm wide, almost hairless; ligules 1–3 mm; inflorescence 12–20 cm, less wide-spreading, branches shorter; *lowest inflorescence node with >2 branches, each with 1–2 spikelets that have hairless scale at base*; spikelets 15–25 mm, 3–5-flowered. HABITAT Shaded woodland, especially Beech woods on calcareous soils. DIST. Native. Scattered throughout Britain; absent from Ireland. (Most of Europe.) FLS Jun–Aug.

Upright Brome
Bromopsis erecta

Tufted, erect perennial to 100 cm. LEAVES *Lower leaves narrow, 2–3 mm wide, inrolled*; upper leaves flat; *margins with equally spaced, spreading hairs as long as leaf is wide*; ligules 1.3–3 mm. INFLORESCENCES *10–15 cm, erect, reddish brown*; branches erect, clustered; spikelets 15–40 mm, 4–14-flowered; lemmas 8–15 mm, awn 3–8 mm. HABITAT Rough undergrazed grassland on infertile calcareous soil, often forming dense stands; also calcareous dunes. DIST. Native. England SE of line from Tees to Severn; scattered and coastal elsewhere in Britain; central and E Ireland. (S, W and central Europe.) FLS Jun–Jul.

Hungarian Brome
Bromopsis inermis

Tall, rhizomatous perennial to 150 cm. Similar to *B. erecta*, but *leaves flat, hairless; lemmas without awn*. HABITAT Naturalised or casual on rough grassland verges, waste ground, on dry sandy soils. DIST. Introduced (native of North America). Scattered throughout lowland England. (Much of Europe.) FLS Jul–Aug.

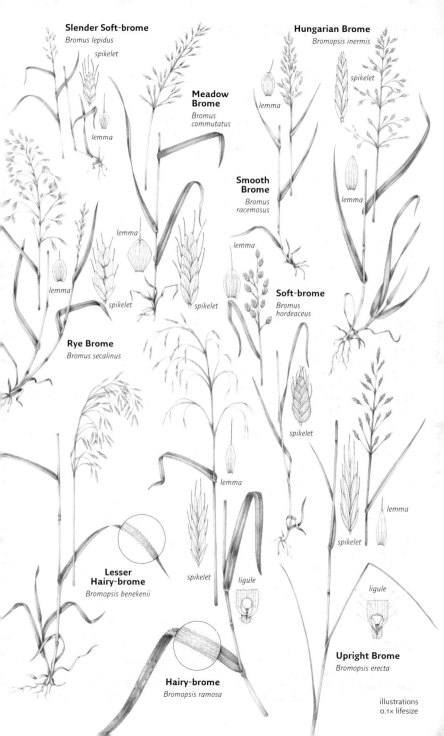

Slender Soft-brome
Bromus lepidus

spikelet

lemma

Meadow Brome
Bromus commutatus

lemma

spikelet

Hungarian Brome
Bromopsis inermis

spikelet

lemma

lemma

Smooth Brome
Bromus racemosus

lemma

lemma

spikelet

Soft-brome
Bromus hordeaceus

lemma

spikelet

Rye Brome
Bromus secalinus

spikelet

lemma

spikelet

lemma

Lesser Hairy-brome
Bromopsis benekenii

lemma

spikelet

ligule

ligule

Hairy-brome
Bromopsis ramosa

Upright Brome
Bromopsis erecta

illustrations
0.1× lifesize

Great Brome *Anisantha diandra*

Loosely tufted annual to 80 cm. LEAVES 4–8 mm wide, loosely hairy; ligules 3–6 mm, jagged. INFLORESCENCES To 25 cm, lax, spreading, nodding, branches in clusters of 2–4; spikelets 7–9 cm (including awns), becoming wedge-shaped, 5–8-flowered; lemmas 20–36 mm, awn 35–65 mm. HABITAT Arable fields, roadsides, waste ground, heathland, on sandy soils. DIST. Introduced. Scattered throughout BI, but widespread in East Anglia, Channel Is. (S and W Europe.) FLS May–Jul.

Ripgut Brome *Anisantha rigida*

Loosely tufted annual to 60 cm. Similar to *A. diandra*, but inflorescence dense, with erect branches; spikelets 2.5–3.5 cm; glumes pale except for veins; lemmas 22–30 mm. HABITAT Rare casual of disturbed ground on sandy soils; naturalised near sea on S coast, Channel Is. DIST. (S and W Europe.) FLS May–Jun.

Barren Brome *Anisantha sterilis*

Loosely tufted or solitary, erect annual to 100 cm. LEAVES Soft, flat, hairy, 2–7 mm wide; ligules 2–4 mm, toothed. INFLORESCENCES Very loose, open, nodding; branches wide-spreading, at least some as long as or longer than spikelets, each with 1 spikelet; spikelets 4–6 cm (including awns), 4–10-flowered; lemmas 13–20 mm, awn 15–30 mm. HABITAT Roadsides, hedge banks, railway banks, waste ground, cereal crops; to 365 m. DIST. Archaeophyte. Naturalised throughout Britain N to central Scotland, E Ireland. (S, W and central Europe.) FLS May–Jul.

Compact Brome *Anisantha madritensis*

Loosely tufted or solitary, erect or spreading annual to 60 cm. Similar to *A. sterilis*, but upper leaf sheaths hairless; inflorescence contracted, branches erect, shorter than spikelets, with 1–2 spikelets; lemmas 12–20 mm. HABITAT Waste ground, roadsides, walls, sand-dunes. DIST. Introduced. Naturalised or casual in scattered sites in S England, S Wales. (S and W Europe.) FLS May–Jul.

California Brome *Ceratochloa carinata*

Short-lived, erect perennial to 80 cm. LEAVES 4–14 mm wide, glabrous or sparsely hairy; ligules *c*.2 mm, apex truncate, torn. INFLORESCENCES Large, 15–30 cm, loose, branches spreading, nodding; spikelets 22–45 mm, 5–9-flowered, strongly compressed; glumes unequal; lemmas 10–18 mm, strongly keeled on back, 7–9-nerved, awn 6–10 mm. HABITAT Naturalised or casual on road verges, field borders, riverbanks, waste ground. DIST. Introduced (native of W North America). FLS Jun–Aug.

False bromes *Brachypodium*

Inflorescence a spike-like raceme, with broader sides of spikelets facing stem; pedicels short, <2 mm, 1 spikelet at each node; lemmas 7-veined, awned.

Tor-grass *Brachypodium pinnatum*

Strongly rhizomatous perennial to 120 cm. STEMS Stiffly erect, usually hairless. LEAVES 2–6 mm wide, yellowish green, rolled or flat, usually stiffly erect, sparsely hairy or glabrous, rough; ligules up to 2 mm. INFLORESCENCES Spike-like, erect, to 25 cm, pedicels 1–2 mm; spikelets 20–40 mm, solitary, cylindrical to lanceolate, alternating in 2 rows or opposite sides of axis, 8–22-flowered; lemmas 6–10 mm, awn short, 1–5 mm. HABITAT Dry, infertile calcareous grassland; to 305 m. Can dominate large areas if undergrazed. DIST. Native. Widespread in England SE of line from Humber to Severn; rare in Ireland. (All Europe except N.) FLS Jun–Aug.

False Brome *Brachypodium sylvaticum*

Densely tufted, weakly rhizomatous perennial to 90 cm. LEAVES Yellowish green, 6–12 mm wide, usually drooping, blades and sheaths loosely hairy; ligules 1–6 mm. INFLORESCENCES Spike-like, 6–20 cm, nodding, pedicels 0.5–2 mm; spikelets 20–40 mm, 8–16-flowered; lemmas 7–12 mm, awn 7–15 mm. HABITAT Woodlands, hedge banks, scrub, limestone grassland and pavement, on well-drained calcareous or neutral soils; to 465 m. DIST. Native. Throughout BI. (Most of Europe.) FLS Jul–Aug.

Couch-grasses and Lyme-grass
Elymus, Elytrigia and *Leymus*

See key on p.601. Inflorescence a spike, with 1–3 sessile spikelets at each node, in 2 opposite and alternate rows on either side of stem, broader side of spikelet facing stem; lemmas 5–7-veined, awned or awnless.

Bearded Couch *Elymus caninus*

Loosely tufted perennial, without rhizomes, to 110 cm. STEMS Flowering stems with short hairs at nodes. LEAVES Bright green, 4–13 mm wide, flat, drooping, sparsely hairy or glabrous; sheaths glabrous or sparsely hairy; ligules to 1.5 mm. INFLORESCENCES A spike, with 1 spikelet at each node, 5–20 cm, nodding; spikelets sessile, 10–20 mm, 2–6-flowered; lemmas 8–13 mm, awn to 20 mm. HABITAT Wood borders, shaded banks of streams and rivers, on well-drained base-rich soils; also mountain gullies, cliff and rock ledges to 810 m in Scotland (var. *donianus*). DIST. Native. Rather local. Throughout BI but rare in Ireland. (All Europe.) FLS Jun–Aug.

Bearded Couch
Elymus caninus

False Brome
Brachypodium sylvaticum

spikelet

ligule

node

spikelet

spikelet

Barren Brome
Anisantha sterilis

spikelet

Great Brome
Anisantha diandra

spikelet

ligule

spikelet

Tor-Grass
Brachypodium pinnatum

Ripgut Brome
Anisantha rigida

California Brome
Ceratochloa carinata

Compact Brome
Anisantha madritensis

illustrations
0.2× lifesize

Common Couch
Elytrigia repens

Robust, tufted perennial to 120 cm, spreading by rhizomes and forming large patches. STEMS Hairless. LEAVES 3–10 mm wide, flat, usually *sparsely hairy above*, sheaths with short, pointed auricles; ligules short, <1 mm. INFLORESCENCES Slender, erect, to 20 cm; *spikelets* 10–20 mm, *overlapping by about ⅓ their length*, in 2 opposite rows on either side of stem; lemmas 6–12 mm, without (var. *repens*) or with (var. *aristata*) an awn. HABITAT Rough grassland, roadsides, railway banks, waste ground, common arable weed of fertile soils; to 430 m. DIST. Native. Widespread throughout BI, but sparse in NW Scotland. (All Europe.) FLS Jun–Aug.

Sea Couch
Elytrigia atherica

Robust *bluish-green* perennial to 120 cm, spreading by long rhizomes and often forming extensive, dense patches. STEMS Hairless. LEAVES 2–6 mm wide, stiff, rolled when dry, *prominently veined above, veins glabrous*; sheaths with short auricles, *lower sheaths with fringe of minute hairs along free margin*; ligules short, <1 mm. INFLORESCENCES 4–20 cm, stiff, erect; spikelets 10–20 mm, closely overlapping; lemmas 7–11 mm, usually without awns. HABITAT Shingle banks, sea walls, edges of brackish creeks, upper levels of salt marshes. DIST. Native. Coasts of BI, N to S Scotland; E and SE Ireland. (W and S Europe.) FLS Jun–Aug.

Sand Couch
Elytrigia juncea

Mat-forming perennial, spreading by long rhizomes. STEMS Flowering stems erect or spreading, to 60 cm. LEAVES Bluish green, 2–6 mm wide, flat or rolled, *upper surface prominently veined, veins densely and shortly hairy*, sheaths without auricles; ligules short, ≤1 mm. INFLORESCENCES 4–20 cm; *spikelets* 15–28 mm, 3–8-flowered, *spaced ± their own length apart, so hardly overlapping*; lemmas 11–20 mm. HABITAT Sandy shores just above strandline, sometimes on fine shingle. DIST. Native. Common all round coasts of BI. (All round coasts of Europe.) FLS Jun–Aug.

Lyme-grass
Leymus arenarius

Tall, robust, rhizomatous perennial to 200 cm. LEAVES Glaucous, 8–20 mm wide, flat or inrolled, sheaths with auricles; ligules short, ≤1 mm. INFLO-RESCENCES *Dense, 15–35 cm long, stiffly erect; spikelets in pairs, 20–32 mm*, 3–6-flowered; lemmas 15–25 mm, densely hairy. HABITAT Coastal sand dunes; widely planted as sand-binder. DIST. Native. All round coasts of BI, but scarce in S and frequent in N. (N and W Europe.) FLS Jul–Aug.

Wood Barley
Hordelymus europaeus *(N

Tall, loosely tufted, short-lived perennial to 120 cm. LEAVES 5–14 mm wide, flat, hairy; lower sheaths with spreading hairs, auricles spreading; ligule short, <1 mm. INFLORESCENCES 5–10 cm, erect, dense, bristly; *3 spikelets at each node, all bisexual, 1-flowered; glumes joined at base, long-awned; lemma 8–10 mm, awn long*, 15–25 mm. HABITAT Wood (especially Beech), copses, old hedgerows, on calcareous soils; to 440 m. DIST. Native. Very local. Scattered throughout England; rare in Wales, Scotland. (Most of Europe except Mediterranean and extreme N.)

Bread Wheat
Triticum aestivum

Erect annual to 150 cm. STEMS Hollow, usually glabrous. LEAVES 6–16 mm wide; sheaths usually glabrous, with auricles; ligules blunt. INFLORES-CENCES 6–18 mm; *1 spikelet per node, 10–15 mm, 3–6-flowered (only 2 fertile); glumes blunt, convex, keeled in upper ⅓ only*, 5–7-veined; lemmas convex, 3-veined, awned or awnless. HABITAT Field borders, roadsides, waste ground. DIST. Introduced. The common cultivated wheat, often persisting as a relic. FLS May–Jul.

Rye
Secale cereale

Similar to wheats. INFLORESCENCES 1 spikelet per node, 2-flowered; glumes narrow, 1-veined; lemma narrow, 5-veined, stiffly hairy on keels, long-awned. DIST. Introduced. Scattered throughout BI as infrequent casual relic of cultivation. FLS May–Jul.

Heath-grass
Danthonia decumbens

Densely tufted perennial to 60 cm. STEMS Flowering stems spreading, slender, stiff. LEAVES Rather glaucous, 2–4 mm wide, stiff, flat or rolled; *ligules a fringe of short hairs*. INFLORESCENCES Narrow panicle with 3–12 spikelets; *spikelets 6–12 mm, rather plump*, 2-flowered, *pale shining purplish or green*; glumes as long as spikelet; lemmas 5–7 mm, margins and base hairy, florets rarely opening. HABITAT Short acid grassland, grass heaths, moorland, chalk and limestone grassland with surface leaching; to 600 m. DIST. Native. Throughout BI. (Most of Europe.) FLS Jun–Aug.

Sand Couch
Elytrigia juncea

spikelet

ligule

Sea Couch
Elytrigia atherica

spikelet

ligule

Heath-grass
Danthonia decumbens

spikelet

ligule

Rye
Secale cereale

spikelet

kelet

spikelet

lemma

spikelet

spikelet

d Barley
delymus
opaeus

Common Couch
Elytrigia repens

Bread Wheat
Triticum aestivum

Lyme-grass
Leymus arenarius

illustrations
0.1× lifesize

Barleys *Hordeum* and *Hordelymus*

Annual or perennial grasses without rhizomes (*see* key on p.601 and *Hordelymus europaeus* on p.638). Inflorescence a spike, with spikelets arranged in groups of 3 (triplets) at each node on inflorescence, the whole dispersed together at maturity; spikelets 1-flowered; each triplet with a central bisexual flower and 2 lateral flowers that are either bisexual (in some cultivated varieties), or male or sterile; glumes and lemmas of bisexual flowers with long awns.

Wall Barley   *Hordeum murinum*

Vigorous annual to 60 cm. STEMS Erect or spreading. LEAVES 2-8 mm wide, usually loosely hairy, with *long-pointed overlapping auricles*, sheaths somewhat inflated; ligules short, to 1 mm. INFLORESCENCES 4-12 cm, erect, dense; glumes bristle-like, with long awns, *glumes of middle spikelet with marginal hairs*; lemmas 7-12 mm, awn 18-50 mm. HABITAT Disturbed ground, rough grassland, walls; to 450 m. DIST. Archaeophyte. Widespread in Britain N to S Scotland; very local in E Ireland. (Most of Europe.) FLS May-Aug.

Sea Barley   *Hordeum marinum* VU.

Loosely tufted or solitary annual to 40 cm. STEMS Erect or spreading. LEAVES 1-3.5 mm wide, bluish green, auricles almost absent, sheaths inflated; ligules short, to 1 mm. INFLORESCENCES 20-60 mm, dense, bristly, awns eventually spreading; glumes narrow, with long awns, *glumes of middle spikelets rough, without marginal hairs*; lemma of middle spikelet 6-8 mm, awn to 24 mm. HABITAT Bare trampled ground close to sea, sea walls, upper parts of salt marshes. DIST. Native. Very local. S coast of Britain from the Wash to S Wales. (Coasts of W and S Europe.) FLS Jun.

Meadow Barley   *Hordeum secalinum* *(R)

Slender, erect, tufted perennial to 80 cm. LEAVES 2-6 mm wide, with *short*, spreading auricles at base, shortly hairy or glabrous, *sheaths not inflated*; ligules <1 mm. INFLORESCENCES Erect, dense, 20-80 mm, awns erect or slightly spreading; glumes bristle-like, awned; lemma 6-9 mm, awn 6-12 mm. HABITAT Old pastures, meadows, alluvial grasslands, on heavy soils; coastal grassland. DIST. Native. Locally common in lowland England; rare further W and in Ireland. (Most of Europe except N.) FLS Jun-Jul.

Two-rowed Barley   *Hordeum distichon*

Erect annual to 90 cm. LEAVES 14-15 mm wide, glabrous, with pointed auricles; ligules very short. INFLORESCENCES 6-12 cm excluding awns; only middle spikelet fertile; lemma *c*.10 mm, *awn very long, to 12 cm; inflorescence not breaking up at maturity, the seed (grain) separating away easily from glumes*. HABITAT

The common cultivated barley, sometimes occurring as a casual relic. DIST. Introduced. FLS May-Jun.

Foxtail Barley   *Hordeum jubatum*

Attractive tufted, short-lived perennial to 60 cm. LEAVES 2-5 mm wide, hairy beneath, sheaths hairy, ligules short, to 1 mm. INFLORESCENCES 3-8 cm, *narrow, dense, nodding, with long purplish awns*; glumes long, narrow, awn-like, those of outer spikelet >30 mm, middle 20-60 mm; lemmas 6-8 mm, awn 50-100 mm. HABITAT Cultivated for ornament. Casual of waste ground and roadsides. DIST. Introduced (native of North America). Scattered throughout BI. FLS May-Aug.

Pampas-grass   *Cortaderia selloana*

Large, tussock-forming perennial to >1 m across. STEMS Flowering stems erect, to >3 m tall. LEAVES 1-3 m, flat, with *fiercely serrated cutting edge*; ligule a row of hairs. INFLORESCENCES Large, spreading panicle, 50-100 cm; spikelets 12-16 mm including awns, silvery; glumes and lemmas awned; base of lemmas with tuft of long, fine hairs. HABITAT Roadsides, rough grassland, sea cliffs, sand-dunes. DIST. Introduced (native of South America). Familiar much-cultivated garden plant, naturalised in S England. FLS Sep-Oct.

Purple Moor-grass   *Molinia caerulea*

Densely tufted perennial, *often forming large, dense tussocks*, especially where there is ground-water movement. STEMS Flowering stems erect, to 130 cm. LEAVES 3-10 mm wide, slightly hairy or glabrous, *ligules a fringe of short hairs*. INFLORESCENCES Loose, open or dense panicle, often with a purplish haze; spikelets 3-7.5 mm, 1-4-flowered; lemmas without awns. HABITAT Heaths, moorland, bogs, wet woodlands, fens, mountain grassland, usually on acid peaty or mineral soils. DIST. Native. Widespread throughout BI, but scarce parts of lowland England. (Most of Europe.) FLS Jul-Sep.

Common Reed   *Phragmites australis*

Tall, robust perennial, spreading by tough, creeping rhizomes and stolons. The tallest native British grass. STEMS *Flowering stems erect, rigid*, to 3 m. LEAVES 10-30 mm wide, greyish green, flat; *ligules a dense fringe of stiff, short hairs*. INFLORESCENCES Large, much-branched, dense or loose purplish panicle to 40 cm; spikelets 10-16 mm, 2-6-flowered; lemmas surrounded by silky white hairs. HABITAT Forms extensive, dense stands (reed-beds) in shallow water of rivers, lakes, ponds, broads, flooded pits, fens, ditches and estuaries. DIST. Throughout BI. (All Europe.) FLS Aug-Oct.

Wall Barley
Hordeum murinum

leaf sheath

ligule

spikelet

Foxtail Barley
Hordeum jubatum

Sea Barley
Hordeum marinum

ligule

spikelet

leaf sheath

Common Reed
Phragmites australis

spikelet

ligule

spikelet

ligule

spikelet

ligule

Purple Moor-grass
Molinia caerulea

leaf sheath

spikelet

Two-rowed Barley
Hordeum distichon

Meadow Barley
Hordeum secalinum

Pampas-grass
Cortaderia selloana

illustrations
0.15× lifesize

Bermuda Grass
Cynodon dactylon

Mat-forming perennial, spreading by scaly rhizomes and much-branched stolons, which produce short, leafy shoots. Stems Flowering shoots to 30 cm. Leaves 2-4 mm wide, flat, sparsely hairy to glabrous; ligules a row of short hairs. Inflorescences *Umbel of 3-6 slender spikes*; spikelets in pairs on one side of inflorescence axis, 1-flowered; lemmas as long as spikelet, boat-shaped, densely and minutely hairy on keel. Habitat Short, sandy grassland, lawns, dunes, close to sea; casual inland. Dist. Introduced or native in W Cornwall. Introduced. Scattered localities in S England, Channel Is, especially near coast. (All Europe.) Fls Aug-Sep.

Common Cord-grass
Spartina anglica

Deep-rooting, rhizomatous perennial. Stems Flowering stems to 130 cm. Leaves Green to greyish green, 6-15 mm wide, erect, flat or inrolled; ligules 1.8-3 mm, consisting of a fringe of silky hairs. Inflorescences 12-40 cm long, a narrow, erect panicle of 2-12 spikes; spikes rigid, to 25 cm, ending in a bristle up to 50 mm long; *spikelets 14-21 mm*, in 2 rows, 1-flowered, softly hairy; *anthers 7-10 mm*. Habitat Coastal and estuarine salt marshes, dominating extensive areas of inter-tidal mud flats. Dist. Native. Coasts of Britain N to central Scotland, all round coasts of Ireland. (W Europe) Fls Jul-Nov.

Small Cord-grass
Spartina maritima EN.

Tufted or patch-forming, rhizomatous perennial. Similar to *S. anglica*, but smaller and more slender; flowering stems stiffly erect, to 50 cm; leaves dark green to purplish, narrower, 3.5-4.5 mm wide; ligules 0.2-0.6 mm; inflorescence 4-10 cm long, a panicle of 1-5 spikes; spikes 3-8 cm, dark green or purplish, ending in a bristle up to 14 mm long; *spikelets 11-17 mm*; *anthers 4-6.5 mm*. Habitat Bare inter-tidal sand or mud, salt-marsh creeks and pans, bare ground behind sea walls. Dist. Native. Very local. The Wash to Southampton Water. (S and W Europe.) Fls Jul-Sep.

Cockspur
Echinochloa crus-galli

Tufted annual to 120 cm. Stems Flowering stems erect or spreading, usually branched. Leaves 10-20 mm wide, flat, hairless; ligules absent. Inflorescences *To 20 cm, green or purplish, comprising a branched panicle of several dense spike-like racemes*; spikelets 3-4 mm, crowded in groups or pairs, 2-flowered; lower lemma with short point or awn up to 5 cm. Habitat Casual of waste ground, rubbish tips, cultivated ground. Dist. Introduced. Scattered throughout England, Wales; rare in Scotland, Ireland. (All Europe.) Fls Aug-Oct.

Common Millet
Panicum miliaceum

Tall, tufted annual to 120 cm. Leaves 8-25 mm wide, flat, *sheaths with long, spreading hairs*; ligules a fringe of hairs, c.1.2 mm. Inflorescences *Large, diffuse panicle*, drooping at tip; spikelets 4-6 mm, 2-flowered; lemmas without awns. Habitat Birdseed casual of waste ground, tips, game-bird feeding areas. Dist. Introduced (native of Asia). Scattered throughout BI. Fls Aug-Oct.

Bristle-grasses *Setaria*

Mostly annuals with dense spike-like inflorescences; spikelets 2-flowered, the upper bisexual, the lower male or sterile; base of each spikelet with a small tuft of minutely toothed bristles, which remain after spikelets have fallen; awns without lemmas. Several similar-looking species occur as casuals of tips and waste ground, usually originating from bird- or oil-seed.

Green Bristle-grass
Setaria viridis

Loosely tufted annual to 60 cm. Leaves 4-10 mm wide, flat, glabrous, sheaths hairy on margins; ligules a fringe of silky hairs. Inflorescences 1-10 cm, greenish or purplish, erect, dense and bristly; *bristles up to 10 mm, 1-3 beneath each spikelet*; spikelets 2-2.5 mm; upper glume much longer than lower glume, ± as long as spikelet. Habitat Birdseed casual of tips and waste ground. Dist. Introduced. Scattered throughout BI. (S Europe.) Fls Aug-Oct.

Yellow Bristle-grass
Setaria pumila

Similar to *S. viridis*, but *5-10 yellowish to reddish-yellow bristles per spikelet*; spikelets 3-33 mm; upper glume scarcely longer than lower glume and ½-⅔ as long as spikelet. Habitat Casual of tips and waste ground. Dist. Introduced. Scattered throughout BI (S Europe.) Fls Jul-Oct.

Smooth Finger-grass
Digitaria ischaemum

Tufted *annual* to 35 cm. Stems Flowering stems prostrate or spreading from bent base. Leaves 2-7 mm wide, tinged purple, flat, glabrous; sheaths glabrous; ligules 1-2 mm, blunt. Inflorescences *2-8 slender, spreading, spike-like racemes arising from near tip of stem*; spikelets 2-2.3 mm, in pairs on one side of axis, 2-flowered; upper glume and lower lemma ± same length. Habitat Rare casual of waste ground, tips. Dist. Introduced. S England. (S Europe.) Fls Aug-Sep. Similar spp. **Hairy Finger grass** *D. sanguinalis* is taller than *D. ischaemum* and differs in the hairy sheaths and the upper glume < as long as lemma. It occurs as a weed of bulb fields in the Channel Is and Scilly Is.

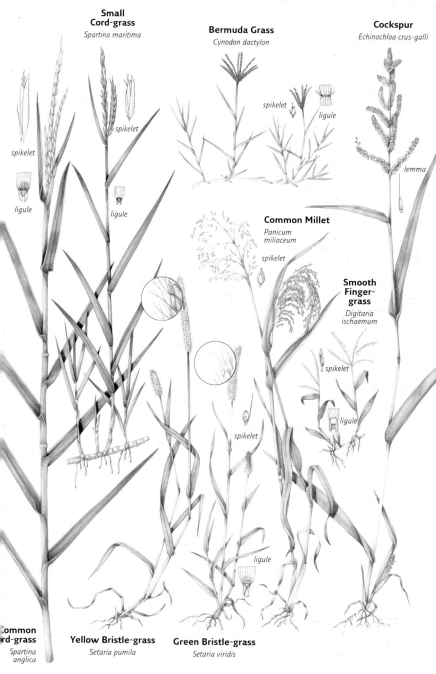

**Small
Cord-grass**
Spartina maritima

spikelet

spikelet

ligule

spikelet

ligule

Bermuda Grass
Cynodon dactylon

spikelet

ligule

Cockspur
Echinochloa crus-galli

lemma

Common Millet
*Panicum
miliaceum*

spikelet

**Smooth
Finger-
grass**
*Digitaria
ischaemum*

spikelet

ligule

spikelet

ligule

**Common
Cord-grass**

*Spartina
anglica*

Yellow Bristle-grass
Setaria pumila

Green Bristle-grass
Setaria viridis

illustrations
0.2× lifesize

SPARGANIACEAE Bur-reeds

Rhizomatous aquatic perennials, with branched or unbranched stems. Leaves long and narrow with sheathing bases. Flowers unisexual, in tight, spherical heads, female heads at base of inflorescence, male heads above; individual flowers minute, with 3–6 scale-like tepals; male flowers with ≥3 stamens, females with a single ovary.

1	Inflorescence branched, male heads on branches and main stem, tepals dark-tipped	*S. erectum*
	Inflorescence unbranched, all male heads on main stem, tepals not dark-tipped	2
2	Stem leaves keeled at base, triangular in section; >3 male heads, well separated	*S. emersum*
	Stem leaves flat; 1–3 male heads, crowded together	3
3	Leaf-like bract of lowest female head >10 cm long, >2× as long as inflorescence; usually 2 male heads	*S. angusti-folium*
	Leaf-like bract of lowest female head <10 cm long, barely longer than inflorescence; usually 1 male head	*S. natans*

Branched Bur-reed
Sparganium erectum

Robust, erect perennial to 150 cm. LEAVES 10–15 mm wide, erect, keeled. INFLORESCENCES *Branched; 6–9 male heads*, mostly on branches above the 1–3 female heads. HABITAT Shallow margins of rivers, dykes, lakes, ponds and canals, in nutrient-rich water; to 425 m. DIST. Native. Common throughout BI, but scarce in NW Scotland. (All Europe.) FLS Jun–Aug. NOTE Separated into 4 subspecies based on the shape of the fruits; there is no apparent habitat difference between these and they often grow together.

Unbranched Bur-reed
Sparganium emersum

Erect or floating perennial to 60 cm. Similar to *S. erectum*, but smaller, usually with both erect and floating leaves; erect leaves 3–12 mm wide, distinctly keeled throughout their length; floating leaves flat, somewhat keeled, base not inflated; *inflorescence unbranched, with 4–7 male heads*, 3–4 female heads. HABITAT Similar to *S. erectum*, but often in deeper water; to 500 m. DIST. Native. Rather local. Throughout BI. (Most of Europe.) FLS Jun–Jul.

Floating Bur-reed
Sparganium angustifolium

Rhizomatous perennial. STEMS Long, slender, submerged or floating, to 100 cm. LEAVES 30–80 cm × 2–4 mm, linear, without midrib or keel, base sheathing and inflated. INFLORESCENCES Unbranched, *bracts inflated at base, lowest >10 cm long, 2.5–4× as long as inflorescence*; 2–3 male heads, crowded into elongated terminal head; 2–4 female heads. HABITAT Clear, nutrient-poor, organic-rich, acid or neutral upland lakes; to 1005 m. Also pools, rivers, streams, canals. DIST. Native. N and W Britain, N and W Ireland. (Most of Europe except S.) FLS Aug–Sep.

Least Bur-reed
Sparganium natans

Submerged or floating, rhizomatous perennial. STEMS To 40 cm. LEAVES 2–6 mm wide, linear, flat, without distinct midrib or keel; sheaths not inflated. INFLORESCENCES Unbranched, *lowest bract somewhat inflated, <10 cm long, scarcely longer than inflorescence; 1 male head*; 1–3 female heads. HABITAT Shallow margins of lakes, ponds and drainage ditches, in acid and calcareous water; to 650 m. DIST. Native. Scattered throughout BI, but rare and declining in lowlands. (All Europe except S.) FLS Jun–Jul.

TYPHACEAE Bulrushes

Bulrushes *Typha*

Tall, robust, rhizomatous perennials growing in shallow water. Stems erect, unbranched. Leaves flat grey-green, arranged on two opposite sides of stem with sheathing bases. Inflorescence a cylindrical spike of closely packed tiny flowers, the lower part brown and with female flowers, the upper narrower and yellow, and consisting of male flowers; perianth consisting of numerous bristles and/or scales.

Bulrush, Reedmace
Typha latifolia

Tall, robust aquatic or semi-aquatic rhizomatous perennial to 3 m. LEAVES *8–25 mm wide*, bluish green. INFLORESCENCES *18–30 mm wide, with male and female parts ± contiguous*, male part 6–14 cm, female part 8–15 cm. HABITAT Shallow, nutrient-rich water or bare mud at margins of lakes, pools, canals, ditches and slow-moving rivers; to 500 m. DIST. Native. Throughout BI, but scarce or absent in NW Scotland. (All Europe.) FLS Jun–Jul.

Lesser Bulrush
Typha angustifolia

Similar to *T. latifolia*, but *leaves narrower, 3–6 mm wide*; *inflorescence narrower, 13–25 mm wide, with male and female parts separated by 3–8 cm of bare stem*. HABITAT Similar to *T. latifolia*, but preferring deeper water and tolerant of less nutrient-rich conditions. DIST. Native. Widespread but local throughout lowland England; rare and scattered in rest of BI. (All Europe.) FLS Jun–Jul.

Branched Bur-reed
Sparganium erectum

Unbranched Bur-reed
Sparganium emersum

Branched
Bur-reed

Least
Bur-reed

Floating
Bur-reed

Unbranched
Bur-reed

Least Bur-reed
Sparganium natans

Floating Bur-reed
Sparganium angustifolium

Lesser Bulrush
Typha angustifolia

Bulrush
Typha latifolia

illustrations
0.1× lifesize

	if	**then**
1	▷ Leaves normally developed	Go to ▷ **2**
	▷ Much-branched perennials or shrubs; leaves reduced to small scales and replaced by flat or needle-like leaf-like stems (cladodes) that arise in leaf axils	Go to ▷ **24**
2	▷ Leaves vertical on 2 opposite sides of stem, Iris- or sword-like, identical on both surfaces and sheathing at base	Go to ▷ **3**
	▷ Leaves not Iris- or sword-like	Go to ▷ **4**
3	▷ Flowers yellow; style 1; filaments densely hairy	*Narthecium* (p.648)
	▷ Flowers whitish; styles 3; filaments glabrous	*Tofieldia* (p.648)
4	▷ Leaves 4, in a whorl on stem below the single flower	*Paris* (p.652)
	▷ Leaves not in whorls of 4, often >1 flower	Go to ▷ **5**
5	▷ Flowers with spathe-like bracts, borne in umbels, umbel-like groups or solitary	Go to ▷ **6**
	▷ Flowers not in umbels, and if solitary without spathe-like bracts	Go to ▷ **11**
6	▷ Flowers entirely replaced by bulbils	*Allium* (p.656)
	▷ At least some flowers present	Go to ▷ **7**
7	▷ Perianth with funnel-like corona (daffodil)	*Narcissus* (p.658)
	▷ Perianth without corona	Go to ▷ **8**
8	▷ Ovary inferior	Go to ▷ **9**
	▷ Ovary superior	Go to ▷ **10**
9	▷ 3 inner tepals much shorter and blunter than outer	*Galanthus* (p.660)
	▷ All tepals similar	*Leucojum* (p.658)
10	▷ Perianth white or pink	*Allium* (p.656)
	▷ Perianth yellow	*Gagea* (p.648)
11	▷ Flowering stem leafy or with leaf-like bracts	Go to ▷ **12**
	▷ Leaves all basal, or leaves absent at flowering, or stem with few scale-like leaves	Go to ▷ **16**
12	▷ Leaves deeply cordate at base; flowers white; tepals 4	*Maianthemum* (p.650)
	▷ Leaves not cordate; tepals 6	Go to ▷ **13**

section of flower

if	**then**
13	▷ Flowers in axils of leaves, greenish white	***Polygonatum*** (p.652)
	▷ Inflorescence terminal, or flowers terminal and solitary	Go to ▷ **14**
14	▷ Inflorescence a raceme; tepals recurved	***Lilium*** (p.650)
	▷ Flowers solitary; tepals not recurved	Go to ▷ **15**
15	▷ Leaves broad; flowers yellow, erect	***Tulipa*** (p.648)
	▷ Leaves filiform; flowers white, erect (N Wales, rare)	***Lloydia*** (p.648)
	▷ Leaves linear; flowers purple-chequered (rarely white), nodding	***Fritillaria*** (p.650)
16	▷ Leaves absent at flowering; flowers solitary, Crocus-like	***Colchicum*** (p.648)
	▷ Leaves present at flowering	Go to ▷ **17**
17	▷ Inflorescence a panicle; filaments densely hairy	***Simethis*** (p.648)
	▷ Inflorescence a raceme; filaments glabrous	Go to ▷ **18**
18	▷ Leaves stalked, ovate-lanceolate	***Convallaria*** (p.650)
	▷ Leaves sessile, linear	Go to ▷ **19**
19	▷ Tepals fused for the greater part of their length; mouth of perianth contracted; upper flowers sterile	***Muscari*** (p.654)
	▷ Tepals free or united only at base; perianth not contracted at mouth; all flowers fertile	Go to ▷ **20**
20	▷ bracts 2 per flower; tepals fused at base	***Hyacinthoides*** (p.654)
	▷ Bracts absent or 1 per flower; tepals free	Go to ▷ **21**
21	▷ Tepals blue to pinkish	***Scilla*** (p.654)
	▷ Tepals white, sometimes striped below	Go to ▷ **22**
22	▷ Plant with bulb; bracts whitish	***Ornithogalum*** (p.652)
	▷ Plant without bulb; bracts thin, brownish	Go to ▷ **23**
23	▷ Base of filaments swollen and covering top of ovary	***Asphodelus*** ● (p.650)
	▷ Base of filaments not swollen	***Anthericum*** ● (p.650)
24	▷ Evergreen shrub; cladodes ovate, sharp-pointed; fruit a berry	***Ruscus*** (p.660)
	▷ Much-branched perennial, cladodes in needle-like clusters	***Asparagus*** (p.660)

LILIACEAE Lily family

A large and very variable family, often split into a number of smaller families (*see* key on p.646). Flowers usually regular, colourful and conspicuous, with 6 petal-like tepals, 6 stamens and a 3-celled inferior or superior ovary. Members of the similar-looking Iridaceae have only 3 stamens.

Bog Asphodel   *Narthecium ossifragum*

Glabrous, rhizomatous perennial to 40 cm. LEAVES *Mostly basal*, up to 30 cm long × 5 mm wide, often curved, similar on both surfaces, *erect and* Iris-*like.* FLOWERS 6-20 in a raceme; *tepals golden yellow;* 1 style; *filaments densely hairy, anthers orange.* FRUITS Capsule. HABITAT Abundant plant of acid bogs, wet heaths, flushes; to 1005 m. DIST. Native. Widespread in N and W Britain; local in S England. (N and W Europe.) FLS Jul-Sep.

Scottish Asphodel   *Tofieldia pusilla*

Similar to a small *Narthecium.* STEMS To 20 cm. LEAVES Mostly basal, to 4 cm × 2 mm. FLOWERS 5-10 in a short, dense inflorescence; *tepals greenish white;* 3 *styles;* filaments glabrous, anthers greenish yellow. HABITAT Wet calcareous hillside flushes, springs, mountain stream sides; to 975 m. DIST. Native. Widespread in central Scottish Highlands; confined to Upper Teesdale (Yorkshire, Durham) in England. (N Europe.) FLS Jun-Aug.

Kerry Lily   *Simethis planifolia* *(R)

Rhizomatous perennial to 40 cm. LEAVES All basal, to 60 cm × 7.5 mm, longer than stem. FLOWERS In a lax *cyme*, bracts shorter than pedicels; *tepals spreading, white inside, purplish beneath;* filaments densely hairy. DIST. Native. Very rare. Confined to a small area in S Kerry, W Co. Cork (SW Ireland). HABITAT Rocky coastal heath among rough gorse. (SW Europe.) FLS May-Jul.

Meadow Saffron   *Colchicum autumnale* *(R)

Glabrous perennial with a spherical corm. STEMS Flowering stem elongating in fruit. LEAVES Developing in spring, up to 35 × 5 cm, bright glossy green; *plant leafless at flowering.* FLOWERS 1-3, Crocus-*like, appearing in late summer-autumn;* perianth tube 5-20 cm, pale purple; ovary subterranean. HABITAT Damp permanent meadows, clearings in open woodland, on rich, fertile soils. DIST. Native. Locally frequent but declining. Central and S Britain, especially around Severn Valley. (S, W and central Europe.) FLS Aug-Oct.

Snowdon Lily   *Lloydia serotina* VU. *(B)

Bulbous and stoloniferous perennial to 15 cm. LEAVES Linear; 2 basal leaves, 2-4 stem leaves. FLOWERS 1-2, *10-15 mm across; tepals free, 9-12 mm, white with purplish veins.* HABITAT Mildly acid damp ledges and vertical fissures on steep cliff faces; 550-760 m. DIST. Native. Very rare. Snowdonia, N Wales. (Arctic Russia, mts of central Europe.) FLS Jun.

Yellow Star-of-Bethlehem   *Gagea lutea*

Bulbous perennial to 25 cm. LEAVES *Single linear-lanceolate basal leaf* with hooded tip, to 45 cm × 15 mm, often curled; 2 stem leaves. FLOWERS 1-7, *in umbel-like inflorescence;* tepals yellow with green band on outside, free, spreading. HABITAT Damp woodland on deep, rich calcareous loams. DIST. Native. Widely scattered throughout Britain; absent from Ireland. (Most of Europe.) FLS Mar-May.

Early Star-of-Bethlehem   *Gagea bohemica* VU. *(B)

Small, bulbous perennial. STEMS 1.2-3.7 cm; flowering stems often replaced by bulbils. LEAVES 2-4 *basal leaves, filiform;* 4 stem leaves, 15-40 × 2-4 mm. FLOWERS *In usually 1-flowered inflorescence;* tepals bright yellow, with greenish veins outside. HABITAT Shallow soils on S- and E-facing cliffs of dolerite. DIST. Native. Very rare. Confined to a single site at Stanner Rocks, Radnorshire (Wales). (W France, central and S Europe.) FLS Early, Jan-Mar.

Wild Tulip   *Tulipa sylvestris*

Bulbous and sometimes stoloniferous perennial to 45 cm. LEAVES 2-3 stem leaves, to 30 × 1.8 cm. FLOWERS 1, rounded at base, 40-90 mm across; tepals yellow. HABITAT Meadows, orchards, open woodlands hedgerows. DIST. Introduced. Declining. Widely scattered throughout BI, mostly in lowland central England. (S and SE Europe.) FLS Apr-May.

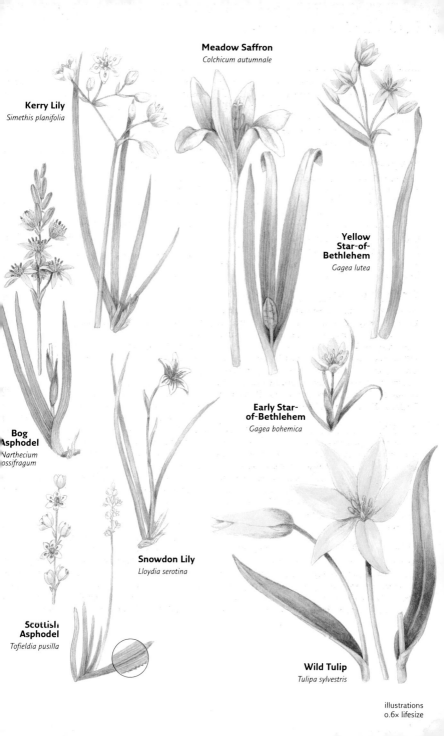

Meadow Saffron
Colchicum autumnale

Kerry Lily
Simethis planifolia

**Yellow
Star-of-
Bethlehem**
Gagea lutea

**Bog
Asphodel**
*Narthecium
ossifragum*

**Early Star-
of-Bethlehem**
Gagea bohemica

Snowdon Lily
Lloydia serotina

**Scottish
Asphodel**
Tofieldia pusilla

Wild Tulip
Tulipa sylvestris

illustrations
0.6× lifesize

Fritillary
Fritillaria meleagris VU.

Bulbous perennial to 50 cm. LEAVES Mostly cauline, linear, to 20 cm long. FLOWERS Solitary at end of stem, pendulous, cup-shaped, 28-40 mm across, chequered dull pink and purple, sometimes white. HABITAT Damp pastures, hay meadows; much cultivated and frequently naturalised. DIST. Probably native. Rare and declining. Mainly Thames Valley, Suffolk. (Central Europe.) FLS Apr-May.

May Lily
Maianthemum bifolium VU.

Rhizomatous perennial to 20 cm. STEMS *Erect, hairy above, with 2 leaves.* LEAVES Basal leaves solitary, with long petioles; stem leaves sessile, 4-6 × 2.5-5 cm, cordate with rounded lobes. FLOWERS White, 8-20 in a terminal raceme; 4 tepals, free; 4 stamens. FRUITS Red berry. HABITAT Oak-birch woodlands on well-drained acid soils. DIST. Probably native. Very rare. Scattered localities in E and N England; naturalised elsewhere. (All Europe except extreme N and S.) FLS May-Jun.

Lily-of-the-valley
Convallaria majalis

Perennial to 35 cm with long, creeping, much-branched rhizomes. LEAVES *In pairs on long stalks*, 5-20 × 3-7 cm. FLOWERS *Nodding, sweet-scented*, 6-12 in a 1-sided raceme. FRUITS Red berry. HABITAT Dry, open woodlands on nutrient-poor, usually base-rich soils, especially Ash woods on limestone; also a frequent garden escape. DIST. Native. Scattered throughout Britain. (Most of Europe except extreme N and S.) FLS May-Jun.

St Bernard's Lily
Anthericum liliago

Glabrous perennial to 70 cm. LEAVES All basal, linear, 12-40 × 3-7 mm. FLOWERS 6-10 in a raceme, sometimes with few branches; *tepals 16-22 mm*, much longer than stamens. FRUITS *Capsule, 8-10 mm.*

HABITAT Open woods, dry calcareous grassland. DIST. *Not BI.* (Most of Europe except N and extreme S.) FLS May-Jul.

Anthericum ramosum

Similar to *A. liliago*, but flowers smaller, in a branched panicle; *tepals 10-14 mm*, a little longer than stamens; *capsule 5-6 mm.* HABITAT Dry calcareous grasslands, scrub. DIST. *Not BI.* (Most of Europe except N and extreme S.) FLS Jun-Jul.

White Asphodel
Asphodelus albus

Tall, glabrous annual to 100 cm. LEAVES All basal, linear, strongly keeled beneath, 15-60 × 1-2 cm. FLOWERS In a dense raceme; tepals 15-20 mm, white with dark midrib; *bracts brown; anthers with filaments expanded at base and covering top of ovary.* HABITAT Meadows, heaths, open woods, rocky mountain pastures. DIST. *Not BI.* (S Europe, N to NW France.) FLS Apr-May.

Martagon Lily
Lilium martagon

Tall, attractive, bulbous perennial to 200 cm. LEAVES *In whorls*, 7-20 cm. FLOWERS 3-10, *pink-purple*, *c.*40 mm across. HABITAT Wood margins, coppice, orchards, derelict gardens. DIST. Introduced. Naturalised as a garden escape in scattered localities throughout Britain. (Most of Europe.) FLS Aug-Sep.

Pyrenean Lily
Lilium pyrenaicum

Tall, bulbous perennial to 90 cm. LEAVES *Spirally arranged on stem*, 3-15 cm, very numerous. FLOWERS 1-8, *yellow with black dots*, *c.*35 mm across. HABITAT Wood margins, hedgerows, roadsides. DIST. Introduced. Naturalised as a garden escape in scattered localities throughout BI. (Pyrenees, Alps, E Europe.) FLS May-Jun.

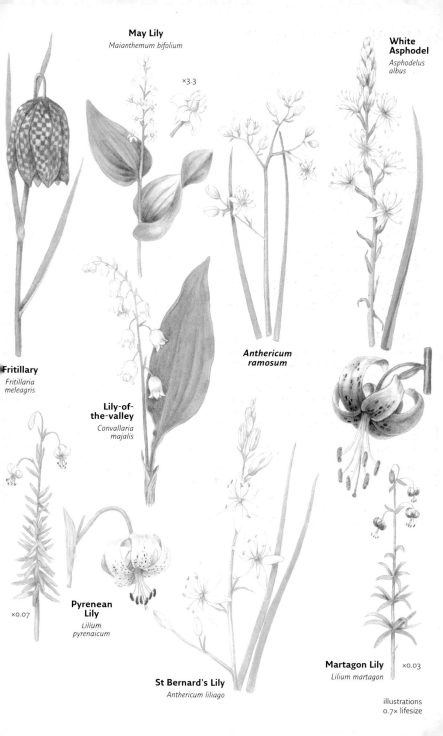

May Lily
Maianthemum bifolium

×3.3

White Asphodel
Asphodelus albus

Fritillary
Fritillaria meleagris

Anthericum ramosum

Lily-of-the-valley
Convallaria majalis

Pyrenean Lily
Lilium pyrenaicum

×0.07

St Bernard's Lily
Anthericum liliago

Martagon Lily
Lilium martagon

×0.03

illustrations
0.7× lifesize

Solomon's-seal
Polygonatum multiflorum

Glabrous, rhizomatous perennial to 80 cm. STEMS *Smooth*, arching. LEAVES 5–12 cm, all cauline, alternate. FLOWERS *Tubular, 9–15 mm, contracted in middle*, in 2–5-flowered axillary clusters; *filaments of stamens hairy*. FRUITS Bluish-black berry. SIMILAR SPP. **Garden Solomon's-seal** *P. × hybridum* (*P. odoratum × P. multiflorum*) is the commonest Solomon's-seal grown in gardens, and frequently occurs as an escape of cultivation throughout BI. It is often confused with *P. multiflorum*, but the stems are ridged or slightly angled and the flowers are 15–22 mm. HABITAT Dry woodlands, usually on chalk or limestone. DIST. Native. Local and scattered N to Lake District, centred on central-S England; introduced elsewhere in BI. (Most of Europe except SW.) FLS May–Jun.

Angular Solomon's-seal
Polygonatum odoratum

Similar to *P. multiflorum*, but *stems distinctly angled*; *flowers 15–30 mm, not contracted in middle*, in clusters of 1–2; *filaments of stamens glabrous*. HABITAT Open deciduous woodland (especially Ash), grikes in limestone pavement; to 485 m. DIST. Native. Very local. Cotswolds, areas of Carboniferous limestone in N England; very scattered elsewhere. (Most of Europe except N and extreme S.) FLS Jun–Jul.

Whorled Solomon's-seal
Polygonatum verticillatum VU. *(B)

Similar to *P. multiflorum* and *P. odoratum*, but with narrow, *linear-lanceolate leaves in whorls of 3–8*, and smaller flowers, 5–10 mm; filaments of stamens glabrous. HABITAT Moist, base-rich mountain woods, wooded gorges. DIST. Native. Very rare. Perthshire (central Scotland). (Arctic Norway, mts of S Europe.) FLS Jun–Jul.

Herb Paris
Paris quadrifolia

Distinctive rhizomatous perennial with erect stems, to 40 cm. LEAVES *Broad, in whorls of 4* at top of stem, 6–12 cm. FLOWERS Solitary; tepals green, outer 4 sepal-like, inner 4 linear; 8 stamens. FRUITS Black, berry-like. HABITAT Damp calcareous woodland, grikes in limestone pavement; to 360 m. DIST. Native. Widely distributed but rather local throughout Britain. (Most of Europe except Mediterranean.) FLS May–Aug.

Spiked Star-of-Bethlehem
Ornithogalum pyrenaicum

Erect, bulbous perennial to 80 cm. LEAVES In a basal rosette, linear, 30–60 cm long, soon withering. FLOWERS 15–22 mm across, *>20 forming elongated raceme*; 1 bract per flower, shorter than pedicels, whitish; tepals free. HABITAT Open woods, scrub, lanesides, hedgerows, on calcareous or base-rich soils. DIST. Native. Very local. Restricted to an area of W England (Somerset, Gloucestershire, Wiltshire); also Bedfordshire, Cambridgeshire. (SW and S-central Europe.) FLS Jun–Jul.

Star-of-Bethlehem
Ornithogalum angustifolium

Similar to *O. pyrenaicum*, but *leaves with white stripe running down midrib*; flowers 30–40 mm across, shorter than or as long as pedicels, 4–12 in *corymbose inflorescence, lower pedicels up to 10 cm, much longer than upper*. HABITAT Rough grassland, open woods, roadside verges. DIST. Introduced; possibly native in Breckland (East Anglia). Throughout BI, but very rare in Ireland. (S and S-central Europe.) FLS Apr–Jun.

Drooping Star-of-Bethlehem
Ornithogalum nutans

Erect, bulbous perennial to 60 cm. Similar to *O. pyrenaicum*, but *leaves channelled with broad white stripe down midrib; flowers larger, 40–60 mm across, drooping, 3–12 in 1-sided raceme*; bracts longer than pedicels; pedicels curved. HABITAT Churchyards, hedgerows, wood margins, rough grassland. DIST. Introduced. Declining. Scattered throughout lowland England as infrequent naturalised or casual escape from cultivation. (S and E Europe.) FLS Apr–May.

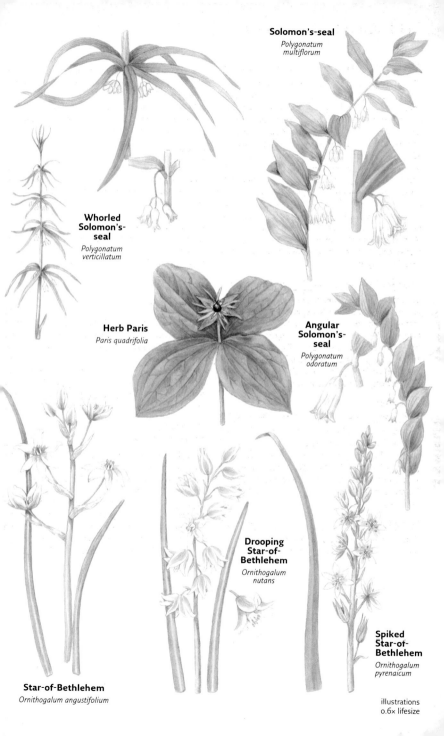

Solomon's-seal
Polygonatum multiflorum

Whorled Solomon's-seal
Polygonatum verticillatum

Herb Paris
Paris quadrifolia

Angular Solomon's-seal
Polygonatum odoratum

Drooping Star-of-Bethlehem
Ornithogalum nutans

Spiked Star-of-Bethlehem
Ornithogalum pyrenaicum

Star-of-Bethlehem
Ornithogalum angustifolium

illustrations 0.6× lifesize

Spring Squill · *Scilla verna*

Glabrous, bulbous perennial to 30 cm. STEMS Smooth. LEAVES 2–7, all basal, long-linear. FLOW-ERS 10–16 mm across, 2–12 forming dense inflores-cence; *1 bract per flower, longer than pedicels*; tepals free. HABITAT Short, dry grassland close to sea, cliff tops, maritime heath. DIST. Native. Rather local. SW and W coasts of BI from Devon to Shetland; E coast of Ireland. (W Europe.) FLS *Apr–May*.

Autumn Squill · *Scilla autumnalis*

Similar to *S. verna*, but *leaves appearing after flowers*; flowers 6–12 mm across, 4–20 forming inflores-cence; *bracts absent*. HABITAT Short, dry turf close to sea. DIST. Native. Very local. SW England, Channel Is, lower Thames Valley. (S and W Europe.) FLS *Jul–Sep*.

Alpine Squill · *Scilla bifolia*

Similar to *S. verna*, but *2 leaves*, broader, slightly sheathing the stem at base; flowers 10–20 mm across, erect, 1–5(–10) in inflorescence; bracts absent or very small. HABITAT Churchyards, grassy banks. DIST. Introduced. Naturalised as infrequent relic or escape of cultivation in scattered localities throughout England. (Central and S Europe.) FLS Mar-Apr.

Bluebell · *Hyacinthoides non-scripta* *(B)
Protected by law against sale

Glabrous, bulbous perennial to 50 cm. LEAVES All basal, 7–15(–20) mm wide. FLOWERS Drooping, 10–28 mm across, 4–16 in 1-sided, drooping inflo-rescence; bracts in pairs, blue; tepals united at base, parallel-sided so *flowers cylindrical, tips revolute; sta-mens unequal in length, anthers cream or yellow*. HABI-TAT Abundant and often forming extensive carpets in deciduous woodland, hedge banks, coastal cliffs, upland acid grassland; to 685 m. DIST. Native. Throughout BI except Orkney, Shetland. (W Europe.) FLS Apr-Jun.

Spanish Bluebell · *Hyacinthoides hispanica*

Similar to *H. non-scripta*, but leaves broader, to 35 mm wide; inflorescence not 1-sided, flowers erect or spreading, 15–22 mm long, 15–25 mm across, becoming saucer-shaped, *tips of petals not revolute,* *stamens equal in length, anthers blue.* DIST. Intro-duced. Cultivated in gardens and occasionally natu-ralised in suitable habitats. (Spain, Portugal.) FLS Apr–May. NOTE Most bluebells commonly cultivated in gardens are the hybrid between *H. non-scripta* and *H. hispanica*, *H. × variabilis*, which is fully fertile and will back-cross with *H. non-scripta*. It is a frequent escape, occurring in woods, hedgerows, church-yards, roadsides and rough ground throughout the BI. It is intermediate in character between the par-ents, but usually more difficult to separate from *H. hispanica*; the flowers are 12–17 mm long and 10–20 mm across, and mauve, pink or white.

Grape-hyacinths *Muscari*

Glabrous, bulbous perennials with basal leaves. Tepals fused into globular flowers, these strongly contracted at the mouth and usually blue with white tips or sometimes brownish; inflorescence is a dense raceme.

Grape-hyacinth · *Muscari neglectum* VU.

STEMS To 30 cm. LEAVES 3–6, linear. FLOWERS Fertile *flowers dark blue, becoming blackish blue* with age, ovoid, longer than wide, 3.5–7.5 mm; lobes spreading, white. HABITAT Grassy roadsides, field borders, hedge banks, plantations; also widely naturalised as garden escape. DIST. Native. Very rare. Cambridgeshire, Suf-folk. (Most of Europe except N.) FLS Apr–May.

Garden Grape-hyacinth · *Muscari armeniacum*

Similar to *M. neglectum*, but *flowers a brighter blue and turning paler with age*, 3.5–5.5 mm. HABITAT Common garden plant, frequently discarded and establishing in grassland, hedge banks, dunes, road-sides, waste ground. DIST. Introduced. (SE Europe.) FLS Apr–May.

Compact Grape-hyacinth · *Muscari botryoides*

Similar to *M. neglectum*, but leaves linear, widening towards tip; *flowers spherical*, bright blue, not ovoid 2.5–5 mm; *lobes white, strongly recurved*. HABITAT Commonly cultivated and occasionally naturalised as garden throw-out or relic of cultivation on road-sides, sand and gravel pits. DIST. Introduced. (S Europe.) FLS Apr-Jun.

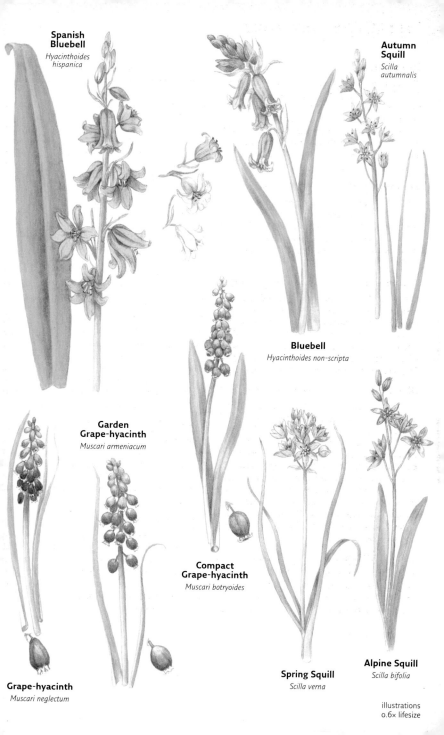

Spanish Bluebell
Hyacinthoides hispanica

Autumn Squill
Scilla autumnalis

Bluebell
Hyacinthoides non-scripta

Garden Grape-hyacinth
Muscari armeniacum

Compact Grape-hyacinth
Muscari botryoides

Grape-hyacinth
Muscari neglectum

Spring Squill
Scilla verna

Alpine Squill
Scilla bifolia

illustrations
0.6× lifesize

Onions *Allium*

Onions, chives and leeks are bulbous perennials that mostly have a characteristic smell of onion or garlic (*see* key on p.664). Leaves usually all basal, linear or cylindrical. Flowers arranged in a terminal umbel, and sometimes replaced by bulbils; whole inflorescence is at first enclosed within a thin, papery spathe, which splits on flowering into 1 or 2 bracts; tepals free; 6 stamens. Fruits a capsule.

Chives   *Allium schoenoprasum* *(R)

STEMS To 50 cm, smooth, hollow. LEAVES To 35 cm, *cylindrical, hollow*. FLOWERS *Purple, in dense, spherical umbel*, 1.5–5 cm across; spathe as long as or shorter than umbel; stamens not protruding. HABITAT Rocky hill pastures, coastal grasslands, on limestone or basic igneous rocks; also widely naturalised as casual escape from cultivation on tips and roadsides. DIST. Native. Rare and very scattered. Cornwall, N England, S Wales, Ireland (E Co. Mayo). (All Europe except S.) FLS Jun–Jul.

Rosy Garlic   *Allium roseum*

STEMS To 65 cm, smooth. LEAVES To 35 cm long, 5–14 mm *wide, flat*, rough. FLOWERS Cup-shaped, pink, in many-flowered umbel to 7 cm across, with (var. *bulbiferum*) or without bulbils; *spathe 3–4-lobed; stamens not protruding*. HABITAT Rough ground, hedge banks, roadsides. DIST. Introduced. Naturalised escape from cultivation. S and SW England (spreading in SW); rare elsewhere. (S Europe, Mediterranean.) FLS May–Jun.

Three-cornered Garlic   *Allium triquetrum*

STEMS To 45 cm, *sharply 3-angled*. LEAVES 2–5, to 40 cm long, 5–17 mm wide, *flat, keeled beneath*. FLOWERS Drooping, in 3–15-flowered umbel, rather lax and 1-sided, without bulbils; *2 bracts*; tepals 10–18 mm, white with longitudinal green stripe; stamens not protruding. HABITAT Roadsides, hedge banks, waste ground. DIST. Introduced. Naturalised escape from cultivation, widespread and increasing. S and SW Britain, S Ireland; scattered but spreading elsewhere. (W Mediterranean.) FLS Apr–Jun.

Few-flowered Garlic   *Allium paradoxum*

STEMS To 30 cm, sharply 3-angled. LEAVES 1, to 30 cm long, 5–15 mm wide, flat. FLOWERS *Absent, or 1-few in umbels with small green bulbils*; 2 bracts, shorter than pedicels; tepals 10–12 mm, white; stamens not protruding. HABITAT Roadsides, field margins, riverbanks, waste ground. DIST. Introduced. Naturalised escape from cultivation throughout Britain, but predominantly in S and E, spreading and locally invasive. (Native of Caucasus.) FLS Apr–May.

Ramsons   *Allium ursinum*

STEMS To 50 cm, 2-angled. LEAVES 2–3, basal, *narrowly ovate, rounded at base*, 10–25 cm long, 4–7 cm broad; petiole to 20 cm, twisted. FLOWERS In 6–20-flowered umbel, without bulbils; 2 bracts, shorter than pedicels; *tepals spreading*, 7–12 mm, white. HABITAT Damp woodlands on rich, loamy, mildly acid to calcareous soils, hedge banks, coastal cliffs, limestone pavement; to 430 m. DIST. Native. Widespread and common throughout BI, but becoming scarce in N Scotland. (Most of Europe except extreme N and S.) FLS Apr–Jun.

Field Garlic   *Allium oleraceum* VU.

STEMS To 100 cm, smooth. LEAVES 2–4, to 30 cm long, *cylindrical, lower part hollow*, ribbed beneath. FLOWERS In 5–40-flowered umbel, with few to many bulbils, or sometimes with bulbils only; *2 bracts, long-pointed, much longer than umbel; pedicels long*, 15–60 mm, *outer drooping*; tepals 5–7 mm, pinkish, greenish or brownish; stamens not protruding. HABITAT Dry, rough calcareous grassland, usually on steep, S-facing slopes. DIST. Native. Scattered throughout England; rare elsewhere. (All Europe except extreme S.) FLS Jul–Aug.

Keeled Garlic   *Allium carinatum*

STEMS To 60 cm, smooth. LEAVES 2–4, linear, 10–20 cm × 1–2.5 mm, flat, slightly channelled above. FLOWERS Cup-shaped, in diffuse umbel; *2 bracts, long-pointed, much longer than umbel*; pedicels 10–25 mm, unequal; tepals 4–6 mm, *purple; stamens conspicuously protruding*. HABITAT Roadsides, waste ground, churchyards. DIST. Introduced. Naturalised escape from cultivation, scattered throughout BI. (N and central Europe.) FLS Aug.

Wild Leek   *Allium ampeloprasum*

Tall, robust perennial to 180 cm. LEAVES 4–10, flat, channelled, to 50 cm long, 5–40 mm wide. FLOWERS Cup-shaped, in *dense, spherical umbel, 5–9 cm across* with or without bulbils; 1 bract; *tepals 4–5.5 mm, dark pink*; stamens slightly protruding. HABITAT Rough vegetation, rocky ground, cliffs, hedge banks, field borders, close to sea. DIST. Archaeophyte. Rare. SW England, Scilly Is, Channel Is, W Ireland; very rare elsewhere. (S and W Europe.) NOTE There are 3 varieties in BI: var. *ampeloprasum*, umbels without bulbils (SW England, Wales); var. *bulbiferum*, umbels with flowers and bulbils, 6–8 mm (Channel Is); and var. *babingtonii*, umbels with flowers and bulbils, 8–15 mm (endemic to SW England, Wales, W Ireland). FL Jul–Aug.

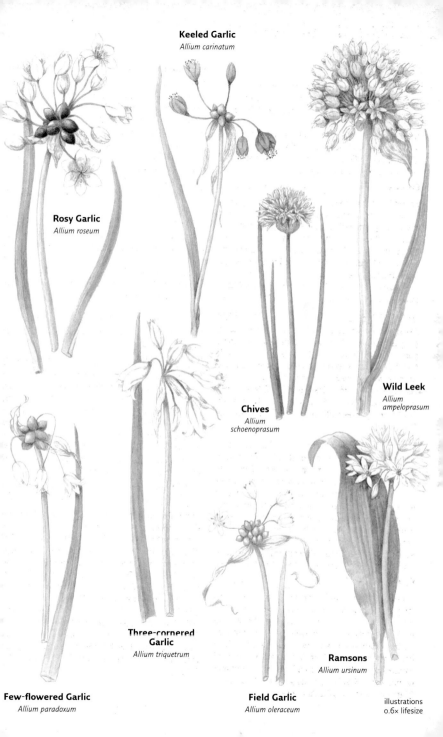

Keeled Garlic
Allium carinatum

Rosy Garlic
Allium roseum

Chives
Allium schoenoprasum

Wild Leek
Allium ampeloprasum

Three-cornered Garlic
Allium triquetrum

Few-flowered Garlic
Allium paradoxum

Field Garlic
Allium oleraceum

Ramsons
Allium ursinum

illustrations
0.6× lifesize

Sand Leek
Allium scorodoprasum

STEMS To 90 cm, smooth. LEAVES 2-5, linear, flat, to 27 cm long × 7-20 mm wide. FLOWERS In few-flowered umbel with purple bulbils; 2 bracts, shorter than umbel; tepals 4-6.5 mm, purple; stamens not protruding. HABITAT Rough grassland, scrub, open woodland, road verges, waste ground, on well-drained soils. DIST. Native. N England to central Scotland; naturalised in scattered localities elsewhere. (Most of Europe except S.) FLS May-Aug.

Wild Onion, Crow Garlic
Allium vineale

STEMS To 120 cm, smooth. LEAVES 2-4, *cylindrical, hollow*. FLOWERS Umbel 2-5 cm across, with bulbils only (var. *compactum*), with flowers and bulbils (var. *vineale*), or rarely with flowers only (var. *capsuliferum*); 1 bract; tepals 2-4.5 mm, pink or greenish white; stamens protruding or not. HABITAT Dry calcareous or neutral grasslands, hedgerows, roadsides, weed of cereal crops, coastal cliffs; to 455 m. DIST. Native. Widespread in Britain N to central Scotland, becoming coastal further N; S Ireland. (Most of Europe except extreme N.) FLS Jun-Jul.

Round-headed Leek
Allium sphaerocephalon VU. *(B)

STEMS To 90 cm, smooth. LEAVES 2-6, to 30 cm long, *half-cylindrical, grooved, hollow*. FLOWERS In *dense*, many-flowered *umbel*, 2-4 cm across, without bulbils; 2-4 bracts, reflexed, much shorter than umbel; tepals 4-5.5 mm, reddish purple; *stamens conspicuously protruding*. DIST. Native. Very rare, in 2 localities only on Carboniferous limestone rocks in Avon Gorge, and St Aubin's Bay, Jersey (Channel Is). (W Europe, Mediterranean.) FLS Jun-Aug. *Not illustrated.*

Summer Snowflake
Leucojum aestivum

Bulbous perennial to 60 cm. STEMS 3-angled, hollow. LEAVES Basal, 30-50 cm × 5-15 mm. FLOWERS 2-5, to 34 mm across; spathe single; tepals free, 10-22 mm, all similar. HABITAT Riverside willow and Alder carr that floods in winter, wet meadows; widely naturalised as garden escape near habitation. DIST. Native. Very local. Central-S England, scattered localities in S Ireland. (W, central and S Europe.) FLS Apr-May.

Spring Snowflake
Leucojum vernum

Similar to *L. aestivum*, but *flowers solitary*, tepals 15-25 mm. HABITAT Woodland, scrub, stream banks. DIST. Introduced. Rare. Naturalised as relic of cultivation in scattered localities throughout lowland Britain. (W, central and E Europe.) FLS Feb-Apr.

Daffodils *Narcissus*
Familiar bulbous perennials (*see* key on p.665). Flowers either solitary or arranged in few-flowered umbels with a single thin, papery bract, the spathe, and with a trumpet-like or ring-like corona inserted between tepals and stamens; 6 tepals, all alike, usually spreading; 6 stamens; ovary inferior. There are numerous varieties, cultivars and hybrids, which are increasingly becoming naturalised on roadsides, banks and waste ground. The only native British daffodil is *N. pseudonarcissus* ssp. *pseudonarcissus*.

Daffodil
Narcissus pseudonarcissus ssp. *pseudonarcissus*

HABITAT Damp, open woods, coppice, heathland, commons, old pastures, on mildly acid soils. DIST. Native and widespread to N England, E Wales; scarce in E England. Widely naturalised in East Anglia, Wales, Scotland; absent from Ireland. (W and central Europe.) FLS Feb-Mar.

Spanish Daffodil
Narcissus pseudonarcissus ssp. *major*

HABITAT Hedgerows, roadsides, waste ground. DIST. Introduced. Formerly much grown in gardens. Naturalised in S England, Wales; scattered elsewhere. (SW Europe.) FLS Mar-May.

Tenby Daffodil
Narcissus pseudonarcissus ssp. *obvallaris*

HABITAT Pastures, churchyards, hedgerows, roadsides, mostly near habitation. DIST. Origin unknown. SW Wales. FLS Feb-Apr.

Pheasant's-eye
Narcissus poeticus

FLOWERS 35-70 mm across; perianth tube (between base of tepals and top of ovary) long, cylindrical, 20-30 mm; tepals white; corona 8-15 mm across, deep yellow with green centre and red rim that has crinkled edge. HABITAT Naturalised as relic of cultivation and garden throw-out on roadsides, hedgerows, waste ground. DIST. Introduced. Scattered throughout Britain; absent from Ireland. (Mts of central, S and E Europe.) FLS Apr-May.

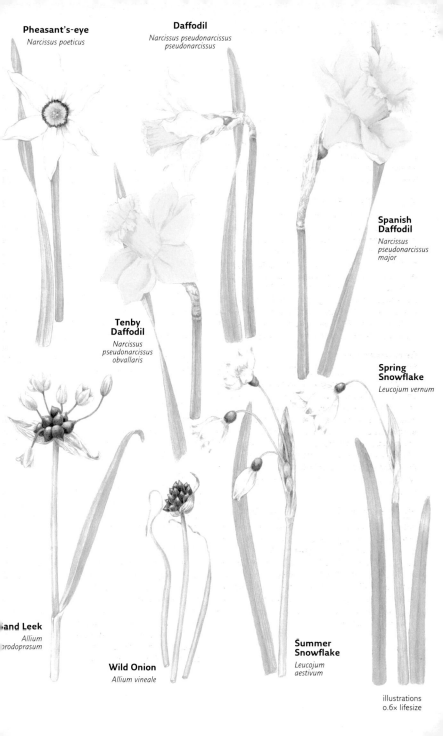

Pheasant's-eye
Narcissus poeticus

Daffodil
*Narcissus pseudonarcissus
pseudonarcissus*

**Spanish
Daffodil**
*Narcissus
pseudonarcissus
major*

**Tenby
Daffodil**
*Narcissus
pseudonarcissus
obvallaris*

**Spring
Snowflake**
Leucojum vernum

and Leek
*Allium
orodoprasum*

Wild Onion
Allium vineale

**Summer
Snowflake**
*Leucojum
aestivum*

illustrations
0.6× lifesize

Snowdrop
Galanthus nivalis

Bulbous perennial to 25 cm. LEAVES 2, glaucous, linear, flat. FLOWERS Solitary, nodding, up to 40 mm across, white; spathe of 2 fused bracts, deeply divided at tip; tepals free, in 2 whorls, inner whorl smaller, emarginate, with green patch near incision. HABITAT Damp woodlands, hedge banks, churchyards, parks; to 370 m. DIST. Probably introduced. Naturalised throughout BI, but rare in N Scotland, Ireland. (Most of Europe except N.) FLS Feb-Mar.

Asparagus
Asparagus officinalis

Rhizomatous perennial, with 2 subspecies: ssp. *officinalis* (Garden Asparagus) and ssp. *prostratus* EN. *(R) (Wild Asparagus). STEMS Much branched; erect, to 1.5 m in ssp. *officinalis*; procumbent, to 30 cm in ssp. *prostratus*. LEAVES Reduced to small scales with clusters of 4-15 needle-like 'cladodes' in their axils that perform the function of leaves, these 10-20 mm, flexible and green in ssp. *officinalis*, and 4-10 mm, rigid and glaucous in ssp. *prostratus*. FLOWERS Unisexual, 1-2 in axils of scale leaves on main stem; pedicels 6-10 mm in ssp. *officinalis*, 2-6 mm in ssp. *prostratus*; tepals fused at base, 4.5-6.5 mm, greenish to pale yellow. FRUITS Red berry. HABITAT Ssp. *officinalis* naturalised as escape from cultivation on sandy heaths, dunes; ssp. *prostratus* on rocky sea cliffs, sand-dunes. DIST. Ssp. *officinalis* archaeophyte; central, S and E England. Ssp. *prostratus* native, very local in SW England, S Wales, SE Ireland, Channel Is. (Coasts of W Europe.) FLS Jul-Sep.

Butcher's-broom
Ruscus aculeatus

Erect, rhizomatous, much-branched evergreen shrub to 80 cm. LEAVES Reduced to minute scales with broad, leaf-like cladodes in their axils; cladodes dark green, 10-30 mm, ovate, thick, spine-tipped. FLOWERS 1, on upper surface of cladode, unisexual, *c*.3 mm across; tepals free, greenish. FRUITS Red berry. HABITAT Dry woods, hedgerows, coastal cliffs. DIST. Native. Rather local. S England, S Wales, Channel Is; sparsely naturalised in similar habitats in rest of BI. (W, S and S-central Europe.) FLS Jan-Mar.

IRIDACEAE Iris family

Differ from the Liliaceae chiefly in having 3 stamens rather than 6; styles are usually 3-branched and ovary is inferior.

Blue-eyed Grass
Sisyrinchium bermudiana *(NI)

Glabrous perennial to 50 cm. STEMS Branched, flattened, winged. LEAVES Grass-like, to 5 mm wide, shorter or as long as stem. FLOWERS 15-20 mm across; spathe 2-4-flowered; tepals pale blue, free. HABITAT Wet meadows, lake shores. DIST. Native. Very local. W Ireland. (In Europe, confined to Ireland.) FLS Jun-Jul.

Spring Crocus
Crocus vernus

The most commonly cultivated garden crocus. LEAVES 2-4, present at flowering, 90-150 × 2-8 mm, shorter than or as long as flowers. FLOWERS Spathe present; perianth tube purple, or white only if rest of flower is white; tepals purple or lavender, white, or striped purple and white. HABITAT Roadsides, parks, churchyards. DIST. Introduced. Naturalised as escape from cultivation throughout Britain. (Central and S Europe.) FLS Feb-Jun.

Early Crocus
Crocus tommasinianus

Similar to *C. vernus*, but 3-4 leaves, 1-3 mm wide, as long as or longer than flowers; perianth tube white; tepals pale lilac to purple. HABITAT Roadsides, parks, woodland, churchyards. DIST. Introduced. Naturalised as escape from cultivation throughout Britain. (SE Europe.) FLS Feb-Mar.

Autumn Crocus
Crocus nudiflorus

Stoloniferous perennial. LEAVES 3-4, not present at flowering, up to 17 cm × 2-4 mm. FLOWERS Solitary, 50-100 mm across; spathe present; perianth tube white, tinged lilac or purple; tepals purple, not prominently veined. HABITAT Meadows, pastures, parks, roadsides. DIST. Introduced. Naturalised as relic of cultivation, scattered throughout Britain. (SW Europe.) FLS Sep-Oct.

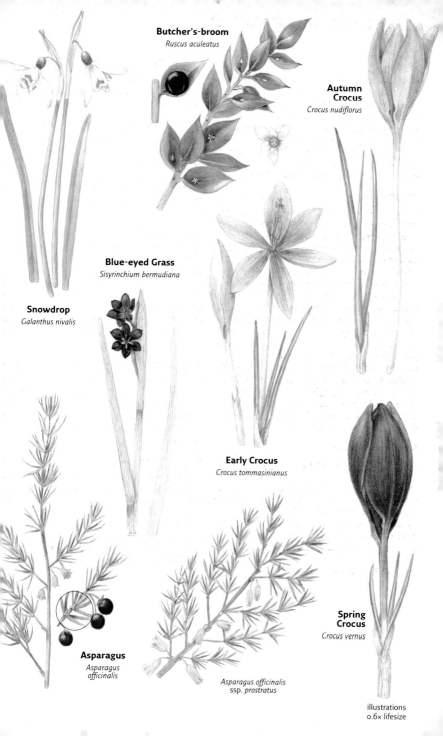

Butcher's-broom
Ruscus aculeatus

Autumn Crocus
Crocus nudiflorus

Blue-eyed Grass
Sisyrinchium bermudiana

Snowdrop
Galanthus nivalis

Early Crocus
Crocus tommasinianus

Asparagus
Asparagus officinalis

Asparagus officinalis
ssp. *prostratus*

Spring Crocus
Crocus vernus

illustrations
0.6× lifesize

Irises *Iris*

Rhizomatous or bulbous perennials, with sword-shaped leaves often arranged in 2 vertical ranks. The characteristic large, showy flower is regular, with tepals in 2 whorls, the outer ('falls') usually deflexed and the smaller inner ones ('standards') often erect, usually consisting of well-marked basal 'claw' and expanded terminal 'limb'. Three style branches ('crest') lie close above falls and are broad, petaloid and notched at tip. Flowers develop within 2 spathes.

Yellow Iris   *Iris pseudacorus*

Tall, erect, glabrous, rhizomatous perennial to 150 cm. STEMS Compressed, smooth, often branched. LEAVES 15–25 mm broad, about as long as flowering stems. FLOWERS 8–10 cm across, *yellow*; pedicels about as long as ovary. HABITAT Shallow margins of ponds, lakes, rivers and dykes, marshes, fens, wet woods; lowland to 480 m. DIST. Native. Widespread and common throughout BI. (Most of Europe.) FLS May–Jul.

Stinking Iris   *Iris foetidissima*

Dark green perennial to 80 cm, with *strong, unpleasant smell* when bruised. STEMS Unbranched, angled on one side. LEAVES As long as or longer than flowering stem. FLOWERS *c*.8 cm across, *purplish livid*, rarely yellowish; spathes 2–3-flowered; pedicels 4–5× as long as ovary. FRUITS *Seeds conspicuous, orange-red*. HABITAT Dry woods, hedge banks, scrubby sea cliffs, usually on calcareous soils. DIST. Native. Locally frequent. S Britain to N Wales. (S and W Europe.) FLS May–Jul.

Blue Iris   *Iris spuria*

Rhizomatous perennial to 90 cm. STEMS Smooth, unbranched. LEAVES 6–20 mm wide, about as long as stems. FLOWERS 60–80 mm across, in 2–4-flowered inflorescence; *outer tepals lilac with violet veins and yellow median streak*, inner tepals violet edged with yellow. FRUITS Ridged capsule, with beak 8–16 mm. HABITAT Commonly grown in gardens; occasionally naturalised on banks, verges, ditches. DIST. Introduced. (Most of Europe.) FLS Jun–Jul.

Sand Crocus   *Romulea columnae* VU. *(B)

Miniature Crocus-*like plant*. STEMS Short. LEAVES Wiry, twisted, 4-grooved; 2 basal leaves, 1–6 stem leaves. FLOWERS 1–3, 9–19 mm; *tepals pale mauve with darker veins*. HABITAT Short sandy turf near sea. DIST. Native. Very rare on Dawlish Warren (Devon); common in Channel Is. (W Europe, Mediterranean.) FLS Mar–May (when sun is out).

Wild Gladiolus   *Gladiolus illyricus* *(B)

Erect, glabrous perennial to 90 cm. LEAVES Glaucous, to 3–10 mm wide. FLOWERS 3–8 in unbranched, spike-like, 1-sided *inflorescence*, 35–40 mm across; tepals 25–40 mm, long-clawed, crimson-purple; perianth tube curved; *anthers shorter than filaments*; style branches abruptly dilated towards tip. HABITAT Acid grass heaths, usually among Bracken. DIST. Native. Very local. New Forest (Hampshire). (S and W Europe.) FLS Jun–Aug.

Italian Gladiolus   *Gladiolus italicus*

Similar to *G. illyricus*, but inflorescence *6–16-flowered*; flowers purplish pink; *anthers longer than filaments*; stigma gradually widening from base upwards. HABITAT Widely grown in gardens; occasionally occurs as casual on tips. DIST. Introduced (S Europe.) FLS Jun–Aug.

Eastern Gladiolus   *Gladiolus communis*

Similar to *G. italicus*, but taller; flowers pink, red or magenta, *10–20 in usually branched inflorescence*; *anthers shorter than filaments*. HABITAT Bulb fields, field margins, rough ground. DIST. Introduced. Naturalised as relic of cultivation in SW England, Scilly Is, Channel Is. (S Europe.) FLS Jun–Aug. *Not illustrated*

Montbretia   *Crocosmia × crocosmiiflora*

Stoloniferous, clump-forming perennial with flattened corms. STEMS To 90 cm, unbranched or with 1–2 branches. LEAVES 5–20 mm wide, shorter than stems, sword-like, *prominently veined on both surfaces*. FLOWERS 10–20 in a one-sided spike, *deep orange*, 2.5–5 cm across, irregular; tepals spreading, lobes about as long as tube. HABITAT Hedge banks, roadsides, woods, waste ground. DIST. Introduced as garden plant in 1880 (native of S Africa). Naturalised throughout BI, especially in W. (W Europe) FLS Sep–Nov.

DIOSCOREACEAE Black Bryony and yams

Black Bryony   *Tamus communis*

Climbing, dioecious perennial with large, subterranean tuber. The only British member of the tropical yam family. STEMS To 20 m or more. LEAVES 3–10 × 2–10 cm, *dark glossy green, ovate, base cordate*. FLOWERS 4–5 mm across, in lax, axillary, spike-like raceme, to 15 cm; tepals pale green. FRUITS *Waxy red berry*. HABITAT Hedgerows, wood margins, on well-drained neutral or calcareous soils. DIST. Native. Widespread and common throughout England, Wales. (S and W Europe.) FLS May–Jul.

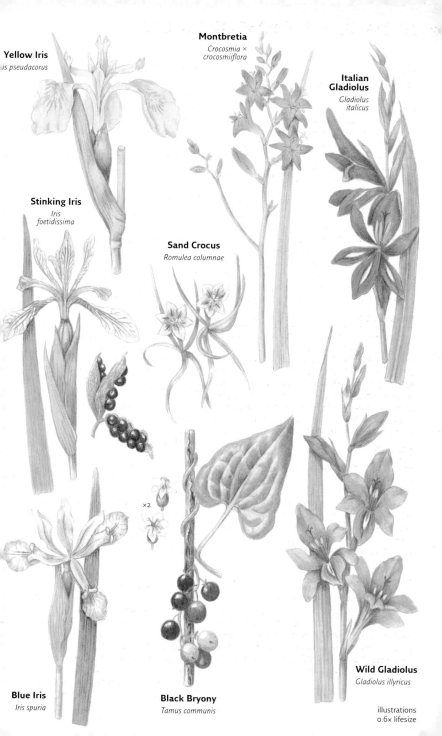

Yellow Iris
Iris pseudacorus

Montbretia
Crocosmia × crocosmiiflora

Italian Gladiolus
Gladiolus italicus

Stinking Iris
Iris foetidissima

Sand Crocus
Romulea columnae

×2

Blue Iris
Iris spuria

Black Bryony
Tamus communis

Wild Gladiolus
Gladiolus illyricus

illustrations
0.6× lifesize

	if	**then**
1	▷ Leaves narrowly ovate, stalked	***A. ursinum*** (p.656)
	▷ Leaves linear or cylindrical, sessile	Go to ▷ **2**
2	▷ Stems smooth, flat or cylindrical	Go to ▷ **3**
	▷ Stems sharply 3-angled	Go to ▷ **11**
3	▷ Leaves cylindrical, hollow	Go to ▷ **4**
	▷ Leaves flat, solid	Go to ▷ **7**
4	▷ Inflorescence with bulbils	Go to ▷ **5**
	▷ Inflorescence without bulbils	Go to ▷ **6**
5	▷ Filaments of inner stamens divided at apex into 3 long points	***A. vineale*** (p.658)
	▷ Filaments of inner stamens not divided at apex into 3 long points	***A. oleraceum*** (p.656)
6	▷ Filaments of inner stamens divided at apex into 3 long points (very rare)	***A. sphaerocephalon*** (p.658)
	▷ Filaments of inner stamens not divided at apex into 3 long points	***A. schoenoprasum*** (p.656)
7	▷ Spathe of 1 bract; plant tall, to 200 cm	***A. ampeloprasum*** (p.656)
	▷ Spathe splitting into ≥2 bracts	Go to ▷ **8**
8	▷ Filaments of inner stamens divided into 3 points	***A. scorodoprasum*** (p.658)
	▷ Filaments of inner stamens not divided into 3 points	Go to ▷ **9**
9	▷ Spathe of 2 unequal bracts with long, slender points, much longer than flowers	Go to ▷ **10**
	▷ Spathe of 2-4 thin, papery bracts, shorter than flowers	***A. roseum*** (p.656)
10	▷ Stamens not protruding from perianth	***A. oleraceum*** (p.656)
	▷ Stamens conspicuously protruding from perianth	***A. carinatum*** (p.656)
11	▷ Leaves 2-5; inflorescence without bulbils	***A. triquetrum*** (p.656)
	▷ 1 leaf; inflorescence with bulbils	***A. paradoxum*** (p.656)

Key to Daffodils *Narcissus*

if	then
1 ▷ Corona about as long as tepals, stamens all same length	Go to ▷ **2**
▷ Corona <¼ as long as tepals, stamens of two lengths	*N. poeticus* (p.658)
2 ▷ Tepals paler than corona	*N. pseudonarcissus* ssp. *pseudonarcissus* (p.658)
▷ Tepals same colour as corona	Go to ▷ **3**
3 ▷ Leaves 20–50 cm × 5–15 mm; tepals as long as corona, twisted at base	*N. p.* ssp. *major* (p.658)
▷ Leaves 20–30 cm × 6–10 mm; tepals shorter than corona, not twisted	*N. p.* ssp. *obvallaris* (p.658)

Key to Orchidaceae Orchids

The distinctive flowers of orchids are strongly irregular and highly modified for insect pollination and are unlikely to be confused with any other group of plants. Flowers are arranged in terminal spikes or racemes, each with a single bract. Perianth consists of 6 free tepals in 2 whorls of 3. Outer 3 (sepals) and 2 of the inner whorl (petals) are more or less similar, while lowest petal or lip (labellum) is large, conspicuous and usually much modified and often extended behind into a hollow 'spur'. Stamens and stigmas are borne on a special structure, the 'column', in middle of flower. There is 1 (2 in *Cypripedium*) stamen with the pollen in 2, often stalked, sticky masses, the 'pollinia'. The 2 (3 in *Cypripedium*) fertile stigmas are located at base of column, the 3rd stigma often forming a sterile protrusion, the 'rostellum', that may function to prevent self-pollination. The ovary is inferior and the fruit is a capsule. The seeds are numerous, minute and dust-like, <0.25 mm in length.

Worldwide, the orchids are one of the largest family of flowering plants, with about 20,000 species; there are currently about 55 species recognised in the British Isles.

Many orchids are very distinctive and will be able to be confidently named by using a combination of the illustrations and the text. However, two groups, the helleborines and those with a spike of predominantly pinkish flowers (mainly *Orchis* and *Dactylorhiza*), are more difficult and keys to assist in the identification of these have been included (*see* p. 667).

if	then
Helleborines *Cephalanthera, Epipactis*	
Orchids with leafy stems. Flowers lack a spur and lower lip is constricted to form 2 halves: a basal, usually cup-like, hypochile; and a terminal epichile.	
▷ Flowers sessile, ± erect	*Cephalanthera* (p.670 and overleaf)
▷ Flowers stalked, spreading or pendent	*Epipactis* (p.670 and overleaf)

CONTINUED OVERLEAF

if	**then**

Cephalanthera

1
▷ Flowers red — **C. rubra** (p.670)
▷ Flowers white — Go to ▷ **2**

2
▷ Lower leaves ovate; bracts longer than ovaries; sepals blunt — **C. damasonium** (p.670)
▷ Leaves lanceolate; bracts shorter than ovaries; sepals acute — **C. longifolia** (p.670)

Epipactis
A difficult group to identify, partly because in some species the flowers are self-pollinated, giving rise to several morphologically similar but genetically distinct plants. The taxonomy of these is confusing and the subject of continuing research.

Epipactis flower

1
▷ Rhizomes creeping and plants often in large colonies; open flowers predominantly white; basal part of lip with erect lobe on each side (fens and marshes) — **E. palustris** (p.670)
▷ Rhizomes short and plants solitary or in small clumps; flowers greenish, purplish or red; basal part of lip without lateral lobes — Go to ▷ **2**

2
▷ Flowers reddish purple, ovaries densely pubescent (limestone rocks and pavement) — **E. atrorubens** (p.670)
▷ Flowers not reddish purple, ovaries glabrous or sparsely pubescent — Go to ▷ **3**

3
▷ Upper leaves spirally arranged; flowers normally with persistent and prominent rostellum — Go to ▷ **4**
▷ Upper leaves 2-ranked; rostellum usually absent in mature flowers — Go to ▷ **5**

4
▷ Plants usually solitary; leaves dark green, the lowest as broad as or broader than long; flowers greenish with pinkish tinge; epichile as broad as or broader than long — **E. helleborine** (p.670)
▷ Plants usually in clumps; leaves greyish green, lowest longer than broad; stems and leaves tinged purplish; flowers predominantly pale green, lip pinkish; epichile as long as or longer than broad — **E. purpurata** (p.670)

if	then

5   ▷ Inflorescence axis glabrous; flowers pendent, often not fully opening — ***E. phyllanthes*** (p.672)

  ▷ Inflorescence axis pubescent; flowers not completely pendent, fully opening — Go to ▷ **6**

6   ▷ Rostellum ≤½ as long as anthers; stigmas with 2 bosses at base; ovary usually pubescent; petals pale green — Go to ▷ **7**

  ▷ Rostellum >½ as long as anthers; stigmas with 2 bosses at base; ovary usually glabrous; epichile wider than long; inner tepals rose — ***E. youngiana*** (p.672)

7   ▷ Epichile longer than wide, not reflexed — ***E. leptochila*** (p.672)

  ▷ Epichile wider than long, reflexed — Go to ▷ **8**

8   ▷ Pedicels purplish (dune slacks) — ***E. dunensis*** (p.672) **(including *E. muelleri* •) (p.670)**

  ▷ Pedicels yellowish green (Holy Island, Northumberland) — ***E. sancta*** (p.672)

Orchids with spikes of predominantly pink flowers

1   ▷ Spurs <3 mm long — ***Neotinea ustulata*** (p.680)

  ▷ Spurs ≤11 mm long — Go to ▷ **2**

  ▷ Spurs >11 mm long — Go to ▷ **6**

2   ▷ At least lower bracts leaf-like, green; labellum 3-lobed, middle lobe often smaller than lateral lobes — ***Dactylorhiza*** (p.676)

  ▷ Lower bracts brown to purplish; labellum not 3-lobed, or if 3-lobed then middle lobe longer than lateral lobes — Go to ▷ **3**

3   ▷ Labellum somewhat 'man-like', with 2 slender lateral lobes (arms) and a central lobe (body) that divides into 2 further lobes (legs) — ***Orchis*** (p.680)

  ▷ Labellum not 'man-like' — Go to ▷ **4**

4   ▷ Lateral sepals with conspicuous green or purplish veins — ***Anacamptis morio*** (p.680)

  ▷ Lateral sepals without conspicuous veins — Go to ▷ **5**

5   ▷ Leaves dark-spotted; labellum 3-lobed, the middle lobe the largest — ***Orchis mascula*** (p.680)

  ▷ Leaves unspotted; labellum 2-lobed or with very short middle lobe — ***Anacamptis laxiflora*** (p.680)

CONTINUED OVERLEAF

		if	then
6		▷ Lower lip flat; inflorescence ± cylindrical; flowers scented	***Gymnadenia*** (*see* text, p.676)
		▷ Base of lower lip with 2 raised parallel ridges; inflorescence ± conical to rounded; flowers not scented	***Anacamptis pyramidalis*** (p.676

Frog Orchid, marsh-orchids and spotted-orchids *Dactylorhiza*

Dactylorhiza flower

		if	then
1		▷ Flowers green to orange-brown	***D. viridis*** (p.676)
		▷ Flowers predominantly pink to purple	Go to ▷ **2**
2		▷ Stem solid; leaves always spotted; lateral sepals spreading; lowest bracts usually not longer than flowers	Go to ▷ **3**
		▷ Stem hollow (do not pick flower to see whether stem is hollow; instead, lightly compress stem between fingers – if hollow it will 'give', or if solid it will resist pressure); usually not spotted; lateral sepals ± erect; lowest bracts usually longer than flowers	Go to ▷ **4**
3		▷ Lobes of labellum ± equal or middle lobe longest	***D. fuchsii*** (p.678)
		▷ Lateral lobes of labellum much larger than small middle lobe	***D. maculata*** (p.678)
4		▷ Leaves yellowish green, hooded at tip; margins of labellum usually reflexed and with 2 parallel loop-shaped marks	***D. incarnata*** (p.678)
		▷ Leaves green to slightly bluish green, not hooded; labellum flat, with irregular loop and spot-like markings	Go to ▷ **5**
5		▷ Usually >5 sheathing leaves, >2 cm wide; central lobe of labellum not longer than laterals	Go to ▷ **6**
		▷ 3–5 sheathing leaves, narrow, <2 cm wide	Go to ▷ **9**
6		▷ Labellum broadly diamond-shaped or with indistinct central lobe; flowers deep purple (N BI, Wales)	***D. purpurella*** (p.678)
		▷ Labellum usually with distinct central lobe	Go to ▷ **7**

	if	then
7	▷ Leaves unspotted or (rarely) with ring-like spots; lower lip roundish, with rather indistinct central lobe, markings predominantly dots that do not reach margins (S Britain, not Ireland)	*D. praetermissa* (p.678)
	▷ Leaves spotted or unspotted; lower lip distinctly 3-lobed, markings, dots and lines extending to margins	Go to ▷ **8**
8	▷ Central lobe of lip pointed, as long as or longer than lateral lobes	*D. majalis* ● (p.678)
	▷ Central lobe of lip blunt, shorter than lateral lobes (Ireland)	*D. occidentalis* (p.678)
9	▷ Labellum with elongated central lobe that is longer than laterals	Go to ▷ **10**
	▷ Labellum distinctly 3-lobed but central lobe not longer than lateral lobes; plant short, squat; leaves heavily marked; flowers deep purple (Outer Hebrides, rare)	*D. ebudensis*
10	▷ Leaves unspotted (widely distributed but scarce)	*D. traunsteinerioides* (p.678)
	▷ Leaves heavily spotted (W Scotland)	*D. t.* ssp. *lapponica* (p.678)

Key to Fragrant Orchids *Gymnadenia*

if	then
▷ Labellum as long as broad with 3 ± equal lobes; sepals linear, angled downwards	*G. conopsea* (p.676)
▷ Labellum longer than broad, middle lobe longer than laterals; sepals ovate-lanceolate	*G. borealis* (p.676)
▷ Labellum broader than long, lateral lobes larger than middle; sepals blunt, horizontal	*G. densiflora* (p.676)

ORCHIDACEAE Orchids

See key on p.665.

Lady's-slipper
Cypripedium calceolus CR. *(B)

Beautiful, unmistakable plant, to about 50 cm. FLOWERS 1-2 forming inflorescence. HABITAT/DIST. Native. Once restricted to open limestone woods in N England; collecting eventually reduced it to one plant in Yorkshire Dales, where it still survives. A reintroduction programme using material from the surviving plant is now underway. (Central and N Europe.) FLS May-Jun.

White Helleborine
Cephalanthera damasonium VU.

STEMS Leafy; flowering stem to 60 cm. LEAVES Ovate, 5-10 cm. FLOWERS *Erect, sessile, remaining closed*, in 3-12-flowered spike; *bracts longer than ovaries*; outer tepals obtuse; labellum shorter than other tepals; hypochile pouched, with orange patch; epichile heart-shaped, with orange keels on upper surface; ovary glabrous. HABITAT Shady chalk and limestone woodlands, especially Beech. DIST. Native. Local but widespread. S England. (Most of Europe except N.) FLS May-Jun.

Narrow-leaved Helleborine
Cephalanthera longifolia VU.

STEMS Flowering stems to 60 cm. LEAVES *Alternate, ± 2-ranked, linear-lanceolate*. FLOWERS Obliquely erect, *partially opening*, in 3-15-flowered spike; *bracts shorter than ovaries*; outer tepals lanceolate, acute; inner tepals shorter, broader, obtuse; labellum shorter than other tepals; epichile with orange ridges, tip turned down; ovary glabrous. HABITAT Open calcareous woodlands; rarely on maritime sands. DIST. Native. Throughout BI but very local and declining. (All Europe except extreme N.) FLS May-Jul.

Red Helleborine
Cephalanthera rubra CR. *(B)

STEMS Flowering stems to 45 cm, glandular above. LEAVES 5-8, lanceolate to narrowly elliptic. FLOWERS *Purplish pink*, large, opening fairly wide, in 2-7-flowered inflorescence; labellum erect, tip acute; ovary glandular. HABITAT Open Beech woodland on chalk and limestone. DIST. Native. Very rare, at 3 sites only in Gloucestershire, Buckinghamshire, Hampshire. (Most of Europe.) FLS Jun-Jul.

Marsh Helleborine
Epipactis palustris *(NI)

Attractive orchid with creeping rhizome. STEMS To 50 cm. LEAVES 5-8, spirally arranged. FLOWERS Stalked, in 7-14-flowered inflorescence; outer tepals brownish or purplish green, hairy on outside; inner tepals whitish with purple veins; labellum strongly constricted; hypochile with erect lobe on each side; epichile white with red veins; rostellum persistent. HABITAT Marshes, fens, wet pastures, dune slacks, often forming large colonies. DIST. Native. Local and declining. Widely distributed in England, Wales, Ireland; very rare in Scotland. (All Europe except extreme N.) FLS Jun-Aug.

Dark-red Helleborine
Epipactis atrorubens

STEMS *Flowering stem* to 60 cm, solitary, erect, violet red below, *densely pubescent above*. LEAVES 5-10, in opposite rows. FLOWERS *Dull reddish purple*, in 8-18-flowered inflorescence; epichile broader than long with 3 large, bright, wrinkled basal bosses; rostellum persistent; ovary pubescent. HABITAT Fissures in bare limestone, scree, grassy slopes, cliff ledges, quarries, grikes in limestone pavement; to 610 m. DIST. Native. Very local. N England, N Wales, N Scotland, W Ireland. (Most of Europe.) FLS Jun-Jul.

Broad-leaved Helleborine
Epipactis helleborine

STEMS 1-3 flowering stems, to 80 cm. LEAVES Spirally arranged, broadly ovate, dull green. FLOWERS Drooping, greenish to dull purplish, in 15-50-flowered inflorescence; *interior of hypochile dark reddish brown; epichile wider than long, with 2 wart-like bosses at base; tip reflexed*; rostellum large, persistent. HABITAT Woods, hedge banks, roadsides, dune slacks, limestone pavement; on mildly acid to calcareous soils. DIST. Native. Widely distributed throughout BI, N & central Scotland. (Most of Europe except extreme N.) FLS Jul-Oct.

Violet Helleborine
Epipactis purpurata

Similar to *E. helleborine*, but *flowering stems often clustered*, tinged violet below; leaves narrower ovate-lanceolate to lanceolate, grey-green or tinged purplish; bracts longer than flowers; flowers pale greenish white; *interior of hypochile mottled violet inside; epichile at least as long as broad, with 2 smoothly ridged basal bosses*. HABITAT Shaded mixed woodlands, coppice, usually on base-rich or calcareous soils. DIST. Native. Rather local but widely distributed in central and S England. (NW and central Europe.) FLS Aug-Sep.

Mueller's Helleborine
Epipactis muelleri

Similar to *E. leptochila*, but outer tepals blunt-tipped; epichile greenish or tinged pink, wider than long, with obtuse, recurved tip; ovary almost glabrous. HABITAT Open woods, woodland clearings. DIST. *Not BI*. (W and central Europe.) FLS Jun-Aug.

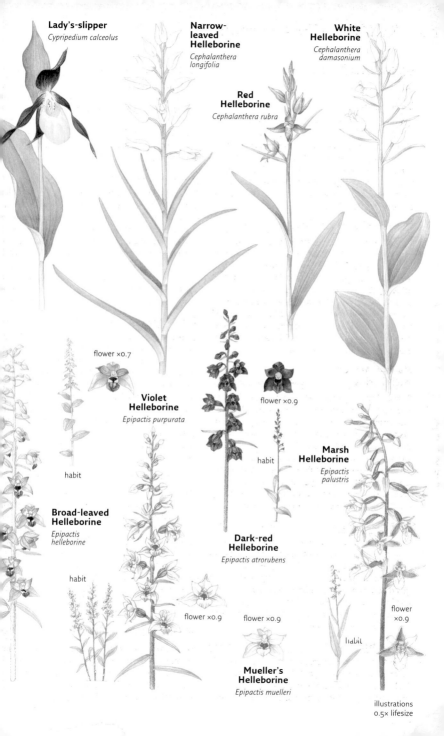

Lady's-slipper
Cypripedium calceolus

Narrow-leaved Helleborine
Cephalanthera longifolia

White Helleborine
Cephalanthera damasonium

Red Helleborine
Cephalanthera rubra

flower ×0.7

Violet Helleborine
Epipactis purpurata

flower ×0.9

habit

Marsh Helleborine
Epipactis palustris

habit

Broad-leaved Helleborine
Epipactis helleborine

habit

Dark-red Helleborine
Epipactis atrorubens

flower ×0.9

flower ×0.9

flower ×0.9

Mueller's Helleborine
Epipactis muelleri

habit

illustrations
0.5× lifesize

Narrow-lipped Helleborine
Epipactis leptochila

STEMS Flowering stems to 70 cm. LEAVES 4–10, in 2 ranks. FLOWERS Rather small, *yellowish green*, spreading or slightly drooping, in 10–25-flowered raceme; bracts ≤2× as long as flowers; *outer tepals acute at apex; epichile longer than wide, cordate-acuminate, yellowish green with white margin*, tip flat; viscidium absent; ovary hairy. HABITAT Very local. Calcareous Beech woods in S England. Native. (N, W and central Europe.) FLS Jun–Aug.

Dune Helleborine
Epipactis dunensis

Plants from coastal dune slacks, metalliferous spoil tips and waste sites in N England with outer tepals obtuse and epichile wider than long and once thought to be a variety of *E. leptochila* are now regarded as a separate species.

Lindisfarne Helleborine
Epipactis sancta EN.

Plants differing from *E. dunensis* with yellowish-green pedicels, slightly toothed margins to the leaves and with a less dense inflorescence from Holy Island (Lindisfarne), Northumberland have recently been named *Epipactis sancta* but require further investigation.

Young's Helleborine
Epipactis youngiana *(B)

Similar to *E. leptochila*, but *stigma with 2 basal bosses and rostellum thus appearing 3-pointed*; ovary glabrous and inner tepals rose. HABITAT Woodland, on heavy soils that are often polluted with metals. DIST. Endemic. Very rare. Northumberland, Lanarkshire. FLS Jul–Oct. NOTE May be a variety of *E. helleborine* (p.670).

Green-flowered Helleborine
Epipactis phyllanthes *(NI)

STEMS Flowering stems to 45 cm. LEAVES 3–6, in 2 ranks, often shorter than internodes, margins often undulate. FLOWERS Rather small, *pendulous, usually hardly opening*, green to yellowish green, ≤30 forming inflorescence, *axis glabrous*; rostellum minute, shrivelling early; *ovary ± glabrous*. HABITAT Sparsely vegetated, shaded habitats on mildly acid soils, woodlands, coppice, roadsides, sand-dunes. DIST. Native. Scattered throughout BI except Scotland. (W France, Denmark, Pyrenees.) FLS Jul–Aug.

Small-leaved Helleborine
Epipactis microphylla

STEMS Flowering stems slender, to 40 cm. LEAVES 3–6, small, 1–2.5 cm, inflorescence densely pubescent; FLOWERS Greenish tinged reddish, epichile with 2 conspicuous wrinkled protuberances at base, ovary densely pubescent. HABITAT Beech and pine woods, calcicole. DIST. *Not BI*. (Central, S Europe, N to Belgium.) FLS May-Aug.

Ghost Orchid
Epipogium aphyllum CR. *(E

Rootless, leafless, saprophytic perennial, lackin chlorophyll. STEMS Flowering stems to 25 cm whitish tinged pink. FLOWERS Pendulous, no inverted, labellum and spur pointing upwards, i 1–2-flowered inflorescence; tepals yellowish, down curving; labellum white with violet spots. HABITA Deep leaf litter in dense, shaded Beech woods wit no associated ground flora. DIST. Native. Onl recorded on a few occasions and not reliably sinc 1986, until refound 2009. Chilterns, Herefordshir (N and central Europe.) FLS Jun–Aug.

Bird's-nest Orchid
Neottia nidus-avis *(N

Rhizomatous, *saprophytic* perennial, *without gree leaves*. Roots in a dense mass resembling a bird nest; *whole plant yellowish brown*. STEMS Flowerin stem to 50 cm, stiffly erect, glandular, densely cov ered by brownish scales. FLOWERS Yellowish brow spur absent, honey-scented, in cylindrical, spike-lik inflorescence; labellum 2× as long as outer tepal with 2 broad, widely spreading lobes. HABITAT Dee humus of shaded calcareous woodlands, especiall Beech woodlands on chalk. DIST. Native. Declinin Throughout BI, but scarce outside S England. (Mo of Europe except extreme N.) FLS May–Jul.

Common Twayblade
Neottia ovata (*Listera ovat*

STEMS Flowering stems solitary, to 75 cm, glabrou below, pubescent above, *with pair of broad, sessi opposite leaves somewhat below middle*. LEAVES 20 cm. FLOWERS *Yellowish green, inconspicuous*, in lax, spike-like raceme, 7–25 mm; tepals ovate, all same length, outer connivent; labellum deep divided at tip into 2 linear lobes. HABITAT Grasslan open woodland, hedgerows, scrub, dune slack limestone pavement, disused quarries, on calcareo or mildly acid soils. DIST. Native. Frequent and som times abundant. Throughout BI. (Most of Euro except extreme N.) FLS Jun–Jul.

Lesser Twayblade
Neottia cordata (*Listera corda*

Small, inconspicuous orchid. STEMS Flowering ste solitary, reddish, 6–10 cm, with *pair of spreadir shiny, ovate leaves about halfway up stem*. FLOWE Tiny, 6–12 forming inflorescence, 1.5–6 cm; out tepals greenish, inner reddish on inside; labellu 3.5–4 mm, reddish, pendulous, divided abc halfway into 2 linear, tapering lobes. HABITAT Dam shaded acid habitats; to 1065 m. DIST. Native. England, N Wales, Scotland, Ireland. (All Euro except S.) FLS Jun–Sep.

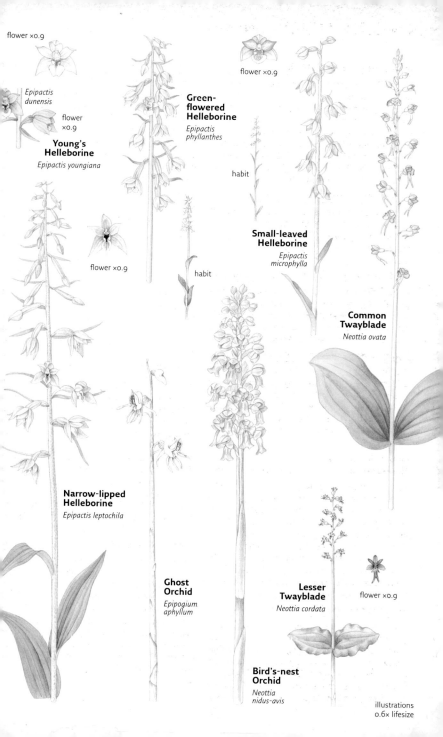

flower ×0.9

Epipactis dunensis

flower ×0.9

Young's Helleborine

Epipactis youngiana

Green-flowered Helleborine

Epipactis phyllanthes

flower ×0.9

habit

Small-leaved Helleborine

Epipactis microphylla

flower ×0.9

habit

Common Twayblade

Neottia ovata

Narrow-lipped Helleborine

Epipactis leptochila

Ghost Orchid

Epipogium aphyllum

Lesser Twayblade

Neottia cordata

flower ×0.9

Bird's-nest Orchid

Neottia nidus-avis

illustrations 0.6× lifesize

Autumn Lady's-tresses — *Spiranthes spiralis*

STEMS Flowering stem to 20 cm, with appressed bract-like scales. LEAVES Ovate-elliptic, glossy green; *those of current season forming lateral overwintering rosette* with or after flowers and withering the following summer before flower spike develops. FLOWERS *Very small, in tightly spiralled 5–15-flowered spike*; bracts 6–7 mm, *tepals all ± equal, lip unlobed*; spur absent. HABITAT Downs, hill pastures, meadows, cliff tops, dunes, lawns, on calcareous soils. DIST. Native. Declining. Widely distributed in S England; scattered in N England, Ireland; coastal in Wales. (All Europe except N.) FLS Aug–Sep.

Summer Lady's-tresses — *Spiranthes aestivalis* EX.

Similar to *S. spiralis*, but flowering stem to 40 cm, bearing true leaves; *leaves linear-lanceolate*, 5–12 cm × 4–9 mm; flowers 6–8 mm, in 6–20-flowered inflorescence, 3–10 cm, in 1 spiral row; bracts 6–9 mm. HABITAT Valley bogs, stream sides. DIST. Native, but extinct; last recorded in 1959 in New Forest (Hampshire). (Central and S Europe, N to Belgium.) FLS Jul–Aug.

Irish Lady's-tresses — *Spiranthes romanzoffiana* *(NI, R)

STEMS Flowering stem to 35 cm. LEAVES *Basal leaves linear-lanceolate*, 5–10 cm × 5–10 mm; cauline leaves brown, erect. FLOWERS 10–14 mm, in 12–35-flowered *inflorescence*, 2.5–5 cm, *in 3 spiral rows*; bracts 10–20 mm. HABITAT Wet, peaty *Molinia* pastures, meadows, peaty margins of rivers, streams and lakes. DIST. Native. N and W Ireland, N Scotland, Devon (1 site). (Only in BI in Europe.) FLS Jul–Aug.

Creeping Lady's-tresses — *Goodyera repens*

Orchid with creeping rhizomes. STEMS Flowering stems to 35 cm, glandular-hairy, scaly. LEAVES *In basal rosette*, ovate-lanceolate, *conspicuously net-veined*, evergreen. FLOWERS Small, sweet-scented, in slender spike, 3–7 cm, with a slight spiral twist; bracts green, 10–15 mm; tepals all ± same length; labellum shorter than tepals, unlobed; spur absent. HABITAT Mature pine woods; to 335 m. DIST. Native in Scotland, especially NE; naturalised on pine plantations in Cumbria, Norfolk. (Central and N Europe.) FLS Jul–Aug.

Fen Orchid — *Liparis loeselii* EN. *(B)

Perennial with 2 above-ground pseudo-bulbs at base of stem. STEMS Flowering stem to 20 cm, 3-angled above. LEAVES 2, ovate, keeled, yellow-green, with greasy appearance. FLOWERS *Small, greenish yellow*, in a lax 4–8-flowered spike; bracts 3–20 mm; *tepals linear, spreading; labellum upward-pointing*, as long as tepals but broader; spur absent. HABITAT Wet fen peat, dune slacks. DIST. Native. Very rare, declining Norfolk Broads, S Wales. (All Europe except N and Mediterranean.) FLS Jun–Jul.

Bog Orchid — *Hammarbya paludosa* *(NI, R

Small rhizomatous perennial with 2 pseudo-bulbs at base of stem. STEMS Flowering stem 3–8 cm. LEAVES 2–3, pale yellow, ovate, 5–10 × 2–5 mm, often fringed with small bulbils. FLOWERS *Small, yellowish green*, ≤20 forming rather dense, spike-like inflorescence 1.5–5 cm; *labellum upward-pointing*, lanceolate, acute; spur absent. HABITAT Wet, open acid *Sphagnum* bogs to 500 m. DIST. Native. Very local, seriously declining N and W Britain, New Forest; scattered in Ireland (Central and N Europe.) FLS Jun–Sep.

Coralroot Orchid — *Corallorhiza trifida* VU

Rootless *saprophytic perennial, without green leaves* rhizome coral-like, with short knobbly branches. STEMS Flowering stem 7–25 cm, slender, yellowish green, with 2–4 long, sheathing scales. FLOWERS *Small, inconspicuous, greenish yellow*, in lax 4–12 flowered spike; labellum *c.*5 mm, white with reddish markings, and with 2 slightly raised longitudinal ridges at base. HABITAT Damp, shaded willow and alder carr on raised bogs and lake margins, dune slacks; to 365 m. DIST. Native. Very rare in N England; scattered in Scotland. (N Europe, S to Pyrenees, N Greece.) FLS May–Aug.

Violet Bird's-nest Orchid — *Limodorum abortivum*

Rhizomatous *saprophytic perennial*, without green leaves; *whole plant violet*. STEMS Flowering stem to 80 cm, clothed with sheathing scales. FLOWERS In 4–25-flowered spike-like raceme; tepals *c.*20 mm free, spreading; labellum triangular, unlobed; spur to 15 mm, cylindrical, curving upwards. HABITAT Open woods, shaded grasslands, on calcareous soils. DIST. Not BI. (Central and S Europe, N to Belgium.) FLS May–Jun.

Musk Orchid — *Herminium monorchis* V

[*See* illustration following page.] Small, inconspicuous orchid. STEMS To 15 cm. LEAVES 2–3 main leaves, low on stem, oblong, 2–7 cm, with 1–3 much smaller bract-like leaves further up stem. FLOWERS Greenish yellow, small, drooping, bell-shaped, sweet-scented, in slender, 1-sided spike; bracts about as long as ovary; tepals converging; labellum 3-lobed, to 4 mm; spur absent. HABITAT Short turf of chalk and limestone grassland. DIST. Native. Very local, declining. S England. (Most of Europe except extreme N and Mediterranean.) FLS Jun–Jul.

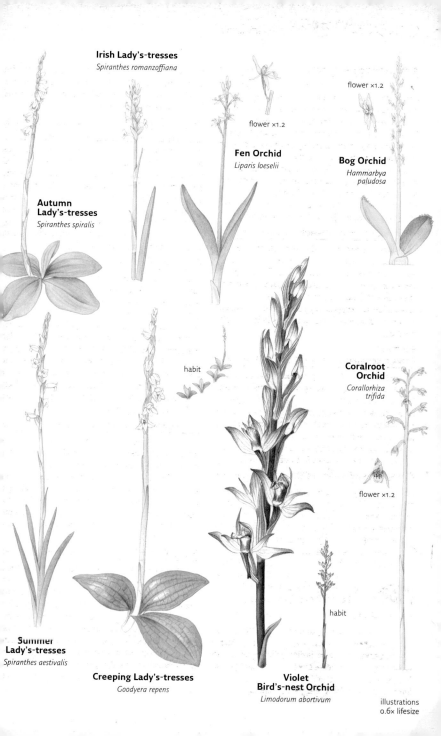

Irish Lady's-tresses
Spiranthes romanzoffiana

flower ×1.2

Fen Orchid
Liparis loeselii

flower ×1.2

Bog Orchid
Hammarbya paludosa

Autumn Lady's-tresses
Spiranthes spiralis

habit

Coralroot Orchid
Corallorhiza trifida

flower ×1.2

Summer Lady's-tresses
Spiranthes aestivalis

Creeping Lady's-tresses
Goodyera repens

Violet Bird's-nest Orchid
Limodorum abortivum

habit

illustrations
0.6× lifesize

Greater Butterfly-orchid *Platanthera chlorantha*

STEMS To 40 cm. LEAVES Usually 2 basal leaves, large, to 15 × 5 cm, elliptic, blunt; upper stem leaves bract-like. FLOWERS 18-23 mm across, greenish white, heavily fragrant at night, in lax spikes to 20 cm; bracts about as long as ovary; outer tepals spreading; labellum long, narrow, to 16 mm; spur long, to 28 mm, curved downwards and forwards; pollinia 3-4 mm, widely diverging below. HABITAT Woods, scrub, meadows, pastures, downs, usually on well-drained calcareous soils; to 460 m. DIST. Native. Throughout BI, but rather local. (Most of Europe, but absent from parts of N, E and SW.) FLS May-Jul.

Lesser Butterfly-orchid *Platanthera bifolia* VU.

Similar to *P. chlorantha*, but stem to 30 cm; leaves to 9 × 3 cm; flowers 11-18 mm across; labellum 6-12 mm; spur 15-20 mm, almost horizontal; pollinia *c*.2 mm, vertical, parallel. HABITAT Heathy grassland, moorland, wood margins, scrub, on acidic to calcareous soils; to 365 m. DIST. Native. Local, declining. Throughout BI, but commoner in N and W. (All Europe, but rare in Mediterranean.) FLS May-Jul.

Pyramidal Orchid *Anacamptis pyramidalis*

STEMS Leafy; flowering stems to 50 cm. LEAVES Lower leaves 8-15 cm, oblong-lanceolate, keeled. FLOWERS Rosy purple, in dense-flowered, ± conical or rounded spike; outer tepals spreading, rest converging into a hood; labellum 3-lobed, with 2 vertical ridges or 'guide-plates' on upper surface; spur 14 mm, as long as or longer than ovary. HABITAT Well-drained calcareous grassland, scrub, roadsides, dunes, dune slacks. DIST. Native. Locally frequent throughout BI, but becoming coastal to N. (Most of Europe except N.) FLS Jun-Aug.

Small-white Orchid *Pseudorchis albida* VU. *(NI, R)

STEMS Flowering stems to 30 cm. LEAVES 3-5 main leaves, oblong-lanceolate. FLOWERS 2-2.5 mm, greenish white, in dense-flowered cylindrical spike; bracts about as long as ovary; tepals converging with 3-lobed labellum, making flowers appear ± tubular; spur short and blunt, shorter than ovary. HABITAT Well-drained hill pastures, mountain grasslands, stream sides; to 550 m. DIST. Native. Widespread in upland Britain but declining. (NW, W and central Europe.) FLS Jun-Jul.

Fragrant Orchids *Gymnadenia* spp.

See key to *Gymnadenia* on p.669. STEMS Flowering stems to 40 cm. LEAVES Lower ones 3-5, narrowly oblong-lanceolate, keeled, to 15 × 3 cm. FLOWERS Inflorescence a ± dense-flowered cylindrical spike; bracts about as long as flowers; flowers small, pinkish-red, very fragrant; outer lateral tepals spreading; labellum 3-lobed; spur 11-16 mm, almost 2× as long as ovary. DIST. Native. Widely distributed throughout BI to 610 m. (Most of Europe.) FLS Jun-Aug. Three closely related species:

Chalk Fragrant Orchid, *G. conopsea*, dry calcareous grassland throughout BI, but commoner in S.
Heath Fragrant Orchid, *G. borealis*, hill pastures, heaths, moors; the commonest species in Scotland, but also scattered in W, S BI.
Marsh Fragrant Orchid, *G. densiflora*, fens, wet meadows, damp calcareous grassland throughout BI, and the commonest species in Ireland.

Short-spurred Fragrant Orchid *Gymnadenia odoratissima*

Similar to *G. conopsea* but smaller. STEMS To 30 cm. LEAVES Linear. FLOWERS Spur 4-5 mm, as long as or slightly shorter than ovary. HABITAT Calcareous grasslands. DIST. Not in BI. (W, central, E Europe.) FLS Jun-Jul.

Frog Orchid, marsh-orchids and spotted-orchids *Dactylorhiza*

A particularly complicated group (*see* key on p.668) largely because of the amount of variation within the species and the ease with which they hybridise. It is often not possible to identify individual plants with certainty. Leaves are spotted or unspotted, the lower with sheathing bases, and the upper intermediate with the bracts and not sheathing, although they may clasp the stem. The flowers have a spur, usually <10 mm long; the 3 upper tepals are incurved; the lateral sepals are spreading, erect or downcurved, and the labellum is usually shallowly 3-lobed. The shape and markings of the labellum are important diagnostic characters, together with the number of sheathing leaves.

Frog Orchid *Dactylorhiza viridis* VU

STEMS Flowering stem to 25 cm, reddish, slightly angled above. LEAVES 2-5. FLOWERS Greenish, tinged brownish purple, in rather lax cylindrical spike, 1.5-6 cm; lowest bracts often longer than flowers; outer tepals converging to form hood; labellum 3.5-6 mm oblong, parallel-sided, 3-lobed at tip; spur short *c*.2 mm. HABITAT Calcareous grasslands, dunes, mires, flushes, limestone pavement, scree, roadsides; to 910 m. DIST. Native. Scattered throughout BI, but declining. (Most of Europe, but only in mts in S.) FLS Jun-Aug.

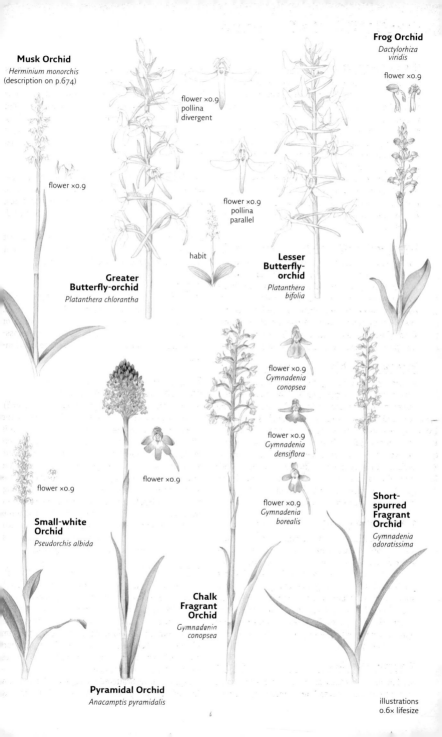

Musk Orchid
Herminium monorchis
(description on p.674)

flower ×0.9

flower ×0.9
pollina
divergent

flower ×0.9
pollina
parallel

habit

Frog Orchid
*Dactylorhiza
viridis*

flower ×0.9

**Greater
Butterfly-orchid**
Platanthera chlorantha

**Lesser
Butterfly-
orchid**
*Platanthera
bifolia*

flower ×0.9
*Gymnadenia
conopsea*

flower ×0.9
*Gymnadenia
densiflora*

flower ×0.9
*Gymnadenia
borealis*

flower ×0.9

flower ×0.9

**Small-white
Orchid**
Pseudorchis albida

**Chalk
Fragrant
Orchid**
*Gymnadenia
conopsea*

**Short-
spurred
Fragrant
Orchid**
*Gymnadenia
odoratissima*

Pyramidal Orchid
Anacamptis pyramidalis

illustrations
0.6× lifesize

Common Spotted-orchid · *Dactylorhiza fuchsii*

The commonest British orchid, often occurring in large numbers. Very variable, with a number of named subspecies and varieties. STEMS Flowering stem to 50 cm. LEAVES With dark, ± transversely elongated spots, oblong-lanceolate; lowest leaves broad, blunt. FLOWERS Pale to deep pink, occasionally white, in dense, cylindrical, many-flowered spike; bracts about as long as ovaries; labellum deeply divided into 3 ± equal lobes, middle lobe slightly longer than lateral; spur 5.5–10 mm. HABITAT Neutral and calcareous grasslands, roadsides, open woodlands, marshes, fens, dune slacks, quarries, embankments; to 530 m. DIST. Native. Widespread throughout most of BI. (Most of Europe except parts of S.) FLS Jun–Aug.

Heath Spotted-orchid · *Dactylorhiza maculata*

Similar to *D. fuchsii*, but leaves with ± circular spots; lowest leaves lanceolate, acute; flowers almost white to pale pink and deep pink; middle lobe of labellum much smaller and usually shorter than broadly rounded lateral lobes. HABITAT Heaths, moors, bogs, mountain grassland, on acid soils; to 915 m. DIST. Native. Throughout BI, but commoner in N and W, and scarce and declining in parts of English lowlands. (Most of Europe except SE.) FLS Jun–Aug.

Early Marsh-orchid · *Dactylorhiza incarnata*

STEMS Flowering, to 60 cm. LEAVES ± erect, yellow-green, hooded at tip. FLOWERS Lowest bracts much longer than flowers; outer tepals ± erect; sides of labellum strongly reflexed soon after flower opens so looks narrow from in front; spur 6–8.5 mm. HABITAT Bogs, fens, marshes, wet meadows, dune slacks. DIST. Throughout BI, declining especially in S. (Most of Europe, rare in Mediterranean.) FLS May-Jul. SSP. 5 well-marked, very variable, with different habitats:

Leaves spotted on both surfaces	ssp. *cruenta*
Leaves unspotted	
Flowers cream	ssp. *ochroleuca*
Flowers flesh pink	ssp. *incarnata*
Flowers purple; bracts purple-tinged	ssp. *pulchella*
Flowers bright crimson-red, stem short 5–20 cm	ssp. *coccinea*

Ssp. *incarnata*: throughout BI. Calcareous fens, marshes, upland flushes to 440 m. Ssp. *pulchella*: throughout BI. Acid *Sphagnum* bogs, wet heathland to 395 m. Ssp. *coccinea*: coasts of BI except S. Dune slacks, machair grassland. Ssp. *cruenta*: NW Scotland, very rare, 2 sites only. Ssp. *ochroleuca*: E Anglia, very rare, calcareous fens, 2 sites only.

Southern Marsh-orchid · *Dactylorhiza praetermissa*

Tall, robust orchid. STEMS To 70 cm tall and 5 mm diam. LEAVES Rather grey-green, unspotted, or rarely ring-spotted (f. *junialis*). FLOWERS Rich pink-ish purple, in rather dense inflorescence; labellum usually wider than long, shortly 3-lobed, slightly concave, markings predominantly fine dots; spur 6–9 mm. HABITAT Damp meadows, marshes, fens, dune slacks. DIST. Native. Widespread in England, Wales, N to Humber. (NW Europe.) FLS Jun–Jul.

Northern Marsh-orchid · *Dactylorhiza purpurella*

STEMS Flowering stems to 30 cm. LEAVES Usually 5–8, ± stiffly spreading, dull green or grey-green, unspotted. FLOWERS Rich deep purple, in short, broad, dense, rather flat-topped inflorescence; bracts purplish; labellum 7–9 mm wide, flat, diamond-shaped, sub-entire or obscurely 3-lobed, markings rather indistinct loops, lines; spur to 9 mm. HABITAT Wet meadows, fens, marshes, road verges, dune slacks. DIST. Native. Britain N of Humber, W Wales, N Ireland. (NW Europe.) FLS Jun–Jul.

Broad-leaved Marsh-orchid · *Dactylorhiza majalis*

STEMS Flowering stems to 60 cm. LEAVES Usually 4–8, with large, irregular spots. FLOWERS Purplish lilac; labellum 9–10 mm, usually 3-lobed, middle lobe without markings. HABITAT Damp meadows, fens. DIST. *Not* BI. (W and central Europe.) FLS May–Jun.

Irish Marsh-orchid · *Dactylorhiza occidentalis*

STEMS Flowering stems to 35 cm. LEAVES Green to slightly glaucous, heavily marked with spots and blotches (f. *occidentalis*) or unmarked (f. *kerryensis*). FLOWERS Deep red-purple, in dense, ovoid inflorescence; labellum 8 × 11 mm, broader than long, 3-lobed, markings predominantly loops, dots; spur to 8.5 mm. HABITAT Marshes, wet meadows, fens. DIST. Endemic to Ireland. Throughout Ireland except NE. FLS May–Jul.

Narrow-leaved Marsh-orchid · *Dactylorhiza traunsteinerioides* *(N

STEMS Flowering stem to 30 cm. LEAVES 2–4 basal leaves, linear-lanceolate, spotted or unspotted. FLOWERS Pale to lilac, in rather lax, few-flowered 1-sided inflorescence; labellum 9 × 11 mm, distinctly 3-lobed, with central lobe much longer than laterals, markings predominantly loops, dashes; spur to 10 mm. HABITAT Base-rich flushed marshes, fens. DIST. Native, or possibly endemic. Scattered throughout BI, but rare and local. FL

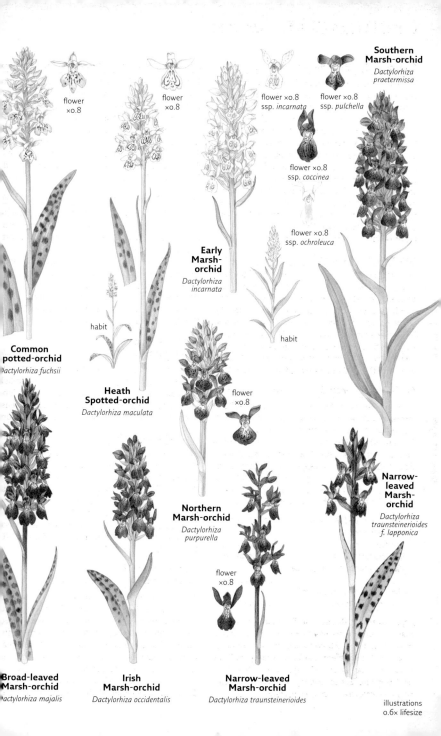

flower
×0.8

flower
×0.8

**Southern
Marsh-orchid**

*Dactylorhiza
praetermissa*

flower ×0.8
ssp. *incarnata*

flower ×0.8
ssp. *pulchella*

flower ×0.8
ssp. *coccinea*

flower ×0.8
ssp. *ochroleuca*

**Early
Marsh-
orchid**

*Dactylorhiza
incarnata*

habit

habit

**Common
Spotted-orchid**

Dactylorhiza fuchsii

**Heath
Spotted-orchid**

Dactylorhiza maculata

flower
×0.8

**Northern
Marsh-orchid**

*Dactylorhiza
purpurella*

flower
×0.8

**Narrow-
leaved
Marsh-
orchid**

*Dactylorhiza
traunsteinerioides
f. lapponica*

**Broad-leaved
Marsh-orchid**

Dactylorhiza majalis

**Irish
Marsh-orchid**

Dactylorhiza occidentalis

**Narrow-leaved
Marsh-orchid**

Dactylorhiza traunsteinerioides

illustrations
0.6× lifesize

May-Jul. **SIMILAR SPP. Lapland Marsh-orchid** *(B), a rather short plant with heavily marked leaves, was originally identified as the Scandinavian *D. lapponica* when it was discovered in 1988, but is now regarded as a form of *D. traunsteinerioides*. It occurs in wet base-rich hill flushes in scattered localities on the W coast of Scotland and Western Isles.

Dense-flowered Orchid — *Neotinea maculata*

STEMS Flowering stems to 30 cm. **LEAVES** 2-3 basal leaves, unspotted or sometimes with small brownish spots. **FLOWERS** Very small, pinkish or white, not fully opening, in dense spike, 2-6 cm; bracts small; tepals converging to form a hood; labellum 3-lobed, about as long as tepals, central lobe notched; spur very short. **HABITAT** Short calcareous grassland, limestone pavement, dunes, road verges. **DIST.** Native. Very local. S and W Ireland, I of Man. (SW Europe, Mediterranean.) **FLS** Apr-Jun.

Burnt Orchid — *Neotinea ustulata* EN

STEMS Flowering stems short, to 20 cm. **LEAVES** Few, mainly basal, unspotted. **FLOWERS** Small, in dense-flowered spike, 2-5 cm, tip dark maroon when flowers first open, becoming paler, then whitish; bracts as long as or longer than ovary; tepals converging to form a hood; labellum 3-lobed, central lobe longer than laterals, notched; spur very short. **HABITAT** Short, grazed, dry, warm chalk and limestone grassland, sand-dunes. **DIST.** Native. Very local, rare, declining. England N to Tees, but centred on chalk of central-S England. (Central Europe.) **FLS** May-Jun, Jul-Aug.

Green-winged Orchid — *Anacamptis morio* *(NI, R)

STEMS Flowering stems to 40 cm. **LEAVES** Unspotted. **FLOWERS** Deep purple, through pale pink to almost white, in rather lax, few-flowered inflorescence, 2.5- 8 cm; tepals converging to form hood, outer tepals with conspicuous greenish or greyish veins; labellum broader than long, 3-lobed, lateral lobes folded back; spur about as long as ovary. **HABITAT** Old permanent pastures, hay meadows, churchyards, sand-dunes. **DIST.** Native. Local and declining, but can form large colonies. Throughout Britain N to Tees; central and W Ireland. (Most of Europe except N.) **FLS** May-Jun.

Loose-flowered Orchid — *Anacamptis laxiflora*

STEMS Flowering stems to 40 cm. **LEAVES** Narrow, unspotted. **FLOWERS** Usually deep purple, in lax, few-flowered, cylindrical spike; outer tepals free, the lateral erect; inner tepals shorter, forming a hood; labellum 6-10 mm, 3-lobed, slightly broader than long, sides reflexed; spur 10-15 mm. **HABITAT** Calcareous or base-rich marshes, wet meadows. **DIST.** Native. Channel Is (Jersey, Guernsey). (W, central and S Europe.) **FLS** May-Jun.

Toothed Orchid — *Orchis tridentata*

STEMS Flowering stem to 45 cm. **LEAVES** 3-4, unspotted. **FLOWERS** Inflorescence ovoid; bracts shorter than or as long as ovary; flowers white to pale violet-lilac, tepals converging to form hood; labellum longer than wide, purple-spotted, 3-lobed, lateral lobes spreading, middle lobe emarginate. **HABITAT** Grassy calcareous hillsides, open woodland. **DIST.** *Not BI.* (Central and S Europe.) **FLS** Apr-Jun.

Early-purple Orchid — *Orchis mascula*

STEMS Flowering stems to 60 cm. **LEAVES** Basal leaves in a rosette, usually with purple-black spots. **FLOWERS** Purplish crimson, in a rather lax spike, 4-15 cm; bracts about as long as ovary; lateral pair of outer tepals (sepals) spreading then folded back; rest of tepals converging; labellum 8-12 mm, sides reflexed, 3-lobed, central lobe longer than laterals, notched; spur as long as or longer than ovary, curved upwards. **HABITAT** Woods, coppice, calcareous grassland, pastures, hedge banks, roadsides, on base-rich soils; to 880 m. **DIST.** Native. Widespread and common throughout BI. (W and W-central Europe.) **FLS** Apr-Jun.

Lady Orchid — *Orchis purpurea* EN

Tall, handsome orchid. **STEMS** Flowering stems to 50(-100) cm. **LEAVES** 3-5, unspotted, shining. **FLOWERS** In dense to rather lax inflorescence, to 15 cm; bracts very small; tepals converging to form a hood (head) over column, dark reddish purple; labellum rose-pink to whitish, lateral lobes linear, curved (arms), central lobe with 2 broad lobes (skirt); spur about as long as ovary. **HABITAT** Open woodland, scrub, on chalk. **DIST.** Native. Very local. Almost confined to N Downs (Kent) and single localities in Herefordshire, Oxfordshire. (W, central and E Europe.) **FLS** May.

Monkey Orchid — *Orchis simia* VU. *(B)

STEMS Flowering stems to 45 cm. **LEAVES** Few, unspotted. **FLOWERS** In dense, rather untidy spike; 'hood' loose, rather long, whitish to rose-pink, spotted; labellum 14-16 mm, lateral lobes narrow, spreading (arms), central lobe longer than laterals (body); tip with 2 long, narrow lobes (legs), as narrow as 'arms' and small central tooth (tail). **HABITAT** Chalk grassland, scrub. **DIST.** Native. Very rare, in Kent (2 sites) and Oxford (1 site) only; all sites managed by active conservation. (Central and S Europe.) **FLS** May-Jun.

Military Orchid — *Orchis militaris* VU. *(B)

Rather similar to *O. simia*, but inflorescence dense to fairly lax, not so 'untidy' as in *O. simia*; tepals o

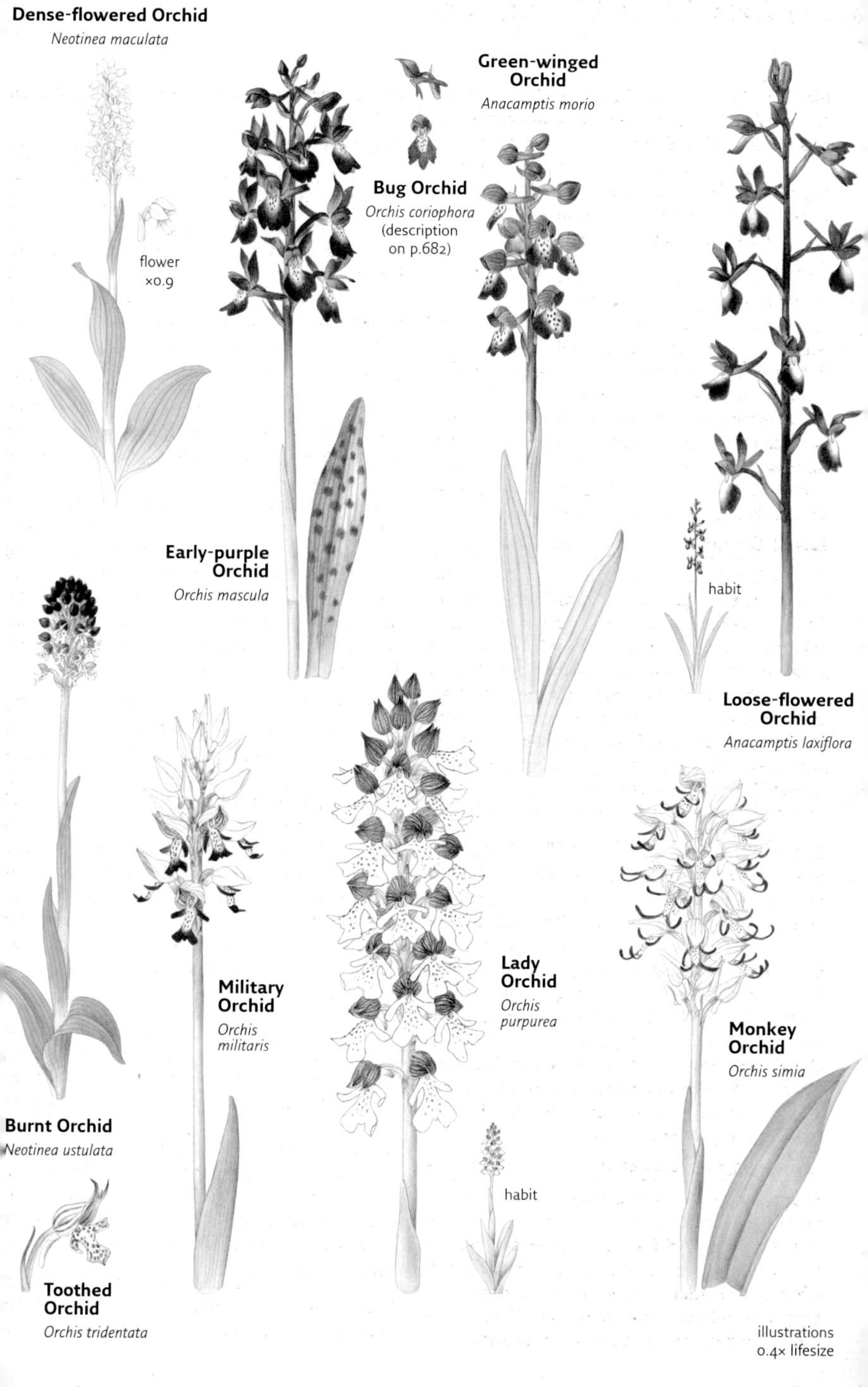

Dense-flowered Orchid
Neotinea maculata

Green-winged Orchid
Anacamptis morio

Bug Orchid
Orchis coriophora
(description
on p.682)

flower
×0.9

Early-purple Orchid
Orchis mascula

Loose-flowered Orchid
Anacamptis laxiflora

habit

Military Orchid
Orchis militaris

Lady Orchid
Orchis purpurea

Monkey Orchid
Orchis simia

Burnt Orchid
Neotinea ustulata

Toothed Orchid
Orchis tridentata

habit

illustrations
0.4× lifesize

hood pale greyish pink; middle lobe of labellum (legs) broader, >2× as wide as lateral lobes. HABITAT/DIST. Native. Very rare. Chalk grassland, scrub, woodland glades (1 site in Buckinghamshire); chalk pit (Suffolk). (Central Europe.) FLS May–Jun.

Bug Orchid
Orchis coriophora

[*See* illustration previous page.] STEMS Flowering stems to 40 cm. LEAVES 4–7, unspotted. FLOWERS Inflorescence rather dense; bracts as long as or longer than ovary; tepals converging to form a sharp-pointed violet-brown hood; labellum 3-lobed, longer than wide, purplish-green, unspotted, middle lobe entire. Whole plant smells of bed bugs. HABITAT Damp grassland. DIST. *Not BI*. (S, central, E Europe, N to Belgium.) FLS Apr–Jun.

Man Orchid
Orchis anthropophora EN.

STEMS Flowering stems to 40 cm. LEAVES Lower leaves crowded, oblong-lanceolate, glossy, keeled. FLOWERS In a rather lax, cylindrical, many-flowered spike; bracts shorter than ovary; tepals all converging to form hood (head), green edged with maroon; *labellum 12–15 mm, hanging vertically, yellow to orange-yellow, distinctly 'man-like'*, narrow lateral lobes forming 'arms' and 'legs'; spur absent. HABITAT Rough chalk and limestone grassland, scrub, roadsides, quarries. DIST. Native. Rare, scattered, declining. SE England, centred on North Downs of Kent, Surrey. (W Europe, Mediterranean.) FLS Jun–Jul.

Lizard Orchid
Himantoglossum hircinum *(B)

Tall, remarkable-looking orchid. STEMS Flowering stems to 90 cm. LEAVES 4–6 lower leaves, large, 6–15 × 3–5 cm, blunt, rather yellow-green, withering from tips before flowering. FLOWERS Numerous, rather untidy-looking, *smelling strongly of goats*, in large, lax spike to 25(–50) cm; tepals greenish, purple-striped beneath, converging to form a hood; *labellum 30–50 mm, whitish with purple spots at base, extended into long, narrow, pale brown, coiled, strap-shaped lobe* (lizard's tail); spur *c*.4 mm. HABITAT Chalk grassland, hedge banks, sand-dunes, shingle, quarries. DIST. Native. Rare, declining, very scattered and unpredictable in appearance. S England, centred on Kent. (S, S-central and W Europe.) FLS May–Jul.

Bee Orchid
Ophrys apifera *(NI)

Attractive, distinctive orchid. STEMS Flowering stems to 45 cm. LEAVES 5–6 basal leaves, greyish green. FLOWERS Rather large, in 2–7-flowered inflorescence; outer tepals (sepals) deep pink, 10–15 mm, oblong; inner tepals linear, greenish; labellum 10–15 mm, resembling abdomen of bumble-bee, strongly convex, velvety, *central lobe ending in long,*

tooth-like appendage, curved back beneath lobe so as to be invisible from above. HABITAT Short, dry calcareous grassland, scrub, dunes, lawns, roadsides, limestone pavement. DIST. Native. Throughout Britain to N England, widespread but local in S; scattered in Ireland. (S, W and central Europe.) FLS Jun–Jul.

Late Spider-orchid
Ophrys fuciflora VU. *(B)

Similar to *O. apifera*, but inner tepals ± triangular, pinkish; labellum ± flat, *central lobe ending in wide, often 3-toothed yellowish, upcurving appendage, clearly visible from above.* HABITAT Short, species-rich chalk grassland. DIST. Native. Very rare, in E Kent only. (Central and S Europe.) FLS Jun–Jul.

Early Spider-orchid
Ophrys sphegodes *(B)

Rather small orchid. STEMS Flowering stems to 20 cm. LEAVES 3–4 basal leaves, bluish green. FLOWERS In 2–10-flowered inflorescence; outer tepals (sepals) green, 6–8 mm, spreading; inner tepals shorter, greeny brown; labellum 9–10 mm, velvety, brown with H-shaped mark, bumble-bee-like. HABITAT Short, species-rich chalk and limestone grassland. DIST. Native. Very local, declining. S coast of England from Kent to Dorset; in a few scattered localities elsewhere. (W, central and S Europe.) FLS Apr–May.

Fly Orchid
Ophrys insectifera VU.

Slender, inconspicuous orchid. STEMS Flowering stems to 60 cm. LEAVES 3 basal leaves. FLOWERS 4–12, small, well spaced, in a slender spike; bracts longer than ovary; *outer tepals (sepals) green, spreading; inner tepals (antennae) brown, linear*; labellum narrow, 9–10 mm, 3-lobed, brown with iridescent blue transverse band, base with 2 shining black 'eyes'. HABITAT Shady woodland, scrub, on dry calcareous soils; to 390 m. In Ireland, occurs in fens, calcareous flushes. DIST. Local and scattered throughout lowland England; very rare in Wales; scattered in central Ireland. (Most of Europe except extreme N.) FLS May–Jul.

Small-flowered Tongue-orchid
Serapias parviflora

Distinctive orchid. STEMS Flowering stems to 35 cm. LEAVES 5–7, linear-lanceolate. FLOWERS Small 1.5–2 cm, pinkish brown, in elongate, spike-like, 3–5-flowered raceme; bracts about as long and partially enclosing flowers; tepals converging; labellum pale to dull red, 14–19 mm with hypochile and epichile, epichile lanceolate, directed downwards or backwards, slightly hairy. HABITAT Rabbit-grazed grassland on coastal cliff. DIST. Possibly native. S Devon discovered in 1989, population kept going artificially (SW Europe, Mediterranean.) FLS Jun–Jul.

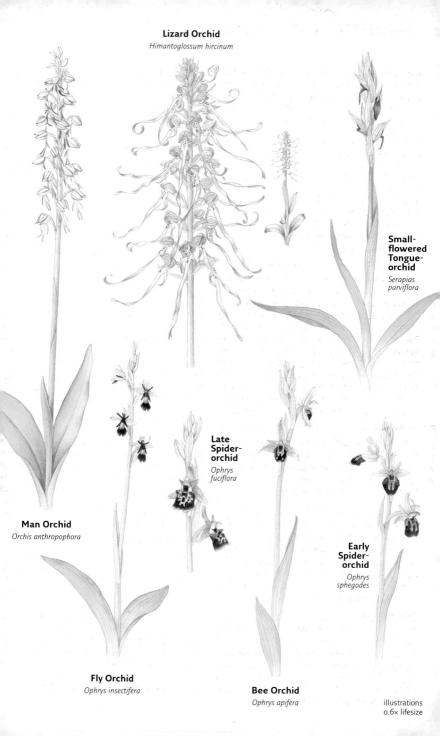

Lizard Orchid
Himantoglossum hircinum

Small-flowered Tongue-orchid

Serapias parviflora

Man Orchid
Orchis anthropophora

Late Spider-orchid

Ophrys fuciflora

Early Spider-orchid

Ophrys sphegodes

Fly Orchid
Ophrys insectifera

Bee Orchid
Ophrys apifera

illustrations
0.6× lifesize

GLOSSARY

Achene Small, dry, single-seeded, indehiscent fruit, e.g. that of butter-cup. (*See* illustration.)

achene

Actinomorphic Flowers that are radially symmetrical (syn. 'Regular'), e.g. Geranium. (*See* illustration.)

Acuminate Gradually tapering to a point. *See* diagram of cordate leaf.

Alternate (of leaves) Individual leaves are neither opposite nor whorled on stem.

Annual A plant that completes its life cycle from germination to seed in a single season.

Anther The pollen-containing part of the stamen, situated at the tip of the filament.

actinomorphic

Apocarpous A plant with individual carpels that are separate and not fused to form a single ovary (*see* p.48).

Apomictic Producing viable seed without fertilisation; in effect, cloning by seed.

Appressed Pressed close to another organ but not fused to it, e.g. hairs on a stem.

Archaeophyte Although not thought to be native, a plant long estab-lished in the British Isles and certainly present since before 1600 (cf. 'Introduced').

Aristate With an awn or stiff bristle.

Ascending Sloping or curving upwards at an oblique angle.

Auricle Small, ear-like projections at the base of a leaf, especially in grasses. (*See* illustration.)

auricle

Awn Bristle-like projection from the tip or back of a lemma or glume in grasses. (*See* illustration.)

awn

Axillary Arising in the axil of a leaf or bract.

Base-rich Soil or water rich in minerals such as calcium or magnesium that produces a non-acid neutral or basic reaction (cf. 'Fertile').

Berry Fleshy fruit with usually several seeds, without a hard stony layer surrounding seeds, e.g. Tomato. (*See* illustration.)

Biennial A plant that completes its life cycle in two growing seasons and does not flower in the first. e.g. Foxglove.

berry

Bifid Deeply split into two.

Bog Vegetation that develops on wet acid peat (cf. 'Fen').

Brackish Refers to water or wet soils that are salty but less saline than sea water; especially marshes and dykes close to the sea.

Bract (*see* p.47).

Bracteole (*see* p.105).

sepal (calyx)

Bulb Underground organ consisting of a short stem bearing a number of fleshy scale leaves, the whole enclosing next year's flower bud, e.g. an onion.

Bulbil A small bulb arising in the axil of a leaf or in an inflorescence.

Calcicole A plant usually found on calcium-rich soils, e.g. over chalk or limestone.

Calcifuge A plant usually found on calcium-poor acid soils, e.g. heath and moorland.

Calyx The sepals of a flower. (*See* illustration.)

Capitulum The head-like inflorescence of a member of the Asteraceae family. (*See* illustration.)

capitulum   capsule

Capsule A dry, dehiscent fruit consisting of more than one carpel. (*See* illustration.)

Carpel A unit composed of the female part of the flower (*see* p.48).

Carr Woodland or scrub that develops on permanently wet soils.

Casual An introduced plant that does not become established.

Cladode A green leaf-like lateral shoot.

Compound (of a leaf) Comprised of several distinct leaflets e.g. palmate, pinnate.

Cone The reproductive structure of a coniferous tree; also of horsetails and some clubmosses (*see* pp.13, 17, 43).

Cordate Refers to base of leaf blade. (*See* illustration.)

cordate

Corm Short, bulb-like underground stem that, unlike a bulb, does not consist of fleshy scale leaves (cf. 'Tuber').

Corolla The petals of a flower.

Corymb An inflorescence in which all the flowers are more or less at the same level but whose stalks arise from different points on the stem (adj. corymbose) (*see* p.48).

Crucifer Name commonly given to members of the Brassicaceae (= Cruciferae).

Cuneate Refers to base of leaf blade. (*See* illustration.)

cuneate

Cuspidate (of a leaf) Abruptly drawn out to a sharp narrow point.

Deciduous Refers to trees and shrubs that lose their leaves in autumn.

Decumbent Refers to stems that lie on the ground or are prostrate and tend to rise up at the tips (cf. 'Ascending').

decurrent

Decurrent (of leaves) With the base prolonged down the petiole or stem as a wing. (*See* illustration.)

Deflexed Bent sharply downwards.

Dioecious Having male and female flowers on separate plants, e.g. Holly.

Discoid (of a member of the Asteraceae) Having flower heads that consist of tubular or disc florets only. (*See* illustration.)

Dominant The plant species that gives vegetation its characteristic appearance; the most abundant species.

drupe   discoid

Drupe A fleshy fruit with one or more seeds, each of which is surrounded by a stony layer, e.g. plum. (*See* illustration.)

Elliptic (*See* illustration.)

Endemic Native to one country or a small area. If used without qualification, then refers here to the British Isles.

Entire (of a leaf) Neither toothed nor serrated. (*See* illustration.)

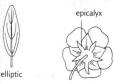
epicalyx
elliptic

Epicalyx A calyx-like whorl outside the true calyx, e.g. as in *Potentilla*. (*See* illustration.)

Eutrophic (of soil or water) Especially rich in nutrients, particularly nitrogen and phosphorus; extremely fertile.

Falcate Sickle-shaped.

Fen Vegetation that develops on wet calcareous peat, usually calcium-rich and with a pH >6.0 (cf. 'Bog').

entire

Fertile (of soil or water) With an adequate supply of plant nutrients, especially nitrogen, phosphorus and potassium (*see also* 'Eutrophic').

Filament The stalk of the stamen.

Filiform Thread-like.

Fimbriate With a fringe like margin.

Floret A highly modified individual small flower, e.g. of grasses or Asteraceae.

Flush Area of wet ground with moving ground water, e.g. margin of upland spring.

Follicle A dry, dehiscent fruit consisting of a single carpel, splitting along one side.

Fruit The ripe seeds together with the structure surrounding them, which may be either dry (e.g. a nut) or fleshy (e.g. a berry).

Glabrous Without hairs.

Gland Small, globular vesicle containing oil or resin, with or without a stalk, on the surface of any part of a plant.

Glandular With glands. (*See* illustration.)

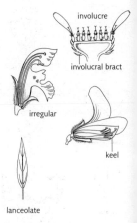
glandular hair

Glaucous With a blue-green or grey-green hue.

Glume A bract enclosing a floret of a grass or sedge.

Heath Lowland vegetation on infertile acid mineral soil, usually dominated by members of the heath family, e.g. Heather (cf. 'Moor').

Herb Any non-woody plant (not same as culinary definition).

Herbaceous Green, soft and with a leafy texture.

Hispid Coarsely and stiffly hairy, e.g. Viper's-bugloss.

Hyaline Thin and translucent.

Hybrid Offspring that results from a cross between two different species.

Incurved Bent gradually inwards.

Indusium Tissue covering or enclosing the sporangia of a fern (*see* p.23).

Inferior (of a flower) With the perianth inserted above the ovary, and the ovary embedded in, and fused with, the receptacle (*see* p.48).

Inflorescence The flowering part of the stem, including the flowers, branches and bracts (*see* p.48).

Internode The part of the stem between two adjacent nodes (*see* p.47).

Introduced Not native. In this book it refers to plants brought into the British Isles either accidentally or intentionally since about 1600 (sometimes referred to as 'neophytes').

Involucral Forming an involucre.

Involucre Bracts that form a more or less calyx-like whorl around or just below a condensed head-like inflorescence, e.g. Asteraceae. (*See* illustration.)

involucre

involucral bract

Irregular (of a flower) Divisible through the centre of the flower in only one longitudinal plane to produce two identical halves that are mirror images of each other (syn. 'Zygomorphic'), e.g. dead-nettles. (*See* illustration.)

irregular

Keel The lower petal or petals when these are shaped like the keel of a boat; sharp edge shaped like the keel of a boat. (*See* illustration.)

keel

Labiate Name commonly given to members of the Lamiaceae (= Labiatae).

Lanceolate (*See* illustration.)

lanceolate

Latex A milky juice, usually poisonous or a skin irritant.

Leaching The process of removing the nutrients from the upper layers of the soil by the downward movement of rain water.

Legume 1. Name commonly given to members of the Fabaceae (= Leguminosae) family.

2. Fruit (pod) of a member of the Fabaceae.

Lemma The lower bract that surrounds the individual floret of a grass (*see* p.586).

Ligulate (of the inflorescence of a Composite). Consisting of ray florets only, e.g. Dandelion; strap-shaped. (*See* illustration.)

ligulate

Ligule 1. The fused petals of a ray floret in a Composite.

2. The scale-like flap at the junction of the leaf blade and leaf sheath in grasses (*see* p.587).

linear

upper lip

lower lip

Limb The flattened, expanded terminal part of a corolla, the base of which is tubular.

Linear (*See* illustration.)

Lip A group of petals or tepals united together and sharply differentiated from the rest. (*See* illustration.)

Lobed (of leaves) Divided, but not into separate leaflets (*see* palmately lobed diagram).

Marsh Vegetation that develops on wet mineral soil, i.e. not on peat (cf. 'Bog' and 'Fen').

Meadow Grassland traditionally cut for hay (cf. 'Pasture').

Mesotrophic Soil or water that is neither extremely fertile (eutrophic) nor extremely infertile (oligotrophic).

Mica A group of minerals forming an important constituent of some igneous rocks, e.g. granite and serpentine.

Mire Vegetation that develops on wet peat; may be a bog or fen (cf. 'Marsh'). All three wetland habitats may intergrade.

Monocarpic (of a perennial) Flowering only once.

Monoecious Having unisexual flowers, but with the male and female flowers on the same plant, e.g. oak trees.

Moor Upland vegetation that develops on acid peat, usually dominated by members of the heath family, e.g. Heather, Bilberry (cf. 'Heath').

Mucronate (of a leaf) With a short bristle-like tip.

Native Thought to have arrived in an area by means of natural dispersal (i.e. not introduced).

Neophyte See 'Introduced'.

Node The point on a stem where leaves are attached (*see* p.47).

Nut Dry, one-seeded, woody, indehiscent fruit, e.g. Hazel.

Ob- (as prefix) Inverted, e.g. obovate, a leaf that is broadest above the middle, as opposed to ovate, a leaf that is broadest below the middle.

Oblong (*See* illustration.)

Obovate (*See* illustration.)

Obtuse Blunt.

Opposite Of two organs that arise at the same level on opposite sides of a stem.

Orbicular Rounded. (*See* illustration.)

Oval (*See* illustration.)

Ovary The part of the carpel containing the ovules (*see* p.48).

Ovate (*See* illustration.)

Ovoid (of a solid object) Egg-shaped.

Ovule The organ inside the ovary containing the egg and seed after fertilisation.

Palea The upper of the two bracts enclosing the individual florets of a grass. (*See* illustration.)

Palmate Divided into separate leaflets, with all the leaflets arising from the tip of the petiole. (*See* illustration.)

Panicle A much-branched inflorescence (*see* p.48).

Papillose Covered by minute protuberances.

Pasture Grassland that is regularly managed by grazing (cf. 'Meadow').

Peat The partially decomposed remains of plants that accumulate in cool, wet conditions.

Pedicel The stalk of a single flower.

Peduncle The stalk of an inflorescence.

oblong

obovate

orbicular

oval

ovate

palea

palmately lobed

palmate

Peltate (of a leaf) Having its lower surface attached to the stalk. (*See* illustration.)

peltate

Perennial A plant that lives for more than two years, flowering in the second year and regularly or irregularly thereafter.

Perianth A collective term for the sepals and petals, or the tepals if these are not differentiated into calyx and corolla.

Petal An individual segment of the corolla.

Petiole The stalk of a leaf.

Pinnate (of a leaf) Having separate leaflets along each side of the leaf stalk. (*See* illustration.)

pinnate

Pollinia The pollen masses of the stamens of orchids.

Prickle A sharp-pointed outgrowth from the stem, e.g. rose (cf. 'Thorn').

Procumbent Lying along the ground.

Proliferous An inflorescence that produces small plantlets instead of flowers.

Prostrate Lying flat.

Prothallus The small, separate, free-living sexual generation of a fern, producing the male and female organs.

Pruinose Having a whitish bloom, e.g. on a plum.

Pubescent Hairy.

Raceme (*see* p.48).

Rachis The axis or midrib of a fern frond.

Radiate (of a Composite inflorescence) Having disc florets in the centre and ray florets around the periphery (daisy-like).

Ray (of an inflorescence) The primary branch of an umbel. (*See* illustration.)

ray

Ray floret An individual flower of a Composite inflorescence, with petals that are united into a strap-shaped ligule. (*See* illustration.)

Receptacle The enlarged tip of the stem that bears the flower parts (*see* p.48).

ray floret

Recurved Curved backwards.

Regular (of a flower) Radially symmetrical (syn. actinomorphic).

Revolute Rolled back from the tip or margin.

Rhizome A horizontal underground root-like stem.

Rotate (of a corolla) With a short tube and spreading lobes.

Runner A creeping stem, rooting and producing plantlets at its nodes.

Salt-marsh Vegetation that develops on soft inter-tidal mud.

Saprophyte A plant lacking chlorophyll and deriving its nourishment from decaying organic matter, usually in association with a fungus.

Scape A leafless flower stalk.

Scarious Thin, dry, pale and membranous.

Scrub Vegetation dominated by shrubs and young trees.

Seed Technically the fertilised ovule. The sexual reproductive structure of the plant, which germinates to produce the plant of the next generation.

Sepal An individual segment of the calyx.

Sessile Without a stalk.

Sheathing (*See* illustration.)

sheathing

Shrub A woody plant like a small tree but with several stems that arise from the base rather than a single trunk.

Simple (of a leaf) Not compound, i.e. not composed of several distinct leaflets.

spur

stellate hair

stipule

subulate

tendril

trifoliate

whorled

zygomorphic

Sorus (of a fern) A group of sporangia.

Spathe A large bract enclosing or subtending a flower or inflorescence.

Spike (*see* p.48).

Sporangium The spore-containing structure of a fern, horsetail or club-moss.

Spore The small reproductive structure of a fern, horsetail or clubmoss.

Spur A slender, tubular, often nectar-secreting projection that usually extends from the rear of a flower. (*See* illustration.)

Stamen The male reproductive structure of a flowering plant (*see* p.48).

Stellate Star-shaped. (*See* illustration.)

Stigma The receptive tip of the style (*see* p.48).

Stipule A leafy outgrowth from base of the petiole. (*See* illustration.)

Stolon A creeping stem, rooting at the nodes and producing young plants along its length.

Style The elongated terminal portion of the carpel, bearing stigma at its tip (*see* p.48).

Subulate Flat and awl-shaped, tapering from base to apex. (*See* illustration.)

Sucker A shoot originating below ground.

Superior (of a flower) With the ovary inserted above the origin of the perianth (cf. 'Inferior' (*see* p.48)).

Tendril A climbing, thread-like, twining tip to a branch, leaf or petiole. (*See* illustration.)

Tepal The individual segment of a perianth when the sepals and petals are not differentiated.

Terete (usually of a stem) Smooth, cylindrical and more or less circular in section.

Thorn A short, pointed branch (cf. 'Prickle').

Tiller A lateral vegetative shoot arising from the base of a grass stem.

Tomentose Densely covered in soft hairs.

Trifoliate (of a leaf) Consisting of three leaflets. (*See* illustration.)

Trigonous (of a stem) Bluntly three-angled.

Triquetrous (of a stem) Sharply three-angled.

Tube (of a flower) The fused basal part of a calyx or corolla.

Tuber A swollen underground stem or root, surviving for one year (cf. 'Corm').

Umbel An inflorescence in which the pedicels all arise from the same point on the peduncle (*see* p.48).

Umbellifer Name commonly given to members of the Apiaceae (= Umbelliferae).

Vein A strand of strengthening and conducting tissue running through a leaf (syn. nerve).

Whorl Three or more organs arranged in a circle around an axis, e.g. a whorl of leaves on a stem, or the corolla as a whorl of petals (adj. whorled). (*See* illustration.)

Zygomorphic See 'Irregular'. (*See* illustration.)

582.130941
STR

04 INDEX